# AUTOCOURSE™

## THE WORLD'S LEADING GRAND PRIX ANNUAL

GRAN PREMIO D'ITALIA

CMG PUBLISHING

# CONTENTS

## AUTOCOURSE 2007–2008

is published by:
Crash Media Group Ltd
Number One
The Innovation Centre
Silverstone Circuit
Silverstone
Northants NN12 8GX
United Kingdom
Tel: +44 (0)870 3505044
Fax: +44 (0)870 3505088
Email: info@crash.net
Website: www.crashmediagroup.com


Printed in Italy by
ALSABA industrie grafiche,
Z.I. Belvedere S. Antonio
53034 Colle Val d'Elsa (SI)
Tel: +39 (0)577 905311
Website: www.alsaba.it

ISBN: 978-1905334-21-6

## DISTRIBUTORS

Gardners Books
1 Whittle Drive, Eastbourne,
East Sussex, BN23 6QH
Tel: +44 (0)1323 521555
email: sales@gardners.com

Menoshire Ltd
Unit 13
21 Wadsworth Road
Perivale
Middlesex UB6 7LQ
Telephone: +44 (0)20 8566 7344
Fax: +44 (0)20 8991 2439

NORTH AMERICA
Motorbooks International
PO Box 1
729 Prospect Avenue
Osceola
Wisconsin 54020, USA
Telephone: 1 715 294 3345
Fax: 1 715 294 4448

**Dust jacket: Finn Kimi Räikkönen
claimed the driver's championship
in his first season for Ferrari.**

**Title page: The three title contenders
Lewis Hamilton, Fernando Alonso
and Kimi Räikkönen, who took their
battle right to the season's end,
share the podium at Monza.**
Photographs: Peter J Fox/www.crash.net

editor
ALAN HENRY

publisher
BRYN WILLIAMS

text editor
SUZANNE ARNOLD

art editor
STEVE SMALL

design and production
ROSANNE DAVIS
MIKE WESTON

results and statistics
DAVID HAYHOE

advertising sales
SIMON MOORE

office manager
WENDY SALISBURY

chief photographer
PETER J FOX

chief contributing photographers
BERNARD ASSET

PAUL-HENRI CAHIER

JEAN-FRANÇOIS GALERON

LUKAS GORYS

PETER NYGAARD

JAD SHERIF

f1 illustrations
ADRIAN DEAN
f1artwork@blueyonder.co.uk

## Acknowledgements

The Editor of AUTOCOURSE wishes to thank the following for their assistance in compiling the 2007–2008 edition.
**France:** ACO; Fédération Française du Sport Automobile; FIA (Max Mosley, Bernie Ecclestone, Alan Donnelly, Richard Woods, Christel Picot, Alexandra Scherin, Charlie Whiting, Herbie Blash and Pat Behar); Renault F1 (Flavio Briatore, Pat Symonds, Patrizia Spinelli and Bradley Lord); **Germany:** Formula 3 Vereinigung; Mercedes-Benz (Norbert Haug, Wolfgang Schattling, Frank Reichert and Tanya Severin); Sabine Kehm; **Great Britain:** Autocar; Mark Blundell; Martin Brundle; Bob Constanduros; Maurice Hamilton; McLaren (Ron Dennis, Martin Whitmarsh, Justine Bowen, Beverley Keynes, Ellen Kolby, Clare Robertson, Claire Bateman, Lyndy Redding, Simon Points, Paddy Lowe, Neil Oatley, Steve Hallam and Peter Stayner); Red Bull Racing (Helmut Marko, Christian Horner, Adrian Newey, Eric Silbermann, Britta Roeske and Katie Tweedle); Nigel Roebuck; Spyker (Colin Kolles, Ian Phillips, Mike Gascoyne and Lucy Nell); Sir Jackie Stewart; Professor Sid Watkins; Jason Swales; Holly Samos; Fiona Winterburn; David Croft; WilliamsF1 (Sir Frank Williams, Patrick Head, Sam Michael, Jonathan Williams, Claire Williams, Silvia Hoffer Frangipane, Katie Aspinall and Liam Clogger); **Italy:** Commissione Sportiva Automobilistica Italiana; Scuderia Ferrari (Jean Todt, Antonio Ghini, Luca Colajanni, Matteo Bonciani and Stefania Bocci); Scuderia Toro Rosso (Gerhard Berger, Franz Tost and Fabiana Valenti); 'George' Piola; **Japan:** Bridgestone (Hirohide Hamashima, Hiroshi Yasukawa, Hisao Suganuma, Andy Stobart and Rachel Ingham); Honda Racing (Nick Fry, Yasahiro Wada, Alastair Watkins, Tracy Novak, Nicola Armstrong, Jules Kulpinski and Robert Watherston); Toyota (Tsutomu Tomita, John Howett, Fernanda Vilas, Marieluise Mammitsch and Alastair Moffat); **Switzerland:** BMW Sauber (Mario Theissen, Peter Sauber, Hanspeter Brack, Ann Bradshaw, Heikke Hinnitsch and Jorg Kottmeier); **USA:** ChampCar, Daytona International Speedway; Indianapolis Motor Speedway; NASCAR; Roger Penske; SportsCar.

**Photographs published in AUTOCOURSE 2007–2008 have been contributed by:**

**Chief photographer:** Peter J Fox of www.crash.net. **Chief contributing photographers:** Bernard Asset; Paul-Henri Cahier; Lucas Gorys; Peter Nygaard of GP Photo; Jad Sherif, Jean François-Galeron, Frits van Eldik, Hirashi Yamamura of WRi2.
**Other photographs contributed by:** A1GP Media Service; Muriel Brousseau of Brousseau Photo; Dirk Klynsmit of Graphic Dak Photos; Jacob Ebrey Motorsport Photography; Andrew Ferraro of GP2 Media Services; LAT Photographic (Phil Abbott, Brian Czobat/LAT South USA; Richard Dole, Hoyer/Ebrey/LAT, Yasushi Ishihara, Nigel Kinrade/LAT South USA, Michael Levitt, Oliver Read, Dan Streck, Terri Taylor, Paul Webb, Kevin Wood, XPB.cc/LAT); John Morris of M-Pix; Steve Small of www.crash.net; Chris Walker/www.kartpix.net; Mike Weston of www.crash.net

www.autocourse.com

# What you put into winning, Kimi, our customers put into their cars

Congratulations, Kimi, on taking your first ever Formula One world title. And to Ferrari for winning the Constructors' Championship in such dramatic style too. Your determination to the very last race has certainly paid off. Determination that we, at Shell, are proud to have shown with you – every exhilarating step of the way.

Such unparalleled success comes only from the kind of passion for performance we've shared together for over 60 years. It's one of the longest-running technical partnerships in Formula One. And yet again – after a truly exciting and challenging season – we've proven it to be the most successful.

But it's not just on the track that our developments come into their own. In fact, the 500,000 hours a year we invest in research together are what give Shell V-Power and Shell Helix such a competitive edge. So thank you, Kimi, and everyone else at Ferrari for an incredibly rewarding season. Having worked so hard to deliver the fuels and lubricants you needed to claim such historic victories, Shell – and all our customers – can feel like winners too.

**Shell**
## V-Power   **Shell** HELIX

**Made to move**

# FOREWORD by KIMI RÄIKKÖNEN

RIGHT back when I was a little kid, I was mad about engines. I always liked to be at the controls of anything powered by an engine and my dream was to be Formula 1 world champion one day.

Today, having come pretty close a couple of times, the dream has come true. Going into the Brazilian Grand Prix, I didn't have much hope that I could do it: seven points to make up and two drivers ahead of me seemed an insurmountable obstacle. However, in the end we did it – the team and I – because we never gave up believing it was possible and we always gave it our all, even when the points gap seemed out of reach. It is not in my character to throw in the towel and, at Ferrari, I have found fantastic people who share my philosophy: never give up!

Coming to Maranello rekindled my passion for driving in Formula 1. I was immediately made to feel at ease and the team tried to ensure that conditions were right for me to give my best, without ever putting me under pressure. Whatever the final outcome, it would have been a positive year anyway. That final victory was the reward for all the hard work, day after day, from all the team, from me, and Felipe, whose help was fundamental, and from our technical and commercial partners. Special thanks go to Jenni, to my family and to everyone who believed in me when I was a nobody.

Now that I have turned my dream into reality, anything else I get from Formula 1 will simply be a bonus. The title will not change my life, just as my success and fame to date changed nothing. I will continue to do what I have always done, loving my racing and spending my spare time with my family and my closest friends. But, on top of that, I know I can count on a new family and new friends: the ones from Maranello.

## The Home of Business

The Bahrain International Circuit is setting new standards in the world of business. Set against a stunning desert landscape, BIC provides a unique and exclusive setting to host conferences, stage seminars, hold media events and organise private functions.

## and Motorsport

What's more, you can even hire the world-famous Formula One track at the circuit to cater to your business needs. All this comes with the globally renowned catering by Käfer. Simply put, welcome to the home of business and motorsport in the Middle East.

For more information: +973 17 45 0000/www.bahraingp.com

# EDITOR'S INTRODUCTION
# UNRAVELLING THE STRANDS

L IVING at the heart of the F1 community through the summer of 2007 was rather like being stranded on a battlefield, the only difference being the extreme difficulty of identifying who were really the bad guys and who the good. By any standards this was a curious experience. There were moments when great deeds were performed out on the circuit, others when one formed the impression that the sport was living out some bizarre high-octane version of Lewis Carroll's *Alice Through the Looking Glass.*

Before attempting to unravel the strands of some of the sport's more enduring mysteries, it would perhaps be best to start by giving credit where credit is due.

Ferrari was perceived as the vindictive bad guy by some factions – perhaps understandably if you were one of the 1,400-strong McLaren workforce – but when the jealousies and intrigue are stripped aside you have to give the team credit for Kimi Räikkönen's world championship-winning efforts.

The Kimster was seeking a degree of rejuvenation when he decided to take on the exacting challenge of becoming Michael Schumacher's de facto successor at the cutting edge of the Maranello brigade. Under the circumstances, bearing in mind Schumacher's seven world championships, you might have expected Räikkönen to make heavy weather of the challenge.

He was 17 points behind Lewis Hamilton with two races to go, then played two stunning wins to grab the title by a single point from McLaren teamsters Hamilton and Fernando Alonso. At the end of the day Räikkönen was a worthy world champion with six wins to his credit. In assessing the Ferrari record, one should also have great respect for the three victories achieved by Felipe Massa, who certainly opened the year as a credible title contender and received his well-merited reward with a contract extension until '10.

Over at McLaren, one would like to believe that that team's '07 season would best be remembered from a purely historical perspective for yielding up the genius of Lewis Hamilton, who oh so nearly became the sport's first rookie world champion, rather than for becoming embroiled in a convoluted and unbelievable saga over allegedly stolen Ferrari technical data, which ended in loss of championship points and a staggering $100-million fine. The key to the depths of talent offered by F1's first black driver has nothing to do with his ethnicity; that counts as much here as it influenced Tiger Woods's skill with a five iron. As with Woods, the keys to Hamilton's success are his rounded personality and composure away from the field of battle.

On the face of it, signing the young British driver to partner the incoming double world champion Fernando Alonso might have been considered a huge risk by some observers. F1 teams are generally unwilling to break the thread of development continuity by changing both drivers at the same moment. But with Juan Pablo Montoya's contract being terminated mid-way through '06 and Kimi Räikkönen's having contracted himself to Ferrari more than a year ago, McLaren boldly committed itself to the lad who – as a ten-year-old kart racer – had originally walked up to Ron Dennis at the 1995 *Autosport* Awards and boldly asked if one day he might drive a McLaren F1 car. Dennis was impressed and took Lewis under the team's wing as a member of its driver development programme.

McLaren had last risked appointing a driver with no previous F1 experience in '93 when it signed Michael Andretti. It was not a happy experience and the team dropped Andretti before the end of the year. The sceptics may have made much of the fact that Hamilton trashed a McLaren during pre-season testing at Valencia, but in reality signing him was a no-risk strategy. His CV already reflected dominant score cards in both Euro F3 and GP2, while the best part of 1,000 hours spent on McLaren's bespoke in-house F1 simulator ensured that he arrived at Melbourne for the Australian GP as the best-prepared freshman of all time.

Hamilton has an easy, flowing driving style that – as with all the great exponents of F1 driving – takes as little out of his lean physical frame as it does the mechanical components of the car. It comes easily to him, talent and control crackling through his fingertips like high-tension static.

There have been a few dissenting voices. The former world champion Nigel Mansell, for instance, believes the 22-year-old Englishman was lucky to be in a 'fabulous' car and to have a fast-tracked apprenticeship in the sport.

'Lewis has lucked into a fabulous car,' he said. 'Mercedes must be very relieved to have a competitive car this year. McLaren is a fantastic race team that has had many, many championship wins with great drivers.'

The other crisis McLaren had to cope with was Fernando Alonso's growing disenchantment with the team, something that grew out of his basic belief that he had been somehow promised priority treatment over Hamilton. By the end of the year he was even being schmoozed by his former team Renault for a possible return.

However, team boss Flavio Briatore made it clear that Renault, for whom Alonso had won consecutive title crowns over the previous two seasons, was not in the business of interfering with other people's contracts – even though he clearly believes that Alonso would thrive emotionally at Renault rather than having to endure a turbulent and uncomfortable team-mate in Lewis Hamilton at McLaren.

'I can't deny that I think Fernando is great but he has a contract with someone,' Briatore said. 'He is very special. We had a special relationship at Renault and it was always transparent. Although he signed for McLaren we continue to be friends. Of course I would love to have him in the team – I think everyone would want Fernando because he is exceptional.'

Briatore would not be drawn into commenting on the problems Alonso has been having at McLaren, nor on whether he thought the driver would see out his contract with the team headed by his own long-time rival Dennis. By the end of the season, Dennis might have been forgiven for thinking Briatore was welcome to Alonso.

The FIA president Max Mosley took a more robust stance than many of those outside the governing body. After the FIA World Motor Sport Council meeting that imposed those draconian penalties, Mosley offered the view that Hamilton and Alonso should have been thrown out of this year's F1 drivers' championship after the British team was fined that staggering amount of money and stripped of its points in the constructors' world championship.

Mosley told BBC radio that he was part of a minority on the council that would have supported the loss of points for both men 'on the grounds that there is a suspicion that they had an advantage that they should not have had'.

He also expressed the view that should either of the McLaren drivers have won the championship then a public question mark would inevitably have hung over their success because the team had Ferrari information in its possession. Only the immunity that Mosley granted to the McLaren drivers – to Fernando Alonso, Lewis Hamilton and also reserve driver Pedro de la Rosa – in return for their information prevented them from being thrown out of the title race after McLaren was found guilty of being in possession of technical data illegally acquired from its rival.

Furthermore Mosley felt that Hamilton, whose championship lead over Alonso was trimmed to two points with three races left and 30 points to race for, would not take as much satisfaction from winning the title in these circumstances as he might have done before the controversy blew up.

'I think he will probably feel more comfortable if he wins a subsequent championship, which I am sure he will, without any of these question marks,' said Mosley.

'There was a big debate in the World Council about whether all the points should go – team and drivers'.

'The lawyers [on the council] felt that everything should go – drivers' points and all – because they argued how can you give the world champions' cup to someone who may have had an unfair advantage over other drivers?'

Mosley's view was set against the backdrop of Ron Dennis's dilemma when it came to deciding whether McLaren should appeal against the penalties handed down by the FIA's World Motor Sport Council.

The McLaren chairman still passionately believed that his team had been the focal point of a gross injustice in the sense

# A NEW STANDARD OF DRIVING PLEASURE.

**3**
**YEARS WARRANTY**
100 000 miles

**NEW RENAULT LAGUNA. YOU CAN NEVER BE TOO DEMANDING.** Looking the part is one thing, feeling the part is another. Drive the new Renault Laguna and you enjoy every curve and contour of the road. You quickly appreciate its precise and direct steering, and its newly developed reactive chassis. Its thicker anti-roll

The official fuel consumption figures for the New Laguna range in mpg (l/100km): Urban 21.7 (13) – 46.3 (6.1),

bars and its innovative reinforced suspension mean less roll around bends too. Combine these with a powerful, yet efficient dCi 150 engine, and you get a car that gives you a special driving experience based on quality, performance and reliability. New Laguna. Discover new standards at www.newlaguna.co.uk or by calling 0800 52 51 50.

RENAULT

Extra Urban 42.2 (6.7) – 61.4 (4.6), Combined 31.7 (8.9) – 57.6 (4.9). $CO_2$ emissions (g/km) 130 – 210.

**Right:** Dario's day of days – the Scotsman gets to 'drink the milk' as he celebrates his win in the Indianapolis 500.
Photograph: Michael Levitt/LAT Photographic

**Below:** BMW Sauber was indisputably the best of the rest. On occasion, Nick Heidfeld managed to break into the top four stranglehold of Ferrari and McLaren.
Photograph: Peter J Fox/www.crash.net

that there was still no evidence to prove that any of Ferrari's intellectual property had been incorporated into the McLaren car's design. Yet he suspected that this might be the best way in which to cool frayed tempers, but was mindful that the consequences of such an appeal might result in the penalty's being increased and the drivers' championship points accrued by Hamilton and Alonso could be forfeit as well.

In the event the McLaren team decided not to proceed with the appeal. Ferrari, meanwhile, was relentlessly unforgiving in its criticism of McLaren. Whatever the rights and wrongs of the issue, the Maranello management believed that its number-one rival had penetrated to the very heart of its F1 operation. Quite rightly, Ferrari demanded a very clear explanation of what on earth was going on and it was clear that the team felt that McLaren's explanation was significantly lacking in many respects. For its part, McLaren offered a detailed time line relating to the troubled episode, which was accepted – though not without reservations – by its loyal band of supporters.

With McLaren and Ferrari carving up the winning cake between them, there was little in the way of consolation to be found in the ranks of the also-rans. BMW Sauber was generally best of the rest, but former world champion Renault was eclipsed for the time being, failing to win a race for the first time since '02. Toyota and Honda continued to languish on the outer fringes of competitiveness, but Williams looked crisper and sharper than before and the new Red Bull-Renaults began to demonstrate genuine promise as the season drew to its close.

On the commercial front, F1 continued to dominate the international motor sport agenda, but the dispute over whether the category should admit so-called 'customer cars' stalled Prodrive founder David Richards' efforts to finalise a deal to run a second pair of McLaren-Mercs from '08.

F1 is also continuing to expand. In '07 it returned to Fuji after a 30-year break and the 18-race '08 calendar will include a round at Valencia and a night race in Singapore.

Outside the orbit of the F1 world championship, Dario Franchitti at least kept a thread of motor racing tradition alive by winning the Indy 500 while NASCAR thrived in the USA, as always, and Peugeot took up the gauntlet to challenge Toyota in the diesel battle at Le Mans.

So what does the future hold? More of the costly same for race organisers, one suspects. Bernie Ecclestone is a trim-looking 77 years old and looks as though he's got plenty more miles on the clock yet. Those who might dream of trading him in for a new commercial rights holder are just that: dreamers. For the moment, anyway.

Alan Henry
Tillingham, Essex, UK
November 2007

## ANGUS GEORGE FLEMING: 1951–2007

Angus Fleming is not a name that many of you will know – he wasn't involved in motor sport or the media industry. However, he was an extremely important person to us all at CMG, but sadly on 1 October 2007 he was cruelly and prematurely taken from us.

We have a great deal to thank Angus for as he was the person who helped steer us towards our ultimate goal, he prepared us for greater things, he was instrumental in the acquisition of AUTOCOURSE and its sister titles and was an ever-present beacon shining brightly, come day or night!

The words 'no' and 'can't do' didn't exist in Angus's vocabulary, his cup was *always* half full, never half empty, and that's the way we shall remember him – a passionate, honourable, generous and honest man.

He was my rock, my confidant, and over the years he became my very best friend. I will miss him terribly...

**Bryn Williams**
**Managing Director**
**Crash Media Group Ltd**

# JACQUES LEMANS
## SPORTS

## SL-Chrono

*solid stainless steel*
*Swarovski crystals*
*high-grade leatherstap or bracelet*
*water resistant up to 10 ATM*
*ø 36mm*

Formula 1
LICENSED PRODUCT

F 5006U

## 116 different F1 models
dealer locator: www.jacques-lemans.com

FIA FORMULA 1
WORLD CHAMPIONSHIP 2007
# TOP TEN DRIVERS

Chosen by the Editor, taking into account their racing
performances and the equipment at their disposal

Photographs by Peter J Fox/www.crash.net

| Born: | **7 January 1985** |
| --- | --- |
| Team: | **Vodafone McLaren Mercedes** |
| Grand prix starts in 2007: | **17** |
| World championship placing: | **2nd** |
| Wins: | **4** |
| Poles: | **6** |
| Points: | **109** |

# LEWIS HAMILTON

ALL the customary superlatives have long since been exhausted when it comes to assessing the driving genius of F1's dazzling new kid on the block. Truth be told, after his previous two years of domination of the F3 Euro Series and GP2, promoting Lewis to F1 was an absolutely zero-risk decision for the McLaren management to take. His form in these two crucial feeder categories had been such as to provide accurate and rock-solid pointers to his future potential. Detractors can talk to their hearts' content about the benefits of the sophisticated McLaren simulator and the number of testing miles Lewis had covered in what turned out to be the best car of the year, but these were trifling footnotes that could in no way undermine the sheer magnitude of this rookie's achievements.

So are those who predicted that Hamilton would be *that* good really being wise after the event? Not at all. Putting aside the fact that he had previously not so much as seen seven of the 17 circuits on which he raced this year, it was entirely logical that he should have performed so impressively from the outset. Setting it all into a historical context, think for a moment what might have happened had Ayrton Senna been at the wheel of a McLaren-TAG rather than a Toleman-Hart in 1984? What might have happened in '91 if Michael Schumacher had gone straight into a Williams-Renault?

Using such a process of substitution, Hamilton's form was 90 percent expected, backed up by a 10 percent blend of staggering talent, composure and utterly remarkable maturity for a guy of such tender years. Yet beneath the surface lurked cold steel. We first saw it in Monaco, where Lewis was obviously highly disappointed that a different fuel strategy played straight into team-mate Fernando Alonso's hands during a race that the British driver rightly believed belonged to him. Yet Lewis did not have to wait long before correcting the record, utterly dominating both the Canadian and US Grands Prix in a manner that unequivocally endorsed the new boy's standing among his peers. From then on, it was simply more of the same. Quite simply, he was the best driver out there. And he is only going to get better.

# 2 KIMIRÄIKKÖNEN

**Born: 17 October 1979**

**Team: Scuderia Ferrari Marlboro**

**Grand prix starts in 2007: 17**

**World championship placing: 1st**

**Wins: 6**

**Poles: 3**

**Points: 110**

KIMI Räikkönen may have been the outsider when it came to battling out the final nerve-racking stages of the world championship, but the taciturn Finn with a taste for partying in many ways looked best-suited of the three contenders to withstand the huge pressure of the momentous occasion.

While Lewis Hamilton tried to keep calm in the face of possibly losing his great chance of becoming the first rookie title holder and his McLaren team-mate Fernando Alonso attempted to control the paranoia that had wrecked his relationship with his new employers in less than a season, Räikkönen went to São Paulo's wild and woolly Interlagos track knowing that all he could do was drive flat-out and let the mathematics look after themselves. He did just that and Kimi, the mathematical outsider, was crowned world champion.

At the start of the 2007 season he took on the unenviable role of trying to fill Michael Schumacher's boots as Ferrari's de facto number-one driver, a role that he initially found hard-going after five years driving for the rival McLaren-Mercedes squad. He won the opening race in Australia then didn't win again until Magny-Cours, round eight of the season's 17 events. He won four more, taking his tally to six victories, one more than either Hamilton or Alonso managed.

Räikkönen is a curiously self-contained individual who marches very much to his own beat. He is the highest-paid driver in the business, on $30 million a year, and early in the season the Ferrari team seemed slightly baffled by his laid-back attitude. Used to Schumacher's staying late into the evenings after practice to pore over endless reams of technical data, they found it unnerving to see Räikkönen and his wife Jenni heading out of the paddock and back to their hotel at around 5 pm.

For the first half of the season Räikkönen struggled to acclimatise to the Bridgestone tyres used by Ferrari and was rather shaded by his team-mate Felipe Massa. After France he successfully reversed the trend, scoring four wins out of nine races to keep his championship hopes alive through to the final round. And there the job was done.

| Born: **29 July 1981** |
| Team: **Vodafone McLaren Mercedes** |
| Grand prix starts in 2007: **17** |
| World championship placing: **3rd** |
| Wins: **4** |
| Poles: **2** |
| Points: **109** |

# FERNANDO ALONSO

WHEN Fernando Alonso first spoke to Ron Dennis about the possibility of joining McLaren, the two men had just shared the podium at Interlagos in 2005, where Alonso had just clinched his first world championship with a third-placed finish for Renault behind the McLaren-Mercedes of Juan Pablo Montoya and Kimi Räikkönen. A month or so later their three-year deal was signed and by the time Alonso first sat in a McLaren at the end of '06 he had added a second title to his impressively expanding CV.

What a difference two years would make. By the time Alonso returned to Interlagos at the end of the '07 season his relationship with McLaren had been terminally blighted after only a single year together and his reputation as possibly the most complete performer in F1 lay in ruins.

Whether he was driven by paranoia or a genuine belief that McLaren had promised him a performance advantage that it failed to deliver is difficult to say. If it was the former, it was probably the result of listening to whispers from his tight-knit coterie of Spanish insiders. If the latter, he must stand guilty of never having probed McLaren's long-established tradition of trying to ensure complete equality of opportunity for its drivers at all times.

Either way, Fernando badly damaged his reputation, although his obvious petulance was positively punctuated by some genuinely first-rate drives to win in Malaysia, Italy and Monaco. There was also his spectacular triumph at the Nürburgring, where he outfoxed Felipe Massa in a dramatic wheel-banging contest over the last four laps. Yet there were other days on which Alonso looked almost average. His drive at Montreal was littered with unforced errors – a performance put into even more painful perspective by the fact that this was the day on which Lewis Hamilton won his maiden victory – he crashed heavily in Japan and wound up third in the championship behind Hamilton, both men having won four races but Hamilton having finished second once more than Alonso had.

Alonso is unquestionably a first-class driver but his brand and image, both inside and outside the sport, have been done huge damage by his behaviour. And other team principals are clearly wary of enduring what Ron Dennis has been through this season.

# FELIPE MASSA

4

THERE is an uncomplicated, twinkling charm about Felipe Massa that somehow tempts you to look past his obvious role as a world championship contender.

The relaxed 26-year-old Brazilian's easy demeanour makes him look like a bloke who likes driving racing cars and somehow can't quite believe he's landed a Ferrari drive as one of the key claimants to the legendary Michael Schumacher's crown.

Yet his hard on-track achievements have served to contradict this slightly soft, rather tactile image. Massa is maturing into a tough customer, as Fernando Alonso found out to his cost when he tried sitting it out, wheel to wheel, with the Ferrari driver going into the first corner in this year's Spanish GP. Massa survived, intact and unrepentant, to lead the race throughout while Alonso slid onto the gravel. 'I think that proves you have to sometimes take some risks if you want to be a competitor for the championship,' Massa said with a knowing grin.

Massa's emergence as a title contender has left the F1 paddock divided. There were those who believed that he would be shaded by the prodigiously talented Kimi Räikkönen, the super-fast Finn who moved from McLaren to succeed Schumacher at Ferrari. Others think that Felipe has retrospectively validated his 2006 performances as Schumacher's running mate and that the pace he demonstrated alongside the seven-times world champion now looks like a genuine reflection of his speed and ability.

Ironically, it was Massa's lowest moment of the '07 season that seems to have been the making of him. In Malaysia he qualified his Ferrari superbly on pole position but lost out to eventual winner Fernando Alonso's McLaren on the sprint down to the first corner before making a series of mistakes battling with Lewis Hamilton and eventually trailing home a crestfallen fifth.

There was only a week's break between Malaysia and the third round in Bahrain, seven days for Massa to wait before gaining the opportunity to atone, seven days during which he bore the brunt of media criticism calling into question his suitability for the exacting role as a Ferrari driver. He answered his critics by winning first in Bahrain, then again in Spain and Turkey. His reward was an extended contract to the end of '10.

**Born: 25 April 1981**

**Team: Scuderia Ferrari Marlboro**

**Grand prix starts in 2007: 17**

**World championship placing: 4th**

**Wins: 3**

**Poles: 6**

**Points: 94**

| | |
|---|---|
| **Born: 10 May 1977** | |
| **Team: BMW Sauber F1 Team** | |
| **Grand prix starts in 2007: 17** | |
| **World championship placing: 5th** | |
| **Wins: 0** | |
| **Poles: 0** | |
| **Points: 61** | |

# NICKHEIDFELD

OVER the past couple of years Nick Heidfeld has built on a reputation for speed and absolute dependability behind the wheel. A decade ago he was a highly regarded McLaren test driver and tipped as one of the sport's most impressive emergent stars, but his hopes of making an early move up the ladder were thwarted when Kimi Räikkönen beat him to take the McLaren seat as Mika Häkkinen's successor at the end of the 2001 season.

Heidfeld's level of achievement then became patchy, to say the least, but his rehabilitation as a potential F1 front runner went into top gear when he landed a Williams-BMW drive in '05. Paired alongside the highly regarded Australian Mark Webber, he shaded his rival – most notably in Monaco. BMW Sauber was determined to secure Heidfeld's services, encouraged by memories of his previous experience with the Hinwil-based team from '01 to '03.

From the start of the '07 season Heidfeld proved himself to be 'best of the rest', opening the year with fourth places in Australia, Malaysia and Bahrain. Consistent almost to a fault, he fully exploited the potential of the BMW-Sauber to great effect. He retired with mechanical trouble on only three occasions and finished 13 of the other 14 races in the top six.

In Hungary there was much speculation that he might get in among the McLarens, something that seemed even more likely after Alonso was given a grid penalty. Come the race, Heidfeld did the perfect job, keeping the McLaren neatly boxed in all the way to the chequered flag while driving with impressive verve and assurance. He drove the whole season with immaculate precision and clearly hopes to be driving for F1's third winning force in '08 if BMW Sauber can take the crucial next step forward that will allow it to go head-to-head with Ferrari and McLaren. If that proves to be the case, there is no doubt that Nick will be able to do himself justice.

# 6

# HEIKKI KOVALAINEN

**Born: 19 October 1981**

**Team: ING Renault F1 Team**

**Grand prix starts in 2007: 17**

**World championship placing: 7th**

**Wins: 0**

**Poles: 0**

**Points: 30**

THERE was a great sense of expectancy surrounding Heikki Kovalainen from the start of the season, his perceived status as a rising star who might just be the equal of Lewis Hamilton based on his speed during the 2005 GP2 championship and his proven pace and accomplishment through '06, when he was the Renault team's official test and reserve driver.

And yet things did not quite gel when it came to his promotion into F1 alongside Giancarlo Fisichella. In truth, it was one of those occasions when you could see that the driver concerned had all the potential in the world yet somehow lacked the ability to unlock it in the shorter term.

The first three races went badly. With team-mate Fisichella posting a fifth, sixth and eighth in Australia, Malaysia and Bahrain, Heikki's score-card ran tenth, eighth and ninth. Before long team boss Flavio Briatore's tinder-dry humour was being deployed to

question whether perhaps the real Finn had been stolen and replaced by an imposter: 'I really hope the real Heikki is back for the next race.'

It was all good tongue-in-cheek stuff, albeit with a serious undertone. Heikki was expected to do better than this and, after a slow start to the year, kicked off with a respectable fourth in Canada, followed a week later by fifth at Indianapolis.

These results gave a firm boost to Renault, yet the best was yet to come, much later in the season. In appalling conditions at Fuji he finished second after a great battle with Felipe Massa's Ferrari. Although he rounded off the season with a disappointing high-speed shunt at Interlagos, the overall verdict on the young Finn's performance was overwhelmingly positive – so much so that when paddock insiders were discussing who might replace Fernando Alonso at McLaren, Kovalainen's name was close to the top of most lists.

THIS engaging Pole embarked on his first full season of F1 buoyed by a promising start to his career when he took over the drive vacated by Jacques Villeneuve during the summer of 2006. Kubica is highly regarded as possible world championship material by many people – including Lewis Hamilton, who was one of his most formidable rivals when they were climbing through the ranks together.

To start with, Kubica lacked the points-scoring consistency of his BMW Sauber team-mate Nick Heidfeld and it was not until the Spanish GP, round four of the title chase, that he began to deliver strong results with a fourth place, followed by a strong fifth at Monaco.

Yet just as Kubica looked as though he was really getting into his stride he faced what, for a few fleeting seconds, was the most lethal challenge of his racing career to date. Under braking for the tightest hairpin on Montreal's Circuit Gilles Villeneuve, a misunderstanding with Jarno Trullli led to his BMW-Sauber's vaulting over the back of the Toyota before cartwheeling to destruction with huge lumps of debris scattering in all directions. It was one of those fearful moments when you hold your breath and just pray that the seat harness does its job to perfection; and in this case it did its job admirably.

Few cars have been so comprehensively destroyed in recent times. As the wreckage skidded to an uncomfortable stop, Kubica initially did not move in the cockpit. But eventually he was given the all-clear and taken to hospital for a check-up. This revealed that he was fitter than anybody might have imagined, given the forces involved in his almighty shunt. By Monday morning he was back on his feet again and by Thursday he was absolutely back to his old form and he was disappointed when the doctor refused to let him compete at Indy as a precaution.

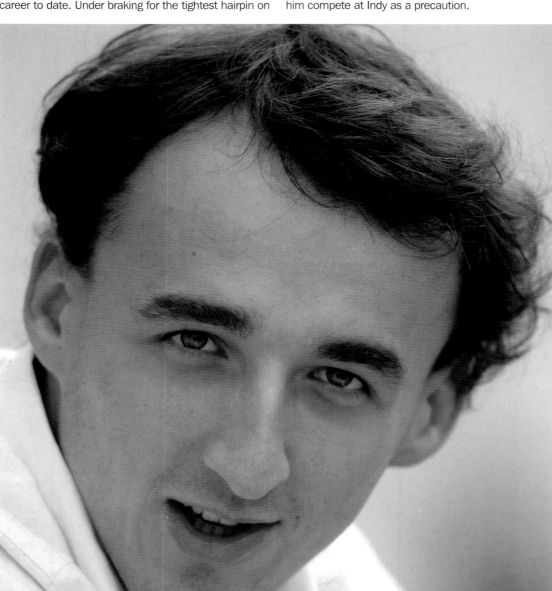

7

**Born: 7 December 1984**

**Team: BMW Sauber F1 Team**

**Grand prix starts in 2007: 16**

**World championship placing: 6th**

**Wins: 0**

**Poles: 0**

**Points: 39**

# ROBERT KUBICA

# NICO
# ROSBERG

8

In his second season of F1 Nico Rosberg developed a sheen of confidence that was justified by his performances on-track. After a somewhat over-anxious freshman season in 2006, Keke's boy emerged as a rounded and complete performer, registering a succession of points-scoring finishes in the second half of the season. It was just a shame that Nico's battle for fourth place at Interlagos with the two BMW-Saubers should be overshadowed by the fuel-cooling controversy, for this was the race in which he finally came of age, demonstrating that he was well capable of delivering hard results after a bare-knuckle fight with some genuinely formidable opposition.

After a difficult first year struggling with unreliability on the last Cosworth V8 to compete in F1, Rosberg relished the dependability of the Toyota V8 now used by Williams and generally out-ran the works Toyotas during the second half of the year. He also generally had the upper hand over his team-mate Alex Wurz, who raced well enough but was never really able to set competitive times in qualifying.

Rosberg was a good qualifier and it is fair to say that he is one of the more marketable assets in the Williams armoury. That's not to say that Sir Frank is thinking about trading him to another team, but there have been rumours that Rosberg, too, might be high on the list of potential future team-mates for Lewis Hamilton at McLaren.

Rosberg scored points in the first race, nipping seventh place at Melbourne, and usually kept well out of trouble on his way to ninth place in the drivers' championship. This well-rounded 22-year-old seems comfortable in his own skin at Williams and increasingly looks as though he fits into their way of doing things in much the same manner as his father did a generation ago.

**Born: 27 June 1985**

**Team: AT&T Williams**

**Grand prix starts in 2007: 18**

**World championship placing: 9th**

**Wins: 0**

**Poles: 0**

**Points: 20**

# MARK WEBBER

9

WEBBER'S two-year stint with Williams delivered mixed results, particularly alongside Heidfeld during 2005, so it was always going to be fascinating to see what the single-minded Australian would deliver in his next F1 berth. During the summer of '06 it was speculated that he would switch to Renault, or possibly even McLaren, but eventually Flavio Briatore's management company brokered him a deal to join Red Bull Racing, where he would enjoy the luxuries of an Adrian Newey-inspired chassis and a Renault engine.

As another dimension of the challenge, Webber found himself measured exactingly against his new team-mate David Coulthard, a veteran of 13 grand prix victories for McLaren and a previous runner-up in the world championship. On paper it looked a stimulating challenge but it got off to a slow start, with neither car scoring points in the first three races of the season. The new Red Bull initially proved frail but Mark scored his first points of the year with seventh in the US GP at Indianapolis. The high spot was third place in the European GP at the Nürburgring, where he joined Fernando Alonso and Felipe Massa on the podium after their epic battle for victory in the closing stages.

Later, two of the last three races of the season should have yielded podium places. An almost-certain second behind Lewis Hamilton at Fuji was thwarted by the freak accident in which Webber was rammed from behind by Sebastian Vettel's Toro Rosso while they were behind the safety car, then a brilliant 'best of the rest' fifth place on the grid at Interlagos resulted in nothing more than an early retirement.

Taking the broad view, there was little for Webber to celebrate in '07. But there were plenty of signals to suggest that '08 might be something really special if Red Bull can spice its performance potential with technical durability at last.

**Born: 27 August 1976**

**Team: Red Bull Racing**

**Grand prix starts in 2007: 17**

**World championship placing: 12th**

**Wins: 0**

**Poles: 0**

**Points: 10**

| Born: **19 January 1980** |
| Team: **Honda Racing F1 Team** |
| Grand prix starts in 2007: **17** |
| World championship placing: **15th** |
| Wins: **0** |
| Poles: **0** |
| Points: **6** |

THERE was a poignant moment in the paddock at the Hungaroring on the Friday afternoon. A flood of photographers and television journalists swept across from the grandly titled McLaren brand centre and surrounded Lewis Hamilton as he strode purposefully towards the team garage.

In the crush, nobody noticed Jenson Button as he ducked and weaved a path through the seething mass of humanity, the winner of last year's race here alone and unacknowledged by the jostling onlookers. It was a stern reminder of just how relentless, unforgiving and hard-edged the F1 business can be when it comes to consuming the careers of the vulnerable.

In 2006, driving superbly on an initially soaking track surface, Button came from 14th on the grid to give the Honda RA106 an impressive victory. It was supposed to trigger a run of sustained success. As he reflects on his '07 achievements, only a fifth place in the tricky wet-dry conditions at Shanghai stands out as a memorable occasion.

Talk closely with Button and he radiates a slightly detached, curiously enigmatic approach to his dilemma. He gives the impression of wanting to skirt around the subject, almost as if reflecting in any more detail on a season that delivered him only six points would somehow drain the reservoir of his personal motivation for good.

Ask him about his future with the Honda team and Button's mood becomes ever so slightly fixed as you sense his powers of diplomacy being stretched taut. 'We've got to continue making sure we improve our car step by step,' he answers. 'And to have the right people around to help us.'

It must be heartbreaking to see your career evaporating in front of your eyes, but his many fans and supporters hope he keeps his focus and powers through to success in the future. If Honda can't deliver in '08 he needs to bail out and find another berth. In terms of hard results it seems that he has given the team rather more than it has given him. He not only deserves better, but needs it urgently.

JENSONBUTTON

# THE ICEMAN COMETH

## By HEIKKI KULTA

The red-hot cauldron of Ferrari has become a comforting environment for Kimi Räikkönen.
Photograph: Peter J Fox/www.crash.net

**Above: Kimi was dominant at Spa-Francorchamps. His win proved to be his launch pad to the championship.**
Photograph: Peter J Fox/www.crash.net

THANKS to Kimi Räikkönen, it's great to be a Finn right now! I have been asked to explain to you how big a deal it is for Finland that Kimi Räikkönen is the new world champion. I'm not trying to blow things out of proportion if I say that it's the greatest Finnish motor racing achievement of all times. Finland has achieved a lot – but the way Räikkönen won this championship makes it the greatest of them all.

It came so unexpectedly. Kimi – the guy who has no luck – was suddenly the luckiest guy in the world. Somehow the year 2007 has been one of pure success for Finnish sports stars. It's been an outstanding year in all our top national sports. It's just incredible.

It was Keke Rosberg who first made F1 popular with us Finns. In fact, you could say the history of Finnish F1 started precisely 25 years ago, when Keke clinched the world title by finishing fifth in the final race in Las Vegas. This new kind of championship woke up almost five million people here in the far north. Cross-country skiing, ski jumping, long-distance running, javelin throwing… these were the top sports in Finland.

Suddenly we realised that F1 can be a sport, too.

Rosberg changed the Finnish way of thinking about F1. We learned that it is not just some kind of motor show for rich people in Monte Carlo. After Keke, his protégé Mika Häkkinen won titles in 1998 and '99. The whole of Finland was cheering for Mika – and cheering for Keke, too.

Now we have a new kind of F1 world champion. Räikkönen has nothing to do with the long tradition of the Rosberg era. He is a self-made Finnish racing driver and hasn't been trained for a certain role. Kimi never acts other than how he really is. For us Finns, Räikkönen is the easiest to identify with – he is of the same mettle as most of us.

There is a saying that a real Finn neither speaks nor smooches – at least, not publicly. Not long ago, we didn't travel that much. If we were planning to go abroad, when we thought about it we anticipated just watching places silently. If somebody came to talk to you, you'd hide behind the others. Then, back in the hotel sitting down with other Finns – who were just as shy as you – and having a couple of beers, you'd enjoy the experiences of the day and tell each other how travelling always beats home.

It is like a competition to see who feels the most shy. It's in our nature – and has been for a long time.

The more we hear foreigners complaining that Räikkönen is so quiet and unconcerned with building a new image for himself, the more we respect him.

The quietest Finnish sports stars have always been the cross-country skiers and javelin throwers. They've made it into an art, keeping their mouths shut after winning big trophies. Now, this year, we have new world champions in skiing and the javelin and both are being very talkative and dealing very well with the international publicity.

Räikkönen has many times said that he was, probably, born 20 years too late. He would have been more comfortable in the F1 of the '70s – the time of James Hunt and his kind of drivers. Kimi loves to drive very fast but he also loves to relax properly after the race. It is no coincidence that he used 'James Hunt' as his pseudonym when he took part in a top-level skidoo competition just before the F1 season began. Räikkönen is the wild one – in his own way. And that makes him even popular with us.

Finnish television doesn't show the grands prix live any more. You have to get a pay-to-view TV card to see a race live. If this season had been shown on a free channel, the viewing figures would have jumped to record levels.

There are 5.2 million people in Finland and more than 20 percent of them – more than a million – have got used to watching F1. This year almost 300,000 paid for F1 coverage. They all watched the Brazilian GP – and the aftermath was

**Below: Body language sometimes says more than words from the taciturn Räikkönen, speaking here at Magny-Cours.**
Photograph: Brousseau Photo

**Bottom: Even as far afield as Shanghai, a loyal band of Finns always turned up to support their hero.**
Photograph: Peter J Fox/www.crash.net

**Below: Räikkönen is happiest when in the cockpit of his Ferrari, doing the job he loves.**
Photograph: Paul-Henri Cahier

**Bottom: Number six becomes number one. Kimi's victorious Ferrari is showered in silver confetti after his win in Brazil.**
Photograph: Lukas Gorys

watched by 947,000 people. The largest TV audience for a grand prix was for Brazil in '99, when 1.9 million Finnish fans watched Mika Häkkinen win the race.

This era of pay-to-view TV is glorious for restaurants. Anywhere that was showing the Brazilian GP this year was full. And there were none of the usual drunken fights – celebrating Kimi's championship united people even more successfully than Finnish giant Nokia manages to connect people.

Sometimes, there have been huge celebration parties in the streets of Helsinki. When Finland won the ice hockey world championship for the first time back in '95 and when the amazing Lordi won the Eurovision Song Contest in '06 tens of thousands of fans joined in the celebrations.

But there are no such plans this time. Kimi relishes his privacy even though he knows how much it means to us to win something big.

Räikkönen himself is a keen fan of all sports. He follows all types of motor sport. He also loves ice hockey and one of his very close friends is Teemu Selanne, who won the ice hockey Stanley Cup for the first (and probably last) time just before the Canadian GP.

It was Selanne who was one of the first to congratulate Kimi in Brazil – just as Kimi had been one of the first to congratulate him back in June from Montreal.

This year has been exceptional in Finnish sporting life – it's been one of our most successful ever. We have a cross-country skiing world champion, we were in the ice hockey

world championship final, Selanne was one the Anaheim Ducks players to win the Stanley Cup... We have the world champion javelin thrower. Marcus Gronholm is fighting to become rally world champion. The list could go on.

But most of all – Finland has the F1 world drivers' champion. Nationwide, obviously, that is the one that is the most prized.

Keke Rosberg was Finland's sportsman of the year back in '82. Mika Häkkinen was elected sportsman of the year in '98.

The title is voted for by Finnish sports journalists. The rest of the world will consider Räikkönen to be the Finnish sportsman of '07, but you never know how things will work out in our own voting. Only a handful of Finnish journalists tour the world with F1, but most Finnish journalists know the other athletes and, when it comes to it, many vote for the people they know personally. There will be quite a harsh debate between the sports media and the everyday sports fans if Räikkönen is not named sportsman of the year.

They say that the only thing that beats the feeling of envying your neighbour is the feeling of sexual heat. At least we have something for everybody – not all Finns are icemen like our new hero.

**Above: Kimi momentarily lost in his own world as he prepares for yet another meeting with the press.**
Photograph: Peter J Fox/www.crash.net

**Left: He sheds a tear on the podium after becoming world champion in Brazil.**
Photograph: Frits van Eldik/WRi2

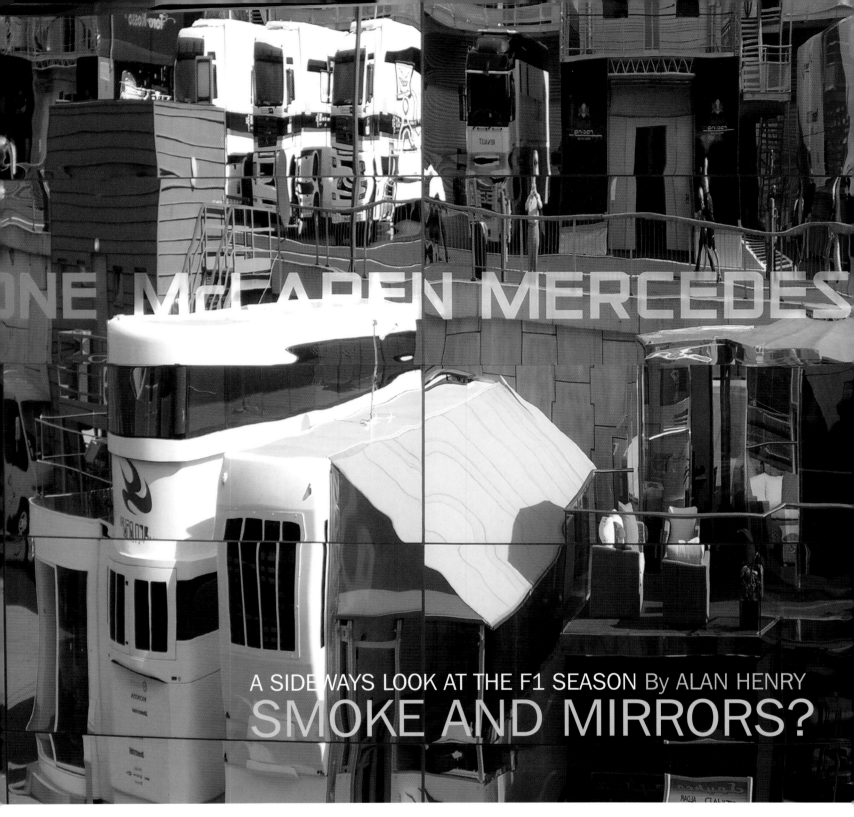

ONE McLAREN MERCEDES

A SIDEWAYS LOOK AT THE F1 SEASON By ALAN HENRY
# SMOKE AND MIRRORS?

**Above: The kaleidoscopic world of the Formula 1 paddock, where nothing is as straightforward as it seems.**
Photograph: Steve Small/www.crash.net

**Above right: Max Mosley and Ron Dennis and the $100-million handshake.**
Photograph: Jad Sherif/WRi2.

**Right: Mosley gives an extensive briefing on the FIA's massive fine to the media scrum in the Spa-Francorchamps paddock.**
Photograph: Peter J Fox/www.crash.net

There was happily no blood, but a lot of sweat and tears were expended during the course of the 2007 FIA Formula 1 world championship and, although it would be wrong to attach too much emotional baggage to any one individual, one's bound to say that the FIA president Max Mosley certainly featured strongly at the head of the pack when it came to shaping the news. He certainly stamped his authority on this year's F1 championship with his unwavering belief that McLaren got off lightly in terms of the penalties applied in the so-called 'spy-gate' affair.

Anybody who witnessed his defiantly confident mood in the paddock over the weekend of the Belgian GP will have realised that he seriously meant business. Max was determined, in his own way, to put the most sharply defined perspective he possibly could on the whole issue – and if that meant humiliating McLaren's Ron Dennis by forcing him into that gruesome staged photo shoot with the two of them shaking hands, so be it.

Later in the season I asked a leading personality in another team why he thought Ron didn't simply tell Max to push off and refuse to pose for the camera. My friend paused for a moment,

then offered this considered response: 'Because McLaren has more than 500 people working on its F1 project. And all of them have got mortgages to pay.' I must admit that this observation rather stopped me in my tracks. Did he really think that the FIA – the governing body – would have risked putting McLaren out of business as the consequence of an adverse ruling from its World Motor Sport Council?

My friend briefly went quiet, then rolled his eyes. Clearly his implied response was an enigmatic 'perhaps'.

In the past, on several occasions, I've described Mosley as having that 'curiously unruffled and distant cordiality of the over-privileged' and I have to confess that he's fascinated me ever since that memorable occasion in July 1970 when he threw me out of his March Engineering factory at Bicester, for what reason I can't readily recall.

However, six years later he did a centre-piece interview with me for *Motoring News* in which he took a somewhat sanguine view of F1 politics, reassuring me that, 'Nobody's been shot and there's not going to be a war.' Well, he was half right, anyway. During Mosley's 17-year tenure as FIA president

nobody has actually been shot – as far as I can recall, anyway – but you could say that F1 has been pretty well continuously at war, arguing some issue or other, for most of that time.

Returning to the Ferrari-McLaren espionage issue, I must say that I didn't initially see the full implications when the whole thing kicked off. The notion of Mike Coughlan, the now-discredited McLaren chief designer, asking his wife to take a 780-page Ferrari design dossier to a copying shop in Surrey seemed so manifestly laughable that it was hard to take it seriously. Similarly the fact that he later apparently burned the document in a garden bonfire – it seemed so surreal that one began to look nervously at the calendar just to check that it wasn't actually 1 April.

Over at Ferrari the situation seemed similarly unlikely with engineer Nigel Stepney's walking out of the factory with all this data – and then meeting up at a Spanish yachting marina to deliver the bumf to Coughlan only for them to be accidentally witnessed by another F1 technical director who just happened to be there on holiday.

I frankly don't believe for a moment that any of the illegally acquired Ferrari intellectual property found its way onto a McLaren. But you are bound to have some sympathy with Ferrari's deep concerns in this matter and I wonder if they really received the convincing reassurance they were after, even though you also have to wonder how good their security is down at Maranello. Back on the McLaren side of the equation, I think it is quite clear that they may not have fully taken aboard the implications of the whole affair quite quickly enough.

If McLaren was guilty of anything it was of being too lax and a little bit sloppy, but not dishonest. But I can quite see why it would be particularly difficult to get Ferrari to accept that view.

As someone who's never been bothered with happy endings I

wasn't in the slightest bit worried that Lewis Hamilton failed to become the first rookie world champion. In my book he'd already done enough to convince the world that he was the best driver in the business and I'm privately quite pleased that Kimi Räikkönen won the title because it rules off decisively at the end of Michael Schumacher's rather dreary run of five successive championships.

In that connection, it was strange to see Schumacher at several grands prix acting in the role of advisor. Those with Machiavellian mindsets immediately concluded that this was designed to offer a psychological and technical leg-up for Felipe Massa, perhaps even at the expense of the incoming Räikkönen. Yet that interpretation assumed that Kimi would play ball. But he is such a self-contained personality that you sometimes wondered whether he even knew who the hell Schumacher was when they rubbed shoulders in the pits. Or cared, come to that.

All of which brings me to the question of team orders, a fluid issue in F1 circles, to say the least. The whole thing reminds me of that wonderful exchange in the *Yes Minister* television series when the harassed minister asks his private secretary, 'Where do we stand on this, Humphrey?'

His aide replies, 'Where one stands, minister, depends on where one sits.' In other words, 'Where would you like us to stand?'

McLaren quite legitimately got away with telling Lewis Hamilton to stay behind the increasingly paranoid Fernando Alonso in Monaco, although later some of the Woking brigade got very sniffy about Felipe Massa's relinquishing the lead to Räikkönen at Interlagos during the final round of refuelling stops. I'm bound to point out that McLaren needs to be wary on this one, bearing in mind the way it forced David Coulthard to yield wins to Mika Häkkinen in both the 1997 European and '98 Australian GPs. A senior McLaren source told me sniffily that the team was 'comfortable' with those decisions. Not a view shared by Coulthard, I might add.

F1 utterly dominates the motor sport scene. Forty years ago sports car racing eclipsed it in terms of status but, away from Le Mans, these days it attracts scant attention. It's just the same for the Indy 500. In '65 Jim Clark missed the Monaco Grand Prix to win at the Brickyard, yet when I listened to my TV commentating friend Peter Windsor recounting that story to Scott Speed, the former Toro Rosso driver replied incredulously, 'Why would he do that?'

I suppose you could ask Dario Franchitti, winner of this year's 500, the same question. Now worth a fortune, the amiable Scot is married to Hollywood A-list super star Ashley Judd and followed his win in the 500 with the overall Indy Racing League championship. Yet, somehow, a decade ago, Franchitti's hopes of making it in F1 never got off the ground. 'I had a run in a McLaren at Jerez in '95 but the opportunities were not really there in F1 at the time,' Dario recalled.

'My subsequent Jaguar test was a complete waste of my time and their money. It was done with the best of intentions,

and I really wanted to do something there, but once I saw how bad the car was, and how the team worked, it just didn't fit.'

He added, 'You always look back and say, "I'd love to have done F1", because that's what you dreamed about as a kid growing up. But I'm pretty happy the way it turned out.' Not too difficult to see why, Dario; not too difficult at all.

The entire UK motor racing fraternity was delighted that this mellow Scot had finally achieved such high-profile success, something that would normally have guaranteed him the front cover of the influential *Autosport* magazine. Unfortunately his success came on the day Lewis Hamilton lost in Monaco to Alonso. So that piece of key editorial coverage was sadly denied to him. Not a surprise, really, under the circumstances.

What looked being like a flat-out sprint to the finish between the two McLaren super stars Lewis Hamilton and Fernando Alonso raised memories of that epic contest 19 years ago that left the Woking squad caught up in a similarly gripping drama, between Alain Prost and the incoming Ayrton Senna.

The more you examine these two particular F1 case histories, the more dramatic and sharply drawn are the similarities. Bestriding both pairings, of course, was the overwhelming McLaren philosophy that it could manage drivers – particularly this kind of high-octane pairing – better than anybody else in the business.

Now, if you were a cynic you would conclude that the McLaren top brass was deluding itself. If you were a realist, however, after monitoring and examining in detail the historic realities of these ongoing feuds, you might well conclude that these partnerships are broadly unmanageable anyway: just like Nigel Mansell/Nelson Piquet and Alan Jones/Carlos Reutemann at Williams in the early '80s. The defining difference was that McLaren – and Williams, to be fair – was sufficiently feisty to

give it a go, accepting all the accompanying aggravation as just part of the background hubbub in the heat of high-octane battle between two top drivers.

Ah yes, I hear you say, but when Senna arrived to rain on Prost's parade at the start of the '88 season, Alain was very much the team's sitting tenant. This year Alonso was the experienced one being embarrassed by the incoming Lewis. Err, well, not quite, your honour. Lewis may have been a freshman to the cockpit of the MP4-22, but he's been a contracted McLaren driver for pretty much the past ten years.

Funny how, in F1, everything and nothing can be exactly the same. At precisely the same moment! Yet watching the deterioration of the relationship between Alonso and McLaren during the course of the season, it was almost as if both of them knew that it was coming adrift yet neither could react quickly or positively enough to correct the damage. Alonso would sit with his coterie of advisors in the McLaren brand centre, increasingly an embarrassed outpost of Spain within an enclave of the British empire. It got so bad that the FIA felt it was necessary to appoint an observer to ensure fair play in the season-ending Brazilian GP at Interlagos.

There are historical ironies attaching to this story, as well. It will not have escaped the attention of regular AUTOCOURSE readers that the FIA never appointed a 'special scrutineer' to look after the interests of Eddie Irvine or Rubens Barrichello when they were serving their stints as Michael Schumacher's assistants at the wheel of the number-two Ferrari.

Ironically, at the end of the day, while Schuey insisted on his *droit de seigneur*, the next man to win a world championship in a Ferrari did it after a fair and unfettered fight with his team-mate. So hats off to Kimi Räikkönen, I say.

I just hope he and the Finnish nation enjoy their celebrations.

**Left:** Fernando Alonso cut a somewhat isolated figure in the aftermath of his relationship breakdown with Ron Dennis.
Photograph: Peter J Fox/www.crash.net

**Below left:** Dario Franchitti's double of the Indianapolis 500 and the IRL title was the culmination of a decade of open-wheel racing. Here, he holds aloft the winner's trophy at Chicagoland.
Photograph: Paul Webb/LAT Photographic

**Below:** Kimi Räikkönen emerged as a worthy champion and his has been a universally well-received victory.
Photograph: Paul Webb/LAT Photographic

PERSONALITY PROFILE
# A STAR IS BORN
by SIMON ARRON

**Previous spread: Lewis Hamilton took the 2007 world championship by storm and only narrowly lost out to KImi Räikkönen in the title battle.**
Photograph: Peter J Fox/www.crash.net

**Below: With his mentor Ron Dennis. A fan of McLaren since the days of Ayrton Senna, Lewis looks likely to be a fixture there far into the future.**
Photograph: Paul-Henri Cahier

**Bottom: Hamilton weighs up his rivals' times during practice. He took six pole positions in his début year.**
Photograph: Peter J Fox/www.crash.net

BUCKMORE PARK, 1997: it's a chilly autumnal morning and the birdsong in the local woods is drowned out by the constant two-stroke yap of passing Junior Yamaha Super One karts. None of the drivers looks capable of reaching the pedals in a road car but here they're in their element. Mostly young boys barely beyond their 11-plus, they exude confidence and precision. There's one, in a distinctive yellow helmet, whom I recognise. I've seen him racing before, in the less-than-opulent surroundings of an indoor hall at Birmingham's National Exhibition Centre. That day he was up against some of Britain's national motor sport stalwarts in a charity kart event – and he drove rings around most of them (partly a function of his lightness, but mostly a reflection of his potential).

In the Buckmore paddock I strike up a conversation with his father and a few morsels of his vocabulary leave me speechless. 'Motor home', for instance. What's wrong with a diesel-powered estate, a roof rack and the odd night in a cheap B&B? Several things, apparently, not least that a motor home provides the budding racer with a retreat in which to

gather his thoughts. And he's able to stay late at the track, poring over every nut and sprocket and contemplating detail improvements. It's all about perfecting mental and practical preparations, I'm told.

How much does this cost? 'We spent £30,000 last year,' says Karting Dad, 'but if you are going to do it properly you need...' and he launches into a catalogue of essential spares and gizmos that complement the perfect, championship-chasing season. I don't know whether to feel impressed or bewildered. A bit of both, probably.

A decade passes before my next conversation with Karting Dad. Again we're in the paddock, but this time the park is Albert rather than Buckmore and the Australian Grand Prix is less than 48 hours away. I step forward to reintroduce myself and apologise for any cynicism that spiked my conversation ten years earlier: the überprofessional methods of Anthony Hamilton and his son Lewis might have seemed extreme within a karting context but the ends have more than justified the means. By the time of our reacquaintance, Hamilton junior's bolthole is no longer a creaky, family-run motor home, but McLaren's inner sanctum.

Anthony chuckles. 'That motor home was an old Bedford,' he says, 'and its purpose was simply to make life as easy as possible for Lewis. It also allowed all of us to go to races to watch him – and family support has always been a crucial part of his career. I thought I'd probably stop coming to watch if and when he got to F1, because I imagined it would be best to leave him to get on with it, but he's asked me to tag along and it's great to be here.'

And how did he feel, watching Lewis nose out of the McLaren pit for the first time? Another huge beam.

'Ecstatically proud,' he says, 'but other than that I'm not really sure. I'm still trying to make sense of the whole thing.'

He wasn't alone. For most of 2007, most of the motor sport industry was trying to make sense of Lewis Hamilton. Vodafone McLaren Mercedes offered him a prime Formula 1 seat but he'd be up against the sport's defending double world champion Fernando Alonso: there could be no finer benchmark, of course, but it was also, potentially, as good a way as any of shredding a reputation before it was properly forged. Any element of risk appeared laid to rest, however, by the time the season was but one corner old.

Fourth on the grid at Melbourne, Hamilton swept around Alonso's outside and went on to lead him for two thirds of the afternoon. It was a move born of primal racing instinct: the McLaren MP4-22 looked like an overgrown kart bent to comply with its driver's will – a theme that would recur throughout the season.

Look at Malaysia, where he outwitted both Ferrari drivers through the first two corners and then duped the potentially faster Felipe Massa into a litany of errors: one was in his second grand prix, the other in his 73rd, but you'd never have guessed as much.

When Hamilton crashed heavily during second free practice in Monaco on Thursday afternoon, everyone anticipated that he might in future temper his approach with a little more caution. Result? He was instantly fast when he returned to the track on Saturday, despite the fact that (a) it was raining and (b) he'd never driven an F1 car around Monaco in the wet before. His ability to get an immediate feel for unfamiliar conditions rapidly became a trademark.

**Above: Speed and style. The mercurial talents of Hamilton produced many moments of outrageous speed from his McLaren-Mercedes.**
Photograph: Bernard Asset

Montreal (dirty, slippery, dry circuit) and Fuji (dirty, slippery, wet circuit with near-zero visibility) provided the most testing conditions of the season and he won both races, despite never having seen either venue previously. Monza was an off-weekend, in relative terms (meaning Alonso was perceptibly quicker throughout), yet Hamilton salvaged second with one of the campaign's finest bits of improvisation: he shouldn't have been able to negotiate the first chicane after outbraking Kimi Räikkönen from a long way back, but having achieved objective number one he simply hurled the MP4-22 sideways to reduce its speed to a level the laws of physics might regard as acceptable. That kart thing again.

And then there was his qualifying lap in China. When Alonso switched to softer Bridgestones for a final run, he pared 0.178s from his previous best time. In identical circumstances, Hamilton found 0.702s. True, Hamilton had a slightly lighter car (to the tune of three laps' fuel), but comparing like with like he was still 0.4s clear of his team-mate.

You had to feel slightly sorry for Alonso, who subsequently threw his crash helmet around and kicked a door from its hinges in McLaren HQ before bleating to Spanish radio about impartial treatment. The truth, unpalatable as it might have seemed from a twice world champion's perspective, was that Hamilton's guilt amounted to no more than having driven an extraordinary, balls-out lap. The look of delighted bewilderment atop McLaren's pit counter was a clue that we'd just witnessed something special. 'There was no

mystery involved in Lewis's lap,' said team principal Ron Dennis, 'but there was a little magic.'

It's a frequently repeated mantra that modern grand prix cars are dull to watch but nobody told Hamilton. His McLaren's body language was rarely less than thrilling – and he was almost as articulate out of the car, despite his relatively tender years. Yes, he's been a part of the McLaren charm academy since he was at primary school, but he combines a polished approach with solid content and rarely shies away from questions. In Japan he was asked whether he thought it possible for him and Alonso to continue as team-mates in '08. Previous McLaren ambassadors would have swatted that one away. Mika Häkkinen might have grunted or grinned but wouldn't have bothered with any words, Kimi Räikkönen would have been less communicative still and David Coulthard would have conjured a measured, plausible response that didn't answer the question.

Hamilton's version ran as follows. 'No, I don't. I mean, if the team wants to keep him it keeps him but I'm here to stay.' Most things appear to be second nature to him but if you asked him to sit on a fence for two minutes he might struggle.

When he wasn't involved in mind games with his team-mate, his easy charm behind the microphone added to his global appeal. It was obvious that he'd be revered at Silverstone and despised in Spain (although the race was a little too early in the campaign for the effects of that to be felt in full – wait until '08), but he was adored, too, in Canada, America, China, Japan and other markets.

On a personal level, I detected a significant shift in the way F1 is perceived. My 13-year-old daughter, who had shown no previous appetite for the sport, asked me to get an autograph for the first time. My son, 16, began watching regularly again after a decade of indifference. My parents, who have always kept their enthusiasm for F1 under tight control and still wonder when I might get a proper job, began asking pertinent questions and, in Dad's case, started to get up at daft o'clock to watch Asian races live on TV. When the post arrived one morning, I automatically opened a magazine that had Lewis's face staring at me from the back cover, because I assumed it was something to do with me, but it turned out to be my wife's copy of *National Geographic*. That's a tiny snapshot of the Lewis Hamilton effect: factor in a global population approaching seven billion and you'll appreciate that the so-called hype is anything but. It's simply reality.

Despite falling agonisingly short in his quest for the world championship, Lewis Hamilton achieved a number of landmarks. He became the first driver of Afro-Caribbean descent to compete in F1, shook the sport from its mild torpor and opened it up to several key new audiences. In the process, he emerged as the most capable rookie to have graced the world championship in its 58 seasons.

More than that, though, his improvisation and car control were terrific to watch – and such important constants often tended to be overlooked beneath the fug of hyperbole.

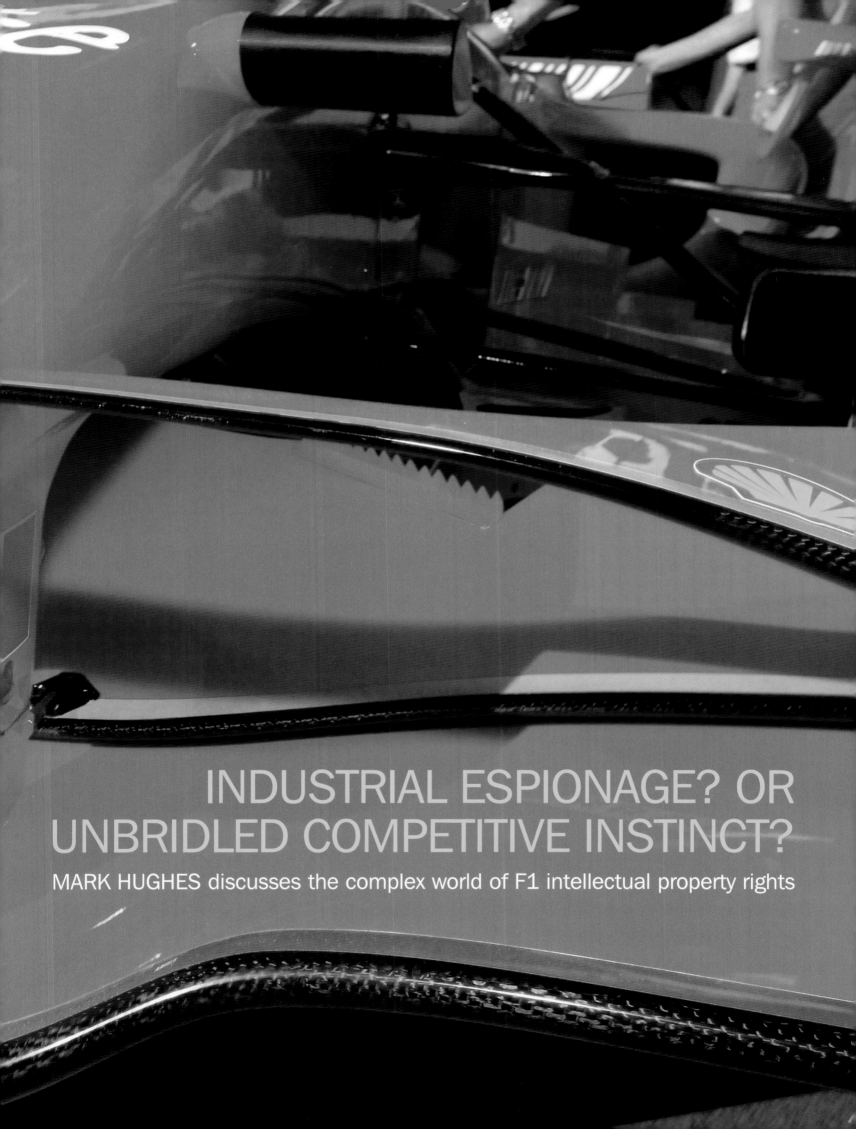

# INDUSTRIAL ESPIONAGE? OR UNBRIDLED COMPETITIVE INSTINCT?

MARK HUGHES discusses the complex world of F1 intellectual property rights

THE industrial espionage charges brought against McLaren by Ferrari centred on the concept of intellectual property rights. In F1, these are not the hard-and-fast things they are in the real world. The concept is a construct of the commercial world and how it deals with ownership of ideas and how profit is made from those ideas. Motor racing doesn't work quite like that and never has.

If it did, we might have a ridiculous situation: teams still using front-engined cars trying to beat Cooper. Or everyone except Ferrari banned from using aerodynamic wings – because, of the current teams, Ferrari was the first to use them in F1.

Take a look at the current grid and some of the design features. Carbon-fibre construction? Sorry, only McLaren can use that because it introduced it in 1981; back to the drawing board, the rest of you. Having the engine form a load-bearing role? Nope. If ever Lancia wishes to return to F1 it could have a load-bearing engine, but no-one else. In F1 terms, that's Lancia's intellectual property, dating to '54. Barge boards, the better to define the airflow and give the under-floor aero a boost? That was Henri Durand's invention for McLaren in '93. No-one else is entitled to it. Not unless they want to pay McLaren some royalty fee, perhaps? But McLaren would be under no obligation to accept such a deal. Cooling chimneys? Shadow-only, old chap ('79 DN9B). Shadow no longer exists? Then, arguably, Ferrari. Paddle sequential shift? Ferrari-only.

Where reasonable adaptation of new knowledge ends and blatant copying begins is a very blurred line in this sport. Back in '79 Tyrrell produced its 009 model and onlookers were astonished at its likeness to the previous year's dominant Lotus 79. It didn't just closely resemble the Lotus – it was visually identical and the likeness continued beneath the skin. There can be no doubt that a certain degree of what would now be called industrial espionage went into the design of that Tyrrell and it was maybe not a coincidence that Tyrrell's designer at the time was an ex-Lotus man.

In that very same year a new marque appeared, Rebaque, with a new car for independent driver and entrant Hector Rebaque. The previous year he had bought and raced a Lotus 78. This time he had gone one better and, just like Tyrrell, had a replica Lotus 79 built. He painted his brown. The Tyrrell was blue. The previous year's Lotus had been black. That really was the only way to tell them apart. The story of how the Rebaque took form is hysterically funny in the light of today's preoccupation with intellectual property (IP). 'We went up to a sub-contracted fabricator,' recalls one of the two men who 'designed' the car, 'and there was the jig for the Lotus 79. So we just used it.' Not only that, but the Rebaque was actually assembled at the British workshop of the American Penske CART team – and a car very like the Lotus 79 gained Penske an awful lot of success in the following couple of seasons in the American CART open-wheel series.

Going farther back than that, it would take a trained eye to tell the difference between a Lotus 25 (introduced in '62) and the BRP of the following year. In this case Lotus boss Colin Chapman actually took legal action for copyright infringement and the matter was settled out of court. In the Lotus 79-copy cases, he reportedly just shook his head in bemusement – the difference was that in early '79 he believed (wrongly) he already had the next big technological leap that would render the copies obsolete.

**Previous spread:** The F2007 Ferrari in Melbourne. Its dominant performance in the opening race of the season soon had rival teams searching for ideas to adapt and incorporate in their own machines.

**Opposite:** McLaren's Martin Whitmarsh and Ron Dennis found themselves unwittingly caught up in the aftermath of the 'Stepney-gate' affair. It cost their team dearly despite the fact that McLaren did not use any of the information.
Photographs: Peter J Fox/www.crash.net

**Centre:** Cooper began the rear-engined revolution that brought Jack Brabham back-to-back championships in 1959 and '60. It was to be the high-water mark of the Surbiton concern, which was quickly overtaken by the genius of Colin Chapman, whose monocoque Lotus 25, driven by Jim Clark, (below left) became *the* machine of the 1.5-litre era in the early '60s.

**Bottom:** The ground-effect Lotus 79 was totally dominant in 1978, helping Mario Andretti to win the world championship. This revolutionary design spawned many imitators, with various levels of success.
Photographs: www.crashpa.net

**Above: Williams and Toyota enjoy
a technical collaboration in which
intellectual property from both sides
is shared under an agreement phrased
in very firm and clear-cut legal terms.**
Photograph: Peter J Fox/www.crash.net

**Opposite: In 1978 the new Arrows
team arrived in Brazil with a replicated
version of Tony Southgate's Shadow DN9.
The courts later ruled that the designer
had breached Shadow's copyright
and a new and unrelated machine
had to be produced.**
Photograph: www.crashpa.net

Way back, before the term 'F1' was invented, grand
prix racing had its first IP row when former Hispano-Suiza
employees Ernest Henry, Paolo Zuccarelli, Georges Boillot and
Jules Goux transferred to Peugeot and created a radical new
twin-cam, 4v-per-cylinder racer that dominated grands prix for
the next couple of seasons. Hispano-Suiza claimed that the
engine technology of the car originated from a sports car
designed by its man Marc Birkigt. A civil action was brought
and a settlement reached.

Just a few months before the release of the 79 clone,
Shadow had taken successful legal action to prevent the
Arrows team from continuing to run its original car, the FA1.
A group of disaffected Shadow employees, including designer
Tony Southgate, had left to set up a new team. Southgate
took the view that he owned the IP in the DN9 he had just
designed for Shadow and he simply replicated it a few weeks
later for Arrows. The court ruled otherwise and Arrows had to
produce an unrelated replacement car, the A1 – which turned
out to be slower. This was one of the rare cases in which F1
resorted to law courts over the matter of ownership of design
and in this case an entire car was involved so it was maybe
not too surprising. But ideas, concepts, components even –
these things run between teams almost as if in the ether, and
always have done.

A fact not widely known is that the first carbon-fibre
McLaren, the MP4/1, ran with a gearbox casing fashioned

from Tyrrell patterns. An engineer who was there at the time
reports, 'Teddy Mayer came in with them under his arm one
day. He said he'd paid Tyrrell for them but no one asked to
see the receipt.'

When McLaren's designer John Barnard left the team, he
reportedly took with him nearly all of the drawings he'd done
during his time there.

He immediately joined Ferrari. In the early '90s, after he
left Ferrari and was running his own consultancy company,
he became technical director for Benetton. How on earth was
he supposed not to use the information in his possession – in
most cases information concerning his own ideas from his
own mind – in his new role? And this is just one high-profile
example. Think how many others there have been at all the
different levels.

This has just been the way of the racing world. It's a small,
incestuous environment, way too small to let a strict definition
of intellectual property rights run rampant. Do that and the
competitive structure of F1 would unravel.

But the concept does have a very important role to play
in the sport. In modern-day F1, intellectual property rights
are more commonly applied in agreements between teams
and partners. For example, Williams, stung by the feeling that
its former partner BMW had used Williams know-how to
design its gearbox, agreed very firm and clear-cut legal terms
with new partner Toyota over who owned design ideas. This

Left: Bobby Unser's Penske battles Mario Andretti's Wildcat for victory in the 1981 Indianapolis 500. The cars drew on both Formula 1 technology and John Barnard's ground-breaking Chaparral (below centre), which won the at the Speedway in '80.
Photographs: IMS

Below: Barnard's '81 McLaren MP4-1 was the first to feature a carbon-fibre tub.
Photograph: www.crashpa.net

has led to a reciprocal agreement whereby Toyota's engine supply to the team is offset against Toyota's using Williams' transmission technology in its own car. In this application, the concept of intellectual property is exactly as in the bigger outside commercial world. But trying to extend that to design ideas used by competing teams is an awkward stretch.

The Williams gearbox case is illuminating in other aspects, too. It incorporated technology initially sourced from a partner supplier, X-trac. There was a reciprocal commercial agreement between these two parties. But when a key Williams man left and joined another team and, soon afterwards, that other team developed a gearbox very similar to Williams', where did that leave X-trac? In such cases, IP law is very relevant in protecting the interests of technology companies involved in the sport. But to try to blanket-apply it throughout would be to destroy the fabric of how the sport works and prospers.

Designers and engineers are constantly changing teams, taking knowledge with them in their heads. It is asking the impossible for them not to apply that knowledge in their new teams. Often, that is precisely why they have been head-hunted. Furthermore, friendships remain between guys who have worked together in the past but are now in competing teams. They meet socially, they talk, are fascinated by the same subject; it's inevitable that they exchange ideas. This is normal – even if exchanging a 780-page document is not.

GIANCLAUDIO 'CLAY' REGAZZONI, one of the iconic figures of Ferrari Formula 1 history, was killed in a car crash in Italy at the age of 67 during December 2006, shortly after the last edition of AUTOCOURSE went to press. The five-times grand prix winner, who twice triumphed at Monza driving for Ferrari, was reported to have collided head-on with a truck on a main road near Parma while driving a Chrysler Voyager.

Nikki Lauda, his team-mate at Ferrari from 1974 to '76, paid tribute to a man whom he described as 'equalled only by James Hunt' in his ability to combine professionalism behind the wheel with the extroverted, fun-loving image of the traditional racing driver. 'Clay was the sort of guy you could never forget,' said Lauda. 'He died as he lived, simply taking life as it came. He was a great blend of the professional and the playboy. He enjoyed life and was never negative.

'Even after the accident in his Ensign in the US Grand Prix at Long Beach in '80, a crash that left him paralysed from the waist down, he made the best of his circumstances and was soon driving again in cars adapted with hand controls. When I joined Ferrari in '74 he was the star and I was the young kid and I learned a great deal from him.'

Regazzoni also won the hearts of British fans when he scored the Williams F1 team's maiden victory in the '79 British Grand Prix at Silverstone, the last such success of the Swiss driver's career.

A rough, tough and uncompromising competitor from the Swiss canton of Ticino, Regazzoni was always something of a maverick. In the late '60s, when the crusade for car and circuit safety was gaining momentum, Regazzoni was interested only in racing – and racing hard. Controversy was snapping at his heels for much of the time. In '68 he was implicated in the fatal accident involving the Englishman Chris Lambert's Brabham after a collision with Regazzoni's Tecno in the Dutch round of the European Formula 2 championship at Zandvoort. Regazzoni was subsequently exonerated.

In '70 he returned to Zandvoort for his F1 début at the wheel of a Ferrari, taking fourth place in a race marred by the death of the British driver Piers Courage, then two months later he scored a superb victory in the Italian Grand Prix after the world champion-elect Jochen Rindt was killed in practice.

He remained at Ferrari until the end of '72, then moved to the British BRM squad for a barren season before returning to Ferrari for another three-year stint. In '77 he drove for Ensign, in '78 for Shadow and then he celebrated his 40th birthday with Williams before returning to Ensign, where he ended his career the following year.

## EMMANUEL DE GRAFFENRIED

## ROBIN MONTGOMERIE-CHARRINGTON

The motor racing career of **BARON EMMANUEL 'TOULO' DE GRAFFENRIED**, who died aged 92 in January, began in the early 1930s and ended in the late '50s. It spanned his victory in the '36 Prix de Berne at the Bremgarten circuit, Switzerland, and effectively concluded with a seventh place in the '56 Italian GP. While he may have been a journeyman F1 driver, his great charm and unfailing courtesy ensured that he remained one of the most popular personalities in motor sport for decades after his retirement.

Born into a well-connected and wealthy Swiss family in Paris, De Graffenried was educated at the Institut Le Rosey in Switzerland, where fellow pupils included the future Shah of Iran. He settled down to enjoy a gilded existence, becoming involved in motor sport in his early 20s.

After his '36 victory – in an Alfa Romeo – he switched to the rival Maserati marque, with which his name was most closely associated for the rest of his career; its highlight was his victory in the '49 British Grand Prix at Silverstone, driving a Maserati 4CLT entered by Enrico Platé's private team. De Graffenried was the first to admit that this was a fortunate victory, with his rivals Luigi Villoresi, Reg Parnell and Prince Bira all taking turns to lead at various times before encountering mechanical misfortunes. In the end, the baron won at an average speed of 77.31 mph, ahead of Bob Gerard's ERA and the French Talbot driven by Louis Rosier.

De Graffenried continued to drive for Platé and in '53 posted his best world championship grand prix result with a fourth in the Belgian race at Spa-Francorchamps. Although De Graffenried was paying Platé for the privilege of driving his car, the two men became good friends and when Platé died after being hit by a spinning car in the pits at Buenos Aires the following year, De Graffenried's thoughts began to turn towards retirement.

In the early '50s, he contested events at the Gavea track in Rio de Janeiro and at Interlagos in São Paulo. He relished describing how he and his colleagues would travel to Brazil in the age before jet aircraft, when 'Christmas at sea on the way to South America was a great treat.' In '55 he emerged from semi-retirement to double for Kirk Douglas in action scenes for the movie *The Racers*. He did well financially out of that work – the production company was bowled over by having a real live F1 driver who was also an aristocrat on its books.

After Monza in '56 De Graffenried's career rather drifted to a halt. Two decades later his relaxed charm served to soften the commercial hard edge of American sponsors from the Philip Morris Marlboro brand. The tobacco multinational's European headquarters were in De Graffenried's home city Lausanne and the baron was quickly recruited for promotional work and glad-handing.

In retirement, De Graffenried continued with his successful Lausanne garage, which sold Alfa Romeos, Rolls-Royces and Ferraris. He was also a major force behind the retrospective meeting at the Dijon-Prenois circuit during the '74 French Grand Prix weekend. This reunited many pre- and postwar drivers and in many ways set the standards by which historic motor racing events have since been judged.

Enthusiastic amateur racer **ROBIN MONTGOMERIE-CHARRINGTON** died in April at the age of 90. He raced an 1100-cc Cooper in the early postwar years and, when his rival Bill Aston set about building his Aston-Butterworth F2 contender for the 1952 season, 'Monty' decided to acquire one of those machines. His only world championship outing was in that year's Belgian GP at Spa, where he retired from the race, but he finished third in the Grand Prix des Frontieres at Chimay before retiring from the sport at the end of that season.

# FORMULA 1 REVIEW

Photograph: Peter J Fox/www.crash.net

Contributors
**BOB CONSTANDUROS**

**MAURICE HAMILTON**

**ALAN HENRY**

F1 illustrations
**ADRIAN DEAN**

# VODAFONE McLAREN MERCEDES

**FERNANDO ALONSO**

**LEWIS HAMILTON**

© ADRIAN DEAN

## McLAREN MERCEDES MP4-22

| | |
|---|---|
| **SPONSORS** | Technology partners: **ExxonMobil • Bridgestone • BAE Systems • SAP** |
| | Corporate partners: **Vodafone • Johnnie Walker • Aigo • Hugo Boss • Santander • Hilton International • Schüco • Tag Heuer • Mutua Madriliña** |
| | Associate partners: **Steinmetz Diamond Group** |
| | Official suppliers: **Henkel • Nescafé Xpress • FedEx • Kenwood • Sonax • Advanced Composites Group • Enkei • Akebono • Kangaroo TV • GS Yuasa • Mazak Machine Tools • Belte • Sports Marketing Surveys • Sparco • SGI • Koni • Charmilles** |
| **ENGINE** | Type: **Mercedes FO 108T** No. of cylinders: **V8** Electronics: **McLaren Electronics Systems** Fuel: **Mobil Unleaded** Lubricants: **Mobil 1 products** |
| **TRANSMISSION** | Gearbox: **7 forward speeds and 1 reverse; semi-auto** Driveshafts: **McLaren** Clutch: **Hand-operated** |
| **CHASSIS** | Front and rear suspension: **Inboard torsion bar/damper system operated by pushrod and bell crank with a double wishbone arrangement** |
| | Suspension dampers: **Koni** Wheels: **Enkei** Tyres: **Bridgestone** Steering: **McLaren power-assisted** Battery: **GS Yuasa** Instruments: **McLaren Electronic Systems** |
| **DIMENSIONS** | Formula weight: **600 kg including driver** |

The McLaren Mercedes squad probably put more effort into the 2007 season than any in the team's history, but that did not prevent what should have been a thoroughly memorable year from turning into an *annus horribilis* that left the team's image tarnished in the eyes of some of its extraordinarily vehement critics.

On-track, McLaren produced a truly formidable contender in the MP4-22 and launched the F1 career of the remarkable Lewis Hamilton, who was paired with the seasoned double world champion Fernando Alonso to make up what most people regarded as the ultimate super-team. Sadly it didn't turn out quite as intended.

Off-track, the '07 season was dominated by the so-called 'spy-gate' controversy that centred on the controversial sequence of events in which a 780-page Ferrari technical dossier ended up in the hands of the now-disgraced McLaren chief designer Mike Coughlan. This led to McLaren's losing its constructors' championship points, being fined a swingeing $100 million and being described by Max Mosley, the FIA president, as having 'polluted' the world championship.

These misfortunes handed the constructors' trophy on a plate to Ferrari, but there were no doubts over Kimi Räikkönen's title-winning efforts on the drivers' front. All 17 races were shared between Ferrari and McLaren, with only BMW Sauber getting close as consistently the most impressive outsider.

McLaren's bruised reputation will surely be quickly repaired, although opinion in the paddock has been divided on this topic. Some hard liners believe that the British team knew full well what it was doing in acquiring the Ferrari data; others accept the team's explanation that the existence of the controversial documents was known only to a handful of individuals, most of whom might have been slow off the mark in understanding their full significance.

What is indisputable is that McLaren's claim that it can manage its driver relations better than almost everybody else in the pit lane now lies in ruins. The collapse of its relationship with Fernando Alonso, coming so soon after the Kimi Räikkönen-Juan Pablo Montoya partnership unravelled in '06, illustrates just how much the team needs to learn when it comes to dealing with its men behind the wheel.

By the end of the year it seemed almost inconceivable that Fernando Alonso could remain with McLaren for '08, even though he had completed just one year of a three-year contract. His acrimonious and non-communicative relationship with Ron Dennis, the McLaren chairman, makes the future look bleak.

Meanwhile, Ferrari has made it very clear that it will continue to press civil court actions against Mike Coughlan, who has been suspended from his role as McLaren chief designer, and its own former senior engineer Nigel Stepney, who leaked the documentation to Coughlan. There are no indications of how long such actions will take to come to final hearings but there must be some lingering concern that, when they do, there could be more uncomfortable revelations.

There could be more stress for McLaren before the start of the next season because the FIA intends to examine the '08 MP4-23 challenger in detail to satisfy itself that there is nothing in the concept that could be traced back to Ferrari. How this process will be initiated, what it will involve and against what time scale it will take place remain to be seen.

McLaren certainly did not stint when it came to developing the MP4-22. Its development period began before its predecessor the MP4-21 had even turned a wheel. Initial sketches of the aerodynamic concepts and discussions about the design of the clutch and gearbox took place back in December '05.

During the design process, each of the car's 11,000 components was reviewed in meticulous detail in the quest for improved performance, reliability and efficiency.

The MP4-22 represents the latest research and development concepts. Initial ideas were developed with computer aided design (CAD) in mid-March '06, with the first computational fluid dynamics (CFD) simulations running later that month. The wind tunnel programme began in May.

The design also incorporated three demanding new pieces of crash protection legislation. The totally new rear crash structure is noticeably wider and blunter than its predecessor. An extra 6-mm-thick laminated panel must now be bonded to the side of the driver cell to guard against penetration from another car or object. Frontal protection for the driver has been improved, with the velocity of impact in the crash test raised from 14 to 15 metres per second, with softer deceleration front and rear.

**Above: Lewis Hamilton took the season by storm, shaking up the Formula 1 hierarchy with his performances in the McLaren-Mercedes MP4-22.**
Photograph: Peter J Fox/www.crash.net

### TEAM McLAREN MERCEDES

Team principal: **Ron Dennis**

CEO, Formula 1: **Martin Whitmarsh**

Vice president Mercedes-Benz Motorsport: **Norbert Haug**

Managing director (McLaren): **Jonathan Neale**

Managing director, Mercedes-Benz: **Ola Källenius**

Design and development director: **Neil Oatley**

Head of engineering: **Paddy Lowe**

Head of vehicle engineering: **Mark Williams**

Head of aerodynamics: **Simon Lacey**

Race team manager: **Dave Ryan**

Chief mechanic: **Peter Vale**

Race engineer, car no. 1, Fernando Alonso: **Mark Slade**

Race engineer, car no. 2, Lewis Hamilton: **Phil Prew**

**Right: It was a season of fantastic success pervaded by a sense of abject failure for (from left to right) Ron Dennis, Martin Whitmarsh and Dave Ryan.**

**Below: Norbert Haug seems undecided about the contents of this edition of the *Red Bulletin*, the paddock's gossip mag.**
Photographs: Peter J Fox/www.crash.net

**Below right: Lewis Hamilton, very much at home in the McLaren family.**
Photograph: Bernard Asset

**Bottom: Reigning world champion Fernando Alonso joined the team full of optimism, but ended the season disenchanted with life at Woking.**
Photographs: Peter J Fox/www.crash.net

Other regulation changes that have affected the design process include the use of a homologated engine for '07 and the switch to a single tyre supplier. Mercedes did pretty much a perfect job in delivering an engine to the new 19,000-rpm rules – an engine that was both powerful and brilliantly reliable.

The construction and profile of the Bridgestone Potenza tyres had a strong influence on the MP4-22's chassis dynamics and, significantly, the aerodynamics. The tyres affect the flow structures downstream of the front wheels and the team's engineers used CFD software – to simulate heat and fluid flow – to devise the optimum solution to harness the new rubber.

With such detailed simulation increasingly vital in Formula 1, the infrastructure, manufacturing capacity and technical tools available to the design team at the McLaren Technology Centre played an important role. The MP4-22's development involved generating 4,500 components and 3,500 tooling drawings and the aerodynamics development was very demanding, with a continuous programme that required an entirely new set of wetted surfaces for the launch car, with around a third updated before the first race. This was followed up with new aero components brought to the car every three or four weeks throughout the season.

The net result of these efforts was a car that won eight of the season's 17 races, just one fewer than the Ferrari. Hamilton failed to finish in the points only twice, when he wound up ninth at the Nürburgring and after he slid into the gravel at Shanghai. Alonso's big shunt in heavy rain at Fuji was his only non-finish.

Nobody doubts McLaren's ability to bounce back. Quite how much damage has been done to its image and perceived integrity will probably take longer to settle into focus than it will take to win the next race. Its most loyal supporters believe the rehabilitation will be both deserved and complete.

Alan Henry

# BOMBARDIER
# LEARJET
# 45
# XR

**THE RACE IS ON.**

LIVE IT FAST. ROCKET YOUR ENTOURAGE TO THE ULTIMATE DESTINATION AT SPEEDS EXCEEDING 460 KNOTS.

LIVE IT LARGE. TREAT YOURSELF AND SEVEN GUESTS TO VOLUMINOUS CABIN COMFORT, FEELING RIGHT AT HOME, AWAY FROM HOME.

LIVE IT HIGH. CLIMB TO 43,000 FEET IN LESS THAN 25 MINUTES*. SOAR ABOVE THE CROWD AT 51,000 FEET.

LIVE IT IN STYLE. TOUCH DOWN ON THE RUNWAY, CREATING ANTICIPATION BEFORE YOUR NEXT RACE.

LIVE IT LIKE FOUR-TIME GRAND PRIX WINNER LEWIS HAMILTON, AND BECOME A LIVING LEGEND.

**WWW.LIVETHERACE.TV**

**BOMBARDIER**

BOMBARDIER
*LEARJET*

## ING RENAULT F1 TEAM

**GIANCARLO FISICHELLA**

**HEIKKI KOVALAINEN**

FORMULA 1's capacity for surprise can be summed up by the 2007 constructors' championship. It makes desperate reading for Renault as the points table shows a dramatic fall from grace by the champion of the previous two years. Having won 16 races across 2005 and '06, Renault struggled onto the podium just once in '07, an extraordinary decline by any standards and an extremely painful one for a team driven by the highest standards of engineering integrity and race-winning strategy.

The only significant question for the Anglo-French team at the end of the season was how it had managed to fail. That, in turn, would define its success in '07 as it relentlessly tracked down the problem and addressed it while coping with continual and excruciating disappointment every other week on the racetrack.

The trouble was two-fold: wind tunnel readings and tyres, a combination that gave Giancarlo Fisichella and Heikki Kovalainen a car that was difficult to drive. But how could a team with Renault's experience allow such fundamental failings? Had the previous success induced a degree of almost cocky self-assurance and a dangerous relaxation of checking procedures, particularly with regard to the wind tunnel?

'When you say it like that, it sounds awfully arrogant, doesn't it?' says Pat Symonds, Renault's executive director of engineering. 'But there is an element of it. The trouble is that over the years the expectations that you have of the wind tunnel have just got better and better and better. Years ago we checked absolutely everything that came out of the wind tunnel. We checked it on the car full size and we got to the point where the correlation was actually so damn good

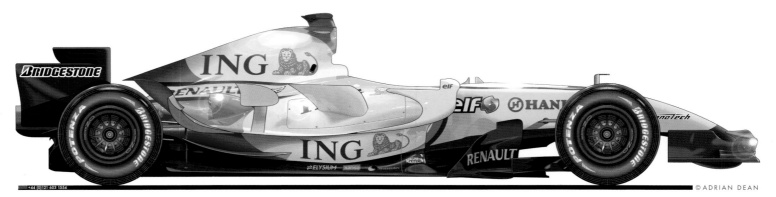

© ADRIAN DEAN

### RENAULT F1 R27

| | |
|---|---|
| **SPONSORS** | **ING • Renault • Elf • Bridgestone • Hanjin • Chronotech** |
| **ENGINE** | **Type: Renault RS27  No. of cylinders (vee angle): V8 (90°)  Sparking plugs: Champion  Electronics: Magneti Marelli Step 11** |
| | **Fuel: Elf  Oil: Elf** |
| **TRANSMISSION** | **Gearbox: Renault F1 7-speed longitudinal 'quickshift' (i.e. Seamless) Semi-auto: Electro-hydraulic actuation of gearchange, clutch and differential** |
| | **Hand-operated: clutch and gearchange  Driveshafts: Renault F1 integrated tri-lobe  Clutch: AP Racing** |
| **CHASSIS** | **Front and rear suspension: Double wishbone/pushrod operating torsion bar  Dampers: Penske** |
| | **Wheel diameter: 13 inch, front and rear  Wheels: OZ  Tyres: Bridgestone  Brake pads: Hitco  Brake discs: Hitco  Brake calipers: AP Racing** |
| | **Steering: Renault F1 hydro-mechanical servo system (power-assisted)  Radiators: Marston  Fuel tanks: ATL  Instruments: Renault F1 Team** |
| **DIMENSIONS** | **Track, front: 1,450 mm  rear: 1,420mm  Gearbox weight: 40kg  Chassis weight (tub): 68kg** |
| | **Formula weight: 605 kg including driver** |

that we just said, "Well, we don't need to check it any more." It slipped away without our realising it.'

Symonds points out that the wind tunnel problem alone would have been tricky but not impossible to solve. But the switch to Bridgestone and a single tyre supplier exacerbated the difficulty.

'They are separate issues and either one of them would have been troublesome,' says Symonds. 'The combination of the two was particularly bad. I have to say, though, that, while investigating this phenomenon, we trawled back an awful long way and discovered that part of the problem of wind tunnel correlation actually started when we were on Michelin tyres. So, we mustn't just point in one direction and look for single answers. Generally when something is this difficult to solve, it's because there isn't a single answer.

'We use pneumatic tyres in the wind tunnel so that these models are real representations of the proper tyres. We used to use carbon-fibre wheels and tyres, which were solid. Now the model tyres are made out of rubber and inflated. The construction of the tyre is such that, when scale loads are applied, it deflects to the same shape as a real tyre under the scale loads. They are immensely sophisticated little things.

'The representation that the Bridgestone model tyre gave in terms of its shape, when loaded, was not a precise replication of the real thing. It deflected differently. And that is an incredibly critical area. You can get very critical aerodynamics where they switch between states. If you can imagine a bit of flow that attaches and detaches repeatedly: it's unstable. You have a car that one minute is quicker than it is another minute. That is a terribly difficult car to drive. That was our problem at the

beginning of the season.'

This was the worst possible news for Kovalainen as he made the step up from test driver into the race team following Fernando Alonso's departure to McLaren. Formula 1 is complicated enough for a novice without having to perform with a car that is unforgiving and unpredictable.

'Rookies make mistakes: that's what it's all about,' says Symonds. 'We gave Heikki a car that was pretty well different at every corner he turned into. It made things very difficult at a time when he was getting on top of the switch from test driver to race driver. As for Fisi, his experience and his coolness, and the fact that he'd been through it all before, actually allowed him to keep calm, not overdrive and get a better result out of the car than Heikki could manage. Fisi knew that the car was going to bite him, so he kept it at a level where that wasn't going to happen and ultimately got a better result with it.'

As Renault began to nail down the problem and react to it, the emphasis shifted as Kovalainen began a strong second phase of the season whereas Fisichella appeared not just to stand still but also to make fundamental mistakes such as crashing because he forgot about cold brakes after starting from the pit lane for the Belgian Grand Prix. In a difficult year such as this, it was the last thing a team needed from a driver with more than 190 grands prix to his credit.

The turning point for Kovalainen came in Canada. Having trashed two cars during practice and the first phase of qualifying, he started from the back of the grid and came through a safety car-riddled race to finish a very fine fourth. It was, according to team principal Flavio Briatore, as if Kovalainen's brother had been driving the car on Friday and

## RENAULT F1 TEAM

**President: Bernard Rey**

**Managing director: Flavio Briatore**

**Deputy managing directors, France: Rob White, André Lainé**

**Technical director: Bob Bell**

**Deputy technical director: James Allison**

**Executive director of engineering: Pat Symonds**

**Head of race engineering (engine): Denis Chevrier**

**Chief race engineer: Ala Permane**

**Chief designer: Tim Densham**

**Engine project leader (RS27): Axel Plasse**

**Head of aerodynamics: Dino Toso**

**Sporting manager: Steve Nielsen**

**Chief mechanic: Gavin Hudson**

**Race engineers, car no. 3, Giancarlo Fisichella: David Greenwood, Phil Charles, Ricardo Penteado**

**Race engineer, car no. 4, Heikki Kovalainen: Adam Carter, Simon Rennie, Rémi Taffin**

**Top: Giancarlo Fisichella failed to register a single podium finish in a disappointing season.**

**Above left: Flavio Briatore, still running the show for Renault.**

**Above far left: Title sponsor ING was a major presence in Formula 1 throughout the 2007 season.**

Photographs: Peter J Fox/www.crash.net

Above: Heikki Kovalainen acquitted himself well in a difficult début season.

Right: Deputy managing director Rob White.

Centre right: Pat Symonds.

Right: Technical director Bob Bell.

Below: Nelson Piquet Jr held the role of test driver, patiently waiting for his chance of a full-time drive.

Opposite: Giancarlo Fisichella and Renault in Malaysia. Early in the season, the team had problems making the R27 chassis work effectively on Bridgestone tyres.

Photographs: Peter J Fox/www.crash.net

Saturday, only for the driver they had been hoping to see all along emerge on race day. Kovalainen went on to score points in eight of the next nine races, the highlight a gutsy and flawless drive into second place in atrocious conditions in Japan. By then, Renault had gone a long way to discovering the source of its technical shortcomings.

'What we had was a car that was now consistent, one that had its major problem solved,' says Symonds. 'What it lacked was the nine months of development that it took us to discover the problem, be rigorous and ensure that we had understood it. So we had a car that was at least easier to drive but lacked the performance by being effectively an out-of-date car. At least Heikki was able to use the car, not make mistakes and produce some reasonable results with it.'

Symonds successfully relinquished part of his day-to-day role to Alan Permane, the chief race engineer. Meanwhile, the Enstone-based technical team led by Bob Bell, Tim Densham and Dino Toso dealt with their chassis and aerodynamic problems. Symonds mentions James Allison in particular for his dogged determination to find a solution. In Paris, Rob White and his engine division continued to provide reliable and, according to Fisichella and Kovalainen, extremely driveable V8s. Apart from an oil leak at Spa, the season was trouble-free. Which is just as well because an unreliable engine would have been a distraction the team did not need as it applied itself to the task of sorting out the car.

'When you've won two championships in a row, it gets exponentially harder to maintain that,' says Symonds. 'The second one is harder than the first one, the third one harder than the second and so on. But, in spite of the reality that to win continually is near-impossible, it's still very, very disappointing to drop from being in a position to near enough challenge for every win to a point where at the start of this season our performance was a good two percent off that of the front runners. That is hard to take.

'Our primary objective is to go out and win races and one can never be satisfied with a season like we've had. But there are a few positives. While we're not proud of the fact that we got into this situation, we should be proud of the very pragmatic approach we've taken to getting out of it. That took longer than I expected. Once we really crashed into it, mid to end of February, when we said, "Look, this is massive," I did hope that we'd get a slightly quicker solution. But you can't rush things like that. I think all of us know that it has happened to plenty of teams over the years and we've seen those who – perhaps because of outside pressure – have had to use the scattergun approach and change everything in the hope that it will work. That's never worked.

'We've been rigorous, we've been honest with ourselves, we've done everything in very logical steps, so that we now approach building an '08 car with a certain knowledge of what went wrong in '07 – and therefore high in confidence that we can get back to challenging at the front again.'

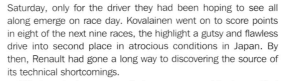

Maurice Hamilton

5

6

**FELIPE MASSA**

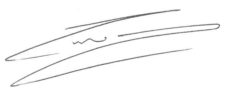

**KIMI RÄIKKÖNEN**

© ADRIAN DEAN

## FERRARI F2007

| | |
|---|---|
| **SPONSORS** | Title sponsor: **Philip Morris**  Major sponsors: **FIAT • Shell • Bridgestone • Alice • Martini • Acer • AMD** |
| **ENGINE** | Type: **Ferrari 056**  No. of cylinders (vee angle): **V8 (90°)**  Total displacement: **2,398 cm³**  Bore: **98 mm**  Weight: **95 kg** <br> Sparking plugs: **NGK**  Electronics: **Magneti Marelli**  Fuel: **Shell V-power ULG 62**  Oil: **Shell SL-0977** |
| **TRANSMISSION** | Gearbox: **Ferrari longitudinal gearbox, limited-slip differential; semi-automatic sequential electronically controlled gearbox – quick shift** <br> Number of gears: **7 plus reverse**  Clutch: **AP Racing** |
| **CHASSIS** | Front and rear suspension: **Independent suspension, pushrod-activated torsion springs front and rear**  Dampers: **Sachs** <br> Wheel diameter: **13" front and rear**  Wheels: **BBS**  Tyres: **Bridgestone**  Brake discs: **Brembo ventilated carbon-fibre disc brakes** <br> Brake pads: **Brembo/Carbon Industry**  Brake calipers: **Brembo** |
| **DIMENSIONS** | Wheelbase: **3,135 mm**  Front track: **1,470 mm**  Rear track: **1,405 mm** <br> Overall length: **4,545 mm**  Overall height: **959 mm**  Overall width: **1,796 mm** <br> Formula weight: **605 kg including driver** |

**Above: Felipe Massa's inclusion provided the Scuderia with two top-line drivers. He was a contender in the four-way battle for the championship until late in the season.**
Photograph: Peter J Fox/www.crash.net

'WE must not forget that in Japan he was 17 points behind and today he is one ahead,' said Jean Todt after Kimi Räikkönen came from behind to clinch the world championship for drivers with a dominant win in Brazil.

'So he took 18 points in two races. I always said that until mathematically it is over, we still believe we can make it. That is what we did. Kimi won the first race so we were strong from the beginning of the championship. We had too many failures but at the end we can be happy tonight.'

It was not just a victory for Ferrari and Kimi Räikkönen – it was a victory for an entirely new regime at Maranello. A year earlier, Brazil had marked the final race for technical director Ross Brawn, multi-champion Michael Schumacher and engine guru Paolo Martinelli, now replaced respectively by Mario Almondo, Räikkönen and Gilles Simon, whose department provided engines to Scuderia Toro Rosso and Spyker as well as the factory team.

It was a change that did not necessarily please everyone. Exactly a year before Räikkönen's championship clincher, the team's race technical manager admitted that he felt unhappy with the prospects of the new regime. It was a dissatisfaction that was to have dramatic consequences.

The biggest change, however, was the loss of Schumacher and Brawn, the former because of his talent on the track and inspirational leadership, the latter because of his all-embracing control and leadership in the factory and on-circuit, covering many aspects of Ferrari's mainly successful championship campaigns for many years. As his replacement, Almondo, explained, 'I am the technical director, but this is not to be confused with the task undertaken by Ross Brawn, who was the chief at the track as well. That task will be undertaken by Luca Baldisseri. Aldo Costa is head of the chassis design; chief designer is Nicolas Tombazis.

'It is not one single person; each person does his own work. It's a well-prepared team and we will work 200 percent with intent and energy; we all want to work together. We will refine this organisation over the next few months and set up this collaboration. We have Felipe [Massa] already and we will introduce Kimi to this organisation.'

Before its launch, Almondo described the new F2007 as innovative. 'We have gone into possible developments with Shell [to maximise the energy/power delivered by the engine and limit friction and engine temperature], as well as a new gearbox. There are a few major technical novelties, not overall, but strong, intelligent, extremely technical novelties in the car – things that have not been done in the past.'

Costa pointed out that 'the car was a good development from the previous year's car. We introduced some new things. One of the more evident modifications was the [longer] wheelbase, which we have done for the specific reason that we wanted better space for aerodynamic development. These characteristics had some positive aspects and no big negative aspects in vehicle dynamics were found, so we decided to go in that direction.'

New tyre regulations meant that everyone was on Bridgestone tyres, as Ferrari had been since 1999. Costa pointed out that there was no advantage from having developed Bridgestone's tyres in the past. 'Last year the game was to try to develop the tyres – we were focusing with Bridgestone on developing new tyres, new tyres, new tyres, new compounds, new constructions.

'This year was completely different. You have got these four tyres, four compounds, and you have to optimise your car around them. That's your fixed constraint; then you have to think about the various possibilities to gain performance from pressure management, from camber settings, toe settings, tyre warmers, everything around the tyres. How can I find performance around the tyres to make the tyres work better?

'It was probably why this year we found our competitor stronger on bumpy circuits and the kerbing because over the past few years we didn't concentrate very much on that because it was much better to invest time in new tyres, new tyres, new tyres.'

The regulation change affected Räikkönen more than Massa, according to Luca Baldisseri. 'We were generally struggling with Kimi a bit at the beginning because he had some trouble to adapt his driving style to our car, to learn all our systems and to learn the Bridgestone tyres, but I have to say that from mid-season onwards he was at the same level as Michael.'

## SCUDERIA MARLBORO FERRARI

**President: Luca di Montezemolo**

**Managing director and team principal: Jean Todt**

**Technical director: Mario Almondo**

**Engine director: Gilles Simon**

**Team manager: Stefano Domenicali**

**Head of car design: Aldo Costa**

**Chief designer: Nikolas Tombazis**

**Chief aerodynamicist: John Iley**

**Electronics: Roberto Dalla**

**Chief race engineer: Luca Baldisserri**

**Race engineer, car no. 5, Felipe Massa: Rob Smedley**

**Race engineer, car no. 6, Kimi Räikkönen: Christopher Dyer**

**Top: The Ferrari team poses for a celebration photograph following Kimi Räikkönen's win in the Chinese Grand Prix.**
Photograph: Jean-François Galeron/WRi2

**Above: Jean Todt wears a smile of quiet satisfaction.**

**Above right: There were plenty of podium visits for both Felipe Massa (centre) and Kimi Räikkönen.**

**Opposite: Kimi Räikkönen at speed in the United States Grand Prix.**
Photographs: Peter J Fox/www.crash.net

**Below: Technical director Mario Almondo.**
Photograph: Jean-François Galeron/WRi2

Ferrari was the pre-season pace-setter, although McLaren was close behind. Ferrari had two drivers of equal status who might perhaps take points off one another; McLaren had a world champion and a rookie, so it might have seemed that everyone's status there was more clear-cut...

Todt constantly pointed to a lack of reliability that cost Ferrari dearly, but that was because the level of reliability in '07 F1 was so high. The roll-call of problems is not long, however crucial they may have been. Felipe Massa suffered a gearbox problem in Australian qualifying and, while Räikkönen won, Massa had an engine change, started last and finished sixth.

It was here that there was a clarification on Ferrari's floor stay, which went against them. Costa said it wasn't a big thing, that it had been around in F1 for many years and wasn't that crucial.

Massa had his revenge for his Australian retirement with pole position in Malaysia but then made a poor start and finished fifth. Räikkönen had suffered a water leak in Australia and drove a relatively restrained race to maintain his third place on the grid in the race.

Stung by criticism of his Malaysian start, Massa put his Ferrari on pole and won in Bahrain, while Kimi was equally consistent with third place. Fernando Alonso, Lewis Hamilton and Räikkönen all had 22 points. There was a big update in terms of aerodynamics for Spain, where Massa again won from pole while Räikkönen retired with an electronic problem.

Massa started and finished third in Monaco but Räikkönen suffered from hitting the barrier exiting the Swimming Pool in qualifying and started 16th. There was also at this point an early indication of poor performance on Bridgestone's super-soft tyre, also used in Canada, Hungary and Brazil, and its performance over kerbs.

'McLaren probably understood better than us how to manage the super-soft tyre in Monaco,' said Costa. 'We also had problems managing it in Canada. At Budapest it was less and in Brazil we demonstrated that we no longer had a problem. So, yes, there was a learning curve.'

It was about this time that the team suffered a breakage of its wind tunnel, which put it out of action for two weeks – not

a huge loss, said Costa. There were however modifications in Canada, perhaps the team's worst race, where Massa was disqualified for rejoining against a red light and Räikkönen finished fifth. They were thrashed by the McLarens at Indy, as well. Ferrari was now 35 points behind McLaren in the constructors' series, Massa 19 behind Hamilton and Räikkönen another seven points back.

Modifications came thick and fast in France and Britain and so did points, as Räikkönen won both, only to suffer a hydraulic failure in the European Grand Prix, although Massa finished second. The pendulum of fortune swung against Massa in Hungary with an odd refuelling mistake in qualifying that left him 13th in the race but Räikkönen was second.

Revenge was sweet with a dominant one-two in Turkey, only for the team to suffer again over the kerbs at Monza. Räikkönen shunted on Saturday morning but finished third while Massa retired with a rear-suspension failure. Räikkönen was 18 points behind Hamilton in the drivers' championship, Ferrari 23 behind McLaren. All that, of course, became academic in Belgium and the drivers' gap came to 13 points with Ferrari's first front row of the year and third one-two finish.

With more updates to the car, in the chaos of Japan they salvaged third and sixth in spite of the extra pit stop to change to the pre-ordained extreme wet-weather tyre – the case of the missing email. The drivers' gap was still 17 but it came down to seven points in China, where Räikkönen won and Massa finished third.

And in Brazil Räikkönen picked up another ten points and was followed home by pole-winning team-mate Massa to clinch the world championship in a dominant display. 'Everything has been perfect,' said Todt. 'Pole position, quickest lap during the race, fantastic job from the team, from the drivers: Kimi, Felipe. In the final result Kimi has been outstanding. The car has been very strong; the team has been very strong. We were not expecting to finish the season like that. Nine wins. Nine pole positions.'

Bob Constanduros

**JENSON BUTTON**

**RUBENS BARRICHELLO**

Photographs: Peter J Fox/www.crash.net

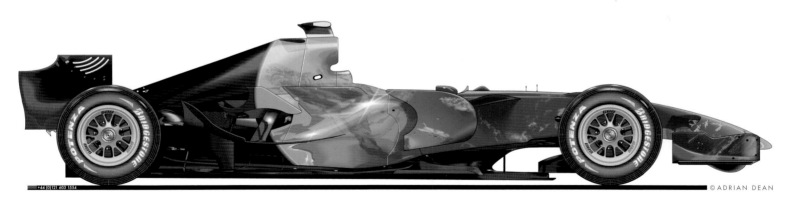

+44 (0)121 603 1554

© ADRIAN DEAN

## HONDA RA107

| PARTNERS | Bridgestone • Celerant • Eneos • Fila • Gatorade • NGK • NTN • Ray Ban • Seiko • Universal Music Group |
|---|---|
| ENGINE | **Type:** Honda RA807E  **No. of cylinders (vee angle):** V10 (90°)  **Ignition:** PGM-IG  **Injection system:** PGM-F1  **Oil:** Eneos |
| TRANSMISSION | **Gearbox:** Carbon composite maincase ; 7-speed unit Honda internals  **Gear selection:** Sequential, semi-automatic, hydraulic activation  **Clutch:** Carbon plate |
| CHASSIS | **Front and rear suspension:** Wishbone and pushrod-activated torsion springs and rockers; mechanical anti-roll bar  **Dampers:** Showa<br>**Wheel diameter, front:** 312 mm **rear:** 340 mm  **Wheels:** BBS forged magnesium  **Tyres:** Bridgestone  **Brake discs:** Alcon carbon  **Brake pads:** Alcon carbon<br>**Steering:** Honda F1 power-assisted rack and pinion  **Fuel tank:** ATL  **Instruments:** Honda steering-wheel F1carbon fibre construction |
| DIMENSIONS | **Overall length:** 4,700mm  **Overall height:** 950mm  **Overall width:** 1,800mm<br>**Formula weight:** 600 kg including driver |

Honda came off the back of the 2006 season of F1 racing in an understandably upbeat mood, Jenson Button having scored the marque's first contemporary grand prix victory in Hungary and followed up with a run of success, scoring regular points through to the end of the year. The team was optimistic that it could sustain this momentum into '07, but although initial wind tunnel testing results from the new RA107 looked promising, they did not correlate with the car's performance from the moment it rolled out onto the track.

'It was quite clear from the start that the RA107 had a pretty serious aerodynamic imbalance, with the centre of pressure effectively shifting backwards and forwards under acceleration and braking,' explained team principal Nick Fry. 'We really identified the problem at the early-season Bahrain test and it was our view that it was a problem that could be overcome. But when it came to addressing it we found it was perhaps a little more complicated than we had originally thought. The figures were fairly horrific but we mistakenly thought we could overcome them.'

Certainly the season's racing got off to a bad start in the first three fly-away races – Australia, Malaysia and Bahrain – with neither Jenson nor Rubens Barrichello getting anywhere in sight of the top ten during qualifying and playing very much bit-part roles in the races themselves.

It was all hugely disheartening but there was nothing for it but simply to slog on and see what might realistically be salvaged from what was already unfolding into a depressing scenario.

'The fixes we originally came up with simply didn't work,' explained Fry. 'So we knuckled down to a pretty intensive programme of development during the first few months of the year. These developments included under-cut sidepods, major changes to the front suspension for aerodynamic reasons and so on. None of those things proved to be totally effective, although they were definitely minor moves in the right direction.

'This sequence of problems moved us towards thinking in terms of taking an early decision to slow development on the current car and effectively use it as a prototype on which to assess ideas and concepts for the '08 car.

'The main problem has been aerodynamics – what we designed was fundamentally a car that, for example, was structurally very good, but that had elements such as the suspension that were not perhaps as aerodynamically efficient as they needed to be.'

Fry believes that it is unfair and unrealistic for Honda's critics to portray the team as an organisation that is floundering and adrift. He believes that the team's problems are quantifiable and have the potential to be rectified through a logical and structured approach.

'You just have to look at the second half of the '06 season to see where we can be relative to the opposition,' he said, 'and it's my task to steer us back towards that competitive level by the start of the '08 season. I think this an entirely reasonable target.'

Fry is also quick to point out that any strategic decisions taken by the race team are by definition approved by the Honda senior management in Japan. He quashes the notion that the F1 team is something of an independent operator that sometimes agrees with the senior management's strategy and sometimes takes an independent line.

'The team is wholly owned by Honda,' he said, 'so any decisions we might take are obviously taken with Honda's approval.'

While the aerodynamic improvements the team is now seeking fall within the responsibility of newly appointed chief aerodynamicist Loïc Bigois, who made the switch from Williams in the middle of the season, Fry is confident that other aspects of the car are suitably robust and competitive – notably the V8 engine and its transmission package.

'I think the spread of power across the range of engines currently competing in F1 is pretty small, although there are variations in quite how they deliver that power, something

**Above: Jenson Button drove with just as much skill as ever, but sadly the RA107 couldn't do justice to his talent.**
Photograph: Peter J Fox/www.crash.net

## HONDA RACING TEAM

**Chief executive officer: Nick Fry**

**President, HRD: Yasuhiro Wada**

**Technical director, HRD: Yosuke Sekino**

**Engine director, HRD: Shuhei Nakamoto**

**Engineering director: Jacky Eeckelaert**

**Deputy technical director: Gary Savage**

**Chief designer: Kevin Taylor**

**Chief race engineer: Craig Wilson**

**Race engineer, car No. 7, Jenson Button: Andrew Shovlin**

**Race engineer, car No. 8, Rubens Barrichello: Jock Clear**

**Race-team manager: Ron Meadows**

**Chief mechanic: Alastair Gibson**

**Opposite: Jenson Button steps into the RA107.**

**Right: Team principal Nick Fry.**

**Centre right: Sporting director Gil de Ferran, who left in mid-season.**

**Far right: Jacky Eeckelaert.**
Photographs: Peter J Fox/www.crash.net

**Above: Rubens Barrichello's season was so disastrous that the popular Brazilian failed to score even a single championship point.**

**Below: Christian Klien spent the season out of the limelight performing testing duties for the team.**
Photographs: Peter J Fox/www.crash.net

that may become a little more significant in '08 when traction control is banned,' he said. 'But for the moment, yes, I think our engine and gearbox are strong elements of the car.'

Rationalising the situation in such positive terms may be good for morale, yet the truth of the matter is that this was a dismal season when it came to hard results. Not until the French GP did Button manage to coax the RA107 over the finishing line to take eighth place and the team's first point of the season. And there were precious few such points waiting farther down the road. Jenson was fifth in China, but unfortunately threw away what looked like a possible podium finish in the torrential rain at Fuji when he dislodged his car's nose cone against a rival in the blinding spray early in the race.

Inevitably the two drivers shouldered the burden of the team's disappointment because the role of driver makes them responsible for carrying the team's public face. Fry admitted that he was impressed by the way they handled the challenge, particularly if you considered the backdrop against which their efforts were set.

Button handled the arrival of Lewis Hamilton on the F1 scene with considerable resilience and good humour, even though journalists have become familiar with the narrowing of his eyes in thinly veiled exasperation when faced with any question starting, 'What do you think of Lewis...'

It is the perception from the touchlines that Button may be tougher and more resilient than Barrichello and perhaps a touch hungrier as he yearns for the sort of success that Rubens enjoyed at Ferrari.

'Jenson is totally committed and flat-out from the first corner, all the time,' said Fry admiringly.

'As for Rubens, I believe he still has all his skill and potential but, by the same token, I fully accept that after 15 years in F1, when we have presented him with a car that is less than fully competitive, it may sometimes be hard for him to maximise his motivation.'

Producing that better car is the overwhelming challenge facing Honda in '08.

Alan Henry

**9**

NICK HEIDFELD

ROBERT KUBICA

**10**

SEBASTIAN VETTEL

© ADRIAN DEAN

## BMW SAUBER F1.07

| | |
|---|---|
| **SPONSORS** | Petronas • Intel • Credit Suisse • Dell • Syntium |
| **TECHNICAL PARTNER** | Bridgestone |
| **SUPPLIERS** | Certina • Dalco • Dräxlmeier • DuPont • Fluent Inc • MAN • NGK • Puma • Walter Meier • Würth • ZF Sachs |
| **ENGINE** | Type: **BMW P86/87**  No. of cylinders: **V8**  Electronics: **BMW**  Oil: **Petronas** |
| **TRANSMISSION** | Gearbox: **7-speed longitudinal, quick shift**  Clutch: **AP Racing** |
| **CHASSIS** | Suspension: :  **Upper and lower wishbones (front and rear), pushrods**  Dampers **Sachs Race Engineering** |
| | Wheel diameter: **330 mm front and rear**  Wheels: **OZ**  Tyres: **Bridgestone**  Brake pads and discs: **Brembo/Carbon Industrie** |
| | Brake calipers: **Brembo**  Steering: **BMW Sauber F1 Team power steering**  Radiators: **Calsonic, Modine**  Instruments: **BMW Sauber F1 Team** |
| **DIMENSIONS** | Length: **4,580 mm**  Width: **1,800 mm**  Height: **1,000 mm**  Wheelbase: **3,110 mm** |
| | Formula weight: **605 kg** |

'WE started from fifth place in the world championship in 2007 – with 36 points earned in our début season [as a BMW-owned team],' said BMW Sauber's team principal Mario Theissen. 'For this season we set ourselves the goal of halving the gap to the leading cars.

'We hit that target in the first three races of the season and in Bahrain we narrowed the margin even farther. We have established ourselves firmly as the third-strongest team on the grid, exceeding our expectations. I'm particularly pleased that the gap to the teams in front is smaller than our advantage over the cars behind.'

Theissen was speaking early in the season and his team didn't disappoint in the races to come. Later, he would admit that the deficit to the top two teams was 'about half a second' but that didn't prevent drivers Nick Heidfeld and Robert Kubica from frequently qualifying in or racing to fourth place – and occasionally better – meaning they had infiltrated the top two teams. Only in the final few races of the '07 season did Ferrari and McLaren lock out the top four places with more success.

Once Renault, Honda and Toyota had handicapped themselves in one way or another, BMW Sauber was there gratefully to grab that third place in the hierarchy. It shouldn't have been a surprise. This was a team on the ascendancy, improving its resources but also enjoying stability in key areas.

As technical director Willy Rampf said mid-season, 'Over the winter we had a development programme and I think it was the first time that we were able to do all the development we planned, because we have more people, we have more resources and we have more time in the wind tunnel. I think we did quite a good job over the winter – even better than we expected. We basically fulfilled our requirements and our targets.'

Theissen explained, 'The workforce in Hinwil is up from 275 previously to just over 400. We have a three-shift system in place in the wind tunnel and our new supercomputer Albert2 is up and running. We will have reached our target of 430 employees by the end of the year. And then there is the new factory, which is scheduled for completion in time to have us operating at full power come the start of the '08 season.'

Rampf expanded on this. 'The wind tunnel, as everybody knows, is the most important tool in Formula 1, but we have increased the wind tunnel hours by a factor of, let's say, 2.5 from about one and a half years ago to now. Similarly the computational fluid dynamics [CFD]: we have increased the capacity by a factor of three to four, which means we can do much more development in this direction.'

Vital to all specialist tools was Albert2, the team's new 21-ton computer lurking in the basement. Five times more powerful than its predecessor, it is capable of 12.3 teraflops – 12.3 billion floating point operations per second – working on endless simulations and both establishing and backing up the CFD and the wind tunnel's findings 'When we started with the wind tunnel, we were quite careful with all the calibration and everything to be 100-percent sure that what we measured in the wind tunnel was what we see on the track and so far we have good correlation,' explained Rampf. 'That also helped us over the winter by changing the tyre and still being ahead of the internal target of aero development.'

It also allowed them to simulate the tyre deformation of the new Bridgestones. 'We knew how critical it was and as soon as we got the tyres we started very early on to try to have a good relationship between the model tyres and then the tyre that we used on the track.

'We have pneumatic tyres for all the development and it was clear to us that there was a big difference [by comparison with the previous tyres]. It was a question of time and effort to come step by step closer to the reality. It was not a surprise that the tyres were different. We expected it and we made a plan to work it out.'

However, the F1.07 was conceived to take into account the Bridgestone monopoly. 'The regulations were more or less the same, apart from some safety features. It was an evolution of last year's car but evolution with a lot of detailed changes compared with last year's car,' continued Rampf. 'The basic dimensions were not so different but we had much more time to develop the car in detail compared with the year before. We also revised, for example, the cooling system drastically.

## BMW SAUBER F1 TEAM

**BMW Motorsport director:**
**Mario Theissen**

**Technical director, chassis:**
**Willy Rampf**

**Technical director, powertrain:**
**Heinz Paschen**

**Head of aerodynamics: Willem Toet**

**Head of track engineering:**
**Mike Krack**

**Team manager: Beat Zehnder**

**Chief mechanic: Urs Kuratle**

**Race engineer, car no. 9, Nick Heidfeld: Andy Borme**

**Race engineer, car no. 10 Robert Kubica & Vettel: Giampaulo Dall'ara**

**Top: Robert Kubica drove well but got slightly less out of the car than team-mate Nick Heidfeld, who out-scored him.**

**Above, from left: Motor sport director Mario Theissen; founder Peter Sauber; test driver Timo Glock, who won the GP2 championship this year and is hoping to make it into F1; technical director with responsibility for the chassis Willy Rampf.**
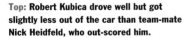
Photographs: Peter J Fox/www.crash.net

That was a very good step forward. The front suspension was also a huge change; the rear suspension as well.

'We also made sure that we were more flexible with this year's car than we were with last year's because of the single tyre supply of standard tyres. Nobody knew exactly how the tyre performance would be and when we did the concept of the car in, say, July to September last year nobody had any information about these tyres. So this was part of the car concept – to be more flexible with weight distribution and aero balance.'

In spite of high tyre temperatures pre-season, the team worked hard to be able to run Bridgestone's softer tyre. 'This is something we also improved over the year, to find the right load and the right management of the tyres to start with the soft tyres. Soft always gives better start performance and if you can do a race start with the new soft compound it's definitely an advantage.'

As was now to be expected from the team as a major manufacturer, development was extensive and consistent during the year. There were five changes of floor, front and rear wings and bodywork during the year, particularly for Monaco and Monza, plus two power steering developments and cooling modifications.

However, things didn't always go perfectly. Early in the season the team suffered problems with its quick-shift gearbox. 'A quick-shift gearbox is a very delicate system,' explained Rampf, 'and you have to do the fine tuning on a racetrack. If you get your shift timing wrong by a few milliseconds, you have to open the gearbox because there is a major mechanical clash.' There were related problems in Spain and Kubica suffered a heartbreaking hydraulics failure when leading in China.

Monaco was a low point, competitively speaking. 'We were a

bit too optimistic. We were biased too much that there might be a safety car, which was the case for the five years before. Okay, we gambled – we tried to win in Monaco because that is possible, that's why we did it, we split the cars. It didn't work out.'

The team tried to work a strategy in which one driver did a short stint while the other went longer. 'We have a certain procedure or philosophy. We discuss beforehand and then we decide this driver goes short, this driver goes long. If one driver goes short, one goes long, we always try to be in the window that both have the same chance to score the same amount of points.'

Happily, the drivers got on well and worked well together. 'There is a fair competition, which is absolutely right,' said Rampf. 'The lap times are very, very close. They have to fight for the best position and qualifying is a bit biased towards Nick.'

Kubica, however, was always tough on himself, declaring at the end of the season that he didn't think he'd got the best out of the car over the year. 'In some races he was really unlucky,' said Rampf. 'You could see he didn't get enough out of it because performance-wise they are very similar but Nick has many more points than Robert.'

Of course, the most dramatic moment of the season was Kubica's accident in Canada but he still bounced back after a one-race lay-off to outqualify and outrace his team-mate in the next two races. With a team like that and concentration on details to eliminate that half-second gap to Ferrari and McLaren, BMW Sauber is surely on course at least to retain third place in the future.

Bob Constanduros

Some think horsepower.

**We think brainpower.**

Investment Banking • Private Banking • Asset Management

We look at things from a different perspective – for the benefit of our clients. Building on our experience and expertise to drive innovation is an approach we share with the BMW Sauber F1 Team. By challenging conventional thinking we help our clients realize new opportunities. This has been our ambition since 1856. www.credit-suisse.com/sponsoring

**Thinking New Perspectives.**

CREDIT SUISSE

**RALF SCHUMACHER**

**JARNO TRULLI**

WITH Jarno Trulli and Ralf Schumacher continuing on Toyota's driving strength it was almost impossible to believe that not only did the team fail to win a single grand prix but it never managed to score a podium finish. After six years of effort, its latest TF107 challenger simply moved no nearer achieving tangible F1 success.

The one casualty to be sacrificed on the back of this poor performance was always going to be Ralf Schumacher. At the end of his third season at a reputed $1 million a race, he had become a luxury they could well do without, even in the context of a $600-million annual spend.

According to Pascal Vasselon, Toyota's senior general manager, there were two abiding problems that consigned the 2007 car to the status of also-ran. One was that it was not quick enough to fight mid-field with Ferrari, McLaren or BMW. The fact that the team was farther back, struggling with Red Bull, Renault and Williams, was all that needed to be said.

'The second problem was that we simply didn't score the points our car was capable of,' said Vasselon.

'Renault, for instance, was a good benchmark and we can conclude that we had roughly the same car performance. And yet they scored a lot more points than we did.'

Several things contributed behind the scenes to this lack of performance. On the one hand there were reliability issues – a lot fewer than in '06 but still a frustrating logjam getting in the way of serious achievement. Jarno encountered what turned out to be a fuel system problem at Barcelona when he was P6 on the grid, for example, and Ralf had that wheel-securing problem at Silverstone.

Toyota had some disastrous pit stops – such as at the Nürburgring when Ralf's pace in the wet and the dry was very impressive. And they had a brake calliper temperature issue in Monaco, where Jarno is always fast but could not race to his full potential.

Vasselon added, 'Probably a bigger issue than any of that in terms of why we could not score the points our pace warranted was our starts. We were struggling there and we can continue the parallel with Renault – usually they gained one, two or three places at the start and we lost one, two or three. They qualified in the mid-field pack and were often ahead of it by Turn One, whereas we were doing the opposite.

'It was not only an issue surrounding the start itself but also up to the first corner. And then, actually, more than once we had a decent start and were involved in an incident at the first corner.'

The homologated V8 engines helped with reliability because

© ADRIAN DEAN

## TOYOTA TF107

| | |
|---|---|
| **SPONSORS** | **Panasonic • Denso • bmc Software • Bridgestone • Dassault Systemes • Ebbon-Dacs • EMC • KDDI • Fly Kingfisher • Magneti Marelli • Time Inc** |
| **ENGINE** | Type: **Toyota RVX-07** No. of cylinders: **V8** Sparking plugs: **Denso** Fuel: **Esso** Oil: **Esso** |
| **TRANSMISSION** | Gearbox: **7-speed plus reverse** |
| **CHASSIS** | Front suspension: **Carbon fibre double wishbone arrangement, with carbon fibre trackrod and pushrod** Rear suspension: **Carbon fibre double wishbone arrangement, with carbon fibre toelink and pushrod** Dampers: **Penske** Wheels: **BBS** Tyres: **Bridgestone** Brake discs: **Hitco** Brake pads: **Hitco** Brake calipers: **Brembo** Steering: **Toyota power-assisted** Fuel tank: **ATL** Instruments: **Toyota/Marelli** |
| **DIMENSIONS** | Wheelbase: **3,090 mm** Overall length **4,530 mm** Overall height **950 mm** Overall width: **1,800 mm** Formula weight: **600 kg including driver and camera** |

manufacturers could not push for power and they were limited to 19,000 rpm. 'We also had an improvement in reliability from the chassis side. In testing, the Toyotas were very reliable and that was satisfying after dedicating more resources and a different structure. And we had no problems with adapting to the Bridgestone control tyres from an aerodynamic perspective. A tyre is highly deformable and the front is steered, so if the car is sensitive to a tyre change it means that the flow structure around the car is not robust enough. The only sensible way to develop an F1 car is to be tyre insensitive but as long as a tyre deforms, that is very difficult.'

What did change very significantly, of course, was the innate character of the tyres. And it was a total change. It is still about extracting the best from the tyres and optimisation is never easy, but it was not as difficult as in '06, for two reasons. First, the compounds this year were less critical – whereas before, they were at the peak of grip and flirting with major performance destructors such as blistering or graining. This season, usually, they were on the safe side.

Second, the competing teams were using the same tyres all year and so had a data base. Last year the tyres were very peaky and were always changing and so teams were always trying to understand the character of the latest compound.

Yet for some of the drivers it was a difficult transition. The major problem was that from the '06 to '07 construction, the tyres went towards oversteer. If you bolted an '07 set of Bridgestones onto an '06 car, you got oversteer – to the point that it forced the teams to develop understeering cars to compensate. That was simply because, with the characteristics of these tyres, if you kept oversteer you got instability and could

not maintain a consistent balance.

'Consequently we all built understeer into the car and for some drivers that was just perfect,' said Vasselon. For others – Fernando Alonso, Kimi Räikkönen, Ralf; those who like a neutral-to-oversteering car – it was not really possible to have stability and consistency. So they had to adapt their styles to avoid overdriving the tyres. For them it was a major change and some coped better than others.

Toyota managed to improve the potential without generating instability and Ralf also changed a bit from his side. Jarno, however, preferred understeer and so the change to the '07 tyres was into a window he felt comfortable with, so he did not really struggle.

Bob Constanduros

**Above: John Howett presided over another season over under-achievement.**

**Top: Ralf Schumacher ended his three-year tenure at Toyota without gaining the victory both parties had hoped for.**

**Centre left: Tadashi Yamashina took over from Tsutomu Tomita (left), who retired as team principal in mid-season.**

**Bottom: Jarno Trulli sometimes shone in qualifying but found decent race results hard to come by.**

Photographs: Peter J Fox/www.crash.net

## PANASONIC TOYOTA RACING

**Team principal:** Tadashi Yamashina

**Team president:** John Howett

**Executive vice president:**
Yoshiaki Kinoshita

**Senior general manager (engine):**
Luca Marmorini

**Senior general manager (chassis):**
Pascal Vasselon

**Director, techical co-ordination:**
Noritoshi Arai

**Team manager:** Richard Cregan

**Chief race and test engineer:**
Dieter Gass

DAVID COULTHARD

15

MARK WEBBER

Photographs: Peter J Fox/www.crash.net

14

+44 (0)121 603 1554

© ADRIAN DEAN

## RED BULL-RENAULT RB3

| | |
|---|---|
| **PARTNERS** | **Alphaform • Avus Racing • Bridgestone • Dataram • DMG • Elf • Highland Spring • Leica Geosystems • Mac Tools • Magneti Marelli • Metro • MSC Software • MTS • P&O • Platform Computing • Quehenberger • Rauch • Renault • Sabelt • Scottish and Newcastle • Standox • UGS • VW Commercial Vehicles** |
| **ENGINE** | Type: **Renault RS27**  No. of cylinders (vee angle): **V8 (90°)**  Sparking plugs: **Champion**  Electronics: **Magneti Marelli**  Fuel: **Elf**  Oil: **Elf** |
| **TRANSMISSION** | Gearbox: **7-speed gearbox, longitudinally mounted with hydraulic system for power shift and clutch operation**  Clutch: **AP Racing clutch** |
| **CHASSIS** | Front suspension: **Aluminium alloy uprights, upper and lower carbon wishbones and pushrods, torsion bar springs and anti-roll bars**<br>Rear suspension: **Aluminium alloy uprights, upper and lower carbon wishbones and pushrods, torsion bar springs and anti-roll bars**<br>Dampers: **Multimatic**  Wheels: **Avus Racing**  Wheel diameter, front: **13"**  rear: **13"**  Tyres: **Bridgestone**  Brake discs: **Hitco**<br>Brake pads: **Hitco**  Brake calipers: **Brembo**  Steering: **Red Bull Racing**  Radiators: **Marston/Red Bull Racing**  Fuel tank: **Red Bull Racing/ATL**<br>Instruments: **Red Bull Racing** |
| **DIMENSIONS** | Overall length: **As regulated by front and rear overhang**  Overall length: **As regulated**  Overall height: **As regulated**<br>Formula weight: **As regulated – 600 kg including driver** |

N the third year of its brief history, Red Bull Racing should finally have been able to come into its element as a rule change bringing in homologated two-race customer engines allowed teams to compete on a relatively level playing field. Red Bull Racing fought in a tight mid-field group that included its new engine supplier, Renault, fellow 'privateers' Williams and automotive giant Toyota and yet the team somehow failed to capitalise on promising materials and performances, even when it was more competitive in the later stages of the year.

As the team continued to build resources and personnel – reaching 540 during the year – and enjoyed a 20-percent rise in budget, it benefited from design guru Adrian Newey's input for the first time. However, he represented a culture change in the way the team worked, so that there was still a 'getting to know you' process within the team. But it was he who first recognised a time-consuming calibration problem with the team's Bedford wind tunnel.

'Adrian is probably one of the most competitive people I've ever met and his track record speaks for itself,' said team principal Christian Horner. 'His methodology, his competitiveness, his drive and his obvious skill have had a colossal impact and the rate at which he's producing drawings more than occupies over 200 engineers' time and more than occupies over 200 people working in the manufacturing process. They struggle to keep up at present with the development rate that he's driving from his drawing board. He's already mentally three races down the road from us, anyway, because he's always working on the next update.

'But we've had to understand how he works. The RB3 was his car and he's applied his development techniques to this car and we've had to adapt our working ways to accommodate Adrian's methodologies because they're proven and they work and they're working for us, it's pushing us in the right direction.

'The effort has been phenomenal and I would challenge any team to work harder than the whole group in Milton Keynes,' said Horner in North America. 'Not only has Adrian introduced a new car, he's introduced a new work ethic in terms of the on-going development that you need to succeed in Formula 1. Whereas the team had previously been used to two updates a year, we're in the sixth race and we're already on our sixth upgrade, so there's been a cultural change in the way that we

operate but everybody's responded tremendously well to that and I really believe that the foundations are now firmly in place.

'We've still got a long way to go but we've got a very good team now. It's not all about one guy. His impact is immeasurable but we've got a very good basis supporting him in Peter Prodromou, who also joined us from McLaren, in Rob Marshall, the chief designer, throughout the group, throughout R&D, throughout the different simulation groups. The group is now really starting to gel and I think that that bodes very well for the future.' Joining the staff late in the season was Newey's former colleague Geoff Willis – but Mark Smith left at the same time.

It was Newey who recognised the problem with the wind tunnel on the plane home from the first Barcelona test. 'I think the increase in scale from 50 to 60 percent and using the opportunity of installing that model to re-look at the calibration enables us to go through it with a fine-tooth comb,' said Horner.

'In saying that, though, we've made very good use of CFD [computational fluid dynamics] and pushed the boundaries of CFD and I think the combination of tunnel and computer should hopefully stand us in good stead for the future.'

But it set the whole team back four weeks – not what they wanted, according to David Coulthard. 'If you start quick, that is pretty much where you stay so I would like to be in a situation where we hit the ground running at the first grand prix, rather than trying to develop during the course of the year. We're still in a transitional stage for Red Bull and we are getting new parts on the car at every test, which is fantastic and did not happen before.'

Coulthard, who usually raced well, scored the team's first points in Spain, round four, after which he said, 'The thing that I take most encouragement from is our race pace in Bahrain, where we had our first set of upgrades. Then in Barcelona, relative to the front runners, we got closer to McLaren and Ferrari. However, we had a lot of problems at the end of that grand prix but we were able to get to the finish.'

By Canada, Horner felt that the team had caught up the four weeks lost at the beginning of the season. 'We've had a very aggressive development cycle and at every race since Australia we've put more performance on the car. I think it's really shown as we've started to get among the bigger teams, really from Bahrain onwards. We've had a few frustrating

**Above: David Coulthard on home turf in Monaco.**
Photograph: Peter J Fox/www.crash.net

**RED BULL RACING**

Team principal: **Dietrich Mateschitz**

Sporting director: **Christian Horner**

Chief technical officer: **Adrian Newey**

Technical director: **Geoff Willis**

Team manager: **Jonathan Wheatley**

Chief designer: **Rob Marshall**

Head of R&D controls and development: **Anton Stipinovich**

Head of aerodynamics: **Ben Agathangelou**

Head of R&D, testing and vehicle dynamics: **Andrew Green**

**Opposite: David Coulthard takes his Red Bull through Parabolica, Monza.**

**Right: Team boss Christian Horner.**

**Centre right: Consultant Dr Helmut Marko.**

**Far right: Chief technical officer Adrian Newey.**

Photographs: Peter J Fox/www.crash.net

**Above: Mark Webber did not enjoy much luck in his début season for the team.**

**Right: The experienced Geoffrey Willis was drafted into the squad as technical director during the season.**

**Below: DC ready for action.**

Photographs: Peter J Fox/www.crash.net

reliability issues, quite simply because the whole car has been so new – the engine, the electronics, the aerodynamics, every factor of the car – but we're rapidly getting on top of those.'

Reliability continued to plague the team, however. Mark Webber would usually qualify in the top ten, didn't score a point until Indianapolis but was on the podium to capitalise on a wild-card race in Germany with Coulthard fifth. However, out of ten races, they had seven mechanically induced retirements. 'We've had a lot of re-occurring problems, which is always the thing in F1 that is not excusable,' admitted Newey. 'Problems do happen but the golden rule is making sure they don't happen again and we didn't achieve that. Is it manufacturing, quality control or packaging? Tick all the boxes, really. It's partly design not being as good as it could be through manufacture, assembly and operational problems.'

At the last test at Jerez, before the final three races, the team made an encouraging breakthrough, even though it didn't change the car enormously. The car ran at the front of its group but, partially due to the changing weather conditions – and Webber's controversial collision in Japan with Sebastian Vettel – the rewards still weren't there, just when the team was challenging Williams for fourth in the constructors' series.

'We're not where we eventually aspire to be but, given the age of the team and where it is, we performed satisfactorily but dropped the ball in terms of reliability,' summed up Newey. 'Even if you have the budget you have to be careful about growing too quickly because that can cause more problems than it solves.'

Alan Henry

# A T&T WILLIAMS

NICO ROSBERG

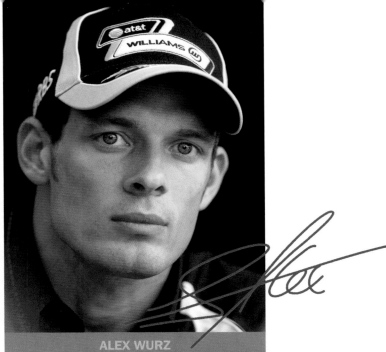

ALEX WURZ

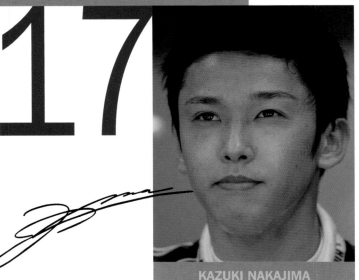

KAZUKI NAKAJIMA

16

17

Photographs: Peter J Fox/www.crash.net

+44 (0)121 603 1554

© ADRIAN DEAN

## WILLIAMS-TOYOTA FW29

| | |
|---|---|
| **SPONSORS** | **AT&T • RBS • Accenture • Allianz • Lenovo • Philips • Petrobras • AirAsia • Bridgestone • Hamleys • Oris • Randstad • Puma • DeWalt • Man PPG • Reuters • Qinetiq • Rays • SKF • Battery** |
| **ENGINE** | Type: **Toyota RVX-07** No. of cylinders (vee angle): **V8 (90°)** |
| **TRANSMISSION** | Gearbox: **WilliamsF1 7-speed sequential semi-automatic, plus reverse** |
| **CHASSIS** | Front and rear suspension: **Carbon fibre double wishbone arrangement, with composite toelink (front) and pushrod-activated torsion springs (and rockers; rear)** Dampers: **WilliamsF1** Wheels: **RAYS forged magnesium** Tyres: **Bridgestone** Brake discs: **Carbone Industrie** Brake pads: **Carbone Industrie** Calipers: **AP Racing** Steering: **WilliamsF1 power-assisted** Fuel: **Petrobras** Lubricants: **Lubrax** |
| **DIMENSIONS** | Wheelbase **3,100 mm** Length: **4,500 mm** Height: **950 mm** Width: **1,800 mm** Formula weight: **605 kg including driver, camera and ballast** |

Above: **Nico Rosberg continued to develop his talents and is now considered a top-line F1 driver.**
Photograph: Peter J Fox/www.crash.net

WILLIAMS was very clear about what needed to be done. Finishing eighth in the 2006 championship had been something of a shock for a team that had won the constructors' title nine times. Patrick Head and his technical department, led by Sam Michael, had established a package of reforms focused on improving reliability and introducing new blood. Jon Tomlinson came on board as head of aerodynamics, Rod Nelson moved from Renault to become chief operations engineer and John Russell, a former race engineer with the team, returned with sole responsibility for reliability and moving Williams on from the 11 mechanical failures that contributed to such a poor record in '06. All of this took place against the fundamental change of engine supply from Cosworth to Toyota and the introduction of a revised seamless-shift gearbox.

Early indications that Williams might be on a successful course came when the team arrived for the first grand prix, in Melbourne, having already completed several race distances on either the test track or Toyota's dyno in Cologne. In '06, Williams' first complete race distance had come at the end of the opening round of the championship in Bahrain.

'That's been very important,' said Michael, speaking just before the Japanese GP. 'With three races to go in '07, we've had just three mechanical DNFs. We managed that with early planning of the engine installation with Toyota and a much simpler – or different – seamless-shift concept from last year's. We also changed a lot of systems and checks in-house at the factory. Last year, unreliability affected us a lot because when you have endemic problems in the car, you can't concentrate on making it go faster. This year's been quite different. We've been able to keep looking at small pieces of performance to improve the car during the year because it was instantly more reliable.'

Having achieved that, a ramp up in performance was the obvious goal. Again, Williams appeared to be heading in the right direction when Nico Rosberg qualified 12th and finished seventh at Melbourne, then started sixth at the next race in Malaysia. In the light of Michael's remark about improved reliability, it was doubly unfortunate that Rosberg should retire with hydraulics trouble when running a very solid sixth after 42 laps. It was to be a similar story at Indianapolis, where another sixth place went with Rosberg's oil pressure.

'We cost ourselves six points in those two races with Nico,' says Michael. 'The points in Malaysia were even more tantalising because, when Nico lost those three points, it gave two extra points to Renault because one [of Renault's cars] was right behind him and the other was outside the points before we went out. So, relative to Renault, we lost eight points [in those two races] because of reliability. Renault and McLaren are the only teams not to have had a mechanical DNF during a race and that's the goal you have to aim for.'

Going into the Japanese GP, Williams was 11 points behind Renault and trying to close the gap in the final three races. It did not happen because of Renault's strong showing at Fuji and an electronics problem for Rosberg. But the fact that Williams had entertained the thought of beating the reigning champion marked a step up in performance and expectation.

Although Michael does not say as much, Williams cannot have ignored the fact that Rosberg brought much more to the party than Alex Wurz, who was promoted from the role of test driver to replace Mark Webber. The points against each driver's name are deceiving, Wurz having given the team its first (and only) podium after a tenacious one-stop run on soft rubber at Montreal and a similar dogged drive into fourth in extreme conditions at the Nürburgring. Otherwise, however, his season – and Williams' point-scoring opportunities – was heavily compromised by poor performances during qualifying, Wurz never making it into the top ten.

Rosberg, on the other hand, developed into the mature driver Head and Sir Frank Williams had obviously hoped to see when they signed the GP2 champion at the beginning of '06. His maiden season had been more disappointing than fulfilling, but '07, particularly the second half, will go down as the making of a confident and quick future star, Rosberg's consistent qualifying performances laying the foundation for a raft of points at the end of very strong races in Turkey, Italy and Belgium. The potential was also there in Japan but for a rare engine failure that cost him ten places after qualifying sixth.

'Our relationship with Toyota has been really good,' said Michael. 'Right from the beginning they have bent over backwards to help us. The thing you always worry about in a relationship with a new engine manufacturer is the packaging implications. We knew the Toyota had always been reliable and

## WILLIAMSF1 TEAM

**Managing director & team principal: Sir Frank Williams**

**Director of engineering: Patrick Head**

**Chief executive officer: Chris Chapple**

**Technical director: Sam Michael**

**Chief operating officer: Alex Burns**

**Chief designer: Ed Wood**

**Head of aerodynamics: Jon Tomlinson**

**Race-team manager: Tim Newton**

**Race engineer: car, no. 16, Nico Rosberg: Tony Ross**

**Race engineer: car, no. 17, Alex Wurz and Nakajima: James Broughton**

**Right: Sir Frank Williams can take satisfaction from moving his team up the constructors' table.**

**Centre right: Sam Michael led a revamped techniclal team which saw the car's reliability greatly improved.**

**Far right: Patrick Head oversaw the operation with his usual pragmatism.**

**Below: Alex Wurz scored the team's only podium in Canada.**

Photographs: Peter J Fox/www.crash.net

**Above: Kazuki Nakajima was given his grand prix début at the season's finale in Brazil.**

Photograph: Peter J Fox/www.crash.net

they tried to make sure that we had enough time to package the engine and understand all the implications of the airbox, exhaust and cooling. We started much earlier than we did with Cosworth to get around potential reliability issues and it paid off.

'We also used Toyota's dynos very heavily to do all our gearbox work. Last year's box took quite a bit of maintenance and attention to keep it running. This year's box is not only a lot lighter but better in every way. And much more reliable. We designed it to comply with '08 regulations. We didn't run the boxes like that [over four faces, as required in '08] in races because we didn't have to in '07. But we felt that if we tried to

meet the '08 gearbox requirements over the coming winter then, if we had a problem, we could be in big trouble at the start of '08. So we decided that we'd make this box from '07 and it's worked well.'

Williams also had less trouble with adapting to the Bridgestones than in '06 following the switch from Michelin at the beginning of that year. 'The '07 tyres were obviously a lot different from the previous year's because Bridgestone was no longer in a tyre war,' said Michael. 'A lot of it comes down to how the tyres work with your car. It took us most of the winter to understand the tyres. A lot of it is judgement and then testing, but we were able to get a handle on it fairly early.

'The bottom line is that we were not fast enough,' concluded Michael. 'On our best track [Monaco] we were 0.6s off and on our worst track [Silverstone] we were about 1.5s off, so the average is one second. We have to find that over the winter. The car did not have any nasty windows of the sort where you'd get to a track and suddenly find yourself in a nightmare. That didn't really happen. We've not been strong relative to McLaren and Ferrari but we have been strong relative to the chasing pack.

'We're effectively fifth in the championship because being fourth is through someone else's downfall [McLaren's disqualification] and not because we have made a better car. Our main target for '08 is to make sure we close that gap to the guys in front and put ourselves in a top-three position. This year has been better than '06. But it's not where we want to be.'

Maurice Hamilton

Driver's gone.

Light's gone.

Crowd's gone.

The work's begun.

# Make it happen.

When you have to deliver, having a strong team behind you is vital, whether you're in Formula One™ or banking. And, at RBS, it's our strong team that allows us to deliver for our customers. That's why, as one of the world's most successful banks, we're able to make it happen.

rbs.com

## Make it happen

**✻ RBS**

*The Royal Bank of Scotland Group*

**SEBASTIAN VETTEL**

## SCUDERIA TORO ROSSO

**VITANTONIO LIUZZI**

**SCOTT SPEED**

R ED BULL'S second-string team moved up a gear in 2007 with last year's rev-limited Cosworth V10s replaced by customer Ferrari V8s – which had originally been held by the main Red Bull squad before its switch to Renault power.

The team continued to be run effectively by co-owner Gerhard Berger's right-hand man Franz Tost and was further strengthened in early April by the recruitment of respected former McLaren and Ferrari engineer Giorgio Ascanelli as technical director. The car was actually manufactured by an associate company – Red Bull Technologies, based close to the main Red Bull team in Milton Keynes – and amounted to a Ferrari-engined version of the sister car, which was permitted by the strict letter of the regulations.

Toro Rosso began the season with American Scott Speed and Italy's Vitantonio Liuzzi in the cars, but it didn't take long for management to tire of Speed's rather abrasive over-confidence. After the European GP, he was replaced. BMW Sauber released its test driver Sebastian Vettel, who joined Toro Rosso and consolidated his reputation as the find of the year with a brilliant fourth place in the Chinese GP, where Liuzzi also finished in a creditable position: fifth. It's fair to say that Liuzzi's form was more obviously showcased in the second half of the year, by which time Champcar ace Sébastien Bourdais had been signed to replace him for '08.

Initially the team seemed a little disappointed about its car's performance. 'Reliability and performance were important and we were neither reliable nor fast,' said Ascanelli. 'I would say that the big struggle was finding reliability, which by the end of the season was quite decent.'

A lot of effort went into getting the best out of the engine installation in the chassis, cooling the exhaust geometry, and the airbox and fuel system in conjunction with Ferrari. In Ascanelli's words, it was fuel system development rather than fuel development. 'People need to be trained to think in a certain way,' he said. 'A classic example happened in Japan. Sebastian Vettel did a fantastic job for us in qualifying and we found ourselves in Q3 and at that point we made a mistake, which was calling him in at the wrong time, with the result that we lost the chance to do a lap time on new rubber. We missed the flag by 13s, so it was not a large mistake, but it probably cost us two places on the grid.

'Then, in the race, Fernando Alonso had a few troubles and we were actually overtaking him. This had never happened! You have to run your race in a completely different way. If you are behind you've got to have limited ambition and take relatively low risk, but when you are in front you have to have a

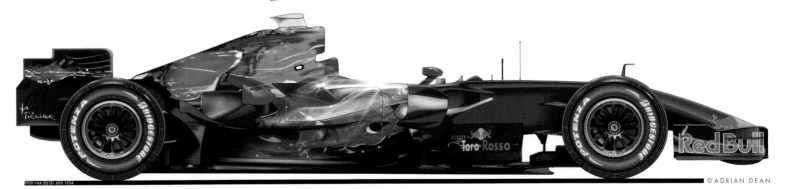

© ADRIAN DEAN

### TORO ROSSO-FERRARI STR2

| | |
|---|---|
| **SPONSOR** | **Red Bull** |
| **OFFICIAL SUPPLIERS** | **Avus Racing • Bridgestone • Magneti Marelli • Ferrari • USAG • Puma • Sabelt • VW Commercial vehicles • AMK** |
| **ENGINE** | Type: **Ferrari 057** No. of cylinders (vee angle): **V8 (90°)** Sparking plugs: **Champion** Electronics: **Magneti Marelli** Fuel: **Shell** Oil: **Shell** |
| **TRANSMISSION** | Gearbox: **7-speed, longitudinally mounted with hydraulic system for power shift and clutch operation** Clutch: **AP Racing** |
| **CHASSIS** | Front and rear suspension: **Aluminium alloy uprights, upper and lower carbon wishbones and pushrods. Torsion bar springs and anti-roll bar** Dampers: **Multimatic** Wheel diameter front: **15"** rear **13"** Wheels: **Avus Racing** Tyres: **Bridgestone** Brake discs and pads: **Hitco & Messier Bugatti** Brake calipers: **AP** Steering: **Red Bull Technology** Radiators: **Red Bull Technology** Fuel Tank: **ATL** Instruments: **Red Bull Technology** |
| **DIMENSIONS** | Overall length: **As regulated by front and rear overhang** Overall length: **As regulated** Overall height: **As regulated** Formula weight: **As regulated – 600 kg including driver** |

totally different perspective.'

Ascanelli is sanguine about the apparent early-season driver problems, basically believing that Vitantonio and Scott and – later – Vitantonio and Sebastian actually had quite decent relationships.

'Scott was extremely decisive on what he wanted to do and generally had a good feeling about the car and I liked him,' said Giorgio. 'But I don't think he was happy with us and I don't think our boss was happy with him. To make a wedding you need two and this one had neither.

'I don't think badly of him as a driver. As much as I enjoyed his company, though, as a human being it was difficult for a young team to accept the challenge of such a character. He was cocky. My rule is that everyone makes mistakes and we try to stick together and I always tell everyone that a mistake from a driver is the same as that of a mechanic or engineer – just more apparent. Scott's expectations were higher than the team could deliver.'

Tonio, he felt, was more committed, although the situation was not that dissimilar because Tonio was not that happy with the situation he was in, either. It was the team's impression, however, that Tonio put in more effort than Speed.

'Vettel, for a young guy, is interesting,' said Ascanelli. 'He's on a steep learning curve but if he keeps learning I think he has some justified ambitions. Bourdais I have not yet worked with but he has won championships, so he knows how to do it.'

That said, his experiences engineering Michael Andretti at McLaren in 1993 left Giorgio a little sceptical about the wisdom of recruiting drivers from Champcar backgrounds: 'Cars in the USA are a bit more robust and you can have a tangle without necessarily destroying them,' he grinned. 'Here, collisions have to be avoided.'

Taken as a whole, Toro Rosso did quite a decent job on a modest budget. It has a small test team but realises that it is not operating at the absolute F1 cutting edge because of financial and equipment constraints. 'We were at every test but we did not run enough miles due to reliability and physically having too few resources,' said Ascanelli. 'That is part of the problem.'

A team such as Toro Rosso has to satisfy the brief of Red Bull co-founder Dietrich Mateschitz. His philosophy and strategy is that Red Bull is there to try to win races and the second team has to promote the brand and train young drivers – but on a limited budget.

Ascanelli summed it up shrewdly: 'Ron Dennis told me in '91 that to win one race is relatively easy, to win one championship is not that difficult but to be consistently at the top of motor racing is incredibly tough. To be honest and reasonable, Toro Rosso had a set-up that allowed us to be about eighth or ninth and if we hadn't had the reliability problems, that's where we could have been aiming.'

Alan Henry

**Above: Vitantonio Liuzzi plugged away throughout the season but was dropped at the year's end.**

**Left: The services of Scott Speed were dispensed with by mid-season.**

**Below left: Franz Tost (centre) and Gerhard Berger ran the team within the constraints placed by Dietrich Mateschitz.**

Photographs: Peter J Fox/www.crash.net

### SCUDERIA TORO ROSSO

**Team principal:** Franz Tost

**Team co-owner:** Gerhard Berger

**Technical director:** Giorgio Ascanelli

**General manager:**
Gianfranco Fantuzzi

**Chief engineer:** Laurent Mekies

**Team manager:** Massimo Rivola

**Race engineer, car no. 18, Tonio Liuzzi:** Brunetto Calderoni

**Race engineer, car no. 19, Speed & Sebastian Vettel:** Stefano Pieranoni

ETIHAD ALDAR SPYKER F1 TEAM

**20**

**21**

ADRIAN SUTIL

CHRISTIJAN ALBERS

MARKUS WINKELHOCK

SAKON YAMAMOTO

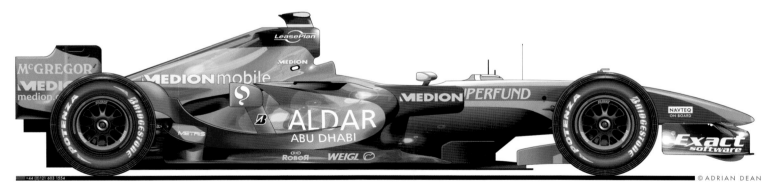

© ADRIAN DEAN

## SPYKER-FERRARI

| | |
|---|---|
| **SPONSORS** | **Title sponsors Etihad Airways • Aldar Abu Dhabi** |
| | **Sponsors Twins Investments • LeasePlan • Superfund • GPupdate.net • Bridgestone • Rotozip • Quick • 4net • Philoderm • Trust • Exact Medion • Dremel • Dream7 • Navteq • Kemppi • AD Sportwereld • MaxCredible** |
| **ENGINE** | **Type: Ferrari F1-056H No. of cylinders (vee angle): V8 (90°) Sparking plugs: NGK** |
| **TRANSMISSION** | **Gearbox: Spyker 7-speed plus reverse longitudinal gearbox with electrohydraulic sequential gear change Clutch: AP Racing triple-plate** |
| **CHASSIS** | **Front and rear suspension: Composite pushrods, dampers and torsion bars; cast uprights Wheels: BBS Tyres: Bridgestone Fuel-tank capacity: over 90 kg** |
| **DIMENSIONS** | **Wheelbase: more than 3,000 mm Front track: 1,480 mm Rear track: 1,418 mm Height: 950 mm Length: 5,000mm Formula weight: 605 kg including driver** |

**Left:** Adrian Sutil scored a valuable point for the team in Japan.

**Below left:** Mechanics and technicians run a final systems check on the car before the race in Malaysia.

**Bottom left:** In an increasingly po-faced paddock, motor racing can still be fun!

**Below:** Christijan Albers lost his place in a mid-season reshuffle.

Photographs: Peter J Fox/www.crash.net

S PYKER'S first championship point of 2007 may have been the subject of dispute but the team's performance in Japan summed up the potential underpinning what appeared to be a poor season. At the end of '06, the team was on the road to recovery when the Dutch firm Spyker bought what had formerly been Jordan from Alex Shnaider. The owner of Midland had invested next to nothing in his latest plaything in '06 and the arrival of Spyker appeared to bring an end to the stagnation. Despite good intentions, the sports car maker found the road to F1 fame paved with the expensive expectation of a team that needed a healthy financial input to remain even remotely competitive. When Spyker NV's shortcomings became obvious, the Silverstone-based team knew it faced another season of going not very far.

Apart from keeping the team alive in the short term, the one positive outcome of the Spyker association had been the hiring of Mike Gascoyne to head the technical group. Gascoyne, cooling his heels after a summary departure from Toyota, was familiar with the team and its potential thanks to a period with Jordan a few years earlier. He made it clear that progress would be limited until suitable investment began to have a long-term effect. In short, Spyker was unlikely to move off the back of the grid. And so it proved. Yet, when circumstances allowed, the orange-and-grey cars managed to embarrass outfits working on five times Spyker's budget.

One of Gascoyne's first moves was to expand wind tunnel potential by striking a deal with Aerolab, the company run by Jean-Claude Migeot. 'We had a plan in place in terms of technical development, wind tunnels and so on,' said Gascoyne. 'The investment in the company didn't turn out as

we expected, which meant the budget was very tight. But we were able to bring Aerolab on board in January. It's not just a wind tunnel but an operation of about 35 people doing a full aerodynamic service including model design that really integrates into our own aerodynamics department. That meant we were able to do an update very early in the year. The car had been produced by James Key and his team before I turned up. They'd done a very good job in difficult circumstances.

'But we knew we'd be starting at the back; we expected that. Our major rivals were receiving cars from other teams and that meant they were going to take a step forward. We wanted to spend the year rebuilding. We didn't do the Bahrain test before the season or the Malaysia test so, although we had updates on the car, we suffered in those races. But it's important to say that F1 was very competitive in '07 and, although we were qualifying at the back, we were also regularly under three seconds off the pole time. In any other season, that would have made you a reasonably competitive mid-field team.'

The problems with insufficient downforce and too much drag were addressed by a B-spec update. But those plans received a set-back when the revised car failed a rear-impact test, a problem that was put right in time for the Italian Grand Prix. The low-downforce requirements of Monza did not allow the aero developments to show but, a week later at Spa, Spyker could measure its step forward more accurately. Added to which, a piece of opportunism inherent in the team since its Jordan days enabled a Spyker to run in the mid-field when the team bucked the trend and started Adrian Sutil on soft tyres.

'I think that other teams missed a trick there,' grinned Gascoyne. 'People were tending to run the hard tyre and be a

## SPYKER FERRARI

Team owner: **Vijay Mallya**

Director of Formula 1 racing: **Michiel Mol**

Team principal: **Dr Colin Kolles**

Director of business affairs: **Ian Phillips**

Technical director: **Mike Gascoyne**

Chief race and test engineer:
**Dominic Harlow**

Chief designer: **John McQuilliam**

Head of aerodynamics: **Simon Phillips**

Head of electronics: **Mike Wroe**

Head of production: **Simon Shinkins**

Technical co-ordinator: **James Key**

Team manager: **Andy Stevenson**

Chief mechanic: **Andy Deeming**

Race engineer, car no. 20,
Adrian Sutil: **Bradley Joyce**

Race engineer, car number 21,
Albers &Winkelhock & Yamamoto:
**Jody Eggington**

**Top: With new owners commited to invest, the Spyker team can look forward to upward progress.**

**Above centre, left to right: Team principal, Colin Kolles; Michiel Mol; Mike Gascoyne; and new owner Vijay Mallya.**

**Above: Technical director James Key.**

**Right: The enthusiastic Sakon Yamamoto raced from Hungary onwards.**

**Opposite: Man and machine and track. The Spyker is rolled into the garage under the Turkish sun.**

Photographs: Peter J Fox/www.crash.net

little bit conservative. We wanted to target a very aggressive first stint and it was a good example of the team functioning well. It was suggested that we made some risky strategy calls but I don't think we made any risky calls; just the right ones.'

Gascoyne was referring particularly to the wet start at the Nürburgring when Markus Winkelhock was brought into the pits at the end of the parade lap, fitted with wet-weather tyres – and went on to lead the race when the rest of the field made the same switch.

'It was good that, towards the end of the year, we were able to start to go racing – even if it was just for 14th or 15th place. At least you're trying to out-think people and that was good for everyone. The entire team has worked very, very well.'

Sutil, in his first season, was one of Spyker's greatest assets, the first hint of this being when he set the fastest time during the wet practice session on Saturday morning at Monaco.

'Adrian has been learning and has got better throughout the year,' said Gascoyne. 'He's a very good, quick driver and mentally he has the ability. He just has to learn to remain focused. We've tried to help him and he's got stronger and stronger. At the start of the season, he'd only done three

morning sessions at grands prix in an F1 car. After Spa, his confidence was definitely on the up. Hitting the walls in Monaco and Canada, and at Copse during practice at Silverstone: that made life difficult for Adrian and the team. But he's learned from that. The guy is a star of the future; no question.'

Sutil's performance indirectly led to the fall of Christijan Albers, whose failure to match his team-mate's pace led to his replacement by Winkelhock at the Nürburgring and Sakon Yamamoto for the rest of the season. 'We've been very impressed with Sakon,' said Gascoyne. 'He's professional in his attitude and has a very good work ethic. He ended up pushing his team-mate quite hard on occasions. It's been a big ask for him in qualifying but he's been teaching himself how to step up to the plate. As for Markus: leading his first grand prix by 30 seconds at home: what a great story! The good thing is we're going be able to do much more in '08 because we have got everything in place. Despite massive financial difficulties, we finished '07 in a very positive frame of mind.'

Maurice Hamilton

## ANTHONY DAVIDSON

### SUPER AGURI RACING

**22**

**23**

**TAKUMA SATO**

IT'S often said that a team's second year is more difficult than its first, but that depends on how well-prepared it was for its début. The Super Aguri team was better prepared for 2007 than for '06.

There were many changes. The team had a new car instead of a four-year-old machine, ran on tyres it was used to, was able to go pre-season testing like everyone else and now had two talented and tough drivers in former Honda team-mates Takuma Sato and Anthony Davidson – and was able to fine-tune its general organisation.

The team was now fully grown and various factors came to its aid. Sporting director Graham Taylor pointed out that 'the playing field has been flattened by the introduction of a single tyre manufacturer'.

And, once again, as in its début year, the team surprised. Tenth and eleventh places on the grid at the first grand prix were followed by a world championship point three races later, in Spain. There were three more in the chaos of Canada – and might have been more.

But then a lack of budget began to bite and, like so many impoverished teams before it, Super Aguri began to slide gently down the order as those with bigger budgets continued to develop. 'We have not been able to put on any really serious development parts since May,' said Ben Wood, head of aerodynamics, 'which has really hurt our on-track performance.'

This was principally down to one sponsor, SS United, a Hong Kong oil company, that, whatever its intentions, simply failed to pay, resulting in several rumours that the team was for sale and in financial trouble. Aguri Suzuki's Japanese contacts bailed it out late in the season but the damage had already been done.

Sato explained that, 'We were always aiming high following our tenth-position result in Brazil last year. We came into this season with high motivation.' Most important, the team was able to come to a sensible arrangement regarding the chassis and engine package.

The SA07 was the result of eight months' collaboration between the Super Aguri team design department lead by chief designer Peter McCool and Honda's R&D centre in Tochigi,

Photographs: Peter J Fox/www.crash.net

© ADRIAN DEAN

## SUPER AGURI-HONDA SA07

| | |
|---|---|
| **PARTNERS** | Honda • Bridgestone • Autobacs • Seiko • Samantha Kingz • Four Leaf with Dreamcubes • Pioneer • NGK • Metris • Speakerbus • Rodac • Takata • NGK • Eneos • Kinotrope • Nexsan |
| **ENGINE** | Type: **Honda RA807-E** No. of cylinders (vee angle): **V8 ( 90°)** Sparking plugs: **NGK** Electronics: **Honda PGM F1** Oil: **Eneos** |
| **TRANSMISSION** | Gearbox: **SAF1 Honda carbon composite maincase. 7 speed sequential "quick shift" electro hydraulically controlled** Clutch: **Sachs** |
| **CHASSIS** | Front and rear suspension: **Wishbones, pushrod operated torsion bars and dampers. Mechanical anti-roll bar** <br> Dampers: **Showa** Wheels: **BBS** Tyres: **Bridgestone** Brakes:**6 piston calipers with carbon pads and discs** <br> Steering: **SAF1 power-assisted** Steering wheel: **SAF1 specification and composite construction** Fuel tank: **ATL** Instruments: **SAF1 specification** |
| **DIMENSIONS** | Front track **1,460mm** Rear track **1,420mm** Wheelbase: **3,135mm** Overall length: **4,680mm** Overall height: **950mm** Overall width: **1800mm** <br> Formula weight: **600 kg including driver** |

**Left: Mechanics work on Takuma Sato's car in the heat of Sepang.**

**Below: Team founder Aguri Suzuki,**
Photographs: Peter J Fox/www.crash.net

**Far left: Chief technical engineer Mark Preston.**

**Left: Managing director Daniele Audetto.**

**Below: Anthony Davidson often qualified superbly, but the races proved more difficult.**
Photographs: Peter J Fox/www.crash.net

Japan. The team's winter test programme allowed it to validate a number of design concepts and test the increased reliability of the new Honda power train.

Honda's homologated engine was also a major step forward in power and reliability. It increased Super Aguri's performance and provided a competitive engine for this period of new rules and stability. A carbon gearbox was now part of the package from Honda, which would allow more flexibility in weight distribution and increased integration, bringing with it the added benefit of reliability.

But that wasn't the only benefit. The personnel remained pretty much on 140 but they had a lot of help from Honda in Japan. 'We had a lot of people come over from the R&D department,' said technical director Mark Preston. 'They are very supportive of Aguri so we do have a fair amount of contact. When you can take a gearbox that's a lovely quick-shift from Honda, that saves maybe 30 people: software people, designers, rig testers. It's a really big resource difference. You can get on with stuff that makes the car go faster.

'But we also now have tyre, aero and strategist specialists, which are some of the areas we have honed in on. That has helped a lot from last year and to run higher up and be in the top ten we'd need to have more of those people who concentrate on one job in detail.'

As Davidson said, 'The team expanded the aero department over the winter and made some pretty impressive steps forward. In Bahrain we found that the new aero package was looking after the tyres quite well, on the longer runs especially.' The team used the ex-McLaren National Physics Lab 50-percent wind tunnel in Teddington and, as Preston points out, 'it's won world championships before.

'This year we brought lots of bits that made the car look different. The biggest change was the floor at Magny-Cours. Probably the new rear wings have been the most visual and we tried a different front wing, one of those that goes up and onto the nose box, but we only ran that a few times in practice. We had a new rear wing for China, which was a bit more efficient.'

The cars were incredibly reliable in pre-season testing and the team did both the Bahrain and Malaysia tests, which put it at an advantage over several of its rivals. 'It helped us arrive at the first race more prepared,' continued Preston.

'We came out of the box well and our tenth and 11th at Melbourne were a big shock. We'd set our goals from the year before and tried to keep them fairly reasonable and said we'd get through Q1 and see where we ended up. But we weren't really that organised.

'We didn't race so well and over the next few races we changed things in terms of strategy and how we organised ourselves. We were constantly making changes to the way we worked and if we look back maybe we could have done better if we'd been a bit older as a group.

'It's amazing how many changes we were still making at the end of the season – just logistics and stuff that the big teams have had years to get right. There's a fair bit of experience on the team but it's about working together.

'Barcelona was the first time that the new step of organisation came into play. One of the examples was that we had had all the engineers out on the pit wall and our radio systems aren't the best in the world. We decided we weren't communicating well and so all the engineers came into the truck, into what we called the battle room. That's one of the things that explains why we went better in Barcelona and got the point.'

However, it worked against them in Canada because they didn't see Davidson coming in (having the first pit in the pit lane – as at two other races). After that, one person went back on the pit wall.

'It was still a learning year but a different kind of learning year. We just put as much downforce on the car as we could. This year has been continuing fine tuning everywhere to try and race better. Last year we didn't really have to race anybody until the last race. We've tightened up procedures and I'm happy we are stepping forward and not being afraid to change things.'

Bob Constanduros

## SUPER AGURI RACING

**Team principal:** Aguri Suzuki

**Managing director:** Daniel Audetto

**Chief operations officer:** Kevin Lee

**Chief technical engineer:** Mark Preston

**Chief designer:** Peter McCool

**Team manager:** Mick Ainsley-Cowlishaw

**Race engineer, car number 22, Takuma Sato:** Gerry Hughes

**Race engineer, car number 23, Anthony Davidson:** Antonio Cuquerella

# CHASSIS LOGBOOK 2007
## Compiled by David Hayhoe

## ROUND 1 AUSTRALIAN GP

**McLAREN-MERCEDES**
| 1 | Fernando Alonso | MP4-22/03 |
| 2 | Lewis Hamilton | MP4-22/04 |
| T-car | | MP4-22/01 |

**RENAULT**
| 3 | Giancarlo Fisichella | R27/02 |
| 4 | Heikki Kovalainen | R27/03 |
| | | (01 Fri) |

**FERRARI**
| 5 | Felipe Massa | F2007/260 |
| 6 | Kimi Räikkönen | F2007/261 |
| T-car | | F2007/258 |

**HONDA**
| 7 | Jenson Button | RA107/04 |
| 8 | Rubens Barrichello | RA107/02 |
| T-car | | RA107/01 |

**BMW-SAUBER**
| 9 | Nick Heidfeld | F1.07/05 |
| 10 | Robert Kubica | F1.07/04 |
| 35 | Sebastian Vettel | F1.07/03 |

**TOYOTA**
| 11 | Ralf Schumacher | TF107/03 |
| 12 | Jarno Trulli | TF107/04 |
| T-car | | TF107/01 |

**RED BULL-RENAULT**
| 14 | David Coulthard | RB3/1 |
| | | (3 Fri 1st practice) |
| 15 | Mark Webber | RB3/2 |

**WILLIAMS-TOYOTA**
| 16 | Nico Rosberg | FW29/03 |
| 17 | Alexander Wurz | FW29/04 |
| 38 | Kazuki Nakajima | FW29/01 |

**TORO ROSSO-FERRARI**
| 18 | Vitantonio Liuzzi | STR02/03 |
| 19 | Scott Speed | STR02/01 |

**SPYKER-FERRARI**
| 20 | Adrian Sutil | F8-VII/03 |
| 21 | Christijan Albers | F8-VII/01 |
| | | (02 Fri & Sat) |

**SUPER AGURI-HONDA**
| 22 | Takuma Sato | SA07/04 |
| 23 | Anthony Davidson | SA07/03 |
| T-car | | SA07/02 |

## ROUND 2 MALAYSIAN GP

**McLAREN-MERCEDES**
| 1 | Fernando Alonso | MP4-22/01 |
| 2 | Lewis Hamilton | MP4-22/05 |
| T-car | | MP4-22/03 |

**RENAULT**
| 3 | Giancarlo Fisichella | R27/04 |
| | | (01 Fri) |
| 4 | Heikki Kovalainen | R27/01 |
| | | (03 Fri) |

**FERRARI**
| 5 | Felipe Massa | F2007/260 |
| 6 | Kimi Räikkönen | F2007/261 |
| T-car | | F2007/258 |

**HONDA**
| 7 | Jenson Button | RA107/04 |
| 8 | Rubens Barrichello | RA107/02 |
| T-car | | RA107/01 |

**BMW-SAUBER**
| 9 | Nick Heidfeld | F1.07/05 |
| 10 | Robert Kubica | F1.07/04 |
| 35 | Sebastian Vettel | F1.07/03 |

**TOYOTA**
| 11 | Ralf Schumacher | TF107/03 |
| 12 | Jarno Trulli | TF107/04 |
| T-car | | TF107/01 |

**RED BULL-RENAULT**
| 14 | David Coulthard | RB3/3 |
| 15 | Mark Webber | RB3/2 |
| T-car | | RB3/1 |

**WILLIAMS-TOYOTA**
| 16 | Nico Rosberg | FW29/03 |
| | | (01 Fri) |
| 17 | Alexander Wurz | FW29/04 |
| 38 | Kazuki Nakajima | FW29/03 |

**TORO ROSSO-FERRARI**
| 18 | Vitantonio Liuzzi | STR02/03 |
| 19 | Scott Speed | STR02/01 |

**SPYKER-FERRARI**
| 20 | Adrian Sutil | F8-VII/03 |
| 21 | Christijan Albers | F8-VII/01 |
| T-car | | F8-VII/02 |

**SUPER AGURI-HONDA**
| 22 | Takuma Sato | SA07/04 |
| 23 | Anthony Davidson | SA07/03 |
| T-car | | SA07/02 |

## ROUND 3 BAHRAIN GP

**McLAREN-MERCEDES**
| 1 | Fernando Alonso | MP4-22/01 |
| 2 | Lewis Hamilton | MP4-22/05 |
| T-car | | MP4-22/03 |

**RENAULT**
| 3 | Giancarlo Fisichella | R27/04 |
| 4 | Heikki Kovalainen | R27/01 |
| | | (03 Sat practice) |

**FERRARI**
| 5 | Felipe Massa | F2007/260 |
| 6 | Kimi Räikkönen | F2007/261 |
| T-car | | F2007/258 |

**HONDA**
| 7 | Jenson Button | RA107/04 |
| 8 | Rubens Barrichello | RA107/02 |
| T-car | | RA107/01 |

**BMW-SAUBER**
| 9 | Nick Heidfeld | F1.07/05 |
| 10 | Robert Kubica | F1.07/03 |
| | | (04 Fri 1st practice) |

**TOYOTA**
| 11 | Ralf Schumacher | TF107/03 |
| 12 | Jarno Trulli | TF107/04 |
| T-car | | TF107/01 |

**RED BULL-RENAULT**
| 14 | David Coulthard | RB3/3 |
| 15 | Mark Webber | RB3/2 |
| T-car | | RB3/1 |

**WILLIAMS-TOYOTA**
| 16 | Nico Rosberg | FW29/03 |
| 17 | Alexander Wurz | FW29/04 |
| T-car | | FW29/01 |

**TORO ROSSO-FERRARI**
| 18 | Vitantonio Liuzzi | STR02/03 |
| 19 | Scott Speed | STR02/01 |
| T-car | | STR02/02 |

**SPYKER-FERRARI**
| 20 | Adrian Sutil | F8-VII/03 |
| 21 | Christijan Albers | F8-VII/01 |
| T-car | | F8-VII/02 |

**SUPER AGURI-HONDA**
| 22 | Takuma Sato | SA07/04 |
| 23 | Anthony Davidson | SA07/03 |
| T-car | | SA07/02 |

## ROUND 4 SPANISH GP

**McLAREN-MERCEDES**
| 1 | Fernando Alonso | MP4-22/06 |
| 2 | Lewis Hamilton | MP4-22/05 |
| T-car | | MP4-22/03 |

**RENAULT**
| 3 | Giancarlo Fisichella | R27/04 |
| | | (02 Fri) |
| 4 | Heikki Kovalainen | R27/03 |

**FERRARI**
| 5 | Felipe Massa | F2007/260 |
| 6 | Kimi Räikkönen | F2007/262 |
| | | (261 Fri) |

**HONDA**
| 7 | Jenson Button | RA107/04 |
| 8 | Rubens Barrichello | RA107/02 |
| T-car | | RA107/01 |

**BMW-SAUBER**
| 9 | Nick Heidfeld | F1.07/05 |
| 10 | Robert Kubica | F1.07/07 |
| T-car | | F1.07/04 |

**TOYOTA**
| 11 | Ralf Schumacher | TF107/05 |
| 12 | Jarno Trulli | TF107/04 |
| T-car | | TF107/01 |

**RED BULL-RENAULT**
| 14 | David Coulthard | RB3/3 |
| 15 | Mark Webber | RB3/2 |
| T-car | | RB3/1 |

**WILLIAMS-TOYOTA**
| 16 | Nico Rosberg | FW29/05 |
| 17 | Alexander Wurz | FW29/04 |
| T-car | | FW29/03 |

**TORO ROSSO-FERRARI**
| 18 | Vitantonio Liuzzi | STR02/03 |
| 19 | Scott Speed | STR02/04 |
| T-car | | STR02/01 |

**SPYKER-FERRARI**
| 20 | Adrian Sutil | F8-VII/03 |
| 21 | Christijan Albers | F8-VII/02 |
| T-car | | F8-VII/01 |

**SUPER AGURI-HONDA**
| 22 | Takuma Sato | SA07/04 |
| 23 | Anthony Davidson | SA07/03 |
| T-car | | SA07/02 |

## ROUND 5 MONACO GP

**McLAREN-MERCEDES**
| | | |
|---|---|---|
| 1 | Fernando Alonso | MP4-22/06 |
| 2 | Lewis Hamilton | MP4-22/05 |
| | T-car | MP4-22/03 |

**RENAULT**
| | | |
|---|---|---|
| 3 | Giancarlo Fisichella | R27/05 |
| | | (04 Thu 1st practice) |
| 4 | Heikki Kovalainen | R27/03 |
| | | (02 Thu) |

**FERRARI**
| | | |
|---|---|---|
| 5 | Felipe Massa | F2007/260 |
| 6 | Kimi Räikkönen | F2007/262 |
| | T-car | F2007/261 |

**HONDA**
| | | |
|---|---|---|
| 7 | Jenson Button | RA107/04 |
| 8 | Rubens Barrichello | RA107/02 |
| | T-car | RA107/01 |

**BMW-SAUBER**
| | | |
|---|---|---|
| 9 | Nick Heidfeld | F1.07/05 |
| 10 | Robert Kubica | F1.07/07 |
| | T-car | F1.07/04 |

**TOYOTA**
| | | |
|---|---|---|
| 11 | Ralf Schumacher | TF107/05 |
| 12 | Jarno Trulli | TF107/04 |
| | T-car | TF107/03 |

**RED BULL-RENAULT**
| | | |
|---|---|---|
| 14 | David Coulthard | RB3/3 |
| 15 | Mark Webber | RB3/2 |
| | T-car | RB3/1 |

**WILLIAMS-TOYOTA**
| | | |
|---|---|---|
| 16 | Nico Rosberg | FW29/05 |
| 17 | Alexander Wurz | FW29/04 |
| | T-car | FW29/03 |

**TORO ROSSO-FERRARI**
| | | |
|---|---|---|
| 18 | Vitantonio Liuzzi | STR02/03 |
| 19 | Scott Speed | STR02/04 |
| | T-car | STR02/01 |

**SPYKER-FERRARI**
| | | |
|---|---|---|
| 20 | Adrian Sutil | F8-VII/03 |
| 21 | Christijan Albers | F8-VII/02 |
| | T-car | F8-VII/01 |

**SUPER AGURI-HONDA**
| | | |
|---|---|---|
| 22 | Takuma Sato | SA07/04 |
| 23 | Anthony Davidson | SA07/03 |
| | T-car | SA07/02 |

## ROUND 7 UNITED STATES GP

**McLAREN-MERCEDES**
| | | |
|---|---|---|
| 1 | Fernando Alonso | MP4-22/06 |
| 2 | Lewis Hamilton | MP4-22/01 |
| | T-car | MP4-22/03 |
| | T-car | MP4-22/05 |

**RENAULT**
| | | |
|---|---|---|
| 3 | Giancarlo Fisichella | R27/05 |
| 4 | Heikki Kovalainen | R27/03 |
| | | (02 Fri) |

**FERRARI**
| | | |
|---|---|---|
| 5 | Felipe Massa | F2007/260 |
| 6 | Kimi Räikkönen | F2007/262 |
| | T-car | F2007/261 |

**HONDA**
| | | |
|---|---|---|
| 7 | Jenson Button | RA107/04 |
| 8 | Rubens Barrichello | RA107/05 |
| | T-car | RA107/02 |

**BMW-SAUBER**
| | | |
|---|---|---|
| 9 | Nick Heidfeld | F1.07/05 |
| 10 | Sebastian Vettel | F1.07/03 |
| | T-car | F1.07/04 |

**TOYOTA**
| | | |
|---|---|---|
| 11 | Ralf Schumacher | TF107/05 |
| 12 | Jarno Trulli | TF107/06 |
| | T-car | TF107/04 |

**RED BULL-RENAULT**
| | | |
|---|---|---|
| 14 | David Coulthard | RB3/3 |
| 15 | Mark Webber | RB3/4 |
| | T-car | RB3/1 |

**WILLIAMS-TOYOTA**
| | | |
|---|---|---|
| 16 | Nico Rosberg | FW29/05 |
| 17 | Alexander Wurz | FW29/04 |
| 38 | Kazuki Nakajima | FW29/03 |

**TORO ROSSO-FERRARI**
| | | |
|---|---|---|
| 18 | Vitantonio Liuzzi | STR02/03 |
| 19 | Scott Speed | STR02/04 |
| | T-car | STR02/01 |

**SPYKER-FERRARI**
| | | |
|---|---|---|
| 20 | Adrian Sutil | F8-VII/03 |
| 21 | Christijan Albers | F8-VII/02 |
| | T-car | F8-VII/01 |

**SUPER AGURI-HONDA**
| | | |
|---|---|---|
| 22 | Takuma Sato | SA07/04 |
| 23 | Anthony Davidson | SA07/02 |
| | | (03 Fri & Sat) |

## ROUND 6 CANADIAN GP

**McLAREN-MERCEDES**
| | | |
|---|---|---|
| 1 | Fernando Alonso | MP4-22/06 |
| 2 | Lewis Hamilton | MP4-22/01 |
| | T-car | MP4-22/03 |
| | T-car | MP4-22/05 |

**RENAULT**
| | | |
|---|---|---|
| 3 | Giancarlo Fisichella | R27/05 |
| | | (02 Fri) |
| 4 | Heikki Kovalainen | R27/03 |
| | | (06 Fri) |

**FERRARI**
| | | |
|---|---|---|
| 5 | Felipe Massa | F2007/260 |
| 6 | Kimi Räikkönen | F2007/262 |
| | T-car | F2007/261 |

**HONDA**
| | | |
|---|---|---|
| 7 | Jenson Button | RA107/04 |
| 8 | Rubens Barrichello | RA107/05 |
| | T-car | RA107/02 |

**BMW-SAUBER**
| | | |
|---|---|---|
| 9 | Nick Heidfeld | F1.07/05 |
| 10 | Robert Kubica | F1.07/07 |
| | T-car | F1.07/04 |

**TOYOTA**
| | | |
|---|---|---|
| 11 | Ralf Schumacher | TF107/05 |
| 12 | Jarno Trulli | TF107/06 |
| | T-car | TF107/04 |

**RED BULL-RENAULT**
| | | |
|---|---|---|
| 14 | David Coulthard | RB3/3 |
| 15 | Mark Webber | RB3/4 |
| | T-car | RB3/1 |

**WILLIAMS-TOYOTA**
| | | |
|---|---|---|
| 16 | Nico Rosberg | FW29/05 |
| 17 | Alexander Wurz | FW29/04 |
| 38 | Kazuki Nakajima | FW29/03 |

**TORO ROSSO-FERRARI**
| | | |
|---|---|---|
| 18 | Vitantonio Liuzzi | STR02/03 |
| 19 | Scott Speed | STR02/04 |
| | T-car | STR02/01 |

**SPYKER-FERRARI**
| | | |
|---|---|---|
| 20 | Adrian Sutil | F8-VII/03 |
| 21 | Christijan Albers | F8-VII/02 |
| | T-car | F8-VII/01 |

**SUPER AGURI-HONDA**
| | | |
|---|---|---|
| 22 | Takuma Sato | SA07/04 |
| 23 | Anthony Davidson | SA07/03 |
| | T-car | SA07/02 |

## ROUND 8 FRENCH GP

**McLAREN-MERCEDES**
| | | |
|---|---|---|
| 1 | Fernando Alonso | MP4-22/06 |
| 2 | Lewis Hamilton | MP4-22/04 |
| | T-car | MP4-22/03 |
| | T-car | MP4-22/05 |

**RENAULT**
| | | |
|---|---|---|
| 3 | Giancarlo Fisichella | R27/05 |
| | | (02 Fri) |
| 4 | Heikki Kovalainen | R27/03 |

**FERRARI**
| | | |
|---|---|---|
| 5 | Felipe Massa | F2007/260 |
| 6 | Kimi Räikkönen | F2007/262 |
| | T-car | F2007/261 |

**HONDA**
| | | |
|---|---|---|
| 7 | Jenson Button | RA107/04 |
| 8 | Rubens Barrichello | RA107/05 |
| | T-car | RA107/02 |

**BMW-SAUBER**
| | | |
|---|---|---|
| 9 | Nick Heidfeld | F1.07/05 |
| 10 | Robert Kubica | F1.07/03 |
| | T-car | F1.07/04 |

**TOYOTA**
| | | |
|---|---|---|
| 11 | Ralf Schumacher | TF107/05 |
| 12 | Jarno Trulli | TF107/06 |
| | T-car | TF107/04 |

**RED BULL-RENAULT**
| | | |
|---|---|---|
| 14 | David Coulthard | RB3/3 |
| 15 | Mark Webber | RB3/4 |
| | T-car | RB3/1 |

**WILLIAMS-TOYOTA**
| | | |
|---|---|---|
| 16 | Nico Rosberg | FW29/05 |
| 17 | Alexander Wurz | FW29/04 |
| | T-car | FW29/03 |

**TORO ROSSO-FERRARI**
| | | |
|---|---|---|
| 18 | Vitantonio Liuzzi | STR02/03 |
| 19 | Scott Speed | STR02/04 |
| | T-car | STR02/01 |

**SPYKER-FERRARI**
| | | |
|---|---|---|
| 20 | Adrian Sutil | F8-VII/04 |
| | | (03 Fri & Sat) |
| 21 | Christijan Albers | F8-VII/01 |
| | | (02 Fri) |

**SUPER AGURI-HONDA**
| | | |
|---|---|---|
| 22 | Takuma Sato | SA07/04 |
| 23 | Anthony Davidson | SA07/03 |
| | T-car | SA07/02 |

## ROUND 9 BRITISH GP

**McLAREN-MERCEDES**
| 1 | Fernando Alonso | MP4-22/06 |
| 2 | Lewis Hamilton | MP4-22/04 |
| | T-car | MP4-22/05 |

**RENAULT**
| 3 | Giancarlo Fisichella | R27/05 |
| | | (02 Fri) |
| 4 | Heikki Kovalainen | R27/03 |

**FERRARI**
| 5 | Felipe Massa | F2007/260 |
| 6 | Kimi Räikkönen | F2007/262 |
| | T-car | F2007/261 |

**HONDA**
| 7 | Jenson Button | RA107/04 |
| 8 | Rubens Barrichello | RA107/05 |
| 34 | Christian Klien | RA107/04 |
| | T-car | RA107/02 |

**BMW-SAUBER**
| 9 | Nick Heidfeld | F1.07/05 |
| 10 | Robert Kubica | F1.07/03 |
| | T-car | F1.07/04 |

**TOYOTA**
| 11 | Ralf Schumacher | TF107/05 |
| 12 | Jarno Trulli | TF107/06 |
| | T-car | TF107/04 |

**RED BULL-RENAULT**
| 14 | David Coulthard | RB3/3 |
| 15 | Mark Webber | RB3/4 |
| | T-car | RB3/1 |

**WILLIAMS-TOYOTA**
| 16 | Nico Rosberg | FW29/05 |
| 17 | Alexander Wurz | FW29/03 |
| | T-car | FW29/04 |

**TORO ROSSO-FERRARI**
| 18 | Vitantonio Liuzzi | STR02/03 |
| 19 | Scott Speed | STR02/04 |
| | T-car | STR02/01 |

**SPYKER-FERRARI**
| 20 | Adrian Sutil | F8-VII/03 |
| 21 | Christijan Albers | F8-VII/04 |
| | T-car | F8-VII/02 |

**SUPER AGURI-HONDA**
| 22 | Takuma Sato | SA07/02 |
| | | (04 Fri & Sat) |
| 23 | Anthony Davidson | SA07/03 |

## ROUND 12 TURKISH GP

**McLAREN-MERCEDES**
| 1 | Fernando Alonso | MP4-22/06 |
| 2 | Lewis Hamilton | MP4-22/01 |
| | T-car | MP4-22/03 |

**RENAULT**
| 3 | Giancarlo Fisichella | R27/05 |
| 4 | Heikki Kovalainen | R27/03 |
| | | (02 Fri) |

**FERRARI**
| 5 | Felipe Massa | F2007/263 |
| 6 | Kimi Räikkönen | F2007/262 |
| | T-car | F2007/261 |

**HONDA**
| 7 | Jenson Button | RA107/04 |
| 8 | Rubens Barrichello | RA107/05 |
| | T-car | RA107/02 |

**BMW-SAUBER**
| 9 | Nick Heidfeld | F1.07/08 |
| 10 | Robert Kubica | F1.07/03 |
| | T-car | F1.07/04 |

**TOYOTA**
| 11 | Ralf Schumacher | TF107/05 |
| 12 | Jarno Trulli | TF107/04 |
| | T-car | TF107/06 |

**RED BULL-RENAULT**
| 14 | David Coulthard | RB3/5 |
| 15 | Mark Webber | RB3/4 |
| | T-car | RB3/1 |

**WILLIAMS-TOYOTA**
| 16 | Nico Rosberg | FW29/05 |
| 17 | Alexander Wurz | FW29/03 |
| | T-car | FW29/04 |

**TORO ROSSO-FERRARI**
| 18 | Vitantonio Liuzzi | STR02/03 |
| 19 | Sebastian Vettel | STR02/04 |
| | T-car | STR02/01 |

**SPYKER-FERRARI**
| 20 | Adrian Sutil | F8-VII/01 |
| 21 | Sakon Yamamoto | F8-VII/02 |

**SUPER AGURI-HONDA**
| 22 | Takuma Sato | SA07/02 |
| 23 | Anthony Davidson | SA07/03 |
| | T-car | SA07/04 |

## ROUND 10 EUROPEAN GP

**McLAREN-MERCEDES**
| 1 | Fernando Alonso | MP4-22/06 |
| 2 | Lewis Hamilton | MP4-22/05 |
| | | (01 Fri & Sat) |
| | T-car | MP4-22/04 |

**RENAULT**
| 3 | Giancarlo Fisichella | R27/05 |
| 4 | Heikki Kovalainen | R27/03 (02 Fri) |

**FERRARI**
| 5 | Felipe Massa | F2007/260 |
| 6 | Kimi Räikkönen | F2007/262 |
| | T-car | F2007/261 |

**HONDA**
| 7 | Jenson Button | RA107/04 |
| 8 | Rubens Barrichello | RA107/05 |
| | T-car | RA107/02 |

**BMW-SAUBER**
| 9 | Nick Heidfeld | F1.07/05 |
| 10 | Robert Kubica | F1.07/03 |
| | T-car | F1.07/04 |

**TOYOTA**
| 11 | Ralf Schumacher | TF107/05 |
| 12 | Jarno Trulli | TF107/04 |
| | | (06 Fri 1st practice) |

**RED BULL-RENAULT**
| 14 | David Coulthard | RB3/3 |
| 15 | Mark Webber | RB3/4 |
| | T-car | RB3/1 |

**WILLIAMS-TOYOTA**
| 16 | Nico Rosberg | FW29/05 |
| 17 | Alexander Wurz | FW29/03 |
| | T-car | FW29/04 |

**TORO ROSSO-FERRARI**
| 18 | Vitantonio Liuzzi | STR02/03 |
| 19 | Scott Speed | STR02/04 |
| | T-car | STR02/01 |

**SPYKER-FERRARI**
| 20 | Adrian Sutil | F8-VII/03 |
| 21 | Markus Winkelhock | F8-VII/04 |
| | T-car | F8-VII/02 |

**SUPER AGURI-HONDA**
| 22 | Takuma Sato | SA07/02 |
| 23 | Anthony Davidson | SA07/03 |
| | T-car | SA07/04 |

## ROUND 13 ITALIAN GP

**McLAREN-MERCEDES**
| 1 | Fernando Alonso | MP4-22/06 |
| 2 | Lewis Hamilton | MP4-22/01 |
| | T-car | MP4-22/03 |

**RENAULT**
| 3 | Giancarlo Fisichella | R27/02 |
| | | (05 Sat practice) |
| 4 | Heikki Kovalainen | R27/03 |

**FERRARI**
| 5 | Felipe Massa | F2007/263 |
| 6 | Kimi Räikkönen | F2007/262 |
| | | (264 Fri & Sat practice) |

**HONDA**
| 7 | Jenson Button | RA107/04 |
| 8 | Rubens Barrichello | RA107/05 |
| | T-car | RA107/02 |

**BMW-SAUBER**
| 9 | Nick Heidfeld | F1.07/08 |
| 10 | Robert Kubica | F1.07/03 |
| | T-car | F1.07/04 |

**TOYOTA**
| 11 | Ralf Schumacher | TF107/05 |
| 12 | Jarno Trulli | TF107/04 |
| | T-car | TF107/03 |

**RED BULL-RENAULT**
| 14 | David Coulthard | RB3/5 |
| 15 | Mark Webber | RB3/4 |
| | T-car | RB3/1 |

**WILLIAMS-TOYOTA**
| 16 | Nico Rosberg | FW29/05 |
| 17 | Alexander Wurz | FW29/03 |
| | T-car | FW29/04 |

**TORO ROSSO-FERRARI**
| 18 | Vitantonio Liuzzi | STR02/03 |
| 19 | Sebastian Vettel | STR02/04 |
| | T-car | STR02/01 |

**SPYKER-FERRARI**
| 20 | Adrian Sutil | F8-VII/03 |
| 21 | Sakon Yamamoto | F8-VII/04 |
| | T-car | F8-VII/01 |

**SUPER AGURI-HONDA**
| 22 | Takuma Sato | SA07/02 |
| 23 | Anthony Davidson | SA07/03 |
| | T-car | SA07/04 |

## ROUND 11 HUNGARIAN GP

**McLAREN-MERCEDES**
| 1 | Fernando Alonso | MP4-22/06 |
| 2 | Lewis Hamilton | MP4-22/05 |
| | T-car | MP4-22/04 |

**RENAULT**
| 3 | Giancarlo Fisichella | R27/05 |
| | | (02 Fri) |
| 4 | Heikki Kovalainen | R27/03 |

**FERRARI**
| 5 | Felipe Massa | F2007/260 |
| 6 | Kimi Räikkönen | F2007/262 |
| | T-car | F2007/261 |

**HONDA**
| 7 | Jenson Button | RA107/04 |
| 8 | Rubens Barrichello | RA107/05 |
| | T-car | RA107/02 |

**BMW-SAUBER**
| 9 | Nick Heidfeld | F1.07/05 |
| 10 | Robert Kubica | F1.07/03 |
| | T-car | F1.07/04 |

**TOYOTA**
| 11 | Ralf Schumacher | TF107/05 |
| 12 | Jarno Trulli | TF107/06 |
| | T-car | TF107/04 |

**RED BULL-RENAULT**
| 14 | David Coulthard | RB3/3 |
| 15 | Mark Webber | RB3/4 |
| | T-car | RB3/1 |

**WILLIAMS-TOYOTA**
| 16 | Nico Rosberg | FW29/05 |
| 17 | Alexander Wurz | FW29/03 |
| | T-car | FW29/04 |

**TORO ROSSO-FERRARI**
| 18 | Vitantonio Liuzzi | STR02/03 |
| 19 | Sebastian Vettel | STR02/04 |
| | T-car | STR02/01 |

**SPYKER-FERRARI**
| 20 | Adrian Sutil | F8-VII/03 |
| 21 | Sakon Yamamoto | F8-VII/04 |
| | T-car | F8-VII/02 |

**SUPER AGURI-HONDA**
| 22 | Takuma Sato | SA07/02 |
| 23 | Anthony Davidson | SA07/03 |
| | T-car | SA07/04 |

## ROUND 14 BELGIAN GP

**McLAREN-MERCEDES**
| 1 | Fernando Alonso | MP4-22/06 |
| 2 | Lewis Hamilton | MP4-22/01 |
| | T-car | MP4-22/03 |

**RENAULT**
| 3 | Giancarlo Fisichella | R27/02 |
| 4 | Heikki Kovalainen | R27/03 |
| | | (05 Fri) |

**FERRARI**
| 5 | Felipe Massa | F2007/263 |
| 6 | Kimi Räikkönen | F2007/262 |
| | T-car | F2007/260 |

**HONDA**
| 7 | Jenson Button | RA107/04 |
| 8 | Rubens Barrichello | RA107/05 |
| | T-car | RA107/02 |

**BMW-SAUBER**
| 9 | Nick Heidfeld | F1.07/08 |
| 10 | Robert Kubica | F1.07/03 |
| | T-car | F1.07/04 |

**TOYOTA**
| 11 | Ralf Schumacher | TF107/05 |
| 12 | Jarno Trulli | TF107/04 |
| | T-car | TF107/03 |

**RED BULL-RENAULT**
| 14 | David Coulthard | RB3/3 |
| 15 | Mark Webber | RB3/4 |
| | T-car | RB3/1 |

**WILLIAMS-TOYOTA**
| 16 | Nico Rosberg | FW29/05 |
| 17 | Alexander Wurz | FW29/03 |
| | T-car | FW29/04 |

**TORO ROSSO-FERRARI**
| 18 | Vitantonio Liuzzi | STR02/03 |
| 19 | Sebastian Vettel | STR02/04 |
| | T-car | STR02/01 |

**SPYKER-FERRARI**
| 20 | Adrian Sutil | F8-VII/03 |
| 21 | Sakon Yamamoto | F8-VII/04 |
| | T-car | F8-VII/02 |

**SUPER AGURI-HONDA**
| 22 | Takuma Sato | SA07/02 |
| 23 | Anthony Davidson | SA07/03 |
| | T-car | SA07/04 |

## ROUND 15 JAPANESE GP

**McLAREN-MERCEDES**
| 1 | Fernando Alonso | MP4-22/06 |
|---|---|---|
| 2 | Lewis Hamilton | MP4-22/05 |
| | T-car | MP4-22/03 |

**RENAULT**
| 3 | Giancarlo Fisichella | R27/02 (05 Fri) |
|---|---|---|
| 4 | Heikki Kovalainen | R27/03 |

**FERRARI**
| 5 | Felipe Massa | F2007/263 |
|---|---|---|
| 6 | Kimi Räikkönen | F2007/262 |
| | T-car | F2007/260 |

**HONDA**
| 7 | Jenson Button | RA107/04 |
|---|---|---|
| 8 | Rubens Barrichello | RA107/02 (05 Fri) |

**BMW-SAUBER**
| 9 | Nick Heidfeld | F1.07/08 |
|---|---|---|
| 10 | Robert Kubica | F1.07/03 |
| | T-car | F1.07/04 |

**TOYOTA**
| 11 | Ralf Schumacher | TF107/05 |
|---|---|---|
| 12 | Jarno Trulli | TF107/04 |
| | T-car | TF107/03 |

**RED BULL-RENAULT**
| 14 | David Coulthard | RB3/5 |
|---|---|---|
| 15 | Mark Webber | RB3/4 |
| | T-car | RB3/1 |

**WILLIAMS-TOYOTA**
| 16 | Nico Rosberg | FW29/05 |
|---|---|---|
| 17 | Alexander Wurz | FW29/03 |
| | T-car | FW29/04 |

**TORO ROSSO-FERRARI**
| 18 | Vitantonio Liuzzi | STR02/01 |
|---|---|---|
| | | (03 Fri & Sat) |
| 19 | Sebastian Vettel | STR02/04 |

**SPYKER-FERRARI**
| 20 | Adrian Sutil | F8-VII/03 |
|---|---|---|
| 21 | Sakon Yamamoto | F8-VII/04 |
| | T-car | F8-VII/02 |

**SUPER AGURI-HONDA**
| 22 | Takuma Sato | SA07/02 |
|---|---|---|
| 23 | Anthony Davidson | SA07/03 |
| | T-car | SA07/04 |

Photographs: Peter J Fox/www.crash.net

## ROUND 16 CHINESE GP

**McLAREN-MERCEDES**
| 1 | Fernando Alonso | MP4-22/03 |
|---|---|---|
| 2 | Lewis Hamilton | MP4-22/05 |
| | T-car | MP4-22/04 |

**RENAULT**
| 3 | Giancarlo Fisichella | R27/02 |
|---|---|---|
| 4 | Heikki Kovalainen | R27/03 |
| | | (05 Fri) |

**FERRARI**
| 5 | Felipe Massa | F2007/263 |
|---|---|---|
| 6 | Kimi Räikkönen | F2007/262 |
| | T-car | F2007/260 |

**HONDA**
| 7 | Jenson Button | RA107/04 |
|---|---|---|
| 8 | Rubens Barrichello | RA107/02 |
| | | (05 Fri) |

**BMW-SAUBER**
| 9 | Nick Heidfeld | F1.07/08 |
|---|---|---|
| 10 | Robert Kubica | F1.07/03 |
| | T-car | F1.07/04 |

**TOYOTA**
| 11 | Ralf Schumacher | TF107/05 |
|---|---|---|
| 12 | Jarno Trulli | TF107/04 |
| | T-car | TF107/03 |

**RED BULL-RENAULT**
| 14 | David Coulthard | RB3/5 |
|---|---|---|
| 15 | Mark Webber | RB3/4 |
| | T-car | RB3/1 |

**WILLIAMS-TOYOTA**
| 16 | Nico Rosberg | FW29/05 |
|---|---|---|
| 17 | Alexander Wurz | FW29/03 |
| 38 | Kazuki Nakajima | FW29/03 |
| | T-car | FW29/04 |

**TORO ROSSO-FERRARI**
| 18 | Vitantonio Liuzzi | STR02/03 |
|---|---|---|
| 19 | Sebastian Vettel | STR02/04 |
| | T-car | STR02/01 |

**SPYKER-FERRARI**
| 20 | Adrian Sutil | F8-VII/03 |
|---|---|---|
| 21 | Sakon Yamamoto | F8-VII/04 |
| | T-car | F8-VII/02 |

**SUPER AGURI-HONDA**
| 22 | Takuma Sato | SA07/02 |
|---|---|---|
| 23 | Anthony Davidson | SA07/03 |
| | T-car | SA07/04 |

## ROUND 17 BRAZILIAN GP

**McLAREN-MERCEDES**
| 1 | Fernando Alonso | MP4-22/03 |
|---|---|---|
| 2 | Lewis Hamilton | MP4-22/05 |
| | T-car | MP4-22/04 |

**RENAULT**
| 3 | Giancarlo Fisichella | R27/02 |
|---|---|---|
| | | (05 Fri 2nd practice) |
| 4 | Heikki Kovalainen | R27/03 |

**FERRARI**
| 5 | Felipe Massa | F2007/263 |
|---|---|---|
| 6 | Kimi Räikkönen | F2007/262 |
| | T-car | F2007/260 |

**HONDA**
| 7 | Jenson Button | RA107/04 |
|---|---|---|
| 8 | Rubens Barrichello | RA107/02 |
| | T-car | RA107/05 |

**BMW-SAUBER**
| 9 | Nick Heidfeld | F1.07/08 |
|---|---|---|
| 10 | Robert Kubica | F1.07/03 |
| | T-car | F1.07/04 |

**TOYOTA**
| 11 | Ralf Schumacher | TF107/05 |
|---|---|---|
| 12 | Jarno Trulli | TF107/04 |
| | T-car | TF107/03 |

**RED BULL-RENAULT**
| 14 | David Coulthard | RB3/5 |
|---|---|---|
| 15 | Mark Webber | RB3/4 |
| | T-car | RB3/1 |

**WILLIAMS-TOYOTA**
| 16 | Nico Rosberg | FW29/05 |
|---|---|---|
| 17 | Kazuki Nakajima | FW29/03 |
| | T-car | FW29/04 |

**TORO ROSSO-FERRARI**
| 18 | Vitantonio Liuzzi | STR02/03 |
|---|---|---|
| 19 | Sebastian Vettel | STR02/04 |
| | T-car | STR02/01 |

**SPYKER-FERRARI**
| 20 | Adrian Sutil | F8-VII/03 |
|---|---|---|
| 21 | Sakon Yamamoto | F8-VII/04 |
| | T-car | F8-VII/02 |

**SUPER AGURI-HONDA**
| 22 | Takuma Sato | SA07/02 |
|---|---|---|
| 23 | Anthony Davidson | SA07/03 |
| | T-car | SA07/04 |

# GRANDS PRIX 2007
## by ALAN HENRY & DAVID TREMAYNE

Taking over the role vacated by Michael Schumacher, Kimi Räikkönen delivers an impressively dominant run to a début victory in the Ferrari F2007.

Photograph: Peter J Fox/www.crash.net

# AUSTRALIAN GP

## MELBOURNE

**Main: After so many false starts in his F1 career, Anthony Davidson at last settles down as a full-time member of the GP community at the wheel of his Super Aguri.**

**Right: After Michelin's withdrawal, Bridgestone is F1's sole tyre supplier.**

**Below right: Robert Kubica, starting his first full season as a member of the BMW Sauber squad, is one of many facing the challenge of adapting to Bridgestones.**

**Below: Spruced up and ready for the start of a new season, the Spyker team is prepared with Adrian Sutil's car.**

Photographs: Peter J Fox/www.crash.net

## NEW RULES FOR 2007

### Bridgestone to manage F1 monopoly

Michelin's withdrawal from F1 left Bridgestone in a supply monopoly situation and, from the outset, the Japanese company worked to ensure that the former Michelin runners would get as much technical back-up as those teams that were well-accustomed to working with the company.

Bridgestone picked two tyre specifications from its range of four for each race, offering differing constructions and compounds to cope with the widest range of weather and track abrasiveness. However, the new rules required the teams to use both types of tyres during the course of the race, introducing a wild card by forcing them to use a nominally less-than-optimum tyre choice for at least one stint.

### New engine rules

From the start of the season engine specifications were frozen until the end of 2009, with only very minor changes permitted within the published rules. In addition, each engine was limited to an operational maximum of 19,000 rpm, capping the traditional quest for extra revs as a means of finding more engine power.

Engine development programmes instead concentrated on improving driveability and efficiency through secondary measures such as engine-mapping software, a sophisticated method of ensuring that the engine is operating to maximum efficiency at all speeds and in all conditions.

### Changes to the Friday format

In the light of an agreement between the teams to limit testing during the season away from GP weekends, the two free practice sessions on Fridays were extended from 60 to 90 minutes. The two-race engine rule was still in force, but it no longer applied to the first two free practice sessions, with the result that the teams were free to cover unlimited mileage on Fridays. This of course obliged teams going into their second engine weekend to fit another unit just for Friday and then revert to the appropriately sealed unit in time for Saturday morning, a requirement that piled an increased workload on the mechanics.

Third drivers were also permitted to participate on Fridays, but only on the condition that they shared cars with one of the two race drivers.

## THE TEAMS

### VODAFONE McLAREN MERCEDES

All-new driver line-up of double world champion Fernando Alonso and emergent star Lewis Hamilton, the latter promoted to the F1 front line after an epic season in GP2. Hopes pinned on the new MP4-22 challenger powered by the latest Mercedes FO 108T V8 engine, a combination that demonstrated promising potential in winter testing.

### ING RENAULT F1 TEAM

Reigning world champion facing life without Fernando Alonso and pinning its hopes on Giancarlo Fisichella as de facto team leader at the wheel of one of the new R27 contenders. Former test driver and 2005 GP2 series runner-up Heikki Kovalainen moved up to the number-two slot as one of the most promising new arrivals on the F1 scene.

### SCUDERIA FERRARI MARLBORO

Much-speculated arrival of Kimi Räikkönen to partner Michael Schumacher's disciple Felipe Massa opened post-Schuey era. They raced with evolutionary F2007 developed by new technical director Mario Almondo's design team. Luca Badoer and Marc Gené retained as test drivers.

### HONDA RACING F1 TEAM

Buoyed up by Jenson Button's late-2006 form, the Brackley-based team stormed into the new season determined to sustain that competitive momentum with Rubens Barrichello still paired with Button in the new RA107s. Former Red Bull racer Christian Klien was recruited as principal test driver to succeed Anthony Davidson, who was promoted to Super Aguri.

### BMW SAUBER F1 TEAM

Aiming to build on steady progress made in 2006 with Nick Heidfeld and Robert Kubica looking for consistent points-scoring finishes in F1.07 contender evolved by Willy Rampf's design team at the operation's Hinwil base. Sebastian Vettel retained as test driver. Hoping that early gearbox electronics problems would be licked in time for the opening race of the year.

### PANASONIC TOYOTA RACING

Struggling to pull itself out of the midfield ruck, this top-heavy operation was looking to make good on its promise to emerge as a potentially winning contender. Ralf Schumacher embarked on the third year of his $19-million-a-season contract, still partnered by Jarno Trulli and with Franck Montagny aboard as test driver.

### RED BULL RACING

First proper Adrian Newey-devised design concept for the Milton Keynes-based team, this year using Renault V8 engines to propel the ambitions of David Coulthard and the incoming Mark Webber. New car designed by third-party sub-contractors Red Bull Technology, thereby exploiting the provision in the rules permitting them to supply materially the same chassis to Scuderia Toro Rosso.

### AT&T WILLIAMS

For their third engine partner in as many seasons, Sir Frank's eponymous team switched from Cosworth to Toyota power for the new FW29. Test driver Alex Wurz was promoted to partner Nico Rosberg; the popular Austrian driver returned full-time to the F1 field after a five-year absence. Narain Karthikeyan and Kazuki Nakajima signed as test drivers.

### SCUDERIA TORO ROSSO

Vitantonio Liuzzi and Scott Speed still partnered together in the former Minardi squad, which switched from using rev-restricted Cosworth V10 engines to the customer Ferrari V8s previously used by Red Bull. Technical director Alex Hitzinger was replaced in the role by Giorgio Ascanelli early in the year.

### ETIHAD ALDAR SPYKER F1 TEAM

Recently rebranded by its Dutch owners, Spyker switched to Ferrari power and recruited Lewis Hamilton's one-time F3 team-mate Adrian Sutil to partner Christijan Albers in 2007. Recently appointed chief technical officer Mike Gascoyne was flexing his muscles for a big challenge.

### SUPER AGURI F1 TEAM

Still struggling to make its mark, Super Aguri relied on the design of the 2006 Honda RA106 as the basis of its new contender, the SA07, driven by Anthony Davidson and Takuma Sato. Sakon Yamamoto was retained as test driver.

## DIARY

NOVEMBER 2006

Ferrari appoints senior manager Mario Almondo to the role of F1 technical director as successor to Ross Brawn, who is leaving Maranello for a year's sabbatical away from the pit wall.

FIA president Max Mosley has a 'peace in our time' meeting with BMW's Burkhard Göschel in his capacity as a leading light in the Grand Prix Manufacturers' Association. Their discussion centres on how F1 should develop while maintaining road car relevance.

Bernie Ecclestone indicates that an Indian GP could be on the cards within the next two or three years. Bernie also says that a 20-race F1 calendar may become inevitable within another four or five years.

DECEMBER 2006

Mika Häkkinen disappoints in a test at the wheel of the McLaren-Mercedes MP4-21.

Former Ferrari F1 driver Clay Regazzoni is killed in a road accident near Parma in northern Italy.

Fernando Alonso has his first McLaren test, wearing unbranded overalls, at Barcelona.

Bruno Senna, nephew of the late Ayrton, makes it clear that his 2007 GP2 programme should be seen as a springboard to an F1 career within the next couple of seasons.

Three pre-Christmas F1 tests attract ten teams split between Barcelona and Jerez over nine days before the holiday shut-down.

Aguri Suzuki insists that his team's new car is a totally different machine from last season's Honda RA106, but many teams remain sceptical and the row over customer cars shows no sign of abating.

JANUARY 2007

Lewis Hamilton walks away from a 130-mph testing accident at Valencia.

Renault admits it is struggling slightly in testing to get the best out of the latest Bridgestone rubber.

Kazuki Nakajima is confirmed as test driver for the Williams-Toyota F1 squad.

FEBRUARY 2007

Michael Schumacher confirms he will continue in a consultancy role with Ferrari, but stops short of outlining his mandate in detail.

## MELBOURNE QUALIFYING

Ferrari's latest recruit, Kimi Räikkönen, wrote his own slice of Maranello history by planting his sleek F2007 on pole position with a best lap of 1m 26.072s in the top-ten shoot-out on his début outing for the team. It was a feat last achieved by the legendary Juan Manuel Fangio, who topped the grid order for the Argentine GP at Buenos Aires at the wheel of a Lancia-Ferrari D50 in 1956.

In truth, Räikkönen's decisive performance came as no surprise. He had been convincingly quick in most of the pre-season tests and the consistency of his lap times during long runs with the latest-generation Bridgestone tyres marked him out as a potential winner long before he arrived in Melbourne.

'It was a great qualifying,' said the obviously satisfied Finn. 'I think our car is more competitive in race trim than over a single lap, but it was a shame for Felipe [Massa], who was not able to get the sort of result he should have done.'

The hapless Brazilian, who'd arrived in Australia aiming to repeat his Interlagos victory from the end of last season, ended up 16th after suffering a gearbox breakage that lost him a lot of track time and prompted the Ferrari squad to install a fresh engine and start him from the back of the grid in an effort to maximise whatever tactical potential he could salvage from this difficult situation.

'Already at the end of free practice we had seen that there was a faulty component in the F2007's gearbox,' explained Luca Baldisserri, head of track operations. 'It was changed as a precaution but, unfortunately, the problem reoccurred and this forced Massa to stop at the side of the track.'

Second and fourth were the McLaren-Mercedes of Fernando Alonso (1m 26.493s) and the impressive Lewis Hamilton (1m 26.755s). The young British driver coolly remained in the

| 1 | J Button | 1:41.647 | 5 | H Kovalainen | +3.03 |
| 2 | F Alonso | +1.231 | 6 | A Sutil | +3.68 |
| 3 | S Vettel | +1.562 | 7 | K Nakajima | +4.23 |
| 4 | J Trulli | +2.483 | | T Sato | |

thick of the battle for fastest time and eventually covered himself in glory with a starting position on the second row. 'I'm overwhelmed to be on the second row for my first grand prix,' he said. 'This weekend is what I've been preparing myself for during the past 13 years and I'm enjoying every moment.'

Alonso seemed a touch cautious. 'I think it has been a difficult day for everybody,' said the reigning world champion. 'In the morning we had some drops of rain again, which was worrying. Qualifying is always difficult and the first qualifying of the year is a little more stressful because you need to get used to the system again and, for me, with a new team, get used to the way your team works. Having said that, I must say that I've felt confident with the car all weekend.'

Despite having battled with on-going gearbox hydraulic problems during winter testing, the BMW Sauber squad was in fine fettle from the start of first free practice and could hardly have asked for more by the end of qualifying, with Nick Heidfeld (1m 26.556s) third on the grid and Robert Kubica (1m 27.347s) fifth.

'It was a fantastic result for us,' enthused Heidfeld. 'We came here having done a race simulation in Bahrain, which worked fine. The car was not perfect and with some fuel on board it was not easy. I think Ferrari has the edge.' Kubica admitted that he might have lapped even quicker had he not missed the chance of an extra lap by one second as the chequered flag came out.

Giancarlo Fisichella confessed that he knew the weekend would be a struggle with the Renault R27, so sixth-fastest on 1m 27.634s wasn't too bad, even allowing for traffic on his best run. Unfortunately Heikki Kovalainen lost time with fuel-pressure problems during Friday free practice and could manage no better than 13th (1m 26.964s). Completing the top ten were Mark Webber's Red Bull (1m 27.934s), the Toyota TF107s of Jarno Trulli (1m 28.404s) and Ralf Schumacher (1m 28.692s) and Takuma Sato, who did an excellent job to line up his Super Aguri tenth with 1m 28.871s, one place ahead of débutant team-mate Anthony Davidson (1m 26.909s).

Jenson Button and Rubens Barrichello struggled abjectly with their Honda RA107s, Button's mood in particular not helped by the nagging memory that he'd been on pole position here 12 months earlier at the wheel of what amounted to this year's 'new' Super Aguri.

Meanwhile, in the Williams camp, Nico Rosberg confessed that his FW29 felt rather on the loose side and he found it difficult to attack really effectively, ending up 12th (1m 26.914s), at least with the satisfaction that he was three places ahead of his team-mate, F1 returnee Alex Wurz (1m 27.393s).

'It was interesting to see how the qualifying sessions worked from a driver's point of view,' said Wurz thoughtfully. 'I'd have to say it is fairly brutal.' Welcome to F1 2007-style, Alex.

**Above:** Honda's Jenson Button immersed in his own thoughts as he waits for the off in the cockpit of his RA107 challenger. Would the controversial 'earth car' livery prove a lucky talisman for the new season?
Photograph: Paul-Henri Cahier

**Left:** Tonio Liuzzi gets the big picture.
Photograph: Jad Sherif/WRi2

**Top left:** Home town heroes together; Mark Webber is joined by the effervescent Kylie Minogue on the Melbourne grid.
Photograph: Peter J Fox/www.crash.net

Above: Fernando Alonso's McLaren MP4-22 lays Bridgestone rubber on the asphalt as Alonso comes up to lap one of the Spykers during his pursuit of Lewis Hamilton.

Inset: Lewis takes time out to exchange words with triple world champion Jackie Stewart.

Right: Nico Rosberg opened his second F1 season with an encouraging seventh place first time out in the new Williams-Toyota.

Photographs: Peter J Fox/www.crash.net

KIMI RÄIKKÖNEN provided the Ferrari team with a seamless transition to the post-Michael Schumacher era when he scored a decisive victory in the Australian Grand Prix, a well-earned success that seemed to endorse the 27-year-old Finn's position as a clear favourite for the 2007 world championship crown. As Räikkönen celebrated his success on the podium, Jean Todt, the Ferrari chief executive and team principal, handed him a mobile phone. The caller was the seven-times world champion who retired at the end of last season. 'I think it was Michael, but the line was pretty bad and I couldn't hear anything,' said Räikkönen with a sly grin.

Yet in so many ways Räikkönen's somewhat predictable success – compromised only by a single fleeting slip when he ran wide up the kerb at the tricky right-hand Turn Three on the sun-drenched Albert Park circuit – was dramatically shaded by a flawless drive from Britain's Lewis Hamilton, who finished third behind his McLaren team-mate Fernando Alonso on his F1 début.

Starting from pole position, Räikkönen edged cleanly into the lead in the opening sprint of the new season, his Ferrari F2007 displaying a small, but decisive, performance edge over the pursuing McLaren-Mercedes MP4-22s, which Alonso and Hamilton had qualified second and fourth.

'It is great to be winning again with my new team, whom I want to thank for giving me a great car,' said Räikkönen. 'The race was not as easy as it might have looked from the outside, partly because shortly after the start the radio failed so it was almost impossible to talk to the pit wall.

'Fortunately we had prepared well for the race and knew what we had to do, but there were a few difficult moments. I was not flat out the whole way, but was adapting my pace to how the race was going.' It was later ascertained that the Ferrari had developed a very slight water leak during the race, but this caused no problem.

Hampered by the failure of his pit-to-car radio, Räikkönen was forced to rely for race information on old-fashioned pit boards held up by his mechanics. He completed the opening lap 1.4s ahead of Nick Heidfeld's BMW-Sauber, with Hamilton dodging through to third place ahead of Alonso in the jostling throng at the first corner.

The fast-starting Heidfeld was running on a very light fuel load and made his first stop only 14 laps into the 58-lap race, eight laps before Alonso brought the first of the McLarens in to refuel for the first time. In the opinion of Ron Dennis, the McLaren team principal, this spell boxed in behind the BMW-Sauber cost Alonso and Hamilton any chance they might have had to challenge Räikkönen for the lead.

'Our race was seriously compromised by the Heidfeld strategy, which we just didn't understand,' said Dennis. 'It smacked of showboating in the opening part of the race. We were boxed in and lost contact with Kimi, after which we had to take a realistic approach because we weren't going to close that gap.'

Dennis was obviously full of praise for Hamilton's performance in his maiden F1 race. 'Both he and Fernando are highly motivational drivers who are a pleasure to work with,' he said.

## THE MOST IMPRESSIVE OF DÉBUTS?

Lewis Hamilton's début in the Australian Grand Prix marked him down as the most impressive F1 freshman to appear on the scene, certainly since Jacques Villeneuve in 1996 and probably since Michael Schumacher five years earlier. More significantly, from the moment the 22-year-old opened his career by setting the fourth-fastest time in Friday's rain-slicked first practice session, the great and the good were queuing up to offer their praise.

'I think that Lewis could well be the best new talent to arrive in F1 that I've ever seen,' said triple world champion Niki Lauda. 'I really don't think I've been as impressed with any new boy as I am with Lewis for as long as I can remember.'

Jackie Stewart added, 'For such a young man he has huge confidence and composure. If he can channel his obvious talent to proper effect, he's clearly got the potential to be absolutely outstanding.' Stewart, not a man to throw compliments around lightly, might also have observed that on Hamilton's fourth flying lap on the Albert Park circuit – in damp conditions – he managed a 1m 40s best lap, quicker than his team-mate Fernando Alonso had done after 12 laps. Of such small indexes are great drivers' reputations made.

In the race Lewis demonstrated great mental acuity. Squeezed out to the right on the run to the first corner by the BMW-Sauber of Robert Kubica – a rival he rates very highly indeed – the new McLaren ace promptly backed out of a rapidly shrinking gap, dodged around the other side of Kubica and neatly despatched him as they slid into the turn. It was a beautifully judged move of near-surgical deftness.

From then on, Hamilton enjoyed a near-perfect run to third place, the only tiny scratch on this canvass of excellence coming when he tweaked a front-wing end plate slightly out of shape over a high kerb. Yet this was the most minor of failings.

'I am absolutely ecstatic,' said Lewis after his first visit to the F1 podium. 'Today's result is more than I ever dreamed of achieving on my grand prix début. The race was intense and I was working very hard. I made a few mistakes, but nothing major, and I really enjoyed myself. It was great to lead the race for a few laps, but I knew it was only a temporary thing.'

Temporary for the moment, perhaps, but not for long.

'I don't think anybody could fail to be impressed with Lewis. About an hour and a half before the race I could see the pressure was getting to him and he was a little nervous, but his steely resolve powered him through.

'When he gets into the car he switches into a very focused and disciplined mindset. Take the first corner; nine times out of ten, drivers who are squeezed like that keep their feet full on the throttle. It takes intelligence to back out of it and go around the other side. But, for Lewis, what a dream weekend. I had more arrogance at every step of my career than he has now. I don't know where he finds the ability to motivate himself and have self-belief without its turning into arrogance. He's so balanced, so on the ground.'

Räikkönen made his first refuelling stop in 9.7s at the end of lap 19, allowing Hamilton to take the lead with Fernando second. On lap 22 Fernando made his first stop in 9.3s and went back into the race third behind Räikkönen and Hamilton. On the next lap Lewis made his first stop in 8.7s and resumed second ahead of his team-mate.

On lap 42 Räikkönen made his second stop, allowing Lewis through into the lead – but Lewis was held up by Takuma Sato's Super Aguri-Honda as he came into the pits for his own second stop (8.2s) at the end of lap 43. Alonso stayed out for another couple of laps before making his second stop in 6.5s and accelerated back into the race in second place ahead of the young British driver.

Heidfeld eventually finished fourth ahead of Giancarlo Fisichella's Renault and Felipe Massa's Ferrari. Massa had started

**Above:** Taken as a whole, Fernando Alonso was pretty satisfied with second on his début outing for McLaren-Mercedes.

**Right:** Felipe Massa recovered superbly from his enforced lowly grid position to wind up a strong fifth at the chequered flag.
Photographs: Peter J Fox/www.crash.net

**Below:** David Coulthard's frayed Red Bull-Renault shudders to a halt in a gravel trap after its collision with the Williams of Alex Wurz.
Photograph: John Morris/M-Pix

last after a gearbox problem disrupted his qualifying efforts.

'The race proved more difficult than I expected,' said Fisichella, who could have been forgiven for reflecting on how easily he had won this race two years earlier. 'From a personal point of view, I got the best I could from the package today, but I was struggling with overall grip from the start.' Despite this, he kept his composure to hang on ahead of the second Ferrari.

'After what happened in qualifying yesterday it would have been difficult to do any better than this sixth place,' shrugged Massa philosophically. 'I was able to run at a good pace even with a full fuel load facing a race that would be one long climb through the field. The F2007 was very competitive, so I am optimistic about the next few races. But here, for sure, if it had not been for the failure in qualifying, I would definitely have been fighting for the win.'

Nico Rosberg (Williams) and Ralf Schumacher (Toyota) completed the ranks of points scorers in seventh and eighth places, while Alex Wurz was fortunate to emerge unhurt after David Coulthard's Red Bull vaulted over his Williams when they collided at Turn Three.

'After his second stop, I was aware that David was close behind me on the track,' said Wurz. 'Suddenly I felt an impact and the next thing I knew, I was his landing pad as the impact had sent him airborne over my car. It looked pretty spectacular, but I'm fine. It's a shame my race ended the way it did, but as soon as we got back to the paddock David came to apologise to me and was a gentleman about the incident.'

Coulthard added, 'I went for the pass but it was over-optimistic on my part. The collision was my fault, not Alex's, so apologies to him for that.'

By any standards Hamilton's was a remarkable performance. It wasn't just that he started the weekend by setting third-fastest time behind the two Ferraris at the end of the first day's practice, but also that the 22-year-old looked as though he'd been handling an F1 car in the heat of race action for years.

At the post-practice media conference Lewis seemed a young man who couldn't put a wheel out of place and his sunny expression contrasted starkly with the morose looks on the faces of Jenson Button and Mark Webber, both of whom had suddenly appreciated the stark reality that their Honda and Red Bull challengers had delivered less than they were hoping for. At least for the moment.

Quite what Button would do to kick-start his career to best possible effect remained something of a mystery. Less than two years ago he had been paying top dollar to buy his way out of a Williams contract and now he must have been wondering what he did it all for.

Jenson's frustration with his ill-handling RA107 reached fever pitch during the race, when he shouted to his pit crew that the car's handling was rubbish and its balance so bad that it was almost impossible to drive. In return, the Honda technicians said that their data suggested Button was mistaken, a response that hardly calmed the mood of the moment.

Things went no better for Button's old karting rival Anthony Davidson on his début for the Super Aguri squad. He ended up spending a night in hospital as a precautionary measure after injuring his back in a heavy landing following a collision with the Spyker of Christijan Albers. Under the circumstances 'Ant' did well to finish 16th.

If Lewis Hamilton was the star of the show, fellow F1 rookie Heikki Kovalainen had a simply dire afternoon on his maiden outing with the Renault R27 – and team boss Flavio Briatore did not shrink from telling the young Finn just how disappointed he was. 'It may have been my grand prix début, but there is very little to remember from it and lots to forget,' said Heikki after finishing tenth.

You could be forgiven for thinking that the same problems as Honda's afflicted the rival Toyota squad, which had yet another disappointing day. Ralf Schumacher scored a single championship point for eighth place and Jarno Trulli came home ninth. 'We had expected to be in the top ten, but to bring two cars home was a good result from this first race,' said Schumacher. 'The conditions were good for the race, but the car was a little difficult, which made it hard work at times.'

*Alan Henry*

**Above:** Kimi Räikkönen enjoyed a relatively unchallenged run to victory for the Prancing Horse.

**Left:** Team boss Flavio Briatore looked bemused and nonplussed by the lack of Renault pace.

Photographs: Peter J Fox/www.crash.net

FIA F1 WORLD CHAMPIONSHIP
ROUND 1

# ING
# AUSTRALIAN GRAND PRIX
MELBOURNE 16–18 MARCH 2007

**ALBERT PARK, MELBOURNE**
Circuit: 3.295 miles / 5.303 km

116/187 mph/kmh

Photograph: Peter J Fox/www.crash.net

---

## RACE RESULTS

| Pos. | Driver | Nat. | No. | Entrant | Car/Engine | Tyres | Laps | Time/Retirement | Speed (mph/km/h) | Gap to leader | Fastest race lap |
|------|--------|------|-----|---------|------------|-------|------|-----------------|------------------|---------------|------------------|
| 1 | Kimi Räikkönen | FIN | 6 | Scuderia Ferrari Marlboro | Ferrari F2007-056 V8 | B | 58 | 1h 25m 28.770s | 134.150/215.893 | | 1m 25.235s 41 |
| 2 | Fernando Alonso | E | 1 | Vodafone McLaren Mercedes | McLaren MP4-22-Mercedes FO 108T V8 | B | 58 | 1h 25m 36.012s | 133.960/215.588 | + 7.242s | 1m 26.314s 20 |
| 3 | Lewis Hamilton | GB | 2 | Vodafone McLaren Mercedes | McLaren MP4-22-Mercedes FO 108T V8 | B | 58 | 1h 25m 47.365s | 133.665/215.113 | + 18.595s | 1m 26.351s 20 |
| 4 | Nick Heidfeld | D | 9 | BMW Sauber F1 Team | BMW Sauber F1.07-BMW P86/7 V8 | B | 58 | 1h 26m 7.533s | 133.143/214.273 | + 38.763s | 1m 26.722s 37 |
| 5 | Giancarlo Fisichella | I | 3 | ING Renault F1 Team | Renault R27-RS27 V8 | B | 58 | 1h 26m 35.239s | 132.432/213.130 | + 1m 6.469s | 1m 26.892s 18 |
| 6 | Felipe Massa | BR | 5 | Scuderia Ferrari Marlboro | Ferrari F2007-056 V8 | B | 58 | 1h 26m 35.575s | 132.424/213.117 | + 1m 6.805s | 1m 27.044s 28 |
| 7 | Nico Rosberg | D | 16 | AT&T Williams | Williams FW29-Toyota RVX-07 V8 | B | 57 | | | + 1 lap | 1m 26.721s 40 |
| 8 | Ralf Schumacher | D | 11 | Panasonic Toyota Racing | Toyota TF107-RVX-07 V8 | B | 57 | | | + 1 lap | 1m 27.796s 42 |
| 9 | Jarno Trulli | I | 12 | Panasonic Toyota Racing | Toyota TF107-RVX-07 V8 | B | 57 | | | + 1 lap | 1m 28.034s 45 |
| 10 | Heikki Kovalainen | FIN | 4 | ING Renault F1 Team | Renault R27-RS27 V8 | B | 57 | | | + 1 lap | 1m 27.592s 44 |
| 11 | Rubens Barrichello | BR | 8 | Honda Racing F1 Team | Honda RA107-RA807E V8 | B | 57 | | | + 1 lap | 1m 28.098s 17 |
| 12 | Takuma Sato | J | 22 | Super Aguri F1 Team | Super Aguri SA07-Honda RA807E V8 | B | 57 | | | + 1 lap | 1m 28.487s 20 |
| 13 | Mark Webber | AUS | 15 | Red Bull Racing | Red Bull RB3-Renault RS27 V8 | B | 57 | | | + 1 lap | 1m 27.501s 21 |
| 14 | Vitantonio Liuzzi | I | 18 | Scuderia Toro Rosso | Toro Rosso STR02-Ferrari 056H V8 | B | 57 | | | + 1 lap | 1m 28.282s 44 |
| 15 | Jenson Button | GB | 7 | Honda Racing F1 Team | Honda RA107-RA807E V8 | B | 57 | | | + 1 lap | 1m 28.387s 42 |
| 16 | Anthony Davidson | GB | 23 | Super Aguri F1 Team | Super Aguri SA07-Honda RA807E V8 | B | 56 | | | + 2 laps | 1m 28.489s 41 |
| 17 | Adrian Sutil | D | 20 | Etihad Aldar Spyker F1 Team | Spyker F8-VII-Ferrari 056H V8 | B | 56 | | | + 2 laps | 1m 28.687s 40 |
| | Alexander Wurz | A | 17 | AT&T Williams | Williams FW29-Toyota RVX-07 V8 | B | 48 | Accident | | | 1m 28.303s 24 |
| | David Coulthard | GB | 14 | Red Bull Racing | Red Bull RB3-Renault RS27 V8 | B | 48 | Accident | | | 1m 27.706s 44 |
| | Robert Kubica | POL | 10 | BMW Sauber F1 Team | BMW Sauber F1.07-BMW P86/7 V8 | B | 36 | Gearbox | | | 1m 26.642s 19 |
| | Scott Speed | USA | 19 | Scuderia Toro Rosso | Toro Rosso STR02-Ferrari 056H V8 | B | 28 | Tyres | | | 1m 28.953s 22 |
| | Christijan Albers | NL | 21 | Etihad Aldar Spyker F1 Team | Spyker F8-VII-Ferrari 056H V8 | B | 10 | Accident | | | 1m 30.899s 9 |

Fastest race lap: Kimi Räikkönen on lap 41, 1m 25.235s, 139.174 mph/223.978 km/h.

Lap record: Michael Schumacher (Ferrari F2004 V10), 1m 24.125s, 141.010 mph/226.933 km/h (2004).

All results and data © FOM 2007

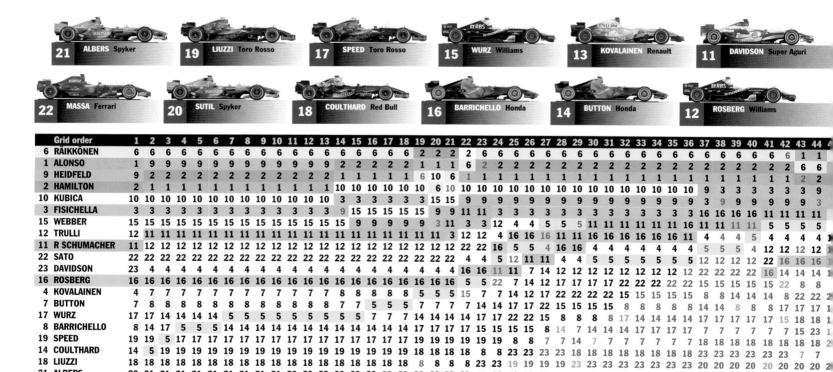

## PRACTICE 1 (FRIDAY)

Overcast, heavy cloud (track 22–24ºC, air 20–22ºC)

| Pos. | Driver | Laps | Time |
|---|---|---|---|
| 1 | Fernando Alonso | 23 | 1m 29.214s |
| 2 | Felipe Massa | 7 | 1m 30.707s |
| 3 | Sebastian Vettel | 22 | 1m 30.857s |
| 4 | Lewis Hamilton | 14 | 1m 30.878s |
| 5 | Jenson Button | 15 | 1m 31.162s |
| 6 | Kazuki Nakajima | 21 | 1m 31.401s |
| 7 | David Coulthard | 9 | 1m 31.528s |
| 8 | Heikki Kovalainen | 20 | 1m 31.571s |
| 9 | Mark Webber | 16 | 1m 31.661s |
| 10 | Rubens Barrichello | 12 | 1m 31.737s |
| 11 | Takuma Sato | 7 | 1m 31.782s |
| 12 | Giancarlo Fisichella | 14 | 1m 32.011s |
| 13 | Alexander Wurz | 18 | 1m 32.194s |
| 14 | Adrian Sutil | 26 | 1m 34.043s |
| 15 | Vitantonio Liuzzi | 8 | 1m 34.627s |
| 16 | Christijan Albers | 10 | 1m 35.055s |
| 17 | Nick Heidfeld | 12 | 1m 37.249s |
| 18 | Anthony Davidson | 6 | 1m 39.221s |
| 19 | Kimi Räikkönen | 7 | 1m 39.242s |
| 20 | Ralf Schumacher | 9 | 1m 39.550s |
| 21 | Scott Speed | 9 | 1m 41.763s |
| 22 | Jarno Trulli | 11 | 1m 44.130s |

## PRACTICE 2 (FRIDAY)

Cloudy/light rain (track 23–27ºC, air 20–21ºC)

| Pos. | Driver | Laps | Time |
|---|---|---|---|
| 1 | Felipe Massa | 32 | 1m 27.353s |
| 2 | Kimi Räikkönen | 33 | 1m 27.750s |
| 3 | Lewis Hamilton | 29 | 1m 27.829s |
| 4 | Giancarlo Fisichella | 33 | 1m 27.941s |
| 5 | Nick Heidfeld | 27 | 1m 27.970s |
| 6 | Alexander Wurz | 31 | 1m 27.981s |
| 7 | Fernando Alonso | 25 | 1m 28.040s |
| 8 | Nico Rosberg | 29 | 1m 28.055s |
| 9 | Robert Kubica | 26 | 1m 28.281s |
| 10 | David Coulthard | 23 | 1m 28.495s |
| 11 | Anthony Davidson | 28 | 1m 28.727s |
| 12 | Jarno Trulli | 33 | 1m 28.921s |
| 13 | Takuma Sato | 23 | 1m 29.009s |
| 14 | Jenson Button | 30 | 1m 29.066s |
| 15 | Rubens Barrichello | 12 | 1m 29.542s |
| 16 | Ralf Schumacher | 26 | 1m 29.574s |
| 17 | Mark Webber | 11 | 1m 29.801s |
| 18 | Heikki Kovalainen | 10 | 1m 30.097s |
| 19 | Scott Speed | 28 | 1m 30.383s |
| 20 | Adrian Sutil | 35 | 1m 31.108s |
| 21 | Christijan Albers | 32 | 1m 31.175s |
| 22 | Vitantonio Liuzzi | 16 | 1m 31.693s |

## QUALIFYING (SATURDAY)

Cloudy, windy, light rain (track 23–27ºC, air 20–21ºC)

| Pos. | Driver | First | Second | Third |
|---|---|---|---|---|
| 1 | Kimi Räikkönen | 1m 26.644s | 1m 25.644s | 1m 26.072s |
| 2 | Fernando Alonso | 1m 26.697s | 1m 25.326s | 1m 26.493s |
| 3 | Nick Heidfeld | 1m 26.895s | 1m 25.358s | 1m 26.556s |
| 4 | Lewis Hamilton | 1m 26.674s | 1m 25.577s | 1m 26.755s |
| 5 | Robert Kubica | 1m 26.696s | 1m 25.882s | 1m 27.347s |
| 6 | Giancarlo Fisichella | 1m 27.270s | 1m 25.944s | 1m 27.634s |
| 7 | Mark Webber | 1m 26.978s | 1m 26.623s | 1m 27.934s |
| 8 | Jarno Trulli | 1m 27.014s | 1m 26.688s | 1m 28.404s |
| 9 | Ralf Schumacher | 1m 27.328s | 1m 26.739s | 1m 28.692s |
| 10 | Takuma Sato | 1m 27.365s | 1m 26.758s | 1m 28.871s |
| 11 | Anthony Davidson | 1m 26.986s | 1m 26.909s | |
| 12 | Nico Rosberg | 1m 27.596s | 1m 26.914s | |
| 13 | Heikki Kovalainen | 1m 27.529s | 1m 26.964s | |
| 14 | Jenson Button | 1m 27.540s | 1m 27.264s | |
| 15 | Alexander Wurz | 1m 27.479s | 1m 27.393s | |
| 16 | Felipe Massa | 1m 26.712s | No time | |
| 17 | Rubens Barrichello | 1m 27.679s | | |
| 18 | Scott Speed | 1m 28.305s | | |
| 19 | David Coulthard | 1m 28.579s | | |
| 20 | Vitantonio Liuzzi | 1m 29.267s | | |
| 21 | Adrian Sutil | 1m 29.339s | | |
| 22 | Christijan Albers | 1m 31.932s | | |

## PRACTICE 3 (SATURDAY)

Overcast (track 23–28ºC, air 21–24ºC)

| Pos. | Driver | Laps | Time |
|---|---|---|---|
| 1 | Kimi Räikkönen | 14 | 1m 26.064s |
| 2 | Giancarlo Fisichella | 18 | 1m 26.454s |
| 3 | Lewis Hamilton | 12 | 1m 26.467s |
| 4 | Anthony Davidson | 17 | 1m 26.491s |
| 5 | Felipe Massa | 14 | 1m 26.547s |
| 6 | Nick Heidfeld | 18 | 1m 26.753s |
| 7 | Fernando Alonso | 10 | 1m 26.786s |
| 8 | Heikki Kovalainen | 13 | 1m 26.937s |
| 9 | Takuma Sato | 12 | 1m 27.266s |
| 10 | Alexander Wurz | 9 | 1m 27.322s |
| 11 | Mark Webber | 13 | 1m 27.390s |
| 12 | Robert Kubica | 19 | 1m 27.753s |
| 13 | Ralf Schumacher | 13 | 1m 27.887s |
| 14 | Jarno Trulli | 16 | 1m 27.897s |
| 15 | Rubens Barrichello | 16 | 1m 28.039s |
| 16 | Nico Rosberg | 5 | 1m 28.061s |
| 17 | Jenson Button | 21 | 1m 28.119s |
| 18 | David Coulthard | 12 | 1m 28.208s |
| 19 | Vitantonio Liuzzi | 15 | 1m 28.332s |
| 20 | Scott Speed | 9 | 1m 28.485s |
| 21 | Adrian Sutil | 19 | 1m 28.678s |
| 22 | Christijan Albers | 7 | 1m 30.547s |

## RACE TYRE STRATEGIES

### BRIDGESTONE

In 2007, the tyre regulations stipulate that the two dry-tyre specifications must be used during the race. At Melbourne the soft compound Bridgestone Potenza tyre was marked with a 3-cm white spot on the sidewall.

The visibility of this marking at speed proved to be unsatisfactory, leading to the introduction of a white stripe in the tyre groove from the Malaysian Grand Prix onwards.

| | Driver | Race stint 1 | Race stint 2 | Race stint 3 |
|---|---|---|---|---|
| 1 | Kimi Räikkönen | Medium: laps 1–19 | Medium: 20–42 | Soft: 43–58 |
| 2 | Fernando Alonso | Medium: 1–22 | Medium: 23–45 | Soft: 46–58 |
| 3 | Lewis Hamilton | Medium: 1–23 | Medium: 24–43 | Hard: 44–58 |
| 4 | Nick Heidfeld | Soft: 1–14 | Medium: 15–38 | Medium: 39–58 |
| 5 | Giancarlo Fisichella | Medium: 1–20 | Medium: 21–44 | Soft: 45–58 |
| 6 | Felipe Massa | Soft: 1–29 | Medium: 30–58 | |
| 7 | Nico Rosberg | Medium: 1–27 | Medium: 28–41 | Soft: 42–58 |
| 8 | Ralf Schumacher | Medium: 1–24 | Medium: 25–45 | Soft: 46–58 |
| 9 | Jarno Trulli | Medium: 1–25 | Medium: 26–46 | Soft: 47–58 |
| 10 | Heikki Kovalainen | Medium: 1–27 | Medium: 28–46 | Soft: 47–58 |
| 11 | Rubens Barrichello | Soft: 1–19 | Medium: 20–39 | Medium: 40–58 |
| 12 | Takuma Sato | Medium: 1–24 | Medium: 25–42 | Soft: 43–58 |
| 13 | Mark Webber | Medium: 1–22 | Medium: 23–42 | Soft: 43–58 |
| 14 | Vitantonio Liuzzi | Medium: 1–23 | Medium: 24–45 | Soft: 46–58 |
| 15 | Jenson Button | Medium: 1–27 | Soft: 28–43 | Medium: 44–58 |
| 16 | Anthony Davidson | Medium: 1–29 | Medium: 30–45 | Soft: 46–58 |
| 17 | Adrian Sutil | Medium: 1–22 | Medium: 23–41 | Soft: 42–58 |
| | Alexander Wurz | Medium: 1–32 | Soft: 33–48 (DNF) | |
| | David Coulthard | Medium: 1–28 | Medium: 29–47 | Soft: 48 (DNF) |
| | Robert Kubica | Medium: 1–21 | Medium: 22–36 (DNF) | |
| | Scott Speed | Medium: 1–25 | Medium: 26–28 (DNF) | |
| | Christijan Albers | Medium: 0 (DNF) | | |

 9 SCHUMACHER Toyota
 7 WEBBER Red Bull
 5 KUBICA BMW-Sauber
 3 HEIDFELD BMW-Sauber
 1 RÄIKKÖNEN Ferrari

 10 SATO Super Aguri
 8 TRULLI Toyota
 6 FISICHELLA Renault
 4 HAMILTON McLaren
 2 ALONSO McLaren

**RACE DISTANCE:**
58 laps,
191.118 miles/307.574 km

**RACE WEATHER:**
Sunny,
(track 33–34ºC, air 21–22ºC)

| 46 | 47 | 48 | 49 | 50 | 51 | 52 | 53 | 54 | 55 | 56 | 57 | 58 | |
|---|---|---|---|---|---|---|---|---|---|---|---|---|---|
| 6 | 6 | 6 | 6 | 6 | 6 | 6 | 6 | 6 | 6 | 6 | 6 | 6 | 1 |
| 1 | 1 | 1 | 1 | 1 | 1 | 1 | 1 | 1 | 1 | 1 | 1 | 1 | 2 |
| 2 | 2 | 2 | 2 | 2 | 2 | 2 | 2 | 2 | 2 | 2 | 2 | 2 | 3 |
| 9 | 9 | 9 | 9 | 9 | 9 | 9 | 9 | 9 | 9 | 9 | 9 | 4 | 4 |
| 3 | 3 | 3 | 3 | 3 | 3 | 3 | 3 | 3 | 3 | 3 | 3 | 3 | 5 |
| 5 | 5 | 5 | 5 | 5 | 5 | 5 | 5 | 5 | 5 | 5 | 5 | 5 | 6 |
| 16 | 16 | 16 | 16 | 16 | 16 | 16 | 16 | 16 | 16 | 16 | 16 | 16 | 7 |
| 4 | 11 | 11 | 11 | 11 | 11 | 11 | 11 | 11 | 11 | 11 | 11 | 11 | 8 |
| 11 | 4 | 4 | 12 | 12 | 12 | 12 | 12 | 12 | 12 | 12 | 12 | 12 | |
| 14 | 12 | 12 | 4 | 4 | 4 | 4 | 4 | 4 | 4 | 4 | 4 | 4 | |
| 12 | 8 | 8 | 8 | 8 | 8 | 8 | 8 | 8 | 8 | 8 | 8 | 8 | |
| 8 | 14 | 22 | 22 | 22 | 22 | 22 | 22 | 22 | 22 | 22 | 22 | 22 | |
| 22 | 11 | 15 | 15 | 15 | 15 | 15 | 15 | 15 | 15 | 15 | 15 | 15 | |
| 17 | 14 | 18 | 18 | 18 | 18 | 18 | 18 | 18 | 18 | 18 | 18 | 18 | |
| 15 | 15 | 15 | 7 | 7 | 7 | 7 | 7 | 7 | 7 | 7 | 7 | 7 | |
| 18 | 18 | 18 | 23 | 23 | 23 | 23 | 23 | 23 | 23 | 23 | 23 | 23 | |
| 7 | 7 | 7 | 20 | 20 | 20 | 20 | 20 | 20 | 20 | 20 | 20 | 20 | |
| 23 | 23 | 23 | | | | | | | | | | | |
| 20 | 20 | 20 | | | | | | | | | | | |

15 Pit stop    20 Drive Thru penalty
20 One lap or more behind leader

## FOR THE RECORD

**FIRST GRAND PRIX START:**
Lewis Hamilton, Heikki Kovalainen, Adrian Sutil

**12,000th LAP LED:** Ferrari

**TENTH WIN:** Kimi Räikkönen

**20th FASTEST LAP:** Kimi Räikkönen

**FIRST LAP LED, FIRST PODIUM, FIRST POINT:** Lewis Hamilton

## POINTS

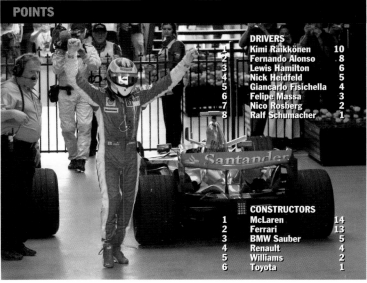

### DRIVERS

| | | |
|---|---|---|
| 1 | Kimi Räikkönen | 10 |
| 2 | Fernando Alonso | 8 |
| 3 | Lewis Hamilton | 6 |
| 4 | Nick Heidfeld | 5 |
| 5 | Giancarlo Fisichella | 4 |
| 6 | Felipe Massa | 3 |
| 7 | Nico Rosberg | 2 |
| 8 | Ralf Schumacher | 1 |

### CONSTRUCTORS

| | | |
|---|---|---|
| 1 | McLaren | 14 |
| 2 | Ferrari | 13 |
| 3 | BMW Sauber | 5 |
| 4 | Renault | 4 |
| 5 | Williams | 2 |
| 6 | Toyota | 1 |

Photographs: Peter J Fox/www.crash.net

FIA F1 WORLD CHAMPIONSHIP/ROUND 2

# MALAYSIAN GP

Bernie Ecclestone expressed the belief at Sepang that Jenson Button should stay loyal to the Honda team and power through his current problems to sustain his reputation as a potentially leading F1 contender.

The sport's commercial rights holder also predicted that 2007 would be a crucial season for the 27-year-old British driver, who needed to work hard in a bid to break his recent cycle of disappointment, no matter how frustrated he may have felt with the Japanese squad in recent months.

'Jenson really must get his act together this year, otherwise he's going to find the future very difficult – that's what it amounts to,' said Ecclestone. 'But he really ought to stick with Honda to make it work, in my view. He needs to stick with Honda, get his head down and make it work.

'Okay, so his current problems may not be his fault, and it's a shame they've happened, but he's just got to get things back on track.'

For his part, Button may have been putting a brave public face on his disappointing start to the 2007 F1 season, but the signs were that the 27-year-old was running out of patience with the Honda team's apparent inability to surmount the technical problems that had bugged the RA107 in the Australian GP and during testing at Sepang in preparation for the second round of the title chase.

There was much speculation in the pit lane that Honda's F1 management – like Toyota's – was hamstrung by bureaucratic logjams between their racing bases in Europe and their corporate headquarters in Japan. The feeling was that neither car maker fully understood the need for F1 teams to have a lean, efficient management chain to maximise their efforts and resources.

'I can't speak for Toyota, but my observation is that probably Toyota – and definitely Honda – are approaching F1 in a somewhat different way from some of the other teams,' said Nick Fry, the Honda team principle. 'The key difference is that Honda is trying to use F1 as a training and learning experience that feeds back into the mainstream research and development of the parent company.

'So, rather than buying ideas, we are learning and trying to develop our own ideas, so this is genuinely an attempt to bring people on through the ranks, with the result that it is perhaps taking longer than it might otherwise do. I think Jenson is impressed with the amount of sheer effort and resources that are being focused on the programme at the moment.'

That may well have been the case, but Button was making no bones about the fact that he was expecting only a very minor performance improvement, at best, over the Sepang weekend after he and his team-mate Rubens Barrichello struggled with braking instability problems during the Australian race.

'We are expecting some big steps forward this year and there are some big changes being made, which we need to do,' Button said. 'There is no point in making small steps forward and finding a couple of hundredths; we need a big change – and that is what we are working on.'

Ecclestone may have believed that Button should stay with Honda and fight his way through this difficult patch, but that was easier said than done. At Sepang Button was celebrating the third anniversary of his first podium finish, with a third place in the BAR-Honda. On the strength of his and Honda's performances so far this season, the possibility of Button's repeating such a result in the foreseeable future seemed depressingly remote.

QUALIFYING in the torrid conditions at Sepang reinforced the message from Melbourne: the 2007 championship contest was already developing into a two-horse race between Ferrari and McLaren Mercedes. After his challenge was blunted in Australia due to gearbox problems in qualifying, Felipe Massa (1m 35.043s) bounced back as a serious title contender with a smooth run to edge out Fernando Alonso's McLaren in a close-fought battle for pole position.

'It was a great lap,' said Massa with an air of obvious satisfaction. 'I just tried everything I could at the last attempt. At the second attempt, I had traffic so I couldn't improve my lap time and then the last one was a clean lap. There was also a slight rain shower, but it held off at the right time. That helped me a lot, but it was still a great lap.'

Just 0.3s behind the Ferrari, Alonso (1m 35.310s) was well pleased to be on the front row again for his second successive race with McLaren, but he acknowledged that the Ferrari F2007 still had a slight performance edge over his McLaren MP4-22. 'I think we have to be realistic,' said the world champion, 'and accept that our pace, particularly on long runs, is not as good as the Ferrari's. But we certainly improved the car during last week's test.'

Kimi Räikkönen qualified a moderately satisfied third on 1m 35.479s, Ferrari opting not to change the engine in his car, which had developed a slight water leak during the Australian race. The Melbourne winner lined up alongside Lewis Hamilton's McLaren (1m 36.045s), the young British driver doing another outstanding job on only his second outing in the sport's senior category.

'The car is working well and I think we could have both been on the front row,' said Hamilton. 'However when I came to Turn Seven it had started spitting with rain a little bit. I experienced this at the test last week and knew it could be slippery, so I eased off a small amount.'

Both BMW Sauber drivers performed well, with Nick Heidfeld (1m 36.543s) lining up fifth, two places ahead of Robert Kubica (1m 36.896s). 'That was the best I could achieve today,' said Nick, who switched to the harder Bridgestone tyres for his final run, 'because the balance of my car is better, but still not ideal, so under the circumstances the result is fine.'

Splitting the BMW-Saubers was Nico Rosberg on 1m 36.829s after a great performance in his Williams-Toyota. 'I don't think we could have hoped for much more than P6 today,' beamed Nico. 'I'm pretty pleased, especially because yesterday we seemed unable to find the form we'd shown here during the test. However, since this morning [Saturday], my car has been feeling better and everything started to go in the right direction. As the grip level rises, so the car gets stronger, just like at Melbourne.' By contrast, team-mate Alex Wurz's car got stuck in gear at the start of qualifying, consigning him to an eventual 20th place.

Completing the top ten were the Toyotas of Jarno Trulli (1m 36.902s) and Ralf Schumacher (1m 37.078s) and Mark Webber's Red Bull-Renault on 1m 37.345s. Schumacher was generally satisfied despite a less-than-ideal handling balance and Trulli lost some crucial preparation time during the Saturday-morning free practice session due to an electrical problem. Webber was well satisfied with his efforts, but team-mate David Coulthard confessed that he didn't quite push hard enough on his best lap, missing a place in the top-ten run-off.

Just outside the top ten were the Renaults of Heikki Kovalainen (1m 35.630s) and Giancarlo Fisichella (1m 35.706s). Behind Coulthard, Takuma Sato shone at the wheel of his Super Aguri in 14th place (1m 35.945s), shading Jenson Button in the Honda on 1m 36.088s.

'I'm obviously very frustrated,' said Button. 'We know where we are at the moment and we're doing our best with what we have, but qualifying 15th is still difficult to accept. We made it through to Q2 but the car isn't good enough to make it through to the final session at the moment. It's unbelievable how much grip I lost towards the end of the second session.'

Team-mate Rubens Barrichello wound up right at the back after suffering a gearbox failure that forced him to switch to the spare RA107, which was not set up for him.

Respected Italian engineer Giorgio Ascanelli (above) is appointed technical director of Scuderia Toro Rosso.

Race stewards at Sepang reject as inadmissible a protest by the Spyker team relating to the eligibility of the Super Aguri cars on the basis that they were not built by the entrant concerned.

LEWIS Hamilton demonstrated his star quality with a brilliant drive to second place in the Malaysian Grand Prix at Sepang, rounding off a superb McLaren Mercedes one-two behind his team-mate Fernando Alonso after another remarkably assured and composed performance in only his second F1 outing.

Only three weeks had passed since Hamilton opened his top-flight career with third place in Australia. His achievement in the second round of the title chase meant that the 22-year-old became the first driver to score podiums in his first two F1 races since Peter Arundell – team-mate to the legendary Jim Clark – in 1964, driving for the now-defunct Lotus team. Hamilton pushed impressively hard from the start of the torrid race, vaulting through from fourth on the grid to second place by the time he'd negotiated the first couple of corners on the opening lap.

Having fended off the Ferrari F2007s of Felipe Massa and Kimi Räikkönen in the opening stages, he found himself thrown dramatically onto the defensive in the closing laps as Räikkönen mounted a ferocious counter-attack, closing to within a second of the McLaren as they took the chequered flag in tight formation. This topped off a memorable afternoon's racing in difficult conditions, which had begun with Lewis forcing Felipe Massa into a mistake.

'It was the most difficult race I have ever had,' confessed F1's most celebrated novice. 'To see two Ferraris behind you, two red blobs in the mirror, knowing they are slightly lighter than you and slightly quicker... it was very, very difficult to keep them behind. Felipe had a couple of moves but fortunately I was able to trick him into outbraking himself. I cut across to the point that he went off, so I apologise for that. Then I had Kimi hunting me down for most of the race.

'I can't explain how tough it is... hot in the cockpit... I ran out of water, so halfway through the race I didn't have enough water. It was getting hotter and hotter. It was nice to have a gap, but I pushed to the end. The team did a great job; they worked long hours, longer than other teams, and they have done a fantastic job. I had to dig as deep as I could by preserving energy to bring the car to the end. I am overwhelmed.'

As the starting signal was given, Massa was first to move but, as the cars drew level with the end of the pit lane, Alonso began to pull alongside Massa's Ferrari and as they went into the braking area for the first, tight right-hander the world champion slipped seamlessly through into the lead. A couple of lengths behind, Hamilton demonstrated again that he is not intimidated in such exalted company, first grabbing third from Räikkönen and then boldly running around the outside of Massa to pop up second as the pack streamed away from the next corner.

At the end of the opening lap the two McLaren-Mercs dominated the stream of cars as they accelerated hard past the pits, Alonso already 1.7s ahead of Hamilton. Second time around, the gap was 2.7s with Massa in third ahead of Räikkönen, then Nick Heidfeld's BMW-Sauber a strong fifth pursued by team-mate Robert Kubica, Nico Rosberg's Williams and the Renault R27 of Giancarlo Fisichella.

At the end of the second lap a frustrated Vitantonio Liuzzi pitted to change the nose section on his Toro Rosso, damaged, ironically enough, when he tapped one of team-mate Scott Speed's rear wheels to avoid what he considered an over-ambitious move by Super Aguri's Takuma Sato.

'Sato pulled a crazy move at Turn Four and compromised my race,' said Liuzzi, who eventually trailed home 17th. 'It was a shame because I felt my race pace was really strong and we could have done better in terms of the result.'

By the end of lap 3 Alonso had clearly made a break and was 3.7s ahead of his team-mate, while Massa could see his chances of translating pole position into a victory slipping away and was looking desperately for a way past Hamilton. After a preliminary attempt on lap three failed to ruffle Hamilton,

**Below: The consistently impressive Lewis Hamilton posted the fastest race lap on his way to second place.**

**Below left: Asian beauties.**

**Below centre: Adrian Sutil, who failed to make it beyond the opening lap.**
Photographs: Peter J Fox/www.crash.net

Massa made a dramatic dive down the inside of the McLaren on lap six going into the tight right-hand Turn Four, running wide onto the grass and allowing Hamilton to dodge back ahead immediately. This dropped him to fifth behind Heidfeld and left the two McLarens running 8.1s ahead of the pack.

Meanwhile, as Heidfeld just about kept in touch with the leaders, Kubica's race was falling apart. He'd touched the back of Nick's sister car in the first-corner scrum, slightly damaging his aerodynamics, so his lap times dropped away in the early stages but his pit crew was unable to discuss things with him because his radio wasn't working. The team brought him in to change tyres at the end of lap 11, then again later to change his nose section.

'In qualifying the pace was good,' said Kubica, 'then in the race nothing worked. My main problem was braking stability. It was impossible to stop the car and I crossed the line at the finish after making many mistakes. I was locking [up] and going straight and had oversteer.'

Alonso continued to lead commandingly but was not without his problems. His radio had packed up from about the ten-lap mark, so he wasn't quite certain that the pit crew would be ready for him at his first scheduled refuelling stop at the end of lap 18. But with manager Ron Dennis himself using a pit board to confirm to Fernando that it was time to stop, all was well and Alonso got in and out with no drama, briefly relinquishing the lead to Hamilton before he made his own stop at the end of lap 20.

Second time around it was Hamilton who stopped first, pitting on lap 38 in 7.6s while Alonso made a 7.4s stop two laps later. After Massa's early mistake, Räikkönen took up the chase from third place and, in the final stint, when they were both using the harder of the two available Bridgestone compounds, began to close in on Lewis's McLaren. From 5.6s adrift on lap 47, he trimmed off half a second next time around. On lap 48 the gap was 4.5s, then 3.8s, 3.3s, 2.8s and 2.3s on consecutive tours. In fact Lewis had things nicely under control, pacing himself perfectly to cross the line 17.557s behind Alonso and 0.782s ahead of the fast-closing Finn.

Alonso was ecstatic at having achieved his first win for his new team. 'I'm so happy and pleased with the progress we've made as a team since we unveiled the MP4-22 in mid-January,' he enthused. 'We knew the key to victory today was to make a good start and get in front to control the race, which we achieved. To have Lewis in second place makes today's result even better.'

Behind Räikkönen, Heidfeld successfully fended off Massa by 2.9s at the chequered flag. 'This is a fantastic experience,' he said. 'To beat one of the Ferraris might not happen again so soon. In the early part of the weekend Felipe was so superior. After we had major problems with the balance of the car in practice, everything was fine in the race. It's a great – and perhaps a little unexpected – result. But we should keep our feet on the ground.'

After taking only third and fifth places from a race that delivered substantially less than it originally promised, Jean Todt spoke for all at Ferrari when he described it as 'definitely a disappointing result'. He added, in reference to McLaren, 'We know we are up against a very strong and battle-ready opponent, who did a better job than us today. Fortunately, in just one week's time we get the chance to make up for it at Sakhir [in Bahrain]. We will do all we can there to get the best possible result.' Prophetic words indeed...

Renault wound up with a solid, slightly improved performance in which Giancarlo Fisichella came home sixth, two places ahead of team-mate Heikki Kovalainen. 'This was the maximum I could do today,' shrugged Fisichella, 'and, with our situation at the moment, it felt like a podium finish. But the pace was better than during the rest of the weekend, the car balance more stable and consistent.' Kovalainen also pushed as hard as he could, surviving a few high-speed wobbles to bring the car home in one piece and score his first F1 championship point.

Separating the two Renaults was Jarno Trulli's Toyota TF107, saving the day for the Japanese car maker after a race in which Ralf Schumacher's sister car trailed home 15th after being initially bogged down in traffic and then further delayed by a slow puncture that brought him in for an unscheduled pit stop shortly after his initial scheduled refuelling visit. 'Jarno's result shows that we have the pace to challenge with both cars,' said Schumacher, putting a rather optimistic interpretation on the way in which events had unfolded.

As Hamilton, his team and his fans celebrated into the early evening, Jenson Button emerged from the cockpit of his Honda RA107 in a dejected frame of mind after another frustrating afternoon battling a difficult-to-drive car. A 12th-place finish behind his team-mate Rubens Barrichello hardly represented the peak of his ambitions.

Ferrari's two drivers had squandered what could have been a winning opportunity from the moment Massa failed to transform that pole position into a leading edge at the first corner. By the time the volatile Brazilian had calmed down and Räikkönen got into a competitive rhythm, the two McLaren drivers had hammered home their winning advantage. Ron Dennis, the McLaren chairman, may have thought 'nobody gifted us anything today' but his drivers' dominant edge was given a free run in the early stages thanks to the Ferrari drivers' chaotic opening laps. Räikkönen and Massa gave them an inch, but Alonso and Hamilton took a mile.

*Alan Henry*

**Left: Nick Heidfeld brought the BMW-Sauber home in fourth place, consolidating a consistent trend that would characterise his season.**

**Bottom left: Giancarlo Fisichella transformed a disappointing qualifying session into a decent sixth place at the chequered flag.**

Photographs: Peter J Fox/www.crash.net

**Below: The first- and second-placed McLarens cool down in *parc fermé* as Fernando Alonso and Lewis Hamilton celebrate on the podium.**

Photograph: Lukas Gorys

# FIA F1 WORLD CHAMPIONSHIP • ROUND 2

# PETRONAS
# MALAYSIAN GRAND PRIX
## KUALA LUMPUR 6–8 APRIL 2007

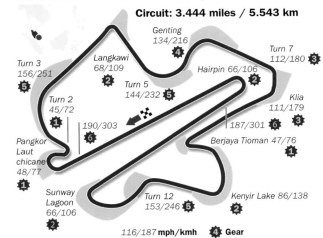

**SEPANG INTERNATIONAL CIRCUIT, KUALA LUMPUR**

**Circuit: 3.444 miles / 5.543 km**

Genting 134/216 — 4
Langkawi 68/109 — 2
Turn 3 156/251 — 5
Turn 7 112/180 — 3
Hairpin 66/106 — 2
Turn 5 144/232 — 5
Klia 111/179 — 3
Turn 2 45/72 — 4
190/303 — 6
187/301 — 6
Pangkor Laut chicane 48/77 — 1
Berjaya Tioman 47/76 — 1
Sunway Lagoon 66/106 — 2
Turn 12 153/246 — 5
Kenyir Lake 86/138 — 2

116/187 mph/kmh — **4** Gear

Photograph: Peter J Fox/www.crash.net

## RACE RESULTS

All results and data © FOM 2007

| Pos. | Driver | Nat. | No. | Entrant | Car/Engine | Tyres | Laps | Time/Retirement | Speed (mph/km/h) | Gap to leader | Fastest race lap | |
|---|---|---|---|---|---|---|---|---|---|---|---|---|
| 1 | Fernando Alonso | E | 1 | Vodafone McLaren Mercedes | McLaren MP4-22-Mercedes FO 108T V8 | B | 56 | 1h 32m 14.930s | 125.451/201.893 | | 1m 36.861s | 42 |
| 2 | Lewis Hamilton | GB | 2 | Vodafone McLaren Mercedes | McLaren MP4-22-Mercedes FO 108T V8 | B | 56 | 1h 32m 32.487s | 130.646/210.255 | + 17.557s | 1m 36.701s | 22 |
| 3 | Kimi Räikkönen | FIN | 6 | Scuderia Ferrari Marlboro | Ferrari F2007-056 V8 | B | 56 | 1h 32m 33.269s | 125.037/201.227 | + 18.339s | 1m 37.228s | 40 |
| 4 | Nick Heidfeld | D | 9 | BMW Sauber F1 Team | BMW Sauber F1.07-BMW P86/7 V8 | B | 56 | 1h 32m 48.707s | 124.690/200.669 | + 33.777s | 1m 37.417s | 55 |
| 5 | Felipe Massa | BR | 5 | Scuderia Ferrari Marlboro | Ferrari F2007-056 V8 | B | 56 | 1h 32m 51.635s | 124.624/200.563 | + 36.705s | 1m 37.199s | 42 |
| 6 | Giancarlo Fisichella | I | 3 | ING Renault F1 Team | Renault R27-RS27 V8 | B | 56 | 1h 33m 20.568s | 123.980/199.527 | + 1m 5.638s | 1m 37.879s | 44 |
| 7 | Jarno Trulli | I | 12 | Panasonic Toyota Racing | Toyota TF107-RVX-07 V8 | B | 56 | 1h 33m 25.062s | 123.881/199.367 | + 1m 10.132s | 1m 38.016s | 40 |
| 8 | Heikki Kovalainen | FIN | 4 | ING Renault F1 Team | Renault R27-RS27 V8 | B | 56 | 1h 33m 26.945s | 123.839/199.300 | + 1m 12.015s | 1m 37.810s | 41 |
| 9 | Alexander Wurz | A | 17 | AT&T Williams | Williams FW29-Toyota RVX-07 V8 | B | 56 | 1h 33m 44.854s | 123.445/198.666 | + 1m 29.924s | 1m 37.864s | 19 |
| 10 | Mark Webber | AUS | 15 | Red Bull Racing | Red Bull RB3-Renault RS27 V8 | B | 56 | 1h 33m 48.486s | 123.366/198.538 | + 1m 33.556s | 1m 38.540s | 55 |
| 11 | Rubens Barrichello | BR | 8 | Honda Racing F1 Team | Honda RA107-RA807E V8 | B | 55 | | | + 1 lap | 1m 38.566s | 32 |
| 12 | Jenson Button | GB | 7 | Honda Racing F1 Team | Honda RA107-RA807E V8 | B | 55 | | | + 1 lap | 1m 38.658s | 54 |
| 13 | Takuma Sato | J | 22 | Super Aguri F1 Team | Super Aguri SA07-Honda RA807E V8 | B | 55 | | | + 1 lap | 1m 38.496s | 37 |
| 14 | Scott Speed | USA | 19 | Scuderia Toro Rosso | Toro Rosso STR02-Ferrari 056H V8 | B | 55 | | | + 1 lap | 1m 39.098s | 54 |
| 15 | Ralf Schumacher | D | 11 | Panasonic Toyota Racing | Toyota TF107-RVX-07 V8 | B | 55 | | | + 1 lap | 1m 39.243s | 52 |
| 16 | Anthony Davidson | GB | 23 | Super Aguri F1 Team | Super Aguri SA07-Honda RA807E V8 | B | 55 | | | + 1 lap | 1m 39.566s | 32 |
| 17 | Vitantonio Liuzzi | I | 18 | Scuderia Toro Rosso | Toro Rosso STR02-Ferrari 056H V8 | B | 55 | | | + 1 lap | 1m 38.447s | 21 |
| 18 | Robert Kubica | POL | 10 | BMW Sauber F1 Team | BMW Sauber F1.07-BMW P86/7 V8 | B | 55 | | | + 1 lap | 1m 38.874s | 53 |
| | Nico Rosberg | D | 16 | AT&T Williams | Williams FW29-Toyota RVX-07 V8 | B | 42 | Hydraulics | | | 1m 37.704s | 18 |
| | David Coulthard | GB | 14 | Red Bull Racing | Red Bull RB3-Renault RS27 V8 | B | 36 | Brake pedal | | | 1m 38.098s | 28 |
| | Christijan Albers | NL | 21 | Etihad Aldar Spyker F1 Team | Spyker F8-VII-Ferrari 056H V8 | B | 7 | Transmission | | | 1m 41.495s | 5 |
| | Adrian Sutil | D | 20 | Etihad Aldar Spyker F1 Team | Spyker F8-VII-Ferrari 056H V8 | B | 0 | Accident | | | No time | – |

**Fastest race lap:** Lewis Hamilton on lap 22, 1m 36.701s, 128.223 mph/206.355 km/h.

**Lap record:** Juan Pablo Montoya (Williams FW26-BMW V10), 1m 34.223s, 131.596 mph/211.782 km/h (2004).

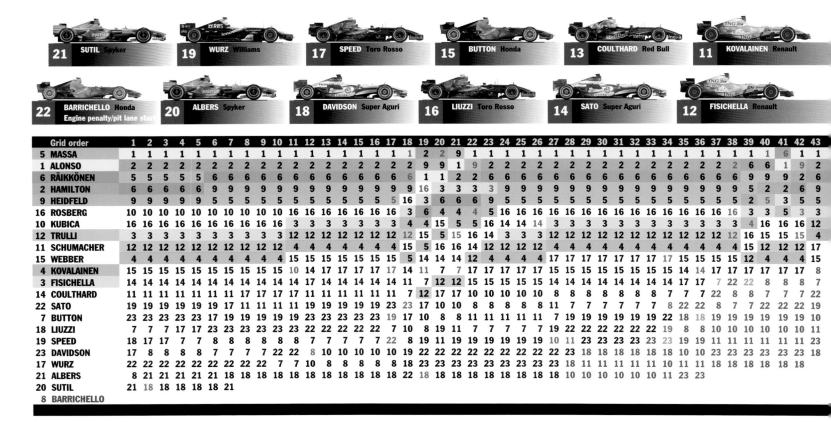

| 21 | SUTIL Spyker |
| 19 | WURZ Williams |
| 17 | SPEED Toro Rosso |
| 15 | BUTTON Honda |
| 13 | COULTHARD Red Bull |
| 11 | KOVALAINEN Renault |
| 22 | BARRICHELLO Honda — Engine penalty/pit lane start |
| 20 | ALBERS Spyker |
| 18 | DAVIDSON Super Aguri |
| 16 | LIUZZI Toro Rosso |
| 14 | SATO Super Aguri |
| 12 | FISICHELLA Renault |

| Grid order | 1 | 2 | 3 | 4 | 5 | 6 | 7 | 8 | 9 | 10 | 11 | 12 | 13 | 14 | 15 | 16 | 17 | 18 | 19 | 20 | 21 | 22 | 23 | 24 | 25 | 26 | 27 | 28 | 29 | 30 | 31 | 32 | 33 | 34 | 35 | 36 | 37 | 38 | 39 | 40 | 41 | 42 | 43 |
|---|---|---|---|---|---|---|---|---|---|---|---|---|---|---|---|---|---|---|---|---|---|---|---|---|---|---|---|---|---|---|---|---|---|---|---|---|---|---|---|---|---|---|---|
| 5 MASSA | 1 | 1 | 1 | 1 | 1 | 1 | 1 | 1 | 1 | 1 | 1 | 1 | 1 | 1 | 1 | 1 | 1 | 1 | 2 | 2 | 9 | | 1 | 1 | 1 | 1 | 1 | 1 | 1 | 1 | 1 | 1 | 1 | 1 | 1 | 1 | 1 | 1 | 1 | 1 | 6 | 1 | 1 |
| 1 ALONSO | 2 | 2 | 2 | 2 | 2 | 2 | 2 | 2 | 2 | 2 | 2 | 2 | 2 | 2 | 2 | 2 | 2 | 2 | 9 | 9 | 1 | 9 | 2 | 2 | 2 | 2 | 2 | 2 | 2 | 2 | 2 | 2 | 2 | 2 | 2 | 2 | 2 | 2 | 2 | 6 | 1 | 9 | 2 |
| 6 RÄIKKÖNEN | 5 | 5 | 5 | 5 | 6 | 6 | 6 | 6 | 6 | 6 | 6 | 6 | 6 | 6 | 6 | 6 | 6 | 6 | 1 | 1 | 2 | 2 | 6 | 6 | 6 | 6 | 6 | 6 | 6 | 6 | 6 | 6 | 6 | 6 | 6 | 6 | 6 | 6 | 6 | 9 | 9 | 1 | 9 |
| 2 HAMILTON | 6 | 6 | 6 | 6 | 9 | 9 | 9 | 9 | 9 | 9 | 9 | 9 | 9 | 9 | 9 | 9 | 9 | 9 | 16 | 3 | 3 | 3 | 3 | 9 | 9 | 9 | 9 | 9 | 9 | 9 | 9 | 9 | 9 | 9 | 9 | 9 | 9 | 9 | 9 | 5 | 2 | 6 | 9 |
| 9 HEIDFELD | 9 | 9 | 9 | 9 | 5 | 5 | 5 | 5 | 5 | 5 | 5 | 5 | 5 | 5 | 5 | 5 | 5 | 16 | 3 | 6 | 6 | 6 | 9 | 5 | 5 | 5 | 5 | 5 | 5 | 5 | 5 | 5 | 5 | 5 | 5 | 5 | 5 | 5 | 5 | 2 | 5 | 3 | 5 | 5 |
| 16 ROSBERG | 10 | 10 | 10 | 10 | 10 | 10 | 10 | 10 | 10 | 10 | 16 | 16 | 16 | 16 | 16 | 16 | 16 | 3 | 6 | 4 | 4 | 4 | 5 | 16 | 16 | 16 | 16 | 16 | 16 | 16 | 16 | 16 | 16 | 16 | 16 | 16 | 16 | 3 | 3 | 5 | 3 | 3 | |
| 10 KUBICA | 16 | 16 | 16 | 16 | 16 | 16 | 16 | 16 | 16 | 3 | 3 | 3 | 3 | 3 | 3 | 4 | 4 | 15 | 5 | 16 | 14 | 14 | 14 | 3 | 3 | 3 | 3 | 3 | 3 | 3 | 3 | 3 | 3 | 3 | 3 | 3 | 4 | 16 | 16 | 16 | 12 | | |
| 12 TRULLI | 3 | 3 | 3 | 3 | 3 | 3 | 3 | 3 | 3 | 12 | 12 | 12 | 12 | 12 | 12 | 12 | 15 | 5 | 15 | 16 | 14 | 12 | 12 | 12 | 12 | 12 | 12 | 12 | 12 | 12 | 12 | 12 | 12 | 12 | 12 | 16 | 15 | 15 | 15 | 4 | | | |
| 11 SCHUMACHER | 12 | 12 | 12 | 12 | 12 | 12 | 12 | 12 | 12 | 4 | 4 | 4 | 4 | 4 | 4 | 15 | 5 | 16 | 16 | 14 | 12 | 12 | 12 | 4 | 4 | 4 | 4 | 4 | 4 | 4 | 4 | 4 | 4 | 4 | 4 | 12 | 12 | 12 | 12 | 12 | | | |
| 15 WEBBER | 4 | 4 | 4 | 4 | 4 | 4 | 4 | 4 | 4 | 15 | 15 | 15 | 15 | 15 | 5 | 14 | 14 | 14 | 12 | 4 | 4 | 17 | 17 | 17 | 17 | 17 | 17 | 17 | 15 | 15 | 15 | 15 | 12 | 4 | 4 | 4 | 15 | | | | | | |
| 4 KOVALAINEN | 15 | 15 | 15 | 15 | 15 | 15 | 15 | 15 | 5 | 10 | 14 | 14 | 14 | 14 | 11 | 7 | 7 | 17 | 17 | 17 | 17 | 17 | 15 | 15 | 15 | 15 | 15 | 15 | 14 | 14 | 17 | 17 | 17 | 17 | 17 | 8 | | | | | | | |
| 3 FISICHELLA | 14 | 14 | 14 | 14 | 14 | 14 | 14 | 14 | 14 | 17 | 17 | 11 | 7 | 12 | 12 | 15 | 15 | 14 | 14 | 14 | 14 | 14 | 14 | 14 | 17 | 17 | 7 | 22 | 22 | 8 | 8 | 8 | 7 | | | | | | | | | | |
| 14 COULTHARD | 11 | 11 | 11 | 11 | 11 | 11 | 11 | 11 | 11 | 11 | 10 | 10 | 10 | 10 | 8 | 8 | 11 | 7 | 7 | 7 | 7 | 7 | 7 | 7 | 7 | 7 | 22 | 7 | 7 | 7 | 22 | 22 | 22 | | | | | | | | | | |
| 22 SATO | 19 | 19 | 19 | 19 | 19 | 11 | 11 | 11 | 11 | 11 | 19 | 19 | 23 | 17 | 10 | 10 | 8 | 8 | 11 | 7 | 7 | 7 | 19 | 19 | 22 | 18 | 19 | 19 | 19 | 19 | 19 | 19 | 10 | | | | | | | | | | |
| 7 BUTTON | 23 | 23 | 23 | 23 | 23 | 19 | 7 | 7 | 7 | 19 | 11 | 11 | 11 | 11 | 19 | 19 | 19 | 22 | 18 | 19 | 19 | 19 | 19 | 11 | | | | | | | | | | | | | | | | | | | |
| 18 LIUZZI | 7 | 7 | 7 | 17 | 17 | 23 | 23 | 22 | 22 | 22 | 7 | 10 | 19 | 11 | 18 | 18 | 10 | 8 | 10 | 10 | 10 | 10 | 11 | | | | | | | | | | | | | | | | | | | | |
| 19 SPEED | 18 | 17 | 17 | 7 | 7 | 8 | 8 | 8 | 8 | 7 | 22 | 23 | 10 | 11 | 23 | 23 | 11 | 11 | 11 | 11 | 23 | | | | | | | | | | | | | | | | | | | | | | |
| 23 DAVIDSON | 22 | 22 | 22 | 22 | 22 | 22 | 22 | 22 | 22 | 23 | 18 | 18 | 18 | 18 | 18 | 18 | 23 | 23 | 23 | 23 | | | | | | | | | | | | | | | | | | | | | | | |
| 17 WURZ | 22 | 22 | 22 | 22 | 22 | 22 | 22 | 22 | 22 | 18 | 18 | 10 | 10 | 10 | 10 | 10 | 11 | 23 | | | | | | | | | | | | | | | | | | | | | | | | | |
| 21 ALBERS | 8 | 21 | 21 | 21 | 21 | 18 | 18 | 18 | 18 | | | | | | | | | | | | | | | | | | | | | | | | | | | | | | | | | | |
| 20 SUTIL | 21 | 18 | 18 | 18 | 18 | 18 | 21 | | | | | | | | | | | | | | | | | | | | | | | | | | | | | | | | | | | | |
| 8 BARRICHELLO | | | | | | | | | | | | | | | | | | | | | | | | | | | | | | | | | | | | | | | | | | | |

## PRACTICE 1 (FRIDAY)

Sunny (track 37–43ºC, air 30–32ºC)

| Pos. | Driver | Laps | Time |
|---|---|---|---|
| 1 | Felipe Massa | 17 | 1m 34.972s |
| 2 | Fernando Alonso | 24 | 1m 35.220s |
| 3 | Lewis Hamilton | 22 | 1m 35.712s |
| 4 | Kimi Räikkönen | 20 | 1m 35.779s |
| 5 | Nico Rosberg | 21 | 1m 36.308s |
| 6 | Mark Webber | 20 | 1m 36.522s |
| 7 | Jarno Trulli | 25 | 1m 36.597s |
| 8 | Kazuki Nakajima | 15 | 1m 36.885s |
| 9 | Ralf Schumacher | 22 | 1m 37.052s |
| 10 | Robert Kubica | 12 | 1m 37.121s |
| 11 | David Coulthard | 7 | 1m 37.484s |
| 12 | Sebastian Vettel | 39 | 1m 37.837s |
| 13 | Vitantonio Liuzzi | 20 | 1m 37.882s |
| 14 | Heikki Kovalainen | 24 | 1m 38.143s |
| 15 | Giancarlo Fisichella | 26 | 1m 38.300s |
| 16 | Adrian Sutil | 29 | 1m 38.720s |
| 17 | Takuma Sato | 10 | 1m 38.966s |
| 18 | Scott Speed | 9 | 1m 39.130s |
| 19 | Rubens Barrichello | 21 | 1m 39.234s |
| 20 | Jenson Button | 17 | 1m 39.331s |
| 21 | Anthony Davidson | 9 | 1m 39.357s |
| 22 | Christijan Albers | 25 | 1m 40.074s |

## PRACTICE 2 (FRIDAY)

Scattered cloud (track 48–50ºC, air 34–35ºC)

| Pos. | Driver | Laps | Time |
|---|---|---|---|
| 1 | Felipe Massa | 34 | 1m 35.780s |
| 2 | Giancarlo Fisichella | 36 | 1m 35.910s |
| 3 | Heikki Kovalainen | 37 | 1m 36.106s |
| 4 | Kimi Räikkönen | 33 | 1m 36.160s |
| 5 | Nico Rosberg | 31 | 1m 36.523s |
| 6 | Alexander Wurz | 21 | 1m 36.621s |
| 7 | Robert Kubica | 18 | 1m 36.717s |
| 8 | Ralf Schumacher | 28 | 1m 36.760s |
| 9 | Lewis Hamilton | 30 | 1m 36.797s |
| 10 | Nick Heidfeld | 25 | 1m 36.862s |
| 11 | Mark Webber | 18 | 1m 36.906s |
| 12 | Fernando Alonso | 26 | 1m 37.041s |
| 13 | David Coulthard | 26 | 1m 37.203s |
| 14 | Takuma Sato | 30 | 1m 37.282s |
| 15 | Jenson Button | 29 | 1m 37.578s |
| 16 | Jarno Trulli | 34 | 1m 37.712s |
| 17 | Vitantonio Liuzzi | 26 | 1m 37.855s |
| 18 | Anthony Davidson | 27 | 1m 38.334s |
| 19 | Adrian Sutil | 28 | 1m 38.419s |
| 20 | Scott Speed | 20 | 1m 38.650s |
| 21 | Rubens Barrichello | 20 | 1m 38.713s |
| 22 | Christijan Albers | 23 | 1m 39.807s |

## QUALIFYING (SATURDAY)

Cloudy (track 45–49ºC, air 34–35ºC)

| Pos. | Driver | First | Second | Third |
|---|---|---|---|---|
| 1 | Felipe Massa | 1m 35.340s | 1m 34.454s | 1m 35.043s |
| 2 | Fernando Alonso | 1m 34.942s | 1m 34.057s | 1m 35.310s |
| 3 | Kimi Räikkönen | 1m 35.138s | 1m 34.687s | 1m 35.479s |
| 4 | Lewis Hamilton | 1m 35.028s | 1m 34.650s | 1m 36.045s |
| 5 | Nick Heidfeld | 1m 35.617s | 1m 35.203s | 1m 36.543s |
| 6 | Nico Rosberg | 1m 35.755s | 1m 35.380s | 1m 36.829s |
| 7 | Robert Kubica | 1m 35.294s | 1m 34.739s | 1m 36.896s |
| 8 | Jarno Trulli | 1m 35.666s | 1m 35.255s | 1m 36.902s |
| 9 | Ralf Schumacher | 1m 35.736s | 1m 35.595s | 1m 37.078s |
| 10 | Mark Webber | 1m 35.727s | 1m 35.579s | 1m 37.345s |
| 11 | Heikki Kovalainen | 1m 36.092s | 1m 35.630s | |
| 12 | Giancarlo Fisichella | 1m 35.879s | 1m 35.706s | |
| 13 | David Coulthard | 1m 35.730s | 1m 35.766s | |
| 14 | Takuma Sato | 1m 36.430s | 1m 35.945s | |
| 15 | Jenson Button | 1m 35.913s | 1m 36.088s | |
| 16 | Vitantonio Liuzzi | 1m 36.140s | 1m 36.145s | |
| 17 | Scott Speed | 1m 36.578s | | |
| 18 | Anthony Davidson | 1m 36.816s | | |
| 19 | Rubens Barrichello | 1m 36.827s | | |
| 20 | Alexander Wurz | 1m 37.326s | | |
| 21 | Christijan Albers | 1m 38.279s | | |
| 22 | Adrian Sutil | 1m 38.415s | | |

## PRACTICE 3 (SATURDAY)

Sunny, scattered cloud (track 44–47ºC, air 32–34ºC)

| Pos. | Driver | Laps | Time |
|---|---|---|---|
| 1 | Lewis Hamilton | 14 | 1m 34.811s |
| 2 | Felipe Massa | 15 | 1m 34.953s |
| 3 | Fernando Alonso | 11 | 1m 35.311s |
| 4 | Robert Kubica | 16 | 1m 35.385s |
| 5 | Kimi Räikkönen | 7 | 1m 35.498s |
| 6 | Nico Rosberg | 16 | 1m 35.770s |
| 7 | Nick Heidfeld | 20 | 1m 36.160s |
| 8 | Anthony Davidson | 19 | 1m 36.195s |
| 9 | Ralf Schumacher | 20 | 1m 36.245s |
| 10 | Mark Webber | 17 | 1m 36.257s |
| 11 | David Coulthard | 13 | 1m 36.273s |
| 12 | Vitantonio Liuzzi | 18 | 1m 36.297s |
| 13 | Giancarlo Fisichella | 15 | 1m 36.434s |
| 14 | Alexander Wurz | 16 | 1m 36.473s |
| 15 | Scott Speed | 14 | 1m 36.501s |
| 16 | Takuma Sato | 18 | 1m 36.545s |
| 17 | Jenson Button | 20 | 1m 36.658s |
| 18 | Heikki Kovalainen | 6 | 1m 36.876s |
| 19 | Rubens Barrichello | 19 | 1m 36.972s |
| 20 | Jarno Trulli | 16 | 1m 37.473s |
| 21 | Adrian Sutil | 20 | 1m 38.018s |
| 22 | Christijan Albers | 20 | 1m 38.225s |

## RACE TYRE STRATEGIES

**BRIDGESTONE**

In 2007, the tyre regulations stipulate that the two dry-tyre specifications must be visibly distinguishable from each other. At the Malaysian Grand Prix, the medium compound Bridgestone Potenza tyre was marked with a white line in the second-from-inside groove.

| | Driver | Race stint 1 | Race stint 2 | Race stint 3 | Race stint 4 |
|---|---|---|---|---|---|
| 1 | Fernando Alonso | Medium: laps 1–18 | Medium: 19–40 | Hard: 41–56 | |
| 2 | Lewis Hamilton | Medium: 1–20 | Medium: 21–38 | Hard: 39–56 | |
| 3 | Kimi Räikkönen | Medium: 1–18 | Medium: 19–41 | Hard: 42–56 | |
| 4 | Nick Heidfeld | Medium: 1–22 | Medium: 23–42 | Hard: 43–56 | |
| 5 | Felipe Massa | Medium: 1–17 | Medium: 18–40 | Hard: 41–56 | |
| 6 | Giancarlo Fisichella | Medium: 1–18 | Medium: 19–41 | Hard: 42–56 | |
| 7 | Jarno Trulli | Hard: 1–27 | Medium: 23–38 | Medium: 39–56 | |
| 8 | Heikki Kovalainen | Medium: 1–22 | Medium: 23–39 | Hard: 40–56 | |
| 9 | Alexander Wurz | Medium: 1–17 | Medium: 18–34 | Hard: 35–56 | |
| 10 | Mark Webber | Hard: 1–21 | Hard: 22–42 | Hard: 43–56 | |
| 11 | Rubens Barrichello | Medium: 1–12 | Medium: 13–34 | Hard: 35–55 | |
| 12 | Jenson Button | Hard: 1–21 | Medium: 22–37 | Medium: 38–55 | |
| 13 | Takuma Sato | Medium: 1–17 | Medium: 18–39 | Hard: 40–55 | |
| 14 | Scott Speed | Medium: 1–17 | Medium: 18–34 | Hard: 35–55 | |
| 15 | Ralf Schumacher | Medium: 1–19 | Medium: 20–28 | Hard: 29–55 | |
| 16 | Anthony Davidson | Medium: 1–18 | Medium: 19–34 | Hard: 35–55 | |
| 17 | Vitantonio Liuzzi | Medium: 1–2 | Medium: 3–19 | Medium: 20–36 | Hard: 37–55 |
| 18 | Robert Kubica | Medium: 1–11 | Medium: 12–27 | Hard: 28–55 | |
| | Nico Rosberg | Medium: 1–19 | Medium: 20–38 | Hard: 39–42 (DNF) | |
| | David Coulthard | Hard: 1–26 | Medium: 27–36 (DNF) | | |
| | Christijan Albers | Medium: 1–7 (DNF) | | | |
| | Adrian Sutil | Medium: 0 (DNF) | | | |

**9** SCHUMACHER Toyota

**7** KUBICA BMW-Sauber

**5** HEIDFELD BMW-Sauber

**3** RÄIKKONEN Ferrari

**1** MASSA Ferrari

**10** WEBBER Red Bull

**8** TRULLI Toyota

**6** ROSBERG Williams

**4** HAMILTON McLaren

**2** ALONSO McLaren

**RACE DISTANCE:**
56 laps,
192.879 miles/310.408 km

**RACE WEATHER:**
Sunny,
track 50–53ºC, air 35–36ºC

| 44 | 45 | 46 | 47 | 48 | 49 | 50 | 50 | 52 | 53 | 54 | 55 | 56 | |
|---|---|---|---|---|---|---|---|---|---|---|---|---|---|
| 1 | 1 | 1 | 1 | 1 | 1 | 1 | 1 | 1 | 1 | 1 | 1 | 1 | 1 |
| 2 | 2 | 2 | 2 | 2 | 2 | 2 | 2 | 2 | 2 | 2 | 2 | 2 | 2 |
| 6 | 6 | 6 | 6 | 6 | 6 | 6 | 6 | 6 | 6 | 6 | 6 | 6 | 3 |
| 9 | 9 | 9 | 9 | 9 | 9 | 9 | 9 | 9 | 9 | 9 | 9 | 9 | 4 |
| 5 | 5 | 5 | 5 | 5 | 5 | 5 | 5 | 5 | 5 | 5 | 5 | 5 | 5 |
| 3 | 3 | 3 | 3 | 3 | 3 | 3 | 3 | 3 | 3 | 3 | 3 | 3 | 6 |
| 12 | 12 | 12 | 12 | 12 | 12 | 12 | 12 | 12 | 12 | 12 | 12 | 12 | 7 |
| 4 | 4 | 4 | 4 | 4 | 4 | 4 | 4 | 4 | 4 | 4 | 4 | 4 | 8 |
| 17 | 17 | 17 | 17 | 17 | 17 | 17 | 17 | 17 | 17 | 17 | 17 | 17 | |
| 15 | 15 | 15 | 15 | 15 | 15 | 15 | 15 | 15 | 15 | 15 | 15 | 15 | |
| 8 | 8 | 8 | 8 | 8 | 8 | 8 | 8 | 8 | 8 | 8 | 8 | | |
| 7 | 7 | 7 | 7 | 7 | 7 | 7 | 7 | 7 | 7 | 7 | 7 | | |
| 22 | 22 | 22 | 22 | 22 | 22 | 22 | 22 | 22 | 22 | 22 | | | |
| 19 | 19 | 19 | 19 | 19 | 19 | 19 | 19 | 19 | 19 | 19 | | | |
| 10 | 10 | 11 | 11 | 11 | 11 | 11 | 11 | 11 | 11 | 11 | | | |
| 11 | 11 | 23 | 23 | 23 | 23 | 23 | 23 | 23 | 23 | 23 | | | |
| 23 | 23 | 18 | 18 | 18 | 18 | 18 | 18 | 18 | 18 | 18 | | | |
| 18 | 18 | 10 | 10 | 10 | 10 | 10 | 10 | 10 | 10 | 10 | | | |

**20** Pit stop

**20** One lap or more behind leader

## FOR THE RECORD

**FIRST POINT:** Heikki Kovalainen
**1,000th LAP LED:** Fernando Alonso
**FIRST FASTEST LAP:** Lewis Hamilton

## POINTS

**CONSTRUCTORS**

| 1 | McLaren | 32 |
|---|---|---|
| 2 | Ferrari | 23 |
| 3 | BMW Sauber | 10 |
| 4 | Renault | 8 |
| 5 | Toyota | 3 |
| 6 | Williams | 2 |

**DRIVERS**

| 1 | Fernando Alonso | 18 |
|---|---|---|
| 2 | Kimi Räikkönen | 16 |
| 3 | Lewis Hamilton | 14 |
| 4 | Nick Heidfeld | 10 |
| 5 | Giancarlo Fisichella | 7 |
| 6 | Felipe Massa | 7 |
| 7 | Nico Rosberg | 2 |
| 8 | Jarno Trulli | 2 |
| 9 | Ralf Schumacher | 1 |
| 10 | Heikki Kovalainen | 1 |

Photographs: Peter J Fox/www.crash.net

# BAHRAIN GP
## SAKHIR

Top: **FIA deputy race director Herbie Blash** seems somewhat apprehensive of the bird of prey.
Photograph: Lukas Gorys

Centre and bottom: Music and traditional pageantry are all part of the Middle Eastern mix.

Right: Felipe Massa atones for his disappointing performance in Malaysia as he edges his Ferrari F2007 ahead of the pack on the sprint away from the grid at Sakhir.
Photographs: Peter J Fox/www.crash.net

**Far left:** Bahrain has embraced Formula 1.
Photograph: Jean-François Galeron/WRi2

**Left:** Gulf Air's 747 holds the paddock's attention during a fly-past.
Photograph: Peter J Fox/www.crash.net

## SAKHIR QUALIFYING

Lewis Hamilton set the tone of the weekend when he qualified alongside Felipe Massa on the front row of the grid with a 1m 32.935s, barely 0.3s away from the Brazilian pacemaker. A consummate effort from the 22-year-old pushed the other Ferrari of Kimi Räikkönen (1m 33.131s) and his own McLaren team-mate Fernando Alonso (1m 33.192s) back onto the second row of the grid, Alonso in particular struggling to work out an ideal handling balance in the first and second sectors of the lap.

'The car is competitive,' confirmed Massa (1m 32.652s) with a grin. 'Today we have shown that we have a very quick car, even in qualifying when we know everybody has the same fuel. For sure the track is not easy because it's always a little bit dirty, especially at the beginning of the race.'

McLaren successfully kept the pressure on Ferrari, privately hoping that its Italian rival would be marginal on engine cooling for the second straight race. But for the Mercedes-backed team there was also a helping of unexpected grief, which started when a crashing sound echoed down the pit lane in the early hours of Saturday morning, sending McLaren's night security guard into a complete panic. He raced into the garage to find that an overhead lighting gantry had slipped from its mounting and fallen onto one of the two MP4-22s below. A telephone call was made to a group of the team's mechanics, waking them from their sleep at 2.30 am with instructions to drive out to the circuit as fast as they could. By the time of that morning's free practice session the lighting gantry had been repaired and the damage to the car – a broken wing end plate on Alonso's – had been repaired.

'To be honest, my lap wasn't that great,' Hamilton said. 'I definitely had better laps early in the session. It was tough. I lost a bit of time in Turn One, but the rest of the lap seemed to go quite well.

'Turn 13 was a little bit hectic and I think the wind is always changing [here] and coming across in different ways, so you always have a tail wind or a crosswind. It's quite tough to put the car on the limit and anticipate what's going to happen, but I'm still very happy to get second for the team.'

Fifth and sixth were the BMW-Saubers of Nick Heidfeld (1m 33.404s) and Robert Kubica (1m 33.710s) after extremely well-matched performances.

'I am very happy and the team did a very good job,' said Heidfeld. 'I had an excellent car and my last run in the final session was really good. The gap [to Ferrari and McLaren] is significant, but again we have shown ourselves to be the third-fastest team. To improve on these positions in the race will only be possible if a Ferrari or a McLaren has been extremely light [on fuel] today or if something unpredictable happens.' Kubica generally shared those sentiments, although he confessed he was still slightly struggling with the handling balance of his machine, but was hoping for a good race.

Over in the Renault camp Giancarlo Fisichella needed a gearbox change on Saturday, while Heikki Kovalainen made a precautionary switch to the spare car following the diagnosis of potential fuel-pump problems on his race chassis. Fisichella lined up seventh on 1m 34.056s while Heikki was 12th on 1m 32.935s.

'I feel I achieved our maximum today,' said Giancarlo. 'It is so tight to get into the top ten for us at the moment and, in fact, I was tenth in Q2 by just a few hundredths of a second. I think we have found a consistent balance for the race and look forward to scoring more points tomorrow.'

Mark Webber did an absolutely outstanding job to qualify eighth on 1m 34.106s in the Red Bull RB3, but David Coulthard's shaky start to the season continued with gearbox sensor trouble in the first stint of qualifying. 'It was a sensor failure, so the team changed something and I went back out,' he explained. 'But then instead of not having seventh gear, I didn't have fifth, sixth or seventh, which wasn't ideal.' Nico Rosberg (1m 34.399s) completed the top ten for Williams just behind Jarno Trulli's Toyota (1m 34.154s), while poor old Coulthard had to be content with a distant 21st.

Alex Wurz (1m 32.915s) just squeezed in 11th ahead of Heikki Kovalainen (1m 32.935s) and the impressive Anthony Davidson (1m 33.082s), who built on a solid Friday practice performance to line up 13th, four places ahead of Super Aguri team-mate Takuma Sato (1m 33.984s).

A broken rear-suspension rocker took a lot of time out of Ralf Schumacher's free practice schedule and he wound up a disappointing 14th on 1m 33.294s, while Honda continued to have a dismal time with the RA107, Jenson Button's progress in free practice being thwarted by an engine failure and his 1m 33.731s best could earn him only 16th on the grid right behind team-mate Rubens Barrichello (1m 33.624s).

Behind Sato came the Toro Rossos of Vitantonio Liuzzi (1m 34.024s) and Scott Speed (1m 34.333s), while the two Spykers of Adrian Sutil (1m 35.280s) and Christijan Albers (1m 33.533s) sandwiched the hapless Coulthard right at the back.

**Right:** Shaikh Salman Bin Hamad Al-Khalifa, the crown prince of Bahrain.

**Below:** Crash test dummies take a breather from their road safety campaign.
Photographs: Peter J Fox/www.crash.net

**Below right:** The calm before the storm. All smiles for the moment from Fernando Alonso and McLaren boss Ron Dennis.
Photograph: Lukas Gorys

**Far left:** Behind-the-scenes analysis in the Spyker team.

**Left:** A Red Bull conference for (from left) team principal Christian Horner, consultant Dr Helmut Marko and chief technical officer Adrian Newey.

Photographs: Peter J Fox/www.crash.net

**Main:** Lewis Hamilton continues his sensational form.

**Left:** Takuma Sato lays rubber as he locks up his Super Aguri.

**Below:** Former BAR head David Richards was back on the F1 beat in Bahrain.

Photographs: Peter J Fox/www.crash.net

## RICHARDS SENDS SIGNS ON McLAREN DEAL

Prodrive boss David Richards made a visit to Bahrain, intensifying speculation that his Banbury-based organisation would be taking the 12th F1 'franchise' in 2008 and that he was close to a deal to run what amounted to a McLaren 'B team', the cars for which would be based between races at McLaren's refurbished premises in Albert Drive, Woking, the team's home from 1987 to 2003.

Richards said he believed that his planned way of tackling the world championship could provide a cost-conscious template for the future development of a sport that he clearly believes has become excessively expensive.

'My first priority to my partner [constructor] would be to say, "Which people would you want to promote, loan or move across to us?"' he said. 'We don't want new people or those with big egos trying to make names for themselves.

'I want to give opportunities to people. Organisations sometimes have fixed ceilings because the lead people have been in those positions for many years and have never moved on. Now we can offer career opportunities to people in a whole raft of roles – that's why we're not rushing off recruiting.'

IT was a measure of Lewis Hamilton's towering status as an emergent F1 star that there was almost a palpable sense of disappointment that he could bring his McLaren-Mercedes MP4-22 home in only second place, a mere 2.36s behind Felipe Massa's winning Ferrari F2007 in the Bahrain Grand Prix at the sun-baked Sakhir circuit. In the process, he put himself on the same points tally as Fernando Alonso and Kimi Räikkönen at the top of the championship table.

After McLaren's young prodigy finished third on his début outing in Australia, then second in Malaysia, there was a sense of fevered expectation that he might actually deliver his first victory in only the third race of his career. This was always a highly improbable outcome, but Hamilton could hardly be judged any less a star performer after putting relentless pressure on Massa's Ferrari from the start of the 57-lap contest.

'I am happy with it. This weekend we have definitely closed the gap to Ferrari and to have another second in only my third race... I could not ask for more,' said Hamilton. 'There is only one more step from here and we will keep on pushing for Barcelona. I think it is a fantastic achievement. I am extremely proud. We have worked extremely hard to get where we are today – me and my family, but also my team in terms of how competitive we are.

'I am looking forward to going home. I have not been home for nine weeks – I'll be back next week. I think the support is growing and I am looking forward to getting to Silverstone [for the British GP in July] and seeing how many fans are there.

'I have not experienced it yet, so it will be new to me. I hope I will still be able to walk the streets!'

Hamilton added, 'Unfortunately I didn't get as good a start as Felipe – he did very well in the first corner. I tried to make sure I stayed as close as possible and maybe have a chance on the first lap but we were evenly matched. I struggled a bit in the second stint but came good in the end.'

At the start Massa accelerated cleanly into the lead, elbowing his way into the first tight right-hander with a confidence that signalled his determination to atone for his disappointing performance in Malaysia, where he translated pole position into fifth place at the chequered flag. In Bahrain qualifying he did the job brilliantly to secure his fourth pole in five races, in the process edging out man-of-the-moment Hamilton's McLaren by 0.3s to line up at the front of the grid.

'The first two races of the season have not gone the way I wanted them to and I really hope that this will reverse the trend,' said Massa after qualifying. He also made it clear that if young Hamilton had ideas about slipping past him into the first corner for the second straight race then he'd better think again. 'We have a very competitive car, both over a single lap and over a longer distance. Now we have to do our best to get the most out of the potential at our disposal.'

He did just that, heading the field at the end of the opening lap from the McLarens of Hamilton and Alonso, the Ferrari of Kimi Räikkönen and the BMW-Saubers of Nick Heidfeld and Robert Kubica. Unfortunately a first-corner collision between Jenson Button's Honda and the Toro Rosso of Scott Speed eliminated Speed, led to further woes for Button and triggered a safety car period that lasted until the end of lap three, while the debris was cleared.

Button could hardly believe what was happening to him. 'I made a good start and made up at least three places, but then

at Turn Two Taku [Sato] ran wide, tried to squeeze me and I had nowhere to go but onto the dirt on the inside,' he said.

'Then in Turn Three I had [David] Coulthard and someone else fighting around me. DC went wide, then cut in again sharply and I had nowhere to go. We touched, I spun around and the anti-stall [mechanism] didn't cut in. I stalled and that was the end of my race after two corners.'

For the first few laps after the restart Hamilton held the gap to Massa at 0.6s, but by lap eight Felipe had steadied his advantage to just a second. Yet Lewis fought back with a couple of fastest laps, trimming it back to 0.9s on lap nine and then 0.8s next time around. Buoyed by the sight of Massa momentarily locking his wheels and running wide a few laps earlier, Hamilton kept up the pressure, but Massa never made another slip and looked totally in command for the rest of the afternoon.

For his part, Räikkönen seemed slow off the mark at the restart, coming across the start line already 2.3s behind Alonso as the signal was given to resume racing. Despite having their aerodynamics slightly compromised by the need to run additional slats on top of the side pods, as they had in Malaysia the previous week, the Ferraris' cooling problems were not so marginal that they needed to reduce the maximum rev limit used by their drivers. That played into Massa's hands as he exploited a slight performance edge over Hamilton's McLaren in the early stages of the race, neither of these nominal 'number-twos' being in any way challenged by their de facto team leaders on this occasion.

Räikkönen might well have remained in touch with the leading twosome had he not been asleep during the opening sprint. By the time he shook himself into life he was boxed in behind a below-par Fernando Alonso, who confessed that he didn't quite have his customary confidence in the feel of his MP4-22.

'I was struggling for pace and grip and just couldn't drive the car as hard as I would have liked,' Alonso explained. 'You always start the race believing you can win, but after six or seven laps I knew it would be tough.' Alonso has a driving style that relies on heavy braking to assist the car's change of direction and, although this was his first competitive outing using Carbone Industrie pads on the McLaren, he simply could not generate the confidence he had felt in the Hitco pads he'd become accustomed to with Renault the previous year.

Hamilton made his first refuelling stop from second place at the end of lap 19 but Massa stayed out until lap 21 and, as the race settled down again after that first flurry of pit lane activity, Massa found himself running a more comfortable 4.6s ahead of Hamilton with Räikkönen now third after vaulting ahead of Alonso by staying out one lap longer than the twice-world champion before making his first stop.

Once he was behind Räikkönen, Alonso just slipped out of contention. With a clear track ahead of him, Räikkönen picked up the pace and began matching – even slightly bettering – Massa's pace.

During this second stint, free from the slight dose of oversteer that had bugged him from the start, Felipe simply

**Above:** Robert Kubica, who eventually finished sixth, leads a queue of cars comprising Giancarlo Fisichella, Mark Webber and Heikki Kovalainen.
Photograph: Peter J Fox/www.crash.net

**Left:** Kimi Räikkönen's Ferrari shows a clean pair of heels to Fernando Alonso.
Photograph: Peter J Fox/www.crash.net

**Centre left:** Jarno Trulli wipes away the endless perspiration.
Photograph: Paul-Henri Cahier

**Centre:** Fisichella took a hard-won eighth place just ahead of Renault team-mate Kovalainen.
Photograph: Jad Sherif/www.WRi2

**Nicolas Lapierre (above centre) scores his maiden GP2 victory in Bahrain.**

**Paul Tracy breaks a bone in his back in an accident practising for the Champcar race at Long Beach.**

**Peugeot's 908 Hdi turbo-diesel claims a début victory in the Monza 1,000-km race driven by Nicolas Minassian and Marc Gené.**

**Opposite: An exultant Felipe Massa delights in his first victory of the 2007 season.**

**Below: Grand prix cars strut their stuff in front of the Bahrain grandstand.**
Photographs: Peter J Fox/www.crash.net

flew. At the start of the stint Hamilton was just 3.5s behind Massa and 6s ahead of Räikkönen. But by the time it came to the second round of stops, Massa coming in on lap 40, Hamilton was 10s down on the leading Ferrari and had Räikkönen right on his gearbox.

While Hamilton struggled slightly in the second stint, Alonso had his work cut out keeping on top of Nick Heidfeld's well-driven BMW-Sauber, Heidfeld displaying a level of confidence and precision that seemed likely to guarantee him a way past the world champion's McLaren in the fullness of time. And so it proved.

'I just tried to stay as close to him as possible, to try and pressure him into a mistake,' said Heidfeld. Eventually Alonso made the slight slip that lost him crucial momentum coming out onto the main straight at the end of the 31st lap. That forced him onto the defensive for the next few corners, Heidfeld stalking him patiently before neatly running right around the outside of the McLaren at Turn Four.

'When we were on the hard tyres in the final stint of the race he was faster than me again,' said an elated Nick after taking the chequered flag, 'but I knew that if I didn't make any mistakes I could stay ahead of him to the end.'

Alonso was left shrugging his shoulders with disappointment after this heady performance. 'After this race I'm left with a bit of a bitter taste for not having been able to climb onto the podium, which was the main target,' he told Spanish television. 'But after these first three races I didn't think I would be sharing the lead in the championship with the Ferraris – we thought they were on another planet. So we'll arrive in Barcelona [for his home grand prix on 13 May] in good condition and leading the championship.'

Alonso finished 14s behind race winner Felipe Massa and admitted, 'I couldn't do more than I did. It's four points and we finished the race. I wasn't very comfortable with the car and in the end I did the best I could.'

McLaren chief executive Martin Whitmarsh explained that Alonso had not really been happy with the braking performance of his car all through the weekend. 'This is a circuit with really heavy braking and I think Fernando is a little less comfortable than Lewis in such a situation. It's a track where it's easy to lock up both front and rear tyres and, while we need to do a little more work on our braking system, this was a continuing issue for Fernando throughout the weekend.'

Rounding off a superb day for the BMW Sauber squad, Robert Kubica came home sixth after battling with an aerodynamic imbalance caused by his refuelling flap's steadfastly refusing to shut, badly disrupting the airflow over the car.

Seventh place fell to Jarno Trulli's Toyota TF107. Trulli battled hard to pass both Renaults during the course of the chase and ended up well satisfied that he had eclipsed team-mate Ralf Schumacher's efforts in a nightmare race from 14th on the grid, struggling home 12th after getting away slowly from the grid and spending much of the afternoon bogged down in traffic.

Separating the two Toyotas as they took the chequered flag were the Renault R27s of Giancarlo Fisichella and Heikki Kovalainen, plus the Williams FW29s of Nico Rosberg and Alex Wurz. It was a busy weekend for the Renault boys. Kovalainen made a great start but lost ground again to Trulli after his R27's rear tyres started to go off under the weight of a heavy fuel load. Despite grappling with similar rear-tyre wear problems, Fisichella eventually pipped his team-mate by 7.7s at the chequered flag while Rosberg, who had grappled with the feel of his Williams' brakes, was the final unlapped runner, crossing the line less than a second behind his old GP2 sparring partner Heikki.

Rubens Barrichello had a rather fruitless run to 13th place in the sole surviving Honda RA107 and the two Spykers of Christijan Albers and Adrian Sutil completed the list of 15 officially classified finishers.

Neither of the Red Bull-Renaults made it to the finish. A feisty drive through the field by David Coulthard was brought to a disappointing end by a driveshaft failure and Mark Webber's sister car succumbed to a broken engine. Both the Toro Rossos and the two Super Aguris also found the pace too gruelling.

*Alan Henry*

# GULF AIR
# BAHRAIN
# GRAND PRIX

SAKHIR 13–15 APRIL 2007

Photograph: Lukas Gorys

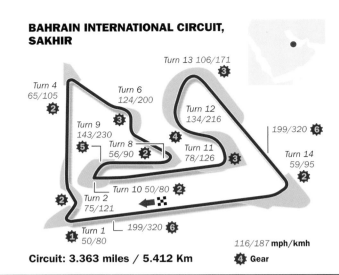

**BAHRAIN INTERNATIONAL CIRCUIT, SAKHIR**

Turn 4 65/105 **2**
Turn 6 124/200
Turn 13 106/171 **3**
Turn 9 143/230 **5**
Turn 12 134/216 **3**
Turn 8 56/90 **2**
Turn 11 78/126 **3**
199/320 **6**
Turn 14 59/95 **2**
Turn 10 50/80 **2**
Turn 2 75/121 **2**
Turn 1 50/80 **4**
199/320 **6**
116/187 **mph/kmh**

**Circuit: 3.363 miles / 5.412 Km**   **4** Gear

## RACE RESULTS

| Pos. | Driver | Nat. | No. | Entrant | Car/Engine | Tyres | Laps | Time/Retirement | Speed (mph/km/h) | Gap to leader | Fastest race lap | |
|---|---|---|---|---|---|---|---|---|---|---|---|---|
| 1 | Felipe Massa | BR | 5 | Scuderia Ferrari Marlboro | Ferrari F2007-056 V8 | B | 57 | 1h 33m 27.515s | 122.961/197.887 | | 1m 34.067s | 42 |
| 2 | Lewis Hamilton | GB | 2 | Vodafone McLaren Mercedes | McLaren MP4-22-Mercedes FO 108T V8 | B | 57 | 1h 33m 29.875s | 122.910/197.804 | + 2.360s | 1m 34.270s | 18 |
| 3 | Kimi Räikkönen | FIN | 6 | Scuderia Ferrari Marlboro | Ferrari F2007-056 V8 | B | 57 | 1h 33m 38.354s | 122.724/197.505 | + 10.839s | 1m 34.357s | 39 |
| 4 | Nick Heidfeld | D | 9 | BMW Sauber F1 Team | BMW Sauber F1.07-BMW P86/7 V8 | B | 57 | 1h 33m 41.346s | 122.659/197.400 | + 13.831s | 1m 34.470s | 38 |
| 5 | Fernando Alonso | E | 1 | Vodafone McLaren Mercedes | McLaren MP4-22-Mercedes FO 108T V8 | B | 57 | 1h 33m 41.941s | 122.646/197.379 | + 14.426s | 1m 34.420s | 46 |
| 6 | Robert Kubica | POL | 10 | BMW Sauber F1 Team | BMW Sauber F1.07-BMW P86/7 V8 | B | 57 | 1h 34m 13.044s | 121.971/196.293 | + 45.529s | 1m 34.819s | 46 |
| 7 | Jarno Trulli | I | 12 | Panasonic Toyota Racing | Toyota TF107-RVX-07 V8 | B | 57 | 1h 34m 48.886s | 121.202/195.056 | + 1m 21.371s | 1m 35.153s | 40 |
| 8 | Giancarlo Fisichella | I | 3 | ING Renault F1 Team | Renault R27-RS27 V8 | B | 57 | 1h 34m 49.216s | 121.195/195.045 | + 1m 21.701s | 1m 35.200s | 51 |
| 9 | Heikki Kovalainen | FIN | 4 | ING Renault F1 Team | Renault R27-RS27 V8 | B | 57 | 1h 34m 56.926s | 121.031/194.781 | + 1m 29.411s | 1m 35.475s | 27 |
| 10 | Nico Rosberg | D | 16 | AT&T Williams | Williams FW29-Toyota RVX-07 V8 | B | 57 | 1h 34m 57.431s | 121.021/194.764 | + 1m 29.916s | 1m 35.556s | 51 |
| 11 | Alexander Wurz | A | 17 | AT&T Williams | Williams FW29-Toyota RVX-07 V8 | B | 56 | | | + 1 lap | 1m 35.992s | 27 |
| 12 | Ralf Schumacher | D | 11 | Panasonic Toyota Racing | Toyota TF107-RVX-07 V8 | B | 56 | | | + 1 lap | 1m 35.845s | 37 |
| 13 | Rubens Barrichello | BR | 8 | Honda Racing F1 Team | Honda RA107-RA807E V8 | B | 56 | | | + 1 lap | 1m 35.842s | 50 |
| 14 | Christijan Albers | NL | 21 | Etihad Aldar Spyker F1 Team | Spyker F8-VII-Ferrari 056H V8 | B | 55 | | | + 2 laps | 1m 37.184s | 40 |
| 15 | Adrian Sutil | D | 20 | Etihad Aldar Spyker F1 Team | Spyker F8-VII-Ferrari 056H V8 | B | 53 | | | + 4 laps | 1m 36.772s | 45 |
| 16 | Anthony Davidson | GB | 23 | Super Aguri F1 Team | Super Aguri SA07-Honda RA807E V8 | B | 51 | Engine | | + 6 laps | 1m 36.111s | 27 |
| | Mark Webber | AUS | 15 | Red Bull Racing | Red Bull RB3-Renault RS27 V8 | B | 41 | Gearbox | | | 1m 35.705s | 37 |
| | David Coulthard | GB | 14 | Red Bull Racing | Red Bull RB3-Renault RS27 V8 | B | 36 | Driveshaft | | | 1m 35.384s | 23 |
| | Takuma Sato | J | 22 | Super Aguri F1 Team | Super Aguri SA07-Honda RA807E V8 | B | 34 | Engine | | | 1m 36.359s | 23 |
| | Vitantonio Liuzzi | I | 18 | Scuderia Toro Rosso | Toro Rosso STR02-Ferrari 056H V8 | B | 26 | Hydraulics | | | 1m 35.723s | 23 |
| | Jenson Button | GB | 7 | Honda Racing F1 Team | Honda RA107-RA807E V8 | B | 0 | Accident | | | No time | – |
| | Scott Speed | USA | 19 | Scuderia Toro Rosso | Toro Rosso STR02-Ferrari 056H V8 | B | 0 | Accident | | | No time | – |

**Fastest race lap:** Felipe Massa on lap 42, 1m 34.067s, 128.699 mph/207.120 km/h.

**Lap record:** Michael Schumacher (Ferrari F2004 V10), 1m 30.252s, 134.263 mph/216.074 km/h (2004) (3.366-mile/5.417-km circuit).

All results and data © FOM 2007

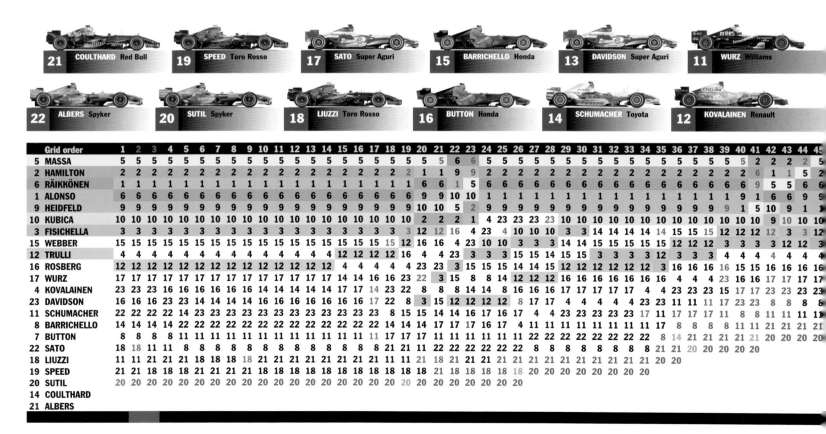

| 21 | COULTHARD Red Bull | 19 | SPEED Toro Rosso | 17 | SATO Super Aguri | 15 | BARRICHELLO Honda | 13 | DAVIDSON Super Aguri | 11 | WURZ Williams |
|---|---|---|---|---|---|---|---|---|---|---|---|
| 22 | ALBERS Spyker | 20 | SUTIL Spyker | 18 | LIUZZI Toro Rosso | 16 | BUTTON Honda | 14 | SCHUMACHER Toyota | 12 | KOVALAINEN Renault |

| Grid order | 1 | 2 | 3 | 4 | 5 | 6 | 7 | 8 | 9 | 10 | 11 | 12 | 13 | 14 | 15 | 16 | 17 | 18 | 19 | 20 | 21 | 22 | 23 | 24 | 25 | 26 | 27 | 28 | 29 | 30 | 31 | 32 | 33 | 34 | 35 | 36 | 37 | 38 | 39 | 40 | 41 | 42 | 43 | 44 | 45 |
|---|---|---|---|---|---|---|---|---|---|---|---|---|---|---|---|---|---|---|---|---|---|---|---|---|---|---|---|---|---|---|---|---|---|---|---|---|---|---|---|---|---|---|---|---|---|
| 5 MASSA | 5 | 5 | 5 | 5 | 5 | 5 | 5 | 5 | 5 | 5 | 5 | 5 | 5 | 5 | 5 | 5 | 5 | 5 | 5 | 5 | 5 | 5 | 6 | 6 | 5 | 5 | 5 | 5 | 5 | 5 | 5 | 5 | 5 | 5 | 5 | 5 | 5 | 5 | 5 | 5 | 5 | 2 | 2 | 2 | 5 |
| 2 HAMILTON | 2 | 2 | 2 | 2 | 2 | 2 | 2 | 2 | 2 | 2 | 2 | 2 | 2 | 2 | 2 | 2 | 2 | 2 | 2 | 1 | 1 | 9 | 2 | 2 | 2 | 2 | 2 | 2 | 2 | 2 | 2 | 2 | 2 | 2 | 2 | 2 | 2 | 2 | 2 | 6 | 1 | 1 | 5 | 2 | |
| 6 RÄIKKÖNEN | 1 | 1 | 1 | 1 | 1 | 1 | 1 | 1 | 1 | 1 | 1 | 1 | 1 | 1 | 1 | 1 | 1 | 1 | 1 | 6 | 6 | 1 | 5 | 5 | 6 | 6 | 6 | 6 | 6 | 6 | 6 | 6 | 6 | 6 | 6 | 6 | 6 | 6 | 6 | 1 | 6 | 5 | 5 | 6 | 6 |
| 1 ALONSO | 6 | 6 | 6 | 6 | 6 | 6 | 6 | 6 | 6 | 6 | 6 | 6 | 6 | 6 | 6 | 6 | 6 | 6 | 6 | 9 | 9 | 10 | 10 | 1 | 1 | 1 | 1 | 1 | 1 | 1 | 1 | 1 | 1 | 1 | 1 | 1 | 1 | 1 | 1 | 9 | 9 | 6 | 6 | 9 | 9 |
| 9 HEIDFELD | 9 | 9 | 9 | 9 | 9 | 9 | 9 | 9 | 9 | 9 | 9 | 9 | 9 | 9 | 9 | 9 | 9 | 9 | 9 | 10 | 10 | 5 | 2 | 9 | 9 | 9 | 9 | 9 | 9 | 9 | 9 | 9 | 9 | 9 | 9 | 9 | 9 | 1 | 5 | 10 | 9 | 1 | 1 | |
| 10 KUBICA | 10 | 10 | 10 | 10 | 10 | 10 | 10 | 10 | 10 | 10 | 10 | 10 | 10 | 10 | 10 | 10 | 10 | 10 | 10 | 2 | 2 | 2 | 4 | 23 | 23 | 23 | 23 | 10 | 10 | 10 | 10 | 10 | 10 | 10 | 10 | 10 | 10 | 10 | 10 | 10 | 9 | 10 | 10 | 10 | |
| 3 FISICHELLA | 3 | 3 | 3 | 3 | 3 | 3 | 3 | 3 | 3 | 3 | 3 | 3 | 3 | 3 | 3 | 3 | 3 | 3 | 3 | 3 | 12 | 12 | 16 | 4 | 23 | 4 | 10 | 10 | 10 | 3 | 3 | 14 | 14 | 14 | 14 | 15 | 15 | 15 | 12 | 12 | 12 | 3 | 3 | 12 | |
| 15 WEBBER | 15 | 15 | 15 | 15 | 15 | 15 | 15 | 15 | 15 | 15 | 15 | 15 | 15 | 15 | 15 | 15 | 15 | 15 | 15 | 12 | 16 | 16 | 4 | 23 | 10 | 10 | 3 | 3 | 15 | 15 | 15 | 15 | 15 | 15 | 15 | 12 | 12 | 12 | 3 | 3 | 3 | 12 | 12 | 12 | |
| 12 TRULLI | 4 | 4 | 4 | 4 | 4 | 4 | 4 | 4 | 4 | 4 | 4 | 4 | 4 | 4 | 4 | 4 | 4 | 12 | 12 | 12 | 12 | 16 | 4 | 23 | 3 | 3 | 15 | 15 | 14 | 14 | 3 | 3 | 3 | 3 | 12 | 3 | 3 | 3 | 4 | 4 | 4 | 4 | 4 | 4 | |
| 16 ROSBERG | 12 | 12 | 12 | 12 | 12 | 12 | 12 | 12 | 12 | 12 | 12 | 12 | 12 | 12 | 4 | 4 | 4 | 4 | 4 | 23 | 23 | 3 | 15 | 15 | 14 | 14 | 15 | 48 | 12 | 12 | 12 | 12 | 3 | 16 | 16 | 16 | 16 | 15 | 15 | 16 | 16 | 16 | 16 | |
| 17 WURZ | 17 | 17 | 17 | 17 | 17 | 17 | 17 | 17 | 17 | 17 | 17 | 17 | 17 | 17 | 14 | 14 | 16 | 16 | 23 | 22 | | 3 | 15 | 8 | 12 | 12 | 12 | 12 | 16 | 16 | 16 | 16 | 16 | 4 | 4 | 4 | 23 | 16 | 16 | 17 | 17 | 17 | 17 | | |
| 4 KOVALAINEN | 23 | 23 | 23 | 16 | 16 | 16 | 16 | 16 | 16 | 14 | 14 | 14 | 14 | 14 | 14 | 14 | 14 | 23 | 22 | 8 | 8 | 4 | 14 | 14 | 8 | 16 | 16 | 16 | 17 | 17 | 17 | 17 | 17 | 4 | 23 | 23 | 23 | 15 | 17 | 17 | 23 | 23 | 23 | | |
| 23 DAVIDSON | 16 | 16 | 16 | 23 | 23 | 14 | 14 | 14 | 14 | 16 | 16 | 16 | 16 | 16 | 23 | 23 | 17 | 22 | 8 | 3 | 15 | 14 | 12 | 12 | 12 | 17 | 16 | 17 | 4 | 4 | 23 | 23 | 23 | 15 | 17 | 11 | 11 | 11 | 17 | 23 | 8 | 8 | 8 | | |
| 11 SCHUMACHER | 22 | 22 | 22 | 22 | 22 | 23 | 23 | 23 | 23 | 23 | 23 | 23 | 23 | 23 | 16 | 16 | 23 | 17 | 16 | 17 | 17 | 16 | 4 | 8 | 17 | 17 | 4 | 4 | 23 | 23 | 17 | 11 | 11 | 17 | 11 | 17 | 17 | 8 | 11 | 11 | 11 | 11 | 11 | | |
| 8 BARRICHELLO | 14 | 14 | 14 | 14 | 14 | 22 | 22 | 22 | 22 | 22 | 22 | 22 | 22 | 22 | 17 | 17 | 17 | 16 | 17 | 4 | 4 | 11 | 11 | 11 | 11 | 11 | 11 | 11 | 11 | 11 | 11 | 17 | 8 | 8 | 8 | 11 | 21 | 21 | 21 | 21 | | | | | |
| 7 BUTTON | 8 | 8 | 8 | 8 | 8 | 11 | 11 | 11 | 11 | 11 | 11 | 11 | 11 | 11 | 8 | 8 | 16 | 17 | 17 | 11 | 22 | 22 | 22 | 22 | 22 | 22 | 22 | 22 | 8 | 14 | 21 | 21 | 21 | 21 | 21 | 20 | 20 | 20 | | | | | | | |
| 22 SATO | 18 | 18 | 11 | 11 | 11 | 8 | 8 | 8 | 8 | 8 | 8 | 8 | 8 | 8 | 11 | 11 | 22 | 8 | 21 | 11 | 21 | 8 | 8 | 8 | 8 | 8 | 8 | 8 | 21 | 21 | 20 | 20 | 20 | 20 | 20 | | | | | | | | | | |
| 18 LIUZZI | 11 | 11 | 18 | 18 | 18 | 18 | 18 | 18 | 18 | 18 | 18 | 18 | 18 | 18 | 21 | 21 | 21 | 21 | 21 | 21 | 21 | 21 | 21 | 21 | 21 | 21 | 20 | 20 | 20 | | | | | | | | | | | | | | | | |
| 19 SPEED | 21 | 21 | 18 | 18 | 21 | 21 | 21 | 21 | 21 | 21 | 21 | 21 | 21 | 21 | 18 | 18 | 18 | 18 | 18 | 18 | 20 | 20 | 20 | 20 | 20 | | | | | | | | | | | | | | | | | | | | | |
| 20 SUTIL | 20 | 20 | 20 | 20 | 20 | 20 | 20 | 20 | 20 | 20 | 20 | 20 | 20 | 20 | 20 | 20 | 20 | 20 | 20 | 20 | | | | | | | | | | | | | | | | | | | | | | | | | |
| 14 COULTHARD | | | | | | | | | | | | | | | | | | | | | | | | | | | | | | | | | | | | | | | | | | | | | |
| 21 ALBERS | | | | | | | | | | | | | | | | | | | | | | | | | | | | | | | | | | | | | | | | | | | | | |

## PRACTICE 1 (FRIDAY)

Sunny (track 36–42ºC, air 30–32ºC)

| Pos. | Driver | Laps | Time |
|---|---|---|---|
| 1 | Kimi Räikkönen | 21 | 1m 33.162s |
| 2 | Felipe Massa | 17 | 1m 33.679s |
| 3 | Lewis Hamilton | 17 | 1m 34.110s |
| 4 | Fernando Alonso | 15 | 1m 34.161s |
| 5 | Jarno Trulli | 26 | 1m 34.896s |
| 6 | Nick Heidfeld | 30 | 1m 35.076s |
| 7 | Robert Kubica | 24 | 1m 35.248s |
| 8 | Vitantonio Liuzzi | 23 | 1m 35.292s |
| 9 | Nico Rosberg | 19 | 1m 35.375s |
| 10 | Alexander Wurz | 20 | 1m 35.398s |
| 11 | Jenson Button | 24 | 1m 35.445s |
| 12 | Heikki Kovalainen | 21 | 1m 35.474s |
| 13 | Ralf Schumacher | 24 | 1m 35.573s |
| 14 | Giancarlo Fisichella | 17 | 1m 35.697s |
| 15 | Scott Speed | 22 | 1m 35.726s |
| 16 | Takuma Sato | 15 | 1m 35.856s |
| 17 | Rubens Barrichello | 20 | 1m 35.911s |
| 18 | Anthony Davidson | 6 | 1m 36.243s |
| 19 | Mark Webber | 18 | 1m 36.483s |
| 20 | David Coulthard | 7 | 1m 36.513s |
| 21 | Adrian Sutil | 27 | 1m 37.084s |
| 22 | Christijan Albers | 29 | 1m 38.258s |

## PRACTICE 2 (FRIDAY)

Sunny (track 43ºC, air 32ºC)

| Pos. | Driver | Laps | Time |
|---|---|---|---|
| 1 | Kimi Räikkönen | 33 | 1m 33.527s |
| 2 | Lewis Hamilton | 33 | 1m 33.540s |
| 3 | Robert Kubica | 37 | 1m 33.732s |
| 4 | Felipe Massa | 28 | 1m 33.772s |
| 5 | Fernando Alonso | 30 | 1m 33.784s |
| 6 | Alexander Wurz | 26 | 1m 33.973s |
| 7 | Nick Heidfeld | 34 | 1m 34.076s |
| 8 | Nico Rosberg | 34 | 1m 34.189s |
| 9 | David Coulthard | 32 | 1m 34.359s |
| 10 | Jarno Trulli | 33 | 1m 34.366s |
| 11 | Rubens Barrichello | 28 | 1m 34.391s |
| 12 | Heikki Kovalainen | 33 | 1m 34.585s |
| 13 | Anthony Davidson | 29 | 1m 34.595s |
| 14 | Mark Webber | 24 | 1m 34.677s |
| 15 | Giancarlo Fisichella | 34 | 1m 34.796s |
| 16 | Takuma Sato | 35 | 1m 35.001s |
| 17 | Vitantonio Liuzzi | 38 | 1m 35.268s |
| 18 | Ralf Schumacher | 29 | 1m 35.427s |
| 19 | Adrian Sutil | 31 | 1m 35.582s |
| 20 | Scott Speed | 34 | 1m 35.687s |
| 21 | Christijan Albers | 30 | 1m 35.835s |
| 22 | Jenson Button | 19 | 1m 36.079s |

## QUALIFYING (SATURDAY)

Hazy sunshine (track 42–45ºC, air 32–33ºC)

| Pos. | Driver | First | Second | Third |
|---|---|---|---|---|
| 1 | Felipe Massa | 1m 32.443s | 1m 31.359s | 1m 32.652s |
| 2 | Lewis Hamilton | 1m 32.580s | 1m 31.732s | 1m 32.935s |
| 3 | Kimi Räikkönen | 1m 33.161s | 1m 31.812s | 1m 33.131s |
| 4 | Fernando Alonso | 1m 33.049s | 1m 32.214s | 1m 33.192s |
| 5 | Nick Heidfeld | 1m 33.164s | 1m 32.154s | 1m 33.404s |
| 6 | Robert Kubica | 1m 33.348s | 1m 32.292s | 1m 33.710s |
| 7 | Giancarlo Fisichella | 1m 33.556s | 1m 32.889s | 1m 34.056s |
| 8 | Mark Webber | 1m 33.496s | 1m 32.808s | 1m 34.106s |
| 9 | Jarno Trulli | 1m 33.218s | 1m 32.429s | 1m 34.154s |
| 10 | Nico Rosberg | 1m 33.349s | 1m 32.815s | 1m 34.399s |
| 11 | Alexander Wurz | 1m 33.759s | 1m 32.915s | |
| 12 | Heikki Kovalainen | 1m 33.467s | 1m 32.935s | |
| 13 | Anthony Davidson | 1m 33.299s | 1m 33.082s | |
| 14 | Ralf Schumacher | 1m 33.923s | 1m 33.294s | |
| 15 | Rubens Barrichello | 1m 33.776s | 1m 33.624s | |
| 16 | Jenson Button | 1m 33.967s | 1m 33.731s | |
| 17 | Takuma Sato | 1m 33.984s | | |
| 18 | Vitantonio Liuzzi | 1m 34.024s | | |
| 19 | Scott Speed | 1m 34.333s | | |
| 20 | Adrian Sutil | 1m 35.280s | | |
| 21 | David Coulthard | 1m 35.341s | | |
| 22 | Christijan Albers | 1m 35.533s | | |

## PRACTICE 3 (SATURDAY)

Cloud, light rain (track 35–37ºC, air 30–31ºC)

| Pos. | Driver | Laps | Time |
|---|---|---|---|
| 1 | Lewis Hamilton | 12 | 1m 32.543s |
| 2 | Kimi Räikkönen | 16 | 1m 32.549s |
| 3 | Nick Heidfeld | 15 | 1m 32.652s |
| 4 | Robert Kubica | 15 | 1m 32.755s |
| 5 | Anthony Davidson | 20 | 1m 32.900s |
| 6 | Felipe Massa | 12 | 1m 32.950s |
| 7 | Fernando Alonso | 11 | 1m 33.235s |
| 8 | Mark Webber | 14 | 1m 33.399s |
| 9 | Giancarlo Fisichella | 17 | 1m 33.602s |
| 10 | Heikki Kovalainen | 21 | 1m 33.605s |
| 11 | Nico Rosberg | 14 | 1m 33.614s |
| 12 | Alexander Wurz | 17 | 1m 33.658s |
| 13 | Vitantonio Liuzzi | 18 | 1m 33.700s |
| 14 | Jarno Trulli | 22 | 1m 33.724s |
| 15 | David Coulthard | 14 | 1m 33.826s |
| 16 | Jenson Button | 20 | 1m 34.023s |
| 17 | Takuma Sato | 21 | 1m 34.082s |
| 18 | Rubens Barrichello | 17 | 1m 34.397s |
| 19 | Scott Speed | 12 | 1m 34.791s |
| 20 | Ralf Schumacher | 11 | 1m 35.144s |
| 21 | Christijan Albers | 22 | 1m 35.395s |
| 22 | Adrian Sutil | 18 | 1m 35.436s |

## RACE TYRE STRATEGIES

BRIDGESTONE

In 2007, the tyre regulations stipulate that the two dry-tyre specifications must be visibly distinguishable from each other. At the Bahrain Grand Prix, the medium compound Bridgestone Potenza tyre was marked with a white line in the second-from-inside groove.

| | Driver | Race stint 1 | Race stint 2 | Race stint 3 | Race stint 4 |
|---|---|---|---|---|---|
| 1 | Felipe Massa | Medium: laps 1–21 | Medium: 22–40 | Hard: 41–57 | |
| 2 | Lewis Hamilton | Medium: 1–19 | Medium: 20–44 | Hard: 45–57 | |
| 3 | Kimi Räikkönen | Medium: 1–23 | Medium: 24–41 | Hard: 42–57 | |
| 4 | Nick Heidfeld | Medium: 1–23 | Medium: 24–41 | Hard: 42–57 | |
| 5 | Fernando Alonso | Medium: 1–22 | Medium: 23–43 | Hard: 44–57 | |
| 6 | Robert Kubica | Medium: 1–23 | Medium: 24–43 | Hard: 44–57 | |
| 7 | Jarno Trulli | Medium: 1–21 | Medium: 22–42 | Hard: 43–57 | |
| 8 | Giancarlo Fisichella | Medium: 1–19 | Medium: 20–44 | Hard: 45–57 | |
| 9 | Heikki Kovalainen | Medium: 1–25 | Medium: 26–42 | Hard: 43–57 | |
| 10 | Nico Rosberg | Medium: 1–22 | Medium: 23–39 | Hard: 40–57 | |
| 11 | Alexander Wurz | Medium: 1–17 | Medium: 18–34 | Hard: 35–57 | |
| 12 | Ralf Schumacher | Medium: 1–17 | Medium: 18–38 | Hard: 39–57 | |
| 13 | Rubens Barrichello | Medium: 1–26 | Medium: 27–46 | Hard: 47–57 | |
| 14 | Christijan Albers | Medium: 1–20 | Medium: 21–41 | Hard: 42–57 | |
| 15 | Adrian Sutil | Medium: 1 | Hard: 2–19 | Medium: 20–37 | Medium: 38–53 |
| 16 | Anthony Davidson | Medium: 1–28 | Medium: 29–39 | Hard: 40–51 (DNF) | |
| | Mark Webber | Medium: 1–18 | Medium: 19–38 | Hard: 39–41 (DNF) | |
| | David Coulthard | Medium: 1–17 | Medium: 18–35 | Hard: 36 (DNF) | |
| | Takuma Sato | Medium: 1–20 | Medium: 21–34 (DNF) | | |
| | Vitantonio Liuzzi | Hard: 1–2 | Medium: 3–21 | Medium: 22–26 (DNF) | |
| | Jenson Button | Medium: 0 (DNF) | | | |
| | Scott Speed | Medium: 0 (DNF) | | | |

 **9** TRULLI Toyota
 **7** FISICHELLA Renault
 **5** HEIDFELD BMW-Sauber
 **3** RÄIKKONEN Ferrari
 **1** MASSA Ferrari

 **10** ROSBERG Williams
 **8** WEBBER Red Bull
 **6** KUBICA BMW-Sauber
 **4** ALONSO McLaren
 **2** HAMILTON McLaren

RACE DISTANCE:
57 laps,
191.530 miles/308.238 km

RACE WEATHER:
Sunny, windy,
track 37–41ºC, air 28–30ºC

| 46 | 47 | 48 | 49 | 50 | 51 | 52 | 53 | 54 | 55 | 56 | 57 | |
|---|---|---|---|---|---|---|---|---|---|---|---|---|
| 5 | 5 | 5 | 5 | 5 | 5 | 5 | 5 | 5 | 5 | 5 | 5 | 1 |
| 2 | 2 | 2 | 2 | 2 | 2 | 2 | 2 | 2 | 2 | 2 | 2 | 2 |
| 6 | 6 | 6 | 6 | 6 | 6 | 6 | 6 | 6 | 6 | 6 | 6 | 3 |
| 9 | 9 | 9 | 9 | 9 | 9 | 9 | 9 | 9 | 9 | 9 | 9 | 4 |
| 1 | 1 | 1 | 1 | 1 | 1 | 1 | 1 | 1 | 1 | 1 | 1 | 5 |
| 10 | 10 | 10 | 10 | 10 | 10 | 10 | 10 | 10 | 10 | 10 | 10 | 6 |
| 12 | 12 | 12 | 12 | 12 | 12 | 12 | 12 | 12 | 12 | 12 | 12 | 7 |
| 3 | 3 | 3 | 3 | 3 | 3 | 3 | 3 | 3 | 3 | 3 | 3 | 8 |
| 4 | 4 | 4 | 4 | 4 | 4 | 4 | 4 | 4 | 4 | 4 | 4 | |
| 16 | 16 | 16 | 16 | 16 | 16 | 16 | 16 | 16 | 16 | 16 | 16 | |
| 17 | 17 | 17 | 17 | 17 | 17 | 17 | 17 | 17 | 17 | 17 | | |
| 23 | 23 | 23 | 23 | 23 | 23 | 11 | 11 | 11 | 11 | 11 | 11 | |
| 8 | 11 | 11 | 11 | 11 | 8 | 8 | 8 | 8 | 8 | 8 | | |
| 11 | 8 | 8 | 8 | 8 | 8 | 21 | 21 | 21 | 21 | | | |
| 21 | 21 | 21 | 21 | 21 | 21 | 20 | 20 | | | | | |
| 20 | 20 | 20 | 20 | 20 | 20 | | | | | | | |

20 Pit stop
20 Drive-through penalty
20 One lap or more behind leader
20 Safety car deployed on laps shown

## FOR THE RECORD

**200th LAP LED:** Felipe Massa
**400th POINT:** Fernando Alonso
**FIRST FRONT ROW:** Lewis Hamilton

## POINTS

### DRIVERS

| | | |
|---|---|---|
| 1 | Fernando Alonso | 22 |
| 2 | Kimi Räikkönen | 22 |
| 3 | Lewis Hamilton | 22 |
| 4 | Felipe Massa | 17 |
| 5 | Nick Heidfeld | 15 |
| 6 | Giancarlo Fisichella | 8 |
| 7 | Jarno Trulli | 4 |
| 8 | Robert Kubica | 3 |
| 9 | Nico Rosberg | 2 |
| 10 | Heikki Kovalainen | 1 |
| 11 | Ralf Schumacher | 1 |

### CONSTRUCTORS

| | | |
|---|---|---|
| 1 | McLaren | 44 |
| 2 | Ferrari | 39 |
| 3 | BMW Sauber | 18 |
| 4 | Renault | 9 |
| 5 | Toyota | 5 |
| 6 | Williams | 2 |

**Main:** After trying to go for broke in a bid to take the lead from second place on the grid, Fernando Alonso finds himself ploughing wide into the gravel at the first corner.
Photograph: Paul-Henri Cahier

**Inset:** Felipe Massa celebrates his second successive victory.
Photograph: Peter J Fox/www.crash.net

FIA F1 WORLD CHAMPIONSHIP/ROUND 4

# SPANISH GP

## BARCELONA

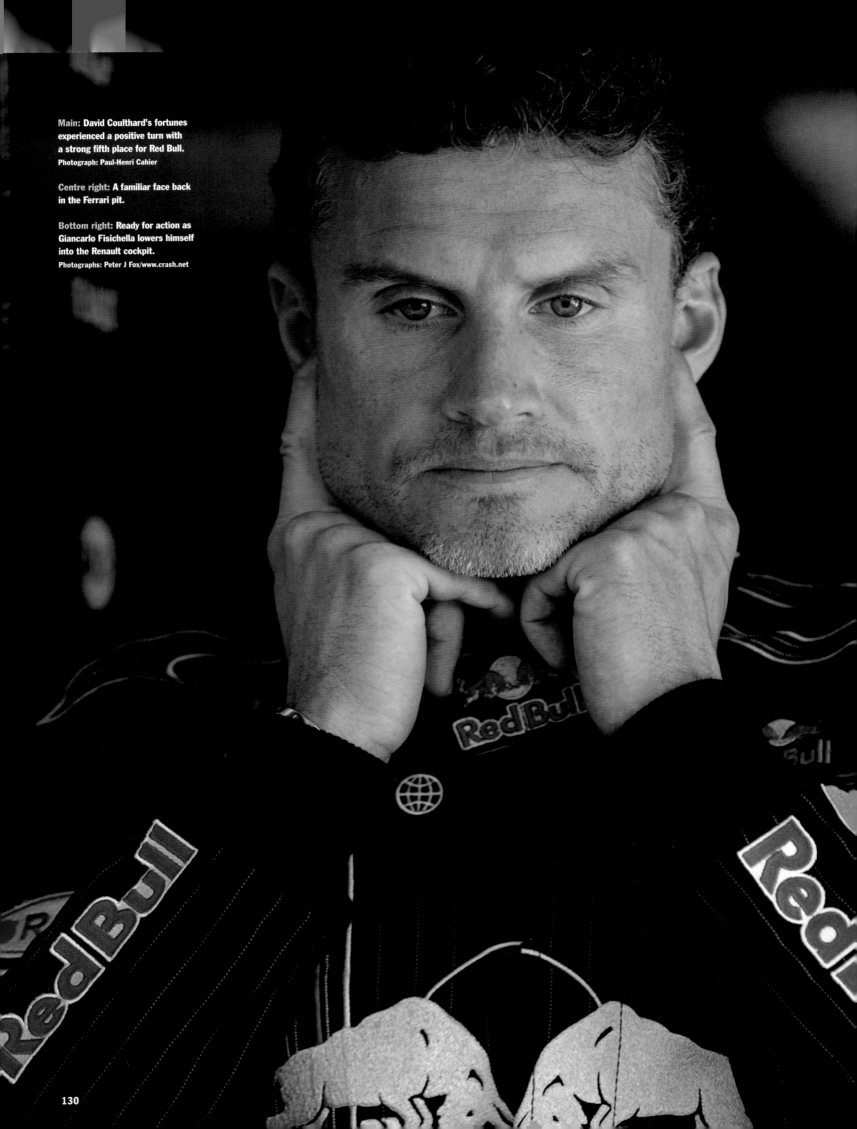

Main: David Coulthard's fortunes experienced a positive turn with a strong fifth place for Red Bull.
Photograph: Paul-Henri Cahier

Centre right: A familiar face back in the Ferrari pit.

Bottom right: Ready for action as Giancarlo Fisichella lowers himself into the Renault cockpit.
Photographs: Peter J Fox/www.crash.net

Michael Schumacher (above) makes a low-key return to the F1 paddock with Ferrari at Barcelona and insists he is not contemplating a return to the cockpit.

Bruno Senna scores his maiden GP2 race win in the Saturday event at Barcelona, beating Timo Glock into second place. Glock wins Sunday's race with Senna fourth.

Helio Castroneves qualifies on pole position for the Indy 500 at 225.817 mph.

Former Honda F1 test driver James Rossiter is recruited to a similar role with the Super Aguri squad.

From the outset, Fernando Alonso was confident that he could grab pole position, but he was pipped in the final moments by Felipe Massa on 1m 21.421s, who thus claimed the prized slot on the front row of the grid for the third race in succession.

'The team told me on the radio that I was three to four tenths in front of everybody after the first [qualifying] attempt,' said Alonso. 'I was thinking that if I could do my second run on new tyres as quickly as I could then I would be on pole position. I did improve the time, but it was obviously not quite enough for pole. But I think as long as you are in the top three it is possible to fight for the win.'

For his part, Massa was clearly elated at seeing off the much-fancied Kimi Räikkönen in the other Ferrari yet again. Räikkönen managed no better than third-fastest time (1m 21.723s) for a place on the second row of the grid. 'It was a very good qualifying lap,' said Massa. 'I think both sets of tyres and both laps were very similar. In the last lap, I improved a bit due to having less fuel, after three or four laps, and there was nothing more I could get from the car.'

One might have expected the Ferrari F2007 to have lost some of its early-season pace after the introduction at this race of revised rules relating to the flexible floor provisions, but the situation was certainly helped by the assistance of Michael Schumacher in his role as consultant to the team. The cars were modified at the circuit and the results duly impressive, although Räikkönen's result was again ever so slightly disappointing.

'It seems that taking third place in qualifying is now becoming a habit,' he said. 'It's not a bad position, but obviously you always hope to be ahead of everybody.'

Lewis Hamilton was satisfied with his 1m 21.785s for fourth, while Robert Kubica lined up his BMW-Sauber fifth. Kubica said that his car still felt a little tail-happy, so his 1m 22.253s represented a pretty special effort.

'I am happy after that because I think the position is good, given that I struggled with the balance of my car,' he explained. 'This morning it was looking better, but then this afternoon I picked up oversteer. But I hope that tomorrow the circuit will be better with more grip.'

Nick Heidfeld, in the other BMW, posted a 1m 22.389s for seventh place, just behind Jarno Trulli (1m 22.324s), who had squeezed a reasonable performance from the aerodynamically upgraded Toyota TF107, which was making its début at this race. By contrast Ralf Schumacher (1m 22.666s) failed to make it

through the first qualifying session and lined up an eventual 17th.

Meanwhile, the Renault squad was enjoying its best qualifying session of the season so far, with Heikki Kovalainen lining up eighth on 1m 22.568s and Giancarlo Fisichella in tenth on 1m 22.881s.

'We went with hard tyres in the final part of qualifying and think that was a good choice because we have a good strategy for the race,' said Fisichella. 'The session this afternoon wasn't perfect for me; I didn't complete my programme this morning during the third free practice session. That meant that I wasn't totally comfortable in the car when I went out for my first laps in qualifying. I thought I had a brake problem on my first run and aborted it, so that made it quite tight getting through into the next session of qualifying.'

Next up was Nico Rosberg's Williams on 1m 21.968s ahead of Rubens Barrichello's Honda (1m 22.097s), Takuma Sato's Super Aguri (1m 22.115s) and the other Honda of Jenson Button (1m 22.120s).

Anthony Davidson was 15th on 1m 22.295s, but reckoned he could have been much quicker had it not been for an unfortunate setback. 'After setting a good time in the morning, I felt confident in the car and that I could do it again in qualifying,' he said. 'Getting through to Q2 was good – and we weren't really expecting it – and [we] thought it was going to be a bit more difficult than it was. But in Q2 I got caught out by the wind at Turn Nine and ended up spinning off.'

Behind Davidson was Vitantonio Liuzzi's Toro Rosso on 1m 22.508s ahead of Ralf Schumacher and Alex Wurz, who could manage only 1m 22.769s in his Williams FW29.

'It was a bit of a disaster. Worse than a traffic jam on the M25,' said Wurz with more good nature as he obviously felt. 'People really slowed down on their in-laps. They seemed to forget there were people all around them doing their quick laps. At the last chicane I actually nearly stopped because five cars in front of me were going slowly, which caused my tyre pressures to drop quite dramatically.'

Mark Webber had to be content with 19th on a 1m 23.398s after experiencing a whole raft of problems, including a driveshaft glitch during the morning's free practice session and a hydraulic failure in qualifying. This all ensured that only the Spykers of Adrian Sutil (1m 23.811s) and Christijan Albers (1m 23.990s) and Scott Speed's Toro Rosso (no time due to a mechanical problem) lined up behind Wurz in the final grid order.

**Above: All goes smoothly during a routine refuelling stop for Lewis Hamilton's second-placed McLaren.**
Photograph: Bernard Asset

**Top right: Fernando Alonso was under pressure after failing to take pole position from Felipe Massa.**
Photograph: Peter J Fox/www.crash.net

**Centre right: Kimi Räikkönen again found himself outpaced by Massa and his Ferrari failed to last the distance.**
Photograph: Jad Sherif/WRi2

LEWIS HAMILTON'S relentless onslaught on the F1 history books continued at full throttle at the Circuit de Catalunya as he stormed to his third second place in as many races, surging majestically into the lead of the drivers' championship, the youngest driver to head the points table.

In front of 140,000 madly enthusiastic Spanish race fans, Hamilton stole local hero Fernando Alonso's thunder by beating him after Alonso ran wide onto the gravel thanks to a first-corner brush with Felipe Massa's Ferrari F2007, which dominated the race from pole position.

With a neat slice of historical symmetry, Hamilton succeeded team founder Bruce McLaren as the youngest championship points leader, being one month and two days younger than McLaren was when he won the 1960 Argentine Grand Prix at Buenos Aires at the wheel of a Cooper.

'I wouldn't really say it fuels my belief that I can win the world championship in my first year, but for sure it is a positive development,' said Hamilton, who also extended his record of podium finishes to four at this early stage in his career. 'This is only my first season and there will obviously be some ups and downs. If I can keep scoring podium finishes I can do well.'

Hamilton qualified fourth, but made a great start to surge past Kimi Räikkönen's Ferrari going down to the first corner. Meanwhile

Alonso, his motivation fuelled by home-track adrenaline, tried to force his way past Massa's Ferrari as they negotiated the first right-left complex at the end of the start-line straight.

The two cars made light contact, but it was enough to drop Alonso to fourth and damage one of the aerodynamic deflectors on the right-hand side of his McLaren's chassis. This also had the effect of serving up another bonus for Hamilton, who slipped through into second place as Alonso was busy wrestling his car back under control.

'The key was to get the best position at the first corner,' said Hamilton. 'It was very close when he [Alonso] came back onto the track, but we got through it. The middle stint of the race [on soft tyres] wasn't great but we certainly had the pace in the closing stages. To come out of my fourth grand prix leading the world championship against all these great drivers is unbelievable.'

For Alonso the weekend delivered less by far than he had been hoping for. The Spanish star had monopolised McLaren's pre-race testing at Barcelona, sharing the aerodynamically revised MP4-22 with test driver Pedro de la Rosa rather than Hamilton, who was given a week's break from driving.

After the race Alonso made it very clear that he had been nosing ahead of Massa going into the first corner and that the

home-town favourite was handed an early bonus after nine laps when Räikkönen slowed suddenly and swung gently into the pit lane, where he retired with a suspected electrical problem.

'Honestly, there's little to say, except that I am very disappointed,' said Kimi as he headed for his rental car in the company of his managers Steve and David Robertson. 'I lost a place to Hamilton at the start, but made the most of the fight between Felipe and Fernando to get back to third place. I was running at a good pace and could have had a good result, but suddenly the car had an electrical problem and all I could do was come back to the garage.' Closer examination revealed that his F2007 had developed a problem with the wiring to the alternator.

Massa, meanwhile, had been taken aback at just how quickly he'd stretched his advantage over the opposition. By the end of the opening lap he'd already opened a 1.6s edge over Hamilton, even though he was confident the McLaren driver was running with a heavier fuel load than his Ferrari's.

'I was surprised by how easily I pulled away from him,' said Felipe. 'I knew he was running more fuel, but I was pulling away sometimes by as much as 0.5s per lap.'

The Ferrari driver later claimed he wasn't aware that the rear of his car had been enveloped in flames as he accelerated back into the race after his first scheduled pit stop, during which a trickle of fuel leaked onto the hot engine. 'I didn't notice the fire,' he said. Thankfully the effect of the slipstream as he raced back down the pit lane extinguished this brief conflagration and he had a trouble-free run from that point on.

As for Hamilton, he drove perfectly. By his own admission, he found himself struggling slightly to get heat into his tyres in the early stages and was grappling with a touch of oversteer as a result. 'Things improved considerably after a few laps,' he went on, 'although by then the gap to Felipe was already

## SPANISH STORM OVER SECOND F1 RACE

F1 commercial rights holder Bernie Ecclestone (below) whipped up a storm of controversy in the run-up to the Spanish GP when he was accused of political interference following the completion of a deal for Valencia to host a round of the championship title chase at the end of 2008.

Ecclestone topped off a quite remarkable week of high-powered negotiations by confirming that not only would the Spanish GP remain at Barcelona until 2016, but new street circuits in Valencia and Singapore would join the existing schedule next year.

Nevertheless, the Valencia announcement attracted much criticism after it emerged that the deal was conditional on the regional government's remaining in power to finalise the contract after a round of local elections that was due shortly after the deal was announced. As a result it was suggested that Ecclestone was trying to influence Spanish political affairs.

Bernie was quick to deny this notion. 'We've made all the arrangements and agreements, so if he [Bernie's contact] doesn't win, then I will have to deal with someone else. There's nothing political about it at all.'

Ferrari driver had squeezed him out. 'I thought I was much in front of him, but he didn't agree,' said Alonso.

Massa added, 'We touched. The cars were very close and Fernando was trying to push me inside, so there was very small contact. It is sure that the most difficult part of the race is the start, but after that the car was responding well and the race was in my hands.'

A little farther around the opening lap there was another slight altercation as Ralf Schumacher braked suddenly in his Toyota TF107 and was hit up the rear by Alex Wurz's Williams FW29, which suffered front suspension damage and was forced to pull in for good at the end of the opening lap.

'A short race and really not the best weekend for me,' shrugged Wurz. 'I had a good start and overtook a few guys, but then I lined up behind Ralf going into Turn Ten and he suddenly had to lift for someone in front. It's such close racing out there that I had zero chance to react and ended up on his wheel.'

Schumacher had to pull in to check for damage at the end of the lap, dropping him right to the tail of the field, where he circulated until the end of lap 44 before retiring when his nose section worked loose.

The opening stages thus settled down with Massa leading from Hamilton, Räikkönen and the frustrated Alonso. The

Photograph: Peter J Fox/www.crash.net

Above: Scott Speed suffered this frightening tyre failure on the main straight, forcing Toro Rosso team-mate Vitantonio Liuzzi into the pit exit lane in avoidance.

Right: Takuma Sato did well to score his first point of the season.
Photographs: Peter J Fox/www.crash.net

Below: Kimi Räikkönen's Ferrari succumbed to electrical failure.
Photograph: Bernard Asset

too big. In the second stint I was a little unlucky in traffic, but that happens sometimes. Overall I'm happy with the outcome of the race and I want to keep on scoring points.'

Behind the high rollers in that exclusive club battling for victory at the front of the field, Robert Kubica drove an excellent race to finish fourth in his BMW-Sauber and David Coulthard did well to keep his Red Bull ahead of the fast-closing Nico Rosberg's Williams to grab fifth at the chequered flag.

Kubica was the sole survivor of the BMW Sauber squad after Nick Heidfeld's pit crew encountered a problem refitting his right-front-wheel securing nut at his first refuelling stop; this was followed by retirement after 46 laps with gearbox failure.

'On top of that, Alonso was not very quick on his harder tyres in his second stint,' said Heidfeld, 'and I believe I had the chance to finish on the podium.'

As for Coulthard, his result put the wind back into the sails of the Red Bull squad after a troubled start to the season. 'Towards the end of the race I lost third gear and thought I was going to have to retire the car,' said Coulthard, '[but] I managed to drive using only fourth gear and above, which lost me time in

the last sector but still enabled me to be quick in the first. We've made more progress than any other team since the beginning of the year and when you're aggressively attacking lap times, sometimes you have to put other areas of the car to one side.'

Nico Rosberg, meanwhile, stormed through to take sixth place and three championship points in his Williams-Toyota after a strong race made tougher by the fact that the supply of fluid from his on-board drinks bottle failed and he was starting to dehydrate in the closing stages.

The final unlapped runner was Heikki Kovalainen in the Renault R27. He finished seventh, this being the best the once-dominant French squad could salvage after both Kovalainen and his team-mate Giancarlo Fisichella had their races badly compromised by refuelling rig malfunctions. At Kovalainen's first stop and Fisichella's second, insufficient fuel went on board for the cars to complete their planned stints so both men had to make additional stops to top up. Despite all these strategic setbacks, Heikki was at least able to garner a couple of championship points as a reward for his efforts.

'This is my best finish so far in F1,' he said with obvious pleasure, 'which is at least something positive for me on a personal level, even though within the team we know that I was quick enough to finish in fifth position today.'

For his part, Fisichella finished ninth just behind Takuma Sato's well-driven Super Aguri. Sato was understandably elated to have scored the team's first world championship point ahead of a competitor of Fisichella's unquestioned status.

Rounding off the list of finishers were the struggling Honda RA107s, Rubens Barrichello tenth and Jenson Button 12th, sandwiching Anthony Davidson's Super Aguri, after a bruising race in which Jenson knocked his wing off against his team-mate's rear wheel and had to pit for a replacement, losing a lot of time. Neither Toro Rosso made it to the chequered flag.

And so it was on to Monaco in two weeks' time. Hamilton had raced through the streets of the Principality on three occasions in F3 and GP2. He had yet to be beaten and didn't intend that that should change on his début in the world's most glamorous grand prix.

*Alan Henry*

**Above: Felipe Massa was totally dominant.**
Photograph: Jad Sherif/WRi2

**Left: Nico Rosberg was delighted to score a career-best sixth place.**
Photograph: Peter J Fox/www.crash.net

**FIA F1 WORLD CHAMPIONSHIP • ROUND 4**

# GRAN PREMIO DE ESPAÑA TELEFÓNICA
### CATALUNYA 11-13 MAY 2007

**CIRCUIT DE CATALUNYA, BARCELONA**

Renault 142/228
Repsol 81/130
Seat 60/97
Campsa 137/220
Europcar 147/237
Banc Sabadell 73/117
Würth 90/145
Elf 85/137
190/305
La Caixa 71/114
New Holland 142/229

**Circuit:**
2.892 miles/ 4.655 km
116/187 mph/kmh
Gear

Photograph: Peter J Fox/www.crash.net

---

## RACE RESULTS

| Pos. | Driver | Nat. | No. | Entrant | Car/Engine | Tyres | Laps | Time/Retirement | Speed (mph/km/h) | Gap to leader | Fastest race lap | |
|---|---|---|---|---|---|---|---|---|---|---|---|---|
| 1 | Felipe Massa | BR | 5 | Scuderia Ferrari Marlboro | Ferrari F2007-056 V8 | B | 65 | 1h 31m 36.230s | 123.095/198.102 | | 1m 22.680s | 14 |
| 2 | Lewis Hamilton | GB | 2 | Vodafone McLaren Mercedes | McLaren MP4-22-Mercedes FO 108T V8 | B | 65 | 1h 31m 43.020s | 122.943/197.857 | + 6.790s | 1m 22.876s | 20 |
| 3 | Fernando Alonso | E | 1 | Vodafone McLaren Mercedes | McLaren MP4-22-Mercedes FO 108T V8 | B | 65 | 1h 31m 53.686s | 122.705/197.475 | + 17.456s | 1m 22.966s | 17 |
| 4 | Robert Kubica | POL | 10 | BMW Sauber F1 Team | BMW Sauber F1.07-BMW P86/7 V8 | B | 65 | 1h 32m 7.845s | 122.391/196.969 | + 31.615s | 1m 23.129s | 20 |
| 5 | David Coulthard | GB | 14 | Red Bull Racing | Red Bull RB3-Renault RS27 V8 | B | 65 | 1h 32m 34.561s | 121.802/196.022 | + 58.331s | 1m 23.524s | 18 |
| 6 | Nico Rosberg | D | 16 | AT&T Williams | Williams FW29-Toyota RVX-07 V8 | B | 65 | 1h 32m 35.768s | 121.776/195.979 | + 59.538s | 1m 23.693s | 60 |
| 7 | Heikki Kovalainen | FIN | 4 | ING Renault F1 Team | Renault R27-RS27 V8 | B | 65 | 1h 32m 38.358s | 121.719/195.888 | + 1m 2.128s | 1m 22.980s | 32 |
| 8 | Takuma Sato | J | 22 | Super Aguri F1 Team | Super Aguri SA07-Honda RA807E V8 | B | 64 | | | + 1 lap | 1m 24.110s | 23 |
| 9 | Giancarlo Fisichella | I | 3 | ING Renault F1 Team | Renault R27-RS27 V8 | B | 64 | | | + 1 lap | 1m 23.560s | 57 |
| 10 | Rubens Barrichello | BR | 8 | Honda Racing F1 Team | Honda RA107-RA807E V8 | B | 64 | | | + 1 lap | 1m 24.287s | 16 |
| 11 | Anthony Davidson | GB | 23 | Super Aguri F1 Team | Super Aguri SA07-Honda RA807E V8 | B | 64 | | | + 1 lap | 1m 24.291s | 59 |
| 12 | Jenson Button | GB | 7 | Honda Racing F1 Team | Honda RA107-RA807E V8 | B | 64 | | | + 1 lap | 1m 24.186s | 64 |
| 13 | Adrian Sutil | D | 20 | Etihad Aldar Spyker F1 Team | Spyker F8-VII-Ferrari 056H V8 | B | 63 | | | + 2 laps | 1m 25.191s | 57 |
| 14 | Christijan Albers | NL | 21 | Etihad Aldar Spyker F1 Team | Spyker F8-VII-Ferrari 056H V8 | B | 63 | | | + 2 laps | 1m 25.260s | 61 |
| | Nick Heidfeld | D | 9 | BMW Sauber F1 Team | BMW Sauber F1.07-BMW P86/7 V8 | B | 46 | Gearbox | | | 1m 23.483s | 22 |
| | Ralf Schumacher | D | 11 | Panasonic Toyota Racing | Toyota TF107-RVX-07 V8 | B | 44 | Accident damage | | | 1m 24.003s | 37 |
| | Vitantonio Liuzzi | I | 18 | Scuderia Toro Rosso | Toro Rosso STR02-Ferrari 056H V8 | B | 19 | Hydraulics | | | 1m 25.207s | 18 |
| | Scott Speed | USA | 19 | Scuderia Toro Rosso | Toro Rosso STR02-Ferrari 056H V8 | B | 9 | Rear tyre | | | 1m 26.238s | 6 |
| | Kimi Räikkönen | FIN | 6 | Scuderia Ferrari Marlboro | Ferrari F2007-056 V8 | B | 9 | Electrics | | | 1m 23.475s | 7 |
| | Jarno Trulli | I | 12 | Panasonic Toyota Racing | Toyota TF107-RVX-07 V8 | B | 8 | Fuel line | | | 1m 26.094s | 6 |
| | Mark Webber | AUS | 15 | Red Bull Racing | Red Bull RB3-Renault RS27 V8 | B | 7 | Transmission | | | 1m 26.323s | 4 |
| | Alexander Wurz | A | 17 | AT&T Williams | Williams FW29-Toyota RVX-07 V8 | B | 1 | Accident | | | No time | – |

**Fastest race lap:** Felipe Massa on lap 14, 1m 22.680s, 125.943 mph/202.685 km/h.

**Lap record:** Giancarlo Fisichella (Renault R25 V10), 1m 15.641s, 136.835 mph/220.213 km/h (2005).

 **21 ALBERS** Spyker
 **19 WEBBER** Williams
 **17 SCHUMACHER** Toyota
 **15 DAVIDSON** Super Aguri
 **13 SATO** Super Aguri
**11 ROSBERG** Williams

 **22 SPEED** Toro Rosso
 **20 SUTIL** Spyker
 **18 WURZ** Williams
 **16 LIUZZI** Toro Rosso
 **14 BUTTON** Honda
**12 BARRICHELLO** Honda

| Grid order | 1 | 2 | 3 | 4 | 5 | 6 | 7 | 8 | 9 | 10 | 11 | 12 | 13 | 14 | 15 | 16 | 17 | 18 | 19 | 20 | 21 | 22 | 23 | 24 | 25 | 26 | 27 | 28 | 29 | 30 | 31 | 32 | 33 | 34 | 35 | 36 | 37 | 38 | 39 | 40 | 41 | 42 | 43 | 44 | 45 | 46 | 47 | 48 | 49 | 50 | |
|---|---|---|---|---|---|---|---|---|---|---|---|---|---|---|---|---|---|---|---|---|---|---|---|---|---|---|---|---|---|---|---|---|---|---|---|---|---|---|---|---|---|---|---|---|---|---|---|---|---|---|---|
| 5 MASSA | 5 | 5 | 5 | 5 | 5 | 5 | 5 | 5 | 5 | 5 | 5 | 5 | 5 | 5 | 5 | 5 | 5 | 5 | 5 | 5 | 2 | 2 | 9 | 9 | 5 | 5 | 5 | 5 | 5 | 5 | 5 | 5 | 5 | 5 | 5 | 5 | 5 | 5 | 5 | 5 | 2 | 2 | 2 | 2 | 2 | 5 | 5 | 5 | | | |
| 1 ALONSO | 2 | 2 | 2 | 2 | 2 | 2 | 2 | 2 | 2 | 2 | 2 | 2 | 2 | 2 | 2 | 2 | 2 | 2 | 2 | 10 | 10 | 9 | 5 | 5 | 2 | 2 | 2 | 2 | 2 | 2 | 2 | 2 | 2 | 2 | 2 | 2 | 2 | 2 | 2 | 2 | 5 | 5 | 5 | 5 | 5 | 1 | 2 | 2 | | | |
| 6 RÄIKKÖNEN | 6 | 6 | 6 | 6 | 6 | 6 | 6 | 6 | 1 | 1 | 1 | 1 | 1 | 1 | 1 | 1 | 1 | 1 | 1 | 9 | 9 | 5 | 2 | 2 | 1 | 1 | 1 | 1 | 1 | 1 | 1 | 1 | 1 | 1 | 1 | 1 | 1 | 1 | 1 | 1 | 1 | 1 | 1 | 1 | 1 | 2 | 1 | 1 | | | |
| 2 HAMILTON | 1 | 1 | 1 | 1 | 1 | 1 | 1 | 1 | 10 | 10 | 10 | 10 | 10 | 10 | 10 | 10 | 10 | 10 | 10 | 5 | 5 | 16 | 16 | | 1 | 10 | 10 | 10 | 10 | 10 | 10 | 10 | 10 | 10 | 10 | 10 | 10 | 10 | 10 | 10 | 10 | 10 | 10 | 10 | 10 | 10 | 10 | 10 | | | |
| 10 KUBICA | 10 | 10 | 10 | 10 | 10 | 10 | 10 | 10 | 9 | 9 | 9 | 9 | 9 | 9 | 9 | 9 | 9 | 9 | 9 | 14 | 16 | 1 | 1 | 10 | 14 | 14 | 14 | 14 | 14 | 14 | 14 | 14 | 14 | 14 | 14 | 14 | 14 | 14 | 14 | 14 | 14 | 16 | 14 | 14 | 14 | 14 | 14 | 14 | | | |
| 12 TRULLI | 9 | 9 | 9 | 9 | 9 | 9 | 9 | 14 | 14 | 14 | 14 | 14 | 14 | 14 | 14 | 14 | 14 | 14 | 16 | 1 | 10 | 10 | 14 | 4 | 4 | 4 | 4 | 4 | 16 | 16 | 16 | 16 | 16 | 16 | 16 | 16 | 16 | 16 | 16 | 16 | 16 | 16 | 16 | 16 | 16 | 16 | 16 | 1 | | | |
| 9 HEIDFELD | 14 | 14 | 14 | 14 | 14 | 14 | 14 | 4 | 4 | 4 | 4 | 4 | 4 | 4 | 4 | 4 | 4 | 4 | 1 | 7 | 22 | 22 | 4 | 16 | 16 | 16 | 16 | 16 | 4 | 4 | 4 | 4 | 4 | 4 | 4 | 4 | 4 | 22 | 22 | 22 | 4 | 4 | 4 | 4 | 4 | 4 | 4 | 4 | | | |
| 4 KOVALAINEN | 4 | 4 | 4 | 4 | 4 | 4 | 4 | 16 | 16 | 16 | 16 | 16 | 16 | 16 | 16 | 16 | 16 | 16 | 7 | 3 | 14 | 14 | 22 | 23 | 23 | 23 | 8 | 8 | 8 | 8 | 8 | 8 | 8 | 8 | 8 | 8 | 8 | 8 | 22 | 4 | 4 | 4 | 22 | 3 | 3 | 3 | | | | |
| 14 COULTHARD | 16 | 16 | 16 | 16 | 16 | 16 | 16 | 8 | 8 | 8 | 8 | 8 | 8 | 8 | 8 | 8 | 7 | 7 | 3 | 22 | 4 | 16 | 8 | 8 | 3 | 3 | 3 | 3 | 3 | 3 | 3 | 3 | 3 | 3 | 22 | 22 | 3 | 3 | 4 | 3 | 22 | 22 | 22 | 2 | | | |
| 3 FISICHELLA | 8 | 8 | 8 | 8 | 8 | 8 | 8 | 7 | 7 | 7 | 7 | 7 | 7 | 7 | 7 | 3 | 3 | 22 | 14 | 23 | 23 | 3 | 3 | 22 | 22 | 22 | 22 | 22 | 22 | 22 | 22 | 22 | 22 | 3 | 3 | 8 | 8 | 8 | 8 | 8 | 8 | 8 | | | | | |
| 16 ROSBERG | 7 | 7 | 7 | 7 | 7 | 7 | 7 | 3 | 3 | 3 | 3 | 3 | 3 | 3 | 8 | 22 | 4 | 4 | 8 | 8 | 22 | 22 | 22 | 23 | 23 | 23 | 23 | 23 | 23 | 23 | 23 | 23 | 23 | 23 | 23 | 23 | 23 | 23 | 23 | 23 | 23 | 23 | 2 | | | | |
| 8 BARRICHELLO | 3 | 3 | 3 | 3 | 3 | 3 | 3 | 22 | 22 | 18 | 22 | 22 | 22 | 22 | 22 | 7 | 22 | 8 | 11 | 11 | 11 | 11 | 11 | 11 | 11 | 11 | 11 | 11 | 11 | 11 | 11 | 11 | 9 | 9 | 7 | 7 | 7 | 7 | | | | | | | | |
| 22 SATO | 22 | 22 | 22 | 22 | 22 | 22 | 22 | 18 | 18 | 18 | 18 | 18 | 18 | 18 | 8 | 8 | 8 | 20 | 20 | 11 | 9 | 20 | 20 | 20 | 9 | 9 | 9 | 9 | 9 | 9 | 9 | 9 | 11 | 9 | 11 | 20 | 7 | 20 | 20 | 20 | 2 | | | | | |
| 7 BUTTON | 19 | 19 | 19 | 19 | 19 | 19 | 19 | 18 | 23 | 23 | 23 | 23 | 23 | 20 | 20 | 21 | 21 | 20 | 20 | 9 | 20 | 20 | 20 | 20 | 20 | 20 | 20 | 20 | 20 | 20 | 20 | 7 | 20 | 20 | 21 | 21 | 2 | | | | | | | | |
| 23 DAVIDSON | 18 | 18 | 15 | 15 | 15 | 15 | 18 | 23 | 20 | 20 | 20 | 20 | 20 | 21 | 11 | 11 | 20 | 9 | 9 | 21 | 21 | 21 | 21 | 7 | 7 | 7 | 7 | 7 | 7 | 7 | 21 | 21 | | | | | | | | | | | | | | |
| 18 LIUZZI | 15 | 15 | 18 | 18 | 18 | 23 | 23 | 20 | 21 | 21 | 21 | 21 | 11 | 11 | 11 | 11 | 7 | 7 | 7 | 7 | 7 | 7 | 7 | 21 | 21 | 21 | 21 | 21 | 21 | 21 | 21 | 21 | | | | | | | | | | | | | | |
| 11 SCHUMACHER | 20 | 23 | 23 | 23 | 12 | 12 | 20 | 11 | 11 | 11 | 11 | 11 | 11 | 11 | 11 | 11 | 18 | | | | | | | | | | | | | | | | | | | | | | | | | | | | | |
| 17 WURZ | 23 | 20 | 12 | 12 | 12 | 20 | 21 | 6 | | | | | | | | | | | | | | | | | | | | | | | | | | | | | | | | | | | | | | |
| 15 WEBBER | 12 | 12 | 12 | 20 | 20 | 20 | 21 | 12 | 11 | | | | | | | | | | | | | | | | | | | | | | | | | | | | | | | | | | | | | |
| 20 SUTIL | 21 | 21 | 21 | 21 | 21 | 21 | 15 | 11 | | | | | | | | | | | | | | | | | | | | | | | | | | | | | | | | | | | | | | |
| 21 ALBERS | 11 | 11 | 11 | 11 | 11 | 11 | 11 | | | | | | | | | | | | | | | | | | | | | | | | | | | | | | | | | | | | | | | |
| 19 SPEED | 17 | | | | | | | | | | | | | | | | | | | | | | | | | | | | | | | | | | | | | | | | | | | | | | |

All results and data © FOM 2007

136

### PRACTICE 1 (FRIDAY)

Sunny (track 36–42ºC, air 30–32ºC)

| Pos. | Driver | Laps | Time |
|---|---|---|---|
| 1 | Lewis Hamilton | 22 | 1m 21.880s |
| 2 | Fernando Alonso | 21 | 1m 22.268s |
| 3 | Kimi Räikkönen | 19 | 1m 22.291s |
| 4 | Robert Kubica | 21 | 1m 22.446s |
| 5 | Felipe Massa | 15 | 1m 22.565s |
| 6 | Anthony Davidson | 21 | 1m 22.665s |
| 7 | Jarno Trulli | 28 | 1m 22.740s |
| 8 | Ralf Schumacher | 23 | 1m 22.843s |
| 9 | Nico Rosberg | 28 | 1m 23.048s |
| 10 | Jenson Button | 22 | 1m 23.114s |
| 11 | Alexander Wurz | 23 | 1m 23.131s |
| 12 | Nick Heidfeld | 26 | 1m 23.170s |
| 13 | Takuma Sato | 22 | 1m 23.316s |
| 14 | Heikki Kovalainen | 24 | 1m 23.322s |
| 15 | Giancarlo Fisichella | 21 | 1m 23.397s |
| 16 | David Coulthard | 21 | 1m 23.428s |
| 17 | Mark Webber | 21 | 1m 23.444s |
| 18 | Rubens Barrichello | 23 | 1m 23.479s |
| 19 | Adrian Sutil | 25 | 1m 23.954s |
| 20 | Vitantonio Liuzzi | 24 | 1m 24.104s |
| 21 | Scott Speed | 19 | 1m 24.179s |
| 22 | Christijan Albers | 25 | 1m 24.396s |

### PRACTICE 2 (FRIDAY)

Sunny (track 43ºC, air 32ºC)

| Pos. | Driver | Laps | Time |
|---|---|---|---|
| 1 | Fernando Alonso | 33 | 1m 21.397s |
| 2 | Giancarlo Fisichella | 39 | 1m 21.684s |
| 3 | Heikki Kovalainen | 38 | 1m 21.966s |
| 4 | Felipe Massa | 31 | 1m 22.048s |
| 5 | Lewis Hamilton | 37 | 1m 22.188s |
| 6 | Kimi Räikkönen | 33 | 1m 22.251s |
| 7 | Nico Rosberg | 29 | 1m 22.415s |
| 8 | Nick Heidfeld | 40 | 1m 22.543s |
| 9 | Mark Webber | 39 | 1m 22.589s |
| 10 | Scott Speed | 35 | 1m 22.617s |
| 11 | Robert Kubica | 43 | 1m 22.710s |
| 12 | David Coulthard | 30 | 1m 22.719s |
| 13 | Jenson Button | 39 | 1m 22.808s |
| 14 | Rubens Barrichello | 40 | 1m 22.926s |
| 15 | Alexander Wurz | 30 | 1m 22.950s |
| 16 | Vitantonio Liuzzi | 29 | 1m 23.143s |
| 17 | Ralf Schumacher | 28 | 1m 23.219s |
| 18 | Jarno Trulli | 42 | 1m 23.307s |
| 19 | Takuma Sato | 40 | 1m 23.493s |
| 20 | Anthony Davidson | 49 | 1m 23.497s |
| 21 | Adrian Sutil | 33 | 1m 23.609s |
| 22 | Christijan Albers | 30 | 1m 23.736s |

### QUALIFYING (SATURDAY)

Sunny (track 39–40ºC, air 28ºC)

| Pos. | Driver | First | Second | Third |
|---|---|---|---|---|
| 1 | Felipe Massa | 1m 21.375s | 1m 20.597s | 1m 21.421s |
| 2 | Fernando Alonso | 1m 21.609s | 1m 20.797s | 1m 21.451s |
| 3 | Kimi Räikkönen | 1m 21.802s | 1m 20.741s | 1m 21.723s |
| 4 | Lewis Hamilton | 1m 21.120s | 1m 20.713s | 1m 21.785s |
| 5 | Robert Kubica | 1m 21.941s | 1m 21.381s | 1m 22.253s |
| 6 | Jarno Trulli | 1m 22.501s | 1m 21.554s | 1m 22.324s |
| 7 | Nick Heidfeld | 1m 21.625s | 1m 21.113s | 1m 22.389s |
| 8 | Heikki Kovalainen | 1m 21.790s | 1m 21.623s | 1m 22.568s |
| 9 | David Coulthard | 1m 22.491s | 1m 21.488s | 1m 22.749s |
| 10 | Giancarlo Fisichella | 1m 22.064s | 1m 21.677s | 1m 22.881s |
| 11 | Nico Rosberg | 1m 21.943s | 1m 21.968s | |
| 12 | Rubens Barrichello | 1m 22.502s | 1m 22.097s | |
| 13 | Takuma Sato | 1m 22.090s | 1m 22.115s | |
| 14 | Jenson Button | 1m 22.503s | 1m 22.120s | |
| 15 | Anthony Davidson | 1m 22.295s | No time | |
| 16 | Vitantonio Liuzzi | 1m 22.508s | No time | |
| 17 | Ralf Schumacher | 1m 22.666s | | |
| 18 | Alexander Wurz | 1m 22.769s | | |
| 19 | Mark Webber | 1m 23.398s | | |
| 20 | Adrian Sutil | 1m 23.811s | | |
| 21 | Christijan Albers | 1m 23.990s | | |
| 22 | Scott Speed | No time | | |

### PRACTICE 3 (SATURDAY)

Sunny, breezy (track 32ºC, air 25–26ºC)

| Pos. | Driver | Laps | Time |
|---|---|---|---|
| 1 | Lewis Hamilton | 13 | 1m 21.233s |
| 2 | Fernando Alonso | 13 | 1m 21.312s |
| 3 | Robert Kubica | 17 | 1m 21.364s |
| 4 | Nick Heidfeld | 17 | 1m 21.464s |
| 5 | David Coulthard | 12 | 1m 21.556s |
| 6 | Felipe Massa | 14 | 1m 21.659s |
| 7 | Kimi Räikkönen | 15 | 1m 21.829s |
| 8 | Anthony Davidson | 15 | 1m 21.845s |
| 9 | Nico Rosberg | 16 | 1m 21.953s |
| 10 | Heikki Kovalainen | 18 | 1m 22.067s |
| 11 | Giancarlo Fisichella | 12 | 1m 22.140s |
| 12 | Jarno Trulli | 25 | 1m 22.174s |
| 13 | Rubens Barrichello | 15 | 1m 22.274s |
| 14 | Takuma Sato | 21 | 1m 22.295s |
| 15 | Scott Speed | 16 | 1m 22.314s |
| 16 | Ralf Schumacher | 21 | 1m 22.570s |
| 17 | Jenson Button | 17 | 1m 22.744s |
| 18 | Mark Webber | 13 | 1m 22.759s |
| 19 | Alexander Wurz | 16 | 1m 23.020s |
| 20 | Vitantonio Liuzzi | 8 | 1m 23.367s |
| 21 | Adrian Sutil | 22 | 1m 23.584s |
| 22 | Christijan Albers | 22 | 1m 23.817s |

### RACE TYRE STRATEGIES

**BRIDGESTONE**

In 2007, the tyre regulations stipulate that the two dry-tyre specifications must be visibly distinguishable from each other. At the Spanish Grand Prix, the medium compound Bridgestone Potenza tyre was marked with a white line in the second-from-inside groove.

| | Driver | Race stint 1 | Race stint 2 | Race stint 3 | Race stint 4 |
|---|---|---|---|---|---|
| 1 | Felipe Massa | Medium: laps 1–19 | Medium: 20–42 | Hard: 43–65 | |
| 2 | Lewis Hamilton | Medium: 1–22 | Medium: 23–47 | Hard: 48–65 | |
| 3 | Fernando Alonso | Medium: 1–19 | Hard: 20–48 | Medium: 49–65 | |
| 4 | Robert Kubica | Medium: 1–21 | Medium: 22–47 | Hard: 48–65 | |
| 5 | David Coulthard | Medium: 1–20 | Medium: 21–42 | Hard: 43–65 | |
| 6 | Nico Rosberg | Medium: 1–23 | Medium: 24–43 | Hard: 44–65 | |
| 7 | Heikki Kovalainen | Medium: 1–19 | Medium: 20–30 | Medium: 31–42 | Hard: 43–65 |
| 8 | Takuma Sato | Medium: 1–24 | Medium: 25–46 | Hard: 47–65 | |
| 9 | Giancarlo Fisichella | Medium: 1–19 | Medium: 20–42 | Hard: 43–65 | |
| 10 | Rubens Barrichello | Medium: 1–18 | Medium: 19–41 | Hard: 42–65 | |
| 11 | Anthony Davidson | Medium: 1–27 | Medium: 28–49 | Hard: 50–65 | |
| 12 | Jenson Button | Medium: 1–21 | Medium: 22 | Medium: 23–48 | Hard: 49–65 |
| 13 | Adrian Sutil | Medium: 1–23 | Medium: 24–46 | Hard: 47–65 | |
| 14 | Christijan Albers | Medium: 1–24 | Medium: 25–47 | Hard: 48–65 | |
| | Nick Heidfeld | Medium: 1–24 | Medium: 25–46 (DNF) | | |
| | Ralf Schumacher | Medium: 1 | Medium: 2–27 | Medium: 28–44 (DNF) | |
| | Vitantonio Liuzzi | Medium: 1–19 (DNF) | | | |
| | Scott Speed | Hard: 1–9 (DNF) | | | |
| | Kimi Räikkönen | Medium: 1–9 (DNF) | | | |
| | Jarno Trulli | Medium: 1–8 (DNF) | | | |
| | Mark Webber | Medium: 1–7 (DNF) | | | |
| | Alexander Wurz | Medium: 0 (DNF) | | | |

**9** COULTHARD Red Bull

**7** HEIDFELD BMW-Sauber

**5** KUBICA BMW-Sauber

**3** RÄIKKÖNEN Ferrari

**1** MASSA Ferrari

**10** FISICHELLA Renault

**8** KOVALAINEN Renault

**6** TRULLI Toyota
Started from pit lane

**4** HAMILTON McLaren

**2** ALONSO McLaren

**RACE DISTANCE:**
65 laps
187.933 miles/302.449 km

**RACE WEATHER:**
Hazy sunshine,
track 38–40ºC, air 28–29ºC

| 52 | 52 | 54 | 55 | 56 | 57 | 58 | 59 | 60 | 61 | 62 | 63 | 64 | 65 | |
|---|---|---|---|---|---|---|---|---|---|---|---|---|---|---|
| 5 | 5 | 5 | 5 | 5 | 5 | 5 | 5 | 5 | 5 | 5 | 5 | 5 | 5 | 1 |
| 2 | 2 | 2 | 2 | 2 | 2 | 2 | 2 | 2 | 2 | 2 | 2 | 2 | 2 | 2 |
| 1 | 1 | 1 | 1 | 1 | 1 | 1 | 1 | 1 | 1 | 1 | 1 | 1 | 1 | 3 |
| 10 | 10 | 10 | 10 | 10 | 10 | 10 | 10 | 10 | 10 | 10 | 10 | 10 | 10 | 4 |
| 14 | 14 | 14 | 14 | 14 | 14 | 14 | 14 | 14 | 14 | 14 | 14 | 14 | 14 | 5 |
| 16 | 16 | 16 | 16 | 16 | 16 | 16 | 16 | 16 | 16 | 16 | 16 | 16 | 16 | 6 |
| 4 | 4 | 4 | 4 | 4 | 4 | 4 | 4 | 4 | 4 | 4 | 4 | 4 | 4 | 7 |
| 3 | 3 | 3 | 3 | 3 | 3 | 3 | 22 | 22 | 22 | 22 | 22 | 22 | 22 | 8 |
| 22 | 22 | 22 | 22 | 22 | 22 | 22 | 3 | 3 | 3 | 3 | 3 | | | |
| 8 | 8 | 8 | 8 | 8 | 8 | 8 | 8 | 8 | 8 | 8 | 8 | | | |
| 23 | 23 | 23 | 23 | 23 | 23 | 23 | 23 | 23 | 23 | 23 | 23 | | | |
| 7 | 7 | 7 | 7 | 7 | 7 | 7 | 7 | 7 | 7 | 7 | 7 | | | |
| 20 | 20 | 20 | 20 | 20 | 20 | 20 | 20 | 20 | 20 | 20 | | | | |
| 21 | 21 | 21 | 21 | 21 | 21 | 21 | 21 | 21 | 21 | 21 | | | | |

20 Pit stop
20 One lap or more behind leader

### FOR THE RECORD

**FIRST POINT:** Super Aguri

**YOUNGEST DRIVER TO LEAD AN F1 WORLD CHAMPIONSHIP:**
Lewis Hamilton

### POINTS

**DRIVERS**

| | | |
|---|---|---|
| 1 | Lewis Hamilton | 30 |
| 2 | Fernando Alonso | 28 |
| 3 | Felipe Massa | 27 |
| 4 | Kimi Räikkönen | 22 |
| 5 | Nick Heidfeld | 15 |
| 6 | Giancarlo Fisichella | 8 |
| 7 | Robert Kubica | 8 |
| 8 | Nico Rosberg | 5 |
| 9 | Jarno Trulli | 4 |
| 10 | David Coulthard | 4 |
| 11 | Heikki Kovalainen | 3 |
| 12 | Ralf Schumacher | 1 |
| 13 | Takuma Sato | 1 |

**CONSTRUCTORS**

| | | |
|---|---|---|
| 1 | McLaren | 58 |
| 2 | Ferrari | 49 |
| 3 | BMW Sauber | 23 |
| 4 | Renault | 11 |
| 5 | Williams | 5 |
| 6 | Toyota | 5 |
| 7 | Red Bull | 4 |
| 8 | Super Aguri | 1 |

Photographs: Peter J Fox/www.crash.net

FIA F1 WORLD CHAMPIONSHIP/ROUND 5

# MONACO GP
## MONTE CARLO

## MONTE CARLO QUALIFYING

Lewis Hamilton received a spectacular reality check early in the weekend when his McLaren-Mercedes plunged off the road into the wall during the second 90-minute free practice session. After he spent most of the day jousting with his team-mate Fernando Alonso for fastest time, it seemed the 22-year-old British driver had mastered the twists and turns of this uniquely challenging circuit with the same aplomb as he deployed to seize the lead of the world championship over the first three races of the season.

Yet Monaco is no respecter of reputations and, braking hard for the tricky second-gear, 60-mph Ste Dévote right-hander, Hamilton shot off the road into the outer barrier, ripping off the left-hand front wheel and shuddering to a halt in a cloud of smoke and debris. Lewis calmly undid his harness, climbed from the cockpit and strolled away from the wreckage, rightly putting the unfortunate excursion down to experience.

'Today was the first time I ever drove a Formula 1 car around Monaco and it was awesome,' said Hamilton. 'I have obviously had experience around Monaco in an F3 and a GP2 car, but in an F1 car it is very different.

'I found out how unforgiving the track can be when I went off in the second session, causing some damage to the car. I'm obviously sorry because there will be a bit of work for the guys [the mechanics], but until then everything had been going smoothly and we had been able to set some competitive lap times.

'I made a small error under braking for Ste Dévote and the tyres hadn't worked up enough grip, so I made a tiny mistake, the back of the car slipped a little and that was it.'

Hamilton was at least in good company. By the end of the second session Ralf Schumacher's Toyota, Anthony Davidson's Super Aguri and the Spyker-Ferrari of Lewis's one-time F3 team-mate Adrian Sutil were scattered around the circuit in varying states of disarray.

During the first free practice session Hamilton simply lapped faster and faster at the head of the timing screens, fleetingly raising memories of the late Ayrton Senna's kerb-shaving genius through the same sunlit streets almost two decades ago.

Come qualifying, Hamilton was out to demonstrate that his accident had in no way dimmed his enthusiasm and commitment to giving his absolute maximum. Heavy rain injected a tantalising element of unpredictability during Saturday morning's practice session, but qualifying turned out to be dry, setting the stage for an epic battle between the two McLaren drivers.

For much of the contest Hamilton seemed to have the upper hand by a wafer-thin margin, but at the end of the day it was Fernando Alonso (1m 15.726s) who just squeezed into pole position by a fraction less than 0.2s. On the inside of the second row, Felipe Massa (1m 15.967s) saved the day for Ferrari with third place despite having one of his qualifying laps ruined when his team-mate Kimi Räikkönen glanced a barrier, breaking his car's rear suspension and skidding to a halt in front of Massa.

Both McLaren drivers lost vital fractions during their battle for pole, Alonso behind Nico Rosberg's Williams and Hamilton when he was momentarily balked by Mark Webber's Red Bull. The two McLaren drivers were incredibly well matched in this exacting and unforgiving environment, but if pit lane speculation was correct and Hamilton was running with more fuel than Alonso to run a longer opening stint, he looked as though he was in a very strong position indeed.

Yet you could say it was Alonso, who won here last year for Renault, who was out to prove a point. The twice-world champion arrived in Monaco trailing Hamilton in the title chase by two points and determined to retake the initiative. A series of impeccable laps put him fastest in Q2 and Q3 after a copybook display of precision high-speed motoring.

'We made good progress and the car feels good,' said Alonso. 'Monaco is a unique circuit with close barriers and traffic. It's very easy to get a lap ruined, but that's the challenge for everybody. I think we are in good shape.'

For much of the first session the BMW Sauber driver Robert Kubica – one of the contemporaries whom Hamilton genuinely rates – was right up in the leading bunch, showing just how much progress has been made by the team over the past few races. In particular, Kubica and team-mate Nick Heidfeld were benefiting from a new power steering system that gave them a more precise and sensitive feel on this track where there are seldom millimetres to spare.

In the end it was Giancarlo Fisichella (1m 16.285s) who grabbed the outside of row two in his Renault R27, while the third row of the grid was shared by Nico Rosberg's Williams (1m 16.439s) and Mark Webber's Red Bull-Renault (1m 16.784s). On the next couple of rows came the two BMW-Saubers and the two Hondas, completing the top ten.

Alex Wurz's Williams (1m 16.662s) lined up in 11th ahead of Vitantonio Liuzzi's Toro Rosso (1m 16.703s). David Coulthard (1m 16.319s) started 13th in his Red Bull-Renault, having been penalised two places for blocking Heikki Kovalainen.

Robert Kubica's BMW-Sauber framed by the unyielding barriers with no obvious escape route should things go wrong.

Photograph: Peter J Fox/www.crash.net

**Right: Lewis Hamilton takes his McLaren smoothly along the waterfront on his way to second place in his first Monaco Grand Prix.**
Photograph: Lukas Gorys

**Below: Kimi Räikkönen finds himself mired in the pack after his qualifying woes. He salvaged eighth place and single point at the end of the day.**
Photograph: Brousseau Photo

**Bottom left: No problem for the shopping.**

**Centre: An anxious-looking Honda trio of Jock Clear (senior race engineer for Rubens Barrichello), Gil de Ferran (sporting director) and Nick Fry (chief executive officer).**

**Bottom right: Nick Heidfeld rounds the hairpin in his Sauber-BMW on the way to sixth place. He started on super-soft Bridgestones, hoping to gain from a safety car intervention that never came.**
Photographs: Peter J Fox/www.crash.net

FERNANDO Alonso delivered a psychologically crucial victory through the unforgiving streets of Monte Carlo, winning the most prestigious race on the F1 calendar for the second successive year and stamping his mastery over his eager young team-mate Lewis Hamilton, who had arrived in the sun-drenched principality determined to score his first win in only the fifth race of his F1 career.

The two McLaren Mercedes drivers totally dominated the weekend from free practice through qualifying, when the twice-world champion pipped the young pretender to pole position. They then settled down to give the rest of the field a relentless high-speed driving lesson, keeping the crowd on the edges of their seats for the entire 78-lap distance.

Alonso led for the lion's share of the contest, Hamilton just popping ahead for short periods coming up to his refuelling stops because he ran slightly farther in each stint, confirming pre-race suspicions that he had qualified with more fuel on board. Yet whatever Hamilton contrived to throw at his team-mate, Alonso had an answer, picking his way through the slower traffic – an ever-present bugbear on this circuit – with a perfectly judged blend of decisiveness and caution. Alonso's success not only put him on the same points tally as Hamilton, but also removed any lingering worries that he had been slightly depressed by his young rival's pace over the past few races.

Hamilton freely admitted that he was very glad that his McLaren was a mechanically robust car because he'd brushed the guard rail on several occasions as he battled to keep the pressure on Alonso. After the second round of refuelling stops the McLaren personnel on the pit wall told both drivers to cool their pace and bring the cars home safely, although Lewis later made it clear that he didn't take too much notice of any instructions to slow down.

'It was really something special for me,' said Alonso. 'The team gave me such a nice car for 78 laps. I had a good race apart from losing several seconds behind Jarno Trulli's Toyota as I came up to the first refuelling stops.' In the end, a succession of very quick laps just before his second refuelling stop on lap 51 ensured that the world champion went into the closing phase of the race maintaining the upper hand.

From the start of the weekend McLaren had been confident that its MP4-22 would have the performance edge over the Ferrari F2007 in which Felipe Massa had won the previous two races. Their predictions turned out to be correct, although many observers were sceptical in the extreme to hear the McLaren team principal Ron Dennis say that the drivers had been paced from an early stage of the race. If that was the case, why did both Alonso and Hamilton lap faster than their qualifying times during their chase?

Massa, who finished a distant third ahead of Giancarlo Fisichella's improving Renault, was impressed by the speed of the McLarens. 'Definitely today they showed incredible pace,' he said. 'Even if I had pushed 150 percent it would have changed nothing.'

Massa had led the pursuit from the start, but even by lap four he was 1.6s down on Hamilton's second-placed McLaren. Giancarlo Fisichella's Renault was next up, leading the rest of the pack from Nick Heidfeld in the BMW-Sauber.

To be fair, Massa gave it his best shot. 'We tried to see if we could change the situation by using the extra-soft tyres in the second stint of the race, but it did not make much difference,' he confessed. 'The main problem today was the traffic; I lost a lot of time behind backmarkers, but I don't think that had any effect on the result. Today Ferrari was the inferior of the two teams, but I hope we have all we need to get back to winning again from the next race.'

Fisichella's fourth place was certainly a morale booster for the Renault squad, although admittedly it was a far cry from Alonso's victory for the team here 12 months ago. Fisichella started from fourth on the grid and gave an error-free, competitive drive to finish 20s ahead of his closest pursuer. Running a two-stop strategy and using hard tyres for his first stint before switching to the softer compound, he was able to build a comfortable gap in the opening stint, maintain it in the second and then conserve the machinery in the closing stages.

'The car had more grip thanks to a new wing,' said Fisichella, 'and the consistency was much better, too. I was happy with the race I drove and it was good to finish ahead of BMW for the first time.'

By contrast, Heikki Kovalainen endured a much more frustrating afternoon in his Renault R27. Starting from 15th on the grid after having his qualifying run spoiled on Saturday, he ran a one-stop strategy using hard tyres followed by the soft. He reckoned he was held up by David Coulthard's Red Bull through much of the first stint and, while he jumped the Scot at the first round of refuelling stops, the cars in front were too far away for him to manage anything better than 13th.

Fisichella finished ahead of the BMW-Saubers of Robert Kubica and Nick Heidfeld and the final championship points were scored by Alex Wurz in the Williams and Kimi Räikkönen in the Ferrari.

Both BMW Sauber drivers ran on one-stop refuelling strategies in anticipation of the safety car's being deployed at some stage or another, but that never happened. 'Looking back now, I think we could have finished better, but I'm glad we at least scored some championship points,' said Kubica. 'I had a small problem with the brakes soon after the start and had to pump them all the time, which did not make me feel confident. Then I was stuck in traffic and at the end had a sensor problem that meant I was without traction control for quite a long time.'

Heidfeld ended the afternoon feeling a little frustrated because he'd been running ahead of his team-mate initially, dropping behind only after he slowed to let the dominant McLarens lap him. It was just sufficient to allow Kubica to nip by during the stops.

Aside from Hamilton, the British contingent had a dismal time. Jenson Button's Honda trailed home 11th, three places

## DIARY

Bill France Jr, son of the legendary founder of NASCAR, dies at the age of 74.

Switzerland moves towards reintroducing circuit racing within its borders, motor sport having been banned there since the 1955 Le Mans disaster.

Dario Franchitti wins a rain-hit Indy 500 that reportedly attracted the second-lowest audience in the USA since the media research agency Nielsen began rating the event in 1993.

The GP2 series announces plans to expand to the Middle East and Asia in 2008 and is scheduled to run as a joint promotion with the newly launched Speedcar series.

## McLAREN GETS GREEN LIGHT

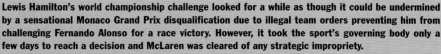

Lewis Hamilton's world championship challenge looked for a while as though it could be undermined by a sensational Monaco Grand Prix disqualification due to illegal team orders preventing him from challenging Fernando Alonso for a race victory. However, it took the sport's governing body only a few days to reach a decision and McLaren was cleared of any strategic impropriety.

Ron Dennis, the McLaren chairman, explained that Hamilton would have been favourite to win the Monaco Grand Prix for the team if the safety car had been deployed during the course of the race, as it had been four times over the past five years. He explained that Hamilton and Fernando Alonso, the eventual winner, started the 78-lap race on different fuel loads in a bid to cover every strategic possibility in this notoriously unpredictable event.

Dennis also defended his decisions, saying they were not tantamount to team orders, which are banned in F1. 'Team strategy is what you use to win a grand prix,' he said. 'Team orders are what you use to manipulate a grand prix. And we do not and have not manipulated grands prix unless there were exceptional circumstances, which occurred, for example, in Australia [in 1998], when someone tapped into our radio and instructed Mika Häkkinen to enter the pits. It was only fair then to ask David Coulthard to allow Häkkinen back into the lead.

'If the safety car is deployed, a one-stop refuelling strategy will almost certainly beat a two-stop strategy,' said Dennis. 'If there is no safety car, then a two-stop strategy is the best. Because of the difficulties involved in passing, Monaco is the only circuit on which the issue of the safety car determines who wins. McLaren has now won an all-time record 14 out of the 65 races at Monaco. And why? Because McLaren understands better than anybody else what's involved in winning there.'

Alonso ran the entire 78-lap race on a two-stop strategy, with Hamilton originally on a one-stop strategy, which meant that he was carrying five laps' more fuel than Alonso in the opening stages. Once he got to his first refuelling stop and was comfortably holding second place, the team switched him to a two-stop strategy because that was the fastest option for the balance of the race.

ahead of David Coulthard's Red Bull, and Anthony Davidson was a distant 18th for the Super Aguri squad, having picked up a penalty for ignoring blue overtaking flags.

Behind Räikkönen's eighth-placed Ferrari and the Toro Rosso of Scott Speed, Rubens Barrichello brought his Honda RA107 home ahead of team-mate Jenson Button. Rubens had made the most of the first corner mêlée to gain two places, easing his way into seventh place from ninth on the grid. On a heavier fuel load, Button lost out at Ste Dévote on the opening lap and had to be content to chase his colleague across the finishing line just a second adrift.

'It was a difficult race today,' said Button. 'I was stuck in traffic in all three stints and never got a clear run, so I couldn't take the best advantage of our strategy. But we have to take some encouragement from our signs of improvement. We have to keep pushing and moving in the right direction.'

For the Red Bull team, for which David Coulthard had finished third here last year, this was a highly disappointing race. Mark Webber was slowed by an early misfire that ultimately caused the gearbox to fail. Coulthard collided with Tonio Liuzzi on the first lap, badly damaging a front-wing end plate, which left him grappling poor handling all the way to a distant 14th.

*Alan Henry*

**Above:** The sight of highly strung F1 cars racing through public streets offers a unique and compelling experience for fans at Monaco.
Photograph: Bernard Asset

**Left:** On this occasion the Ferrari F2007s were decisively eclipsed by the McLarens. Here Felipe Massa leans into the Massenet left-hander just before Casino Square on his way to a distant third place.
Photograph: Jad Sherif/WRi2

**Far left:** Thumbs up and a spontaneous grin from Lewis Hamilton after he finishes a close-fought second.

**Top left:** Scott Speed just missed out on a point for Toro Rosso.
Photographs: Peter J Fox/www.crash.net

# FIA F1 WORLD CHAMPIONSHIP • ROUND 5
## GRAND PRIX DE
# MONACO
### MONTE-CARLO 24–27 MAY 2007

Photograph: Peter J Fox/www.crash.net

**CIRCUIT DE MONACO,**
Circuit: 2.075 miles /
3.340 km

Mirabeau Haute 50/80
Mirabeau Bas 55/88
Casino 79/127 Square
Loews 30/48
Massenet 60/97
Ste Devote 58/93
165/265
Portier 54/87
Tabac 96/154
Nouvelle Chicane 40/64
Tunnel 150/241
Louis Chiron 123/198
Piscine 120/193
116/187 mph/kmh
Anthony Noghes 55/88
Gear
La Rascasse 35/56

## RACE RESULTS

All results and data © FOM 2007

| Pos. | Driver | Nat. | No. | Entrant | Car/Engine | Tyres | Laps | Time/Retirement | Speed (mph/km/h) | Gap to leader | Fastest race lap | |
|---|---|---|---|---|---|---|---|---|---|---|---|---|
| 1 | Fernando Alonso | E | 1 | Vodafone McLaren Mercedes | McLaren MP4-22-Mercedes FO 108T V8 | B | 78 | 1h 40m 29.329s | 96.655/155.551 | | 1m 15.284s | 44 |
| 2 | Lewis Hamilton | GB | 2 | Vodafone McLaren Mercedes | McLaren MP4-22-Mercedes FO 108T V8 | B | 78 | 1h 40m 33.424s | 96.590/155.446 | + 4.095s | 1m 15.372s | 28 |
| 3 | Felipe Massa | BR | 5 | Scuderia Ferrari Marlboro | Ferrari F2007-056 V8 | B | 78 | 1h 41m 38.443s | 95.559/153.788 | + 1m 9.114s | 1m 16.183s | 47 |
| 4 | Giancarlo Fisichella | I | 3 | ING Renault F1 Team | Renault R27-RS27 V8 | B | 77 | | | + 1 lap | 1m 16.254s | 54 |
| 5 | Robert Kubica | POL | 10 | BMW Sauber F1 Team | BMW Sauber F1.07-BMW P86/7 V8 | B | 77 | | | + 1 lap | 1m 16.006s | 39 |
| 6 | Nick Heidfeld | D | 9 | BMW Sauber F1 Team | BMW Sauber F1.07-BMW P86/7 V8 | B | 77 | | | + 1 lap | 1m 17.041s | 30 |
| 7 | Alexander Wurz | A | 17 | AT&T Williams | Williams FW29-Toyota RVX-07 V8 | B | 77 | | | + 1 lap | 1m 16.658s | 40 |
| 8 | Kimi Räikkönen | FIN | 6 | Scuderia Ferrari Marlboro | Ferrari F2007-056 V8 | B | 77 | | | + 1 lap | 1m 16.592s | 62 |
| 9 | Scott Speed | USA | 19 | Scuderia Toro Rosso | Toro Rosso STR02-Ferrari 056H V8 | B | 77 | | | + 1 lap | 1m 16.867s | 73 |
| 10 | Rubens Barrichello | BR | 8 | Honda Racing F1 Team | Honda RA107-RA807E V8 | B | 77 | | | + 1 lap | 1m 17.080s | 69 |
| 11 | Jenson Button | GB | 7 | Honda Racing F1 Team | Honda RA107-RA807E V8 | B | 77 | | | + 1 lap | 1m 16.802s | 40 |
| 12 | Nico Rosberg | D | 16 | AT&T Williams | Williams FW29-Toyota RVX-07 V8 | B | 77 | | | + 1 lap | 1m 16.991s | 70 |
| 13 | Heikki Kovalainen | FIN | 4 | ING Renault F1 Team | Renault R27-RS27 V8 | B | 76 | Engine | | + 2 laps | 1m 17.100s | 72 |
| 14 | David Coulthard | GB | 14 | Red Bull Racing | Red Bull RB3-Renault RS27 V8 | B | 76 | | | + 2 laps | 1m 16.786s | 75 |
| 15 | Jarno Trulli | I | 12 | Panasonic Toyota Racing | Toyota TF107-RVX-07 V8 | B | 76 | | | + 2 laps | 1m 17.495s | 53 |
| 16 | Ralf Schumacher | D | 11 | Panasonic Toyota Racing | Toyota TF107-RVX-07 V8 | B | 76 | | | + 2 laps | 1m 17.231s | 47 |
| 17 | Takuma Sato | J | 22 | Super Aguri F1 Team | Super Aguri SA07-Honda RA807E V8 | B | 76 | | | + 2 laps | 1m 17.183s | 74 |
| 18 | Anthony Davidson | GB | 23 | Super Aguri F1 Team | Super Aguri SA07-Honda RA807E V8 | B | 76 | | | + 2 laps | 1m 17.223s | 63 |
| 19 | Christijan Albers | NL | 21 | Etihad Aldar Spyker F1 Team | Spyker F8-VII-Ferrari 056H V8 | B | 70 | Driveshaft | | + 8 laps | 1m 17.689s | 70 |
| | Adrian Sutil | D | 20 | Etihad Aldar Spyker F1 Team | Spyker F8-VII-Ferrari 056H V8 | B | 53 | Accident | | | 1m 17.678s | 34 |
| | Mark Webber | AUS | 15 | Red Bull Racing | Red Bull RB3-Renault RS27 V8 | B | 17 | Misfire/gearbox | | | 1m 18.998s | 17 |
| | Vitantonio Liuzzi | I | 18 | Scuderia Toro Rosso | Toro Rosso STR02-Ferrari 056H V8 | B | 1 | Accident | | | No time | – |

**Fastest race lap:** Fernando Alonso on lap 44, 1m 15.284s, 99.242 mph/159.715 km/h.

**Lap record:** Michael Schumacher (Ferrari F2004 V10), 1m 14.439s, 100.369 mph/161.528 km/h (2004).

| 22 ALBERS Spyker | 20 R. SCHUMACHER Toyota | 18 SPEED Toro Rosso | 16 RÄIKKÖNEN Ferrari | 14 TRULLI Toyota | 12 LIUZZI Toro Rosso |
|---|---|---|---|---|---|
| 21 SATO Super Aguri | 19 SUTIL Spyker | 17 DAVIDSON Super Aguri | 15 KOVALAINEN Renault | 13 COULTHARD Red Bull Penalty - demoted 2 places | 11 WURZ Williams |

| Grid order | 1 2 3 4 5 6 7 8 9 10 11 12 13 14 15 16 17 18 19 20 21 22 23 24 25 26 27 28 29 30 31 32 33 34 35 36 37 38 39 40 41 42 43 44 45 46 47 48 49 50 51 52 53 54 55 56 57 58 59 60 |
|---|---|
| 1 ALONSO | 1 1 1 1 1 1 1 1 1 1 1 1 1 1 1 1 1 1 1 1 1 1 1 1 1 2 2 1 1 1 1 1 1 1 1 1 1 1 1 1 1 1 1 1 1 1 1 1 1 1 2 2 1 1 1 1 1 1 1 1 |
| 2 HAMILTON | 2 2 2 2 2 2 2 2 2 2 2 2 2 2 2 2 2 2 2 2 2 2 2 2 2 1 1 2 2 2 2 2 2 2 2 2 2 2 2 2 2 2 2 2 2 2 2 2 2 2 1 1 2 2 2 2 2 2 2 2 |
| 5 MASSA | 5 5 5 5 5 5 5 5 5 5 5 5 5 5 5 5 5 5 5 5 5 5 5 5 5 5 5 5 5 5 5 5 5 5 5 5 5 5 5 5 5 5 5 5 5 5 5 5 5 5 5 5 5 5 5 5 5 5 5 5 |
| 3 FISICHELLA | 3 3 3 3 3 3 3 3 3 3 3 3 3 3 3 3 3 3 3 3 3 3 3 9 9 9 9 9 9 9 3 3 3 3 3 3 3 3 3 3 3 3 3 3 3 3 3 3 3 3 3 3 3 3 3 3 3 3 3 3 |
| 16 ROSBERG | 9 9 9 9 9 9 9 9 9 9 9 9 9 9 9 9 9 9 9 9 9 9 3 3 3 3 3 3 3 8 8 8 8 8 10 10 10 10 10 10 10 10 10 10 10 10 10 10 10 10 10 10 10 10 10 10 10 10 10 10 |
| 15 WEBBER | 16 16 16 16 16 16 16 16 16 16 16 16 16 16 16 16 16 16 16 8 8 8 8 8 8 8 8 8 10 10 10 10 17 17 17 17 17 17 9 9 9 9 9 9 9 9 9 9 9 9 9 9 9 9 9 9 9 9 9 9 |
| 9 HEIDFELD | 8 8 8 8 8 8 8 8 8 8 8 8 8 8 8 8 8 8 8 10 10 10 10 10 10 10 10 10 17 17 17 17 7 7 7 9 9 6 6 6 17 17 17 17 17 17 17 17 17 17 17 17 17 17 17 17 17 17 17 7 |
| 10 KUBICA | 15 15 15 15 15 15 15 15 15 15 15 15 15 15 15 10 10 10 10 17 17 17 17 17 17 17 17 9 7 7 7 9 9 9 9 6 6 6 17 17 8 8 8 8 8 8 8 8 8 8 8 8 8 8 8 8 8 8 8 |
| 8 BARRICHELLO | 10 10 10 10 10 10 10 10 10 10 10 10 10 10 10 10 10 17 17 17 17 7 7 7 7 7 7 7 9 9 9 9 6 6 6 7 19 19 19 8 8 7 7 7 7 7 7 7 7 7 7 7 6 |
| 7 BUTTON | 17 17 17 17 17 17 17 17 17 17 17 17 17 17 17 17 7 7 7 7 6 6 6 6 6 6 6 6 6 6 6 8 19 19 19 8 8 8 7 16 16 16 16 16 16 16 16 16 6 19 |
| 17 WURZ | 7 7 7 7 7 7 7 7 7 7 7 7 7 7 7 6 6 6 19 19 19 19 19 19 19 19 19 19 19 19 8 8 8 8 7 7 7 16 16 6 6 6 6 6 6 6 6 6 19 9 |
| 18 LIUZZI | 6 6 6 6 6 6 6 6 6 6 6 6 6 6 6 19 19 19 16 16 16 16 16 16 16 16 16 16 16 16 16 16 16 16 19 19 19 19 19 19 19 19 19 19 19 19 19 19 16 16 |
| 14 COULTHARD | 18 19 19 19 19 19 19 19 19 19 19 19 19 19 4 4 4 4 4 14 14 14 14 14 14 14 14 14 14 14 14 4 4 4 4 14 14 4 4 4 4 4 4 4 4 4 4 4 4 4 |
| 12 TRULLI | 19 14 14 14 14 14 14 14 14 14 14 14 14 14 14 4 4 4 14 4 4 4 4 4 4 4 4 4 4 4 4 14 14 14 14 4 4 14 14 14 14 14 14 14 14 14 14 14 14 14 |
| 4 KOVALAINEN | 14 4 4 4 4 4 4 4 4 4 4 4 4 4 12 12 22 22 22 12 12 12 12 12 12 12 12 12 12 12 12 12 12 12 12 11 11 22 22 22 22 22 22 22 12 12 12 |
| 6 RÄIKKÖNEN | 4 22 22 22 22 22 12 12 12 12 12 12 12 12 22 12 12 12 23 23 23 23 23 23 20 20 20 20 20 20 11 11 11 11 22 12 12 12 12 12 12 11 11 11 |
| 23 DAVIDSON | 22 12 12 12 12 12 12 22 22 22 22 22 22 22 23 23 23 23 23 20 20 20 20 11 11 11 11 11 11 11 22 22 22 12 12 12 11 11 11 11 11 11 22 22 22 |
| 19 SPEED | 12 23 23 23 23 23 23 23 20 20 20 20 20 20 22 11 11 11 11 11 23 23 23 22 22 22 12 20 20 20 20 20 20 23 23 23 23 23 23 23 |
| 20 SUTIL | 23 20 20 20 20 20 20 20 23 23 23 23 23 23 20 20 20 20 11 11 11 11 11 22 22 22 23 3 23 23 23 23 23 21 21 |
| 11 SCHUMACHER | 20 21 21 21 21 21 21 21 21 21 21 21 21 21 21 11 11 11 11 22 22 22 22 23 23 23 21 21 21 21 21 21 21 21 |
| 22 SATO | 21 11 11 11 11 11 11 11 11 11 11 11 11 11 11 11 11 11 |
| 21 ALBERS | 11 |

146

## PRACTICE 1 (THURSDAY)

Sunny (track 33–41ºC, air 26–29ºC)

| Pos. | Driver | Laps | Time |
|------|--------|------|------|
| 1 | Fernando Alonso | 33 | 1m 16.973s |
| 2 | Lewis Hamilton | 14 | 1m 17.601s |
| 3 | Nick Heidfeld | 31 | 1m 17.616s |
| 4 | Giancarlo Fisichella | 27 | 1m 17.758s |
| 5 | Kimi Räikkönen | 28 | 1m 17.918s |
| 6 | Mark Webber | 19 | 1m 17.956s |
| 7 | Nico Rosberg | 27 | 1m 18.074s |
| 8 | Felipe Massa | 29 | 1m 18.189s |
| 9 | Robert Kubica | 28 | 1m 18.675s |
| 10 | Rubens Barrichello | 22 | 1m 18.676s |
| 11 | Alexander Wurz | 29 | 1m 18.869s |
| 12 | Scott Speed | 27 | 1m 18.967s |
| 13 | David Coulthard | 16 | 1m 19.095s |
| 14 | Takuma Sato | 27 | 1m 19.203s |
| 15 | Vitantonio Liuzzi | 24 | 1m 19.285s |
| 16 | Heikki Kovalainen | 27 | 1m 19.321s |
| 17 | Jenson Button | 27 | 1m 19.332s |
| 18 | Anthony Davidson | 22 | 1m 19.337s |
| 19 | Jarno Trulli | 22 | 1m 19.496s |
| 20 | Ralf Schumacher | 25 | 1m 19.799s |
| 21 | Adrian Sutil | 19 | 1m 21.634s |
| 22 | Christijan Albers | 5 | 1m 23.235s |

## PRACTICE 2 (THURSDAY)

Sunny (track 41–42ºC, air 27–28ºC)

| Pos. | Driver | Laps | Time |
|------|--------|------|------|
| 1 | Fernando Alonso | 40 | 1m 15.940s |
| 2 | Kimi Räikkönen | 43 | 1m 16.215s |
| 3 | Lewis Hamilton | 19 | 1m 16.296s |
| 4 | Jarno Trulli | 39 | 1m 16.354s |
| 5 | Giancarlo Fisichella | 41 | 1m 16.753s |
| 6 | Felipe Massa | 37 | 1m 16.784s |
| 7 | Robert Kubica | 48 | 1m 16.848s |
| 8 | Nico Rosberg | 34 | 1m 16.852s |
| 9 | Mark Webber | 16 | 1m 17.292s |
| 10 | David Coulthard | 16 | 1m 17.414s |
| 11 | Rubens Barrichello | 40 | 1m 17.449s |
| 12 | Jenson Button | 45 | 1m 17.457s |
| 13 | Takuma Sato | 47 | 1m 17.459s |
| 14 | Nick Heidfeld | 43 | 1m 17.486s |
| 15 | Alexander Wurz | 34 | 1m 17.516s |
| 16 | Vitantonio Liuzzi | 42 | 1m 17.898s |
| 17 | Heikki Kovalainen | 41 | 1m 18.086s |
| 18 | Scott Speed | 40 | 1m 18.233s |
| 19 | Anthony Davidson | 25 | 1m 18.328s |
| 20 | Ralf Schumacher | 38 | 1m 18.662s |
| 21 | Christijan Albers | 35 | 1m 18.820s |
| 22 | Adrian Sutil | 29 | 1m 19.358s |

## QUALIFYING (SATURDAY)

Overcast, light rain (track 28–30ºC, air 25–26ºC)

| Pos. | Driver | First | Second | Third |
|------|--------|-------|--------|-------|
| 1 | Fernando Alonso | 1m 16.059s | 1m 15.431s | 1m 15.726s |
| 2 | Lewis Hamilton | 1m 15.685s | 1m 15.479s | 1m 15.905s |
| 3 | Felipe Massa | 1m 16.786s | 1m 16.034s | 1m 15.967s |
| 4 | Giancarlo Fisichella | 1m 17.596s | 1m 16.054s | 1m 16.285s |
| 5 | Nico Rosberg | 1m 16.870s | 1m 16.100s | 1m 16.439s |
| 6 | Mark Webber | 1m 17.816s | 1m 16.420s | 1m 16.784s |
| 7 | Nick Heidfeld | 1m 17.385s | 1m 15.733s | 1m 16.832s |
| 8 | Robert Kubica | 1m 17.584s | 1m 15.576s | 1m 16.955s |
| 9 | Rubens Barrichello | 1m 17.244s | 1m 16.454s | 1m 17.498s |
| 10 | Jenson Button | 1m 17.297s | 1m 16.457s | 1m 17.939s |
| 11 | David Coulthard | 1m 17.204s | 1m 16.319s* | |
| 12 | Alexander Wurz | 1m 17.874s | 1m 16.662s | |
| 13 | Vitantonio Liuzzi | 1m 16.720s | 1m 16.703s | |
| 14 | Jarno Trulli | 1m 17.686s | 1m 16.988s | |
| 15 | Heikki Kovalainen | 1m 17.836s | 1m 17.125s | |
| 16 | Kimi Räikkönen | 1m 16.251s | No time | |
| 17 | Anthony Davidson | 1m 18.250s | | |
| 18 | Scott Speed | 1m 18.390s | | |
| 19 | Adrian Sutil | 1m 18.418s | | |
| 20 | Ralf Schumacher | 1m 18.539s | | |
| 21 | Takuma Sato | 1m 18.554s | | |
| 22 | Christijan Albers | No time | | |

* Received a penalty for impeding Kovalainen

## PRACTICE 3 (SATURDAY)

Rain, overcast (track 25–27ºC, air 23–24ºC)

| Pos. | Driver | Laps | Time |
|------|--------|------|------|
| 1 | Adrian Sutil | 12 | 1m 36.612s |
| 2 | Kimi Räikkönen | 13 | 1m 36.739s |
| 3 | Lewis Hamilton | 15 | 1m 36.767s |
| 4 | Giancarlo Fisichella | 16 | 1m 36.784s |
| 5 | Scott Speed | 15 | 1m 36.954s |
| 6 | Fernando Alonso | 16 | 1m 37.020s |
| 7 | Heikki Kovalainen | 15 | 1m 37.214s |
| 8 | Nico Rosberg | 15 | 1m 37.388s |
| 9 | Jenson Button | 12 | 1m 37.442s |
| 10 | Rubens Barrichello | 14 | 1m 37.463s |
| 11 | Mark Webber | 13 | 1m 37.732s |
| 12 | Felipe Massa | 12 | 1m 37.997s |
| 13 | Takuma Sato | 14 | 1m 38.121s |
| 14 | Anthony Davidson | 17 | 1m 38.180s |
| 15 | David Coulthard | 6 | 1m 38.302s |
| 16 | Robert Kubica | 13 | 1m 38.463s |
| 17 | Alexander Wurz | 14 | 1m 38.876s |
| 18 | Nick Heidfeld | 18 | 1m 38.899s |
| 19 | Christijan Albers | 14 | 1m 38.935s |
| 20 | Ralf Schumacher | 17 | 1m 40.677s |
| 21 | Vitantonio Liuzzi | 8 | 1m 41.108s |
| 22 | Jarno Trulli | 22 | 1m 43.417s |

## RACE TYRE STRATEGIES

**BRIDGESTONE**

In 2007, the tyre regulations stipulate that the two dry-tyre specifications must be visibly distinguishable from each other. At the Monaco Grand Prix, the super-soft compound Bridgestone Potenza tyre was marked with a white line in the second-from-inside groove.

| | Driver | Race stint 1 | Race stint 2 | Race stint 3 |
|---|--------|--------------|--------------|--------------|
| 1 | Fernando Alonso | Soft: laps 1–26 | Soft: 27–51 | Super-soft: 52–78 |
| 2 | Lewis Hamilton | Soft: 1–29 | Soft: 30–53 | Super-soft: 54–78 |
| 3 | Felipe Massa | Soft: 1–26 | Super-soft: 27–55 | Super-soft: 56–78 |
| 4 | Giancarlo Fisichella | Soft: 1–23 | Soft: 24–55 | Super-soft: 56–77 |
| 5 | Robert Kubica | Soft: 1–45 | Super-soft: 46–77 | |
| 6 | Nick Heidfeld | Super-soft: 1–32 | Soft: 33–77 | |
| 7 | Alexander Wurz | Soft: 1–44 | Super-soft: 45–77 | |
| 8 | Kimi Räikkönen | Soft: 1–47 | Super-soft: 48–77 | |
| 9 | Scott Speed | Soft: 1–45 | Super-soft: 46–77 | |
| 10 | Rubens Barrichello | Soft: 1–37 | Soft: 38–60 | Super-soft: 61–77 |
| 11 | Jenson Button | Soft: 1–41 | Soft: 42–61 | Super-soft: 62–77 |
| 12 | Nico Rosberg | Soft: 1–23 | Soft: 24–59 | Super-soft: 60–77 |
| 13 | Heikki Kovalainen | Soft: 1–55 | Super-soft: 56–76 | |
| 14 | David Coulthard | Soft: 1–42 | Super-soft: 43–76 | |
| 15 | Jarno Trulli | Soft: 1–47 | Super-soft: 48–76 | |
| 16 | Ralf Schumacher | Soft: 1–49 | Soft: 50–76 | |
| 17 | Takuma Sato | Super-soft: 1–24 | Soft: 25–57 | Super-soft: 58–76 |
| 18 | Anthony Davidson | Soft: 1–36 | Super-soft: 37–76 | |
| 19 | Christijan Albers | Super-soft: 1–24 | Soft: 25–51 | Super-soft: 52–70 (DNF) |
| | Adrian Sutil | Soft: 1–44 | Super-soft: 45–53 (DNF) | |
| | Mark Webber | Soft: 1–15 (DNF) | | |
| | Vitantonio Liuzzi | Soft: 1 (DNF) | | |

 **10** BUTTON Honda
 **8** KUBICA BMW-Sauber
 **6** WEBBER Red Bull
 **4** FISICHELLA Renault
 **2** HAMILTON McLaren

 **9** BARRICHELLO Honda
 **7** HEIDFELD BMW-Sauber
 **5** ROSBERG Williams
 **3** MASSA Ferrari
 **1** ALONSO McLaren

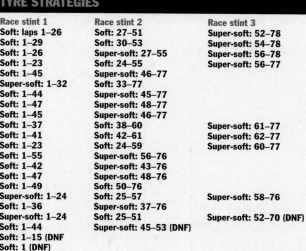

RACE DISTANCE:
78 laps
161.880 miles/260.520 km

RACE WEATHER:
Sunny
track 31-41º C, air 23-26º C

| | 62 | 63 | 64 | 65 | 66 | 67 | 68 | 69 | 70 | 71 | 72 | 73 | 74 | 75 | 76 | 77 | 78 | |
|--|----|----|----|----|----|----|----|----|----|----|----|----|----|----|----|----|----|--|
| 1 | 1 | 1 | 1 | 1 | 1 | 1 | 1 | 1 | 1 | 1 | 1 | 1 | 1 | 1 | 1 | 1 | 1 | |
| 2 | 2 | 2 | 2 | 2 | 2 | 2 | 2 | 2 | 2 | 2 | 2 | 2 | 2 | 2 | 2 | 2 | 2 | 2 |
| 5 | 5 | 5 | 5 | 5 | 5 | 5 | 5 | 5 | 5 | 5 | 5 | 5 | 5 | 5 | 5 | 5 | 5 | 3 |
| 3 | 3 | 3 | 3 | 3 | 3 | 3 | 3 | 3 | 3 | 3 | 3 | 3 | 3 | 3 | 3 | 3 | 3 | 4 |
| 10 | 10 | 10 | 10 | 10 | 10 | 10 | 10 | 10 | 10 | 10 | 10 | 10 | 10 | 10 | 10 | 10 | 10 | 5 |
| 9 | 9 | 9 | 9 | 9 | 9 | 9 | 9 | 9 | 9 | 9 | 9 | 9 | 9 | 9 | 9 | 9 | 9 | 6 |
| 7 | 17 | 17 | 17 | 17 | 17 | 17 | 17 | 17 | 17 | 17 | 17 | 17 | 17 | 17 | 17 | 17 | 17 | 7 |
| 6 | 6 | 6 | 6 | 6 | 6 | 6 | 6 | 6 | 6 | 6 | 6 | 6 | 6 | 6 | 6 | 6 | 6 | 8 |
| 9 | 19 | 19 | 19 | 19 | 19 | 19 | 19 | 19 | 19 | 19 | 19 | 19 | 19 | 19 | 19 | 19 | 19 | |
| 7 | 8 | 8 | 8 | 8 | 8 | 8 | 8 | 8 | 8 | 8 | 8 | 8 | 8 | 8 | 8 | 8 | 8 | |
| 8 | 7 | 7 | 7 | 7 | 7 | 7 | 7 | 7 | 7 | 7 | 7 | 7 | 7 | 7 | 7 | 7 | 7 | |
| 6 | 16 | 16 | 16 | 16 | 16 | 16 | 16 | 16 | 16 | 16 | 16 | 16 | 16 | 16 | 16 | 16 | 16 | |
| 4 | 4 | 4 | 4 | 4 | 4 | 4 | 4 | 4 | 4 | 4 | 4 | 4 | 4 | 4 | | | | |
| 4 | 14 | 14 | 14 | 14 | 14 | 14 | 14 | 14 | 14 | 14 | 14 | 14 | 14 | 14 | | | | |
| 2 | 12 | 12 | 12 | 12 | 12 | 12 | 12 | 12 | 12 | 12 | 12 | 12 | 12 | 12 | | | | |
| 1 | 11 | 11 | 11 | 11 | 11 | 11 | 11 | 11 | 11 | 11 | 11 | 11 | 11 | 11 | | | | |
| 2 | 22 | 22 | 22 | 22 | 22 | 22 | 22 | 22 | 22 | 22 | 22 | 22 | | | | | | |
| 3 | 23 | 23 | 23 | 23 | 23 | 23 | 23 | 23 | 23 | 23 | 23 | 23 | 23 | | | | | |
| 1 | 21 | 21 | 21 | 21 | 21 | 21 | 21 | 21 | | | | | | | | | | |

**0** Pit stop   **20** One lap or more behind leader
**23** Drive-through penalty

## FOR THE RECORD

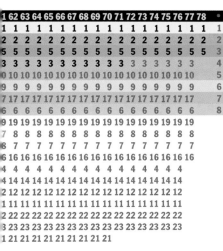

150th GRAND PRIX WIN: McLaren

## POINTS

**DRIVERS**

| | | |
|---|---|---|
| 1 | Fernando Alonso | 38 |
| 2 | Lewis Hamilton | 38 |
| 3 | Felipe Massa | 33 |
| 4 | Kimi Räikkönen | 23 |
| 5 | Nick Heidfeld | 18 |
| 6 | Giancarlo Fisichella | 13 |
| 7 | Robert Kubica | 12 |
| 8 | Nico Rosberg | 5 |
| 9 | Jarno Trulli | 4 |
| 10 | David Coulthard | 4 |
| 11 | Heikki Kovalainen | 3 |
| 12 | Alexander Wurz | 2 |
| 13 | Ralf Schumacher | 1 |
| 14 | Takuma Sato | 1 |

**CONSTRUCTORS**

| | | |
|---|---|---|
| 1 | McLaren | 76 |
| 2 | Ferrari | 56 |
| 3 | BMW Sauber | 30 |
| 4 | Renault | 16 |
| 5 | Williams | 7 |
| 6 | Toyota | 5 |
| 7 | Red Bull | 4 |
| 8 | Super Aguri | 1 |

**150**

Photograph: Peter J Fox/www.crash.net

Photograph: Lukas Gorys

# CANADIAN GP

## MONTREAL

A seminal F1 moment that will go down in the history book. Visor slightly open and forefinger raised in celebration, Lewis Hamilton cruises on his slowing-down lap at the Circuit Gilles Villeneuve after scoring his maiden victory in the Canadian Grand Prix.
Photograph: Paul-Henri Cahier

## MONTREAL QUALIFYING

**Above:** Heikki Kovalainen's Renault is leaking oil, as the haze following the R27 on the pit clearly indicates.

**Top right:** Pole position for Lewis Hamilton.

**Centre right:** Girls, girls, girls.

**Opposite:** Nick Heidfeld took a strong second place behind Hamilton.
Photographs: Peter J Fox/www.crash.net

**Below:** Ralf Schumacher, sanguine over his problems with his Toyota.
Photograph: Jean-François Galeron/WRi2

With the first pole position of his F1 career, Lewis Hamilton was perfectly poised to score his maiden grand prix victory and expunge the disappointment of Monaco. And success would pour balm on the first signs of potential internal friction – arising from the controversy over Fernando Alonso's win in Monaco and suggestions that he had been favoured over Hamilton – that threatened to unseat McLaren.

In Montreal Hamilton admitted that he might now be more guarded in his post-race comments. 'I think it's always a learning experience,' he said. 'Maybe next time I might watch what I say, but I just said what I felt. I'm only human. Sometimes your feelings need to be expressed and you need to let everyone know how you feel. It's all right putting a big smile on your face but maybe next time I might control it a little better.'

Already there were whispers that the Hamiltons – Lewis and father Anthony – might be moved to look elsewhere for a ride for 2008 and Dennis was clearly well aware that the season would continue to develop into a juggling act that would require all the finesse he could muster to avoid an Ayrton Senna-Alain Prost situation.

'I don't feel there is a need to get a special message across,' Hamilton said. 'The team can see I'm doing a good job. I think when I do win, they'll be excited.'

On Saturday he did make a special statement, however, by becoming the second-youngest pole sitter in history, at 22 years, five months and two days old (Rubens Barrichello retained that particular record with 22 years, three months and five days). Alonso had been on a quicker lap but later conceded that an error in the hairpin left dirt on his tyres and ruined his chances.

'It's been a fantastic day,' Hamilton said, wearing a bigger smile than ever. 'We've got the pace on the rest and it came down to this, pulling it out in the last minute. I owe this all to the team and I'm very happy with it.

'It took a while to learn the circuit yesterday. Even though it looks quite simple, it's technical and demanding physically and mentally. Yesterday I stayed out of the barrier, which is always a good thing, went home, had time to think about practice and what I needed to do to improve and I was able to go into the final qualifying session and on the final lap the car was sweet. The tyres were perfect and I was able to pull it all out; each sector was consistent, I didn't make any mistakes and I got the time, so I'm just thrilled.

'The last corner is difficult, especially when you have done a neat lap and you are approaching the corner and you are thinking, "Don't mess it up..." It came up quicker than ever and I nearly brushed it, but I was so chuffed when I crossed the line and they told me I was P1.'

Hamilton lapped in 1m 15.707s. Alonso had to be content with 1m 16.163s for the other front-row slot.

A dramatic final improvement for Nick Heidfeld put him ahead of the Ferraris, with 1m 16.266s for BMW Sauber, leaving Kimi Räikkönen fourth on 1m 16.411s and Felipe Massa fifth on 1m 16.570s.

Mark Webber was sixth with 1m 16.913s for Red Bull, narrowly beating Nico Rosberg's 1m 16.919s for Williams. Robert Kubica was eighth for BMW Sauber on 1m 16.993s. The fifth row belonged to Giancarlo Fisichella on 1m 17.229s for Renault and Jarno Trulli on 1m 17.747s for Toyota.

Takuma Sato was the fastest runner to miss out on Q3 after lapping his Super Aguri in 1m 16.743s to head Tonio Liuzzi (1m 16.760s), Rubens Barrichello (1m 17.116s), David Coulthard (1m 17.304s), Jenson Button (1m 17.541s) and Scott Speed (1m 17.571s).

The principal incident in the second session came when Heidfeld missed the last corner and had a time of 1m 16.519s disallowed by the stewards. He rectified that with a 1m 15.960s that left him third in Q2, but the price was a brush with the outside wall, which necessitated inspection of his BMW-Sauber prior to Q3.

The first session weeded out Anthony Davidson (1m 17.542s), Ralf Schumacher (1m 17.634s), the unfortunate Heikki Kovalainen (1m 17.806s), Alex Wurz (1m 18.089s), Adrian Sutil (1m 18.536s) and Christijan Albers (1m 19.196s). Kovalainen was in the wars yet again, sliding his Renault backwards into the wall on the exit to the back chicane. That wiped off its rear wing and damaged the right-rear suspension, but Renault's mechanics did a brilliant job to get him going again as the session was red-flagged temporarily while the debris was swept away. Kovalainen improved by almost two seconds on his previous time, but the midfield was so close that it wasn't enough.

Hamilton savoured his success, feeling very confident. 'I have never been fortunate enough to start from pole, so that's another new experience. We have got the car, we've got the strategy, so it's up to me to make sure I get a good start and reach the first corner first.' Alonso, however, had other ideas...

LEWIS Hamilton's maiden grand prix triumph was duly delivered in style after a tumultuous race with no fewer than four interventions by the safety car.

The Englishman was in command all the way, winning at only his sixth attempt, but behind him chaos reigned as a series of incidents, the most serious a very nasty crash involving Polish driver Robert Kubica, shuffled the order time and again in his wake.

Hamilton's most perilous moment came right at the start, as team-mate Fernando Alonso burst alongside him but then ran wide trying to outbrake him into the first corner, a left-hander that then tightens into a tight right. The Spaniard slid haplessly over the run-off area and then for the second time in three races sliced right across Hamilton's bows as he tried to regain the track. It would be far from his only mistake in an afternoon during which Hamilton's driving, and Alonso's own errors, made Alonso seem the rookie.

'I made a poor getaway,' Hamilton admitted. 'I don't know what happened. I should have had a certain amount of revs but it went over, so I backed off a bit and it went under. I was able to close the door on Nick [Heidfeld], then I saw Fernando go flying past but get onto the marbles. I just took the corners as normal and when Fernando went flying past it was quite exciting... I just thought, "This is my opportunity," and got on with it. To be honest, it was a fairly simple race apart from the restarts and making sure I pulled a good gap from Nick.'

As Alonso fell back to third place behind Hamilton and the fast-starting Nick Heidfeld in the BMW-Sauber, Kimi Räikkönen dropped behind team-mate Felipe Massa and the two Ferraris were running only fourth and sixth as Nico Rosberg split them in his Williams.

Hamilton reeled off a series of fast laps to build a comfortable lead of almost 20s in the opening stages, looking calm and totally self-assured. Heidfeld had no trouble keeping Alonso at bay and at this stage the champion appeared to be in trouble with his brakes as twice more he ran wide over the run-off area in the first corner. It transpired, however, that there were no problems in that department. A year ago Alonso seemed the perfect driver, as quick as Michael Schumacher, making fewer mistakes than Kimi Räikkönen. But Hamilton's emergence had begun to highlight hitherto unsuspected flaws and in Montreal they were embarrassingly evident as a hint of desperation crept into his driving.

Hamilton pitted for the first time on lap 22, two laps later than Heidfeld, and Massa moved temporarily into the lead. Then Hamilton's former Formula 3 team-mate, Adrian Sutil, hit the wall hard around the back of the circuit, necessitating deployment of the safety car. At that moment, by ill luck, Alonso and Rosberg made their pit stops, in contravention of a new rule banning stops under the safety car but before the pit lane has been declared opened. Both were given 10s stop-and-go penalties. The Ferraris, meanwhile, had also lost out in the mêlée and Massa could not pit until lap 25. He dropped to 12th, Räikkönen to 16th.

Just after the safety car went back into the pits at the end of the 26th lap, the complexion of the race changed again: Kubica had a very heavy high-speed accident on the fastest part of the course, in the flat-out left-hander leading down to the hairpin. Trying to go around the outside of Jarno Trulli's Toyota, he lost control and slammed hard into the outside wall before his car barrel-rolled all the way down to the hairpin itself. The 22-year-old from Krakow was taken to the medical centre at the circuit, where he was described as conscious, stable and able to talk before a helicopter flight to the Sacre Coeur Hospital in Montreal for further examination.

Once again the safety car was deployed, staying out until the 34th lap. As Hamilton resumed racing in the lead, Alonso and Rosberg came in to serve their penalties on the 36th lap. Alonso dropped to 14th, his race now hopelessly compromised as Ferrari was handed a sudden gift. Rosberg dropped to 17th, but his race more or less ended two laps later when he and Trulli spun in unison in the first corner. The BMW was temporarily beached and Rosberg's once so promising race ruined.

Up front, Hamilton continued on his way. In second place Heidfeld posed no threat, though he was moving along quickly

enough to stay well clear of Mark Webber who, despite an early spin, had been able to exploit the various dramas to work his Red Bull into third place ahead of Massa. Giancarlo Fisichella was fifth but, after sliding wide in the hairpin, Räikkönen had been overtaken by Takuma Sato's Super Aguri and was only seventh.

By the 42nd lap Alonso had worked his way back up to eighth, the final points-scoring position, but, as it had been since the start, it was clearly Hamilton's race to lose. It was, however, a long way from over.

Hamilton's final pit stop came and went smoothly on the 48th lap, after closest challenger Heidfeld had come in a lap earlier, but shortly after Hamilton rejoined Christijan Albers triggered another safety car deployment after missing the back chicane and wiping off his Spyker's front wing. It now lay forlornly on the track. Just in case this wasn't all exciting enough, both Fisichella and Massa were shown the black flag and disqualified for having earlier left the pit lane against a red light after their pit stops. Rookie errors from two experienced men.

As the race entered its final third, Hamilton thus led from Webber and Heidfeld, while Räikkönen in fourth place was getting no peace from Alonso and Rubens Barrichello. Further pit stops shuffled that order again and Alonso jumped Räikkönen as they exited the pits after their final stops – but just after he had slithered wide yet again in Turn One and lost a place to Räikkönen, a crash by Tonio Liuzzi triggered yet another safety car period as his broken Toro Rosso was carted off.

This incident brought to a head the animosity that had been festering between Liuzzi, a likable character, and team owner

## DIARY

**Dario Franchitti becomes the first Scot to win the Indianapolis 500 since Jim Clark in 1965.**

**Bernie Ecclestone's wealth is estimated at £2.25 billion in the annual Rich List compiled by the *Sunday Times* newspaper. Former Allsport Management co-owner Paddy McNally's worth is rated at £623 million.**

**Pirelli reveals that it came very close to finalising a deal to supply F1 tyres from the start of the 2008 season, but could not agree with the FIA over the most appropriate wheel dimensions.**

**Lewis Hamilton's driving style at race starts comes under fire from former world champion Jacques Villeneuve, who thinks the FIA has been too lenient. Villeneuve thinks the F1 rookie is too inclined to chop his rivals abruptly.**

## KUBICA SURVIVES UNSCATHED

The 185-mph accident that befell Robert Kubica at Montreal was so horrific that there were some uncomfortable moments initially when it seemed that 10 June 2007 might be the next black date to be remembered in F1's litany of horrors. Thus there was cheering when it was revealed that the popular Pole had sustained no injury beyond shock and bruising.

'I had a bit of pain in my ankle the first day,' he revealed at Indianapolis the following weekend, 'but now it's 100 percent okay. No headache, nearly like brand new.'

Asked whether he had seen the accident on TV he caused much laughter as he replied, 'Yeah, I have seen it also live when I was there. What I remember is what you see. I was racing with Jarno, the corner was going to the left, I show up before the corner to the left-hand side of Jarno, then as the corner was a left-hander, I thought Jarno would go there and I went on the right-hand side, but apparently he ran a bit wider. I was not expecting it, we touched, the front wing went under the car and I have no more control. When I was on the outside of the track on the grass, suddenly I hit something that lifted my car pretty much and I hit the wall. When I stop, I stop.'

Team personnel revealed that he later reported, 'The steering is really light when you are in the air.'

'I realised I was not in bad shape,' Kubica continued. 'That was very important for me. I mean, I have been involved already in one accident a few years ago. It was in a road car and I knew straight away that something was really bad. But this time when I stopped I was moving. I felt a bit of ankle pain and that was all. It shows that the push of the FIA for the safety, you know, the crash tests and everything, has been a big improvement. A big thanks to the FIA, because in the end they are pushing for this. Probably ten years ago we would not be speaking here and this time I'm like nothing has happened.'

**Main:** The explosive force of Robert Kubica's shunt in the BMW-Sauber had to be seen to be believed.

**Insets:** Every component seemed to be ripped off in the huge impact, but the monocoque tub survived intact and the talented young Pole was able to escape without injury.

Photographs: Peter Nygaard/GP Photo

Gerhard Berger and manager Franz Tost, both of whom blamed him squarely for the loss of what could have been third place. On-board footage clearly showed that he was very lucky to miss one of Kubica's wheels, debris from the earlier crash. 'I think I ran over 40 percent of his car!' Liuzzi said. 'I avoided a complete wheel and tyre, but it was dangerous for me with the heat shields because a couple went under the front-right wheel and one of them got stuck between the tyre and the brake duct. The complete front of my car was not touching the ground, the right-front wheel was locked and I had sparks coming out from underneath.'

A pit stop seemed inevitable, but Liuzzi wanted points and managed to dislodge the offending debris and keep going. 'In any case we were under the safety car, so I thought I'd try one more lap and see what happened. My strategy had already been spoiled by the first safety car and to recover any positions I had to push as hard as I could, not pit. So I kept going. The car was not perfectly stable after running over all that debris. In right-handers it was fine but it was moving around in left-handers and was a bit uncertain. Because we had a problem with the radio I couldn't communicate anything to the team, so when I stopped finally for the tyre change I had to tell them with my hands to check the car. They gave a look quickly but could not check it properly. I went back out and the car was still behaving a little bit strangely in the left corners. I was able to push and I was fighting after the restart with [Alex] Wurz and the only thing that didn't allow me to overtake was that we lose a lot of time without the seamless shift on the straights. But I did have good traction, which is very important in Montreal. The issue in the left corners was weird, but I was still able to push.

'After Robert's accident and the way the car felt so inconsistent, I was really worried that the suspension might explode, because carbon suspension, once it gets a little bit cracked, is really, really dangerous. I was really worried in Turn Five that it could happen there because of all the load you put in. Fortunately it happened on a slower part of the circuit where it was less dangerous.

'I went into the last chicane and it was not a problem of tyre pressure because everything was on target and when I started braking and turning in I braked 10 m earlier than my usual point. When I went into the corner the car went into the right part of it okay, but when I tried to turn to the left it just went straight into the wall. Usually there you go into the cement wall if you screw up but because I had no grip I went straight towards the tyre wall.

'For sure from the outside when you crash like that, and there are no other people involved, it can look really weird. But I was pretty sure that something happened to the car – I feel that a toe link or something like that broke, because there was no reaction and the car didn't turn at all. It was impossible for me to do anything. I was just a passenger.'

It would have been all too easy for Hamilton to lose his nerve now, especially with Heidfeld hungering after his own maiden triumph, but he showed no sign of anxiety as he handled the final restart brilliantly and then calmly reeled off the final laps of this extraordinary race in his usual unflurried manner on his date with destiny.

Farther back, Alonso's disaster continued as Takuma Sato overtook him for sixth place on the 68th lap. Ahead of them Alex Wurz took a survivors' third for Williams, in front of Heikki Kovalainen, who did his cause at Renault no end of good by fighting up to fourth after his qualifying disaster. Räikkönen was an unimpressive fifth ahead of Sato, Alonso and Ralf Schumacher.

While Hamilton put in a pluperfect performance, Alonso's left many question marks and Räikkönen's troubled afternoon – which began with that first-corner bump with Massa – included a prolonged and bumpy trip over the grass in the back chicane and then excessive understeer caused by debris from Kubica's accident jammed under his car. So while McLaren garnered ten points from Hamilton and two from Alonso, Ferrari got only four from Räikkönen. The tide was certainly running with McLaren at this point in the season.

BMW Sauber celebrated Heidfeld's strong second place, which he would probably have secured even if Alonso had not been penalised, but it was tempered by the scare of Kubica's accident. Heidfeld's eight-point haul lifted BMW Sauber further clear of Renault in the constructors' table. It also gave Ferrari a scare as BMW made a big jump forwards on this low-downforce track. Heidfeld ran ahead of the F2007s all race – except for the first pit stops – and set the third-fastest lap, ahead of them and right behind the Silver Arrows. For the record, this is how the five fastest laps stacked up: Alonso 1m 16.367s; Hamilton 1m 16.494s; Heidfeld 1m 16.696s; Massa 1m 16.849s; Räikkönen 1m 16.861s.

Renault scored another five points, however, courtesy of Kovalainen, so now it had 21 to BMW Sauber's 38.

Wurz's third place for Williams really should have been the property of team-mate Rosberg, who drove superbly all weekend but, like Alonso, lost out badly when his lap-23 refuelling stop was penalised. At this stage the independent team was able to show the works Toyota team the way home as Schumacher put in an undramatic drive to score the final point. Jarno Trulli sustained a puncture in the Kubica accident and later admitted that his heart wasn't in the contest afterwards. He crashed his Toyota exiting the pits under the safety car on lap 57.

Scoring its first point at Barcelona had been a big deal for Super Aguri, but Montreal was even better. The team made a clever choice of the soft Bridgestone tyres for Takuma Sato's last stint after single-stopping team-mate Anthony Davidson reported that the super-softs were graining horribly on his sister car. Thus the feisty little racer was able not just to catch and pass Schumacher but also to pass Alonso

**Top: A good race strategy helped Takuma Sato finish an impressive sixth for Super Aguri.**
Photograph: Peter J Fox/www.crash.net

**Above: Alex Wurz looks understandably elated about taking third place.**
Photograph: Lukas Gorys

**Centre right: Wurz put in a gritty drive despite rear-wing damage from an early collision.**

**Top right: The ever-improving Heikki Kovalainen was in the points for Renault once again.**
Photographs: Peter J Fox/www.crash.net

**Right: Fernando Alonso did his best to salvage something from a messy afternoon that began with an off-track moment at the first corner. He wound up taking two points for seventh place.**
Photograph: Peter Nygaard/GP Photo

with two laps to go. The three-point haul left Super Aguri eighth on four points, just behind Red Bull.

Davidson's chances of adding to that tally ended when a collision with a beaver on lap 37 so damaged his front wing that he locked up the front tyres approaching the last corner and was obliged to head for the pits instead of getting around it. The team wasn't ready for him so he lost a lot of time and finished 11th.

At one stage, when Mark Webber was running second to Hamilton, a healthy dose of points seemed on the cards for Webber, even though he had spun down from ninth to 14th on lap four. But the safety cars did him no favours and his final pit stop on lap 54 put him back down to 12th. By the finish he was alongside Schumacher but he just failed to get the final point. Red Bull team-mate David Coulthard's race ended much sooner, when his RB3 was struck down with yet more gearbox problems while running 15th on lap 36.

Honda, too, looked good for a while with Rubens Barrichello running third from lap 54 to 62, but he needed a final pit stop and fell back to 12th by the finish.

It took Tony Brooks four races to win, Jackie Stewart eight. And now Lewis Hamilton had split them and done it in six.

'This is a fantastic day; this is history,' he said, a huge smile spread across his face. 'To come here for my first time in Canada and to win… I've had five podiums already and I have been ready for quite some time for the win – it was just a matter of when and where. I had absolutely no problems at all in the race. The safety car made it a bit boring at times. I heard about Robert, who is a good friend of mine. I hope he is okay and send my best wishes to his family. It's good to hear he is well.

'I seemed to sit behind the safety car for quite some time this afternoon, so each time I had to build it [my lead] back up after things dulled down each time. The team did a great job before the first safety car; I had good pace and could keep a good gap and over the last few laps I just counted them down. I'm the type of guy who likes to push to the end, but this is a tricky circuit; you make one mistake on the marbles and you are into the wall, so I just calmed it down.'

On the track, maybe. But around the world, people went crazy at the news that the rookie had won. His life in the UK was changed forever.

'I want to dedicate this to my dad [Anthony], because without him all this would not be possible,' Hamilton ended and clearly this was only going to be the start for the new world championship leader.

*David Tremayne*

**CIRCUIT GILLES VILLENEUVE, MONTRÉAL**

Island Hairpin **1** 44/71
Turn 3 92/148 **2**
Turn 5 160/257 **5**
Pont de la Concorde 88/142 **2**
Senna 83/134
Turn 6 56/90 **2**
Start/finish Chicane **2** 89/143
185/298 **5**
Turn 9 70/113 **2**
208/335 **6**
Droite du Casino
L'epingle 36/58 **1**

**Circuit: 2.709 miles/4.361 km**
116/187 mph/kmh
**4** Gear

## FIA F1 WORLD CHAMPIONSHIP • ROUND 6
# GRAND PRIX DU CANADA
### MONTREAL 8–10 JUNE 2007

## RACE RESULTS

| Pos. | Driver | Nat. | No. | Entrant | Car/Engine | Tyres | Laps | Time/Retirement | Speed (mph/km/h) | Gap to leader | Fastest race lap | |
|---|---|---|---|---|---|---|---|---|---|---|---|---|
| 1 | Lewis Hamilton | GB | 2 | Vodafone McLaren Mercedes | McLaren MP4-22-Mercedes FO 108T V8 | B | 70 | 1h 44m 11.292s | 109.237/175.799 | | 1m 16.494s | 37 |
| 2 | Nick Heidfeld | D | 9 | BMW Sauber F1 Team | BMW Sauber F1.07-BMW P86/7 V8 | B | 70 | 1h 44m 15.635s | 109.161/175.677 | + 4.343s | 1m 16.696s | 19 |
| 3 | Alexander Wurz | A | 17 | AT&T Williams | Williams FW29-Toyota RVX-07 V8 | B | 70 | 1h 44m 16.617s | 109.143/175.649 | + 5.325s | 1m 17.947s | 67 |
| 4 | Heikki Kovalainen | FIN | 4 | ING Renault F1 Team | Renault R27-RS27 V8 | B | 70 | 1h 44m 18.021s | 109.119/175.610 | + 6.729s | 1m 18.368s | 67 |
| 5 | Kimi Räikkönen | FIN | 6 | Scuderia Ferrari Marlboro | Ferrari F2007-056 V8 | B | 70 | 1h 44m 24.299s | 109.010/175.434 | + 13.007s | 1m 16.861s | 21 |
| 6 | Takuma Sato | J | 22 | Super Aguri F1 Team | Super Aguri SA07-Honda RA807E V8 | B | 70 | 1h 44m 27.990s | 108.945/175.330 | + 16.698s | 1m 18.035s | 47 |
| 7 | Fernando Alonso | E | 1 | Vodafone McLaren Mercedes | McLaren MP4-22-Mercedes FO 108T V8 | B | 70 | 1h 44m 33.228s | 108.854/175.184 | + 21.936s | 1m 16.367s | 46 |
| 8 | Ralf Schumacher | D | 11 | Panasonic Toyota Racing | Toyota TF107-RVX-07 V8 | B | 70 | 1h 44m 34.180s | 108.838/175.157 | + 22.888s | 1m 17.910s | 38 |
| 9 | Mark Webber | AUS | 15 | Red Bull Racing | Red Bull RB3-Renault RS27 V8 | B | 70 | 1h 44m 34.252s | 108.836/175.155 | + 22.960s | 1m 17.618s | 47 |
| 10 | Nico Rosberg | D | 16 | AT&T Williams | Williams FW29-Toyota RVX-07 V8 | B | 70 | 1h 44m 35.276s | 108.819/175.127 | + 23.984s | 1m 17.156s | 42 |
| 11 | Anthony Davidson | GB | 23 | Super Aguri F1 Team | Super Aguri SA07-Honda RA807E V8 | B | 70 | 1h 44m 35.610s | 108.813/175.117 | + 24.318s | 1m 18.780s | 36 |
| 12 | Rubens Barrichello | BR | 8 | Honda Racing F1 Team | Honda RA107-RA807E V8 | B | 70 | 1h 44m 41.731s | 108.707/174.947 | + 30.439s | 1m 18.543s | 62 |
| | Jarno Trulli | I | 12 | Panasonic Toyota Racing | Toyota TF107-RVX-07 V8 | B | 58 | Accident | | | 1m 19.092s | 12 |
| | Vitantonio Liuzzi | I | 18 | Scuderia Toro Rosso | Toro Rosso STR02-Ferrari 056H V8 | B | 54 | Accident | | | 1m 19.375s | 9 |
| DQ | Felipe Massa | BR | 5 | Scuderia Ferrari Marlboro | Ferrari F2007-056 V8 | B | 51 | Left pit-lane against red light | | | 1m 16.849s* | 22 |
| DQ | Giancarlo Fisichella | I | 3 | ING Renault F1 Team | Renault R27-RS27 V8 | B | 51 | Left pit-lane against red light | | | 1m 17.411s* | 22 |
| | Christijan Albers | NL | 21 | Etihad Aldar Spyker F1 Team | Spyker F8-VII-Ferrari 056H V8 | B | 47 | accident/ handling | | | 1m 19.254s | 21 |
| | David Coulthard | GB | 14 | Red Bull Racing | Red Bull RB3-Renault RS27 V8 | B | 36 | Gearbox | | | 1m 18.981s | 19 |
| | Robert Kubica | POL | 10 | BMW Sauber F1 Team | BMW Sauber F1.07-BMW P86/7 V8 | B | 26 | Accident | | | 1m 17.529s | 19 |
| | Adrian Sutil | D | 20 | Etihad Aldar Spyker F1 Team | Spyker F8-VII-Ferrari 056H V8 | B | 21 | Accident | | | 1m 19.452s | 20 |
| | Scott Speed | USA | 19 | Scuderia Toro Rosso | Toro Rosso STR02-Ferrari 056H V8 | B | 8 | Accident/ front suspension | | | 1m 20.092s | 6 |
| | Jenson Button | GB | 7 | Honda Racing F1 Team | Honda RA107-RA807E V8 | B | 0 | Gear selection on grid | | | No time | |

\* Fastest laps disallowed, due to disqualification

Fastest race lap: Fernando Alonso on lap 46, 1m 16.367s, 127.742 mph/205.580 km/h.

Lap record: Rubens Barrichello (Ferrari F2004 V10), 1m 13.622s, 132.505 mph/213.246 km/h (2004).

21 **ALBERS** Spyker
Started from pit lane

19 **WURZ** Williams

17 **DAVIDSON** Super Aguri

15 **BUTTON** Honda

13 **BARRICHELLO** Honda

11 **SATO** Super Aguri

22 **KOVALAINEN** Renault
Engine penalty

20 **SUTIL** Spyker

18 **SCHUMACHER** Toyota

16 **SPEED** Toro Rosso

14 **COULTHARD** Red Bull

12 **LIUZZI** Toro Rosso

| Grid order | 1 | 2 | 3 | 4 | 5 | 6 | 7 | 8 | 9 | 10 | 11 | 12 | 13 | 14 | 15 | 16 | 17 | 18 | 19 | 20 | 21 | 22 | 23 | 24 | 25 | 26 | 27 | 28 | 29 | 30 | 31 | 32 | 33 | 34 | 35 | 36 | 37 | 38 | 39 | 40 | 41 | 42 | 43 | 44 | 45 | 46 | 47 | 48 | 49 | 50 | 51 | 52 | 53 | 54 |
|---|---|---|---|---|---|---|---|---|---|---|---|---|---|---|---|---|---|---|---|---|---|---|---|---|---|---|---|---|---|---|---|---|---|---|---|---|---|---|---|---|---|---|---|---|---|---|---|---|---|---|---|---|---|---|
| 2 HAMILTON | 2 | 2 | 2 | 2 | 2 | 2 | 2 | 2 | 2 | 2 | 2 | 2 | 2 | 2 | 2 | 2 | 2 | 2 | 2 | 2 | 2 | 2 | 5 | 5 | 5 | 2 | 2 | 2 | 2 | 2 | 2 | 2 | 2 | 2 | 2 | 2 | 2 | 2 | 2 | 2 | 2 | 2 | 2 | 2 | 2 | 2 | 2 | 2 | 2 | 2 | 2 | 2 | 2 | 2 |
| 1 ALONSO | 9 | 9 | 9 | 9 | 9 | 9 | 9 | 9 | 9 | 9 | 9 | 9 | 9 | 9 | 9 | 9 | 9 | 9 | 9 | 5 | 5 | 2 | 2 | 2 | 9 | 9 | | | | | | | | | | | | | | | | | | | | | | | 9 | 15 | 15 | 15 | 15 | 15 |
| 9 HEIDFELD | 1 | 1 | 1 | 1 | 1 | 1 | 1 | 1 | 1 | 1 | 1 | 1 | 1 | 1 | 1 | 1 | 1 | 1 | 1 | 5 | 1 | 1 | 1 | 6 | 6 | 1 | 1 | 1 | 1 | 1 | 1 | 1 | 1 | 1 | 23 | 11 | 11 | 11 | 15 | 15 | 15 | 15 | 15 | 15 | 15 | 15 | 15 | 9 | 9 | 9 | 9 | 9 | 9 | 9 |
| 6 RÄIKKÖNEN | 5 | 5 | 5 | 5 | 5 | 5 | 5 | 5 | 5 | 5 | 5 | 5 | 5 | 5 | 5 | 5 | 1 | 16 | 16 | 16 | 3 | 3 | 16 | 16 | 16 | 16 | 16 | 16 | 16 | 16 | 16 | 11 | 15 | 15 | 5 | 5 | 5 | 5 | 5 | 5 | 5 | 5 | 5 | 5 | 5 | 5 | 6 | 8 | 17 | | | | | |
| 5 MASSA | 16 | 16 | 16 | 16 | 16 | 16 | 16 | 16 | 16 | 16 | 16 | 16 | 16 | 16 | 16 | 16 | 6 | 6 | 6 | 9 | 9 | 8 | 8 | 8 | 8 | 23 | 23 | 23 | 23 | 23 | 15 | 5 | 5 | 3 | 3 | 3 | 3 | 3 | 3 | 22 | 22 | 6 | 6 | 1 | 17 | | | | | | | | | |
| 15 WEBBER | 6 | 6 | 6 | 6 | 6 | 6 | 6 | 6 | 6 | 6 | 6 | 6 | 6 | 6 | 6 | 6 | 3 | 3 | 10 | 10 | 14 | 14 | 17 | 17 | 17 | 11 | 11 | 11 | 11 | 11 | 5 | 3 | 3 | 22 | 22 | 22 | 22 | 22 | 22 | 6 | 6 | 1 | 1 | 8 | 18 | 12 | | | | | | | | |
| 16 ROSBERG | 3 | 3 | 3 | 3 | 3 | 3 | 3 | 3 | 3 | 3 | 3 | 10 | 3 | 3 | 3 | 3 | 9 | 9 | 1 | 1 | 4 | 23 | 23 | 23 | 15 | 15 | 15 | 15 | 15 | 3 | 22 | 22 | 22 | 6 | 6 | 6 | 6 | 6 | 6 | 1 | 1 | 3 | 3 | 11 | 12 | | | | | | | | | |
| 10 KUBICA | 10 | 10 | 10 | 10 | 10 | 10 | 10 | 10 | 10 | 10 | 10 | 3 | 10 | 10 | 10 | 10 | 10 | 10 | 16 | 16 | 17 | 17 | 11 | 11 | 5 | 5 | 5 | 5 | 22 | 6 | 6 | 6 | 6 | 4 | 1 | 1 | 1 | 1 | 1 | 3 | 8 | 18 | | | | | | | | | | | | |
| 3 FISICHELLA | 15 | 15 | 15 | 22 | 22 | 22 | 22 | 22 | 22 | 22 | 22 | 22 | 22 | 22 | 22 | 22 | 22 | 22 | 23 | 23 | 15 | 15 | 15 | 3 | 3 | 3 | 3 | 6 | 4 | 4 | 4 | 21 | 1 | 4 | 4 | 8 | 8 | 8 | 8 | 8 | 11 | 11 | 18 | 1 | | | | | | | | | |
| 12 TRULLI | 22 | 22 | 22 | 12 | 12 | 12 | 12 | 12 | 12 | 12 | 12 | 12 | 12 | 12 | 12 | 12 | 11 | 11 | 5 | 5 | 5 | 6 | 6 | 6 | 22 | 22 | 21 | 21 | 21 | 1 | 21 | 8 | 21 | 11 | 11 | 11 | 11 | 11 | 17 | 22 | 6 | 11 | | | | | | | | | | | | |
| 22 SATO | 12 | 12 | 12 | 18 | 18 | 18 | 18 | 18 | 18 | 18 | 18 | 18 | 18 | 18 | 18 | 18 | 3 | 3 | 22 | 22 | 22 | 6 | 6 | 4 | 8 | 8 | 21 | 21 | 21 | 17 | 21 | 21 | 21 | 17 | 18 | 12 | 11 | 12 | 11 | 22 | 4 | 22 | 11 | 12 | | | | | | | | | |
| 18 LIUZZI | 18 | 18 | 18 | 15 | 15 | 15 | 15 | 15 | 15 | 15 | 15 | 15 | 15 | 15 | 15 | 15 | 5 | 3 | 12 | 12 | 21 | 21 | 21 | 17 | 17 | 17 | 17 | 18 | 18 | 18 | 18 | 12 | 22 | 22 | 4 | 22 | 11 | 18 | | | | | | | | | | | | | | | | |
| 8 BARRICHELLO | 8 | 8 | 8 | 14 | 14 | 14 | 14 | 14 | 14 | 14 | 14 | 14 | 14 | 14 | 14 | 14 | 14 | 14 | 3 | 12 | 12 | 22 | 8 | 21 | 17 | 17 | 18 | 18 | 18 | 12 | 12 | 12 | 12 | | | | | | | | | | | | | | | | | | | | | |
| 14 COULTHARD | 14 | 14 | 14 | 15 | 14 | 14 | 14 | 14 | 14 | 14 | 14 | 14 | 14 | 4 | 4 | 10 | 12 | 22 | 22 | 21 | 8 | 8 | 8 | 8 | 1 | 18 | 18 | 18 | 18 | 12 | 12 | 12 | | 4 | 4 | 4 | 23 | 23 | | | | | | | | | | | | | | | | |
| 7 BUTTON | 17 | 17 | 17 | 17 | 17 | 17 | 17 | 17 | 17 | 4 | 4 | 4 | 4 | 17 | 17 | 17 | 12 | 10 | 21 | 14 | 17 | 17 | 17 | 17 | 14 | 12 | 12 | 12 | 12 | 4 | 4 | 4 | 4 | 16 | 16 | 16 | | | | | | | | | | | | | | | | | |
| 19 SPEED | 19 | 19 | 19 | 19 | 19 | 19 | 19 | 4 | 4 | 4 | 17 | 17 | 17 | 17 | 17 | 17 | 23 | 23 | 6 | 6 | 14 | 14 | 14 | 18 | 16 | 16 | 16 | 16 | 16 | 16 | 16 | 16 | 16 | 23 | 23 | 23 | | | | | | | | | | | | | | | | | |
| 23 DAVIDSON | 23 | 23 | 4 | 4 | 4 | 4 | 23 | 23 | 23 | 23 | 23 | 23 | 23 | 23 | 23 | 23 | 11 | 11 | 18 | 18 | 18 | 4 | 18 | 14 | 14 | 14 | 16 | 23 | 23 | 23 | 23 | 23 | 23 | | | | | | | | | | | | | | | | | | | | |
| 11 SCHUMACHER | 4 | 4 | 23 | 23 | 23 | 23 | 11 | 11 | 11 | 11 | 11 | 11 | 11 | 11 | 11 | 11 | 15 | 15 | 22 | 22 | 4 | 12 | 12 | 14 | 18 | 18 | 18 | 18 | | | | | | | | | | | | | | | | | | | | | | | | | | |
| 17 WURZ | 11 | 11 | 11 | 11 | 11 | 11 | 11 | 11 | 20 | 20 | 20 | 20 | 20 | 20 | 20 | 20 | 20 | 20 | 21 | 21 | | | | | | | | | | | | | | | | | | | | | | | | | | | | | | | | | |
| 20 SUTIL | 20 | 20 | 20 | 20 | 20 | 20 | 20 | 21 | 21 | 21 | 21 | 21 | 21 | 21 | 21 | 21 | | | | | | | | | | | | | | | | | | | | | | | | | | | | | | | | | | | | | | |
| 21 ALBERS | 21 | 21 | 21 | 21 | 21 | 21 | 21 | 21 | | | | | | | | | | | | | | | | | | | | | | | | | | | | | | | | | | | | | | | | | | | | | | |
| 4 KOVALAINEN | | | | | | | | | | | | | | | | | | | | | | | | | | | | | | | | | | | | | | | | | | | | | | | | | | | | | | |

## PRACTICE 1 (FRIDAY)

Overcast (track 27–31ºC, air 22–25ºC)

| Pos. | Driver | Laps | Time |
|---|---|---|---|
| 1 | Fernando Alonso | 17 | 1m 17.759s |
| 2 | Lewis Hamilton | 20 | 1m 17.967s |
| 3 | Kimi Räikkönen | 21 | 1m 18.136s |
| 4 | Felipe Massa | 21 | 1m 18.167s |
| 5 | Mark Webber | 21 | 1m 18.301s |
| 6 | Giancarlo Fisichella | 24 | 1m 18.620s |
| 7 | Nick Heidfeld | 20 | 1m 18.634s |
| 8 | Ralf Schumacher | 32 | 1m 18.652s |
| 9 | David Coulthard | 24 | 1m 18.717s |
| 10 | Anthony Davidson | 16 | 1m 18.896s |
| 11 | Takuma Sato | 20 | 1m 18.898s |
| 12 | Jarno Trulli | 25 | 1m 18.925s |
| 13 | Jenson Button | 24 | 1m 18.932s |
| 14 | Heikki Kovalainen | 26 | 1m 18.997s |
| 15 | Alexander Wurz | 22 | 1m 19.189s |
| 16 | Scott Speed | 29 | 1m 19.234s |
| 17 | Kazuki Nakajima | 30 | 1m 19.273s |
| 18 | Rubens Barrichello | 18 | 1m 19.937s |
| 19 | Vitantonio Liuzzi | 12 | 1m 20.331s |
| 20 | Christijan Albers | 17 | 1m 21.251s |
| 21 | Adrian Sutil | 25 | 1m 21.630s |
| 22 | Robert Kubica | 2 | No time |

## PRACTICE 2 (FRIDAY)

Sunny (track 39–40ºC, air 28–29ºC)

| Pos. | Driver | Laps | Time |
|---|---|---|---|
| 1 | Fernando Alonso | 37 | 1m 16.550s |
| 2 | Felipe Massa | 34 | 1m 17.090s |
| 3 | Lewis Hamilton | 36 | 1m 17.307s |
| 4 | Kimi Räikkönen | 37 | 1m 17.515s |
| 5 | Nick Heidfeld | 42 | 1m 17.827s |
| 6 | Nico Rosberg | 25 | 1m 17.992s |
| 7 | Rubens Barrichello | 38 | 1m 18.108s |
| 8 | Giancarlo Fisichella | 40 | 1m 18.130s |
| 9 | Mark Webber | 40 | 1m 18.181s |
| 10 | Takuma Sato | 38 | 1m 18.309s |
| 11 | David Coulthard | 40 | 1m 18.316s |
| 12 | Robert Kubica | 29 | 1m 18.399s |
| 13 | Jenson Button | 36 | 1m 18.474s |
| 14 | Vitantonio Liuzzi | 33 | 1m 18.493s |
| 15 | Anthony Davidson | 35 | 1m 18.545s |
| 16 | Scott Speed | 37 | 1m 18.602s |
| 17 | Alexander Wurz | 25 | 1m 18.871s |
| 18 | Jarno Trulli | 16 | 1m 18.895s |
| 19 | Ralf Schumacher | 16 | 1m 19.331s |
| 20 | Christijan Albers | 38 | 1m 19.453s |
| 21 | Adrian Sutil | 25 | 1m 19.662s |
| 22 | Heikki Kovalainen | 13 | 1m 20.519s |

## QUALIFYING (SATURDAY)

Sunny, scattered cloud (track 38–40ºC, air 24–25ºC)

| Pos. | Driver | First | Second | Third |
|---|---|---|---|---|
| 1 | Lewis Hamilton | 1m 16.576s | 1m 15.486s | 1m 15.707s |
| 2 | Fernando Alonso | 1m 16.562s | 1m 15.522s | 1m 16.163s |
| 3 | Nick Heidfeld | 1m 17.006s | 1m 15.960s | 1m 16.266s |
| 4 | Kimi Räikkönen | 1m 16.468s | 1m 16.592s | 1m 16.411s |
| 5 | Felipe Massa | 1m 16.756s | 1m 16.138s | 1m 16.570s |
| 6 | Mark Webber | 1m 17.315s | 1m 16.257s | 1m 16.913s |
| 7 | Nico Rosberg | 1m 17.016s | 1m 16.190s | 1m 16.919s |
| 8 | Robert Kubica | 1m 17.267s | 1m 16.368s | 1m 16.993s |
| 9 | Giancarlo Fisichella | 1m 16.805s | 1m 16.288s | 1m 17.229s |
| 10 | Jarno Trulli | 1m 17.324s | 1m 16.600s | 1m 17.747s |
| 11 | Takuma Sato | 1m 17.490s | 1m 16.743s | |
| 12 | Vitantonio Liuzzi | 1m 17.541s | 1m 16.760s | |
| 13 | Rubens Barrichello | 1m 17.011s | 1m 17.116s | |
| 14 | David Coulthard | 1m 17.436s | 1m 17.304s | |
| 15 | Jenson Button | 1m 17.522s | 1m 17.541s | |
| 16 | Scott Speed | 1m 17.433s | 1m 17.571s | |
| 17 | Anthony Davidson | 1m 17.542s | | |
| 18 | Ralf Schumacher | 1m 17.634s | | |
| 19 | Heikki Kovalainen | 1m 17.806s | | |
| 20 | Alexander Wurz | 1m 18.089s | | |
| 21 | Adrian Sutil | 1m 18.536s | | |
| 22 | Christijan Albers | 1m 19.196s | | |

## PRACTICE 3 (SATURDAY)

Sunny (track 24–30ºC, air 23–24ºC)

| Pos. | Driver | Laps | Time |
|---|---|---|---|
| 1 | Lewis Hamilton | 12 | 1m 16.071s |
| 2 | Kimi Räikkönen | 14 | 1m 16.459s |
| 3 | Fernando Alonso | 9 | 1m 16.465s |
| 4 | Felipe Massa | 13 | 1m 16.666s |
| 5 | Takuma Sato | 12 | 1m 16.864s |
| 6 | Nico Rosberg | 14 | 1m 16.975s |
| 7 | Mark Webber | 11 | 1m 17.071s |
| 8 | Rubens Barrichello | 16 | 1m 17.329s |
| 9 | David Coulthard | 11 | 1m 17.391s |
| 10 | Anthony Davidson | 15 | 1m 17.391s |
| 11 | Giancarlo Fisichella | 12 | 1m 17.454s |
| 12 | Jenson Button | 15 | 1m 17.468s |
| 13 | Robert Kubica | 12 | 1m 17.601s |
| 14 | Jarno Trulli | 17 | 1m 17.624s |
| 15 | Scott Speed | 12 | 1m 17.742s |
| 16 | Ralf Schumacher | 13 | 1m 17.748s |
| 17 | Vitantonio Liuzzi | 14 | 1m 17.799s |
| 18 | Adrian Sutil | 13 | 1m 18.270s |
| 19 | Nick Heidfeld | 5 | 1m 18.428s |
| 20 | Alexander Wurz | 11 | 1m 18.489s |
| 21 | Heikki Kovalainen | 10 | 1m 18.758s |
| 22 | Christijan Albers | 13 | 1m 18.933s |

## RACE TYRE STRATEGIES

**BRIDGESTONE**

In 2007, the tyre regulations stipulate that the two dry-tyre specifications must be visibly distinguishable from each other. At the Canadian Grand Prix, the super-soft compound Bridgestone Potenza tyre was marked with a white line in the second-from-inside groove.

| | Driver | Race stint 1 | Race stint 2 | Race stint 3 | Race stint 4 |
|---|---|---|---|---|---|
| 1 | Lewis Hamilton | Soft: laps 1–22 | Soft: 23–48 | Super-soft: 49–70 | |
| 2 | Nick Heidfeld | Soft: 1–20 | Soft: 21–47 | Super-soft: 48–70 | |
| 3 | Alexander Wurz | Soft: 1–30 | Super-soft: 31–70 | | |
| 4 | Heikki Kovalainen | Soft: 1–27 | Super-soft: 28–44 | Soft: 45–70 | |
| 5 | Kimi Räikkönen | Soft: 1–25 | Soft: 26–53 | Super-soft: 54–70 | |
| 6 | Takuma Sato | Soft: 1–25 | Soft: 26–50 | Super-soft: 51–53 | Soft: 54–70 |
| 7 | Fernando Alonso | Soft: 1–23 | Soft: 24–53 | Super-soft: 54–70 | |
| 8 | Ralf Schumacher | Soft: 1–40 | Soft: 41–53 | Super-soft: 54–70 | |
| 9 | Mark Webber | Soft: 1–22 | Soft: 23–54 | Super-soft: 55–70 | |
| 10 | Nico Rosberg | Soft: 1–23 | Soft: 24–49 | Super-soft: 50–70 | |
| 11 | Anthony Davidson | Soft: 1–37 | Super-soft: 38–40 | Soft: 41–70 | |
| 12 | Rubens Barrichello | Soft: 1–30 | Soft: 31–63 | Super-soft: 64–70 | |
| | Jarno Trulli | Soft: 1–25 | Soft: 26–58 | Super-soft: 59–70 | |
| | Vitantonio Liuzzi | Soft: 1–25 | Soft: 26–30 | Super-soft: 31–32 | Soft: 33–52 (DNF) |
| | Felipe Massa | Soft: 1–25 | Soft: 26–51 (DSQ) | | |
| | Giancarlo Fisichella | Soft: 1–25 | Soft: 26–48 | Super-soft: 49–51 (DSQ) | |
| | Christijan Albers | Soft: 1–25 | Soft: 26–47 (DNF) | | |
| | David Coulthard | Soft: 1–27 | Soft: 28–30 | Super-soft: 30–31 | Soft: 32–36 (DNF) |
| | Robert Kubica | Soft: 1–25 | Soft: 26–27 (DNF) | | |
| | Adrian Sutil | Soft: 1–21 (DNF) | | | |
| | Scott Speed | Soft: 1–8 (DNF) | | | |
| | Jenson Button | Soft: 0 (DNF) | | | |

9 FISICHELLA Renault · 7 ROSBERG Williams · 5 MASSA Ferrari · 3 HEIDFELD BMW-Sauber · 1 HAMILTON McLaren

10 TRULLI Toyota · 8 KUBICA BMW-Sauber · 6 WEBBER Red Bull · 4 RÄIKKÖNEN Ferrari · 2 ALONSO McLaren

**RACE DISTANCE:**
70 laps
189.686 miles/305.270 km

**RACE WEATHER:**
Sunny, scattered cloud, track 39–43ºC, air 25–27ºC

### Lap chart (laps 55–70)

| 55 | 56 | 57 | 58 | 59 | 60 | 61 | 62 | 63 | 64 | 65 | 66 | 67 | 68 | 69 | 70 | • |
|---|---|---|---|---|---|---|---|---|---|---|---|---|---|---|---|---|
| 2 | 2 | 2 | 2 | 2 | 2 | 2 | 2 | 2 | 2 | 2 | 2 | 2 | 2 | 2 | 1 | 1 |
| 9 | 9 | 9 | 9 | 9 | 9 | 9 | 9 | 9 | 9 | 9 | 9 | 9 | 9 | 9 | 2 | 2 |
| 8 | 8 | 8 | 8 | 8 | 8 | 8 | 8 | 17 | 17 | 17 | 17 | 17 | 17 | 17 | 17 | 3 |
| 17 | 17 | 17 | 17 | 17 | 17 | 17 | 17 | 4 | 4 | 4 | 4 | 4 | 4 | 4 | 4 | 4 |
| 4 | 4 | 4 | 4 | 4 | 4 | 4 | 6 | 6 | 6 | 6 | 6 | 6 | 6 | 6 | 5 | 5 |
| 12 | 12 | 12 | 6 | 6 | 6 | 1 | 1 | 1 | 1 | 1 | 22 | 22 | 22 | 22 | 22 | 6 |
| 6 | 6 | 11 | 11 | 11 | 1 | 1 | 1 | 11 | 11 | 11 | 11 | 22 | 22 | 1 | 1 | 7 |
| 6 | 11 | 11 | 1 | 1 | 11 | 11 | 22 | 22 | 22 | 11 | 11 | 11 | 11 | 11 | 11 | 8 |
| 1 | 1 | 1 | 22 | 22 | 22 | 22 | 15 | 15 | 15 | 15 | 15 | 15 | 15 | 15 | 15 | |
| 22 | 22 | 22 | 15 | 15 | 15 | 15 | 16 | 16 | 16 | 16 | 16 | 16 | 16 | 16 | 16 | |
| 15 | 15 | 15 | 16 | 16 | 16 | 16 | 23 | 23 | 23 | 23 | 23 | 23 | 23 | 23 | | |
| 16 | 16 | 16 | 12 | 23 | 23 | 23 | 8 | 8 | 8 | 8 | 8 | 8 | | | | |
| 23 | 23 | 23 | 23 | | | | | | | | | | | | | |

20 Pit stop
20 One lap or more behind leader
16 Stop-and-go penalty
20 Safety car deployed on laps shown

## FOR THE RECORD

**FIRST POLE AND FIRST WIN:**
Lewis Hamilton

**1,000th POINT:** Renault

**100th POINT:** Nick Heidfeld

**TENTH FASTEST LAP:** Fernando Alonso

## POINTS

| | DRIVERS | | | CONSTRUCTORS | |
|---|---|---|---|---|---|
| 1 | Lewis Hamilton | 48 | 1 | McLaren | 88 |
| 2 | Fernando Alonso | 40 | 2 | Ferrari | 60 |
| 3 | Felipe Massa | 33 | 3 | BMW Sauber | 38 |
| 4 | Kimi Räikkönen | 27 | 4 | Renault | 21 |
| 5 | Nick Heidfeld | 26 | 5 | Williams | 13 |
| 6 | Giancarlo Fisichella | 13 | 6 | Toyota | 6 |
| 7 | Robert Kubica | 12 | 7 | Red Bull | 4 |
| 8 | Heikki Kovalainen | 8 | 8 | Super Aguri | 4 |
| 9 | Alexander Wurz | 8 | | | |
| 10 | Nico Rosberg | 5 | | | |
| 11 | Jarno Trulli | 4 | | | |
| 12 | David Coulthard | 4 | | | |
| 13 | Takuma Sato | 4 | | | |
| 14 | Ralf Schumacher | 2 | | | |

On top of his world. Lewis Hamilton cuts
a victorious stance on the front of his
McLaren MP4-22 after scoring his second
grand prix victory in as many weeks.
Photograph: Peter J Fox/www.crash.net

# UNITED STATES GP

## INDIANAPOLIS

## INDIANAPOLIS QUALIFYING

Fernando Alonso had arrived at Indianapolis determined to
expunge the disappointing memories of the previous Sunday's
race in Canada, where he had finished a distant and frustrated
seventh. The American circuit had never been one of his
favourites – his best result here thus far was fifth for Renault
in 2006 – but Alonso initially set the qualifying pace in torrid
conditions. The track temperature soared to levels more
usually seen in Bahrain and Malaysia. Yet history was about to
repeat itself.

As in Montreal, just as it seemed the world champion would
get the upper hand, Lewis Hamilton stole pole in the closing
moments of the final session, rubbing in his advantage by
projecting a surprised innocent delight that he had again
managed to outflank his more experienced colleague.

'Yes, it was quite a surprise, to be honest,' said Hamilton,
who managed a 1m 12.331s best. 'Going into qualifying,
we hadn't really found the best, the optimal, set-up and I knew
Fernando was extremely quick here. But it's great to see that the
team is so quick and ahead of the Ferraris, obviously. So I could
not be happier. I did not really expect to be on pole. I thought
Fernando [who did a 1m 12.500s] would have been quicker, but
obviously not.'

Felipe Massa (1m 12.703s) and his team-mate Kimi Räikkönen
(1m 12.839s) monopolised the second row of the grid in their
Ferrari F2007s, while Nick Heidfeld in the BMW-Sauber
(1m 12.847s) shared the third row with Heikki Kovalainen's
Renault (1m 13.308s). In seventh place, 19-year-old Sebastian
Vettel became the second-youngest driver to qualify for a world
championship grand prix after taking over the second BMW-Sauber
from Robert Kubica, who was refused permission to compete on
medical grounds following his 185-mph accident in Canada.

Kubica was obviously hugely taken aback when the medical
authorities at Indianapolis made known their decision. 'Naturally
I'm disappointed because I felt absolutely ready to race,' said
Kubica. 'But I respect the decision. It was made because there is
too much risk in letting me race in this grand prix in case I have
another impact so soon after Montreal. I will go home now. I
wish Sebastian all the best. It is good for him and I am pretty
sure he will do a good job.'

For his part, Massa was already anticipating that this would
be a difficult weekend after managing no better than
1m 12.703s to secure his berth ahead of Räikkönen on the
inside of the second row.

'Well, for sure, a bit closer but not enough – we need to be
in front, not just closer,' he said. 'But for sure the situation is
better than in Canada. That was a pretty difficult weekend for
us. Here, starting third, on the second row, is not a disaster.'

On the third row, Heidfeld had not been totally happy with the
handling balance of the BMW-Sauber, but things improved a lot
for qualifying and Nick reflected that he thought he might well
have ended up third had it not been for losing 0.4s on a really
hot lap in sector three. Stand-in Vettel did a super job, lapping
in 1m 13.513s to line up seventh just ahead of Jarno Trulli
(1m13.789s) in the Toyota TF107 and Mark Webber's Red
Bull (1m 13.871s).

In the other Red Bull, David Coulthard's qualifying efforts
were thwarted by a spin in the first stint, so an eventual
11th-fastest 1m 12.873s was far from a disaster under the
circumstances. He lined up just ahead of Ralf Schumacher's
Toyota (1m 12.920s); a late front-wing adjustment probably cost
Ralf a shot at a place in the top ten. Come the race, of course,
he would be out at the first corner.

Jenson Button posted a 1m 12.998s to take 13th, ahead of
Nico Rosberg's Williams (1m 13.060s), Rubens Barrichello
in the other Honda (1m 13.201s) and Anthony Davidson
(1m 13.259s), who needed a switch to the Super Aguri T-car for
qualifying after brushing the wall at Turn 13 during Saturday's
free practice. Then followed Alex Wurz's Williams (1m 13.441s)
and Takuma Sato's Super Aguri (1m 13.477s), and the last two
rows were completed by the two Toro Rossos and a couple of
Spykers lining up in Noah's ark formation.

**Above: Indy owner Tony George (top) and Bernie Ecclestone failed to reach agreement to continue holding the US Grand Prix at the Indianapolis Motor Speedway.**

Photographs: Peter J Fox/www.crash.net

**Below: Jenson Button's Honda is damaged in the first-corner fracas that eliminates team-mate Rubens Barrichello, Ralf Schumacher and David Coulthard.**

Photograph: Peter Nygaard/GP Photo

LEWIS Hamilton's magic carpet ride towards the championship crown in his first year of F1 continued in flawless style when he dominated the US Grand Prix, roundly beating his McLaren Mercedes team-mate Fernando Alonso after a tense wheel-to-wheel battle in which they briefly came inches from touching as they weaved at each other at 195 mph on the main pit straight.

It was Hamilton's second win in as many weekends, following his maiden victory in Montreal, and extended his championship lead to 10 points with seven of the season's 17 races completed. Third and fourth were the Ferrari F2007s of Felipe Massa and Kimi Räikkönen, with Heikki Kovalainen's Renault and Jarno Trulli's Toyota completing the top half dozen.

Facing a 600-m sprint to the first corner, the McLaren team did its best to forget painful memories of last year's race, in which team-mates Kimi Räikkönen and Juan Pablo Montoya were eliminated from the race in a multiple collision only a few seconds after the starting signal was given.

Happily, on this occasion, the front half of the field got away cleanly, with Hamilton just easing ahead of Alonso as the two McLarens accelerated off ahead of the rest of the pack. Straining every sinew as he went into the braking area for the first tight right-hander, Alonso pulled level with Hamilton on the outside line. For a moment the two cars jinked towards each other as Alonso momentarily considered taking a lunge around the outside of his team-mate, but then he thought better of it and dutifully slotted in behind.

By the end of the opening lap Hamilton was already 0.4s ahead of Alonso with Felipe Massa's Ferrari leading the pursuit and Nick Heidfeld's BMW-Sauber, Heikki Kovalainen's Renault and Kimi Räikkönen's Ferrari stringing out behind them. Down at the tail of the field the inevitable first-corner mêlée claimed Ralf Schumacher's Toyota, which slithered off the track, bouncing into David Coulthard's Red Bull. New boy Sebastian Vettel's BMW-Sauber went sailing over the grass in avoidance but Vettel regained the circuit without further incident.

Unfortunately that first-corner chaos mangled the Honda RA107s of Jenson Button and Rubens Barrichello, the Brazilian limping straight to the pits, where his car was immediately retired with a broken wishbone and push-rod. Even more frustratingly, in his efforts to avoid Schumacher's Toyota, Barrichello had managed to bounce his car into Button's machine, the impact immediately taking the edge off the surviving Honda's performance. Coulthard was also out on the spot, with a fractured oil cooler on his Red Bull.

'I think it was just an unlucky first-corner racing incident,' shrugged a philosophical Barrichello. 'I tried to avoid a spinning Ralf and unfortunately hit two cars, one of which was Jenson's. The contact broke my front suspension and that was it for me today.'

For his part, Button was left with fairly extensive damage to the front of his car, the right-hand side pod and the aerodynamic 'flick up' and this inevitably compromised its aerodynamic performance. He was running a one-stop strategy in a bid to salvage something worthwhile from his lowly grid position but during the stop the team suffered a fuel rig relief-valve failure that caused him to receive 15 kg too much fuel, much to the detriment of his lap times in the second half of the race. He eventually limped home an inconsequential 12th.

Giancarlo Fisichella's similar one-stop strategy was also badly compromised, by a mistake on the second lap: he spun his Renault R27 going into Turn Four, dropping from eighth to 19th. It was certainly a missed opportunity, for he reckoned that otherwise he could have taken sixth place at the very least. That early mistake put the pressure on Heikki Kovalainen to do battle for the reigning constructors' champion and he certainly rose to the occasion when the pressure was on.

The McLarens were clearly the class of the field and, with Hamilton again driving at the absolute peak of his form, Alonso could do little more than follow in his team-mate's wheeltracks and hope that the 22-year-old might make a crucial slip and enable him to seize the initiative. Yet the fact that Hamilton was racing for the first time at Indianapolis in no way flustered

his composure and he continued to reel off the laps with metronomic consistency.

In third place Felipe Massa had a good run and led team-mate Kimi Räikkönen by 2.58s at the chequered flag, though Räikkönen closed the gap during the final stint by running the softer of the two Bridgestone tyres.

'Yeah, there was big pressure,' said Massa, coyly not revealing the detail of the different tyre choice – which was freely available from Bridgestone anyway. 'Kimi was on different tyres from mine and for sure he had better grip, better track grip as well at the end of the race. So he was able to close the gap. But for sure, you know, I did a good start; he didn't.'

Massa admitted that on this occasion there was precious little prospect of the Ferraris' beating the McLarens in a straight fight. 'In the first stint maybe I was a bit closer, but they were pulling away slowly, lap by lap,' he said. 'So they just created the gap – especially Lewis, who was going away quite quickly. And I just couldn't push my car sufficiently because it was sliding around so much. So for sure it would have been quite difficult for us to beat them today. But it's good to finish third and fourth.'

Hamilton had built up a 3.5s lead by the time he came in for his first refuelling stop with 21 of the 73 laps completed.

Above: **Jarno Trulli earned Toyota a strong sixth place, much more respectable a result than the meaningless 2005 pole, which never mattered because the Michelin runners pulled out after the formation lap.**
Photograph: Peter J Fox/www.crash.net

**Right:** Heikki Kovalainen enjoyed his second successive points finish, a strong fourth place at the Speedway emphasising that he was finding his feet as an F1 contender.

**Below:** Mark Webber finally notched up some points for Red Bull with seventh.

**Centre:** No doubt about the allegiances of this supporter.

**Below right:** Well, if so, he'll be enjoying his commission on the McLaren deal!

**Bottom:** Sebastian Vettel did an excellent job to finish eighth on his GP début subbing for Robert Kubica, who was not permitted by the medical officials to compete at Indy.

Photographs: Peter J Fox/www.crash.net

SATO OWNS ALONSO

Alonso stopped next time around, but when the race settled down again Lewis was just over a second ahead of the hapless Alonso.

Then suddenly it seemed as though Hamilton was in trouble. Slowed in traffic, he found that Alonso was coming back at him. Out of the last banked corner on lap 38, the world champion slipstreamed up onto Hamilton's tail and moved to surge past, only for the young British driver to swerve across and keep him boxed out.

'There was pressure all the way,' said Hamilton later. 'I think in the first stint, the first couple of laps, it was extremely close and then obviously I managed to pull out a slight gap, but going into the middle stint the first two laps were very good and then my tyres just decided to grain. Maybe I pushed a little too hard on them a little too soon, so immediately Fernando was right on my tail and it was extremely difficult.

'Obviously he was in my slipstream the whole time, so he would always catch me down the straight, so whatever I made up on the infield I lost there. It was very, very tough.'

From then on Hamilton kept the upper hand through the second round of refuelling stops and all the way to the chequered flag, the two McLarens crossing the finishing line a few lengths apart after a totally dominant display of technical firepower and driving excellence.

Alonso was obviously frustrated by the experience but at least consoled himself with the fact that this was his first podium finish at the American circuit.

'I didn't win but I finally managed to leave Indianapolis with a trophy,' he smiled after it was all over. 'I think the race was decided after the first corner and I didn't manage to get past. All I could do was stay as close to Lewis as possible. We were side by side on one occasion but it was all fair and square and it was good racing.'

Farther back, Kovalainen drove a fine race, leaping ahead of Räikkönen as the pack accelerated away from the grid and staying ahead of his fellow Finn up to the first round of refuelling stops, by which time Heikki was actually leading the race as he peeled off into the pit lane. Switching to the super-soft Bridgestone tyre for the middle stint proved not to be the answer and he was jumped by Nick Heidfeld in the BMW-Sauber and Räikkönen as he rejoined the circuit.

'I tried to pass Nick on the way into Turn Four,' he said later, 'but I couldn't make it stick and the tyres started graining as I was sliding around in the slipstream. But I kept pushing him and when he retired it was just a question of pushing the car and keeping the lap times consistent.'

The first sign of trouble for Heidfeld came when he braked for the first turn only to have his BMW-Sauber's rear wheels momentarily lock up and pitch him into a spin. 'When I wanted to get going again I couldn't get a gear, which is why Kovalainen was able to pass me,' explained Nick. 'The spin caused a flat-spotted tyre and I made my first pit stop a little early. After the second stop I got stuck behind Mark Webber but then the hydraulic problems occurred anyway.'

Leaking hydraulic fluid eventually caused Nick Heidfeld's retirement after 55 laps, indirectly helping new boy Vettel through to score a point on his F1 début with eighth place behind Jarno Trulli's Toyota and Mark Webber's Red Bull.

'It was fantastic – a lot of fun, but a much longer race than I ever imagined it to be,' grinned Vettel. 'The car was working well and I could have been quicker, but I was often stuck in traffic. And it is extremely difficult to pass here because the other guys know how to defend.'

Webber was pleased with the performance of his Red Bull-Renault, the team's sole representative in the thick of the battle after Coulthard checked out at the first corner. 'The race for me was pretty much a scrap with Jarno from start to finish,' he enthused. 'I would have liked slightly better car balance in the middle stint, but it's certainly good to get those two points in the bag.'

Giancarlo Fisichella was the first finisher to be lapped, in ninth place ahead of Alex Wurz's Williams FW29, his one-stop refuelling strategy compromised by his being boxed in behind Vitantonio Liuzzi's Toro Rosso early in the race. Team-mate Nico Rosberg looked as though he was on course for sixth place, also on a one-stop strategy, but his car suffered an oil

leak and subsequent engine failure that cruelly sidelined him five laps from the chequered flag.

Anthony Davidson's Super Aguri convincingly pipped Button's Honda for 11th and Scott Speed's Toro Rosso was two laps down in 13th ahead of the Spyker-Ferraris of Adrian Sutil and Christijan Albers. Rosberg was classified 16th and Liuzzi last, having battled severe rear-tyre wear for most of the race before being called in to retire with water-pressure problems just five laps from the finish.

Overwhelmingly, the day had belonged to Lewis Hamilton. In the period of one week he had notched up no fewer than 20 world championship points, dramatically strengthening his prospects of winning the F1 world championship in his first season. Yet you could see by the introspective expression on Alonso's face that this was one race victory he should really have prised from Hamilton's grasp. In that respect, the race beneath the long shadows of those legendary Indianapolis grandstands provided another key pointer over precisely which direction the title battle was moving.

*Alan Henry*

## DIARY

Ferrari denies media speculation that it has targeted Nico Rosberg as a possible replacement for Kimi Räikkönen in the event of Räikkönen's failing to deliver consistently competitive performances over the balance of the season.

F1 continues evaluating the possibility of night racing under lights with a trial at Indianapolis over the grand prix weekend.

Michael Schumacher is tipped to make a competitive return to the cockpit in the all-star Race of Champions, which is scheduled to be held at Wembley stadium on 16 December. The event was previously run at the Stade de France in Paris.

## FERRARI ROCKED BY STEPNEY INVESTIGATION

Photograph: www.crashpa.net

We couldn't have known it at the time, but it was the start of something seismic. The Ferrari F1 team was rocked only days after the US GP by the news that its long-time employee Nigel Stepney (above) was to be the subject of a criminal investigation for so-called 'sabotage' as a result of an ongoing internal investigation. That process went a step further during the course of the week and Stepney was formally dismissed from his position with the most famous F1 team.

Stepney, who until the end of last year held the key post of race and test team technical manager for Ferrari, was regarded as a major contributor to the élite group of personnel who helped Michael Schumacher win five of his record seven world championships while driving for the Scuderia. The investigation into his behaviour came only a few months after two former Ferrari employees were found guilty of passing aerodynamic information to F1 rival Toyota.

The suggestion was that the British engineer somehow sought to contaminate the oil systems of the F2007s driven by Kimi Räikkönen and Felipe Massa ahead of the Monaco Grand Prix. Stepney said he would be vindicated by any legal action that might follow.

To many F1 insiders, the whole thing sounded utterly baffling. On the one hand, why would Stepney jeopardise his £750,000 annual salary by getting involved in a half-baked escapade that would look out of place in a child's magazine, so absurd did it appear? On the other hand, why would Ferrari take such extreme action if it weren't pretty sure of its position? The F1 community awaited the outcome of the legal case in a mood of fascinated disbelief.

'Ferrari has taken action against Nigel Stepney and there is now an investigation,' said a company spokesman on the Thursday after Indianapolis, declining to elaborate further.

Sources close to the team indicated that the Modena district attorney had launched a criminal investigation after receiving Ferrari's complaint with accompanying documents. A public defence lawyer was appointed to represent Stepney in the investigation in his absence.

Stepney worked with Ayrton Senna at Lotus in the 1980s and then moved to Benetton before being head-hunted by Ferrari a decade ago. A loyal disciple of respected technical director Ross Brawn, he was moved to a new factory-based role at the start of the season after his request to follow Brawn into a year's sabbatical was refused.

Speaking to *Autosport* magazine earlier in 2007, he had said, 'I am looking at spending a year away from Ferrari. I'm not happy with the situation within the team – I really want to move forward with my career and that's something that's not happening right now.

'Ideally, I'd like to move into a new environment here at Ferrari – but if an opportunity arose with another team, I would definitely consider it.'

# UNITED STATES GRAND PRIX

INDIANAPOLIS 15–17 JUNE 2007

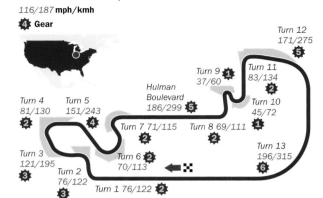

**INDIANAPOLIS MOTOR SPEEDWAY, INDIANAPOLIS**

Circuit: 2.605 miles/4.192 km

*116/187* mph/kmh

🔧 Gear

Turn 12 171/275

Turn 11 83/134

Turn 9 37/60

Turn 10 45/72

Turn 4 81/130

Turn 5 151/243

Hulman Boulevard 186/299

Turn 7 71/115

Turn 8 69/111

Turn 13 196/315

Turn 3 121/195

Turn 6 70/113

Turn 2 76/122

Turn 1 76/122

Photograph: Peter Nygaard/GP Photo

## RACE RESULTS

| Pos. | Driver | Nat. | No. | Entrant | Car/Engine | Tyres | Laps | Time/Retirement | Speed (mph/km/h) | Gap to leader | Fastest race lap | |
|---|---|---|---|---|---|---|---|---|---|---|---|---|
| 1 | Lewis Hamilton | GB | 2 | Vodafone McLaren Mercedes | McLaren MP4-22-Mercedes FO 108T V8 | B | 73 | 1h 31m 9.965s | 125.145/201.401 | | 1m 13.222s | 20 |
| 2 | Fernando Alonso | E | 1 | Vodafone McLaren Mercedes | McLaren MP4-22-Mercedes FO 108T V8 | B | 73 | 1h 31m 11.483s | 125.110/201.345 | + 1.518s | 1m 13.257s | 21 |
| 3 | Felipe Massa | BR | 5 | Scuderia Ferrari Marlboro | Ferrari F2007-056 V8 | B | 73 | 1h 31m 22.807s | 124.851/200.929 | + 12.842s | 1m 13.380s | 50 |
| 4 | Kimi Räikkönen | FIN | 6 | Scuderia Ferrari Marlboro | Ferrari F2007-056 V8 | B | 73 | 1h 31m 25.387s | 124.792/200.834 | + 15.422s | 1m 13.117s | 49 |
| 5 | Heikki Kovalainen | FIN | 4 | ING Renault F1 Team | Renault R27-RS27 V8 | B | 73 | 1h 31m 51.367s | 124.205/199.888 | + 41.402s | 1m 13.998s | 67 |
| 6 | Jarno Trulli | I | 12 | Panasonic Toyota Racing | Toyota TF107-RVX-07 V8 | B | 73 | 1h 32m 16.668s | 123.637/198.974 | +1m 6.703s | 1m 14.016s | 30 |
| 7 | Mark Webber | AUS | 15 | Red Bull Racing | Red Bull RB3-Renault RS27 V8 | B | 73 | 1h 32m 17.296s | 123.623/198.952 | +1m 7.331s | 1m 14.004s | 57 |
| 8 | Sebastian Vettel | D | 10 | BMW Sauber F1 Team | BMW Sauber F1.07-BMW P86/7 V8 | B | 73 | 1h 32m 17.748s | 123.613/198.936 | + 1m 7.783s | 1m 13.862s | 53 |
| 9 | Giancarlo Fisichella | I | 3 | ING Renault F1 Team | Renault R27-RS27 V8 | B | 72 | | | + 1 lap | 1m 14.009s | 67 |
| 10 | Alexander Wurz | A | 17 | AT&T Williams | Williams FW29-Toyota RVX-07 V8 | B | 72 | | | + 1 lap | 1m 14.486s | 41 |
| 11 | Anthony Davidson | GB | 23 | Super Aguri F1 Team | Super Aguri SA07-Honda RA807E V8 | B | 72 | | | + 1 lap | 1m 14.066s | 55 |
| 12 | Jenson Button | GB | 7 | Honda Racing F1 Team | Honda RA107-RA807E V8 | B | 72 | | | + 1 lap | 1m 14.703s | 42 |
| 13 | Scott Speed | USA | 19 | Scuderia Toro Rosso | Toro Rosso STR02-Ferrari 056H V8 | B | 71 | | | + 2 laps | 1m 15.092s | 66 |
| 14 | Adrian Sutil | D | 20 | Etihad Aldar Spyker F1 Team | Spyker F8-VII-Ferrari 056H V8 | B | 71 | | | + 2 laps | 1m 14.858s | 49 |
| 15 | Christijan Albers | NL | 21 | Etihad Aldar Spyker F1 Team | Spyker F8-VII-Ferrari 056H V8 | B | 70 | | | + 3 laps | 1m 15.902s | 65 |
| 16 | Nico Rosberg | D | 16 | AT&T Williams | Williams FW29-Toyota RVX-07 V8 | B | 68 | Oil leak/fire | | + 5 laps | 1m 14.066s | 34 |
| 17 | Vitantonio Liuzzi | I | 18 | Scuderia Toro Rosso | Toro Rosso STR02-Ferrari 056H V8 | B | 68 | Water pressure | | + 5 laps | 1m 15.426s | 64 |
| | Nick Heidfeld | D | 9 | BMW Sauber F1 Team | BMW Sauber F1.07-BMW P86/7 V8 | B | 55 | Hydraulic leak | | | 1m 13.414s | 20 |
| | Takuma Sato | J | 22 | Super Aguri F1 Team | Super Aguri SA07-Honda RA807E V8 | B | 13 | Spin | | | 1m 16.680s | 8 |
| | David Coulthard | GB | 14 | Red Bull Racing | Red Bull RB3-Renault RS27 V8 | B | 0 | Accident/oil cooler | | | No time | – |
| | Ralf Schumacher | D | 11 | Panasonic Toyota Racing | Toyota TF107-RVX-07 V8 | B | 0 | Accident | | | No time | – |
| | Rubens Barrichello | BR | 8 | Honda Racing F1 Team | Honda RA107-RA807E V8 | B | 0 | Accident/suspension | | | No time | – |

**Fastest race lap:** Kimi Räikkönen on lap 49, 1m 13.117s, 128.250 mph/206.397 km/h.

**Lap record:** Rubens Barrichello (Ferrari F2004 V10), 1m 10.399s, 133.201 mph/214.366 km/h (2004).

All results and data © FOM 2007

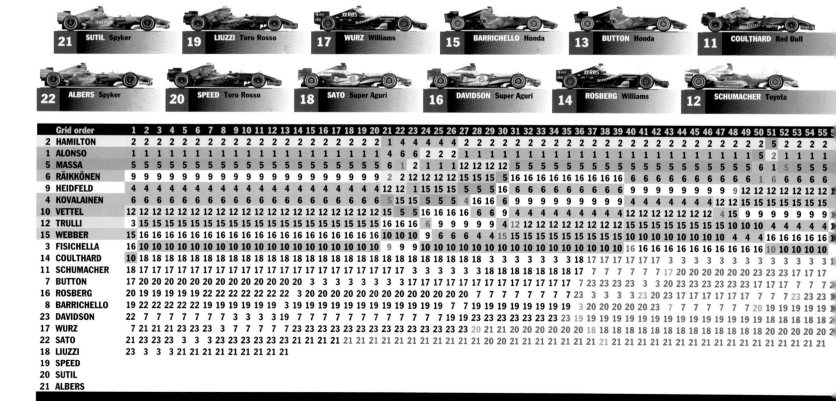

| 21 | SUTIL Spyker | 19 | LIUZZI Toro Rosso | 17 | WURZ Williams | 15 | BARRICHELLO Honda | 13 | BUTTON Honda | 11 | COULTHARD Red Bull |
| 22 | ALBERS Spyker | 20 | SPEED Toro Rosso | 18 | SATO Super Aguri | 16 | DAVIDSON Super Aguri | 14 | ROSBERG Williams | 12 | SCHUMACHER Toyota |

| Grid order | 1 | 2 | 3 | 4 | 5 | 6 | 7 | 8 | 9 | 10 | 11 | 12 | 13 | 14 | 15 | 16 | 17 | 18 | 19 | 20 | 21 | 22 | 23 | 24 | 25 | 26 | 27 | 28 | 29 | 30 | 31 | 32 | 33 | 34 | 35 | 36 | 37 | 38 | 39 | 40 | 41 | 42 | 43 | 44 | 45 | 46 | 47 | 48 | 49 | 50 | 51 | 52 | 53 | 54 | 55 |
|---|---|---|---|---|---|---|---|---|---|---|---|---|---|---|---|---|---|---|---|---|---|---|---|---|---|---|---|---|---|---|---|---|---|---|---|---|---|---|---|---|---|---|---|---|---|---|---|---|---|---|---|---|---|---|---|
| **2 HAMILTON** | 2 | 2 | 2 | 2 | 2 | 2 | 2 | 2 | 2 | 2 | 2 | 2 | 2 | 2 | 2 | 2 | 2 | 2 | 2 | 2 | 2 | 1 | 4 | 4 | 4 | 4 | 2 | 2 | 2 | 2 | 2 | 2 | 2 | 2 | 2 | 2 | 2 | 2 | 2 | 2 | 2 | 2 | 2 | 2 | 2 | 2 | 2 | 2 | 2 | 5 | 2 | 2 | 2 | 2 | |
| **1 ALONSO** | 1 | 1 | 1 | 1 | 1 | 1 | 1 | 1 | 1 | 1 | 1 | 1 | 1 | 1 | 1 | 1 | 1 | 1 | 1 | 1 | 1 | 4 | 6 | 2 | 2 | 2 | 1 | 1 | 1 | 1 | 1 | 1 | 1 | 1 | 1 | 1 | 1 | 1 | 1 | 1 | 1 | 1 | 1 | 1 | 1 | 1 | 1 | 1 | 5 | 2 | 1 | 1 | 1 | 1 | |
| **5 MASSA** | 5 | 5 | 5 | 5 | 5 | 5 | 5 | 5 | 5 | 5 | 5 | 5 | 5 | 5 | 5 | 5 | 5 | 5 | 5 | 5 | 5 | 6 | 1 | 2 | 1 | 1 | 12 | 12 | 12 | 12 | 5 | 5 | 5 | 5 | 5 | 5 | 5 | 5 | 5 | 5 | 5 | 5 | 5 | 5 | 5 | 5 | 5 | 5 | 1 | 1 | 5 | 5 | 5 | 5 | |
| **6 RÄIKKÖNEN** | 9 | 9 | 9 | 9 | 9 | 9 | 9 | 9 | 9 | 9 | 9 | 9 | 9 | 9 | 9 | 9 | 9 | 9 | 9 | 9 | 9 | 2 | 2 | 12 | 12 | 12 | 15 | 15 | 15 | 5 | 16 | 16 | 16 | 16 | 16 | 16 | 16 | 16 | 6 | 6 | 6 | 6 | 6 | 6 | 6 | 6 | 6 | 6 | 6 | 6 | 6 | 6 | 6 | 6 | |
| **9 HEIDFELD** | 4 | 4 | 4 | 4 | 4 | 4 | 4 | 4 | 4 | 4 | 4 | 4 | 4 | 4 | 4 | 4 | 4 | 4 | 4 | 4 | 12 | 12 | 1 | 15 | 15 | 15 | 5 | 5 | 16 | 6 | 6 | 6 | 6 | 6 | 6 | 6 | 9 | 9 | 9 | 9 | 9 | 9 | 9 | 9 | 12 | 12 | 12 | 12 | 12 | 12 | |
| **4 KOVALAINEN** | 6 | 6 | 6 | 6 | 6 | 6 | 6 | 6 | 6 | 6 | 6 | 6 | 6 | 6 | 6 | 6 | 6 | 6 | 6 | 6 | 5 | 15 | 15 | 5 | 5 | 5 | 4 | 16 | 16 | 9 | 9 | 9 | 9 | 9 | 9 | 9 | 4 | 4 | 4 | 4 | 4 | 4 | 12 | 15 | 15 | 15 | 15 | 15 | 15 | 15 | |
| **10 VETTEL** | 12 | 12 | 12 | 12 | 12 | 12 | 12 | 12 | 12 | 12 | 12 | 12 | 12 | 12 | 12 | 12 | 12 | 12 | 12 | 15 | 5 | 5 | 16 | 16 | 16 | 16 | 6 | 6 | 9 | 4 | 4 | 4 | 4 | 4 | 4 | 12 | 12 | 12 | 12 | 12 | 4 | 15 | 9 | 9 | 9 | 9 | 9 | 9 | |
| **12 TRULLI** | 15 | 15 | 15 | 15 | 15 | 15 | 15 | 15 | 15 | 15 | 15 | 15 | 15 | 15 | 15 | 15 | 15 | 15 | 16 | 6 | 9 | 9 | 9 | 9 | 4 | 12 | 12 | 12 | 12 | 12 | 12 | 12 | 12 | 15 | 15 | 15 | 15 | 15 | 10 | 10 | 4 | 4 | 4 | 4 | |
| **15 WEBBER** | 16 | 16 | 16 | 16 | 16 | 16 | 16 | 16 | 16 | 16 | 16 | 16 | 16 | 16 | 16 | 16 | 16 | 16 | 10 | 10 | 6 | 6 | 6 | 4 | 15 | 15 | 15 | 15 | 15 | 15 | 15 | 10 | 10 | 10 | 10 | 4 | 4 | 16 | 16 | 16 | 16 | 16 | |
| **3 FISICHELLA** | 16 | 10 | 10 | 10 | 10 | 10 | 10 | 10 | 10 | 10 | 10 | 10 | 10 | 10 | 10 | 10 | 10 | 10 | 9 | 9 | 10 | 10 | 10 | 10 | 10 | 10 | 10 | 10 | 10 | 10 | 16 | 16 | 16 | 16 | 16 | 16 | 16 | 16 | 10 | 10 | 10 | 10 | |
| **14 COULTHARD** | 10 | 18 | 18 | 18 | 18 | 18 | 18 | 18 | 18 | 18 | 18 | 18 | 18 | 18 | 18 | 18 | 18 | 18 | 3 | 3 | 3 | 3 | 3 | 18 | 17 | 17 | 17 | 17 | 17 | 3 | 3 | 3 | 3 | 3 | 3 | 3 | 3 | 3 | 3 | |
| **11 SCHUMACHER** | 17 | 17 | 17 | 17 | 17 | 17 | 17 | 17 | 17 | 17 | 17 | 17 | 17 | 17 | 17 | 17 | 3 | 3 | 18 | 18 | 18 | 18 | 18 | 7 | 7 | 7 | 7 | 7 | 17 | 20 | 20 | 20 | 20 | 23 | 23 | 17 | 17 | 17 | |
| **7 BUTTON** | 20 | 20 | 20 | 20 | 19 | 19 | 22 | 22 | 22 | 22 | 3 | 20 | 20 | 20 | 20 | 20 | 7 | 7 | 17 | 17 | 17 | 7 | 23 | 23 | 23 | 23 | 17 | 17 | 7 | 7 | 7 | 2 | |
| **16 ROSBERG** | 20 | 19 | 19 | 19 | 22 | 22 | 22 | 3 | 20 | 20 | 20 | 20 | 20 | 7 | 7 | 7 | 7 | 23 | 3 | 20 | 20 | 20 | 23 | 7 | 7 | 7 | 7 | 7 | 20 | 19 | 19 | 19 | 19 | 1 | |
| **8 BARRICHELLO** | 19 | 22 | 22 | 22 | 3 | 19 | 19 | 19 | 19 | 19 | 19 | 19 | 19 | 19 | 19 | 3 | 20 | 20 | 20 | 23 | 7 | 7 | 7 | 7 | 7 | 20 | 19 | 19 | 19 | 19 | 1 | |
| **23 DAVIDSON** | 22 | 7 | 7 | 7 | 7 | 7 | 7 | 3 | 3 | 3 | 19 | 7 | 7 | 7 | 7 | 23 | 23 | 23 | 19 | 19 | 19 | 19 | 19 | 19 | 19 | 19 | 19 | 18 | 18 | 18 | 18 | |
| **17 WURZ** | 7 | 21 | 21 | 21 | 23 | 23 | 23 | 3 | 7 | 7 | 7 | 7 | 23 | 23 | 23 | 21 | 21 | 20 | 20 | 20 | 20 | 20 | 18 | 18 | 18 | 18 | 18 | 18 | 18 | 18 | 20 | 20 | 20 | 20 | |
| **22 SATO** | 21 | 23 | 23 | 23 | 3 | 3 | 3 | 23 | 23 | 23 | 23 | 23 | 21 | 21 | 21 | 7 | 21 | 21 | 21 | 21 | 21 | 21 | 21 | 21 | 21 | 21 | 21 | 21 | 21 | 21 | 21 | 21 | 21 | 21 | |
| **18 LIUZZI** | 23 | 3 | 3 | 3 | 21 | 21 | 21 | 21 | 21 | 21 | | | | | | | | | | | | | | | | | | | | | | | | | |
| **19 SPEED** | | | | | | | | | | | | | | | | | | | | | | | | | | | | | | | | | | | |
| **20 SUTIL** | | | | | | | | | | | | | | | | | | | | | | | | | | | | | | | | | | | |
| **21 ALBERS** | | | | | | | | | | | | | | | | | | | | | | | | | | | | | | | | | | | |

## TIME SHEETS

### PRACTICE 1 (FRIDAY)

Hazy sunshine (track 28–36ºC, air 23–25ºC)

| Pos. | Driver | Laps | Time |
|---|---|---|---|
| 1 | Fernando Alonso | 16 | 1m 11.925s |
| 2 | Nick Heidfeld | 24 | 1m 12.391s |
| 3 | Lewis Hamilton | 21 | 1m 12.628s |
| 4 | Sebastian Vettel | 33 | 1m 12.869s |
| 5 | Kimi Räikkönen | 21 | 1m 12.966s |
| 6 | Nico Rosberg | 24 | 1m 13.020s |
| 7 | Felipe Massa | 22 | 1m 13.040s |
| 8 | David Coulthard | 22 | 1m 13.159s |
| 9 | Jenson Button | 23 | 1m 13.597s |
| 10 | Mark Webber | 26 | 1m 13.682s |
| 11 | Jarno Trulli | 32 | 1m 13.777s |
| 12 | Kazuki Nakajima | 27 | 1m 13.786s |
| 13 | Ralf Schumacher | 27 | 1m 13.819s |
| 14 | Vitantonio Liuzzi | 28 | 1m 13.907s |
| 15 | Scott Speed | 24 | 1m 13.990s |
| 16 | Giancarlo Fisichella | 19 | 1m 14.000s |
| 17 | Takuma Sato | 20 | 1m 14.037s |
| 18 | Rubens Barrichello | 23 | 1m 14.052s |
| 19 | Heikki Kovalainen | 18 | 1m 14.189s |
| 20 | Anthony Davidson | 10 | 1m 14.632s |
| 21 | Christijan Albers | 28 | 1m 14.636s |
| 22 | Adrian Sutil | 27 | 1m 14.810s |

### PRACTICE 2 (FRIDAY)

Sunny (track 43–46ºC, air 30–31ºC)

| Pos. | Driver | Laps | Time |
|---|---|---|---|
| 1 | Fernando Alonso | 35 | 1m 12.156s |
| 2 | Lewis Hamilton | 34 | 1m 12.309s |
| 3 | Felipe Massa | 36 | 1m 12.435s |
| 4 | Kimi Räikkönen | 38 | 1m 12.587s |
| 5 | Nick Heidfeld | 43 | 1m 13.026s |
| 6 | David Coulthard | 41 | 1m 13.042s |
| 7 | Nico Rosberg | 35 | 1m 13.057s |
| 8 | Heikki Kovalainen | 48 | 1m 13.110s |
| 9 | Rubens Barrichello | 40 | 1m 13.144s |
| 10 | Jenson Button | 46 | 1m 13.202s |
| 11 | Sebastian Vettel | 50 | 1m 13.217s |
| 12 | Mark Webber | 21 | 1m 13.263s |
| 13 | Vitantonio Liuzzi | 41 | 1m 13.332s |
| 14 | Anthony Davidson | 46 | 1m 13.364s |
| 15 | Giancarlo Fisichella | 44 | 1m 13.394s |
| 16 | Alexander Wurz | 29 | 1m 13.539s |
| 17 | Jarno Trulli | 42 | 1m 13.692s |
| 18 | Scott Speed | 34 | 1m 13.712s |
| 19 | Takuma Sato | 46 | 1m 13.753s |
| 20 | Ralf Schumacher | 39 | 1m 13.765s |
| 21 | Christijan Albers | 30 | 1m 14.225s |
| 22 | Adrian Sutil | 33 | 1m 14.513s |

### QUALIFYING (SATURDAY)

Sunny, scattered cloud, breezy (track 45–47ºC, air 31–32ºC)

| Pos. | Driver | First | Second | Third |
|---|---|---|---|---|
| 1 | Lewis Hamilton | 1m 12.563s | 1m 12.065s | 1m 12.331s |
| 2 | Fernando Alonso | 1m 12.416s | 1m 11.926s | 1m 12.500s |
| 3 | Felipe Massa | 1m 12.731s | 1m 12.180s | 1m 12.703s |
| 4 | Kimi Räikkönen | 1m 12.732s | 1m 12.111s | 1m 12.839s |
| 5 | Nick Heidfeld | 1m 12.543s | 1m 12.188s | 1m 12.847s |
| 6 | Heikki Kovalainen | 1m 12.998s | 1m 12.599s | 1m 13.308s |
| 7 | Sebastian Vettel | 1m 12.711s | 1m 12.644s | 1m 13.513s |
| 8 | Jarno Trulli | 1m 13.186s | 1m 12.828s | 1m 13.789s |
| 9 | Mark Webber | 1m 13.425s | 1m 12.788s | 1m 13.871s |
| 10 | Giancarlo Fisichella | 1m 13.168s | 1m 12.603s | 1m 13.953s |
| 11 | David Coulthard | 1m 13.424s | 1m 12.873s | |
| 12 | Ralf Schumacher | 1m 12.851s | 1m 12.920s | |
| 13 | Jenson Button | 1m 13.306s | 1m 12.998s | |
| 14 | Nico Rosberg | 1m 13.128s | 1m 13.060s | |
| 15 | Rubens Barrichello | 1m 13.203s | 1m 13.201s | |
| 16 | Anthony Davidson | 1m 13.164s | 1m 13.259s | |
| 17 | Alexander Wurz | 1m 13.441s | | |
| 18 | Takuma Sato | 1m 13.477s | | |
| 19 | Vitantonio Liuzzi | 1m 13.484s | | |
| 20 | Scott Speed | 1m 13.712s | | |
| 21 | Adrian Sutil | 1m 14.122s | | |
| 22 | Christijan Albers | 1m 14.597s | | |

### PRACTICE 3 (SATURDAY)

Sunny (track 34–39ºC, air 27–29ºC)

| Pos. | Driver | Laps | Time |
|---|---|---|---|
| 1 | Fernando Alonso | 12 | 1m 12.150s |
| 2 | Sebastian Vettel | 27 | 1m 12.321s |
| 3 | Lewis Hamilton | 14 | 1m 12.378s |
| 4 | Heikki Kovalainen | 21 | 1m 12.574s |
| 5 | Nick Heidfeld | 24 | 1m 12.646s |
| 6 | Kimi Räikkönen | 16 | 1m 12.692s |
| 7 | Felipe Massa | 17 | 1m 12.709s |
| 8 | Giancarlo Fisichella | 20 | 1m 12.710s |
| 9 | David Coulthard | 17 | 1m 12.940s |
| 10 | Nico Rosberg | 18 | 1m 13.031s |
| 11 | Jarno Trulli | 23 | 1m 13.057s |
| 12 | Ralf Schumacher | 23 | 1m 13.061s |
| 13 | Anthony Davidson | 20 | 1m 13.069s |
| 14 | Mark Webber | 14 | 1m 13.289s |
| 15 | Jenson Button | 20 | 1m 13.318s |
| 16 | Vitantonio Liuzzi | 23 | 1m 13.415s |
| 17 | Takuma Sato | 19 | 1m 13.476s |
| 18 | Rubens Barrichello | 17 | 1m 13.573s |
| 19 | Alexander Wurz | 18 | 1m 13.626s |
| 20 | Scott Speed | 18 | 1m 13.979s |
| 21 | Adrian Sutil | 24 | 1m 14.142s |
| 22 | Christijan Albers | 24 | 1m 14.402s |

### RACE TYRE STRATEGIES

BRIDGESTONE

In 2007, the tyre regulations stipulate that the two dry-tyre specifications must be visibly distinguishable from each other. At the United States Grand Prix, the soft compound Bridgestone Potenza tyre was marked with a white line in the second-from-inside groove.

| | Driver | Race stint 1 | Race stint 2 | Race stint 3 |
|---|---|---|---|---|
| 1 | Lewis Hamilton | Soft: laps 1–21 | Soft: 22–51 | Medium: 52–73 |
| 2 | Fernando Alonso | Soft: 1–22 | Soft: 23–50 | Medium: 51–73 |
| 3 | Felipe Massa | Soft: 1–21 | Soft: 22–52 | Medium: 53–73 |
| 4 | Kimi Räikkönen | Medium: 1–24 | Soft: 25–51 | Soft: 52–73 |
| 5 | Heikki Kovalainen | Soft: 1–27 | Soft: 28–47 | Medium: 48–73 |
| 6 | Jarno Trulli | Soft: 1–31 | Soft: 32–56 | Medium: 57–73 |
| 7 | Mark Webber | Soft: 1–30 | Soft: 31–59 | Medium: 60–73 |
| 8 | Sebastian Vettel | Soft: 1–24 | Soft: 25–51 | Medium: 52–73 |
| 9 | Giancarlo Fisichella | Soft: 1–36 | Medium: 37–72 | |
| 10 | Alexander Wurz | Soft: 1–43 | Medium: 44–72 | |
| 11 | Anthony Davidson | Medium: 1–41 | Soft: 42–53 | Soft: 54–72 |
| 12 | Jenson Button | Soft: 1–43 | Medium: 44–72 | |
| 13 | Scott Speed | Soft: 1–36 | Medium: 37–71 | |
| 14 | Adrian Sutil | Medium: 1–28 | Soft: 29–50 | Soft: 51–71 |
| 15 | Christijan Albers | Medium: 1–38 | Soft: 39–70 | |
| 16 | Nico Rosberg | Soft: 1–40 | Medium: 41–68 (DNF) | |
| 17 | Vitantonio Liuzzi | Medium: 1–37 | Soft: 38–68 (DNF) | |
| | Nick Heidfeld | Soft: 1–21 | Medium: 22–48 | Medium: 49–55 (DNF) |
| | Takuma Sato | Soft: 1–13 (DNF) | | |
| | David Coulthard | Soft: 0 (DNF) | | |
| | Ralf Schumacher | Soft: 0 (DNF) | | |
| | Rubens Barrichello | Soft: 0 (DNF) | | |

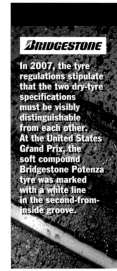

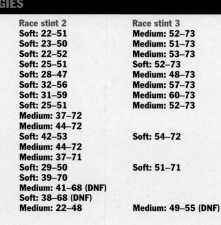

9 WEBBER Red Bull

7 VETTEL BMW-Sauber

5 HEIDFELD BMW-Sauber

3 MASSA Ferrari

1 HAMILTON McLaren

10 FISICHELLA Renault

8 TRULLI Toyota

6 KOVALAINEN Renault

4 RÄIKKÖNEN Ferrari

2 ALONSO McLaren

**RACE DISTANCE:**
73 laps
190.150 miles/306.016 km

**RACE WEATHER:**
Sunny, scattered cloud, track 45–46ºC, air 34–36ºC

### Lap chart

| 57 | 58 | 59 | 60 | 61 | 62 | 63 | 64 | 65 | 66 | 67 | 68 | 69 | 70 | 71 | 72 | 73 | |
|---|---|---|---|---|---|---|---|---|---|---|---|---|---|---|---|---|---|
| 2 | 2 | 2 | 2 | 2 | 2 | 2 | 2 | 2 | 2 | 2 | 2 | 2 | 2 | 2 | 2 | 1 | |
| 1 | 1 | 1 | 1 | 1 | 1 | 1 | 1 | 1 | 1 | 1 | 1 | 1 | 1 | 1 | 1 | 2 | |
| 5 | 5 | 5 | 5 | 5 | 5 | 5 | 5 | 5 | 5 | 5 | 5 | 5 | 5 | 5 | 5 | 3 | |
| 6 | 6 | 6 | 6 | 6 | 6 | 6 | 6 | 6 | 6 | 6 | 6 | 6 | 6 | 6 | 6 | 4 | |
| 15 | 15 | 4 | 4 | 4 | 4 | 4 | 4 | 4 | 4 | 4 | 4 | 4 | 4 | 4 | 4 | 5 | |
| 4 | 4 | 15 | 16 | 16 | 16 | 16 | 16 | 16 | 16 | 16 | 12 | 12 | 12 | 12 | 12 | 6 | |
| 16 | 16 | 12 | 12 | 12 | 12 | 12 | 12 | 12 | 12 | 15 | 15 | 15 | 15 | 15 | 15 | 7 | |
| 12 | 12 | 15 | 15 | 15 | 15 | 15 | 15 | 15 | 15 | 10 | 10 | 10 | 10 | 10 | 10 | 8 | |
| 10 | 10 | 10 | 10 | 10 | 10 | 10 | 10 | 10 | 10 | 3 | 3 | 3 | 3 | | | | |
| 3 | 3 | 3 | 3 | 3 | 3 | 3 | 3 | 3 | 17 | 17 | 17 | 17 | | | | | |
| 17 | 17 | 17 | 17 | 17 | 17 | 17 | 17 | 17 | 23 | 23 | 23 | 23 | | | | | |
| 7 | 7 | 7 | 7 | 7 | 23 | 23 | 23 | 23 | 7 | 7 | 7 | 7 | | | | | |
| 23 | 23 | 23 | 23 | 23 | 7 | 7 | 7 | 7 | 7 | | | | | | | | |
| 19 | 19 | 19 | 19 | 19 | 19 | 19 | 19 | 19 | 20 | 20 | 20 | | | | | | |
| 18 | 18 | 18 | 18 | 18 | 18 | 18 | 18 | 18 | 21 | 21 | | | | | | | |
| 20 | 20 | 20 | 20 | 20 | 20 | 20 | 20 | 20 | | | | | | | | | |
| 21 | 21 | 21 | 21 | 21 | 21 | 21 | 21 | 21 | | | | | | | | | |

20 Pit stop
20 One lap or more behind leader

### FOR THE RECORD

**FIRST GRAND PRIX START:** Sebastian Vettel (above)

**100TH LAP LED:** Lewis Hamilton

**FIRST POINT (YOUNGEST F1 POINT SCORER):** Sebastian Vettel

**FIRST LAP LED:** Heikki Kovalainen

**GERMAN DRIVERS:** 5 (the most since Germany 1953)

### POINTS

**DRIVERS**

| | | |
|---|---|---|
| 1 | Lewis Hamilton | 58 |
| 2 | Fernando Alonso | 58 |
| 3 | Felipe Massa | 39 |
| 4 | Kimi Räikkönen | 32 |
| 5 | Nick Heidfeld | 26 |
| 6 | Giancarlo Fisichella | 13 |
| 7 | Robert Kubica | 12 |
| 8 | Heikki Kovalainen | 12 |
| 9 | Alexander Wurz | 8 |
| 10 | Jarno Trulli | 7 |
| 11 | Nico Rosberg | 5 |
| 12 | David Coulthard | 4 |
| 13 | Takuma Sato | 4 |
| 14 | Ralf Schumacher | 2 |
| 15 | Mark Webber | 2 |
| 16 | Sebastian Vettel | 1 |

**CONSTRUCTORS**

| | | |
|---|---|---|
| 1 | McLaren | 106 |
| 2 | Ferrari | 71 |
| 3 | BMW Sauber | 39 |
| 4 | Renault | 25 |
| 5 | Williams | 13 |
| 6 | Toyota | 9 |
| 7 | Red Bull | 6 |
| 8 | Super Aguri | 4 |

Photographs: Peter J Fox/www.crash.net

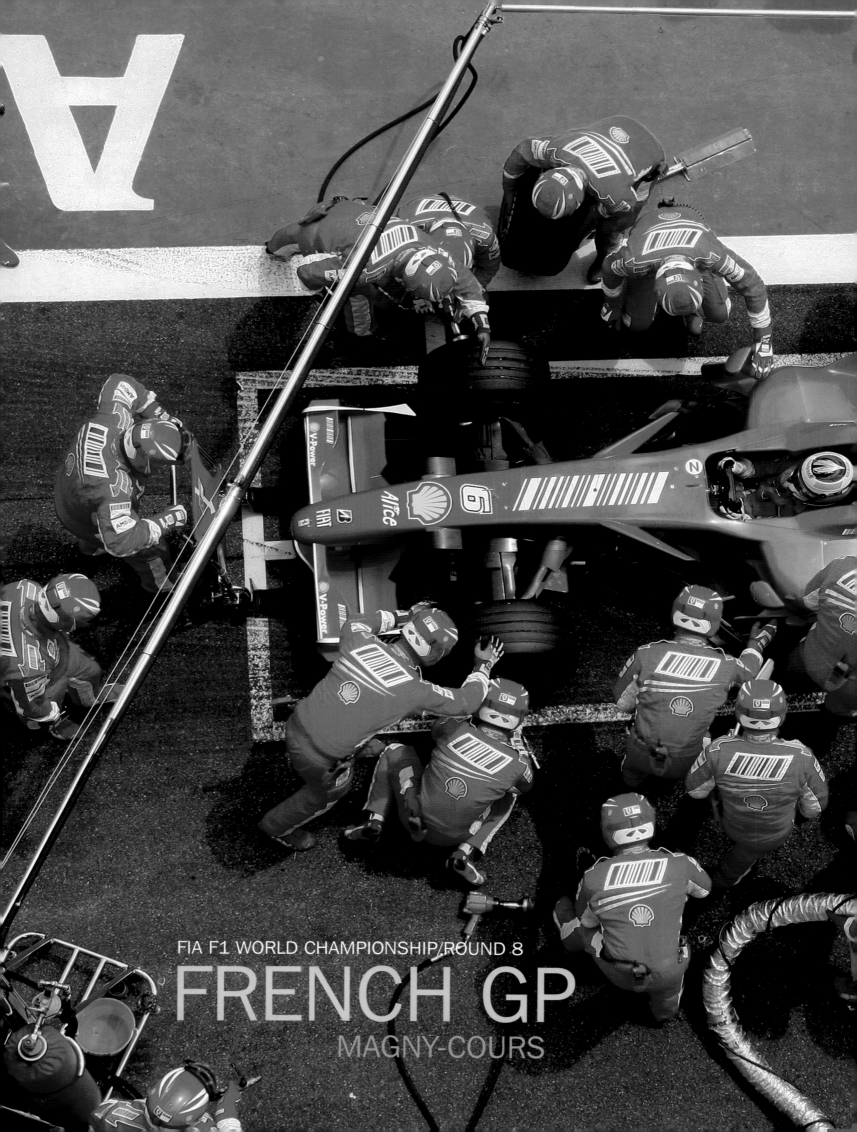

FIA F1 WORLD CHAMPIONSHIP/ROUND 8
# FRENCH GP
MAGNY-COURS

A perfect pit stop for Kimi Räikkönen, who turned the tables on his team-mate Felipe Massa to take victory at Magny-Cours.
Photograph: Peter Nygaard/GP Photo

The long corners of the Circuit de Nevers played to the strengths of the Ferrari F2007 chassis and Felipe Massa and Kimi Räikkönen relished the consequent enhanced grip generated by the higher operating temperatures of their Bridgestone tyres. Both cars had an uprated clutch specification and repairs had been completed on Maranello's F1 wind tunnel, which had suffered a breakage of its rolling road belt just before Barcelona and had been pretty much *hors de combat* ever since.

Come the serious business of qualifying, Fernando Alonso dropped out of contention at the start of the top-ten shoot-out when his McLaren emitted an ominous-looking puff of smoke. The world champion steered straight into the pit lane, shouting over the radio that his engine had failed. In fact, five minutes' detailed investigation established that the gearbox had suffered a massive internal breakage and the car was stranded in its garage for the rest of the day.

Even before qualifying, McLaren Mercedes' well-polished gloss seemed to have been mildly ruffled by technical glitches: Lewis Hamilton's engine shut-down system was activated in Friday's free practice when it detected that the Mercedes V8 was running too cold and a brake sensor problem on Fernando Alonso's car lost him time on Saturday morning.

Alonso thus found himself lining up tenth on the grid, leaving Hamilton (1m 15.104s) to battle the Ferraris alone. The 22-year-old strained every sinew, but Massa just pipped him for pole on 1m 15.034s with Räikkönen (1m 15.257s) grabbing third place ahead of the impressive Robert Kubica's BMW-Sauber (1m 15.493s), the young Pole doing a great job on his return to the cockpit after his horrifying 185-mph accident in the previous month's Canadian Grand Prix.

'The car was pretty sweet for the qualifying session,' said Hamilton. 'It was good enough for pole but I lost a bit of time in Turn 15. I braked a little late and ran a little wide, but still I managed to do a good time. I lost a bit of time, but that's the way the game goes, but I'm very, very happy. I'm on the front row and I believe I have a good strategy for tomorrow, so I'll be very strong.'

In the Ferrari camp, Massa was totally elated. 'On my first try I managed to do quite a good lap,' he said, 'but then it became progressively more difficult to manage any worthwhile improvement. We had a promising test at Silverstone, so that was really encouraging from the moment we accelerated out onto the circuit.'

Räikkönen confessed that his lap felt pretty good but he stood up and took the blame for screwing up the final corner. 'They are never perfect,' he shrugged. 'I lost [it] on one corner on the last try but that was my fault and there's nothing else to complain about.'

Giancarlo Fisichella (1m 15.674s) and Heikki Kovalainen (1m 15.826s) proved the Renault R27s were finally back in business by qualifying fifth and sixth, the team having finally and successfully correlated the aerodynamic qualities of Bridgestone's tyres, registered in the wind tunnel, with its on-track experience.

'The simple answer is that McLaren has done a better job than us in the past year in generating performance developments,' said Bob Bell, Renault's technical director. 'It's no secret that the Bridgestone tyres need a farther-forward weight distribution and thus farther-forward aero balance and, for its own reason, McLaren had already developed in that direction last year while running the Michelin tyres.'

In the Toyota camp Jarno Trulli (1m 15.935s) qualified eighth separated from team-mate Ralf Schumacher (1m 15.534s) by Nico Rosberg's Williams (1m 16.328s) and the hapless Alonso. Jenson Button (1m 15.584s) was 12th ahead of Rubens Barrichello (1m 15.761s), with the Red Bulls of Mark Webber (1m 15.806s) and David Coulthard (no time, apparently due to an oil-pressure issue) behind them.

Scott Speed's Toro Rosso (1m 16.049s) split the two Bulls while Vitantonio Liuzzi (1m 16.142s) was 17th, ahead of Alex Wurz's disappointingly slow Williams (1m 16.241s), no fewer than nine places adrift of the impressive Rosberg.

Yet Wurz would not permit himself to be downcast. 'If you ignore the fact that I was eliminated in the first round, and I'm in 18th place, I'm actually much closer to my team-mate here than I've been at other races and was only one tenth away from making it into Q2.' Well, yes, I suppose we take the point.

## McLAREN ROCKED BY SCANDAL

Only five days before the British GP at Silverstone, McLaren was forced to suspend chief designer Mike Coughlan (below) following allegations from Ferrari that one of its own engineers had leaked crucial technical information to Coughlan.

The 48-year-old British engineer was suspected of illegally collaborating with Ferrari's former race and test team manager Nigel Stepney, who was dismissed after an internal team investigation suggested that he had tried to sabotage the Ferrari F2007s of Kimi Räikkönen and Felipe Massa before the Monaco Grand Prix by putting damaging additives into the cars' lubrication systems.

In a search carried out at Coughlan's house near the McLaren headquarters, documents allegedly belonging to Ferrari were discovered, immediately leading to McLaren's decision to suspend him. Ferrari applied for the search warrant through the British courts, in a parallel process to the investigation of Stepney, and said it reserved the right to take further legal action.

It was a highly embarrassing development for McLaren and looked certain to take the gloss off Lewis Hamilton's efforts to win the British GP at his first attempt. It seemed inevitable that Ferrari would revel in McLaren's discomfort, although there was no hint from Ferrari that it believed McLaren to be in any way complicit in Coughlan's alleged wrongdoing.

'We have proof that Stepney had been supplying technical information to a McLaren employee and we found evidence of that fact in his [Coughlan's] home,' said a spokesman for Ferrari, who would not identify Coughlan as the culprit. 'This is a very serious situation. We are talking about a lot of information being given to a prominent McLaren engineer. We are not talking here about rumours or speculation.'

McLaren confirmed that a member of its staff was being investigated by Ferrari for possibly having obtained technical secrets from a Ferrari employee. The team, which was leading the constructors' championship ahead of Ferrari, said it would cooperate with the investigation. 'McLaren became aware that a senior member of its technical organisation was the subject of a Ferrari investigation regarding the receipt of technical information,' said an official statement.

'The team has learned that this individual had personally received a package of technical information from a Ferrari employee at the end of April. While McLaren has no involvement in the matter and condemns such actions, we will fully cooperate with any investigation. The individual has, in the meanwhile, been suspended by the company pending a full and proper investigation of the matter. No further comment will be made.'

For his part, Stepney maintained his innocence of all charges and vowed to prove that he was not involved in such subterfuge when he returned from a mid-season holiday. Coughlan and Stepney worked together at Benetton in the early 1990s and later at Ferrari's UK design studio, which was based in Surrey until 1996.

of 50,000 sponsors who had pledged money via myearthdream.com to benefit the environment.
Photograph: Lukas Gorys

**Main:** Kimi Räikkönen and Fernando Alonso were in a happy mood at one of the weekend's many media conferences.
Photograph: Lukas Gorys

LEWIS Hamilton's record of finishing on the podium in his every grand prix remained impressively intact after the Magny-Cours weekend, but a distant third place was rather less than expected. This was one race in which the 22-year-old star's McLaren-Mercedes was comprehensively outclassed by the Ferrari F2007s of Kimi Räikkönen and Felipe Massa, who finished in one-two formation out front.

Massa had qualified commandingly on pole position and led the race from the start, building up a 3.7s lead on Räikkönen over the first ten laps. Hamilton's McLaren was neatly bottled up in third place while Massa seemingly made good his escape.

However, Räikkönen piled on the pressure in the run-up to the second round of refuelling stops, hammering home a sequence of very quick laps to vault ahead of his team-mate coming out of the pits for the last time. He duly hung on to score his second win of the season by 2.4s from the hapless Massa. Hamilton, who had switched to a three-stop strategy, with an extra stop on lap 51, had to settle for third place.

'This win certainly helps,' grinned Räikkönen with obvious relief. 'I think the car was good all the time – brakes and handling – and we were able to be quick when we needed to be. I couldn't ask for more. It was nice to win, because people always think you have lost it when you don't have a good result, but we have been working hard to improve things.'

Massa freely admitted that he felt he had lost what would have been his third win of the year thanks to being held up by crowds of jostling backmarkers. 'I lost too much time during the second stint,' he said. 'Whenever I had a clear track I was certainly very quick. But for sure if you have three or four [slower] cars in front of you, all racing, then you are going to lose time.'

For Hamilton, it was all highly disappointing. His McLaren was fuelled for a short early stint in the hope that he could out-gun any Ferrari that might be near him on the starting grid. But he dropped from second to third on the run to the first corner. 'I didn't get the best of starts and Kimi came flying past me,' he said. 'As Felipe said, even if you are seconds quicker than the car in front, you still can't pass.'

McLaren had set its cars up for a predicted 90-percent chance of a wet race, but a change in wind direction kept the track dry and prevented the team from capitalising on its potential.

Hamilton came home 9.574s ahead of Robert Kubica's BMW-Sauber, with which he had a spectacular wheel-to-wheel joust after his second refuelling stop, a battle that was every bit as absorbing as the contest between Nick Heidfeld in the

other BMW and Fernando Alonso in his McLaren; they finished fifth and seventh, sandwiching Giancarlo Fisichella's Renault.

Kubica finished the day feeling upbeat and positive about the progress BMW had made with its F1.07 and regarded his battle with Hamilton, however brief, as proof positive that he was now totally fit after that huge accident in the Canadian GP.

'It was a good race for the team, finishing fourth and fifth,' he said. 'It was also a very good weekend for me personally. I made quite a good start but was on the dirty side of the track with Lewis and it was therefore difficult to overtake. After that I was close to him just once, when he was coming out of the pits, and we had a short fight but he had new tyres, braked later going into the hairpin and overtook me again. The last 20 laps were simply about bringing the car home because Lewis was a long way ahead and Nick well behind me. The car was very good. Physically I am 100 percent, and mentally too. I could do another race right now!'

The opening lap had been a busy affair, flagging up what promised to be a difficult race for Toyota in particular. Jarno Trulli tanked into the back of Heikki Kovalainen's Renault at the Adelaide hairpin, spinning the Renault and damaging the front of his Toyota. He retired immediately with front-suspension damage. Kovalainen had to stop to change a punctured rear tyre, after which he spent the rest of the race making the best of a bad job to finish 15th.

Meanwhile, Giancarlo Fisichella was accused by Heidfeld of weaving unpredictably as the pack scrambled away from the grid. 'That was not correct,' said Heidfeld crisply. In the end, 'Fisi' came home 3.4s behind Heidfeld but ahead of Alonso.

'Our pace was close to BMW's,' said Fisichella. 'I was able to keep Fernando behind me on equal fuel loads at the end of the race. The main problem was understeer with the high fuel load in the second stint, which cost me too much time. I had a small battle with Fernando early in the race, but he was much lighter and got past. We were running together at the end, though, and it was much closer. The soft tyres grained a little in the first few laps of the final stint and then he was much faster than me through Turn Three, so we had a good battle for a few laps. Then the tyre situation improved and I was able to build a little gap.'

After his qualifying setbacks, Fernando found himself forced to start the race from tenth place saddled with a fuel load better suited to a front-row position. There was precious little scope for tactical creativity so it was just a question of getting his head down and delivering the best job possible.

'I had to do whatever I could today,' he shrugged once the race was over. 'I wasn't worried about the risks.'

There was palpable relief in the Honda camp when Jenson Button scored his – and the team's – first championship point of the season, crossing the finishing line just a couple of seconds behind Alonso's McLaren.

Both Jenson and his team-mate Rubens Barrichello used the harder of Bridgestone's two compounds in the opening two stints and Jenson drove a very strong middle stint, in which he set personal best times lap after lap. As a result

he was able to leapfrog Nico Rosberg's Williams to take eighth place after the final round of stops.

'It was an enjoyable race today and we've shown that the car has improved a lot,' said Button. 'It's nice to have a car that gives me the confidence to push and I'm pleased with our fastest lap relative to our competitors'. A good weekend and I'm looking forward to another one at the British Grand Prix next week.'

Unfortunately Barrichello suffered from braking problems and found it impossible to match Button's pace, finishing 11th behind Ralf Schumacher's Toyota.

Neither of the Toro Rossos made it to the finish. Scott Speed battled a handling imbalance probably caused by an incorrect choice of nose wing setting before stopping with what appeared to be a failure of the car's new 'seamless shift' gearbox. Tonio Liuzzi was hit from behind on the first lap by Anthony Davidson's Super Aguri, spinning him around before the two cars collided again. And with Mark Webber and David Coulthard managing no better than 12th and 13th in their sister-team Red Bulls, it was a disappointing day for the Austrian energy-drink manufacturer.

'The race was going quite well at the beginning and normally, with my longer strategy, I should have been able to jump some people,' said Coulthard. 'I'm not sure if my in-laps weren't quick enough or the pit stops weren't quick enough but I didn't gain any advantage at the stops.'

Webber had a frustrating time bogged down in heavy traffic in what team principal Christian Horner freely confessed was the team's least competitive race of the season so far. The only consolation was that both cars displayed bullet-proof mechanical reliability.

*Alan Henry*

**Above: Having taken pole position, Felipe Massa was unable to make it count in the race and had to settle for second place.**
Photograph: Peter J Fox/www.crash.net

**Centre: How many more? A banner flags up the impending loss of another F1 fixture in Europe's motor racing heartland.**
Photograph: Jean-François Galeron/WRi2

**Left: Lewis Hamilton clatters his McLaren across the kerbing. Despite being outpaced by the Ferraris, Lewis clocked up his eighth successive podium.**
Photograph: Peter J Fox/www.crash.net

Opposite: Relief for Jenson Button, who finally manages to score a point for Honda with a much-improved performance car.
Photograph: Jean-François Galeron/WRi2.

Right: The latest calamity in Christijan Albers' troubled Spyker career occurred when he dragged his refuelling rig with him out of the pits, a slip that contributed to the end of his tenure with the team.

Below: Nick Heidfeld again impressed with a good run for BMW Sauber, keeping a race-long edge over Fernando Alonso.
Photographs: Peter J Fox/www.crash.net

Right: Kimi Räikkönen and Lewis Hamilton share out the bubbly. Unfortunately for the Ferrari team, the winner's bottle crashes to the ground.
Photographs: Peter J Fox/www.crash.net

# GRAND PRIX DE FRANCE
MAGNY-COURS 29 JUNE–1 JULY 2007

### CIRCUIT DE NEVERS, MAGNY-COURS

**Circuit: 2.741 miles/4.411 km**

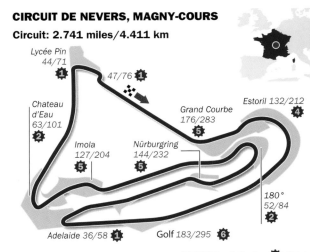

Lycée Pin 44/71 **1**

47/76 **1**

Chateau d'Eau 63/101 **2**

Grand Courbe 176/283 **5**

Estoril 132/212 **4**

Imola 127/204 **5**

Nürburgring 144/232 **5**

180° 52/84 **2**

Adelaide 36/58 **1**

Golf 183/295 **6**

116/187 **mph/kmh**   **4** Gear

## RACE RESULTS

| Pos. | Driver | Nat. | No. | Entrant | Car/Engine | Tyres | Laps | Time/Retirement | Speed (mph/km/h) | Gap to leader | Fastest race lap | |
|---|---|---|---|---|---|---|---|---|---|---|---|---|
| 1 | Kimi Räikkönen | FIN | 6 | Scuderia Ferrari Marlboro | Ferrari F2007-056 V8 | B | 70 | 1h 30m 54.200s | 126.560/203.679 | | 1m 16.207s | 20 |
| 2 | Felipe Massa | BR | 5 | Scuderia Ferrari Marlboro | Ferrari F2007-056 V8 | B | 70 | 1h 30m 56.614s | 126.504/203.589 | + 2.414s | 1m 16.099s | 42 |
| 3 | Lewis Hamilton | GB | 2 | Vodafone McLaren Mercedes | McLaren MP4-22-Mercedes FO 108T V8 | B | 70 | 1h 31m 26.353s | 125.818/202.485 | + 32.153s | 1m 16.587s | 39 |
| 4 | Robert Kubica | POL | 10 | BMW Sauber F1 Team | BMW Sauber F1.07-BMW P86/7 V8 | B | 70 | 1h 31m 35.927s | 125.600/202.133 | + 41.727s | 1m 17.153s | 44 |
| 5 | Nick Heidfeld | D | 9 | BMW Sauber F1 Team | BMW Sauber F1.07-BMW P86/7 V8 | B | 70 | 1h 31m 43.001s | 125.438/201.873 | + 48.801s | 1m 16.875s | 70 |
| 6 | Giancarlo Fisichella | I | 3 | ING Renault F1 Team | Renault R27-RS27 V8 | B | 70 | 1h 31m 46.410s | 125.360/201.748 | + 52.210s | 1m 16.703s | 70 |
| 7 | Fernando Alonso | E | 1 | Vodafone McLaren Mercedes | McLaren MP4-22-Mercedes FO 108T V8 | B | 70 | 1h 31m 50.716s | 125.262/201.590 | + 56.516s | 1m 16.495s | 36 |
| 8 | Jenson Button | GB | 7 | Honda Racing F1 Team | Honda RA107-RA807E V8 | B | 70 | 1h 31m 53.085s | 125.209/201.504 | + 58.885s | 1m 16.770s | 70 |
| 9 | Nico Rosberg | D | 16 | AT&T Williams | Williams FW29-Toyota RVX-07 V8 | B | 70 | 1h 32m 2.705s | 124.991/201.153 | + 1m 8.505s | 1m 17.011s | 69 |
| 10 | Ralf Schumacher | D | 11 | Panasonic Toyota Racing | Toyota TF107-RVX-07 V8 | B | 69 | | | + 1 lap | 1m 16.966s | 68 |
| 11 | Rubens Barrichello | BR | 8 | Honda Racing F1 Team | Honda RA107-RA807E V8 | B | 69 | | | + 1 lap | 1m 17.220s | 68 |
| 12 | Mark Webber | AUS | 15 | Red Bull Racing | Red Bull RB3-Renault RS27 V8 | B | 69 | | | + 1 lap | 1m 17.249s | 69 |
| 13 | David Coulthard | GB | 14 | Red Bull Racing | Red Bull RB3-Renault RS27 V8 | B | 69 | | | + 1 lap | 1m 17.447s | 68 |
| 14 | Alexander Wurz | A | 17 | AT&T Williams | Williams FW29-Toyota RVX-07 V8 | B | 69 | | | + 1 lap | 1m 17.240s | 69 |
| 15 | Heikki Kovalainen | FIN | 4 | ING Renault F1 Team | Renault R27-RS27 V8 | B | 69 | | | + 1 lap | 1m 17.206s | 69 |
| 16 | Takuma Sato | J | 22 | Super Aguri F1 Team | Super Aguri SA07-Honda RA807E V8 | B | 68 | | | + 2 laps | 1m 17.796s | 39 |
| 17 | Adrian Sutil | D | 20 | Etihad Aldar Spyker F1 Team | Spyker F8-VII-Ferrari 056H V8 | B | 68 | | | + 2 laps | 1m 18.091s | 27 |
| | Scott Speed | USA | 19 | Scuderia Toro Rosso | Toro Rosso STR02-Ferrari 056H V8 | B | 55 | Hydraulics | | | 1m 17.934s | 51 |
| | Christijan Albers | NL | 21 | Etihad Aldar Spyker F1 Team | Spyker F8-VII-Ferrari 056H V8 | B | 28 | Refuelling hose attached | | | 1m 18.955s | 27 |
| | Anthony Davidson | GB | 23 | Super Aguri F1 Team | Super Aguri SA07-Honda RA807E V8 | B | 1 | Accident damage | | | No time | – |
| | Jarno Trulli | I | 12 | Panasonic Toyota Racing | Toyota TF107-RVX-07 V8 | B | 1 | Accident | | | No time | – |
| | Vitantonio Liuzzi | I | 18 | Scuderia Toro Rosso | Toro Rosso STR02-Ferrari 056H V8 | B | 0 | Accident | | | No time | – |

Fastest race lap: Felipe Massa on lap 42, 1m 16.099s, 129.662 mph/208.670 km/h.

Lap record: Michael Schumacher (Ferrari F2004 V10), 1m 15.377s, 130.904 mph/210.669 km/h (2004).

**22 SATO** Super Aguri
Ten-place penalty

**20 ALBERS** Spyker

**18 WURZ** Williams

**16 COULTHARD** Red Bull

**14 WEBBER** Red Bull

**12 BUTTON** Honda

**21 SUTIL** Spyker

**19 DAVIDSON** Super Aguri

**17 LIUZZI** Toro Rosso

**15 SPEED** Toro Rosso

**13 BARRICHELLO** Honda

**11 SCHUMACHER** Toyota

| Grid order | 1 | 2 | 3 | 4 | 5 | 6 | 7 | 8 | 9 | 10 | 11 | 12 | 13 | 14 | 15 | 16 | 17 | 18 | 19 | 20 | 21 | 22 | 23 | 24 | 25 | 26 | 27 | 28 | 29 | 30 | 31 | 32 | 33 | 34 | 35 | 36 | 37 | 38 | 39 | 40 | 41 | 42 | 43 | 44 | 45 | 46 | 47 | 48 | 49 | 50 | 51 | 52 | 53 | 54 |
|---|---|---|---|---|---|---|---|---|---|---|---|---|---|---|---|---|---|---|---|---|---|---|---|---|---|---|---|---|---|---|---|---|---|---|---|---|---|---|---|---|---|---|---|---|---|---|---|---|---|---|---|---|---|---|
| **5 MASSA** | 5 | 5 | 5 | 5 | 5 | 5 | 5 | 5 | 5 | 5 | 5 | 5 | 5 | 5 | 5 | 5 | 5 | 5 | 5 | 6 | 6 | 6 | 5 | 5 | 5 | 5 | 5 | 5 | 5 | 5 | 5 | 5 | 5 | 5 | 5 | 5 | 5 | 5 | 5 | 5 | 5 | 5 | 6 | 6 | 6 | 6 | 6 | 6 | 6 | 6 | 6 | 6 | 6 | 6 |
| **2 HAMILTON** | 6 | 6 | 6 | 6 | 6 | 6 | 6 | 6 | 6 | 6 | 6 | 6 | 6 | 6 | 6 | 6 | 6 | 6 | 6 | 5 | 5 | 5 | 6 | 6 | 6 | 6 | 6 | 6 | 6 | 6 | 6 | 6 | 6 | 6 | 6 | 6 | 6 | 6 | 6 | 6 | 6 | 6 | 5 | 5 | 5 | 5 | 5 | 5 | 5 | 5 | 5 | 5 | 5 | 5 |
| **6 RÄIKKÖNEN** | 2 | 2 | 2 | 2 | 2 | 2 | 2 | 2 | 2 | 2 | 2 | 2 | 2 | 2 | 2 | 10 | 10 | 10 | 9 | 9 | 9 | 2 | 2 | 2 | 2 | 2 | 2 | 2 | 2 | 2 | 2 | 2 | 2 | 2 | 2 | 2 | 2 | 2 | 2 | 2 | 2 | 2 | 2 | 2 | 2 | 2 | 2 | 2 | 2 | 2 | 2 | 2 | 2 | 2 |
| **10 KUBICA** | 10 | 10 | 10 | 10 | 10 | 10 | 10 | 10 | 10 | 10 | 10 | 10 | 10 | 10 | 10 | 3 | 3 | 3 | 2 | 2 | 2 | 10 | 10 | 10 | 10 | 10 | 10 | 10 | 10 | 10 | 10 | 10 | 10 | 10 | 10 | 10 | 10 | 10 | 10 | 10 | 10 | 10 | 9 | 9 | 3 | 3 | 3 | 10 | 10 | 10 | 10 | 10 | 10 | 10 |
| **3 FISICHELLA** | 3 | 3 | 3 | 3 | 3 | 3 | 3 | 3 | 3 | 3 | 3 | 3 | 3 | 3 | 3 | 9 | 9 | 9 | 16 | 10 | 10 | 7 | 7 | 7 | 7 | 7 | 7 | 7 | 7 | 1 | 1 | 1 | 1 | 1 | 9 | 9 | 9 | 9 | 9 | 9 | 9 | 9 | 3 | 3 | 7 | 7 | 7 | 9 | 9 | 9 | 9 | 9 | 9 | 9 |
| **4 KOVALAINEN** | 9 | 9 | 9 | 9 | 9 | 9 | 9 | 9 | 9 | 9 | 9 | 9 | 9 | 9 | 9 | 16 | 16 | 16 | 10 | 7 | 7 | 9 | 9 | 9 | 9 | 9 | 9 | 9 | 9 | 9 | 9 | 9 | 9 | 9 | 3 | 3 | 3 | 3 | 3 | 3 | 3 | 16 | 7 | 10 | 10 | 10 | 3 | 3 | 3 | 3 | 3 | 3 | 3 | 3 |
| **9 HEIDFELD** | 16 | 1 | 1 | 1 | 1 | 1 | 1 | 1 | 1 | 1 | 1 | 1 | 1 | 1 | 1 | 1 | 2 | 2 | 2 | 7 | 3 | 3 | 1 | 1 | 1 | 1 | 1 | 1 | 1 | 3 | 3 | 3 | 3 | 16 | 16 | 16 | 16 | 16 | 16 | 16 | 7 | 10 | 9 | 9 | 9 | 1 | 1 | 1 | 1 | 1 | 1 | 1 | 1 | 1 |
| **12 TRULLI** | 1 | 16 | 16 | 16 | 16 | 16 | 16 | 16 | 16 | 16 | 16 | 16 | 16 | 16 | 16 | 7 | 7 | 7 | 3 | 1 | 1 | 3 | 3 | 3 | 3 | 3 | 3 | 3 | 3 | 16 | 16 | 16 | 16 | 7 | 7 | 7 | 7 | 7 | 7 | 10 | 1 | 1 | 1 | 1 | 7 | 7 | 7 | 7 | 7 | 7 | 7 | 7 | 7 | 7 |
| **16 ROSBERG** | 7 | 7 | 7 | 7 | 7 | 7 | 7 | 7 | 7 | 7 | 7 | 7 | 7 | 7 | 7 | 1 | 1 | 1 | 16 | 16 | 16 | 16 | 16 | 16 | 16 | 16 | 16 | 16 | 16 | 7 | 7 | 7 | 7 | 1 | 1 | 1 | 1 | 1 | 1 | 1 | 16 | 16 | 16 | 16 | 16 | 16 | 16 | 16 | 16 | 16 | 16 | 16 | 16 | 16 |
| **1 ALONSO** | 8 | 8 | 8 | 8 | 8 | 8 | 8 | 8 | 8 | 8 | 8 | 8 | 8 | 8 | 8 | 8 | 8 | 8 | 8 | 8 | 8 | 8 | 8 | 8 | 8 | 8 | 8 | 8 | 8 | 8 | 8 | 11 | 11 | 11 | 11 | 11 | 11 | 11 | 11 | 11 | 11 | 11 | 11 | 11 | 11 | 11 | 11 | 11 | 11 | 11 | 11 | 11 | 11 | 11 |
| **11 SCHUMACHER** | 11 | 11 | 11 | 11 | 11 | 11 | 11 | 11 | 11 | 11 | 11 | 11 | 11 | 11 | 11 | 11 | 11 | 11 | 11 | 11 | 11 | 11 | 11 | 11 | 15 | 15 | 15 | 14 | 14 | 14 | 11 | 8 | 8 | 8 | 8 | 8 | 8 | 8 | 8 | 8 | 8 | 8 | 8 | 8 | 8 | 8 | 8 | 8 | 8 | 8 | 19 | 8 | | |
| **7 BUTTON** | 15 | 15 | 15 | 15 | 15 | 15 | 15 | 15 | 15 | 15 | 15 | 15 | 15 | 15 | 15 | 15 | 15 | 15 | 15 | 14 | 14 | 15 | 11 | 11 | 15 | 15 | 15 | 15 | 15 | 15 | 15 | 15 | 15 | 15 | 15 | 15 | 15 | 14 | 14 | 14 | 17 | 17 | 19 | 8 | 15 | 15 | | | | | | | | |
| **8 BARRICHELLO** | 14 | 14 | 14 | 14 | 14 | 14 | 14 | 14 | 14 | 14 | 14 | 14 | 14 | 14 | 14 | 14 | 14 | 14 | 14 | 17 | 19 | 19 | 15 | 15 | 14 | 14 | 14 | 17 | 17 | 17 | 17 | 17 | 17 | 17 | 14 | 14 | 14 | 15 | 17 | 17 | 19 | 19 | 15 | 15 | 14 | 14 | 14 | 17 | 17 | | | | | |
| **15 WEBBER** | 19 | 19 | 19 | 17 | 17 | 17 | 17 | 17 | 17 | 17 | 17 | 17 | 17 | 17 | 17 | 17 | 17 | 17 | 17 | 17 | 17 | 17 | 17 | 17 | 17 | 19 | 11 | 11 | 17 | 17 | 17 | 17 | 17 | 17 | 17 | 17 | 17 | 17 | 17 | 17 | 17 | 19 | 19 | 15 | 15 | 14 | 14 | 17 | | | | | | |
| **19 SPEED** | 17 | 17 | 17 | 19 | 22 | 22 | 22 | 22 | 22 | 22 | 22 | 22 | 22 | 22 | 22 | 22 | 19 | 19 | 19 | 19 | 19 | 20 | 17 | 19 | 19 | 19 | 19 | 19 | 19 | 19 | 19 | 19 | 19 | 19 | 19 | 19 | 19 | 19 | 19 | 19 | 15 | 15 | 14 | 14 | 17 | 17 | 4 | 19 | | | | | | |
| **14 COULTHARD** | 22 | 22 | 22 | 22 | 19 | 19 | 19 | 19 | 19 | 19 | 19 | 19 | 19 | 19 | 19 | 19 | 20 | 20 | 20 | 20 | 20 | 11 | 22 | 22 | 22 | 22 | 22 | 22 | 22 | 22 | 22 | 22 | 22 | 4 | 4 | 4 | 4 | 4 | 4 | 4 | 4 | 4 | 4 | 19 | | | | | | | | | | |
| **18 LIUZZI** | 21 | 21 | 21 | 21 | 21 | 21 | 21 | 21 | 21 | 21 | 21 | 21 | 21 | 21 | 21 | 21 | 21 | 21 | 21 | 21 | 20 | 20 | 20 | 20 | 20 | 4 | 4 | 4 | 4 | 4 | 22 | 22 | 22 | 22 | 22 | 22 | 22 | 22 | 22 | 22 | 22 | 22 | 22 | 22 | | | | | | | | | | |
| **17 WURZ** | 20 | 20 | 20 | 20 | 20 | 20 | 20 | 20 | 20 | 20 | 20 | 20 | 20 | 20 | 20 | 4 | 4 | 4 | 4 | 4 | 4 | 4 | 22 | 4 | 4 | 20 | 20 | 20 | 20 | 20 | 20 | 20 | 20 | 20 | 20 | 20 | 20 | 20 | 20 | 20 | 20 | 20 | 20 | 20 | | | | | | | | | | |
| **23 DAVIDSON** | 23 | 4 | 4 | 4 | 4 | 4 | 4 | 4 | 4 | 4 | 4 | 4 | 4 | 4 | 4 | 22 | 22 | 22 | 22 | 22 | 22 | 22 | 4 | 4 | | | | | | | | | | | | | | | | | | | | | | | | | | | | | | |
| **21 ALBERS** | 4 | | | | | | | | | | | | | | | | | | | | | | | | | | | | | | | | | | | | | | | | | | | | | | | | | | | | | |
| **20 SUTIL** | 12 | | | | | | | | | | | | | | | | | | | | | | | | | | | | | | | | | | | | | | | | | | | | | | | | | | | | | |
| **22 SATO** | | | | | | | | | | | | | | | | | | | | | | | | | | | | | | | | | | | | | | | | | | | | | | | | | | | | | |

## PRACTICE 1 (FRIDAY)

Cloudy (track 22–26ºC, air 17–19ºC)

| Pos. | Driver | Laps | Time |
|---|---|---|---|
| 1 | Kimi Räikkönen | 22 | 1m 15.382s |
| 2 | Felipe Massa | 22 | 1m 15.447s |
| 3 | Fernando Alonso | 19 | 1m 16.154s |
| 4 | Nico Rosberg | 24 | 1m 16.214s |
| 5 | David Coulthard | 24 | 1m 16.268s |
| 6 | Lewis Hamilton | 20 | 1m 16.277s |
| 7 | Nick Heidfeld | 25 | 1m 16.338s |
| 8 | Alexander Wurz | 23 | 1m 16.407s |
| 9 | Robert Kubica | 19 | 1m 16.441s |
| 10 | Jarno Trulli | 26 | 1m 16.603s |
| 11 | Vitantonio Liuzzi | 32 | 1m 16.895s |
| 12 | Takuma Sato | 22 | 1m 16.967s |
| 13 | Rubens Barrichello | 25 | 1m 16.990s |
| 14 | Jenson Button | 24 | 1m 17.047s |
| 15 | Scott Speed | 33 | 1m 17.103s |
| 16 | Anthony Davidson | 26 | 1m 17.166s |
| 17 | Ralf Schumacher | 26 | 1m 17.168s |
| 18 | Giancarlo Fisichella | 20 | 1m 17.226s |
| 19 | Heikki Kovalainen | 21 | 1m 17.348s |
| 20 | Mark Webber | 26 | 1m 17.435s |
| 21 | Christijan Albers | 28 | 1m 18.178s |
| 22 | Adrian Sutil | 15 | 1m 18.419s |

## PRACTICE 2 (FRIDAY)

Cloudy (track 26–28ºC, air 19–22ºC)

| Pos. | Driver | Laps | Time |
|---|---|---|---|
| 1 | Felipe Massa | 38 | 1m 15.453s |
| 2 | Kimi Räikkönen | 28 | 1m 15.488s |
| 3 | Scott Speed | 21 | 1m 15.773s |
| 4 | Lewis Hamilton | 36 | 1m 15.780s |
| 5 | Vitantonio Liuzzi | 40 | 1m 15.952s |
| 6 | David Coulthard | 36 | 1m 15.958s |
| 7 | Nico Rosberg | 39 | 1m 16.003s |
| 8 | Fernando Alonso | 32 | 1m 16.049s |
| 9 | Anthony Davidson | 25 | 1m 16.162s |
| 10 | Ralf Schumacher | 41 | 1m 16.184s |
| 11 | Giancarlo Fisichella | 43 | 1m 16.205s |
| 12 | Robert Kubica | 42 | 1m 16.236s |
| 13 | Alexander Wurz | 38 | 1m 16.260s |
| 14 | Jarno Trulli | 46 | 1m 16.285s |
| 15 | Jenson Button | 43 | 1m 16.395s |
| 16 | Mark Webber | 17 | 1m 16.562s |
| 17 | Heikki Kovalainen | 40 | 1m 16.735s |
| 18 | Rubens Barrichello | 47 | 1m 16.950s |
| 19 | Nick Heidfeld | 18 | 1m 16.968s |
| 20 | Takuma Sato | 49 | 1m 17.165s |
| 21 | Adrian Sutil | 32 | 1m 18.213s |
| 22 | Christijan Albers | 9 | 1m 18.708s |

## QUALIFYING (SATURDAY)

Sunny (track 23–34ºC, air 22–23ºC)

| Pos. | Driver | First | Second | Third |
|---|---|---|---|---|
| 1 | Felipe Massa | 1m 15.303s | 1m 14.822s | 1m 15.034s |
| 2 | Lewis Hamilton | 1m 14.805s | 1m 14.795s | 1m 15.104s |
| 3 | Kimi Räikkönen | 1m 14.872s | 1m 14.828s | 1m 15.257s |
| 4 | Robert Kubica | 1m 15.778s | 1m 15.066s | 1m 15.493s |
| 5 | Giancarlo Fisichella | 1m 16.047s | 1m 15.227s | 1m 15.674s |
| 6 | Heikki Kovalainen | 1m 15.524s | 1m 15.272s | 1m 15.826s |
| 7 | Nick Heidfeld | 1m 15.783s | 1m 15.149s | 1m 15.900s |
| 8 | Jarno Trulli | 1m 16.118s | 1m 15.379s | 1m 15.935s |
| 9 | Nico Rosberg | 1m 16.092s | 1m 15.331s | 1m 16.328s |
| 10 | Fernando Alonso | 1m 15.322s | 1m 15.084s | No time |
| 11 | Ralf Schumacher | 1m 15.760s | 1m 15.534s | |
| 12 | Jenson Button | 1m 16.113s | 1m 15.584s | |
| 13 | Rubens Barrichello | 1m 16.140s | 1m 15.761s | |
| 14 | Mark Webber | 1m 15.746s | 1m 15.806s | |
| 15 | Scott Speed | 1m 15.980s | 1m 16.049s | |
| 16 | David Coulthard | 1m 15.915s | No time | |
| 17 | Vitantonio Liuzzi | 1m 16.142s | | |
| 18 | Alexander Wurz | 1m 16.241s | | |
| 19 | Takuma Sato | 1m 16.244s | | |
| 20 | Anthony Davidson | 1m 16.366s | | |
| 21 | Christijan Albers | 1m 17.826s | | |
| 22 | Adrian Sutil | 1m 17.915s | | |

## PRACTICE 3 (SATURDAY)

Cloudy (track 28–29ºC, air 20–21ºC)

| Pos. | Driver | Laps | Time |
|---|---|---|---|
| 1 | Lewis Hamilton | 8 | 1m 14.843s |
| 2 | Felipe Massa | 16 | 1m 14.906s |
| 3 | Kimi Räikkönen | 15 | 1m 15.276s |
| 4 | Heikki Kovalainen | 19 | 1m 15.404s |
| 5 | Giancarlo Fisichella | 20 | 1m 15.489s |
| 6 | Robert Kubica | 20 | 1m 15.535s |
| 7 | Nico Rosberg | 18 | 1m 15.735s |
| 8 | Fernando Alonso | 4 | 1m 15.742s |
| 9 | Jarno Trulli | 19 | 1m 15.801s |
| 10 | David Coulthard | 15 | 1m 15.802s |
| 11 | Vitantonio Liuzzi | 22 | 1m 15.872s |
| 12 | Jenson Button | 16 | 1m 15.902s |
| 13 | Anthony Davidson | 20 | 1m 15.925s |
| 14 | Ralf Schumacher | 22 | 1m 15.944s |
| 15 | Nick Heidfeld | 18 | 1m 16.060s |
| 16 | Rubens Barrichello | 19 | 1m 16.102s |
| 17 | Alexander Wurz | 16 | 1m 16.104s |
| 18 | Scott Speed | 18 | 1m 16.161s |
| 19 | Takuma Sato | 18 | 1m 16.221s |
| 20 | Mark Webber | 14 | 1m 16.573s |
| 21 | Adrian Sutil | 21 | 1m 17.517s |
| 22 | Christijan Albers | 23 | 1m 17.705s |

## RACE TYRE STRATEGIES

**BRIDGESTONE**

In 2007, the tyre regulations stipulate that the two dry-tyre specifications must be visibly distinguishable from each other. At the French Grand Prix, the soft compound Bridgestone Potenza tyre was marked with a white line in the second-from-inside groove.

| | Driver | Race stint 1 | Race stint 2 | Race stint 3 | Race stint 4 |
|---|---|---|---|---|---|
| 1 | Kimi Räikkönen | Medium: laps 1–22 | Medium: 23–46 | Soft: 47–70 | |
| 2 | Felipe Massa | Medium: 1–19 | Medium: 20–43 | Soft: 44–70 | |
| 3 | Lewis Hamilton | Medium: 1–16 | Medium: 17–37 | Medium: 38–51 | Soft: 52–70 |
| 4 | Robert Kubica | Medium: 1–19 | Medium: 20–45 | Soft: 46–70 | |
| 5 | Nick Heidfeld | Medium: 1–22 | Medium: 23–47 | Soft: 48–70 | |
| 6 | Giancarlo Fisichella | Medium: 1–19 | Medium: 20–50 | Soft: 51–70 | |
| 7 | Fernando Alonso | Soft: 1–16 | Medium: 17–37 | Medium: 38–70 | |
| 8 | Jenson Button | Medium: 1–32 | Medium: 33–50 | Soft: 51–70 | |
| 9 | Nico Rosberg | Medium: 1–20 | Medium: 21–46 | Soft: 47–70 | |
| 10 | Ralf Schumacher | Medium: 1–27 | Medium: 28–52 | Soft: 53–70 | |
| 11 | Rubens Barrichello | Medium: 1–33 | Medium: 34–50 | Soft: 51–70 | |
| 12 | Mark Webber | Medium: 1–30 | Medium: 31–46 | Soft: 47–70 | |
| 13 | David Coulthard | Medium: 1–32 | Medium: 33–48 | Soft: 49–70 | |
| 14 | Alexander Wurz | Medium: 1–28 | Medium: 29–50 | Medium: 51–70 | |
| 15 | Heikki Kovalainen | Medium: 1 | Medium: 2–26 | Medium: 27–54 | Soft: 55–70 |
| 16 | Takuma Sato | Soft: 1–18 | Medium: 19–40 | Medium: 41–70 | |
| 17 | Adrian Sutil | Soft: 1–28 | Soft: 29–34 | Medium: 35–70 | |
| | Scott Speed | Medium: 1–30 | Medium: 31–52 | Soft: 53–70 | |
| | Christijan Albers | Soft: 1–28 | Soft: 29 (DNF) | | |
| | Anthony Davidson | Medium: 1 (DNF) | | | |
| | Jarno Trulli | Medium: 1 (DNF) | | | |
| | Vitantonio Liuzzi | Medium: 0 (DNF) | | | |

10 ALONSO McLaren

8 TRULLI Toyota

6 KOVALAINEN Renault

4 KUBICA BMW-Sauber

2 HAMILTON McLaren

9 ROSBERG Williams

7 HEIDFELD BMW-Sauber

5 FISICHELLA Renault

3 RÄIKKÖNEN Ferrari

1 MASSA Ferrari

RACE DISTANCE:
70 laps
191.746 miles/308.586 km

RACE WEATHER:
Sunny, cloudy, track 31–32ºC, air 24–25ºC

| 55 | 56 | 57 | 58 | 59 | 60 | 61 | 62 | 63 | 64 | 65 | 66 | 67 | 68 | 69 | 70 | • |
|---|---|---|---|---|---|---|---|---|---|---|---|---|---|---|---|---|
| 6 | 6 | 6 | 6 | 6 | 6 | 6 | 6 | 6 | 6 | 6 | 6 | 6 | 6 | 6 | 6 | 1 |
| 5 | 5 | 5 | 5 | 5 | 5 | 5 | 5 | 5 | 5 | 5 | 5 | 5 | 5 | 5 | 5 | 2 |
| 2 | 2 | 2 | 2 | 2 | 2 | 2 | 2 | 2 | 2 | 2 | 2 | 2 | 2 | 2 | 2 | 3 |
| 10 | 10 | 10 | 10 | 10 | 10 | 10 | 10 | 10 | 10 | 10 | 10 | 10 | 10 | 10 | 10 | 4 |
| 9 | 9 | 9 | 9 | 9 | 9 | 9 | 9 | 9 | 9 | 9 | 9 | 9 | 9 | 9 | 9 | 5 |
| 3 | 3 | 3 | 3 | 3 | 3 | 3 | 3 | 3 | 3 | 3 | 3 | 3 | 3 | 3 | 3 | 6 |
| 1 | 1 | 1 | 1 | 1 | 1 | 1 | 1 | 1 | 1 | 1 | 1 | 1 | 1 | 1 | 1 | 7 |
| 7 | 7 | 7 | 7 | 7 | 7 | 7 | 7 | 7 | 7 | 7 | 7 | 7 | 7 | 7 | 7 | 8 |
| 16 | 16 | 16 | 16 | 16 | 16 | 16 | 16 | 16 | 16 | 16 | 16 | 16 | 16 | 16 | 16 | |
| 11 | 11 | 11 | 11 | 11 | 11 | 11 | 11 | 11 | 11 | 11 | 11 | 11 | 11 | 11 | 11 | |
| 8 | 8 | 8 | 8 | 8 | 8 | 8 | 8 | 8 | 8 | 8 | 8 | 8 | 8 | | | |
| 15 | 15 | 15 | 15 | 15 | 15 | 15 | 15 | 15 | 15 | 15 | 15 | 15 | 15 | 15 | | |
| 14 | 14 | 14 | 14 | 14 | 14 | 14 | 14 | 14 | 14 | 14 | 14 | 14 | 14 | | | |
| 17 | 17 | 17 | 17 | 17 | 17 | 17 | 17 | 17 | 17 | 17 | 17 | 17 | 17 | | | |
| 19 | 4 | 4 | 4 | 4 | 4 | 4 | 4 | 4 | 4 | 4 | 4 | 4 | | | | |
| 4 | 22 | 22 | 22 | 22 | 22 | 22 | 22 | 22 | 22 | 22 | 22 | | | | | |
| 22 | 20 | 20 | 20 | 20 | 20 | 20 | 20 | 20 | 20 | 20 | 20 | | | | | |
| 20 | | | | | | | | | | | | | | | | |

**20** Pit stop
**20** One lap or more behind leader

## FOR THE RECORD

**FIRST POINTS OF THE SEASON:**
Jenson Button and Honda

**700th LAP LED:** Kimi Räikkönen

## POINTS

**DRIVERS**

| | | |
|---|---|---|
| 1 | Lewis Hamilton | 64 |
| 2 | Fernando Alonso | 50 |
| 3 | Felipe Massa | 47 |
| 4 | Kimi Räikkönen | 42 |
| 5 | Nick Heidfeld | 30 |
| 6 | Robert Kubica | 17 |
| 7 | Giancarlo Fisichella | 16 |
| 8 | Heikki Kovalainen | 12 |
| 9 | Alexander Wurz | 8 |
| 10 | Jarno Trulli | 7 |
| 11 | Nico Rosberg | 5 |
| 12 | David Coulthard | 4 |
| 13 | Takuma Sato | 4 |
| 14 | Mark Webber | 2 |
| 15 | Ralf Schumacher | 2 |
| 16 | Sebastian Vettel | 1 |
| 17 | Jenson Button | 1 |

**CONSTRUCTORS**

| | | |
|---|---|---|
| 1 | McLaren | 114 |
| 2 | Ferrari | 89 |
| 3 | BMW Sauber | 48 |
| 4 | Renault | 28 |
| 5 | Williams | 13 |
| 6 | Toyota | 9 |
| 7 | Red Bull | 6 |
| 8 | Super Aguri | 4 |
| 9 | Honda | 1 |

Photographs: Peter J Fox/www.crash.net

At the start, pole sitter Lewis Hamilton moves over to block Kimi Räikkönen's fast-starting Ferrari as the pack sprints away from the grid towards Copse corner. On the left, Felipe Massa's Ferrari waits to join in from the end of the pit lane.
Photograph: Peter J Fox/www.crash.net

FIA F1 WORLD CHAMPIONSHIP/ROUND 8

# BRITISH GP
## SILVERSTONE

## DIARY

The biggest crowd of police and security men in the Silverstone paddock is attracted by footballer David Beckham and his wife Victoria (above), guests of Honda.

Red Bull boss Dietrich Mateschitz quashes paddock rumours that Scuderia Toro Rosso is for sale but again signals his enthusiasm for recruiting BMW Sauber test driver Sebastian Vettel to the team.

BBC Radio 5 Live confirms that Murray Walker will be back on his old radio beat, joining the commentary team for the European GP at the Nürburgring.

Jörg Zander is signed as Honda F1's deputy technical director, moving from BMW.

Kimi Räikkönen later admitted that he knew life would have been easier had he started from pole position, but a mistake coming out of Woodcote just as Lewis Hamilton was delivering the perfect lap in his McLaren-Mercedes dropped him to the outside of the front row.

Hamilton's 1m 19.997s marked him out as the only runner to break the 1m 20s barrier; he also earned the 50th pole position of the McLaren-Mercedes partnership. By any standards it was a great effort and Lewis generously attributed it, in part, to the support of his huge army of fans.

'I'd been losing about two-tenths to Fernando [Alonso], particularly in sector one,' he recalled, 'so this time [on my best lap] I went up to the first corner [Copse] trying to keep it flat. I didn't do it flat, but I nearly did and so I knew that I had already gained a tenth and a half, nearly two tenths. Then trying to maintain it for the rest of the lap was obviously extremely difficult. When you've got that sort of pressure on you it's great to see so many fans out there [supporting you] and the support they gave me today was unreal. So I pulled out the lap. It's great to be home and I truly got an extra buzz.'

Räikkönen ended up second on 1m 20.099s with world champion Fernando Alonso posting a 1m 20.147s to edge Felipe Massa's Ferrari (1m 20.265s) on the second row. 'Yesterday [Friday] I was not completely happy with our car and our pace,' he admitted, 'but overnight we made some changes to the set-up and today I found a completely different car, much quicker, and I was able to be quickest in nearly all the sessions, so there is no reason not to be optimistic for tomorrow.'

Behind Massa, Robert Kubica did another fine job to earn fifth place on 1m 20.401s with the BMW-Sauber. 'We struggled with my set-up on Friday, but overnight we made some changes for qualifying and it looks as though this made all the difference,' he grinned. 'If I was joking I would say we are the first of the B championship. It looks like Ferrari and McLaren here are too far away to fight with them, but it is important to be there if someone has a failure so we can gain positions.'

By contrast, his team-mate Nick Heidfeld was left seething with frustration after managing only a ninth-fastest 1m 20.894s. 'It was my worst qualifying result so far this season,' he said. 'I couldn't get the most out of the tyres, either at the beginning of the lap or towards the end, when they started graining.'

The two BMW-Saubers were split by an on-form Ralf Schumacher's Toyota TF107 (1m 20.516s) and the Renaults of Heikki Kovalainen (1m 20.721s) and Giancarlo Fisichella (1m 20.775s), while Jarno Trulli completed the top ten in the other Toyota on 1m 21.240s.

Sharing the sixth row of the grid were the two Red Bull-Renaults of Mark Webber (1m 20.235s) and David Coulthard (1m 20.329s), both struggling for pace and handling balance.

Having missed one of Friday's free practice sessions, due to a pain in his back that appeared to be consistent with the after-effects of his collision at Indianapolis, Jenson Button was frustrated that his eventual 1m 21.335s was good enough only for 18th, four places behind team-mate Rubens Barrichello (1m 20.364s). Between them were the Toro Rossos of Scott Speed (1m 20.515s) and Tonio Liuzzi (1m 20.823s) and the Williams of Nico Rosberg (1m 21.219s).

The penultimate row was shared by Anthony Davidson's Super Aguri (1m 21.448s) and Adrian Sutil's Spyker (1m 22.019s), with Takuma Sato (1m 22.045s) and Spyker's Christijan Albers (1m 22.589s) right at the back.

EWIS Hamilton's hopes of winning the British Grand Prix at his first attempt evaporated disappointingly over 59 high-speed laps of Silverstone's daunting swerves, his perfectly judged efforts to take pole position on Saturday translating into a distant third place at the end in front of a capacity crowd of approving – if slightly disappointed – fans.

Instead it was Kimi Räikkönen who became the first driver to win three races in the 2007 season – and it was his second in eight days – by grabbing the lead from Fernando Alonso at the final round of refuelling stops. In the closing laps Räikkönen rammed home his advantage to send a firm message to the world champion that this battle was over, beating him by 2.459s.

Hamilton retained his record of appearing on the podium in every F1 race he contested, finishing in the top three for the ninth time in as many races. Yet there was no concealing his disappointment with this result, coming as it did at the end of a week in which the McLaren Mercedes team had been under siege and distracted following the well-publicised revelations of alleged industrial sabotage involving its chief designer.

For Räikkönen this was a particularly satisfying success at a circuit he loves but where he has been unlucky over the years. 'It was a very nice feeling to win the race,' he said. 'I have been close here several times; now finally I got the win.'

Räikkönen took the victory even though Alonso emerged on top after the first round of refuelling stops: a longer second stint allowed him to pass Alonso in the pits. 'We had a little traffic but we had a good car all day and all weekend,' he said. 'I just tried to save some fuel and look after the tyres and the car and when Lewis pitted I pushed to gain some time and Fernando did a very short stop so I knew I was going to run longer in my second stint. So I tried to push as hard as I could when he came in and that was enough.'

In the first stint Kimi concentrated on saving fuel and conserving tyres, secure in the knowledge that he could run for longer before his first refuelling stop than his British rival. Coming up to the second stops he did the same to Alonso before establishing a winning edge. On the face of it this may have seemed a processional and rather predictable race but in reality it unfolded into a finely balanced and intensely tactical affair with refuelling strategies and tyre choices combining to define the outcome for the top three contenders.

Not since the halcyon days of Nigel Mansell and Damon Hill

had Silverstone's grandstands been packed with such a partisan crowd but now Lewis-mania came to the former RAF base on a breezy summer's day beneath clusters of scudding clouds. Hamilton's qualifying effort had rocked his rivals on Saturday afternoon as he slammed through the 170-mph Stowe corner with a deft flick of opposite lock to the delight of the traditionalists in the spectator enclosures. As the chequered flag fluttered, Hamilton vaulted from third-fastest to pole position, pushing Räikkönen back into second place just as the Ferrari driver was congratulating himself on outclassing the rest of the field. That meant that Räikkönen – after a slight slip coming out of Woodcote on his best lap – had to move to the dirty right-hand side of the circuit, leaving Alonso to line up immediately behind Hamilton with Felipe Massa sustaining the front-running symmetry by putting the other Ferrari fourth ahead of Robert Kubica's BMW-Sauber.

There was a spine-tingling sense of anticipation as Hamilton led the 22 cars briskly around on the pre-race formation lap but that sense of expectation was deflated when Massa stalled his Ferrari, was sent to the back of the grid for the restart and triggered a second formation lap before the race finally got under way.

Away from the line Hamilton eased neatly into Copse corner a couple of lengths ahead of Räikkönen, who briefly toyed with a lunge to the outside of the McLaren. To the delight of his supporters Hamilton completed the opening lap 0.6s ahead of Räikkönen's Ferrari while Alonso kept a watching brief from third place, content for the moment to permit the other two to set the pace.

After six laps or so it became clear that Hamilton was struggling for balance, as indeed he had been all weekend. 'I spent too much time trying to drive around the problem,' he said later. 'I wanted to use the softer [Bridgestone] tyre choice for the first stint of the race, but it was too much of a gamble.'

Hamilton made his first stop at the end of lap 16, almost getting off to a false restart as he accelerated away before the warning lollipop had been raised to signal him back into the race. Lewis just checked it but the moment cost him a couple of extra seconds. Räikkönen went through into the lead, but then stopped on lap 18, allowing Alonso to go ahead. Alonso piled on the pressure before making a very quick 6.3s stop, taking on a relatively small amount of fuel, which he hoped would allow him to build up enough of a lead to stay ahead at

**Above: Johnny Herbert, who won the British Grand Prix in 1995 for Benetton.**

**Below: Red Bull carried this multi-photo-image livery for just one race. Sadly Mark Webber's exposure lasted only eight laps.**
Photographs: Peter J Fox/www.crash.net

his second stop, after a short middle stint. But Räikkönen was too quick for him; after Alonso made his second stop on lap 37, the Ferrari driver pulled out a second a lap through to his own second stop six laps later, after which he comfortably resumed with his lead unchallenged and reeled off the remaining miles to his third chequered flag of the year.

Even in defeat, Hamilton could count himself fortunate. Had Felipe Massa not stalled his Ferrari on the grid he would almost certainly have finished third at the McLaren driver's expense: Massa fought back through the field to take fifth behind an impressively composed Robert Kubica in the BMW. For the last 13 laps of the race Kubica drove with matchless precision

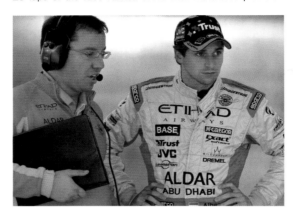

to fend off a relentless attack from Massa. He certainly kept his cool but modestly played down the level of his achievement.

'Being behind here is tough – Felipe lost a lot of downforce [because of following in the BMW's dirty air],' said Kubica. 'He had a harder job than me because I just had to control the situation, not push too much, and I was pretty sure I would hold him.'

Massa had obviously hoped for very much more. Ferrari team chief Jean Todt may have described Räikkönen's performance as 'simply majestic' but he did not underplay Massa's long slog through the pack. 'Felipe drove an extraordinary race,' said Todt. 'but was penalised by a technical problem that meant he had to start the race from the pit lane. Considering this handicap, finishing fifth is really impressive.'

Lewis Hamilton demonstrated the Michael Schumacher touch as he calmly came to terms with his very obvious disappointment at failing to win. There was no rancour or overt frustration about his reaction. Instead, displaying his instinctive feel for the situation and considerable common sense, he blamed himself for any shortfall in his performance, taking a leaf very obviously out of the seven-times world champion's book by making it clear that little or no responsibility could attach to his team.

Hamilton and Alonso shared technical data but were free to make their own choices when it came to their race set-ups. Moreover, the intensity of McLaren's competition with Ferrari meant that both teams were pushing every aspect of their cars' performance to the absolute limit, so the occasional minor error of judgement is only to be expected.

The real imponderable raised by this grand prix for McLaren was whether Räikkönen's victories at Magny-Cours and

Silverstone heralded a return to Ferrari's early-season marked performance edge over its toughest rivals: the Silver Arrows.

'I don't think so,' said Martin Whitmarsh, McLaren's chief operating officer. 'We have got to lift our game, though. We have a test starting on Tuesday and we have got a range of upgrades on the car.

'Ferrari won't stand still, either, but at the moment the circuits will vary the competitive performances of each team and we will see it swing backwards and forwards.'

McLaren remained determined to separate its cars' on-track performance from the continuing controversy surrounding its suspended chief designer Mike Coughlan, in whose home many Ferrari design drawings had been found the previous week.

'Ferrari is a strong team and so is McLaren,' said Whitmarsh. 'Obviously I believe we are going to improve the car. We are in a great points position, despite what has happened here and last weekend. We have to make sure we build upon that and fight for this championship.'

To Renault, Alonso's 2006 triumph must have seemed like a distant memory. Yet again, the team was unable to reproduce its qualifying form in the race and Heikki Kovalainen complained early on that his rear-tyre performance was losing its edge.

'This was a race of two halves for me,' he explained after finishing a lapped seventh, just 4.7s ahead of team-mate Giancarlo Fisichella. 'Quite quickly I began to struggle with the car, especially in the slow corners. I used hard tyres for the second stint and the same thing happened. It was only after I got onto the soft tyres for the final stint that the car felt more consistent on a long run.'

Curiously, this was the absolute reverse of Fisichella's experience – he found that the soft tyres were much less consistent in terms of pure grip. 'It was almost as if I had a problem with the car,' he explained. 'The situation was very unusual but I was not under threat for my position so I could just bring it home.'

Rubens Barrichello and Jenson Button translated 14th and 18th places on the starting grid to ninth and tenth at the chequered flag in the only two cars running on a one-stop strategy, which meant they were very heavy in the opening stages of the race. 'They were the most improved drivers in the race, having made up five and eight places respectively,' said a team statement. Not bad considering that Jenson had to miss Friday's practice due to back problems dating to his first-corner collision in the US GP.

Things were little better in the rival Japanese camp. After Ralf Schumacher and Jarno Trulli qualified their Toyota TF107s promisingly in sixth and tenth positions, the team was hoping for a decent result. Unfortunately Ralf dropped back to eighth after the start and eventually retired after a front wheel began to work loose due to an unexplained attachment problem. Trulli, who had been frustrated by higher tyre-wear levels than his team-mate, quit with handling problems after 43 laps.

Not that Nico Rosberg or Alex Wurz could offer much hope to the Toyota brigade, either. In their Toyota-powered Williams they could manage only 12th and 13th in the team's home race. Wurz admitted that the 'risky combination' of the option tyre and a heavy fuel load meant that traction would be difficult, but because he made a poor start the strategy didn't pay off. Rosberg was frustrated by the way David Coulthard bundled him onto the grass and Wurz survived a collision with Scott Speed's Toro Rosso, which eliminated Speed from the race.

*Alan Henry*

**Above: After taking pole position, Lewis Hamilton was understandably a touch disappointed with third place, although it might well have been fourth if Massa had started the race from his qualifying position on the second row.**
Photograph: Peter J Fox/www.crash.net

## COUGHLAN DOES DEAL WITH FERRARI

McLaren's chief designer agreed to help Ferrari in its legal quest to determine how a cache of confidential technical information came into his hands, bringing to an end a High Court action that had lasted only a day.

Mike Coughlan and his wife Trudy, whose visit to a photocopying shop near Woking to copy more than 780 pages of data alerted Ferrari to the matter, agreed to submit a sworn affidavit to the Italian team. This would contain details of all they knew about the affair and they agreed to continue to cooperate with Ferrari's investigation.

Ferrari's lawyers were due to question Coughlan in court again on 10 July, but after detailed negotiations the previous night a compromise was agreed. As a consequence, the second hearing was cancelled.

In return, Ferrari agreed to withdraw its own request to the High Court to use such information and material collected, including the affidavit, in its application against Coughlan to the Modena district attorney in Italy.

Meanwhile, speculation was building over whether the FIA, international motor sport's governing body, might intervene to review the dispute by convening a meeting of its World Motor Sport Council to examine the issues involved. It was duly convened just days after the British GP.

The FIA made it clear that its only interest related to any possible breach of the F1 regulations or sporting code. However, the World Motor Sport Council has a range of wider penalties at its disposal – such as disqualification or loss of points – that could be applied in the event of its rules' being infringed.

McLaren offered up its MP4-22 to the governing body to carry out a full technical inspection in a bid to prove that there was no facet of its design that could be linked to the Ferrari data. This move was well received, but shortly afterwards the FIA wanted to clarify exactly when Jonathan Neale, McLaren's managing director, was informed that Coughlan had the Ferrari data in his possession. Ferrari also wanted to know.

McLaren made no comment on the issue but a source close to the team said it was 'confident' that there were no problems vindicating the team's position. Ferrari spokesman Luca Colajanni said, 'All we can tell you today is that there was an agreement on outstanding procedural matters and we will not be making the [Coughlan] affidavit available to the Italian courts. We don't know when we will be back in court again.'

Meanwhile in Italy the Modena district attorney opened a criminal investigation against Ferrari's former race and test team manager Nigel Stepney after Ferrari filed a formal complaint against him. Stepney, who was sacked early in July, was suspected of misappropriating the technical data and supplying it to Coughlan. He vigorously denied both allegations.

# FIA F1 WORLD CHAMPIONSHIP • ROUND 8
## SANTANDER
# BRITISH GRAND PRIX
### SILVERSTONE 6–8 JULY 2007

**SILVERSTONE GRAND PRIX CIRCUIT**

116/187 mph/kmh
4 Gear

Club 139/224 ④
Vale 58/93 ②
Luffield 65/105 ④
Bridge ⑤ 157/253
Stowe 114/183 ④
Abbey ② 73/117
Woodcote 168/270 ⑤
Priory 103/166 ③
Brooklands 63/101 ②
Hangar straight 193/311 ⑥
Maggotts 163/262 ⑥
Chapel 110/177 ③
Copse 140/225 ⑤
Becketts 126/203 ④

Photograph: Peter J Fox/www.crash.net

Circuit: 3.194 miles/5.141 km

## RACE RESULTS

All results and data © FOM 2007

| Pos. | Driver | Nat. | No. | Entrant | Car/Engine | Tyres | Laps | Time/Retirement | Speed (mph/km/h) | Gap to leader | Fastest race lap | |
|---|---|---|---|---|---|---|---|---|---|---|---|---|
| 1 | Kimi Räikkönen | FIN | 6 | Scuderia Ferrari Marlboro | Ferrari F2007-056 V8 | B | 59 | 1h 21m 43.074s | 138.335/222.629 | | 1m 20.638s | 17 |
| 2 | Fernando Alonso | E | 1 | Vodafone McLaren Mercedes | McLaren MP4-22-Mercedes FO 108T V8 | B | 59 | 1h 21m 45.533s | 138.266/222.518 | + 2.459s | 1m 21.117s | 35 |
| 3 | Lewis Hamilton | GB | 2 | Vodafone McLaren Mercedes | McLaren MP4-22-Mercedes FO 108T V8 | B | 59 | 1h 22m 22.447s | 137.234/220.856 | + 39.373s | 1m 21.675s | 11 |
| 4 | Robert Kubica | POL | 10 | BMW Sauber F1 Team | BMW Sauber F1.07-BMW P86/7 V8 | B | 59 | 1h 22m 36.393s | 136.847/220.234 | + 53.319s | 1m 22.105s | 14 |
| 5 | Felipe Massa | BR | 5 | Scuderia Ferrari Marlboro | Ferrari F2007-056 V8 | B | 59 | 1h 22m 37.137s | 136.827/220.201 | + 54.063s | 1m 20.858s | 17 |
| 6 | Nick Heidfeld | D | 9 | BMW Sauber F1 Team | BMW Sauber F1.07-BMW P86/7 V8 | B | 59 | 1h 22m 39.410s | 136.764/220.100 | + 56.336s | 1m 21.991s | 17 |
| 7 | Heikki Kovalainen | FIN | 4 | ING Renault F1 Team | Renault R27-RS27 V8 | B | 58 | | | + 1 lap | 1m 22.552s | 11 |
| 8 | Giancarlo Fisichella | I | 3 | ING Renault F1 Team | Renault R27-RS27 V8 | B | 58 | | | + 1 lap | 1m 22.136s | 13 |
| 9 | Rubens Barrichello | BR | 8 | Honda Racing F1 Team | Honda RA107-RA807E V8 | B | 58 | | | + 1 lap | 1m 23.387s | 23 |
| 10 | Jenson Button | GB | 7 | Honda Racing F1 Team | Honda RA107-RA807E V8 | B | 58 | | | + 1 lap | 1m 23.581s | 29 |
| 11 | David Coulthard | GB | 14 | Red Bull Racing | Red Bull RB3-Renault RS27 V8 | B | 58 | | | + 1 lap | 1m 23.118s | 40 |
| 12 | Nico Rosberg | D | 16 | AT&T Williams | Williams FW29-Toyota RVX-07 V8 | B | 58 | | | + 1 lap | 1m 22.896s | 49 |
| 13 | Alexander Wurz | A | 17 | AT&T Williams | Williams FW29-Toyota RVX-07 V8 | B | 58 | | | + 1 lap | 1m 22.693s | 57 |
| 14 | Takuma Sato | J | 22 | Super Aguri F1 Team | Super Aguri SA07-Honda RA807E V8 | B | 57 | | | + 2 laps | 1m 23.413s | 42 |
| 15 | Christijan Albers | NL | 21 | Etihad Aldar Spyker F1 Team | Spyker F8-VII-Ferrari 056H V8 | B | 57 | | | + 2 laps | 1m 24.390s | 56 |
| 16 | Vitantonio Liuzzi | I | 18 | Scuderia Toro Rosso | Toro Rosso STR02-Ferrari 056H V8 | B | 53 | Gearbox | | + 6 laps | 1m 23.628s | 46 |
| | Jarno Trulli | I | 12 | Panasonic Toyota Racing | Toyota TF107-RVX-07 V8 | B | 43 | Handling | | | 1m 23.708s | 17 |
| | Anthony Davidson | GB | 23 | Super Aguri F1 Team | Super Aguri SA07-Honda RA807E V8 | B | 35 | Mechanical | | | 1m 24.144s | 26 |
| | Scott Speed | USA | 19 | Scuderia Toro Rosso | Toro Rosso STR02-Ferrari 056H V8 | B | 29 | Accident | | | 1m 23.570s | 19 |
| | Ralf Schumacher | D | 11 | Panasonic Toyota Racing | Toyota TF107-RVX-07 V8 | B | 22 | Front wheel | | | 1m 22.510s | 12 |
| | Adrian Sutil | D | 20 | Etihad Aldar Spyker F1 Team | Spyker F8-VII-Ferrari 056H V8 | B | 16 | Engine | | | 1m 25.015s | 16 |
| | Mark Webber | AUS | 15 | Red Bull Racing | Red Bull RB3-Renault RS27 V8 | B | 8 | Hydraulics | | | 1m 23.767s | 6 |

Fastest race lap: Kimi Räikkönen on lap 17, 1m 20.638s, 142.614 mph/229.514 km/h.

Lap record: Michael Schumacher (Ferrari F2004 V10), 1m 18.739s, 146.053 mph/235.049 km/h (2004).

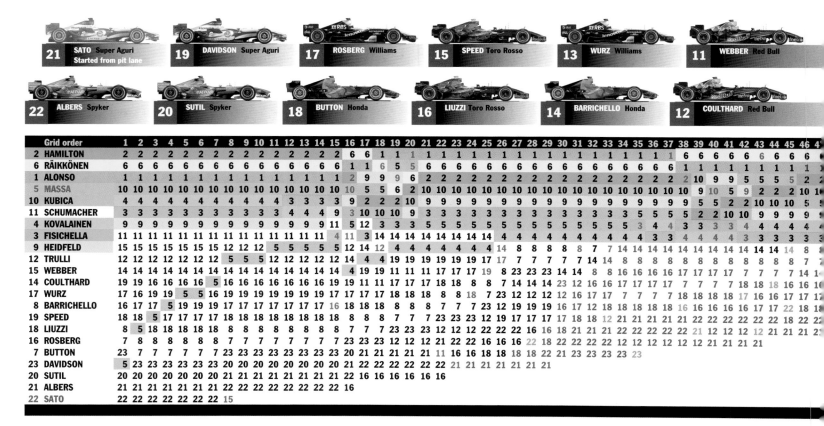

| 21 | SATO Super Aguri Started from pit lane |
| 19 | DAVIDSON Super Aguri |
| 17 | ROSBERG Williams |
| 15 | SPEED Toro Rosso |
| 13 | WURZ Williams |
| 11 | WEBBER Red Bull |
| 22 | ALBERS Spyker |
| 20 | SUTIL Spyker |
| 18 | BUTTON Honda |
| 16 | LIUZZI Toro Rosso |
| 14 | BARRICHELLO Honda |
| 12 | COULTHARD Red Bull |

| Grid order | 1 | 2 | 3 | 4 | 5 | 6 | 7 | 8 | 9 | 10 | 11 | 12 | 13 | 14 | 15 | 16 | 17 | 18 | 19 | 20 | 21 | 22 | 23 | 24 | 25 | 26 | 27 | 28 | 29 | 30 | 31 | 32 | 33 | 34 | 35 | 36 | 37 | 38 | 39 | 40 | 41 | 42 | 43 | 44 | 45 | 46 | 47 |
|---|---|---|---|---|---|---|---|---|---|---|---|---|---|---|---|---|---|---|---|---|---|---|---|---|---|---|---|---|---|---|---|---|---|---|---|---|---|---|---|---|---|---|---|---|---|---|---|
| 2 HAMILTON | 2 | 2 | 2 | 2 | 2 | 2 | 2 | 2 | 2 | 2 | 2 | 2 | 2 | 2 | 2 | 6 | 1 | 1 | 1 | 1 | 1 | 1 | 1 | 1 | 1 | 1 | 1 | 1 | 1 | 1 | 1 | 1 | 1 | 1 | 1 | 1 | 1 | 6 | 6 | 6 | 6 | 6 | 6 | 6 | 6 | 6 | 6 |
| 6 RÄIKKÖNEN | 6 | 6 | 6 | 6 | 6 | 6 | 6 | 6 | 6 | 6 | 6 | 6 | 6 | 6 | 6 | 1 | 6 | 5 | 6 | 6 | 6 | 6 | 6 | 6 | 6 | 6 | 6 | 6 | 6 | 6 | 6 | 6 | 6 | 6 | 6 | 6 | 6 | 1 | 1 | 1 | 1 | 1 | 1 | 1 | 1 | 1 | 1 |
| 1 ALONSO | 1 | 1 | 1 | 1 | 1 | 1 | 1 | 1 | 1 | 1 | 1 | 1 | 1 | 1 | 1 | 2 | 9 | 9 | 9 | 6 | 2 | 2 | 2 | 2 | 2 | 2 | 2 | 2 | 2 | 2 | 2 | 2 | 2 | 2 | 2 | 2 | 2 | 2 | 10 | 9 | 9 | 5 | 5 | 5 | 5 | 2 | 2 |
| 5 MASSA | 10 | 10 | 10 | 10 | 10 | 10 | 10 | 10 | 10 | 10 | 10 | 10 | 10 | 10 | 10 | 10 | 5 | 5 | 6 | 2 | 10 | 10 | 10 | 10 | 10 | 10 | 10 | 10 | 10 | 10 | 10 | 10 | 10 | 10 | 10 | 10 | 10 | 9 | 10 | 5 | 9 | 2 | 2 | 2 | 10 | 10 | |
| 10 KUBICA | 4 | 4 | 4 | 4 | 4 | 4 | 4 | 4 | 4 | 4 | 3 | 3 | 3 | 3 | 9 | 2 | 2 | 2 | 10 | 9 | 9 | 9 | 9 | 9 | 9 | 9 | 9 | 9 | 9 | 9 | 9 | 9 | 9 | 9 | 9 | 9 | 9 | 5 | 5 | 2 | 10 | 10 | 10 | 5 | 5 | | |
| 11 SCHUMACHER | 3 | 3 | 3 | 3 | 3 | 3 | 3 | 3 | 3 | 4 | 4 | 4 | 9 | 3 | 10 | 10 | 10 | 3 | 3 | 3 | 3 | 3 | 3 | 3 | 3 | 3 | 3 | 3 | 3 | 3 | 3 | 3 | 3 | 3 | 3 | 5 | 5 | 2 | 2 | 10 | 10 | 9 | 9 | 9 | 9 | | |
| 4 KOVALAINEN | 9 | 9 | 9 | 9 | 9 | 9 | 9 | 9 | 9 | 9 | 9 | 11 | 5 | 4 | 3 | 14 | 14 | 14 | 14 | 14 | 14 | 14 | 5 | 5 | 5 | 5 | 5 | 5 | 5 | 5 | 4 | 4 | 4 | 3 | 3 | 3 | 4 | 4 | 4 | 4 | 4 | 4 | 4 | | | | |
| 3 FISICHELLA | 11 | 11 | 11 | 11 | 11 | 11 | 11 | 11 | 11 | 11 | 11 | 11 | 11 | 4 | 11 | 3 | 14 | 14 | 14 | 14 | 14 | 14 | 4 | 4 | 4 | 4 | 4 | 4 | 4 | 4 | 3 | 3 | 3 | 4 | 4 | 4 | 3 | 3 | 3 | 3 | 3 | 3 | 3 | | | | |
| 9 HEIDFELD | 15 | 15 | 15 | 15 | 15 | 15 | 15 | 12 | 12 | 5 | 5 | 5 | 5 | 5 | 12 | 14 | 12 | 4 | 4 | 4 | 4 | 4 | 14 | 8 | 8 | 8 | 8 | 7 | 7 | 14 | 14 | 14 | 14 | 14 | 14 | 14 | 14 | 14 | 14 | 8 | | | | | | | |
| 12 TRULLI | 12 | 12 | 12 | 12 | 12 | 12 | 5 | 5 | 5 | 12 | 12 | 12 | 12 | 12 | 14 | 4 | 4 | 19 | 19 | 19 | 19 | 19 | 17 | 7 | 7 | 7 | 7 | 14 | 14 | 8 | 8 | 8 | 8 | 8 | 8 | 8 | 8 | 8 | 7 | | | | | | | | |
| 15 WEBBER | 14 | 14 | 14 | 14 | 14 | 14 | 14 | 14 | 14 | 14 | 14 | 14 | 14 | 4 | 19 | 19 | 11 | 11 | 11 | 17 | 17 | 19 | 8 | 23 | 23 | 23 | 14 | 14 | 8 | 16 | 16 | 16 | 17 | 17 | 17 | 7 | 7 | 7 | 14 | 14 | | | | | | | |
| 14 COULTHARD | 19 | 19 | 19 | 16 | 16 | 5 | 16 | 16 | 16 | 16 | 16 | 16 | 4 | 11 | 11 | 11 | 17 | 17 | 7 | 14 | 14 | 23 | 23 | 12 | 12 | 16 | 17 | 17 | 17 | 7 | 7 | 18 | 16 | 16 | 16 | | | | | | | | | | | | |
| 17 WURZ | 17 | 16 | 19 | 19 | 5 | 5 | 19 | 19 | 19 | 19 | 17 | 17 | 7 | 7 | 7 | 8 | 7 | 8 | 23 | 12 | 12 | 16 | 16 | 17 | 17 | 7 | 7 | 7 | 18 | 18 | 16 | 16 | 16 | | | | | | | | | | | | | | |
| 8 BARRICHELLO | 16 | 17 | 17 | 5 | 19 | 19 | 17 | 17 | 17 | 17 | 17 | 16 | 18 | 18 | 8 | 8 | 7 | 23 | 12 | 12 | 16 | 12 | 12 | 18 | 7 | 7 | 7 | 16 | 16 | 16 | 16 | 17 | 17 | 22 | 18 | | | | | | | | | | | | |
| 19 SPEED | 18 | 18 | 5 | 17 | 17 | 17 | 16 | 18 | 18 | 18 | 18 | 18 | 8 | 8 | 23 | 7 | 23 | 12 | 18 | 16 | 18 | 18 | 12 | 21 | 21 | 21 | 22 | 22 | 22 | 22 | 22 | 18 | 22 | | | | | | | | | | | | | |
| 18 LIUZZI | 8 | 5 | 18 | 18 | 18 | 18 | 18 | 8 | 8 | 8 | 8 | 8 | 7 | 7 | 23 | 12 | 16 | 18 | 21 | 21 | 22 | 22 | 22 | 21 | 12 | 12 | 12 | 21 | 21 | 21 | | | | | | | | | | | | | | | | | |
| 16 ROSBERG | 7 | 8 | 8 | 8 | 8 | 8 | 7 | 7 | 7 | 7 | 7 | 7 | 23 | 23 | 16 | 16 | 22 | 18 | 22 | 22 | 12 | 12 | 12 | 12 | 21 | 21 | 21 | | | | | | | | | | | | | | | | | | | | |
| 7 BUTTON | 23 | 7 | 7 | 7 | 7 | 7 | 23 | 20 | 20 | 23 | 23 | 20 | 21 | 11 | 18 | 18 | 18 | 23 | 23 | 23 | 23 | | | | | | | | | | | | | | | | | | | | | | | | | | |
| 23 DAVIDSON | 5 | 23 | 23 | 23 | 23 | 23 | 20 | 20 | 20 | 20 | 20 | 22 | 22 | 22 | 22 | 21 | 21 | 21 | 21 | 21 | | | | | | | | | | | | | | | | | | | | | | | | | | | |
| 20 SUTIL | 20 | 20 | 20 | 20 | 20 | 20 | 21 | 21 | 21 | 21 | 22 | 22 | 16 | 16 | 16 | 16 | 16 | | | | | | | | | | | | | | | | | | | | | | | | | | | | | | |
| 21 ALBERS | 21 | 21 | 21 | 21 | 21 | 22 | 22 | 22 | 22 | 22 | 22 | 16 | | | | | | | | | | | | | | | | | | | | | | | | | | | | | | | | | | | |
| 22 SATO | 22 | 22 | 22 | 22 | 22 | 22 | 22 | 15 | | | | | | | | | | | | | | | | | | | | | | | | | | | | | | | | | | | | | | | |

### PRACTICE 1 (FRIDAY)

Overcast, windy
(track 19–20ºC, air 15–16ºC)

| Pos. | Driver | Laps | Time |
|---|---|---|---|
| 1 | Lewis Hamilton | 24 | 1m 21.100s |
| 2 | Kimi Räikkönen | 26 | 1m 21.211s |
| 3 | Felipe Massa | 26 | 1m 21.285s |
| 4 | Fernando Alonso | 21 | 1m 21.675s |
| 5 | Nico Rosberg | 24 | 1m 22.006s |
| 6 | Robert Kubica | 25 | 1m 22.107s |
| 7 | Nick Heidfeld | 13 | 1m 22.176s |
| 8 | Alexander Wurz | 23 | 1m 22.216s |
| 9 | Ralf Schumacher | 21 | 1m 22.878s |
| 10 | Rubens Barrichello | 27 | 1m 22.956s |
| 11 | Jarno Trulli | 26 | 1m 23.030s |
| 12 | Anthony Davidson | 24 | 1m 23.037s |
| 13 | Heikki Kovalainen | 25 | 1m 23.099s |
| 14 | Giancarlo Fisichella | 21 | 1m 23.179s |
| 15 | Jenson Button | 17 | 1m 23.517s |
| 16 | Takuma Sato | 18 | 1m 23.548s |
| 17 | Mark Webber | 21 | 1m 23.564s |
| 18 | David Coulthard | 15 | 1m 23.618s |
| 19 | Scott Speed | 20 | 1m 23.854s |
| 20 | Adrian Sutil | 25 | 1m 23.954s |
| 21 | Vitantonio Liuzzi | 23 | 1m 24.154s |
| 22 | Christijan Albers | 30 | 1m 24.172s |

### PRACTICE 2 (FRIDAY)

Overcast, windy, light rain
(track 20–21ºC, air 17ºC)

| Pos. | Driver | Laps | Time |
|---|---|---|---|
| 1 | Kimi Räikkönen | 35 | 1m 20.639s |
| 2 | Felipe Massa | 30 | 1m 21.138s |
| 3 | Ralf Schumacher | 34 | 1m 21.381s |
| 4 | Lewis Hamilton | 39 | 1m 21.381s |
| 5 | Jarno Trulli | 35 | 1m 21.467s |
| 6 | Fernando Alonso | 35 | 1m 21.616s |
| 7 | Nico Rosberg | 40 | 1m 21.619s |
| 8 | Alexander Wurz | 37 | 1m 21.650s |
| 9 | Mark Webber | 31 | 1m 22.137s |
| 10 | Anthony Davidson | 40 | 1m 22.143s |
| 11 | Heikki Kovalainen | 42 | 1m 22.189s |
| 12 | Giancarlo Fisichella | 39 | 1m 22.257s |
| 13 | Robert Kubica | 41 | 1m 22.372s |
| 14 | David Coulthard | 23 | 1m 22.428s |
| 15 | Nick Heidfeld | 34 | 1m 22.486s |
| 16 | Takuma Sato | 38 | 1m 22.487s |
| 17 | Rubens Barrichello | 39 | 1m 22.511s |
| 18 | Christian Klien | 45 | 1m 22.833s |
| 19 | Scott Speed | 42 | 1m 22.840s |
| 20 | Vitantonio Liuzzi | 35 | 1m 23.105s |
| 21 | Christijan Albers | 35 | 1m 23.113s |
| 22 | Adrian Sutil | 30 | 1m 23.720s |

### QUALIFYING (SATURDAY)

Scattered cloud (track 31–32ºC, air 21ºC)

| Pos. | Driver | First | Second | Third |
|---|---|---|---|---|
| 1 | Lewis Hamilton | 1m 19.885s | 1m 19.400s | 1m 19.997s |
| 2 | Kimi Räikkönen | 1m 19.753s | 1m 19.252s | 1m 20.099s |
| 3 | Fernando Alonso | 1m 19.330s | 1m 19.152s | 1m 20.147s |
| 4 | Felipe Massa | 1m 19.790s | 1m 19.421s | 1m 20.265s |
| 5 | Robert Kubica | 1m 20.294s | 1m 20.054s | 1m 20.401s |
| 6 | Ralf Schumacher | 1m 20.513s | 1m 19.860s | 1m 20.516s |
| 7 | Heikki Kovalainen | 1m 20.570s | 1m 20.077s | 1m 20.721s |
| 8 | Giancarlo Fisichella | 1m 20.842s | 1m 20.042s | 1m 20.775s |
| 9 | Nick Heidfeld | 1m 20.534s | 1m 20.178s | 1m 20.894s |
| 10 | Jarno Trulli | 1m 21.150s | 1m 20.133s | 1m 21.240s |
| 11 | Mark Webber | 1m 20.583s | 1m 20.235s | |
| 12 | David Coulthard | 1m 21.154s | 1m 20.329s | |
| 13 | Alexander Wurz | 1m 20.830s | 1m 20.350s | |
| 14 | Rubens Barrichello | 1m 21.169s | 1m 20.364s | |
| 15 | Scott Speed | 1m 20.834s | 1m 20.515s | |
| 16 | Vitantonio Liuzzi | 1m 21.160s | 1m 20.823s | |
| 17 | Nico Rosberg | 1m 21.219s | | |
| 18 | Jenson Button | 1m 21.335s | | |
| 19 | Anthony Davidson | 1m 21.448s | | |
| 20 | Adrian Sutil | 1m 22.019s | | |
| 21 | Takuma Sato | 1m 22.045s | | |
| 22 | Christijan Albers | 1m 22.589s | | |

### PRACTICE 3 (SATURDAY)

Scattered cloud (track 24–25ºC, air 18–19ºC)

| Pos. | Driver | Laps | Time |
|---|---|---|---|
| 1 | Kimi Räikkönen | 17 | 1m 19.751s |
| 2 | Fernando Alonso | 12 | 1m 19.920s |
| 3 | Felipe Massa | 17 | 1m 19.969s |
| 4 | Lewis Hamilton | 12 | 1m 20.344s |
| 5 | Nico Rosberg | 17 | 1m 20.666s |
| 6 | Ralf Schumacher | 21 | 1m 20.770s |
| 7 | Vitantonio Liuzzi | 21 | 1m 20.876s |
| 8 | Heikki Kovalainen | 17 | 1m 20.882s |
| 9 | Nick Heidfeld | 19 | 1m 20.882s |
| 10 | Anthony Davidson | 23 | 1m 20.915s |
| 11 | Giancarlo Fisichella | 19 | 1m 20.983s |
| 12 | Mark Webber | 16 | 1m 21.002s |
| 13 | Scott Speed | 19 | 1m 21.039s |
| 14 | Rubens Barrichello | 22 | 1m 21.140s |
| 15 | Alexander Wurz | 17 | 1m 21.148s |
| 16 | Robert Kubica | 17 | 1m 21.156s |
| 17 | Jarno Trulli | 18 | 1m 21.321s |
| 18 | David Coulthard | 16 | 1m 21.343s |
| 19 | Jenson Button | 24 | 1m 21.583s |
| 20 | Takuma Sato | 23 | 1m 21.745s |
| 21 | Christijan Albers | 23 | 1m 22.101s |
| 22 | Adrian Sutil | 24 | 1m 22.180s |

20 Pit stop
20 One lap or more behind leader

### RACE TYRE STRATEGIES

**BRIDGESTONE**

In 2007, the tyre regulations stipulate that the two dry-tyre specifications must be visibly distinguishable from each other. At the British Grand Prix, the medium compound Bridgestone Potenza tyre was marked with a white line in the second-from-inside groove.

| | Driver | Race stint 1 | Race stint 2 | Race stint 3 |
|---|---|---|---|---|
| 1 | Kimi Räikkönen | Medium: laps 1–18 | Medium: 19–43 | Hard: 44–59 |
| 2 | Fernando Alonso | Hard: 1–20 | Medium: 21–37 | Hard: 38–59 |
| 3 | Lewis Hamilton | Hard: 1–16 | Hard: 17–37 | Medium: 38–59 |
| 4 | Robert Kubica | Hard: 1–16 | Hard: 17–40 | Medium: 41–59 |
| 5 | Felipe Massa | Medium: 1–20 | Medium: 21–43 | Hard: 44–59 |
| 6 | Nick Heidfeld | Hard: 1–19 | Hard: 20–42 | Medium: 43–59 |
| 7 | Heikki Kovalainen | Hard: 1–15 | Hard: 16–37 | Medium: 38–59 |
| 8 | Giancarlo Fisichella | Hard: 1–16 | Hard: 17–37 | Medium: 38–59 |
| 9 | Rubens Barrichello | Medium: 1–31 | Hard: 32–59 | |
| 10 | Jenson Button | Medium: 1–33 | Hard: 34–59 | |
| 11 | David Coulthard | Hard: 1–26 | Hard: 27–45 | Medium: 46–59 |
| 12 | Nico Rosberg | Medium: 1–15 | Medium: 16–38 | Hard: 39–59 |
| 13 | Alexander Wurz | Medium: 1–26 | Medium: 27–42 | Medium: 43–59 |
| 14 | Takuma Sato | Hard: 1–28 | Hard: 29–45 | Medium: 46–59 |
| 15 | Christijan Albers | Hard: 1–23 | Hard: 24–39 | Medium: 40–59 |
| 16 | Vitantonio Liuzzi | Hard: 1–24 | Hard: 25–44 | Medium: 45–59 |
| | Jarno Trulli | Hard: 1–18 | Hard: 19–33 | Medium: 34–43 (DNF) |
| | Anthony Davidson | Hard 1–30 | Medium: 31–35 (DNF) | |
| | Scott Speed | Hard: 1–25 | Hard: 26–29 (DNF) | |
| | Ralf Schumacher | Hard: 1–16 | Medium: 17–22 (DNF) | |
| | Adrian Sutil | Hard: 1–16 (DNF) | | |
| | Mark Webber | Hard: 1–8 (DNF) | | |

**9** HEIDFELD BMW-Sauber

**7** KOVALAINEN Renault

**5** KUBICA BMW-Sauber

**3** ALONSO McLaren

**1** HAMILTON McLaren

**10** TRULLI Toyota

**8** FISICHELLA Renault

**6** SCHUMACHER Toyota

**4** MASSA Ferrari
Started from pit lane

**2** RÄIKKÖNEN Ferrari

**RACE DISTANCE:**
59 laps
188.408 miles/303.214 km

**RACE WEATHER:**
Scattered cloud,
(track 31–32ºC, air 20–21ºC

| 48 | 49 | 50 | 51 | 52 | 53 | 54 | 55 | 56 | 57 | 58 | 59 | |
|---|---|---|---|---|---|---|---|---|---|---|---|---|
| 6 | 6 | 6 | 6 | 6 | 6 | 6 | 6 | 6 | 6 | 6 | 6 | 1 |
| 1 | 1 | 1 | 1 | 1 | 1 | 1 | 1 | 1 | 1 | 1 | 1 | 2 |
| 2 | 2 | 2 | 2 | 2 | 2 | 2 | 2 | 2 | 2 | 2 | 2 | 3 |
| 10 | 10 | 10 | 10 | 10 | 10 | 10 | 10 | 10 | 10 | 10 | 10 | 4 |
| 5 | 5 | 5 | 5 | 5 | 5 | 5 | 5 | 5 | 5 | 5 | 5 | 5 |
| 9 | 9 | 9 | 9 | 9 | 9 | 9 | 9 | 9 | 9 | 9 | 9 | 6 |
| 4 | 4 | 4 | 4 | 4 | 4 | 4 | 4 | 4 | 4 | 4 | | 7 |
| 3 | 3 | 3 | 3 | 3 | 3 | 3 | 3 | 3 | 3 | 3 | | 8 |
| 8 | 8 | 8 | 8 | 8 | 8 | 8 | 8 | 8 | 8 | | | |
| 7 | 7 | 7 | 7 | 7 | 7 | 7 | 7 | 7 | 7 | | | |
| 14 | 14 | 14 | 14 | 14 | 14 | 14 | 14 | 14 | 14 | 14 | | |
| 16 | 16 | 16 | 16 | 16 | 16 | 16 | 16 | 16 | 16 | 16 | | |
| 17 | 17 | 17 | 17 | 17 | 17 | 17 | 17 | 17 | 17 | 17 | | |
| 18 | 18 | 18 | 18 | 18 | 18 | 22 | 22 | 22 | 22 | | | |
| 22 | 22 | 22 | 22 | 22 | 22 | 21 | 21 | 21 | 21 | | | |
| 21 | 21 | 21 | 21 | 21 | 21 | | | | | | | |

### FOR THE RECORD

200th FASTEST LAP: Ferrari

9,000th LAP LED: McLaren

### POINTS

| | DRIVERS | | | CONSTRUCTORS | |
|---|---|---|---|---|---|
| 1 | Lewis Hamilton | 70 | 1 | McLaren | 128 |
| 2 | Fernando Alonso | 58 | 2 | Ferrari | 103 |
| 3 | Kimi Räikkönen | 52 | 3 | BMW Sauber | 56 |
| 4 | Felipe Massa | 51 | 4 | Renault | 31 |
| 5 | Nick Heidfeld | 33 | 5 | Williams | 13 |
| 6 | Robert Kubica | 22 | 6 | Toyota | 9 |
| 7 | Giancarlo Fisichella | 17 | 7 | Red Bull | 6 |
| 8 | Heikki Kovalainen | 14 | 8 | Super Aguri | 4 |
| 9 | Alexander Wurz | 8 | 9 | Honda | 1 |
| 10 | Jarno Trulli | 7 | | | |
| 11 | Nico Rosberg | 5 | | | |
| 12 | David Coulthard | 4 | | | |
| 13 | Takuma Sato | 4 | | | |
| 14 | Mark Webber | 2 | | | |
| 15 | Ralf Schumacher | 2 | | | |
| 16 | Sebastian Vettel | 1 | | | |
| 17 | Jenson Button | 1 | | | |

Photographs: Peter J Fox/www.crash.net

**Right:** A furious Massa's eyes betray just how angry he is following a race in which he clearly feels Alonso has been excessively aggressive.

FIA F1 WORLD CHAMPIONSHIP/ROUND 10
# EUROPEAN GP
## NÜRBURGRING

## DIARY

Former BAR technical director Geoff Willis joins Red Bull Racing as chief designer.

Helio Castroneves equals the record for the most pole positions in an IRL season by taking his sixth pole of 2007 at Mid-Ohio.

Sébastien Bourdais is close to an F1 deal with Scuderia Toro Rosso for 2008.

Plans to stage the 2008 Australian GP as a night race are abandoned.

Top: McLaren's Ron Dennis brushes away the scrum of photographers as he and Lewis Hamilton return from Lewis's hospital check-up after his crash in qualifying.

Above: Markus Winkelhock settles into the grand prix weekend.
Photographs: Peter J. Fox/www.crash.net

Below: Happy together! Robert Kubica and BMW spokesperson Ann Bradshaw face the camera.
Photograph: Jean-François-Galeron/WRi2

## NÜRBURGRING QUALIFYING

Television viewers across the world may have had grandstand seats for Lewis Hamilton's white-knuckle ride into the barriers during Saturday qualifying, but what they won't have known is that his team-mate Fernando Alonso came within a whisker of suffering the same fate when his McLaren MP4-22 was found to have a similarly loose right-front wheel nut when it arrived in the pit lane seconds after Lewis plunged off the road.

On closer examination Alonso's right-front wheel turned out to have been damaged and was leaking air. The McLaren mechanics worked until midnight getting to the bottom of the problems with the air guns, after which they prepared the monocoque from the spare car in preparation for fitting the engine from Lewis's race car when the wreckage was returned from *parc fermé* on Sunday morning.

Alonso had been on course for pole position, but had a big moment in Turn Five, which caused him to drop behind Kimi Räikkönen, who put pole beyond doubt for Ferrari with a 1m 31.450s best, just 0.3s inside the best Alonso could manage.

Fernando said, 'I lost the rear a little bit in Turn Five and I lost control in the oversteer until Turn Six. For 50 or 60 metres the car was not in my control, so I was lucky to put it back on the asphalt because I think I nearly touched the grass.

'So from that moment I thought for sure that pole position was not possible any more and I tried to do a good rest of the lap, tried to be fifth or sixth. I really thought I had lost too much time and then when I realised I was second I was pretty pleased because I had been lucky in that moment.'

Felipe Massa had looked favourite to bag pole, but confessed later that he 'lost a bit of the right feeling' after the break following Hamilton's accident. He wound up third on 1m 31.778s, squeezing in ahead of the impressive BMW-Sauber F1.07s of Nick Heidfeld (1m 31.840s) and Robert Kubica (1m 32.123s). 'I was satisfied with fourth until I saw I missed the front row by only one tenth,' shrugged Heidfeld with a self-deprecatory grin.

Over in the Red Bull-Renault camp there were grins of quiet satisfaction after Mark Webber lined up sixth on 1m 32.476s, but team-mate David Coulthard was less fortunate. In Q1 his efforts were spoiled by Webber's locking up his brakes in front of him, after which there was insufficient time remaining for a second run, so he failed to make the cut and had to be content with a 20th-fastest 1m 33.151s.

Renault had a new aerodynamic package available for this race and Heikki Kovalainen reported that the front wing was a definite step forward, even though the R27 was still lacking somewhat when it came to overall grip. He qualified a respectable seventh on 1m 32.478s, but team-mate Giancarlo Fisichella pushed too hard and, as a result, had to handle the frustration of lining up 13th on 1m 32.010s.

Toyota, meanwhile, enjoyed a trouble-free practice and Jarno Trulli was feeling in a particularly buoyant frame of mind, having run his troublesome Silverstone chassis (number 06) back-to-back against his older chassis (04) and reached the conclusion that the older chassis was better. 'Maybe there is something we cannot see, but the new car proved slower and worse on the tyres as well,' said Jarno after lining up eighth on 1m 32.501s.

He was one place ahead of his team-mate Ralf Schumacher (1m 32.570s), who was at least content to be on the clean side of the starting grid. Next up was Hamilton on 1m 33.833s, followed by the keenly matched Williams duo, Nico Rosberg (1m 31.978s) and Alex Wurz (1m 31.996s).

Honda kicked off the weekend by confirming that Jenson Button and Rubens Barrichello would remain on the driving strength. On this occasion it was Rubens who spearheaded the qualifying effort, setting a 14th-fastest 1m 32.221s while a disbelieving Button failed to register a decent time, ending up 17th on 1m 32.983s. 'I just didn't have the grip and balance that I've had on new tyres all weekend,' said Jenson. At least he would go on to show storming speed in the early rain-soaked laps of the race.

The Super Aguris of Anthony Davidson (1m 32.451s) and Takuma Sato (1m 32.838s) split the two Hondas and the rest of the grid was made up of the Toro Rossos of Scott Speed (1m 33.038s) and Vitantonio Liuzzi (1m 33.148s), Coulthard and the two Spykers of Adrian Sutil and Markus Winkelhock, who was due to write his own modest slice of F1 history come the race.

IT was the race of the year. The new Nürburgring may not be everybody's cup of tea but on this occasion it delivered a terrific race by any exacting standards. After a torrential rain shower sent most of the competitors skating in all directions early on, the European Grand Prix settled into an admittedly close-fought but rather routine event, with Felipe Massa's Ferrari F2007 just sustaining a marginal edge over Fernando Alonso's McLaren MP4-22. Then another rain shower in the closing stages kicked the advantage into Alonso's favour. With four laps to go, after the two cars banged wheels repeatedly, Alonso elbowed his way ahead of the Ferrari to score what he must surely regard as one of the very best victories of his F1 career. His winning margin was 8.2s.

'It was an exciting race both to drive and, I hope, to watch,' said Alonso. 'The Ferraris had a slight edge in the dry but perhaps our car worked slightly better in the wet. The rain at the end helped us a lot. I had six laps to pass Felipe. We touched twice but I enjoyed the race hugely. I like changing conditions and when the rain came I knew I had to go for it.'

Massa, though, felt the reigning world champion's technique was a little questionable, but tried to keep his cool during the post-race press conference. It was later reported, however, that away from the microphones Massa had told Alonso that he ought to learn how to drive in traffic, to which Alonso responded by telling Massa to push off. Only he didn't say 'push'. 'You should learn to drive,' said Alonso dismissively, just before the podium ceremony. Massa fired back, 'Hey, maybe you should.' Alonso tried to ignore his rival but Felipe still had more to say. 'This is the second time this year with you. You banged wheels with me at Barcelona, too, remember?' Alonso by this time was more interested in the plaudits of the crowds. 'Yes, yes,' he replied, again dismissively, as they went out onto the podium proper. Alonso quickly apologised for his lapse and looked rather sheepish about it.

'Hey, I'm sorry if you thought I said anything wrong,' said Alonso, 'but maybe you've still got a bit to learn,' adding for good measure that if Massa ever pulls a stunt like that again, he'll put him into the barrier.

Felipe bridled at this. 'Well, if you want to apologise, then it's not only to me, because there are rules about these things and I've done nothing wrong!' Michael Schumacher stepped in then to calm the situation – he'd got his own problems, having been

**Below left: David Coulthard chats with Red Bull's consultant Dr Helmut Marko.**

**Bottom: Lucky boy. Lewis Hamilton is winched from the gravel trap to rejoin the field in the race.**
Photographs: Peter J Fox/www.crash.net

**Above: Alex Wurz once again brought the Williams team precious points.**
Photograph: Peter J Fox/www.crash.net

invited by the organisers to present the constructors' cup to the winning entrant on the podium. Handing over the silverware to McLaren team principal Ron Dennis was really a bit more than he could stand. But he gritted his teeth and got the job done.

Meanwhile Massa was becoming a little more reflective and calm. 'Towards the end I fitted a set of tyres that were vibrating a lot and I could not keep the pace,' he pondered. 'Before that, I was controlling the race, but then came the rain and I could not stay ahead.'

By contrast, Lewis Hamilton's world championship hopes received an unwelcome cold shower after torrential rain transformed the circuit into a precarious skating rink and the race was red-flagged to a temporary halt after only four of its scheduled 60 laps had been completed.

Although Hamilton's McLaren seemed to be one of the victims left firmly embedded in a gravel trap, the youngster was rescued from his embarrassment by the intervention of a trackside crane and lifted back onto the track, removed from a potential position of danger and therefore free to continue racing.

Although the race was restarted, Hamilton was consigned to the back of the field and eventually finished ninth, missing out on a point by a single place, a result that slashed his championship lead from 12 points to two.

Minutes before the start a light rain shower had brushed the circuit, but the cars accelerated away for their formation lap without any undue delay. Yet within seconds most of the drivers were frantically radioing their pits warning their teams that they would be stopping for intermediate or dry-weather tyres at the end of the opening lap. As it transpired, events turned out to be a whole lot more spectacular than that.

As the starting signal was given, Kimi Räikkönen just edged ahead of Massa going into the first corner and, though

everybody edged through the tight right-hander quite successfully, the two BMW Sauber drivers collided in Turn Two, causing the rest of the pack to scatter in all directions. Hamilton and Jenson Button made terrific starts, but Lewis just tagged the pirouetting Robert Kubica and punctured his McLaren's left-rear tyre. It left him with a frustrating and time-consuming crawl back to the pits to change the wheel, just as Nick Heidfeld had to limp home with a frayed nose cone after pitching Kubica into that unnecessary spin.

'My start was not as good as usual,' said Heidfeld, 'and, unfortunately, in the first corner Robert forced me out onto the dirt.' Kubica added, 'In the second corner I think Nick arrived a bit too fast, he touched me and I spun. I was then last.' Both cars suffered minor damage, Heidfeld's sustaining a bent right-front track rod, Kubica's a damaged rear-wing end plate.

Within a few moments, a huge downpour hit the track and several drivers crashed helplessly as a river formed at the first corner. Jenson Button, Tonio Liuzzi, Scott Speed, Nico Rosberg and Adrian Sutil retired – and Liuzzi was lucky not to hit the safety car, though his Toro Rosso did make slight contact with one of the cranes. Formula 1 rookie Markus Winkelhock benefited from having started with wet-weather tyres from the pit lane and moved into the lead as the others pitted when the rain started to fall. The safety car was deployed but the race was red-flagged moments later.

It was an impressive performance from the son of the late, highly popular Manfred Winkelhock, who was killed when he crashed a Porsche 956 sports car during an endurance race at Canada's Mosport Park circuit in the summer of 1985. His father would have been extremely proud.

At the eventual restart the field was boxed in behind the safety car to feel its way and become acclimatised to the

treacherous conditions. The cars were finally unleashed to resume the racing proper at the end of lap seven and Massa eased away from the pack.

When the race was red-flagged, events had begun to get a little complicated. Due to a slight procedural glitch the timing screens showed that Hamilton had been lapped, even though McLaren was adamant that he hadn't. Eventually race director Charlie Whiting informed all the teams that Hamilton could come through and unlap himself, so McLaren gambled on a quick change to dry-weather rubber at the end of the first lap behind the safety car. This turned out to be a premature call and it took another five laps or so before Lewis felt totally at ease on the slow-to-dry track surface.

After Räikkönen retired with a transmission failure on his Ferrari the way was clear for Mark Webber to come storming through to claim third and a place on the rostrum, his Red Bull

**Below:** David Coulthard delivered a welcome result for the Red Bull Renault squad, netting a good fifth place two spots behind Mark Webber's sister car.
Photograph: Peter J Fox/www.crash.net

**Bottom:** Mark Webber did a great job fending off Alex Wurz's Williams to take third place – and only his second podium finish – on the sprint to the flag.
Photograph: Jean-François Galeron/WRi2

World champion Fernando Alonso came off the Nürburgring podium vowing to win the next race in Hungary to show McLaren had made progress with its car. He took his third win of the season at the Nürburgring but moved into the race lead only when the rain fell. Alonso said he now wanted to win in Hungary the following week to prove McLaren could also beat Ferrari in dry conditions.

'In Hungary it would be good to win in the dry,' said the double world champion. 'More than anything to see that we have improved the car a bit and because Hungary suits the McLaren very well. It's a slower circuit, like Monaco. In the past few races they [Ferrari] have been three tenths per lap quicker.'

The Spaniard gained ten points on championship leader Lewis Hamilton after his victory and was now just two behind the Briton. However, he reckoned his victory was not the turning point of his season.

'I don't think so,' he said. 'As I always said, the championship is long and whoever is more consistent or stronger in the 17 races will win the title. Sometimes things go right, other times they don't. This time everything worked well and we took advantage of it, unlike other times. I will remain the same. I'll try to be on the podium and finish ahead of everybody else.'

**Above: Fernando Alonso ploughs a straight furrow while Jenson Button aquaplanes off the track.**
Photograph: Peter J Fox/www. crash.net

team-mate David Coulthard coming home fifth behind Alex Wurz's Williams, which was only 0.3s behind Webber as they crossed the finishing line. For Webber, it was only the second podium finish of his F1 career.

'The FIA took the right decisions in bringing out the safety car and then suspending [red-flagging] the race,' said Webber. 'I did struggle a little with my rear tyres in the middle stint of the race and I have to say that I wasn't too disappointed to see Kimi Räikkönen retire.'

Wurz excelled on a day when team-mate Nico Rosberg was caught out by the torrential rain storm. 'I kept the pressure on, hoping that Mark might make a mistake at some stage,' said Wurz. 'He made one on the last lap, but not a big enough one for me to be able to launch an attack. I almost tasted the champagne but I was happy with fourth. '

Nick Heidfeld and Robert Kubica finished strongly in sixth and seventh places, both managing to remain relatively gentlemanly and restrained despite their earlier collision. But BMW Motorsport chief Mario Theissen noted crisply, 'Finishing sixth and seventh was not because of the weather; the collision on the first lap was responsible for that.'

Renault came to the Nürburgring hoping for a respectable performance from its R27s, but the outcome fell well short of expectations. Heikki Kovalainen drove an energetic race to finish eighth, two places ahead of his highly disappointed team-mate Giancarlo Fisichella. Team principal Flavio Briatore didn't mince his words: 'This was a bad race for the team,' he said. 'We arrived here optimistic that our new developments would help us gain in performance, but we failed to take advantage of the changing conditions and lost more ground to our rivals.'

With elder brother Michael spectating from the Ferrari pit, Ralf Schumacher had hopes of delivering a vaguely respectable result for the Toyota squad – hopes that evaporated when he drove into Nick Heidfeld's BMW as Heidfeld attempted to overtake on the right-hander before the pits. Schumacher reckoned that Heidfeld had tried to push through where there was simply not enough room, but from the touchlines it simply looked as though the Toyota driver wasn't paying enough attention to the job in hand. It all seemed a far cry from Ralf's majestic victory here at the wheel of a Williams-BMW in 2003.

*Alan Henry*

**Above: Something tangible at last for Mark Webber.**
Photograph: Peter J Fox/www.crash.net

**Left:** Ron Dennis must have been delighted at receiving the winner's trophy for McLaren from sometime rival Michael Schumacher.
Photograph: Jad Sherif/WRi2

**Bottom:** BMW-Sauber train. Robert Kubica slipstreams team-mate Nick Heidfeld.
Photograph: Paul-Henri Cahier

# GRAND PRIX OF EUROPE

## NÜRBURGRING 20–22 JULY 2007

**NÜRBURGRING, NÜRBURG/EIFEL**
Circuit: 3.199 miles / 5.148 km

Dunlop-Kurve 58/93 **2**
Ford-Kurve 70/113 **2**
122/196 **4**
Audi-S 160/257 **5**
Castrol-S 47/76 **1**
Michelin 92/148 **3**
Bit-Kurve 100/161 **3**
Coca-Cola Kurve 70/113 **2**
Mercedes-Arena 65/105 **2**
NGK- 66/106 Schikane **2**
Hatzenbach-Bogen 180/290 **6**

116/187 mph/kmh **4** Gear

Photograph: Peter J Fox/www.crash.net

## RACE RESULTS

| Pos. | Driver | Nat. | No. | Entrant | Car/Engine | Tyres | Laps | Time/Retirement | Speed (mph/km/h) | Gap to leader | Fastest race lap | |
|---|---|---|---|---|---|---|---|---|---|---|---|---|
| 1 | Fernando Alonso | E | 1 | Vodafone McLaren Mercedes | McLaren MP4-22-Mercedes FO 108T V8 | B | 60 | 2h 6m 26.358s | 91.072/146.566 | | 1m 33.231s | 35 |
| 2 | Felipe Massa | BR | 5 | Scuderia Ferrari Marlboro | Ferrari F2007-056 V8 | B | 60 | 2h 6m 34.513s | 90.974/146.409 | + 8.155s | 1m 32.853s | 34 |
| 3 | Mark Webber | AUS | 15 | Red Bull Racing | Red Bull RB3-Renault RS27 V8 | B | 60 | 2h 7m 32.032s | 90.290/145.308 | + 1m 5.674s | 1m 34.449s | 29 |
| 4 | Alexander Wurz | A | 17 | AT&T Williams | Williams FW29-Toyota RVX-07 V8 | B | 60 | 2h 7m 32.295s | 90.287/145.303 | + 1m 5.937s | 1m 34.235s | 33 |
| 5 | David Coulthard | GB | 14 | Red Bull Racing | Red Bull RB3-Renault RS27 V8 | B | 60 | 2h 7m 40.014s | 90.196/145.157 | + 1m 13.656s | 1m 34.316s | 48 |
| 6 | Nick Heidfeld | D | 9 | BMW Sauber F1 Team | BMW Sauber F1.07-BMW P86/7 V8 | B | 60 | 2h 7m 46.656s | 90.118/145.031 | + 1m 20.298s | 1m 34.354s | 49 |
| 7 | Robert Kubica | POL | 10 | BMW Sauber F1 Team | BMW Sauber F1.07-BMW P86/7 V8 | B | 60 | 2h 7m 48.773s | 90.093/144.991 | + 1m 22.415s | 1m 34.451s | 49 |
| 8 | Heikki Kovalainen | FIN | 4 | ING Renault F1 Team | Renault R27-RS27 V8 | B | 59 | | | + 1 lap | 1m 34.603s | 48 |
| 9 | Lewis Hamilton | GB | 2 | Vodafone McLaren Mercedes | McLaren MP4-22-Mercedes FO 108T V8 | B | 59 | | | + 1 lap | 1m 33.401s | 29 |
| 10 | Giancarlo Fisichella | I | 3 | ING Renault F1 Team | Renault R27-RS27 V8 | B | 59 | | | + 1 lap | 1m 34.893s | 48 |
| 11 | Rubens Barrichello | BR | 8 | Honda Racing F1 Team | Honda RA107-RA807E V8 | B | 59 | | | + 1 lap | 1m 35.632s | 37 |
| 12 | Anthony Davidson | GB | 23 | Super Aguri F1 Team | Super Aguri SA07-Honda RA807E V8 | B | 59 | | | + 1 lap | 1m 35.282s | 46 |
| 13 | Jarno Trulli | I | 12 | Panasonic Toyota Racing | Toyota TF107-RVX-07 V8 | B | 59 | | | + 1 lap | 1m 34.496s | 29 |
| | Kimi Räikkönen | FIN | 6 | Scuderia Ferrari Marlboro | Ferrari F2007-056 V8 | B | 34 | Hydraulics | | | 1m 33.904s | 32 |
| | Takuma Sato | J | 22 | Super Aguri F1 Team | Super Aguri SA07-Honda RA807E V8 | B | 19 | Hydraulics | | | 1m 37.401s | 18 |
| | Ralf Schumacher | D | 11 | Panasonic Toyota Racing | Toyota TF107-RVX-07 V8 | B | 18 | Accident | | | 1m 36.195s | 18 |
| | Markus Winkelhock | D | 21 | Etihad Aldar Spyker F1 Team | Spyker F8-VII-Ferrari 056H V8 | B | 13 | Electronics | | | 1m 42.783s | 13 |
| | Jenson Button | GB | 7 | Honda Racing F1 Team | Honda RA107-RA807E V8 | B | 2 | Accident | | | 2m 20.041s | 2 |
| | Adrian Sutil | D | 20 | Etihad Aldar Spyker F1 Team | Spyker F8-VII-Ferrari 056H V8 | B | 2 | Accident | | | 2m 25.798s | 2 |
| | Nico Rosberg | D | 16 | AT&T Williams | Williams FW29-Toyota RVX-07 V8 | B | 2 | Spin | | | 2m 50.950s | 2 |
| | Scott Speed | USA | 19 | Scuderia Toro Rosso | Toro Rosso STR02-Ferrari 056H V8 | B | 2 | Spin | | | 3m 1.900s | 2 |
| | Vitantonio Liuzzi | I | 18 | Scuderia Toro Rosso | Toro Rosso STR02-Ferrari 056H V8 | B | 2 | Accident | | | 3m 22.300s | 2 |

All results and data © FOM 2007

**Fastest race lap:** Felipe Massa on lap 34, 1m 32.853s, 124.021 mph/199.592 km/h.

**Lap record:** Michael Schumacher (Ferrari F2004 V10), 1m 29.468s, 128.714 mph/207.144 km/h (2004)

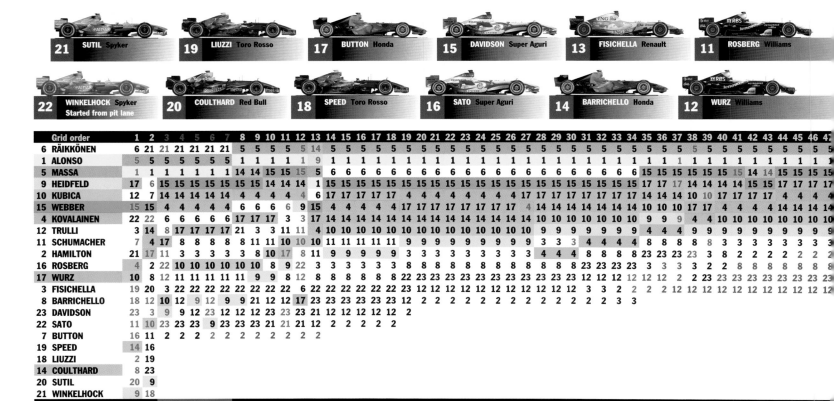

| 21 | SUTIL | Spyker |
| 19 | LIUZZI | Toro Rosso |
| 17 | BUTTON | Honda |
| 15 | DAVIDSON | Super Aguri |
| 13 | FISICHELLA | Renault |
| 11 | ROSBERG | Williams |
| 22 | WINKELHOCK Spyker — Started from pit lane |
| 20 | COULTHARD | Red Bull |
| 18 | SPEED | Toro Rosso |
| 16 | SATO | Super Aguri |
| 14 | BARRICHELLO | Honda |
| 12 | WURZ | Williams |

**Grid order**

| Grid order | 1 | 2 | 3 | 4 | 5 | 6 | 7 | 8 | 9 | 10 | 11 | 12 | 13 | 14 | 15 | 16 | 17 | 18 | 19 | 20 | 21 | 22 | 23 | 24 | 25 | 26 | 27 | 28 | 29 | 30 | 31 | 32 | 33 | 34 | 35 | 36 | 37 | 38 | 39 | 40 | 41 | 42 | 43 | 44 | 45 | 46 | 47 |
|---|---|---|---|---|---|---|---|---|---|---|---|---|---|---|---|---|---|---|---|---|---|---|---|---|---|---|---|---|---|---|---|---|---|---|---|---|---|---|---|---|---|---|---|---|---|---|---|
| 6 RÄIKKÖNEN | 6 | 21 | 21 | 21 | 21 | 21 | 21 | 5 | 5 | 5 | 5 | 5 | 14 | 5 | 5 | 5 | 5 | 5 | 5 | 5 | 5 | 5 | 5 | 5 | 5 | 5 | 5 | 5 | 5 | 5 | 5 | 5 | 5 | 5 | 5 | 5 | 5 | 5 | 5 | 5 | 5 | 5 | 5 | 5 | 5 | 5 | 5 |
| 1 ALONSO | 5 | 5 | 5 | 5 | 5 | 5 | 5 | 1 | 1 | 1 | 1 | 1 | 9 | 1 | 1 | 1 | 1 | 1 | 1 | 1 | 1 | 1 | 1 | 1 | 1 | 1 | 1 | 1 | 1 | 1 | 1 | 1 | 1 | 1 | 1 | 1 | 1 | 1 | 1 | 1 | 1 | 1 | 1 | 1 | 1 | 1 | 1 |
| 5 MASSA | 1 | 1 | 1 | 1 | 1 | 1 | 1 | 14 | 14 | 15 | 15 | 15 | 5 | 6 | 6 | 6 | 6 | 6 | 6 | 6 | 6 | 6 | 6 | 6 | 6 | 6 | 6 | 6 | 6 | 6 | 6 | 6 | 6 | 6 | 6 | 6 | 6 | 15 | 15 | 15 | 15 | 15 | 15 | 14 | 14 | 15 | 15 |
| 9 HEIDFELD | 17 | 6 | 15 | 15 | 15 | 15 | 15 | 15 | 15 | 14 | 14 | 14 | 1 | 15 | 15 | 15 | 15 | 15 | 15 | 15 | 15 | 15 | 15 | 15 | 15 | 15 | 15 | 15 | 15 | 15 | 17 | 17 | 14 | 14 | 14 | 14 | 15 | 17 | 17 | 17 | 17 |
| 10 KUBICA | 12 | 7 | 14 | 14 | 14 | 14 | 14 | 4 | 4 | 4 | 4 | 4 | 6 | 17 | 17 | 17 | 17 | 4 | 4 | 4 | 4 | 4 | 17 | 17 | 17 | 17 | 17 | 17 | 14 | 14 | 10 | 10 | 17 | 17 | 17 | 17 | 4 | 4 | 4 | 4 | 4 |
| 15 WEBBER | 15 | 15 | 4 | 4 | 4 | 6 | 6 | 6 | 9 | 15 | 4 | 14 | 14 | 14 | 14 | 14 | 14 | 14 | 14 | 14 | 14 | 10 | 10 | 10 | 9 | 4 | 4 | 14 | 14 | 14 | 14 | 14 |
| 4 KOVALAINEN | 22 | 22 | 6 | 6 | 6 | 6 | 17 | 17 | 3 | 3 | 17 | 14 | 14 | 14 | 14 | 14 | 14 | 10 | 10 | 10 | 9 | 9 | 4 | 10 | 10 | 10 | 10 | 10 | 10 |
| 12 TRULLI | 3 | 14 | 8 | 17 | 17 | 17 | 17 | 21 | 3 | 3 | 11 | 11 | 4 | 10 | 10 | 10 | 10 | 10 | 10 | 10 | 10 | 10 | 10 | 10 | 9 | 9 | 9 | 9 | 9 | 9 | 9 | 9 | 4 | 4 | 9 | 9 | 9 | 9 | 9 | 9 | 9 | 9 | 9 |
| 11 SCHUMACHER | 7 | 4 | 17 | 8 | 8 | 8 | 8 | 8 | 11 | 11 | 10 | 10 | 10 | 11 | 11 | 11 | 11 | 11 | 9 | 9 | 9 | 9 | 9 | 9 | 9 | 9 | 3 | 3 | 3 | 4 | 4 | 4 | 4 | 8 | 3 | 3 | 3 | 3 | 3 | 3 | 3 |
| 2 HAMILTON | 21 | 17 | 11 | 3 | 3 | 3 | 3 | 8 | 10 | 17 | 8 | 11 | 9 | 9 | 9 | 9 | 3 | 3 | 3 | 3 | 3 | 4 | 4 | 4 | 8 | 8 | 8 | 23 | 23 | 23 | 23 | 3 | 3 | 2 | 2 | 2 | 2 | 2 | 2 |
| 16 ROSBERG | 4 | 2 | 22 | 10 | 10 | 10 | 10 | 10 | 6 | 8 | 9 | 22 | 8 | 8 | 8 | 8 | 8 | 8 | 8 | 8 | 8 | 8 | 8 | 23 | 23 | 23 | 3 | 3 | 3 | 2 | 2 | 8 | 8 | 8 | 8 | 8 | 8 |
| 17 WURZ | 10 | 8 | 12 | 11 | 11 | 11 | 11 | 9 | 8 | 8 | 8 | 23 | 23 | 23 | 23 | 23 | 23 | 23 | 12 | 12 | 12 | 2 | 2 | 3 | 23 | 23 | 23 | 23 | 23 | 23 | 23 | 12 |
| 3 FISICHELLA | 19 | 20 | 3 | 22 | 22 | 22 | 22 | 22 | 22 | 6 | 22 | 22 | 22 | 12 | 12 | 12 | 12 | 12 | 2 | 2 | 2 | 12 | 12 | 12 | 12 | 12 | 12 | 12 | 12 | 12 | 12 | 12 | 12 | 12 | 12 |
| 8 BARRICHELLO | 18 | 12 | 10 | 12 | 9 | 12 | 9 | 9 | 21 | 12 | 12 | 17 | 23 | 23 | 23 | 23 | 2 | 2 | 2 | 2 | 2 | 2 | 2 | 2 | 2 | 2 | 3 | 3 |
| 23 DAVIDSON | 23 | 9 | 9 | 12 | 23 | 12 | 12 | 12 | 23 | 23 | 21 | 12 | 12 | 12 | 2 |
| 22 SATO | 11 | 10 | 23 | 23 | 23 | 9 | 23 | 23 | 23 | 21 | 21 | 12 | 2 | 2 | 2 | 2 |
| 7 BUTTON | 16 | 11 | 2 | 2 | 2 | 2 | 2 | 2 | 2 | 2 | 2 | 2 |
| 19 SPEED | 14 | 16 |
| 18 LIUZZI | 2 | 19 |
| 14 COULTHARD | 8 | 23 |
| 20 SUTIL | 20 | 9 |
| 21 WINKELHOCK | 9 | 18 |

## PRACTICE 1 (FRIDAY)

Hazy sunshine, cloudy
(track 23–25ºC, air 19–21ºC)

| Pos. | Driver | Laps | Time |
|---|---|---|---|
| 1 | Lewis Hamilton | 26 | 1m 32.515s |
| 2 | Kimi Räikkönen | 24 | 1m 32.751s |
| 3 | Fernando Alonso | 27 | 1m 32.932s |
| 4 | Nick Heidfeld | 35 | 1m 32.975s |
| 5 | Robert Kubica | 34 | 1m 33.205s |
| 6 | Felipe Massa | 24 | 1m 33.605s |
| 7 | Ralf Schumacher | 32 | 1m 33.825s |
| 8 | Jenson Button | 28 | 1m 33.936s |
| 9 | David Coulthard | 25 | 1m 34.062s |
| 10 | Rubens Barrichello | 25 | 1m 34.142s |
| 11 | Jarno Trulli | 34 | 1m 34.152s |
| 12 | Alexander Wurz | 32 | 1m 34.345s |
| 13 | Nico Rosberg | 32 | 1m 34.563s |
| 14 | Anthony Davidson | 30 | 1m 34.567s |
| 15 | Mark Webber | 22 | 1m 34.683s |
| 16 | Takuma Sato | 36 | 1m 34.708s |
| 17 | Vitantonio Liuzzi | 31 | 1m 34.907s |
| 18 | Heikki Kovalainen | 21 | 1m 34.921s |
| 19 | Giancarlo Fisichella | 22 | 1m 35.077s |
| 20 | Scott Speed | 15 | 1m 35.643s |
| 21 | Adrian Sutil | 22 | 1m 36.340s |
| 22 | Markus Winkelhock | 30 | 1m 37.116s |

## PRACTICE 2 (FRIDAY)

Sunny, cloudy
(track 23–25ºC, air 20ºC)

| Pos. | Driver | Laps | Time |
|---|---|---|---|
| 1 | Kimi Räikkönen | 28 | 1m 33.339s |
| 2 | Lewis Hamilton | 28 | 1m 33.478s |
| 3 | Felipe Massa | 27 | 1m 33.590s |
| 4 | Fernando Alonso | 30 | 1m 33.637s |
| 5 | Ralf Schumacher | 18 | 1m 33.668s |
| 6 | Jarno Trulli | 22 | 1m 33.746s |
| 7 | Nico Rosberg | 24 | 1m 33.845s |
| 8 | Jenson Button | 36 | 1m 33.880s |
| 9 | Nick Heidfeld | 22 | 1m 34.146s |
| 10 | Robert Kubica | 19 | 1m 34.221s |
| 11 | Mark Webber | 29 | 1m 34.235s |
| 12 | Alexander Wurz | 21 | 1m 34.264s |
| 13 | Takuma Sato | 26 | 1m 34.357s |
| 14 | Rubens Barrichello | 26 | 1m 34.411s |
| 15 | Giancarlo Fisichella | 28 | 1m 34.431s |
| 16 | Heikki Kovalainen | 25 | 1m 34.446s |
| 17 | David Coulthard | 19 | 1m 34.504s |
| 18 | Anthony Davidson | 26 | 1m 34.554s |
| 19 | Scott Speed | 26 | 1m 35.320s |
| 20 | Vitantonio Liuzzi | 24 | 1m 35.653s |
| 21 | Adrian Sutil | 25 | 1m 36.527s |
| 22 | Markus Winkelhock | 19 | 1m 37.319s |

## QUALIFYING (SATURDAY)

Cloudy (track 31–35ºC, air 20–22ºC)

| Pos. | Driver | First | Second | Third |
|---|---|---|---|---|
| 1 | Kimi Räikkönen | 1m 31.522s | 1m 31.237s | 1m 31.450s |
| 2 | Fernando Alonso | 1m 31.074s | 1m 30.983s | 1m 31.741s |
| 3 | Felipe Massa | 1m 31.447s | 1m 30.912s | 1m 31.778s |
| 4 | Nick Heidfeld | 1m 31.889s | 1m 31.652s | 1m 31.840s |
| 5 | Robert Kubica | 1m 31.961s | 1m 31.444s | 1m 32.123s |
| 6 | Mark Webber | 1m 32.629s | 1m 31.661s | 1m 32.476s |
| 7 | Heikki Kovalainen | 1m 32.594s | 1m 31.783s | 1m 32.478s |
| 8 | Jarno Trulli | 1m 32.381s | 1m 31.859s | 1m 32.501s |
| 9 | Ralf Schumacher | 1m 32.446s | 1m 31.843s | 1m 32.570s |
| 10 | Lewis Hamilton | 1m 31.587s | 1m 31.185s | 1m 33.833s |
| 11 | Nico Rosberg | 1m 32.117s | 1m 31.978s | |
| 12 | Alexander Wurz | 1m 32.173s | 1m 31.996s | |
| 13 | Giancarlo Fisichella | 1m 32.378s | 1m 32.010s | |
| 14 | Rubens Barrichello | 1m 32.674s | 1m 32.221s | |
| 15 | Anthony Davidson | 1m 32.793s | 1m 32.451s | |
| 16 | Takuma Sato | 1m 32.678s | 1m 32.838s | |
| 17 | Jenson Button | 1m 32.983s | | |
| 18 | Scott Speed | 1m 33.038s | | |
| 19 | Vitantonio Liuzzi | 1m 33.148s | | |
| 20 | David Coulthard | 1m 33.151s | | |
| 21 | Adrian Sutil | 1m 34.500s | | |
| 22 | Markus Winkelhock | 1m 35.940s | | |

## PRACTICE 3 (SATURDAY)

Sunny (track 27–31ºC, air 19–21ºC)

| Pos. | Driver | Laps | Time |
|---|---|---|---|
| 1 | Kimi Räikkönen | 18 | 1m 31.396s |
| 2 | Lewis Hamilton | 12 | 1m 31.627s |
| 3 | Fernando Alonso | 11 | 1m 32.039s |
| 4 | Robert Kubica | 18 | 1m 32.039s |
| 5 | Felipe Massa | 18 | 1m 32.217s |
| 6 | Nico Rosberg | 16 | 1m 32.344s |
| 7 | Nick Heidfeld | 20 | 1m 32.581s |
| 8 | Mark Webber | 16 | 1m 32.632s |
| 9 | David Coulthard | 18 | 1m 32.679s |
| 10 | Ralf Schumacher | 21 | 1m 32.788s |
| 11 | Vitantonio Liuzzi | 20 | 1m 32.841s |
| 12 | Jenson Button | 18 | 1m 32.869s |
| 13 | Jarno Trulli | 20 | 1m 32.936s |
| 14 | Scott Speed | 14 | 1m 32.974s |
| 15 | Alexander Wurz | 16 | 1m 33.154s |
| 16 | Giancarlo Fisichella | 17 | 1m 33.214s |
| 17 | Rubens Barrichello | 19 | 1m 33.229s |
| 18 | Heikki Kovalainen | 13 | 1m 33.484s |
| 19 | Anthony Davidson | 20 | 1m 33.792s |
| 20 | Takuma Sato | 19 | 1m 33.945s |
| 21 | Adrian Sutil | 20 | 1m 34.423s |
| 22 | Markus Winkelhock | 19 | 1m 36.090s |

## RACE TYRE STRATEGIES

**BRIDGESTONE**

In 2007, the tyre regulations stipulate that the two dry-tyre specifications must be visibly distinguishable from each other. At the European Grand Prix, the soft compound Bridgestone Potenza tyre was marked with a white line in the second-from-inside groove. Wet and extreme wet tyres were used during the European Grand Prix.

Race stopped at end of lap 4. Restarted at lap 5 with a change of tyres allowed.

| | Driver | Stint 1 | Stint 2 | Stint 3 | Stint 4 | Stint 5 | Stint 6 | Stint 7 | Stint 8 |
|---|---|---|---|---|---|---|---|---|---|
| 1 | Alonso | Med: lap 1 | Wet: 2–4 | Wet: 5–12 | Med: 13–37 | Med: 38–53 | Wet: 54–60 | | |
| 2 | Massa | Med: 1 | Wet: 2–4 | Wet: 5–12 | Med: 13–38 | Med: 39–53 | Wet: 54–60 | | |
| 3 | Webber | Med: 1 | Wet: 2–4 | Wet: 5–12 | Med: 13–41 | Med: 42–53 | Wet: 54–60 | | |
| 4 | Wurz | Med: 1–2 | Ex wet: 3–4 | Wet: 5–11 | Med: 12–37 | Med: 38–53 | Wet: 54–60 | | |
| 5 | Coulthard | Med: 1 | Wet: 2–4 | Wet: 5–13 | Med: 14–43 | Med: 44–52 | Wet: 53–60 | | |
| 6 | Heidfeld | Med: 1 | Wet: 2 | Ex wet: 3–4 | Ex wet: 5–13 | Wet: 14–37 | Med: 38–53 | Wet: 54–60 | |
| 7 | Kubica | Med: 1–2 | Ex wet: 3–4 | Wet: 5–12 | Med: 13–39 | Med: 40–52 | Wet: 53–60 | | |
| 8 | Kovalainen | Med: 1 | Wet: 2–4 | Wet: 5–12 | Med: 13–27 | Med: 28–49 | Wet: 50–60 | | |
| 9 | Hamilton | Med: 1 | Wet: 2–4 | Wet: 5–6 | Med: 7–34 | Med: 35–54 | Wet: 55–60 | | |
| 10 | Fisichella | Med: 1–2 | Wet: 3–4 | Wet: 5–12 | Med: 13–27 | Med: 28–49 | Wet: 50–60 | | |
| 11 | Barrichello | Med: 1 | Wet: 2 | Ex wet: 3–4 | Wet: 5–12 | Med: 13–39 | Med: 40–52 | Wet: 53–60 | |
| 12 | Davidson | Med: 1 | Wet: 2–3 | Ex wet: 4 | Ex wet: 5–6 | Wet: 7–11 | Med: 12–38 | Med: 39–51 | Wet: 52–60 |
| 13 | Trulli | Med: 1–2 | Wet: 3 | Ex wet: 4–6 | Wet: 7–12 | Med: 13–34 | Med: 35–53 | Wet: 54–60 | |
| | Räikkönen | Med: 1–2 | Wet: 3–4 | Wet: 5–11 | Med: 12–34 (DNF) | | | | |
| | Sato | Med: 1–2 | Wet: 3 | Wet: 4 | Wet: 5–12 | Med: 13–19 (DNF) | | | |
| | Schumacher | Med: 1 | Wet: 2–3 | Ex wet: 4 | Wet: 5–12 | Med: 13–18 (DNF) | | | |
| | Winkelhock | Wet: 1–3 | Ex wet: 4 | Ex wet: 5–11 | Wet: 12–13 (DNF) | | | | |
| | Button | Med: 1 | Wet: 2 (DNF) | | | | | | |
| | Sutil | Med: 1 | Wet: 2 (DNF) | | | | | | |
| | Rosberg | Med: 1 | Wet: 2 (DNF) | | | | | | |
| | Speed | Med: 1 | Wet: 2 (DNF) | | | | | | |
| | Liuzzi | Med: 1 | Wet: 2 | Ex wet 2 (DNF) | | | | | |

**9 SCHUMACHER** Toyota

**7 KOVALAINEN** Renault

**5 KUBICA** BMW-Sauber

**3 MASSA** Ferrari

**1 RÄIKKÖNEN** Ferrari

**10 HAMILTON** McLaren

**8 TRULLI** Toyota

**6 WEBBER** Red Bull

**4 HEIDFELD** BMW-Sauber

**2 ALONSO** McLaren

**RACE DISTANCE:**
60 laps
191.919 miles/308.863 km

**RACE WEATHER:**
Brief heavy rain, cloudy, sunny,
(track 22–30ºC, air 16–19ºC)

| 48 | 49 | 50 | 51 | 52 | 53 | 54 | 55 | 56 | 57 | 58 | 59 | 60 | • |
|---|---|---|---|---|---|---|---|---|---|---|---|---|---|
| 5 | 5 | 5 | 5 | 5 | 5 | 5 | 5 | 1 | 1 | 1 | 1 | 1 | 1 |
| 1 | 1 | 1 | 1 | 1 | 1 | 1 | 1 | 5 | 5 | 5 | 5 | 5 | 2 |
| 15 | 15 | 15 | 15 | 15 | 15 | 15 | 15 | 15 | 15 | 15 | 15 | 15 | 3 |
| 17 | 17 | 17 | 17 | 17 | 17 | 17 | 17 | 17 | 17 | 17 | 17 | 17 | 4 |
| 4 | 4 | 14 | 14 | 14 | 9 | 14 | 14 | 14 | 14 | 14 | 14 | 14 | 5 |
| 14 | 14 | 10 | 10 | 9 | 14 | 10 | 10 | 10 | 10 | 10 | 9 | 9 | 6 |
| 10 | 10 | 9 | 9 | 10 | 10 | 9 | 9 | 9 | 9 | 9 | 10 | 10 | 7 |
| 9 | 9 | 4 | 3 | 2 | 2 | 4 | 4 | 4 | 4 | 4 | 4 | 4 | 8 |
| 3 | 3 | 3 | 4 | 3 | 4 | 3 | 3 | 3 | 3 | 3 | 3 | 3 | |
| 2 | 2 | 2 | 4 | 4 | 3 | 2 | 2 | 2 | 2 | 2 | 3 | | |
| 8 | 8 | 8 | 8 | 8 | 8 | 8 | 8 | 8 | 8 | 8 | | | |
| 23 | 23 | 23 | 23 | 12 | 23 | 23 | 23 | 23 | 23 | 23 | 23 | | |
| 12 | 12 | 12 | 12 | 23 | 12 | 12 | 12 | 12 | 12 | 12 | | | |

**20** Pit stop
**20** One lap or more behind leader
**20** Safety car deployed on laps shown

## FOR THE RECORD

**FIRST GRAND PRIX AND FIRST LAP LED:**
Markus Winkelhock (above)

**400th GRAND PRIX:** Renault engine

## POINTS

| | DRIVERS | | | CONSTRUCTORS | |
|---|---|---|---|---|---|
| 1 | Lewis Hamilton | 70 | 1 | McLaren | 138 |
| 2 | Fernando Alonso | 68 | 2 | Ferrari | 111 |
| 3 | Felipe Massa | 59 | 3 | BMW Sauber | 61 |
| 4 | Kimi Räikkönen | 52 | 4 | Renault | 32 |
| 5 | Nick Heidfeld | 36 | 5 | Williams | 18 |
| 6 | Robert Kubica | 24 | 6 | Red Bull | 16 |
| 7 | Giancarlo Fisichella | 17 | 7 | Toyota | 9 |
| 8 | Heikki Kovalainen | 15 | 8 | Super Aguri | 4 |
| 9 | Alexander Wurz | 13 | 9 | Honda | 1 |
| 10 | Mark Webber | 8 | | | |
| 11 | David Coulthard | 8 | | | |
| 12 | Jarno Trulli | 7 | | | |
| 13 | Nico Rosberg | 5 | | | |
| 14 | Takuma Sato | 4 | | | |
| 15 | Ralf Schumacher | 2 | | | |
| 16 | Sebastian Vettel | 1 | | | |
| 17 | Jenson Button | 1 | | | |

Photograph: Peter J Fox/www.crash.net

Photograph: Lukas Gorys

Lewis Hamilton leads Kimi Räikkönen into the first corner while their team-mates are left farther down in the pack.
Photograph: Peter J Fox/www.crash.net

FIA F1 WORLD CHAMPIONSHIP/ROUND 11

# HUNGARIAN GP
## HUNGARORING

## HUNGARORING QUALIFYING

Just when Ron Dennis had his hands really full with McLaren's war with Ferrari, his champion Fernando Alonso heaped a whole load of internal strife on his shoulders after snatching the critical pole position from Lewis Hamilton in the final moments of qualifying at the Hungaroring. Nine hours later, the stewards took it away, triggering the situation that ultimately would lead to the team's disqualification from the world championship for constructors.

In qualifying, McLaren owned the track. The MP4-22 had a speed advantage over the Ferraris for the first time since Indianapolis and this was enhanced further when, in Q2, Ferrari's Felipe Massa bumped to a stop as he tried to leave the pits. In a misunderstanding, the team hadn't refuelled him and as time ran out the frustrated Brazilian was left down in 14th place. Just what you want on a track where overtaking is well-nigh impossible.

That left Alonso, Hamilton and Kimi Räikkönen to fight it out in Q3, with Nick Heidfeld again dangerously close in the BMW-Sauber. Hamilton set the pace with 1m 19.781s and one set of tyres left to use. Alonso had chosen the harder Bridgestone compound, unable to get the super-soft option tyre to last a whole lap without graining, but Hamilton had perfected that trick and gone for that tyre. Alonso's best, by comparison, was only 1m 20.133s.

In their final pit stops Alonso came in first, but instead of leaving in good time on his last set of tyres he was still there when Hamilton arrived. By the time Alonso left, to begin a last run that would yield a 1m 19.674s that was sufficient to win him the pole, Hamilton had lost his chance of a final lap. The balloon was about to go up.

Meanwhile, Räikkönen was forced to admit that, in qualifying at least, the Ferrari simply wasn't fast enough. He had too much understeer. So much, in fact, that he was outqualified by Heidfeld, 1m 20.259s to 1m 20.410s. Robert Kubica, in the other F1.07 was seventh on 1m 20.876s.

Nico Rosberg grabbed fifth for Williams on 1m 20.632s, to his surprise, but again team-mate Alex Wurz had too much understeer and was 13th on 1m 20.865s.

The Toyota TF107s had been qualifying well of late and Ralf Schumacher and Jarno Trulli made the top ten with 1m 20.714s and 1m 21.206s for sixth and ninth respectively.

Giancarlo Fisichella was a happy boy to squeeze through Q2 after getting caught in traffic. He managed 1m 21.079s in

Q3 for eighth and the top ten was completed by Mark Webber, who took his Red Bull around in 1m 21.256s. Team-mate David Coulthard was close behind in 11th on 1m 20.718s from Q2, then came Heikki Kovalainen on 1m 20.779s in a Renault that did not feel as poised on the prime tyre as it had earlier.

Behind Wurz and Massa, Anthony Davidson was happy that he got the most from his Super Aguri on his way to 15th place with 1m 21.127s, but team-mate Takuma Sato was way behind down in 19th on 1m 22.143s after his run on the option tyre was stymied by a weight check.

At Toro Rosso, Tonio Liuzzi did the business with a lap of 1m 21.730s to get through Q1 and 16th overall, but he was struggling to make the super-soft tyres last on his STR02. New team-mate Sebastian Vettel, who had replaced Scott Speed, struggled in the sister car and a mistake in the final sector ruined his chances. He lined up 20th on 1m 22.177s for his second GP start.

Honda had another tough weekend. Jenson Button said his RA107 had decent balance and felt consistent but it just wasn't quick enough to better 1m 21.737s and 17th place. Rubens Barrichello said his car felt completely different on the two types of tyre and was 18th with 1m 21.877s. Adrian Sutil was happier with his Spyker after set-up changes since morning practice and took the 21st slot with 1m 22.737s. Sakon Yamamoto brought up the rear on 1m 23.774s after hitting traffic.

Much later, after the stewards had considered a number of complaints they moved Alonso five places down the grid for deliberately holding up Hamilton in the pits, totally shuffling key positions. Now Lewis had pole position, which meant that Heidfeld started not from the clean line but on the dirty side of the grid. Räikkönen went from dirty to clean and Rosberg was moved from the good side to the bad.

Many weeks later, it transpired that on the morning of the race Alonso had approached McLaren chief Ron Dennis and, others alleged, threatened to inform the FIA that he and Pedro de la Rosa knew about the information that McLaren's Mike Coughlan had received from Ferrari's Nigel Stepney unless Dennis favoured him over Hamilton for the rest of the season. Unknown to anyone else at that time, Dennis felt morally obliged to call FIA president Max Mosley and blow the whistle on his own team.

## DIARY

Breaking his self-imposed silence on the 'Stepney-gate' saga, McLaren chief Ron Dennis writes a strong letter to Luigi Macaluso of the CSAI, outlining the team's position.

Toro Rosso confirms mid-month that it has signed Champcar star Sébastien Bourdais to partner Sebastian Vettel in 2008, leaving former F3000 champion Vitantonio Liuzzi out in the cold.

Jean Rédélé dies at the age of 85. Via his Alpine concern he was a key figure in the history of Renault's competition activities and played an important role in the company's entry into F1 in 1977.

## QUALIFYING DRAMA SPLITS THE McLAREN TEAM ASUNDER

According to Fernando Alonso, it was Lewis Hamilton who triggered the controversy in qualifying by failing to let Alonso go ahead in the all-important Q3. According to Hamilton, Alonso hung back so much that Hamilton would almost have had to stop to let him catch up.

Neither man was happy, each believing the team had ruined his chances. 'Nothing was said to me on the radio,' Hamilton said evenly. 'I was told on my way into the pits that Fernando was doing his stop, so I backed off so I wouldn't end up in a queue. But when I came into the pits, for some reason he was just held there. I really don't understand why he was held back, so you should ask the team. I definitely will be asking them in the debrief.'

Asked to quantify the amount by which the chequered flag prevented him from starting a final all-out lap, he added, 'I missed my second quick lap by about the same amount of time I was held back in the pit stop.'

'I was waiting for instructions after the second stop,' Alonso said. 'It was the same as the first: someone times the gaps between us and cars on the track. On the first stop they told me to go, but we had the blanket thing [a tyre warmer got caught and delayed Alonso's departure]. And there was a delay while we were changing the front wing because I had a bit of understeer. The second time, we didn't lose anything.'

Observers counted at least five seconds between the lollipop's being raised – the signal that the driver is free to go – and Alonso's leaving. That was in addition to the delay up to that point. McLaren explained that this was because Alonso's engineer was still studying the GPSs of rival cars to choose the optimal moment to release him.

'You can ask the team this question,' Alonso said, 'because although I am always monitoring the stops by the radio and they do the calculations and find the gaps, I just drive the car. I am always ready to go; when they put on the tyres, I go when I have to. Sometimes we wait for five seconds, ten, 40.'

'Two or four seconds, maybe,' Hamilton responded trenchantly. 'Not 40.' Team principal Ron Dennis later admitted that he and Hamilton had had a 'spirited' exchange over the radio.

Hamilton had upset the strategy by failing to let Alonso go ahead of him on the road in the session: it was Alonso's turn to get a longer fuel burn. And that created the tension. Subsequently, Dennis, Alonso and Hamilton were called before the stewards. Just before midnight the stewards ruled that Alonso had impeded Hamilton even if the latter had not obeyed team policy and docked him five grid places. On paper, it thus became Hamilton's race to lose.

**Above:** At the end of the day it was Fernando Alonso who got the worst of the pit lane fracas with team-mate Lewis Hamilton.
Photograph: Lukas Gorys

**Top left:** Lewis Hamilton's final attempt at pole position was thwarted by Alonso's delaying tactics.
Photograph: Peter J Fox/www.crash.net

HISTORY will remember the 2007 Hungarian Grand Prix as the race at which the wheels began to fall off the relationship between Lewis Hamilton and Fernando Alonso – and as the race in which Hamilton demonstrated a champion's resilience.

Their problems began in qualifying when Alonso delayed Hamilton in the pits as a tit-for-tat payback for Hamilton's disobeying team orders on running order in Q3. They were exacerbated when the FIA intervened, in the form of the race stewards, who put Alonso back five grid places from pole and denied McLaren any constructors' points for its Sunday afternoon's work. Hamilton put everything behind him to score his third victory of the season as Alonso could finish only fourth, separated from him by Kimi Räikkönen and Nick Heidfeld.

The race would also become notable, many weeks later, as the point at which the relationship between Alonso and team principal Ron Dennis really hit rock bottom.

It would have been easy for Hamilton to gloat in victory, since he clearly regarded Alonso as the real villain of the piece. Instead, he sat calmly afterwards, disguised whatever inward glee he might have felt over a win that boosted his championship lead once again and maintained his customary dignity. It was, he said, a tough race, especially in the circumstances. As if all the intra-team flak hadn't been bad enough, he had to cope for much of the race with Räikkönen breathing down his neck. Yet he made it all seem easy, as if all the adversity merely served to sharpen his spurs.

Hamilton took the lead immediately but, as expected, behind him drivers on the dirtier inside part of the track struggled. Räikkönen easily beat front-row starter Heidfeld away and

farther back Rosberg put paid to Alonso's idea of sneaking down the inside. Rosberg annexed fourth ahead of Ralf Schumacher, a fast-starting Robert Kubica, Alonso, Mark Webber and Heikki Kovalainen, who pulled a great move on David Coulthard during the opening lap.

Hamilton quickly pulled away. Only the Renault drivers and Rubens Barrichello had chosen to start on Bridgestone's super-soft tyres. Hamilton's soft rubber was working well and after ten laps he had 3.1s over Räikkönen. Farther back Alonso had showed his steel after getting on the marbles on the outside of Turn 14 at the end of the opening lap. Hung out to dry, he had lost a place to Webber but cut back sharply across Kovalainen's bows to avoid losing another. They were so close in Turn One that Kovalainen actually hit the back of his car, puncturing his Renault's nose.

As expected, the Ferrari was highly competitive in race trim, but on the 13th lap Räikkönen lost 1.6s, later sheepishly admitting, 'I ran wide in two corners in the last sector.'

The two leaders refuelled for the first time on lap 19, resuming still in first and second places as others – notably Alonso, who had begun a strong recovery – had stopped earlier. In the second stint Räikkönen carried less fuel and was therefore faster. And Hamilton had a problem.

'In the first stint I managed to pull out a gap and control the pace, look after the tyres and the fuel, and in the second I had an idea we might be slightly stronger than Kimi because we

had good pace considering we were slightly heavier,' Hamilton said. 'But then the front wheels began locking up under braking because of a steering problem. The front end felt a lot different from in the first stint. The car was steering to the right and that enabled Kimi to catch up. I decided to stay off the kerbs and though the team said that it was not too much of a problem, it still affected me. It was difficult.'

At times now the gap between him and Räikkönen shrank to as little as six-tenths of a second. And the biggest threat loomed as Hamilton came up to lap Felipe Massa, who had started 14th with (ironically, given the reason he had been so far back on the grid) a big fuel load. The aerodynamic effect of following a car closely steals front-end downforce and that was the problem Räikkönen had every time he got too close to Hamilton. But now Hamilton experienced it before Massa finally moved over after at least five minutes. In the past people have been penalised for impeding for much less than that. By lap 45 Hamilton and Räikkönen were 1.3s apart, but then Kimi refuelled for the second and final time a lap later. Hamilton got the hammer down for four laps before making his own stop and by the time he emerged from the pits, now on the same super-soft tyres as Räikkönen, he was 4.4s clear. But soon they ran into lapped traffic again on this fundamentally tedious track, where the one real overtaking point is the entry to the first corner. By lap 57 Räikkönen was half a second behind again – and definitely hungry.

'For sure I would have tried if I'd had the chance,' he said when he was asked why he hadn't taken a run at Hamilton. 'But I didn't have a chance and there was no point being stupid.'

'It was tricky all through to the last lap,' Hamilton admitted. 'Kimi was getting closer and closer in traffic so it was important to get good exits from the corners and not to damage my tyres. Once I got a clean gap in traffic I was able to manage the situation and not to push too hard. Once I got the gap out to a second I just managed it at that. There was no point pushing too hard and falling off.'

And so they finished 0.715s apart but it was Hamilton who got the crucial ten points.

Alonso's afternoon was far less rewarding. He was stuck until the last stops behind several of the runners who were doing three stops and then he really started to haul in Heidfeld, who stopped on laps 17, 41 and 54.

'We knew the option tyre could be difficult, so we wanted to start in the front for the race and qualified a bit light,' Heidfeld said. 'The option tyre was actually quite good, but I tried not to push it too hard, to ensure that we didn't get any graining, especially with Fernando behind. The last corner is the most important one here to be quick through. He was quicker than me everywhere, then I saw he backed off a bit, but with him you can never be sure. I tried to pick up the pace but there was a backmarker ahead and I didn't want to get into his dirty air, but as you know it is not so easy to overtake here so I was okay.'

Above: Ralf Schumacher had a strong weekend in a largely moribund season, claiming sixth place for Toyota.
Photograph: Peter J Fox/www.crash.net

'I am quite pleased with the race today, which was a difficult one,' Alonso said. 'The maximum we could have reached from sixth position on the grid was a podium finish – especially on this circuit, which is comparable to Monaco in terms of overtaking opportunities. This didn't work out in the end, but fourth is better than fifth and at the final stage of the race I did not push too much to save my engine for the Turkish Grand Prix. Without the penalty after yesterday's qualifying the victory would have been possible today, as you can see from my lap times when I had a clear track. I am now seven points behind Lewis. The fight for the championship is still open and I will try my best to close the gap.'

A combination of that great start, a hard drive and excellent pit work earned Kubica fifth place in the second BMW-Sauber. 'I am happy with the pace,' he said. 'Today the car worked well and my race was pretty good.'

After holding off Alonso for a long time, Ralf Schumacher hung in there for sixth ahead of Nico Rosberg and Heikki Kovalainen. He was very happy with his car once some front wing flap adjustments during his first stop had eliminated some nervousness and was content that his two-stop strategy was the right one. Team-mate Jarno Trulli, however, faded down to tenth and was highly disappointed to find himself stuck in traffic almost all race.

Rosberg had seemed destined for more than the two points that he eventually picked up for Williams, but his three-stop strategy just didn't quite work out. Kovalainen did better in the race than in qualifying, pushing hard all the way through and doing an impressive 27 laps on the super-soft tyres on which he started. He took a second set of them for his middle stint and didn't run the softs until the end, yet he never had any problem with graining.

Team-mate Giancarlo Fisichella should have been with him, but lost a place to Trulli and later had a collision with Anthony Davidson as he left the pits after his second stop. He said his race was decided by the penalty he had received for blocking Sakon Yamamoto in qualifying, which he still believed was undeserved.

Ninth place for Mark Webber meant no more points for Red Bull, but he took heart from his RB3's new-found reliability and reckoned nothing better was possible on the day, while team-mate David Coulthard, who finished 11th behind Trulli, said his car's behaviour was very inconsistent between tyre sets.

Behind him, 12th place was the subject of an intense fight between Fisichella (who won it), Massa and Alex Wurz. 'It was a horrible race; there are no other words to describe it,' said Massa glumly. 'At the start I passed some cars but at the exit to Turn One I lost position again. It's been a weekend to forget.'

'What can I say?' asked Button, 12 months after he had been the toast of Budapest following his long-awaited maiden F1 victory. Honda's lamentable performance said it all.

Hamilton's third victory pushed his championship points tally to 80 and boosted his lead to seven over Alonso, while the eight that Räikkönen garnered put him back ahead of the unfortunate Massa with 60 to Massa's 59. In the constructors' championship, meanwhile, McLaren still led even though it didn't score the 15 points it deserved, with 138 points to Ferrari's 119.

Without question, this was the toughest weekend of Hamilton's career so far. He had upset his team, argued with mentor Ron Dennis and unwittingly set in motion the events that triggered not just Alonso's penalty but also the FIA's seemingly vindictive insistence that McLaren should not score any points.

'Going into the race it was like there was a big cloud over my mind,' Hamilton admitted. 'It was difficult to stay focused and with the team not getting any points I didn't know whether they blamed me or not, or just the situation. I just tried to come in with a smile on my face and do the same procedures as always, so I went around to all of the team and only one person didn't wish me good luck. That didn't really affect me; I just got in the car and did my job.'

Despite everything that circumstance threw at him, he did that supremely well.

*David Tremayne*

**Below: Lewis Hamilton drove impeccably to score his third GP victory of the season and strengthen his championship hopes in the process.**
Photograph: Peter J Fox/www.crash.net

Wurz got stuck behind Davidson's Super Aguri for the first 29 laps and by the time he got ahead after the first stops it was too late to hope for much. He also had a run-in with Adrian Sutil, to whom he flicked a vee sign after Sutil let Fisichella and Massa past before pushing him onto the grass.

After Davidson's brush with Fisichella, Takuma Sato was Super Aguri's only finisher. He struggled with low grip on a heavy fuel load and it was not until he ran the super-soft tyres in his third stint that his SA07's balance improved. He nearly distinguished himself by tripping up Hamilton in Turn One as he rejoined after a pit stop; fortunately Hamilton just missed him.

Toro Rosso débutant Sebastian Vettel took 16th after a tough afternoon in which he found the STR02 to be a very different proposition from the BMW-Sauber F1.07 he was used to. He ran a lot more fuel than team-mate Tonio Liuzzi, who was annoyed to find himself bottled up behind Massa's heavier Ferrari when his own strategy required him to be pushing as hard as he could. His race ended with an electronic problem. Sutil had a few off-track adventures in his Spyker on his way to 17th, but Spyker was delighted to beat the mighty Honda, which had a simply awful afternoon: Jenson Button retired after 35 laps with a throttle sensor problem while Rubens Barrichello soldiered on to 18th, two embarrassing laps down.

FIA F1 WORLD CHAMPIONSHIP · ROUND 11

# MAGYAR NAGYDÍJ
## BUDAPEST 3–5 AUGUST 2007

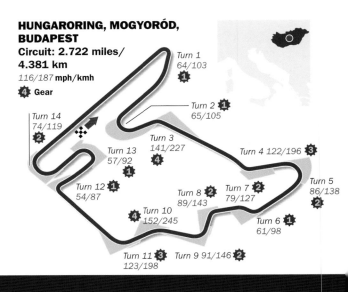

**HUNGARORING, MOGYORÓD, BUDAPEST**
Circuit: 2.722 miles/ 4.381 km
*116/187* mph/kmh

**4** Gear

Turn 1 64/103
Turn 2 65/105
Turn 3 141/227
Turn 4 122/196
Turn 5 86/138
Turn 6 61/98
Turn 7 79/127
Turn 8 89/143
Turn 9 91/146
Turn 10 152/245
Turn 11 123/198
Turn 12 54/87
Turn 13 57/92
Turn 14 74/119

Photograph: Peter J Fox/www.crash.net

## RACE RESULTS

| Pos. | Driver | Nat. | No. | Entrant | Car/Engine | Tyres | Laps | Time/Retirement | Speed (mph/km/h) | Gap to leader | Fastest race lap | |
|---|---|---|---|---|---|---|---|---|---|---|---|---|
| 1 | Lewis Hamilton | GB | 2 | Vodafone McLaren Mercedes | McLaren MP4-22-Mercedes FO 108T V8 | B | 70 | 1h 35m 52.991s | 119.239/191.897 | | 1m 20.171s | 13 |
| 2 | Kimi Räikkönen | FIN | 6 | Scuderia Ferrari Marlboro | Ferrari F2007-056 V8 | B | 70 | 1h 35m 53.706s | 119.225/191.874 | + 0.715s | 1m 20.047s | 70 |
| 3 | Nick Heidfeld | D | 9 | BMW Sauber F1 Team | BMW Sauber F1.07-BMW P86/7 V8 | B | 70 | 1h 36m 36.120s | 118.352/190.469 | + 43.129s | 1m 20.582s | 16 |
| 4 | Fernando Alonso | E | 1 | Vodafone McLaren Mercedes | McLaren MP4-22-Mercedes FO 108T V8 | B | 70 | 1h 36m 37.849s | 118.317/190.413 | + 44.858s | 1m 20.324s | 49 |
| 5 | Robert Kubica | POL | 10 | BMW Sauber F1 Team | BMW Sauber F1.07-BMW P86/7 V8 | B | 70 | 1h 36m 40.607s | 118.261/190.322 | + 47.616s | 1m 20.419s | 40 |
| 6 | Ralf Schumacher | D | 11 | Panasonic Toyota Racing | Toyota TF107-RVX-07 V8 | B | 70 | 1h 36m 40.660s | 118.198/190.222 | + 50.669s | 1m 20.961s | 68 |
| 7 | Nico Rosberg | D | 16 | AT&T Williams | Williams FW29-Toyota RVX-07 V8 | B | 70 | 1h 36m 52.130s | 118.027/189.945 | + 59.139s | 1m 20.672s | 68 |
| 8 | Heikki Kovalainen | FIN | 4 | ING Renault F1 Team | Renault R27-RS27 V8 | B | 70 | 1h 37m 1.095s | 117.845/189.652 | + 1m 8.104s | 1m 20.935s | 69 |
| 9 | Mark Webber | AUS | 15 | Red Bull Racing | Red Bull RB3-Renault RS27 V8 | B | 70 | 1h 37m 9.322s | 117.678/189.385 | + 1m 16.331s | 1m 20.915s | 63 |
| 10 | Jarno Trulli | I | 12 | Panasonic Toyota Racing | Toyota TF107-RVX-07 V8 | B | 69 | | | + 1 lap | 1m 21.253s | 48 |
| 11 | David Coulthard | GB | 14 | Red Bull Racing | Red Bull RB3-Renault RS27 V8 | B | 69 | | | + 1 lap | 1m 21.553s | 67 |
| 12 | Giancarlo Fisichella | I | 3 | ING Renault F1 Team | Renault R27-RS27 V8 | B | 69 | | | + 1 lap | 1m 21.695s | 66 |
| 13 | Felipe Massa | BR | 5 | Scuderia Ferrari Marlboro | Ferrari F2007-056 V8 | B | 69 | | | + 1 lap | 1m 20.981s | 37 |
| 14 | Alexander Wurz | A | 17 | AT&T Williams | Williams FW29-Toyota RVX-07 V8 | B | 69 | | | + 1 lap | 1m 21.264s | 49 |
| 15 | Takuma Sato | J | 22 | Super Aguri F1 Team | Super Aguri SA07-Honda RA807E V8 | B | 69 | | | + 1 lap | 1m 20.980s | 66 |
| 16 | Sebastian Vettel | D | 19 | Scuderia Toro Rosso | Toro Rosso STR02-Ferrari 056H V8 | B | 69 | | | + 1 lap | 1m 21.915s | 65 |
| 17 | Adrian Sutil | D | 20 | Etihad Aldar Spyker F1 Team | Spyker F8-VII-Ferrari 056H V8 | B | 68 | | | + 2 laps | 1m 22.263s | 67 |
| 18 | Rubens Barrichello | BR | 8 | Honda Racing F1 Team | Honda RA107-RA807E V8 | B | 68 | | | + 2 laps | 1m 22.004s | 34 |
| | Vitantonio Liuzzi | I | 18 | Scuderia Toro Rosso | Toro Rosso STR02-Ferrari 056H V8 | B | 42 | Electronics | | | 1m 22.410s | 35 |
| | Anthony Davidson | GB | 23 | Super Aguri F1 Team | Super Aguri SA07-Honda RA807E V8 | B | 41 | Accident | | | 1m 22.166s | 39 |
| | Jenson Button | GB | 7 | Honda Racing F1 Team | Honda RA107-RA807E V8 | B | 35 | Throttle sensor | | | 1m 22.906s | 25 |
| | Sakon Yamamoto | J | 21 | Etihad Aldar Spyker F1 Team | Spyker F8-VII-Ferrari 056H V8 | B | 4 | Spin | | | 1m 26.741s | 4 |

**Fastest race lap:** Kimi Räikkönen on lap 70, 1m 20.047s, 122.428 mph/197.029 km/h.

Lap record: Michael Schumacher (Ferrari F2004 V10), 1m 19.071s, 123.939 mph/199.461 km/h (2004).

All results and data © FOM 2007

| 21 | SUTIL Spyker | 19 | SATO Super Aguri | 17 | BUTTON Honda | 15 | DAVIDSON Super Aguri | 13 | FISICHELLA Renault Five-place penalty | 11 | KOVALAINEN Renault |
| 22 | YAMAMOTO Spyker | 20 | VETTEL Toro Rosso | 18 | BARRICHELLO Honda | 16 | LIUZZI Toro Rosso | 14 | MASSA Ferrari | 12 | WURZ Williams |

| Grid order | 1 2 3 4 5 6 7 8 9 10 11 12 13 14 15 16 17 18 19 20 21 22 23 24 25 26 27 28 29 30 31 32 33 34 35 36 37 38 39 40 41 42 43 44 45 46 47 48 49 50 51 52 53 5 |
|---|---|
| **2 HAMILTON** | 2 2 2 2 2 2 2 2 2 2 2 2 2 2 2 2 2 2 2 2 2 2 2 2 2 2 2 2 2 2 2 2 2 2 2 2 2 2 2 2 2 2 2 2 2 2 2 2 2 2 2 2 2 2 2 |
| **9 HEIDFELD** | 6 6 6 6 6 6 6 6 6 6 6 6 6 6 6 6 6 6 6 6 6 6 6 6 6 6 6 6 6 6 6 6 6 6 6 6 6 6 6 6 6 6 6 6 6 6 6 6 6 6 6 6 6 6 6 |
| **6 RÄIKKÖNEN** | 9 9 9 9 9 9 9 9 9 9 9 9 9 9 9 9 9 11 10 15 9 9 9 9 9 9 9 9 9 9 9 9 9 9 9 9 9 9 9 9 9 9 9 10 9 9 9 9 9 9 9 9 9 9 9 |
| **16 ROSBERG** | 16 16 16 16 16 16 16 16 16 16 16 16 16 16 11 10 15 9 4 4 4 4 4 4 16 16 16 16 16 10 10 10 10 10 10 10 10 9 11 11 11 11 11 1 1 1 10 10 10 1 |
| **11 SCHUMACHER** | 11 11 11 11 11 11 11 11 11 11 11 11 11 11 11 16 15 16 4 16 16 16 16 16 10 10 10 11 11 11 11 11 11 11 11 11 11 1 1 1 1 1 11 10 10 16 16 16 1 |
| **1 ALONSO** | 10 10 10 1 1 1 1 1 1 1 1 1 1 1 1 10 9 4 16 14 14 14 14 14 10 11 11 11 11 11 1 1 1 1 1 10 10 10 10 10 16 1 1 1 |
| **10 KUBICA** | 15 15 1 10 10 10 10 10 10 10 10 10 10 10 1 14 10 10 10 10 11 1 1 1 15 15 15 15 15 15 16 16 16 16 4 11 11 11 11 1 |
| **12 TRULLI** | 1 1 15 15 15 15 15 15 15 15 15 15 15 16 14 10 11 11 11 11 1 15 15 15 16 16 16 16 16 16 4 4 4 4 4 11 15 15 15 1 |
| **15 WEBBER** | 4 4 4 4 4 4 4 4 4 4 4 4 4 14 12 12 1 1 1 1 1 15 4 4 4 4 4 4 4 15 15 15 15 15 15 12 12 4 4 |
| **14 COULTHARD** | 14 14 14 14 14 14 14 14 14 14 14 14 12 11 11 15 15 15 15 23 23 23 14 14 14 14 14 14 14 14 12 12 12 12 4 4 12 12 12 1 |
| **4 KOVALAINEN** | 3 3 3 3 3 3 3 3 3 12 12 12 12 12 12 3 1 23 23 23 23 23 17 17 14 22 5 5 3 3 3 3 3 12 12 17 17 17 17 17 17 14 14 1 |
| **17 WURZ** | 12 12 12 12 12 12 12 12 12 12 12 12 12 17 17 22 22 22 22 22 5 3 22 12 12 12 12 12 17 17 15 5 14 14 14 14 14 3 17 17 1 |
| **3 FISICHELLA** | 23 23 23 23 23 23 23 23 23 23 23 23 1 17 17 17 22 22 22 22 5 3 12 12 17 17 17 5 14 14 14 14 14 3 17 1 |
| **5 MASSA** | 17 17 17 17 17 17 17 17 17 17 17 17 17 5 3 1 12 12 17 17 17 17 5 3 3 3 3 3 5 5 3 3 3 5 5 5 5 1 |
| **23 DAVIDSON** | 22 22 22 22 22 22 22 22 22 22 22 22 5 5 3 3 3 12 19 17 23 23 23 23 23 23 23 22 22 22 22 22 22 22 22 2 |
| **18 LIUZZI** | 5 5 5 5 5 5 5 5 5 5 5 5 3 3 12 19 27 23 22 22 22 22 22 22 22 18 19 19 19 19 19 19 19 19 19 1 |
| **7 BUTTON** | 18 18 18 18 18 18 18 18 18 18 18 18 7 7 7 7 7 7 19 17 23 19 19 19 19 19 19 19 18 20 20 20 20 20 20 20 8 8 |
| **8 BARRICHELLO** | 19 19 19 19 19 19 19 19 19 19 19 19 7 7 20 20 20 20 20 20 20 8 8 8 8 8 8 8 8 |
| **22 SATO** | 7 7 7 7 7 7 7 7 7 7 7 7 20 20 20 20 20 18 18 18 7 7 8 8 8 20 20 20 20 20 8 |
| **19 VETTEL** | 20 20 20 20 20 20 20 20 20 20 20 20 18 18 18 18 18 18 8 8 8 8 8 7 7 7 8 8 8 |
| **20 SUTIL** | 8 8 8 8 8 8 8 8 8 8 8 8 8 8 8 8 8 8 8 20 20 20 20 20 20 20 |
| **21 YAMAMOTO** | 21 21 21 21 |

206

## PRACTICE 1 (FRIDAY)

Sunny (track 35–38ºC, air 26–28ºC)

| Pos. | Driver | Laps | Time |
|---|---|---|---|
| 1 | Robert Kubica | 25 | 1m 22.390s |
| 2 | Felipe Massa | 18 | 1m 22.519s |
| 3 | Kimi Räikkönen | 21 | 1m 22.540s |
| 4 | Fernando Alonso | 18 | 1m 22.585s |
| 5 | Lewis Hamilton | 19 | 1m 22.654s |
| 6 | Nick Heidfeld | 24 | 1m 22.891s |
| 7 | Nico Rosberg | 19 | 1m 22.983s |
| 8 | Jenson Button | 20 | 1m 23.294s |
| 9 | Rubens Barrichello | 20 | 1m 23.601s |
| 10 | Ralf Schumacher | 27 | 1m 23.802s |
| 11 | Anthony Davidson | 13 | 1m 24.102s |
| 12 | Jarno Trulli | 30 | 1m 24.318s |
| 13 | Alexander Wurz | 12 | 1m 24.321s |
| 14 | David Coulthard | 17 | 1m 24.474s |
| 15 | Heikki Kovalainen | 18 | 1m 24.733s |
| 16 | Sebastian Vettel | 26 | 1m 24.905s |
| 17 | Giancarlo Fisichella | 19 | 1m 24.920s |
| 18 | Vitantonio Liuzzi | 20 | 1m 24.976s |
| 19 | Takuma Sato | 13 | 1m 25.307s |
| 20 | Mark Webber | 14 | 1m 25.584s |
| 21 | Adrian Sutil | 29 | 1m 26.332s |
| 22 | Sakon Yamamoto | 30 | 1m 28.118s |

## PRACTICE 2 (FRIDAY)

Scattered cloud, light rain, cloudy (track 38–41ºC, air 29–31ºC)

| Pos. | Driver | Laps | Time |
|---|---|---|---|
| 1 | Fernando Alonso | 29 | 1m 20.919s |
| 2 | Heikki Kovalainen | 39 | 1m 21.283s |
| 3 | Lewis Hamilton | 32 | 1m 21.338s |
| 4 | Nico Rosberg | 40 | 1m 21.485s |
| 5 | Nick Heidfeld | 37 | 1m 21.517s |
| 6 | Kimi Räikkönen | 29 | 1m 21.589s |
| 7 | Felipe Massa | 29 | 1m 21.620s |
| 8 | Giancarlo Fisichella | 36 | 1m 21.698s |
| 9 | Jarno Trulli | 35 | 1m 21.857s |
| 10 | Robert Kubica | 37 | 1m 21.906s |
| 11 | Ralf Schumacher | 29 | 1m 21.912s |
| 12 | Alexander Wurz | 35 | 1m 21.987s |
| 13 | Mark Webber | 28 | 1m 22.325s |
| 14 | David Coulthard | 33 | 1m 22.483s |
| 15 | Anthony Davidson | 41 | 1m 22.510s |
| 16 | Jenson Button | 47 | 1m 22.550s |
| 17 | Takuma Sato | 42 | 1m 22.556s |
| 18 | Rubens Barrichello | 29 | 1m 22.727s |
| 19 | Vitantonio Liuzzi | 42 | 1m 23.136s |
| 20 | Sebastian Vettel | 39 | 1m 23.148s |
| 21 | Adrian Sutil | 34 | 1m 23.673s |
| 22 | Sakon Yamamoto | 29 | 1m 26.307s |

## QUALIFYING (SATURDAY)

Scattered cloud (track 34–35ºC, air 24–26ºC)

| Pos. | Driver | First | Second | Third |
|---|---|---|---|---|
| 1 | Fernando Alonso | 1m 20.425s | 1m 19.661s | 1m 19.674s |
| 2 | Lewis Hamilton | 1m 19.570s | 1m 19.301s | 1m 19.781s |
| 3 | Nick Heidfeld | 1m 20.751s | 1m 20.322s | 1m 20.259s |
| 4 | Kimi Räikkönen | 1m 20.435s | 1m 20.107s | 1m 20.410s |
| 5 | Nico Rosberg | 1m 20.547s | 1m 20.188s | 1m 20.632s |
| 6 | Ralf Schumacher | 1m 20.449s | 1m 20.455s | 1m 20.714s |
| 7 | Robert Kubica | 1m 20.366s | 1m 20.703s | 1m 20.876s |
| 8 | Giancarlo Fisichella | 1m 21.645s | 1m 20.590s | 1m 21.079s |
| 9 | Jarno Trulli | 1m 20.481s | 1m 19.951s | 1m 21.206s |
| 10 | Mark Webber | 1m 20.794s | 1m 20.439s | 1m 21.256s |
| 11 | David Coulthard | 1m 21.291s | 1m 20.718s | |
| 12 | Heikki Kovalainen | 1m 20.285s | 1m 20.779s | |
| 13 | Alexander Wurz | 1m 21.243s | 1m 20.865s | |
| 14 | Felipe Massa | 1m 20.408s | 1m 21.021s | |
| 15 | Anthony Davidson | 1m 21.018s | 1m 21.127s | |
| 16 | Vitantonio Liuzzi | 1m 21.730s | 1m 21.993s | |
| 17 | Jenson Button | 1m 21.737s | | |
| 18 | Rubens Barrichello | 1m 21.877s | | |
| 19 | Takuma Sato | 1m 22.143s | | |
| 20 | Sebastian Vettel | 1m 22.177s | | |
| 21 | Adrian Sutil | 1m 22.737s | | |
| 22 | Sakon Yamamoto | 1m 23.774s | | |

## PRACTICE 3 (SATURDAY)

Scattered cloud, cloudy (track 29–34ºC, air 24–25ºC)

| Pos. | Driver | Laps | Time |
|---|---|---|---|
| 1 | Felipe Massa | 15 | 1m 20.183s |
| 2 | Fernando Alonso | 11 | 1m 20.414s |
| 3 | Lewis Hamilton | 11 | 1m 20.461s |
| 4 | Nick Heidfeld | 18 | 1m 20.565s |
| 5 | Kimi Räikkönen | 15 | 1m 20.741s |
| 6 | Nico Rosberg | 16 | 1m 20.868s |
| 7 | Jarno Trulli | 22 | 1m 20.878s |
| 8 | Ralf Schumacher | 21 | 1m 20.933s |
| 9 | Mark Webber | 13 | 1m 21.220s |
| 10 | Alexander Wurz | 15 | 1m 21.323s |
| 11 | Anthony Davidson | 20 | 1m 21.501s |
| 12 | Robert Kubica | 18 | 1m 21.652s |
| 13 | Heikki Kovalainen | 22 | 1m 21.666s |
| 14 | David Coulthard | 15 | 1m 21.752s |
| 15 | Takuma Sato | 18 | 1m 21.839s |
| 16 | Vitantonio Liuzzi | 21 | 1m 21.909s |
| 17 | Giancarlo Fisichella | 22 | 1m 22.131s |
| 18 | Jenson Button | 23 | 1m 22.202s |
| 19 | Sebastian Vettel | 20 | 1m 22.394s |
| 20 | Rubens Barrichello | 18 | 1m 22.596s |
| 21 | Adrian Sutil | 22 | 1m 23.560s |
| 22 | Sakon Yamamoto | 24 | 1m 24.062s |

## RACE TYRE STRATEGIES

*BRIDGESTONE*

In 2007, the tyre regulations stipulate that the two dry-tyre specifications must be visibly distinguishable from each other. At the Hungarian Grand Prix, the super-soft compound Bridgestone Potenza tyre was marked with a white line in the second-from-inside groove.

| | Driver | Race stint 1 | Race stint 2 | Race stint 3 | Race stint 4 |
|---|---|---|---|---|---|
| 1 | Lewis Hamilton | Soft: laps 1–19 | Soft: 20–50 | Super-soft: 51–70 | |
| 2 | Kimi Räikkönen | Soft: 1–19 | Soft: 20–46 | Super-soft: 47–70 | |
| 3 | Nick Heidfeld | Soft: 1–17 | Soft: 18–41 | Soft: 42–54 | Super-soft: 55–70 |
| 4 | Fernando Alonso | Soft: 1–17 | Soft: 18–50 | Super-soft: 51–70 | |
| 5 | Robert Kubica | Soft: 1–19 | Soft: 20–42 | Soft: 43–56 | Super-soft: 57–70 |
| 6 | Ralf Schumacher | Soft: 1–18 | Soft: 19–48 | Super-soft: 49–70 | |
| 7 | Nico Rosberg | Soft: 1–17 | Soft: 18–32 | Soft: 33–55 | Super-soft: 56–70 |
| 8 | Heikki Kovalainen | Super-soft: 1–27 | Super-soft: 28–49 | Soft: 50–70 | |
| 9 | Mark Webber | Soft: 1–20 | Soft: 21–40 | Soft: 41–58 | Super-soft: 59–70 |
| 10 | Jarno Trulli | Soft: 1–20 | Soft: 21–51 | Super-soft: 52–70 | |
| 11 | David Coulthard | Soft: 1–26 | Soft: 27–43 | Super-soft: 44–70 | |
| 12 | Giancarlo Fisichella | Super-soft: 1–19 | Soft: 20–41 | Soft: 42–70 | |
| 13 | Felipe Massa | Soft: 1–35 | Super-soft: 36–50 | Super-soft: 51–70 | |
| 14 | Alexander Wurz | Soft: 1–29 | Soft: 30–51 | Super-soft: 52–70 | |
| 15 | Takuma Sato | Soft: 1–32 | Soft: 33–55 | Super-soft: 56–70 | |
| 16 | Sebastian Vettel | Soft: 1–31 | Soft: 32–49 | Super-soft: 50–70 | |
| 17 | Adrian Sutil | Soft: 1–27 | Soft: 28–45 | Super-soft: 46–70 | |
| 18 | Rubens Barrichello | Super-soft: 1–17 | Soft: 18–35 | Soft: 36–70 | |
| | Vitantonio Liuzzi | Soft: 1–20 | Soft: 21–42 (DNF) | | |
| | Anthony Davidson | Soft: 1–30 | Soft: 31–41 (DNF) | | |
| | Jenson Button | Soft: 1–30 | Soft: 31–35 (DNF) | | |
| | Sakon Yamamoto | Soft: 1–4 (DNF) | | | |

9 WEBBER Red Bull

7 KUBICA BMW-Sauber

5 SCHUMACHER Toyota

3 RÄIKKÖNEN Ferrari

1 HAMILTON McLaren

10 COULTHARD Red Bull

8 TRULLI Toyota

6 ALONSO McLaren
Five-place penalty

4 ROSBERG Williams

2 HEIDFELD BMW-Sauber

**RACE DISTANCE:**
70 laps
190.552 miles/306.663 km

**RACE WEATHER:**
Scattered cloud, track 38–40ºC, air 27–28ºC

### Lap chart

| | 55 | 56 | 57 | 58 | 59 | 60 | 61 | 62 | 63 | 64 | 65 | 66 | 67 | 68 | 69 | 70 | |
|---|---|---|---|---|---|---|---|---|---|---|---|---|---|---|---|---|---|
| | 2 | 2 | 2 | 2 | 2 | 2 | 2 | 2 | 2 | 2 | 2 | 2 | 2 | 2 | 2 | 1 | 1 |
| | 6 | 6 | 6 | 6 | 6 | 6 | 6 | 6 | 6 | 6 | 6 | 6 | 6 | 6 | 6 | 2 | 2 |
| | 10 | 10 | 9 | 9 | 9 | 9 | 9 | 9 | 9 | 9 | 9 | 9 | 9 | 9 | 9 | 9 | 3 |
| | 9 | 9 | 1 | 1 | 1 | 1 | 1 | 1 | 1 | 1 | 1 | 1 | 1 | 1 | 1 | 4 | 4 |
| | 1 | 1 | 10 | 10 | 10 | 10 | 10 | 10 | 10 | 10 | 10 | 10 | 10 | 10 | 10 | 10 | 5 |
| | 11 | 11 | 11 | 11 | 11 | 11 | 11 | 11 | 11 | 11 | 11 | 11 | 11 | 11 | 11 | 11 | 6 |
| | 15 | 15 | 15 | 15 | 16 | 16 | 16 | 16 | 16 | 16 | 16 | 16 | 16 | 16 | 16 | 16 | 7 |
| | 16 | 16 | 16 | 4 | 4 | 4 | 4 | 4 | 4 | 4 | 4 | 4 | 4 | 4 | 4 | 4 | 8 |
| | 4 | 4 | 4 | 15 | 15 | 15 | 15 | 15 | 15 | 15 | 15 | 15 | 15 | 15 | 15 | 15 | |
| | 12 | 12 | 12 | 12 | 12 | 12 | 12 | 12 | 12 | 12 | 12 | 12 | 12 | | | | |
| | 14 | 14 | 14 | 14 | 14 | 14 | 14 | 14 | 14 | 14 | 14 | 14 | 14 | | | | |
| | 3 | 3 | 3 | 3 | 3 | 3 | 3 | 3 | 3 | 3 | 3 | 3 | 3 | | | | |
| | 17 | 17 | 17 | 5 | 5 | 5 | 5 | 5 | 5 | 5 | 5 | 5 | 5 | | | | |
| | 5 | 5 | 5 | 17 | 17 | 17 | 17 | 17 | 17 | 17 | 17 | 17 | 17 | | | | |
| | 22 | 22 | 22 | 22 | 22 | 22 | 22 | 22 | 22 | 22 | 22 | 22 | 22 | | | | |
| | 19 | 19 | 19 | 19 | 19 | 19 | 19 | 19 | 19 | 19 | 19 | 19 | 19 | | | | |
| | 20 | 20 | 20 | 20 | 20 | 20 | 20 | 20 | 20 | 20 | 20 | 20 | 20 | | | | |
| | 8 | 8 | 8 | 8 | 8 | 8 | 8 | 8 | 8 | 8 | 8 | 8 | 8 | | | | |

**20** Pit stop
**20** One lap behind leader

## FOR THE RECORD

**400TH POINT:** Kimi Räikkönen

## POINTS

**VODAFONE McLAREN MERCEDES**

| | DRIVERS | | | CONSTRUCTORS | |
|---|---|---|---|---|---|
| 1 | Lewis Hamilton | 80 | 1 | McLaren | 138 |
| 2 | Fernando Alonso | 73 | 2 | Ferrari | 119 |
| 3 | Kimi Räikkönen | 60 | 3 | BMW Sauber | 71 |
| 4 | Felipe Massa | 59 | 4 | Renault | 33 |
| 5 | Nick Heidfeld | 42 | 5 | Williams | 20 |
| 6 | Robert Kubica | 28 | 6 | Red Bull | 16 |
| 7 | Giancarlo Fisichella | 17 | 7 | Toyota | 12 |
| 8 | Heikki Kovalainen | 16 | 8 | Super Aguri | 4 |
| 9 | Alexander Wurz | 13 | 9 | Honda | 1 |
| 10 | Mark Webber | 8 | | (McLaren was not | |
| 11 | David Coulthard | 8 | | awarded constructor | |
| 12 | Nico Rosberg | 7 | | points in this race) | |
| 13 | Jarno Trulli | 7 | | | |
| 14 | Ralf Schumacher | 5 | | | |
| 15 | Takuma Sato | 4 | | | |
| 16 | Sebastian Vettel | 1 | | | |
| 17 | Jenson Button | 1 | | | |

Photographs: Peter J Fox/www.crash.net

# TURKISH GP
## ISTANBUL PARK

ISTA

Felipe Massa beams with delight as
he celebrates his second successive
Turkish victory at the wheel of a
Ferrari – and his third GP victory
of the 2007 season.
Photograph: Peter J Fox/www.crash.net

### DIARY

During his customary Sunday-evening
media debrief at Istanbul, Ferrari
president Jean Todt makes it clear that
he is not yet prepared to retire and
that he is motivated to continue in F1.
His comments seem to indicate that he
has come under pressure to quit from
Ferrari chairman Luca di Montezemolo.

Rumours in the Istanbul paddock
suggest that Toyota plans to replace
Ralf Schumacher with GP2 front-runner
Timo Glock for the 2008 season.

Meanwhile, Dutch sources are adamant
that Renault has agreed terms for
Nelson Piquet Jr to replace Giancarlo
Fisichella in 2008. Piquet's half-Dutch
ancestry is attractive to sponsor ING
but the situation is complicated by the
uncertainty over Fernando Alonso's
situation at McLaren.

Spanish entrepreneur Alejandro Agag's
name is linked with the Super Aguri
F1 and Prodrive teams during the
Turkish GP weekend.

Felipe Massa was very happy after snatching pole position from
Lewis Hamilton. His face lit up with a big smile as he admitted,
'It was very tough, very tight, always a big fight between all
four drivers.'

With Massa and Hamilton on the front row, Kimi Räikkönen
and Fernando Alonso on the second, things were neatly poised.
Massa put the perfect lap together in 1m 27.329s while
Hamilton lost a fraction in the slippery final Turn 14 on his way
to 1m 27.373s and Räikkönen made an error between 13 and
14 that sapped his speed and left him on 1m 27.546s. Alonso
was right behind him on 1m 27.574s.

The Ferrari drivers were easy to quantify, the McLaren pilots
less so. Where Hamilton was busy digging deep to find six tenths
over his first Q3 run on Bridgestone's medium tyre, Alonso, on
the harder compound, was on a strategy that called for a very
late run in which he would reach the chequered flag only
seconds before it fell. As it was he caught traffic, which made it
an even closer call and he failed to better his previous time.

He and Hamilton had sat down on Thursday to air their
grievances over the Hungarian débâcle and as Hamilton
apologised Alonso told him his beef was with the team, not him.
On Friday, there was more from Alonso when he told BBC Radio
5 Live, 'That is always very clear in any team, you know, to have
equal opportunities to everybody and to have an equal car to
your team-mate's. What I think sometimes is that I gave the
team a lot. When I arrived in December, I remember the car I
drove; I remember the results they had in 2006. And now, you
know, I brought to the team half a second, six tenths, whatever,
and I don't see anything being given back to me.'

It was hard not to feel for him, even if you didn't agree
with that simplistic opinion. Up until '07 he had been the new
yardstick of the sport, the one man who seemed flawless. Oh,
how the arrival of Hamilton had revised that view.

Robert Kubica was BMW Sauber's ace this weekend, running
light for 1m 27.722s to leave team-mate Nick Heidfeld sixth on
1m 28.037s. Neither expected to challenge the top four
on sheer pace but they were well clear of the rest. Heikki
Kovalainen got the closest, for Renault, with his lap of
1m 28.491s. That other young lion, Nico Rosberg, also got the

top-ten position he wanted, taking eighth with 1m 28.501s in
the Williams FW29. Ninth was the preserve of Jarno Trulli, who
took his Toyota around in 1m 28.740s, and Giancarlo Fisichella
completed the first five rows with 1m 29.322s in the second
Renault, in which he struggled to achieve a decent balance all
through an understeering final session.

Anthony Davidson put in a great performance to push his
Super Aguri to 11th overall on 1m 28.002s after missing out on
Q3 by less than two tenths of a second. Most impressive.

The Red Bulls were 12th and 13th courtesy of Mark Webber
and David Coulthard. Webber lapped in 1m 28.013s, Coulthard
1m 28.100s, but both complained of lack of downforce or the
need for a reduction in drag. The two Hondas were likewise at
the limit of their aero performance. This time Rubens
Barrichello just edged out Jenson Button with 14th on
1m 28.188s against Button's 15th on 1m 28.220s.

Alex Wurz struggled again and was only 16th on 1m 28.390s
set in Q2. Tonio Liuzzi again showed rookie Sebastian Vettel
the way around, lapping his Toro Rosso confidently in
1m 28.798s for 17th and just losing out in Q1 to Barrichello by
six thousandths of a second. His overriding problem was that he
was sent out in traffic, couldn't quite warm the front tyres
quickly enough and thus lost out despite the rest of the lap's
being perfect. Ralf Schumacher could manage no better than
18th-fastest on 1m 28.809s, which weeded him out in Q1.
Locking rear wheels hampered him initially and a change of front
wing and tyres then generated oversteer. Takuma Sato was less
happy, languishing in 19th place on 1m 28.953s after Q1. He
said the balance was as good as Davidson's but his car simply
lacked grip.

Sebastian Vettel lost time on the weighbridge and thus the
team had to revise his strategy and as last car out he struggled
with tyre pressures and temperatures as he recorded 1m
29.408s for 20th.

Adrian Sutil got worryingly close to that for Spyker with 1m
29.861s, comfortably outpacing team-mate Sakon Yamamoto,
whose eventual best was 1m 31.479s. First Yamamoto spun,
then he had a gear-selection problem that prevented him from
making a final run.

## THE PRICE OF FAME

It was the barest of touches, nothing approaching a handshake at all, and perhaps it gave the lie to the newly re-established empathy between Lewis Hamilton (right) and his McLaren team-mate Fernando Alonso.

It came at the end of qualifying as they climbed from their cars and Hamilton savoured a hard-won second place on the grid. Alonso had run ahead of him in the previous two sessions but now the tables had been turned and the disappointment was writ large on the Spaniard's face.

The intra-team battle with Alonso notwithstanding, the racetrack really was Hamilton's 'happy place'. Away from it, he admitted, things were not so comfortable after Hungary. The world of celebrity was not one he really wanted to inhabit.

'It's quite disappointing, all the media attention,' he said, alluding to the paparazzi's interest in his recent holiday break. 'It's a lot of rubbish, all those stories about me and Sara Ojjeh. I was supposed to go away with my friends, have a lads' holiday, but I thought it was a bad idea in the middle of a season fighting for the world championship. Instead I was invited along to Mansour [Ojjeh, part-owner of TAG]'s boat and there were 13 of us, including all three of the Ojjeh daughters and their boyfriends. I wasn't expecting to have pictures taken and what you didn't see in that one [Hamilton throwing Sara Ojjeh into the water] was that there were 11 other people there. It's not as if I was in with all those women. The thing with my ex-girlfriend is that we made a mutual decision to move on and are still great friends. Now I'm supposedly dating one of the Ojjeh daughters, which is completely untrue.'

As he came to terms with his new life, the championship leader was smart enough to know that fame comes at a high price and to appreciate the bittersweet irony that further success would only increase media interest in him.

FELIPE Massa's confidence from qualifying translated into his second Turkish GP victory. As Massa led Ferrari team-mate Kimi Räikkönen home to a dominant triumph for the Scuderia, Fernando Alonso scooped third place after McLaren team-mate Lewis Hamilton was stymied by the dramatic failure of his right-front Bridgestone tyre on the 43rd lap when a podium position was his for the taking. It was the miracle that Fernando Alonso had been praying for.

In what would prove a highly successful calculated gamble, both Ferraris went to the line on Bridgestone's medium option tyre. They got away strongly on the cleaner side of the grid as the McLarens struggled away on the dirty side on their hard compound rubber. Räikkönen easily beat Hamilton to Turn One to take second place in Massa's wake and the BMW-Saubers of Robert Kubica (medium) and Nick Heidfeld (hard) likewise got the drop on Alonso.

Through the first round of pits stops the status quo remained, with Massa leading confidently from pole for the second year in succession, Räikkönen riding shotgun and Hamilton pacing himself, waiting for his chance.

They stopped on laps 19, 18 and 20 respectively, all three opting to repeat their initial tyre choices. At that point, Alonso seemed doomed as he struggled along in sixth place behind the white-and-blue cars.

During the second stint, Räikkönen launched a strong challenge on Massa, reducing what was once a 2.5s gap to as little as four tenths of a second by the time the second stops fell due. But the flow remained with Massa. Räikkönen refuelled and had the harder tyres fitted on lap 41. Massa did the same a lap later. That left Hamilton in the lead on the 43rd lap, but that was when his race – and his right-front tyre – literally came apart.

'It happened with no warning,' he revealed. 'I'd just gone through the really quick corner, Turn Eight, and as I braked for Turn Nine, I saw bits of tyre flying off and then it exploded...'

It was a tough blow for the championship leader.

'As soon as it happened I hit the brakes and locked up the front-right trying to make Turn Nine,' he added. 'I was very lucky to get the car stopped as I ran right into the run-off area. The tyre was flapping around but I thought I could get back to the pits. The whole wheel and tyre stopped going around by Turn 12 and then I nearly hit the wall when I got to the pits.'

Fortunately, McLaren was able to fit a new set of tyres – in this case the softer rubber – and Hamilton resumed the race. But, crucially, his misfortune had handed a lifeline to Alonso, who had moved ahead of both BMW-Saubers during the first pit stops but had been 14s adrift of Hamilton. Now he swept up to third place, with Heidfeld also moving ahead of the stricken McLaren. The MP4-22's front wing was damaged and Hamilton was forced to drive for a finish while trying to hustle a less-than-perfect machine sufficiently hard to keep ahead of a hungry Heikki Kovalainen in the sixth-placed Renault.

'Without the front-wing problem I could have challenged Heidfeld,' Hamilton said. He was lucky to be running at all, however, and at least to salvage fifth place and four crucial championship points from the possible eight he might have taken without the drama.

In the final laps none of the leaders was pushing. Indeed, Räikkönen let himself fall as much as 7.4s behind Massa by the 56th of the 58 laps, before slashing the fastest lap to 1m 27.295s on the penultimate tour. By the finish he was only 2.275s adrift but everyone knew it was window dressing and that he was simply bored.

Alonso counted it a gift when his 100th race yielded third. 'Nick was very consistent and driving very well and I was lucky to overtake him at the first pit stop,' he admitted, 'and my race started then. I just tried to be consistent and not make mistakes and wait for a miracle. That happened with Hamilton, for me to take the place on the podium.'

Massa was absolutely delighted with his second consecutive Turkish victory, especially because his parents were at the track to see him in action. Räikkönen apart, his only problem was the need to tear off a helmet cooling duct that had worked loose and was disturbing his concentration because of the turbulence it created.

His success meant that the four men fighting for the title had now each won three races. Hamilton still led with 84 points, but Alonso now had 79, Massa 69 and Räikkönen 68. It was still far too close to call.

Out of the main spotlight, the ever-reliable Heidfeld drove another great but unobtrusive race. To begin with he played second fiddle to fast-starting team-mate Robert Kubica, who had a lighter fuel load and the softer tyres. Kubica was the first to pit, however, after only 12 laps. Heidfeld was the next one in, five laps later, and up until then he had yet again held off Alonso just as he did in France.

Whereas Kubica struggled with his car and a lack of speed that negated his adventurous strategy, Heidfeld said everything – strategy, team performance, car and tyres – was perfect. The result was yet further confirmation of the great job that BMW's Dr Mario Theissen and his men had been doing all season.

Where Heidfeld held on for fourth place and five points, Kubica struggled to challenge Nico Rosberg and had to be content with one point for eighth place, but the total of six took BMW Sauber to 77 overall, further cementing its third place in the constructors' championship chase.

Behind the recovered Hamilton, Kovalainen again drove a charging race for Renault to comfortably outpace team-mate Giancarlo Fisichella. Both drivers were in the thick of the first-corner action at the start, Kovalainen getting pushed wide by

Heidfeld and Fisichella tapping Jarno Trulli into a spin. While Fisi was left to rue the bodged getaway (he claimed that Trulli braked suddenly), Heikki said everything about his race was like Heidfeld's once the tyres had come in: perfect.

'Ever since the Nürburgring, when we introduced some new developments, we have been looking for the chance to prove they were a step forward,' he said, 'and I think this race has done that.'

After some of his recent bad luck, Nico Rosberg and Williams deserved a good run. He had gone into qualifying hoping for a top-ten slot and believing that seventh or eighth would be a great result from the race – and he got the seventh, fending off Kubica from the second pit stops onwards. 'I didn't expect him to pit before us and we beat him fair and square,' he said.

Team-mate Alex Wurz was trapped in traffic most of the time and finished a distant 11th, separated from Fisichella by David Coulthard, who made the better start of the Red Bull duo and was in the thick of the battle for ninth all the way through. But he said his RB3's behaviour was 'inconsistent'. Mark Webber's race in the other RB3 was over after a wobble going into Turn Five turned out to be caused by a hydraulic problem that interfered with the downshift.

Ralf Schumacher's 12th place gave Toyota the upper hand over fellow Japanese contenders Honda and Super Aguri, but Schumacher was unhappy about his TF107's performance on the hard tyres and didn't particularly care for his one-stop strategy. He fared better than Trulli, whose race was ruined by the first-corner knock from Fisichella.

The Honda drivers were also frustrated, having had to start at the back after they required post-qualifying engine changes. Rubens Barrichello was already 18th by the end of the opening

**Above: Timed to synchronised perfection, the Ferrari pit delivers a superbly slick refuelling stop for Kimi Räikkönen.**
Photograph: Frits van Eldik/WRi2

**Centre: David Coulthard, still looking for more speed from his Red Bull-Renault.**
Photograph: Paul-Henri Cahier

**Left: Nick Heidfeld once again battles with Fernando Alonso, but this time the BMW Sauber driver misses the final podium position.**
Photograph: Peter J Fox/www.crash.net

lap, but gradually Jenson Button hauled him in and Rubens was instructed over the radio to let Jenson past because the latter felt he was much quicker. That happened just as the television feed picked up the team's instruction to the Brazilian – and his retort: 'You've gotta be kidding me...' Respective fastest laps of 1m 28.873s and 1m 29.513s tended to bear witness to their performance differential.

While Barrichello battled a car that he said moved about a lot from corner to corner, Button got his head down and pushed very hard, getting involved in several good skirmishes. 'It was a lot of fun passing ten cars!' he said cheerfully. 'If you put to one side where we finished – because 13th position is still far from a good result – I think we had a reasonable race compared with the last one.'

Had Anthony Davidson not got trapped behind Tonio Liuzzi's Toro Rosso early on, he might have been in a better position to challenge Button, his old Buckmore Park karting rival. But Liuzzi had a blinding first lap to jump up to 12th place and drove superbly to keep a poor car in play, losing out to the Super Aguri only after the final stops.

'It was a good start but then I got sandwiched going into Turn One between Coulthard and Fisichella,' Davidson said. 'Fisichella and Trulli touched, Trulli spun and I had to go on the outside of him off the track and when I rejoined I touched another car and damaged my front end, which definitely affected the balance of the car. It was a tough race from there on, really. We had a good strategy. We got ahead of the Toro Rosso, which was who I was fighting with all race, so it is a shame to have had a bit of contact at the start. After that, it was a good clean race and it felt good to finish another grand prix.'

Team-mate Takuma Sato was less cheerful, losing places hand over fist at the start after having to brake very hard to avoid colliding with the Toyotas when Trulli was spun in Turn One. After that, he was virtually doomed thanks to his single-stop strategy and, whereas Davidson brought his SA07 home 14th, Taku had to settle for 18th.

Liuzzi continued to flog the Toro Rosso all the way home to 15th, handing out another drubbing to team-mate Scott Speed's replacement, Sebastian Vettel. Liuzzi's sole problem was a harsh upshift and for once Gerhard Berger found it in himself to pay him some compliments and acknowledge the shortcomings of the STR02 package. Vettel didn't help himself by stalling in his first pit stop. He finished 19th, his best lap almost half a second shy of his team-mate's.

Sakon Yamamoto's Spyker was the only car running behind Vettel at the finish and the Japanese driver achieved his aim of finishing the race even though low fuel pressure delayed him by stalling the engine in one pit stop. While he was running, Adrian Sutil had given Vettel a hard time, but stalling in the pits and getting stuck in gear during his first stop obliged the team to push him into the garage for a restart because Yamamoto was due in. That cost him dearly and he later retired in sight of the flag when he, too, suffered fuel-pressure problems.

This was not a great race, notwithstanding the battles down in the lower midfield, especially among the Toyotas and Hondas, but it put the Ferrari drivers back in play, threw Alonso a lifeline and gave Hamilton a lot to think about. He looked remarkably calm for someone who had just seen his team-mate close to within five points of him.

'I certainly don't count myself lucky,' he said of his ability to get to the finish despite the puncture, which Bridgestone thought was just one of those things. 'I was the only one who had a delaminated tyre. I knew when the Ferraris stopped that I had five or six laps of fuel left, so I hoped I would have the opportunity to use those laps to close the gap to the Ferraris and jump at least one of them. But that's racing.

'I'm not worried about the championship. We were strong testing in Belgium and I am confident for the next race in Italy. It's possible the fight will go all the way down to Brazil but at the end of the day it doesn't matter if I get it early or late, so long as I get it.'

*David Tremayne*

**Left: A witty banner summing up the ever-evolving McLaren spying row.**
Photograph: Peter J Fox/www.crash.net

**Below: The victorious Felipe Massa is the toast of his mechanics.**
Photograph: Jean-François Galeron/WRi2

**Bottom: Kimi Räikkönen was outpaced by his team-mate over the weekend and had to settle for second place.**
Photograph: Paul-Henri Cahier

## ISTANBUL KURTKOY

**Circuit: 3.317 miles/5.338 km**

*116/187* mph/kmh

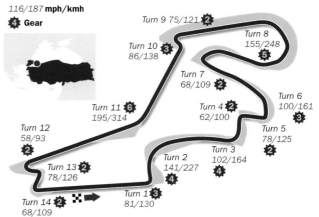

Photograph: Peter J Fox/www.crash.net

# FIA F1 WORLD CHAMPIONSHIP • ROUND 12

## PETROL OFISI
# TURKISH GRAND PRIX

## ISTANBUL 24–26 AUGUST 2007

---

## RACE RESULTS

| Pos. | Driver | Nat. | No. | Entrant | Car/Engine | Tyres | Laps | Time/Retirement | Speed (mph/km/h) | Gap to leader | Fastest race lap | |
|---|---|---|---|---|---|---|---|---|---|---|---|---|
| 1 | Felipe Massa | BR | 5 | Scuderia Ferrari Marlboro | Ferrari F2007-056 V8 | B | 58 | 1h 26m 42.161s | 133.041/214.108 | | 1m 27.922s | 18 |
| 2 | Kimi Räikkönen | FIN | 6 | Scuderia Ferrari Marlboro | Ferrari F2007-056 V8 | B | 58 | 1h 26m 44.436s | 132.982/214.014 | + 2.275s | 1m 27.295s | 57 |
| 3 | Fernando Alonso | E | 1 | Vodafone McLaren Mercedes | McLaren MP4-22-Mercedes F0 108T V8 | B | 58 | 1h 27m 8.342s | 132.374/213.036 | + 26.181s | 1m 28.070s | 39 |
| 4 | Nick Heidfeld | D | 9 | BMW Sauber F1 Team | BMW Sauber F1.07-BMW P86/7 V8 | B | 58 | 1h 27m 21.835s | 132.033/212.487 | + 39.674s | 1m 28.319s | 39 |
| 5 | Lewis Hamilton | GB | 2 | Vodafone McLaren Mercedes | McLaren MP4-22-Mercedes F0 108T V8 | B | 58 | 1h 27m 27.246s | 131.897/212.268 | + 45.085s | 1m 27.963s | 17 |
| 6 | Heikki Kovalainen | FIN | 4 | ING Renault F1 Team | Renault R27-RS27 V8 | B | 58 | 1h 27m 28.330s | 131.870/212.224 | + 46.169s | 1m 28.603s | 20 |
| 7 | Nico Rosberg | D | 16 | AT&T Williams | Williams FW29-Toyota RVX-07 V8 | B | 58 | 1h 27m 37.939s | 131.629/211.836 | + 55.778s | 1m 28.536s | 37 |
| 8 | Robert Kubica | POL | 10 | BMW Sauber F1 Team | BMW Sauber F1.07-BMW P86/7 V8 | B | 58 | 1h 27m 38.868s | 131.606/211.799 | + 56.707s | 1m 28.918s | 11 |
| 9 | Giancarlo Fisichella | I | 3 | ING Renault F1 Team | Renault R27-RS27 V8 | B | 58 | 1h 27m 41.652s | 131.536/211.687 | + 59.491s | 1m 28.793s | 56 |
| 10 | David Coulthard | GB | 14 | Red Bull Racing | Red Bull RB3-Renault RS27 V8 | B | 58 | 1h 27m 53.170s | 131.249/211.225 | + 1m 11.009s | 1m 29.068s | 54 |
| 11 | Alexander Wurz | A | 17 | AT&T Williams | Williams FW29-Toyota RVX-07 V8 | B | 58 | 1h 28m 1.789s | 131.035/210.880 | + 1m 19.628s | 1m 28.737s | 55 |
| 12 | Ralf Schumacher | D | 11 | Panasonic Toyota Racing | Toyota TF107-RVX-07 V8 | B | 57 | | | + 1 lap | 1m 28.924s | 55 |
| 13 | Jenson Button | GB | 7 | Honda Racing F1 Team | Honda RA107-RA807E V8 | B | 57 | | | + 1 lap | 1m 28.873s | 34 |
| 14 | Anthony Davidson | GB | 23 | Super Aguri F1 Team | Super Aguri SA07-Honda RA807E V8 | B | 57 | | | + 1 lap | 1m 29.658s | 38 |
| 15 | Vitantonio Liuzzi | I | 18 | Scuderia Toro Rosso | Toro Rosso STR02-Ferrari 056H V8 | B | 57 | | | + 1 lap | 1m 29.563s | 56 |
| 16 | Jarno Trulli | I | 12 | Panasonic Toyota Racing | Toyota TF107-RVX-07 V8 | B | 57 | | | + 1 lap | 1m 29.459s | 39 |
| 17 | Rubens Barrichello | BR | 8 | Honda Racing F1 Team | Honda RA107-RA807E V8 | B | 57 | | | + 1 lap | 1m 29.513s | 35 |
| 18 | Takuma Sato | J | 22 | Super Aguri F1 Team | Super Aguri SA07-Honda RA807E V8 | B | 57 | | | + 1 lap | 1m 29.916s | 56 |
| 19 | Sebastian Vettel | D | 19 | Scuderia Toro Rosso | Toro Rosso STR02-Ferrari 056H V8 | B | 57 | | | + 1 lap | 1m 29.983s | 39 |
| 20 | Sakon Yamamoto | J | 21 | Etihad Aldar Spyker F1 Team | Spyker F8-VII-Ferrari 056H V8 | B | 56 | | | + 2 laps | 1m 30.951s | 21 |
| 21 | Adrian Sutil | D | 20 | Etihad Aldar Spyker F1 Team | Spyker F8-VII-Ferrari 056H V8 | B | 53 | Fuel pressure | | + 5 laps | 1m 30.617s | 52 |
| | Mark Webber | AUS | 15 | Red Bull Racing | Red Bull RB3-Renault RS27 V8 | B | 9 | Differential/ hydraulics | | | 1m 30.808s | 4 |

Fastest race lap: Kimi Räikkönen on lap 57, 1m 27.295s, 136.786 mph/220.136 km/h.

Lap record: Juan Pablo Montoya (McLaren MP4-20-Mercedes Benz V10), 1m 24.770s, 140.861 mph/226.693 km/h (2005).

| Grid order | 1 | 2 | 3 | 4 | 5 | 6 | 7 | 8 | 9 | 10 | 11 | 12 | 13 | 14 | 15 | 16 | 17 | 18 | 19 | 20 | 21 | 22 | 23 | 24 | 25 | 26 | 27 | 28 | 29 | 30 | 31 | 32 | 33 | 34 | 35 | 36 | 37 | 38 | 39 | 40 | 41 | 42 | 43 | 44 | 4 |
|---|---|---|---|---|---|---|---|---|---|---|---|---|---|---|---|---|---|---|---|---|---|---|---|---|---|---|---|---|---|---|---|---|---|---|---|---|---|---|---|---|---|---|---|---|---|
| 5 MASSA | 5 | 5 | 5 | 5 | 5 | 5 | 5 | 5 | 5 | 5 | 5 | 5 | 5 | 5 | 5 | 5 | 5 | 5 | 5 | 2 | 4 | 5 | 5 | 5 | 5 | 5 | 5 | 5 | 5 | 5 | 5 | 5 | 5 | 5 | 5 | 5 | 5 | 5 | 5 | 5 | 5 | 5 | 1 | 5 | 5 |
| 2 HAMILTON | 6 | 6 | 6 | 6 | 6 | 6 | 6 | 6 | 6 | 6 | 6 | 6 | 6 | 6 | 6 | 6 | 6 | 6 | 2 | 4 | 5 | 6 | 6 | 6 | 6 | 6 | 6 | 6 | 6 | 6 | 6 | 6 | 6 | 6 | 6 | 6 | 6 | 6 | 6 | 2 | 5 | 6 | | |
| 6 RÄIKKÖNEN | 2 | 2 | 2 | 2 | 2 | 2 | 2 | 2 | 2 | 2 | 2 | 2 | 2 | 2 | 2 | 2 | 2 | 2 | 4 | 5 | 6 | 2 | 2 | 2 | 2 | 2 | 2 | 2 | 2 | 2 | 2 | 2 | 2 | 2 | 2 | 2 | 2 | 2 | 2 | 1 | 6 | 1 | | |
| 1 ALONSO | 10 | 10 | 10 | 10 | 10 | 10 | 10 | 10 | 10 | 10 | 10 | 10 | 9 | 9 | 9 | 9 | 9 | 1 | 6 | 6 | 2 | 3 | 1 | 1 | 1 | 1 | 1 | 1 | 1 | 1 | 1 | 1 | 1 | 1 | 1 | 1 | 1 | 1 | 1 | 6 | 2 | 9 | | |
| 10 KUBICA | 9 | 9 | 9 | 9 | 9 | 9 | 9 | 9 | 9 | 9 | 9 | 9 | 1 | 1 | 1 | 1 | 1 | 4 | 3 | 3 | 3 | 1 | 9 | 9 | 9 | 9 | 9 | 9 | 9 | 9 | 9 | 9 | 9 | 9 | 9 | 9 | 9 | 9 | 9 | 4 | 3 | 2 | | |
| 9 HEIDFELD | 1 | 1 | 1 | 1 | 1 | 1 | 1 | 1 | 1 | 1 | 1 | 1 | 4 | 4 | 4 | 4 | 4 | 17 | 1 | 1 | 1 | 9 | 4 | 4 | 4 | 4 | 4 | 4 | 4 | 4 | 4 | 4 | 4 | 4 | 4 | 4 | 4 | 4 | 4 | 3 | 9 | 4 | | |
| 4 KOVALAINEN | 4 | 4 | 4 | 4 | 4 | 4 | 4 | 4 | 4 | 4 | 4 | 4 | 16 | 16 | 16 | 16 | 16 | 3 | 9 | 9 | 4 | 10 | 10 | 10 | 10 | 10 | 10 | 10 | 10 | 10 | 10 | 10 | 10 | 10 | 10 | 16 | 16 | 3 | 3 | 9 | 4 | 16 | 1 | | |
| 16 ROSBERG | 16 | 16 | 16 | 16 | 16 | 16 | 16 | 16 | 16 | 16 | 16 | 16 | 14 | 14 | 14 | 14 | 14 | 9 | 10 | 10 | 10 | 16 | 16 | 16 | 16 | 16 | 16 | 16 | 16 | 16 | 16 | 16 | 16 | 16 | 16 | 3 | 3 | 14 | 14 | 14 | 16 | 10 | 1 | | |
| 12 TRULLI | 14 | 14 | 14 | 14 | 14 | 14 | 14 | 14 | 14 | 14 | 14 | 14 | 17 | 17 | 17 | 17 | 17 | 10 | 16 | 16 | 16 | 18 | 18 | 3 | 3 | 3 | 3 | 3 | 3 | 3 | 3 | 3 | 3 | 3 | 14 | 14 | 16 | 16 | 16 | 10 | 17 | | | |
| 3 FISICHELLA | 15 | 15 | 15 | 15 | 15 | 15 | 15 | 15 | 17 | 17 | 17 | 17 | 3 | 3 | 3 | 3 | 3 | 16 | 18 | 18 | 18 | 3 | 3 | 23 | 14 | 14 | 14 | 14 | 14 | 14 | 14 | 14 | 14 | 14 | 10 | 10 | 10 | 10 | 10 | 17 | 3 | | | |
| 23 DAVIDSON | 17 | 17 | 17 | 17 | 17 | 17 | 17 | 17 | 3 | 3 | 3 | 3 | 10 | 10 | 10 | 10 | 10 | 18 | 23 | 23 | 23 | 23 | 23 | 14 | 11 | 11 | 11 | 11 | 11 | 17 | 17 | 17 | 17 | 17 | 17 | 17 | 17 | 14 | 14 | 1 | | | |
| 15 WEBBER | 18 | 18 | 3 | 3 | 3 | 3 | 18 | 18 | 18 | 18 | 18 | 18 | 18 | 18 | 18 | 18 | 18 | 23 | 14 | 14 | 7 | 14 | 14 | 11 | 17 | 17 | 17 | 17 | 7 | 7 | 7 | 18 | 18 | 23 | 23 | 23 | 23 | 11 | 11 | 1 | | | |
| 14 COULTHARD | 3 | 3 | 18 | 18 | 18 | 18 | 3 | 3 | 23 | 23 | 23 | 23 | 23 | 23 | 23 | 14 | 7 | 14 | 14 | 11 | 17 | 17 | 17 | 19 | 19 | 19 | 7 | 7 | 7 | 7 | 18 | 18 | 23 | 23 | 23 | 23 | 11 | 11 | 12 | 12 | | | |
| 17 WURZ | 23 | 23 | 23 | 23 | 23 | 23 | 23 | 23 | 11 | 11 | 11 | 11 | 11 | 11 | 11 | 11 | 11 | 8 | 17 | 19 | 18 | 7 | 7 | 18 | 7 | 7 | 7 | 18 | 18 | 23 | 23 | 23 | 11 | 11 | 11 | 11 | 11 | 12 | 12 | | | | |
| 18 LIUZZI | 11 | 11 | 11 | 11 | 11 | 11 | 11 | 11 | 8 | 8 | 8 | 8 | 8 | 8 | 8 | 8 | 8 | 7 | 11 | 8 | 8 | 17 | 19 | 18 | 23 | 23 | 23 | 23 | 23 | 11 | 11 | 11 | 8 | 12 | 7 | 7 | 12 | 7 | 23 | 11 | | | |
| 11 SCHUMACHER | 8 | 8 | 8 | 8 | 8 | 8 | 8 | 8 | 2 | 12 | 7 | 7 | 7 | 7 | 7 | 7 | 12 | 12 | 17 | 17 | 7 | 7 | 22 | 22 | 22 | 8 | 8 | 12 | 7 | 18 | 18 | 18 | 18 | 18 | 18 | 18 | 18 | | | | | | |
| 22 SATO | 19 | 19 | 7 | 7 | 12 | 12 | 12 | 12 | 12 | 7 | 12 | 12 | 12 | 12 | 17 | 12 | 19 | 19 | 7 | 22 | 22 | 22 | 8 | 8 | 8 | 12 | 12 | 7 | 8 | 8 | 8 | 8 | 8 | | | | | | | | | | |
| 19 VETTEL | 20 | 7 | 12 | 12 | 7 | 7 | 7 | 15 | 19 | 19 | 19 | 19 | 19 | 19 | 19 | 20 | 2 | 22 | 22 | 12 | 12 | 12 | 19 | 19 | 19 | 19 | 19 | 19 | 19 | 19 | 19 | 19 | 19 | 19 | 22 | 22 | | | | | | | |
| 20 SUTIL | 21 | 20 | 19 | 19 | 19 | 19 | 19 | 20 | 20 | 20 | 20 | 20 | 20 | 20 | 20 | 20 | 21 | 12 | 12 | 12 | 19 | 19 | 19 | 22 | 22 | 22 | 22 | 22 | 22 | 22 | 22 | 22 | 22 | 22 | 22 | 22 | 22 | 22 | | | | | |
| 21 YAMAMOTO | 7 | 12 | 20 | 20 | 20 | 20 | 20 | 19 | 21 | 21 | 21 | 21 | 21 | 21 | 21 | 21 | 21 | 21 | 21 | 21 | 21 | 21 | 22 | 21 | 21 | 21 | 21 | 21 | 21 | 21 | 21 | 21 | | | | | | | | | | | |
| 7 BUTTON | 12 | 21 | 22 | 22 | 22 | 22 | 22 | 22 | 22 | 22 | 21 | 21 | 21 | 21 | 21 | 21 | 21 | 20 | 20 | 20 | 20 | 20 | 20 | | | | | | | | | | | | | | | | | | | | | |
| 8 BARRICHELLO | 22 | 22 | 21 | 21 | 21 | 21 | 21 | 21 | 21 | | | | | | | | | | | | | | | | | | | | | | | | | | | | | | | | | | | |

### PRACTICE 1 (FRIDAY)

Sunny (track 36–43ºC, air 30–31ºC)

| Pos. | Driver | Laps | Time |
|---|---|---|---|
| 1 | Kimi Räikkönen | 22 | 1m 27.988s |
| 2 | Felipe Massa | 20 | 1m 28.391s |
| 3 | Fernando Alonso | 20 | 1m 29.222s |
| 4 | Lewis Hamilton | 10 | 1m 29.261s |
| 5 | Heikki Kovalainen | 19 | 1m 29.346s |
| 6 | Nico Rosberg | 23 | 1m 29.403s |
| 7 | Ralf Schumacher | 24 | 1m 29.414s |
| 8 | Giancarlo Fisichella | 19 | 1m 29.541s |
| 9 | Nick Heidfeld | 20 | 1m 29.641s |
| 10 | Jarno Trulli | 26 | 1m 29.685s |
| 11 | Robert Kubica | 23 | 1m 29.710s |
| 12 | Anthony Davidson | 17 | 1m 30.384s |
| 13 | David Coulthard | 23 | 1m 30.398s |
| 14 | Jenson Button | 17 | 1m 30.483s |
| 15 | Rubens Barrichello | 25 | 1m 30.580s |
| 16 | Vitantonio Liuzzi | 21 | 1m 30.612s |
| 17 | Takuma Sato | 15 | 1m 30.624s |
| 18 | Alexander Wurz | 12 | 1m 30.876s |
| 19 | Mark Webber | 22 | 1m 30.917s |
| 20 | Sebastian Vettel | 22 | 1m 31.383s |
| 21 | Adrian Sutil | 31 | 1m 31.445s |
| 22 | Sakon Yamamoto | 35 | 1m 32.270s |

### PRACTICE 2 (FRIDAY)

Sunny (track 36–48ºC, air 34–36ºC)

| Pos. | Driver | Laps | Time |
|---|---|---|---|
| 1 | Lewis Hamilton | 28 | 1m 28.469s |
| 2 | Kimi Räikkönen | 21 | 1m 28.762s |
| 3 | Ralf Schumacher | 23 | 1m 28.773s |
| 4 | Jarno Trulli | 28 | 1m 28.874s |
| 5 | Felipe Massa | 25 | 1m 28.884s |
| 6 | Fernando Alonso | 24 | 1m 28.947s |
| 7 | Nico Rosberg | 27 | 1m 28.995s |
| 8 | Heikki Kovalainen | 28 | 1m 29.025s |
| 9 | Alexander Wurz | 27 | 1m 29.093s |
| 10 | Robert Kubica | 31 | 1m 29.368s |
| 11 | David Coulthard | 12 | 1m 29.435s |
| 12 | Giancarlo Fisichella | 28 | 1m 29.456s |
| 13 | Nick Heidfeld | 30 | 1m 29.792s |
| 14 | Jenson Button | 26 | 1m 29.945s |
| 15 | Rubens Barrichello | 31 | 1m 30.055s |
| 16 | Takuma Sato | 27 | 1m 30.104s |
| 17 | Mark Webber | 25 | 1m 30.315s |
| 18 | Anthony Davidson | 24 | 1m 30.530s |
| 19 | Vitantonio Liuzzi | 24 | 1m 30.702s |
| 20 | Sebastian Vettel | 16 | 1m 30.801s |
| 21 | Adrian Sutil | 32 | 1m 31.153s |
| 22 | Sakon Yamamoto | 32 | 1m 31.175s |

### QUALIFYING (SATURDAY)

Cloudy (track 45–49ºC, air 34–35ºC)

| Pos. | Driver | First | Second | Third |
|---|---|---|---|---|
| 1 | Felipe Massa | 1m 27.488s | 1m 27.039s | 1m 27.329s |
| 2 | Lewis Hamilton | 1m 27.513s | 1m 26.936s | 1m 27.373s |
| 3 | Kimi Räikkönen | 1m 27.294s | 1m 26.902s | 1m 27.546s |
| 4 | Fernando Alonso | 1m 27.328s | 1m 26.841s | 1m 27.574s |
| 5 | Robert Kubica | 1m 27.997s | 1m 27.253s | 1m 27.722s |
| 6 | Nick Heidfeld | 1m 28.099s | 1m 27.253s | 1m 28.037s |
| 7 | Heikki Kovalainen | 1m 28.127s | 1m 27.784s | 1m 28.491s |
| 8 | Nico Rosberg | 1m 28.275s | 1m 27.750s | 1m 28.501s |
| 9 | Jarno Trulli | 1m 28.318s | 1m 27.801s | 1m 28.740s |
| 10 | Giancarlo Fisichella | 1m 28.313s | 1m 27.880s | 1m 29.322s |
| 11 | Anthony Davidson | 1m 28.304s | 1m 28.002s | |
| 12 | Mark Webber | 1m 28.500s | 1m 28.013s | |
| 13 | David Coulthard | 1m 28.395s | 1m 28.100s | |
| 14 | Rubens Barrichello | 1m 28.792s | 1m 28.188s | |
| 15 | Jenson Button | 1m 28.373s | 1m 28.220s | |
| 16 | Alexander Wurz | 1m 28.360s | 1m 28.390s | |
| 17 | Vitantonio Liuzzi | 1m 28.798s | | |
| 18 | Ralf Schumacher | 1m 28.809s | | |
| 19 | Takuma Sato | 1m 28.953s | | |
| 20 | Sebastian Vettel | 1m 29.408s | | |
| 21 | Adrian Sutil | 1m 29.861s | | |
| 22 | Sakon Yamamoto | 1m 31.479s | | |

### PRACTICE 3 (SATURDAY)

Sunny (track 41–45ºC, air 33ºC)

| Pos. | Driver | Laps | Time |
|---|---|---|---|
| 1 | Lewis Hamilton | 12 | 1m 27.325s |
| 2 | Felipe Massa | 15 | 1m 27.366s |
| 3 | Kimi Räikkönen | 16 | 1m 27.506s |
| 4 | Fernando Alonso | 13 | 1m 27.743s |
| 5 | Nico Rosberg | 16 | 1m 28.056s |
| 6 | Nick Heidfeld | 18 | 1m 28.184s |
| 7 | Robert Kubica | 21 | 1m 28.224s |
| 8 | Giancarlo Fisichella | 20 | 1m 28.261s |
| 9 | Mark Webber | 15 | 1m 28.337s |
| 10 | Heikki Kovalainen | 17 | 1m 28.364s |
| 11 | Alexander Wurz | 16 | 1m 28.413s |
| 12 | David Coulthard | 14 | 1m 28.448s |
| 13 | Ralf Schumacher | 20 | 1m 28.481s |
| 14 | Jarno Trulli | 21 | 1m 28.520s |
| 15 | Jenson Button | 16 | 1m 28.548s |
| 16 | Rubens Barrichello | 18 | 1m 28.715s |
| 17 | Anthony Davidson | 16 | 1m 28.755s |
| 18 | Vitantonio Liuzzi | 20 | 1m 28.937s |
| 19 | Sebastian Vettel | 19 | 1m 29.408s |
| 20 | Takuma Sato | 14 | 1m 29.436s |
| 21 | Adrian Sutil | 22 | 1m 30.044s |
| 22 | Sakon Yamamoto | 21 | 1m 30.712s |

## RACE TYRE STRATEGIES

**BRIDGESTONE**

In 2007, the tyre regulations stipulate that the two dry-tyre specifications must be visibly distinguishable from each other. At the Turkish Grand Prix, the medium compound Bridgestone Potenza tyre was marked with a white line in the second-from-inside groove.

| | Driver | Race stint 1 | Race stint 2 | Race stint 3 |
|---|---|---|---|---|
| 1 | Felipe Massa | Medium: laps 1–19 | Medium: 20–42 | Hard: 43–58 |
| 2 | Kimi Räikkönen | Medium: 1–18 | Medium: 19–41 | Hard: 42–58 |
| 3 | Fernando Alonso | Hard: 1–18 | Hard: 19–43 | Medium: 44–58 |
| 4 | Nick Heidfeld | Hard: 1–17 | Hard: 18–41 | Medium: 42–58 |
| 5 | Lewis Hamilton | Hard: 1–20 | Hard: 21–43 | Medium: 44–58 |
| 6 | Heikki Kovalainen | Hard: 1–21 | Hard: 22–42 | Medium: 43–58 |
| 7 | Nico Rosberg | Hard: 1–17 | Hard: 18–39 | Medium: 40–58 |
| 8 | Robert Kubica | Medium: 1–12 | Medium: 13–37 | Hard: 38–58 |
| 9 | Giancarlo Fisichella | Hard: 1–22 | Hard: 23–43 | Medium: 44–58 |
| 10 | David Coulthard | Medium: 1–17 | Medium: 18–42 | Hard: 43–58 |
| 11 | Alexander Wurz | Hard: 1–18 | Hard: 19–44 | Medium: 45–58 |
| 12 | Ralf Schumacher | Hard: 1–32 | Medium: 33–57 | |
| 13 | Jenson Button | Hard: 1–22 | Hard: 23–35 | Medium: 36–57 |
| 14 | Anthony Davidson | Hard: 1–26 | Medium: 27–42 | Hard: 43–57 |
| 15 | Vitantonio Liuzzi | Medium: 1–24 | Medium: 25–37 | Hard: 38–57 |
| 16 | Jarno Trulli | Hard: 1–20 | Hard: 21–44 | Medium: 45–57 |
| 17 | Rubens Barrichello | Hard: 1–23 | Medium: 24–36 | Medium: 37–57 |
| 18 | Takuma Sato | Hard: 1–32 | Medium: 33–57 | |
| 19 | Sebastian Vettel | Hard: 1–28 | Medium: 29–43 | Medium: 44–57 |
| 20 | Sakon Yamamoto | Medium: 1–22 | Medium: 23–36 | Hard: 37–56 |
| 21 | Adrian Sutil | Medium: 1–21 | Medium: 22–33 | Hard: 34–53 (DNF) |
| | Mark Webber | Medium: 1–9 (DNF) | | |

**10 FISICHELLA Renault**

**8 ROSBERG Williams**

**6 HEIDFELD BMW-Sauber**

**4 ALONSO McLaren**

**2 HAMILTON McLaren**

**9 TRULLI Toyota**

**7 KOVALAINEN Renault**

**5 KUBICA BMW-Sauber**

**3 RÄIKKÖNEN Ferrari**

**1 MASSA Ferrari**

RACE DISTANCE:
58 laps,
192.250 miles/309.396 km

RACE WEATHER:
Sunny,
47–49ºC, air 34–35ºC

| 46 | 47 | 48 | 49 | 50 | 51 | 52 | 53 | 54 | 55 | 56 | 57 | 58 | |
|---|---|---|---|---|---|---|---|---|---|---|---|---|---|
| 5 | 5 | 5 | 5 | 5 | 5 | 5 | 5 | 5 | 5 | 5 | 5 | 5 | 1 |
| 6 | 6 | 6 | 6 | 6 | 6 | 6 | 6 | 6 | 6 | 6 | 6 | 6 | 2 |
| 1 | 1 | 1 | 1 | 1 | 1 | 1 | 1 | 1 | 1 | 1 | 1 | 1 | 3 |
| 9 | 9 | 9 | 9 | 9 | 9 | 9 | 9 | 9 | 9 | 9 | 9 | 4 | 4 |
| 2 | 2 | 2 | 2 | 2 | 2 | 2 | 2 | 2 | 2 | 2 | 2 | 5 | 5 |
| 4 | 4 | 4 | 4 | 4 | 4 | 4 | 4 | 4 | 4 | 4 | 4 | 6 | 6 |
| 16 | 16 | 16 | 16 | 16 | 16 | 16 | 16 | 16 | 16 | 16 | 16 | 17 | 7 |
| 10 | 10 | 10 | 10 | 10 | 10 | 10 | 10 | 10 | 10 | 10 | 10 | 10 | 8 |
| 3 | 3 | 3 | 3 | 3 | 3 | 3 | 3 | 3 | 3 | 3 | 3 | 3 | |
| 14 | 14 | 14 | 14 | 14 | 14 | 14 | 14 | 14 | 14 | 14 | 14 | | |
| 17 | 17 | 17 | 17 | 17 | 17 | 17 | 17 | 17 | 17 | 17 | 17 | | |
| 11 | 11 | 11 | 11 | 11 | 11 | 11 | 11 | 11 | 11 | 11 | 11 | | |
| 7 | 7 | 7 | 7 | 7 | 7 | 7 | 7 | 7 | 7 | | | | |
| 23 | 23 | 23 | 23 | 23 | 23 | 23 | 23 | 23 | 23 | 23 | 23 | | |
| 18 | 18 | 18 | 18 | 18 | 18 | 18 | 18 | 18 | 18 | 18 | 18 | | |
| 8 | 8 | 8 | 12 | 12 | 12 | 12 | 12 | 12 | 12 | 12 | 12 | | |
| 12 | 12 | 12 | 8 | 8 | 8 | 8 | 8 | 8 | 8 | 8 | 8 | | |
| 22 | 22 | 22 | 22 | 22 | 22 | 22 | 22 | 22 | 22 | 22 | 22 | | |
| 19 | 19 | 19 | 19 | 19 | 19 | 19 | 19 | 19 | 19 | | | | |
| 21 | 21 | 21 | 21 | 21 | 21 | 21 | 21 | 21 | 21 | | | | |
| 20 | 20 | 20 | 20 | 20 | 20 | 20 | 20 | | | | | | |

12 Pit stop          18 One lap or more behind leader

## FOR THE RECORD

## POINTS

| | DRIVERS | |
|---|---|---|
| 1 | Lewis Hamilton | 84 |
| 2 | Fernando Alonso | 79 |
| 3 | Felipe Massa | 69 |
| 4 | Kimi Räikkönen | 68 |
| 5 | Nick Heidfeld | 47 |
| 6 | Robert Kubica | 29 |
| 7 | Heikki Kovalainen | 19 |
| 8 | Giancarlo Fisichella | 17 |
| 9 | Alexander Wurz | 13 |
| 10 | Nico Rosberg | 9 |
| 11 | Mark Webber | 8 |
| 12 | David Coulthard | 8 |
| 13 | Jarno Trulli | 7 |
| 14 | Ralf Schumacher | 5 |
| 15 | Takuma Sato | 4 |
| 16 | Sebastian Vettel | 1 |
| 17 | Jenson Button | 1 |

| | CONSTRUCTORS | |
|---|---|---|
| 1 | McLaren | 148 |
| 2 | Ferrari | 137 |
| 3 | BMW Sauber | 77 |
| 4 | Renault | 36 |
| 5 | Williams | 22 |
| 6 | Red Bull | 16 |
| 7 | Toyota | 12 |
| 8 | Super Aguri | 4 |
| 9 | Honda | 1 |

Photographs: Peter J Fox/www.crash.net

FIA F1 WORLD CHAMPIONSHIP/ROUND 13

# ITALIAN GP

MONZA

MARTINI

Past and present at Monza. Fernando Alonso speeds to victory from under the disused banking, the historic park circuit dappled through the trees by an autumnal sun.
Photograph: Peter J Fox/www.crash.net

**Above:** Eddie Irvine's (above) return to the Formula 1 paddock certainly reflected a certain *dégagé* image.
Photograph: Peter Nygaard/GP Photo

**Right:** Spyker mechanics work on their newly updated cars

**Far right:** One of Monza's lovely Santander grid girls.
Photographs: Peter J Fox/www.crash.net

**Centre:** Kimi Räikkönen reflects on his driving error in Saturday's free practice, which left his F2007 badly damaged (centre right) and his neck painfully strained.
Photographs: Bernard Asset

**Below:** Fernando Alonso's McLaren rides across the kerbing in his failed attempt to better the Ferraris in qualifying.
Photograph: Lukas Gorys

## MONZA QUALIFYING

After all the feuding that had sullied the season, McLaren took a measure of revenge in qualifying at Monza by rubbing Ferrari's nose in it. The MP4-22 had been good all year on fast tracks and in low-downforce trim and that, allied to the car's behaviour over the Italian circuit's notorious kerbs, sealed the matter firmly in the Anglo-German team's favour.

And Monza was the venue for something of a renaissance by Fernando Alonso, who put it over team-mate Lewis Hamilton to snatch pole position. Alonso turned in a best lap of 1m 21.997s, leaving Hamilton second with 1m 22.034s. By contrast, the Ferraris seemed a trifle breathless as Felipe Massa managed 1m 22.549s and Kimi Räikkönen 1m 23.183s.

Alonso was very happy with his car and had few complaints, but Hamilton said his single-lap balance left something to be desired. He did not expect that to be a problem over the race distance, however.

Though Ferrari had always been better over the long haul this year, Massa was detuned in third place and was clearly impressed with the McLarens' pace. Räikkönen, meanwhile, was nursing a very sore neck after a major shunt at the entry to Ascari during the morning's practice session. At the time it seemed that he had suffered some sort of suspension failure – the car twitched to the right, slammed into the barriers and then slid head-on into the tyre wall. Later, however, Kimi suggested that he might have got a wheel too close to the outer kerb. He gingerly pushed as hard as he could in qualifying, but Räikkönen admitted that the pain made his top five of painful experiences. His neck was very stiff, but he could count himself lucky not to have sustained further damage. The F2007 was junk, so his race engine was transferred to the spare car, which, understandably, was not fully set up to his liking.

BMW Sauber expressed the view that Nick Heidfeld lost two-tenths on his best lap, a 1m 23.174s, but it was nothing that could have made a difference to his grid place. Robert Kubica made a mistake on his best lap, but 1m 23.446s was still good enough for sixth. As had become usual in 2007, there was an air of quiet confidence in the Swiss-German camp.

Renault's fortunes picked up slightly as Heikki Kovalainen settled into seventh place with 1m 24.102s – and Kovalainen said he was relieved to get through from Q2 after losing time when Rubens Barrichello went off the road and came back on right in front of him.

Barrichello's manoeuvre also hurt Giancarlo Fisichella, who did not make it through and had to start only 15th on 1m 23.325s.

Renault's sudden spurt was a bit of a surprise for Williams, who had looked strong all weekend thanks to the flair of Nico Rosberg. He was really happy with the way things went, nevertheless, and lapped in 1m 24.382s for eighth in Q3, but team-mate Alex Wurz again lost time in Q2, locking his front wheels in the first chicane, and started only 13th on 1m 23.209s.

Toyota and Honda each helped to make it a fascinating top ten that contained seven marques. Neither Jarno Trulli nor Ralf Schumacher had any particular problems, but whereas Trulli made it through to Q3 and eventually qualified ninth on 1m 24.555s, Schumacher missed the cut in Q1 and faced a start from 18th place with 1m 23.787s. Jenson Button was very pleased to plant his Honda tenth on the grid with 1m 25.165s, especially because it took him time to get to grips with the car during the three sessions. Revised front and rear suspension helped, allied to the low-downforce aero package, and he believed that the team had made a significant step forward at last. Barrichello, however, besides making himself unpopular with Renault, blamed worn tyres for his off-track moment in the second Lesmo. He qualified 12th (1m 23.176s).

Mark Webber was annoyed to miss out on the top ten with a lap of 1m 23.166s in his Red Bull, but 11th was a whole lot better than team-mate David Coulthard's 20th place. Coulthard posted a lap of 1m 24.019s but then lost control under braking for the first chicane in Q1 and spun to a standstill. He climbed out and bowed to the appreciative crowd. He blamed the incident on low oil pressure in the gearbox, which locked the rear axle just as he was changing down through the gears.

Anthony Davidson once again beat Super Aguri team-mate Takuma Sato with a lap in 1m 23.274s compared with 1m 23.749s. They were 14th and 17th. Davidson was pleased to have been able to work through to a decent set-up on his SA07, but Sato said he lost time, especially over the bump in the second chicane.

Sebastian Vettel got the upper hand at Toro Rosso for the first time in his three race outings, lapping in 1m 23.351s for 16th after making it through to Q2. Team-mate Tonio Liuzzi lost a couple of tenths with an engine on its second race, which was consistently 3 mph down on straight-line speed, and also blamed Wurz for impeding him in the Parabolica on his best lap. His lap of 1m 23.886s left him 19th.

Spyker ran its long-awaited updated B-spec F8-VII, but still its drivers Adrian Sutil and Sakon Yamamoto were in 21st and 22nd places, on 1m 24.699s and 1m 25.084s respectively. The team had hoped for more but Yamamoto spun and broke his front wing.

## FERRARI STILL SEEKS JUSTICE

Ferrari team principal Jean Todt said after Monza that if McLaren was exonerated over the spying scandal that had plagued Formula 1 for the previous three months, Ferrari would move into the civil courts to pursue its claim that the English team benefited from its intellectual property.

His comments came after McLaren soundly beat Ferrari on its home ground at Monza. 'For us it is something that is too important and we will move forwards in Italy,' Todt said. 'I'm not going to comment on what the decisions will be – I don't know what will be the decision or then what can happen once the decision will be taken – and we will move on then with a civil court in the UK as well.'

He added that he had no influence over any penalty that might be handed down if McLaren were to be found guilty. 'It's not a menu where we get, "Would you prefer number one? Number two?" We are not to choose. That's the FIA, the World [Motor Sport] Council, who will have to decide with the evidence that they will have in hand and our duty is to make available as much evidence as possible for the World Council to understand exactly what happened.

'We did not accept it [the previous verdict] because we felt that the decision was not appropriate and then if you see the wording of the decision, "in case of new evidence" things will be different. We have new evidence.'

Todt pointed out that there was no chance of an agreement between Ferrari and McLaren before the hearing the following Thursday. 'It's nothing to do with an agreement between Ferrari and McLaren. It's a case that is going to be taken in front of the World Council. It was normally a hearing before the International Court of Appeal. Then the FIA has decided to stop this International Court of Appeal in the light of new evidence and to present that to the World Council, so that's the problem.'

He admitted that the scandal had been damaging for Formula 1. 'It's affecting the sport. We are sorry that it happens, but unfortunately we are in a position where we want the truth to appear.'

**Right:** Happy at work. Tonio Liuzzi in the Toro Rosso.
Photograph: Jean-Francois Galeron

**Below:** James Hogan, CEO of Etihad Airways, (left) with drivers Sakon Yamamoto and Adrian Sutil and Ron Barrott, CEO of Aldar, on the Monza grid.
Photograph: Peter J Fox/www.crash.net

AMAZINGLY, McLaren had never scored a one-two at Monza in its 41-year history. Fernando Alonso and Lewis Hamilton put that right as they dished out a crushing defeat to Ferrari on its home ground. As the racing engines drowned out all of the interminable hoopla of an acrimonious weekend and the political machinations could no longer interfere with what the sport is really about, Ron Dennis's beleaguered team did its work where it mattered most: on the racetrack.

As Alonso led Hamilton across the finish line, Dennis finally showed the strain he had been under for the previous three months as the emotion of the moment got to him. Behind the litany of allegations of theft, deceit, fraud, cheating and sabotage, such passion is what drives the sport. During the course of a bitter weekend Dennis had been offered a deal whereby, if he agreed to retire from the sport, all of McLaren's problems would disappear. He made his reply in the sporting arena on the Sunday afternoon, rather than in a court room, and it was more deafening than the cheers of the *tifosi* and the endless noise of their air horns.

Alonso dominated the race from start to finish. He never looked remotely ruffled after he had beaten Hamilton on the run down to the first corner and defended there against him and the fast-starting Felipe Massa, who seemed on a mission from God to break the McLarens. When David Coulthard's Red Bull crashed hard at the Curva Grande as a result of a front-wing failure, the safety car was deployed and Alonso had to be canny on the restart six laps in – and this time it was Hamilton coming hard at him in his mirrors. He deflected that attack, too, and after that it was plain sailing as he drew to within three points of Hamilton's championship lead.

This time Hamilton had no answer for the world champion's relentless pace. But at least he didn't have to worry about

Massa after the opening nine laps. Massa had practically been in the cockpit with him and Hamilton had had to be robust in his defence at times but then the red car suddenly swooped into the pits at the end of the ninth lap, did one more slow lap and then came in for good. A rear damper was malfunctioning, affecting the behaviour of the rear suspension and, to the dismay of the crowd, one of the Ferraris was through.

'I am very disappointed,' said the crestfallen Massa. 'It's horrible to see your chances go in the early stages because of a reliability problem. There was something not working with the rear suspension: coming into Ascari I could feel it under braking and I came into the pits, thinking it might be due to a puncture. However, once the tyres were changed the car was still undriveable and I had to retire.'

Hamilton now had only Alonso to worry about but he never quite had the pace to challenge him. 'Obviously I didn't get the best getaway from the dirty side of the grid and Felipe went past,' he said, 'but I outbraked both him and Fernando in the chicane. I was close to taking Fernando, too, but Felipe clipped me so I lost that opportunity. I had a second chance at the restart but Fernando did a great job and made sure he pulled out enough of a gap.'

Hamilton stayed second during the first pit stops on lap 18 for him and 20 for Alonso. The timing clearly indicated that they were on two stops and when Kimi Räikkönen stayed out until lap 25 it was equally clear that he was on a one-stopper.

He had taken the lead when the McLarens stopped, then lost it when he refuelled. During the McLarens' second stops, Hamilton fell behind the Ferrari.

He had flat-spotted his tyres under braking in the middle stint and thus pitted earlier than planned, worried that an increasingly vibrating tyre might fail as the right-front had in Turkey. When he resumed behind Räikkönen, who was on the more durable harder compound Bridgestones, he knew he had two laps at best in which to exploit his softer compounds to make a passing move. When it came, its simplicity, confidence and execution were breathtaking. If anyone still harboured doubts about Hamilton's greatness, that move surely dispelled them for good. Under braking from 205 mph, he pushed to the inside of the Ferrari, grabbed some opposite lock as the back end started to come around and slithered audaciously back into second place. Job done, more salt rubbed into the Scuderia's open wounds.

'The key was to try to optimise the in- and out-laps and the pit entry and exit,' he said later. 'I managed to pull out a couple of good laps, the car felt good and I took the opportunity I had and made sure I stuck it in there. I wanted to do it for the team. It was very important that I got those two extra points. We had got the one-two in qualifying and a one-two in the race would put the icing on the cake.'

This was not the greatest race Monza had hosted in its 85 years, but nonetheless that was a wonderful move.

Räikkönen finished a humiliating 27.325s behind Alonso, 21.263s behind Hamilton, but was philosophical. 'We knew we were heavier than McLaren and that we weren't quick enough today,' he admitted – and his hefty shunt the previous morning had seriously hurt his neck and was clearly also a significant factor. Under braking, he could hardly control his head. 'Because of that I couldn't keep my head up under the brakes. I knew after qualifying it wasn't going to be any fun. After Lewis passed me, I just slowed down and drove to the finish.'

Fourth and fifth places for BMW Sauber, courtesy of Nick Heidfeld and Robert Kubica, were to be expected on this fast circuit. The underrated Heidfeld, in particular, drove his usual impeccable race. Kubica, as so often seemed to be the case in a tricky 2007 season, had a rather more eventful race that included a bodged first pit stop: 'In the first laps when the car was lighter we were really quick but I think we could have had a better performance when the car was heavy, so perhaps this is something we have to work on. For the pit stop I didn't arrive straight so the car slid down from the jack when the guys were changing the tyres. Then we couldn't get the jack out from under the front wing, so it cost me a lot of time, but fortunately in the end it didn't change anything for the team. '

Nico Rosberg pulled off some stunning moves as he battled early on with Jenson Button. The Williams and the Honda swapped places several times before the RA107 lost out: it was running more fuel and was therefore a little heavier.

Above: **Kimi Räikkönen drove strongly to finish third, although this was hardly a result calculated to delight the car-mad *tifosi* who, as always, were banking on a Ferrari victory.**
Photograph: Jean-François Galeron/WRi2

**Below: Nico Rosberg again collected points for Williams.**
Photograph: Peter J Fox/www.crash.net

**Bottom: DC investigates the damage after his Red Bull crashes out.**
Photograph: Peter Nygaard/GP Photo

'It was a good weekend for us,' Rosberg said. 'We showed a competitive pace and we've been happy with our performance all weekend. The team's made good progress following the test here last week and the hard work paid off with a really big step forward. Well done to Toyota, as well, because Monza's an engine track and we held our own.'

In the end, Kovalainen was able to get his Renault between Rosberg and Button to snatch seventh place, reporting that he was on the limit all race and complaining about his Renault's lack of pace. 'I got a fantastic start, passed Kubica and was fighting with Heidfeld going into the Curva Grande, but he put me on the grass and I had to back off, which meant I lost a place to Kubica as well. After that, it was quite a lonely race. I passed Robert at the first stop and kept him behind me for the middle stint, but I just didn't have enough pace to come out ahead of Rosberg after my last pit stop. Everybody did a good job today and there were no mistakes at all. But, unfortunately, this was the maximum we could do.'

It was a tough break that Button ended up with only one point, his second in a dismal season, but he accepted it gratefully after a feisty race that served to remind his critics that, in a decent car, he would again be the front-runner that he was in '04.

'It was nice to get a point today but it was a frustrating race for me because I had so much understeer in the first stint,'

Above: A well-executed pit stop for Robert
Kubica on his way to fifth place.
Photograph: Jad Sherif/WRi2

he said. 'We run such low front wing around this circuit that it is
very easy to lock the front tyres, particularly at Parabolica, and I
flat-spotted the front right, which meant I was losing grip
through every right-hander. That meant I couldn't fend off
Rosberg and the long first stint of 33 laps compromised me
even further. So it was frustrating because I could have had a
better result, but we did our very best this weekend and a point
is definitely some reward. The team has done a great job and
everyone is in good spirits, so I'm pleased to have got another
point for them. They really deserve it.'

Rubens Barrichello in the second Honda battled all the
way through with Mark Webber's Red Bull over ninth and
tenth places – Webber finished ahead – and they were
chased home by Jarno Trulli, who lost many places on the
opening lap.

Giancarlo Fisichella had a dismal day. He made a superb
start but then got blocked by the inevitable traffic in the first
chicane. That was where Coulthard ran into the back of him
on lap two, damaging the Red Bull's front wing. Ultimately, the
unhappy Fisichella finished a lapped 12th ahead of Alex Wurz,
whose aggressive strategy didn't work out, Anthony Davidson
and Ralf Schumacher. Davidson had run ahead of Fisichella for
a while and was pleased to beat Schumacher's faster Toyota,
especially because an attack by Sebastian Vettel in the first
corner damaged one of his Super Aguri's dampers.

Team-mate Takuma Sato was hampered by a brake problem
and struggled home 16th ahead of the Toro Rossos of Tonio
Liuzzi and Vettel. Once again Liuzzi beat his rookie team-mate
Vettel despite his tired engine. Vettel lost a bit of time early on
when he needed repairs after a brush with Davidson while trying
to avoid Coulthard in the first corner, but got most of it back
thanks to the safety car. In the Spyker race, Sakon Yamamoto
actually passed team-mate Adrian Sutil on lap eight but was
quickly repassed. Sutil was unhappy with his revised car's
balance and neither benefited from their two-stop strategies.

At least they finished. Coulthard's second-lap brush with
Fisichella proved costly: it broke his front wing and led to his
nasty shunt at Curva Grande. 'When I accelerated, the
downforce pushed the wing underneath the front of the car and
broke the steering,' he said. 'I went straight off the track
and into the tyres and that was the end of my weekend.'

Long after all the victory celebrations, Ron Dennis was still
clearly emotional and struggled to make coherent comment.
'It's been a very challenging weekend, but motor racing is all
about passion, highs and lows,' he managed to say. 'I just feel
appreciative of the fans, the vast majority of whom seemed
to enjoy a great motor race.'

After all the acrimony off the track, that was a welcome
development.

*David Tremayne*

FIA F1 WORLD CHAMPIONSHIP • ROUND 13

# GRAN PREMIO D'ITALIA

MONZA 7–9 SEPTEMBER 2007

**AUTODROMO NAZIONALE DI MONZA**

Circuit: 3.600 miles / 5.793 km

Lesmo 2 98/158
Lesmo 1 83/134
Curva del Serraglio 177/285
Curva Vialone 92/148
Curva Parabolica 101/163
Variante della Roggia 62/100
Variante Ascari 124/200
Variante del Rettifilo 67/108
Curva Grande 174/280
Rettifilo Tribune 224/360

116/187 **mph/kmh**   **Gear**

Photograph: Peter J Fox/www.crash.net

## RACE RESULTS

| Pos. | Driver | Nat. | No. | Entrant | Car/Engine | Tyres | Laps | Time/Retirement | Speed (mph/km/h) | Gap to leader | Fastest race lap | |
|------|--------|------|-----|---------|------------|-------|------|-----------------|------------------|---------------|------------------|---|
| 1 | Fernando Alonso | E | 1 | Vodafone McLaren Mercedes | McLaren MP4-22-Mercedes FO 108T V8 | B | 53 | 1h 18m 37.806s | 145.430/234.047 | | 1m 22.871s | 15 |
| 2 | Lewis Hamilton | GB | 2 | Vodafone McLaren Mercedes | McLaren MP4-22-Mercedes FO 108T V8 | B | 53 | 1h 18m 43.868s | 145.244/233.747 | + 6.062s | 1m 22.936s | 17 |
| 3 | Kimi Räikkönen | FIN | 6 | Scuderia Ferrari Marlboro | Ferrari F2007-056 V8 | B | 53 | 1h 19m 5.131s | 144.592/232.699 | + 27.325s | 1m 23.370s | 21 |
| 4 | Nick Heidfeld | D | 9 | BMW Sauber F1 Team | BMW Sauber F1.07-BMW P86/7 V8 | B | 53 | 1h 19m 34.368s | 143.707/231.274 | + 56.562s | 1m 23.681s | 19 |
| 5 | Robert Kubica | POL | 10 | BMW Sauber F1 Team | BMW Sauber F1.07-BMW P86/7 V8 | B | 53 | 1h 19m 38.364s | 143.587/231.081 | + 1m 0.558s | 1m 23.908s | 22 |
| 6 | Nico Rosberg | D | 16 | AT&T Williams | Williams FW29-Toyota RVX-07 V8 | B | 53 | 1h 19m 43.616s | 143.429/230.827 | + 1m 5.810s | 1m 24.472s | 52 |
| 7 | Heikki Kovalainen | FIN | 4 | ING Renault F1 Team | Renault R27-RS27 V8 | B | 53 | 1h 19m 44.557s | 143.401/230.782 | + 1m 6.751s | 1m 24.226s | 53 |
| 8 | Jenson Button | GB | 7 | Honda Racing F1 Team | Honda RA107-RA807E V8 | B | 53 | 1h 19m 49.974s | 143.239/230.521 | + 1m 12.168s | 1m 24.532s | 32 |
| 9 | Mark Webber | AUS | 15 | Red Bull Racing | Red Bull RB3-Renault RS27 V8 | B | 53 | 1h 19m 53.685s | 143.129/230.343 | + 1m 15.879s | 1m 24.824s | 46 |
| 10 | Rubens Barrichello | BR | 8 | Honda Racing F1 Team | Honda RA107-RA807E V8 | B | 53 | 1h 19m 54.764s | 143.096/230.291 | + 1m 16.958s | 1m 24.767s | 52 |
| 11 | Jarno Trulli | I | 12 | Panasonic Toyota Racing | Toyota TF107-RVX-07 V8 | B | 53 | 1h 19m 55.542s | 143.073/230.253 | + 1m 17.736s | 1m 24.622s | 49 |
| 12 | Giancarlo Fisichella | I | 3 | ING Renault F1 Team | Renault R27-RS27 V8 | B | 52 | | | + 1 lap | 1m 24.849s | 32 |
| 13 | Alexander Wurz | A | 17 | AT&T Williams | Williams FW29-Toyota RVX-07 V8 | B | 52 | | | + 1 lap | 1m 25.000s | 42 |
| 14 | Anthony Davidson | GB | 23 | Super Aguri F1 Team | Super Aguri SA07-Honda RA807E V8 | B | 52 | | | + 1 lap | 1m 25.116s | 46 |
| 15 | Ralf Schumacher | D | 11 | Panasonic Toyota Racing | Toyota TF107-RVX-07 V8 | B | 52 | | | + 1 lap | 1m 24.951s | 49 |
| 16 | Takuma Sato | J | 22 | Super Aguri F1 Team | Super Aguri SA07-Honda RA807E V8 | B | 52 | | | + 1 lap | 1m 24.669s | 49 |
| 17 | Vitantonio Liuzzi | I | 18 | Scuderia Toro Rosso | Toro Rosso STR02-Ferrari 056H V8 | B | 52 | | | + 1 lap | 1m 25.373s | 45 |
| 18 | Sebastian Vettel | D | 19 | Scuderia Toro Rosso | Toro Rosso STR02-Ferrari 056H V8 | B | 52 | | | + 1 lap | 1m 25.313s | 47 |
| 19 | Adrian Sutil | D | 20 | Etihad Aldar Spyker F1 Team | Spyker F8-VII-Ferrari 056H V8 | B | 52 | | | + 1 lap | 1m 25.377s | 30 |
| 20 | Sakon Yamamoto | J | 21 | Etihad Aldar Spyker F1 Team | Spyker F8-VII-Ferrari 056H V8 | B | 52 | | | + 1 lap | 1m 25.478s | 34 |
| | Felipe Massa | BR | 5 | Scuderia Ferrari Marlboro | Ferrari F2007-056 V8 | B | 10 | Rear suspension | | | 1m 23.971s | 8 |
| | David Coulthard | GB | 14 | Red Bull Racing | Red Bull RB3-Renault RS27 V8 | B | 1 | Accident/front wing/steering | | | No time | – |

**Fastest race lap:** Fernando Alonso on lap 15, 1m 22.871s, 156.370 mph/251.653 km/h.

**Lap record:** Rubens Barrichello (Ferrari F2004 V10), 1m 21.046s, 159.892 mph/257.320 km/h (2004).

All results and data © FOM 2007

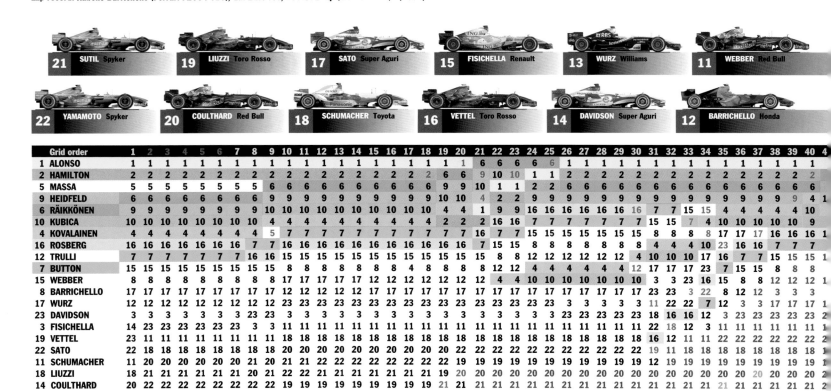

| 21 | SUTIL Spyker | 19 | LIUZZI Toro Rosso | 17 | SATO Super Aguri | 15 | FISICHELLA Renault | 13 | WURZ Williams | 11 | WEBBER Red Bull |
| 22 | YAMAMOTO Spyker | 20 | COULTHARD Red Bull | 18 | SCHUMACHER Toyota | 16 | VETTEL Toro Rosso | 14 | DAVIDSON Super Aguri | 12 | BARRICHELLO Honda |

| Grid order | 1 | 2 | 3 | 4 | 5 | 6 | 7 | 8 | 9 | 10 | 11 | 12 | 13 | 14 | 15 | 16 | 17 | 18 | 19 | 20 | 21 | 22 | 23 | 24 | 25 | 26 | 27 | 28 | 29 | 30 | 31 | 32 | 33 | 34 | 35 | 36 | 37 | 38 | 39 | 40 | 4 |
|---|---|---|---|---|---|---|---|---|---|---|---|---|---|---|---|---|---|---|---|---|---|---|---|---|---|---|---|---|---|---|---|---|---|---|---|---|---|---|---|---|---|
| 1 ALONSO | 1 | 1 | 1 | 1 | 1 | 1 | 1 | 1 | 1 | 1 | 1 | 1 | 1 | 1 | 1 | 1 | 1 | 1 | 1 | 1 | 6 | 6 | 6 | 6 | 6 | 1 | 1 | 1 | 1 | 1 | 1 | 1 | 1 | 1 | 1 | 1 | 1 | 1 | 1 | 1 | 1 |
| 2 HAMILTON | 2 | 2 | 2 | 2 | 2 | 2 | 2 | 2 | 2 | 2 | 2 | 2 | 2 | 2 | 2 | 2 | 2 | 2 | 2 | 2 | 9 | 10 | 10 | 1 | 1 | 2 | 2 | 2 | 2 | 2 | 2 | 2 | 2 | 2 | 2 | 2 | 2 | 2 | 2 | 2 | 2 |
| 5 MASSA | 5 | 5 | 5 | 5 | 5 | 5 | 5 | 5 | 6 | 6 | 6 | 6 | 6 | 6 | 6 | 6 | 6 | 6 | 9 | 9 | 10 | 1 | 1 | 2 | 2 | 6 | 6 | 6 | 6 | 6 | 6 | 6 | 6 | 6 | 6 | 6 | 6 | 6 | 6 | 6 | 6 |
| 9 HEIDFELD | 6 | 6 | 6 | 6 | 6 | 6 | 6 | 9 | 9 | 9 | 9 | 9 | 9 | 9 | 9 | 9 | 9 | 9 | 10 | 10 | 4 | 2 | 2 | 9 | 9 | 9 | 9 | 9 | 9 | 9 | 9 | 9 | 9 | 9 | 9 | 9 | 9 | 9 | 9 | 4 | 1 |
| 6 RÄIKKÖNEN | 9 | 9 | 9 | 9 | 9 | 9 | 9 | 10 | 10 | 10 | 10 | 10 | 10 | 10 | 10 | 10 | 10 | 4 | 4 | 1 | 9 | 16 | 16 | 16 | 16 | 16 | 16 | 7 | 7 | 15 | 15 | 4 | 4 | 4 | 4 | 4 | 10 | | | | |
| 10 KUBICA | 10 | 10 | 10 | 10 | 10 | 10 | 10 | 4 | 4 | 4 | 4 | 4 | 4 | 4 | 4 | 4 | 4 | 2 | 2 | 16 | 16 | 7 | 7 | 7 | 7 | 7 | 7 | 15 | 15 | 7 | 4 | 10 | 10 | 10 | 10 | 10 | 9 | | | | |
| 4 KOVALAINEN | 4 | 4 | 4 | 4 | 4 | 4 | 5 | 7 | 7 | 7 | 7 | 7 | 7 | 7 | 7 | 7 | 7 | 16 | 7 | 7 | 15 | 15 | 15 | 15 | 15 | 15 | 8 | 8 | 8 | 8 | 17 | 17 | 16 | 16 | 16 | 1 | | | | | |
| 16 ROSBERG | 16 | 16 | 16 | 16 | 16 | 16 | 7 | 16 | 16 | 16 | 16 | 16 | 16 | 16 | 16 | 16 | 7 | 15 | 15 | 8 | 8 | 8 | 8 | 8 | 8 | 4 | 4 | 4 | 10 | 23 | 16 | 16 | 7 | 7 | 7 | | | | | | |
| 12 TRULLI | 7 | 7 | 7 | 7 | 7 | 7 | 16 | 15 | 15 | 15 | 15 | 15 | 15 | 15 | 15 | 15 | 15 | 8 | 8 | 12 | 12 | 12 | 12 | 12 | 4 | 10 | 10 | 10 | 17 | 16 | 7 | 7 | 15 | 15 | 1 | | | | | | |
| 7 BUTTON | 15 | 15 | 15 | 15 | 15 | 15 | 15 | 8 | 8 | 8 | 8 | 8 | 8 | 4 | 8 | 4 | 8 | 12 | 12 | 4 | 4 | 4 | 4 | 4 | 12 | 17 | 17 | 17 | 23 | 7 | 15 | 15 | 8 | 8 | 8 | | | | | | |
| 15 WEBBER | 8 | 8 | 8 | 8 | 8 | 8 | 8 | 17 | 17 | 17 | 17 | 17 | 12 | 12 | 12 | 12 | 12 | 4 | 4 | 10 | 10 | 10 | 10 | 10 | 10 | 3 | 3 | 23 | 16 | 15 | 8 | 12 | 12 | 12 | 1 | | | | | | |
| 8 BARRICHELLO | 17 | 17 | 17 | 17 | 17 | 17 | 17 | 12 | 12 | 12 | 12 | 12 | 17 | 17 | 17 | 17 | 17 | 17 | 17 | 17 | 23 | 23 | 3 | 22 | 8 | 12 | 12 | 3 | 3 | 3 | | | | | | | | | | | |
| 17 WURZ | 12 | 12 | 12 | 12 | 12 | 12 | 12 | 23 | 23 | 23 | 23 | 23 | 23 | 23 | 23 | 23 | 23 | 23 | 3 | 3 | 11 | 22 | 22 | 7 | 12 | 3 | 17 | 17 | 17 | 1 | | | | | | | | | | | |
| 23 DAVIDSON | 3 | 3 | 3 | 3 | 3 | 3 | 3 | 23 | 3 | 3 | 3 | 3 | 3 | 3 | 3 | 3 | 3 | 3 | 23 | 23 | 23 | 23 | 16 | 16 | 12 | 23 | 23 | 23 | 23 | 2 | | | | | | | | | | | |
| 3 FISICHELLA | 14 | 23 | 23 | 23 | 23 | 23 | 3 | 11 | 11 | 11 | 11 | 11 | 11 | 11 | 11 | 11 | 11 | 11 | 11 | 11 | 11 | 22 | 18 | 12 | 3 | 11 | 11 | 11 | 11 | 1 | | | | | | | | | | | |
| 19 VETTEL | 23 | 11 | 11 | 11 | 11 | 11 | 11 | 1 | 18 | 18 | 18 | 18 | 18 | 18 | 18 | 18 | 18 | 18 | 18 | 18 | 16 | 12 | 11 | 22 | 22 | 22 | 22 | 22 | 2 | | | | | | | | | | | | |
| 22 SATO | 22 | 18 | 18 | 18 | 18 | 18 | 18 | 18 | 20 | 20 | 20 | 20 | 20 | 20 | 20 | 20 | 20 | 20 | 19 | 11 | 18 | 18 | 18 | 18 | 18 | 18 | 18 | 18 | 1 | | | | | | | | | | | | |
| 11 SCHUMACHER | 11 | 20 | 20 | 20 | 20 | 20 | 20 | 20 | 22 | 22 | 22 | 22 | 22 | 22 | 22 | 22 | 22 | 22 | 12 | 19 | 19 | 19 | 19 | 19 | 19 | 19 | 19 | 19 | 1 | | | | | | | | | | | | |
| 18 LIUZZI | 18 | 21 | 21 | 21 | 21 | 21 | 21 | 21 | 21 | 21 | 21 | 22 | 22 | 22 | 22 | 21 | 21 | 20 | 20 | 20 | 20 | 20 | 20 | 20 | 20 | 20 | 20 | 20 | 2 | | | | | | | | | | | | |
| 14 COULTHARD | 20 | 22 | 22 | 22 | 22 | 22 | 22 | 19 | 19 | 19 | 19 | 19 | 19 | 19 | 19 | 21 | 21 | 21 | 21 | 21 | 21 | 21 | 21 | 21 | 21 | 21 | 21 | 21 | 2 | | | | | | | | | | | | |
| 20 SUTIL | 21 | 19 | 19 | 19 | 19 | 19 | 19 | 19 | 5 | | | | | | | | | | | | | | | | | | | | | | | | | | | | | | | | |
| 21 YAMAMOTO | 19 | | | | | | | | | | | | | | | | | | | | | | | | | | | | | | | | | | | | | | | | |

**3**  Safety car deployed on laps show

226

### PRACTICE 1 (FRIDAY)

Sunny (track 25–29°C, air 18–22°C)

| Pos. | Driver | Laps | Time |
|------|--------|------|------|
| 1 | Kimi Räikkönen | 20 | 1m 22.446s |
| 2 | Felipe Massa | 17 | 1m 22.590s |
| 3 | Lewis Hamilton | 18 | 1m 22.618s |
| 4 | Fernando Alonso | 12 | 1m 22.840s |
| 5 | Nico Rosberg | 21 | 1m 23.472s |
| 6 | Jenson Button | 21 | 1m 23.668s |
| 7 | Giancarlo Fisichella | 22 | 1m 23.671s |
| 8 | Robert Kubica | 22 | 1m 23.703s |
| 9 | Nick Heidfeld | 17 | 1m 23.886s |
| 10 | Jarno Trulli | 29 | 1m 23.965s |
| 11 | Heikki Kovalainen | 21 | 1m 24.076s |
| 12 | Rubens Barrichello | 19 | 1m 24.564s |
| 13 | Takuma Sato | 15 | 1m 24.587s |
| 14 | Mark Webber | 22 | 1m 24.595s |
| 15 | Ralf Schumacher | 20 | 1m 24.660s |
| 16 | Alexander Wurz | 29 | 1m 24.689s |
| 17 | Anthony Davidson | 17 | 1m 24.694s |
| 18 | David Coulthard | 19 | 1m 24.810s |
| 19 | Adrian Sutil | 24 | 1m 25.130s |
| 20 | Sebastian Vettel | 25 | 1m 25.439s |
| 21 | Sakon Yamamoto | 25 | 1m 25.448s |
| 22 | Vitantonio Liuzzi | 25 | 1m 25.762s |

### PRACTICE 2 (FRIDAY)

Sunny (track 36–38°C, air 26–27°C)

| Pos. | Driver | Laps | Time |
|------|--------|------|------|
| 1 | Fernando Alonso | 30 | 1m 22.386s |
| 2 | Lewis Hamilton | 33 | 1m 23.209s |
| 3 | Giancarlo Fisichella | 38 | 1m 23.584s |
| 4 | Robert Kubica | 44 | 1m 23.599s |
| 5 | Nico Rosberg | 33 | 1m 23.679s |
| 6 | Felipe Massa | 27 | 1m 23.722s |
| 7 | Nick Heidfeld | 38 | 1m 23.821s |
| 8 | Kimi Räikkönen | 12 | 1m 23.833s |
| 9 | Heikki Kovalainen | 32 | 1m 23.848s |
| 10 | Alexander Wurz | 32 | 1m 23.881s |
| 11 | Jarno Trulli | 39 | 1m 23.919s |
| 12 | Ralf Schumacher | 29 | 1m 23.922s |
| 13 | Jenson Button | 36 | 1m 24.137s |
| 14 | Mark Webber | 31 | 1m 24.328s |
| 15 | Rubens Barrichello | 40 | 1m 24.462s |
| 16 | David Coulthard | 31 | 1m 24.605s |
| 17 | Takuma Sato | 27 | 1m 25.328s |
| 18 | Sebastian Vettel | 36 | 1m 25.459s |
| 19 | Adrian Sutil | 24 | 1m 25.531s |
| 20 | Vitantonio Liuzzi | 26 | 1m 25.567s |
| 21 | Sakon Yamamoto | 40 | 1m 25.863s |
| 22 | Anthony Davidson | 6 | 1m 26.021s |

### QUALIFYING (SATURDAY)

Sunny (track 36–37°C, air 25–26°C)

| Pos. | Driver | First | Second | Third |
|------|--------|-------|--------|-------|
| 1 | Fernando Alonso | 1m 21.718s | 1m 21.356s | 1m 21.997s |
| 2 | Lewis Hamilton | 1m 21.956s | 1m 21.746s | 1m 22.034 |
| 3 | Felipe Massa | 1m 22.309s | 1m 21.993s | 1m 22.549 |
| 4 | Nick Heidfeld | 1m 23.107s | 1m 22.466s | 1m 23.174 |
| 5 | Kimi Räikkönen | 1m 22.673s | 1m 22.369s | 1m 23.183 |
| 6 | Robert Kubica | 1m 23.088s | 1m 22.400s | 1m 23.446 |
| 7 | Heikki Kovalainen | 1m 23.505s | 1m 23.134s | 1m 24.102 |
| 8 | Nico Rosberg | 1m 23.333s | 1m 22.748s | 1m 24.382 |
| 9 | Jarno Trulli | 1m 23.724s | 1m 23.107s | 1m 24.555 |
| 10 | Jenson Button | 1m 23.639s | 1m 23.021s | 1m 25.165 |
| 11 | Mark Webber | 1m 23.575s | 1m 23.166s | |
| 12 | Rubens Barrichello | 1m 23.474s | 1m 23.176s | |
| 13 | Alexander Wurz | 1m 23.739s | 1m 23.209s | |
| 14 | Anthony Davidson | 1m 23.646s | 1m 23.274s | |
| 15 | Giancarlo Fisichella | 1m 23.559s | 1m 23.325s | |
| 16 | Sebastian Vettel | 1m 23.578s | 1m 23.351s | |
| 17 | Takuma Sato | 1m 23.749s | | |
| 18 | Ralf Schumacher | 1m 23.787s | | |
| 19 | Vitantonio Liuzzi | 1m 23.886s | | |
| 20 | David Coulthard | 1m 24.019s | | |
| 21 | Adrian Sutil | 1m 24.699s | | |
| 22 | Sakon Yamamoto | 1m 25.084s | | |

### PRACTICE 3 (SATURDAY)

Sunny (track 29–32°C, air 22–23°C)

| Pos. | Driver | Laps | Time |
|------|--------|------|------|
| 1 | Fernando Alonso | 10 | 1m 22.054s |
| 2 | Lewis Hamilton | 11 | 1m 22.200s |
| 3 | Felipe Massa | 11 | 1m 22.615s |
| 4 | Nick Heidfeld | 15 | 1m 22.855s |
| 5 | Robert Kubica | 14 | 1m 23.287s |
| 6 | Nico Rosberg | 13 | 1m 23.454s |
| 7 | Alexander Wurz | 15 | 1m 23.596s |
| 8 | Jarno Trulli | 16 | 1m 23.672s |
| 9 | Heikki Kovalainen | 12 | 1m 23.672s |
| 10 | Mark Webber | 13 | 1m 23.708s |
| 11 | Jenson Button | 15 | 1m 23.803s |
| 12 | Rubens Barrichello | 14 | 1m 23.830s |
| 13 | Sebastian Vettel | 14 | 1m 23.853s |
| 14 | Giancarlo Fisichella | 12 | 1m 23.877s |
| 15 | Anthony Davidson | 12 | 1m 23.942s |
| 16 | Takuma Sato | 16 | 1m 24.022s |
| 17 | David Coulthard | 12 | 1m 24.055s |
| 18 | Ralf Schumacher | 13 | 1m 24.167s |
| 19 | Vitantonio Liuzzi | 15 | 1m 24.208s |
| 20 | Kimi Räikkönen | 3 | 1m 24.442s |
| 21 | Sakon Yamamoto | 17 | 1m 24.736s |
| 22 | Adrian Sutil | 18 | 1m 24.943s |

## RACE TYRE STRATEGIES

**BRIDGESTONE**

In 2007, the tyre regulations stipulate that the two dry-tyre specifications must be visibly distinguishable from each other. At the Italian Grand Prix, the soft compound Bridgestone Potenza tyre was marked with a white line in the second-from-inside groove.

| | Driver | Race stint 1 | Race stint 2 | Race stint 3 |
|---|--------|-------------|-------------|-------------|
| 1 | Fernando Alonso | Medium: laps 1–20 | Medium: 21–43 | Soft: 44–53 |
| 2 | Lewis Hamilton | Medium: 1–18 | Medium: 19–40 | Soft: 41–53 |
| 3 | Kimi Räikkönen | Soft: 1–25 | Medium: 26–53 | |
| 4 | Nick Heidfeld | Medium: 1–18 | Medium: 19–40 | Soft: 41–53 |
| 5 | Robert Kubica | Medium: 1–23 | Medium: 24–43 | Soft: 44–53 |
| 6 | Nico Rosberg | Medium: 1–30 | Soft: 31–53 | |
| 7 | Heikki Kovalainen | Medium: 1–21 | Medium: 22–41 | Soft: 42–53 |
| 8 | Jenson Button | Medium: 1–33 | Soft: 34–53 | |
| 9 | Mark Webber | Medium: 1–34 | Soft: 35–53 | |
| 10 | Rubens Barrichello | Medium: 1–34 | Soft: 35–53 | |
| 11 | Jarno Trulli | Medium: 1–31 | Soft: 32–53 | |
| 12 | Giancarlo Fisichella | Medium: 1–33 | Soft: 34–52 | |
| 13 | Alexander Wurz | Medium: 1–37 | Soft: 38–52 | |
| 14 | Anthony Davidson | Medium: 1–35 | Soft: 36–52 | |
| 15 | Ralf Schumacher | Medium: 1–31 | Soft: 32–52 | |
| 16 | Takuma Sato | Medium: 1–34 | Soft: 35–52 | |
| 17 | Vitantonio Liuzzi | Medium: 1–32 | Soft: 33–52 | |
| 18 | Sebastian Vettel | Medium: 1 | Medium: 2–31 | Soft: 32–52 |
| 19 | Adrian Sutil | Soft: 1–21 | Medium: 22–37 | Soft: 38–52 |
| 20 | Sakon Yamamoto | Soft: 1–20 | Soft: 21–35 | Medium: 36–52 |
| | Felipe Massa | Medium: 1–9 | Medium: 10 (DNF) | |
| | David Coulthard | Soft: 1 (DNF) | | |

**9** TRULLI Toyota

**7** KOVALAINEN Renault

**5** RÄIKKÖNEN Ferrari

**3** MASSA Ferrari

**1** ALONSO McLaren

**10** BUTTON Honda

**8** ROSBERG Williams

**6** KUBICA BMW-Sauber

**4** HEIDFELD BMW-Sauber

**2** HAMILTON McLaren

**RACE DISTANCE:**
58 laps, 192.250 miles/309.396 km

**RACE WEATHER:**
Sunny, 47–49°C, air 34–35°C

| 42 | 43 | 44 | 45 | 46 | 47 | 48 | 49 | 50 | 51 | 52 | 53 | ● | |
|----|----|----|----|----|----|----|----|----|----|----|----|----|----|
| 1 | 1 | 1 | 1 | 1 | 1 | 1 | 1 | 1 | 1 | 1 | 1 | 1 | 1 |
| 6 | 2 | 2 | 2 | 2 | 2 | 2 | 2 | 2 | 2 | 2 | 2 | 2 | 2 |
| 2 | 6 | 6 | 6 | 6 | 6 | 6 | 6 | 6 | 6 | 6 | 6 | 3 | 3 |
| 10 | 10 | 9 | 9 | 9 | 9 | 9 | 9 | 9 | 9 | 9 | 9 | 9 | 4 |
| 9 | 9 | 16 | 16 | 10 | 10 | 10 | 10 | 10 | 10 | 10 | 10 | 5 | 5 |
| 16 | 16 | 10 | 10 | 16 | 16 | 16 | 16 | 16 | 16 | 16 | 16 | 6 | 6 |
| 4 | 4 | 4 | 4 | 4 | 4 | 4 | 4 | 4 | 4 | 4 | 4 | 7 | 7 |
| 7 | 7 | 7 | 7 | 7 | 7 | 7 | 7 | 7 | 7 | 7 | 7 | 8 | 8 |
| 15 | 15 | 15 | 15 | 15 | 15 | 15 | 15 | 15 | 15 | 15 | 15 | | |
| 8 | 8 | 8 | 8 | 8 | 8 | 8 | 8 | 8 | 8 | 8 | 8 | | |
| 12 | 12 | 12 | 12 | 12 | 12 | 12 | 12 | 12 | 12 | 12 | 12 | | |
| 3 | 3 | 3 | 3 | 3 | 3 | 3 | 3 | 3 | 3 | 3 | | | |
| 17 | 17 | 17 | 17 | 17 | 17 | 17 | 17 | 17 | 17 | 17 | | | |
| 23 | 23 | 23 | 23 | 23 | 23 | 23 | 23 | 23 | 23 | 23 | | | |
| 11 | 11 | 11 | 11 | 11 | 11 | 11 | 11 | 11 | 11 | 11 | | | |
| 22 | 22 | 22 | 22 | 22 | 22 | 22 | 22 | 22 | 22 | 22 | | | |
| 18 | 18 | 18 | 18 | 18 | 18 | 18 | 18 | 18 | 18 | 18 | | | |
| 19 | 19 | 19 | 19 | 19 | 19 | 19 | 19 | 19 | 19 | 19 | | | |
| 20 | 20 | 20 | 20 | 20 | 20 | 20 | 20 | 20 | 20 | 20 | | | |
| 21 | 21 | 21 | 21 | 21 | 21 | 21 | 21 | 21 | 21 | 21 | | | |

**20** Pit stop  **20** One lap or more behind leader

## FOR THE RECORD

GRAN PREMIO D'ITALIA

**100th GRAND PRIX START:**
Fernando Alonso

**100th GRAND PRIX:** Toyota

## POINTS

### CONSTRUCTORS

| | | |
|---|---|---|
| 1 | McLaren | 166 |
| 2 | Ferrari | 143 |
| 3 | BMW Sauber | 86 |
| 4 | Renault | 38 |
| 5 | Williams | 25 |
| 6 | Red Bull | 16 |
| 7 | Toyota | 12 |
| 8 | Super Aguri | 4 |
| 9 | Honda | 2 |

### DRIVERS

| | | |
|---|---|---|
| 1 | Lewis Hamilton | 92 |
| 2 | Fernando Alonso | 89 |
| 3 | Kimi Räikkönen | 74 |
| 4 | Felipe Massa | 69 |
| 5 | Nick Heidfeld | 52 |
| 6 | Robert Kubica | 33 |
| 7 | Heikki Kovalainen | 21 |
| 8 | Giancarlo Fisichella | 17 |
| 9 | Alexander Wurz | 13 |
| 10 | Nico Rosberg | 12 |
| 11 | Mark Webber | 8 |
| 12 | David Coulthard | 8 |
| 13 | Jarno Trulli | 7 |
| 14 | Ralf Schumacher | 5 |
| 15 | Takuma Sato | 4 |
| 16 | Jenson Button | 2 |
| 17 | Sebastian Vettel | 1 |

Photographs: Peter J Fox/www.crash.net

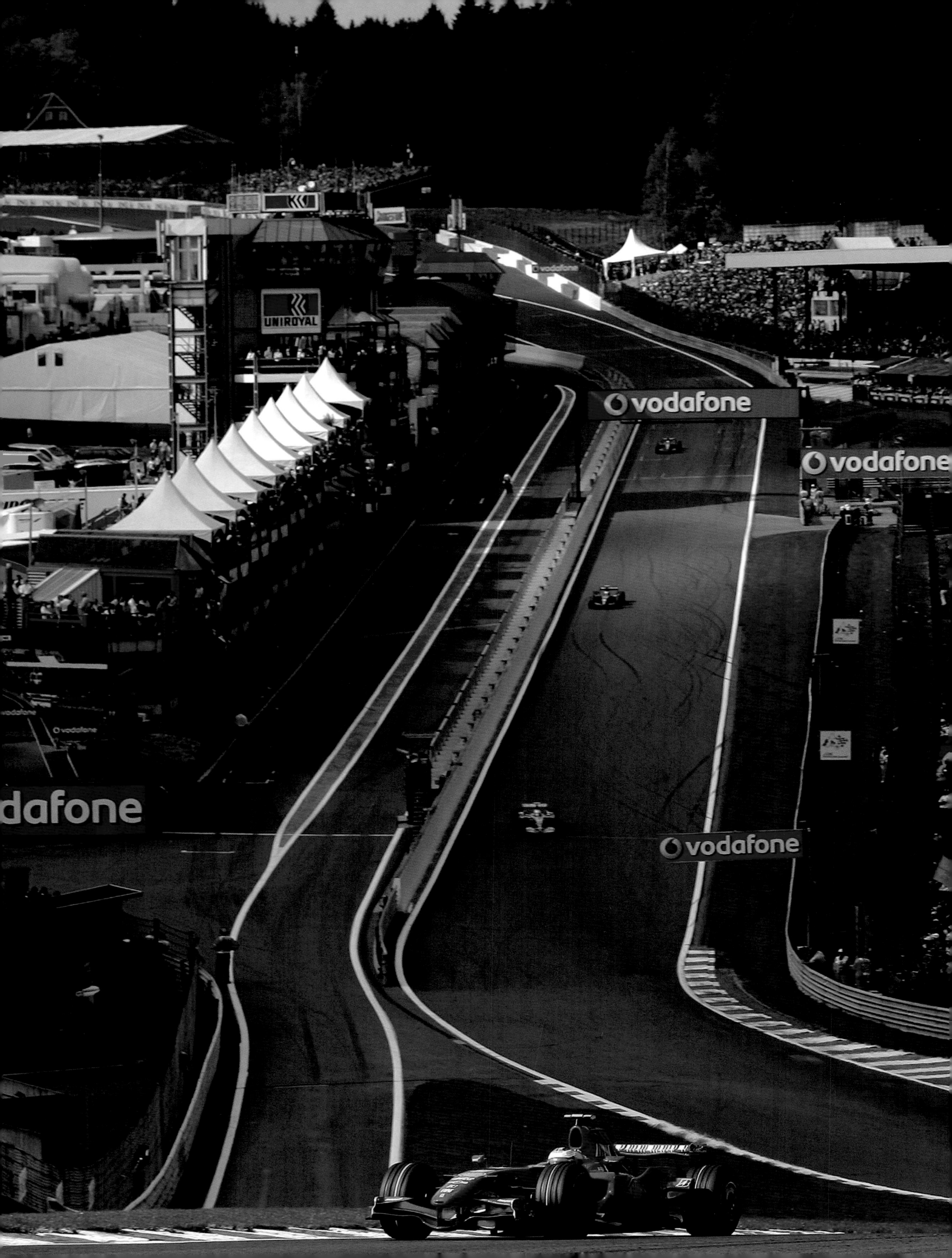
UNIROYAL
vodafone
vodafone
dafone
vodafone

**Kimi Räikkönen marked F1's return to the
splendid Spa-Francorchamps circuit after a year's
absence by scoring his third straight Belgian GP
victory, his first at the wheel of a Ferrari.**
Photograph: Peter J Fox/www.crash.net

## SPA-FRANCORCHAMPS QUALIFYING

The sweeps and turns of Spa-Francorchamps suited Ferrari perfectly and the result was the Scuderia's first all-red front row of the season. The team's season-long difficulty with generating sufficient heat in the Bridgestone tyres over a single lap was less of a problem here thanks to the length of the lap and thus pole sitter Kimi Räikkönen and Felipe Massa went into the race satisfied that they had got everything out of their F2007s when it really mattered and brimful of confidence.

Räikkönen's lap of 1m 45.994s, set like all of the others on Bridgestone's soft 'option' tyre, was just sufficient to beat Massa's 1m 46.011s. Massa said the difference was because he locked his brakes in the final chicane.

McLaren was relegated to the second row of the grid. Fernando Alonso didn't help things by spinning at Rivage on his penultimate run but he recovered very quickly and was able to make the final run, which was fast enough to oust Lewis Hamilton from third place. He lapped in 1m 46.091s, compared with Hamilton's 1m 46.406s.

This was, of course, an extremely tough weekend for McLaren after the FIA World Motor Sport Council had cancelled all its points in the world championship for constructors and fined it a swingeing $100 million on Thursday – what with that and the revelation that in Hungary Fernando Alonso had attempted to blackmail team boss Ron Dennis into favouring him over Hamilton for the rest of the season, it was hardly surprising that the air in the camp was very strained. But despite the speed of the Ferraris, which had been expected, McLaren felt it had the pace and strategy to compete for victory.

BMW Sauber should have taken fifth place on the grid courtesy of a lap in 1m 46.996s by Robert Kubica but an engine change after a failure in the morning's final practice session dropped him ten grid places. That promoted Nico Rosberg, who was again on strong form for Williams. He was clearly on a relatively light fuel load but his 1m 47.334s was nevertheless a good effort. He said he was surprised to be so quick; having struggled the previous day, the team had come up with good solutions. Kubica's partner Nick Heidfeld, meanwhile, was obviously running heavy, given the speed the BMW-Sauber had shown here in the July test, and was seventh-fastest – sixth on the grid – on 1m 47.409s.

Rosberg's team-mate Alex Wurz struggled as usual and complained of poor straight-line speed on his way to a lap of 1m 47.394s in Q2, which left him 16th.

There was a degree of satisfaction *chez* Red Bull with Mark Webber's eighth place after minor changes to the car had beneficial effects, though Webber as usual did not seem particularly pleased with the result and said he would have liked to get more out of the RB3 than a lap of 1m 47.524s. David Coulthard, 13th on a 1m 46.800s from Q2 in the second RB3, would have been happy with that. As it was, an off-line moment when pushing hard cost him his shot at getting through to Q3.

Yet again Jarno Trulli put a Toyota in the top ten – ninth on 1m 47.798s – and he was quite happy with that as a frustrated Ralf Schumacher missed out again and took 12th with a lap of 1m 46.618s. Once again, there was an interesting representation of marques in the top ten, with Ferrari, McLaren, BMW Sauber, Williams, Red Bull, Toyota and Renault all up there.

Heikki Kovalainen was satisfied with the final top-ten slot after lapping his Renault in 1m 48.505s but Giancarlo Fisichella struggled with his R27 in both morning and afternoon sessions and confessed that he just didn't feel comfortable because it was sliding around a lot. Unable to carry speed through the corners, he lapped in 1m 46.603s in Q2 for 11th.

Honda felt confident of a good grid position at one stage in the weekend, but its best turned out to be Jenson Button's 14th with a lap of 1m 46.955s from Q2. The RA107 was just not suited to Spa aerodynamically and the resultant understeer hampered both cars. Rubens Barrichello was very unhappy with 18th on 1m 47.954s, set in Q1.

Tonio Liuzzi's performance in getting through to Q2 and outqualifying Wurz with a lap of 1m 47.115s was a sound effort, especially because he was feeling very unwell due to sickness. He just made it through to Q2 at team-mate Sebastian Vettel's expense, who lapped his STR02 in 1m 47.581s to beat Barrichello for 17th.

The Super Aguris and Spykers were quite evenly matched. Takuma Sato won their battle with 19th place in 1m 47.908s, followed by Spyker's Adrian Sutil on 1m 48.044s. Anthony Davidson did 1m 48.199s and Sakon Yamamoto 1m 49.577s. Sato was happier with his SA07's set-up after a night of engineering head-scratching but Davidson suffered graining rear tyres and was still unhappy. Yamamoto lost time with a brake problem in the morning, then had to bed new pads in with the medium tyres when Q1 began. He then lost time in a mandatory weight check and managed only one run on the softer rubber.

**Above:** The gleaming red Ferraris of Kimi Räikkönen and Felipe Massa head the pack around La Source hairpin.

**Above left:** No matter how disappointing the season may become, Jarno Trulli can never suppress a smile for long.
Photographs: Peter Nygaard/GP Photo

**Left:** Proud fathers. Anthony Hamilton looks as though he's heard it all before from John Button.
Photograph: Peter J Fox/www.crash.net

**Right:** FIA communications chief Richard Woods with the governing body's president Max Mosley and McLaren's Ron Dennis on the steps of the Vodafone McLaren Mercedes brand centre.
Photograph: Jad Sherif/WRi2

## McLAREN RECEIVES HEFTY PUNISHMENT

McLaren's worst fears were realised at the reconvened hearing of the FIA's World Motor Sport Council in Paris on the Thursday before practice for the Belgian Grand Prix began. The WMSC cancelled all of the team's points in the world championship for constructors and fined it $100 million, the biggest penalty in motor sport history by a factor of 20.

The new evidence that had persuaded the FIA to reconvene the WMSC meeting of 26 July (rather than hear an appeal against that hearing's findings on behalf of Ferrari) was a series of emails and SMS messages between disgraced McLaren chief designer Mike Coughlan — who received stolen intellectual property from former Ferrari head of performance Nigel Stepney — and McLaren drivers Fernando Alonso and Pedro de la Rosa.

It transpired that the new evidence had emanated from McLaren chief Ron Dennis himself after Fernando Alonso attempted to intimidate him on the morning of the Hungarian GP to gain favourable treatment for the remainder of the season in return for not bringing his knowledge to the FIA. Disgusted, Dennis told the FIA himself.

The information that Coughlan imparted to De la Rosa, who in turn passed it on to Alonso, comprised details of the Ferrari's weight distribution, braking system, tyre inflation gas, flexible rear wing and pit stop strategy in Australia. The new evidence suggested that at least 288 SMS messages and 35 telephone calls passed between Coughlan and Stepney between 11 March 2007 and 3 July 2007.

The evidence was purely circumstantial but, though it could not prove that such information had actually been used to improve the McLaren, the WMSC took the view that De la Rosa's evidence indicated that there was no reluctance or hesitation about testing the Ferrari information for potential benefit.

The WMSC agreed there was no evidence that the information had been disseminated to others at McLaren and that Coughlan was a single rogue employee. However, it said it was not necessary to demonstrate that any confidential Ferrari information was directly copied by McLaren or put to direct use in the McLaren car to justify a finding that article 151(c) of the international sporting code was breached or that a penalty was merited.

FERRARI ran away and hid from McLaren in the Belgian Grand Prix as Kimi Räikkönen scored his fourth win of the season ahead of Felipe Massa. As the reds ran riot, the Silver Arrows were left to reflect on a bruising and costly weekend of fines and disqualification compounded by an on-track spat between third- and fourth-placed finishers Fernando Alonso and Lewis Hamilton.

The two Ferraris had simply taken off from their front-row positions, leaving Alonso, on the inside, and Hamilton ducking into La Source hairpin side by side. Somehow they avoided making contact, but it was close. Then on the exit as they ran down the hill towards Eau Rouge Alonso pushed his team-mate wide onto the run-off area as they battled for third place. It was quite deliberate and afterwards Hamilton did not hold back.

'For the past few years I've been watching Formula 1 and Fernando is always complaining about other people being unfair,' he said. 'But he pushed me wide quite deliberately. For someone who looks up to someone who is trying to set a standard and be someone for a youngster to look up to, I think he's not really standing up to his position.

'I outbraked him into Turn One, I was on the outside, there was enough room for him to get around. But he really cut across and pushed me wide. It was quite deliberate. I could see it. If I had held my position we would have collided. In fact, I think we did touch.'

A little later, when he had been got at by McLaren's PR staff, he toned that down. 'It was a racing incident, I guess, but I didn't feel it was fair. I felt there was room for all of us but somehow I ran out of it.'

Hamilton lost a bit of traction on the dirt but was still alongside Alonso as he regained the track and they sped towards Eau Rouge, still one of the most majestic and challenging corners in F1. There, he was finally obliged to concede the place and run behind Alonso, apart from during the various pit stops, to the finish.

'The first incident was the difficult one,' he said. 'I'd hoped to come back on and get in the slipstream of one of the Ferraris. But at Eau Rouge it was just common sense to ease off a fraction. Fernando had the momentum and was quicker going into it. It would have been stupid of me to keep it flat, but I was tempted. That worked in Formula 3 in the wet, but I'm not sure it would in a Formula 1 car...'

Team principal Ron Dennis is no stranger to having his drivers – 'competitive animals', as he had described racers earlier in the weekend – battle it out. 'We give them the opportunity to race themselves,' he said. 'I was not concerned. They were racing. If it were two different cars, you wouldn't think twice about it. It was absolutely no problem.'

Alonso thus kept his third place, but the very desperation of his manoeuvre was an indication of his mindset during a tough weekend.

Up the road, Räikkönen stayed in front all the way through apart from during his pit stops. By the end of the race Massa was coming at him like a runaway train, but it was window dressing and it was clear that there would never be a serious challenge. Such racing among team-mates is not the way of F1 these days. Nobody was ever going to throw away a one-two finish, especially because Räikkönen's new score of 84 points brought him within 13 of Hamilton and 11 of Alonso in the title fight. The drivers' title was far from decided, even if the FIA World Motor Sport Council's ruling on Thursday had made sure that Ferrari had done enough to win a hollow constructors' crown.

'That was a great day!' said a delighted Räikkönen, who was able to forget all about the neck strain he suffered in his shunt at Monza. 'I had some doubts about the handling after yesterday's qualifying but everything went well. The car worked very well for the whole race: I was quick enough in the first part to control things after that. It is nice to win here on my favourite track for the third time in a row. Now we must continue to push. We are still a long way off in the championship but we are not giving up and we will keep going right to the very end.'

Massa had his head down and set the fastest lap in his pursuit as he closed to within 1.4s on the penultimate lap,

before easing back. He'd made his point. 'It was a good race,' he said. 'I just had a bit of oversteer in the first stint but at the stop we made a change to the front wing. The soft tyres worked very well and it might have been better to use them even for the first stint, but you can only see things like that after the race. I am very happy for the team because we really wanted this one-two! Now, the situation in the championship is a bit better and we will continue to fight to the end, believe it!'

Alonso was philosophical on a day when McLaren could offer no significant challenge to Ferrari. But his version of the Hamilton incident was interesting, to say the least – especially because he claimed he'd had to avoid Massa's Ferrari, which was already well clear of his own car. 'Unfortunately Lewis ran wide,' he said. 'There was no space left and I knew there was plenty of run-off area.'

Regarding his third place, he continued, 'Unfortunately Ferrari was just too quick for us today. I tried quite hard to keep pace with Felipe in the first stint, hoping that I could make up a position in the pit stops, but they were slowly moving ahead. After the first stop it was impossible to catch them.'

Hamilton's candour extended to his own performance. 'The car wasn't perfect,' he said, rueing his decision to go a different route from Alonso on set-up, 'but neither was I. I did the best job I could but I need to improve. What I always find when I'm behind Fernando is that he's very fortunate when he catches a backmarker. He catches them at the right time and just slipstreams past on the straight, whereas I catch them mid-field.

'To be honest, my race was frustrating and quite boring. It was just one of those races you need to bring it home and finish.'

His lead in the championship went down another point, now 97 to Alonso's 95, as slowly the tide seemed to be turning in Alonso's favour.

**Above:** Jenson Button locks up a wheel as he guides his Honda into La Source hairpin ahead of Robert Kubica's BMW-Sauber. Button put in his usual dogged performance in an ill-handling car before retirement.
Photograph: Frits van Eldik/WRi2

**Top left:** To celebrate their attendance at more than 500 grands prix, F1 rights holder Bernie Ecclestone (second from right) presents medals to veteran journalists Alan Henry (left), Frederick af Petersons, Renaud De la Borderie and Enrico Cardao.
Photograph: Jean-Francois Galeron WRi2

**Centre:** Rubens Barrichello's season of misery continued and he was still yet to register a single point.
Photograph: Peter J Fox/www.crash.net

**Left:** Lewis Hamilton finds himself unceremoniously edged off the track by team-mate Fernando Alonso at the start.
Photograph: Paul-Henri Cahier

Once again, Nick Heidfeld drove strongly for BMW Sauber on his way to fifth place, but it was a big fight after he lost ground, having run wide at La Source at the start avoiding the duelling McLarens. He lost places to Nico Rosberg, Heikki Kovalainen and Mark Webber and had to battle back up to fifth.

'This time my start wasn't good at all,' he admitted. 'In the first corner I tried to make up for it, but it didn't work out. I was braking too late and in the end lost out and was on the outside of the pack. I knew I had to overtake Heikki because he was on a one-stop strategy. It wasn't easy, but it was possible. When Nico and Mark refuelled a lot earlier than me it was clear that I could finish ahead of them. Also my lap times were good when I had nobody in front of me and drove in clean air. Towards the end I was under no pressure, so I reduced the engine's revs.'

Rosberg's Williams lacked the pace to challenge Heidfeld's BMW and he pitted early, as expected, but he had the grunt to keep out of the clutches of Webber's Red Bull. That was important because Williams was again the fourth-best team. Sadly the second car continued to be under-utilised as Alex Wurz spun down to the tail of the field, later lost a place to Sakon Yamamoto after another mistake and retired with fading fuel pressure.

Webber was pleased with the two points he garnered for seventh and thanked team-mate David Coulthard for keeping Robert Kubica at bay behind him for many laps, helping to preserve his chance of points. But it was an unhappy day for Coulthard, who was deeply affected by the death of his friend and rally world champion Colin McRae and his son and friends in a helicopter accident. David's RB3 stopped with a hydraulic problem that affected the power steering and throttle.

In an otherwise remarkably dull race Kovalainen and Kubica fought tooth and nail for the final point. Kovalainen had his Renault set up for low downforce and drag and that proved crucial on Spa's long straights because the BMW simply could not exploit its superior cornering speed when it mattered.

As Kovalainen once again starred, his Renault team-mate Giancarlo Fisichella had a lousy race. He needed an engine change after qualifying and thus started from the back of the grid instead of his rightful 11th place and elected to start from the pits with a lower-downforce set-up to try and enhance his chance of making up places. On the first lap, however, he locked up his cold brakes on the entry to Les Combes, ran off the road and broke the front-left pushrod. Game over.

Kovalainen, one of F1's new breed of characters, was delighted with his performance. 'It felt like I drove half of the race with my mirrors,' he said. 'And when I had a clear track, the car was too heavy to be able to do the lap times we needed to make our strategy work. To be honest, with a different strategy, I think we could have achieved a better result today because the car was definitely more competitive than it looked.'

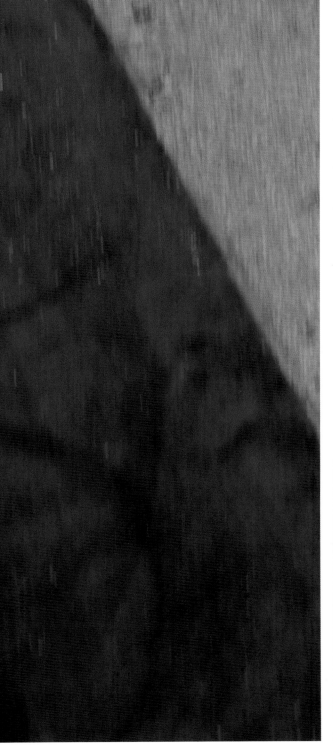

the B-spec Spyker. He and team-mate Sakon Yamamoto were the only two drivers to start on the soft Bridgestone rubber and Sutil was flying as he challenged and passed several names and was running a strong 12th before his pit stop. The team was delighted with 14th, though Yamamoto was hampered by understeer initially and lost time. A switch to harder rubber and a front-wing adjustment helped but he still finished only 17th.

Super Aguri, like Honda, expected a tough race. Takuma Sato battled with Button on his way to 15th and Anthony Davidson started from the pit lane after experiencing a front-end problem on the grid out-lap. He was half a minute behind his team-mate by the finish.

The Belgian GP was arguably one of the dullest of the season, but Ferrari's renaissance put Räikkönen and Massa back into contention for the drivers' title and they smelled blood in the water. Hamilton, however, wasn't ready to give up despite a disappointing result.

'I don't believe the last three races are going to be like this one,' he said. 'Anything can happen. But I need to improve. I will go away this week and figure out how to do that. I don't fear anyone – I hope you can see that. I've just got to keep on pushing. For sure it is not going as well as we planned and the gap is closing but there are still three races left and they are still three races we can win.'

*David Tremayne*

DIARY

**Motor sport mourns the death of former rally champion Colin McRae, who is killed with his five-year-old son Johnny and two friends in a helicopter accident near his home in Jerviswood, Scotland.**

**Coincidentally, on the same evening David Richards and his wife Karen escape unharmed when their helicopter crashes near Stansted Airport as they travel home from the Belgian GP**

**Shortly after the Belgian Grand Prix, McLaren chief Ron Dennis indicates that, in a desire for closure, the team will not contest the $100-million fine levied by the World Motor Sport Council.**

**Spyker team principal Colin Kolles says at Spa that the team is continuing with its arbitration case against Toro Rosso and Super Aguri over the use of customer chassis.**

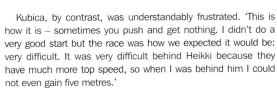

Kubica, by contrast, was understandably frustrated. 'This is how it is – sometimes you push and get nothing. I didn't do a very good start but the race was how we expected it would be: very difficult. It was very difficult behind Heikki because they have much more top speed, so when I was behind him I could not even gain five metres.'

Toyota's race was miserable, with Jarno Trulli immediately falling from eighth on the grid to 11th on the opening lap – and finishing there. Ralf Schumacher did only one place better.

Toro Rosso lost Sebastian Vettel early on when a steering problem afflicted his STR02 in right-hand corners, so he was finding it difficult to keep team-mate Tonio Liuzzi in sight. Liuzzi drove a great race, marred only by a small moment when his right-front wheel caused the team a few problems during his single pit stop. He finished 12th, on Honda's pace, which was as good a result as the team had any right to expect on such a quick circuit.

Honda expected to struggle at Spa with the unloved RA107's inherent aerodynamic shortcomings – and struggle it did. Button as usual drove the wheels off his car as it vacillated between understeer and oversteer all around the lap. Then the clutch started slipping, the power steering failed and he finally had to quit seven laps from the end with a hydraulic problem. Rubens Barrichello, meanwhile, crept home 13th, barely ahead of the hard-driving Adrian Sutil, who was on excellent form in

# ING
# BELGIAN GRAND PRIX
SPA-FRANCORCHAMPS 14–16 SEPTEMBER 2007

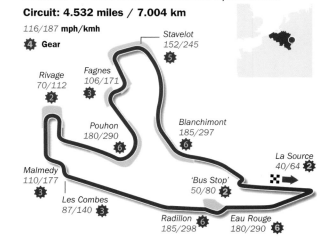

## CIRCUIT DE SPA FRANCORCHAMPS, BELGIUM

**Circuit: 4.532 miles / 7.004 km**

*116/187* mph/kmh

**4** Gear

Stavelot 152/245 **5**

Rivage 70/112 **2**

Fagnes 106/171 **3**

Pouhon 180/290 **6**

Blanchimont 185/297 **6**

La Source 40/64 **2**

Malmedy 110/177 **3**

'Bus Stop' 50/80 **2**

Les Combes 87/140 **3**

Radillon 185/298 **6**

Eau Rouge 180/290 **6**

Photograph: Peter J Fox/www.crash.net

All results and data © FOM 2007

## RACE RESULTS

| Pos. | Driver | Nat. | No. | Entrant | Car/Engine | Tyres | Laps | Time/Retirement | Speed (mph/km/h) | Gap to leader | Fastest race lap | |
|---|---|---|---|---|---|---|---|---|---|---|---|---|
| 1 | Kimi Räikkönen | FIN | 6 | Scuderia Ferrari Marlboro | Ferrari F2007-056 V8 | B | 44 | 1h 20m 39.066s | 142.402/229.174 | | 1m 48.095s | 12 |
| 2 | Felipe Massa | BR | 5 | Scuderia Ferrari Marlboro | Ferrari F2007-056 V8 | B | 44 | 1h 20m 43.761s | 142.264/228.952 | + 4.695s | 1m 48.036s | 34 |
| 3 | Fernando Alonso | E | 1 | Vodafone McLaren Mercedes | McLaren MP4-22-Mercedes FO 108T V8 | B | 44 | 1h 20m 53.409s | 141.981/228.497 | + 14.343s | 1m 48.182s | 44 |
| 4 | Lewis Hamilton | GB | 2 | Vodafone McLaren Mercedes | McLaren MP4-22-Mercedes FO 108T V8 | B | 44 | 1h 21m 2.681s | 141.711/228.061 | + 23.615s | 1m 48.215s | 41 |
| 5 | Nick Heidfeld | D | 9 | BMW Sauber F1 Team | BMW Sauber F1.07-BMW P86/7 V8 | B | 44 | 1h 21m 30.945s | 140.892/226.743 | + 51.879s | 1m 48.663s | 33 |
| 6 | Nico Rosberg | D | 16 | AT&T Williams | Williams FW29-Toyota RVX-07 V8 | B | 44 | 1h 21m 55.942s | 140.175/225.590 | + 1m 16.876s | 1m 49.769s | 29 |
| 7 | Mark Webber | AUS | 15 | Red Bull Racing | Red Bull RB3-Renault RS27 V8 | B | 44 | 1h 21m 59.705s | 140.068/225.418 | + 1m 20.639s | 1m 50.049s | 12 |
| 8 | Heikki Kovalainen | FIN | 4 | ING Renault F1 Team | Renault R27-RS27 V8 | B | 44 | 1h 22m 4.172s | 139.941/225.213 | + 1m 25.106s | 1m 49.600s | 21 |
| 9 | Robert Kubica | POL | 10 | BMW Sauber F1 Team | BMW Sauber F1.07-BMW P86/7 V8 | B | 44 | 1h 22m 4.727s | 139.925/225.188 | + 1m 25.661s | 1m 48.894s | 32 |
| 10 | Ralf Schumacher | D | 11 | Panasonic Toyota Racing | Toyota TF107-RVX-07 V8 | B | 44 | 1h 22m 7.640s | 139.843/225.055 | + 1m 28.574s | 1m 50.022s | 43 |
| 11 | Jarno Trulli | I | 12 | Panasonic Toyota Racing | Toyota TF107-RVX-07 V8 | B | 44 | 1h 22m 22.719s | 139.416/224.368 | + 1m 43.653s | 1m 48.990s | 43 |
| 12 | Vitantonio Liuzzi | I | 18 | Scuderia Toro Rosso | Toro Rosso STR02-Ferrari 056H V8 | B | 43 | | | + 1 lap | 1m 50.730s | 40 |
| 13 | Rubens Barrichello | BR | 8 | Honda Racing F1 Team | Honda RA107-RA807E V8 | B | 43 | | | + 1 lap | 1m 50.678s | 43 |
| 14 | Adrian Sutil | D | 20 | Etihad Aldar Spyker F1 Team | Spyker F8-VII-Ferrari 056H V8 | B | 43 | | | + 1 lap | 1m 50.902s | 29 |
| 15 | Takuma Sato | J | 22 | Super Aguri F1 Team | Super Aguri SA07-Honda RA807E V8 | B | 43 | | | + 1 lap | 1m 50.886s | 32 |
| 16 | Anthony Davidson | GB | 23 | Super Aguri F1 Team | Super Aguri SA07-Honda RA807E V8 | B | 43 | | | + 1 lap | 1m 51.391s | 43 |
| 17 | Sakon Yamamoto | J | 21 | Etihad Aldar Spyker F1 Team | Spyker F8-VII-Ferrari 056H V8 | B | 43 | | | + 1 lap | 1m 51.648s | 30 |
| | Jenson Button | GB | 7 | Honda Racing F1 Team | Honda RA107-RA807E V8 | B | 36 | Hydraulics | | | 1m 51.141s | 22 |
| | Alexander Wurz | A | 17 | AT&T Williams | Williams FW29-Toyota RVX-07 V8 | B | 34 | Fuel pressure | | | 1m 51.270s | 18 |
| | David Coulthard | GB | 14 | Red Bull Racing | Red Bull RB3-Renault RS27 V8 | B | 29 | Hydraulics | | | 1m 51.156s | 24 |
| | Sebastian Vettel | D | 19 | Scuderia Toro Rosso | Toro Rosso STR02-Ferrari 056H V8 | B | 8 | Steering | | | 1m 52.724s | 4 |
| | Giancarlo Fisichella | I | 3 | ING Renault F1 Team | Renault R27-RS27 V8 | B | 1 | Brakes/accident/front suspension | | | No time | – |

**Fastest race lap:** Felipe Massa on lap 34, 1m 48.036s, 145.021 mph/233.388 km/h.

**Lap record:** Kimi Räikkönen (McLaren MP4-19B-Mercedes V10), 1m 45.108s, 148.465 mph/238.931 km/h (2004) (4.335-mile/6.976-km circuit).

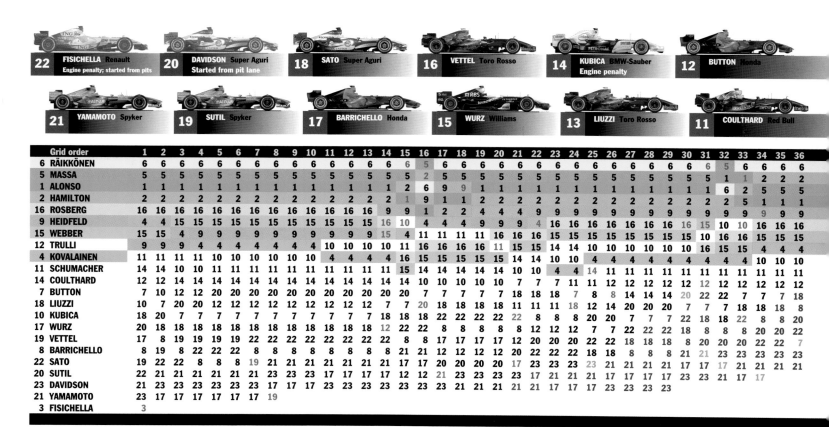

| 22 | FISICHELLA Renault | Engine penalty; started from pits |
| 20 | DAVIDSON Super Aguri | Started from pit lane |
| 18 | SATO Super Aguri | |
| 16 | VETTEL Toro Rosso | |
| 14 | KUBICA BMW-Sauber | Engine penalty |
| 12 | BUTTON Honda | |
| 21 | YAMAMOTO Spyker | |
| 19 | SUTIL Spyker | |
| 17 | BARRICHELLO Honda | |
| 15 | WURZ Williams | |
| 13 | LIUZZI Toro Rosso | |
| 11 | COULTHARD Red Bull | |

| Grid order | 1 | 2 | 3 | 4 | 5 | 6 | 7 | 8 | 9 | 10 | 11 | 12 | 13 | 14 | 15 | 16 | 17 | 18 | 19 | 20 | 21 | 22 | 23 | 24 | 25 | 26 | 27 | 28 | 29 | 30 | 31 | 32 | 33 | 34 | 35 | 36 |
|---|---|---|---|---|---|---|---|---|---|---|---|---|---|---|---|---|---|---|---|---|---|---|---|---|---|---|---|---|---|---|---|---|---|---|---|---|
| 6 RAÏKKÖNEN | 6 | 6 | 6 | 6 | 6 | 6 | 6 | 6 | 6 | 6 | 6 | 6 | 6 | 6 | 6 | 6 | 5 | 6 | 6 | 6 | 6 | 6 | 6 | 6 | 6 | 6 | 6 | 6 | 6 | 6 | 6 | 6 | 5 | 6 | 6 | 6 |
| 5 MASSA | 5 | 5 | 5 | 5 | 5 | 5 | 5 | 5 | 5 | 5 | 5 | 5 | 5 | 5 | 5 | 5 | 6 | 5 | 5 | 5 | 5 | 5 | 5 | 5 | 5 | 5 | 5 | 5 | 5 | 5 | 5 | 1 | 1 | 2 | 2 | 2 |
| 1 ALONSO | 1 | 1 | 1 | 1 | 1 | 1 | 1 | 1 | 1 | 1 | 1 | 1 | 1 | 1 | 2 | 6 | 9 | 9 | 1 | 1 | 1 | 1 | 1 | 1 | 1 | 1 | 1 | 1 | 1 | 1 | 1 | 6 | 2 | 5 | 5 | 5 |
| 2 HAMILTON | 2 | 2 | 2 | 2 | 2 | 2 | 2 | 2 | 2 | 2 | 2 | 2 | 2 | 2 | 1 | 9 | 1 | 1 | 2 | 2 | 2 | 2 | 2 | 2 | 2 | 2 | 2 | 2 | 2 | 2 | 2 | 5 | 1 | 1 | 1 | 1 |
| 16 ROSBERG | 16 | 16 | 16 | 16 | 16 | 16 | 16 | 16 | 16 | 16 | 16 | 16 | 16 | 9 | 9 | 1 | 2 | 4 | 4 | 4 | 9 | 9 | 9 | 9 | 9 | 9 | 9 | 9 | 9 | 9 | 9 | 9 | 9 | 9 | 9 | 9 |
| 9 HEIDFELD | 4 | 4 | 15 | 15 | 15 | 15 | 15 | 15 | 15 | 15 | 15 | 15 | 15 | 16 | 10 | 4 | 4 | 4 | 9 | 9 | 4 | 16 | 16 | 16 | 16 | 16 | 16 | 16 | 16 | 15 | 10 | 10 | 16 | 16 | 16 |
| 15 WEBBER | 15 | 15 | 4 | 9 | 9 | 9 | 9 | 9 | 9 | 9 | 9 | 9 | 9 | 15 | 9 | 11 | 11 | 11 | 16 | 16 | 16 | 15 | 15 | 15 | 15 | 15 | 15 | 15 | 15 | 10 | 16 | 16 | 15 | 15 | 15 |
| 12 TRULLI | 9 | 9 | 9 | 4 | 4 | 4 | 4 | 4 | 4 | 10 | 10 | 10 | 10 | 11 | 11 | 16 | 16 | 16 | 11 | 15 | 15 | 14 | 14 | 10 | 10 | 10 | 10 | 10 | 16 | 15 | 15 | 4 | 4 | 4 |
| 4 KOVALAINEN | 11 | 11 | 11 | 11 | 10 | 10 | 10 | 10 | 10 | 4 | 4 | 4 | 4 | 16 | 15 | 15 | 15 | 15 | 14 | 14 | 10 | 10 | 4 | 4 | 4 | 4 | 4 | 4 | 4 | 4 | 10 | 10 | 10 |
| 11 SCHUMACHER | 14 | 14 | 10 | 10 | 11 | 11 | 11 | 11 | 11 | 11 | 11 | 11 | 11 | 15 | 14 | 14 | 14 | 14 | 10 | 10 | 4 | 4 | 14 | 11 | 11 | 11 | 11 | 11 | 11 | 11 | 11 | 11 | 11 |
| 14 COULTHARD | 12 | 12 | 14 | 14 | 14 | 14 | 14 | 14 | 14 | 14 | 14 | 14 | 14 | 10 | 10 | 10 | 10 | 7 | 7 | 7 | 11 | 12 | 12 | 12 | 12 | 12 | 12 | 12 | 12 | 12 |
| 7 BUTTON | 7 | 10 | 12 | 12 | 20 | 20 | 20 | 12 | 20 | 20 | 20 | 20 | 20 | 7 | 7 | 7 | 7 | 18 | 18 | 8 | 14 | 14 | 14 | 20 | 22 | 22 | 7 | 7 | 7 | 18 |
| 18 LIUZZI | 10 | 7 | 20 | 20 | 12 | 12 | 12 | 20 | 12 | 12 | 12 | 12 | 7 | 20 | 18 | 18 | 18 | 11 | 11 | 11 | 18 | 12 | 12 | 18 | 7 | 7 | 18 | 18 | 18 | 8 |
| 10 KUBICA | 18 | 20 | 7 | 7 | 7 | 7 | 7 | 7 | 7 | 7 | 7 | 18 | 18 | 12 | 22 | 22 | 22 | 22 | 3 | 8 | 20 | 20 | 7 | 7 | 22 | 18 | 18 | 22 | 8 | 20 |
| 17 WURZ | 20 | 18 | 18 | 18 | 18 | 18 | 18 | 18 | 18 | 18 | 18 | 7 | 12 | 12 | 8 | 8 | 8 | 12 | 12 | 7 | 7 | 22 | 22 | 22 | 8 | 8 | 20 | 20 | 22 |
| 19 VETTEL | 17 | 8 | 19 | 19 | 19 | 22 | 22 | 22 | 22 | 22 | 22 | 8 | 17 | 17 | 17 | 12 | 20 | 20 | 20 | 22 | 22 | 18 | 18 | 8 | 20 | 20 | 22 | 22 | 7 |
| 8 BARRICHELLO | 8 | 19 | 8 | 22 | 22 | 8 | 8 | 8 | 8 | 8 | 8 | 22 | 22 | 22 | 12 | 20 | 22 | 22 | 8 | 8 | 8 | 21 | 21 | 23 | 23 | 23 | 23 | 23 |
| 22 SATO | 19 | 22 | 22 | 8 | 8 | 19 | 21 | 21 | 21 | 21 | 21 | 21 | 21 | 20 | 20 | 20 | 17 | 23 | 23 | 21 | 21 | 21 | 21 | 17 | 17 | 21 | 21 | 21 |
| 20 SUTIL | 22 | 21 | 21 | 21 | 21 | 21 | 21 | 19 | 21 | 23 | 21 | 21 | 12 | 12 | 20 | 20 | 20 | 17 | 17 | 17 | 17 | 17 | 23 | 23 | 21 | 17 |
| 23 DAVIDSON | 21 | 23 | 23 | 23 | 23 | 17 | 17 | 17 | 23 | 23 | 23 | 23 | 23 | 23 | 17 | 17 | 17 | 17 | 17 | 23 | 23 | 21 | 17 |
| 21 YAMAMOTO | 23 | 17 | 17 | 17 | 17 | 17 | 17 | 19 |
| 3 FISICHELLA | 3 |

## PRACTICE 1 (FRIDAY)

Sunny (track 16–23ºC, air 13–17ºC)

| Pos. | Driver | Laps | Time |
|---|---|---|---|
| 1 | Kimi Räikkönen | 16 | 1m 47.339s |
| 2 | Lewis Hamilton | 19 | 1m 47.881s |
| 3 | Fernando Alonso | 17 | 1m 47.994s |
| 4 | Nick Heidfeld | 20 | 1m 48.052s |
| 5 | Nico Rosberg | 18 | 1m 48.372s |
| 6 | Robert Kubica | 20 | 1m 48.605s |
| 7 | Alexander Wurz | 20 | 1m 48.920s |
| 8 | Jarno Trulli | 19 | 1m 48.994s |
| 9 | Heikki Kovalainen | 22 | 1m 49.138s |
| 10 | Jenson Button | 22 | 1m 49.330s |
| 11 | Giancarlo Fisichella | 25 | 1m 49.380s |
| 12 | Ralf Schumacher | 21 | 1m 49.548s |
| 13 | Mark Webber | 23 | 1m 49.894s |
| 14 | David Coulthard | 19 | 1m 49.931s |
| 15 | Rubens Barrichello | 22 | 1m 50.264s |
| 16 | Sebastian Vettel | 27 | 1m 50.482s |
| 17 | Takuma Sato | 16 | 1m 50.640s |
| 18 | Anthony Davidson | 20 | 1m 50.648s |
| 19 | Adrian Sutil | 22 | 1m 50.768s |
| 20 | Vitantonio Liuzzi | 12 | 1m 51.628s |
| 21 | Sakon Yamamoto | 21 | 1m 52.379s |
| 22 | Felipe Massa | 2 | No time |

## PRACTICE 2 (FRIDAY)

Scattered cloud (track 28–30ºC, air 19–20ºC)

| Pos. | Driver | Laps | Time |
|---|---|---|---|
| 1 | Fernando Alonso | 29 | 1m 46.654s |
| 2 | Lewis Hamilton | 29 | 1m 46.765s |
| 3 | Felipe Massa | 27 | 1m 46.953s |
| 4 | Kimi Räikkönen | 26 | 1m 47.166s |
| 5 | Jarno Trulli | 33 | 1m 47.491s |
| 6 | Ralf Schumacher | 34 | 1m 47.946s |
| 7 | Giancarlo Fisichella | 30 | 1m 48.086s |
| 8 | Mark Webber | 29 | 1m 48.271s |
| 9 | Robert Kubica | 37 | 1m 48.279s |
| 10 | Heikki Kovalainen | 38 | 1m 48.567s |
| 11 | Nick Heidfeld | 36 | 1m 48.606s |
| 12 | Nico Rosberg | 32 | 1m 48.840s |
| 13 | David Coulthard | 17 | 1m 48.883s |
| 14 | Jenson Button | 29 | 1m 48.919s |
| 15 | Rubens Barrichello | 31 | 1m 49.364s |
| 16 | Alexander Wurz | 28 | 1m 49.393s |
| 17 | Sakon Yamamoto | 32 | 1m 49.697s |
| 18 | Sebastian Vettel | 34 | 1m 49.720s |
| 19 | Takuma Sato | 23 | 1m 50.168s |
| 20 | Adrian Sutil | 24 | 1m 50.399s |
| 21 | Anthony Davidson | 24 | 1m 50.542s |
| 22 | Vitantonio Liuzzi | 9 | 1m 50.865s |

## QUALIFYING (SATURDAY)

Cloudy (track 23–24ºC, air 16–18ºC)

| Pos. | Driver | First | Second | Third |
|---|---|---|---|---|
| 1 | Kimi Räikkönen | 1m 46.242s | 1m 45.070s | 1m 45.994s |
| 2 | Felipe Massa | 1m 46.060s | 1m 45.173s | 1m 46.011s |
| 3 | Fernando Alonso | 1m 46.058s | 1m 45.442s | 1m 46.091s |
| 4 | Lewis Hamilton | 1m 46.437s | 1m 45.132s | 1m 46.406s |
| 5 | Robert Kubica | 1m 46.707s | 1m 45.885s | 1m 46.996s |
| 6 | Nico Rosberg | 1m 46.950s | 1m 46.469s | 1m 47.334s |
| 7 | Nick Heidfeld | 1m 46.923s | 1m 45.994s | 1m 47.409s |
| 8 | Mark Webber | 1m 47.084s | 1m 46.426s | 1m 47.524s |
| 9 | Jarno Trulli | 1m 47.143s | 1m 46.480s | 1m 47.798s |
| 10 | Heikki Kovalainen | 1m 46.971s | 1m 46.240s | 1m 48.505s |
| 11 | Giancarlo Fisichella | 1m 47.143s | 1m 46.603s | |
| 12 | Ralf Schumacher | 1m 47.300s | 1m 46.618s | |
| 13 | David Coulthard | 1m 47.340s | 1m 46.800s | |
| 14 | Jenson Button | 1m 47.474s | 1m 46.955s | |
| 15 | Vitantonio Liuzzi | 1m 47.576s | 1m 47.115s | |
| 16 | Alexander Wurz | 1m 47.522s | 1m 47.394s | |
| 17 | Sebastian Vettel | 1m 47.581s | | |
| 18 | Rubens Barrichello | 1m 47.954s | | |
| 19 | Takuma Sato | 1m 47.980s | | |
| 20 | Adrian Sutil | 1m 48.044s | | |
| 21 | Anthony Davidson | 1m 48.199s | | |
| 22 | Sakon Yamamoto | 1m 49.577s | | |

## PRACTICE 3 (SATURDAY)

Cloudy (track 21–23ºC, air 15–17ºC)

| Pos. | Driver | Laps | Time |
|---|---|---|---|
| 1 | Kimi Räikkönen | 17 | 1m 46.137s |
| 2 | Felipe Massa | 17 | 1m 46.388s |
| 3 | Fernando Alonso | 10 | 1m 46.507s |
| 4 | Lewis Hamilton | 14 | 1m 46.782s |
| 5 | Heikki Kovalainen | 13 | 1m 47.065s |
| 6 | Jarno Trulli | 11 | 1m 47.218s |
| 7 | Nico Rosberg | 16 | 1m 47.251s |
| 8 | Nick Heidfeld | 16 | 1m 47.359s |
| 9 | Ralf Schumacher | 19 | 1m 47.454s |
| 10 | Mark Webber | 15 | 1m 47.527s |
| 11 | Giancarlo Fisichella | 16 | 1m 47.564s |
| 12 | Jenson Button | 18 | 1m 47.767s |
| 13 | David Coulthard | 10 | 1m 47.806s |
| 14 | Sebastian Vettel | 19 | 1m 47.838s |
| 15 | Alexander Wurz | 16 | 1m 47.902s |
| 16 | Takuma Sato | 16 | 1m 48.129s |
| 17 | Vitantonio Liuzzi | 21 | 1m 48.163s |
| 18 | Adrian Sutil | 18 | 1m 48.348s |
| 19 | Rubens Barrichello | 16 | 1m 48.528s |
| 20 | Anthony Davidson | 16 | 1m 48.955s |
| 21 | Sakon Yamamoto | 14 | 1m 49.179s |
| 22 | Robert Kubica | 2 | No time |

## RACE TYRE STRATEGIES

**BRIDGESTONE**

In 2007, the tyre regulations stipulate that the two dry-tyre specifications must be visibly distinguishable from each other. At the Belgian Grand Prix, the soft compound Bridgestone Potenza tyre was marked with a white line in the second-from-inside groove.

| | Driver | Race stint 1 | Race stint 2 | Race stint 3 |
|---|---|---|---|---|
| 1 | Kimi Räikkönen | Medium: laps 1–15 | Medium: 16–31 | Soft: 32–44 |
| 2 | Felipe Massa | Medium: 1–16 | Medium: 17–32 | Soft: 33–44 |
| 3 | Fernando Alonso | Medium: 1–15 | Medium: 16–33 | Soft: 34–44 |
| 4 | Lewis Hamilton | Medium: 1–16 | Medium: 17–37 | Soft: 38–44 |
| 5 | Nick Heidfeld | Medium: 1–18 | Medium: 19–34 | Soft: 35–44 |
| 6 | Nico Rosberg | Medium: 1–14 | Medium: 15–30 | Soft: 31–44 |
| 7 | Mark Webber | Medium: 1–14 | Medium: 15–31 | Soft: 32–44 |
| 8 | Heikki Kovalainen | Medium: 1–22 | Soft: 23–44 | |
| 9 | Robert Kubica | Medium: 1–15 | Medium: 16–30 | Soft: 31–44 |
| 10 | Ralf Schumacher | Medium: 1–20 | Soft: 21–44 | |
| 11 | Jarno Trulli | Medium: 1–14 | Medium: 15–31 | Soft: 32–44 |
| 12 | Vitantonio Liuzzi | Medium: 1–18 | Soft: 19–44 | |
| 13 | Rubens Barrichello | Medium: 1–26 | Soft: 27–44 | |
| 14 | Adrian Sutil | Soft: 1–16 | Soft: 17–30 | Medium: 31–44 |
| 15 | Takuma Sato | Medium: 1–21 | Soft: 22–33 | Soft: 34–44 |
| 16 | Anthony Davidson | Medium: 1–25 | Soft: 26–44 | |
| 17 | Sakon Yamamoto | Soft: 1–17 | Medium: 18–31 | Medium: 32–44 |
| | Jenson Button | Medium: 1–24 | Soft: 25–36 (DNF) | |
| | Alexander Wurz | Medium: 1–21 | Soft: 22–32 | Medium: 33–34 (DNF) |
| | David Coulthard | Medium: 1–14 | Soft: 15–29 (DNF) | |
| | Sebastian Vettel | Medium: 1–7 | Medium: 8 (DNF) | |
| | Giancarlo Fisichella | Medium: 1 (DNF) | | |

10 SCHUMACHER Toyota

8 TRULLI Toyota

6 HEIDFELD BMW-Sauber

4 HAMILTON McLaren

2 MASSA Ferrari

9 KOVALAINEN Renault

7 WEBBER Red Bull

5 ROSBERG Williams

3 ALONSO McLaren

1 RÄIKKÖNEN Ferrari

**RACE DISTANCE:**
44 laps
191.415 miles/308.053 km

**RACE WEATHER:**
Sunny,
track 27–28ºC, air 20–21ºC

| 37 | 38 | 39 | 40 | 41 | 42 | 43 | 44 | • |
|---|---|---|---|---|---|---|---|---|
| 6 | 6 | 6 | 6 | 6 | 6 | 6 | 6 | 1 |
| 5 | 5 | 5 | 5 | 5 | 5 | 5 | 5 | 2 |
| 2 | 1 | 1 | 1 | 1 | 1 | 1 | 1 | 3 |
| 1 | 2 | 2 | 2 | 2 | 2 | 2 | 2 | 4 |
| 9 | 9 | 9 | 9 | 9 | 9 | 9 | 9 | 5 |
| 16 | 16 | 16 | 16 | 16 | 16 | 16 | 16 | 6 |
| 15 | 15 | 15 | 15 | 15 | 15 | 15 | 15 | 7 |
| 4 | 4 | 4 | 4 | 4 | 4 | 4 | 4 | 8 |
| 10 | 10 | 10 | 10 | 10 | 10 | 10 | 10 | |
| 11 | 11 | 11 | 11 | 11 | 11 | 11 | 11 | |
| 12 | 12 | 12 | 12 | 12 | 12 | 12 | 12 | |
| 18 | 18 | 18 | 18 | 18 | 18 | 18 | | |
| 8 | 8 | 8 | 8 | 8 | 8 | 8 | | |
| 20 | 20 | 20 | 20 | 20 | 20 | 20 | | |
| 22 | 22 | 22 | 22 | 22 | 22 | 22 | | |
| 23 | 23 | 23 | 23 | 23 | 23 | 23 | | |
| 21 | 21 | 21 | 21 | 21 | 21 | 21 | | |

20 Pit stop
20 One lap or more behind leader

## FOR THE RECORD

**40th F1 GRAND PRIX:**
Spa-Francorchamps

**15th CONSTRUCTORS'**
**WORLD CHAMPIONSHIP:** Ferrari

**TENTH WIN AT SPA:** Ferrari

**100TH GRAND PRIX START:**
Mark Webber

## POINTS

### DRIVERS

| | | |
|---|---|---|
| 1 | Lewis Hamilton | 97 |
| 2 | Fernando Alonso | 95 |
| 3 | Kimi Räikkönen | 84 |
| 4 | Felipe Massa | 77 |
| 5 | Nick Heidfeld | 56 |
| 6 | Robert Kubica | 33 |
| 7 | Heikki Kovalainen | 22 |
| 8 | Giancarlo Fisichella | 17 |
| 9 | Nico Rosberg | 15 |
| 10 | Alexander Wurz | 13 |
| 11 | Mark Webber | 10 |
| 12 | David Coulthard | 8 |
| 13 | Jarno Trulli | 7 |
| 14 | Ralf Schumacher | 5 |
| 15 | Takuma Sato | 4 |
| 16 | Jenson Button | 2 |
| 17 | Sebastian Vettel | 1 |

### CONSTRUCTORS

| | | |
|---|---|---|
| 1 | Ferrari | 161 |
| 2 | BMW Sauber | 90 |
| 3 | Renault | 39 |
| 4 | Williams | 28 |
| 5 | Red Bull | 18 |
| 6 | Toyota | 12 |
| 7 | Super Aguri | 4 |
| 8 | Honda | 2 |

The FIA World Motor Sport Council ruled on 13 September that McLaren is ineligible for constructors' points in 2007 because of the espionage scandal.

Photographs: Perer J Fox/www.crash.net

Main: Lewis Hamilton expertly steers
his McLaren on the flooded track.
Photograph: Paul-Henri Cahier

Inset: Lewis is ecstatic at his best
victory to date.
Photograph: Peter J Fox/www.crash.net

FIA F1 WORLD CHAMPIONSHIP/ROUND 15

# JAPANESE GP

## MOUNT FUJI

## FUJI QUALIFYING

**Above:** Adrian Sutil gained huge satisfaction from securing the Spyker team's first championship point of the season after Vitantonio Liuzzi was penalised for passing under a yellow flag.

**Below right:** A Sato banner urges Takuma to go and fight.
Photographs: Peter J Fox/www.crash.net

**Bottom right:** Renault's new president Bernard Rey paid a visit to the race.
Photograph: Bernard Asset

### DIARY

Yet another emotional outburst from Fernando Alonso to the Spanish media at Fuji prompts further speculation that he will not be staying with McLaren for 2008.

Following the near miss between David Coulthard and Alex Wurz in Australia, the FIA's Technical Working Group announces plans, subject to ratification by the World Motor Sport Council, to raise cockpit sides by 25 mm for 2008 to offer drivers greater head protection.

Ralf Schumacher reveals in Japan that he will not be staying with Toyota for 2008, despite optimistic comments all season.

Lewis Hamilton's score of 107 points after the Japanese GP makes him the fastest driver ever to amass his first 100 championship points: he achieved it in just 15 races. Jacques Villeneuve took 22 races to do the same.

Yet again, McLaren dominated a qualifying session but Ferrari remained convinced that it would be competitive come the race.

The three sessions at Fuji were tricky for everybody after low cloud cover had prevented any serious running in the morning because the medical helicopter could not stay aloft due to the poor visibility. For the engineers and drivers it was thus a matter of guesstimating suitable chassis settings based on Friday's running, when the Ferraris had dominated the morning session and McLaren the afternoon. Adding to the conundrum were Fuji's mile-long front straight and the need to bear in mind straight-line speed at the expense of grip over the rest of the lap.

For the fifth time this year, Lewis Hamilton took pole position, pipping Fernando Alonso to it with a lap of 1m 25.368s compared with Alonso's 1m 25.438s. While both said they were happy with their McLarens, Kimi Räikkönen, in third place on 1m 25.516s, complained of a faulty gearbox sensor on his Ferrari that, he said, cost him a little bit of time. Felipe Massa, fourth on 1m 25,765s, was less happy with the balance of his F2007 when it mattered – on new tyres and low fuel – and battled with too much oversteer.

The tricky conditions simply made it more difficult for all of them as they battled to stay in the reckoning for the title.

Behind them, BMW Sauber took its habitual 'best of the rest' position courtesy of Nick Heidfeld. He lapped his F1.07 in 1m 26.505s but admitted that initial hopes of jumping one of the red cars had soon faded. Robert Kubica started only ninth, unhappy with graining tyres and the team's strategy for the all-important Q3 session. His best lap was 1m 27.225s.

Between the two BMW drivers were Nico Rosberg, Jenson Button, Mark Webber and Sebastian Vettel. But the unfortunate Rosberg had to lose ten grid places after his Williams FW29 needed its race engine changed at the end of Friday. That was a major blow because he was again very quick on his way to the sixth-fastest Q3 time of 1m 26.728s. Team-mate Alex Wurz ran foul of an FIA weight check and then hit traffic. He had been the fastest (of three drivers who ventured out) on Saturday morning, but was left down in 18th place on 1m 27.454s.

Button's sixth place on the grid was a major boost for Honda, especially in rival Toyota's backyard but also because the revised RA107 that had been intended to race here was deemed even worse than the unloved RA107 with which the Englishman lapped in 1m 26.913s. He was as neat and smooth as ever and the performance served as a reminder to those with short memories just how under-utilised his talent had been all season. Like Wurz at Williams, Rubens Barrichello was unable to match his team-mate and he languished down in 17th place on 1m 27.323s, having missed out on Q2 by a frustrating 0.1s.

At Red Bull, Webber was happy with his RB3 after lapping it in 1m 26.914s for eighth place. Clearly, the team's subtle weight-distribution changes had had a beneficial effect on the car's performance. David Coulthard, however, complained of poor stability under braking and excessive understeer and his 1m 26.247s left him 12th overall.

Vettel's fine performance in taking his Toro Rosso through to Q3 – a first for the team – pushed him to 1m 26.973s. That left him ninth – eighth after Rosberg's penalty – but he believed he could have done even better had a change of strategy not cost him his final run.

The weight-distribution changes that had been effected *chez* Red Bull had also helped the STR02. Across the garage, team-mate Tonio Liuzzi, normally a wet-weather ace, was only 15th (and 14th on the grid) on 1m 26.948s. In his case, the team decided to hedge its bets given that the forecast of rain for the race was not universally accepted. He ran with dry aero settings in the hope that better conditions would prevail on Sunday.

Heikki Kovalainen and Giancarlo Fisichella were very disappointed with only tenth and 11th places on the grid because both felt their Renault R27s were nicely balanced. The problem was that they lacked grip. There was nothing to cheer for Toyota, either, on its home ground. Jarno Trulli managed only 1m 26.253s for 13th on the grid and Ralf Schumacher crashed into Sakon Yamamoto, ensuring that he was unable to make use of having got through into Q2. His car was rebuilt but he never managed to challenge for a new time in the session and was thus 16th.

At the back, honours were evenly distributed between Super Aguri and Spyker. Anthony Davidson headed the quartet with 1m 27.564s, chased by Adrian Sutil on 1m 28.628s, Takuma Sato on 1m 28.792s and Yamamoto on 1m 29.668s. Both Super Aguri drivers reported lack of grip and Sato also lost crucial time on the FIA weighbridge. At Spyker, Sutil thought Friday had been much better because his set-up was not optimised on Saturday. Yamamoto's assault by Schumacher did not affect his running.

FOR the first 19 of its 67 laps the Japanese GP looked like the publicity nightmare to end all publicity nightmares as the field circulated behind the safety car in dire conditions. But finally, when the race exploded into life on the 20th lap, it developed into the most exciting encounter of the season as Lewis Hamilton earned his spurs on a day when Fernando Alonso put his McLaren into the wall and a costly tyre-choice error by Ferrari all but handed the 22-year-old Hamilton the title on a plate.

It was, Hamilton reported afterwards, the most difficult race of his career. It was also the best.

There were always going to be comparisons between the 1976 classic race at Fuji, which cemented James Hunt's world championship, and the return in 2007. But just to make sure, the weather gods staged similar conditions. As Mount Fuji stood like a silent sentinel in the background, things out on the track were as hospitable as a Mexican prison and the race was started behind the safety car. Thus began the tedious chugging around that threatened to render F1 a laughing stock across the world.

Even while this was happening, Ferrari was instructed to bring in Kimi Räikkönen and Felipe Massa to switch from the intermediate Bridgestone wets on which they alone had started to the extreme wets mandated by the stewards in an email circulated to all teams before the race. Ferrari claimed not to have received the email.

When the race finally went green at the start of the 20th lap, Hamilton burst into the lead from Alonso and soon opened a comfortable lead over his team-mate.

Hamilton's stop on lap 28 cost him only two places, leaving him behind Toro Rosso's young charger Sebastian Vettel and Red Bull's veteran Mark Webber, but Alonso's a lap earlier had left him behind those two and Hamilton plus the Renaults of Giancarlo Fisichella and Heikki Kovalainen, Robert Kubica's BMW-Sauber and David Coulthard's Red Bull.

As the first round of fuel stops developed, Vettel led from lap 29 to 31, Webber from 32 to 36, Heikki Kovalainen from 37 to 39 and Giancarlo Fisichella on lap 40, until each in turn made his stop. Then Hamilton resumed the lead and held it to the finish. But he'd had the biggest scare of his race on the 34th lap, when he got sideways in Turn Ten and was tapped into a spin by Kubica.

'The last stint I was heavy with fuel,' Hamilton explained. 'It was easy to grain the tyres and I'd asked [the team] why don't I let them pass me if they have to pit soon? I couldn't see anything in my mirrors, my visor was fogged up and I couldn't see Robert inside me. I'm not taking the blame for that incident, though. When you are behind you have to take it easy, especially in these conditions. He was not fully up the inside to make the move and I couldn't see him or hear him. He should have taken me down the straight.'

Kubica was perplexed, and angered, by the whole thing, especially because he received a drive-through penalty. 'I was doing a good pace but unfortunately I touched Lewis, had my pit stop, then a drive-through, which I was surprised to get,' he said. 'I was running much quicker than him and in one corner he was doing a completely different line or made a mistake, so he was completely wide. I stayed on the inside, he cut into the apex and I was there and unfortunately we touched. I think it was a race accident.'

Hamilton half spun but was able to get going before anyone else went past, Kovalainen having passed him earlier. 'After that brush I felt a vibration and I just thought, "Shoot – a tyre is going down." That big vibration continued all the way to the finish but the team said the car seemed okay so I just had to keep it on the track.'

The lap after that, Hamilton got his big break when Alonso cut across Vettel going into Turn One as they fought over eighth place. The McLaren driver spun and dropped down to tenth. Worse was yet to come, however. Going through Turn Five on the 42nd lap he lost control as his McLaren aquaplaned and thumped hard into the bank. He was unharmed but the

**Above: Heikki Kovalainen on the podium celebrates a best-ever second place.**

**Below: It was also Renault's best result of the year, further enhancing Kovalainen's reputation.**

Photographs: Peter J Fox/www.crash.net

**Above:** Mark Webber steps from his badly damaged Red Bull after being involved in that freak accident behind the safety car.

**Top left:** Lewis Hamilton's manoeuvres behind the safety car were later to be scrutinised by the FIA.

Photographs: Peter J Fox/www.crash.net

**Right:** Red Bulls minus wings. Toro Rosso's Sebastian Vettel after hitting Webber's Red Bull machine.

Photograph: Studio Colombo/WRi2

While Mark Webber was raging about impetuous youth in the aftermath of the Japanese Grand Prix – referring to the shunt behind the safety car on the 46th lap in which Toro Rosso's Sebastian Vettel smashed into the back of his Red Bull – Ferrari was declaiming the FIA and the stewards' failure to notify it in time that all teams were required to race on Bridgestone's extreme-wet-weather tyres.

The two incidents generated yet further controversy in a season during which scandal had become commonplace.

The safety car fiasco occurred as the field bunched behind Bernd Maylander in the Mercedes-Benz CLK safety car. Normally the 6.3-litre, 500-bhp V8 has sufficient pace to stay ahead of a GP field, but in the wet it was struggling. As race leader Lewis Hamilton tried to keep the heat in his tyres and brakes, the field continually concertinaed behind him and it was at one of these points that Webber felt he had to dive inside Hamilton to avoid the McLaren, after Hamilton had had to back off to give Maylander the chance to pull away, and Vettel got caught out and struck the back of the Red Bull.

'It's kids, isn't it?' an angry Webber said. 'They haven't got enough experience. They do a good job and then they fuck it all up.'

Vettel received a ten-place grid penalty for China.

Down at Ferrari, there was anger after all teams were sent an email before the start about which tyres were mandatory in the conditions and the Scuderia claimed not to have received the information. It was instructed to bring in Kimi Räikkönen and Felipe Massa early in the race, which was still running under the safety car, to switch from the intermediates on which they had been sent to the grid.

safety car was deployed again as the wreckage was cleared away. His title aspirations appeared all but over.

'It was very difficult to see anything because of the spray, especially when you were coming down the straight,' he said. 'As a result I did not see Vettel in my mirrors and was surprised when he hit me. I think the car was damaged quite a bit by that, but I was able to continue. However, when I was braking for Turn Five I just aquaplaned and spun. Unfortunately the walls at that corner are very close to the track, so I hit the barrier heavily and that was it. Of course, it is a difficult situation for me now in the championship. However, I will keep fighting until the end – as last year's battle showed, anything can happen.'

Now Hamilton faced the final test as he prepared for another race restart.

'When we were behind the safety car for the second time I was constantly on to my engineers [on the radio], telling them to tell Red Bull to get Mark [Webber] to make a bit more of a gap between us. I couldn't go any faster because of the safety car ahead of me. Then one time Mark just appeared alongside me when he braked so late. He was just too close, then he braked really hard. I don't know what happened but my instinct said something was going to happen.'

It did. Vettel was caught unawares and removed the two Red Bull cars – Webber's and his own Red Bull-backed Toro Rosso – when he hit the back of Webber's RB3 hard.

It was a great shame because both had been driving extremely well. Webber was feeling unwell, having been sick early in the morning, on the grid and again during the initial stop-start running behind the safety car. Yet none of this had been reflected in his performance as he kept Hamilton in sight and waited for his chance to strike. Now he found himself punted out just when a potential victory – and at least a podium finish – was in sight.

'That was a completely disastrous finish,' he growled. 'We were in very, very good shape to challenge Lewis for first today. We were strong and I didn't make any mistakes despite the tricky conditions. Vettel was a bit wild behind me during the first safety car period and then did a very good job of hitting me very hard under the second.'

You had to feel sorry for poor Vettel, who in a moment went from hero to zero. From being the first man to lead a race in a Toro Rosso to the guy who had cost his team a strong points finish and taken out a Red Bull stable-mate.

The stewards later gave him a ten-place grid penalty for China.

Now Hamilton just had to pull away from the duelling Kovalainen and Räikkönen. The two Finns fought tooth and nail, Kimi doing everything he could and Heikki withstanding all the pressure and barely making any mistakes. They went on to form the first-ever twin-Finn podium.

'It's been a rollercoaster year for us,' Kovalainen said. 'We gambled with the car yesterday, hoping it would be dry today, then this morning it was raining more than yesterday! But I never give up, I always keep going and our strategies worked well today. The team deserves one podium this year.'

Räikkönen was philosophical about a possible victory lost and the fact that he was now within three points of being out of the title fight: 'We made the decision to start on intermediates and when we were running behind the safety car the real issue was to see anything on the straight. You could see nothing. Some new rule forced everyone to start on wets but the FIA or race control forgot to tell us and they forced us to pit to change them. That cost us a lot.'

Behind them, David Coulthard picked up a good fourth place after his most convincing performance of the season, having kept the faster Räikkönen behind him from lap 49 to 56. Fisichella took an unobtrusive fifth ahead of a fabulous duel between Massa and Kubica, which electrified the sodden spectators.

Massa had an up-and-down race after the tyre problem early on, went off the road several times and came back at the delayed Kubica as they staged an old-fashioned wheel-rubbing, side-by-side scrap for sixth place on the final lap. It reminded many of the great fight between Gilles Villeneuve and René

Arnoux at Dijon in 1979. Time and again they rubbed bodywork and swapped places and the issue was decided only as they exited the last corner when Robert edged Felipe wide. As the BMW struggled for traction on the wet kerb, Felipe found more on the grippy run-off area and just got the place. They embraced afterwards, just as Gilles and René had.

'I knew that, given the championship positions, I could take the risk of running different tyres from our rivals, but it was not the right choice, on top of which there was the decision of the stewards that we were unaware of and which is nevertheless serious,' Massa said, now out of the title hunt. 'I managed to get up to the front places again but I had to pit again because I did not have enough fuel to get to the end. Winning the duel with Kubica on the final lap was the best moment of this race for me.'

The final point fell to Tonio Liuzzi. He might have been overshadowed by Vettel on this occasion, because of their differing qualifying strategies, but he made as much as he could from a pit lane start in the spare STR02 (in which the team got the rules wrong and let him go a lap down) and a clever early refuelling stop and was simply electric during the second safety car start, when he gained five places in one lap. In his second stop on lap 44 he was given a set of grained wets instead of his scheduled set, but he was still a points contender from then on, though he made things difficult for himself when, having passed Adrian Sutil, he spun through 360 degrees in Turn One on lap 58. He gathered it up and started all over again and repassed the Spyker on lap 64. When Nick Heidfeld's BMW-Sauber stopped just by the pit entrance on the 65th lap, he moved up the place he needed to score Toro Rosso's first world championship point. Later, however, he was docked 25s for passing Sutil under a yellow flag, so the point passed to Spyker instead.

Heidfeld's race was compromised right from the first start behind the safety car, when he was jumped by a whole bunch of guys and fell from third to 10th thanks to a combination of a faulty radio and a misfire. Then Button tried to dive inside him in Turn One and the resultant collision damaged both cars. He was still headed for sixth when his engine began to sound rough and his F1.07 stopped.

Sutil took ninth on the road and led home the Hondas of Rubens Barrichello (who ran in the points until his final stop on lap 60) and Button. Button was fourth as the safety car pulled in for the first time but lost his front wing in the clash with Heidfeld. He carried on without it until his first stop on the 23rd lap but was further delayed by a throttle problem. He passed Barrichello for 11th place on lap 61 but then Takuma Sato savaged him in his Super Aguri on the final lap and he did not make the flag.

It was a disappointing day for the Japanese drivers and teams. Toyota got Jarno Trulli home only in 13th place, after he downshifted at the wrong time and spun behind the first safety car, and Ralf Schumacher retired after suffering drowned electronics and then a puncture. Apparently, Toyota's management had been promised a podium finish.

Sato took 15th place for Super Aguri but team-mate Anthony Davidson retired after 54 laps with a throttle sensor failure. Sakon Yamamoto survived a spin and nearly stalling after his first stop to take 12th.

The race was also a disaster for Williams. Rosberg ran well initially before a spin but was halted by an electronic problem that robbed him of traction control and a consistent gearshift. Team-mate Alex Wurz was shunted from behind by Sato on the first restart, spun all the way down to Turn One and collected the hapless Massa.

F1's return to Fuji proved, against the initial odds, a great success and the best man won a brilliant race. 'Towards the end lots of thoughts were going through my mind,' Hamilton admitted. 'On the last lap I was thinking of some of the races that Ayrton Senna and Alain Prost were in and it made me feel that perhaps I was on my way to achieving something similar to them.'

For many, his style was an echo of Senna's at its very best.

*David Tremayne*

**Right:** David Coulthard delivered in a disappointing season by bringing his Red Bull-Renault home in fourth place.
Photograph: Jad Sherif/WRi2

**Centre:** The fans may have taken a soaking at Fuji but they witnessed a splendid race.
Photograph: Peter J Fox/www.crash.net

**Far right:** Fernando Alonso hit the barriers with considerable force.
Photographs: Lukas Gorys

**Main photgraph:** Felipe Massa and Robert Kubica became embroiled in a thrilling side-by-side battle for sixth place on the final lap.
Photograph: Hiroshi Yamamura/WRi2

# FIA F1 WORLD CHAMPIONSHIP • ROUND 15
## FUJI TELEVISION
# JAPANESE GRAND PRIX
### FUJI 28–30 SEPTEMBER 2007

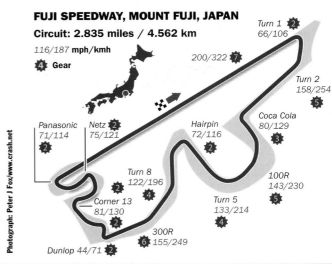

**FUJI SPEEDWAY, MOUNT FUJI, JAPAN**

Circuit: 2.835 miles / 4.562 km

116/187 mph/kmh

**⚙ Gear**

Turn 1 66/106 ②
Turn 2 158/254 ⑤
200/322 ⑦
Coca Cola 80/129 ③
Hairpin 72/116 ②
100R 143/230 ⑤
Netz 75/121 ②
Panasonic 71/114 ②
Turn 8 122/196 ②
Turn 5 133/214 ④
Corner 13 81/130 ②
300R 155/249 ⑥
Dunlop 44/71 ②

Photograph: Peter J Fox/www.crash.net

## RACE RESULTS

| Pos. | Driver | Nat. | No. | Entrant | Car/Engine | Tyres | Laps | Time/Retirement | Speed (mph/km/h) | Gap to leader | Fastest race lap | |
|---|---|---|---|---|---|---|---|---|---|---|---|---|
| 1 | Lewis Hamilton | GB | 2 | Vodafone McLaren Mercedes | McLaren MP4-22-Mercedes FO 108T V8 | B | 67 | 2h 0m 34.579s | 94.435/151.978 | | 1m 28.193s | 27 |
| 2 | Heikki Kovalainen | FIN | 4 | ING Renault F1 Team | Renault R27-RS27 V8 | B | 67 | 2h 0m 42.956s | 94.325/151.802 | + 8.377s | 1m 29.655s | 34 |
| 3 | Kimi Räikkönen | FIN | 6 | Scuderia Ferrari Marlboro | Ferrari F2007-056 V8 | B | 67 | 2h 0m 44.057s | 94.311/151.779 | + 9.478s | 1m 29.619s | 29 |
| 4 | David Coulthard | GB | 14 | Red Bull Racing | Red Bull RB3-Renault RS27 V8 | B | 67 | 2h 0m 54.876s | 94.170/151.552 | + 20.297s | 1m 30.086s | 56 |
| 5 | Giancarlo Fisichella | I | 3 | ING Renault F1 Team | Renault R27-RS27 V8 | B | 67 | 2h 1m 13.443s | 93.930/151.166 | + 38.864s | 1m 30.387s | 33 |
| 6 | Felipe Massa | BR | 5 | Scuderia Ferrari Marlboro | Ferrari F2007-056 V8 | B | 67 | 2h 1m 23.621s | 93.798/150.954 | + 49.042s | 1m 29.588s | 32 |
| 7 | Robert Kubica | POL | 10 | BMW Sauber F1 Team | BMW Sauber F1.07-BMW P86/7 V8 | B | 67 | 2h 1m 23.864s | 93.795/150.949 | + 49.285s | 1m 29.021s | 32 |
| 8 | Adrian Sutil | D | 20 | Etihad Aldar Spyker F1 Team | Spyker F8-VII-Ferrari 056H V8 | B | 67 | 2h 1m 34.708s | 93.656/150.725 | + 1m 0.129s | 1m 31.891s | 54 |
| 9 | Vitantonio Liuzzi | I | 18 | Scuderia Toro Rosso | Toro Rosso STR02-Ferrari 056H V8 | B | 67 | 2h 1m 55.201s* | 93.394/150.303 | + 1m 20.622s | 1m 30.653s | 35 |
| 10 | Rubens Barrichello | BR | 8 | Honda Racing F1 Team | Honda RA107-RA807E V8 | B | 67 | 2h 2m 2.921s | 93.295/150.144 | + 1m 28.342s | 1m 31.060s | 57 |
| 11 | Jenson Button | GB | 7 | Honda Racing F1 Team | Honda RA107-RA807E V8 | B | 66 | Accident | | + 1 lap | 1m 31.951s | 58 |
| 12 | Sakon Yamamoto | J | 21 | Etihad Aldar Spyker F1 Team | Spyker F8-VII-Ferrari 056H V8 | B | 66 | | | + 1 lap | 1m 32.130s | 33 |
| 13 | Jarno Trulli | I | 12 | Panasonic Toyota Racing | Toyota TF107-RVX-07 V8 | B | 66 | | | + 1 lap | 1m 32.414s | 55 |
| 14 | Nick Heidfeld | D | 9 | BMW Sauber F1 Team | BMW Sauber F1.07-BMW P86/7 V8 | B | 65 | Accident damage | | + 2 laps | 1m 29.084s | 28 |
| 15 | Takuma Sato | J | 22 | Super Aguri F1 Team | Super Aguri SA07-Honda RA807E V8 | B | 65 | Accident/tyre | | + 2 laps | 1m 31.507s | 54 |
| | Ralf Schumacher | D | 11 | Panasonic Toyota Racing | Toyota TF107-RVX-07 V8 | B | 55 | Tyre | | | 1m 30.865s | 33 |
| | Anthony Davidson | GB | 23 | Super Aguri F1 Team | Super Aguri SA07-Honda RA807E V8 | B | 54 | Throttle sensor | | | 1m 31.803s | 27 |
| | Nico Rosberg | D | 16 | AT&T Williams | Williams FW29-Toyota RVX-07 V8 | B | 49 | Electronics | | | 1m 29.926s | 27 |
| | Sebastian Vettel | D | 19 | Scuderia Toro Rosso | Toro Rosso STR02-Ferrari 056H V8 | B | 46 | Accident | | | 1m 29.057s | 31 |
| | Mark Webber | AUS | 15 | Red Bull Racing | Red Bull RB3-Renault RS27 V8 | B | 45 | Accident | | | 1m 28.940s | 30 |
| | Fernando Alonso | E | 1 | Vodafone McLaren Mercedes | McLaren MP4-22-Mercedes FO 108T V8 | B | 41 | Accident | | | 1m 28.511s | 25 |
| | Alexander Wurz | A | 17 | AT&T Williams | Williams FW29-Toyota RVX-07 V8 | B | 19 | Accident | | | 2m 5.636s | 19 |

\* Liuzzi finished 8th but classification includes a 25s penalty for overtaking under yellow flags.

**Fastest race lap:** Lewis Hamilton on lap 27, 1m 28.193s, 115.736 mph/186.259 km/h.

**Lap record:** Jody Scheckter (Wolf WR3-Ford Cosworth), 1m 14.300s on lap 72, 131.236 mph/211.203 km/h (1977) (2.709-mile/4.359-km circuit).

All results and data © FOM 2007

**21** SATO Super Aguri  **19** DAVIDSON Super Aguri  **17** BARRICHELLO Honda  **15** SCHUMACHER Toyota  **13** TRULLI Toyota  **11** KOVALAINEN Renault

**22** YAMAMOTO Spyker  **20** SUTIL Spyker  **18** WURZ Williams  **16** ROSBERG Williams Engine penalty  **14** LIUZZI Toro Rosso  **12** COULTHARD Red Bull

| Grid order | 1 2 3 4 5 6 7 8 9 10 11 12 13 14 15 16 17 18 19 20 21 22 23 24 25 26 27 28 29 30 31 32 33 34 35 36 37 38 39 40 41 42 43 44 45 46 47 48 49 50 51 52 5 |
|---|---|
| 2 HAMILTON | 2 2 2 2 2 2 2 2 2 2 2 2 2 2 2 2 2 2 2 2 2 2 2 2 2 2 2 2 2 2 19 19 19 15 15 15 15 15 4 4 4 3 2 2 2 2 2 2 2 2 2 2 |
| 1 ALONSO | 1 1 1 1 1 1 1 1 1 1 1 1 1 1 1 1 1 1 1 1 19 15 15 19 2 4 4 3 2 3 15 15 15 15 4 4 4 4 4 4 |
| 6 RÄIKKÖNEN | 6 6 9 9 9 9 9 9 9 9 9 9 9 9 9 9 9 9 9 19 19 19 19 19 19 19 19 15 2 2 2 10 10 10 14 14 2 15 3 19 19 19 19 5 5 5 5 5 5 |
| 5 MASSA | 5 9 7 7 7 7 7 7 7 7 7 7 7 7 7 7 7 15 15 15 15 15 15 15 15 3 3 4 4 10 4 2 2 2 15 19 19 18 18 4 14 14 14 14 14 14 |
| 9 HEIDFELD | 9 7 15 15 15 15 15 15 15 15 15 15 15 15 15 15 15 7 7 3 3 3 3 3 3 4 10 10 4 3 3 3 14 15 15 14 1 1 4 18 5 3 3 3 6 6 6 6 |
| 7 BUTTON | 7 15 19 19 19 19 19 19 19 19 10 19 19 10 19 19 19 19 3 4 4 4 4 4 10 10 3 3 14 14 2 19 19 19 6 18 5 5 14 9 9 9 9 |
| 15 WEBBER | 15 19 10 10 10 10 10 10 10 10 10 10 10 10 10 10 10 4 14 14 14 14 1 9 19 19 6 6 6 6 8 14 14 14 3 6 6 9 9 9 |
| 19 VETTEL | 19 10 6 3 3 3 3 3 3 3 3 3 3 3 3 3 3 3 10 10 10 14 14 14 14 1 1 1 1 9 1 6 6 1 1 1 3 3 9 8 8 8 8 |
| 10 KUBICA | 10 5 3 4 4 4 4 4 4 4 4 4 4 4 4 4 4 14 14 20 20 20 9 9 9 9 9 9 1 18 18 18 5 14 20 20 6 10 10 10 10 10 1 |
| 3 FISICHELLA | 3 3 4 14 14 14 14 14 14 14 14 14 14 14 14 14 9 20 20 9 9 20 6 6 6 6 6 6 1 18 16 16 16 14 20 9 9 8 11 11 18 18 20 |
| 4 KOVALAINEN | 4 14 12 12 12 12 12 12 12 11 11 11 11 11 11 16 20 9 11 11 6 20 20 20 20 20 18 16 20 5 20 9 6 6 6 10 19 21 16 21 20 18 1 |
| 14 COULTHARD | 14 14 11 11 11 11 11 11 11 16 16 16 16 16 16 1 6 11 11 11 23 23 23 23 18 18 18 16 16 6 8 8 11 21 16 7 21 21 21 21 |
| 12 TRULLI | 12 12 11 16 16 16 16 16 16 16 16 16 16 23 23 23 5 23 23 23 23 23 23 18 18 18 8 9 10 10 11 21 16 16 7 12 17 7 |
| 18 LIUZZI | 11 11 16 8 8 8 8 8 8 8 8 23 23 20 6 6 7 18 18 18 16 16 16 23 23 5 20 10 10 11 11 11 16 7 18 12 12 12 12 |
| 11 SCHUMACHER | 16 16 8 23 23 23 23 5 23 23 23 8 21 18 18 16 16 11 21 21 21 5 5 23 9 23 9 21 21 21 12 18 20 23 23 23 |
| 16 ROSBERG | 8 8 23 20 20 20 20 20 20 20 20 20 22 20 21 6 18 21 16 16 21 21 21 8 8 21 16 16 12 18 20 11 11 11 11 11 |
| 8 BARRICHELLO | 23 23 20 22 22 22 22 22 22 22 22 5 16 20 5 23 8 8 8 8 8 5 8 8 8 8 23 11 11 11 16 7 7 7 18 23 23 16 22 22 22 |
| 17 WURZ | 20 20 22 21 21 21 21 21 21 21 17 21 8 7 18 22 8 12 12 11 11 12 12 12 12 7 7 7 7 7 18 22 22 22 |
| 23 DAVIDSON | 22 22 21 17 17 17 17 17 17 17 5 21 17 6 12 11 21 12 12 12 12 12 12 7 12 12 23 23 23 23 |
| 20 SUTIL | 21 21 17 5 5 5 5 5 5 5 6 6 5 5 6 5 12 12 12 12 5 7 7 7 7 7 7 12 23 23 23 22 22 22 |
| 22 SATO | 17 17 5 6 6 6 6 6 6 6 21 21 6 5 17 17 18 5 5 5 22 22 22 22 22 22 22 22 22 22 22 22 |
| 21 YAMAMOTO | 18 18 18 18 18 18 18 18 18 18 18 18 18 18 18 18 12 |

**246**

## PRACTICE 1 (FRIDAY)

Cloudy (track 30–34°C, air 24–27°C)

| Pos. | Driver | Laps | Time |
|---|---|---|---|
| 1 | Kimi Räikkönen | 26 | 1m 19.119s |
| 2 | Felipe Massa | 27 | 1m 19.498s |
| 3 | Fernando Alonso | 27 | 1m 19.667s |
| 4 | Lewis Hamilton | 24 | 1m 19.807s |
| 5 | Nico Rosberg | 26 | 1m 20.058s |
| 6 | Robert Kubica | 26 | 1m 20.297s |
| 7 | Alexander Wurz | 24 | 1m 20.411s |
| 8 | Jarno Trulli | 32 | 1m 20.483s |
| 9 | Adrian Sutil | 29 | 1m 20.516s |
| 10 | Anthony Davidson | 22 | 1m 20.601s |
| 11 | Rubens Barrichello | 24 | 1m 20.686s |
| 12 | Heikki Kovalainen | 27 | 1m 20.718s |
| 13 | Nick Heidfeld | 26 | 1m 20.728s |
| 14 | Vitantonio Liuzzi | 29 | 1m 20.808s |
| 15 | Ralf Schumacher | 28 | 1m 20.828s |
| 16 | Giancarlo Fisichella | 23 | 1m 20.851s |
| 17 | Takuma Sato | 15 | 1m 21.186s |
| 18 | Mark Webber | 18 | 1m 21.437s |
| 19 | Jenson Button | 22 | 1m 21.541s |
| 20 | Sebastian Vettel | 18 | 1m 21.854s |
| 21 | David Coulthard | 18 | 1m 22.436s |
| 22 | Sakon Yamamoto | 17 | 1m 22.902s |

## PRACTICE 2 (FRIDAY)

Cloudy (track 35–37°C, air 26–27°C)

| Pos. | Driver | Laps | Time |
|---|---|---|---|
| 1 | Lewis Hamilton | 38 | 1m 18.734s |
| 2 | Fernando Alonso | 34 | 1m 18.948s |
| 3 | Felipe Massa | 36 | 1m 19.483s |
| 4 | Jarno Trulli | 35 | 1m 19.711s |
| 5 | Kimi Räikkönen | 29 | 1m 19.714s |
| 6 | Heikki Kovalainen | 40 | 1m 19.789s |
| 7 | Giancarlo Fisichella | 39 | 1m 19.926s |
| 8 | David Coulthard | 33 | 1m 19.949s |
| 9 | Ralf Schumacher | 40 | 1m 19.969s |
| 10 | Robert Kubica | 45 | 1m 20.069s |
| 11 | Mark Webber | 35 | 1m 20.069s |
| 12 | Alexander Wurz | 37 | 1m 20.233s |
| 13 | Nico Rosberg | 43 | 1m 20.270s |
| 14 | Jenson Button | 44 | 1m 20.336s |
| 15 | Nick Heidfeld | 36 | 1m 20.462s |
| 16 | Adrian Sutil | 37 | 1m 20.736s |
| 17 | Rubens Barrichello | 33 | 1m 20.889s |
| 18 | Vitantonio Liuzzi | 44 | 1m 20.985s |
| 19 | Sebastian Vettel | 38 | 1m 20.997s |
| 20 | Anthony Davidson | 34 | 1m 21.007s |
| 21 | Sakon Yamamoto | 38 | 1m 21.305s |
| 22 | Takuma Sato | 34 | 1m 21.352s |

## QUALIFYING (SATURDAY)

Light rain (track 16–17°C, air 14–15°C)

| Pos. | Driver | First | Second | Third |
|---|---|---|---|---|
| 1 | Lewis Hamilton | 1m 25.489s | 1m 24.753s | 1m 25.368s |
| 2 | Fernando Alonso | 1m 25.379s | 1m 24.806s | 1m 25.438s |
| 3 | Kimi Räikkönen | 1m 25.390s | 1m 24.988s | 1m 25.516s |
| 4 | Felipe Massa | 1m 25.359s | 1m 25.049s | 1m 25.765s |
| 5 | Nick Heidfeld | 1m 25.971s | 1m 25.248s | 1m 26.505s |
| 6 | Nico Rosberg | 1m 26.579s | 1m 25.816s | 1m 26.728s |
| 7 | Jenson Button | 1m 26.614s | 1m 25.454s | 1m 26.913s |
| 8 | Mark Webber | 1m 25.970s | 1m 25.535s | 1m 26.914s |
| 9 | Sebastian Vettel | 1m 26.025s | 1m 25.909s | 1m 26.973s |
| 10 | Robert Kubica | 1m 26.300s | 1m 25.530s | 1m 27.225s |
| 11 | Giancarlo Fisichella | 1m 26.909s | 1m 26.033s | |
| 12 | Heikki Kovalainen | 1m 27.223s | 1m 26.232s | |
| 13 | David Coulthard | 1m 26.904s | 1m 26.247s | |
| 14 | Jarno Trulli | 1m 26.711s | 1m 26.253s | |
| 15 | Vitantonio Liuzzi | 1m 27.234s | 1m 26.948s | |
| 16 | Ralf Schumacher | 1m 27.191s | No time | |
| 17 | Rubens Barrichello | 1m 27.323s | | |
| 18 | Alexander Wurz | 1m 27.454s | | |
| 19 | Anthony Davidson | 1m 27.564s | | |
| 20 | Adrian Sutil | 1m 28.628s | | |
| 21 | Takuma Sato | 1m 28.792s | | |
| 22 | Sakon Yamamoto | 1m 29.668s | | |

## PRACTICE 3 (SATURDAY)

Light rain (track 17–18°C, air 15°C)

| Pos. | Driver | Laps | Time |
|---|---|---|---|
| 1 | Alexander Wurz | 3 | 1m 32.746s |
| 2 | Nico Rosberg | 3 | 1m 34.758s |
| 3 | Jarno Trulli | 3 | 1m 36.150s |
| 4 | Sebastian Vettel | 1 | No time |
| 5 | Adrian Sutil | 1 | No time |
| 6 | Sakon Yamamoto | 1 | No time |
| 7 | Vitantonio Liuzzi | 1 | No time |
| 8 | Robert Kubica | 1 | No time |
| 9 | Giancarlo Fisichella | 1 | No time |
| 10 | Heikki Kovalainen | 1 | No time |
| 11 | Ralf Schumacher | 2 | No time |
| 12 | Nick Heidfeld | 1 | No time |
| 13 | Takuma Sato | 2 | No time |
| 14 | Mark Webber | 1 | No time |
| 15 | Anthony Davidson | 2 | No time |
| 16 | Jenson Button | 2 | No time |
| 17 | David Coulthard | 1 | No time |
| 18 | Fernando Alonso | 2 | No time |
| 19 | Rubens Barrichello | 2 | No time |
| 20 | Lewis Hamilton | 1 | No time |
| 21 | Felipe Massa | 1 | No time |
| 22 | Kimi Räikkönen | 0 | No time |

## RACE TYRE STRATEGIES

In 2007, the tyre regulations stipulate that the two dry-tyre specifications must be visibly distinguishable from each other. At the Japanese Grand Prix, the soft compound Bridgestone Potenza tyre was marked with a white line in the second-from-inside groove. Wet and extreme-wet tyres were used during the Japanese Grand Prix.

| | Driver | Stint 1 | Stint 2 | Stint 3 | Stint 4 | Stint 5 |
|---|---|---|---|---|---|---|
| 1 | Lewis Hamilton | Ex-wet: laps 1–28 | Ex-wet: 29–67 | | | |
| 2 | Heikki Kovalainen | Ex-wet: 1–39 | Wet: 40–67 | | | |
| 3 | Kimi Räikkönen | Wet: 1–3 | Ex-wet: 4–14 | Ex-wet: 15–40 | Ex-wet: 41–67 | |
| 4 | David Coulthard | Ex-wet: 1–39 | Ex-wet: 40–67 | | | |
| 5 | Giancarlo Fisichella | Ex-wet: 1–41 | Ex-wet: 42–67 | | | |
| 6 | Felipe Massa | Wet: 1–3 | Ex-wet: 4–14 | Ex-wet: 15–20 | Ex-wet: 21–58 | Ex-wet: 59–67 |
| 7 | Robert Kubica | Ex-wet: 1–36 | Ex-wet: 37–40 | Ex-wet: 41–67 | | |
| 8 | Adrian Sutil | Ex-wet: 1–44 | Ex-wet: 45–67 | | | |
| 9 | Vitantonio Liuzzi | Ex-wet: 1–10 | Ex-wet: 11–44 | Ex-wet: 45–67 | | |
| 10 | Rubens Barrichello | Ex-wet: 1–10 | Ex-wet: 11–44 | Ex-wet: 45–67 | | |
| 11 | Jenson Button | Ex-wet: 1–23 | Ex-wet: 24–66 | | | |
| 12 | Sakon Yamamoto | Ex-wet: 1–13 | Ex-wet: 14–57 | Ex-wet: 58–67 | | |
| 13 | Jarno Trulli | Ex-wet: 1–18 | Ex-wet: 19–60 | Ex-wet: 61–66 | | |
| 14 | Nick Heidfeld | Ex-wet: 1–35 | Ex-wet: 36–66 (DNF) | | | |
| 15 | Takuma Sato | Ex-wet: 1–18 | Ex-wet: 19–22 | Ex-wet: 23–43 | Ex-wet: 44–65 (DNF) | |
| | Ralf Schumacher | Ex-wet: 1–28 | Ex-wet: 29–48 | Ex-wet: 49–55 (DNF) | | |
| | Anthony Davidson | Ex-wet: 1–37 | Ex-wet: 38–54 (DNF) | | | |
| | Nico Rosberg | Ex-wet: 1–40 | Ex-wet: 41–48 | Ex-wet: 49 (DNF) | | |
| | Sebastian Vettel | Ex-wet: 1–32 | Ex-wet: 33–46 (DNF) | | | |
| | Mark Webber | Ex-wet: 1–36 | Ex-wet: 37–45 (DNF) | | | |
| | Fernando Alonso | Ex-wet: 1–27 | Ex-wet: 28–41 (DNF) | | | |
| | Alexander Wurz | Ex-wet: 1–16 | Ex-wet: 17–19 (DNF) | | | |

**9** KUBICA BMW-Sauber

**7** WEBBER Red Bull

**5** HEIDFELD BMW-Sauber

**3** RÄIKKÖNEN Ferrari

**1** HAMILTON McLaren

**10** FISICHELLA Renault

**8** VETTEL Toro Rosso

**6** BUTTON Honda

**4** MASSA Ferrari

**2** ALONSO McLaren

**RACE DISTANCE:** 67 laps, 189.777 miles/305.416 km

**RACE WEATHER:** Rain, track 19–20°C, air 15°C

| 54 | 55 | 56 | 57 | 58 | 59 | 60 | 61 | 62 | 63 | 64 | 65 | 66 | 67 | |
|---|---|---|---|---|---|---|---|---|---|---|---|---|---|---|
| 2 | 2 | 2 | 2 | 2 | 2 | 2 | 2 | 2 | 2 | 2 | 2 | 2 | 2 | 1 |
| 4 | 4 | 4 | 4 | 4 | 4 | 4 | 4 | 4 | 4 | 4 | 4 | 4 | 4 | 2 |
| 5 | 5 | 5 | 5 | 6 | 6 | 6 | 6 | 6 | 6 | 6 | 6 | 6 | 6 | 3 |
| 14 | 14 | 14 | 6 | 14 | 14 | 14 | 14 | 14 | 14 | 14 | 14 | 14 | 14 | 4 |
| 6 | 6 | 6 | 14 | 5 | 3 | 3 | 3 | 3 | 3 | 3 | 3 | 3 | 3 | 5 |
| 3 | 3 | 3 | 3 | 9 | 9 | 9 | 9 | 9 | 9 | 10 | 10 | 5 | | 6 |
| 9 | 9 | 9 | 9 | 8 | 10 | 10 | 10 | 10 | 10 | 5 | 5 | 10 | | 7 |
| 8 | 8 | 8 | 8 | 10 | 5 | 5 | 5 | 5 | 5 | 9 | 18 | 18 | | 8 |
| 10 | 10 | 10 | 10 | 10 | 5 | 8 | 20 | 20 | 20 | 18 | 18 | 20 | 20 | |
| 20 | 20 | 18 | 18 | 20 | 20 | 20 | 18 | 18 | 18 | 20 | 20 | 7 | 8 | |
| 18 | 18 | 20 | 20 | 18 | 18 | 18 | 7 | 7 | 7 | 7 | 7 | 8 | | |
| 21 | 21 | 21 | 7 | 7 | 7 | 7 | 8 | 8 | 8 | 8 | 8 | 21 | | |
| 7 | 7 | 7 | 12 | 12 | 12 | 12 | 12 | 21 | 21 | 21 | 21 | 21 | 12 | |
| 12 | 12 | 12 | 21 | 21 | 21 | 21 | 12 | 12 | 12 | 12 | 12 | 12 | | |
| 23 | 22 | 22 | 22 | 22 | 22 | 22 | 22 | 22 | 22 | 22 | 22 | | | |
| 22 | 11 | | | | | | | | | | | | | |
| 11 | | | | | | | | | | | | | | |

**20** Pit stop
**20** One lap or more behind leader
**20** Drive-through penalty
**20** Safety car deployed on laps shown

## FOR THE RECORD

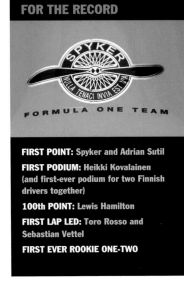

SPYKER — MULTA TENACI INVIA EST VIA — FORMULA ONE TEAM

**FIRST POINT:** Spyker and Adrian Sutil

**FIRST PODIUM:** Heikki Kovalainen (and first-ever podium for two Finnish drivers together)

**100th POINT:** Lewis Hamilton

**FIRST LAP LED:** Toro Rosso and Sebastian Vettel

**FIRST EVER ROOKIE ONE-TWO**

## POINTS

**CONSTRUCTORS**

| 1 | Ferrari | 170 |
|---|---|---|
| 2 | BMW Sauber | 92 |
| 3 | Renault | 51 |
| 4 | Williams | 28 |
| 5 | Red Bull | 23 |
| 6 | Toyota | 12 |
| 7 | Super Aguri | 4 |
| 8 | Honda | 2 |
| 9 | Spyker | 1 |

**DRIVERS**

| 1 | Lewis Hamilton | 107 |
|---|---|---|
| 2 | Fernando Alonso | 95 |
| 3 | Kimi Räikkönen | 90 |
| 4 | Felipe Massa | 80 |
| 5 | Nick Heidfeld | 56 |
| 6 | Robert Kubica | 35 |
| 7 | Heikki Kovalainen | 30 |
| 8 | Giancarlo Fisichella | 21 |
| 9 | Nico Rosberg | 15 |
| 10 | David Coulthard | 13 |
| 11 | Alexander Wurz | 13 |
| 12 | Mark Webber | 10 |
| 13 | Jarno Trulli | 7 |
| 14 | Ralf Schumacher | 5 |
| 15 | Takuma Sato | 4 |
| 16 | Jenson Button | 2 |
| 17 | Sebastian Vettel | 1 |
| 18 | Adrian Sutil | 1 |

Photographs: Peter J Fox www.crash.net

**Main:** Disaster for Lewis Hamilton. The big screen gives Hamilton's view of his calamitous situation stuck in the gravel on the pit lane entry.

**Inset:** Victory for Kimi Räikkönen keeps his slim championship hopes alive.
Photographs: Peter J Fox/www.crash.net

FIA F1 WORLD CHAMPIONSHIP/ROUND 16
# CHINESE GP
## SHANGHAI

## SHANGHAI QUALIFYING

Right: Ralf Schumacher (centre) and his manager Hans Mahr (left) locked in conference with Toyota's John Howett over the possibility of extending the driver's contract. But no deal would be reached.
Photograph: Peter J Fox/www.crash.net

Opposite: Calmness pervades the circuit as the cars stand in *parc fermé* after qualifying.
Photograph: Bernard Asset

Below: Colin Kolles (left), Adrian Sutil and Michiel Mol toast Spyker's first ever point.
Photograph: Peter J Fox/www.crash.net

## DIARY

After the Chinese GP, Alex Wurz announces his immediate retirement from active race driving.

Shortly afterwards, Williams confirms that its Friday test driver Kazuki Nakajima, the son of former Team Lotus and Tyrrell F1 racer Satoru, will make his F1 début for the team in the Brazilian GP at Interlagos.

David Richards admits that, because the company's self-imposed date (1 October) has passed without anything being firmed up regarding its 2008 F1 entry, Prodrive is considering its options.

Lewis Hamilton was delighted with his sixth pole position of the season after an inch-perfect lap, for he (and others) had been uncertain which Bridgestone tyre offered the best options for Q3. In the end he gambled and went with the softer tyre, on which others had been struggling. And this time he gave himself a decent cushion over his rivals by being the first to pit before his final run. He made best use of that to lap in 1m 35.908s.

'On my first visit here I kept chopping away at the time and I'm thrilled to get pole,' Hamilton said. 'I went into qualifying knowing I didn't have the pace of Fernando [Alonso], but I knew if I just worked at it and didn't put in too much effort I might be able to do it and I did, so I'm very happy.'

It seemed highly likely that he was running lighter than Fernando Alonso, who was only fourth on 1m 36.576s. And so it proved: Alonso would run three laps longer the next day. The plan was that running light would stand him in good stead if, as predicted, Typhoon Korsa, which was sweeping through the region, brought rain on the morrow. As he knew from Fuji, it's better to be the one making the spray than the one imbibing it.

Both Ferrari drivers were quite happy with their cars, in second and third places on the grid. The F2007 was always stronger in the race than in qualifying and with laps of 1m 36.044s and 1m 36.221s respectively, Kimi Räikkönen (who had a hydraulic failure in the morning) and Felipe Massa didn't have much to complain about, though Massa admitted that losing the back end of his car hurt his lap time.

Red Bull's recent upswing in performance continued as David Coulthard built on his Fuji performance with fifth place (1m 37.619s) and Mark Webber was seventh (1m 38.153s). Coulthard was, frankly, surprised to be that quick and to take his best grid position in a while and Webber felt that the team had a strong chance of catching Williams in the fight for fourth place in the constructors' championship.

Ralf Schumacher was sixth for Toyota on 1m 38.013s but team-mate Jarno Trulli was only 13th on 1m 36.959s. While Schumacher found grip and balance in his TF107, Trulli did not and was so fed up with his car's behaviour that he considered switching to the spare car and starting from the pit lane.

There was an air of despondency at BMW Sauber because Nick Heidfeld was only eighth (1m 38.455s) and Robert Kubica ninth (1m 38.472s). Both were on high fuel loads, but the numerous hydraulic failures that had struck down Heidfeld in practice were weighing things down. And worse was to come, it transpired. Heidfeld was happy with his car in Q2 when he was sixth but said the balance deteriorated with the race fuel load in Q3. Kubica echoed this.

Jenson Button was another man to be surprised by the performance of his car after qualifying his unloved Honda RA107 tenth on 1m 39.285s. He was happy about that and spoke of the team's 'over-achieving'. Rubens Barrichello was the first to lose out in Q1, though, taking 17th with 1m 37.251s, and understandably did not share his team-mate's pleasure.

Eleventh and 12th places on the grid were a major boost for Toro Rosso, courtesy of Tonio Liuzzi (1m 36.862s) and Sebastian Vettel (1m 36.891s). Liuzzi was bumped at the end of Q2 only by Jenson Button's final lap and blamed some understeer that took the edge off his STR02 on his last run. Vettel said he was surprised by his car's pace. He was also surprised when, having had his ten-place grid penalty from Fuji rescinded, he got a five-place penalty for impeding Heikki Kovalainen on his best lap and dropped from 12th to 17th.

Getting the tyres to work was the key to fast times at Shanghai and neither Renault nor Williams managed the trick. The former struggled all through practice and ended qualifying with Kovalainen 14th on 1m 36.991s and Giancarlo Fisichella 18th on 1m 37.290s. Kovalainen admitted that he slid off the road pushing too hard in Turn 13 on his final run and then again trying to make up for that in Turn 16, while Fisi grained his set of soft tyres and then went off, also in Turn 16.

Down at Williams there was despair as, no matter what it tried with tyre pressures and weight distribution, the FW29s could generate the right temperatures but no grip on the soft tyre. Nico Rosberg was 16th on 1m 37.483s and Alex Wurz 19th on 1m 37.456s.

Once again Anthony Davidson was Super Aguri's lead qualifier, in 15th place with 1m 37.247s. He was happy with his car's balance and felt that the grip improved as more rubber went down. Takuma Sato, however, was so unhappy with his SA07 in the morning that he asked his engineers for a radical change of set-up for qualifying. The result was the same: no grip and only 20th place on the grid with 1m 38.218s. At the back were the Spykers of Adrian Sutil (1m 38.668s) and Sakon Yamamoto (1m 39.336s).

## A PRE-RACE NIGHTMARE FOR HAMILTON

Photograph: Bernard Asset

On his arrival in China, Lewis Hamilton (left, with team boss Ron Dennis) found himself embroiled in controversy when the row about the safety car incident from Fuji flared up again. Toro Rosso's Franz Tost had seen an amateur video film posted on the YouTube website that, he claimed, showed that Hamilton's driving caused the crash between his driver Sebastian Vettel and Red Bull's Mark Webber. Webber and Vettel were critical of Hamilton in Thursday's press conference.

The row dragged into Friday, with much spin doctoring from Paris leading the gullible to believe that Hamilton might be docked points. That seemed unlikely given that Vettel, who had been held liable by the stewards in Fuji, got only a ten-place grid penalty.

Before the stewards finally decided on Friday to take no further action Hamilton told Radio 5 Live, 'It's just a shame for the sport and if this is the way it's going to keep going then it's probably not somewhere I really want to be. Formula 1 is supposed to be about hard competition, fair, and that's what I've tried to do this year – just be fair.'

The FIA expressed surprise that the new controversy had attracted such worldwide interest amid suggestions that the whole thing had carefully been leaked by its spin doctors.

In the end, Hamilton took his sixth pole of the season, but it was not easy.

'This weekend has been a bit of a rollercoaster and quite an emotional trip,' he admitted. 'After last weekend was so great in Fuji we came here nice and early on Thursday and found out they were investigating me from that race. I thought immediately, "I'm gonna get a penalty for sure, otherwise why would they investigate?" but thankfully with the team's support I got through. It wasn't easy yesterday, but I had to forget about the possibility that I might get some points taken away. But it was a good decision by the FIA last night.'

Many paddock observers believed that the decision had as much to do with the FIA's surprise at the anger the whole unnecessary incident had generated as it did with the common sense of the stewards.

LEWIS Hamilton made his first real mistake of the season in China – and it cost him dear. He had just lost the lead of the race to eventual winner Kimi Räikkönen as he struggled to keep going on tyres that were worn to the canvas and just as he made the haven of the pits the error came. His McLaren slid wide onto the gravel bed on the outside of the tight left-hand entry and became beached.

As Ferrari sped home to a superb victory, its 200th, Hamilton was forced to abandon his car and watch his 12-point title lead eroded as Fernando Alonso brought his McLaren home second ahead of Felipe Massa in the second red car.

It could scarcely have been a worse ending for the day on which he could have clinched the title.

Fifty-four minutes earlier it had all looked good. Hamilton sped confidently into the lead as the race began on a wet and slippery track, opening up a 10s lead over Räikkönen by the time he made his first scheduled pit stop on lap 15. That handed Räikkönen the lead, which he maintained until his own stop on lap 19. Hamilton, pushing hard, retook the initiative as the Ferrari driver rejoined. Farther back, Massa was locked in battle with Alonso, though neither appeared at that stage to be in a position to challenge Hamilton and Räikkönen.

All four front runners kept their original intermediate Bridgestone wet-weather tyres through their stops.

It rained a little more around the 26-lap mark and suddenly Räikkönen was eating into Hamilton's lead as the latter's rear tyres were finished. From 4.6s on lap 25 the gap was down to 3.1s on lap 26 and a mere 0.8s by lap 27. The two drivers then spent much of the 28th side by side but after Hamilton had fended off one move he slid wide and the Ferrari driver pounced. Immediately Räikkönen opened up a significant advantage as the scale of Hamilton's tyre-wear problem became apparent. The previous day he had spoken of the Ferrari's characteristic of being kinder to its tyres in a race and here that was proving crucial.

McLaren's problem was the weather. 'We believed that it was a lower risk to leave Lewis on those tyres until we had more information on a new threat of rain,' explained managing director Martin Whitmarsh. 'We didn't want to put him on to dry tyres too early and risk his going off if it rained again. The reality is that we made the decision a lap too late. Being Lewis, I'm sure he will blame himself, but it was a mistake by the team. We said for him to stay out.'

Bridgestone had been calling for the team to bring Hamilton in sooner, too, but if he could have carried on to his scheduled stop, he might still have had a chance. It was crystal clear he was struggling for grip as Alonso had closed right onto his tail as he finally swept into the pits on lap 31. And that was when he slid into the gravel and his race came to its ignominious end.

'The tyres were finished,' he said. 'It was like driving on ice.'

Later, about to leave the circuit before the race was even over, he shook the hand of every McLaren team member in the garage. And he took it on the chin. 'It's my first mistake all year and to do it on the way into the pits is not something I usually do,' he said. 'You cannot go through life without making mistakes.'

His dramatic demise had suddenly thrown Räikkönen and Alonso the lifelines their own championship aspirations so desperately needed. Now it was a matter of whether Räikkönen could maximise his or whether Alonso could his by catching and passing the Ferrari. The weather stabilised shortly after Hamilton's retirement, however, and stalemate set in as the Ferrari reeled off the remaining laps and the McLaren chased it home. Farther back, Massa set a string of fastest laps in his pursuit of Alonso, but without getting in a position to challenge him.

'I am very happy!' Räikkönen smiled. 'It is a really great result for me and the whole team. We needed this win. At the start of the race, I had a lot of understeer but then the situation improved. I was one of the last to switch to dry tyres but this was a help because after a little while the rain began to fall again. Even after the second stop I had a bit of

understeer, but, as before, the situation improved in the final stages. I knew Alonso was very quick but I was in full control of the situation. Last week, in Fuji, we were unlucky but today things went right for us. We have had yet another example that in this sport anything can happen.'

Alonso seemed happy, too, for once, though clearly victory would have pushed him even closer to Hamilton. 'Today was a very good result for me,' he said. 'It was difficult towards the end on the wet Bridgestone tyres because they were practically slick, but we stayed out as long as possible to get through the final shower, which was the right decision because I was able to come out ahead of Felipe on my final stop. Although this result is a boost to my chances in the championship, it is still not going to be easy. However, I will not be giving up until the chequered flag in two weeks' time.'

Massa had hoped to be fighting for the win, 'but the race was affected by the changing weather conditions. At the moment I switched to dry tyres, the timing was not ideal. The rain came back immediately and it was really difficult to stay on the track. In any case, in these instances, it can pay off to take risks: sometimes it works out and sometimes not. After a few difficulties with graining, the situation improved to the extent that, in the final part of the race, I was going very well.'

Some way behind them, fourth place fell to a delighted Sebastian Vettel, who more than made up for his Fuji gaffe. He was fortunate that his single-stop strategy worked better than team-mate Tonio Liuzzi's two-stopper, because he did not lose out so much when the weather changed mid-race.

Nevertheless, his was a great performance.

'P4! A fantastic race,' he said happily. 'In the beginning it was quite difficult, starting in the mid-field. For a couple of metres the visibility was okay and then you got all the spray. After the start, I used my momentum to go around the outside of several cars. Even though it was really slippery I took the risk. I kept pushing as hard as I could. After I passed [Heikki] Kovalainen I had a clear track ahead of me and was able to push harder. Just as I changed to dry tyres the rain came, but fortunately it went away quickly. I fought with Jenson [Button] but when we realised he was on a two-stopper, I didn't worry.'

Liuzzi was the star of the early going, climbing past Mark Webber on lap one and Nick Heidfeld on lap four. He was fifth when he made his first pit stop on lap 19 but thereafter, like Massa, he got caught out by the rain and began to lose valuable ground. His initial set of wets grained at the rear and his replacement dries grained at the front, but he was happy to finish a good sixth, especially because he fended off Heidfeld's BMW-Sauber for the last 17 laps.

'This was a great race from start to finish with everything going perfectly,' he said. 'I think Sebastian's one-stop strategy was better but that does not matter now. It is fantastic for the team that we both scored points. I made no mistakes and had some great fights with Williams, Renault and BMW. I don't think we could have done more than this. I am really happy for the team, who really deserve these points. Many times this year we have shown that we were capable of scoring, but somehow we never did. Now everyone can be happy.' The result

**Above: Kimi Räikkönen's final pit stop – Ferrari leaves him on the same set of used Bridgestones.**
Photograph: Jad Sherif/WRi2

**Centre: Felipe Massa had to settle for third place.**

**Left: Fernando Alonso played himself back into championship contention after finishing second.**
Photographs: Peter J Fox/www.crash.net

catapulted Toro Rosso from last place to seventh in the constructors' championship.

Like Massa, Jenson Button set a string of fastest laps during a fighting race, which netted him fifth place for Honda between the Toro Rossos.

'A fantastic race today and I'm very happy to come away with four points and our best result of the season,' he said. 'I struggled at the start because the car was not working well in the wet conditions and I had no grip, so I ended up slipping back. When the track dried out we decided to go for the dry option tyre and a light fuel load.'

Team-mate Rubens Barrichello's race was much less convincing. He hit Anthony Davidson in Turn One on the second lap, spinning them both, and finished only 15th.

China was one of those 'what if' races for BMW Sauber. Robert Kubica in particular was headed for a strong result. He was leading on the 33rd lap when his F1.07 suffered another hydraulic failure, robbing the team of a likely third place, possibly more because he would not have needed to refuel.

'I found myself with no power steering and no gears,' he said glumly. 'It was looking pretty good up to then.'

Heidfeld clung on to finish seventh right behind Liuzzi, but he wasn't happy either. 'I am very disappointed because fourth was possible for us today,' he said. 'In hindsight it was a mistake to take a second set of wets after 28 laps. At this time my first set was completely finished and I lost about 12 seconds a lap. On top of that it looked like we would have more rain. But after

32 laps I had to pit again for dry tyres. The race started well – I managed to gain two positions at the start and it was almost three. On lap four I made a mistake under braking before the hairpin and Liuzzi passed me. Later in the race we met again but I couldn't overtake him. I was very close in the corners but couldn't catch him on the straights.'

David Coulthard put Red Bull in the points again with eighth place, but that counted as a disappointment because he'd started fifth. It didn't help that the team's Toro Rosso stablemates were ahead of him. Coulthard was another one who was unlucky with the timing of his stops: he changed to dries just before it rained again. At the end he held off a charging Heikki Kovalainen for the last point, with Mark Webber in tenth leading home a challenging Giancarlo Fisichella. Like Coulthard, Webber rued going back to the pits for wet tyres as the rain ended.

It was Renault's first failure to score since Hungary 2006. Kovalainen reported lack of grip early on and Fisichella's second pit stop robbed him of a better finish. By the end, however, the R27s were flying and Kovalainen firmly believed they had the pace to finish fourth with better fortune.

'The start of the race was a disaster for me,' he said. 'I made a good start and climbed three positions but the understeer was just really bad, with low grip. Four cars passed me and I lost too much time. We changed to dry tyres at exactly the right time and after that the car was pretty good. In the middle of the race, I lost time in a very strange way: Kimi had just lapped me but he was on old wet tyres, while my dry tyres were new. I

couldn't pass off-line because it was wet and I didn't want to have an accident with a front-runner, so I lost about seven or eight seconds until I could overtake him. After that, I pushed as hard as possible but I couldn't get past David at the end: I was quicker, but not by enough.'

Williams' awful weekend continued in the race. Nico Rosberg made an indifferent start, fought back hard, then picked up a puncture on lap 29 as he got pincered by the Renaults in a dramatic double overtaking move going into Turn One. Rosberg went off with Kovalainen. That ended his hope of points. Team-mate Alex Wurz was running well in the wet, set a fastest lap when he was the first to change to dries, but struggled towards the end of the race as the track dried out. Afterwards, he announced his retirement.

Toyota's day began badly. Sixth-fastest qualifier Ralf Schumacher spun in the first corner, staged a great comeback as he for once looked like the man who won races for Williams in 2001 and got back up to 13th after a great move around the outside of Kovalainen in Turn One. But then, on lap 25, he pulled alongside Liuzzi and stupidly tried to turn in with the Toro Rosso still beside him. He bounced off, did a great job to hold the resultant slide and then spun foolishly on the kerb. Later he went off in Turn 16 and failed to finish. Jarno Trulli finished a race in which he barely featured but could do no better than 13th.

*David Tremayne*

**Above: Sebastian Vettel marked himself out as a real talent with a great run to fourth for the Toro Rosso squad.**
Photograph: Peter J Fox/www.crash.net

**Centre left: The carcass of Lewis Hamilton's rear tyre can be clearly seen.**

**Centre: Out of the race, Lewis makes a brief visit to the pit wall before leaving.**
Photographs: Jad Sherif/WRi2

**Far left: Tonio Liuzzi brought his Toro Rosso into the points with sixth place.**
Photograph: Peter J Fox/www.crash.net

**Left: Rising stars Liuzzi (left) and Vettel congratulate each other on finishing in the points.**
Photograph: Lukas Gorys/www.crash.net

FIA F1 WORLD CHAMPIONSHIP · ROUND 16

# SINOPEC
# CHINESE GRAND PRIX

## FUJI 5–7 OCTOBER 2007

Photograph: Peter J Fox/www.crash.net

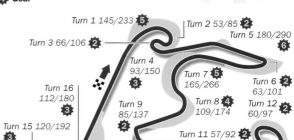

## SHANGHAI INTERNATIONAL CIRCUIT

**Circuit: 3.387 miles / 5.451 km**

*116/187* **mph/kmh**

**4** Gear

Turn 1 145/233 **5**
Turn 2 53/85 **2**
Turn 5 180/290 **6**
Turn 3 66/106 **2**
Turn 4 93/150 **4**
Turn 7 165/266 **5**
Turn 6 63/101 **4**
Turn 16 112/180 **3**
Turn 9 85/137 **2**
Turn 8 109/174 **4**
Turn 12 60/97 **2**
Turn 15 120/192 **3**
Turn 11 57/92 **2**
Turn 10 100/161 **3**
Turn 14 55/89 **2**
Turn 13 125/201 **4**

## RACE RESULTS

| Pos. | Driver | Nat. | No. | Entrant | Car/Engine | Tyres | Laps | Time/Retirement | Speed (mph/km/h) | Gap to leader | Fastest race lap | |
|---|---|---|---|---|---|---|---|---|---|---|---|---|
| 1 | Kimi Räikkönen | FIN | 6 | Scuderia Ferrari Marlboro | Ferrari F2007-056 V8 | B | 56 | 1h 37m 58.395s | 116.088/186.826 | | 1m 38.285s | 52 |
| 2 | Fernando Alonso | E | 1 | Vodafone McLaren Mercedes | McLaren MP4-22-Mercedes FO 108T V8 | B | 56 | 1h 38m 8.201s | 115.894/186.514 | + 9.806s | 1m 37.991s | 54 |
| 3 | Felipe Massa | BR | 5 | Scuderia Ferrari Marlboro | Ferrari F2007-056 V8 | B | 56 | 1h 38m 11.286s | 115.834/186.417 | + 12.891s | 1m 37.454s | 56 |
| 4 | Sebastian Vettel | D | 19 | Scuderia Toro Rosso | Toro Rosso STR02-Ferrari 056H V8 | B | 56 | 1h 38m 51.904s | 115.041/185.140 | + 53.509s | 1m 39.890s | 52 |
| 5 | Jenson Button | GB | 7 | Honda Racing F1 Team | Honda RA107-RA807E V8 | B | 56 | 1h 39m 7.061s | 114.748/184.668 | + 1m 8.666s | 1m 38.913s | 39 |
| 6 | Vitantonio Liuzzi | I | 18 | Scuderia Toro Rosso | Toro Rosso STR02-Ferrari 056H V8 | B | 56 | 1h 39m 12.068s | 114.651/184.513 | + 1m 13.673s | 1m 39.654s | 53 |
| 7 | Nick Heidfeld | D | 9 | BMW Sauber F1 Team | BMW Sauber F1.07-BMW P86/7 V8 | B | 56 | 1h 39m 12.619s | 114.641/184.496 | + 1m 14.224s | 1m 39.325s | 55 |
| 8 | David Coulthard | GB | 14 | Red Bull Racing | Red Bull RB3-Renault RS27 V8 | B | 56 | 1h 39m 19.145s | 114.515/184.294 | + 1m 20.750s | 1m 39.640s | 55 |
| 9 | Heikki Kovalainen | FIN | 4 | ING Renault F1 Team | Renault R27-RS27 V8 | B | 56 | 1h 39m 19.581s | 114.507/184.281 | + 1m 21.186s | 1m 39.331s | 52 |
| 10 | Mark Webber | AUS | 15 | Red Bull Racing | Red Bull RB3-Renault RS27 V8 | B | 56 | 1h 39m 23.080s | 114.439/184.172 | + 1m 24.685s | 1m 39.371s | 55 |
| 11 | Giancarlo Fisichella | I | 3 | ING Renault F1 Team | Renault R27-RS27 V8 | B | 56 | 1h 39m 25.078s | 114.402/184.111 | + 1m 26.683s | 1m 38.900s | 39 |
| 12 | Alexander Wurz | A | 17 | AT&T Williams | Williams FW29-Toyota RVX-07 V8 | B | 55 | | | + 1 lap | 1m 39.743s | 54 |
| 13 | Jarno Trulli | I | 12 | Panasonic Toyota Racing | Toyota TF107-RVX-07 V8 | B | 55 | | | + 1 lap | 1m 39.911s | 55 |
| 14 | Takuma Sato | J | 22 | Super Aguri F1 Team | Super Aguri SA07-Honda RA807E V8 | B | 55 | | | + 1 lap | 1m 40.126s | 54 |
| 15 | Rubens Barrichello | BR | 8 | Honda Racing F1 Team | Honda RA107-RA807E V8 | B | 55 | | | + 1 lap | 1m 40.516s | 55 |
| 16 | Nico Rosberg | D | 16 | AT&T Williams | Williams FW29-Toyota RVX-07 V8 | B | 54 | | | + 2 laps | 1m 39.233s | 54 |
| 17 | Sakon Yamamoto | J | 21 | Etihad Aldar Spyker F1 Team | Spyker F8-VII-Ferrari 056H V8 | B | 53 | | | + 3 laps | 1m 40.764s | 52 |
| | Robert Kubica | POL | 10 | BMW Sauber F1 Team | BMW Sauber F1.07-BMW P86/7 V8 | B | 33 | Hydraulics | | | 1m 40.926s | 32 |
| | Lewis Hamilton | GB | 2 | Vodafone McLaren Mercedes | McLaren MP4-22-Mercedes FO 108T V8 | B | 30 | Spin | | | 1m 43.131s | 22 |
| | Ralf Schumacher | D | 11 | Panasonic Toyota Racing | Toyota TF107-RVX-07 V8 | B | 25 | Spin | | | 1m 44.062s | 25 |
| | Adrian Sutil | D | 20 | Etihad Aldar Spyker F1 Team | Spyker F8-VII-Ferrari 056H V8 | B | 24 | Accident | | | 1m 47.063s | 22 |
| | Anthony Davidson | GB | 23 | Super Aguri F1 Team | Super Aguri SA07-Honda RA807E V8 | B | 11 | Accident/brakes | | | 1m 51.765s | 9 |

All results and data © FOM 2007

Fastest race lap: Felipe Massa on lap 56, 1m 37.454s, 125.121 mph/201.362 km/h.

Lap record: Michael Schumacher (Ferrari F2004 V10), 1m 32.238s, 132.196 mph/212.749 km/h (2004).

**21** SUTIL Spyker

**19** WURZ Williams

**17** VETTEL Toro Rosso
Five-place penalty

**15** ROSBERG Williams

**13** KOVALAINEN Renault

**11** LIUZZI Toro Rosso

**22** YAMAMOTO Spyker

**20** SATO Super Aguri

**18** FISICHELLA Renault

**16** BARRICHELLO Honda

**14** DAVIDSON Super Aguri

**12** TRULLI Toyota

| Grid order | 1 | 2 | 3 | 4 | 5 | 6 | 7 | 8 | 9 | 10 | 11 | 12 | 13 | 14 | 15 | 16 | 17 | 18 | 19 | 20 | 21 | 22 | 23 | 24 | 25 | 26 | 27 | 28 | 29 | 30 | 31 | 32 | 33 | 34 | 35 | 36 | 37 | 38 | 39 | 40 | 41 | 42 | 43 |
|---|---|---|---|---|---|---|---|---|---|---|---|---|---|---|---|---|---|---|---|---|---|---|---|---|---|---|---|---|---|---|---|---|---|---|---|---|---|---|---|---|---|---|---|
| 2 HAMILTON | 2 | 2 | 2 | 2 | 2 | 2 | 2 | 2 | 2 | 2 | 2 | 2 | 2 | 2 | 2 | 6 | 6 | 6 | 6 | 2 | 2 | 2 | 2 | 2 | 2 | 2 | 2 | 2 | 2 | 6 | 6 | 6 | 10 | 6 | 6 | 6 | 6 | 6 | 6 | 6 | 6 | 6 | 6 |
| 6 RÄIKKÖNEN | 6 | 6 | 6 | 6 | 6 | 6 | 6 | 6 | 6 | 6 | 6 | 6 | 6 | 6 | 6 | 5 | 1 | 2 | 6 | 6 | 6 | 6 | 6 | 6 | 6 | 6 | 2 | 2 | 1 | 1 | 1 | 1 | 1 | 1 | 1 | 1 | 1 | 1 | 1 | 1 | 1 | 1 | 1 |
| 5 MASSA | 5 | 5 | 5 | 5 | 5 | 5 | 5 | 5 | 5 | 5 | 5 | 5 | 5 | 5 | 5 | 1 | 5 | 2 | 14 | 5 | 5 | 5 | 5 | 5 | 1 | 10 | 10 | 1 | 5 | 5 | 5 | 5 | 5 | 5 | 5 | 5 | 5 | 5 | 5 | 5 | 5 | 5 | 5 |
| 1 ALONSO | 1 | 1 | 1 | 1 | 1 | 1 | 1 | 1 | 1 | 1 | 1 | 1 | 1 | 1 | 1 | 2 | 2 | 14 | 5 | 1 | 1 | 1 | 1 | 1 | 9 | 9 | 9 | 18 | 18 | 18 | 5 | 19 | 7 | 7 | 7 | 7 | 7 | 7 | 7 | 19 | | |
| 14 COULTHARD | 14 | 14 | 14 | 14 | 14 | 14 | 14 | 14 | 14 | 14 | 14 | 14 | 14 | 14 | 14 | 18 | 1 | 9 | 9 | 9 | 9 | 9 | 5 | 18 | 18 | 9 | 9 | 9 | 9 | 19 | 7 | 19 | 19 | 19 | 19 | 19 | 19 | 19 | 3 | | | |
| 11 SCHUMACHER | 9 | 9 | 9 | 18 | 18 | 18 | 18 | 18 | 18 | 18 | 18 | 18 | 18 | 18 | 18 | 5 | 18 | 10 | 10 | 10 | 10 | 10 | 10 | 19 | 5 | 10 | 10 | 10 | 5 | 19 | 7 | 18 | 18 | 18 | 3 | 3 | 3 | 3 | 7 | | | | |
| 15 WEBBER | 18 | 18 | 18 | 9 | 9 | 9 | 9 | 9 | 9 | 9 | 9 | 9 | 9 | 9 | 9 | 9 | 15 | 15 | 19 | 19 | 18 | 10 | 5 | 19 | 7 | 18 | 17 | 17 | 17 | 3 | 18 | 18 | 18 | 18 | 18 | | | | | | | |
| 9 HEIDFELD | 15 | 15 | 15 | 15 | 10 | 10 | 10 | 10 | 10 | 15 | 15 | 15 | 15 | 15 | 15 | 19 | 19 | 19 | 14 | 14 | 14 | 15 | 15 | 15 | 15 | 7 | 18 | 17 | 3 | 3 | 17 | 9 | 9 | 9 | 9 | 9 | | | | | | |
| 10 KUBICA | 10 | 10 | 10 | 10 | 15 | 15 | 15 | 15 | 15 | 10 | 10 | 10 | 10 | 10 | 14 | 14 | 14 | 14 | 12 | 12 | 18 | 19 | 19 | 7 | 17 | 9 | 9 | 14 | 14 | 14 | 14 | 14 | | | | | | | | | | |
| 7 BUTTON | 4 | 4 | 4 | 4 | 4 | 19 | 19 | 19 | 19 | 19 | 19 | 19 | 19 | 19 | 19 | 12 | 12 | 12 | 18 | 12 | 12 | 12 | 10 | 17 | 7 | 7 | 17 | 3 | 9 | 14 | 14 | 9 | 14 | 15 | 15 | 15 | 15 | | | | | | |
| 18 LIUZZI | 7 | 19 | 19 | 19 | 19 | 4 | 12 | 12 | 12 | 12 | 12 | 12 | 12 | 12 | 4 | 22 | 4 | 18 | 18 | 18 | 16 | 16 | 12 | 7 | 7 | 17 | 3 | 14 | 15 | 15 | 15 | 4 | 4 | 4 | 4 | | | | | | | |
| 12 TRULLI | 19 | 12 | 12 | 12 | 12 | 12 | 4 | 4 | 4 | 4 | 4 | 4 | 4 | 4 | 12 | 11 | 11 | 11 | 11 | 11 | 11 | 3 | 17 | 14 | 14 | 3 | 14 | 15 | 4 | 4 | 17 | 17 | 17 | 17 | 17 | | | | | | | |
| 4 KOVALAINEN | 12 | 7 | 7 | 7 | 7 | 7 | 7 | 7 | 7 | 7 | 7 | 7 | 7 | 7 | 11 | 4 | 4 | 11 | 11 | 11 | 11 | 16 | 16 | 4 | 3 | 14 | 14 | 4 | 12 | 12 | 12 | 12 | 12 | 12 | 12 | | | | | | | |
| 23 DAVIDSON | 23 | 22 | 22 | 22 | 22 | 22 | 16 | 16 | 16 | 16 | 16 | 16 | 16 | 16 | 7 | 7 | 11 | 4 | 4 | 4 | 4 | 7 | 4 | 3 | 7 | 16 | 12 | 12 | 12 | 12 | 22 | 22 | 22 | 22 | | | | | | | | |
| 16 ROSBERG | 8 | 17 | 17 | 17 | 16 | 16 | 17 | 17 | 17 | 11 | 11 | 11 | 11 | 11 | 7 | 7 | 7 | 7 | 3 | 22 | 3 | 4 | 12 | 22 | 22 | 22 | 8 | 8 | 8 | 8 | 8 | 8 | 8 | | | | | | | | | |
| 8 BARRICHELLO | 22 | 3 | 3 | 16 | 17 | 17 | 11 | 11 | 11 | 17 | 17 | 17 | 17 | 17 | 17 | 17 | 17 | 4 | 22 | 22 | 8 | 8 | 8 | 16 | 16 | 16 | 16 | 16 | 16 | 16 | | | | | | | | | | | | |
| 19 VETTEL | 17 | 16 | 16 | 3 | 3 | 11 | 11 | 3 | 3 | 3 | 3 | 3 | 3 | 3 | 17 | 11 | 22 | 7 | 8 | 22 | 8 | 16 | 16 | 16 | 21 | 21 | 21 | 21 | 21 | 21 | | | | | | | | | | | | |
| 3 FISICHELLA | 3 | 20 | 11 | 11 | 11 | 3 | 3 | 17 | 4 | 22 | 8 | 16 | 16 | 16 | 21 | 21 | | | | | | | | | | | | | | | | | | | | | | | | | | |
| 17 WURZ | 16 | 21 | 23 | 8 | 8 | 22 | 22 | 22 | 22 | 22 | 17 | 11 | 11 | 21 | 21 | 21 | | | | | | | | | | | | | | | | | | | | | | | | | | |
| 22 SATO | 20 | 11 | 8 | 23 | 23 | 23 | 23 | 23 | 20 | 20 | 20 | 20 | 20 | 20 | 21 | | | | | | | | | | | | | | | | | | | | | | | | | | | |
| 20 SUTIL | 21 | 23 | 20 | 20 | 21 | 20 | 20 | 20 | 21 | 21 | 21 | 21 | 21 | | | | | | | | | | | | | | | | | | | | | | | | | | | | | |
| 21 YAMAMOTO | 11 | 8 | 21 | 21 | 20 | 20 | 21 | 21 | 21 | 21 | | | | | | | | | | | | | | | | | | | | | | | | | | | | | | | | |

## PRACTICE 1 (FRIDAY)

Cloudy/sunny (track 32–35ºC, air 27–29ºC)

| Pos. | Driver | Laps | Time |
|---|---|---|---|
| 1 | Kimi Räikkönen | 24 | 1m 37.024s |
| 2 | Fernando Alonso | 18 | 1m 37.108s |
| 3 | Felipe Massa | 21 | 1m 37.128s |
| 4 | Lewis Hamilton | 20 | 1m 37.210s |
| 5 | Nico Rosberg | 23 | 1m 37.707s |
| 6 | Robert Kubica | 23 | 1m 38.055s |
| 7 | Jarno Trulli | 30 | 1m 38.208s |
| 8 | Giancarlo Fisichella | 16 | 1m 38.217s |
| 9 | Kazuki Nakajima | 30 | 1m 38.270s |
| 10 | Nick Heidfeld | 13 | 1m 38.445s |
| 11 | Heikki Kovalainen | 17 | 1m 38.551s |
| 12 | Ralf Schumacher | 23 | 1m 38.661s |
| 13 | David Coulthard | 25 | 1m 38.700s |
| 14 | Jenson Button | 18 | 1m 38.942s |
| 15 | Rubens Barrichello | 22 | 1m 38.945s |
| 16 | Takuma Sato | 23 | 1m 39.238s |
| 17 | Vitantonio Liuzzi | 22 | 1m 39.497s |
| 18 | Mark Webber | 23 | 1m 39.535s |
| 19 | Anthony Davidson | 20 | 1m 39.539s |
| 20 | Sebastian Vettel | 24 | 1m 39.898s |
| 21 | Sakon Yamamoto | 27 | 1m 40.126s |
| 22 | Adrian Sutil | 26 | 1m 40.149s |

## PRACTICE 2 (FRIDAY)

Cloudy (track 38–39ºC, air 28–29ºC)

| Pos. | Driver | Laps | Time |
|---|---|---|---|
| 1 | Kimi Räikkönen | 31 | 1m 36.607s |
| 2 | Fernando Alonso | 28 | 1m 36.613s |
| 3 | Felipe Massa | 29 | 1m 36.630s |
| 4 | Lewis Hamilton | 33 | 1m 36.876s |
| 5 | Jarno Trulli | 36 | 1m 37.151s |
| 6 | Mark Webber | 34 | 1m 37.450s |
| 7 | Ralf Schumacher | 32 | 1m 37.524s |
| 8 | David Coulthard | 27 | 1m 37.617s |
| 9 | Nico Rosberg | 36 | 1m 37.646s |
| 10 | Giancarlo Fisichella | 32 | 1m 37.970s |
| 11 | Heikki Kovalainen | 21 | 1m 38.062s |
| 12 | Jenson Button | 41 | 1m 38.205s |
| 13 | Rubens Barrichello | 40 | 1m 38.304s |
| 14 | Robert Kubica | 39 | 1m 38.379s |
| 15 | Nick Heidfeld | 16 | 1m 38.388s |
| 16 | Alexander Wurz | 32 | 1m 38.531s |
| 17 | Anthony Davidson | 38 | 1m 38.975s |
| 18 | Vitantonio Liuzzi | 36 | 1m 39.065s |
| 19 | Adrian Sutil | 37 | 1m 39.224s |
| 20 | Takuma Sato | 37 | 1m 39.360s |
| 21 | Sebastian Vettel | 34 | 1m 39.404s |
| 22 | Sakon Yamamoto | 38 | 1m 40.051s |

## QUALIFYING (SATURDAY)

Cloudy (track 35–37ºC, air 28–29ºC)

| Pos. | Driver | First | Second | Third |
|---|---|---|---|---|
| 1 | Lewis Hamilton | 1m 35.798s | 1m 35.898s | 1m 35.908s |
| 2 | Kimi Räikkönen | 1m 35.692s | 1m 35.381s | 1m 36.044s |
| 3 | Felipe Massa | 1m 35.792s | 1m 35.796s | 1m 36.221s |
| 4 | Fernando Alonso | 1m 35.809s | 1m 35.845s | 1m 36.576s |
| 5 | David Coulthard | 1m 36.930s | 1m 36.252s | 1m 37.619s |
| 6 | Ralf Schumacher | 1m 37.135s | 1m 36.709s | 1m 38.013s |
| 7 | Mark Webber | 1m 37.199s | 1m 36.602s | 1m 38.153s |
| 8 | Nick Heidfeld | 1m 36.737s | 1m 36.217s | 1m 38.455s |
| 9 | Robert Kubica | 1m 36.309s | 1m 36.116s | 1m 38.472s |
| 10 | Jenson Button | 1m 37.092s | 1m 36.771s | 1m 39.285s |
| 11 | Vitantonio Liuzzi | 1m 37.047s | 1m 36.862s | |
| 12 | Sebastian Vettel* | 1m 37.006s | 1m 36.891s | |
| 13 | Jarno Trulli | 1m 37.209s | 1m 36.959s | |
| 14 | Heikki Kovalainen | 1m 37.225s | 1m 36.991s | |
| 15 | Anthony Davidson | 1m 37.203s | 1m 37.247s | |
| 16 | Nico Rosberg | 1m 37.144s | 1m 37.483s | |
| 17 | Rubens Barrichello | 1m 37.251s | | |
| 18 | Giancarlo Fisichella | 1m 37.290s | | |
| 19 | Alexander Wurz | 1m 37.456s | | |
| 20 | Takuma Sato | 1m 38.218s | | |
| 21 | Adrian Sutil | 1m 38.668s | | |
| 22 | Sakon Yamamoto | 1m 39.336s | | |

* Vettel received a five-place penalty for impeding Kovalainen.

## PRACTICE 3 (SATURDAY)

Sunny (track 37ºC, air 28–29ºC)

| Pos. | Driver | Laps | Time |
|---|---|---|---|
| 1 | Kimi Räikkönen | 15 | 1m 36.100s |
| 2 | Fernando Alonso | 13 | 1m 36.126s |
| 3 | Lewis Hamilton | 14 | 1m 36.227s |
| 4 | Felipe Massa | 14 | 1m 36.405s |
| 5 | Ralf Schumacher | 18 | 1m 36.959s |
| 6 | David Coulthard | 13 | 1m 36.964s |
| 7 | Robert Kubica | 23 | 1m 37.024s |
| 8 | Heikki Kovalainen | 14 | 1m 37.106s |
| 9 | Nick Heidfeld | 18 | 1m 37.176s |
| 10 | Mark Webber | 13 | 1m 37.315s |
| 11 | Nico Rosberg | 16 | 1m 37.323s |
| 12 | Vitantonio Liuzzi | 18 | 1m 37.463s |
| 13 | Jenson Button | 19 | 1m 37.564s |
| 14 | Jarno Trulli | 20 | 1m 37.679s |
| 15 | Anthony Davidson | 15 | 1m 37.732s |
| 16 | Sebastian Vettel | 19 | 1m 37.759s |
| 17 | Giancarlo Fisichella | 17 | 1m 37.791s |
| 18 | Rubens Barrichello | 20 | 1m 37.920s |
| 19 | Alexander Wurz | 16 | 1m 37.926s |
| 20 | Takuma Sato | 16 | 1m 38.577s |
| 21 | Adrian Sutil | 20 | 1m 38.868s |
| 22 | Sakon Yamamoto | 21 | 1m 39.517s |

## RACE TYRE STRATEGIES

BRIDGESTONE

In 2007, the tyre regulations stipulate that the two dry-tyre specifications must be visibly distinguishable from each other. At the Chinese Grand Prix, the soft compound Bridgestone Potenza tyre was marked with a white line in the second-from-inside groove. Wet and extreme-wet tyres were used during the Chinese Grand Prix.

| | Driver | Stint 1 | Stint 2 | Stint 3 | Stint 4 | Stint 5 |
|---|---|---|---|---|---|---|
| 1 | Kimi Räikkönen | Wet: 1-19 | Wet: 20-32 | Medium: 33-56 | | |
| 2 | Fernando Alonso | Wet: 1-18 | Wet: 19-32 | Hard: 33-56 | | |
| 3 | Felipe Massa | Wet: 1-17 | Wet: 18-26 | Medium: 27-56 | | |
| 4 | Sebastian Vettel | Wet: 1-26 | Medium: 27-56 | | | |
| 5 | Jenson Button | Wet: 1-24 | Medium: 25-42 | Medium: 43-56 | | |
| 6 | Vitantonio Liuzzi | Wet: 1-19 | Wet: 20-31 | Medium: 32-56 | | |
| 7 | Nick Heidfeld | Wet: 1-28 | Wet: 29-32 | Hard: 33-56 | | |
| 8 | David Coulthard | Wet: 1-26 | Wet: 19-26 | Medium: 27-56 | | |
| 9 | Heikki Kovalainen | Wet: 1-24 | Medium: 25-56 | | | |
| 10 | Mark Webber | Wet: 1-23 | Hard: 24-27 | Wet: 28-31 | Hard: 32-56 | |
| 11 | Giancarlo Fisichella | Wet: 1-25 | Medium: 26-45 | Medium: 46-56 | | |
| 12 | Alex Wurz | Wet: 1-22 | Medium: 23-37 | Medium: 38-56 | | |
| 13 | Jarno Trulli | Wet: 1-25 | Medium: 26-56 | | | |
| 14 | Takuma Sato | Wet: 1-25 | Medium: 26-56 | | | |
| 15 | Rubens Barrichello | Wet: 1-25 | Medium: 26 | Wet: 27-31 | Medium: 32-56 | |
| | Nico Rosberg | Wet: 1-25 | Medium: 26-28 | Wet: 29-31 | Medium: 32-56 | |
| | Sakon Yamamoto | Ex Wet: 1-7 | Wet: 8-24 | Medium: 25-26 | Wet: 27-30 | Medium: 31-56 |
| | Robert Kubica | Wet: 1-25 | Hard: 26-33 (DNF) | | | |
| | Lewis Hamilton | Wet: 1-15 | Wet: 16-30 (DNF) | | | |
| | Ralf Schumacher | Wet: 1-23 | Medium: 24-25 (DNF) | | | |
| | Adrian Sutil | Ex Wet: 1-6 | Wet: 7-24 | Medium: 25 (DNF) | | |
| | Anthony Davidson | Wet: 1-11 | Wet: 12 (DNF) | | | |

9 KUBICA BMW-Sauber

7 WEBBER Red Bull

5 COULTHARD Red Bull

3 MASSA Ferrari

1 HAMILTON McLaren

10 BUTTON Honda

8 HEIDFELD BMW-Sauber

6 SCHUMACHER Toyota

4 ALONSO McLaren

2 RÄIKKÖNEN Ferrari

RACE DISTANCE:
56 laps
189.559 miles/305.066 km

RACE WEATHER:
Light rain/overcast,
track 28–29ºC, air 28–29ºC

| | 45 | 46 | 47 | 48 | 49 | 50 | 51 | 52 | 53 | 54 | 55 | 56 | |
|---|---|---|---|---|---|---|---|---|---|---|---|---|---|
| 6 | 6 | 6 | 6 | 6 | 6 | 6 | 6 | 6 | 6 | 6 | 6 | 6 | 1 |
| 1 | 1 | 1 | 1 | 1 | 1 | 1 | 1 | 1 | 1 | 1 | 1 | 1 | 2 |
| 5 | 5 | 5 | 5 | 5 | 5 | 5 | 5 | 5 | 5 | 5 | 5 | 5 | 3 |
| 9 | 19 | 19 | 19 | 19 | 19 | 19 | 19 | 19 | 19 | 19 | 19 | 19 | 4 |
| 3 | 3 | 7 | 7 | 7 | 7 | 7 | 7 | 7 | 7 | 7 | 7 | 7 | 5 |
| 7 | 7 | 18 | 18 | 18 | 18 | 18 | 18 | 18 | 18 | 18 | 18 | 18 | 6 |
| 8 | 18 | 9 | 9 | 9 | 9 | 9 | 9 | 9 | 9 | 9 | 9 | 9 | 7 |
| 9 | 9 | 14 | 14 | 14 | 14 | 14 | 14 | 14 | 14 | 14 | 14 | 14 | 8 |
| 4 | 14 | 15 | 15 | 4 | 4 | 4 | 4 | 4 | 4 | 4 | 4 | 4 | |
| 5 | 15 | 4 | 4 | 15 | 15 | 15 | 15 | 15 | 15 | 15 | 15 | 15 | |
| 4 | 4 | 3 | 3 | 3 | 3 | 3 | 3 | 3 | 3 | 3 | 3 | 3 | |
| 7 | 17 | 17 | 17 | 17 | 17 | 17 | 17 | 17 | 17 | 17 | 17 | 17 | |
| 2 | 12 | 12 | 12 | 12 | 12 | 12 | 12 | 12 | 12 | 12 | 12 | | |
| 2 | 22 | 22 | 22 | 22 | 22 | 22 | 22 | 22 | 22 | 22 | 22 | | |
| 8 | 8 | 8 | 8 | 8 | 8 | 8 | 8 | 8 | 8 | 8 | | | |
| 6 | 16 | 16 | 16 | 16 | 16 | 16 | 16 | 16 | 16 | 16 | | | |
| 1 | 21 | 21 | 21 | 21 | 21 | 21 | 21 | 21 | 21 | | | | |

20 Pit stop
20 One lap or more behind leader

## FOR THE RECORD

BEST CAREER RESULT:
Vitantonio Liuzzi and
Sebastian Vettel (above)

FIRST POINTS: Toro Rosso

200th WIN: Ferrari

## POINTS

| | DRIVERS | |
|---|---|---|
| 1 | Lewis Hamilton | 107 |
| 2 | Fernando Alonso | 103 |
| 3 | Kimi Räikkönen | 100 |
| 4 | Felipe Massa | 86 |
| 5 | Nick Heidfeld | 58 |
| 6 | Robert Kubica | 35 |
| 7 | Heikki Kovalainen | 30 |
| 8 | Giancarlo Fisichella | 21 |
| 9 | Nico Rosberg | 15 |
| 10 | David Coulthard | 14 |
| 11 | Alexander Wurz | 13 |
| 12 | Mark Webber | 10 |
| 13 | Jarno Trulli | 7 |
| 14 | Sebastian Vettel | 6 |
| 15 | Jenson Button | 6 |
| 16 | Ralf Schumacher | 5 |
| 17 | Takuma Sato | 4 |
| 18 | Vitantonio Liuzzi | 3 |
| 19 | Adrian Sutil | 1 |

| | CONSTRUCTORS | |
|---|---|---|
| 1 | Ferrari | 186 |
| 2 | BMW Sauber | 94 |
| 3 | Renault | 51 |
| 4 | Williams | 28 |
| 5 | Red Bull | 24 |
| 6 | Toyota | 12 |
| 7 | Toro Rosso | 8 |
| 8 | Honda | 6 |
| 9 | Super Aguri | 4 |
| 10 | Spyker | 1 |

Photographs: Peter J Fox www.crash.net

# BRAZILIAN GP
## INTERLAGOS

The party starts here. Kimi Räikkönen takes a mighty swig of champagne and the defeated champion Fernando Alonso doesn't look too displeased at the outcome.
Photograph: Paul-Henri Cahier

Right: As the drivers depart on their final pre-race parade lap of the season their teams' exhausted press and PR officers put on a smile for the end-of-term group photograph.
Photograph: Lukas Gorys

Below: Veteran journalist Jacques Deschenaux signs in for the last time. His distinguished career in Formula 1 began when he acted as personal assistant to Jo Siffert back in the late 1960s.
Photograph: Bernard Asset

Above: Ralf Schumacher sheepishly rounds off at the end of his three-year tenure at Toyota with a signed rear-wing end plate as a memento.
Photograph: Peter J Fox/www.crash.net

Right: Rubens Barrichello poses with his two sons – a future Brazilian racing dynasty, perhaps?
Photograph: Lukas Gorys

Opposite: The crucial first corner, with Felipe Massa away in the lead and Kimi Räikkönen momentarily balking Lewis Hamilton. Fernando Alonso is about to take advantage and pounce on his team-mate.
Photograph: Studio Colombo/WRi2

## INTERLAGOS QUALIFYING

For the second year in succession Felipe Massa gave his adoring countrymen precisely what they wanted as he put his Ferrari on pole position for his home grand prix. In difficult track conditions – there was less grip than there had been in the morning's free practice session – the little Brazilian said he was very satisfied with his first run… and his second was better still, yielding 1m 11.931s. He admitted that he'd made a slight mistake on it, however.

Team-mate Kimi Räikkönen was clearly disappointed with his best of 1m 12.322s from his first run, but on his second he had to go around Lewis Hamilton as Hamilton left the pits and that cost him a little bit of momentum and led momentarily to more bad feelings between Ferrari and McLaren. Thankfully, the stewards wisely decided that Hamilton had no case to answer; it was just one of those things.

Hamilton came very close to snatching pole away from Massa, but said he'd been slightly conservative in the final part of the lap to avoid risking what he had already gained over the first part of it. His best was 1m 12.082s.

Fernando Alonso's 1m 12.356s best left him fourth and he said that some set-up changes hadn't worked and had sapped his confidence in his MP4-22's handling.

Red Bull continued its impressive progress at Interlagos as Mark Webber took fifth place with a lap of 1m 12.928s and David Coulthard pushed his RB3 into the top ten with a lap of 1m 13.272s for ninth.

It was unusual to see BMW Sauber lose its customary 'best of the rest' slot, but Nick Heidfeld said he was 'extremely happy' with his sixth-fastest time of 1m 13.081s, suggesting he had a reasonable fuel load. He said he was lucky to make Q3, however, after a big slide and a near spin in Turn Six during Q2 left him right on the bubble. Team-mate Robert Kubica was seventh on 1m 13.129s, annoyed that he'd got dirt on his tyres going off-line to go around a slow Alonso on his final lap. As a result, in the last corner he locked a front wheel under braking, slid wide and lost time.

Jarno Trulli planted the spare Toyota TF107 in eighth place with 1m 13.195s, having rejected his race car, whose handling felt 'spooky'. He was much happier, but having been quick on Friday team-mate Ralf Schumacher went backwards and was only 15th on 1m 13.315s for what some believed was his final grand prix.

Nico Rosberg said he was surprised to make Q3 in a Williams FW29 that had been transformed since the morning's practice session and was grateful to take tenth overall with a lap of 1m 13.477s. He still wasn't overly happy with the balance and admitted to a small error without which he thought he might have beaten Coulthard. He had a new team-mate for this race, GP2 racer Kazuki Nakajima, whose father Satoru raced for Lotus and Tyrrell in the 1980s. Nakajima had a tough time getting 19th place with 1m 14.417s.

Retirement rumours continued to dog Rubens Barrichello, but he was on good form to take his Honda RA107 to 11th place on 1m 12.932s. He was relieved to have a strong run in front of his countrymen but disappointed to miss out on Q3. Team-mate Jenson Button struggled to 16th-fastest time on 1m 14.054s, suffering for lack of grip.

Twelfth and 17th positions, courtesy of Giancarlo Fisichella (1m 12.968s) and Heikki Kovalainen (1m 14.078s) were not at all what Renault had expected. Fisichella reported that he was right on the limit, struggling for grip, and missed Q3 by a small margin. Likewise, Kovalainen missed Q2 by a tiny amount, admitting to a mistake when he went too deep into Turn 12 and locked the front tyres.

Toro Rosso again looked respectable, with Sebastian Vettel 13th on 1m 13.058s and Tonio Liuzzi 14th on 1m 13.251s. Vettel was happier with his car after the team played around with tyre pressures, while Liuzzi's time was from his first run after understeer and graining cost him too much in the first sector to register improvement on the second. The change in Vettel's tyre pressures serendipitously had a beneficial effect on his car's understeer, which made all the difference.

Takuma Sato qualified 18th for Super Aguri on 1m 14.098s and Anthony Davidson was 20th on 1m 14.596s, both struggling for grip.

Adrian Sutil's qualifying at Spyker was hampered by a fuel-pressure problem, which he had already encountered in the morning. It left him stranded out on the circuit after he had recorded 1m 15.217s for 21st place, while Sakon Yamamoto was close behind on 1m 15.487s.

AMID controversy that somehow summarised an acrimonious season, the 2007 title fight was resolved in an echo of 1986 as underdog Kimi Räikkönen came from behind to snatch the world championship crown from McLaren's Lewis Hamilton and Fernando Alonso by one point.

On a day when everything went right for Ferrari and nothing went right for McLaren, Räikkönen grabbed the lead towards the end from pole-sitting team-mate Felipe Massa, leaving Alonso a frustrated and powerless third and Hamilton fighting up to an insufficient seventh after opening-lap dramas and then a crucial gear-selection problem had at one stage dropped him to 18th place.

Then, barely had the spray of champagne subsided when yet another controversy arose, one that threatened the positions of three cars that had finished ahead of Hamilton, opening up potential salvation if their drivers – Nico Rosberg, Robert Kubica and Nick Heidfeld – were disqualified.

Should that have happened, and the drivers lost their points, Hamilton would have moved from seventh to fourth, from earning two points to earning five, to scoring 112 instead of 109. And that would have been sufficient to beat Räikkönen's championship-winning tally of 110.

All weekend the English rookie looked like a man ready to embrace his destiny. But things went wrong almost the moment the race started. Massa made a great start from pole position, to Hamilton's right, and immediately moved across to protect the inside line. At the same time Räikkönen boiled up from the second row, also on Hamilton's right. By the first corner the two Ferraris were ahead and as Hamilton had to back off momentarily to avoid making contact with Räikkönen, Alonso snatched his chance. He squeezed down the inside of his team-mate and, as they all but rubbed wheels, he grabbed third place. Hamilton's response, an attempt to go around the outside at the next corner, proved his undoing as he slid wide and dropped to eighth.

At the end of the lap, Räikkönen, running second to Massa, had 108 potential points. Alonso, third, had 109, Hamilton, eighth, 108. A lap later Hamilton passed Jarno Trulli's Toyota. Five laps later he pulled a move down the inside of Nick Heidfeld to snatch sixth place in the first corner, appropriately named after the late Ayrton Senna. Now it was Alonso 109, Räikkönen 108, Hamilton 110. But then came disaster on the eighth lap. For agonising moments the McLaren number-two car stumbled and banged along in neutral until Hamilton finally managed to persuade it into gear again, but by then he was down in 18th place with a mountain to climb

'The start wasn't that great and I got boxed in behind Kimi, then Fernando came past me and I locked up a bit behind him and lost some ground in Turn Four,' Hamilton said. 'But I knew that we had the pace to get that back. But then when I was downshifting for Turn Four on lap eight the gearbox just went into neutral. And I coasted for an awful long time. I still don't know how but I managed to coax it back into operation and get going again, but I had to be careful to manage the engine because the revs were very low.

'When that was happening, coming so soon after China, I just found myself thinking that for sure somebody didn't want me to win the championship.'

He had 63 laps in which to launch a salvage operation.

It didn't take Alonso long to realise that the Ferraris were uncatchable. 'I could hold them initially, until they really started to push,' he reported. 'After that there was nothing I could do.'

After 13 laps Massa was 1.7s ahead of Räikkönen, with Alonso 8.3s farther back. Hamilton, up to 16th, was stuck firmly in mid-field traffic. He was back up to 11th by the 17th lap, however, as the pit stops started, but when both McLaren drivers made their first calls on the 22nd lap, Hamilton dropped back to 14th. Alonso's car was fitted with another set of harder-compound tyres, but Hamilton's crew opted for the softer

## DIARY

**In Brazil, it transpires that McLaren has instigated legal action in Italy against Ferrari for alleged illegal use of Italian legal documents in the FIA World Motor Sport Council meeting in September.**

**Jarno Trulli, Ralf Schumacher, Tonio Liuzzi and Sakon Yamamoto are all due to test for Spyker in mid-November, with a view to filling the vacant seat for 2008 alongside Adrian Sutil. Toyota sources say mention of Trulli's name is a plant to gee up the Italian driver. Meanwhile Spyker's new owner, Vijay Mallya, is successful in applying to the FIA to have the team's name changed for '08 to Force India F1, with the cars known as Force Indias.**

**In an emotional 'trick' ceremony in the McLaren garage in Interlagos, Ron Dennis finds himself being presented with a cut-glass trophy when he expects to give his troops a pep talk. It is inscribed with the words, '2007 constructors' champion, from the team'.**

**In the week after the Brazilian GP, the FIA World Motor Sport Council meets in Paris and announces plans for a total freeze on engine development for ten years, starting in 2008. The intention is to give teams more time to develop things such as regenerative braking systems instead.**

rubber and a light fuel load to try and catapult him past the slower cars immediately ahead.

Meanwhile, Robert Kubica in the BMW-Sauber was challenging Alonso for third place – and he moved ahead in Turn One at the start of the 33rd lap. That dropped the champion's score to 108, while farther back Hamilton overtook Vettel and gained another place when Ralf Schumacher pitted. That left him ninth, just outside the points, still on 107 overall. Räikkönen, still second but catching Massa, still had 108. Half distance loomed. Hamilton's next pit stop, on lap 36, dropped him a lap down on the Ferraris, but he retained ninth place and a chance of points. It wasn't over yet.

By lap 40, Kubica's second pit stop had put Alonso back to third, giving him 109 points to Räikkönen's 108 and Hamilton's

107, but all Ferrari had to do was get Räikkönen into the lead – past his own team-mate – and he would have 110 points. Alonso was thus far from safe.

Hamilton came back into the picture when David Coulthard pitted from eighth place on lap 42. Now he was eighth and had another point and his sights set on Trulli's Toyota. He and Räikkönen now had 108 to Alonso's 109. But then Massa ran wide in one corner, losing a lot of ground to Räikkönen, on the 44th lap. Ferrari's game was unravelling.

Massa pitted for the last time on lap 50 but, crucially, Räikkönen went three laps longer. This time he kept the lead and with ten points now in his grasp he led the title chase with 110. Alonso, who pitted on lap 52, was back to fifth behind Räikkönen, Massa, Rosberg and Kubica and thus had 107

points. Hamilton, now unlapped in eighth, still had 108. But then Rosberg's stop on lap 54 moved Alonso back up a place, on to 108, too, and when Hamilton made a third stop on lap 56 he dropped back to ninth behind Coulthard again. He was thus down to 107 again but only until the 57th lap, when he grabbed eighth back from the Scot. Now he was back to 108 but still needed three more points to become champion. Just to complicate things further, Kubica's third stop on lap 58 let Alonso back to third and 109 points. It was dizzying.

Now Hamilton's hopes lay in the duelling BMW-Saubers and Rosberg's Williams' doing something nasty to one another, because Trulli in seventh seemed well beyond his reach. On lap 61 Rosberg dived inside Heidfeld in the first corner, forcing Nick to widen his line to avoid contact. Both ran wide and Trulli closed in as Kubica gratefully jumped back to fourth. But none of it helped Hamilton – until Trulli pitted on lap 63.

Now it was Räikkönen 110, Alonso 109, Hamilton 109 – and that was how they stayed. Game over. Against the odds and the expectations, Räikkönen had done it. He and Ferrari had come from behind to grab the big prize at the 11th hour.

It was small consolation for a shattered McLaren team that its drivers had equal points, underlying the team's philosophy of equality once and for all – but taking second places into account Hamilton got the nod for the runner-up slot, with five to Alonso's four. That seemed just, for many felt that a third title for Alonso would have been rubbing salt into McLaren's wounds, given all that had happened this year.

Williams came to Brazil under serious pressure from Red Bull for its fourth place overall, yet rose to the occasion magnificently as Rosberg battled with – and beat – the BMW-Saubers in a fantastic tussle that was sadly overshadowed by the world championship fight.

In the end, Rosberg outsmarted both of his challengers to score his best F1 result yet with fourth place and he was absolutely delighted to have done it the hard way and to have protected his team's valuable position in the constructors' championship.

At one stage Kubica had seemed likely to challenge Alonso for third, until it transpired he was running on a three-stop strategy. He nevertheless looked very strong until he was instructed to wind down the revs because his engine was showing signs of overheating. Heidfeld, meanwhile, struggled with graining tyres front and rear. Overall, however, BMW garnered 101 points for second place overall, reaching and just exceeding its season target of the round century.

Not that far behind them, Kazuki Nakajima's début was overshadowed by an incident in the pits on lap 31, when he came in a little too fast and hit three of his mechanics. One was sent to the circuit medical centre. After that, Nakajima settled down and actually set the fifth-fastest lap of 1m 13.116s. That compared with Räikkönen's fastest lap of 1m 12.445s, and Rosberg's 1m 13.159s, which was seventh.

Trulli had a strong three-stop race for Toyota, which earned him the final point. Team-mate Ralf Schumacher, in his last race for Toyota, could do no better than 11th.

With Mark Webber fifth on the grid and David Coulthard ninth, Red Bull went into the race with high hopes of taking the five points it needed to overhaul Williams for fourth in the constructors' stakes. However, it came away with nothing. Webber ran fourth until Kubica got by, then the on-board telemetry revealed an electronic disconnection between the engine and gearbox on his RB3 – and that was that after only 14 laps. Coulthard was in the running for eighth at one stage, but after his final pit stop slid into the back of Nakajima in the first corner and damaged his front suspension. He finished ninth, well behind Trulli and just ahead of Nakajima.

There was a fair degree of intra-team skirmishing *chez* Super Aguri. Anthony Davidson was not only attacked by Adrian Sutil when the German's brakes failed going into Turn One, but got

**Above: The hapless Sakon Yamamoto is an innocent victim after Giancarlo Fisichella careers back onto the circuit out of control.**
Photograph: Peter Nygaard/GP Photo

**Centre left: Joy for Ferrari personnel as the championship is snatched at the death.**
Photograph: Lukas Gorys

**Centre: A despondent McLaren boss Ron Dennis is powerless to help either Lewis Hamilton or Fernando Alonso.**
Photograph: Paul-Henri Cahier

**Left: Lewis Hamilton gives everything in his attempt to gain fifth place, but a third pit stop will effectively put him out of the championship chase.**
Photograph: Jad Sherif/WRi2

put on the marbles as team-mate Takuma Sato overtook him. They went on to finish 12th and 14th.

Toro Rosso had hoped for rather more than Tonio Liuzzi's eventual 13th-placed finish, especially given that Sebastian Vettel was at one stage in the thick of the fight for the minor points. But then his STR2 began experiencing gearshift problems and lost its power steering after 34 laps. Liuzzi, meanwhile, got his nose damaged in the first corner mêlée and his two-stop strategy was therefore ruined by the need to stop for a replacement at the end of the lap.

Renault had an awful Brazilian Grand Prix. Heikki Kovalainen got pushed off the track in the first corner – ironically it was because somebody pushed team-mate Giancarlo Fisichella into him. He sustained a puncture, made a stop at the end of the lap, then later felt a vibration at the rear just as the back end snapped around on him in Turn One and pitched him off the road.

After that first-lap brush, Fisichella got involved with Nakajima in Turn One on the second lap, slid off the road and then hacked back right in front of the unfortunate Sakon Yamamoto, who could not avoid running straight into the back of him. Both cars retired.

Honda also got nothing from this race. Jenson Button was running tenth after 20 laps but then retired with an overheated engine. Rubens Barrichello was never really in contention and retired on the 41st lap when his engine blew up.

Adrian Sutil shunted his Spyker into Davidson's Super Aguri in Turn One on lap 23 as his brakes failed. He carried on, served a drive-through penalty and made four more stops before his race ended after 43 laps as the brake pressure faded further and further and obliged him to pump the pedal on the straight. Team-mate Sakon Yamamoto was the unwitting victim as Fisichella rejoined the track in front of him and left him nowhere to go but into the back of the Renault.

In victory, Räikkönen looked happy but slightly bemused.

'We were not in the strongest position but we always believed that we could recover and do a better job than the others and even with the hard times everyone was sticking together and we did not give up,' he said. 'I need to thank the team – they did a great job. We worked hard to improve the situation. We had perfect team work, with Felipe helping all the time. He has been a big help. For sure I am going to enjoy today.

'I got a very good start and was side by side with Felipe but we did not want to race too hard. The main thing was to get past Hamilton and I saw him go off and I knew we had a good chance. We were taking it easy. We could have gone much faster, but it paid off very well.

'I was not really 100-percent sure if someone would stop but there were people who needed to finish and we did not know 100-percent and it took a long time to hear that we had finally won it. It has been a good finish to the season and I am really happy. An amazing day!'

After losing by a solitary point, having led the chase since Spain in May, Hamilton was philosophical and dignified.

'It's been a crazy year, but I can't really say that I'm gutted or that I feel I was robbed,' he said. 'It was just unfortunate. We've all of us had some bad luck this year; it's just a shame that mine seemed to come all at the end of it.

'All along I said to myself that, whatever happens today, who would ever have thought that I would lead the championship? It's been a great feeling, having the possibility to win it. The team has done a fantastic job for me all season and of course I wanted to win. But I guess it wasn't our turn, after all, this year. But I will come back next year stronger, for sure.

'Even after that, though, I refused to believe that it was over. The first time I thought that was when I saw the chequered flag. I never stopped thinking it was still possible.

'Our pace wasn't bad today. Not quite the same as Ferrari's, but we could have been a little bit quicker with more luck.'

*David Tremayne*

## FUEL IRREGULARITIES BRING McLAREN APPEAL

There have been fuel crises before in Formula 1, but the argument that broke out after the Brazilian GP was surely one of the most esoteric. Data inspection by FIA technical delegate Jo Bauer revealed that the cars of Williams and BMW Sauber breached article 6.5.5 of the Formula 1 technical regulations, which states that, 'no fuel on board the car may be more than 10°C below ambient temperature.' This is to avoid teams' freezing fuel and thus reducing its volume so as to get more into the tank and thus gain a potential performance advantage. According to Bauer, telemetry revealed that at various points during the race all four cars exceeded that figure. His report stated that Nick Heidfeld's fuel temperature was measured during his two stops at 24°C and 25°C, when the ambient temperature was 37°C. The other cars – of Robert Kubica, Nico Rosberg and Kazuki Nakajima, featured similar discrepancies.

McLaren appealed against the stewards' decision not to disqualify the Williams and BMW cars but Lewis Hamilton said he wouldn't want to win the championship in the court room.

# FIA F1 WORLD CHAMPIONSHIP • ROUND 17
## GRANDE PRÊMIO DO
# BRASIL

SÃO PAULO 19–21 OCTOBER 2007

**AUTODROMO JOSÉ CARLOS PACE, INTERLAGOS**

Reta Oposta 90/145    116/187 **mph/kmh**
4    4 **Gear**
Junção 77/124    193/311 6
1
Pinheirinho 61/98
Murgulho 146/235    2
3    Curva do Sol 144/232 3
Laranja 58/93    Ferradura 127/204
1    3    Senna-S 89/143
196/315 6    2
Bico de Pato 50/80 1    Arquibancadas 188/303 5    Descida do Sol 64/103 1

Photograph: Peter J Fox/www.crash.net

**Circuit: 2.677 miles/4.309 km**

## RACE RESULTS

| Pos. | Driver | Nat. | No. | Entrant | Car/Engine | Tyres | Laps | Time/Retirement | Speed (mph/km/h) | Gap to leader | Fastest race lap | |
|---|---|---|---|---|---|---|---|---|---|---|---|---|
| 1 | Kimi Räikkönen | FIN | 6 | Scuderia Ferrari Marlboro | Ferrari F2007-056 V8 | B | 71 | 1h 28m 15.270s | 129.228/207.972 | | 1m 12.445s | 66 |
| 2 | Felipe Massa | BR | 5 | Scuderia Ferrari Marlboro | Ferrari F2007-056 V8 | B | 71 | 1h 28m 16.763s | 129.192/207.914 | + 1.493s | 1m 12.584s | 71 |
| 3 | Fernando Alonso | E | 1 | Vodafone McLaren Mercedes | McLaren MP4-22-Mercedes FO 108T V8 | B | 71 | 1h 29m 12.289s | 127.851/205.757 | + 57.019s | 1m 13.150s | 59 |
| 4 | Nico Rosberg | D | 16 | AT&T Williams | Williams FW29-Toyota RVX-07 V8 | B | 71 | 1h 29m 18.118s | 127.712/205.533 | + 1m 2.848s | 1m 13.159s | 56 |
| 5 | Robert Kubica | POL | 10 | BMW Sauber F1 Team | BMW Sauber F1.07-BMW P86/7 V8 | B | 71 | 1h 29m 26.227s | 127.519/205.222 | + 1m 10.957s | 1m 12.686s | 61 |
| 6 | Nick Heidfeld | D | 9 | BMW Sauber F1 Team | BMW Sauber F1.07-BMW P86/7 V8 | B | 71 | 1h 29m 26.587s | 127.511/205.209 | + 1m 11.317s | 1m 13.452s | 53 |
| 7 | Lewis Hamilton | GB | 2 | Vodafone McLaren Mercedes | McLaren MP4-22-Mercedes FO 108T V8 | B | 70 | | | + 1 lap | 1m 12.506s | 58 |
| 8 | Jarno Trulli | I | 12 | Panasonic Toyota Racing | Toyota TF107-RVX-07 V8 | B | 70 | | | + 1 lap | 1m 13.361s | 68 |
| 9 | David Coulthard | GB | 14 | Red Bull Racing | Red Bull RB3-Renault RS27 V8 | B | 70 | | | + 1 lap | 1m 14.195s | 22 |
| 10 | Kazuki Nakajima | J | 17 | AT&T Williams | Williams FW29-Toyota RVX-07 V8 | B | 70 | | | + 1 lap | 1m 13.116s | 69 |
| 11 | Ralf Schumacher | D | 11 | Panasonic Toyota Racing | Toyota TF107-RVX-07 V8 | B | 70 | | | + 1 lap | 1m 13.368s | 65 |
| 12 | Takuma Sato | J | 22 | Super Aguri F1 Team | Super Aguri SA07-Honda RA807E V8 | B | 69 | | | + 2 laps | 1m 14.914s | 39 |
| 13 | Vitantonio Liuzzi | I | 18 | Scuderia Toro Rosso | Toro Rosso STR02-Ferrari 056H V8 | B | 69 | | | + 2 laps | 1m 13.643s | 56 |
| 14 | Anthony Davidson | GB | 23 | Super Aguri F1 Team | Super Aguri SA07-Honda RA807E V8 | B | 68 | | | + 3 laps | 1m 14.329s | 64 |
| | Adrian Sutil | D | 20 | Etihad Aldar Spyker F1 Team | Spyker F8-VII-Ferrari 056H V8 | B | 43 | Brakes | | | 1m 15.202s | 13 |
| | Rubens Barrichello | BR | 8 | Honda Racing F1 Team | Honda RA107-RA807E V8 | B | 40 | Engine | | | 1m 14.742s | 32 |
| | Heikki Kovalainen | FIN | 4 | ING Renault F1 Team | Renault R27-RS27 V8 | B | 35 | Rear vibration/accident | | | 1m 14.891s | 31 |
| | Sebastian Vettel | D | 19 | Scuderia Toro Rosso | Toro Rosso STR02-Ferrari 056H V8 | B | 34 | Hydraulics | | | 1m 14.423s | 18 |
| | Jenson Button | GB | 7 | Honda Racing F1 Team | Honda RA107-RA807E V8 | B | 20 | Engine | | | 1m 14.039s | 20 |
| | Mark Webber | AUS | 15 | Red Bull Racing | Red Bull RB3-Renault RS27 V8 | B | 14 | Transmission | | | 1m 14.398s | 13 |
| | Sakon Yamamoto | J | 21 | Etihad Aldar Spyker F1 Team | Spyker F8-VII-Ferrari 056H V8 | B | 2 | Accident | | | 1m 50.404s | 2 |
| | Giancarlo Fisichella | I | 3 | ING Renault F1 Team | Renault R27-RS27 V8 | B | 2 | Accident damage | | | 2m 2.680s | 2 |

**Fastest race lap:** Kimi Räikkönen on lap 66, 1m 12.445s, 133.052 mph/214.126 km/h.

**Lap record:** Juan Pablo Montoya (Williams FW26-BMW V10), 1m 11.473s, 134.862 mph/217.038 km/h (2004).

All results and data © FOM 2007

22 YAMAMOTO Spyker

20 DAVIDSON Super Aguri

18 SATO Super Aguri

16 BUTTON Honda

14 LIUZZI Toro Rosso

12 FISICHELLA Renault

21 SUTIL Spyker

19 NAKAJIMA Williams

17 KOVALAINEN Renault

15 SCHUMACHER Toyota

13 VETTEL Toro Rosso

11 BARRICHELLO Honda

| Grid order | 1 | 2 | 3 | 4 | 5 | 6 | 7 | 8 | 9 | 10 | 11 | 12 | 13 | 14 | 15 | 16 | 17 | 18 | 19 | 20 | 21 | 22 | 23 | 24 | 25 | 26 | 27 | 28 | 29 | 30 | 31 | 32 | 33 | 34 | 35 | 36 | 37 | 38 | 39 | 40 | 41 | 42 | 43 | 44 | 45 | 46 | 47 | 48 | 49 | 50 | 51 | 52 | 53 | 54 | 55 |
|---|---|---|---|---|---|---|---|---|---|---|---|---|---|---|---|---|---|---|---|---|---|---|---|---|---|---|---|---|---|---|---|---|---|---|---|---|---|---|---|---|---|---|---|---|---|---|---|---|---|---|---|---|---|---|---|
| **5 MASSA** | 5 | 5 | 5 | 5 | 5 | 5 | 5 | 5 | 5 | 5 | 5 | 5 | 5 | 5 | 5 | 5 | 5 | 5 | 5 | 5 | 6 | | 1 | 5 | 5 | 5 | 5 | 5 | 5 | 5 | 5 | 5 | 5 | 5 | 5 | 5 | 5 | 5 | 5 | 5 | 5 | 5 | 5 | 5 | 5 | 5 | 5 | 5 | 5 | 6 | 6 | 6 | 6 | 6 | 6 |
| **2 HAMILTON** | 6 | 6 | 6 | 6 | 6 | 6 | 6 | 6 | 6 | 6 | 6 | 6 | 6 | 6 | 6 | 6 | 6 | 6 | 6 | 6 | 5 | 6 | 5 | 6 | 6 | 6 | 6 | 6 | 6 | 6 | 6 | 6 | 6 | 6 | 6 | 6 | 6 | 6 | 6 | 6 | 6 | 6 | 6 | 6 | 6 | 6 | 6 | 6 | 6 | 5 | 5 | 5 | 5 | 5 | 5 |
| **6 RÄIKKÖNEN** | 1 | 1 | 1 | 1 | 1 | 1 | 1 | 1 | 1 | 1 | 1 | 1 | 1 | 1 | 1 | 1 | 1 | 1 | 1 | 1 | 1 | 5 | 6 | 9 | 9 | 9 | 1 | 1 | 1 | 1 | 1 | 1 | 10 | 10 | 10 | 10 | 1 | 1 | 1 | 1 | 1 | 1 | 1 | 1 | 1 | 1 | 1 | 1 | 1 | 1 | 1 | 16 | 16 | 10 | |
| **1 ALONSO** | 15 | 15 | 15 | 15 | 15 | 15 | 15 | 10 | 10 | 10 | 10 | 10 | 10 | 10 | 10 | 10 | 10 | 10 | 9 | 9 | 9 | 16 | | 1 | 1 | 10 | 10 | 10 | 10 | 10 | 10 | 1 | 1 | 1 | 1 | 1 | 10 | 12 | 12 | 12 | 9 | 9 | 9 | 9 | 9 | 9 | 9 | 9 | 16 | 16 | 10 | 10 | 1 | |
| **15 WEBBER** | 10 | 10 | 10 | 10 | 10 | 10 | 10 | 15 | 15 | 15 | 15 | 15 | 15 | 9 | 9 | 9 | 9 | 9 | 12 | 12 | 14 | 10 | 14 | 10 | 12 | 12 | 12 | 12 | 12 | 12 | 12 | 12 | 12 | 12 | 12 | 12 | 12 | 9 | 9 | 16 | 16 | 16 | 16 | 16 | 16 | 16 | 16 | 9 | 10 | 1 | 1 | 9 | |
| **9 HEIDFELD** | 9 | 9 | 9 | 9 | 9 | 9 | 2 | 9 | 9 | 9 | 9 | 9 | 9 | 12 | 12 | 12 | 12 | 16 | 16 | 14 | 1 | 12 | 9 | 9 | 9 | 9 | 9 | 9 | 9 | 9 | 9 | 9 | 16 | 16 | 16 | 12 | 10 | 10 | 10 | 10 | 10 | 10 | 10 | 9 | 9 | 9 | 16 | | | | | | | |
| **10 KUBICA** | 12 | 12 | 12 | 12 | 2 | 2 | 9 | 12 | 12 | 12 | 12 | 12 | 12 | 16 | 16 | 14 | 14 | 14 | 14 | 19 | 12 | 14 | 16 | 16 | 16 | 16 | 16 | 16 | 16 | 16 | 16 | 16 | 9 | 9 | 9 | 16 | 16 | 16 | 16 | 9 | 9 | 9 | 9 | 10 | 10 | 10 | 10 | 10 | 9 | 9 | 9 | 10 | | | |
| **12 TRULLI** | 2 | 12 | 12 | 12 | 12 | 12 | 12 | 16 | 16 | 16 | 16 | 16 | 16 | 14 | 14 | 16 | 16 | 19 | 19 | 9 | 10 | 19 | 12 | 14 | 14 | 14 | 14 | 14 | 14 | 14 | 14 | 14 | 14 | 14 | 14 | 14 | | 2 | 2 | 2 | 2 | 2 | 2 | 2 | 2 | 2 | 2 | 2 | 2 | 2 | 2 | 2 | 2 | 2 |
| **14 COULTHARD** | 16 | 16 | 16 | 16 | 16 | 16 | 16 | 14 | 14 | 14 | 14 | 14 | 14 | 19 | 19 | 19 | 19 | 10 | 10 | 10 | 19 | 17 | 17 | 17 | 17 | 17 | 17 | 17 | 11 | 2 | 2 | 2 | 2 | 2 | 2 | 2 | 14 | 14 | 14 | 14 | 14 | 14 | 14 | 14 | 14 | 14 | 14 | 14 | 14 | 14 | 14 | | | |
| **16 ROSBERG** | 14 | 14 | 14 | 14 | 14 | 14 | 14 | 8 | 19 | 19 | 19 | 19 | 19 | 7 | 7 | 7 | 7 | 7 | 2 | 2 | 22 | 22 | 11 | 11 | 11 | 11 | 11 | 11 | 19 | 19 | 17 | 17 | 17 | 17 | 17 | 17 | 17 | 17 | 17 | 17 | 17 | 17 | 17 | 17 | 17 | 17 | 17 | 17 | 17 | 17 | 17 | 17 | | | |
| **8 BARRICHELLO** | 8 | 8 | 8 | 8 | 8 | 8 | 19 | 22 | 22 | 22 | 22 | 7 | 7 | 17 | 17 | 2 | 2 | 2 | 2 | 17 | 11 | 11 | 19 | 19 | 19 | 19 | 19 | 19 | 2 | 11 | 8 | 8 | 8 | 8 | 8 | 8 | 11 | 11 | 11 | 11 | 11 | 11 | 11 | 11 | 11 | 11 | 11 | 11 | 11 | 11 | 11 | 11 | | | |
| **3 FISICHELLA** | 19 | 19 | 19 | 19 | 19 | 19 | 22 | 7 | 7 | 7 | 7 | 22 | 22 | 2 | 2 | 17 | 17 | 22 | 22 | 22 | 19 | 19 | 8 | 2 | 2 | 2 | 17 | 17 | 17 | 17 | 22 | 22 | 22 | 22 | 22 | 22 | 22 | 22 | 22 | 22 | 22 | 22 | 22 | 22 | 22 | 22 | 22 | 22 | 22 | 22 | | | | | |
| **19 VETTEL** | 22 | 22 | 22 | 22 | 22 | 22 | 7 | 8 | 17 | 17 | 17 | 22 | 2 | 22 | 22 | 23 | 11 | 8 | 8 | 2 | 2 | 8 | 2 | 2 | 8 | 8 | 8 | 8 | 8 | 11 | 22 | 22 | 18 | 18 | 18 | 18 | 18 | | | | | | | | | | | | | | | | | | |
| **18 LIUZZI** | 7 | 7 | 7 | 7 | 7 | 7 | 17 | 17 | 23 | 23 | 23 | 23 | 23 | 23 | 23 | 11 | 8 | 2 | 22 | 22 | 22 | 19 | | 4 | 18 | 18 | 18 | 18 | 18 | 18 | 23 | 23 | 23 | 23 | 23 | 23 | 23 | 23 | 23 | 23 | | | | | | | | | | | | | | | |
| **11 SCHUMACHER** | 3 | 17 | 17 | 17 | 17 | 17 | 23 | 11 | 11 | 11 | 11 | 11 | 11 | 23 | 23 | 20 | 20 | 18 | 18 | 18 | 4 | 4 | 4 | 4 | 23 | 23 | 23 | 20 | 20 | 20 | | | | | | | | | | | | | | | | | | | | | | | | |
| **7 BUTTON** | 17 | 23 | 23 | 23 | 23 | 23 | 11 | 11 | 20 | 20 | 2 | 2 | 20 | 20 | 20 | 20 | 20 | 20 | 8 | 20 | 18 | 18 | 20 | 4 | 4 | 18 | 18 | 18 | 23 | 20 | 20 | 20 | 20 | | | | | | | | | | | | | | | | | | | | | |
| **4 KOVALAINEN** | 23 | 11 | 11 | 11 | 11 | 11 | 11 | 20 | 20 | 2 | 20 | 20 | 20 | 8 | 8 | 8 | 8 | 8 | 18 | 4 | 4 | 4 | 23 | 23 | 23 | 23 | 23 | 23 | 23 | | | | | | | | | | | | | | | | | | | | | | | | | |
| **22 SATO** | 21 | 20 | 20 | 20 | 20 | 20 | 2 | 2 | 2 | 8 | 8 | 8 | 8 | 18 | 18 | 18 | 18 | 4 | 4 | 23 | 23 | 23 | 20 | 20 | 20 | 20 | 20 | 20 | | | | | | | | | | | | | | | | | | | | | | | | | | |
| **17 NAKAJIMA** | 11 | 21 | 18 | 18 | 18 | 18 | 18 | 18 | 18 | 18 | 18 | 18 | 18 | 4 | 4 | 4 | 4 | 18 | | | | | | | | | | | | | | | | | | | | | | | | | | | | | | | | | | | | |
| **23 DAVIDSON** | 20 | 18 | 4 | 4 | 4 | 4 | 4 | 4 | 4 | 4 | 4 | 4 | | | | | | | | | | | | | | | | | | | | | | | | | | | | | | | | | | | | | | | | | | |
| **20 SUTIL** | 18 | 3 | | | | | | | | | | | | | | | | | | | | | | | | | | | | | | | | | | | | | | | | | | | | | | | | | | | | |
| **21 YAMAMOTO** | 4 | 4 | | | | | | | | | | | | | | | | | | | | | | | | | | | | | | | | | | | | | | | | | | | | | | | | | | | | |

20 Pit stop
20 One lap or more behind leader
20 Drive-through penalty

266

## PRACTICE 1 (FRIDAY)

Rain (track 18–21ºC, air 16–19ºC)

| Pos. | Driver | Laps | Time |
|---|---|---|---|
| 1 | Kimi Räikkönen | 9 | 1m 19.580s |
| 2 | Felipe Massa | 10 | 1m 20.062s |
| 3 | Heikki Kovalainen | 19 | 1m 20.829s |
| 4 | Nico Rosberg | 14 | 1m 21.064s |
| 5 | Lewis Hamilton | 10 | 1m 21.121s |
| 6 | Ralf Schumacher | 22 | 1m 21.243s |
| 7 | Sebastian Vettel | 22 | 1m 21.598s |
| 8 | Mark Webber | 12 | 1m 22.104s |
| 9 | Jarno Trulli | 26 | 1m 22.104s |
| 10 | Vitantonio Liuzzi | 17 | 1m 22.250s |
| 11 | Rubens Barrichello | 23 | 1m 22.434s |
| 12 | Jenson Button | 22 | 1m 22.477s |
| 13 | David Coulthard | 16 | 1m 22.667s |
| 14 | Takuma Sato | 19 | 1m 22.929s |
| 15 | Adrian Sutil | 30 | 1m 23.248s |
| 16 | Kazuki Nakajima | 26 | 1m 23.261s |
| 17 | Anthony Davidson | 20 | 1m 23.551s |
| 18 | Sakon Yamamoto | 25 | 1m 24.366s |
| 19 | Nick Heidfeld | 1 | No time |
| 20 | Robert Kubica | 1 | No time |
| 21 | Fernando Alonso | 1 | No time |
| 22 | Giancarlo Fisichella | 2 | No time |

## PRACTICE 2 (FRIDAY)

Damp, cloud (track 20–21ºC, air 18–19ºC)

| Pos. | Driver | Laps | Time |
|---|---|---|---|
| 1 | Lewis Hamilton | 27 | 1m 12.767s |
| 2 | Fernando Alonso | 28 | 1m 12.889s |
| 3 | Felipe Massa | 30 | 1m 13.075s |
| 4 | Kimi Räikkönen | 30 | 1m 13.112s |
| 5 | Giancarlo Fisichella | 22 | 1m 13.549s |
| 6 | Robert Kubica | 34 | 1m 13.587s |
| 7 | Nico Rosberg | 33 | 1m 13.655s |
| 8 | Kazuki Nakajima | 38 | 1m 13.664s |
| 9 | David Coulthard | 30 | 1m 13.706s |
| 10 | Nick Heidfeld | 44 | 1m 13.785s |
| 11 | Ralf Schumacher | 29 | 1m 13.829s |
| 12 | Heikki Kovalainen | 28 | 1m 13.879s |
| 13 | Rubens Barrichello | 45 | 1m 13.892s |
| 14 | Jenson Button | 44 | 1m 14.095s |
| 15 | Vitantonio Liuzzi | 33 | 1m 14.152s |
| 16 | Jarno Trulli | 25 | 1m 14.179s |
| 17 | Sebastian Vettel | 37 | 1m 14.409s |
| 18 | Takuma Sato | 27 | 1m 14.431s |
| 19 | Anthony Davidson | 31 | 1m 14.477s |
| 20 | Mark Webber | 35 | 1m 14.543s |
| 21 | Adrian Sutil | 35 | 1m 15.095s |
| 22 | Sakon Yamamoto | 32 | 1m 15.715s |

## QUALIFYING (SATURDAY)

Sunny (track 47–49ºC, air 30–33ºC)

| Pos. | Driver | First | Second | Third |
|---|---|---|---|---|
| 1 | Felipe Massa | 1m 12.303s | 1m 12.374s | 1m 11.931s |
| 2 | Lewis Hamilton | 1m 13.033s | 1m 12.296s | 1m 12.082s |
| 3 | Kimi Räikkönen | 1m 13.016s | 1m 12.161s | 1m 12.322s |
| 4 | Fernando Alonso | 1m 12.895s | 1m 12.637s | 1m 12.356s |
| 5 | Mark Webber | 1m 13.081s | 1m 12.683s | 1m 12.928s |
| 6 | Nick Heidfeld | 1m 13.472s | 1m 12.888s | 1m 13.081s |
| 7 | Robert Kubica | 1m 13.085s | 1m 12.641s | 1m 13.129s |
| 8 | Jarno Trulli | 1m 13.470s | 1m 12.832s | 1m 13.195s |
| 9 | David Coulthard | 1m 13.264s | 1m 12.846s | 1m 13.272s |
| 10 | Nico Rosberg | 1m 13.707s | 1m 12.752s | 1m 13.477s |
| 11 | Rubens Barrichello | 1m 13.661s | 1m 12.932s | |
| 12 | Giancarlo Fisichella | 1m 13.482s | 1m 12.968s | |
| 13 | Sebastian Vettel | 1m 13.853s | 1m 13.058s | |
| 14 | Vitantonio Liuzzi | 1m 13.607s | 1m 13.251s | |
| 15 | Ralf Schumacher | 1m 13.767s | 1m 13.315s | |
| 16 | Jenson Button | 1m 14.054s | 1m 13.469s | |
| 17 | Heikki Kovalainen | 1m 14.078s | | |
| 18 | Takuma Sato | 1m 14.098s | | |
| 19 | Kazuki Nakajima | 1m 14.417s | | |
| 20 | Anthony Davidson | 1m 14.596s | | |
| 21 | Adrian Sutil | 1m 15.217s | | |
| 22 | Sakon Yamamoto | 1m 15.487s | | |

## PRACTICE 3 (SATURDAY)

Sunny (track 36–42ºC, air 25–27ºC)

| Pos. | Driver | Laps | Time |
|---|---|---|---|
| 1 | Felipe Massa | 22 | 1m 11.810s |
| 2 | Lewis Hamilton | 18 | 1m 11.934s |
| 3 | Kimi Räikkönen | 21 | 1m 11.942s |
| 4 | Mark Webber | 14 | 1m 12.446s |
| 5 | Jarno Trulli | 23 | 1m 12.461s |
| 6 | Rubens Barrichello | 24 | 1m 12.478s |
| 7 | Nick Heidfeld | 25 | 1m 12.579s |
| 8 | Fernando Alonso | 12 | 1m 12.594s |
| 9 | Sebastian Vettel | 18 | 1m 12.767s |
| 10 | Nico Rosberg | 20 | 1m 12.823s |
| 11 | Vitantonio Liuzzi | 20 | 1m 12.893s |
| 12 | Giancarlo Fisichella | 20 | 1m 12.913s |
| 13 | Jenson Button | 22 | 1m 13.015s |
| 14 | Ralf Schumacher | 23 | 1m 13.046s |
| 15 | Heikki Kovalainen | 20 | 1m 13.090s |
| 16 | David Coulthard | 12 | 1m 13.117s |
| 17 | Anthony Davidson | 16 | 1m 13.299s |
| 18 | Takuma Sato | 16 | 1m 13.331s |
| 19 | Kazuki Nakajima | 17 | 1m 13.474s |
| 20 | Robert Kubica | 14 | 1m 13.525s |
| 21 | Adrian Sutil | 21 | 1m 13.684s |
| 22 | Sakon Yamamoto | 21 | 1m 13.872s |

## RACE TYRE STRATEGIES

**BRIDGESTONE**

In 2007, the tyre regulations stipulate that the two dry-tyre specifications must be visibly distinguishable from each other. At the Brazilian Grand Prix, the super-soft compound Bridgestone Potenza tyre was marked with a white line in the second-from-inside groove.

| | Driver | Race stint 1 | Race stint 2 | Race stint 3 | Race stint 4 |
|---|---|---|---|---|---|
| 1 | Räikkönen | Soft: laps 1–21 | Soft: 22–53 | Super-soft: 54–71 | |
| 2 | Massa | Soft: 1–20 | Soft: 21–50 | Super-soft: 51–71 | |
| 3 | Alonso | Soft: 1–22 | Soft: 23–52 | Super-soft: 53–71 | |
| 4 | Rosberg | Soft: 1–23 | Soft: 24–54 | Super-soft: 55–71 | |
| 5 | Kubica | Soft: 1–19 | Soft: 20–38 | Soft: 39–58 | Super-soft: 59–71 |
| 6 | Heidfeld | Soft: 1–25 | Soft: 26–51 | Super-soft: 52–71 | |
| 7 | Hamilton | Soft: 1–22 | Soft: 23–36 | Super-soft: 37–56 | Soft: 57–71 |
| 8 | Trulli | Soft: 1–22 | Soft: 23–43 | Soft: 44–63 | Super-soft: 64–71 |
| 9 | Coulthard | Soft: 1–23 | Soft: 24–42 | Super-soft: 43–71 | |
| 10 | Nakajima | Soft: 1–31 | Soft: 32–61 | Super-soft: 62–71 | |
| 11 | Schumacher | Soft: 1–33 | Soft: 34–61 | Super-soft: 62–71 | |
| 12 | Sato | Soft: 1–25 | Super-soft: 26–44 | Super-soft: 45–71 | |
| 13 | Liuzzi | Soft: 1 | Soft: 2–30 | Soft: 31–54 | Super-soft: 55–71 |
| 14 | Davidson | Soft: 1–22 | Soft: 23–48 | Super-soft: 49–71 | |
| 15 | Sutil | Soft: 1–22 | Soft: 23–24 | Soft: 25–38 | Super-soft: 39–43 (DNF) |
| 16 | Barrichello | Soft: 1–30 | Soft: 31–40 (DNF) | | |
| 17 | Kovalainen | Super-soft: 1 | Soft: 2–35 (DNF) | | |
| 18 | Vettel | Soft: 1–22 | Soft: 23–34 (DNF) | | |
| 19 | Button | Soft: 1–20 (DNF) | | | |
| | Webber | Soft: 1–7 (DNF) | | | |
| | Yamamoto | Soft: 1–2 (DNF) | | | |
| | Fisichella | Soft: 1–2 (DNF) | | | |

**10 ROSBERG** Williams

**8 TRULLI** Toyota

**6 HEIDFELD** BMW Sauber

**4 ALONSO** McLaren

**2 HAMILTON** McLaren

**9 COULTHARD** Red Bull

**7 KUBICA** BMW Sauber

**5 WEBBER** Red Bull

**3 RÄIKKÖNEN** Ferrari

**1 MASSA** Ferrari

**RACE DISTANCE:**
71 laps
190.083 miles/305.909 km

**RACE WEATHER:**
Sunny,
track 51–53ºC, air 34–36ºC

| 56 | 57 | 58 | 59 | 60 | 61 | 62 | 63 | 64 | 65 | 66 | 67 | 68 | 69 | 70 | 71 | |
|---|---|---|---|---|---|---|---|---|---|---|---|---|---|---|---|---|
| 6 | 6 | 6 | 6 | 6 | 6 | 6 | 6 | 6 | 6 | 6 | 6 | 6 | 6 | 6 | 6 | 1 |
| 5 | 5 | 5 | 5 | 5 | 5 | 5 | 5 | 5 | 5 | 5 | 5 | 5 | 5 | 5 | 5 | 2 |
| 10 | 10 | 10 | 1 | 1 | 1 | 1 | 1 | 1 | 1 | 1 | 1 | 1 | 1 | 1 | 1 | 3 |
| 1 | 1 | 1 | 9 | 9 | 10 | 10 | 10 | 10 | 10 | 10 | 10 | 16 | 16 | 16 | | 4 |
| 9 | 9 | 9 | 16 | 16 | 16 | 16 | 16 | 16 | 16 | 16 | 16 | 10 | 10 | 10 | | 5 |
| 16 | 16 | 16 | 10 | 10 | 9 | 9 | 9 | 9 | 9 | 9 | 9 | 9 | 9 | 9 | | 6 |
| 12 | 12 | 12 | 12 | 12 | 12 | 12 | 12 | 2 | 2 | 2 | 2 | 2 | 2 | 2 | | 7 |
| 2 | 2 | 2 | 2 | 2 | 2 | 2 | 12 | 12 | 12 | 12 | 12 | 12 | 12 | 12 | | 8 |
| 14 | 14 | 14 | 14 | 14 | 17 | 14 | 14 | 14 | 14 | 14 | 14 | 14 | 14 | | | |
| 17 | 17 | 17 | 17 | 17 | 14 | 17 | 17 | 17 | 17 | 17 | 17 | 17 | 17 | | | |
| 11 | 11 | 11 | 11 | 11 | 11 | 11 | 11 | 11 | 11 | 11 | 11 | 11 | 11 | | | |
| 22 | 22 | 22 | 22 | 22 | 22 | 22 | 22 | 22 | 22 | 22 | 22 | 22 | 22 | | | |
| 18 | 18 | 18 | 18 | 18 | 18 | 18 | 18 | 18 | 18 | 18 | 18 | 18 | 18 | | | |
| 23 | 23 | 23 | 23 | 23 | 23 | 23 | 23 | 23 | 23 | 23 | 23 | 23 | 23 | | | |

## FOR THE RECORD

**FIRST DRIVERS' WORLD CHAMPIONSHIP:** Kimi Räikkönen (above)

**200th POINT:** Felipe Massa

**15th DRIVERS' WORLD CHAMPIONSHIP:** Ferrari

**250th GRAND PRIX START:** Rubens Barrichello

**RECORD 11 RETIREMENTS AT HOME GRAND PRIX:** Rubens Barrichello

**FIRST GRAND PRIX START:** Kazuki Nakajima

## POINTS

### CONSTRUCTORS

| | | |
|---|---|---|
| 1 | Ferrari | 204 |
| 2 | BMW Sauber | 101 |
| 3 | Renault | 51 |
| 4 | Williams | 33 |
| 5 | Red Bull | 24 |
| 6 | Toyota | 13 |
| 7 | Toro Rosso | 8 |
| 8 | Honda | 6 |
| 9 | Super Aguri | 4 |
| 10 | Spyker | 1 |

### DRIVERS

| | | |
|---|---|---|
| 1 | Kimi Räikkönen | 110 |
| 2 | Lewis Hamilton | 109 |
| 3 | Fernando Alonso | 109 |
| 4 | Felipe Massa | 94 |
| 5 | Nick Heidfeld | 61 |
| 6 | Robert Kubica | 39 |
| 7 | Heikki Kovalainen | 30 |
| 8 | Giancarlo Fisichella | 21 |
| 9 | Nico Rosberg | 20 |
| 10 | David Coulthard | 14 |
| 11 | Alexander Wurz | 13 |
| 12 | Mark Webber | 10 |
| 13 | Jarno Trulli | 8 |
| 14 | Sebastian Vettel | 6 |
| 15 | Jenson Button | 6 |
| 16 | Ralf Schumacher | 5 |
| 17 | Takuma Sato | 4 |
| 18 | Vitantonio Liuzzi | 3 |
| 19 | Adrian Sutil | 1 |

Photographs: Peter J Fox/www.crash.net

GRANDE PRÊMIO DO BRASIL — SÃO PAULO 2007
FIA Formula 1 WORLD CHAMPIONSHIP

STATISTICS FIA F1 WORLD CHAMPIONSHIP 2007

# DRIVERS' POINTS TABLE Compiled by DAVID HAYHOE

| Place | Driver | Nationality | Date of birth | Car | Australia | Malaysia | Bahrain | Spain | Monaco | Canada | USA | France | Britain | Europe | Hungary | Turkey | Italy | Belgium | Japan | China | Brazil | Points total |
|---|---|---|---|---|---|---|---|---|---|---|---|---|---|---|---|---|---|---|---|---|---|---|
| 1 | Kimi RÄIKKÖNEN | FIN | 17/10/79 | Ferrari | 1pf | 3 | 3 | R | 8 | 5 | 4f | 1 | 1f | Rp | 2f | 2f | 3 | 1p | 3 | 1 | 1f | 110 |
| 2 | Lewis HAMILTON | GB | 7/1/85 | McLaren-Mercedes | 3 | 2f | 2 | 2 | 2 | 1p | 1p | 3 | 3p | 9 | 1p | 5 | 2 | 4 | 1pf | Rp | 7 | 109 |
| 3 | Fernando ALONSO | E | 29/7/81 | McLaren-Mercedes | 2 | 1 | 5 | 3 | 1pf | 7f | 2 | 7 | 2 | 1 | 4 | 3 | 1pf | 3 | R | 2 | 3 | 109 |
| 4 | Felipe MASSA | BR | 25/4/81 | Ferrari | 6 | 5p | 1pf | 1pf | 3 | DQ | 3 | 2pf | 5 | 2f | 13 | 1p | R | 2f | 6 | 3f | 2p | 94 |
| 5 | Nick HEIDFELD | D | 10/5/77 | BMW Sauber | 4 | 4 | 4 | R | 6 | 2 | R | 5 | 6 | 6 | 3 | 4 | 4 | 5 | 14* | 7 | 6 | 61 |
| 6 | Robert KUBICA | POL | 7/12/84 | BMW Sauber | R | 18 | 6 | 4 | 5 | R | - | 4 | 4 | 7 | 5 | 8 | 5 | 9 | 7 | R | 5 | 39 |
| 7 | Heikki KOVALAINEN | FIN | 19/10/81 | Renault | 10 | 8 | 9 | 7 | 13* | 4 | 5 | 15 | 7 | 8 | 8 | 6 | 7 | 8 | 2 | 9 | R | 30 |
| 8 | Giancarlo FISICHELLA | I | 14/1/73 | Renault | 5 | 6 | 8 | 9 | 4 | DQ | 9 | 6 | 8 | 10 | 12 | 9 | 12 | R | 5 | 11 | R | 21 |
| 9 | Nico ROSBERG | D | 27/6/85 | Williams-Toyota | 7 | R | 10 | 6 | 12 | 10 | 16* | 9 | 12 | R | 7 | 7 | 6 | 6 | R | 16 | 4 | 20 |
| 10 | David COULTHARD | GB | 27/3/71 | Red Bull-Renault | R | R | R | 5 | 14 | R | 13 | 11 | 5 | 11 | 10 | R | R | 4 | 8 | 9 |  | 14 |
| 11 | Alexander WURZ | A | 15/2/74 | Williams-Toyota | R | 9 | 11 | R | 7 | 3 | 10 | 14 | 13 | 4 | 14 | 11 | 13 | R | R | 12 | - | 13 |
| 12 | Mark WEBBER | AUS | 27/8/76 | Red Bull-Renault | 13 | 10 | R | R | R | 9 | 7 | 12 | R | 3 | 9 | R | 9 | 7 | R | 10 | R | 10 |
| 13 | Jarno TRULLI | I | 13/7/74 | Toyota | 9 | 7 | 7 | R | 15 | R | 6 | R | R | 13 | 10 | 16 | 11 | 11 | 13 | 13 | 8 | 8 |
| 14 | Sebastian VETTEL | D | 3/7/87 | BMW Sauber | - | - | - | - | - | - | 8 | - | - | - |  |  |  |  |  |  |  |  |
|  |  |  |  | Toro Rosso-Ferrari | - | - | - | - | - | - | - | - | - | - | 16 | 19 | 18 | R | R | 4 | R | 6 |
| 15 | Jenson BUTTON | GB | 19/1/80 | Honda | 15 | 12 | R | 12 | 11 | R | 12 | 8 | 10 | R | R | 13 | 8 | R | 11* | 5 | 6 | 6 |
| 16 | Ralf SCHUMACHER | D | 30/6/75 | Toyota | 8 | 15 | 12 | R | 16 | 8 | R | 10 | R | 6 | 12 | 15 | 10 | R | R | 11 |  | 5 |
| 17 | Takuma SATO | J | 28/1/77 | Super Aguri-Honda | 12 | 13 | R | 8 | 17 | 6 | R | 16 | 14 | R | 15 | 18 | 16 | 15 | 15* | 14 | 12 | 4 |
| 18 | Vitantonio LIUZZI | I | 6/8/80 | Toro Rosso-Ferrari | 14 | 17 | R | R | R | 17* | R | 16* | R | R | 15 | 17 | 12 | 9 | 6 | 13 |  | 3 |
| 19 | Adrian SUTIL | D | 11/1/83 | Spyker-Ferrari | 17 | R | 15 | 13 | R | 14 | 17 | R | R | 17 | 21* | 19 | 14 | 8 | R | R |  | 1 |
| 20 | Rubens BARRICHELLO | BR | 23/5/72 | Honda | 11 | 11 | 13 | 10 | 10 | 12 | R | 11 | 9 | 11 | 18 | 17 | 10 | 13 | 10 | 15 | R | 0 |
| 21 | Scott SPEED | USA | 24/1/83 | Toro Rosso-Ferrari | R | 14 | R | R | 9 | R | 13 | R | R | - | - | - | - | - | - | - | - | 0 |
| 22 | Anthony DAVIDSON | GB | 18/4/79 | Super Aguri-Honda | 16 | 16 | 16* | 11 | 18 | 11 | 11 | R | R | 12 | R | 14 | 14 | 16 | R | R | 14 | 0 |
| 23 | Sakon YAMAMOTO | J | 9/7/82 | Spyker-Ferrari | - | - | - | - | - | - | - | - | - | - | R | 20 | 20 | 17 | 12 | 17 | R | 0 |
| 24 | Christijan ALBERS | NL | 16/4/79 | Spyker-Ferrari | R | R | 14 | 14 | 19* | R | 15 | R | 15 | - | - | - | - | - | - | - | - | 0 |
| 25 | Kazuki NAKAJIMA | J | 11/1/85 | Williams-Toyota | - | - | - | - | - | - | - | - | - | - | - | - | - | - | - | - | 10 | 0 |
| 26 | Markus WINKELHOCK | D | 13/6/80 | Spyker-Ferrari | - | - | - | - | - | - | - | - | - | R | - | - | - | - | - | - | - | 0 |

**The following driver only took part in Friday private testing at grand prix meetings:**

| | | | |
|---|---|---|---|
| Christian KLIEN | A | 7/2/83 | Honda |

**The following driver took part in test sessions and also in grands prix:**

Sebastian VETTEL

| KEY | | | |
|---|---|---|---|
| p | pole position | DQ | disqualified |
| f | fastest lap | * | classified, but not running at the finish |
| R | retired | | |

# POINTS & PERCENTAGES

Compiled by DAVID HAYHOE

Photograph: Peter J Fox/www.crash.net

## GRID POSITIONS: 2007

| Pos. | Driver | Starts | Best | Worst | Average |
|---|---|---|---|---|---|
| 1 | Lewis Hamilton | 17 | 1 | 10 | 2.59 |
| 2 | Fernando Alonso | 17 | 1 | 10 | 3.18 |
| 3 | Kimi Räikkönen | 17 | 1 | 16 | 3.53 |
| 4 | Felipe Massa | 17 | 1 | 22 | 4.24 |
| 5 | Nick Heidfeld | 17 | 2 | 9 | 5.41 |
| 6 | Robert Kubica | 16 | 4 | 14 | 6.88 |
| 7 | Mark Webber | 17 | 5 | 19 | 9.06 |
| 8 | Jarno Trulli | 17 | 6 | 14 | 9.18 |
| 9 | Nico Rosberg | 17 | 4 | 17 | 9.88 |
| 10 | Heikki Kovalainen | 17 | 6 | 22 | 10.71 |
| 11 | Giancarlo Fisichella | 17 | 4 | 22 | 10.82 |
| 12 | Ralf Schumacher | 17 | 5 | 20 | 12.35 |
| 13 | David Coulthard | 17 | 5 | 21 | 13.35 |
| 14 | Jenson Button | 17 | 6 | 21 | 13.88 |
| 15 | Sebastian Vettel | 8 | 7 | 20 | 14.37 |
| 16 | Rubens Barrichello | 17 | 9 | 22 | 15.06 |
| 17 | Alexander Wurz | 16 | 11 | 19 | 15.25 |
| 18 | Vitantonio Liuzzi | 17 | 11 | 19 | 15.65 |
| 19 | Anthony Davidson | 17 | 11 | 20 | 16.06 |
| 20 | Takuma Sato | 17 | 10 | 22 | 17.29 |
| 21 | Scott Speed | 10 | 15 | 22 | 17.70 |
| 22 | Kazuki Nakajima | 1 | 19 | 19 | 19.00 |
| 23 | Adrian Sutil | 17 | 19 | 21 | 20.29 |
| 24 | Christijan Albers | 9 | 20 | 22 | 21.11 |
| 25 | Sakon Yamamoto | 7 | 20 | 22 | 21.57 |
| 26 | Markus Winkelhock | 1 | 22 | 22 | 22.00 |

## CAREER PERFORMANCES: 2007 DRIVERS

| Driver | Nationality | Races | Championships | Wins | 2nd places | 3rd places | 4th places | 5th places | 6th places | 7th places | 8th places | Pole positions | Fastest laps | Points |
|---|---|---|---|---|---|---|---|---|---|---|---|---|---|---|
| Christijan Albers | NL | 46 | - | - | - | - | - | 1 | - | - | - | - | - | 4 |
| Fernando Alonso | E | 104 | 2 | 19 | 18 | 12 | 9 | 6 | 2 | 4 | 1 | 17 | 11 | 490 |
| Rubens Barrichello | BR | 250 | - | 9 | 26 | 26 | 17 | 15 | 9 | 10 | 5 | 13 | 15 | 519 |
| Jenson Button | GB | 135 | - | 1 | 4 | 10 | 12 | 16 | 5 | 7 | 10 | 3 | - | 229 |
| David Coulthard | GB | 228 | - | 13 | 26 | 22 | 12 | 19 | 13 | 15 | 7 | 12 | 18 | 527 |
| Anthony Davidson | GB | 20 | - | - | - | - | - | - | - | - | - | - | - | - |
| Giancarlo Fisichella | I | 194 | - | 3 | 6 | 9 | 14 | 14 | 17 | 11 | 13 | 3 | 2 | 267 |
| Lewis Hamilton | GB | 17 | - | 4 | 5 | 3 | 1 | 1 | - | 1 | - | 6 | 2 | 109 |
| Nick Heidfeld | D | 132 | - | - | 3 | 4 | 8 | 4 | 13 | 10 | 9 | 1 | - | 140 |
| Heikki Kovalainen | FIN | 17 | - | - | 1 | - | 1 | 1 | 1 | 3 | 4 | - | - | 30 |
| Robert Kubica | POL | 22 | - | - | - | 1 | 3 | 4 | 1 | 2 | 1 | - | - | 45 |
| Vitantonio Liuzzi | I | 39 | - | - | - | - | - | - | 1 | - | 2 | - | - | 5 |
| Felipe Massa | BR | 87 | - | 5 | 7 | 5 | 4 | 7 | 5 | 4 | 5 | 9 | 8 | 201 |
| Kazuki Nakajima | J | 1 | - | - | - | - | - | - | - | - | - | - | - | - |
| Kimi Räikkönen | FIN | 121 | 1 | 15 | 17 | 16 | 9 | 8 | 4 | 4 | 4 | 14 | 25 | 456 |
| Nico Rosberg | D | 35 | - | - | - | 1 | - | 3 | 5 | - | - | 1 | | 24 |
| Takuma Sato | J | 86 | - | - | - | 1 | 2 | 3 | 5 | - | 4 | - | - | 44 |
| Ralf Schumacher | D | 180 | - | 6 | 6 | 15 | 19 | 17 | 12 | 11 | 9 | 6 | 8 | 329 |
| Scott Speed | USA | 28 | - | - | - | - | - | - | - | - | - | - | - | - |
| Adrian Sutil | D | 17 | - | - | - | - | - | - | - | 1 | - | - | - | 1 |
| Jarno Trulli | I | 181 | - | 1 | 3 | 3 | 13 | 12 | 12 | 11 | 10 | 3 | - | 183 |
| Sebastian Vettel | D | 8 | - | - | - | - | 1 | - | - | - | 1 | - | - | 6 |
| Mark Webber | AUS | 103 | - | - | - | 2 | 2 | 3 | 8 | 10 | 4 | - | - | 79 |
| Markus Winkelhock | D | 1 | - | - | - | - | - | - | - | - | - | - | - | - |
| Alexander Wurz | A | 69 | - | - | - | 3 | 6 | 3 | 1 | 8 | 1 | - | 1 | 45 |
| Sakon Yamamoto | J | 14 | - | - | - | - | - | - | - | - | - | - | - | - |

**Note:** As is now common practice, drivers retiring on the formation lap are not counted as having started. Where races have been subject to a restart, those retiring during an initial race are included as having started.

## UNLAPPED: 2007

**Number of cars on same lap as leader**

| Grand Prix | Starters | at 1/4 distance | at 1/2 distance | at 3/4 distance | at full distance |
|---|---|---|---|---|---|
| Australia | 22 | 21 | 15 | 8 | 6 |
| Malaysia | 22 | 20 | 18 | 11 | 10 |
| Bahrain | 22 | 19 | 17 | 10 | 10 |
| Spain | 22 | 17 | 10 | 8 | 7 |
| Monaco | 22 | 15 | 9 | 4 | 3 |
| Canada | 22 | 20 | 18 | 13 | 12 |
| USA | 22 | 17 | 12 | 10 | 8 |
| France | 22 | 18 | 10 | 10 | 9 |
| Britain | 22 | 21 | 15 | 9 | 6 |
| Europe | 22 | 16 | 14 | 9 | 7 |
| Hungary | 22 | 20 | 14 | 10 | 9 |
| Turkey | 22 | 21 | 18 | 13 | 11 |
| Italy | 22 | 20 | 20 | 8 | 11 |
| Belgium | 22 | 20 | 18 | 13 | 11 |
| Japan | 22 | 22 | 18 | 16 | 10 |
| China | 22 | 19 | 15 | 13 | 11 |
| Brazil | 22 | 17 | 9 | 8 | 6 |

## LAP LEADERS: 2007

| Grand Prix | L Hamilton | F Massa | K Räikkönen | Fernando Alonso | H Kovalainen | M Winkelhock | M Webber | N Heidfeld | S Vettel | D Coulthard | G Fisichella | R Kubica | Total |
|---|---|---|---|---|---|---|---|---|---|---|---|---|---|
| Australia | 4 | - | 52 | 2 | - | - | - | - | - | - | - | - | 58 |
| Malaysia | 2 | - | 1 | 52 | - | - | - | 1 | - | - | - | - | 56 |
| Bahrain | 4 | 51 | 2 | - | - | - | - | - | - | - | - | - | 57 |
| Spain | 8 | 55 | - | - | - | - | 2 | - | - | - | - | - | 65 |
| Monaco | 5 | - | - | 73 | - | - | - | - | - | - | - | - | 78 |
| Canada | 67 | 3 | - | - | - | - | - | - | - | - | - | - | 70 |
| USA | 66 | 1 | - | 1 | 5 | - | - | - | - | - | - | - | 73 |
| France | - | 40 | 30 | - | - | - | - | - | - | - | - | - | 70 |
| Britain | 15 | - | 24 | 20 | - | - | - | - | - | - | - | - | 59 |
| Europe | - | 47 | 1 | 5 | - | 6 | - | - | - | 1 | - | - | 60 |
| Hungary | 70 | - | - | - | - | - | - | - | - | - | - | - | 70 |
| Turkey | 1 | 55 | - | - | 1 | - | 1 | - | - | - | - | - | 58 |
| Italy | - | - | 5 | 48 | - | - | - | - | - | - | - | - | 53 |
| Belgium | - | 2 | 42 | - | - | - | - | - | - | - | - | - | 44 |
| Japan | 55 | - | - | - | 3 | - | 5 | - | 3 | - | 1 | - | 67 |
| China | 24 | - | 31 | - | - | - | - | - | - | - | - | 1 | 56 |
| Brazil | - | 46 | 24 | 1 | - | - | - | - | - | - | - | - | 71 |
| Total | 321 | 300 | 212 | 203 | 9 | 6 | 5 | 3 | 3 | 1 | 1 | 1 | 1065 |
| (Per cent) | 30.1 | 28.2 | 19.9 | 19.1 | 0.8 | 0.6 | 0.5 | 0.3 | 0.3 | 0.1 | 0.1 | 0.1 | 100.0 |

## RETIREMENTS: 2007

**Number of cars to have retired**

| Grand Prix | Starters | at 1/4 distance | at 1/2 distance | at 3/4 distance | at full distance | % of finishers |
|---|---|---|---|---|---|---|
| Australia | 22 | 1 | 2 | 3 | 5 | 77.3 |
| Malaysia | 22 | 2 | 2 | 4 | 4 | 81.8 |
| Bahrain | 22 | 2 | 3 | 6 | 7 | 68.2 |
| Spain | 22 | 5 | 6 | 8 | 8 | 63.6 |
| Monaco | 22 | 2 | 2 | 3 | 5 | 77.3 |
| Canada | 22 | 2 | 4 | 8 | 10 | 54.5 |
| USA | 22 | 4 | 4 | 4 | 7 | 68.2 |
| France | 22 | 3 | 4 | 4 | 5 | 77.3 |
| Britain | 22 | 1 | 4 | 6 | 7 | 68.2 |
| Europe | 22 | 6 | 8 | 9 | 9 | 59.1 |
| Hungary | 22 | 1 | 2 | 4 | 4 | 81.8 |
| Turkey | 22 | 1 | 1 | 1 | 2 | 90.9 |
| Italy | 22 | 2 | 2 | 2 | 2 | 90.9 |
| Belgium | 22 | 2 | 2 | 3 | 5 | 77.3 |
| Japan | 22 | 0 | 1 | 5 | 10 | 54.5 |
| China | 22 | 1 | 3 | 5 | 5 | 77.3 |
| Brazil | 22 | 3 | 5 | 8 | 8 | 63.6 |

Timo Glock was the undoubted star of
the series and a worthy successor to
Lewis Hamilton. He certainly deserves
another chance in Formula 1.
Photographs: Peter J Fox/www.crash.net

# A CAREER REBUILT...

GP2 REVIEW by CHARLES BRADLEY

POST-Lewis Hamilton, season three of GP2 was always going to have a tough act to follow. But in Timo Glock it produced a champion of Formula 1 quality who sits comfortably alongside Hamilton and 2005 winner Nico Rosberg.

There were some remarkable happenings in GP2 this year, not least those that involved Glock. He had perhaps the fastest-ever shunt at Magny-Cours, when he collided with iSport team-mate Andi Zuber seconds after the lights went out, and was even taken out on the installation lap at Spa-Francorchamps by a rival just when his title hopes hung in the balance.

Despite these pitfalls – and the many reliability issues that afflicted him (GP2 continued to struggle in this area) – Glock and iSport deserved this title. Having joined iSport mid-way through last year, Glock outscored Hamilton for much of the second half of '06 – and he carried that form into pre-season testing and the start of '07. Indeed, early on it looked likely to be a cakewalk: after a handful of rounds he extended a 16-point lead

at the head of the championship, but then came Magny-Cours…

That ridiculous start-line shunt undoubtedly damaged Glock's reputation in the F1 paddock's eyes and he spent the rest of the season rebuilding it. Ironically, the way he battled the adversity that followed probably did him the world of good. By the final race weekend in Valencia he was just two points ahead of Lucas di Grassi, who was trying to make it a hat-trick of titles for ART Grand Prix.

Di Grassi had fought something of a guerrilla war, realising early that ART had been overtaken in terms of speed by iSport. He wasn't helped by a revolving door of team-mates, as Michael Ammermüller broke his wrist in Bahrain and was replaced by a succession of Red Bull *protégés*, none of whom packed his experience of the category.

In the end, Glock's speed shone through. A crazy last feature race at Valencia, which was affected by a heavy rain shower shortly before the start, left Glock scrabbling around for a couple

**Top left: Trident's Pastor Maldonado scored a majestic win at Monaco, but his season was cut short by a broken collarbone sustained in training.**

**Centre left: Karun Chandhok's win at Spa was popular across the paddock.**

**Centre: The 19-year-old Javier Villa scored three sprint-race wins. Former team-mate Adam Carroll hoists him aloft on the Hungaroring podium.**

**Left: Giorgio Pantano helped the Campos Grand Prix team to become a race-winning organisation.**

Photographs: Peter J Fox/www.crash.net

**Above:** Drafted into the Fisichella Motorsport team in mid-season, Adam Carroll soon repaid the team with a superbly stylish win at Silverstone.

**Left:** Kazuki Nakajima was very fast but error-prone for the DAMS team. However, it didn't prevent him from stepping up into the grand prix ranks at season's end.

Photographs: Peter J Fox/www.crash.net

of points, while Di Grassi was involved in a start-line clash and then spun out while running on the right tyres at the wrong time.

The following day's final sprint was always going to be a formality for Glock to wrap up the title and he did so by taking a dominant fifth victory of the season. In contrast, Di Grassi had won only one race all year, in Turkey, an event where his rivals seemed intent on gifting him the win.

The level of unpredictability that has appeared to stalk GP2 since its inception produced no fewer than 12 race winners this year. Besides Glock, the most prolific winner was a huge surprise: Racing Engineering's 19-year-old starlet Javier Villa. His three wins came in the reversed-grid sprint races but he developed an uncanny knack of finishing eighth in the Saturday feature races to give him pole position for Sunday – he did it four times from

10 attempts. On the two occasions he didn't win from reverse pole, he was beaten by Glock – and there's no shame in that.

Giorgio Pantano won more feature races than anyone else, at Magny-Cours and Monza, but it was the way he led the Campos Grand Prix team that was most impressive. Last year, the Valencia-based outfit, run by ex-Minardi F1 racer Adrian Campos, was rarely anything other than a backmarker, but '07 brought a turnaround of dramatic proportions.

With new technical director Chris Murphy getting a handle on the car's pace, it was reliability that really struck down Pantano's title chances. He'd scored only one point before a solid drive to second in Monaco, which was followed by a breakthrough win for the team at Magny-Cours. Engine failure next time out at Silverstone brought his momentum to an end and his next

high point, second in Turkey, was followed by a clash with Di Grassi, which sent Giorgio into apoplexy.

A dominant performance in the feature race at Monza, where he's been winning sub-F1 races since '01, was followed by his throwing away a certain win in the sprint thanks to an over-impetuous passing attempt for the lead. He bravely continued, with his front wing hanging off alarmingly, to race at speeds of around 200 mph and would have scored points but for being black-flagged by the race stewards, who feared for his life. A complete heart-on-his-sleeve racer, Pantano has been tipped for a future in American single-seaters, where he would undoubtedly become a star.

Pantano finished third in the championship thanks to those two victories and a strong weekend in the Valencia finale. His fellow Italian Luca Filippi was the man who lost out. He started the season strongly, taking pole position and feature race honours in the Bahrain season-opener for Super Nova. He was Glock's closest rival in the points early on but suffered when taken out in the first corner at both Barcelona and the Nürburgring, while a huge shunt in Hungary – violent enough to stretch the belts on his HANS device – failed to put him off his stride. He bounced back with runner-up finishes at Monza and Spa before a broken fuel pump in the Valencia feature race put him out of the reckoning, which cost him third in the points race.

Fifth in the championship was Kazuki Nakajima (DAMS), who laid down his marker pace-wise with fastest laps in the first two feature races of the season. It took until Silverstone for him to put together a serious race weekend and it seemed whenever he raced on a track where he'd tested for Williams in its F1 car

he was a force to be reckoned with. That he didn't win a race all season was mainly down to his propensity for silly mistakes but when he stayed focused on the job in hand he was as quick as anyone out there.

Of the other race winners, Adam Carroll did a great job for FMS after it dispensed with Antonio Pizzonia's services after five races. Carroll, who ducked out of an uncompetitive DTM drive, took opportunistic wins at Silverstone and Hungary and remains one of the best overtakers around. Nicolas Lapierre was the other multiple winner for DAMS, at Bahrain and Spa, but was dogged by poor fortune as usual elsewhere – none more so than at Magny-Cours, where he lost a likely sprint-race win to brake failure.

Bruno Senna scored a majestic victory at Barcelona when he nursed his Arden machine home on well-worn tyres in baking temperatures. Zuber won at Silverstone from pole position with fastest lap, but gearbox woes were the bane of his season. He should have won again in Turkey but threw the race away and his head seemed to drop after that.

Pastor Maldonado was peerless in Monaco for Trident Racing, winning with ease, but ragged elsewhere. A broken collarbone (sustained in a mountain bike shunt) put him out of the last eight races. Vitaly Petrov won at Valencia for Campos thanks to an inspired tyre choice and a lightning start, while Karun Chandhok (Durango) improved all through the year and won the sprint race at Spa after a sparkling drive.

Next year, the series gets a makeover in the shape of a new GP2/08 Dallara-Renault. The new car is reckoned to be two seconds a lap quicker than the current machine, which will be pensioned off in the new-for-'08 GP2 Asia Series.

**Above: Brazilian Lucas di Grassi won in Turkey, but relied on his consistency to mount a title challenge.**

**Top left: iSport's Andreas Zuber was fast but inconsistent. he did win at Silverstone, however, and shares the podium here with Mike Conway (left) and Kazuki Nakajima.**

**Centre: Luca Filippi won the season's opener in Bahrain and generally shone in his début year.**
Photographs: Peter J Fox/www.crash.net

**Left: Bruno Senna bore the weight of expectation well and an early-season victory was a boost to his confidence. At Monza (pictured) he took a podium in the sprint race.**
Photograph: Andrew Ferraro/GP2 Media Services

A1GP 'WORLD CUP OF MOTORSPORT' REVIEW

# GERMANY ON TOP
# OF THE WORLD

by OLLIE BARSTOW

Germany on top – down under. Nico Hülkenberg leads the pack at he start of the race at Taupo, New Zealand.

Far left: **Nico Hülkenberg revels in the wet conditions in Malaysia, crushing the opposition with ease.**

Left: **Allam Khodair in the Team Lebanon entry gets out of shape on the kerbing in Shanghai.**
Photographs: A1GP Media Service

Above: **On the Mexico podium following race one are third-placed Ian Dyk (left), driver of A1 Team Australia with winner Team Malaysia's Alex Yoong and Oliver Jarvis of A1 Team Great Britain, who took the second spot.**

Left: **A1 Team France driver Nicolas Lapierre leads the Netherlands entry of Jeroen Bleekemolen in the fourth round of the championship at Sepang in November 2006.**
Photographs: A1GP Media Service

I f the first season of A1GP went a long way to proving wrong the countless cynics who had sounded the series' death knell before it had even begun, the second 'World Cup of Motorsport' undoubtedly served to push it further up the motor sport hierarchy.

Although qualms about finances and a change of ownership mid-season may have rung alarm bells, those difficulties could not overshadow a season of encouraging spectator levels, competitive racing and the discovery of a precocious talent now tipped for superstardom.

His name? Nico Hülkenberg.

Although the champion's trophy would have 'Germany' engraved beneath first-season winner France, it was Hülkenberg who really emerged as the big winner from the 2006–07 A1GP season.

He didn't take long to signal his potential. The 19-year-old earned the seat by virtue of his manager Willi Weber, famed for his work with a certain Michael Schumacher. However, while Weber's team-owner role certainly massaged Hülkenberg's passage into the German seat, it could not take away from Hülkenberg's genuine pace from the first round onwards.

That first round was held at Zandvoort, in the Netherlands, one of a handful of new venues gracing the calendar as the A1GP's ethos of taking motor sport to new markets led to Portugal's and Germany's being dropped and replaced by a round in New Zealand and a second race in China.

But perhaps the loss of the German round was a rather premature move, given the early signs of how the season was going to progress as Hülkenberg ensured that Germany would be making up for its rather lacklustre showing in the inaugural season of competition.

Heading to the Netherlands, the usual suspects remained: reigning champion France was rejoined by closest rivals Switzerland, Great Britain, New Zealand, Malaysia and Brazil as well as lesser-heralded nations such as Lebanon, India and Pakistan. While Japan, Austria and Russia failed to return for year two, the series gained Greece and Singapore (initially...) for a 22-car entry list.

Zandvoort produced two first-time A1GP winners in the shapes of South Africa and Germany with Adrian Zaugg and Hülkenberg taking a victory apiece. They were gained in different ways, though: Zaugg came through a somewhat confusing qualifying system to secure pole position and simply drove away to victory, while Hülkenberg on the other hand came through the pack in rainy conditions to deny the USA and home favourites the Netherlands (led by Jeroen Bleekemolen after national hero Jos Verstappen pulled out just days before the first round) a famous win.

From there the series moved east to Brno, another new venue on the calendar by virtue of the Czech Republic's success in the first season and its emergence as a breeding ground for accomplished drivers – namely Tomas Enge.

Enge had been a race winner in the first season and was among the drivers tipped to shine on familiar ground – something he duly managed when he earned the title of the best result for a home nation with a second-placed finish in the feature race.

The meeting, however, was all about Malaysia and Alex Yoong, the former Minardi F1 driver who had shown good form towards the end of A1GP's first season of racing and who now romped to both race wins around the undulating circuit in the Czech countryside.

His cause was aided in the first race by front-row sitters New Zealand and Germany coming together as they sprinted off the line, sending both into the barriers and promoting Yoong into a lead he retained thereafter.

He thus took pole position for the second race and, although he did come away victorious again, it was only after a superb drive back into contention after Yoong fell several seconds behind Canada's James Hinchcliffe following his pit stop. Hinchcliffe, a Champcar Atlantic driver, was having a stellar A1GP début after being drafted into the seat just before qualifying to replace an out-of-favour Sean McIntosh, taking the lead of the feature race and edging towards the nation's second win in the series.

However, Hinchcliffe's fading tyres were bringing Yoong back into contention and, with only a few laps remaining, Yoong's yellow machine was crawling over the back of the Maple-leaf-branded car. When Yoong made his move, Hinchcliffe misjudged his lunge and bounced off the side of the Malaysian car's side pod, sending him into a spin. It left Malaysia celebrating a double win, ahead of Enge and Mexico's Salvador Duran, while Hinchcliffe finished a rather disgruntled fifth.

With the season's racing coming to a close elsewhere, A1GP was just getting started. It headed out of Europe for the first of two rounds to be held in China, the streets of the capital city Beijing hosting the third round.

This was an exciting street venue intended to replicate the success of South Africa's Durban the previous year, but things started off badly when the layout was criticised for being too tricky for the powerful cars – in particular, there was a hairpin that was proving almost impossible to navigate.

Circuit revisions followed, but then qualifying was cancelled because drain covers became dislodged, raising doubts over whether the round would even go ahead. Nonetheless, after the organisers decided grid positions according to where the drivers had finished in practice, the weekend went ahead with no more problems.

Still, with overtaking barely possible, the sprint race rewarded those who had done well in practice, especially Bleekemolen, who recorded a surprise victory for the Netherlands from pole position, finishing ahead of Mexico and Italy. Indeed, with Canada, Germany and Brazil coming up next, the top six had not deviated from their grid positions.

Things picked up for the feature race, the points on offer apparently leading to a more daring approach to the race. Inevitably, though, with daring come errors and just nine drivers finished on the same lap as the winner.

The ultimate survivor was A1 Team Italy returnee Enrico Toccacelo, who romped to the nation's first A1GP victory with a comfortable margin of four seconds over second-placed Great Britain, Oliver Jarvis granting that nation its best result of the season on his début. The high attrition rate prompted more surprising results behind: Karl Reindler scored an impressive second podium of the season for Australia and newcomer Singapore got off the mark thanks to Christian Murchison's eighth-placed finish.

Alongside Toccacelo, other high-profile returnees to the A1GP field were Matt Halliday – drafted in, somewhat surprisingly, for New Zealand because of his greater street circuit experience over Jonny Reid's – and Switzerland's star of the first season, Neel Jani, the then Scuderia Toro Rosso F1 test driver looking to propel the nation to victory after finishing second in year one.

A couple of minor results did not form a great comeback for Jani in China, but the trip to Sepang in Malaysia proved far more fruitful: he claimed an easy sprint-race victory ahead of Germany and New Zealand, the latter having Reid back in the car.

The feature race was a different matter, however, as Malaysia's infamous micro-climate threw a curve ball into proceedings. While the treacherous conditions prompted a few tentative revolutions in the early laps, Hülkenberg was revelling in them up at the front, having overtaken Switzerland by the end of the first lap.

At times almost three seconds a lap faster than anyone else, Hülkenberg disappeared into the distance as those behind scrabbled for grip on the deluged surface and was 11 seconds up on Jani after just five laps.

Stalling in the pit lane was his only error on the way to Germany's second victory of the season, a crushing 42 seconds up on the next driver over just 28 laps. Second place went the way of Great Britain, Robbie Kerr battling up from fifth on the grid to hold back the advances of France's Nicolas Lapierre, who scored his team's third podium of the season. Sprint-race winner Jani, struggling in the conditions, finished fourth, with North American duo Canada and the USA – with McIntosh and Phil Giebler in the cockpits – fifth and sixth.

Although Indonesia was considered one of the more obscure venues on the A1GP calendar, its maiden international race

Above: Portugal leads Indonesia through the streets of Durban, South Africa.

Right: Ho-Pin Tung scored a marvellous maiden podium for China at Eastern Creek, Australia.

Centre: South Africa's entry provides a sumptuous splash of colour in the Durban sun during its home race.

Opposite page, top to bottom: The brilliant performances of Niko Hülkenberg ensured that he clinched the 2006–07 championship for Germany at the British Brands Hatch round in April; Loïc Duval impresses for France in the wet conditions in Indonesia; Jeroen Bleekemolen stepped into the cockpit vacated by Jos Verstappen (the young Dutchman is pictured with team principal Jan Lammers); Robbie Kerr kicks up the dirt at Brands Hatch in the Great Britain entry.

Photographs: A1GP Media Service

in A1GP's first season had been successful, so the championship headed back to Sentul for the fifth round in year two. By that time Germany had a comfortable advantage in the standings after previous leaders Mexico had gone empty-handed in Malaysia.

However, while the battle at the top intensified as Mexico pulled back some points in the sprint race by finishing second and Germany did exactly the same in the feature race, the weekend was all about New Zealand and Reid.

Having qualified on pole position for the sprint race, Reid simply romped away from the lights to claim New Zealand's maiden win comfortably ahead of Mexico and Great Britain. Behind them, Germany was only fifth after getting a poor start from third.

Hülkenberg put up a far sterner challenge in the feature race, though, the summer storms making their way south of the border to provide an extra challenge for the drivers. As had been the case in Malaysia, the tougher the conditions, the better things were for Hülkenberg as he quickly established a lead, with New Zealand slipping back in second.

However, unlike at Sepang, the circuit began to dry and, as it did so, the pendulum began to swing back in favour of New Zealand. Reid beat down the gap to Hülkenberg, who didn't help his cause when he took a trip through the gravel after his pit stop.

Taking the lead again midway through the race, Reid sprinted off but then had his advantage negated by a safety car period an effective two laps from the end. Inevitably, the safety car backed up the field and allowed Germany and France – which thus benefited from Great Britain's off-track moment that had prompted the safety car – onto his tail.

Nonetheless, at the restart Reid surged away in the two laps before the chequered flag to win by over a second, with Hülkenberg coming through to record his and German's fourth podium of the season. France was on the rostrum again, ahead of Italy's Toccacelo, who staged a stunning drive through the field that was defined by his passing three cars in the final two laps.

As the Christmas break beckoned and with almost half of the season completed, the statistics showed that Germany led the way after five of the 11 rounds, 12 points up on the consistent but still-winless Great Britain, while Mexico, France and New Zealand followed closely. In all, 14 of the 22 nations had already finished on the podium; and only Lebanon, India, Pakistan and Greece were yet to get on the scorers' sheet, although Greece had failed to reappear after the second round.

Germany's position already looked strong but when the teams gathered for the sixth round of the season at New Zealand's Taupo circuit Hülkenberg kick-started

a devastating run of form that all but put the title out of reach for anyone else.

Redeveloped and upgraded to meet A1GP standards, Taupo was an exciting new venue to be welcomed onto the calendar and the crowds turned out in force to cheer on their driver, Reid, who was fresh from his double win in Indonesia. However, despite the extra support he was unable to reproduce that form on home soil – Hülkenberg simply proved too hard to beat from the moment the racing began.

Scoring the perfect weekend of pole position and two race wins, Germany forged farther ahead in the points – and again proved the class of the field with double-victory feats at the Eastern Creek (Sydney, Australia) and Durban rounds that followed Taupo.

Each time, Hülkenberg won from pole position and the six victories were enough to all but guarantee that Germany would come away from the second season of A1GP clutching the winner's trophy.

If things up front were easy – and rather uneventful – for Germany, the battle for second place in the standings was proving rather more exciting.

Great Britain's hopes of challenging Germany for the championship lead took a major knock in the next two rounds, with Kerr managing just one point-scoring finish in the four races – and even that was only a tenth place at Eastern Creek. He had been running second in the first race at Sydney when a puncture put him out of contention for the rest of the weekend.

Instead, France and New Zealand were the on-form nations behind Germany, France proving particularly impressive at Taupo in the hands of Loïc Duval, the little-known but successful Formula Nippon racer who made an impressive début by scoring a pair of second places. Reid didn't disgrace himself on home soil, either: he scored two third-placed finishes.

It was the same story in Australia, with Germany winning the first race comfortably, New Zealand in second place and France having to settle for third.

Maintaining the status quo from Taupo, Switzerland – now with promising youngster Sébastien Buemi back at the wheel of its car – and the Netherlands appeared in the top five once again.

The feature race prompted few changes at the sharp end of the field, with Germany scoring a fourth win in a row and New Zealand in a lonely second place.

Instead, the headlines went the way of China, which scored a marvellous maiden podium thanks to Ho-Pin Tung, who had been drafted in to replace the equally promising Congfu Cheng from the Sentul round onwards. Just behind, the ever-

consistent Netherlands finished fourth and the Czech Republic's patchy season reached a high again with fifth for Enge.

From the wide and fast stretches of Eastern Creek, A1GP moved to the tight and twisty streets of Durban but, while the surroundings could hardly be more different, the result at the front was less so.

Indeed, pole position, victory in the sprint race and victory again in the feature race formed Germany's third consecutive perfect weekend and Hülkenberg was now the most coveted A1GP driver after wins seven and eight surpassed Alex Prémat's best of the previous season.

Given their recent form, France's and New Zealand's appearances on the podium, with the Netherlands and Switzerland fourth and fifth, were less surprising, although New Zealand had had to manage it with Halliday after the team again decided to take advantage of his more extensive street racing experience.

The feature race, on the other hand, was a more unpredictable affair, with the fearsome walls punishing drivers who strayed beyond the appropriate boundaries. Those walls and a number of mechanical dramas meant that only nine cars finished the race, although ten were classified.

Hülkenberg seemed to be the only driver to experience few problems, keeping cool despite a late safety car period that destroyed what had been a comprehensive lead. Nonetheless, he survived to record a comfortable win over Great Britain, which put in a fine performance following a run of poor form to finish second from ninth place on the grid.

New Zealand completed the podium, ahead of Switzerland and – remarkably – Portugal, which made a return to action for the first time, having raised the budget needed for the rest of the season. Fifth place by former British Formula 3 champion Alvaro Parente was an impressive feat given that the car had been hastily put together and even had to have its pit stops carried out by the Australian team.

From Africa to central America: Mexico City was next up for the teams but, significantly, there was one name missing from the entry list – Hülkenberg's. With the title all but a foregone conclusion and Hülkenberg's having F3 commitments, Weber's other young protégé Christian Vietoris was drafted in for the first time. Given his first experience of powerful machinery, the Formula BMW Germany champion embarked on a steep learning curve, bringing Germany's run of spectacular successes to an abrupt end and putting just a single ninth place on the scoreboard.

Yet while France and New Zealand were considered the likely candidates to assume the role of domination, the team to beat instead became Great Britain, which finally got onto the winners' list thanks to Oliver Jarvis. Back in the car for his second outing of the year, Jarvis finished second behind Malaysia – scoring its third win of the season – in the sprint event but made no mistakes in the feature race and thus broke Britain's A1GP duck.

From that moment, the results began to flood in and, while Jarvis's exploits didn't earn him a stay of execution for the final two rounds of the season at Shanghai (China) and Brands Hatch (Britain), Kerr maintained the form to score two more wins and two more second places over the course of the four races.

This changed the appearance of the standings, with a number of nations having to revise their driver line-ups as the end of the A1GP season began to clash with the start of a new one in GP2, the World Series by Renault, F3 and Champcar, among other series.

Most notably, France's form dropped in the last three rounds after it enlisted the services of promising youngster Jean-Karl Vernay, who proved quick but nowhere near as consistent as predecessor Duval. France slipped well behind New Zealand in the battle for the runner-up spot in the standings. But Great Britain filled that slot and set about chasing down its rivals in the closing races.

In the end, it came down to just a single point. Great Britain's superb recovery from a lacklustre mid-season was not quite enough to wrestle second place from a delighted New Zealand.

Above: In sunny conditions, Team South Africa's Adrian Zaugg heads the colourful pack on the Sunday race.

Right: The 2004 Indianapolis 500 winner Buddy Rice is a surprise choice to represent the USA entry in Europe.

Centre right: The experienced Neel Jani continues to represent Switzerland with distinction.

Bottom right: Italy's team boss Piercarlo Ghinzani with his driver Enrico Toccacello.

Opposite page, top: Jonny Reid scored a double win for New Zealand at Brno, Czech Republic.

Opposite page, bottom: Reid leads the pack into the first corner at the start of the first race at Brno. Adam Carroll in the Team Ireland entry smokes his way around the outside line.

Photographs: Allsport-Getty Images

The clear winner, however, was Germany. Hülkenberg's crushing six consecutive wins did enough to secure the title. Hülkenberg returned for the final two rounds in China and Great Britain, ending the season in style by claiming victory in the feature race after an enjoyable battle with Kerr.

Reigning champion France ended up a distant fourth, while the consistent Netherlands just got the better of the inconsistent Malaysia to take fifth place. Italy, Switzerland, the USA – helped in the latter stages of the season by good drives from Jonathan Summerton – and Mexico rounded out the top ten.

## 2007–08 SEASON
As the second season of A1GP came to a close, plans were already being put in place for its third running, the first few rounds of which have already taken place.

Naturally, there have been changes to ensure that things remain competitive and Hülkenberg has moved on to compete in the European F3 championship, leaving the way for Vietoris to return to the cockpit and experience a full season of A1GP.

New Zealand and Great Britain are persevering with Reid, Kerr and Jarvis – who will drive more frequently this season – while Lapierre, Bleekemolen and Zaugg are back for France, the Netherlands and South Africa.

Elsewhere, the USA has entrusted its car to former Indy 500 winner Buddy Rice, while Brazil and Ireland have looked towards the GP2 series for their choices: Sérgio Jimenez and Adam Carroll.

However, with 58 drivers having made race starts in the 2006–07 season – plus those who took part in the practice rookie sessions – expect the grids at the start of the season to differ from those at its end.

The range of drivers for the first round in the Netherlands was typically diverse. The 22 nations that ended the previous season returned for another year, although several sported different liveries. Nonetheless, the first round bore a striking similarity to the first round of the previous season when South Africa claimed the spoils in the opening race. Winning the sprint race from pole position, having gained the top spot through a simpler interpretation of the aggregate system used the year before, Zaugg went on to finish second in the feature race to give the nation a comprehensive lead in the standings after just a single round.

It was Great Britain that denied South Africa a double win as Jarvis powered to victory in the feature race. Making up for a disappointing first race, his third place on the grid put Jarvis into contention from the off and he proceeded to jump Zaugg during the pit-stops and score the nation's fourth-ever win.

Just behind, France got its season off to a good start courtesy of Duval with second and fifth places, while Jani represented the Champcar series for Switzerland with a fifth and a third. Bleekemolen pleased the tens of thousands of home fans with third and eighth, while the ever-consistent Duran got Mexico's season off to a good start with a pair of fourths.

After an anonymous start to the year at Zandvoort, New Zealand got going at the second round in the Czech Republic, where Reid surged to two victories.

South Africa had looked on course to continue its strong start to the season with a third pole in a row around the Brno circuit, but when Zaugg got off the line poorly Reid jumped him into the lead, followed closely by Great Britain – now with Kerr again at the wheel – and Ireland, which had Carroll in the seat for the first time. This led to Ireland's second-ever podium, the GP2 race winner showing off his and the team's credentials as front runners this season with a marvellous début performance.

Even so, Brno was all about New Zealand, with Reid winning the feature race from seventh on the grid after a stirring drive through the order. Bleekemolen had qualified on pole position but was unable to give the Netherlands its third A1GP victory and could manage no better than second when put up against Reid.

Switzerland's solid start to the year continued with third after

Great Britain's chances were destroyed by a puncture, while South Africa too experienced myriad problems in the race – problems that forced it to give up the championship lead to New Zealand.

There was then a prolonged gap before the next round at Sepang after the third meeting – which had been expected to be held at Sentul – was cancelled. Indeed, this year's calendar is barely altered from that of last year, with only Beijing dropped and replaced with the Zhuhai International Circuit.

Still, with an increasing number of sponsors gracing the sides of the cars and more respected names pledging their support to the quirky but successful world cup notion, the third season of the series is looking to be the most competitive yet.

But this year A1GP could face its biggest task yet: a rival for the first time in the form of the GP2 Asia series, which has been created out of F1 rights holder Bernie Ecclestone's desire to make motor racing a year-long activity and to tap untouched nations.

While A1GP could have seen this as a threat to what it has created, it instead recognises the founding of a rival series as a compliment to what it has achieved. Furthermore, A1GP is about to challenge Bernie's brainchild with a formidable partner in the shape of Ferrari, which has announced that it will supply engines to the series from next season for the next six years and the latest chassis is also likely to benefit from elements of Ferrari's F1 efforts.

With Ferrari on board, global recognition growing with every season and an entry list of increasing calibre, A1GP is very much establishing its own niche.

Arai
www.A1GP.com
A1GP
World Cup of Motorsport
SKY SPORTS
RAB CAPITAL
A1GP.com

AS IF 4G WASN'T ENOUGH, HE ALSO HAS THE

WEIGHT OF THE NATION ON HIS SHOULDERS.

22 countries, 5 continents, 10 events

A1GP™

World Cup of Motorsport™

## FORMULA 3 REVIEW by CRAIG LLEWELLYN
# EXPERIENCE THE KEY TO SUCCESS

**Above: Pole sitter Nico Hülkenberg takes the lead of the F3 Euro Series race at the Nürburgring. The ASM driver heads the Mücke Motorsport duo Edoardo Piscopo (8) and Sébastien Buemi (7) on his way to a victory in race one.**

**Right: Champion Romain Grosjean holds aloft a pit board to signify the ASM team's four consecutive titles.**
Photographs: XPB.cc/LAT Photographic

THE two principal Formula 3 series provided very different finishes to their seasons but proved one thing: that experience remains the key to success in this category.

As in 2006, the F3 Euro Series provided the closer competition of the two, with Romain Grosjean and Sébastien Buemi mirroring Paul di Resta and Sebastian Vettel in taking their fight right to the last round.

With only Kamui Kobayashi surviving from the previous season's top ten – Jonathan Summerton reappeared late on with VW's experimental engine – the way was once again open for a previously unheralded name to move into the spotlight and Grosjean and Buemi – 13th and 11th respectively in '06 – were quick to seize the initiative.

Buemi, with added A1GP experience to call on after backing up Neel Jani and Marcel Fässler in the '06–07 campaign, was fastest out of the blocks, claiming pole position and victory in the first race of the year at Hockenheim (Germany). Grosjean took fifth place to open with but turned the tables in race two, making the most of the top eight finishers' being reversed on the grid to claim top spot at the chequered flag. Buemi's third, however, ensured that he left with the early points lead.

Bizarrely, however, he then didn't win another race until the penultimate round at Nogaro (France), but a string of podium finishes kept Buemi – who added GP2 to his F3 and A1GP activities during the year – in contention until the finale. Grosjean, meanwhile, took top spot on five further occasions for ASM, piling on the early pressure with feature-race wins at Brands Hatch (Britain) and the Norisring (Germany) but failing to capitalise fully after registering no-scores in the corresponding sprints.

Buemi was restricted to second place in both the races where his rival missed out, victories going to rookies Edoardo

Mortara and Nico Hülkenberg respectively, and neither contender saw the chequer first at Magny-Cours (France), where Kobayashi finally got his act together and Britain's James Jakes opened his Euro Series victory account.

Grosjean, having finished second and sixth on home soil, was back on top form at Mugello (Italy), taking pole – for which drivers earned a bonus point – and race-one victory, before following up with second place in race two. With Buemi managing only eight points to Grosjean's 16, this proved the turning point of the season. Once he was leading the points table, Grosjean would not be headed again.

The ASM pilot added pole, victory and third next time out at Zandvoort (the Netherlands) to increase his advantage to nine points, but both title contenders were left scrapping for points at the next couple of rounds, at the Nürburgring (Germany) and Barcelona (Spain), with a second apiece in Germany the best they could offer as Hülkenberg and the unfancied Harald Schlegelmilch took the honours.

Barcelona proved even less fruitful, with Grosjean and Buemi emerging with just a single point each. Grosjean suffered a ten-place grid penalty for changing an engine, which left him down in 14th, but Buemi was unable to capitalise after struggling to get the Mücke Dallara sorted to his liking.

Grosjean braved the tricky conditions to work his way back to third in race one – only to be slapped with a 1m penalty that initially left him score-less. Buemi, however, was again unable to take advantage, being caught out by the conditions shortly after half-distance and posting a rare retirement.

With Grosjean's appeal pending, he started sixth for race two but saw his chance to make amends scuppered by a series of first-lap incidents that delayed him badly. Buemi, meanwhile, was doing his best to salvage some points from 21st on the

grid, eventually making it back to sixth as Renger van der Zande added his name to the winners' roster.

At Nogaro the top two were back on form and sharing the wins between them although, crucially, Grosjean seized the more valuable feature from pole to extend the gap back to Buemi. Buemi finally returned to the top of the podium in race two, clawing back four points as his rival managed only fifth spot.

That meant the two protagonists went back to Hockenheim separated by seven points, which became eight before racing started after the organisers commuted Grosjean's 1m penalty to 30s, allowing him to add eighth in race one at the Spanish Circuit de Catalunya to his tally.

Grosjean further extended his advantage with the pole bonus but allowed Hülkenberg to steal a march at the start. The pair then battled – a little too closely for ASM's liking at times – to the flag before Grosjean accepted second and a double-figure cushion that put the championship beyond doubt. Pressure off, Buemi claimed the final race of the year, overhauling long-time leader Mortara with three laps to go.

Mortara proved to be one of the finds of the season, taking two wins, but a string of non-scores belied his pace and left him down in eighth overall. Instead it was another rookie, A1GP 'champion' Hülkenberg, who led the pursuit of Grosjean and Buemi, claiming four race wins and a brace of poles as he beat the more seasoned Kobayashi to third in the points. Kobayashi, meanwhile, secured fourth at the final round only by overhauling the mercurial Jakes, who failed to score at either Nogaro or Hockenheim.

Fellow Manor Motorsport runners Yelmer Buurman and Franck Mailleux also headed Mortara in the end-of-season table, with the promising Tom Dillman and Jean-Karl Vernay rounding out the top ten. Neither took a race win, leaving Van der Zande and Schlegelmilch as the surprises courtesy of the reversed-grid system.

If the Euro Series was a tense affair, however, the British campaign was less so as Marko Asmer proved the adage that racing improves the breed.

Indeed, he had more experience than most as he embarked on his fourth F3 campaign, ambitiously attempting to chase titles in both Britain and Japan. Returning to the Hitech team with which he had made his category début in '04, Asmer was on the

**Below: Sébastien Buemi ended the year as runner-up in the Euro Series. It was a busy year for the Red Bull-backed Swiss driver, who also competed in the GP2 and A1GP series.**
Photograph: XPB.cc/LAT Photographic

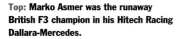

**Top: Marko Asmer was the runaway British F3 champion in his Hitech Racing Dallara-Mercedes.**

**Above: Double R team-mates Jonathan Kennard and Stephen Jelley.**
Photographs: Jacob Ebrey Motorsport Photography

**Centre: Carlin Motorsport's Maro Engel was the principal challenger to Asmer, but ended the season nearly 90 points adrift of the champion.**
Photograph: Hoyer/Ebrey/LAT Photographic

**Centre right: The 2007 F3 Masters was held in Zolder. Victory went to German hotshot Nico Hülkenberg (centre) in his ASM F3 Dallara Mercedes, with the podium completed by Yann Clairay (left) and Jean Karl Vernay.**
Photograph: Hoyer/Ebrey/LAT Photographic

pace from the start, winning at least one race at each of the opening six rounds and missing out only at Spa-Francorchamps and Thruxton over the course of the 11-round campaign.

If anything, the biggest threat to Asmer's title came from within, as the Japanese calendar clashed on more than one occasion with its British rival. Such was his start to the year in the UK, however, that he managed to find a way out of his Three Bond deal (to race in Japan) to concentrate on chasing just one trophy.

Asmer's triumph went hand in hand with Hitech's break-through as a title-winning outfit, David Hayle's operation finally getting the better of old rival Carlin Motorsport and hijacking Räikkönen Robertson Racing's ambitions of back-to-back titles in only its second year. What is more, Asmer had been Hayle's choice of pilot, the decision aided by a pre-season partnership with Walter Grubmüller Jr's wealthy family that led to young Grubmüller's installation alongside whomever Hitech wished to lead the team. Grubmüller, for the record, finished the year 16th with seven points to his name.

Asmer's domination was such that the destiny of the crown was decided at the penultimate round, at Croft, and left him with an 85-point cushion over his nearest rival at the end of the year. Runner-up honours eventually went to the other driver on Hitech's wish-list, Maro Engel, who returned to Carlin for his second season in the series.

The partnership got off to the best possible start, winning the season-opener at Oulton Park, but Engel suffered inconsistent results by comparison with the pace-setting Asmer. First and

second in the two races at Monza (Italy) in June hinted at a return to form, but three straight second places and victory in the final race of the year at Rockingham were as good as it got.

After its success with Mike Conway in '06, Double R had to make do with third this time around, having hired two known quantities to lead its three-car entry. While young gun Atte Mustonen – a Kimi Räikkönen *protégé* – was expected to come to the fore as the year went on, it was another fourth-year man, Stephen Jelley, who ended up best-placed overall.

After three years of building, Jelley finally broke through with wins at Thruxton and Croft late in the season, while consistency allowed him to secure third overall, albeit 110 points off Asmer. By contrast, Mustonen proved mercurial, clearly quick in qualifying but prone to errors on race day. The Finn, still a teenager at season's end, did manage a win at Thruxton but trailed the third Double R car of Jonathan Kennard – who took victory at Spa mid-season – in the standings.

Between Jelley and Kennard, Carlin's latest rookie crop filled fourth and fifth overall. Again, both Sam Bird and Niall Breen took race wins – Bird, the Formula Renault graduate, on foreign soil in Bucharest (Romania) and Belgium, and Breen at Snetterton – but neither proved to have the season-long consistency to challenge those above them.

Asmer's return to the UK and Volkswagen's to the Euro Series made headlines but neither matched the press devoted to the return of the Mansell name to F3. Having performed reasonably well in Formula BMW in '06 – their first full season of car racing after a part-season of karting – Nigel's sons Greg and Leo were thrust into the limelight after a deal was struck for them to run with Fortec Motorsport.

It proved to be a mixed blessing for the family as, while Leo appeared overawed by the step up, younger brother Greg showed enough potential for a career on four wheels. On the podium in only his third outing, at Donington Park in April, he was a regular in the top ten and then returned to the top three at Silverstone and Croft late on.

Greg finished tenth overall but perhaps his most notable storyline came off the track, when he clashed with Fortec team-mate Sebastian Hohenthal. Mansell felt Hohenthal had forced him off the road while they were battling and confronted him after the race, allegedly punching his rival. No charges were brought but the Fortec trucks were notably separated for the rest of the season…

Hohenthal extracted some measure of revenge by edging Mansell for ninth in the standings, courtesy of a podium second time out, a victory on Brands Hatch's GP layout and a brace of thirds at the Rockingham finale, but both were beaten to eighth by the seasoned Brazilian Alberto Valerio, who enjoyed a purple patch mid-season but otherwise failed to shine with Carlin.

The biggest improvement shown during the season came from the new Mygale chassis, which made its début with the ambitious Ultimate Motorsport outfit. Veteran Esteban Guerrieri was paired with Ireland's Michael Devaney and the team worked diligently to iron out the many gremlins that beset the car early on. By the end of the year, both drivers had managed bests of fourth on the road, having sliced into the performance gap between the MO7 and its Dallara rivals.

The national class (for older cars) once again proved the domain of the overseas visitors, with the Americas again claiming the crown, courtesy of Mexico's Sergio Perez. Despite missing out at the first round, he took first or second in all except one of the other races, comfortably seeing off the challenge of Franky Cheng.

Fourth overall Michael Meadows took class wins with Master Motorsport and Double R, while Iceland's Viktor Jensen claimed the other race not won by the top two.

The annual Masters of F3 blue-riband event had to be switched from Zandvoort to Zolder (Belgium) to accommodate the addition of A1GP among Zandvoort's permitted 'noise days', but even that failed to reverse Britain's fortunes. Kumho supplied a different compound of tyre specifically for the Masters but Nico Hülkenberg claimed the biggest win of his season as the Euro Series again ruled the roost.

He was the only ASM driver running in contention, however, as poleman Grosjean managed just 14th after stalling at the start and Kobayashi and Dillman crashed out before the opening lap was complete. With Buemi absent on one of his GP2 forays, Red Bull/Mücke honour was taken up by F3 débutant Brendon Hartley, the long-haired Kiwi teenager claiming an impressive fourth behind two Signature-Plus rookies, Yann Clairay and Vernay.

The change of venue also did little for the racing: it was another processional Masters event. As if to prove just how difficult the UK series finds conquering the Masters, Asmer was its best representative in tenth while Mustonen and Engel were the only others to make the top 15.

There was better news for Britain around the world, with Oliver Jarvis riding high in Japan, James Winslow and Charlie Hollings doing likewise in Australia and Dillon Battistini following in Winslow's footsteps as Asian champion.

Jarvis surprised many by eschewing potential opportunities in the World Series by Renault to take up TOM's offer to lead its Japanese assault but showed his judgement to be accurate by winning on début at Fuji and adding two further victories to his tally before the end of October.

A long period without winning, however, meant that the more experienced Roberto Streit and local favourites Kazuya Oshima, Hiroaki Ishiura and Kodai Tsukakoshi all got in on the act. Jarvis' TOM's team-mate Oshima joined the Briton and Streit in holding title aspirations ahead of the Motegi (Japan) finale as the series' dropped-scores policy came into play. Despite trailing Streit by 25 points on unadjusted totals, Oshima overcame an 11-point deficit to claim the crown from third in the standings after Jarvis's first DNF in race one ruled him out and Streit clashed with Ishiura on lap one of the final race.

Hollings, meanwhile, finds himself in a mighty scrap for Kumho Tyres Australian honours with one round to run at Oran Park. The Briton, a late addition to the field, ties fellow contender Tim Macrow and countryman Winslow as the most successful drivers in terms of wins, with three apiece, but the trio find themselves trailing Leanne Tander, who has notched up two victories of her own.

Winslow abandoned his slim chances of adding a second F3 crown in as many years to concentrate on pursuing the Asian V6 title, while Marco Mapelli, Stuart Kostera and returnee Barton Mawer each claimed a win during a close-fought campaign.

As AUTOCOURSE goes to press, only the Spanish championship also remains to be decided, with TEC Auto duo Máximo Cortés and Marco Barba leading the way from Nicolas Prost, son of four-times F1 champion Alain.

In South America, the title went the way of highly rated Clemente Faria with two races remaining, the Cesario F3 driver leading team-mate Mario Romancini by 25 points ahead of December's double-header in São Paulo (Brazil).

The Italian national series was claimed by Paolo Nocera after main rival Efisio Marchese clashed with Nicola de Marco in the final race. Rising Mexican star Pablo Sánchez López claimed third overall despite combining his campaign with the new Formula Master series.

In Finland, Tomi Limmonen beat Jesse Krohn by three points, while Dutchman Carlo van Dam comfortably followed Ho-Pin Tung as champion in Germany's renamed ATS Cup. Finally, in the burgeoning Asian series Battistini overcame a robust challenge from Finn Henri Karjalainen to clinch the crown at the Zhuhai (China) finale.

**Below: The 2007 All-Japan F3 title was claimed by Kazuya Oshima. The TOM's Toyota driver celebrates his win at the Okayama International circuit, Japan.**

**Bottom: Oliver Jarvis continued his upward career path in the far east. The young British driver wrapped up his season with a win at Sendai (Japan).**

**Photographs: Yasushi Ishihara/LAT Photographic**

# AUDI BEATS PEUGEOT IN LE MANS

# BATTLE OF THE DIESELS

The victorious Audi R10 TDI of Emanuele
Pirro, Marco Werner and Frank Biela
stalked by the number 7 Peugeot.
Photograph: Mike Weston/www.crash.net

**Above:** Stéphane Sarrazin put the Peugeot on pole position but he and his co-drivers Sébastien Bourdais and Pedro Lamy were unable to match Audi's race pace and had to settle for the runner's-up position.

**Right:** Rickard Rydell and David Brabham (along with Darren Turner) took Prodrive's Aston Martin to fifth place overall, securing the win in the GT1 class.
Photographs: Mike Weston/www.crash.net

**Centre top:** A night-time pit stop for the Courage of Bruce Jouanny, Jacques Nicolet and Alain Filhol.

**Centre:** The unlucky Audi trio Rinaldo Capello, Tom Kristensen and Allan McNish was sidelined from the race after losing a wheel when well in command.
Photographs: Mike Weston/www.crash.net

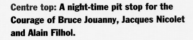

RARELY has a battle at the Le Mans 24 Hours been so eagerly anticipated. From the moment Peugeot announced its return just before the 2005 event, the sports car world knew that Audi had a real rival on its hands. The French marque, remember, had spent big and left no stone unturned on its way to dominating the big race in 1992–93. The only question was when the newcomer would be ready to challenge the German manufacturer's dominance. Not in '07 for the 75th running of the 24 Hours, it turned out.

Peugeot's new 908 HDi turbo-diesel coupé may have been fast – it took pole position for Stéphane Sarrazin – but it wasn't nearly fast enough in race trim to keep pace with Audi's year-old take on the diesel LMP1 prototype regulations, the R10 TDI. Which is why Audi continued its winning ways with Emanuele Pirro, Marco Werner and Frank Biela.

It became clear that the two Peugeots were unable to race the trio of Audis from the moment the cars crossed the start-finish line at 4pm on Saturday. By the first round of pit stops, the best Peugeot was in third place, already 25s behind the leading R10.

Audi set little store by qualifying and the R10, like the all-conquering R8 before it, could race much nearer to its qualifying pace than its rivals. Peugeot, on the other hand, was forced to back off the pace of a car that it wasn't convinced had the reliability to complete 24 hours. It wasn't really a contest.

Audi may have been unchallenged in the race, but its motor sport boss Wolfgang Ullrich still described this Le Mans victory as its most difficult yet. The reason? Two of its three cars retired. That's unheard of. Never before had a factory Joest Racing-run Audi failed to finish at the 24 Hours.

Given that one car went out after losing a wheel nut for unexplained reasons, Audi had a nerve-racking final six and a half hours. Heavy rain before the finish only multiplied those nerves. So bad were the conditions that the race officials were forced to send out the safety car just after the start of the final hour. And so slow was the pace that Audi's engineers were concerned about the leading car's gearbox because Werner was using so few revs in his efforts to keep the car on the track.

Audi's problems began early. The third R10, driven by Mike Rockenfeller, Lucas Luhr and Alexandre Prémat, was running between the Peugeots when Rockenfeller took over for the first time on a damp track. His times were coming down when he got it wrong at Tertre Rouge and clouted the barrier. His efforts to get the car going again were always going to be in

vain considering the extent of the damage.

Things got worse just after 7.30am on Sunday. Rinaldo Capello was rounding the near-flat right-hander at Indianapolis when the left-rear wheel parted company with the rest of the car. Not surprisingly for an accident that started at 160 mph, the car was too badly damaged, even for an Audi, to make it back to the pits.

It was caused by the wheel nut's coming off, but why this had happened remained unexplained. It should be pointed out that Capello was on his 15th lap on the same set of Michelin tyres: his previous stop, three laps before the incident, had been for fuel only.

It was a heavy blow for Capello and team mates Allan McNish and Tom Kristensen, who was returning from injuries sustained in the DTM touring car championship in Germany. If the Audi stood head and shoulders ahead of the Peugeot, this particular Audi crew made those of its sister cars look average. By the time they went out, they were three full laps up on Pirro and co, who admittedly lost time with two incidents. Put simply, Capello, McNish and Kristensen dominated.

'It was our race,' said Capello. 'The gap to the rest was down to our speed and there wasn't one scratch on the car.'

The retirement of the Capello car left the winning Audi with a four-lap margin over the best of the Peugeots, which was driven by Nicolas Minassian, Marc Gené and Le Mans débutant Jacques Villeneuve.

The in-house Peugeot Sport squad, managed by ex-F3 team owner Serge Saulnier, had what has to be described as a strong début with the 908 HDi. Few expected either Pug to run through the race without problem, yet both cars were in podium positions at the 22-hour mark. At that stage the only major delay encountered by either Peugeot was a wheel-bearing failure on the car driven by Sébastien Bourdais, Sarrazin and Pedro Lamy late in the seventh hour.

Engine problems reared their head at Peugeot in the closing stages. An oil pressure warning light brought second-placed Minassian into the pits shortly after 12.30pm. The team spent more than 40 minutes trying to rectify the problem. Minassian went back out on-track and managed one lap before the car was retired with what was diagnosed as a cam-drive failure. In the final hour, the remaining 908 had what Peugeot Sport technical director Bruno Famin described as 'an engine scare'.

**Above: Jacques Villeneuve in the Peugeot, which retired with an engine failure just 31 laps from the finish.**

**Main: Sunset at Le Mans as the winning Audi heads under the Dunlop Bridge.**
Photographs: Mike Weston/www.crash.net

Below: **Martin Short, João Barbosa and Stuart Hall took their privately entered Pescarolo-Judd to an impressive fourth-placed finish at Le Mans.**

Photograph: Mike Weston/www.crash.net

Above: **Alex Gurney and Jon Fogarty were deserved winners of the Grand American Road Racing Series.**

Photograph: Richard Dole/LAT Photographic

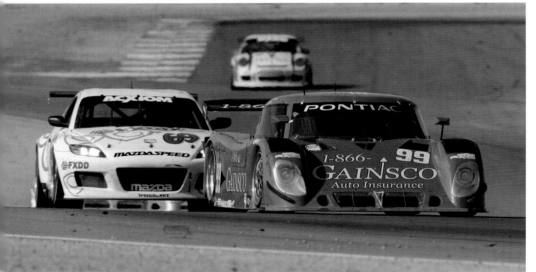

Opposite top: **The works Pescarolo made the podium at Le Mans in the hands of Emmanuel Collard, Jean-Christophe Boullion and Romain Dumas.**

Photograph: Mike Weston/www.crash.net

Opposite: **Team Penske Porsche's, Romain Dumas and Timo Bernhard took outright ALMS wins against the Audis, but had to be content with their title victory in a fiercely competitive LMP2 division.**

Photograph: Michael Levitt/LAT Photographic

This problem was fixed during a 20-minute stop, but Bourdais decided to wait at the final corner for the leader to save a lap's worth of wear on the engine. That left the car just one lap up on the third-placed car at the finish.

Best of the rest went to the lead Pescarolo Sport entry driven by Emmanuel Collard, Jean-Christophe Boullion and Romain Dumas. The French trio ran as high as second during the initial safety car periods and then settled in a position between the two Peugeots. The Judd-powered Pescarolo 01 had a clean run that was interrupted only by a sizeable off on oil for Collard and a subsequent seven-minute stop for repairs.

Pescarolo may have finished on the podium for the third successive year, but team boss Henri was quick to point out what he perceived as the inequity in the balance between diesel and petrol cars. He argued that the 100-bhp-plus power disadvantage of the diesel machinery meant his team went to the grid with no chance of winning the race.

The plucky British Rollcentre team finished an impressive fourth with its privately entered Pescarolo-Judd, albeit 11 laps behind the works version. Team owner Martin Short, João Barbosa and sports car newcomer Stuart Hall had a trouble-free run with only a couple of loose wheels and some errant wiring from the on-board camera in the cockpit.

The LMP2 prototype division was won by the Britain-based Binnie Motorsports team. Its Lola-Zytek driven by Bill Binnie, Chris Buncombe and Allen Timpany came through a race of attrition without major problem until the closing stages,

when the team was effectively forced to hotwire the car after it failed to restart.

The factory Aston Martin team got its revenge on arch-rivals Chevrolet in a classic GT1 confrontation. The Prodrive Astons had a shade more pace than Pratt & Miller's Chevy Corvette C6.Rs and gained an advantage early in the race that they would never relinquish. An internecine Aston battle was eventually decided in favour of David Brabham, Darren Turner and Rickard Rydell when Johnny Herbert went off in the other car and damaged the front splitter.

Jan Magnussen, Johnny O'Connell and Ron Fellows chased the Astons all the way but didn't have quite enough in the tank to get on terms. Aston's cause was helped by the early retirement of one of the two factory Chevys. Oliver Gavin, who shared with Olivier Beretta and Max Papis, retired after only 22 laps when the propshaft broke, stranding him out on the circuit. Amazingly, it was the first retirement posted by a Pratt & Miller Corvette at Le Mans.

Audi raced to another title in the American Le Mans Series for McNish and Capello, but neither they nor Werner and Pirro won many races because the heavily revised '07 version of Porsche's RS Spyder LMP2 contender had the legs of the R10 around the tight and twisty circuits that made up much of the American schedule. So much so that the turbo-diesel car didn't notch up an overall victory from round two of the championship on the streets of St Petersburg in March to the Petit Le Mans enduro at Road Atlanta in October.

Had there been an overall prototype classification, Porsche's stand-out pairing Romain Dumas and Timo Bernhard would have walked it. As it was, they had to be content with victory in a fiercely competitive LMP2 division. They had the measure of their team mates Ryan Briscoe and Sascha Maassen as well as three cars entered under Honda's Acura banner.

GT1 honours went to Chevrolet, which more or less raced alone over the course of the season. The General Motors brand decided to stay in the series even when it became clear that Prodrive and Aston would not be back. Gavin and Beretta retained the GT1 title with a race to go. Some of the best racing was in the GT2 category, in which Ferrari's factory representative Risi Competizione claimed the title at the Laguna Seca (California) finale with former grand prix driver Mika Salo and Jaime Melo.

The Le Mans Series over in Europe had no representation from Audi for a second season, but Peugeot did commit to the championship. It was the icing on the cake of an ever-improving grid. That said, none of the petrol-powered cars could remotely challenge the French turbo-diesels, though Peugeot's inability to get both its cars to the finish regularly ensured that reigning champions Pescarolo Sport went to the finale, a fly-away event in Brazil, still in the hunt for the championship.

The FIA GT Championship had been supposed to race at the Interlagos (Brazil) event, but a revolt from the teams at the back end of the previous season resulted in a much more Europe-centric series with only one long-haul race. The teams' concerns over rising budgets also resulted in a reduction of the regular race duration from three to two hours and a raft of cost-cutting measures.

These changes ensured that the championship enjoyed arguably its best season for some time. The GT1 grid expanded to upwards of 15 cars, while GT2 remained strong. Maserati, Chevrolet, Lamborghini and Aston Martin were all represented in the winner's circle but a close-fought championship was won by Thomas Biagi from the Vitaphone Racing team. GT2 honours went to Dirk Müller after an equally close contest.

The Grand American Road Racing Series produced another close finish. Three teams went to the series finale at Salt Lake City in with a chance of the Daytona Prototype title, which went to the GAINSCO/Bob Stallings Racing team and driver Alex Gurney, son of US racing legend Dan, and Jon Fogarty. They were deserved winners, having scored no fewer than seven race wins through the season.

Seven is also the number of Audi's Le Mans victories. Given Peugeot's impressive return and the amount of testing it did over the second half of the season, an eighth Audi win is far from a formality.

# FIGHTING TO THE FINISH

**Above: Andy Priaulx was once again at the forefront of BMW's WTCC challenge and looking to take the title for a third successive year.**

Photograph: Jakob Ebrey Motorsport Photography

THE fight between Kimi Räikkönen, Lewis Hamilton and Fernando Alonso for the Formula 1 drivers' crown may have grabbed many of the headlines during 2007 but it wasn't the only title battle that went all the way to the wire – the touring car brigade more than matched F1 in the drama stakes throughout the year. On the track, anyway...

As this edition of AUTOCOURSE goes to press, the World Touring Car Championship (WTCC) still has one round left to run, on the streets of Macau (China), with six drivers holding a mathematical chance of securing the title, while a titanic battle between Fabrizio Giovanardi and Jason Plato went all the way to the 30th and final round of the British Touring Car Championship (BTCC). Surviving some off-track politics between arch rivals Audi and Mercedes, Mattias Ekström reclaimed the German DTM touring car crown while, down under, the scene is set for an action-packed conclusion to another V8 Supercar Championship season full of thrills and spills.

For the third consecutive season, it is the most challenging touring car circuit of them all that will decide the destiny of the WTCC title, as drivers representing all four leading marques head to Macau hoping to secure the crown. Not surprisingly, double champion Andy Priaulx is leading the way, although a disastrous weekend at Monza (Italy) means that the Guernsey-man has no room for error, with SEAT's Yvan Muller having turned a 14-point deficit before the Italian round into nothing going to the finale. The two drivers have got 81 points apiece.

'Monza was obviously a big disappointment for the whole team,' Priaulx reflected. 'Definitely two races to forget. We'll be doing everything we can to test and develop and have as good

a car as possible for Macau. Anything can happen in motor racing but I'll do my best to make sure I'm in the best possible shape to secure my third consecutive title.'

Behind the two leaders, Augusto Farfus, in his first season with the BMW Team Germany outfit, is ten points farther back while James Thompson is 12 points off the title lead after a stunning campaign in an Alfa Romeo that is far from being the newest machine on the grid. Farfus' team-mate Jörg Müller and Chevrolet's Nicola Larini are also still in with a shout, although in Larini's case it is the slimmest of slim chances.

As was the case in '06, the regulations – with success ballast and reverse grids – have provided a championship battle that is wide open and a season that nobody has been able to dominate. Going into the final two races, 11 drivers have taken to the top step of the podium, with Chevrolet's Alain Menu having take four wins in the ever-improving Lacetti, Farfus three and Priaulx, Jörg Müller, Yvan Muller and Thompson two apiece. Five other drivers have a single win to their name.

Despite the introduction of rolling starts in something of an effort to remove some of the advantage the rear-wheel-drive BMWs had off the line, the 320si has still been the car to have, having picked up eight wins thus far. Behind them, Chevrolet has six wins, SEAT four and Alfa Romeo two.

New to the calendar this year, the streets of Pau (France) and Porto (Portugal) reverberated to the sound of a bumper field containing some of the leading lights of the touring car world; the famous Zandvoort circuit (the Netherlands) and the Swedish venue at Anderstorp also made their first appearances on the WTCC stage. The latter also hosted the first appearance

of alternative fuels in the series: the Polestar Racing team competed on home soil with a bio-fuelled Volvo and SEAT announced that it was switching Muller and Jordi Gené to diesel-powered Leóns. Despite the added weight of the diesel engine, the extra torque has proved something of a talking point and three of the four SEAT wins have come with the new car – including a double success at Monza.

With other Le&#243;n TDIs appearing on the grid, alternative fuels are becoming more prevalent in the touring car world and, with the series' having announced that it will switch to bio-fuels in '09, it looks like the WTCC could become a showcase for the FIA as the governing body seeks to make motor sport go green.

Regardless of who leaves Macau as the champion, the '07 season has once again shown what touring car racing is all about at the highest level and rumours already abound about what '08 may hold. One thing for certain is that the series will continue to become more global, with the addition of a trip to Japan – a move that in turn has increased speculation of more manufacturer involvement.

**Below: Andy Priaulx took an emotional win on home soil at Brands Hatch.**
Photograph: Jakob Ebrey Motorsport Photography

**Below: Going into the final round of the WTCC, Yvan Muller and Andy Priaulx are both on 81 points. Another four drivers are in with a shot at the title.**
Photograph: Oliver Read/LAT Photographic

**Above: Gutted. Jason Plato is consoled by his wife Sophie after his heroic efforts to take the BTCC title at Thruxton.**
Photograph: Kevin Wood/LAT Photographic

**Below: Colin Turkington took the independent's title in his Team RAC BMW 320si.**
Photograph: Jakob Ebrey Motorsport Photography

Manufacturer involvement is possibly the only thing missing from the Dunlop MSA British Touring Car Championship, but that didn't prevent the '07 season from turning into one of the best seen by tin-top fans in recent years.

With the BTCC implementing the Super 2000 rules (for modified production cars) found in the WTCC, of those expected to fight for the title only SEAT Sport UK started the season with the car it would use all year. Defending champion Matt Neal got his hands on his new Honda Civic only a week before the opening round of the year at Brands Hatch.

When Jason Plato stormed to a double win in the season opener, it added further fuel to the argument that SEAT had an advantage over its rivals – but it soon became apparent that that wasn't the case as VX Racing and Fabrizio Giovanardi came storming back in the second round of the year at Rockingham with the all-new Vectra.

From there, the battle for the title became a titanic fight between two of the most experienced drivers on the grid, with Giovanardi turning what had been a 24-points deficit after the opening round into a one-point lead at the mid-way point. A tough weekend for Giovanardi at Donington Park allowed Plato to open his lead back up to 25 points, but by the time the pair arrived at Thruxton for the season finale, Giovanardi had whittled it back to just nine points – setting up a tense weekend of racing.

An accident for Plato while filming TV show *Fifth Gear* left him with burns to his face, neck and hands that threatened to overshadow the race weekend, but he followed Giovanardi home in the first two races to leave the pair split by just one point going into the final race. As it was, Giovanardi managed to get ahead of Plato off the line and second place to Plato's fourth was enough to add a BTCC title to his already impressive resumé.

'I won ten races this season but Plato didn't leave me any space to be free to win the title,' he said. 'There was a lot of pressure to work hard and keep close to Jason through the season, so it was very tough. But one person has to win and one person has to lose. Everybody wants to have

their name on the BTCC trophy because it is very hard and very tough. This is a special title to win.'

Vauxhall also reclaimed the manufacturers' title from SEAT, although Plato and his team could console themselves with the teams' title at the end of a campaign in which he won six times and scored points in every race. Of the 'rear-gunners' for the title duo, Darren Turner enjoyed the more successful season for SEAT, with three wins, while Giovanardi's team-mate Tom Chilton ended his year – and his time with the team – without a win.

Elsewhere, Gordon Shedden made the most of the ever-improving Team Halfords Civic to finish the year in third place after a solid second season that included four wins, a popular home victory at Knockhill among them. Team-mate Neal also won a race during the opening round of the year, although the team was aware that it was something of a false dawn, with the car needing more time to become a proper title challenger.

Team RAC finally waved goodbye to the venerable MG ZS, which was replaced by a pair of BMW 320sis for the new season. Although it took time for the team to fully realise the car's potential on the Dunlop tyres and British circuits, Colin Turkington won three times en route to the independents' title, while rookie team-mate Tom Onslow-Cole showed an impressive turn of speed in the sister car and was rewarded for his strong efforts with a maiden win at Snetterton. The team also showed it could mix it with the world's best with an outing in the WTCC event at Brands Hatch, where Turkington picked up a podium.

The other two wins went to another rookie, Mat Jackson, who had used his prize money for winning the SEAT Cupra Championship to purchase the very car that carried Andy Priaulx to the '06 WTCC title. It proved a good purchase for Jackson and his family-run team, with wins against the big boys coming at Oulton Park and Thruxton.

Elsewhere, there were impressive performances from the likes of Mike Jordan in the Team Eurotech Honda Integra, with the experienced racer showing there is still life in the older BTC-spec machinery to fight regularly near the front of the field. Adam Jones was another to impress, having switched to a SEAT

**Left:** Defending champion Matt Neal did not enjoy the best of times with his Honda Civic and moves to Vauxhall for 2008.

**Top centre:** A welcome victory at last for Darren Turner at Rockingham.

**Centre:** Vauxhall's Fabrizio Giovanardi (left) and Tom Chilton (centre) are joined at the Thruxton finale by the experienced Alain Menu.

**Below:** Fabrizio Giovanardi wrings the most from his title-winning Vauxhall Vectra.
Photographs: Jakob Ebrey Motorsport Photography

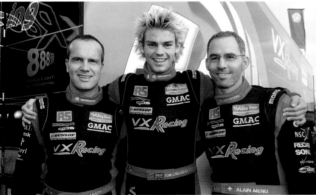

Toledo run by leading WTCC independents Team Air Cool. Despite missing 12 races during the season, he still finished a highly impressive fifth in the independents' standings. Special mention should also go to one of the smallest teams on the grid as the BTCC welcomed its first diesel-powered car, with Rick Kerry and his little AFM Racing team taking on the challenge of trying to develop a BMW 120D. It may not be the only diesel-powered team on the grid next season…

With series director Alan Gow and his team continuing to pull out the stops to take the BTCC back to the heights of the 1990s, there is little doubt that the series will be one to keep an eye on in '08. The announcement that two-times champion Neal will switch to Vauxhall to partner the man who took away his title has already dominated the post-season headlines and with young chargers such as Turkington, Jackson, Onslow-Cole

and Jones aiming to take the fight to the old guard, it promises to be another mouth-watering campaign for the growing number of fans to enjoy.

In the DTM, Mattias Ekström prevailed in a three-way shoot-out for the title in the final round of the season at Hockenheim, taking a second title to go with the one he secured in '04 and taking the title back to Audi after two seasons of success for arch rivals Mercedes.

Ekström started his season in fine style with a victory in the season opener at Hockenheim but it was to be his only win, his championship challenge instead being built on a fine run of six podium finishes in the final seven races. Indeed, the only time he was off the podium in that period came in the highly controversial penultimate round of the season at Barcelona (Spain), when Audi elected to withdraw all its cars from the race in protest at a number of incidents that had forced out its drivers after contact from a Mercedes. Daniel la Rosa was the man who brought Ekström's run of podium finishes to an abrupt end.

The Barcelona event was the second to draw headlines for the wrong reasons, with the third round of the year at the EuroSpeedway Lausitz having been hit by a safety car problem that led to half points' being awarded. While the decision not to award full points was probably the correct one, it was lucky that it didn't affect the final standings.

In the season finale, third place was good enough to ensure that Ekström took the title ahead of Mercedes' Bruno Spengler, who also took just one win during the season, while Ekström's team-mate Martin Tomczyk claimed third. For him, it was a case of what might have been, with two wins but five zero scores during the season.

Wins also went to Mika Häkkinen and Jamie Green, with two apiece – the latter finally breaking his DTM duck – while outgoing champion Bernd Schneider and the returning Gary Paffett won one race each. Paffett's win came at the wheel of a year-old car – and he wasn't the only person to impress with older machinery as another Briton, Paul di Resta, finished fifth in the standings in his début year – despite running in an '05-spec Mercedes.

In the Australian V8 Supercar Championship Series, Toll HSV Dealer Team driver Rick Kelly clinched the '06 title, which was

unfinished when AUTOCOURSE printed last year, but only after a contentious season finale in which he clashed on-track with main rival Craig Lowndes. It was an incident that meant a nervous wait for Kelly before he was confirmed as champion following a stewards' meeting on the Monday after the event.

As AUTOCOURSE closes for press this time around, both Lowndes and Kelly remain in contention for the '07 title – although they are playing second fiddle to their team-mates at the head of the standings.

With 11 of the 14 rounds in the can, Lowndes' team-mate Jamie Whincup heads the standings, the highlights of his season being victories at Sandown and Bathurst – alongside Lowndes – in the two big endurance races. He has no room for error, however, with Garth Tander breathing down his neck only nine points behind. A clean sweep of victories in the Big Pond 400 at Perth early in the year marked him out as real contender for honours and, as things stand, it looks like a straight fight between four drivers from two teams for the title.

The '08 title fight is likely to be decided once again over 14 championship rounds, with a further non-championship event supporting the Australian Grand Prix in Melbourne. Hamilton in New Zealand will make its first appearance on the calendar and Sandown will revert to a sprint-round format as Phillip Island gets the nod to host the 500-km (300-mile) endurance event held before the blue-riband race at Bathurst.

In a further emotional move, Sydney's Oran Park – one of the most historic venues on the calendar – will host the season finale before closing down in '09.

'We wanted to do something special for Oran Park and the people of Sydney,' V8 Supercars Australia chairman Tony Cochrane said. 'The place has so much history and culture that we really want to send it out with a big bang.'

Judging by current form, the V8 Supercar Championship should do just that.

**Above: Rick Kelly and Garth Tander in their Toll HSV Holden Commodore faced a tough battle with Ford throughout the season.**

**Left: Craig Lowndes and Jamie Whincup won the Bathurst 1,000 race outright in their Vodafone Ford.**

**Photographs: Graphic Dak Photos/Dirk Klynsmit**

IT'S difficult to explain to anyone living outside the United States, Canada and Mexico how big NASCAR (National Association for Stock Car Auto Racing) has become during the opening decade of the 21st century. Thanks to an unswerving business development program conceived and implemented half a century ago by Bill France Sr and seriously refined and tweaked by his son Bill Jr during his reign as NASCAR's boss from 1972 to 2003, NASCAR has established itself as a major-league sport in America and over the past few years the France empire has begun drawing the final breaths of commercial oxygen out of the rest of American motor racing.

Today, America's mass market is constantly exposed to NASCAR's top 20 or more drivers. This happens not only through a never-ending, 36-race campaign each year, but also with darn-near 24-hour television coverage on Speed TV and, most important, in TV commercial after TV commercial and in print media ads of all kinds. Many of the top drivers such as Jeff Gordon, Tony Stewart, Jimmie Johnson and Dale Earnhardt Jr, as well as old stagers such as Dale Jarrett and Michael Waltrip, are powerfully tied to their major sponsors as personalities and pitchmen in a continuing series of national advertising campaigns on TV, radio and billboards and in the print media. They are among the best-known and -recognised characters in American sport and four-times champion Gordon and second-generation superstar Earnhardt Jr command a massive income from merchandising sales and endorsing products – considerably more than any Formula 1 driver, Michael Schumacher included.

Thirty years ago in this space I wrote that NASCAR represented the pinnacle of American racing. 'The successful package that is NASCAR's Winston Cup continues to roll happily along,' I wrote. 'The grandstands continue to be as full as ever, Winston Cigarettes continues to be as active and pleased as ever in sponsoring the championship and more and more stock races are televised nationally… NASCAR remains the model for all other motor racing groups to measure themselves against.'

Three decades later NASCAR has built on that base to become the definition of racing in America. After 33 years, series sponsor Winston was replaced in '04 by Nextel, which has merged with rival Sprint so that NASCAR's top division becomes the Sprint Cup series in '08. A new TV deal began this year with ABC/ESPN, Fox and TNT, replacing the previous NBC/Fox package. The new multi-network contract is worth $4.8 billion over eight years. TV ratings actually peaked in '05, declining slightly overall in '06 and '07, although most NASCAR races attract as many viewers as, and often more than, the Indy 500, and the season-opening Daytona 500 continues to draw a huge audience, three and four times bigger than that of the Indy 500. There's also been a decline in attendance at many races in recent years as ticket prices and travel and hotel costs have continued to rise.

But NASCAR's basic strengths remain well established and far ahead of those of any other form of American racing, with room for growth in unfamiliar ways – such as the arrival of Toyota in the first-division Cup series this year and the flood of 'open-wheel' drivers into NASCAR, led by Juan Pablo Montoya and including Jacques Villeneuve, Dario Franchitti, Sam Hornish, AJ Allmendinger and Scott Speed. Some people grumble that the combination of Toyota and foreign drivers is destroying the all-American essence of stock car racing but NASCAR is delighted to have the chance to appeal to a wider audience. It will be interesting to see over the next few years if the arrival of Toyota, Montoya, Villeneuve, Franchitti et al proves to be a positive or a negative for NASCAR.

Former F1 and CART (Championship Auto Racing Teams; Champcar open-wheel racing) superstar Montoya is the poster boy for NASCAR's new global marketing expansion. Montoya's move near the end of '06 from Formula 1 to Chip Ganassi's NASCAR team was a first for racing. No F1 driver had ever made such a move and even though he's had a tough time getting to the front of the field, Juan is enjoying life in NASCAR and helped convince old CART rival Franchitti that a move to NASCAR would be a rejuvenating experience. Montoya was able to make history in '07 by becoming the first foreign driver to win a major-league NASCAR race since Canadian Earl Ross turned the trick back in '74. Juan Pablo scored his first NASCAR victory in a second-division Busch race at the Mexico City road course in March, then came through to take his first Cup win in June at the Infineon Raceway (Sears Point) road course in California.

The two wins paid off big-time for Ganassi, his sponsors and NASCAR as a whole and even though he has yet to make himself a regular top-ten competitor, Montoya couldn't be happier with his move into the 850-bhp, 3,400-lb beasts. 'I'm having fun,' Juan says. 'You get to race every week. The races are awesome and the cars are a handful. It makes it interesting. I wouldn't change it for anything.'

Montoya loves the pure pleasure of racing in NASCAR. 'It's good because you're always racing. In open-wheel you get frustrated because you can't pass people. Here, you can – and if you don't do it, you can try again and try again and you will pass him. There are always different patterns and grooves and every week it's a different track and a different set-up.'

Juan readily admits there are politics in NASCAR – but nothing like in Formula 1. 'There are some politics, but I think it's a well-balanced environment,' he remarked.

The most difficult adjustment Montoya has had to make in NASCAR is not in his driving but in learning to live with being out to lunch on some weekends. 'I think the biggest thing you've got to learn when you come from open-wheel is that some weeks you're going to run 30th or 35th,' he observed. 'And that is so hard to understand, especially when you ran 30th and did a good job! It's hard to explain because there are races where you did a worse job and you finished fifth.'

Juan thinks it can be argued that there are more details for the driver and team to play with and dial in during a race weekend than there are in F1. 'You play with geometries every week and in open-wheel racing you never do that,' he said. 'In open-wheel, you've got bars and springs and the front wing and that's it. Here, you've got shocks and steering and suspension geometries that you're always messing with. So in many ways there are more things for the drivers and the teams to either get right or screw up.

'There are a lot of things we've still got to learn as a team,' Montoya added about his adventure with Ganassi's team. 'We've got to be better and be more consistent as a whole organisation. I think when we're good, we're as good as anybody. We've just got to be that good every week.'

Left: From Richmond to Charlotte... From Bristol to Daytona... NASCAR consistently packs in the fans like no other motor sport category in the United States.
Photographs: LAT South USA

Below: Kyle Busch plays to the audience after his win at Bristol Motor Speedway
Photograph: Nigel Kinrade/LAT South USA

UNITED STATES RACING REVIEW
# NASCAR RULES
by GORDON KIRBY

In October, Ganassi announced that he had signed Indy 500 winner and IRL (Indy Racing League open-wheel racing) champion Franchitti to join Montoya in his Cup team for '08. Franchitti immediately began running a series of ARCA and second-level Busch races in Ganassi's cars to prepare for his rookie NASCAR season, just as Montoya had 12 months earlier. In fact, Montoya's enthusiasm for NASCAR helped convince the 34-year-old Franchitti that it was the right move.

'Juan said, "You'll love the racing and the schedule is busy but it's fun,"' Franchitti remarked. 'He was very enthusiastic. He couldn't recommend it highly enough and that certainly helped point me in this direction.'

Franchitti listened closely in all ways to Montoya's analysis of NASCAR. 'I'm under no illusions here,' he said. 'It's the toughest challenge in my career but that's probably the reason I'm doing it. I was lucky this year to achieve everything I wanted in the IndyCar series and life without a challenge can be kind of boring.

'I'm well aware of the magnitude of this,' he added. 'There are a lot of great drivers and teams out there and Juan has told me it's necessary to take a different mind-set where a tenth, or even a 20th, can be a good day.'

Indeed, with as many as 50 cars showing up for many races and only 43 starting places, it's often a big scramble just to make the field, as former Champcar Atlantic series champion and Champcar star AJ Allmendinger found out this past year.

He made the jump to NASCAR last winter with the new Red Bull Toyota Cup team and qualified for fewer than a third of the races in his rookie NASCAR season.

Of course, just as in every other form of racing, it's all about your car and equipment. With plenty of sponsorship, the top NASCAR teams spend a lot of money on engineering and wind tunnel work. In fact, an increasingly large number of engineers have left F1, IRL, Champcar or sports car racing to work in stock car racing and when you take a close look at NASCAR it's really not much different from F1 in that a handful of big teams dominated play.

At the top of the heap is Rick Hendrick's four-car Chevrolet operation led by multiple champion Jeff Gordon and '06 champ Jimmie Johnson. Gordon and Johnson were the men to beat in '07, heading the championship points for most of the season. The other leading Chevrolet teams in recent years have been Joe Gibbs Racing's three cars led by '02 and '05 champion Tony Stewart and the trio of Chevrolets fielded by Richard Childress Racing and Dale Earnhardt Inc, although Gibbs' team becomes the first high-profile operation to switch to Toyota in '08. Ford's top NASCAR team is the five-car Roush-Fenway operation, which includes '03 champion Matt Kenseth and '07's second-division Busch champion Carl Edwards.

Next in NASCAR's pecking order are Roger Penske's pair of Dodges, which will expand to a three-car team in '08, and Chip

**Above: Multi-car team owner Rick Hendrick, who runs championship favourites Jeff Gordon and Jimmie Johnson.**
Photograph: LAT South Photographic

**Above left: Jack Roush, who heads up Ford's challenge.**
Photograph: Nigel Kinrade/LAT South USA

**Left: Dale Earnhardt Jr, who will leave his family team for Hendrick in 2008.**
Photograph: Nigel Kinrade/LAT South USA

**Below left: Juan Pablo Montoya with his family at Charlottesville.**
Photograph: Michael Levitt/LAT Photographic

**Below: Montoya (car number 42) took a maiden NASCAR win on the road course at Sonoma, California.**
Photograph: Phil Abbot/LAT Photographic

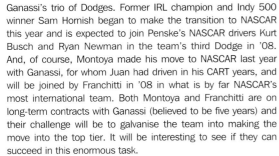

Ganassi's trio of Dodges. Former IRL champion and Indy 500 winner Sam Hornish began to make the transition to NASCAR this year and is expected to join Penske's NASCAR drivers Kurt Busch and Ryan Newman in the team's third Dodge in '08. And, of course, Montoya made his move to NASCAR last year with Ganassi, for whom Juan had driven in his CART years, and will be joined by Franchitti in '08 in what is by far NASCAR's most international team. Both Montoya and Franchitti are on long-term contracts with Ganassi (believed to be five years) and their challenge will be to galvanise the team into making the move into the top tier. It will be interesting to see if they can succeed in this enormous task.

The big story in NASCAR in '07, of course, was Dale Earnhardt Jr's decision to leave the family team – Dale Earnhardt Inc (DEI) – and move to the mighty Hendrick team for '08 beside Gordon, Johnson and Casey Mears. Earnhardt has also left long-time sponsor Budweiser behind for a new alliance with PepsiCo power drink Amp Energy and the Army National Guard. His move has left some long-time Earnhardt fans cold because Hendrick's team and Gordon and Johnson are considered to be antichrists – squeaky clean, politically correct Californians, fer crying out loud! But, in the bigger picture, it will be interesting to see how Dale Jr stacks up against Gordon and Johnson in identical equipment. In the wake of his father's death at Daytona in '01, 'Little E' has become NASCAR's biggest star

**Above: Jeff Gordon was back at his best in 2007, overhauling the late Dale Earnhardt's total of 75 Cup victories.**
Photograph: Brian Czobat/LAT South USA

and most popular driver but he has yet to seriously contend for a championship and failed to qualify for the chase for the cup in his last year with DEI.

The chase for the cup: since '04, NASCAR has determined its champion through what is essentially a play-off over the season's last ten races among the year's top 12 drivers. The format makes it a bit of a crapshoot because a single bad race can ruin the chances of an otherwise dominant driver. You can dispute the validity of Kurt Busch's '04 championship, for example, but nobody argues that either Tony Stewart or Jimmie Johnson didn't deserve their titles in '05 and '06. In '07, Hendrick team-mates Gordon and Johnson were the men to beat all year and the championship came down to a battle between them. Here was a complete contrast to Formula 1 – a pair of team-mates who are very close and equally respectful on and off the track.

Gordon is a part-owner of Johnson's car, in fact, and he enjoyed his best season since taking his fourth title in '01. Early in the year Gordon passed the late Dale Earnhardt's tally of 75 Cup wins and next year he should establish himself as NASCAR's third-most-successful driver of all time behind Richard Petty and David Pearson. Gordon was as good as ever in '07 and his pursuit of his fifth NASCAR championship emphasised the point that he is the only truly great driver racing in America today.

A big bone of contention in NASCAR in '07 was the switch to what's called the 'car of tomorrow' (CoT). It is an attempt to make a safer car and to define a near-identical, essentially spec, car, but the larger, bulkier CoT has been criticised by everyone from drivers and teams to the fans and media. For sure, the cars are less attractive and visual differences between manufacturers have been essentially eliminated. Nor do many drivers like the feel of the new cars and it may well be shown over time that the CoT doesn't race as well as the old car because it makes only half the downforce created by the old

car. But the logistics of the switch to the CoT appear to have gone much better than predicted, which is a testament to the teams, most of which build their own cars and engines.

It will be interesting to see if the CoT proves to be more raceable as the teams sort it out and also to see if NASCAR achieves its goals of making a more level playing field and encouraging the teams to have a smaller, cheaper inventory of cars. For years the top teams have maintained fleets of between 16 and 20 cars per driver – many of them custom-built to suit specific tracks – and NASCAR hopes the CoT will reduce that number and permit small teams to be more competitive.

And Toyota's first year in NASCAR's first division was one of frustration. Qualifying for the races was the first hurdle to clear as most Toyota drivers struggled to make the field. In the autumn, Joe Gibbs' team announced that it will switch to Toyotas for '08. This is the first of NASCAR's multi-car super-teams to make the move to Toyota, which is building a new development facility in North Carolina. As everyone knows, Toyota's financial and technical resources are huge and there's little doubt that the company will start winning Cup races over the next two years.

## OPEN-WHEEL BLUES

At an *Autosport* Awards dinner 11 years ago, I had the pleasure of sharing a table with Bill France Jr, Dale Earnhardt and my colleague Nigel Roebuck. That evening, France and I discussed many things, including the CART/IRL split, and France asked me to keep our CART/IRL conversation off the record, an agreement I honoured during his lifetime. 'You're really worried about Tony [George, owner of Indianapolis Motor Speedway and head of the IRL] pulling the trigger on his new formula, aren't you?' France asked rhetorically. 'You think it's going to end up destroying Indy car racing, don't you?'

He paused for a second, glanced down, then looked me straight in the eye. 'Well, I agree with you,' France declared. 'I think it will. You know my father and I always believed there's got to be one man in control. You can't have any competitors. You've got to have one series with a solid name and brand. Those guys are putting themselves in danger of losing all that. Of course, the more damage they do to themselves, it's only going to help us grow.'

Indeed, after 12 years of civil war between CART/Champcar and the IRL, American open-wheel racing has been reduced to a curiosity at the far-distant margins of the national consciousness. Many people in the United States know the top ten NASCAR drivers but the country's open-wheel drivers don't exist in the national media or mind.

While NASCAR is attracting most of the remaining, big open-wheel names, the IRL's and Champcar's futures remain clouded, at best. One thing that is clear is that the IRL has pretty well won the war of attrition for dominance of American open-wheel racing. In the past few years, Champcar's TV ratings and overall media coverage have dwindled to barely measurable numbers, a tenth or less of NASCAR's. The IRL's ratings are hanging in there, but there's nothing to be proud of in its poor overall media numbers, either.

At least the IRL enjoyed an exciting and compelling championship battle this year with a great grandstand finish between Franchitti and Scott Dixon. The Indy 500 winner and runner-up battled for the IRL title down to the last lap of the year's last race, when Dixon ran out of fuel while leading and Franchitti jinked around him to win the race and the championship. Both drivers won four races and Franchitti's Andretti-Green team-mate Tony Kanaan scored a season-high five wins. Franchitti was particularly strong on the big speedways such as Indianapolis and Michigan. He should have won both races but crashed spectacularly near the end of the Michigan race after colliding with Dan Wheldon. Dario had another flying incident at Kentucky the following weekend and was lucky to escape unscathed from both flips.

But both the IRL and Champcar face serious problems in attracting more ink and air time and in rebuilding and retaining their fan bases. The loss of both series' biggest stars will make things even more difficult. In Champcar, the big question is who will replace four-times champion Sébastien Bourdais at Newman/Haas? For better or worse, Bourdais finally has his F1

Left: Dario Franchitti followed in the footsteps of the late, great, Jim Clark by winning the Indianapolis 500 race. The Scotsman poses for a traditional photograph with his wife Ashley Judd. Also pictured (from left to right) are AGR team manager Kim Green, Honda's Robert Clarke and Dan Layton, Michael Andretti and AGR's Kevin Savoree.
Photograph: Dan Streck/LAT Photographic

Below: With one lap to go Dario Franchitti still tails Scott Dixon in his quest for the IRL title.
Photograph: Michael Levitt/LAT Photographic

Bottom: The four Team Penske and Ganassi drivers squabble for the lead position after a pit stop at the Chicagoland finale.
Photographs: Michael Levitt/LAT Photograpic

chance in '08 with Scuderia Toro Rosso. Justin Wilson was Newman/Haas's first choice but Justin and sponsor CDW are departing the beleaguered Champcar series for the ALMS (American Le Mans Series), where Wilson will drive for Andretti-Green next year. There are no other obvious star drivers available for Newman/Haas and certainly nobody to spark the interest of sponsors, the public or the media.

And if Paul Tracy and the Forsythe team continue to struggle in '08 as they did this past year and the now-ageing Canadian is no longer a front-runner, who will be Champcar's star attractions? It's a little much to expect it all to fall on the shoulders of young Graham Rahal, who did a respectable job at 18 years of age in his rookie Champcar season with Newman/Haas but didn't set the world on fire.

A lot of effort went into the organisation's new Panoz DP01 spec car that replaced the ageing Lola B2/00 chassis in '07. There was lots of talk about the DP01's helping attract new teams to Champcar but hopes for 20 or more cars were dashed as the winter wore on and it became clear that there would be no more than the usual rather motley collection of 17 or 18 cars on the grid. Champcar's big problem is not the car; it's the fact that sponsorship is all but impossible to sell.

Another thing that's occurred over the past two years is that Champcar has lost the last of its oval races and now runs only on road and street circuits. While Champcar has walked away from the ovals, the IRL has taken on a few road and temporary circuits so that it's much closer to the broad-based challenge of the old CART Indy Car World Series than today's Champcar series is.

Champcar now finds itself in the invidious position of turning to Europe for growth and income and therefore placing a good part of its future in the hands of the FIA (Fédération internationale de l'automobile, which runs much international motor sport). The dream of the series' becoming a North American street racing festival has faded with Denver (Colorado) going out of business in '06, this year's hoped-for Phoenix (Arizona) season-closer failing to get off the ground, San José (California) getting the axe in September and many people questioning the future of the new Las Vegas (Nevada) street race.

So Champcar is hoping to run more European races in '08. There are plenty of tracks in Europe looking for cheaper, promotable alternatives to F1. Zolder (Belgium) and Assen (the Netherlands) ran experimental Champcar races in the late summer of '07 and there may be as many as five European races on Champcar's '08 calendar. Even at bargain-basement rates, these tracks can afford to pay Champcar more than the organisation can command for most of its home races. And there's the attraction of a field more than half-full with European drivers who haven't quite made it to F1 – or can't quite afford it – but enjoy European or international sponsorship.

Of course, the more overseas races, the less saleable Champcar is in the United States – and it already has no saleability. There are no major American companies sponsoring Champcars and most of the teams live in fear of the sponsorship well's running dry. The McDonald's sponsorship on Sébastien Bourdais's car over the past three years has been there only because of Paul Newman, who supplies the burger chain with his healthy salad dressings. But even Newman's immense pulling power can't make McDonald's do any kind of marketing programme using the Newman/Haas Champcar. Nor has Newman been able to attract any other sponsorship to his team in recent years. 'I'm afraid we're fucked, my friend,' a glum Newman remarked a number of times in '07.

This past year there were only seven American races on the Champcar schedule – a record low – and by abandoning oval tracks and having fewer American races overall, Champcar is losing any claim to being the American national driving championship. In fact, it's laughable to make that suggestion now. Sadly, in '07, this was something the IRL was more qualified to claim than Champcar. Of course, to the average American there's not the slightest question that NASCAR's Nextel Cup series is the country's national auto racing championship because they don't even know the IRL or Champcar exist.

An almost intractable issue facing both Champcar and the IRL is how to attract more regular print and major media coverage. So much of it has drained away over the years that the press rooms at many races are almost ghost towns. The fact is that in terms of column inches and media recognition, American open-wheel racing is among the smallest – if not the smallest – sports in the nation, hence the sad TV ratings.

Today, NASCAR enjoys a powerful nationwide press corps with newspapers from almost every state of the union covering all 36 Nextel Cup races while Champcar and IRL function without mainstream press corps, relying primarily on websites and a handful of small-circulation enthusiast publications to get the news out. The interest in open-wheel racing from American newspapers and magazines has vanished, a clear indication that the sport is in deep trouble.

'Let's face it,' IRL and NASCAR team owner Chip Ganassi observed, 'when you look at the commercial sponsorship side or the business model of open-wheel racing, I'm afraid to say it doesn't exist. There is no business model and the fact of the matter is that until American open-wheel racing is made a viable business by the powers that be, it's simply dying a slow death.'

## PENSKE'S PORSCHES ET AL

For many years the American Le Mans Series has been dominated by the factory Audi R8s and more recently the turbo-diesel R10s, but the turbo-diesels were beaten consistently in '07 by the pair of more conventional Penske Porsche RS Spyders. The lighter LMP2 Porsches were much improved after a year of development and were able to beat the more powerful LMP1 Audis in race after race with Romain Dumas and Timo Bernard in one car and Sascha Maassen and Ryan Briscoe aboard the other.

Honda also made its début in the ALMS in '07 with its Acura brand. With the IRL becoming a de facto spec car series, Honda was looking for an alternative place to race in America against other manufacturers. Three teams were selected to run one car each and the lead Andretti-Green Acura scored a well-deserved but surprise LMP2 class win and second overall in Acura's ALMS début at the season-opening Sebring 12 hours. The Porsches had alternator problems at Sebring but the trio of Acuras struggled for speed and competitiveness as the Penske operation came on song over the balance of the year.

A big effort is going into the '08 Acura ALMS program but Honda's racing people are unhappy with the ALMS for making in-season rule changes and the Automobile Club de l'Ouest (ACO) for taking a different tack on its vision for the Le Mans 24-hour rules. By the end of the season, Honda's racing bosses and Roger Penske were saying it was unlikely their ALMS cars would ever race in the French classic.

The rival, NASCAR-affiliated Grand-Am sports car series was won by Dan Gurney's youngest son Alex and Jon Fogarty, who combined to win seven races driving Bob Stallings' Riley-Pontiac. Gurney and Fogarty beat Scott Pruett and Memo Rojas in one of Chip Ganassi's pair of Riley-Lexuses and defending champion Max Angelelli aboard Wayne Taylor's Riley-Pontiac.

The revitalised Champcar Atlantic series and its $2-million prize was won by Brazilian Raphael Matos, who expects to follow '06 Atlantic champion Simon Pagenaud into Champcar next season. Brit Alex Lloyd took the IRL's Indy Pro Series championship for Sam Schmidt Racing. Lloyd dominated the series, winning eight of 16 races.

And former Champcar and Atlantic driver Andrew Ranger turned his back on open-wheel racing and made a reluctant move to the new NASCAR Canadian Tire Series. NASCAR bought the Canadian CASCAR stock car organisation in '06 and the 20-year-old Ranger went on to become NASCAR's inaugural Canadian champion. Ranger has become a powerful convert to stock car racing and will continue in the series another year, hoping to make the break into the big-time south of the border in '09 or '10.

Many people grumble about NASCAR's dominance and hope

that the stock car organisation is beginning to struggle with a combination of things such as less-than-sell-out crowds at many Cup races and the problems encountered by the drivers and teams in adapting to the hulking, unattractive car of tomorrow. But the fact is that, in addition to enjoying a very large, highly committed fan base, NASCAR has built a tremendous infrastructure and ladder system way beyond anything ever imagined by any of the open-wheel or sports car sanctioning bodies. If you want to be a professional racer in North America today, the road to NASCAR is irresistible.

**Below: Raphael Matos won the Champcar Atlantic series and should move up to the senior series in 2008.**
Photograph: Terri Taylor/LAT Photographic

**Below left: Alex Lloyd took the IRL Indy Pro Series title with eight wins from 16 starts.**
Photograph: Paul Webb/LAT Photographic

**Above: The Sascha Maassen/Ryan Briscoe Penske Porsche RS Spyder makes a pit stop at Lexington Mid-Ohio.**
Photograph: Paul Webb/LAT Photographic

**Left: The Highcroft Acura proved to be a very competitive package in the hands of veteran drivers David Brabham and Stefan Johansson, seen here at Bowmanville, Ontario.**
Photograph: Richard Dole/LAT Photographic

**Main:** Pippa Coleman (86) leads the BRDC Stars of Tomorrow Mini Max pack out for action. Stars and Super 1 champion Ashley Sutton (3) joins the field from the right.

**Right:** Max Goff, who shone in both BRDC Stars of Tomorrow and the Italian Open Masters before sealing the crowning glory of an impressive campaign – victory in the prestigious Monaco Kart Cup.

Photographs: Chris Walker/www.kartpix.net

KARTING REVIEW

# STARS IN THEIR EYES

by RUSSELL ATKINS

**Left: Italian Open Masters and CIK-FIA European Champion Jack Harvey.**
Photograph: Chris Walker/www.kartpix.net

**Centre: Leading MSA British cadet championship runners (from left to right) Alex Albon, Jake Dennis and Brett Wykes.**
Photograph: Mike Weston/www.crash.net

WITH Lewis Hamilton's dramatic arrival on the Formula 1 scene in 2007, his startling success has thrust karting – the category in which Lewis first made his name more than a decade ago – into the public consciousness and raised its profile beyond all recognition.

BRDC Stars of Tomorrow – or McLaren-Mercedes Champions of the Future, as it was known back when Hamilton raced in it in the mid-to-late 1990s – is the UK's premier karting series and, aside from the '07 F1 vice-champion, has also produced talent of the calibre of DTM king Gary Paffett, fellow tin-top stars Paul di Resta and Susie Stoddart and GP2 ace Christian Bakkerud. So, you may ask, who were this year's cream of the crop?

Brett Wykes followed in Hamilton's wheeltracks by ending the campaign as MSA British cadet (for drivers over nine years old) champion, following a spirited battle with Alex Walker – who recovered from a terrible opening two rounds to stake his claim as a title contender – Hazz Truelove and pre-season tip Alex Albon. All four are clearly names to keep an eye on in years to come.

One gear up in the Lewis Hamilton-sponsored Mini Max class (for 11- to 16-year-olds), Ashley Sutton proved unstoppable on his way to the end-of-season honours. The Bishops Stortford ace was almost 60 points clear of his nearest rival at the close of play and added the prestigious 'O' Plate trophy to his repertoire along the way for good measure, seeing off a determined challenge from Pippa Coleman, another to impress in '07. Macaulay Walsh finished as runner-up in the Mini Max title chase in front of Pat Fletcher and Ben Palmer.

In Junior Max (for 13- to 16-year-olds), meanwhile, Kenny Andrews wrapped up the laurels at the end of a season-long tussle with Max Hawkins. The latter's NJR Motorsports team-mate Daniel Lloyd Jr was also expected to be a contender for honours, but the Huddersfield ace suffered horrendous bad luck in the early rounds and missing the final meeting dropped him back to ninth in the standings, behind '06 Mini Max champion

Tom Ingram, who once again impressed by outpacing many older, more experienced and better-funded rivals during his maiden Junior Max campaign in his small, family-run team. What's more, the 14-year-old picked up the High Wycombe and Marlow Sports Personality of the Year award *en route*, a prestigious accolade formerly received by no less than five-times Olympic gold medallist Sir Steve Redgrave CBE. Others to shine in the class included Scots Robert Gilmore and Ross Dougan, Kalvin Quinn, Gemma Stephenson and Jack Goff.

The JICA (KF3 on the continent; for 12- to 16-year-olds) class battle went all the way down to the wire in the final race of the year, as double MSA British cadet champion Sam Jenkins made history by becoming the first driver to win three Stars titles in a row. The recently turned-13-year-old sealed his success, however, only at the end of a titanic scrap with rivals Max Goff and Luke Wright, and a three-way shoot-out in the final round at Three Sisters near Wigan began with Goff and Jenkins separated by little more than a handful of points in the former's favour, with Wright ready to pick up the pieces should it all end in tears. It culminated in something of an anti-climax, though, after Saturday's winner Goff was excluded from the second heat on the Sunday over a faulty transponder, leaving him mid-grid for the all-important final with too much work to do.

The Brigstock ace, however, made amends for that disappointment by triumphing in the prestigious Monaco Kart Cup later in the year, up against the *crème de la crème* of international opposition from 14 countries. Overcoming earlier woes that had left him down in 30th place on a 34-kart grid, the 13-year-old – one of the youngest drivers in the field – produced a superb performance to see off the challenges of McLaren and Mercedes-Benz Young Driver Support Programme member Oliver Rowland and former British Junior Karting champion and reigning Kartmasters king Jack Harvey to clinch the coveted trophy. Just a week later Max emerged victorious in

**Above: Leading BRDC Stars of Tomorrow and Super 1 JICA ace Max McGuire.**
Photograph: Chris Walker/www.kartpix.net

**Centre left: BRDC Stars of Tomorrow Junior Max champion Kenny Andrews.**
Photograph: Mike Weston/www.crash.net

**Above left: BRDC Stars of Tomorrow Junior Max front-runner and Wycombe and Marlow Sports Personality of the Year Tom Ingram.**
Photograph: Chris Walker/www.kartpix.net

**Left: BRDC Stars of Tomorrow Super ICC champion Frank Wrathall.**
Photograph: Mike Weston/www.crash.net

**Above:** Lewis Hamilton meets the leading ten MSA British cadet championship contenders on a return to his karting roots at Daytona Raceway near Milton Keynes before the British Grand Prix.

**Left:** Gearbox racer Jack Hawksworth – one to keep an eye on in years to come.
Photographs: Chris Walker/www.kartpix.net

**Top centre:** Typically close-fought cadet action in the BRDC Stars of Tomorrow series – Roy Johnson leads eventual champion Brett Wykes, Jake Dennis and Alex Albon at Kimbolton.
Photograph: Mike Weston/www.crash.net

**Left:** BRDC Stars of Tomorrow JICA champion Sam Jenkins.
Photograph: Mike Weston/www.crash.net

the Bridgestone Cup at Garda in Italy, too, cementing his status as one of the most promising young British hopes around. Another to show well in JICA was cadet graduate Max McGuire, who despite the leap by the end of the year was consistently on the leading pace.

In Stars' ultra-fast Super ICC category (for over-16s), meanwhile, Frank Wrathall finally succeeded in lifting the laurels after having come agonisingly close on a number of previous occasions. A popular result, it came at the end of a season-long duel with '06 Junior Max runner-up Jack Hawksworth, who took to the gearbox class like the proverbial duck to water to become a championship challenger in only his first season and, like Wrathall – who similarly impressed in the open-top sports car Ginetta Championship – is undoubtedly one to keep an eye on as he makes his way up the racing ranks.

Many of the same names were racing in Super 1 – the other top-level British karting series – with Truelove and Albon conspiring to deny Wykes a national double as they finished first and second in the cadet championship to leave the Northampton ace third. Truelove triumphed by the slender margin of just five points while others up at the sharp end were early Stars pace-setter Jake Dennis, Daniel Sweeney and James Appleton.

Sutton again prevailed in Mini Max, successfully seeing off the challenges of Billy Albone, Ben Palmer and Bill Cowley on his way to the crown, while Callum Bowyer also made an impression after stepping up from cadets, where he had

finished third in '06. In Junior Max Luke Varley proved to be the dominant force, with only Andrew Tooley offering much of a concerted season-long resistance to the Protrain Racing ace, and JICA/KF3 honours went the way of Rowland – signed up by McLaren in much the same manner as Hamilton was nine years ago – though Tom Joyner, Gary Thompson, Goff, Jordon Lennox-Lamb and Harvey all had their say with some stand-out performances along the way to mark themselves out as men to watch in years to come.

Benjy Russell improved three places on the fourth position he had achieved last year to clinch the Rotax Senior Max class, but fellow '06 protagonists Chris Lock, Dan Holland and reigning champion Michael Simpson all gave him a good run for his money as the quartet ended the year split by just over 60 points – or two race wins, in karting terms. Holland gained revenge by triumphing in Rotax Max 177, comfortably ahead of principal rivals Tom Limer and last season's runner-up Dave Wooder, while in Rotax Max DD2 it was the turn of the ladies to impress, Tiffany Chittenden seeing off all comers to take the crown. Sister Tamsin also shone with a number of strong outings, while former Stars' front-runner Amanda Lassu came in for the last two rounds, securing a rostrum finish in the first of them and blitzing the opposition in the second to mark herself out as a serious title contender for '08.

Sam Tordoff, Greg Harper and Rob Foster ended proceedings separated by a mere four points in the battle for Formula

**Above:** Leading female star Amanda Lassu, who made the jump from Junior Max to DD2 with remarkable success.
Photograph: Chris Walker/www.kartpix.net

Right: Super 1 JICA champion Oliver Rowland, whose future now seems assured because McLaren Mercedes has signed him up to the driver development programme that Lewis Hamilton was placed on nine years ago.

Below: JICA/KF3 ace Jordon Lennox-Lamb, who so impressed his Italian squad that he was swiftly signed up to a two-year European contract.

Photographs: Chris Walker/www.kartpix.net

Above right: Multiple European champion Marco Ardigo (foreground) sprays the podium champagne, joined by Tonykart duo Gary Catt and Alban Varutti. The Italian would also claim the Italian Open Masters KZ2 honours, KF1 World Cup and KF1 World Championship over the course of a spectacular 2007 campaign.

Above far right: British ace Will Stevens, who shone on the European stage by lifting both the European and Italian Open Masters KF2 laurels.

Below: KZ1 World Cup winner and WSK International Series Champion Jonathan Thonon.

Photographs: Chris Walker/www.kartpix.net

Intercontinental A (ICA) honours, with the Formula A title – another trophy won by Hamilton, albeit on the world stage – going the way of Chris Rogers after he repelled the challenges of close rivals Danny Cruttenden and Mark Litchfield.

British drivers also made considerable waves over on the European scene, as Harvey stormed to Italian Open Masters KF3 honours, with a brace of victories from the first two rounds making him unbeatable. Home favourite Matteo Viganò, fellow Brit Tom Grice and Kevin Ceccon ran Harvey closest for the crown, but it may have been a different story had Goff switched over from his BRM mount to Maranello earlier in the campaign. After failing to register so much as a single point over the opening three meetings, Max comfortably outscored every one of his rivals in the final two to vault up into sixth position in the standings out of some 46 drivers and lay down a marker for '08.

The KF2 title was claimed by Will Stevens, the '06 WSK International Series 100 ICA Jr champion thoroughly trouncing the opposition led by Italian Flavio Camponeschi, Austrian Patrick Fontner and German Maring Burkhard en route to the crown. KF1 was a similarly British preserve, Gary Catt proving even more dominant as he ended the year with almost double the points of his nearest competitor, Davide Fore, and triumphing in half of the rounds contested. KZ2, finally, had a

tight three-way scrap between Italians Marco Ardigo, Manuel Cozzaglio and Roberto Toninelli. They shared all but one of the final wins between them, but Ardigo's four victories – despite a no-score at Lonato in June – proved the deciding factor as the defending Formula A European Champion sealed his success by just 15 points.

In the WSK International Series, Viganò prevailed in the KF3 title battle, following a season-long challenge from countryman Alessandro Kouzkin and Harvey, despite the Italian's triumphing only once along the way compared with his rivals' three victories apiece. Belgian Yannik De Brabander lifted the laurels in KF2, a scant three points clear of Spanish ace Javier Tarancon, with Miki Monrás the only other driver to break the 100 points barrier in third. Jonathan Thonon, meanwhile, proved unstoppable in KZ1, winning five of the ten finals to establish a comfortable advantage over closest competitor Kazimieras Vasiliauskas, himself some way clear of Juan Nieves Alvarez in third.

Britain emerged victorious again in the prestigious CIK-FIA European Championships held at Sarno in southern Italy, as Harvey, Grice and James Thorp locked out the KF3 podium. There was an encouraging performance, too, from Lennox-Lamb, who so impressed his new Top Kart team that they swooped to sign him up on a two-year European deal to contest the KF2 and KF1 series. The KF2 European laurels this year were claimed by Stevens – adding yet another trophy to his ever-burgeoning collection – while Monrás and Tarancon joined him up on the rostrum at Salbris in France. Belgian Michael Ryall, meanwhile, delighted the partisan supporters at his home circuit of Mariembourg by seeing off Scott Jenkins – elder brother of Stars JICA champion Sam – and Italian Camponeschi to seal the KF2 World Cup.

Thonon triumphed in the KZ1 World Cup – again held at Sarno – ahead of Italians Ardigo and Francesco Laudato, with Thomas Knopper seeing off the threats of both Rick Dreezen and Michele Santolini for the European KZ2 Championship at the same meeting.

Ardigo pipped Catt to the CIK-FIA European KF1 crown, winning four races to the Britain's two as the pair left third-placed Dane Michael Christensen quite literally trailing in their wheeltracks. Indeed, Ardigo's success was cause for a triple celebration, adding to his triumph in the KF1 World Cup back in May – when he had fought off the challenges of local hero Tatsuya Hattori, Catt and Fore at Suzuka in Japan – and KF1 World Championship at Mariembourg, beating Tony Kart Racing team-mate Catt and Dane Nikolaj Bollingtoft to arguably the greatest trophy in international karting.

# MAJOR RESULTS

## OTHER CHAMPIONSHIP RACING SERIES WORLDWIDE

Compiled by DAVID HAYHOE

## GP2 Series

All cars are Dallara GP2-Renault.

**GP2 SERIES, Bahrain International Circuit, Sakhir, Bahrain, 14/15 April. Round 1. 33 and 23 laps of the 3.363-mile/5.412-km circuit.**
**Race 1 (110.822 miles/178.350 km).**
**1** Luca Filippi, I, 58m 34.676s, 113.512 mph/182.679 km/h; **2** Timo Glock, D, 58m 42.838s; **3** Andreas Zuber, A, 58m 46.579s; **4** Bruno Senna, BR, 58m 51.049s; **5** Lucas di Grassi, BR, 58m 52.750s; **6** Adrian Zaugg, ZA, 59m 13.811s; **7** Nicolas Lapierre, F, 59m 14.138s; **8** Borja García, E, 59m 14.798s; **9** Karun Chandhok, IND, 59m 18.181s; **10** Michael Ammermüller, D, 59m 26.559s; **11** Sakon Yamamoto, J, 59m 36.758s; **12** Andy Soucek, E, 59m 38.818s; **13** Christian Bakkerud, DK, 59m 39.085s; **14** Vitaly Petrov, RUS, 59m 43.965s; **15** Ho-Pin Tung, CHN/NL, 59m 46.792s; **16** Antônio Pizzonia, BR, 32 laps; **17** Kazuki Nakajima, J, 32; **18** Kohei Hirate, J, 32; **19** Sérgio Jimenez, BR, 31 (DNF-engine); **20** Alexandre (Xandinho) Negrão, BR, 14 (DNF-accident); **21** Javier Villa, E, 7 (DNF-engine); **22** Jason Tahinci, TR, 3 (DNF-gearbox); **23** Roldán Rodríguez, E, 1 (DNF-engine); **24** Mike Conway, GB, 0 (DNF-gearbox); **25** Giorgio Pantano, I, 0 (DNF-clutch); **26** Pastor Maldonado, YV, 0 (DNF-gearbox).
**Fastest race lap:** Nakajima, 1m 43.226s, 117.280 mph/188.743 km/h.
**Fastest qualifying lap:** Filippi, 1m 40.873s, 120.015 mph/193.145 km/h.

**Race 2 (77.193 miles/124.230 km).**
**1** Nicolas Lapierre, F, 43m 30.252s, 106.463 mph/171.335 km/h; **2** Timo Glock, D, 43m 33.435s; **3** Luca Filippi, I, 43m 36.938s; **4** Borja García, E, 43m 38.668s; **5** Mike Conway, GB, 43m 40.430s; **6** Kazuki Nakajima, J, 43m 41.341s; **7** Michael Ammermüller, D, 43m 42.511s; **8** Bruno Senna, BR, 43m 52.679s; **9** Andy Soucek, E, 43m 56.109s; **10** Javier Villa, E, 43m 56.972s; **11** Vitaly Petrov, RUS, 44m 02.913s; **12** Roldán Rodríguez, E, 44m 09.229s; **13** Jason Tahinci, TR, 44m 16.725s; **14** Sakon Yamamoto, J, 44m 48.148s; **15** Alexandre (Xandinho) Negrão, BR, 22 laps; **16** Pastor Maldonado, YV, 21; **17** Adrian Zaugg, ZA, 20; **18** Giorgio Pantano, I, 15 (DNF-gearbox); **19** Kohei Hirate, J, 12 (DNF-accident); **20** Sérgio Jimenez, BR, 10 (DNF-engine); **21** Karun Chandhok, IND, 7 (DNF-spin); **22** Ho-Pin Tung, CHN/NL, 3 (DNF-accident); **23** Antônio Pizzonia, BR, 2 (DNF-accident); **24** Lucas di Grassi, BR, 0 (DNF-accident); **25** Andreas Zuber, A, 0 (DNF-accident); **26** Christian Bakkerud, DK, 0 (DNF-accident).
**Fastest lap:** Glock, 1m 44.172s, 116.215 mph/187.029 km/h.
**Pole position:** García.
**Championship points**
**Drivers: 1** Filippi, 16; **2** Glock, 14; **3** Lapierre, 8; **4** Zuber, 6; **5** Senna, 5; **6** di Grassi, 4.
**Teams: 1** iSport International, 20; **2** Super Nova, 18; **3** DAMS, 10.

**GP2 SERIES, Circuit de Catalunya, Montmeló, Barcelona, Spain, 12/13 May. Round 2. 38 and 25 laps of the 2.892-mile/4.655-km circuit.**
**Race 1 (109.836 miles/176.764 km).**
**1** Bruno Senna, BR, 1h 2m 15.237s, 105.859 mph/170.364 km/h; **2** Timo Glock, D, 1h 2m 20.570s; **3** Lucas di Grassi, BR, 1h 2m 44.447s; **4** Roldán Rodríguez, E, 1h 2m 45.441s; **5** Borja García, E, 1h 3m 03.490s; **6** Mikhail Aleshin, RUS, 1h 3m 07.511s; **7** Sérgio Jimenez, BR, 1h 3m 11.231s; **8** Javier Villa, E, 1h 3m 12.052s; **9** Sakon Yamamoto, J, 1h 3m 17.506s; **10** Vitaly Petrov, RUS, 1h 3m 29.350s; **11** Ho-Pin Tung, CHN/NL, 1h 3m 30.287s; **12** Christian Bakkerud, DK, 1h 3m 42.798s; **13** Kohei Hirate, J, 1h 3m 43.159s; **14** Andy Soucek, E, 1h 3m 56.452s; **15** Kazuki Nakajima, J, 36 laps; **16** Adrian Zaugg, ZA, 21 (DNF-spin); **17** Nicolas Lapierre, F, 21 (DNF-engine); **18** Pastor Maldonado, YV, 18 (DNF-engine); **19** Antônio Pizzonia, BR, 11 (DNF-accident damage); **20** Andreas Zuber, A, 0 (DNF-gearbox); **21** Mike Conway, GB, 0 (DNF-accident); **22** Giorgio Pantano, I, 0 (DNF-accident); **23** Luca Filippi, I, 0 (DNF-accident); **24** Karun Chandhok, IND, 0 (DNF-accident); **25** Alexandre (Xandinho) Negrão, BR, 0 (DNF-accident); **26** Jason Tahinci, TR, 0 (DNF-gearbox).
**Fastest race lap:** Nakajima, 1m 29.989s, 115.713 mph/186.222 km/h.
**Fastest qualifying lap:** Glock, 1m 27.713s, 118.716 mph/191.054 km/h.

**Race 2 (72.234 miles/116.249 km).**
**1** Timo Glock, D, 38m 8.585s, 113.625 mph/182.862 km/h; **2** Javier Villa, E, 38m 17.164s; **3** Lucas di Grassi, BR, 38m 17.724s; **4** Bruno Senna, BR, 38m 17.899s; **5** Sérgio Jimenez, BR, 38m 31.282s; **6** Giorgio Pantano, I, 38m 32.042s; **7** Kazuki Nakajima, J, 38m 33.690s; **8** Antônio Pizzonia, BR, 38m 36.611s; **9** Andreas Zuber, A, 38m 37.262s; **10** Kohei Hirate, J, 38m 39.563s; **11** Luca Filippi, I, 38m 45.539s; **12** Mike Conway, GB, 38m 48.983s; **13** Adrian Zaugg, ZA, 38m 49.844s; **14** Borja García, E, 38m 51.518s; **15** Karun Chandhok, IND, 38m 52.442s; **16** Vitaly Petrov, RUS, 24 laps (DNF-fuel pressure); **17** Pastor Maldonado, YV, 24 (DNF-accident); **18** Sakon Yamamoto, J, 22 (DNF-lost drive); **19** Mikhail Aleshin, RUS, 15 (DNF-spin); **20** Christian Bakkerud, DK, 12 (DNF-driver discomfort); **21** Ho-Pin Tung, CHN/NL, 8 (DNF-accident damage); **22** Andy Soucek, E, 1 (DNF-accident damage); **23** Roldán Rodríguez, E, 0 (DNF-accident); **24** Nicolas Lapierre, F, 0 (DNF-engine); **25** Jason Tahinci, TR, 0 (DNF-accident).
**Did not start:** Alexandre (Xandinho) Negrão, BR (injury).
**Fastest race lap:** Glock, 1m 30.269s, 115.355 mph/185.645 km/h.
**Pole position:** Villa.
**Championship points**
**Drivers: 1** Glock, 31; **2** Senna, 18; **3** Filippi, 16; **4** Di Grassi, 14; **5** Lapierre, 8; **6** García, 8.
**Teams: 1** iSport International, 37; **2** Arden International, 21; **3** Super Nova International, 18.

**GP2 SERIES, Monte-Carlo Steet Circuit, Monaco, 26 May. Round 3. 45 laps of the 2.075-mile/3.340-km circuit, 93.392 miles/150.300 km.**
**1** Pastor Maldonado, YV, 1h 6m 49.495s, 83.854 mph/134.949 km/h; **2** Giorgio Pantano, I, 1h 6m 57.934s; **3** Timo Glock, D, 1h 7m 00.431s; **4** Luca Filippi, I, 1h 7m 0.797s; **5** Lucas di Grassi, BR, 1h 7m 3.781s; **6** Vitaly Petrov, RUS, 1h 7m 4.554s; **7** Sébastien Buemi, CH, 1h 7m 06.117s; **8** Antônio Pizzonia, BR, 1h 7m 7.599s; **9** Adrian Zaugg, ZA, 1h 7m 8.209s; **10** Kazuki Nakajima, J, 1h 7m 12.634s; **11** Bruno Senna, BR, 1h 7m 13.021s; **12** Kohei Hirate, J, 1h 7m 31.647s; **13** Ho-Pin Tung, CHN/NL, 1h 7m 35.329s; **14** Andy Soucek, E, 1h 7m 57.900s; **15** Alexandre (Xandinho) Negrão, BR, 44 laps; **16** Borja García, E, 40 (DNF-accident); **17** Sérgio Jimenez, BR, 40 (DNF-accident); **18** Christian Bakkerud, DK, 28 (DNF-suspension); **19** Jason Tahinci, TR, 26 (DNF-accident); **20** Javier Villa, E, 23 (DNF-accident); **21** Nicolas Lapierre, F, 16 (DNF-accident); **22** Roldán Rodríguez, E, 14 (DNF-accident); **23** Sakon Yamamoto, J, 9 (DNF-accident); **24** Mike Conway, GB, 6 (DNF-accident); **25** Andreas Zuber, A, 0 (DNF-gearbox); **26** Karun Chandhok, IND, 0 (DNF-accident).
**Fastest race lap:** Negrão, 1m 22.584s, 90.470 mph/145.597 km/h.
**Fastest qualifying lap:** Maldonado, 1m 20.820s, 92.445 mph/148.775 km/h.
**Championship points**
**Drivers: 1** Glock, 37; **2** Filippi, 21; **3** Senna, 18; **4** Di Grassi, 18; **5** Maldonado, 12; **6** Pantano, 9.
**Teams: 1** iSport International, 43; **2** Super Nova International, 23; **3** ART Grand Prix, 23.

**GP2 SERIES, Circuit de Nevers, Magny-Cours, France, 30 June/1 July. Round 4. 41 and 28 laps of the 2.741-mile/4.411-km circuit.**
**Race 1 (112.261 miles/180.667 km).**
**1** Giorgio Pantano, I, 1h 52m 32.513s, 59.850 mph/96.319 km/h; **2** Lucas di Grassi, BR, 1h 52m 41.290s; **3** Bruno Senna, BR, 1h 52m 54.989s; **4** Luca Filippi, I, 1h 52m 57.098s; **5** Vitaly Petrov, RUS, 1h 53m 12.675s; **6** Adrian Zaugg, ZA, 1h 53m 13.212s; **7** Javier Villa, E, 1h 53m 13.719s; **8** Nicolas Lapierre, F, 1h 53m 20.759s; **9** Mike Conway, GB, 1h 53m 24.944s; **10** Pastor Maldonado, YV, 1h 53m 28.403s; **11** Sakon Yamamoto, J, 1h 53m 31.545s; **12** Andy Soucek, E, 1h 53m 37.205s; **13** Ho-Pin Tung, CHN/NL, 1h 53m 40.907s; **14** Borja García, E, 1h 53m 59.473s*; **15** Jason Tahinci, TR, 1h 53m 59.616s; **16** Roldán Rodríguez, E, 40 laps; **17** Kazuki Nakajima, J, 40; **18** Alexandre (Xandinho) Negrão, BR, 31 (DNF-accident); **19** Kohei Hirate, J, 31 (DNF-spin); **20** Christian Bakkerud, DK, 18 (DNF-steering); **21** Karun Chandhok, IND, 6 (DNF-accident); **22** Timo Glock, D, 0 (DNF-accident); **23** Andreas Zuber, A, 0 (DNF-accident); **24** Michael Ammermüller, D, 0 (DNF-accident); **25** Ernesto Viso, YV, 0 (DNF-accident).
**Disqualified:** Left pit lane on red light - Adam Carroll, GB.
* Finished 12th but given 25s penalty for speeding in the pit lane.
**Fastest race lap:** Rodríguez, 1m 23.405s, 118.304 mph/190.391 km/h.
**Fastest qualifying lap:** Glock, 1m 21.895s, 120.485 mph/193.901 km/h.

**Race 2 (76.630 miles/123.324 km).**
**1** Javier Villa, E, 39m 46.184s, 115.611 mph/186.057 km/h; **2** Luca Filippi, I, 39m 46.787s; **3** Giorgio Pantano, I, 39m 47.446s; **4** Lucas di Grassi, BR, 40m 1.496s; **5** Vitaly Petrov, RUS, 40m 6.318s; **6** Kazuki Nakajima, J, 40m 6.704s; **7** Bruno Senna, BR, 40m 12.079s; **8** Pastor Maldonado, YV, 40m 14.806s; **9** Roldán Rodríguez, E, 40m 20.592s; **10** Andy Soucek, E, 40m 21.895s; **11** Kohei Hirate, J, 40m 25.136s; **12** Christian Bakkerud, DK, 40m 26.905s; **13** Sakon Yamamoto, J, 40m 29.795s; **14** Adam Carrolll GB, 40m 30.433s; **15** Andreas Zuber, A, 40m 30.783s; **16** Karun Chandhok, IND, 40m 33.446s; **17** Ho-Pin Tung, CHN/NL, 40m 37.385s; **18** Jason Tahinci, TR, 41m 5.378s; **19** Michael Ammermüller, D, 27 laps; **20** Borja García, E, 26 (DNF-accident); **21** Mike Conway, GB, 20 (DNF-hydraulics); **22** Nicolas Lapierre, F, 16 (DNF-brakes/accident); **23** Alexandre (Xandinho) Negrão, BR, 9 (DNF-accident); **24** Timo Glock, D, 3 (DNF-gearbox); **25** Adrian Zaugg, ZA, 1 (DNF-accident).
**Did not start:** Ernesto Viso, YV (injured in practice).
**Fastest lap:** Zuber, 1m 23.614s, 118.008 mph/189.915 km/h.
**Pole position:** Lapierre.
**Championship points**
**Drivers: 1** Glock, 39; **2** Filippi, 31; **3** Di Grassi, 29; **4** Senna, 24; **5** Pantano, 23; **6** Villa, 14.
**Teams: 1** iSport International, 45; **2** ART Grand Prix, 35; **3** Super Nova International, 33.

**GP2 SERIES, Silverstone Grand Prix Circuit, Towcester, Northamptonshire, Great Britain, 7/8 July. Round 5. 35 and 24 laps of the 3.194-mile/5.141-km circuit.**
**Race 1 (111.741 miles/179.830 km).**
**1** Andreas Zuber, A, 54m 21.118s, 123.353 mph/198.517 km/h; **2** Mike Conway, GB, 54m 22.933s; **3** Kazuki Nakajima, J, 54m 38.034s; **4** Lucas di Grassi, BR, 54m 49.483s; **5** Luca Filippi, I, 54m 57.599s; **6** Adam Carroll, GB, 55m 8.510s; **7** Pastor Maldonado, YV, 55m 9.418s; **8** Roldán Rodríguez, E, 55m 12.799s; **9** Vitaly Petrov, RUS, 55m 15.332s; **10** Michael Ammermüller, D, 55m 19.963s; **11** Bruno Senna, BR, 55m 20.073s; **12** Karun Chandhok, IND, 55m 21.928s; **13** Javier Villa, E, 55m 22.361s; **14** Adrian Zaugg, ZA, 55m 24.065s; **15** Felipe Albuquerque, P, 55m 26.220s; **16** Sakon Yamamoto, J, 55m 27.475s; **17** Ho-Pin Tung, CHN/NL, 55m 29.117s; **18** Kohei Hirate, J, 55m 43.456s; **19** Jason Tahinci, TR, 55m 44.373s; **20** Borja García, E, 31 laps (DNF-engine); **21** Timo Glock, D, 26 (DNF-alternator drive); **22** Nicolas Lapierre, F, 19 (DNF-accident); **23** Giorgio Pantano, I, 17 (DNF-engine); **24** Alexandre (Xandinho) Negrão, BR, 8 (DNF-clutch); **25** Christian Bakkerud, DK, 1 (DNF-clutch); **26** Andy Soucek, E, 0 (DNF-engine).
**Fastest race lap:** Glock, 1m 30.952s, 126.441 mph/203.487 km/h.
**Fastest qualifying lap:** Zuber, 1m 28.043s, 130.619 mph/210.210 km/h.

**Race 2 (76.602 miles/123.279 km).**
**1** Adam Carroll, GB, 36m 41.162s, 125.283 mph/201.622 km/h; **2** Pastor Maldonado, YV, 36m 46.030s; **3** Kazuki Nakajima, J, 36m 46.403s; **4** Lucas di Grassi, BR, 36m 54.910s; **5** Mike Conway, GB, 36m 55.066s; **6** Andreas Zuber, A, 36m 55.443s; **7** Luca Filippi, I, 37m 0.647s; **8** Giorgio Pantano, I, 37m 3.004s; **9** Vitaly Petrov, RUS, 37m 5.332s; **10** Bruno Senna, BR, 37m 5.495s; **11** Roldán Rodríguez, E, 37m 16.547s; **12** Michael Ammermüller, D, 37m 18.914s; **13** Karun Chandhok, IND, 37m 20.088s; **14** Felipe Albuquerque, P, 37m 21.245s; **15** Ho-Pin Tung, CHN/NL, 37m 24.658s; **16** Jason Tahinci, TR, 37m 33.356s; **17** Borja García, E, 37m 36.599s; **18** Alexandre (Xandinho) Negrão, BR, 37m 38.504s; **19** Adrian Zaugg, ZA, 37m 38.766s; **20** Andy Soucek, E, 37m 41.552s; **21** Christian Bakkerud, DK, 37m 44.438s; **22** Javier Villa, E, 22 laps (DNF-overheating); **23** Kohei Hirate, J, 19 (DNF-gearbox); **24** Timo Glock, D, 6 (DNF-accident); **25** Sakon Yamamoto, J, 2 (DNF-suspension).
**Did not start:** Nicolas Lapierre, F (injured).
**Fastest lap:** Nakajima, 1m 30.590s, 126.947 mph/204.300 km/h.
**Pole position:** Pantano.
**Championship points**
**Drivers: 1** Glock, 39; **2** Di Grassi, 37; **3** Filippi, 35; **4** Senna, 24; **5** Pantano, 23; **6** Zuber, 20.
**Teams: 1** iSport International, 59; **2** Super Nova International, 47; **3** ART Grand Prix, 43.

**GP2 SERIES, Nürburgring, Nürburg/Eifel, Germany, 21/22 July. Round 6. 35 and 24 laps of the 3.199-mile/5.148-km circuit.**
**Race 1 (111.948 miles/180.163 km).**
**1** Timo Glock, D, 1h 1m 32.032s, 109.158 mph/175.672 km/h; **2** Lucas di Grassi, BR, 1h 1m 34.306s; **3** Kazuki Nakajima, J, 1h 1m 34.755s; **4** Giorgio Pantano, I, 1h 1m 50.969s; **5** Kohei Hirate, J, 1h 1m 51.738s; **6** Pastor Maldonado, YV, 1h 2m 5.712s; **7** Adrian Zaugg, ZA, 1h 2m 7.811s; **8** Javier Villa, E, 1h 2m 8.992s; **9** Nicolas Lapierre, F, 1h 2m 9.510s; **10** Roldán Rodríguez, E, 1h 2m 28.580s; **11** Vitaly Petrov, RUS, 1h 2m 32.921s; **12** Alexandre (Xandinho) Negrão, BR, 1h 2m 33.452s; **13** Sakon Yamamoto, J, 1h 2m 33.957s; **14** Ernesto Viso, YV, 1h 2m 34.881s; **15** Bruno Senna, BR, 1h 2m 35.221s; **16** Ho-Pin Tung, CHN/NL, 1h 2m 40.492s; **17** Jason Tahinci, TR, 34 laps; **18** Mike Conway, GB, 34; **19** Borja García, E, 33; **20** Andy Soucek, E, 29 (DNF-brakes); **21** Karun Chandhok, IND, 26 (DNF-engine); **22** Adam Caroll, GB, 18 (DNF-accident); **23** Andreas Zuber, A, 5 (DNF-engine); **24** Christian Bakkerud, DK, 2 (DNF-accident damage); **25** Luca Filippi, I, 1 (DNF-accident damage); **26** Sébastien Buemi, CH, 1 (DNF-accident damage).
**Fastest race lap:** Conway, 1m 43.006s, 111.797 mph/179.919 km/h.
**Fastest qualifying lap:** Glock, 1m 40.977s, 114.043 mph/183.534 km/h.

**Race 2 (76.761 miles/123.535 km).**
**1** Javier Villa, E, 41m 36.640s, 110.685 mph/178.129 km/h; **2** Kohei Hirate, J, 41m 40.229s; **3** Kazuki Nakajima, J, 41m 40.696s; **4** Pastor Maldonado, YV, 41m 44.350s; **5** Timo Glock, D, 41m 45.941s; **6** Lucas di Grassi, BR, 41m 47.148s; **7** Giorgio Pantano, I, 41m 51.015s; **8** Ernesto Viso, YV, 41m 56.041s; **9** Roldán Rodríguez, E, 41m 57.912s; **10** Alexandre (Xandinho) Negrão, BR, 41m 58.851s; **11** Sakon Yamamoto, J, 42m 4.139s; **12** Borja García, E, 42m 6.810s; **13** Andy Soucek, E, 42m 7.225s; **14** Adam Caroll, GB, 42m 7.894s; **15** Mike Conway, GB, 42m 7.925s; **16** Karun Chandhok, IND, 42m 17.730s; **17** Vitaly Petrov, RUS, 42m 18.936s; **18** Christian Bakkerud, DK, 42m 33.030s; **19** Jason Tahinci, TR, 42m 34.133s; **20** Sébastien Buemi, CH, 43m 6.460s; **21** Andreas Zuber, A, 43m 13.156s; **22** Ho-Pin Tung, CHN/NL, 21 laps (DNF-accident); **23** Adrian Zaugg, ZA, 15 (DNF-accident); **24** Luca Filippi, I, 9 (DNF-accident); **25** Bruno Senna, BR, 1 (DNF-suspension damage); **26** Nicolas Lapierre, F, 0 (DNF-accident).
**Fastest lap:** Buemi, 1m 42.512s, 112.336 mph/180.786 km/h.
**Pole position: Villa.**
**Championship points**
**Drivers: 1** Glock, 53; **2** Di Grassi, 46; **3** Filippi, 35; **4** Pantano, 28; **5** Maldonado, 25; **6** Nakajima, 25.
**Teams: 1** iSport International, 73; **2** ART Grand Prix, 53; **3** Super Nova International, 48.

**GP2 SERIES, Hungaroring, Mogyorod, Budapest, Hungary, 4/5 August. Round 7. 41 and 28 laps of the 2.722-mile/4.381-km circuit.**
**Race 1 (111.607 miles/179.614 km).**
**1** Adam Caroll, GB, 1h 6m 39.582s, 100.457 mph/161.669 km/h; **2** Kazuki Nakajima, J, 1h 6m 40.296s; **3** Andreas Zuber, A, 1h 6m 40.738s; **4** Lucas di Grassi, BR, 1h 6m 51.786s; **5** Borja García, E, 1h 6m 52.654s; **6** Roldán Rodríguez, E, 1h 6m 57.095s; **7** Adrian Zaugg, ZA, 1h 7m 10.720s; **8** Javier Villa, E, 1h 7m 11.037s; **9** Ho-Pin Tung, CHN/NL, 1h 7m 11.576s; **10** Timo Glock, D, 1h 7m 11.981s; **11** Kohei Hirate, J, 1h 7m 12.408s; **12** Andy Soucek, E, 1h 7m 17.808s; **13** Bruno Senna, BR, 1h 7m 18.518s; **14** Karun Chandhok, IND, 1h 7m 29.120s; **15** Sébastien Buemi, CH, 37 laps; **16** Giorgio Pantano, I, 34 (DNF-alternator); **17** Christian Bakkerud, DK, 28 (DNF-injury); **18** Jason Tahinci, TR, 22 (DNF-alternator); **19** Vitaly Petrov, RUS, 12 (DNF-accident); **20** Alexandre (Xandinho) Negrão, BR, 12 (DNF-accident); **21** Luca Filippi, I, 12 (DNF-accident); **22** Markus Niemelä, FIN, 11 (DNF-injury); **23** Pastor Maldonado, YV, 8 (DNF-accident); **24** Nicolas Lapierre, F, 8 (DNF-accident); **25** Mike Conway, GB, 0 (DNF-accident).
**Did not qualify:** Marcos Martinez, E.
**Fastest race lap:** Buemi, 1m 29.578s, 109.402 mph/176.065 km/h.
**Fastest qualifying lap:** Glock, 1m 27.566s, 111.916 mph/180.111 km/h.

**Race 2 (76.218 miles/122.661 km).**
**1** Javier Villa, E, 42m 29.159s, 107.637 mph/173.225 km/h; **2** Adam Caroll, GB, 42m 29.821s; **3** Roldán Rodríguez, E, 42m 33.614s; **4** Lucas di Grassi, BR, 42m 42.459s; **5** Borja García, E, 42m 45.657s; **6** Andreas Zuber, A, 42m 46.466s; **7** Giorgio Pantano, I, 42m 48.230s; **8** Mike Conway, GB, 42m 49.073s; **9** Vitaly Petrov, RUS, 42m 56.748s; **10** Kohei Hirate, J, 43m 1.588s; **11** Jason Tahinci, TR, 43m 21.096s; **12** Bruno Senna, BR, 43m 22.085s; **13** Alexandre (Xandinho) Negrão, BR, 43m 25.382s; **14** Nicolas Lapierre, F, 43m 43.678s; **15** Karun Chandhok, IND, 27 laps (DNF-accident); **16** Luca Filippi, I, 27; **17** Sébastien Buemi, CH, 27; **18** Timo Glock, D, 24 (DNF-gearbox); **19** Andy Soucek, E, 21 (DNF-gearbox); **20** Kazuki Nakajima, J, 20 (DNF-accident damage); **21** Adrian Zaugg, ZA, 16 (DNF-accident damage); **22** Pastor Maldonado, YV, 9 (DNF-accident damage); **23** Ho-Pin Tung, CHN/NL, 0 (DNF-driveshaft).
**Did not qualify:** Marcos Martinez, E.
**Did not start:** Markus Niemelä, FIN (injury from race 1); Christian Bakkerud, DK (injury from race 1).
**Fastest race lap:** Buemi, 1m 28.968s, 110.152 mph/177.272 km/h.
**Pole position: Villa.**
**Championship points**
**Drivers: 1** Glock, 55; **2** Di Grassi, 54; **3** Filippi, 35; **4** Nakajima, 33; **5** Villa, 28; **6** Pantano, 28.
**Teams: 1** iSport International, 82; **2** ART Grand Prix, 62; **3** Super Nova International, 48.

**GP2 SERIES, Istanbul Speed Park, Tuzla, Turkey, 25/26 August. Round 8. 34 and 23 laps of the 3.317-mile/ 5.338-km circuit.**
**Race 1 (112.645 miles/181.284 km).**
**1** Lucas di Grassi, BR, 57m 11.277s, 118.184 mph/ 190.198 km/h; **2** Giorgio Pantano, I, 57m 12.648s; **3** Adam Caroll, GB, 57m 17.107s; **4** Timo Glock, D, 57m 17.440s; **5** Borja García, E, 57m 21.460s; **6** Kazuki Nakajima, J, 57m 22.051s; **7** Alexandre (Xandinho) Negrão, BR, 57m 25.972s; **8** Karun Chandhok, IND, 57m 31.033s; **9** Ho-Pin Tung, CHN/NL, 57m 31.906s; **10** Bruno Senna, BR, 57m 34.221s; **11** Roldán Rodríguez, E, 57m 38.504s; **12** Javier Villa, E, 57m 38.866s; **13** Marcos Martinez, E, 58m 5.303s; **14** Jason Tahinci, TR, 58m 20.781s; **15** Nicolas Lapierre, F, 58m 26.471s; **16** Ricardo Risatti, RA, 58m 44.093s; **17** Vitaly Petrov, RUS, 33 laps; **18** Sébastien Buemi, CH, 27 (DNF-gearbox); **19** Andreas Zuber, A, 20 (DNF-accident); **20** Kohei Hirate, J, 18 (DNF-gearbox); **21** Henri Karjalainen, FIN, 15 (DNF-accident); **22** Mike Conway, GB, 2 (DNF-accident damage); **23** Andy Soucek, E, 1 (DNF-accident damage); **24** Luca Filippi, I, 0 (DNF-accident); **25** Adrian Zaugg, ZA, 0 (DNF-accident).
**Did not start:** Christian Bakkerud, DK (injured).
**Fastest race lap:** Lapierre, 1m 35.551s, 124.967 mph/ 201.115 km/h.
**Fastest qualifying lap:** Filippi, 1m 34.278s, 126.655 mph/203.831 km/h.

**Race 2 (76.159 miles/122.566 km).**
**1** Timo Glock, D, 37m 21.489s, 122.317 mph/196.850 km/h; **2** Alexandre (Xandinho) Negrão, BR, 37m 30.958s; **3** Adam Caroll, GB, 37m 32.373s; **4** Borja García, E, 37m 40.094s; **5** Vitaly Petrov, RUS, 37m 40.657s; **6** Bruno Senna, BR, 37m 41.571s; **7** Luca Filippi, I, 37m 42.640s; **8** Roldán Rodríguez, E, 37m 45.718s; **9** Ho-Pin Tung, CHN/NL, 37m 46.198s; **10** Ricardo Risatti, RA, 38m 2.453s; **11** Lucas di Grassi, BR, 38m 28.564s; **12** Giorgio Pantano, I, 38m 40.671s; **13** Sébastien Buemi, CH, 22 laps; **14** Andreas Zuber, A, 22; **15** Adrian Zaugg, ZA, 20; **16** Javier Villa, E, 19 (DNF-accident); **17** Kazuki Nakajima, J, 17 (DNF-accident damage); **18** Andy Soucek, E, 16 (DNF-accident); **19** Karun Chandhok, IND, 11 (DNF-accident); **20** Jason Tahinci, TR, 7 (DNF-accident damage); **21** Marcos Martinez, E, 5 (DNF-accident); **22** Nicolas Lapierre, F, 1 (DNF-accident damage); **23** Kohei Hirate, J, 1 (DNF-accident damage); **24** Henri Karjalainen, FIN, 0 (DNF-accident); **25** Mike Conway, GB, 0 (DNF-accident damage).
**Did not start:** Christian Bakkerud, DK (DNF-injured).
**Fastest lap:** Zuber, 1m 35.733s, 124.730mph/200.733km/h.
**Pole position:** Chandhok.
**Championship points**
**Drivers: 1** Glock, 66; **2** Di Grassi, 64; **3** Filippi, 37; **4** Pantano, 36; **5** Nakajima, 36; **6** Carroll, 34.
**Teams: 1** iSport International, 94; **2** ART Grand Prix, 72; **3** Super Nova International, 50.

**GP2 SERIES, Autodromo Nazionale di Monza, Milan, Italy, 8/9 September. Round 9. 32 and 21 laps of the 3.600-mile/5.793-km circuit.**
**Race 1 (114.995 miles/185.067 km).**
**1** Giorgio Pantano, I, 55m 32.531s, 124.225 mph/ 199.920 km/h; **2** Luca Filippi, I, 55m 40.493s; **3** Timo Glock, D, 55m 42.212s; **4** Bruno Senna, BR, 55m 46.103s; **5** Karun Chandhok, IND, 55m 50.924s; **6** Javier Villa, E, 55m 51.710s; **7** Sébastien Buemi, CH, 55m 52.967s; **8** Ricardo Risatti, RA, 55m 57.631s; **9** Markus Niemelä, FIN, 55m 58.135s; **10** Nicolas Lapierre, F, 55m 58.687s; **11** Jason Tahinci, TR, 55m 59.644s; **12** Vitaly Petrov, RUS, 56m 0.428s; **13** Lucas di Grassi, BR, 56m 45.667s; **14** Alexandre (Xandinho) Negrão, BR, 31 laps; **15** Ho-Pin Tung, CHN/NL, 21 (DNF-accident); **16** Andy Soucek, E, 17 (DNF-accident); **17** Andreas Zuber, A, 17 (DNF-accident); **18** Adam Caroll, GB, 17 (DNF-accident); **19** Roldán Rodríguez, E, 13 (DNF-accident); **20** Kohei Hirate, J, 3 (DNF-accident); **21** Borja García, E, 1 (DNF-accident); **22** Adrian Zaugg, ZA, 0 (DNF-accident); **23** Mike Conway, GB, 0 (DNF-accident); **24** Marcos Martinez, E, 0 (DNF-gearbox); **25** Olivier Pla, F, 0 (DNF-accident).
**Disqualified:** Caused accident - Kazuki Nakajima, J, finished 13th in 56m 38.687s.
**Fastest race lap:** Pantano, 1m 31.442s, 141.714 mph/ 228.065 km/h.
**Fastest qualifying lap:** Pantano, 1m 30.546s, 143.116 mph/230.322 km/h.

**Race 2 (75.400 miles/121.344 km).**
**1** Timo Glock, D, 32m 32.346s, 139.032 mph/223.750 km/h; **2** Luca Filippi, I, 32m 34.160s; **3** Bruno Senna, BR, 32m 40.816s; **4** Lucas di Grassi, BR, 32m 44.900s; **5** Andreas Zuber, A, 32m 51.586s; **6** Karun Chandhok, IND, 32m 53.988s; **7** Andy Soucek, E, 32m 55.199s; **8** Roldán Rodríguez, E, 32m 57.994s; **9** Mike Conway, GB, 32m 58.085s; **10** Markus Niemelä, FIN, 33m 05.853s; **11** Vitaly Petrov, RUS, 33m 11.638s; **12** Olivier Pla, F, 33m 13.696s; **13** Sébastien Buemi, CH, 33m 14.652s; **14** Kohei Hirate, J, 33m 23.655s*; **15** Adam Caroll, GB, 33m 52.209s; **16** Ho-Pin Tung, CHN/NL, 20 laps (DNF-accident); **17** Nicolas Lapierre, F, 20 (DNF-gearbox); **18** Kazuki Nakajima, J, 20; **19** Borja García, E, 20; **20** Jason Tahinci, TR, 20; **21** Ricardo Risatti, RA, 10 (DNF-accident damage); **22** Javier Villa, E, 9 (DNF-clutch); **23** Adrian Zaugg, ZA, 2 (DNF-accident damage); **24** Alexandre (Xandinho) Negrão, BR, 1 (DNF-suspension); **25** Marcos Martinez, E, 0 (DNF-accident).
* Includes a 25s penalty for causing a race incident.
**Disqualified:** Ignored flags for dangerous bodywork - Giorgio Pantano, I, finished 6th in 32m 53.819s.
**Fastest lap:** Carroll, 1m 31.595s, 141.477 mph/227.684 km/h.
**Pole position:** Risatti.
**Championship points**
**Drivers: 1** Glock, 78; **2** Di Grassi, 67; **3** Filippi, 50; **4** Pantano, 50; **5** Nakajima, 36; **6** Carroll, 35.
**Teams: 1** iSport International, 108; **2** ART Grand Prix, 77; **3** Super Nova International, 63.

**GP2 SERIES, Circuit de Spa-Francorchamps, Stavelot, Belgium, 15/16 September. Round 10. 26 and 18 laps of the 4.352-mile/7.004-km circuit.**
**Race 1 (113.078 miles/181.981 km).**
**1** Nicolas Lapierre, F, 53m 1.842s, 127.938 mph/ 205.896 km/h; **2** Luca Filippi, I, 53m 06.678s; **3** Lucas di Grassi, BR, 53m 09.836s; **4** Javier Villa, E, 53m 10.624s; **5** Mike Conway, GB, 53m 18.999s; **6** Andy Soucek, E, 53m 30.858s; **7** Karun Chandhok, IND, 53m 32.260s; **8** Ho-Pin Tung, CHN/NL, 53m 33.741s; **9** Vitaly Petrov, RUS, 53m 44.595s; **10** Sébastien Buemi, CH, 53m 49.948s; **11** Markus Niemelä, FIN, 53m 50.507s; **12** Christian Bakkerud, DK, 53m 58.976s; **13** Adrian Zaugg, ZA, 54m 4.193s; **14** Jason Tahinci, TR, 54m 10.717s; **15** Roldán Rodríguez, E, 54m 15.665s; **16** Borja García, E, 54m 17.503s; **17** Timo Glock, D, 54m 32.428s; **18** Andreas Zuber, A, 25 laps; **19** Alexandre (Xandinho) Negrão, BR, 24 (DNF-radiator); **20** Ricardo Risatti, RA, 23 (DNF-engine); **21** Adam Caroll, GB, 19 (DNF-accident); **22** Kazuki Nakajima, J, 17 (DNF-suspension); **23** Marcos Martinez, E, 16 (DNF-radiator); **24** Bruno Senna, BR, 11 (DNF-accident); **25** Giorgio Pantano, I, 0 (DNF-clutch); **26** Kohei Hirate, J, 0 (DNF-stalled).
**Fastest race lap:** Glock, 1m 58.572s, 132.135 mph/ 212.650 km/h.
**Fastest qualifying lap:** Lapierre, 1m 56.884s, 134.043 mph/215.721 km/h.

**Race 2 (78.261 miles/125.949 km).**
**1** Karun Chandhok, IND, 36m 19.454s, 129.271 mph/ 208.041 km/h; **2** Andy Soucek, E, 36m 20.985s; **3** Lucas di Grassi, BR, 36m 22.136s; **4** Ho-Pin Tung, CHN/NL, 36m 22.429s; **5** Mike Conway, GB, 36m 23.182s; **6** Adam Caroll, GB, 36m 25.090s; **7** Luca Filippi, I, 36m 26.161s; **8** Bruno Senna, BR, 36m 28.291s; **9** Kazuki Nakajima, J, 36m 28.759s; **10** Roldán Rodríguez, E, 36m 32.373s; **11** Vitaly Petrov, RUS, 36m 39.695s; **12** Andreas Zuber, A, 36m 39.883s; **13** Kohei Hirate, J, 36m 40.550s; **14** Giorgio Pantano, I, 36m 42.219s; **15** Javier Villa, E, 36m 42.487s; **16** Alexandre (Xandinho) Negrão, BR, 36m 47.986s; **17** Borja García, E, 36m 53.976s; **18** Ricardo Risatti, RA, 36m 59.471s; **19** Adrian Zaugg, ZA, 37m 12.862s; **20** Jason Tahinci, TR, 37m 20.931s; **21** Nicolas Lapierre, F, 37m 59.455s; **22** Christian Bakkerud, DK, 12 laps (DNF-accident); **23** Sébastien Buemi, CH, 4 (DNF-accident damage); **24** Marcos Martinez, E, 3 (DNF-accident); **25** Markus Niemelä, FIN, 0 (DNF-accident); **26** Timo Glock, D (DNF-accident on installation lap).
**Fastest race lap:** Lapierre, 1m 58.748s, 131.939 mph/ 212.335 km/h.
**Pole position:** Tung.
**Championship points**
**Drivers: 1** Glock, 79; **2** Di Grassi, 77; **3** Filippi, 58; **4** Pantano, 49; **5** Villa, 36; **6** Carroll, 36.
**Teams: 1** iSport International, 109; **2** ART Grand Prix, 87; **3** Super Nova International, 77.

**GP2 SERIES, Circuit de la Comunitat Valenciana Ricardo Tormo, Cheste, Valencia, Spain, 29/30 September. Round 11. 45 and 29 laps of the 2.489-mile/4.005-km circuit.**
**Race 1 (111.987 miles/180.225 km).**
**1** Vitaly Petrov, RUS, 1h 5m 20.497s, 102.832 mph/ 165.491 km/h; **2** Giorgio Pantano, I, 1h 5m 22.992s; **3** Kazuki Nakajima, J, 1h 5m 23.038s; **4** Marcos Martinez, E, 1h 6m 12.155s; **5** Borja García, E, 1h 6m 41.329s; **6** Andy Soucek, E, 44 laps; **7** Timo Glock, D, 44; **8** Javier Villa, E, 44; **9** Mikhail Aleshin, RUS, 44; **10** Filipe Albuquerque, P, 44; **11** Mike Conway, GB, 44; **12** Ho-Pin Tung, CHN/NL, 44; **13** Andreas Zuber, A, 44; **14** Jason Tahinci, TR, 44; **15** Markus Niemelä, FIN, 44; **16** Alexandre (Xandinho) Negrão, BR, 44; **17** Karun Chandhok, IND, 43; **18** Luca Filippi, I, 40 (DNF-accident); **19** Bruno Senna, BR, 23 (DNF-accident); **20** Sergio Hernández, E, 16 (DNF-suspension); **21** Adam Caroll, GB, 8 (DNF-wheel nut); **22** Kohei Hirate, J, 7 (DNF-accident); **23** Lucas di Grassi, BR, 5 (DNF-accident); **24** Roldán Rodríguez, E, 4 (DNF-accident); **25** Christian Bakkerud, DK, 3 (DNF-accident); **26** Nicolas Lapierre, F, 0 (DNF-wheel).
**Fastest race lap:** Chandhok, 1m 22.336s, 108.809 mph/ 175.111 km/h.
**Fastest qualifying lap:** Nakajima, 1m 19.312s, 112.958 mph/181.788 km/h.

**Race 2 (72.169 miles/116.145 km).**
**1** Timo Glock, D, 40m 29.814s, 106.925 mph/172.079 km/h; **2** Javier Villa, E, 40m 35.288s; **3** Andy Soucek, E, 40m 36.913s; **4** Borja García, E, 40m 37.444s; **5** Giorgio Pantano, I, 40m 46.409s; **6** Luca Filippi, I, 40m 48.147s; **7** Kazuki Nakajima, J, 40m 48.379s; **8** Vitaly Petrov, RUS, 40m 49.682s; **9** Mike Conway, GB, 40m 52.747s; **10** Filipe Albuquerque, P, 40m 54.712s; **11** Ho-Pin Tung, CHN/NL, 41m 0.562s; **12** Andreas Zuber, A, 41m 1.321s; **13** Lucas di Grassi, BR, 41m 2.019s; **14** Bruno Senna, BR, 41m 2.206s; **15** Adam Caroll, GB, 41m 13.432s; **16** Kohei Hirate, J, 41m 14.589s; **17** Roldán Rodríguez, E, 41m 16.093s; **18** Alexandre (Xandinho) Negrão, BR, 41m 21.847s; **19** Sergio Hernández, E, 41m 22.426s; **20** Mikhail Aleshin, RUS, 41m 23.162s; **21** Nicolas Lapierre, F, 41m 40.392s; **22** Marcos Martinez, E, 27 laps; **23** Markus Niemelä, FIN, 20 (DNF-accident); **24** Karun Chandhok, IND, 20 (DNF-accident); **25** Christian Bakkerud, DK, 9 (DNF-accident); **26** Jason Tahinci, TR, 0 (DNF-accident).
**Fastest lap:** Glock, 1m 22.313s, 108.840 mph/175.160 km/h.
**Pole position:** Villa.

**Final championship points**
**Drivers**
**1** Timo Glock, D, 88; **2** Lucas di Grassi, BR, 77; **3** Giorgio Pantano, I, 59; **4** Luca Filippi, I, 59; **5** Kazuki Nakajima, J, 44; **6** Javier Villa, E, 42; **7** Adam Caroll, GB, 36; **8** Bruno Senna, BR, 34; **9** Andreas Zuber, A, 30; **10** Borja García, E, 28; **11** Pastor Maldonado, YV, 25; **12** Nicolas Lapierre, F, 23; **13** Vitaly Petrov, RUS, 21; **14** Mike Conway, GB, 19; **15** Karun Chandhok, IND, 16; **16** Andy Soucek, E, 15; **17** Roldán Rodríguez, E, 14; **18** Adrian Zaugg, ZA, 10; **19** Kohei Hirate, J, 9; **20** Alexandre (Xandinho) Negrão, BR, 8; **21** Sébastien Buemi, CH, 6; **22** Marcos Martinez, E, 5; **23** Sérgio Jimenez, BR, 4; **24** Ho-Pin Tung, CHN/NL, 4; **25** Mikhail Aleshin, RUS, 3; **26** Michael Ammermüller, D, 1; **27** Antonio Pizzonia, BR, 1; **28** Ricardo Risatti, RA, 1.

**Teams**
**1** iSport International, 118; **2** ART Grand Prix, 87; **3** Campos Grand Prix, 80; **4** Super Nova International, 78; **5** DAMS, 67; **6** Racing Engineering, 51; **7** Arden International, 44; **8** Durango, 44; **9** Petrol Ofisi FMS International, 37; **10** Trident Racing, 35; **11** Minardi Piquet Sports, 22; **12** DPR, 15; **13** BCN Competicion, 4.

## Euro 3000 Championship

All cars are Lola B02/50-Zytek KV.

**EURO 3000 CHAMPIONSHIP, Autodromo di Vallelunga, Campagnano di Roma, Italy, 22 April. 18 and 23 laps of the 2.538-mile/4.085-km circuit.**
**Round 1 (45.689 miles/73.530 km).**
**1** Oliver Martini, I, 25m 58.332s, 105.550 mph/169.866 km/h; **2** Davide Rigon, I, 25m 59.666s; **3** Diego Nunes, BR, 26m 11.937s; **4** Luiz Razia, BR, 26m 13.295s; **5** Vladimir Arabadjiev, BG, 26m 18.682s; **6** Alx Danielsson, S, 26m 20.621s; **7** Mehdi Bennani, MA, 26m 35.898s; **8** Sebastián Merchán, EC, 26m 46.695s; **9** Francesco Dracone, I, 26m 46.876s; **10** Ómar Leal, CO, 26m 59.040s.
**Fastest race lap:** Martini, 1m 25.544s, 106.821 mph/ 171.911 km/h.
**Fastest qualifying lap:** Rigon, 1m 24.698s, 107.888 mph/173.628 km/h.

**Round 2 (53.381 miles/93.955 km).**
**1** Alx Danielsson, S, 33m 14.496s, 105.376 mph/ 169.585 km/h; **2** Davide Rigon, I, 33m 23.086s; **3** Oliver Martini, I, 33m 31.699s; **4** Vladimir Arabadjiev, BG, 33m 36.479s; **5** Diego Nunes, BR, 33m 40.500s; **6** Sebastián Merchán, EC, 33m 54.849s; **7** Mehdi Bennani, MA, 34m 0.942s; **8** Luiz Razia, BR, 34m 02.366s; **9** Francesco Dracone, I, 34m 14.525s; **10** Ómar Leal, CO, 34m 37.379s.
**Fastest race lap:** Danielsson, 1m 25.674s, 106.659 mph/171.650 km/h.
**Pole position:** Merchán.

**EURO 3000 CHAMPIONSHIP, Hungaroring, Mogyorod, Budapest, Hungary, 16/17 June. 16 and 21 laps of the 2.722-mile/4.381-km circuit.**
**Round 3 (43.556 miles/70.096 km).**
**1** Pastor Maldonado, YV, 26m 24.797s, 98.940 mph/ 159.228 km/h; **2** Diego Nunes, BR, 26m 30.535s; **3** Davide Rigon, I, 26m 31.679s; **4** Alx Danielsson, S, 26m 32.104s; **5** Luiz Razia, BR, 26m 39.971s; **6** Sebastián Merchán, EC, 26m 49.231s; **7** Oliver Martini, I, 26m 50.806s; **8** Jason Tahinci, TR, 27m 01.189s; **9** Mehdi Bennani, MA, 27m 5.476s; **10** Ómar Leal, CO, 28m 3.330s.
**Fastest race lap:** Maldonado, 1m 38.008s, 99.992 mph/ 160.921 km/h.
**Fastest qualifying lap:** Maldonado, 1m 36.432s, 101.626 mph/163.551 km/h.

**Round 4 (57.167 miles/92.001 km).**
**1** Oliver Martini, I, 34m 47.908s, 98.568 mph/158.629 km/h; **2** Luiz Razia, BR, 34m 58.893s; **3** Davide Rigon, I, 34m 59.515s; **4** Sebastián Merchán, EC, 35m 1.710s; **5** Diego Nunes, BR, 35m 2.428s; **6** Alx Danielsson, S, 35m 3.071s; **7** Vladimir Arabadjiev, BG, 35m 32.553s; **8** Jason Tahinci, TR, 35m 45.239s; **9** Ómar Leal, CO, 35m 56.535s; **10** Mehdi Bennani, MA, 20 laps.
**Fastest race lap:** Danielsson, 1m 38.256s, 99.740 mph/ 160.515 km/h.
**Pole position:** Tahinci.

**EURO 3000 CHAMPIONSHIP, Circuit de Nevers, Magny-Cours, France, 15 July. and 16 and 21 laps of the 2.741-mile/4.411-km circuit.**
**Round 5 (43.740 miles/70.392 km).**
**1** Davide Rigon, I, 24m 7.006s, 108.819 mph/175.128 km/h; **2** Diego Nunes, BR, 16 laps; **3** Jason Tahinci, TR, 16; **4** Luiz Razia, BR, 16; **5** Sebastián Merchán, EC, 16; **6** Vladimir Arabadjiev, BG, 16; **7** Giandomenico Sposito, I, 16; **8** Ómar Leal, CO, 16; **9** Valentino Sebastiani, I, 16; **10** Francesco Dracone, I, 16.
**Fastest race lap:** Rigon, 1m 29.453s, 110.305 mph/ 177.518 km/h.
**Fastest qualifying lap:** Alx Danielsson, S, 1m 28.478s, 111.521 mph/179.475 km/h.

**Round 6 (57.444 miles/92.447 km).**
**1** Diego Nunes, BR, 31m 47.873s, 108.392 mph/ 174.440 km/h; **2** Luiz Razia, BR, 21 laps; **3** Alx Danielsson, S, 21; **4** Davide Rigon, I, 21; **5** Jason Tahinci, TR, 21; **6** Oliver Martini, I, 21; **7** Mehdi Bennani, MA, 21; **8** Sebastián Merchán, EC, 21; **9** Francesco Dracone, I, 21; **10** Ómar Leal, CO, 21.
**Fastest race lap:** Danielsson, 1m 29.523s, 110.219 mph/177.380 km/h.
**Pole position:** Leal.

**EURO 3000 CHAMPIONSHIP, Autodromo Internazionale del Mugello, Scarperia, Firenze (Florence), Italy, 21/22 July. 14 and 18 laps of the 3.259-mile/5.245-km circuit.**
**Round 7 (45.627 miles/73.430 km).**
**1** Davide Rigon, I, 23m 40.918s, 115.600 mph/186.040 km/h; **2** Alx Danielsson, S, 23m 45.171s; **3** Diego Nunes, BR, 23m 47.248s; **4** Vladimir Arabadjiev, BG, 24m 1.626s; **5** Ananda Mikola, RI, 24m 2.787s; **6** Luiz Razia, BR, 24m 3.821s; **7** Sebastián Merchán, EC, 24m 21.315s; **8** Mehdi Bennani, MA, 24m 22.055s; **9** Giandomenico Sposito, I, 24m 34.721s; **10** Francesco Dracone, I, 24m 42.147s.
**Fastest race lap:** Nunes, 1m 40.240s, 117.046 mph/ 188.367 km/h.
**Fastest qualifying lap:** Rigon, 1m 38.526s, 119.083 mph/191.644 km/h.

**Round 8 (58.664 miles/94.410 km).**
**1** Diego Nunes, BR, 30m 40.662s, 114.735 mph/ 184.649 km/h; **2** Davide Rigon, I, 30m 41.220s; **3** Ananda Mikola, RI, 30m 58.049s; **4** Luiz Razia, BR, 31m 0.633s; **5** Sebastián Merchán, EC, 31m 12.853s; **6** Ómar Leal, CO, 31m 12.968s; **7** Vladimir Arabadjiev, BG, 31m 13.877s; **8** Andrea Fausti, I, 17 laps; **9** Oliver Martini, I, 15; **10** Alx Danielsson, S, 10.
**Fastest race lap:** Danielsson, 1m 40.589s, 116.640 mph/187.714 km/h.
**Pole position:** Bennani.

**EURO 3000 CHAMPIONSHIP, Nürburgring, Nürburg/ Eifel, Germany, 26 August. 20 and 25 laps of the 2.248-mile/3.618-km circuit.**
**Round 9 (44.962 miles/72.360 km).**
**1** Davide Rigon, I, 27m 9.342s, 99.344 mph/159.878 km/h; **2** Luiz Razia, BR, 20 laps; **3** Diego Nunes, BR, 20; **4** Manuel Saez Merino, E, 20; **5** Oliver Martini, I, 20; **6** Mehdi Bennani, MA, 20; **7** Celso Miguez, E, 20; **8** Francesco Dracone, I 20; **9** Vladimir Arabadjiev, BG, 20; **10** Ómar Leal, CO, 15.
**Fastest race lap:** Rigon, 1m 20.781s, 100.187 mph/ 161.236 km/h.
**Fastest qualifying lap:** Razia, 1m 20.427, 100.628 mph/161.946 km/h.

**Round 10 (56.203 miles/90.450 km).**
**1** Manuel Saez Merino, E, 34m 30.969s, 97.699 mph/ 157.231 km/h; **2** Davide Rigon, I, 25 laps; **3** Celso Miguez, E, 25; **4** Mehdi Bennani, MA, 25; **5** Vladimir Arabadjiev, BG, 25; **6** Diego Nunes, BR, 25; **7** Ómar Leal, CO, 25; **8** Sebastián Merchán, EC, 25; **9** Luiz Razia, BR, 23; **10** Oliver Martini, I, 6.
**Fastest race lap:** Razia, 1m 21.242s, 99.619 mph/ 160.321 km/h.
**Pole position:** Dracone.

**EURO 3000 CHAMPIONSHIP, Circuit de Spa-Francorchamps, Stavelot, Belgium, 14 October. 10 and 13 laps of the 2.875-mile/4.627-km circuit.**
**Round 11 (28.751 miles/46.270 km).**
**1** Giacomo Ricci, I, 21m 34.939s, 79.929 mph/128.633 km/h; **2** Davide Rigon, I, 10 laps; **3** Kasper Andersen, DK, 10; **4** Luiz Razia, BR, 10; **5** Oliver Martini, I, 10; **6** Diego Nunes, BR, 10; **7** Ómar Leal, CO, 10; **8** Tuka Rocha, BR, 10; **9** Jimmy Auby, ZA, 10; **10** Emilia de Villota, E, 10.
**Fastest race lap:** Rigon, 2m 8.127s, 80.782 mph/ 130.005 km/h.
**Fastest qualifying lap:** Rigon, 2m 5.893s, 82.215 mph/132.312 km/h.

**Round 12 (37.376 miles/60.151 km).**
**1** Diego Nunes, BR, 28m 20.438s, 79.129 mph/127.346 km/h; **2** Tuka Rocha, BR, 13 laps; **3** Jimmy Auby, ZA, 13; **4** Emilia de Villota, E, 13; **5** Vladimir Arabadjiev, BG, 13; **6** Francesco Dracone, I, 13; **7** Luiz Razia, BR, 13; **8** Davide Rigon, I, 13; **9** Oliver Martini, I, 12; **10** Giacomo Ricci, I, 6.
**Fastest race lap:** Rigon, 2m 7.836s, 80.965 mph/ 130.301 km/h.
**Pole position:** Rocha.

**EURO 3000 CHAMPIONSHIP, Autodromo Nazionale di Monza, Milan, Italy, 20/21 October. 13 and 16 laps of the 3.600-mile/5.793-km circuit.**
**Round 13 (46.795 miles/75.309 km).**
**1** Davide Rigon, I, 22m 3.111s, 127.322 mph/204.905 km/h; **2** Giacomo Ricci, I, 22m 5.898s; **3** Luiz Razia, BR, 22m 6.960s; **4** Martin Kudzak, S, 22m 24.544s; **5** Ómar Leal, CO, 22m 24.754s; **6** Vladimir Arabadjiev, BG, 22m 27.714s; **7** Francesco Dracone, I, 5 laps; **8** Johnny Cecotto Jr, YV, 4; **9** Jimmy Auby, ZA, 1; **10** Diego Nunes, BR, 1.
**Fastest race lap:** Rigon, 1m 40.467s, 128.983 mph/ 207.578 km/h.
**Fastest qualifying lap:** Nunes, 1m 38.494, 131.567 mph/211.736 km/h.

**Round 14 (57.594 miles/92.688 km).**
**1** Davide Rigon, I, 26m 53.352s, 128.513 mph/206.822 km/h; **2** Giacomo Ricci, I, 27m 01.946s; **3** Johnny Cecotto Jr YV, 27m 12.823s; **4** Ómar Leal, CO, 27m 16.377s; **5** Jimmy Auby, ZA, 27m 18.904s; **6** Vladimir Arabadjiev, BG, 27m 22.512s; **7** Francesco Dracone, I, 27m 43.965s; **8** Diego Nunes, BR, 5 laps; **9** Luiz Razia, BR, 4; **10** Kasper Andersen, DK, 2.
**Disqualified:** Ignored drive-through penalty - Martin Kudzak, S, completed 11 laps.
**Fastest race lap:** Rigon, 1m 39.875s, 129.748 mph/ 208.809 km/h.
**Pole position:** Cecotto Jr.

**Provisional championship points**
**1** Davide Rigon, I, 99; **2** Diego Nunes, BR, 62; **3** Luiz Razia, BR, 51; **4** Oliver Martini, I, 32; **5** Alx Danielsson, S, 32; **6** Giacomo Ricci, I, 23; **7** Vladimir Arabadjiev, BG, 23; **8** Sebastián Merchán, EC, 16; **9** Pastor Maldonado, YV, 12; **10** Manuel Saez Merino, E, 11; **11** Ómar Leal, CO, 11; **12** Jason Tahinci, TR, 9; **13** Mehdi Bennani, MA, 9; **14** Ananda Mikola, RI, 8; **15** Tuka Rocha, BR, 6; **16** Celso Miguez, E, 6; **17** Kasper Andersen, DK, 6; **18** Jimmy Auby, ZA, 6; **19** Martin Kudzak, S, 5; **20** Johnny Cecotto Jr, YV, 4; **21** Emilio de Villota, E, 3; **22** Giandomenico Sposito, I, 2; **23** Francesco Dracone, I, 2.

*Results of the Barcelona race will be given in AUTOCOURSE 2008–2009.*

## All-Japan Formula Nippon Championship

All cars are Lola FN06

## 2006

The following race was run after AUTOCOURSE 2006–2007 went to press.

**ALL-JAPAN FORMULA NIPPON CHAMPIONSHIP, Suzuka International Racing Course, Suzuka-shi, Mie Prefecture, Japan, 19 November. Round 9. 51 laps of the 3.608-mile/5.807-km circuit, 184.023 miles/296.157 km.**
**1** Andre Lotterer, D (-Toyota), 1h 46m 11.459s, 103.977 mph/167.334 km/h; **2** Tsugio Matsuda, J (-Toyota), 1h 46m 16.515s; **3** Tatsuya Kataoka, J (-Toyota), 1h 46m 51.543s; **4** Takashi Kogure, J (-Honda), 1h 46m 58.982s; **5** Takeshi Tsuchiya, J (-Toyota), 1h 47m 03.641s; **6** Loïc Duval, F (-Honda), 1h 47m 4.222s; **7** Toshihiro Kaneishi, J (-Honda), 1h 47m 16.371s; **8** João Paulo de Oliveira, BR (-Honda), 1h 47m 42.542s; **9** Björn Wirdheim, S (-Honda), 1h 47m 42.883s; **10** Yuji Ide, J (-Honda), 1h 47m 45.251s.
**Fastest race lap:** Benoît Tréluyer, F, 2m 2.422s, 106.107 mph/170.763 km/h.
**Fastest qualifying lap:** Matsuda, 1m 42.133s, 127.186 mph/204.686 km/h.

**Final championship points**
**Drivers**
**1** Benoît Tréluyer, F, 51; **2** Tsugio Matsuda, J, 37; **3** Andre Lotterer, D, 30; **4** Loïc Duval, F, 25; **5** Satoshi Motoyama, J, 16; **6** Björn Wirdheim, S, 13.5; **7** Tatsuya Kataoka, J, 13; **8** Yuji Tachikawa, J, 10; **9** Toshihiro Kaneishi, J, 9; **10** Ronnie Quintarelli, I, 6; **11** Sakon Yamamoto, J, 3.5; **12** Takashi Kogure, J, 3; **13** Takeshi Tsuchiya, J, 2; **14** Hideki Mutoh, J, 1; 15 Masataka Yanagida, J, 1.

**Teams**
**1** mobilecast Team Impul, 88; **2** DHG Tom's Racing, 32; **3** PIAA Nakajima Racing, 26.

## 2007

**ALL-JAPAN FORMULA NIPPON CHAMPIONSHIP, Fuji International Speedway, Sunto-gun, Shizuoka Prefecture, Japan, 1 April. Round 1. 65 laps of the 2.835-mile/4.563-km circuit, 184.296 miles/296.595 km.**
**1** Benoît Tréluyer, F (-Toyota), 1h 38m 4.095s, 112.756 mph/181.462 km/h; **2** Tsugio Matsuda, J (-Toyota), 1h 38m 9.938s; **3** Loïc Duval, F (-Honda), 1h 38m 38.780s; **4** Björn Wirdheim, S (-Honda), 1h 38m 39.796s; **5** Ronnie Quintarelli, I (-Toyota), 1h 38m 45.128s; **6** Michael Krumm, D (-Toyota), 1h 38m 56.302s; **7** Tatsuya Kataoka, J (-Toyota), 1h 39m 14.521s; **8** Takashi Kogure, J (-Honda), 1h 39m 15.061s; **9** Masataka Yanagida, J (-Honda), 1h 39m 22.968s; **10** Naoki Yokomizo, J (-Toyota), 1h 39m 24.494s.
**Fastest race lap:** Tréluyer, 1m 28.795s, 114.952 mph/184.997 km/h.
**Fastest qualifying lap:** Tréluyer, 1m 25.525s, 119.347 mph/192.070 km/h.

**ALL-JAPAN FORMULA NIPPON CHAMPIONSHIP, Suzuka International Racing Course, Suzuka-shi, Mie Prefecture, Japan, 15 April. Round 2. 43 laps of the 3.608-mile/5.807-km circuit, 155.157 miles/249.701 km.**
**1** Satoshi Motoyama, J (-Toyota), 1h 18m 23.552s, 118.754 mph/191.115 km/h; **2** Tsugio Matsuda, J (-Toyota), 1h 18m 23.904s; **3** Takashi Kogure, J (-Honda), 1h 18m 32.666s; **4** Loïc Duval, F (-Honda), 1h 18m 41.534s; **5** Andre Lotterer, D (-Toyota), 1h 18m 41.710s; **6** Ronnie Quintarelli, I (-Toyota), 1h 18m 44.676s; **7** Michael Krumm, D (-Toyota), 1h 18m 49.456s; **8** Yuji Tachikawa, J (-Toyota), 1h 19m 31.689s; **9** Naoki Yokomizo, J (-Toyota), 1h 19m 31.987s; **10** Yuji Ide (-Honda), 1h 19m 39.923s.
**Fastest race lap:** Hiroki Yoshimoto, J (-Honda), 1m 48.180s, 120.077 mph/193.244 km/h.
**Fastest qualifying lap:** Matsuda, 1m 41.115s, 128.466 mph/206.746 km/h.

**ALL-JAPAN FORMULA NIPPON CHAMPIONSHIP, Twin Ring Motegi, Motegi-machi, Haga-gun, Tochigi Prefecture, Japan, 20 May. Round 3. 62 laps of the 2.983-mile/4.801-km circuit, 184.959 miles/297.662 km.**
**1** Takashi Kogure, J (-Honda), 1h 44m 32.258s, 106.158 mph/170.844 km/h; **2** Andre Lotterer, D (-Toyota), 1h 44m 51.650s; **3** Tsugio Matsuda, J (-Toyota), 1h 44m 53.198s; **4** Benoît Tréluyer, F (-Toyota), 1h 44m 54.428s; **5** Ronnie Quintarelli, I (-Toyota), 1h 45m 18.029s; **6** Satoshi Motoyama, J (-Toyota), 1h 45m 20.092s; **7** Michael Krumm, D (-Toyota), 1h 45m 20.321s; **8** João Paulo de Oliveira, BR (-Toyota), 1h 45m 33.624s; **9** Toranosuke Takagi, J (-Toyota), 1h 45m 49.081s; **10** Toshihiro Kaneishi, J (-Honda), 1h 45m 50.905s.
**Fastest race lap:** Kogure, 1m 38.785s, 108.716 mph/174.962 km/h.
**Fastest qualifying lap:** Matsuda, 1m 34.775s, 113.316 mph/182.364 km/h.

**ALL-JAPAN FORMULA NIPPON CHAMPIONSHIP, Okayama International Circuit (TI Circuit Aida), Aida Gun, Okayama Prefecture, Japan, 10 June. Round 4. 68 laps of the 2.301-mile/3.703-km circuit, 156.464 miles/251.804 km.**
**1** Ronnie Quintarelli, I (-Toyota), 1h 36m 19.523s, 97.460 mph/156.845 km/h; **2** Benoît Tréluyer, F (-Toyota), 1h 36m 20.441s; **3** Tsugio Matsuda, J (-Toyota), 1h 36m 22.275s; **4** João Paulo de Oliveira, BR (-Toyota), 1h 36m 35.687s; **5** Takashi Kogure, J (-Honda), 1h 37m 0.992s; **6** Yuji Tachikawa, J (-Toyota), 1h 37m 3.646s; **7** Seiji Ara, J (-Toyota), 1h 37m 4.839s; **8** Michael Krumm, D (-Toyota), 1h 37m 7.151s; **9** Tatsuya Kataoka, J (-Toyota), 1h 37m 7.581s; **10** Satoshi Motoyama, J (-Toyota), 1h 37m 10.939s.
**Fastest race lap:** Matsuda, 1m 19.811s, 103.787 mph/167.030 km/h.
**Fastest qualifying lap:** Loïc Duval, F (-Honda), 1m 17.409s, 107.008 mph/172.212 km/h.

**ALL-JAPAN FORMULA NIPPON CHAMPIONSHIP, Suzuka International Racing Course, Suzuka-shi, Mie Prefecture, Japan, 8 July. Round 5. 43 laps of the 3.608-mile/5.807-km circuit, 155.157 miles/249.701 km.**
**1** Satoshi Motoyama, J (-Toyota), 1h 47m 43.524s, 86.418 mph/139.076 km/h; **2** Björn Wirdheim, S (-Honda), 1h 47m 48.029s; **3** Yuji Ide, J (-Honda), 1h 47m 55.571s; **4** Tsugio Matsuda, J (-Toyota), 1h 47m 56.325s; **5** Michael Krumm, D (-Toyota), 1h 47m 56.425s; **6** Fabio Carbone, BR (-Honda), 1h 48m 2.153s; **7** João Paulo de Oliveira, BR (-Toyota), 1h 48m 3.895s; **8** Toranosuke Takagi, J (-Toyota), 1h 48m 5.871s; **9** Toshihiro Kaneishi, J (-Honda), 1h 48m 6.067s; **10** Seiji Ara, J (-Toyota), 1h 48m 9.350s.
**Fastest race lap:** Matsuda, 1m 46.640s, 121.811 mph/196.035 km/h.
**Fastest qualifying lap:** Matsuda, 1m 43.041s, 126.065 mph/202.882 km/h.

**ALL-JAPAN FORMULA NIPPON CHAMPIONSHIP, Fuji International Speedway, Sunto-gun, Shizuoka Prefecture, Japan, 26 August. Round 6. 65 laps of the 2.835-mile/4.563-km circuit, 184.296 miles/296.595 km.**
**1** Andre Lotterer, D (-Toyota), 1h 44m 16.662s, 106.041 mph/170.656 km/h; **2** Benoît Tréluyer, F (-Toyota), 1h 44m 22.273s; **3** Loïc Duval, F (-Honda), 1h 44m 25.225s; **4** Seiji Ara, J (-Toyota), 1h 44m 31.108s; **5** Yuji Tachikawa, J (-Toyota), 1h 44m 32.601s; **6** João Paulo de Oliveira, BR (-Toyota), 1h 44m 33.353s; **7** Ronnie Quintarelli, I (-Toyota), 1h 44m 33.793s; **8** Björn Wirdheim, S (-Honda), 1h 44m 51.471s; **9** Toranosuke Takagi, J (-Toyota), 1h 44m 52.093s; **10** Naoki Yokomizo, J (-Toyota), 1h 44m 55.349s.
**Fastest race lap:** Duval, 1m 28.798s, 114.948 mph/184.991 km/h.
**Fastest qualifying lap:** Satoshi Motoyama, J (-Toyota), 1m 26.901s, 117.457 mph/189.028 km/h.

**ALL-JAPAN FORMULA NIPPON CHAMPIONSHIP, Sportsland-SUGO International Course, Shibata-gun, Miyagi Prefecture, Japan, 16 September. Round 7. 62 laps of the 2.302-mile/3.704-km circuit, 142.697 miles/229.648 km.**
**1** Takashi Kogure, J (-Honda), 1h 21m 42.519s, 104.784 mph/168.634 km/h; **2** Benoît Tréluyer, F (-Toyota), 1h 21m 44.956s; **3** Loïc Duval, F (-Honda), 1h 21m 46.301s; **4** Satoshi Motoyama, J (-Toyota), 1h 21m 51.995s; **5** Tsugio Matsuda, J (-Toyota), 1h 21m 55.663s; **6** Yuji Tachikawa, J (-Toyota), 1h 21m 56.315s; **7** Andre Lotterer, D (-Toyota), 1h 21m 57.252s; **8** Ronnie Quintarelli, I (-Toyota), 1h 22m 0.775s; **9** Fabio Carbone, BR (-Honda), 1h 22m 3.314s; **10** Toranosuke Takagi, J (-Toyota), 61 laps.
**Fastest race lap:** Naoki Yokomizo, J (-Toyota), 1m 10.663s, 117.255 mph/188.704 km/h.
**Fastest qualifying lap:** Kogure, 1m 7.827s, 122.158 mph/196.594 km/h.

**ALL-JAPAN FORMULA NIPPON CHAMPIONSHIP, Twin Ring Motegi, Motegi-machi, Haga-gun, Tochigi Prefecture, Japan, 21 October. Round 8. 52 laps of the 2.983-mile/4.801-km circuit, 155.127 miles/249.652 km.**
**1** Takashi Kogure, J (-Honda), 1h 25m 1.278s, 109.474 mph/176.180 km/h; **2** Loïc Duval, F (-Honda), 1h 25m 12.591s; **3** Benoît Tréluyer, F (-Toyota), 1h 25m 22.936s; **4** Andre Lotterer, D (-Toyota), 1h 25m 29.472s; **5** Tsugio Matsuda, J (-Toyota), 1h 25m 52.310s; **6** Ronnie Quintarelli, I (-Toyota), 1h 25m 52.778s; **7** Björn Wirdheim, S (-Honda), 1h 25m 56.811s; **8** João Paulo de Oliveira, BR (-Toyota), 1h 25m 57.738s; **9** Yuji Tachikawa, J (-Toyota), 1h 25m 59.742s; **10** Tatsuya Kataoka, J (-Toyota), 1h 26m 17.258s.
**Fastest race lap:** Kogure, 1m 35.775s, 112.133 mph/180.460 km/h.
**Fastest qualifying lap:** Kogure, 1m 33.259s, 115.158 mph/185.329 km/h.

**Provisional championship points**
**Drivers**
**1** Benoît Tréluyer, F, 45; **2** Takashi Kogure, J, 41; **3** Tsugio Matsuda, J, 41; **4** Loïc Duval, F, 31; **5** Andre Lotterer, D, 29; **6** Satoshi Motoyama, J, 28; **7** Ronnie Quintarelli, I, 27; **8** Björn Wirdheim, S, 16; **9** João Paulo de Oliveira, BR, 12; **10** Michael Krumm, D, 12; **11** Yuji Tachikawa, J, 11; **12** Seiji Ara, J, 7; **13** Yuji Ide, J, 6; **14** Fabio Carbone, BR, 3; **15** Tatsuya Kataoka, J, 2; **16** Toranosuke Takagi, J, 1.

**Teams**
**1** mobilecast Impul, 86; **2** PIAA Nakajima, 72; **3** Arabian Oasis Impul,40; **4** DHG TOM'S,36; **5** Boss Inging, 27.

*Result of the Suzuka race will be given in AUTOCOURSE 2008–2009.*

## British Formula 3 International Series

**BRITISH FORMULA 3 INTERNATIONAL SERIES, Oulton Park Circuit, Tarporley, Cheshire, Great Britain, 9 April. 18 and 10 laps of the 2.692-mile/4.332-km circuit.**
**Round 1 (48.452 miles/77.976 km).**
**1** Maro Engel, D (Dallara F307-Mercedes Benz), 30m 48.229s, 94.375 mph/151.882 km/h; **2** Marko Asmer, EST (Dallara F307-Mercedes Benz), 30m 49.204s; **3** Stephen Jelley, GB (Dallara F307-Mercedes Benz), 30m 49.808s; **4** Sam Bird, GB (Dallara F307-Mercedes Benz), 30m 52.457s; **5** Sebastian Hohenthal, S (Dallara F307-Mercedes Benz), 30m 53.526s; **6** Jonathan Kennard, GB (Dallara F307-Mercedes Benz), 31m 05.908s; **7** Rodolfo Gonzalez, YV (Dallara F307-Mugen Honda), 31m 8.878s; **8** Atte Mustonen, FIN (Dallara F307-Mercedes Benz), 31m 8.971s; **9** Niall Breen, IRL (Dallara F307-Mercedes Benz), 31m 9.313s; **10** Greg Mansell, GB (Dallara F307-Mercedes Benz), 31m 9.992s.
**National class winner:** Cong Fu Cheng, CHN (Dallara F304-Mugen Honda), 31m 32.629s (14th).
**Fastest race lap:** Hohenthal, 1m 29.491s, 108.284 mph/174.266 km/h.
**Fastest qualifying lap:** Engel, 1m 28.594s, 109.380 mph/176.030 km/h.

**Round 2 (26.918 miles/43.320 km).**
**1** Marko Asmer, EST (Dallara F307-Mercedes Benz), 15m 10.101s, 106.476 mph/171.357 km/h; **2** Stephen Jelley, GB (Dallara F307-Mercedes Benz), 15m 10.553s; **3** Sebastian Hohenthal, S (Dallara F307-Mercedes Benz), 15m 11.107s; **4** Jonathan Kennard, GB (Dallara F307-Mercedes Benz), 15m 12.285s; **5** Maro Engel, D (Dallara F307-Mercedes Benz), 15m 19.443s; **6** Sam Bird, GB (Dallara F307-Mercedes Benz), 15m 20.553s; **7** Greg Mansell, GB (Dallara F307-Mercedes Benz), 15m 20.990s; **8** Walter Grubmüller, A (Dallara F307-Mercedes Benz), 15m 24.000s; **9** Rodolfo Gonzalez, YV (Dallara F307-Mugen Honda), 15m 25.054s; **10** Niall Breen, IRL (Dallara F307-Mercedes Benz), 15m 27.118s.
**National class winner:** Cheng, 15m 41.109s (13th).
**Fastest race lap:** Kennard, 1m 29.491, 108.284 mph/174.266 km/h.
**Fastest qualifying lap:** Kennard, 1m 28.794s, 109.134 mph/175.633 km/h.

**BRITISH FORMULA 3 INTERNATIONAL SERIES, Donington Park National Circuit, Castle Donington, Great Britain, 22 April. 25 and 26 laps of the 1.957-mile/3.149-km circuit.**
**Round 3 (48.917 miles/78.725 km).**
**1** Marko Asmer, EST (Dallara F307-Mercedes Benz), 30m 33.255s, 96.060 mph/154.594 km/h; **2** Stephen Jelley, GB (Dallara F307-Mercedes Benz), 30m 33.800s; **3** Greg Mansell, GB (Dallara F307-Mercedes Benz), 30m 36.441s; **4** Sebastian Hohenthal, S (Dallara F307-Mercedes Benz), 30m 38.978s; **5** Jonathan Kennard, GB (Dallara F307-Mercedes Benz), 30m 39.815s; **6** Esteban Guerrieri, RA (Mygale M-07-Mercedes Benz), 30m 53.460s; **7** Maro Engel, D (Dallara F307-Mercedes Benz), 30m 53.784s; **8** Mário Moraes, BR (Dallara F307-Mercedes Benz), 30m 53.924s; **9** Atte Mustonen, FIN (Dallara F307-Mercedes Benz), 30m 54.049s; **10** Sam Bird, GB (Dallara F307-Mercedes Benz), 30m 54.916s.
**National class winner:** Michael Meadows, GB (Dallara F304-Mugen Honda), 31m 10.229s (13th).
**Fastest race lap:** Asmer, 1m 1.594s, 114.364 mph/184.050 km/h.
**Fastest qualifying lap:** Asmer, 1m 1.200s, 115.100 mph/185.235 km/h.

**Round 4 (50.874 miles/81.874 km).**
**1** Marko Asmer, EST (Dallara F307-Mercedes Benz), 27m 55.340s, 109.319 mph/175.932 km/h; **2** Niall Breen, IRL (Dallara F307-Mercedes Benz), 27m 59.756s; **3** Jonathan Kennard, GB (Dallara F307-Mercedes Benz), 28m 0.172s; **4** Maro Engel, D (Dallara F307-Mercedes Benz), 28m 4.050s; **5** Alberto Valério, BR (Dallara F307-Mercedes Benz), 28m 6.524s; **6** Rodolfo Gonzalez, YV (Dallara F307-Mugen Honda), 28m 7.753s; **7** Michael Devaney, IRL (Mygale M-07-Mercedes Benz), 28m 16.075s; **8** Atte Mustonen, FIN (Dallara F307-Mercedes Benz), 28m 16.630s; **9** Sam Bird, GB (Dallara F307-Mercedes Benz), 28m 17.056s; **10** Sergio Pérez, MEX (Dallara F304-Mugen Honda), 28m 42.778s (1st national class).
**Fastest race lap:** Hohenthal, 1m 2.283s, 113.098 mph/182.014 km/h.
**Fastest qualifying lap:** Asmer, 1m 1.565s, 114.417 mph/184.137 km/h.

**BRITISH FORMULA 3 INTERNATIONAL SERIES, Bucharest Street Circuit, Romania, 19/20 May. 17 and 20 laps of the 1.933-mile/3.111-km circuit.**
**Round 5 (32.861 miles/52.885 km).**
**1** Marko Asmer, EST (Dallara F307-Mercedes Benz), 30m 10.891s, 65.327 mph/105.133 km/h; **2** Alberto Valério, BR (Dallara F307-Mercedes Benz), 30m 11.434s; **3** Sam Bird, GB (Dallara F307-Mercedes Benz), 30m 12.394s; **4** Niall Breen, IRL (Dallara F307-Mercedes Benz), 30m 13.285s; **5** Maro Engel, D (Dallara F307-Mercedes Benz), 30m 13.933s; **6** Atte Mustonen, FIN (Dallara F307-Mercedes Benz), 30m 14.306s; **7** Stephen Jelley, GB (Dallara F307-Mercedes Benz), 30m 16.669s; **8** Esteban Guerrieri, RA (Mygale M-07-Mercedes Benz), 30m 17.092s; **9** Jonathan Kennard, GB (Dallara F307-Mercedes Benz), 30m 17.565s; **10** Rodolfo Gonzalez, YV (Dallara F307-Mugen Honda), 30m 17.862s.
**National class winner:** Michael Meadows, GB (Dallara F304-Mugen Honda), 30m 19.697s (12th).
**Fastest race lap:** Asmer, 1m 13.645s, 94.491 mph/152.069 km/h.
**Fastest qualifying lap:** Asmer, 1m 11.681s, 97.080 mph/156.235 km/h.

**Round 6 (38.660 miles/62.217 km).**
**1** Sam Bird, GB (Dallara F307-Mercedes Benz), 31m 14.395s, 74.251 mph/119.496 km/h; **2** Niall Breen, IRL (Dallara F307-Mercedes Benz), 31m 16.343s; **3** Stephen Jelley, GB (Dallara F307-Mercedes Benz), 31m 17.205s; **4** John Martin, AUS (Dallara F307-Mugen Honda), 31m 18.019s; **5** Marko Asmer, EST (Dallara F307-Mercedes Benz), 31m 20.309s; **6** Michael Devaney, IRL (Mygale M-07-Mercedes Benz), 31m 20.855s; **7** Sebastian Hohenthal, S (Dallara F307-Mercedes Benz), 31m 22.054s; **8** Jonathan Kennard, GB (Dallara F307-Mercedes Benz), 31m 22.478s; **9** Mário Moraes, BR (Dallara F307-Mercedes Benz), 31m 23.178s; **10** Rodolfo Gonzalez, YV (Dallara F307-Mugen Honda), 31m 24.497s *.
* Finished 5th in 31m 19.497s, but was penalised 5s for dangerous driving.
**National class winner:** Sergio Pérez, MEX (Dallara F304-Mugen Honda), 31m 31.646s (11th).
**Fastest race lap:** Devaney, 1m 14.951s, 92.845 mph/149.419 km/h.
**Fastest qualifying lap:** Jelley, 1m 21.172s, 85.729 mph/137.968 km/h.

**BRITISH FORMULA 3 INTERNATIONAL SERIES, Snetterton Circuit, Thetford, Norfolk, Great Britain, 3 June. 28 and 26 laps of the 1.9517-mile/3.141-km circuit.**
**Round 7 (54.648 miles/87.947 km).**
**1** Niall Breen, IRL (Dallara F307-Mercedes Benz), 29m 22.610s, 111.614 mph/179.626 km/h; **2** Sam Bird, GB (Dallara F307-Mercedes Benz), 29m 23.027s; **3** Alberto Valério, BR (Dallara F307-Mercedes Benz), 29m 23.747s; **4** Stephen Jelley, GB (Dallara F307-Mercedes Benz), 29m 25.339s; **5** Rodolfo Gonzalez, YV (Dallara F307-Mugen Honda), 29m 32.596s; **6** Jonathan Kennard, GB (Dallara F307-Mercedes Benz), 29m 34.013s; **7** Maro Engel, D (Dallara F307-Mercedes Benz), 29m 36.257s; **8** Sebastian Hohenthal, S (Dallara F307-Mercedes Benz), 29m 37.514s; **9** Greg Mansell, GB (Dallara F307-Mercedes Benz), 29m 37.950s; **10** Michael Devaney, IRL (Mygale M-07-Mercedes Benz), 29m 38.553s.
**Invitation class winner:** Max Chilton, GB (Dallara F307-Mercedes Benz), 29m 51.204s (11th).
**National class winner:** Sergio Pérez, MEX (Dallara F304-Mugen Honda), 29m 57.854s (13th).
**Fastest race lap:** Jelley, 1m 1.995s, 113.334 mph/182.393 km/h.
**Fastest qualifying lap:** Mustonen, 1m 1.539s, 114.173 mph/183.744 km/h.

**Round 8 (50.744 miles/81.665 km).**
**1** Marko Asmer, EST (Dallara F307-Mercedes Benz), 30m 8.184s, 101.029 mph/162.590 km/h; **2** Alberto Valério, BR (Dallara F307-Mercedes Benz), 30m 9.872s; **3** Sam Bird, GB (Dallara F307-Mercedes Benz), 30m 14.589s; **4** Maro Engel, D (Dallara F307-Mercedes Benz), 30m 15.380s; **5** Stephen Jelley, GB (Dallara F307-Mercedes Benz), 30m 15.700s; **6** Sebastian Hohenthal, S (Dallara F307-Mercedes Benz), 30m 16.287s; **7** Niall Breen, IRL (Dallara F307-Mercedes Benz), 30m 16.921s; **8** Atte Mustonen, FIN (Dallara F307-Mercedes Benz), 30m 17.670s; **9** Greg Mansell, GB (Dallara F307-Mercedes Benz), 30m 19.385s; **10** Mário Moraes, BR (Dallara F307-Mercedes Benz), 30m 20.954s.
**Invitation class winner:** Max Chilton, GB (Dallara F307-Mercedes Benz), 30m 26.941s (14th).
**National class winner:** Viktor Jensen, IS (Dallara F304-Mugen Honda), 30m 36.563s (16th).
**Fastest race lap:** Asmer, 1m 2.015s, 113.297 mph/182.334 km/h.
**Fastest qualifying lap:** Asmer, 1m 1.558s, 114.138 mph/183.688 km/h.

**BRITISH FORMULA 3 INTERNATIONAL SERIES, Autodromo Nazionale di Monza, Milan, Italy, 24 June. 2 x 16 laps of the 3.600-mile/5.793-km circuit.**
**Round 9 (57.594 miles/92.688 km).**
**1** Maro Engel, D (Dallara F307-Mercedes Benz), 28m 43.419s, 120.306 mph/193.613 km/h; **2** Sam Bird, GB (Dallara F307-Mercedes Benz), 28m 46.345s; **3** Alberto Valério, BR (Dallara F307-Mercedes Benz), 28m 48.226s; **4** Marko Asmer, EST (Dallara F307-Mercedes Benz), 28m 49.344s; **5** Jonathan Kennard, GB (Dallara F307-Mercedes Benz), 28m 51.019s; **6** Esteban Guerrieri, RA (Mygale M-07-Mercedes Benz), 29m 4.813s; **7** Niall Breen, IRL (Dallara F307-Mercedes Benz), 29m 4.948s; **8** Michael Devaney, IRL (Mygale M-07-Mercedes Benz), 29m 5.386s; **9** Mário Moraes, BR (Dallara F307-Mercedes Benz), 29m 6.294s; **10** Sergio Pérez, MEX (Dallara F304-Mugen Honda), 29m 6.786s (1st National class).
**Fastest race lap:** Stephen Jelley, GB (Dallara F307-Mercedes Benz), 1m 46.546s, 121.624 mph/195.735 km/h.
**Fastest qualifying lap:** Engel, 1m 46.241s, 121.973 mph/196.297 km/h.

**Round 10 (57.594 miles/92.688 km).**
**1** Marko Asmer, EST (Dallara F307-Mercedes Benz), 28m 43.534s, 120.298 mph/193.600 km/h; **2** Maro Engel, D (Dallara F307-Mercedes Benz), 28m 44.214s; **3** Sam Bird, GB (Dallara F307-Mercedes Benz), 28m 52.455s; **4** Niall Breen, IRL (Dallara F307-Mercedes Benz), 29m 0.133s; **5** Jonathan Kennard, GB (Dallara F307-Mercedes Benz), 29m 1.607s; **6** Sebastian Hohenthal, S (Dallara F307-Mercedes Benz), 29m 4.030s; **7** Sergio Pérez, MEX (Dallara F304-Mugen Honda), 29m 4.958s (1st national class); **8** Michael Devaney, IRL (Mygale M-07-Mercedes Benz), 29m 5.265s; **9** Greg Mansell, GB (Dallara F307-Mercedes Benz), 29m 6.206s; **10** Cong Fu Cheng, CHN (Dallara F304-Mugen Honda), 29m 6.984s.
**Fastest race lap:** Valério, 1m 46.073s, 122.167 mph/196.608 km/h.
**Fastest qualifying lap:** Engel, 1m 46.335s, 121.866 mph/196.124 km/h.

**BRITISH FORMULA 3 INTERNATIONAL SERIES, Brands Hatch Grand Prix Circuit, West Kingsdown, Dartford, Kent, Great Britain, 15 July. 2 x 22 laps of the 2.300-mile/3.703-km circuit.**
**Round 11 (50.620 mph/81.465 km).**
**1** Marko Asmer, EST (Dallara F307-Mercedes Benz), 30m 8.961s, 100.738 mph/162.123 km/h; **2** Stephen Jelley, GB (Dallara F307-Mercedes Benz), 30m 17.309s; **3** Jonathan Kennard, GB (Dallara F307-Mercedes Benz), 30m 18.909s; **4** Rodolfo Gonzalez, YV (Dallara F307-Mugen Honda), 30m 21.506s; **5** Maro Engel, D (Dallara

F307-Mercedes Benz), 30m 29.020s; **6** Niall Breen, IRL (Dallara F307-Mercedes Benz), 30m 30.346s; **7** Michael Devaney, IRL (Mygale M-07-Mercedes Benz), 30m 39.874s; **8** Mário Moraes, BR (Dallara F307-Mercedes Benz), 30m 43.285s; **9** Greg Mansell, GB (Dallara F307-Mercedes Benz), 30m 43.630s; **10** Walter Grubmüller, A (Dallara F307-Mercedes Benz), 30m 49.346s.
**National class winner:** Cong Fu Cheng, CHN (Dallara F304-Mugen Honda), 30m 52.976s (12th).
**Fastest race lap:** Asmer, 1m 18.639s, 105.332 mph/169.516 km/h.
**Fastest qualifying lap:** Asmer, 1m 17.891s, 106.344 mph/171.144 km/h.

**Round 12 (50.620 miles/81.465 km).**
**1** Sebastian Hohenthal, S (Dallara F307-Mercedes Benz), 29m 45.061s, 102.087 mph/164.294 km/h; **2** Atte Mustonen, FIN (Dallara F307-Mercedes Benz), 29m 45.585s; **3** Marko Asmer, EST (Dallara F307-Mercedes Benz), 29m 46.090s; **4** Michael Devaney, IRL (Mygale M-07-Mercedes Benz), 29m 54.842s; **5** Niall Breen, IRL (Dallara F307-Mercedes Benz), 29m 57.145s; **6** Stephen Jelley, GB (Dallara F307-Mercedes Benz), 29m 57.790s; **7** Maro Engel, D (Dallara F307-Mercedes Benz), 29m 59.741s; **8** Alberto Valério, BR (Dallara F307-Mercedes Benz), 30m 0.384s; **9** Walter Grubmüller, A (Dallara F307-Mercedes Benz), 30m 1.540s; **10** Jonathan Kennard, GB (Dallara F307-Mercedes Benz), 30m 2.620s.
**National class winner:** Cong Fu Cheng, CHN (Dallara F304-Mugen Honda), 30m 21.099s (14th).
**Fastest race lap:** Sam Bird, GB (Dallara F307-Mercedes Benz), 1m 19.623s, 104.031 mph/167.421 km/h.
**Fastest qualifying lap:** Asmer, 1m 18.097s, 106.063 mph/170.693 km/h.

**BRITISH FORMULA 3 INTERNATIONAL SERIES, Circuit de Spa-Francorchamps, Stavelot, Belgium, 27/28 July. 12 and 8 laps of the 4.352-mile/7.004-km circuit.**
**Round 13 (52.225 miles/84.048 km).**
**1** Sam Bird, GB (Dallara F307-Mercedes Benz), 27m 15.453s, 114.959 mph/185.008 km/h; **2** Jonathan Kennard, GB (Dallara F307-Mercedes Benz), 27m 18.921s; **3** Stephen Jelley, GB (Dallara F307-Mercedes Benz), 27m 20.045s; **4** Atte Mustonen, FIN (Dallara F307-Mercedes Benz), 27m 20.833s; **5** Rodolfo Gonzalez, YV (Dallara F307-Mugen Honda), 27m 27.070s; **6** Marko Asmer, EST (Dallara F307-Mercedes Benz), 27m 29.161s; **7** Niall Breen, IRL (Dallara F307-Mercedes Benz), 27m 31.412s; **8** Esteban Guerrieri, RA (Mygale M-07-Mercedes Benz), 27m 33.967s; **9** Sergio Pérez, MEX (Dallara F304-Mugen Honda), 27m 34.691s (1st National class); **10** Greg Mansell, GB (Dallara F307-Mercedes Benz), 27m 34.854s.
**Fastest race lap:** Kennard, 2m 15.140s, 115.935 mph/186.579 km/h.
**Fastest qualifying lap:** Jelley, 2m 14.076s, 116.855 mph/188.060 km/h.

**Round 14 (34.817 miles/56.032 km).**
**1** Jonathan Kennard, GB (Dallara F307-Mercedes Benz), 31m 27.172s, 66.417 mph/106.887 km/h; **2** Maro Engel, D (Dallara F307-Mercedes Benz), 31m 27.772s; **3** Sam Bird, GB (Dallara F307-Mercedes Benz), 31m 28.396s; **4** Stephen Jelley, GB (Dallara F307-Mercedes Benz), 31m 28.872s; **5** Mário Moraes, BR (Dallara F307-Mercedes Benz), 31m 29.057s; **6** Atte Mustonen, FIN (Dallara F307-Mercedes Benz), 31m 29.435s; **7** Alberto Valério, BR (Dallara F307-Mercedes Benz), 31m 30.188s; **8** Marko Asmer, EST (Dallara F307-Mercedes Benz), 31m 31.178s; **9** Niall Breen, IRL (Dallara F307-Mercedes Benz), 31m 33.755s; **10** Rodolfo Gonzalez, YV (Dallara F307-Mugen Honda), 31m 33.795s.
**National class winner:** Pérez, 31m 41.663s (15th).
**Fastest race lap:** Kennard, 2m 37.646s, 99.384 mph/159.943 km/h.
**Fastest qualifying lap:** Kennard, 2m 13.896s, 117.012 mph/188.313 km/h.

**BRITISH FORMULA 3 INTERNATIONAL SERIES, Silverstone International Circuit, Towcester, Northamptonshire, Great Britain, 12 August. 22 and 24 of the 2.249-mile/3.619-km circuit.**
**Round 15 (49.478 miles/79.627 km).**
**1** Marko Asmer, EST (Dallara F307-Mercedes Benz), 30m 13.633s, 98.212 mph/158.057 km/h; **2** Maro Engel, D (Dallara F307-Mercedes Benz), 30m 15.289s; **3** Atte Mustonen, FIN (Dallara F307-Mercedes Benz), 30m 18.333s; **4** Greg Mansell, GB (Dallara F307-Mercedes Benz), 30m 20.897s; **5** Stephen Jelley, GB (Dallara F307-Mercedes Benz), 30m 27.532s; **6** Sam Bird, GB (Dallara F307-Mercedes Benz), 30m 29.015s; **7** Niall Breen, IRL (Dallara F307-Mercedes Benz), 30m 38.980s; **8** Michael Devaney, IRL (Mygale M-07-Mercedes Benz), 30m 39.941s; **9** Sebastian Hohenthal, S (Dallara F307-Mercedes Benz), 30m 40.347s; **10** Jonathan Kennard, GB (Dallara F307-Mercedes Benz), 30m 44.670s.
**National class winner:** Sergio Pérez, MEX (Dallara F304-Mugen Honda), 30m 53.228s (11th).
**Fastest race lap:** Asmer, 1m 15.943s, 106.612 mph/171.575 km/h.
**Fastest qualifying lap:** Asmer, 1m 15.312s, 107.505 mph/173.012 km/h.

**Round 16 (53.976 miles/86.866 km).**
**1** Marko Asmer, EST (Dallara F307-Mercedes Benz), 30m 47.439s; 105.180 mph/169.271 km/h; **2** Maro Engel, D (Dallara F307-Mercedes Benz), 30m 54.210s; **3** Greg Mansell, GB (Dallara F307-Mercedes Benz), 30m 56.844s; **4** Michael Devaney, IRL (Mygale M-07-Mercedes Benz), 31m 0.164s; **5** Alberto Valério, BR (Dallara F307-Mercedes Benz), 31m 8.054s; **6** Sam Bird, GB (Dallara F307-Mercedes Benz), 31m 12.214s; **7** Rodolfo Gonzalez, YV (Dallara F307-Mugen Honda), 31m 13.995s; **8** Sebastian Hohenthal, S (Dallara F307-Mercedes Benz), 31m 14.640s; **9** Niall Breen, IRL (Dallara F307-Mercedes Benz), 31m 15.667s; **10** Stephen Jelley, GB (Dallara F307-Mercedes Benz), 31m 15.831s.
**National class winner:** Pérez, 31m 29.184s (12th).
**Fastest race lap:** Asmer, 1m 16.094s, 106.400 mph/171.234 km/h.
**Fastest qualifying lap:** Asmer, 1m 15.428s, 107.339 mph/172.746 km/h.

**BRITISH FORMULA 3 INTERNATIONAL SERIES, Thruxton Circuit, Andover, Hampshire, Great Britain, 26 August. 2 x 24 laps of the 2.356-mile/3.792-km circuit.**
**Round 17 (56.544 miles/90.999 km).**
**1** Stephen Jelley, GB (Dallara F307-Mercedes Benz), 29m 58.967s, 113.153 mph/182.102 km/h; **2** Jonathan Kennard, GB (Dallara F307-Mercedes Benz), 30m 0.777s; **3** Maro Engel, D (Dallara F307-Mercedes Benz), 30m 1.463s; **4** Esteban Guerrieri, RA (Mygale M-07-Mercedes Benz), 30m 2.786s; **5** Alberto Valério, BR (Dallara F307-Mercedes Benz), 30m 4.318s; **6** Greg Mansell, GB (Dallara F307-Mercedes Benz), 30m 5.107s; **7** Rodolfo Gonzalez, YV (Dallara F307-Mugen Honda), 30m 5.117s*; **8** Michael Devaney, IRL (Mygale M-07-Mercedes Benz), 30m 5.183s; **9** Marko Asmer, EST (Dallara F307-Mercedes Benz), 30m 6.145s; **10** Sergio Pérez, MEX (Dallara F304-Mugen Honda), 30m 9.308s (1st national class).
* Finished 4th but given a penalty for cutting a corner to overtake Valério.
**Fastest race lap:** Mustonen, 1m 06.827s, 126.919 mph/204.256 km/h.
**Fastest qualifying lap:** Sebastian Hohenthal, S (Dallara F307-Mercedes Benz), 1m 6.346s, 127.839 mph/205.737 km/h.

**Round 18 (56.544 miles/90.999 km).**
**1** Atte Mustonen, FIN (Dallara F307-Mercedes Benz), 30m 7.208s, 112.637 mph/181.272 km/h; **2** Niall Breen, IRL (Dallara F307-Mercedes Benz), 30m 12.040s; **3** Rodolfo Gonzalez, YV (Dallara F307-Mugen Honda), 30m 13.766s; **4** Maro Engel, D (Dallara F307-Mercedes Benz), 30m 15.440s; **5** Marko Asmer, EST (Dallara F307-Mercedes Benz), 30m 19.102s; **6** Mário Moraes, BR (Dallara F307-Mercedes Benz), 30m 22.929s; **7** Stephen Jelley, GB (Dallara F307-Mercedes Benz), 30m 23.584s; **8** Greg Mansell, GB (Dallara F307-Mercedes Benz), 30m 26.608s; **9** Esteban Guerrieri, RA (Mygale M-07-Mercedes Benz), 30m 28.269s; **10** Alberto Valério, BR (Dallara F307-Mercedes Benz), 30m 29.214s.
**National class winner:** Pérez, 30m 42.096s (13th).
**Fastest race lap:** Gonzalez, 1m 7.137s, 126.333 mph/203.313 km/h.
**Fastest qualifying lap:** Mustonen, 1m 6.593s, 127.365 mph/204.974 km/h.

**BRITISH FORMULA 3 INTERNATIONAL SERIES, Croft Racing Circuit, Croft-on-Tees, North Yorkshire, Great Britain, 9 September. 2 x 24 laps of the 2.125-mile/3.420-km circuit.**
**Round 19 (51.000 miles/82.077 km).**
**1** Stephen Jelley, GB (Dallara F307-Mercedes Benz), 30m 50.597s, 99.211 mph/159.665 km/h; **2** Sam Bird, GB (Dallara F307-Mercedes Benz), 30m 52.548s; **3** Greg Mansell, GB (Dallara F307-Mercedes Benz), 30m 53.052s. **4** Atte Mustonen, FIN (Dallara F307-Mercedes Benz), 30m 53.895s; **5** Alberto Valério, BR (Dallara F307-Mercedes Benz), 30m 58.515s; **6** Mário Moraes, BR (Dallara F307-Mercedes Benz), 31m 2.059s; **7** Michael Devaney, IRL (Mygale M-07-Mercedes Benz), 31m 3.642s; **8** Rodolfo Gonzalez, YV (Dallara F307-Mugen Honda), 31m 4.062s; **9** Cong Fu Cheng, CHN (Dallara F304-Mugen Honda), 31m 7.632s (1st national class); **10** Leo Mansell, GB (Dallara F307-Mercedes Benz), 31m 8.232s.
**Fastest race lap:** Asmer, 1m 14.409s, 102.810 mph/165.457 km/h.
**Fastest qualifying lap:** Asmer, 1m 13.232s, 104.463 mph/168.116 km/h.

**Round 20 (51.000 miles/82.077 km).**
**1** Marko Asmer, EST (Dallara F307-Mercedes Benz), 30m 8.115s, 101.542 mph/163.416 km/h; **2** Niall Breen, IRL (Dallara F307-Mercedes Benz), 30m 11.404s; **3** Atte Mustonen, FIN (Dallara F307-Mercedes Benz), 30m 17.162s; **4** Alberto Valério, BR (Dallara F307-Mercedes Benz), 30m 22.757s; **5** Maro Engel, D (Dallara F307-Mercedes Benz), 30m 22.934s; **6** Greg Mansell, GB (Dallara F307-Mercedes Benz), 30m 24.317s; **7** Esteban Guerrieri, RA (Mygale M-07-Mercedes Benz), 30m 25.669s; **8** Stephen Jelley, GB (Dallara F307-Mercedes Benz), 30m 27.436s; **9** Rodolfo Gonzalez, YV (Dallara F307-Mugen Honda), 30m 28.956s; **10** Sebastian Hohenthal, S (Dallara F307-Mercedes Benz), 30m 29.821s.
**National class winner:** Sergio Pérez, MEX (Dallara F304-Mugen Honda), 30m 56.845s (13th).
**Fastest race lap:** Asmer, 1m 14.555s, 102.609 mph/165.133 km/h.
**Fastest qualifying lap:** Asmer, 1m 13.699s, 103.801 mph/167.051 km/h.

**BRITISH FORMULA 3 INTERNATIONAL SERIES, Rockingham International Circuit, Northamptonshire, Great Britain, 30 September. 2 X 24 laps of the 1.940-mile/3.122-km circuit.**
**Round 21 (46.560 miles/74.931 km).**
**1** Marko Asmer, EST (Dallara F307-Mercedes Benz), 29m 23.941s, 95.024 mph/152.926 km/h; **2** Atte Mustonen, FIN (Dallara F307-Mercedes Benz), 29m 36.868s; **3** Sebastian Hohenthal, S (Dallara F307-Mercedes Benz), 29m 38.437s; **4** Rodolfo Gonzalez, YV (Dallara F307-Mugen Honda), 29m 43.507s; **5** Mário Moraes, BR (Dallara F307-Mercedes Benz), 29m 44.780s; **6** Niall Breen, IRL (Dallara F307-Mercedes Benz), 29m 45.576s; **7** John Martin, AUS (Dallara F307-Mugen Honda), 29m 49.675s; **8** Alberto Valério, BR (Dallara F307-Mercedes Benz), 29m 50.398s; **9** Stephen Jelley, GB (Dallara F307-Mercedes Benz), 29m 51.762s; **10** Maro Engel, D (Dallara F307-Mercedes Benz), 29m 52.576s.
**National class winner:** Sergio Pérez, MEX (Dallara F304-Mugen Honda), 30m 18.555s (14th).
**Fastest race lap:** Asmer, 1m 12.620s, 96.172 mph/154.774 km/h.
**Fastest qualifying lap:** Asmer, 1m 15.320s, 92.724 mph/149.225 km/h.

**Round 22 (46.560 miles/74.931 km).**
**1** Maro Engel, D (Dallara F307-Mercedes Benz), 29m 31.443s, 94.621 mph/152.278 km/h; **2** Sam Bird, GB (Dallara F307-Mercedes Benz), 29m 41.709s; **3** Sebastian Hohenthal, S (Dallara F307-Mercedes Benz), 29m 42.759s; **4** Esteban Guerrieri, RA (Mygale M-07-Mercedes Benz), 29m 48.570s; **5** Atte Mustonen, FIN (Dallara F307-Mercedes Benz), 29m 48.952s; **6** Alberto Valério, BR (Dallara F307-Mercedes Benz), 29m 52.520s; **7** Mário Moraes, BR (Dallara F307-Mercedes Benz), 29m 54.975s; **8** Stephen Jelley, GB (Dallara F307-Mercedes Benz), 29m 56.427s; **9** Niall Breen, IRL (Dallara F307-Mercedes Benz), 29m 57.142s; **10** Greg Mansell, GB (Dallara F307-Mercedes Benz), 29m 59.825s.
**National class winner:** Pérez, 30m 12.408s (13th).
**Fastest race lap:** Engel, 1m 13.057s, 95.597 mph/153.848 km/h.
**Fastest qualifying lap:** Engel, 1m 11.616s, 97.520 mph/156.943 km/h.

**Final championship points**
**1** Marko Asmer, EST, 293; **2** Maro Engel, D, 208; **3** Stephen Jelley, GB, 183; **4** Sam Bird, GB, 180; **5** Niall Breen, IRL, 145; **6** Jonathan Kennard, GB, 130; **7** Atte Mustonen, FIN, 126; **8** Alberto Valério, BR, 119; **9** Sebastian Hohenthal, S, 101; **10** Greg Mansell, GB, 79; **11** Rodolfo Gonzalez, YV, 77; **12** Michael Devaney, IRL, 54; **13** Esteban Guerrieri, RA, 46; **14** Mário Moraes, BR, 43; **15** John Martin, AUS, 16; **16** Walter Grubmüller, A, 7; **17** Leo Mansell, GB, 2.

**National Class**
**1** Sergio Pérez, MEX, 376; **2** Cong Fu Cheng, CHN, 267; **3** Hamad Al Farden, BRN, 182; **4** Michael Meadows, GB, 153; **5** Salman Al-Khalifa, BRN, 149.

## Formula 3 Euro Series

**FORMULA 3 EURO SERIES, Hockenheimring Grand Prix Circuit, Heidelberg, Germany, 21/22 April. 2 x 25 laps of the 2.842-mile/4.574-km circuit.**
**Round 1 (71.054 miles/114.350 km).**
**1** Sébastien Buemi, CH (Dallara F305-Mercedes Benz), 39m 47.412s, 107.143 mph/172.429 km/h; **2** Nicolas Hülkenberg, D (Dallara F305-Mercedes Benz), 39m 51.347s; **3** Franck Mailleux, F (Dallara F305-Mercedes Benz), 39m 55.214s; **4** Renger van der Zande, NL (Dallara F306-Mercedes Benz), 39m 58.055s; **5** Romain Grosjean, F (Dallara F305-Mercedes Benz), 39m 58.549s; **6** Edoardo Mortara, I (Dallara F305-Mercedes Benz), 40m 6.426s; **7** Jean-Karl Vernay, F (Dallara F306-Mercedes Benz), 40m 7.052s; **8** Yelmer Buurman, NL (Dallara F305-Mercedes Benz), 40m 10.408s; **9** Daniel Clos, E (Dallara F305-Mercedes Benz), 40m 11.361s; **10** Kamui Kobayashi, J (Dallara F305-Mercedes Benz), 40m 11.989s.
**Fastest race lap:** Buemi, 1m 34.666s, 108.083 mph/173.942 km/h.
**Fastest qualifying lap:** Buemi, 1m 33.702s, 109.195 mph/175.731 km/h.

**Round 2 (71.054 miles/114.350 km).**
**1** Romain Grosjean, F (Dallara F305-Mercedes Benz), 40m 39.889s, 104.838 mph/168.720 km/h; **2** Yelmer Buurman, NL (Dallara F305-Mercedes Benz), 40m 44.753s; **3** Sébastien Buemi, CH (Dallara F305-Mercedes Benz), 40m 45.344s; **4** Jean-Karl Vernay, F (Dallara F306-Mercedes Benz), 40m 46.331s; **5** James Jakes, GB (Dallara F305-Mercedes Benz), 40m 47.797s; **6** Franck Mailleux, F (Dallara F305-Mercedes Benz), 40m 48.547s; **7** Nicolas Hülkenberg, D (Dallara F305-Mercedes Benz), 40m 48.998s; **8** Edoardo Mortara, I (Dallara F305-Mercedes Benz), 40m 49.399s; **9** Daniel Clos, E (Dallara F305-Mercedes Benz), 40m 56.119s; **10** Kamui Kobayashi, J (Dallara F305-Mercedes Benz), 41m 0.332s.
**Fastest race lap:** Buemi, 1m 34.407s, 108.379 mph/174.419 km/h.
**Pole position:** Buurman.

**FORMULA 3 EURO SERIES, Brands Hatch Indy Circuit, West Kingsdown, Dartford, Kent, Great Britain, 9/10 June. 54 and 55 laps of the 1.199-mile/1.929-km circuit.**
**Round 3 (64.726 miles/104.166 km).**
**1** Romain Grosjean, F (Dallara F305-Mercedes Benz), 40m 40.093s, 95.493 mph/153.681 km/h; **2** James Jakes, GB (Dallara F305-Mercedes Benz), 40m 41.232s; **3** Kamui Kobayashi, J (Dallara F305-Mercedes Benz), 40m 48.634s; **4** Nicolas Hülkenberg, D (Dallara F305-Mercedes Benz), 40m 49.393s; **5** Tim Sandtler, D (Dallara F306-Mercedes Benz), 40m 54.239s; **6** Yelmer Buurman, NL (Dallara F305-Mercedes Benz), 40m 54.658s; **7** Sébastien Buemi, CH (Dallara F305-Mercedes Benz), 40m 55.199s; **8** Edoardo Mortara, I (Dallara F305-Mercedes Benz), 41m 5.916s; **9** Yann Clairay, F (Dallara F305-Mercedes Benz), 41m 6.804s; **10** Tom Dillmann, F (Dallara F307-Mercedes Benz), 41m 7.618s.
**Fastest race lap:** Grosjean, 42.423s, 101.715 mph/163.694 km/h.
**Fastest qualifying lap:** Jakes, 41.704s, 103.468 mph/166.516 km/h.

**Round 4 (65.924 miles/106.095 km).**
**1** Edoardo Mortara, I (Dallara F305-Mercedes Benz), 40m 25.471s, 97.848 mph/157.471 km/h; **2** Sébastien Buemi, CH (Dallara F305-Mercedes Benz), 40m 26.102s; **3** Kamui Kobayashi, J (Dallara F305-Mercedes Benz), 40m 27.087s; **4** Yelmer Buurman, NL (Dallara F305-Mercedes Benz), 40m 34.251s; **5** Tim Sandtler, D (Dallara F306-Mercedes Benz), 40m 35.007s; **6** Nicolas Hülkenberg, D (Dallara F305-Mercedes Benz), 40m 35.336s; **7** Yann Clairay, F (Dallara F305-Mercedes Benz), 40m 39.969s; **8** James Jakes, GB (Dallara F305-Mercedes Benz), 40m 41.500s; **9** Tom Dillmann, F (Dallara F307-Mercedes Benz), 40m 45.242s; **10** Edoardo Piscopo, I (Dallara F305-Mercedes Benz), 40m 49.134s.
**Fastest race lap:** Franck Mailleux, F (Dallara F305-Mercedes Benz), 42.576s, 101.349 mph/163.105 km/h.
**Pole position:** Mortara.

**FORMULA 3 EURO SERIES, Norisring, Nürnberg (Nuremberg), Germany, 23/24 July. 32 and 46 laps of the 1.429-mile/2.300-km circuit.**
**Round 5 (45.733 miles/73.600 km).**
**1** Romain Grosjean, F (Dallara F305-Mercedes Benz), 40m 21.592s, 67.988 mph/109.415 km/h; **2** Sébastien Buemi, CH (Dallara F305-Mercedes Benz), 40m 24.804s; **3** Edoardo Mortara, I (Dallara F305-Mercedes Benz), 40m 28.021s; **4** Tom Dillmann, F (Dallara F307-Mercedes Benz), 40m 30.385s; **5** Jean-Karl Vernay, F (Dallara F306-Mercedes Benz), 40m 37.535s; **6** James Jakes, GB (Dallara F305-Mercedes Benz), 40m 37.819s; **7** Yelmer Buurman, NL (Dallara F305-Mercedes Benz), 31 laps; **8** Kamui Kobayashi, J (Dallara F305-Mercedes Benz), 31; **9** Tim Sandtler, D (Dallara F306-Mercedes Benz), 31; **10** Harald Schlegelmilch, LV (Dallara F306-Mercedes Benz), 30.
**Disqualified:** Ignored flags for loosening engine cover - Filip Salaquarda, CZ (Dallara F306-Mercedes Benz), finished 5th in 40m 37.462s.
**Fastest race lap:** Grosjean, 49.464s, 104.014 mph/167.394 km/h.
**Fastest qualifying lap:** Buemi, 49.416s, 104.115 mph/167.557 km/h.

**Round 6 (65.741 miles/105.800 km).**
**1** Nicolas Hülkenberg, D (Dallara F305-Mercedes Benz), 40m 45.567s, 96.774 mph/155.743 km/h; **2** Sébastien Buemi, CH (Dallara F305-Mercedes Benz), 40m 52.175s; **3** Tom Dillmann, F (Dallara F307-Mercedes Benz), 40m 59.731s; **4** Yelmer Buurman, NL (Dallara F305-Mercedes Benz), 41m 1.535s; **5** James Jakes, GB (Dallara F305-Mercedes Benz), 41m 21.534s; **6** Michael Patrizi, AUS (Dallara F306-Mercedes Benz), 41m 22.074s; **7** Marco Holzer, D (Dallara F305-Opel), 41m 22.707s; **8** Franck Mailleux, F (Dallara F305-Mercedes Benz), 41m 23.218s; **9** Harald Schlegelmilch, LV (Dallara F306-Mercedes Benz), 41m 24.455s; **10** Daniel Clos, E (Dallara F305-Mercedes Benz), 41m 30.859s.
**Fastest race lap:** Hülkenberg, 49.361s, 104.231 mph/167.743 km/h.
**Pole position:** Buurman.

**FORMULA 3 EURO SERIES, Circuit de Nevers, Magny-Cours, France, 30 June/1 July. 16 and 15 laps of the 2.741-mile/4.411-km circuit.**
**Round 7 (43.740 miles/70.392 km).**
**1** Kamui Kobayashi, J (Dallara F305-Mercedes Benz), 25m 1.620s, 104.862 mph/168.759 km/h; **2** Romain Grosjean, F (Dallara F305-Mercedes Benz), 25m 8.184s; **3** Sébastien Buemi, CH (Dallara F305-Mercedes Benz), 25m 8.498s; **4** Yann Clairay, F (Dallara F305-Mercedes Benz), 25m 15.404s; **5** Franck Mailleux, F (Dallara F305-Mercedes Benz), 25m 15.831s; **6** James Jakes, GB (Dallara F305-Mercedes Benz), 25m 16.251s; **7** Yelmer Buurman, NL (Dallara F305-Mercedes Benz), 25m 16.682s; **8** Jean-Karl Vernay, F (Dallara F306-Mercedes Benz), 25m 21.148s; **9** Tom Dillmann, F (Dallara F306-Mercedes Benz), 25m 24.353s; **10** Tim Sandtler, D (Dallara F306-Mercedes Benz), 25m 32.269s.
**Fastest race lap:** Grosjean, 1m 33.141s, 105.938 mph/170.489 km/h.
**Fastest qualifying lap:** Kobayashi, 1m 33.323s, 105.731 mph/170.157 km/h.

**Round 8 (40.999 miles/65.981 km).**
**1** James Jakes, GB (Dallara F305-Mercedes Benz), 25m 39.141s, 95.895 mph/154.327 km/h; **2** Jean-Karl Vernay, F (Dallara F306-Mercedes Benz), 25m 42.529s; **3** Yelmer Buurman, NL (Dallara F305-Mercedes Benz), 25m 42.880s; **4** Franck Mailleux, F (Dallara F305-Mercedes Benz), 25m 43.583s; **5** Esteban Guerrieri, RA (Mygale M-07-Mercedes Benz), 25m 44.741s; **6** Tim Sandtler, D (Dallara F306-Mercedes Benz), 25m 46.175s; **7** Romain Grosjean, F (Dallara F305-Mercedes Benz), 25m 46.588s; **8** Renger van der Zande, NL (Dallara F306-Mercedes Benz), 25m 47.035s; **9** Kamui Kobayashi, J (Dallara F305-Mercedes Benz), 25m 50.144s; **10** Daniel Clos, E (Dallara F305-Mercedes Benz), 25m 50.793s.
**Fastest race lap:** Buemi, 1m 32.972s, 106.130 mph/170.799 km/h.
**Pole position:** Vernay.

**FORMULA 3 EURO SERIES, Autodromo Internazionale del Mugello, Italy, 14/15 July. 2 x 21 laps of the 3.259-mile/5.245-km circuit.**
**Round 9 (68.441 miles/110.145 km).**
**1** Romain Grosjean, F (Dallara F305-Mercedes Benz), 36m 45.924s, 111.693 mph/179.753 km/h; **2** Kamui Kobayashi, J (Dallara F305-Mercedes Benz), 37m 2.236s; **3** Sébastien Buemi, CH (Dallara F305-Mercedes Benz), 37m 4.937s; **4** James Jakes, GB (Dallara F305-Mercedes Benz), 37m 5.596s; **5** Jean-Karl Vernay, F (Dallara F306-Mercedes Benz), 37m 6.888s; **6** Franck Mailleux, F (Dallara F305-Mercedes Benz), 37m 8.048s; **7** Daniel Clos, E (Dallara F305-Mercedes Benz), 37m 12.485s; **8** Renger van der Zande, NL (Dallara F306-Mercedes Benz), 37m 14.097s; **9** Edoardo Mortara, I (Dallara F305-Mercedes Benz), 37m 15.957s; **10** Cyndie Allemann, CH (Dallara F306-Mercedes Benz), 37m 19.982s.
**Fastest race lap:** Nicolas Hülkenberg, D (Dallara F305-Mercedes Benz), 1m 44.003s, 112.811 mph/181.552 km/h.
**Fastest qualifying lap:** Grosjean, 1m 41.485s, 115.610 mph/186.057 km/h.

**Round 10 (68.441 miles/110.145 km).**
**1** Franck Mailleux, F (Dallara F305-Mercedes Benz), 39m 43.703s, 103.363 mph/166.347 km/h; **2** Romain Grosjean, F (Dallara F305-Mercedes Benz), 39m 47.148s; **3** Renger van der Zande, NL (Dallara F306-Mercedes Benz), 39m 53.959s; **4** Kamui Kobayashi, J (Dallara F305-Mercedes Benz), 39m 56.572s; **5** Sébastien Buemi, CH (Dallara F305-Mercedes Benz), 40m 2.060s; **6** Yelmer Buurman, NL (Dallara F305-Mercedes Benz), 40m 5.176s; **7** Yann Clairay, F (Dallara F306-Mercedes Benz), 40m 7.252s; **8** Tom Dillmann, F (Dallara F307-Mercedes Benz), 40m 8.291s; **9** Edoardo Piscopo, I (Dallara F305-Mercedes Benz), 40m 12.907s; **10** Tim Sandtler, D (Dallara F306 Mercedes Benz), 40m 14.961s.
**Fastest race lap:** Grosjean, 1m 45.593s, 111.113 mph/178.818 km/h.
**Pole position:** van der Zande.

**FORMULA 3 EURO SERIES, Circuit Park Zandvoort, Netherlands, 28/29 July. 26 and 23 laps of the 2.676-mile/4.307-km circuit.**
**Round 11 (69.582 miles/111.982 km).**
**1** Romain Grosjean, F (Dallara F305-Mercedes Benz), 40m 59.489s, 101.849 mph/163.910 km/h; **2** Kamui Kobayashi, J (Dallara F305-Mercedes Benz), 41m 0.339s; **3** Sébastien Buemi, CH (Dallara F305-Mercedes Benz), 41m 8.320s; **4** Yann Clairay, F (Dallara F305-Mercedes Benz), 41m 15.364s; **5** Franck Mailleux, F (Dallara F305-Mercedes Benz), 41m 16.659s; **6** Nicolas Hülkenberg, D (Dallara F305-Mercedes Benz), 41m 17.115s; **7** Yelmer Buurman, NL (Dallara F305-Mercedes Benz), 41m 19.353s; **8** James Jakes, GB (Dallara F305-Mercedes Benz), 41m 19.659s; **9** Renger van der Zande, NL (Dallara F306-Mercedes Benz), 41m 37.369s; **10** Filip Salaquarda, CZ (Dallara F306-Mercedes Benz), 41m 43.243s.
**Fastest race lap:** Mailleux, 1m 33.638s, 102.891 mph/165.586 km/h.
**Fastest qualifying lap:** Grosjean, 1m 32.290s, 104.394 mph/168.005 km/h.

**Round 12 (61.554 miles/99.061 km).**
**1** Nicolas Hülkenberg, D (Dallara F305-Mercedes Benz), 41m 23.407s, 89.229 mph/143.600 km/h; **2** Sébastien Buemi, CH (Dallara F305-Mercedes Benz), 41m 33.394s; **3** Romain Grosjean, F (Dallara F305-Mercedes Benz), 41m 39.780s; **4** Tom Dillmann, F (Dallara F307-Mercedes Benz), 41m 54.536s; **5** Renger van der Zande, NL (Dallara F306-Mercedes Benz), 41m 56.696s; **6** James Jakes, GB (Dallara F305-Mercedes Benz), 41m 58.648s; **7** Jean-Karl Vernay, F (Dallara F306-Mercedes Benz), 42m 6.664s; **8** Harald Schlegelmilch, LV (Dallara F306-Mercedes Benz), 42m 53.733s; **9** Edoardo Mortara, I (Dallara F305-Mercedes Benz), 42m 57.131s; **10** Filip Salaquarda, CZ (Dallara F306-Mercedes Benz), 43m 13.714s.
**Fastest race lap:** Mailleux, 1m 35.021s, 101.393 mph/163.176 km/h.
**Pole position:** Jakes.

**FORMULA 3 EURO SERIES, Nürburgring, Nürburg/Eifel, Germany, 1/2 September. 29 and 28 laps of the 2.255-mile/3.629-km circuit.**
**Round 13 (65.394 miles/105.241 km).**
**1** Nicolas Hülkenberg, D (Dallara F305-Mercedes Benz), 40m 56.388s, 95.839 mph/154.237 km/h; **2** Sébastien Buemi, CH (Dallara F305-Mercedes Benz), 41m 5.636s; **3** Edoardo Piscopo, I (Dallara F305-Mercedes Benz), 41m 8.119s; **4** James Jakes, GB (Dallara F305-Mercedes Benz), 41m 9.060s; **5** Romain Grosjean, F (Dallara F305-Mercedes Benz), 41m 27.455s; **6** Maximilian Götz, D (Dallara F306-Volkswagen), 41m 28.272s; **7** Daniel Clos, E (Dallara F305-Mercedes Benz), 41m 29.031s; **8** Harald Schlegelmilch, LV (Dallara F306-MercedesBenz), 41m 30.105s; **9** Filip Salaquarda, CZ (Dallara F306-Mercedes Benz), 41m 34.867s; **10** Franck Mailleux, F (Dallara F305-Mercedes Benz), 41m 35.313s.
**Fastest race lap:** Hülkenberg, 1m 24.091s, 96.536 mph/155.360 km/h.
**Fastest qualifying lap:** Hülkenberg, 1m 22.911s, 97.910 mph/157.571 km/h.

**Round 14 (63.139 miles/101.612 km).**
**1** Harald Schlegelmilch, LV (Dallara F306-Mercedes Benz), 40m 1.354s, 94.655 mph/152.332 km/h; **2** Romain Grosjean, F (Dallara F305-Mercedes Benz), 40m 1.706s; **3** Sébastien Buemi, CH (Dallara F305-Mercedes Benz), 40m 2.464s; **4** Nicolas Hülkenberg, D (Dallara F305-Mercedes Benz), 40m 3.078s; **5** Daniel Clos, E (Dallara F305-Mercedes Benz), 40m 7.162s; **6** Yelmer Buurman, NL (Dallara F305-Mercedes Benz), 40m 8.522s; **7** James Jakes, GB (Dallara F305-Mercedes Benz), 40m 9.041s; **8** Renger van der Zande, NL (Dallara F306-Mercedes Benz), 40m 9.324s; **9** Maximilian Götz, D (Dallara F306-Volkswagen), 40m 10.293s; **10** Jean-Karl Vernay, F (Dallara F306-Mercedes Benz), 40m 14.047s.
**Fastest race lap:** Yann Clairay, F (Dallara F305-Mercedes Benz), 1m 24.439s, 96.139 mph/154.719 km/h.
**Pole position:** Schlegelmilch.

**FORMULA 3 EURO SERIES, Circuit de Catalunya, Montmeló, Barcelona, Spain, 22/23 September. 2 x 30 laps of the 1.850-mile/2.977-km circuit.**
**Round 15 (55.495 miles/89.310 km).**
**1** Edoardo Mortara, I (Dallara F305-Mercedes Benz), 40m 3.576s, 83.118 mph/133.765 km/h; **2** Nicolas Hülkenberg, D (Dallara F305-Mercedes Benz), 40m 4.784s; **3** Tom Dillmann, F (Dallara F307-Mercedes Benz), 40m 11.851s; **4** James Jakes, GB (Dallara F305-Mercedes Benz), 40m 16.488s; **5** Franck Mailleux, F (Dallara F305-Mercedes Benz), 40m 23.917s; **6** Renger van der Zande, NL (Dallara F306-Mercedes Benz), 40m 31.942s; **7** Edoardo Piscopo, I (Dallara F305-Mercedes Benz), 40m 33.266s; **8** Romain Grosjean, F (Dallara F305-Mercedes Benz), 40m 38.570s*; **9** Harald Schlegelmilch, LV (Dallara F306-Mercedes Benz), 40m 40.787s; **10** Yann Clairay, F (Dallara F305-Mercedes Benz), 40m 45.507s.
* Grosjean finished 3rd, but was given a 30s penalty due to mechanics working too long on the grid).
**Fastest race lap:** Grosjean, 1m 18.130s, 85.234 mph/137.171 km/h.
**Fastest qualifying lap:** Hülkenberg, 1m 6.599s, 99.992 mph/160.921 km/h.

**Round 16 (55.495 miles/89.310 km).**
**1** Renger van der Zande, NL (Dallara F306-Mercedes Benz), 40m 34.663s, 82.057 mph/132.057 km/h; **2** Tom Dillmann, F (Dallara F307-Mercedes Benz), 40m 40.223s; **3** Franck Mailleux, F (Dallara F305-Mercedes Benz), 40m 41.178s; **4** Daniel Clos, E (Dallara F305-Mercedes Benz), 40m 47.581s; **5** Filip Salaquarda, CZ (Dallara F306-Mercedes Benz), 40m 54.259s; **6** Sébastien Buemi, CH (Dallara F305-Mercedes Benz), 40m 54.926s; **7** James Jakes, GB (Dallara F305-Mercedes Benz), 40m 55.037s; **8** Nicolas Hülkenberg, D (Dallara F305-Mercedes Benz), 40m 55.363s; **9** Harald Schlegelmilch, LV (Dallara F306-Mercedes Benz), 40m 57.961s; **10** Maximilian Götz, D (Dallara F306-Volkswagen), 40m 58.770s.
**Disqualified:** Grosjean - started from incorrect grid position.
**Fastest race lap:** Mailleux, 1m 7.243s, 99.034 mph/159.380 km/h.
**Pole position:** Piscopo.

**FORMULA 3 EURO SERIES, Circuit Paul Armagnac, Nogaro, France, 29/30 September. 2 x 29 laps of the 2.259-mile/3.636-km circuit.**
**Round 17 (65.520 miles/105.444 km).**
**1** Romain Grosjean, F (Dallara F305-Mercedes Benz), 40m 43.144s, 96.544 mph/155.372 km/h; **2** Kamui Kobayashi, J (Dallara F305-Mercedes Benz), 40m 43.628s; **3** Nicolas Hülkenberg, D (Dallara F305-Mercedes Benz), 40m 44.578s; **4** Sébastien Buemi, CH (Dallara F305-Mercedes Benz), 40m 45.473s; **5** Yelmer Buurman, NL (Dallara F305-Mercedes Benz), 40m 46.184s; **6** Edoardo Mortara, I (Dallara F305-Mercedes Benz), 40m 48.640s; **7** Franck Mailleux, F (Dallara F305-Mercedes Benz), 40m 50.710s; **8** Jean-Karl Vernay, F (Dallara F306-Mercedes Benz), 41m 2.074s; **9** Yann Clairay, F (Dallara F305-Mercedes Benz), 41m 2.689s; **10** Harald Schlegelmilch, LV (Dallara F306-Mercedes Benz), 41m 6.187s.
**Fastest race lap:** Grosjean, 1m 22.226s, 98.916 mph/159.190 km/h.
**Fastest qualifying lap:** Grosjean, 1m 20.990s, 100.426 mph/161.619 km/h.

**Round 18 (65.520 miles/105.444 km).**
**1** Sébastien Buemi, CH (Dallara F305-Mercedes Benz), 40m 48.483s, 96.334 mph/155.034 km/h; **2** Kamui Kobayashi, J (Dallara F305-Mercedes Benz), 40m 48.971s; **3** Nicolas Hülkenberg, D (Dallara F305-Mercedes Benz), 40m 49.664s; **4** Jean-Karl Vernay, F (Dallara F306-Mercedes Benz), 40m 50.958s; **5** Romain Grosjean, F (Dallara F305-Mercedes Benz), 40m 51.521s; **6** Yann Clairay, F (Dallara F305-Mercedes Benz), 40m 53.024s; **7** Yelmer Buurman, NL (Dallara F305-Mercedes Benz), 40m 53.591s; **8** Edoardo Mortara, I (Dallara F305-Mercedes Benz), 40m 54.354s; **9** Maximilian Götz, D (Dallara F306-Volkswagen), 40m 54.822s; **10** Daniel Clos, E (Dallara F305-Mercedes Benz), 40m 55.677s.
**Fastest race lap:** Mortara, 1m 22.543s, 98.537 mph/158.579 km/h.
**Pole position:** Vernay.

**FORMULA 3 EURO SERIES, Hockenheimring Grand Prix Circuit, Heidelberg, Germany, 13/14 October. 24 and 25 laps of the 2.842-mile/4.574-km circuit.**
**Round 19 (68.212 miles/109.776 km).**
**1** Nicolas Hülkenberg, D (Dallara F305-Mercedes Benz), 37m 53.393s, 108.016 mph/173.834 km/h; **2** Romain Grosjean, F (Dallara F305-Mercedes Benz), 37m 54.661s; **3** Yelmer Buurman, NL (Dallara F305-Mercedes Benz), 37m 57.199s; **4** Kamui Kobayashi, J (Dallara F305-Mercedes Benz), 38m 3.754s; **5** Sébastien Buemi, CH (Dallara F305-Mercedes Benz), 38m 6.993s; **6** Edoardo Mortara, I (Dallara F305-Mercedes Benz), 38m 8.139s; **7** Yann Clairay, F (Dallara F305-Mercedes Benz), 38m 8.904s; **8** Daniel Clos, E (Dallara F305-Mercedes Benz), 38m 19.264s; **9** Tim Sandtler, D (Dallara F306-Mercedes Benz), 38m 19.961s; **10** Jean-Karl Vernay, F (Dallara F306-Mercedes Benz), 38m 28.315s.
**Fastest race lap:** Grosjean, 1m 33.701s, 109.196 mph/175.733 km/h.
**Fastest qualifying lap:** Grosjean, 1m 32.805s, 110.250 mph/177.430 km/h.

**Round 20 (71.054 miles/114.350 km).**
**1** Sébastien Buemi, CH (Dallara F305-Mercedes Benz), 39m 47.193s, 107.152 mph/172.445 km/h; **2** Edoardo Mortara, I (Dallara F305-Mercedes Benz), 39m 48.662s; **3** Romain Grosjean, F (Dallara F305-Mercedes Benz), 39m 49.397s; **4** Yelmer Buurman, NL (Dallara F305-Mercedes Benz), 39m 50.810s; **5** Daniel Clos, E (Dallara F305-Mercedes Benz), 39m 54.275s; **6** Franck Mailleux, F (Dallara F305-Mercedes Benz), 39m 55.042s; **7** Nicolas Hülkenberg, D (Dallara F305-Mercedes Benz), 39m 56.120s; **8** Yann Clairay, F (Dallara F305-Mercedes Benz), 40m 0.548s; **9** Harald Schlegelmilch, LV (Dallara F306-Mercedes Benz), 40m 11.180s; **10** Tim Sandtler, D (Dallara F306-Mercedes Benz), 40m 12.432s.
**Fastest race lap:** Buemi, 1m 34.357s, 108.437 mph/174.512 km/h.
**Pole position:** Clos.

**Final championship points**
**Drivers**
**1** Romain Grosjean, F, 106; **2** Sébastien Buemi, CH, 95; **3** Nicolas Hülkenberg, D, 72; **4** Kamui Kobayashi, J, 59; **5** James Jakes, GB, 42; **6** Yelmer Buurman, NL, 40; **7** Franck Mailleux, F, 38; **8** Edoardo Mortara, I, 37; **9** Tom Dillmann, F, 23; **10** Jean-Karl Vernay, F, 23; **11** Renger van der Zande, NL, 21; **12** Yann Clairay, F, 13; **13** Daniel Clos, E, 13; **14** Harald Schlegelmilch, LV, 8; **15** Edoardo Piscopo, I, 8; **16** Tim Sandtler, D, 8; **17** Filip Salaquarda, CZ, 3; **18** Michael Patrizi, AUS, 1.

**Rookies**
**1** Romain Grosjean, F, 106; **2** Sébastien Buemi, CH, 95; **3** Nicolas Hülkenberg, D, 72.

**Teams**
**1** ASM Formula 3, 229; **2** Manor Motorsport, 119; **3** Mücke Motorsport, 104.

**Nations**
**1** France, 176; **2** Switzerland, 93; **3** Germany, 83.

## ATS Formel-3 Cup

**JIM CLARK REVIVAL, Hockenheimring Grand Prix Circuit, Heidelberg, Germany, 28/29 April. 2 x 16 laps of the 2.842-mile/4.574-km circuit.**
**Round 1 (45.474 miles/73.184 km).**
**1** Frédéric Vervisch, B (Lola B06/30-Opel), 25m 59.308s, 104.988 mph/168.961 km/h; **2** Carlo van Dam, NL (Dallara F306-Opel), 26m 06.886s; **3** Récardo Bruins, ROK/NL (Dallara F306-Opel), 26m 8.114s; **4** Nico Verdonck, B (Lola B06/30-Opel), 26m 09.114s; **5** Christian Vietoris, D (Ligier JS47-Opel), 26m 17.638s; **6** Patrick Cicchiello, CH (Dallara F306-Opel), 26m 19.196s; **7** Marcel Schuler, D (Dallara F304-Opel), 26m 23.092s; **8** Matteo Chinosi, I (Dallara F306-Mugen Honda), 26m 34.961s; **9** Max Nilsson, S (Dallara F306-Opel), 26m 35.592s; **10** Ross Zwolsman, NL (Dallara F306-Opel), 26m 36.471s.
**Fastest race lap:** Vervisch, 1m 36.522s, 106.004 mph/170.597 km/h.
**Fastest qualifying lap:** Van Dam, 1m 36.220s, 106.337 mph/171.132 km/h.

**Round 2 (45.474 miles/73.184 km).**
**1** Carlo van Dam, NL (Dallara F306-Opel), 26m 17.963s, 103.746 mph/166.963 km/h; **2** Frédéric Vervisch, B. (Lola B06/30-Opel), 26m 18.997s; **3** Nico Verdonck, B (Lola B06/30-Opel), 26m 22.169s; **4** Récardo Bruins, ROK/NL (Dallara F306-Opel), 26m 23.894s; **5** Matteo Chinosi, I (Dallara F306-Mugen Honda), 26m 30.050s; **6** Max Nilsson, S (Dallara F306-Opel), 26m 41.321s; **7** Christian Vietoris, D (Ligier JS47-Opel), 26m 44.086s; **8** Marcel Schuler, D (Dallara F304-Opel), 26m 44.885s; **9** Ross Zwolsman, NL (Dallara F306-Opel), 26m 46.652s; **10** Michael Klein, D (Dallara F304-Opel), 26m 50.370s.
**Fastest race lap:** Vervisch, 1m 37.441s, 105.005 mph/168.988 km/h.
**Fastest qualifying lap:** Van Dam, 1m 36.334s, 106.211 mph/170.930 km/h.

**ATS FORMEL-3-CUP, Motorsport Arena Oschersleben, Germany, 12/13 May. 14 and 18 laps of the 2.297-mile/3.696-km circuit.**
**Round 3 (32.152 miles/51.744 km).**
**1** Nico Verdonck, B (Lola B06/30-Opel), 26m 23.579s, 73.093 mph/117.631 km/h; **2** Frédéric Vervisch, B (Lola B06/30-Opel), 26m 24.337s; **3** Carlo van Dam, NL (Dallara F306-Opel), 26m 31.152s; **4** Récardo Bruins, ROK/NL (Dallara F306-Opel), 26m 38.757s; **5** ChristianVvietoris, D (Ligier JS47-Opel), 26m 44.203s; **6** Matteo Chinosi, I (Dallara F306-Mugen Honda), 26m 51.503s; **7** Max Nilsson, S (Dallara F306-Opel), 26m 58.193s; **8** Marcel Schuler, D (Dallara F304-Opel), 27m 8.567s; **9** Federico Glorioso, I (Dallara F306-Mugen Honda), 27m 15.615s; **10** Simon Solgat, D (Dallara F304-Opel), 27m 33.928s.
**Fastest race lap:** Bruins, 1m 23.864s, 98.585 mph/158.656 km/h.
**Fastest qualifying lap:** Verdonck, 1m 24.215s, 98.174 mph/157.995 km/h.

**Round 4 (41.339 miles/66.528 km).**
**1** Carlo van Dam, NL (Dallara F306-Opel), 25m 38.739s, 96.715 mph/155.647 km/h; **2** Frédéric Vervisch, B (Lola B06/30-Opel), 25m 40.311s; **3** Michael Klein, D (Dallara F304-Opel), 26m 5.053s; **4** Matteo Chinosi, I (Dallara F306-Mugen Honda), 26m 5.619s; **5** Récardo Bruins, ROK/NL (Dallara F306-Opel), 26m 13.476s; **6** Nico Verdonck, B (Lola B06/30-Opel), 26m 13.777s; **7** Max Nilsson, S (Dallara F306-Opel), 26m 14.255s; **8** Simon Solgat, D (Dallara F304-Opel), 26m 17.898s; **9** Federico Glorioso, I (Dallara F306-Mugen Honda), 26m 18.135s; **10** Norman Knop, D (Dallara F306-Opel), 26m 43.493s.
**Fastest race lap:** Van Dam, 1m 24.191s, 98.202 mph/158.040 km/h.
**Fastest qualifying lap:** Van Dam, 1m 23.407s, 99.125 mph/159.526 km/h.

**ATS FORMEL-3-CUP, Nürburgring, Nürburg/Eifel, Germany, 9 June. 12 and 15 laps of the 2.882-mile/4.638-km circuit.**
**Round 5 (34.583 miles/55.656 km).**
**1** Carlo van Dam, NL (Dallara F306-Opel), 26m 13.034s, 79.146 mph/127.372 km/h; **2** Nico Verdonck, B (Lola B06/30-Opel), 26m 16.358s; **3** Christian Vietoris, D (Dallara F306-Opel), 26m 19.672s; **4** Matteo Chinosi, I (Dallara F306-Mugen Honda), 26m 22.210s; **5** Federico Glorioso, I (Dallara F306-Mugen Honda), 26m 28.705s; **6** Frédéric Vervisch, B (Lola B06/30-Opel), 26m 30.922s; **7** Marcello Thomaz, BR (Dallara F306-Opel), 26m 32.995s; **8** Marcel Schuler, D (Dallara F304-Opel), 26m 35.865s; **9** Johannes Theobald, D (Ligier JS47-Opel), 26m 38.457s; **10** Simon Solgat, D (Dallara F304-Opel), 26m 39.392s.
**Fastest race lap:** Van Dam, 1m 39.545s, 104.223 mph/167.731 km/h.
**Fastest qualifying lap:** Van Dam, 1m 39.764s, 103.995 mph/167.362 km/h.

**Round 6 (43.229 miles/69.570 km).**
**1** Frédéric Vervisch, B (Lola B06/30-Opel), 25m 16.107s, 102.647 mph/165.194 km/h; **2** Christian Vietoris, D (Dallara F306-Opel), 25m 24.382s; **3** Récardo Bruins, ROK/NL (Dallara F306-Opel), 25m 24.898s; **4** Nico Verdonck, B (Lola B06/30-Opel), 25m 25.258s; **5** Marcello Thomaz, BR (Dallara F306-Opel), 25m 33.724s; **6** Matteo Chinosi, I (Dallara F306-Mugen Honda), 25m 34.700s; **7** Michael Klein, D (Dallara F304-Opel), 25m 35.317s; **8** Carlo van Dam, NL (Dallara F306-Opel), 25m 35.565s; **9** Federico Glorioso, I (Dallara F306-Mugen Honda), 25m 42.672s; **10** Max Nilsson, S (Dallara F306-Opel), 25m 46.301s.
**Fastest race lap:** Vervisch, 1m 40.012s, 103.737 mph/166.947 km/h.
**Fastest qualifying lap:** Van Dam, 1m 39.539s, 104.230 mph/167.741 km/h.

**ATS FORMEL-3-CUP, Nürburgring, Nürburg/Eifel, Germany, 7/8 July. 18 and 17 laps of the 2.248-mile/3.618-km circuit.**
**Round 7 (40.466 miles/65.124 km).**
**1** Récardo Bruins, ROK/NL (Dallara F306-Opel), 25m 10.658s, 96.434 mph/155.194 km/h; **2** Carlo van Dam, NL (Dallara F306-Opel), 25m 13.138s; **3** Nico Verdonck, B (Lola B06/30-Opel), 25m 15.939s; **4** Frédéric Vervisch, B (Lola B06/30-Opel), 25m 25.590s; **5** Christian Vietoris, D (Dallara F306-Opel), 25m 30.194s; **6** Michael Klein, D (Dallara F304-Opel), 25m 37.372s; **7** Max Nilsson, S (Dallara F306-Opel), 25m 38.785s; **8** Ross Zwolsman, NL (Dallara F306-Opel), 25m 40.535s; **9** Federico Glorioso, I (Dallara F306-Mugen Honda), 25m 41.392s; **10** Matteo Chinosi, I (Dallara F306-Mugen Honda), 25m 41.959s.
**Fastest race lap:** Van Dam, 1m 23.033s, 97.470 mph/156.862 km/h.
**Fastest qualifying lap:** Vietoris, 1m 21.784s, 98.959 mph/159.258 km/h.

**Round 8 (38.218 miles/61.506 km).**
**1** Christian Vietoris, D (Dallara F306-Opel), 25m 15.991s, 90.756 mph/146.057 km/h; **2** Récardo Bruins, ROK/NL (Dallara F306-Opel), 25m 16.688s; **3** Carlo van Dam, NL (Dallara F306-Opel), 25m 17.342s; **4** Nico Verdonck, B (Lola B06/30-Opel), 25m 19.124s; **5** Matteo Chinosi, I (Dallara F306-Mugen Honda), 25m 27.277s; **6** Frédéric Vervisch, B (Lola B06/30-Opel), 25m 27.374s; **7** Michael Klein, D (Dallara F304-Opel), 25m 36.321s; **8** Federico Glorioso, I. (Dallara F306-Mugen Honda), 256m 45.764s; **9** Marika Diana, I (Dallara F304-Mugen Honda), 26m 9.211s; **10** Leonardo Valois, SK (Dallara F304-Opel), 26m 14.677s.
**Fastest race lap:** Vervisch, 1m 23.525s, 96.896 mph/155.938 km/h.
**Fastest qualifying lap:** Van Dam, 1m 21.455s, 99.358 mph/159.901 km/h.

**ATS FORMEL-3-CUP, EuroSpeedway Lausitz, Klettwitz, Dresden, Germany, 4/5 August. 17 and 20 laps of the 2.139-mile/3.442-km circuit.**
**Round 9 (36.359 miles/58.514 km).**
**1** Frédéric Vervisch, B (Lola B06/30-Opel), 25m 14.322s, 86.436 mph/139.105 km/h; **2** Nico Verdonck, B (Lola B06/30-Opel), 25m 15.714s; **3** Christian Vietoris, D (Dallara F306-Opel), 25m 17.874s; **4** Carlo van Dam, NL (Dallara F306-Opel), 25m 19.835s; **5** Récardo Bruins, ROK/NL (Dallara F306-Opel), 25m 22.900s; **6** Matteo Chinosi, I (Dallara F306-Mugen Honda), 25m 23.496s; **7** Michael Klein, D (Dallara F304-Opel), 25m 31.304s; **8** Dominick Muermans, NL (Dallara F306-Opel), 25m 35.301s; **9** Max Nilsson, S (Dallara F306-Opel), 25m 38.671s; **10** Marcel Schuler, D (Dallara F304-Opel), 25m 38.836s.
**Fastest race lap:** Vervisch, 1m 17.560s, 99.272 mph/159.762 km/h.
**Fastest qualifying lap:** Vietoris, 1m 16.634s, 100.472 mph/161.693 km/h.

**Round 10 (42.775 miles/68.840 km).**
**1** Carlo van Dam, NL. (Dallara F306-Opel), 26m 19.076s, 97.519 mph/156.942 km/h; **2** Christian Vietoris, D (Dallara F306-Opel), 26m 22.963s; **3** Nico Verdonck, B (Lola B06/30-Opel), 26m 23.480s; **4** Matteo Chinosi, I (Dallara F306-Mugen Honda), 26m 27.387s; **5** Récardo Bruins, ROK/NL (Dallara F306-Opel), 26m 27.973s; **6** Dominick Muermans, NL (Dallara F306-Opel), 26m 28.961s; **7** Max Nilsson, S (Dallara F306-Opel), 26m 43.557s; **8** Marcel Schuler, D (Dallara F304-Opel), 26m 48.296s; **9** Michael Klein, D (Dallara F304-Opel), 26m 49.873s; **10** Simon Solgat, D (Dallara F304-Opel), 27m 0.687s.
**Fastest race lap:** Vervisch, 1m 17.673s, 99.128 mph/159.530 km/h.
**Fastest qualifying lap:** Van Dam, 1m 16.367s, 100.823 mph/162.258 km/h.

**ATS FORMEL-3-CUP, Nationale Circuit Assen, Netherlands, 11/12 August. 2 x 16 laps of the 2.830-mile/4.555-km circuit.**
**Round 11 (45.286 miles/72.880 km).**
**1** Carlo van Dam, NL (Dallara F306-Opel), 25m 33.588s, 106.305 mph/171.081 km/h; **2** Frédéric Vervisch, B (Lola B06/30-Opel), 25m 34.153s; **3** Nico Verdonck, B (Lola B06/30-Opel), 25m 35.077s; **4** Matteo Chinosi, I (Dallara F306-Mugen Honda), 25m 45.326s; **5** Michael Klein, D. (Dallara F304-Opel), 25m 49.950s; **6** Récardo Bruins, ROK/NL (Dallara F306-Opel), 25m 54.999s; **7** Christian Vietoris, D (Dallara F306-Opel), 25m 57.274s; **8** Dominick Muermans, NL (Dallara F306-Opel), 26m 09.219s; **9** Federico Glorioso, I (Dallara F306-Mugen Honda), 26m 9.831s; **10** Max Nilsson, S (Dallara F306-Opel), 26m 15.078s.
**Fastest race lap:** Verdonck, 1m 34.869s, 107.403 mph/172.848 km/h.
**Fastest qualifying lap:** Van Dam, 1m 34.054s, 108.334 mph/174.346 km/h.

**Round 12 (45.286 miles/72.880 km).**
**1** Carlo van Dam, NL (Dallara F306-Opel), 25m 33.118s, 106.337 mph/171.133 km/h; **2** Récardo Bruins, ROK/NL

(Dallara F306-Opel), 25m 33.551s; **3** Christian Vietoris, D (Dallaar F306-Opel), 25m 40.441s; **4** Frédéric Vervisch, B (Lola B06/30-Opel), 25m 43.174s; **5** Matteo Chinosi, I (Dallara F306-Mugen Honda), 25m 49.130s; **6** Dominick Muermans, NL (Dallara F306-Opel), 25m 56.162s; **7** Michael Klein, D (Dallara F304-Opel), 25m 57.020s; **8** Federico Glorioso, I. (Dallara F306-Mugen Honda), 25m 57.326s; **9** Nico Verdonck, B (Lola B06/30-Opel), 25m 57.771s; **10** Marcel Schuler, D (Dallara F304-Opel), 26m 13.826s.
**Fastest race lap:** Van Dam, 1m 34.936s, 107.328 mph/172.726 km/h.
**Fastest qualifying lap:** Van Dam, 1m 33.185s, 109.344 mph/175.972 km/h.

**ATS FORMEL-3-CUP, Nationale Circuit Assen, Netherlands, 1/2 September. 2 x 16 laps of the 2.830-mile/4.555-km circuit.**
**Round 13 (45.286 miles/72.880 km).**
**1** Carlo van Dam, NL (Dallara F306-Opel), 25m 15.181s, 107.596 mph/173.159 km/h; **2** Matteo Chinosi, I (Dallara F306-Mugen Honda), 25m 26.260s; **3** Nico Verdonck, B (Lola B06/30-Opel), 25m 27.437s; **4** Frédéric Vervisch, B (Lola B06/30-Opel), 25m 28.439s; **5** Récardo Bruins, ROK/NL (Dallara F306-Opel), 25m 29.619s; **6** Christian Vietoris, D (Dallara F306-Opel), 25m 30.027s; **7** Max Nilsson, S (Dallara F306-Opel), 25m 50.219s; **8** Michael Klein, D (Dallara F304-Opel), 25m 50.563s; **9** Marcel Schuler, D (Dallara F304-Opel), 25m 51.807s; **10** Simon Solgat, D (Dallara F304-Opel), 26m 2.488s.
**Fastest race lap:** Van Dam, 1m 33.473s, 109.007 mph/175.430 km/h.
**Fastest qualifying lap:** Bruins, 1m 48.281s, 94.100 mph/151.439 km/h.

**Round 14 (45.286 miles/72.880 km).**
**1** Récardo Bruins, ROK/NL (Dallara F306-Opel), 25m 22.461s, 107.082 mph/172.331 km/h; **2** Matteo Chinosi, I (Dallara F306-Mugen Honda), 25m 36.869s; **3** Carlo van Dam, NL (Dallara F306-Opel), 25m 37.402s; **4** Nico Verdonck, B (Lola B06/30-Opel), 25m 37.821s; **5** Frédéric Vervisch, B (Lola B06/30-Opel), 25m 38.128s; **6** Christian Vietoris, D (Dallara F306-Opel), 25m 38.817s; **7** Max Nilsson, S (Dallara F306-Opel), 25m 53.502s; **8** Marcel Schuler, D (Dallara F304-Opel), 26m 2.900s; **9** Simon Solgat, D (Dallara F304-Opel), 26m 15.623s; **10** Jonathan Hirschi, CH (Dallara F306-Opel), 26m 16.377s.
**Fastest race lap:** Bruins, 1m 34.389s, 107.949 mph/173.727 km/h.
**Fastest qualifying lap:** Bruins, 1m 46.060s, 96.071 mph/154.610 km/h.

**ATS FORMEL-3-CUP, Sachsenring, Oberlungwitz, Germany, 15/16 September. 18 and 20 laps of the 2.265-mile/3.645-km circuit.**
**Round 15 (40.768 miles/65.610 km).**
**1** Christian Vietoris, D (Dallara F306-Opel), 22m 48.352s, 107.257 mph/172.613 km/h; **2** Frédéric Vervisch, B (Lola B06/30-Opel), 22m 55.438s; **3** Carlo van Dam, NL (Dallara F306-Opel), 22m 59.119s; **4** Récardo Bruins, ROK/NL (Dallara F306-Opel), 22m 59.625s; **5** Michael Klein, D (Dallara F304-Opel), 23m 19.781s; **6** Simon Solgat, D (Dallara F304-Opel), 23m 20.237s; **7** Marcel Schuler, D (Dallara F304-Opel), 23m 20.682s; **8** Jonathan Hirschi, CH (Dallara F306-Opel), 23m 38.826s; **9** Norman Knop, D (Dallara F306-Opel), 23m 54.490s; **10** Matteo Chinosi, I (Dallara F306-Mugen Honda), 17 laps.
**Fastest race lap:** Vietoris, 1m 14.980s, 108.744 mph/175.006 km/h.
**Fastest qualifying lap:** Vietoris, 1m 14.728s, 109.111 mph/175.596 km/h.

**Round 16 (45.298 miles/72.900 km).**
**1** Carlo van Dam, NL (Dallara F306-Opel), 25m 12.549s, 107.813 mph/173.508 km/h; **2** Frédéric Vervisch, B (Lola B06/30-Opel), 25m 13.007s; **3** Matteo Chinosi, I (Dallara F306-Mugen Honda), 25m 19.565s; **4** Nico Verdonck, B (Lola B06/30-Opel), 25m 19.667s; **5** Récardo Bruins, ROK/NL (Dallara F306-Opel), 25m 23.034s; **6** Michael Klein, D (Dallara F304-Opel), 25m 28.357s; **7** Dominick Muermans, NL (Dallara F306-Opel), 25m 29.571s; **8** Marcel Schuler, D (Dallara F304-Opel), 25m 36.498s; **9** Simon Solgat, D (Dallara F304-Opel), 25m 45.782s; **10** Jonathan Hirschi, CH (Dallara F306-Opel), 25m 53.092s.
**Fastest race lap:** Van Dam, 1m 14.976s, 108.750 mph/175.016 km/h.
**Fastest qualifying lap:** Vietoris, 1m 14.346s, 109.671 mph/176.499 km/h.

**ATS FORMEL-3-CUP, Motorsport Arena Oschersleben, Germany, 29/30 September. 11 and 18 laps of the 2.297-mile/3.696-km circuit.**
**Round 17 (25.262 miles/40.656 km).**
**1** Frédéric Vervisch, B (Lola B06/30-Opel), 19m 37.095s, 77.262 mph/124.341 km/h; **2** Nico Verdonck, B (Lola B06/30-Opel), 19m 50.189s; **3** Carlo van Dam, NL (Dallara F306-Opel), 20m 4.441s; **4** Matteo Chinosi, I (Dallara F306-Mugen Honda), 20m 10.954s; **5** Simon Solgat, D (Dallara F304-Opel), 20m 55.801s; **6** Marcel Schuler, D (Dallara F304-Opel), 21m 4.213s; **7** Jonathan Hirschi, CH (Dallara F306-Opel), 21m 13.146s; **8** Dominick Muermans, NL (Dallara F306-Opel), 21m 24.091s; **9** Falk Künster, D (Dallara F304-Opel), 10 laps; **10** Michael Klein, D (Dallara F304-Opel), 10.
**Fastest race lap:** Vervisch, 1m 45.489s, 78.375 mph/126.132 km/h.
**Fastest qualifying lap:** van Dam, 1m 45.358s, 78.473 mph/126.289 km/h.

**Round 18 (41.339 miles/66.528 km).**
**1** Carlo van Dam, NL (Dallara F306-Opel), 25m 31.713s, 97.158 mph/156.361 km/h; **2** Matteo Chinosi, I (Dallara F306-Mugen Honda), 25m 39.950s; **3** Frédéric Vervisch, B (Lola B06/30-Opel), 25m 42.088s; **4** Récardo Bruins, ROK/NL (Dallara F306-Opel), 25m 42.797s; **5** Nico Verdonck, B (Lola B06/30-Opel), 25m 53.089s; **6** Federico Glorioso, I (Dallara F306-Mugen Honda), 26m 07.749s; **7** Simon Solgat, D. (Dallara F304-Opel), 26m 24.721s; **8** Dominick Muermans, NL (Dallara F306-Opel), 26m 24.936s; **9** Jonathan Hirschi, CH (Dallara F306-Opel), 26m 26.571s; **10** Norman Knop, D (Dallara F306-Opel), 26m 34.218s.
**Fastest race lap:** Van Dam, 1m 24.143s, 98.258 mph/158.130 km/h.
**Fastest qualifying lap:** Vervisch, 1m 46.657s, 77.517 mph/124.751 km/h.

**Final championship points**
**Formel-3-Cup**
**1** Carlo van Dam, NL, 159; **2** Frédéric Vervisch, B, 127; **3** Nico Verdonck, B, 98; **4** Récardo Bruins, ROK/NL, 95; **5** Christian Vietoris, D, 81; **6** Matteo Chinosi, I, 77; **7** Michael Klein, D, 29; **8** Max Nilsson, S, 15; **9** Marcel Schuler, D, 13; **10** Dominick Muermans, NL, 12; **11** Simon Solgat, D, 10; **12** Federico Glorioso, I, 9; **13** Marcello Thomaz, BR, 6; **14** Patrick Cicchiello, CH, 3; **15** Jonathan Hirschi, CH, 3; **16** Ross Zwolsman, NL, 1.

**Rookie Cup**
**1** Carlo van Dam, NL, 150; **2** Frederic Vervisch, B, 124; **3** Nico Verdonck, B, 107; **4** Matteo Chinosi, I, 93; **5** Christian Vietoris, D, 86; **6** Michael Klein, D, 52; **7** Simon Solgat, D, 43; **8** Jonathan Hirschi, CH, 13; **9** Leonardo Valois, SK, 9; **10** Massimo Rossi, I, 8.

**Formel-3-Trophy**
**1** Michael Klein, D, 141; **2** Marcel Schuler, D, 130; **3** Simon Solgat, D, 120; **4** Luca Iannaccone, I, 57; **5** Marika Diana, I, 53.

## Italian Formula 3 Championship

**ITALIAN FORMULA 3 CHAMPIONSHIP, Autodromo Adria International Raceway, Adria, Italy, 1 April. Round 1. 19 and 20 laps of the 1.679-mile/2.702-km circuit.**
**Race 1 (31.900 miles/51.338 km).**
**1** Paolo Nocera, I (Dallara F304-Opel), 23m 59.383s, 79.784 mph/128.400 km/h; **2** Efisio Marchese, I (Dallara F303-Opel), 23m 59.768s; **3** Mirko Bortolotti, I (Dallara F304-Opel), 24m 8.574s; **4** Giuseppe Termine, I (Dallara F302-Mugen Honda), 24m 10.209s; **5** Nicola de Marco, I (Dallara F304-Opel), 24m 16.798s; **6** Paolo Bossini, I (Dallara F302-Mugen Honda), 24m 28.785s; **7** Augusto Scalbi, RA (Dallara F304-Opel), 24m 31.003s; **8** Jacopo Faccioni, I (Dallara F304-Opel), 24m 33.650s; **9** Mauro Brozzi, I (Dallara F394-FIAT), 24m 52.411s; **10** Matteo Cozzari, I (Dallara F302-Opel), 24m 52.709s.
**Disqualified:** Failed to observe stop & go penalty after jumping the start - Pablo Sánchez, MEX (Dallara F304-Opel), finished 5th in 24m 14.897s.
**Fastest race lap:** Marchese, 1m 11.736s, 84.256 mph/135.597 km/h.
**Fastest qualifying lap:** Nocera, 1m 11.256s, 84.824 mph/136.510 km/h.

**Race 2 (33.579 miles/54.040 km).**
**1** Paolo Nocera, I (Dallara F304-Opel), 25m 40.982s, 78.446 mph/126.246 km/h; **2** Efisio Marchese, I (Dallara F303-Opel), 25m 41.275s; **3** Fabrizio Crestani, I (Dallara F304-Opel), 25m 41.541s; **4** Pablo Sánchez, MEX (Dallara F304-Opel), 25m 41.879s; **5** Mirko Bortolotti, I (Dallara F304-Opel), 25m 42.322s; **6** Giuseppe Termine, I (Dallara F302-Mugen Honda), 25m 42.839s; **7** Nicola de Marco, I (Dallara F304-Opel), 25m 43.425s; **8** Augusto Scalbi, RA (Dallara F304-Opel), 25m 43.627s; **9** Jacopo Faccioni, I (Dallara F304-Opel), 25m 46.229s; **10** Paolo Bossini, I (Dallara F302-Mugen Honda), 25m 46.886s.
**Fastest race lap:** Marchese, 1m 11.918s, 84.043 mph/135.254 km/h.
**Fastest qualifying lap:** Nocera, 1m 11.397s, 84.656 mph/136.241 km/h.

**ITALIAN FORMULA 3 CHAMPIONSHIP, Autodromo Internazionale di Misano, Misano Adriatico, Rimini, Italy, 5/6 May. Round 2. 2 x 16 laps of the 2.597-mile/4.180-km circuit.**
**Race 1 (41.557 miles/66.880 km).**
**1** Paolo Nocera, I (Dallara F304-Opel), 25m 15.183s, 98.738 mph/158.903 km/h; **2** Pablo Sánchez, MEX (Dallara F304-Opel), 25m 16.632s; **3** Fabrizio Crestani, I (Dallara F304-Opel), 25m 19.448s; **4** Giuseppe Termine, I (Dallara F302-Mugen Honda), 25m 27.184s; **5** Mirko Bortolotti, I (Dallara F304-Opel), 25m 27.918s; **6** Efisio Marchese, I (Dallara F303-Opel), 25m 30.832s; **7** Paolo Bossini, I (Dallara F302-Mugen Honda), 25m 44.379s; **8** Nicola de Marco, I (Dallara F304-Opel), 25m 48.915s; **9** Augusto Scalbi, RA (Dallara F304-Opel), 25m 52.800s; **10** Marco Cencetti, I (Dallara 398-FIAT), 26m 12.065s.
**Fastest race lap:** Crestani, 1m 32.924s, 100.624 mph/161.938 km/h.
**Fastest qualifying lap:** Crestani, 1m 31.392s, 102.311 mph/164.653 km/h.

**Race 2 (41.557 miles/66.880 km).**
**1** Pablo Sánchez, MEX (Dallara F304-Opel), 24m 58.061s, 99.867 mph/160.719 km/h; **2** Fabrizio Crestani, I (Dallara F304-Opel), 24m 58.336s; **3** Nicola de Marco, I (Dallara F304-Opel), 25m 6.302s; **4** Mirko Bortolotti, I (Dallara F304-Opel), 25m 6.648s; **5** Efisio Marchese, I (Dallara F303-Opel), 25m 7.260s; **6** Giuseppe Termine, I (Dallara F302-Mugen Honda), 25m 8.009s; **7** Paolo Bossini, I (Dallara F302-Mugen Honda), 25m 29.278s; **8** Augusto Scalbi, RA (Dallara F304-Opel), 25m 30.523s; **9** Jacopo Faccioni, I (Dallara F304-Opel), 26m 21.653s; **10** Massimo Ballestri, I (Dallara F300-FIAT), 15 laps.
**Fastest race lap:** Sánchez, 1m 32.196s, 101.419 mph/163.217 km/h.
**Fastest qualifying lap:** Crestani, 1m 31.451s, 102.245 mph/164.547 km/h.

**ITALIAN FORMULA 3 CHAMPIONSHIP, Autodromo Mario Umberto Borzacchini, Magione, Perugia, Italy, 20 May. Round 3. 20 and 22 laps of the 1.558-mile/2.507-km circuit.**
**Race 1 (31.156 miles/50.140 km).**
**1** Efisio Marchese, I (Dallara F303-Opel), 24m 33.070s, 76.140 mph/122.535 km/h; **2** Mirko Bortolotti, I (Dallara F304-Opel), 24m 34.469s; **3** Nicola de Marco, I (Dallara F304-Opel), 24m 35.681s; **4** Fabrizio Crestani, I (Dallara F304-Opel), 24m 37.202s; **5** Paolo Nocera, I (Dallara F304-Opel), 24m 37.455s; **6** Paolo Bossini, I (Dallara F302-Mugen Honda), 24m 44.626s; **7** Augusto Scalbi, RA (Dallara F304-Opel), 24m 46.667s; **8** Mauro Brozzi, I (Dallara F301-Opel), 24m 52.603s; **9** Jacopo Faccioni, I (Dallara F304-Opel), 24m 55.121s; **10** Matteo Cozzari, I (Dallara F302-Opel), 24m 55.373s.
**Fastest race lap:** Marchese, 1m 08.087s, 82.365 mph/132.553 km/h.
**Fastest qualifying lap:** Marchese, 1m 07.154s, 83.510 mph/134.395 km/h.

**Race 2 (34.271 miles/55.154 km).**
**1** Efisio Marchese, I (Dallara F303-Opel), 25m 07.794s, 81.825 mph/131.685 km/h; **2** Mirko Bortolotti, I (Dallara F304-Opel), 25m 9.852s; **3** Nicola de Marco, I (Dallara F304-Opel), 25m 13.942s; **4** Paolo Nocera, I (Dallara F304-Opel), 25m 25.776s; **5** Augusto Scalbi, RA (Dallara F304-Opel), 25m 26.645s; **6** Giuseppe Termine, I (Dallara F302-Mugen Honda), 25m 32.582s; **7** Paolo Bossini, I (Dallara F302-Mugen Honda), 25m 37.259s; **8** Fabrizio Crestani, I (Dallara F304-Opel), 25m 37.589s; **9** Jacopo Faccioni, I (Dallara F304-Opel), 25m 48.766s; **10** Matteo Cozzari, I (Dallara F302-Opel), 26m 2.742s.
**Fastest race lap:** Marchese, 1m 7.916s, 82.573 mph/132.887 km/h.
**Pole position:** Marchese.

**ITALIAN FORMULA 3 CHAMPIONSHIP, Autodromo Internazionale del Mugello, Scarperia, Firenze (Florence), Italy, 30 June/1 July. Round 4. 2 x 14 laps of the 3.259-mile/5.245-km circuit.**
**Race 1 (45.627 miles/73.430 km).**
**1** Fabrizio Crestani, I (Dallara F304-Opel), 25m 18.522s, 108.170 mph/174.082 km/h; **2** Mirko Bortolotti, I (Dallara F304-Opel), 25m 20.071s; **3** Pablo Sánchez, MEX (Dallara F304-Opel), 25m 22.016s; **4** Nicola de Marco, I (Dallara F304-Opel), 25m 22.464s; **5** Efisio Marchese, I (Dallara F303-Opel), 25m 42.245s; **6** Paolo Bossini, I (Dallara F302-Mugen Honda), 25m 48.641s; **7** Matteo Cozzari, I (Dallara F302-Opel), 25m 48.911s; **8** Augusto Scalbi, RA (Dallara F304-Opel), 26m 0.275s; **9** Jacopo Faccioni, I (Dallara F304-Opel), 26m 14.702s; **10** Luciano Baldazzi, I (Dallara F302-Opel), 26m 53.343s.
**Fastest race lap:** Bortoletti, 1m 47.061s, 109.589 mph/176.366 km/h.
**Fastest qualifying lap:** Sánchez, 1m 44.659s, 112.104 mph/180.414 km/h.

**Race 2 (45.627 miles/73.430 km).**
**1** Fabrizio Crestani, I (Dallara F304-Opel), 25m 30.404s, 107.330 mph/172.730 km/h; **2** Mirko Bortolotti, I (Dallara F304-Opel), 25m 38.469s; **3** Nicola de Marco, I (Dallara F304-Opel), 25m 40.845s; **4** Paolo Nocera, I (Dallara F304-Opel), 25m 47.539s; **5** Giuseppe Termine, I (Dallara F302-Mugen Honda), 25m 48.306s; **6** Pablo Sánchez, MEX (Dallara F304-Opel), 25m 52.191s; **7** Paolo Bossini, I (Dallara F302-Mugen Honda), 25m 56.751s; **8** Efisio Marchese, I (Dallara F303-Opel), 25m 57.592s; **9** Augusto Scalbi, RA (Dallara F304-Opel), 26m 1.433s; **10** Matteo Cozzari, I (Dallara F302-Opel), 26m 06.821s.
**Fastest race lap:** Sánchez, 1m 47.905s, 108.732 mph/174.987 km/h.
**Fastest qualifying lap:** Sánchez, 1m 44.719s, 112.040 mph/180.311 km/h.

**ITALIAN FORMULA 3 CHAMPIONSHIP, Autodromo Internazionale del Mugello, Scarperia, Firenze (Florence), Italy, 22 July. Round 5. 2 x 14 laps of the 3.259-mile/5.245-km circuit.**
**Race 1 (45.627 miles/73.430 km).**
**1** Mirko Bortolotti, I (Dallara F304-Opel), 25m 4.897s, 109.149 mph/175.658 km/h; **2** Pablo Sánchez, MEX (Dallara F304-Opel), 25m 6.003s; **3** Nicola de Marco, I (Dallara F304-Opel), 25m 10.852s; **4** Efisio Marchese, I (Dallara F303-Opel), 25m 11.187s; **5** Augusto Scalbi, RA (Dallara F304-Opel), 25m 17.169s; **6** Giuseppe Termine, I (Dallara F302-Mugen Honda), 25m 23.802s; **7** Paolo Bossini, I (Dallara F302-Mugen Honda), 25m 26.902s; **8** Matteo Cozzari, I (Dallara F302-Opel), 25m 27.239s; **9** Marco Cencetti, I (Dallara 398-FIAT), 25m 43.359s; **10** Jacopo Faccioni, I (Dallara F304-Opel), 26m 07.150s.
**Fastest race lap:** Nocera, 1m 45.974s, 110.713 mph/178.175 km/h.
**Fastest qualifying lap:** Bortolotti, 1m 45.679s, 111.022 mph/178.673 km/h.

**Race 2 (45.627 miles/73.430 km).**
**1** Pablo Sánchez, MEX (Dallara F304-Opel), 25m 14.153s, 108.482 mph/174.584 km/h; **2** Paolo Nocera, I (Dallara F304-Opel), 25m 16.010s; **3** Nicola de Marco, I (Dallara F304-Opel), 25m 17.178s; **4** Efisio Marchese, I (Dallara F303-Opel), 25m 22.911s; **5** Augusto Scalbi, RA (Dallara F304-Opel), 25m 25.584s; **6** Paolo Bossini, I (Dallara F302-Mugen Honda), 25m 30.980s; **7** Matteo Cozzari, I (Dallara F302-Opel), 25m 32.408s; **8** Mirko Bortolotti, I (Dallara F304-Opel), 25m 41.574s; **9** Jacopo Faccioni, I (Dallara F304-Opel), 26m 12.166s; **10** Giuseppe Termine, I (Dallara F302-Mugen Honda), 3 laps (DNF).
**Fastest race lap:** De Marco, 1m 47.140s, 109.508 mph/176.236 km/h.
**Fastest qualifying lap:** Bortolotti, 1m 46.061s, 110.622 mph/178.029 km/h.

**ITALIAN FORMULA 3 CHAMPIONSHIP, Autodromo Riccardo Paletti, Varano dei Melegari, Parma, Italy, 2 September. Round 6. 2 x 23 laps of the 1.476-mile/2.375-km circuit.**
**Race 1 (33.942 miles/54.625 km).**
**1** Efisio Marchese, I (Dallara F303-Opel), 24m 43.029s, 82.394 mph/132.600 km/h; **2** Paolo Nocera, I (Dallara F304-Opel), 24m 47.846s; **3** Pablo Sánchez, MEX (Dallara F304-Opel), 24m 48.223s; **4** Nicola de Marco, I (Dallara F304-Opel), 24m 57.278s; **5** Giuseppe Termine, I (Dallara F302-Mugen Honda), 25m 5.916s; **6** Paolo Bossini, I (Dallara F302-Mugen Honda), 25m 9.308s; **7** Augusto Scalbi, RA (Dallara F304-Opel), 25m 10.365s; **8** Jacopo Faccioni, I (Dallara F304-Opel), 25m 17.929s; **9** Marco Cencetti, I (Dallara 398-FIAT), 25m 25.834s; **10** Mirko Bortolotti, I (Dallara F304-Opel), 25m 26.179s.
**Fastest race lap:** Marchese, 1m 3.674s, 83.436 mph/134.277 km/h.
**Fastest qualifying lap:** Marchese, 1m 3.377s, 83.827 mph/134.906 km/h.

**Race 2 (33.942 miles/54.625 km).**
**1** Pablo Sánchez, MEX (Dallara F304-Opel), 24m 43.499s, 82.368 mph/132.558 km/h; **2** Paolo Nocera, I (Dallara F304-Opel), 24m 45.942s; **3** Efisio Marchese, I (Dallara F304-Opel), 24m 55.202s; **4** Nicola de Marco, I (Dallara F304-Opel), 24m 56.531s; **5** Fabrizio Crestani, I (Dallara F304-Opel), 24m 59.676s; **6** Giuseppe Termine, I (Dallara F304-Mugen Honda), 25m 10.418s; **7** Augusto Scalbi, RA (Dallara F304-Opel), 25m 12.741s; **8** Paolo Bossini, I (Dallara F304-Mugen Honda), 25m 19.012s; **9** Jacopo Faccioni, I (Dallara F304-Opel), 25m 29.240s; **10** Mirko Bortolotti, I (Dallara F304-Opel), 20 laps.
**Fastest race lap:** Sánchez, 1m 3.978s, 83.040 mph/133.639 km/h.
**Fastest qualifying lap:** Sánchez, 1m 3.448s, 83.734 mph/134.756 km/h.

**ITALIAN FORMULA 3 CHAMPIONSHIP, Autodromo di Vallelunga, Campagnano di Roma, Italy, 15/16 September. Round 7. 2 x 16 laps of the 2.538-mile/4.085-km circuit.**
**Race 1 (40.613 miles/65.360 km).**
**1** Paolo Nocera, I (Dallara F304-Opel), 24m 57.564s, 97.629 mph/157.119 km/h; **2** Giuseppe Termine, I (Dallara F304-Mugen Honda), 25m 4.645s; **3** Mirko Bortolotti, I (Dallara F304-Opel), 25m 5.071s; **4** Nicola de Marco, I (Dallara F304-Opel), 25m 14.503s; **5** Jacopo Faccioni, I (Dallara F304-Opel), 25m 16.907s; **6** Paolo Bossini, I (Dallara F304-Mugen Honda), 25m 18.331s; **7** Efisio Marchese, I (Dallara F304-Opel), 25m 21.261s; **8** Federico Delrosso, I (Dallara F398-Opel), 26m 8.838s; **9** Luigi Folloni, I (Dallara F300-FIAT), 26m 32.483s; **10** Fabrizio Crestani, I (Dallara F304-Opel), 6 laps (DNF).
**Fastest race lap:** Nocera, 1m 32.628s, 98.651 mph/158.764 km/h.
**Fastest qualifying lap:** Nocera, 1m 30.913s, 100.512 mph/161.759 km/h.

**Race 2 (40.613 miles/65.360 km).**
**1** Fabrizio Crestani, I (Dallara F304-Opel), 24m 55.687s, 97.752 mph/157.316 km/h; **2** Paolo Nocera, I (Dallara F304-Opel), 24m 58.830s; **3** Pablo Sánchez, MEX (Dallara F304-Opel), 25m 0.467s; **4** Augusto Scalbi, RA (Dallara F304-Opel), 25m 7.515s; **5** Mirko Bortolotti, I (Dallara F304-Opel), 25m 7.806s; **6** Efisio Marchese, I (Dallara F304-Opel), 25m 11.122s; **7** Giuseppe Termine, I (Dallara F304-Mugen Honda), 25m 22.893s; **8** Jacopo Faccioni, I (Dallara F304-Opel), 25m 23.164s; **9** Paolo Bossini, I (Dallara F304-Mugen Honda), 25m 44.998s; **10** Federico del Rosso, I (Dallara F398-Opel), 26m 6.961s.
**Fastest race lap:** Crestani, 1m 32.648s, 98.630 mph/158.729 km/h.
**Fastest qualifying lap:** De Marco, 1m 31.077s, 100.331 mph/161.467 km/h.

**ITALIAN FORMULA 3 CHAMPIONSHIP, Autodromo Nazionale di Monza, Milan, Italy, 21 October. Round 8. 2 x 14 laps of the 3.600-mile/5.793-km circuit.**
**Race 1 (50.394 miles/81.102 km).**
**1** Paolo Nocera, I (Dallara F304-Opel), 25m 30.484s, 118.538 mph/190.767 km/h; **2** Fabrizio Crestani, I (Dallara F304-Opel), 25m 35.120s; **3** Pablo Sánchez, MEX (Dallara F304-Opel), 25m 44.194s; **4** Augusto Scalbi, RA (Dallara F304-Opel), 25m 49.098s; **5** Giuseppe Termine, I (Dallara F302-Mugen Honda), 25m 54.476s; **6** Paolo Bossini, I (Dallara F302-Mugen Honda), 26m 3.656s; **7** Matteo Cozzari, I (Dallara F302-Opel), 26m 5.538s; **8** Nicola de Marco, I (Dallara F304-Opel), 27m 2.544s; **9** Luciano Baldazzi, I (Dallara F302-Opel), 13 laps; **10** Salvatore Cardullo, I (Dallara F394-Opel), 13.
**Fastest race lap:** Crestani, 1m 48.074s, 119.905 mph/192.967 km/h.
**Fastest qualifying lap:** Nocera, 1m 46.843s, 121.286 mph/195.191 km/h.

**Race 2 (50.394 miles/81.102 km).**
**1** Paolo Nocera, I (Dallara F304-Opel), 25m 33.858s, 118.277 mph/190.348 km/h; **2** Augusto Scalbi, RA (Dallara F304-Opel), 25m 41.696s; **3** Efisio Marchese, I (Dallara F303-Opel), 25m 45.308s; **4** Giuseppe Termine, I (Dallara F302-Mugen Honda), 25m 51.031s; **5** Mirko Bortolotti, I (Dallara F304-Opel), 26m 2.023s; **6** Paolo Bossini, I (Dallara F302-Mugen Honda), 26m 3.594s; **7** Pablo Sánchez, MEX (Dallara F304-Opel), 9 laps; **8** Fabrizio Crestani, I (Dallara F304-Opel), 5; **9** Nicola de Marco, I (Dallara F304-Opel), 1; **10** Sergey Mokshantsev, RUS, 0.
**Fastest race lap:** Nocera, 1m 48.243s, 119.718 mph/192.667 km/h.
**Fastest qualifying lap:** Nocera, 1m 47.333s, 120.732 mph/194.299 km/h.

**Final championship points**
**1** Paolo Nocera, I, 114; **2** Efisio Marchese, I, 93; **3** Pablo Sánchez, MEX, 84; **4** Mirko Bortolotti, I, 81; **5** Fabrizio Crestani, I, 73; **6** Nicola de Marco, I, 67; **7** Giuseppe Termine, I, 52; **8** Augusto Scalbi, RA, 42; **9** Paolo Bossini, I, 35; **10** Jacopo Faccioni, I, 11.

## All-Japan Formula 3 Championship

**ALL-JAPAN FORMULA 3 CHAMPIONSHIP, Fuji International Speedway, Sunto-gun, Shizuoka Prefecture, Japan, 31 March/1 April. 15 and 21 laps of the 2.835-mile/4.563-km circuit.**
**Round 1 (42.530 miles/68.445 km).**
**1** Oliver Jarvis, GB (Dallara F306-Toyota), 24m 30.497s, 104.119 mph/167.563 km/h; **2** Hiroaki Ishiura, J (Dallara F307-Toyota), 24m 34.470s; **3** Kazuya Oshima, J (Dallara F306-Toyota), 24m 35.592s; **4** Roberto Streit, BR (Dallara F306-Toyota), 24m 40.960s; **5** Yuhi Sekiguchi, J (Dallara F305-Toyota), 24m 43.359s; **6** Marko Asmer, EE (Dallara F307-Nissan), 24m 44.299s; **7** Koudai Tsukakoshi, J (Dallara F307-Mugen Honda), 24m 46.901s; **8** Hironobu Yasuda, J (Dallara F306-Nissan), 24m 51.760s; **9** Kouki Saga, J (Dallara F306-Toyota), 24m 56.759s; **10** Motoaki Ishikawa, J (Dallara F306-Toyota), 14 laps.
**Fastest race lap:** Jarvis, 1m 36.599s, 105.665 mph/170.051 km/h.
**Fastest qualifying lap:** Oshima, 1m 35.212s, 107.204 mph/172.528 km/h.

**Round 2 (59.542 miles/95.823 km).**
**1** Kazuya Oshima, J (Dallara F306-Toyota), 34m 24.467s, 103.828 mph/167.095 km/h; **2** Roberto Streit, BR (Dallara F306-Toyota), 34m 29.377s; **3** Oliver Jarvis, GB (Dallara F306-Toyota), 34m 32.722s; **4** Hiroaki Ishiura, J (Dallara F307-Toyota), 34m 35.185s; **5** Koudai Tsukakoshi, J (Dallara F307-Mugen Honda), 34m 43.329s; **6** Marko Asmer, EE (Dallara F307-Nissan), 34m 44.208s; **7** Hironobu Yasuda, J (Dallara F306-Nissan), 34m 54.193s; **8** Takuya Izawa, J (Dallara F307-Mugen Honda), 34m 57.200s; **9** Yuhi Sekiguchi, J (Dallara F305-Toyota), 34m 58.882s; **10** Kouki Saga, J (Dallara F306-Toyota), 35m 13.497s.
**Fastest race lap:** Oshima, 1m 37.872s, 104.291 mph/167.839 km/h.
**Fastest qualifying lap:** Oshima, 1m 35.173s, 107.248 mph/172.599 km/h.

**ALL-JAPAN FORMULA 3 CHAMPIONSHIP, Suzuka International Racing Course, Suzuka-shi, Mie Prefecture, Japan, 14/15 April. 12 and 17 laps of the 3.608-mile/5.807-km circuit.**
**Round 3 (43.300 miles/69.684 km).**
**1** Kazuya Oshima, J (Dallara F306-Toyota), 23m 13.714s, 111.844 mph/179.995 km/h; **2** Oliver Jarvis, GB (Dallara F306-Toyota), 23m 18.394s; **3** Roberto Streit, BR (Dallara F306-Toyota), 23m 21.098s; **4** Hiroaki Ishiura, J (Dallara F307-Toyota), 23m 22.672s; **5** Koudai Tsukakoshi, J (Dallara F307-Mugen Honda), 23m 30.555s; **6** Yuhi Sekiguchi, J (Dallara F305-Toyota), 23m 36.184s; **7** Takuya Izawa, J (Dallara F307-Mugen Honda), 23m 37.393s; **8** Kouki Saga, J (Dallara F306-Toyota), 23m 42.969s; **9** Marko Asmer, EE (Dallara F307-Nissan), 24m 03.110s; **10** Yuki Nakayama, J (Dallara F307-Mugen Honda), 24m 20.339s.
**Fastest race lap:** Oshima, 1m 55.515s, 112.452 mph/180.973 km/h.
**Fastest qualifying lap:** Oshima, 1m 54.235s, 113.712 mph/183.001 km/h.

**Round 4 (61.341 miles/98.719 km).**
**1** Roberto Streit, BR (Dallara F306-Toyota), 33m 5.266s, 111.234 mph/179.012 km/h; **2** Hiroaki Ishiura, J (Dallara F307-Toyota), 33m 6.982s; **3** Oliver Jarvis, GB (Dallara F306-Toyota), 33m 9.204s; **4** Kazuya Oshima, J (Dallara F306-Toyota), 33m 9.919s; **5** Marko Asmer, EE (Dallara F307-Nissan), 33m 22.957s; **6** Koudai Tsukakoshi, J (Dallara F307-Mugen Honda), 33m 23.880s; **7** Yuhi Sekiguchi, J (Dallara F305-Toyota), 33m 30.212s; **8** Takuya Izawa, J (Dallara F307-Mugen Honda), 33m 35.833s; **9** Hironobu Yasuda, J (Dallara F306-Nissan), 33m 38.653s; **10** Kouki Saga, J (Dallara F306-Toyota), 33m 51.609s.
**Fastest race lap:** Oshima, 1m 55.944s, 112.036 mph/180.304 km/h.
**Fastest qualifying lap:** Streit, 1m 54.187s, 113.760 mph/183.078 km/h.

**ALL-JAPAN FORMULA 3 CHAMPIONSHIP, Twin Ring Motegi, Motegi-machi, Haga-gun, Tochigi Prefecture, Japan, 19/20 May. 14 and 20 laps of the 2.983-mile/4.801-km circuit.**
**Round 5 (41.765 miles/67.214 km).**
**1** Oliver Jarvis, GB (Dallara F306-Toyota), 25m 13.870s, 99.317 mph/159.835 km/h; **2** Roberto Streit, BR (Dallara F306-Toyota), 25m 18.035s; **3** Koudai Tsukakoshi, J (Dallara F307-Mugen Honda), 25m 21.678s; **4** Hiroaki Ishiura, J (Dallara F307-Toyota), 25m 22.973s; **5** Takuya Izawa, J (Dallara F307-Mugen Honda), 25m 26.932s; **6** Kazuya Oshima, J (Dallara F306-Toyota), 25m 27.464s; **7** Yuhi Sekiguchi, J (Dallara F305-Toyota), 25m 35.671s; **8** Ben Clucas, GB (Dallara F307-Nissan), 25m 36.112s; **9** Hironobu Yasuda, J (Dallara F306-Nissan), 25m 37.262s; **10** Yuki Nakayama, J (Dallara F307-Mugen Honda), 25m 43.977s.
**Fastest race lap:** Jarvis, 1m 47.447s, 99.952 mph/160.856 km/h.
**Fastest qualifying lap:** Tsukakoshi, 1m 47.622s, 99.789 mph/160.595 km/h.

**Round 6 (59.664 miles/96.020 km).**
**1** Roberto Streit, BR (Dallara F306-Toyota), 36m 24.945s, 98.305 mph/158.206 km/h; **2** Hiroaki Ishiura, J (Dallara F307-Toyota), 36m 27.885s; **3** Takuya Izawa, J (Dallara F307-Mugen Honda), 36m 31.481s; **4** Koudai Tsukakoshi, J (Dallara F307-Mugen Honda), 36m 34.297s; **5** Oliver Jarvis, GB (Dallara F306-Toyota), 36m 35.284s; **6** Ben Clucas, GB. (Dallara F307-Nissan), 36m 51.940s; **7** Yuhi Sekiguchi, J (Dallara F305-Toyota), 36m 52.859s; **8** Hironobu Yasuda, J (Dallara F306-Nissan), 36m 53.397s; **9** Kazuya Oshima, J (Dallara F306-Toyota), 36m 58.559s; **10** Kouki Saga, J (Dallara F306-Toyota), 37m 12.165s.
**Fastest race lap:** Jarvis, 1m 47.835s, 99.592 mph/160.278 km/h.
**Fastest qualifying lap:** Jarvis, 1m 46.512s, 100.829 mph/162.269 km/h.

**ALL-JAPAN FORMULA 3 CHAMPIONSHIP, Okayama International Circuit (TI Circuit Aida), Aida Gun, Okayama Prefecture, Japan, 9/10 June. 18 and 25 laps of the 2.301-mile/3.703-km circuit.**
**Round 7 (41.417 miles/66.654 km).**
**1** Hiroaki Ishiura, J (Dallara F307-Toyota), 25m 56.643s, 95.784 mph/154.148 km/h; **2** Oliver Jarvis, GB (Dallara F306-Toyota), 26m 01.560s; **3** Koudai Tsukakoshi, J (Dallara F307-Mugen Honda), 26m 6.689s; **4** Roberto Streit, BR (Dallara F306-Toyota), 26m 8.524s; **5** Takuya Izawa, J (Dallara F307-Mugen Honda), 26m 11.844s; **6** Yuhi Sekiguchi, J (Dallara F305-Toyota), 26m 15.725s; **7** Kazuya Oshima, J (Dallara F306-Toyota), 26m 18.051s; **8** Hironobu Yasuda, J (Dallara F306-Nissan), 26m 20.499s; **9** Kouki Saga, J (Dallara F306-Toyota), 26m 31.676s; **10** Yuki Nakayama, J (Dallara F307-Mugen Honda), 26m 32.556s.
**Fastest race lap:** Ishiura, 1m 25.860s, 96.475 mph/155.262 km/h.
**Fastest qualifying lap:** Ishiura, 1m 25.178s, 97.248 mph/156.505 km/h.

**Round 8 (57.523 miles/92.575 km).**
**1** Koudai Tsukakoshi, J (Dallara F307-Mugen Honda), 44m 46.916s, 77.071 mph/124.034 km/h; **2** Kazuya Oshima, J (Dallara F306-Toyota), 44m 54.654s; **3** Roberto Streit, BR (Dallara F306-Toyota), 45m 56.904s; **4** Takuya Izawa, J (Dallara F307-Mugen Honda), 45m 57.324s; **5** Oliver Jarvis, GB (Dallara F306-Toyota), 45m 57.462s; **6** Yuhi Sekiguchi, J (Dallara F305-Toyota), 46m 00.187s; **7** Hiroaki Ishiura, J (Dallara F307-Toyota), 46m 00.751s; **8** Marko Asmer, EE (Dallara F307-Nissan), 46m 13.283s; **9** Kouki Saga, J (Dallara F306-Toyota), 46m 17.587s; **10** Hironobu Yasuda, J (Dallara F306-Nissan), 44 laps.
**Fastest race lap:** Tsukakoshi, 1m 27.896s, 94.241 mph/151.665 km/h.
**Fastest qualifying lap:** Ishiura, 1m 24.879s, 97.590mph/157.056 km/h.

**ALL-JAPAN FORMULA 3 CHAMPIONSHIP, Suzuka International Racing Course, Suzuka City, Mie Prefecture, Japan, 7/8 July. 12 and 17 laps of the 3.608-mile/5.807-km circuit.**
**Round 9 (43.330 miles/69.684 km).**
**1** Roberto Streit, BR (Dallara F306-Toyota), 23m 41.453s, 109.662 mph/176.483 km/h; **2** Kazuya Oshima, J (Dallara F306-Toyota), 23m 41.995s; **3** Koudai Tsukakoshi, J (Dallara F307-Mugen Honda), 23m 44.136s; **4** Oliver Jarvis, GB (Dallara F306-Toyota), 23m 50.434s; **5** Hironobu Yasuda, J (Dallara F306-Nissan), 23m 57.345s; **6** Marko Asmer, EE (Dallara F307-Nissan), 23m 59.492s; **7** Yuhi Sekiguchi, J (Dallara F305-Toyota), 24m 0.736s; **8** Yuki Nakayama, J (Dallara F307-Mugen Honda), 24m 8.474s; **9** Takuya Izawa, J (Dallara F307-Mugen Honda), 24m 9.232s; **10** Hiroaki Ishiura, J (Dallara F307-Toyota), 24m 14.111s.
**Fastest race lap:** Tsukakoshi, 1m 57.763s, 110.305 mph/177.519 km/h.
**Fastest qualifying lap:** Streit, 2m 7.623s, 101.783 mph/163.804 km/h.

**Round 10 (61.341 miles/98.719 km).**
**1** Koudai Tsukakoshi, J (Dallara F307-Mugen Honda), 33m 50.129s, 108.775 mph/175.057 km/h; **2** Oliver Jarvis, GB (Dallara F306-Toyota), 33m 52.035s; **3** Kazuya Oshima, J (Dallara F306-Toyota), 33m 52.614s; **4** Roberto Streit, BR (Dallara F306-Toyota), 34m 3.670s; **5** Yuhi Sekiguchi, J (Dallara F305-Toyota), 34m 9.949s; **6** Takuya Izawa, J (Dallara F307-Mugen Honda), 34m 10.473s; **7** Hironobu Yasuda, J (Dallara F306-Nissan), 34m 11.254s; **8** Hiroaki Ishiura, J (Dallara F307-Toyota), 34m 11.760s; **9** Yuki Nakayama, J (Dallara F307-Mugen Honda), 34m 28.068s; **10** Kouki Saga, J (Dallara F306-Toyota), 34m 34.709s.
**Fastest race lap:** Oshima, 1m 58.615s, 109.513 mph/176.244 km/h.
**Fastest qualifying lap:** Tsukakoshi, 2m 0.921s, 107.425 mph/172.883 km/h.

**ALL-JAPAN FORMULA 3 CHAMPIONSHIP, Autopolis International Racing Course, Kamit-sue-mura, Hita-gun, Oita Prefecture, Japan, 4/5 August. 14, 20 and 20 laps of the 2.904-mile/4.674-km circuit.**
**Round 11 (40.660 miles/65.436 km).**
**1** Roberto Streit, BR (Dallara F306-Toyota), 24m 41.820s, 98.781 mph/158.973 km/h; **2** Oliver Jarvis, GB (Dallara F306-Toyota), 24m 43.551s; **3** Kazuya Oshima, J (Dallara F306-Toyota), 24m 45.043s; **4** Takuya Izawa, J (Dallara F307-Mugen Honda), 24m 58.368s; **5** Koudai Tsukakoshi, J (Dallara F307-Mugen Honda), 24m 59.515s; **6** Hiroaki Ishiura, J (Dallara F307-Toyota), 25m 0.709s; **7** Yuhi Sekiguchi, J (Dallara F305-Toyota), 25m 3.668s; **8** Hironobu Yasuda, J (Dallara F306-Nissan), 25m 5.316s; **9** Yuki Nakayama, J (Dallara F307-Mugen Honda), 25m 8.558s; **10** Kouki Saga, J (Dallara F306-Toyota), 25m 16.408s.
**Fastest race lap:** Oshima, 1m 45.009s, 99.567 mph/160.237 km/h.
**Fastest qualifying lap:** Streit, 1m 43.955s, 100.577 mph/161.862 km/h.

**Round 12 (58.086 miles/93.480 km).**
**1** Roberto Streit, BR (Dallara F306-Toyota), 35m 24.422s, 98.431 mph/158.409 km/h; **2** Kazuya Oshima, J (Dallara F306-Toyota), 35m 25.928s; **3** Oliver Jarvis, GB (Dallara F306-Toyota), 35m 26.920s; **4** Takuya Izawa, J (Dallara F307-Mugen Honda), 35m 36.819s; **5** Koudai Tsukakoshi, J (Dallara F307-Mugen Honda), 35m 37.890s; **6** Yuhi Sekiguchi, J (Dallara F305-Toyota), 35m 42.860s; **7** Hironobu Yasuda, J (Dallara F306-Nissan), 35m 47.674s; **8** Yuki Nakayama, J (Dallara F307-Mugen Honda), 35m 54.475s; **9** Taku Bamba, J (Dallara F307-Nissan), 36m 3.188s; **10** Kouki Saga, J (Dallara F306-Toyota), 36m 29.589s.
**Fastest race lap:** Ishiura, 1m 44.319s, 100.226 mph/161.297 km/h.
**Fastest qualifying lap:** Oshima, 1m 43.131s, 101.380 mph/163.155 km/h.

**Round 13 (58.086 miles/93.480 km).**
**1** Kazuya Oshima, J (Dallara F306-Toyota), 35m 28.427s, 98.246 mph/158.111 km/h; **2** Oliver Jarvis, GB (Dallara F306-Toyota), 35m 29.714s; **3** Takuya Izawa, J (Dallara F307-Mugen Honda), 35m 43.041s; **4** Hiroaki Ishiura, J (Dallara F307-Toyota), 35m 43.952s; **5** Yuhi Sekiguchi, J (Dallara F305-Toyota), 36m 2.555s; **6** Roberto Streit, BR (Dallara F306-Toyota), 36m 3.612s; **7** Yuki Nakayama, J (Dallara F307-Mugen Honda), 36m 9.417s; **8** Kouki Saga, J (Dallara F306-Toyota), 36m 17.557s; **9** Taku Bamba, J (Dallara F307-Nissan), 36m 18.294s; **10** Hironobu Yasuda, J (Dallara F306-Nissan), 36m 30.506s.
**Fastest race lap:** Oshima, 1m 45.472s, 99.130 mph/159.534 km/h.
**Fastest qualifying lap:** Oshima, 1m 43.150s, 101.362 mph/163.125 km/h.

**ALL-JAPAN FORMULA 3 CHAMPIONSHIP, Fuji International Speedway, Sunto-gun, Shizuoka Prefecture, Japan, 25/26 August. 15 and 21 laps of the 2.835-mile/4.563-km circuit.**
**Round 14 (42.530 miles/68.445 km).**
**1** Kazuya Oshima, J (Dallara F306-Toyota), 24m 23.435s, 104.622 mph/168.372 km/h; **2** Koudai Tsukakoshi, J (Dallara F307-Mugen Honda), 24m 33.537s; **3** Oliver Jarvis, GB (Dallara F306-Toyota), 24m 34.380s; **4** Takuya Izawa, J (Dallara F307-Mugen Honda), 24m 41.776s; **5** Roberto Streit, BR (Dallara F306-Toyota), 24m 42.490s; **6** Hiroaki Ishiura, J (Dallara F307-Toyota), 24m 43.068s; **7** Hironobu Yasuda, J (Dallara F306-Nissan), 24m 47.103s; **8** Yuhi Sekiguchi, J (Dallara F305-Toyota), 24m 49.286s; **9** Taku Bamba, J (Dallara F307-Nissan), 24m 58.370s; **10** Kouki Saga, J (Dallara F306-Toyota), 25m 10.268s.
**Fastest race lap:** Oshima, 1m 37.215s, 104.996 mph/168.973 km/h.
**Fastest qualifying lap:** Oshima, 1m 37.582s, 104.601 mph/168.338 km/h.

**Round 15 (59.542 miles/95.823 km).**
**1** Kazuya Oshima, J (Dallara F306-Toyota), 34m 33.494s, 103.376 mph/166.367 km/h; **2** Koudai Tsukakoshi, J (Dallara F307-Mugen Honda), 34m 40.109s; **3** Oliver Jarvis, GB (Dallara F306-Toyota), 34m 43.824s; **4** Roberto Streit, BR (Dallara F306-Toyota), 34m 47.837s; **5** Hiroaki Ishiura, J (Dallara F307-Toyota), 34m 51.486s; **6** Takuya Izawa, J (Dallara F307-Mugen Honda), 45m 55.251s; **7** Hironobu Yasuda, J (Dallara F306-Nissan), 35m 0.606s; **8** Taku Bamba, J (Dallara F307-Nissan), 35m 14.125s; **9** Yuki Nakayama, J (Dallara F307-Mugen Honda), 35m 23.918s; **10** Kouki Saga, J (Dallara F306-Toyota), 36m 18.941s.
**Fastest race lap:** Oshima, 1m 38.198s, 103.944 mph/167.282 km/h.
**Fastest qualifying lap:** Oshima, 1m 37.659s, 104.518 mph/168.205 km/h.

**ALL-JAPAN FORMULA 3 CHAMPIONSHIP, Sendai Hi-land Raceway, Aoba-ku, Sendai-shi, Miyagi Prefecture, Japan, 6/7 October. 17, 24 and 24 laps of the 2.525-mile/4.063-km circuit.**
**Round 16 (42.919 miles/69.071 km).**
**1** Roberto Streit, BR (Dallara F306-Toyota), 28m 05.460s, 91.671 mph/147.529 km/h; **2** Hiroaki Ishiura, J (Dallara F307-Toyota), 28m 7.204s; **3** Oliver Jarvis, GB (Dallara F306-Toyota), 28m 9.838s; **4** Hironobu Yasuda, J (Dallara F306-Nissan), 28m 27.532s; **5** Yuki Nakayama, J (Dallara F307-Mugen Honda), 28m 32.079s; **6** Koudai Tsukakoshi, J (Dallara F307-Mugen Honda), 28m 35.532s; **7** Kouki Saga, J (Dallara F306-Toyota), 28m 51.648s; **8** Motoaki Ishikawa, J (Dallara F306-Toyota), 16 laps; **9** Kazuya Oshima, J (Dallara F306-Toyota), 0 (DNF); **10** Yuhi Sekiguchi, J (Dallara F305-Toyota), 0 (DNF).
**Fastest race lap:** Streit, 1m 38.544s, 92.230 mph/148.429 km/h.
**Fastest qualifying lap:** Streit, 1m 37.466s, 93.250 mph/150.070 km/h.

**Round 17 (60.591 miles/97.512 km).**
**1** Oliver Jarvis, GB (Dallara F306-Toyota), 39m 40.791s, 91.620 mph/147.448 km/h; **2** Hiroaki Ishiura, J (Dallara F307-Toyota), 39m 50.830s; **3** Kazuya Oshima, J (Dallara F306-Toyota), 39m 56.786s; **4** Roberto Streit, BR (Dallara F306-Toyota), 39m 57.887s; **5** Takuya Izawa, J (Dallara F307-Mugen Honda), 40m 4.626s; **6** Yuhi Sekiguchi, J (Dallara F305-Toyota), 40m 12.944s; **7** Yuki Nakayama, J (Dallara F307-Mugen Honda), 40m 25.783s; **8** Koudai Tsukakoshi, J (Dallara F307-Mugen Honda), 40m 26.247s; **9** Kouki Saga, J (Dallara F306-Toyota), 40m 36.335s; **10** Hironobu Yasuda, J (Dallara F306-Nissan), 23 laps.
**Fastest race lap:** Jarvis, 1m 38.573s, 92.202 mph/148.385 km/h.
**Fastest qualifying lap:** Jarvis, 1m 37.475s, 93.241 mph/150.056 km/h.

**Round 18 (60.591 miles/97.512 km).**
**1** Hiroaki Ishiura, J (Dallara F307-Toyota), 39m 33.020s, 91.920 mph/147.930 km/h; **2** Oliver Jarvis, GB (Dallara F306-Toyota), 39m 37.263s; **3** Roberto Streit, BR (Dallara F306-Toyota), 39m 42.685s; **4** Koudai Tsukakoshi, J (Dallara F307-Mugen Honda), 39m 43.440s; **5** Yuhi Sekiguchi, J (Dallara F305-Toyota), 39m 57.623s; **6** Hironobu Yasuda, J (Dallara F306-Nissan), 40m 3.595s; **7** Takuya Izawa, J (Dallara F307-Mugen Honda), 40m 27.273s; **8** Kouki Saga, J (Dallara F306-Toyota), 40m 48.254s; **9** Motoaki Ishikawa, J (Dallara F306-Toyota), 23 laps; **10** Yuki Nakayama, J (Dallara F307-Mugen Honda), 20 (DNF).
**Fastest race lap:** Ishiura, 1m 38.080s, 92.666 mph/149.131 km/h.
**Fastest qualifying lap:** Ishiura, 1m 37.428s, 93.286 mph/150.129 km/h.

**ALL-JAPAN FORMULA 3 CHAMPIONSHIP, Twin Ring Motegi, Motegi-machi, Haga-gun, Tochigi Prefecture, Japan, 20/21 October. 14 and 20 laps of the 2.983-mile/4.801-km circuit.**
**Round 19 (41.765 miles/67.214 km).**
**1** Roberto Streit, BR (Dallara F306-Toyota), 25m 11.043s, 99.503 mph/160.134 km/h; **2** Kazuya Oshima, J (Dallara F306-Toyota), 25m 11.397s; **3** Oliver Jarvis, GB (Dallara F306-Toyota), 25m 12.016s; **4** Hiroaki Ishiura, J (Dallara F307-Toyota), 25m 14.170s; **5** Koudai Tsukakoshi, J (Dallara F307-Mugen Honda), 25m 21.242s; **6** Hironobu Yasuda, J (Dallara F306-Nissan), 25m 22.781s; **7** Yuhi Sekiguchi, J (Dallara F305-Toyota), 25m 34.244s; **8** Kouki Saga, J (Dallara F306-Toyota), 25m 43.652s; **9** Motoaki Ishikawa, J (Dallara F306-Toyota), 26m 26.345s; **10** Takuya Izawa, J (Dallara F307-Mugen Honda), 1 lap (DNF).
**Fastest race lap:** Oshima, 1m 47.122s, 100.255 mph/161.345 km/h.
**Fastest qualifying lap:** Streit, 1m 47.003s, 100.367 mph/161.254 km/h.

**Round 20 (59.664 miles/96.020 km).**
**1** Kazuya Oshima, J (Dallara F306-Toyota), 35m 53.867s, 99.723 mph/160.489 km/h; **2** Yuhi Sekiguchi, J (Dallara F305-Toyota), 36m 3.453s; **3** Hiroaki Ishiura, J (Dallara F307-Toyota), 36m 4.168s; **4** Hironobu Yasuda, J (Dallara F306-Nissan), 36m 11.582s; **5** Roberto Streit, BR (Dallara F306-Toyota), 36m 25.652s; **6** Takuya Izawa, J (Dallara F307-Mugen Honda), 36m 32.382s; **7** Yuki Nakayama, J (Dallara F307-Mugen Honda), 36m 35.790s; **8** Koudai Tsukakoshi, J (Dallara F307-Mugen Honda), 36m 36.198s; **9** Motoaki Ishikawa, J (Dallara F306-Toyota), 37m 35.345s; **10** Kouki Saga, J (Dallara F306-Toyota), 17 laps (DNF).
**Fastest race lap:** Oshima, 1m 46.903s, 100.461 mph/161.675 km/h.
**Fastest qualifying lap:** Oshima, 1m 45.983s, 101.333 mph/163.078 km/h.

**Final championship points (best 16 scores)**
**1** Kazuya Oshima, J, 262; **2** Roberto Streit, BR, 252; **3** Oliver Jarvis, GB, 238; **4** Hiroaki Ishiura, J, 201; **5** Koudai Tsukakoshi, J, 182; **6** Takuya Izawa, J, 120; **7** Yuhi Sekiguchi, J, 101; **8** Hironobu Yasuda, J, 76; **9** Yuki Nakayama, J, 35; **10** Marko Asmer, EE, 31; **11** Kouki Saga, J, 31; **12** Motoaki Ishikawa, J, 10; **13** Ben Clucas, GB, 9; **14** Taku Bamba, J, 9.

## Major Non-Championship Formula 3 2006

The following race was run after AUTOCOURSE 2006–2007 went to press.

**FIA F3 WORLD CUP, 53rd MACAU GP, Circuito Da Guia, Macau, 19 November. 10 and 15 laps of the 3.803-mile/6.120-km circuit, 100.279 miles/161.383 km.**
**Qualification Race (38.028 miles/61.200 km).**
**1** Kamui Kobayashi, J (Dallara F306-Mercedes Benz), 22m 45.199s, 100.279 mph/161.383 km/h; **2** Marko Asmer, EE (Dallara F306-Mercedes Benz), 22m 48.532s; **3** Kohei Hirate, J (Dallara F306-Mercedes Benz), 22m 49.134s; **4** Paul di Resta, GB (Dallara F306-Mercedes Benz), 22m 51.914s; **5** Koudai Tsukokashi, J (Dallara F306-Mercedes Benz), 22m 54.913s; **6** Adrian Sutil, D (Dallara F306-Toyota), 22m 55.527s; **7** Mike Conway, GB (Dallara F306-Mercedes Benz), 22m 56.091s; **8** Kazuki Nakajima, J (Dallara F306-Mercedes Benz), 22m 57.885s; **9** Richard Antinucci, USA (Dallara F306-Mercedes Benz), 23m 0.716s; **10** Charlie Kimball, USA (Dallara F306-Mercedes Benz), 23m 1.149s.
**Fastest race lap:** Conway, 2m 13.457s 102.580 mph/165.087 km/h.
**Fastest qualifying lap:** Kobayashi, 2m 13.449s, 102.586 mph/165.097 km/h.

**Feature Race (57.042 miles/91.800 km).**
**1** Mike Conway, GB (Dallara F306-Mercedes Benz), 39m 35.404s, 86.449 mph/139.125 km/h; **2** Richard Antinucci, USA (Dallara F306-Mercedes Benz), 39m 36.893s; **3** Adrian Sutil, D (Dallara F305-Toyota), 39m 37.459s; **4** Sébastien Buemi, CH (Dallara F305-Mugen Honda), 39m 42.813s; **5** Romain Grosjean, CH (Dallara F305-Mercedes Benz), 39m 44.156s; **6** James Jakes, GB (Dallara F305-Mercedes Benz), 39m 59.367s; **7** Kazuya Oshima, J (Dallara F305-Toyota), 40m 5.352s; **8** Yelmer Buurman, NL (Dallara F305-Mercedes Benz), 40m 11.382s; **9** Maro Engel, D (Dallara F305-Mugen Honda), 40m 11.898s; **10** Fabio Carbone, BR (Dallara F305-Nissan), 40m 12.308s.
**Fastest race lap:** Roberto Streit, BR (Dallara F306-Mercedes Benz), 2m 12.527s, 103.300 mph/166.245 km/h.
**Pole position:** Kobayashi.

## 2007

**ZANDVOORT MASTERS OF FORMULA 3, Circuit Zolder, Heusden-Zolder, Belgium, 5 August. 28 laps of the 2.471-mile/3.977-km circuit, 69.193 miles/111.356 km.**
**1** Nicolas Hülkenberg, D (Dallara F305-Mercedes Benz), 40m 45.974s, 101.839 mph/163.895 km/h; **2** Yann Clairay, F (Dallara F305-Mercedes Benz), 40m 52.664s; **3** Jean-Karl Vernay, F (Dallara F306-Mercedes Benz), 40m 53.359s; **4** Brendon Hartley, NZ (Dallara F305-Mercedes Benz), 40m 53.636s; **5** Edoardo Piscopo, I (Dallara F305-Mercedes Benz), 40m 58.140s; **6** Edoardo Mortara, I (Dallara F305-Mercedes Benz), 40m 58.855s; **7** Yelmer Buurman, NL (Dallara F305-Mercedes Benz), 41m 1.114s; **8** Harald Schlegelmilch, LV (Dallara F306-Mercedes Benz), 41m 1.330s; **9** Renger Van Der Zande, NL (Dallara F306-Mercedes Benz), 41m 5.654s; **10** Marko Asmer, EST (Dallara F307-Mercedes Benz), 41m 07.861s.
**Fastest race lap:** James Jakes, GB (Dallara F305-Mercedes Benz), 1m 25.680s, 103.832 mph/167.101 km/h.
**Fastest qualifying lap:** Romain Grosjean, F (Dallara F305-Mercedes Benz), 1m 23.631s, 106.376 mph/171.195 km/h.

*Result of the Macau race will be given in AUTOCOURSE 2008–2009.*

# FIA GT Championship

## 2006

The following race was run after AUTOCOURSE 2006–2007 went to press.

**FIA GT CHAMPIONSHIP, Dubai Autodrome, United Arab Emirates, 18 November. Round 10. 89 laps of the 3.352-mile/5.394-km circuit, 298.299 miles/480.066 km.**
**1** Andrea Piccini/Jean-Denis Deletraz, I/CH (Aston Martin DBR9), 3h 1m 50.016s, 98.430 mph/158.408 km/h; **2** Mike Hezemans/Anthony Kumpen/Bert Longin, NL/B/B (Chevrolet Corvette C6.R), 3h 2m 39.980s; **3** Jamie Davies/Thomas Biagi/Vincent Vosse, GB/I/B (Maserati MC12 GT1), 3h 3m 3.587s; **4** Fabio Babini/Matteo Malucelli, I/I (Aston Martin DBR9), 3h 3m 38.317s; **5** Karl Wendlinger/Philipp Peter/Jaroslav 'Jarek' Janis, A/A/CZ (Aston Martin DBR9), 88 laps; **6** Fabrizio Gollin/Miguel Ramos, I/P (Aston Martin DBR9), 88; **7** Gabriele Gardel/Steve Zacchia/Frédéric Makowiecki, CH/CH/F (Ferrari 550 Maranello Evo), 86 (1st GT2 class); **8** Tim Mullen/Chris Niarchos, GB/CDN (Ferrari 430 GT2), 85; **9** Jaime Melo Jr/Toni Vilander, BR/FIN (Ferrari 430 GT2), 85; **10** Mika Salo/Rui Aguas, FIN/P (Ferrari 430 GT2), 85.
**Fastest race lap:** Deletraz, 1m 55.621s, 104.359 mph/167.948 km/h.
**Fastest qualifying lap:** Malucelli/Babini, 1m 56.067s, 103.957 mph/167.303 km/h (Gardel/Zacchia/Makowiecki, qualified fastest in 1m 55.987s, but car found to be underweight and sent to back of grid, so placed behind the other GT1 cars on the grid).

**Final championship points**
**GT1 Drivers**
**1=** Andrea Bertolini, I, 71; **1=** Michael Bartels, D, 71; **2=** Jean-Denis Deletraz, CH, 62; **2=** Andrea Piccini, I, 62; **3** Jaroslav 'Jarek' Janis, CZ, 58; **4** Sascha Bert, D, 56; **5=** Thomas Biagi, I, 54; **5=** Jamie Davies, GB, 54; **6** Fabio Babini, I, 51; **7=** Mike Hezemans, NL, 48; **7=** Anthony Kumpen, B, 48; **7=** Bert Longin, B, 48; **8** Fabrizio Gollin, I, 33.5; **9=** Karl Wendlinger, A, 32.5; **9=** Philipp Peter, A, 32.5; **10** Christian Pescatori, I, 29; **11** Andrea Montermini, I, 24; **12** Miguel Ramos, P, 22.5; **13** Eric van de Poele, B, 20; **14=** Stéphane Lemeret, B, 18; **14=** Marcel Fässler, CH, 18; **15** Jos Menten, NL, 14.5.

**GT1 Teams**
**1** Vitaphone Racing Team, 125; **2** Aston Martin Racing BMS, 73.5; **3** Phoenix Racing, 62; **4** Zakspeed Racing, 56; **5** GLPK-Carsport, 48.

**GT1 Manufacturers**
**1** Aston Martin, 173; **2** Maserati, 119; **3** Corvette, 65.

**GT2 Drivers**
**1** Jaime Melo Jr, BR, 79; **2** Matteo Bobbi, I, 71; **3=** Mika Salo, FIN, 61; **3=** Rui Aguas, P, 61; **4** Tim Mullen, GB, 60.5; **5=** Nathan Kinch, GB, 43; **5=** Andrew Kirkaldy, GB, 43; **6=** Tim Sugden, GB, 42; **6=** Iradj Alexander-David, CH, 42; **7** Emmanuel Collard, F, 34; **8** Luca Ricitelli, I, 33; **9** Marino Franchitti, GB, 28; **10=** Horst Felbemayr Jr, A, 25.5; **10=** Christian Ried, D, 25.5.

**GT2 Teams**
**1** AF Corse, 140; **2** Scuderia Ecosse, 10.5; **3** Ebimotors, 59.

**GT2 Manufacturers**
**1** Ferrari, 288; **2** Porsche, 98.5; **3** Spyker, 25.

## 2007

**FIA GT CHAMPIONSHIP, Zhuhai International Circuit, Jin Ding, Zhuhai City, China, 25 March. Round 1. 69 laps of the 2.683-mile/4.318-km circuit, 185.133 miles/297.942 km.**
**1** Christophe Bouchut/Stefan Mücke, F/D (Lamborghini Murcielago), 2h 0m 47.212s, 91.963 mph/148.000 km/h; **2** Philipp Peter/Luke Hines, A/GB (Chevrolet Corvette C6.R), 2h 0m 49.665s; **3** Anthony Kumpen/Bert Longin, B/B (Chevrolet Corvette C5.R), 2h 0m 51.322s; **4** Fabio Babini/Jamie Davies, I/GB (Aston Martin DBR9), 2h 0m 57.442s; **5** Mike Hezemans/Jean-Denis Deletraz, NL/CH (Chevrolet Corvette C6.R), 2h 0m 59.045s; **6** Thomas Biagi*, I (Maserati MC12), 2h 1m 1.194s; **7** Christian Montanari/Miguel Ramos, RSM/P (Maserati MC12), 2h 1m 2.738s; **8** Jonny Kane/Jonathan Cocker, GB/GB (Aston Martin DBR9), 68 Laps; **9** Karl Wendlinger/Ryan Sharp, A/GB (Aston Martin DBR9), 68; **10** Dirk Müller/Toni Vilander, D/FIN (Ferrari 430 GT2), 68 (1st GT2 class).
* Shared car with Michael Bartels, who was disqualified for not driving at least 35 minutes in a session.
**Fastest race lap:** Biagi, 1m 32.581s, 104.331 mph/167.905 km/h.
**Fastest qualifying lap:** Biagi, 1m 31.339s 105.750 mph/170.187 km/h.

**FIA GT CHAMPIONSHIP, Silverstone Grand Prix Circuit, Towcester, Northamptonshire, Great Britain, 6 May. Round 2. 66 laps of the 3.194-mile/5.141-km circuit, 210.835 miles/339.306 km.**
**1** Thomas Biagi/Mika Salo, I/FIN (Maserati MC12), 2h 1m 27.020s, 104.159 mph/167.627 km/h; **2** Mike Hezemans/Jean-Denis Deletraz, NL/CH (Chevrolet Corvette C6.R), 2h 1m 34.485s; **3** Anthony Kumpen/Bert Longin, B/B (Chevrolet Corvette C5.R), 2h 2m 01.279s; **4** Karl Wendlinger/Ryan Sharp, A/GB (Aston Martin DBR9), 2h 2m 11.288s; **5** Andrea Bertolini/Andrea Piccini, I/I (Maserati MC12), 2h 2m 15.730s; **6** Christian Montanari/Miguel Ramos, RSM/P (Maserati MC12), 65 laps; **7** Jamie Davies/Fabio Babini, GB/I (Aston Martin DBR9), 65; **8** Alessandro Pier Guidi/Giambattista Giannoccaro, I/I (Maserati MC12), 65; **9** Marc Basseng/Stefan Mücke, D/D (Lamborghini Murcielago), 65; **10** Jonathan Cocker/Piers Johnson, GB/GB (Aston Martin DBR9), 65.
**Fastest race lap:** Hezemans, 1m 46.253s, 108.233 mph/174.184 km/h.
**Fastest qualifying lap:** Hezemans, 1m 43.504s, 111.108 mph/178.810 km/h.

**FIA GT CHAMPIONSHIP, Bucharest, Romania, 20 May. Round 3. 72 laps of the 1.933-mile/3.111-km circuit, 139.182 miles/223.992 km.**
**1** Andrea Bertolini/Andrea Piccini, I/I (Maserati MC12), 2h 0m 56.811s, 69.046 mph/111.119 km/h; **2** Christophe Bouchut/Stefan Mücke, F/D (Lamborghini Murcielago), 2h 1m 36.524s; **3** Christian Montanari/Miguel Ramos, RSM/P (Maserati MC12), 2h 2m 1.420s; **4** Karl Wendlinger/Ryan Sharp, A/GB (Aston Martin DBR9), 2h 2m 16.406s; **5** Anthony Kumpen/Bert Longin, B/B (Chevrolet Corvette C5.R), 71 laps; **6** Dirk Müller/Toni Vilander, D/FIN (Ferrari 430 GT2), 71 (1st GT2 Class); **7** Fabrizio Gollin/Thomas Biagi, I/I (Maserati MC12), 70; **8** Emmanuel Collard/Matteo Malucelli, F/I (Porsche 997 GT3-RSR), 70; **9** Jamie Davies/Fabio Babini, GB/I (Aston Martin DBR9), 69; **10** Marc Lieb/Horst Felbermayr Jr, D/A (Porsche 996 GT3-RS), 69.
**Fastest race lap:** Alessandro Pier Guidi, I (Maserati MC12), 1m 27.784s, 79.275 mph/127.581 km/h.
**Fastest qualifying lap:** Pier Guidi, 1m 14.214s, 93.771 mph/150.909 km/h.

**FIA GT CHAMPIONSHIP, Autodromo Nazionale di Monza, Milan, Italy, 24 June. Round 4. 66 laps of the 3.600-mile/5.793-km circuit, 237.574 miles/382.338 km.**
**1** Karl Wendlinger/Ryan Sharp, A/GB (Aston Martin DBR9), 2h 0m 19.905s, 118.459 mph/190.641 km/h; **2** Christian Montanari/Miguel Ramos, RSM/P (Maserati MC12), 2h 0m 25.524s; **3** Mike Hezemans/Jean-Denis Deletraz, NL/CH (Chevrolet Corvette C6.R), 2h 0m 28.424s; **4** Thomas Biagi/Michael Bartels, I/D (Maserati MC12), 2h 0m 35.080s; **5** Anthony Kumpen/Bert Longin, B/B (Chevrolet Corvette C5.R), 2h 0m 48.829s; **6** Jamie Davies/Fabio Babini, GB/I (Aston Martin DBR9), 2h 1m 06.414s; **7** Robert Lechner/Lukas Lichtner-Hoyer, A/A (Aston Martin DBR9), 2h 2m 05.168s; **8** Andrea Bertolini/Andrea Piccini, I/I (Maserati MC12), 2h 2m 06.252s; **9** Alessandro Pier Guidi/Giambattista Giannoccaro, I/I (Maserati MC12), 65 laps; **10** Peter Kox/Jos Menten, NL/NL (Lamborghini Murcielago), 65.
**Fastest race lap:** Montanari, 1m 45.610s, 122.702 mph/197.470 km/h.
**Fastest qualifying lap:** Wendlinger, 1m 44.945s, 123.480 mph/198.721 km/h.

**FIA GT CHAMPIONSHIP, Motorsport Arena Oschersleben, Germany, 8 July. Round 5. 81 laps of the 2.279-mile/3.696-km circuit, 186.024 miles/299.376 km.**
**1** Thomas Biagi/Michael Bartels, I/D (Maserati MC12), 2h 2m 22.704s, 91.204 mph/146.778 km/h; **2** Andrea Bertolini/Andrea Piccini, I/I (Maserati MC12), 80 laps; **3** Jamie Davies/Fabio Babini, GB/I (Aston Martin DBR9), 80; **4** Alessandro Pier Guidi/Giambattista Giannoccaro, I/I (Maserati MC12), 80; **5** Peter Kox/Jos Menten, NL/NL (Lamborghini Murcielago), 80; **6** Diego Alessi/Ferdinando Monfardini, I/I (Aston Martin DBR9), 78; **7** Gianmaria Bruni/Stéphane Ortelli, I/MC (Ferrari 430 GT2), 78 (1ST GT2 class); **8** Ben Aucott/Joe Macari, GB/GB (Maserati MC12), 77; **9** Emmanuel Collard/Matteo Malucelli, F/I (Porsche 997 GT3-RSR), 77; **10** Tim Mullen/Jaroslav 'Janek' Janis, GB/CZ (Ferrari 430 GT2), 77.
**Disqualified:** Failed scrutineering - Anthony Kumpen/Bert Longin, B/B (Chevrolet Corvette C6.R), finished 1st in 2h 1m 16.768s; Christophe Bouchut/Stefan Mücke, F/D (Lamborghini Murcielago), finished 3rd, 80 laps.
**Fastest race lap:** Kumpen, 1m 26.357s, 95.739 mph/154.077 km/h.
**Fastest qualifying lap:** Kumpen, 1m 24.492s, 97.852 mph/157.477 km/h.

**SPA 24-HOURS, Circuit de Spa-Francorchamps, Stavelot, Belgium, 28-29 July. Round 6. 532 laps of the 4.352-mile/7.004-km circuit, 2315.309 miles/3726.128 km.**
**1** Marcel Fässler/Mike Hezemans/Jean-Denis Deletraz/Fabrizio Gollin, CH/NL/CH/I (Chevrolet Corvette C6.R), 24h 0m 20.547s, 96.448 mph/155.218 km/h; **2** Thomas Biagi/Michael Bartels/Pedro Lamy/Eric van de Poele, I/D/P/B (Maserati MC12), 24h 1m 38.303s; **3** Anthony Kumpen/Bert Longin/Kurt Mollekens/Frédéric Bouvy, B/B/B/B (Chevrolet Corvette C5.R), 529 laps; **4** Christian Montanari/Miguel Ramos/Stéphane Lemeret/Matteo Bobbi, RSM/P/B/I (Maserati MC12), 529; **5** Andrea Bertolini/Andrea Piccini/Fabrizio de Simone/Alessandro Pier Guidi, I/I/I/I (Maserati MC12), 527; **6** Oliver Gavin/Vincent Vosse/Greg Franchi/Olivier Beretta, GB/B/B/MC (Chevrolet Corvette C6.R), 521; **7** Philipp Peter/Joe Macari/Ben Aucott/Marino Franchitti, A/GB/GB/GB (Maserati MC12), 515; **8** Emmanuel Collard/Matteo Malucelli/Marc Lieb, F/I/D (Porsche 997 GT3-RSR), 511 (1st GT2 class); **9** Patrick Long/Richard Lietz/Raymond Narac, USA/A/F (Porsche 997 GT3-RSR), 507; **10** Maxime Soulet/Damien Coens/Marc Duez/Steve van Bellingen, B/B/B/B (Chevrolet Corvette C5.R), 502.
**Fastest race lap:** Lamy, 2m 16.452s, 114.821 mph/184.786 km/h.
**Fastest qualifying lap:** Marcel Fässler/Jean-Denis Deletraz/Mike Hezemans/Fabrizio Gollin, CH/CH/NL/I (Chevrolet Corvette C6.R), 2m 14.554s, 116.440 mph/187.392 km/h.

**FIA GT CHAMPIONSHIP, Autodromo Adria International Raceway, Adria, Italy, 8 September. Round 7. 95 laps of the 1.679-mile/2.702-km circuit, 159.500 miles/256.690 km.**
**1** Karl Wendlinger/Ryan Sharp, A/GB (Aston Martin DBR9), 2h 0m 55.343s, 79.142 mph/127.365 km/h; **2** Andrea Bertolini/Andrea Piccini, I/I (Maserati MC12), 2h 0m 58.859s; **3** Fabio Babini/Jamie Davies, I/GB (Aston Martin DBR9), 2h 1m 03.610s; **4** Christian Montanari/Miguel Ramos, RSM/P (Maserati MC12), 2h 1m 29.202s; **5** Mike Hezemans/Jean-Denis Deletraz, NL/CH (Chevrolet Corvette C6.R), 2h 1m 31.284s; **6** Peter Kox/Jos Menten, NL/NL (Lamborghini Murcielago), 94 laps; **7** Ferdinando Monfardini/Enrico Toccacelo, I/I (Aston Martin DBR9), 94; **8** Robert Lechner/Lukas Lichtner-Hoyer, A/A (Aston Martin DBR9), 93; **9** Christophe Bouchut/Stefan Mücke, F/D (Lamborghini Murcielago), 93; **10** Anthony Kumpen/Bert Longin, B/B (Chevrolet Corvette C5.R), 92.
**Fastest race lap:** Wendlinger, 1m 13.790s, 81.911 mph/131.823 km/h.
**Fastest qualifying lap:** Wendlinger, 1m 12.051s, 83.888 mph/135.004 km/h.

**FIA GT CHAMPIONSHIP, Automotodrom Brno Masaryk Circuit, Brno, Czech Republic, 23 September. Round 8. 59 laps of the 3.357-mile/5.403-km circuit, 198.079 miles/318.777 km.**
**1** Christian Montanari/Miguel Ramos, RSM/P (Maserati MC12), 2h 0m 7.643s, 98.934 mph/159.219 km/h; **2** Karl Wendlinger/Ryan Sharp, A/GB (Aston Martin DBR9), 2h 0m 25.198s; **3** Anthony Kumpen/Bert Longin, B/B (Chevrolet Corvette C5.R), 2h 1m 2.105s; **4** Andrea Bertolini/Andrea Piccini, I/I (Maserati MC12), 2h 1m 3.113s; **5** Alessandro Pier Guidi/Giambattista Giannoccaro, I/I (Maserati MC12), 2h 1m 03.457s; **6** Christophe Bouchut/Stefan Mücke, F/D (Lamborghini Murcielago), 2h 1m 04.556s; **7** Thomas Biagi/Michael Bartels, I/D (Maserati MC12), 2h 1m 19.525s; **8** Peter Kox/Jos Menten, NL/NL (Lamborghini Murcielago), 2h 1m 20.337s; **9** Mike Hezemans/Jean-Denis Deletraz, NL/CH (Chevrolet Corvette C6.R), 2h 1m 46.230s; **10** Robert Lechner/Lukas Lichtner-Hoyer, A/A (Aston Martin DBR9), 2h 2m 5.808s.
**Fastest race lap:** Kox, 1m 57.750s, 102.643 mph/165.187 km/h.
**Fastest qualifying lap:** Bartels, 1m 54.064s, 105.960 mph/170.525 km/h.

**FIA GT CHAMPIONSHIP, Circuit Paul Armagnac, Nogaro, France, 30 September. Round 9. 81 laps of the 2.259-mile/3.636-km circuit, 183.004 miles/294.516 km.**
**1** Mike Hezemans/Jean-Denis Deletraz, NL/CH (Chevrolet Corvette C6.R), 2h 0m 51.550s, 90.851 mph/146.211 km/h; **2** Thomas Biagi/Michael Bartels, I/D (Maserati MC12), 2h 1m 08.221s; **3** Christian Montanari/Miguel Ramos, RSM/P (Maserati MC12), 2h 1m 12.721s; **4** Fabio Babini/Jamie Davies, I/GB (Aston Martin DBR9), 2h 1m 19.664s; **5** Karl Wendlinger/Ryan Sharp, A/GB (Aston Martin DBR9), 2h 1m 20.136s; **6** Andrea Bertolini/Andrea Piccini, I/I (Maserati MC12), 2h 1m 45.325s; **7** Alessandro Pier Guidi/Giambattista Giannoccaro, I/I (Maserati MC12), 2h 1m 47.664s; **8** Anthony Kumpen/Bert Longin, B/B (Chevrolet Corvette C5.R), 80 laps; **9** Robert Lechner/Lukas Lichtner-Hoyer, A/A (Aston Martin DBR9), 80; **10** Ferdinando Monfardini/Jean-Marc Gounon, I/F (Aston Martin DBR9), 80.
**Fastest race lap:** Pier Guidi, 1m 25.735s, 94.868 mph/152.675 km/h.
**Fastest qualifying lap:** Biagi, 1m 23.763s, 97.101 mph/156.269 km/h.

**FIA GT CHAMPIONSHIP, Circuit Zolder, Heusden-Zolder, Belgium, 21 October. Round 10. 79 laps of the 2.489-mile/4.006-km circuit, 196.648 miles/316.474 km.**
**1** Karl Wendlinger/Ryan Sharp, A/GB (Aston Martin DBR9), 2h 0m 31.246s, 97.899 mph/157.553 km/h; **2** Anthony Kumpen/Bert Longin, B/B (Chevrolet Corvette C5.R), 2h 1m 4.215s; **3** Thomas Biagi/Michael Bartels, I/D (Maserati MC12), 2h 1m 4.896s; **4** Mike Hezemans/Jean-Denis Deletraz, NL/CH (Chevrolet Corvette C6.R), 2h 1m 7.267s; **5** Christian Montanari/Miguel Ramos, RSM/P (Maserati MC12), 2h 1m 15.103s; **6** Peter Kox/Jos Menten, NL/NL (Lamborghini Murcielago), 2h 1m 25.453s; **7** Ferdinando Monfardini/Jean-Marc Gounon, I/F (Aston Martin DBR9), 2h 1m 33.096s; **8** Andrea Bertolini/Andrea Piccini, I/I (Maserati MC12), 78 laps; **9** Robert Lechner/Lukas Lichtner-Hoyer, A/A (Aston Martin DBR9), 77; **10** Ben Aucott/Stéphane Daoudi, GB/F (Maserati MC12), 76.
**Fastest race lap:** Alessandro Pier Guidi/Giambattista Giannoccaro, I/I (Maserati MC12), 1m 27.508s, 102.404 mph/164.803 km/h.
**Fastest qualifying lap:** Wendlinger, 1m 25.812s, 104.428 mph/168.060 km/h.

**Final championship points**
**GT1 Drivers**
**1** Thomas Biagi, I, 61; **2** Ryan Sharp/Karl Wendlinger, GB/A, 57; **3** Mike Hezemans/Jean-Denis Deletraz, F/CH, 55; **4** Christian Montanari/Miguel Ramos, RSM/P, 54; **5** Andrea Bertolini/Andrea Piccini, I/I, 51; **6** Michael Bartels, D, 45; **7** Anthony Kumpen/Bert Longin, B/B, 43.5; **8** Jamie Davies/Fabio Babini, GB/I, 30; **9** Alessandro Pier Guidi, I, 23; **10** Fabrizio Gollin/Stefan Mücke/Christophe Bouchut, I/D/F, 21; **11** Marcel Fässler, CH, 18; **12** Pedro Lamy/Eric van de Poele, P/B, 14; **13** Giambattista Giannoccaro, I, 12; **14** Jos Menten/Peter Kox/Fabrizio de Simone, NL/NL/I, 11; **15** Philipp Peter, A, 10.5.

**GT1 Teams**
**1** Vitaphone Racing Team, 115; **2** Scuderia Playteam Sarafree, 63; **3** Jetalliance Racing, 60; **4** Carsport Holland, 55; **5** PK Carsport, 43.5.

**GT1 Manufacturers**
**1** Maserati, 182.5; **2** Corvette, 115.5; **3** Aston Martin, 98; **4** Lamborghini, 32.

**GT2 Drivers**
**1** Toni Vilander/Dirk Müller, FIN/D, 73; **2** Stéphane Ortelli/Gianmaria Bruni, MC/I, 66; **3** Matteo Malucelli/Emmanuel Collard, F, 64; **4** Marcello Zani, I, 43.5; **5** Tim Mullen, GB, 36; **6** Paolo Ruberti, I, 33.5; **7** Andrew Kirkaldy/Damien Pasini, GB/F, 29.5; **8** Matteo Cressoni, I, 28.5; **9** Xavier Pompidou, F, 27.5; **10** Marc Lieb, D, 27.

**GT2 Teams**
**1** AF Corse Motorola, 139; **2** BMS Scuderia Italia, 64; **3** Scuderia Ecosse, 60.5.

**GT2 Manufacturers**
**1** Ferrari, 251.5; **2** Porsche, 156.5.

*Result of the non-championship GT race in Dubai will be given in AUTOCOURSE 2008–2009.*

# Le Mans Series

**1,000 km of MONZA, Autodromo Nazionale di Monza, Milan, Italy, 15 April. Round 1. 173 laps of the 3.600-mile/5.793-km circuit, 622.731 miles/1002.189 km.**
**1** Marc Gené/Nicolas Minassian, E/F (Peugeot 908 HDi), 4h 59m 20.735s, 124.819 mph/200.876 km/h; **2** Jean-Christophe Boullion/Emmanuel Collard, F/F (Pescarolo 01-Judd), 172 laps; **3** Pedro Lamy/Stéphane Sarrazin, P/F (Peugeot 908 HDi), 171; **4** Christophe Tinseau/Harold Primat, F/CH (Pescarolo 01-Judd), 170; **5** Jean-Marc Gounon/Guillaume Moreau, F/F (Courage LC70-AER), 168; **6** Eric van de Poele/Didier Theys/Fredy Lienhard, B/B/CH (Lola B05/40-Judd), 165; **7** João Barboza/Phil Keen/Stuart Hall, P/GB/GB (Pescarolo 01-Judd), 163; **8** Thomas Erdos/Mike Newton, BR/GB (MG Lola EX264-AER), 161 (1st LMP2 class); **9** Jérôme Policand/Luc Alphand/Patrice Goueslard, F/F/F (Chevrolet Corvette C6.R), 160 (1st LMGT1 class); **10** Christophe Bouchut/Gabriele Gardel/Fabrizio Gollin, F/CH/I (Aston Martin DBR9), 159.
**Fastest race lap:** Sarrazin, 1m 36.500s, 134.286 mph/216.112 km/h.
**Fastest qualifying lap:** Minassian, 1m 34.503s, 137.123 mph/220.679 km/h.

**1,000 km of VALENCIA, Circuit de la Comunitat Valenciana Ricardo Tormo, Cheste, Valencia, Spain, 6 May. Round 2. 235 laps of the 2.489-km/4.005-mile circuit, 584.819 miles/941.175 km.**
**1** Pedro Lamy/Stéphane Sarrazin, P/F (Peugeot 908 HDi), 6h 1m 22.255s, 97.099 mph/156.265 km/h (1st LMP1 class); **2** Stefan Mücke/Jan Charouz/Alex Yoong, D/CZ/MAL (Lola B07/10-Judd), 232 laps; **3** Jean-Denis Deletraz/Marcel Fässler/Iradj Alexander, CHCH/CH (Lola B07/10-Judd), 231; **4** João Barboza/Stuart Hall/Martin Short, P/GB/GB (Pescarolo 01-Judd), 230; **5** Jean-Christophe Boullion/Romain Dumas, F/F (Pescarolo 01-Judd), 229; **6** Christophe Tinseau/Harold Primat, F/CH (Pescarolo 01-Judd), 229; **7** Miguel de Castro/Angel Burgeño/Miguel Amaral, E/P/E (Lola B05/40-AER), 224 (1st LMP2 class); **8** Jacques Nicolet/Alan Filhol/Bruce Jouanny, F/F/F (Courage LC75-AER), 222; **9** Stuart Moseley/Tim Greaves/Robin Liddell, GB/GB/GB (Radical SR9-AER), 222; **10** Stéphane Ortelli/Soheil Ayari, MC/F (Saleen S7R), 222 (1st LMGT1 class), 222.
**Fastest race lap:** Sarrazin, 1m 25.234s, 105.110 mph/169.158 km/h.
**Fastest qualifying lap:** Marc Gené, E (Peugeot 908 HDi), 1m 23.489s, 107.307 mph/172.693 km/h.

**1,000 km of NÜRBURGRING, Nürburgring, Nürburg/Eifel, Germany, 1 July. Round 3. 195 laps of the 3.192-mile/5.137-km circuit, 622.437 miles/1001.715 km.**
**1** Pedro Lamy/Stéphane Sarrazin, P/F (Peugeot 908 HDi), 6h 1m 13.828s, 103.386 mph/166.384 km/h; **2** Nicolas Minassian/Jordi Gené, F/E (Peugeot HDi), 194 laps; **3** Jean-Christophe Boullion/Emmanuel Collard, F/F (Pescarolo 01-Judd), 191; **4** Stefan Mücke/Alex Yoong/Jan Charouz, D/MAL/CZ (Lola B07/17-Judd), 188; **5** Jamie Campbell-Walter/Felipe Ortiz/Shinji Nakano, GB/CH/J (Creation CA07-Judd), 188; **6** Thomas Erdos/Mike Newton, BR/GB (MG Lola EX264-AER), 188 (1st LMP2 class); **7** Juan Barazi/Michael Vergers/Karim Ojjeh, DK/NL/ZA (Zytek 07S), 187; **8** Tom Chilton/Hayanari Shimoda, GB/J (Zytek 07S), 187; **9** Jan Lammers/David Hart/Jeroen Bleekemolen, NL/NL/NL (Dome S101.5-Judd), 187; **10** Miguel de Castro/Angel Burgeño/Miguel Amaral, E/E/P (Lola B05/40-AER), 187 (1st LMP2 class).
**Fastest race lap:** Minassian, 1m 44.046s, 110.443 mph/177.741 km/h.
**Fastest qualifying lap:** Gené, 1m 41.867s, 112.805 mph/181.543 km/h.

**1,000 km of SPA, Circuit de Spa-Francorchamps, Stavelot, Belgium, 19 August. Round 4. 143 laps of the 4.352-mile/7.004-km circuit, 622.348 miles/1001.572 km.**
**1** Pedro Lamy/Stéphane Sarrazin, P/F (Peugeot 908 HDi),

5h 47m 47.313s, 107.367 mph/172.790 km/h; **2** Jean-Christophe Boullion/Emmanuel Collard, F/F (Pescarolo 01-Judd), 141 laps; **3** Thomas Erdos/Mike Newton, BR/GB (MG Lola EX264-AER), 140 (1st LMP2 class); **4** Christophe Tinseau/Harold Primat, F/CH (Pescarolo 01-Judd), 138; **5** Miguel de Castro/Angel Burgeño/Miguel Amaral, E/E/P (Lola B05/40-AER), 137; **6** Stéphane Ortelli/Soheil Ayari, MC/F (Saleen S7R), 137 (1st LMGT1 class); **7** Eric van de Poele/Didier Theys/Fredy Lienhard, B/B/CH (Lola B05/40-Judd), 136; **8** Christophe Bouchut/Gabriele Gardel/Fabrizio Gollin, F/CH/I (Aston Martin DBR9), 136; **9** Jérôme Policand/Luc Alphand/Patrice Goueslard, F/F/F (Chevrolet Corvette C6.R), 134; **10** Antonio Garcia/Christian Fittipaldi, E/BR (Aston Martin DBR9), 134.
**Fastest race lap:** Lamy, 2m 3.316s, 127.052 mph/204.470 km/h.
**Fastest qualifying lap:** Nicolas Minassian, F (Peugeot 908 HDi), 2m 00.105s, 130.448 mph/209.936 km/h.

**1,000 km of SILVERSTONE, Silverstone Grand Prix Circuit, Towcester, Northamptonshire, Great Britain, 16 September. Round 5. 195 laps of the 3.194-mile/5.141-km circuit, 622.922 miles/1002.495 km.**
**1** Marc Gené/Nicolas Minassian, E/F (Peugeot 908 HDi), 5h 41m 45.230s, 109.363 mph/176.003 km/h; **2** Jean-Christophe Boullion/Emmanuel Collard, F/F (Pescarolo 01-Judd), 193 laps; **3** João Barboza/Stuart Hall, P/GB (Pescarolo 01-Judd), 191; **4** Jamie Campbell-Walter/Felipe Ortiz/Haruki Kurosawa, GB/CH/J (Creation CA07-Judd), 188; **5** Juan Barazi/Michael Vergers/Karim Ojjeh, DK/NL/ZA (Zytek 07S), 187 (1st LMP2 class); **6** Tom Chilton/Max Chilton, GB/GB (Zytek 07S), 187; **7** Danny Watts/Tom Kimber-Smith, GB/GB (Zytek 07S), 186; **8** Miguel de Castro/Angel Burgeño/Miguel Amaral, E/E/P (Lola B05/40-AER), 185; **9** Thomas Erdos/Mike Newton, BR/GB (MG Lola EX264-AER), 184; **10** Chris Buncombe/Bill Binnie/Allen Timpany, GB/USA/GB (Lola B05/40-Zytek). 182.
**Fastest race lap:** Gené, 1m 34.935s, 121.136 mph/194.950 km/h.
**Fastest qualifying lap:** Minassian, 1m 31.692s, 125.421 mph/201.845 km/h.

**Provisional championship points**
**LMP1 Drivers**
**1** Pedro Lamy/Stéphane Sarrazin, P/F, 36; **2** Jean-Christophe Boullion, F, 34; **3** Emmanuel Collard, F, 30; **4** Marc Gené/Nicolas Minassian, E/F, 28; **5** João Barboza/Stuart Hall, P/GB, 19; **6** Stefan Mücke/Jan Charouz, D/CZ, 15; **7** Christophe Tinseau/Harold Primat, F/CH, 14; **8** Alex Yoong, MAL, 13; **9** Jamie Campbell-Walter/Felipe Ortiz, GB/CH, 12; **10** Tom Chilton, GB, 7; **11** Jean-Denis Deletraz/Marcel Fassler/Iradj Alexander, CH/CH/CH, 6; **12** Bob Berridge/Gareth Evans/Peter Owen, GB/GB/GB, 6.

**LMP2 Drivers**
**1** Thomas Erdos/Mike Newton, BR/GB, 36; **2** Miguel Amaral/Miguel de Castro/Angel Burgeño, P/E/E, 30; **3** Jacques Nicolet/Alain Filhol/Bruce Jouanny, F/F/F, 23; **4** Fredy Lienhard/Didier Theys/Eric van de Poele, CH/B/B, 21; **5** Juan Barazi/Karim Ojjeh/Michael Vergers, DK/ZA/NL, 20.

**GT1 Drivers**
**1** Soheil Ayari/Stéphane Ortelli, F/MC, 40; **2** Patrice Goueslard/Jérôme Policand, F/F, 33; **3** Christophe Bouchut/Gabriele Gardel/Fabrizio Gollin, F/CH/I, 30.

**GT2 Drivers**
**1** Robert Bell, GB, 42; **2** Allan Simonsen, AUS, 32; **3** Marc Lieb/Xavier Pompidou, D/F, 29.

**LMP1 Teams**
**1** Team Peugeot Total (car 8), 36; **2** Pescarolo Sport (car 16), 34; **3** Team Peugeot Total (car 7), 28.

**LMP2 Teams**
**1** RML, 36; **2** Quifel-ASM Team, 30; **3** Saulnier Racing, 23.

**LMGT1 Teams**
**1** Team Oreca, 40; **2** Luc Alphand Aventures, 33; **3** AMR Larbre Competition, 30.

**LMGT2 Teams**
**1** Virgo Motorsport, 42; **2** Team Felbemayr-Proton, 29; **3** GPC-Sport, 27.

*Result of the Interlagos race will be given in AUTOCOURSE 2008–2009.*

## American Le Mans Series

**MOBIL 1 TWELVE HOURS OF SEBRING, Sebring International Raceway, Florida, USA, 17 March. Round 1. 364 laps of the 3.700-mile/5.955-km circuit, 1346.800 miles/2167.464 km.**
**1** Frank Biela/Emanuele Pirro/Marco Werner, D/I/D (Audi R10 TDI), 12h 1m 14.838s, 112.039 mph/180.310 km/h; (1st LMP1 class); **2** Dario Franchitti/Bryan Herta/Tony Kanaan, GB/USA/BR (Acura ARX-01a), 358 Laps (1st LMP2 class); **3** Luis Diaz/Adrian Fernandez, MEX/MEX (Lola-Acura B06/43), 356; **4** Rinaldo Capello/Allan McNish/Tom Kristensen, I/GB/DK (Audi R10 TDI), 353; **5** Timo Bernhard/Romain Dumas/Helio Castroneves, D/F/BR (Porsche RS Spyder), 351; **6** David Brabham/Stefan Johansson/Duncan Dayton, AUS/S/USA (Acura ARX-01a), 346; **7** Oliver Gavin/Olivier Beretta/Max Papis, GB/MC/I (Chevrolet Corvette C6.R), 341 (1st LMGT1 class); **8** Ron Fellows/Johnny O'Connell/Jan Magnussen, CDN/USA/DK (Chevrolet Corvette C6.R), 341; **9** Andy Wallace/Butch Leitzinger/Andy Lally, GB/USA/USA (Porsche RS Spyder), 340; **10** Chris Dyson/Guy Smith, USA/GB (Porsche RS Spyder), 333.
**Fastest race lap:** Kristensen, 1m 46.634s, 124.913 mph/201.028 km/h.
**Fastest qualifying lap:** Werner, 1m 44.974s, 126.889 mph/204.207 km/h.

**ACURA SPORTS CAR CHALLENGE OF ST PETERSBURG, St Petersburg, Florida, USA, 31 March. Round 2. 114 laps of the 1.800-mile/2.897-km circuit, 205.200 miles/330.237 km.**
**1** Rinaldo Capello/Allan McNish, I/GB (Audi R10 TDI), 2h 45m 8.111s, 74.557 mph/119.988 km/h (1st LMP1 class); **2** Marco Werner/Emanuele Pirro, D/I (Audi R10 TDI), 2h 45m 8.537s; **3** Ryan Briscoe/Sascha Maassen, AUS/D (Porsche RS Spyder), 2h 45m 34.461s (1st LMP2 class); **4** Timo Bernhard/Romain Dumas, D/F (Porsche RS Spyder), 2h 45m 34.577s; **5** David Brabham/Stefan Johansson, AUS/S (Acura ARX-01a), 2h 45m 42.190s; **6** Luis Diaz/Adrian Fernandez, MEX/MEX (Lola-Acura B06/43), 113 laps; **7** Clint Field/Jon Field/Richard Berry, USA/USA/USA (Creation CA06/H-Judd), 112; **8** Oliver Gavin/Olivier Beretta, GB/MC (Chevrolet Corvette C6.R), 111 (1st LMGT1 class); **9** Jaime Melo/Mika Salo, BR/FIN (Ferrari 430 GT), 109 (1st LMGT2 class); **10** Johannes Van Overbeek/Jörg Bergmeister, USA/D (Porsche 911 GT3-RSR), 108.
**Fastest race lap:** Briscoe, 1m 4.340s, 100.715 mph/162.085 km/h.
**Fastest qualifying lap:** Dumas, 1m 3.039s, 102.794 mph/165.430 km/h.

**GRAND PRIX OF LONG BEACH, Long Beach Street Circuit, California, USA, 14 April. Round 3. 74 laps of the 1.968-mile/3.167-km circuit, 145.632 miles/234.372 km.**
**1** Timo Bernhard/Romain Dumas, D/F (Porsche RS Spyder), 1h 41m 15.908s, 86.288 mph/138.866 km/h (1st LMP2 class); **2** Ryan Briscoe/Sascha Maassen, AUS/D (Porsche RS Spyder), 1h 41m 16.668s; **3** Andy Wallace/Butch Leitzinger, GB/USA (Porsche RS Spyder), 1h 41m 29.375s; **4** David Brabham/Stefan Johansson, AUS/S (Acura ARX-01a), 1h 41m 51.019s; **5** Chris Dyson/Guy Smith, USA/GB (Porsche RS Spyder), 1h 42m 4.289s; **6** Dario Franchitti/Bryan Herta, GB/USA (Acura ARX-01a), 1h 42m 15.349s; **7** Rinaldo Capello/Allan McNish, I/GB (Audi R10 TDI), 1h 42m 20.212s (1st LMP1 class); **8** Luis Diaz/Adrian Fernandez, MEX/MEX (Lola-Acura B06/43), 73 laps (DNF); **9** Emanuele Pirro/Marco Werner, I/D (Audi R10 TDI), 73; **10** Oliver Gavin/Olivier Beretta, GB/MC (Chevrolet Corvette C6.R), 71 (1st LMGT1 class).
**Fastest race lap:** Briscoe/Maassen, 1m 13.504s, 96.387 mph/155.119 km/h.
**Fastest qualifying lap:** Herta/Franchitti, 1m 11.838s, 98.622 mph/158.717 km/h.

**LONE STAR GRAND PRIX, Reliant Park Circuit, Houston, Texas, USA, 21 April. Round 4. 146 laps of the 1.683-mile/2.709-km circuit, 245.718 miles/395.445 km.**
**1** Timo Bernhard/Romain Dumas, D/F (Porsche RS Spyder), 2h 45m 5.216s, 89.305 mph/143.722 km/h (1st LMP2 class); **2** Marino Franchitti/Bryan Herta, GB/USA (Acura ARX-01a), 2h 45m 5.706s; **3** Rinaldo Capello/Allan McNish, I/GB (Audi R10 TDI), 2h 45m 6.557s (1st LMP1 class); **4** Ryan Briscoe/Sascha Maassen, AUS/D (Porsche RS Spyder), 2h 45m 19.326s; **5** David Brabham/Stefan Johansson, AUS/S (Acura ARX-01a), 145 laps; **6** Chris Dyson/Guy Smith, USA/GB (Porsche RS Spyder), 144; **7** Andy Wallace/Butch Leitzinger, GB/USA (Porsche RS Spyder), 144; **8** Luis Diaz/Adrian Fernandez, MEX/MEX (Lola-Acura B06/43), 144; **9** Jamie Bach/Ben Devlin, USA/GB (Lola B07/40-Mazda), 140; **10** Johnny O'Connell/Jan Magnussen, USA/DK (Chevrolet Corvette C6.R), 138 (1st LMGT1 class).
**Fastest race lap:** Bernhard, 1m 2.893s, 96.335 mph/155.036 km/h.
**Fastest qualifying lap:** Brabham, 1m 1.824s, 98.001 mph/157.717 km/h.

**UTAH GRAND PRIX, Miller Motorsports Park, Tooele, Utah, USA, 19 May. Round 5. 66 laps of the 4.486–mile/7.722-km circuit, 296.076 miles/476.488 km.**
**1** Ryan Briscoe/Sascha Maassen, AUS/D (Porsche RS Spyder), 2h 46m 49.942s, 106.481 mph/171.365 km/h (1st LMP2 class); **2** Rinaldo Capello/Allan McNish, I/GB (Audi R10 TDI), 2h 46m 59.874s (1st LMP1 class); **3** Timo Bernhard/Romain Dumas, D/F (Porsche RS Spyder), 2h 47m 47.133s; **4** Andy Wallace/Butch Leitzinger, GB/USA (Porsche RS Spyder), 2h 48m 18.505s; **5** Chris Dyson/Guy Smith, USA/GB (Porsche RS Spyder), 2h 48m 40.579s; **6** Emanuele Pirro/Marco Werner, I/D (Audi R10 TDI), 2h 48m 47.204s; **7** Luis Diaz/Adrian Fernandez, MEX/MEX (Lola-Acura B06/43), 61 (DNF); **8** Oliver Gavin/Olivier Beretta, GB/MC (Chevrolet Corvette C6.R), 61 (1st LMGT1 class); **9** Johnny O'Connell/Jan Magnussen, USA/DK (Chevrolet Corvette C6.R), 61; **10** Richard Berry/Jon Field/Clint Field, USA/USA/USA (Creation CA06/H-Judd), 60.
**Fastest race lap:** Bernhard, 2m 21.749s, 113.931 mph/183.354 km/h.
**Fastest qualifying lap:** Bernhard, 2m 18.128s, 116.918 mph/188.161 km/h.

**AMERICAN LE MANS NORTHEAST GRAND PRIX, Lime Rock Park, Lakeville, Connecticut, USA, 7 July. Round 6. 174 laps of the 1.540-mile/2.478-km circuit, 267.960 miles/431.240 km.**
**1** Ryan Briscoe/Sascha Maassen, AUS/D (Porsche RS Spyder), 2h 45m 16.651s, 97.276 mph/156.551 km/h (1st LMP2 class); **2** Timo Bernhard/Romain Dumas, D/F (Porsche RS Spyder), 2h 45m 24.096s; **3** David Brabham/Stefan Johansson, AUS/S (Acura ARX-01a), 2h 45m 32.710s; **4** Chris Dyson/Guy Smith, USA/GB (Porsche RS Spyder), 173 laps; **5** Rinaldo Capello/Allan McNish, I/GB (Audi R10 TDI), 173 (1st LMP1 class); **6** Andy Wallace/Butch Leitzinger, GB/USA (Porsche RS Spyder), 172; **7** Marino Franchitti/Bryan Herta, GB/USA (Acura ARX-01a), 170; **8** Oliver Gavin/Olivier Beretta, GB/MC (Chevrolet Corvette C6.R), 165 (1st LMGT1 class); **9** Johnny O'Connell/Jan Magnussen, USA/DK (Chevrolet Corvette C6.R), 165; **10** Adam Pecorari/Gunnar van der Steur, USA/USA (Radical SR9-AER), 162.
**Fastest race lap:** Briscoe, 45.371s, 122.193 mph/196.650 km/h.

**Pole position:** Bernhard/Dumas, 44.659s, 124.141 mph/199.785 km/h (qualifying rained off, grid determined by first free practice).

**ACURA SPORTS CAR CHALLENGE, Mid-Ohio Sports Car Course, Lexington, Ohio, USA, 21 July. Round 7. 134 laps of the 2.258-mile/3.634-km circuit, 302.572 miles/486.942 km.**
**1** Timo Bernhard/Romain Dumas, D/F (Porsche RS Spyder), 2h 46m 1.062s, 109.352 mph/175.985 km/h (1st LMP2 class); **2** Ryan Briscoe/Sascha Maassen, AUS/D (Porsche RS Spyder), 2h 46m 3.422s; **3** Emanuele Pirro/Marco Werner, I/D (Audi R10 TDI), 2h 46m 16.135s (1st LMP1 class); **4** Luis Diaz/Adrian Fernandez, MEX/MEX (Lola-Acura B06/43), 2h 46m 40.414s; **5** Rinaldo Capello/Allan McNish, I/GB (Audi R10 TDI), 2h 47m 05.695s; **6** Andy Wallace/Butch Leitzinger, GB/USA (Porsche RS Spyder), 133 laps; **7** Chris Dyson/Guy Smith, USA/GB (Porsche RS Spyder), 133; **8** David Brabham/Stefan Johansson, AUS/S (Acura ARX-01a), 132; **9** Greg Pickett/Klaus Graf, USA/D (Lola B06/10-AER), 128; **10** Marino Franchitti/Bryan Herta, GB/USA (Acura ARX-01a), 126.
**Fastest race lap:** Dumas, 1m 10.113s, 115.939 mph/186.585 km/h.
**Fastest qualifying lap:** Bernhard, 1m 08.510s, 118.651 mph/190.951 km/h.

**GENERAC 500 AT ROAD AMERICA, Road America, Elkhart Lake, Wisconsin, USA, 11 August. Round 8. 96 laps of the 4.048-mile/6.515-km circuit, 388.608 miles/625.404 km**
**1** Timo Bernhard/Romain Dumas, D/F (Porsche RS Spyder), 4h 1m 17.701s, 96.631 mph/155.512 km/h (1st LMP2 class); **2** Rinaldo Capello/Allan McNish, I/GB (Audi R10 TDI), 4h 1m 19.484s (1st LMP1 class); **3** Marco Werner/Emanuele Pirro, D/I (Audi R10 TDI), 4h 1m 20.190s; **4** Ryan Briscoe/Sascha Maassen, AUS/D (Porsche RS Spyder), 4h 2m 18.428s; **5** David Brabham/Stefan Johansson, AUS/S (Acura ARX-01a), 94 laps; **6** Chris Dyson/Guy Smith, USA/GB (Porsche RS Spyder), 94; **7** Andy Wallace/Butch Leitzinger, GB/USA (Porsche RS Spyder), 94; **8** Luis Diaz/Adrian Fernandez, MEX/MEX (Lola-Acura B06/43), 94; **9** Marino Franchitti/Bryan Herta, GB/USA (Acura ARX-01a), 94; **10** Greg Pickett/Klaus Graf, USA/D (Lola B06/10-AER), 91.
**Fastest race lap:** McNish, 1m 49.303s, 133.325 mph/214.565 km/h.
**Fastest qualifying lap:** McNish, 1m 47.665s, 135.353 mph/217.830 km/h.

**GRAND PRIX OF MOSPORT, Mosport International Raceway, Bowmanville, Ontario, Canada, 26 August. Round 9. 125 laps of the 2.459-mile/3.957-km circuit, 307.375 miles/494.672 km.**
**1** Timo Bernhard/Romain Dumas, D/F (Porsche RS Spyder), 2h 45m 43.043s, 111.289 mph/179.102 km/h (1st LMP2 class); **2** Rinaldo Capello/Allan McNish, I/GB (Audi R10 TDI), 2h 46m 2.619s (1st LMP1 class); **3** Ryan Briscoe/Sascha Maassen, AUS/D (Porsche RS Spyder), 2h 46m 13.641s; **4** Emanuele Pirro/Marco Werner, I/D (Audi R10 TDI), 2h 46m 16.935s; **5** Marino Franchitti/Bryan Herta, GB/USA (Acura ARX-01a), 2h 46m 43.683s; **6** Jamie Bach/Ben Devlin, USA/GB (Lola B07/46-Mazda), 124 laps; **7** Chris Dyson/Guy Smith, USA/GB (Porsche RS Spyder), 124; **8** Luis Diaz/Adrian Fernandez, MEX/MEX (Lola-Acura B06/43), 124; **9** Andy Wallace/Butch Leitzinger, GB/USA (Porsche RS Spyder), 124; **10** Johnny O'Connell/Jan Magnussen, USA/DK (Chevrolet Corvette C6.R), 116 (1st LMGT1 class).
**Fastest race lap:** Werner, 1m 06.371s, 133.378 mph/214.650 km/h.
**Fastest qualifying lap:** Capello, 1m 05.829s, 134.476 mph/216.418 km/h.

**DETROIT SPORTS CAR CHALLENGE, The Raceway at Belle Isle, Detroit, Michigan, USA, 1 September. Round 10. 106 laps of the 2.070-mile/3.331-km circuit, 219.420 miles/353.122 km.**
**1** Timo Bernhard/Romain Dumas, D/F (Porsche RS Spyder), 2h 45m 36.179s, 79.499 mph/127.941 km/h (1st LMP2 class); **2** Marco Werner/Emanuele Pirro, D/I (Audi R10 TDI), 2h 45m 42.127s (1st LMP1 class); **3** Rinaldo Capello/Allan McNish, I/GB (Audi R10 TDI), 2h 45m 54.149s; **4** Andy Wallace/Butch Leitzinger, GB/USA (Porsche RS Spyder), 2h 45m 58.421s; *5* David Brabham/Stefan Johansson, AUS/S (Acura ARX-01a), 2h 45m 58.748s; **6** Luis Diaz/Adrian Fernandez, MEX/MEX (Lola-Acura B06/43), 2h 46m 0.066s; **7** Chris Dyson/Guy Smith, USA/GB (Porsche RS Spyder), 2h 46m 17.692; **8** Jamie Bach/Ben Devlin, USA/GB (Lola B07/46-Mazda), 105 laps; **9** Ryan Briscoe/Sascha Maassen, AUS/D (Porsche RS Spyder), 104; **10** Johnny O'Connell/Jan Magnussen, USA/DK (Chevrolet Corvette C6.R), 103 (1st LMGT1 class).
**Fastest race lap:** Briscoe, 1m 14.993s, 99.369 mph/159.919 km/h.
**Fastest qualifying lap:** Briscoe, 1m 13.357s, 101.585 mph/163.486 km/h.

**PETITE LE MANS, Road Atlanta Motorsports Center, Braselton, Georgia, USA, 6 October. Round 11. 394 laps of the 2.540-mile/4.088-km circuit, 1000.760 miles/1610.567 km.**
**1** Rinaldo Capello/Allan McNish, I/GB (Audi R10 TDI), 9h 18m 58.275s, 107.422 mph/172.878 km/h (1st LMP1 class); **2** Timo Bernhard/Romain Dumas/Patrick Long, D/F/USA (Porsche RS Spyder), 9h 18m 59.198s (1st LMP2 class); **3** Chris Dyson/Guy Smith, USA/GB (Porsche RS Spyder), 386 laps; **4** Stefan Mücke/Danny Watts/Jan Charouz, D/GB/CZ (Zytek 07S), 383; **5** Jamie Campbell-Walter/Harold Primat/Christophe Tinseau, GB/CH/F (Creation CA07-Judd), 377; **6** Andy Wallace/Butch Leitzinger/Andy Lally, GB/USA/USA (Porsche RS Spyder), 372; **7** Ryan Briscoe/Sascha Maassen/Emmanuel Collard, AUS/D/F (Porsche RS Spyder),370; **8** David Brabham/Stefan Johansson/Robbie Kerr, AUS/S/GB (Acura ARX-01a), 365; **9** Oliver Gavin/Olivier Beretta/Max Papis, GB/MC/I (Chevrolet Corvette C6.R), 364 (1st GT1 class); **10** Johannes Van Overbeek/Jörg Bergmeister/Marc Lieb, USA/D/D (Porsche 911 GT3-RSR), 353.
**Fastest race lap:** McNish, 1m 9.195s, 132.148 mph/212.672 km/h.
**Fastest qualifying lap:** Marco Werner, D (Audi R10 TDI), 1m 08.906s, 132.703 mph/213.564 km/h (received grid penalty, resulting in Bernhard starting from pole position).

**MONTEREY SPORTS CAR CHAMPIONSHIPS, Mazda Raceway Laguna Seca, Monterey, California, USA, 20 October. Round 12. 157 laps of the 2.238-mile/3.602-km circuit, 351.366 miles/565.469 km.**
**1** Rinaldo Capello/Allan McNish, I/GB (Audi R10 TDI), 4h 0m 14.224s, 87.755 mph/141.228 km/h; **2** Timo Bernhard/Romain Dumas, D/F (Porsche RS Spyder), 4h 0m 14.634s (1st LMP2 class); **3** Marco Werner/Mike Rockenfeller, D/D (Audi R10 TDI), 4h 0m 35.722s; **4** Ryan Briscoe/Sascha Maassen, AUS/D (Porsche RS Spyder), 4h 0m 36.137s; **5** Luis Diaz/Adrian Fernandez, MEX/MEX (Lola-Acura B06/43), 4h 0m 39.077s; **6** Bryan Herta/Tony Kanaan, USA/BR (Acura ARX-01a), 4h 0m 39.827s; **7** Chris Dyson/Guy Smith, USA/GB (Porsche RS Spyder), 4h 1m 10.659s; **8** Andy Wallace/Butch Leitzinger, GB/USA (Porsche RS Spyder), 156; **9** Jamie Campbell-Walter/Harold Primat, GB/CH (Creation CA07-Judd), 153; **10** Tom Chilton/Darren Manning, GB/GB (Zytek 07S), 153.
**Fastest race lap:** Maassen, 1m 12.127s, 111.703 mph/179.769 km/h.
**Fastest qualifying lap:** Masseen, 1m 10.528s, 114.235 mph/183.844 km/h.

**Final championship points**
**P1 Drivers**
**1** Rinaldo Capello/Allan McNish, I/GB, 246; **2** Marco Werner, D, 210; **3** Emanuele Pirro, I, 175; **4** Clint Field, USA, 95; **5** Chris McMurry, USA, 89; **6** Jon Field, USA, 82; **7** Michael Lewis, USA, 76; **8** Greg Pickett/Klaus Graf, USA/D, 72; **9** Bryan Willman, USA, 63; **10** Richard Berry, USA, 61; **11** Jamie Campbell-Walter/Harold Primat, GB/CH, 38; **12** Frank Biela, D, 26; **13** Tom Chilton/Darren Manning, GB/GB, 25; **14** Tom Kristensen/Christophe Tinseau, DK/F, 22; **15** Memo Gidley/Mike Rockenfeller, USA/D, 19.

**P2 Drivers**
**1** Romain Dumas/Timo Bernhard, F/D, 239; **2** Sascha Maassen/Ryan Briscoe, D/AUS, 186; **3** Andy Wallace/Butch Leitzinger, GB/USA, 128; **4** Chris Dyson/Guy Smith, USA/GB, 124; **5** David Brabham/Stefan Johansson, AUS/S, 115.

**GT1 Drivers**
**1** Oliver Gavin/Olivier Beretta, GB/MC, 246; **2** Jan Magnussen/Johnny O'Connell, DK/USA, 184; **3** Max Papis, I, 52.

**GT2 Drivers**
**1** Mika Salo/Jaime Melo Jr, FIN/BR, 202; **2** Johannes van Overbeeck/Jörg Bergmeister, USA/D, 170; **3** Wolf Henzler, D, 126.

## Japanese Super GT Championship

## 2006

The following race was run after AUTOCOURSE 2006–2007 went to press.

**FUJI GT 500 km, Fuji International Speedway, Sunto-gun, Shizuoka Prefecture, Japan, 5 November. Round 9. 66 laps of the 2.835-mile/4.563-km circuit, 187.131 miles/301.158 km.**
**1** Loïc Duval/Hideki Mutoh, F/J (Honda NSX), 1h 48m 6.601s, 103.856 mph/167.140 km/h; **2** Peter Dumbreck/Naoki Hattori, GB/J (Lexus SC430), 1h 48m 39.258s; **3** Masataka Yanagida/Seji Ara, J/J (Nissan Fairlady Z), 1h 48m 39.580s; **4** Juichi Wakisaka/Andre Lotterer, J/D (Lexus SC430), 1h 48m 48.378s; **5** Akira Iida/Tatsuya Kataoka, J/J (Lexus SC430), 1h 48m 48.553s; **6** Richard Lyons/Michael Krumm, GB/D (Nissan Fairlady Z), 1h 49m 03.443s; **7** Ryo Michigami/Takashi Kogure, J/J (Honda NSX), 1h 49m 4.942s; **8** Naoki Yokomizo/João Paulo de Oliveira, J/BR (Nissan Fairlady Z), 1h 49m 11.385s; **9** Manabu Orido/Takeshi Tsuchiya, J/J (Toyota Supra), 1h 49m 12.041s; **10** André Couto/Katsuyuki Hiranaka, MAC/J (Toyota Supra), 1h 49m 32.169s.
**Fastest race lap:** Duval, 1m 34.716s, 107.766 mph/173.432 km/h.
**Fastest qualifying lap:** Duval/Mutoh, 1m 33.668s, 108.971 mph/175.373 km/h.

**Final championship points**
**1** Juichi Wakisaka/Andre Lotterer, J/D, 80; **2** Sébastien Philippe/Shinya Hosokawa, F/J, 79; **3** Ryo Michigami/Takashi Kogure, J/J, 76; **4** Michael Krumm, D, 75; **5** Yuji Tachikawa/Toranosuke Takagi, J/J, 71; **6** Satoshi Motoyama/Tsugio Matsuda, J/J, 69; **7** Daisuke Ito/Ralph Firman, J/GB, 68; **8** Benoît Tréluyer/Kazuki Hosahino, F/J, 67; **9** Naoki Hattori/Peter Dumbreck, J/GB, 64; **10** Richard Lyons, GB, 62.

## 2007

**SUZUKA GT 300 km, Suzuka International Racing Course, Ino-Cho, Suzuka-shi, Mie Prefecture, Japan, 18 March. Round 1. 52 laps of the 3.608-mile/5.807-km circuit, 187.632 miles/301.964 km.**
**1** Yuji Tachikawa/Toranosuke Takagi, J/J (Lexus SC430), 1h 43m 25.744s, 108.847 mph/175.172 km/h; **2** Richard Lyons/Satoshi Motoyama, GB/J (Nissan Fairlady Z), 1h 43m 29.171s; **3** Loïc Duval/Fabio Carbone, F/BR (Honda NSX), 1h 43m 54.046s; **4** Tatsuya Kataoka/Björn Wirdheim, J/S (Lexus SC430), 1h 44m 0.271s; **5** Michael Krumm/Tsugio Matsuda, J/J (Nissan Fairlady Z), 1h 44m 0.775s;

6 Katsutomo Kaneishi/Toshihiro Kaneishi, J/J (Honda NSX), 1h 44m 1.146s; 7 Juichi Wakisaka/Andre Lotterer, J/D (Lexus SC430), 1h 44m 3.977s; 8 Peter Dumbreck/Naoki Hattori, GB/J (Lexus SC430), 1h 44m 25.008s; 9 Manabu Orido/Takeshi Tsuchiya, J/J (Lexus SC430), 1h 44m 32.443s; 10 Sébastien Philippe/Masataka Yanagida, F/J (Nissan Fairlady Z), 1h 44m 32.856s.
**Fastest race lap:** Firman, 1m 53.118s, 114.835 mph/184.809 km/h.
**Fastest qualifying lap:** Daisuke Ito/Ralph Firman, J/GB (Honda NSX), 1m 49.842s, 118.260 mph/190.321 km/h.

**OKAYAMA GT300 km, Okayama International Circuit (TI Circuit Aida), Aida Gun, Okayama Prefecture, Japan, 8 April. Round 2. 82 laps of the 2.301-mile/3.703-km circuit, 188.677 miles/303.646 km.**
1 Ralph Firman/Daisuke Ito, GB/J (Honda NSX), 2h 1m 14.759s, 93.369 mph/150.263 km/h; 2 Dominik Schwager/Shinya Hosokawa, D/J (Honda NSX), 2h 1m 29.945s; 3 Michael Krumm/Tsugio Matsuda, J/J (Nissan Fairlady Z), 2h 1m 36.908s; 4 Loïc Duval/Fabio Carbone, F/BR (Honda NSX), 2h 1m 44.120s; 5 Juichi Wakisaka/Andre Lotterer, J/D (Lexus SC430), 2h 1m 46.355s; 6 Manabu Orido/Takeshi Tsuchiya, J/J (Lexus SC430), 2h 2m 15.059s; 7 Ryo Michigami/Takashi Kogure, J/J (Honda NSX), 2h 2m 15.422s; 8 Benoît Tréluyer/Kazuki Hoshino, F/J (Nissan Fairlady Z), 2h 2m 15.729s; 9 Peter Dumbreck/Naoki Hattori, GB/J (Lexus SC430), 81 laps; 10 Katsutomo Kaneishi/Toshihiro Kaneishi, J/J (Honda NSX), 81.
**Fastest race lap:** Firman, 1m 24.388s, 98.158 mph/157.970 km/h.
**Fastest qualifying lap:** Michigami/Kogure, 1m 22.881s, 99.943 mph/160.843 km/h.

**FUJI GT 500 km, Fuji International Speedway, Sunto-gun, Shizuoka Prefecture, Japan, 4 May. Round 3. 110 laps of the 2.835-mile/4.563-km circuit, 311.885 miles/501.930 km.**
1 Richard Lyons/Satoshi Motoyama, GB/J (Nissan Fairlady Z), 3h 19m 52.613s, 93.623 mph/150.672 km/h; 2 Michael Krumm/Tsugio Matsuda, J/J (Nissan Fairlady Z), 3h 19m 54.727s; 3 Tatsuya Kataoka/Björn Wirdheim, J/S (Lexus SC430), 3h 20m 7.513s; 4 Sébastien Philippe/Masataka Yanagida, F/J (Nissan Fairlady Z), 3h 21m 7.204s; 5 Dominik Schwager/Shinya Hosokawa, D/J (Honda NSX), 3h 21m 20.255s; 6 Yuji Tachikawa/Toranosuke Takagi, J/J (Lexus SC430), 108 laps; 7 Peter Dumbreck/Naoki Hattori, GB/J (Lexus SC430), 108; 8 Andre Couto/Katsuyuki Hiranaka, MAC/J (Lexus SC430), 108; 9 Ralph Firman/Daisuke Ito, GB/J (Honda NSX), 108; 10 Benoît Tréluyer/Kazuki Hoshino, F/J (Nissan Fairlady Z), 102.
**Fastest race lap:** Kogure, 1m 35.689s, 106.670 mph/171.669 km/h.
**Fastest qualifying lap:** Ryo Michigami/Takashi Kogure, J/J (Honda NSX), 1m 33.066s, 109.676 mph/176.507 km/h.

**SUPER GT INTERNATIONAL SERIES MALAYSIA, Sepang International Circuit, Jalan Pekeliling, Kuala Lumpur, Malaysia, 24 June. Round 4. 54 laps of the 3.444-mile/5.543-km circuit, 185.990 miles/299.322 km.**
1 João Paulo de Oliveira/Seihi Ara, BR/J (Nissan Fairlady Z), 1h 49m 13.210s, 102.173 mph/164.432 km/h; 2 Dominik Schwager/Shinya Hosokawa, D/J (Honda NSX), 1h 49m 24.461s; 3 Benoît Tréluyer/Kazuki Hoshino, F/J (Nissan Fairlady Z), 1h 49m 31.643s; 4 Yuji Tachikawa/Toranosuke Takagi, J/J (Lexus SC430), 1h 49m 40.591s; 5 Manabu Orido/Takeshi Tsuchiya, J/J (Lexus SC430), 1h 49m 41.104s; 6 Ralph Firman/Daisuke Ito, GB/J (Honda NSX), 1h 49m 45.935s; 7 Juichi Wakisaka/Andre Lotterer, J/D (Lexus SC430), 1h 49m 46.425s; 8 Sébastien Philippe/Masataka Yanagida, F/J (Nissan Fairlady Z), 1h 49m 53.177s; 9 Tatsuya Kataoka/Björn Wirdheim, J/S (Lexus SC430), 1h 49m 58.623s; 10 Michael Krumm/Tsugio Matsuda, J/J (Nissan Fairlady Z), 1h 50m 33.330s.
**Fastest race lap:** Tachikawa/Takagi, 1m 57.062s, 105.921 mph/170.464 km/h.
**Fastest qualifying lap:** Ryo Michigami/Takashi Kogure, J/J (Honda NSX), 1m 54.306s, 108.475 mph/174.574 km/h.

**SUGO GT 300 km, Sportsland-SUGO International Course, Shibata-gun, Miyagi Prefecture, Japan, 29 July. Round 5. 81 laps of the 2.302-mile/3.704-km circuit, 186.426 miles/300.024 km.**
1 Ralph Firman/Daisuke Ito, GB/J (Honda NSX), 2h 1m 17.063s, 92.226 mph/148.423 km/h; 2 Ryo Michigami/Takashi Kogure, J/J (Honda NSX), 2h 1m 17.345s; 3 Loïc Duval/Fabio Carbone, F/BR (Honda NSX), 2h 1m 40.365s; 4 Sébastien Philippe/Masataka Yanagida, F/J (Nissan Fairlady Z), 2h 1m 40.879s; 5 Juichi Wakisaka/Andre Lotterer, J/D (Lexus SC430), 2h 1m 57.461s; 6 André Couto/Katsuyuki Hiranaka, MAC/J (Lexus SC430), 2h 2m 37.169s; 7 Jérémie Dufour/Kazuki Hoshino, F/J (Nissan Fairlady Z), 80 laps; 8 Manabu Orido/Takeshi Tsuchiya, J/J (Lexus SC430), 80; 9 Ronnie Quintarelli/Naoki Hattori, I/J (Lexus SC430), 80; 10 João Paulo de Oliveira/Seiji Ara, BR/J (Nissan Fairlady Z), 78.
**Fastest race lap:** Hiranaka, 1m 17.493s, 106.921 mph/172.072 km/h.
**Fastest qualifying lap:** Michigami/Kogure, 1m 15.120s, 110.298 mph/177.508 km/h.

**36th INTERNATIONAL POKKA 1,000 km, Suzuka International Racing Course, Ino-Cho, Suzuka-shi, Mie Prefecture, Japan, 19 August. Round 6. 173 laps of the 3.608-mile/5.807-km circuit, 624.236 miles/1004.611 km.**
1 Juichi Wakisaka/Andre Lotterer/Oliver Jarvis, J/D/GB (Lexus SC430), 6h 4h 10.983s, 102.844 mph/165.512 km/h; 2 Ralph Firman/Daisuke Ito/Yuji Ide, GB/J/J (Honda NSX), 6h 4m 20.923s; 3 Richard Lyons/Satoshi Motoyama, GB/J (Nissan Fairlady Z), 172 laps; 4 Dominik Schwager/Shinya Hosokawa, D/J (Honda NSX), 172; 5 Katsutomo Kaneishi/Toshihiro Kaneishi/Takuya Izawa, J/J/J (Honda NSX), 171; 6 Michael Krumm/Tsugio Matsuda, J/J (Nissan Fairlady Z), 171; 7 Yuji Tachikawa/Toranosuke Takagi, J/J (Lexus SC430), 170; 8 Sébastien Philippe/Masataka Yanagida, F/J (Nissan Fairlady Z), 170; 9 Tatsuya Kataoka/Björn Wirdheim, J/S (Lexus SC430), 170; 10 João Paulo de Oliveira/Seiji Ara, BR/J (Nissan Fairlady Z), 170.
**Fastest race lap:** Motoyama, 1m 57.998s, 110.086 mph/177.166 km/h.
**Fastest qualifying lap:** Philippe/Yanagida, 1m 55.781s, 112.194 mph/180.558 km/h.

**MOTEGI GT 300 km, Twin Ring Motegi, Motegi-machi, Haga-gun, Tochigi Prefecture, Japan, 9 September. Round 7. 63 laps of the 2.983-mile/4.801-km circuit, 187.942 miles/302.463 km.**
1 Ryo Michigami/Takashi Kogure, J/J (Honda NSX), 1h 56m 35.569s, 96.717 mph/155.651 km/h; 2 Michael Krumm/ Tsugio Matsuda, J/J (Nissan Fairlady Z), 1h 56m 54.167s; 3 Tatsuya Kataoka/Björn Wirdheim, J/S (Lexus SC430), 1h 57m 5.785s; 4 Loïc Duval/Fabio Carbone, F/BR (Honda NSX), 1h 57m 43.524s; 5 João Paulo de Oliveira/Seiji Ara, BR/J (Nissan Fairlady Z), 1h 57m 44.040s; 6 Juichi Wakisaka/ Andre Lotterer, J/D (Lexus SC430), 1h 57m 50.045s; 7 Katsutomo Kaneishi/Toshihiro Kaneishi, J/J (Honda NSX), 1h 57m 50.231s; 8 Manabu Orido/Takeshi Tsuchiya, J/J (Lexus SC430), 1h 58m 20.430s; 9 Peter Dumbreck/Naoki Hattori, GB/J (Lexus SC430), 1h 58m 23.832s; 10 André Couto/Katsuyuki Hiranaka, MAC/J (Lexus SC430), 62 laps.
**Fastest race lap:** Kogure, 1m 47.437s, 99.961 mph/160.872 km/h.
**Fastest qualifying lap:** Michigami/Kogure, 1m 45.720s, 101.585 mph/163.485 km/h.

**KYUSHU 300 km, Autopolis International Racing Course, Kamit-sue-mura, Hita-gun, Oita Prefecture, Japan, 14 October. Round 8. 65 laps of the 2.904-mile/4.674-km circuit, 188.779 miles/303.810 km.**
1 Ralph Firman/Daisuke Ito, GB/J (Honda NSX), 1h 55m 57.024s, 97.686 mph/157.210 km/h; 2 Dominik Schwager/Shinya Hosokawa, D/J (Honda NSX), 1h 56m 7.169s; 3 André Couto/Katsuyuki Hiranaka, MAC/J (Lexus SC430), 1h 56m 16.911s; 4 Michael Krumm/Tsugio Matsuda, J/J (Nissan Fairlady Z), 1h 56m 34.149s; 5 Ryo Michigami/Takashi Kogure, J/J (Honda NSX), 1h 56m 34.431s; 6 Juichi Wakisaka/Andre Lotterer, J/D (Lexus SC430), 1h 56m 40.074s; 7 Sébastien Philippe/Masataka Yanagida, F/J (Nissan Fairlady Z), 1h 56m 40.733s; 8 Tatsuya Kataoka/Björn Wirdheim, J/S (Lexus SC430), 1h 57m 3.276s; 9 Loïc Duval/Fabio Carbone, F/BR (Honda NSX), 1h 57m 19.777s; 10 Manabu Orido/Takeshi Tsuchiya, J/J (Lexus SC430), 64 laps.
**Fastest race lap:** Duval, 1m 42.759s, 101.747 mph/163.746 km/h.
**Fastest qualifying lap:** Yuji Tachikawa/Toranosuke Takagi, J/J (Lexus SC430), 1m 39.424s, 105.160 mph/169.239 km/h.

**Provisional championship points**
1 Ralph Firman/Daisuke Ito, GB/GB, 91; 2 Ryo Michigami/Takashi Kogure, J/J, 62; 3 Michael Krumm/Tsugio Matsuda, D/J, 61; 4 Dominik Schwager/Shinya Hosokawa, D/J, 60; 5 Andre Lotterer/Juichi Wakisaka, D/J, 49; 6 Fabio Carbone/Loïc Duval, BR/F, 49; 7 Richard Lyons/Satoshi Motoyama, GB/J, 48; 8 Toranosuke Takagi/Yuji Tachikawa, J/J, 45; 9 Björn Wirdheim/Tatsuya Kataoka, S/J, 38; 10 Sébastien Philippe/Masataka Yanagida, F/J, 30.

*Result of the Fuji race will be given in AUTOCOURSE 2008–2009.*

## Other Sports Car Races

**DAYTONA 24-HOURS, Daytona International Speedway, Daytona Beach, Florida, U.S.A., 27-28 January. 668 laps of the 3.560-mile/5.729-km circuit, 2378.080 miles/3827.149 km.**
1 Scott Pruett/Salvador Duran/Juan Pablo Montoya, USA/MEX/CO (Riley MkXI-Lexus), 24h 0m 55.002s, 99.024 mph/159.363 km/h; 2 Patrick Carpentier/Darren Manning/Ryan Dalziel/Milka Duno, CDN/GB/GB/YV (Riley MkXI-Pontiac), 24h 2m 9.749s; 3 Max Angelelli/Wayne Taylor/Jeff Gordon/Jan Magnussen, I/USA/USA/DK (Riley MkXI-Pontiac), 666 laps; 4 Hurlety Haywood/JC France/João Barbosa/Roberto Moreno/David Donohue, USA/USA/P/BR/USA (Riley MkXI-Porsche), 662; 5 Mark Wilkins/Brian Frisselle/Burt Frisselle/David Empringham, CDN/USA/USA/CDN (Riley MkXI-Lexus), 657; 6 Tomás Enge/Roger Yasukawa/Chris Festa/Christian Montanari/Kris Szekeres, CZ/USA/USA/I/USA (Riley MkXI-Pontiac), 655; 7 Memo Gidley/Fabrizio Gollin/Michel Jourdain/Oriol Servià, USA/I/MEX/E (Doran E4-Ford), 655; 8 Timo Bernhard/Charles Morgan/Rob Morgan/BJ Zacharias, D/USA/USA/USA (Riley MkXI-Porsche), 636; 9 Oswaldo Negri Jr/Mark Patterson/Helio Castroneves/Sam Hornish Jr, BR/ZA/BR/USA (Riley MkXI-Lexus), 628; 10 Michael Valiante/Rob Finlay/Bobby Labonte/Michael McDowell, CDN/USA/USA/USA (Crawford DP03-Ford), 627.
**Fatest race lap:** Darren Law, USA (Riley MkXI-Porsche), 1m 44.057s, 123.163 mph/198.212 km/h.
**Fastest qualifying lap:** Alex Gurney/Jon Fogarty/Jimmy Vasser, USA/USA/USA (Riley MkXI-Pontiac), 1m 43.475s, 123.856 mph/199.327 km/h.

**35th ADAC ZÜRICH 24h RENNEN, Nürburgring Nordschleife Circuit, Nürburg/Eifel, Germany, 9-10 June. 112 laps of the 15.769-mile/25.378-km circuit, 1766.146 miles/2842.336 km.**
**Race stopped early due to fog.**
1 Timo Bernhard/Marc Lieb/Romain Dumas/Marcel Tiemann, D/D/CH/D (Porsche 911 GT3-RSR), 18h 1m 30.009s, 97.983 mph/157.689 km/h; 2 Duncan Huisman/Tom Coronel/Patrick Simon/Christophe Bouchut, NL/NL/D/F (Dodge Viper GTS-R), 111 laps; 3 Marc Basseng/Marc Hennerici/Dirk Adorf/Frank Stippler, D/D/D/D (Porsche 911 GT3-RSR), 111; 4 Uwe Alzen/Jürgen Alzen/Christian Menzel/Christian Mamerow, D/D/D/D (Porsche Cayman), 108; 5 Claudia Hürtgen/Hans-Joachim Stuck/Johannes Stuck/Richard Göransson, D/D/D/S (BMW Z4 M-Coupé), 106; 6 Klaus Frers/Patrik Bernhardt/Pierre Kaffer/Jörg Hardt, D/D/D/D (Porsche 997 RSR), 104; 7 Shane Fox/Wolfgang Weber/Lothar Diedrich/Uwe Nittel, D/D/D/D (Porsche RGT), 103; 8 Rene Rast/Jimmy Johansen/Florian Gruber/Dieter Depping, D/S/D/D (Volkswagen Golf Mk5), 101; 9 Otto Fritschze/Jürgen Fritschze/Rainer Bastuck/Stefan Kissling, D/D/D/D (Opel Astra GTC), 101; 10 Rudi Adams/Gregor Volger/Arnd Meier/Reiner Dörr, D/D/D/D (BMW 130 I), 101.
**Fastest race lap:** Huisman/Coronel/Simon/Bouchut, 8m 49.631s, 107.186 mph/172.499 km/h.

**75th 24 HEURES DU MANS, Circuit International Du Mans, Les Raineries, Le Mans, France, 16-17 June. 369 laps of the 8.469-mile/13.629-km circuit, 3124.938 miles/5029.101 km.**
1 Frank Biela/Emanuele Pirro/Marco Werner, D/I/D (Audi R10 TD1), 24h 2m 42.628s, 129.961 mph/209.152 km/h (1st LMP1 class); 2 Sébastien Bourdais/Pedro Lamy/Stéphane Sarrazin, F/P/F (Peugeot 908 HDi), 359 laps; 3 Emmanuel Collard/Jean-Christophe Boullion/Romain Dumas, F/F/F (Pescarolo 01-Judd), 358; 4 João Barbosa/Stuart Hall/Martin Short, P/GB/GB (Pescarolo 01-Judd), 347; 5 David Brabham/Rickard Rydell/Darren Turner, AUS/S/GB (Aston Martin DBR9), 343 (1st LMGT1 class); 6 Jan Magnussen/Ron Fellows/Johnny O'Connell, DK/CDN/USA (Chevrolet Corvette C6.R), 342; 7 Christophe Bouchut/Fabrizio Gollin/Caspar Elgaard, F/I/DK (Aston Martin DBR9), 341; 8 Alex Young/Stefan Mücke/Jan Charouz, MAL/D/CZ (Lola B07/17-Judd), 338; 9 Peter Kox/Tomás Enge/Johnny Herbert, NL/CZ/GB (Aston Martin DBR9), 337; 10 Laurent Groppi/Nicolas Prost/Jean-Philippe Belloc, F/F/F (Saleen S7-R), 336; 11 Jamie Davis/Fabio Babini/Matteo Malucelli, GB/I/I (Aston Martin DBR9), 336; 12 Jérôme Policand/Patrice Goueslard/Luc Alphand, F/F/F (Chevrolet Corvette C6.R), 326; 13 Christophe Tinseau/Harold Primat/Benoit Tréluyer, F/CH/F (Pescarolo 01-Judd), 324; 14 Robert Pergl/Tomás Kostka/Alexi Vasiliev, CZ/CZ/RUS (Ferrari 550 Maranello), 321; 15 Patrick Long/Richard Lietz/Raymond Narac, USA/A/F (Porsche 997 GT3-RSR), 319 (1st LMGT2 class); 16 Soheil Ayari/Stéphane Ortelli/Nicolas Lapierre, F/MC/F (Saleen S7-R), 318; 17 Antonio Garcia/Christian Fittipaldi/Jos Menten, E/BR/NL (Aston Martin DBR9), 318; 18 Bill Binnie/Chris Buncombe/Allen Timpani, USA/GB/GB (Lola B05/40-Zytek), 317 (1st LMP2 class); 19 Tracy Krohn/Nic Jonsson/Colin Braun, USA/S/USA (Ferrari 430 GT), 313; 20 Bob Berridge/Gareth Evans/Peter Owen, GB/GB/GB (Lola B06/10-AER), 309; 21 Allan Simonsen/Lars Erik Nielsen/Pierre Ehret, AUS/DK/D (Porsche 997 GT3-RSR), 309; 22 Joe Macari/Ben Aucott/Adrian Newey, GB/GB/GB (Ferrari F430 GT), 307; 23 Richard Dean/Lawrence Tomlinson/Rob Bell, GB/GB/GB (Panoz Esperante GTLM), 307; 24 Didier Andre/Jean-Luc Blanchemain/Vincent Vosse, F/F/B (Chevrolet Corvette C5.R), 305; 25 Jan Lammers/David Hart/Jeroen Bleekemolen, NL/NL/NL (Dome S101.5-Judd), 305; 26 Jonathan Cochet/Alexander Frei/Bruno Besson, F/CH/F (Courage LC70-AER), 304; 27 Adrian Fernandez/Haruki Kurosawa/Robbie Kerr, MEX/J/GB (Zytek 07S/2), 301; 28 D Smet/Philipp Peter/Claude-Yves Gosselin, A/A/F (Chevrolet Corvette C6.R), 288; 29 Patrick Bornhauser/Roland Berville/Gregor Fisken, F/F/GB (Aston Martin DBR9), 271; 30 Nicolas Minassian/Marc Gené/Jacques Villeneuve, F/E/CDN (Peugeot 908 HDi), 338 (DNF-engine); 31 Rinaldo Capello/Tom Kristensen/Allan McNish, I/DK/GB (Audi R10 TDI), 262 (DNF-accident); 32 Michael Vergers/Juan Barazi/Karim Ojjeh, NL/DK/ZA (Zytek 07S/2), 252 (DNF-accident); 33 Carl Rosenblad/Matthew Marsh/Jesus Diez Villarroel, S/GB/E (Ferrari F430 GT), 252 (DNF-mechanical); 34 Tommy Erdos/Mike Newton/Andy Wallace, BR/GB/GB (MG Lola EX264-AER), 251 (DNF-piston); 35 Tim Mullen/Chris Niarchos/Andrew Kirkaldy, GB/CDN/GB (Ferrari F430 GT), 241 (DNF-transmission); 36 Bruce Jouanny/Jacques Nicolet/Alain Filhol, F/F/F (Courage LC75-AER), 224 (DNF-engine); 37 Jaime Melo/Mika Salo/Johnny Mowlem, BR/FIN/GB (Ferrari F430 GT), 223 (DNF-water pump); 38 Liz Halliday/Vitaly Petrov/Romain Iannetta, USA/RUS/F (Courage LC75-AER), 198 (DNF-gearbox); 39 Jean-Marc Gounon/Guillaume Moreau/Stefan Johannson, F/F/S (Courage LC70-AER), 175 (DNF-engine); 40 Andrea Chiesa/Andrea Belicchi/Alex Caffi, CH/I/I (Spyker C8 Spyder GT2-R), 145 (DNF-transmission); 41 Warren Hughes/Miguel Amaral/Miguel De Castro, GB/P/E (Lola B05/40-AER), 137 (DNF-accident); 42 Marc Rostan/Chris MacAllister/Gavin Pickering, F/USA/GB (Pilbeam MP93-Judd), 126 (DNF-spin); 43 Johannes van Overbeek/Jörg Bergmeister/Seth Neiman, USA/D/USA (Porsche 997 GT3-RSR), 124 (DNF-gearbox); 44 Norbert Siedler/Tony Burgess/Jean de Pourtales, A/CDN/F (Pescarolo 01-Judd), 98 (DNF-engine); 45 Johnny Kane/Jaroslav 'Jarek' Janis/Mike Hezemans, GB/CZ/NL (Spyker C8 Spyder GT2-R), 70 (DNF-mechanical); 46 Horst Felbermayer Jr./Philip Collin/Horst Felbermayr, A/USA/A (Porsche 997 GT3-RSR), 68 (DNF-electrics); 47 Marcel Fässler/Jean-Denis Deletraz/Iradj Alexander, CH/CH/CH (Lola B07/10-Audi), 62 (DNF-electrics); 48 Tom Kimber-Smith/Danny Watts/Tom Milner Jr, GB/GB/USA (Panoz Esperante GTLM), 60 (DNF-mechanical); 49 Yutaka Yamagishi/Robin Longechal/Yojiro Terada, J/F/J (Dome S101.5-Mader), 56 (DNF-overheating); 50 Jamie Campbell-Walter/Felipe Ortiz/Shinji Nakano, GB/CH/J (Creation CA07-Judd), 55 (DNF-overheating); 51 Lucas Luhr/Mike Rockenfeller/Alexandre Prémat, D/D/F (Audi R10 TDI), 23 (DNF-accident); 52 Oliver Gavin/Olivier Beretta/Max Papis, GB/MC/I (Chevrolet Corvette C6.R), 22 (DNF-propshaft); 53 Stuart Moseley/Tim Greaves/Robin Liddell, GB/GB/GB (Radical SR9-AER), 16 (DNF-accident); 54 Koji Yamanishi/Atsushi Yogo, J/J (Lamborghini Murcielago R-GT), 1 (DNF-transmission).
**Fastest race lap:** McNish, 3m 27.176s, 147.156 mph/236.825 km/h.
**Fastest qualifying lap:** Bourdais, 3m 26.344s, 147.749 mph/237.780 km/h.

## V8 Supercar Championship Series 2006

The following races were run after AUTOCOURSE 2006–2007 went to press.

**FERODO TASMANIA CHALLENGE, Symmons Plains Raceway, Launceston, Tasmania, Australia, 11/12 November. Round 11. 42, 58 and 58 laps of the 1.498-mile/2.411-km circuit.**
**Race 1 (62.921 miles/101.262 km).**
1 Jason Bright, AUS (Ford Falcon BA), 44m 32.8863s, 84.746 mph/136.385 km/h; 2 Mark Winterbottom, AUS (Ford Falcon BA), 44m 35.5680s; 3 Rick Kelly, AUS (Holden Commodore VZ), 44m 36.7458s; 4 Garth Tander, AUS (Holden Commodore VZ), 44m 40.0734s; 5 James Courtney, AUS (Ford Falcon BA), 44m 42.5496s; 6 Steven Richards, NZ (Holden Commodore VZ), 44m 44.2557s; 7 Todd Kelly, AUS (Holden Commodore VZ), 44m 44.4896s; 8 Paul Dumbrell, AUS (Holden Commodore VZ), 44m 54.9923s; 9 Will Davison, AUS (Ford Falcon BA), 44m 55.1534s; 10 Dean Canto, AUS (Holden Commodore VZ), 44m 57.6139s.
**Fastest race lap:** Tander, 52.4193s, 102.887 mph/165.580 km/h.
**Pole position:** Mark Skaife, AUS (Holden Commodore VZ), 52.0372s, 103.642 mph/166.796 km/h.

**Race 2 (86.891 miles/139.838 km).**
1 Garth Tander, AUS (Holden Commodore VZ), 1h 2m 46.1704s, 83.057 mph/133.668 km/h; 2 Mark Winterbottom, AUS (Ford Falcon BA), 1h 2m 46.6683s; 3 Jason Bright, AUS (Ford Falcon BA), 1h 2m 48.1501s; 4 Todd Kelly, AUS (Holden Commodore VZ), 1h 2m 48.6629s; 5 Rick Kelly, AUS (Holden Commodore VZ), 1h 2m 56.7712s; 6 Will Davison, AUS (Ford Falcon BA), 1h 2m 56.9462s; 7 Paul Dumbrell, AUS (Holden Commodore VZ), 1h 3m 0.4244s; 8 Jason Bargwanna, AUS (Ford Falcon BA), 1h 3m 1.7711s; 9 Craig Lowndes, AUS (Ford Falcon BA), 1h 3m 02.2800s; 10 Russell Ingall, AUS (Ford Falcon BA), 1h 3m 02.6307s.
**Fastest race lap:** Kelly (Todd), 52.9716s, 101.814 mph/163.853 km/h.
**Pole position:** Brad Jones, AUS (Ford Falcon BA).

**Race 3 (86.891 miles/139.838 km).**
1 Garth Tander, AUS (Holden Commodore VZ), 1h 7m 39.8942s, 77.048 mph/123.997 km/h; 2 Jason Bright, AUS (Ford Falcon BA), 1h 7m 40.4184s; 3 Mark Winterbottom, AUS (Ford Falcon BA), 1h 07m 43.6214s; 4 Rick Kelly, AUS (Holden Commodore VZ), 1h 7m 44.4577s; 5 Todd Kelly, AUS (Holden Commodore VZ), 1h 7m 44.8768s; 6 Steven Richards, NZ (Holden Commodore VZ), 1h 7m 45.8581s; 7 Craig Lowndes, AUS (Ford Falcon BA), 1h 7m 47.7941s; 8 Paul Dumbrell, AUS (Holden Commodore VZ), 1h 7m 48.5163s; 9 Cameron McConville, AUS (Holden Commodore VZ), 1h 7m 48.8715s; 10 Russell Ingall, AUS (Ford Falcon BA), 1h 7m 49.1823s.
**Fastest race lap:** Bright, 52.5952s, 102.543 mph/165.026 km/h.
**Pole position:** Tander.

**DESERT GRAND PRIX, Bahrain International Circuit, Sakhir, Bahrain, 24/25 November. Round 12. 27, 37 and 37 laps of the 2.386-mile/3.840-km circuit.**
**Race 1 (64.424 miles/103.680 km).**
1 Jason Bright, AUS (Ford Falcon BA), 41m 38.0397s, 92.843 mph/149.416 km/h; 2 Garth Tander, AUS (Holden Commodore VZ), 41m 38.4050s; 3 Todd Kelly, AUS (Holden Commodore VZ), 41m 45.6824s; 4 Rick Kelly, AUS (Holden Commodore VZ), 41m 53.8595s; 5 James Courtney, AUS (Ford Falcon BA), 41m 55.2371s; 6 Steven Richards, NZ (Holden Commodore VZ), 41m 56.0655s; 7 Mark Skaife, AUS (Holden Commodore VZ), 41m 57.8901s; 8 Mark Winterbottom, AUS (Ford Falcon BA), 41m 59.0777s; 9 Craig Lowndes, AUS (Ford Falcon BA), 42m 03.1288s; 10 Jamie Whincup, AUS (Ford Falcon BA), 42m 05.0565s.
**Fastest race lap:** Bright, 1m 24.9102s, 101.164 mph/162.807 km/h.
**Pole position:** Tander, 1m 24.1060s, 102.131 mph/164.364 km/h.

**Race 2 (88.284 miles/142.080 km).**
1 Garth Tander, AUS (Holden Commodore VZ), 53m 55.1641s, 98.240 mph/158.102 km/h; 2 Jason Bright, AUS (Ford Falcon BA), 54m 07.2589s; 3 Mark Winterbottom, AUS (Ford Falcon BA), 54m 10.0127s; 4 Todd Kelly, AUS (Holden Commodore VZ), 54m 22.1468s; 5 Craig Lowndes, AUS (Ford Falcon BA), 54m 30.9338s; 6 Jamie Whincup, AUS (Ford Falcon BA), 54m 31.1720s; 7 Greg Murphy, NZ (Holden Commodore VZ), 54m 38.5918s; 8 Steven Richards, NZ (Holden Commodore VZ), 54m 41.0309s; 9 Cameron McConville, AUS (Holden Commodore VZ), 54m 47.3863s; 10 Jason Richards, NZ (Holden Commodore VZ), 54m 47.7402s.
**Fastest race lap:** Tander, 1m 25.044s, 101.004 mph/162.550 km/h.
**Pole position:** Andrew Jones, AUS (Holden Commodore VZ).

**Race 3 (88.284 miles/142.080 km).**
1 Todd Kelly, AUS (Holden Commodore VZ), 54m 15.8752s, 97.616 mph/157.096 km/h; 2 Jason Bright, AUS (Ford Falcon BA), 54m 17.1559s; 3 Craig Lowndes, AUS (Ford Falcon BA), 54m 24.8715s; 4 Mark Skaife, AUS (Holden Commodore VZ), 54m 37.8844s; 5 Rick Kelly, AUS (Holden Commodore VZ), 54m 41.9815s; 6 Steven Johnson, AUS (Ford Falcon BA), 54m 45.5960s; 7 James Courtney, AUS (Ford Falcon BA), 54m 48.8941s; 8 Garth Tander, AUS (Holden Commodore VZ), 54m 51.7602s;

**9** Cameron McConville, AUS (Holden Commodore VZ), 54m 54.8590s; **10** Russell Ingall, AUS (Ford Falcon BA), 54m 58.9954s.
**Fastest race lap:** Tander, 1m 25.4886s, 100.479 mph/161.705 km/h.
**Pole position:** Tander.

**CATERPILLAR GRAND FINALE, Phillip Island Grand Prix Circuit, Cowes, Victoria, Australia, 9/10 December. Round 13. 23, 32 and 31 laps of the 2.764-mile/4.448-km circuit.**
**Race 1 (63.569 miles/102.304 km).**
**1** Todd Kelly, AUS (Holden Commodore VZ), 38m 0.1350s, 100.366 mph/161.523 km/h; **2** Garth Tander, AUS (Holden Commodore VZ), 38m 1.5818s; **3** Mark Skaife, AUS (Holden Commodore VZ), 38m 11.3835s; **4** Craig Lowndes, AUS (Ford Falcon BA), 38m 12.0027s; **5** Rick Kelly, AUS (Holden Commodore VZ), 38m 13.9472s; **6** Will Davison, AUS (Ford Falcon BA), 38m 14.3859s; **7** Mark Winterbottom, AUS (Ford Falcon BA), 38m 14.9093s; **8** Steven Richards, NZ (Holden Commodore VZ), 38m 17.7460s; **9** James Courtney, AUS (Ford Falcon BA), 38m 18.3798s; **10** Jason Bright, AUS (Ford Falcon BA), 38m 21.5336s.
**Fastest race lap:** Kelly (Todd), 1m 36.1290s, 103.506 mph/166.576 km/h.
**Pole position:** Kelly (Todd), 1m 34.1747s, 105.654 mph/170.032 km/h.

**Race 2 (88.443 miles/142.336 km).**
**1** Todd Kelly, AUS (Holden Commodore VZ), 52m 49.3663s, 100.461 mph/161.675 km/h; **2** Mark Winterbottom, AUS (Ford Falcon BA), 52m 55.5314s; **3** Craig Lowndes, AUS (Ford Falcon BA), 53m 03.2592s; **4** Rick Kelly, AUS (Holden Commodore VZ), 53m 5.1079s; **5** Steven Richards, NZ (Holden Commodore VZ), 53m 6.2734s; **6** Mark Skaife, AUS (Holden Commodore VZ), 53m 6.6135s; **7** Will Davison, AUS (Ford Falcon BA), 53m 6.9358s; **8** Jason Bright, AUS (Ford Falcon BA), 53m 14.4239s; **9** Jamie Whincup, AUS (Ford Falcon BA), 53m 14.5843s; **10** Cameron McConville, AUS (Holden Commodore VZ), 53m 16.5073s.
**Fastest race lap:** Winterbottom, 1m 36.0653s, 103.574 mph/166.686 km/h.
**Pole position:** Kelly (Todd).

**Race 3 (85.680 miles/137.888 km).**
**1** Mark Winterbottom, AUS (Ford Falcon BA), 50m 47.1883s, 101.223 mph/162.903 km/h; **2** Garth Tander, AUS (Holden Commodore VZ), 50m 47.3126s; **3** Jason Richards, NZ (Holden Commodore VZ), 50m 48.4341s; **4** Jason Bright, AUS (Ford Falcon BA), 51m 1.6146s; **5** Todd Kelly, AUS (Holden Commodore VZ), 51m 1.9081s; **6** Cameron McConville, AUS (Holden Commodore VZ), 51m 5.8815s; **7** Jamie Whincup, AUS (Ford Falcon BA), 51m 6.0541s; **8** Steven Richards, NZ (Holden Commodore VZ), 51m 10.3896s; **9** Greg Murphy, NZ (Holden Commodore VZ), 51m 11.2542s; **10** Dean Canto, AUS (Holden Commodore VZ), 51m 12.7207s.
**Fastest race lap:** Tander, 1m 35.5114s, 104.175 mph/167.653 km/h.
**Pole position:** Kelly (Todd).

**Final championship points**
**1** Rick Kelly, AUS, 3,308; **2** Craig Lowndes, AUS, 3,271; **3** Mark Winterbottom, AUS, 3,089; **4** Garth Tander, AUS, 2,965; **5** Jason Bright, AUS, 2,868; **6** Todd Kelly, AUS, 2,815; **7** Steven Richards, NZ, 2,740; **8** Russell Ingall, AUS, 2,708; **9** Steven Johnson, AUS, 2,378; **10** Jamie Whincup, AUS, 2,357; **11** James Courtney, AUS, 2,347; **12** Paul Dumbrell, AUS, 2,332; **13** Cameron McConville, AUS, 2,099; **14** Jason Bargwanna, AUS, 2,053; **15** Max Wilson, BR, 2,038; **16** Mark Skaife, AUS, 2,036; **17** Dean Canto, AUS, 2,024; **18** Jason Richards, NZ, 1,993; **19** Will Davison, AUS, 1,943; **20** Lee Holdsworth, AUS, 1,811.

## 2007

**CLIPSAL 500, Adelaide Steet Circuit, South Australia, Australia, 3/4 March. Round 1. 2 x 78 laps of the 2.001-mile/3.220-km circuit.**
**Race 1 (156.064 miles/251.160 km).**
**1** Todd Kelly, AUS (Holden Commodore VE), 1h 50m 40.5932s, 84.605 mph/136.158 km/h; **2** James Courtney, AUS (Ford Falcon BF), 1h 50m 42.6798s; **3** Jamie Whincup, AUS (Ford Falcon BF), 1h 50m 45.7351s; **4** Rick Kelly, AUS (Holden Commodore VE), 1h 50m 46.8826s; **5** Mark Winterbottom, AUS (Ford Falcon BF), 1h 50m 51.3036s; **6** Garth Tander, AUS (Holden Commodore VE), 1h 51m 01.9833s; **7** Greg Murphy, NZ (Holden Commodore VE), 1h 51m 3.5996s; **8** Russell Ingall, AUS (Ford Falcon BF), 1h 51m 5.0283s; **9** Steven Johnson, AUS (Ford Falcon BF), 1h 51m 13.1466s; **10** Jason Bright, AUS (Ford Falcon BF), 1h 51m 26.0671s.
**Fastest race lap:** Courtney, 1m 22.8075s, 86.984 mph/139.987 km/h.
**Pole position:** Courtney, 1m 22.3584s, 87.458 mph/140.750 km/h.

**Race 2 (156.064 miles/251.160 km).**
**1** Rick Kelly, AUS (Holden Commodore VE), 1h 58m 54.1927s, 78.752 mph/126.738 km/h; **2** Todd Kelly, AUS (Holden Commodore VE), 1h 58m 55.8926s; **3** James Courtney, AUS (Ford Falcon BF), 1h 58m 56.6606s; **4** Russell Ingall, AUS (Ford Falcon BF), 1h 58m 57.2401s; **5** Jamie Whincup, AUS (Ford Falcon BF), 1h 58m 58.6630s; **6** Steven Johnson, AUS (Ford Falcon BF), 1h 58m 59.1330s; **7** Mark Skaife, AUS (Holden Commodore VE), 1h 59m 1.2657s; **8** Steven Richards, NZ (Ford Falcon BF), 1h 59m 5.1644s; **9** Will Davison, AUS (Ford Falcon BF), 1h 59m 5.5333s; **10** Garth Tander, AUS (Holden Commodore VE), 1h 59m 7.9757s.
**Fastest race lap:** Courtney, 1m 22.4348s, 87.377 mph/140.620 km/h.
**Pole position:** Kelly (Todd).

**BIG POND 400, Barbagallo Raceway Wanneroo, Perth, Western Australia, Australia, 24/25 March. Round 2. 3 x 50 laps of the 1.498-mile/2.410-km circuit.**
**Race 1 (74.875 miles/120.500 km).**
**1** Garth Tander, AUS (Holden Commodore VE), 51m 31.2237s, 87.199 mph/140.332 km/h; **2** Rick Kelly, AUS (Holden Commodore VE), 51m 31.5223s; **3** Mark Skaife, AUS (Holden Commodore VE), 51m 34.9894s; **4** Craig Lowndes, AUS (Ford Falcon BF), 51m 38.2507s; **5** Steven Johnson, AUS (Ford Falcon BF), 51m 38.8770s; **6** Will Davison, AUS (Ford Falcon BF), 51m 39.3563s; **7** Jamie Whincup, AUS (Ford Falcon BF), 51m 41.4421s; **8** Greg Murphy, NZ (Holden Commodore VE), 51m 43.0532s; **9** Lee Holdsworth, AUS (Holden Commodore VE), 51m 45.1363s; **10** Mark Winterbottom, AUS (Ford Falcon BF), 51m 48.0137s.
**Fastest race lap:** Tander, 57.4237s, 93.881 mph/151.087 km/h.
**Pole position:** Tander, 56.0511s, 96.180 mph/154.787 km/h.

**Race 2 (74.875 miles/120.500 km).**
**1** Garth Tander, AUS (Holden Commodore VE), 52m 22.0384s, 85.789 mph/138.063 km/h; **2** Rick Kelly, AUS (Holden Commodore VE), 52m 23.1044s; **3** Mark Skaife, AUS (Holden Commodore VE), 52m 23.4678s; **4** Steven Johnson, AUS (Ford Falcon BF), 52m 26.5073s; **5** Will Davison, AUS (Ford Falcon BF), 52m 27.2583s; **6** Mark Winterbottom, AUS (Ford Falcon BF), 52m 28.1307s; **7** Greg Murphy, NZ (Holden Commodore VE), 52m 28.3393s; **8** Craig Lowndes, AUS (Ford Falcon BF), 52m 29.2160s; **9** Lee Holdsworth, AUS (Holden Commodore VZ), 52m 29.4284s; **10** Todd Kelly, AUS (Holden Commodore VE), 52m 29.6015s.
**Fastest race lap:** Tander, 57.7996s, 93.271 mph/150.104 km/h.
**Pole position:** Tander.

**Race 3 (74.875 miles/139.780 km).**
**1** Garth Tander, AUS (Holden Commodore VE), 52m 25.6340s, 85.690 mph/137.905 km/h; **2** Mark Skaife, AUS (Holden Commodore VE), 52m 26.2528s; **3** Rick Kelly, AUS (Holden Commodore VE), 52m 35.9644s; **4** Steven Johnson, AUS (Ford Falcon BF), 52m 36.1482s; **5** Mark Winterbottom, AUS (Ford Falcon BF), 52m 39.0992s; **6** Will Davison, AUS (Ford Falcon BF), 52m 39.3833s; **7** Todd Kelly, AUS (Holden Commodore VE), 52m 39.5552s; **8** Craig Lowndes, AUS (Ford Falcon BF), 52m 39.7683s; **9** Steven Richards, NZ (Ford Falcon BF), 52m 40.0982s; **10** Russell Ingall, AUS (Ford Falcon BF), 52m 42.3041s.
**Fastest race lap:** Skaife, 57.3010s, 94.082 mph/151.410 km/h.
**Pole position:** Tander.

**PLACEMAKERS V8 SUPERCARS, Pukekohe Park Raceway, Auckland, New Zealand, 21/22 April. Round 3. 43, 43 and 36 laps of the 1.765-mile/2.841-km circuit.**
**Race 1 (75.909 miles/122.163 km).**
**1** Garth Tander, AUS (Holden Commodore VE), 43m 46.0087s, 104.063 mph/167.473 km/h; **2** Mark Winterbottom, AUS (Ford Falcon BF), 43m 47.2417s; **3** Rick Kelly, AUS (Holden Commodore VE), 43m 48.6231s; **4** Jamie Whincup, AUS (Ford Falcon BF), 43m 51.2534s; **5** Steven Richards, NZ (Ford Falcon BF), 43m 52.8155s; **6** Todd Kelly, AUS (Holden Commodore VE), 43m 56.5427s; **7** Jason Richards, NZ (Holden Commodore VE), 44m 02.3069s; **8** Russell Ingall, AUS (Ford Falcon BF), 44m 03.6798s; **9** James Courtney, AUS (Ford Falcon BF), 44m 04.0612s; **10** Mark Skaife, AUS (Holden Commodore VE), 44m 11.2799s.
**Fastest race lap:** Kelly (Rick), 56.4068s, 112.666 mph/181.318 km/h.
**Pole position:** Winterbottom, 55.6704s, 114.156 mph/183.717 km/h.

**Race 2 (75.909 miles/122.163 km).**
**1** Garth Tander, AUS (Holden Commodore VE), 47m 28.1385s, 95.947 mph/154.412 km/h; **2** Jamie Whincup, AUS (Ford Falcon BF), 47m 28.9983s; **3** Rick Kelly, AUS (Holden Commodore VE), 47m 29.6674s; **4** Todd Kelly, AUS (Holden Commodore VE), 47m 30.0536s; **5** James Courtney, AUS (Ford Falcon BF), 47m 30.6372s; **6** Mark Skaife, AUS (Holden Commodore VE), 47m 31.6580s; **7** Craig Lowndes, AUS (Ford Falcon BF), 47m 31.9032s; **8** Will Davison, AUS (Ford Falcon BF), 47m 32.2083s; **9** Russell Ingall, AUS (Ford Falcon BF), 47m 33.3930s; **10** Paul Radisich, NZ (Holden Commodore VE), 47m 33.8272s.
**Fastest race lap:** Winterbottom, 56.5605s, 112.360 mph/180.825 km/h.
**Pole position:** Tander.

**Race 3 (63.551 miles/102.276 km).**
**1** Rick Kelly, AUS (Holden Commodore VE), 47m 13.1552s, 80.753 mph/129.958 km/h; **2** Todd Kelly, AUS (Holden Commodore VE), 47m 13.4551s; **3** James Courtney, AUS (Ford Falcon BF), 47m 13.9130s; **4** Craig Lowndes, AUS (Ford Falcon BF), 47m 14.3445s; **5** Jamie Whincup, AUS (Ford Falcon BF), 47m 14.9348s; **6** Will Davison, AUS (Ford Falcon BF), 47m 15.2659s; **7** Paul Radisich, NZ (Holden Commodore VE), 47m 16.2105s; **8** Garth Tander, AUS (Holden Commodore VE), 47m 16.3689s; **9** Mark Skaife, AUS (Holden Commodore VE), 47m 16.7654s; **10** Russell Ingall, AUS (Ford Falcon BF), 47m 17.0361s.
**Fastest race lap:** Kelly (Rick), 56.4550s, 112.570 mph/181.163 km/h.
**Pole position:** Tander.

**V8 SUPERCAR CHAMPIONSHIP SERIES, Winton Motor Raceway, Benalla, Victoria, Australia, 19/20 May. Round 4. 3 x 40 laps of the 1.864-mile/3.000-km circuit.**
**Race 1 (74.565 miles/120.000 km).**
**1** Jamie Whincup, AUS (Ford Falcon BF), 1h 11m 43.2503s, 62.379 mph/100.389 km/h; **2** Steven Richards, NZ (Ford Falcon BF), 1h 11m 45.3468s; **3** Rick Kelly, AUS (Holden Commodore VE), 1h 11m 50.9129s; **4** Garth Tander, AUS (Holden Commodore VE), 1h 11m 51.1351s; **5** Lee Holdsworth, AUS (Holden Commodore VZ), 1h 11m 52.1317s; **6** Steven Johnson, AUS (Ford Falcon BF), 1h 11m 57.4145s; **7** Jason Bright, AUS (Ford Falcon BF), 1h 12m 3.5986s; **8** Paul Morris, AUS (Holden Commodore VE), 1h 12m 04.9056s; **9** Max Wilson, BR (Ford Falcon BF), 1h 12m 05.1451s; **10** Shane Price, AUS (Holden Commodore VE), 1h 12m 06.7956s.
**Fastest race lap:** James Courtney, AUS (Ford Falcon BF), 1m 28.0655s, 76.202 mph/122.635 km/h.
**Pole position:** Todd Kelly, AUS (Holden Commodore VE), 1m 23.4793s, 80.389 mph/129.373 km/h.

**Race 2 (74.565 miles/120.000 km).**
**1** Garth Tander, AUS (Holden Commodore VE), 1h 9m 36.3676s, 64.274 mph/103.439 km/h; **2** Jamie Whincup, AUS (Ford Falcon BF), 1h 9m 36.7130s; **3** Rick Kelly, AUS (Holden Commodore VE), 1h 9m 42.3241s; **4** Greg Murphy, NZ (Holden Commodore VE), 1h 9m 44.3217s; **5** Steven Johnson, AUS (Ford Falcon BF), 1h 9m 45.3711s; **6** Craig Lowndes, AUS (Ford Falcon BF), 1h 9m 45.5195s; **7** Steve Owen, AUS (Holden Commodore VZ), 1h 9m 48.2380s; **8** Russell Ingall, AUS (Ford Falcon BF), 1h 9m 48.3311s; **9** Jason Bright, AUS (Ford Falcon BF), 1h 9m 49.5353s; **10** Andrew Jones, AUS (Ford Falcon BF), 1h 10m 56.0772s.
**Fastest race lap:** Dean Canto, AUS (Holden Commodore VE), 1m 25.2075s, 78.758 mph/126.749 km/h.
**Pole position:** Whincup.

**Race 3 (74.565 miles/120.000 km).**
**1** Garth Tander, AUS (Holden Commodore VE), 1h 0m 45.9377s, 73.625 mph/118.488 km/h; **2** Jamie Whincup, AUS (Ford Falcon BF), 1h 0m 47.8329s; **3** Rick Kelly, AUS (Holden Commodore VE), 1h 0m 48.3726s; **4** Todd Kelly, AUS (Holden Commodore VE), 1h 0m 49.0579s; **5** Craig Lowndes, AUS (Ford Falcon BF), 1h 0m 52.6991s; **6** Russell Ingall, AUS (Ford Falcon BF), 1h 0m 53.3373s; **7** Greg Murphy, NZ (Holden Commodore VE), 1h 1m 0.1310s; **8** James Courtney, AUS (Ford Falcon BF), 1h 1m 0.5383s; **9** Will Davison, AUS (Ford Falcon BF), 1h 1m 0.8474s; **10** Mark Winterbottom, AUS (Ford Falcon BF), 1h 1m 1.3093s.
**Fastest race lap:** Tander, 1m 24.7218s, 79.210 mph/127.476 km/h.
**Pole position:** Tander.

**V8 SUPERCAR CHAMPIONSHIP SERIES, Eastern Creek International Raceway, Sydney, New South Wales, Australia, 10/11 June. Round 5. 3 x 31. laps of the 2.442-mile/3.930-km circuit.**
**Race 1 (75.702 miles/121.830 km).**
**1** Mark Skaife, AUS (Holden Commodore VE), 51m 54.2697s, 87.509 mph/140.831 km/h; **2** Jamie Whincup, AUS (Ford Falcon BF), 51m 55.8324s; **3** Rick Kelly, AUS (Holden Commodore VE), 52m 0.9338s; **4** Todd Kelly, AUS (Holden Commodore VE), 52m 1.8964s; **5** Garth Tander, AUS (Holden Commodore VE), 52m 2.1231s; **6** Steven Richards, NZ (Ford Falcon BF), 52m 3.6364s; **7** Russell Ingall, AUS (Ford Falcon BF), 52m 3.9116s; **8** Jason Bright, AUS (Ford Falcon BF), 52m 8.6133s; **9** Craig Lowndes, AUS (Ford Falcon BF), 52m 8.7337s; **10** Steven Johnson, AUS (Ford Falcon BF), 52m 8.9946s.
**Fastest race lap:** Skaife, 1m 33.3802s, 94.144 mph/151.509 km/h.
**Pole position:** Kelly (Todd), 1m 31.6332s, 95.939 mph/154.398 km/h.

**Race 2 (75.702 miles/121.830 km).**
**1** Mark Skaife, AUS (Holden Commodore VE), 57m 2.5256s, 79.627 mph/128.147 km/h; **2** Rick Kelly, AUS (Holden Commodore VE), 57m 4.3406s; **3** Jamie Whincup, AUS (Ford Falcon BF), 57m 4.5407s; **4** Craig Lowndes, AUS (Ford Falcon BF), 57m 5.9312s; **5** Todd Kelly, AUS (Holden Commodore VE), 57m 7.6567s; **6** Steven Richards, NZ (Ford Falcon BF), 57m 8.1127s; **7** Mark Winterbottom, AUS (Ford Falcon BF), 57m 8.9836s; **8** Steven Johnson, AUS (Ford Falcon BF), 57m 10.6839s; **9** Will Davison, AUS (Ford Falcon BF), 57m 11.2798s; **10** Paul Morris, AUS (Holden Commodore VE), 57m 11.6340s.
**Fastest race lap:** Skaife, 1m 33.8239s, 93.699 mph/150.793 km/h.
**Pole position:** Skaife.

**Race 3 (75.702 miles/121.830 km).**
**1** Todd Kelly, AUS (Holden Commodore VE), 50m 42.8679s, 89.562 mph/144.136 km/h; **2** Craig Lowndes, AUS (Ford Falcon BF), 50m 43.1582s; **3** Mark Skaife, AUS (Holden Commodore VE), 50m 43.5014s; **4** Rick Kelly, AUS (Holden Commodore VE), 50m 47.4787s; **5** Garth Tander, AUS (Holden Commodore VE), 50m 52.0659s; **6** Mark Winterbottom, AUS (Ford Falcon BF), 50m 52.8176s; **7** Steven Richards, NZ (Ford Falcon BF), 50m 58.5153s; **8** James Courtney, AUS (Ford Falcon BF), 50m 58.7526s; **9** Steven Johnson, AUS (Ford Falcon BF), 51m 8.9445s; **10** Will Davison, AUS (Ford Falcon BF), 51m 9.1717s.
**Fastest race lap:** Lowndes, 1m 33.6419s, 93.881 mph/151.086 km/h.
**Pole position:** Skaife.

**SKYCITY TRIPLE CROWN, Hidden Valley Raceway, Darwin, Northern Territory, Australia, 23/24 June. Round 6. 3 x 42 laps of the 1.783-mile/2.870-km circuit.**
**Race 1 (74.900 miles/120.540 km).**
**1** Mark Skaife, AUS (Holden Commodore VE), 56m 15.2338s, 79.888 mph/128.567 km/h; **2** Rick Kelly, AUS (Holden Commodore VE), 56m 22.0626s; **3** Craig Lowndes, AUS (Ford Falcon BF), 56m 25.5824s; **4** Todd Kelly, AUS (Holden Commodore VE), 56m 26.4382s; **5** Jamie Whincup, AUS (Ford Falcon BF), 56m 26.6841s; **6** Garth Tander, AUS (Holden Commodore VE), 56m 27.8871s; **7** Steven Richards, NZ (Ford Falcon BF), 56m 33.1850s; **8** Max Wilson, BR (Ford Falcon BF), 56m 40.9622s; **9** Dean Canto, AUS (Holden Commodore VE), 56m 41.8481s; **10** Jason Richards, NZ (Holden Commodore VE), 56m 42.1350s.
**Fastest race lap:** Kelly (Todd), 1m 10.5528s, 90.996 mph/146.443 km/h.
**Pole position:** Kelly (Rick), 1m 9.4539s, 92.436 mph/148.760 km/h.

**Race 2 (74.900 miles/120.540 km).**
**1** Craig Lowndes, AUS (Ford Falcon BF), 56m 15.5500s, 79.880 mph/128.555 km/h; **2** Rick Kelly, AUS (Holden Commodore VE), 56m 16.6266s; **3** Garth Tander, AUS (Holden Commodore VE), 56m 17.9297s; **4** Jamie Whincup, AUS (Ford Falcon BF), 56m 18.3962s; **5** Mark Skaife, AUS (Holden Commodore VE), 56m 19.0084s; **6** Mark Winterbottom, AUS (Ford Falcon BF), 56m 19.4601s; **7** Will Davison, AUS (Ford Falcon BF), 56m 20.0352s; **8** Todd Kelly, AUS (Holden Commodore VE), 56m 24.5356s; **9** Steven Richards, NZ (Ford Falcon BF), 56m 25.7781s; **10** Jason Richards, NZ (Holden Commodore VE), 56m 26.7586s.
**Fastest race lap:** Tander, 1m 10.5091s, 91.052 mph/146.534 km/h.
**Pole position:** Skaife.

**Race 3 (74.999 miles/120.540 km).**
**1** Craig Lowndes, AUS (Ford Falcon BF), 54m 26.3310s, 82.551 mph/132.853 km/h; **2** Rick Kelly, AUS (Holden Commodore VE), 54m 29.2181s; **3** Garth Tander, AUS (Holden Commodore VE), 54m 29.8214s; **4** Todd Kelly, AUS (Holden Commodore VE), 54m 30.4215s; **5** Mark Skaife, AUS (Holden Commodore VE), 54m 30.8029s; **6** Mark Winterbottom, AUS (Ford Falcon BF), 54m 35.5098s; **7** Will Davison, AUS (Ford Falcon BF), 54m 36.2020s; **8** Steven Richards, NZ (Ford Falcon BF), 54m 39.0679s; **9** Jason Richards, NZ (Holden Commodore VE), 54m 39.7603s; **10** Lee Holdsworth, AUS (Holden Commodore VZ), 54m 40.3701s.
**Fastest race lap:** Lowndes, 1m 10.5819s, 90.958 mph/146.383 km/h.
**Pole position:** Lowndes.

**V8 SUPERCAR CHAMPIONSHIP SERIES, Queensland Raceway, Ipswich, Queensland, Australia, 21/22 July. Round 7. 3 x 38 laps of the 1.942-mile/3.126-km circuit.**
**Race 1 (73.811 miles/118.788 km).**
**1** Garth Tander, AUS (Holden Commodore VE), 46m 12.5325s, 95.841 mph/154.240 km/h; **2** Mark Skaife, AUS (Holden Commodore VE), 46m 14.5269s; **3** James Courtney, AUS (Ford Falcon BF), 46m 16.7334s; **4** Jamie Whincup, AUS (Ford Falcon BF), 46m 20.6772s; **5** Craig Lowndes, AUS (Ford Falcon BF), 46m 24.6151s; **6** Will Davison, AUS (Ford Falcon BF), 46m 25.5488s; **7** Rick Kelly, AUS (Holden Commodore VE), 46m 31.0811s; **8** Todd Kelly, AUS (Holden Commodore VE), 46m 32.2927s; **9** Russell Ingall, AUS (Ford Falcon BF), 46m 34.6969s; **10** Mark Winterbottom, AUS (Ford Falcon BF), 46m 35.1483s.
**Fastest race lap:** Tander, 1m 11.1314s, 98.306 mph/158.208 km/h.
**Pole position:** Whincup, 1m 10.1489s, 99.683 mph/160.424 km/h.

**Race 2 (73.811 miles/118.788 km).**
**1** Garth Tander, AUS (Holden Commodore VE), 48m 39.2172s, 91.025 mph/146.490 km/h; **2** Jamie Whincup, AUS (Ford Falcon BF), 48m 41.6569s; **3** Craig Lowndes, AUS (Ford Falcon BF), 48m 43.3829s; **4** James Courtney, AUS (Ford Falcon BF), 48m 46.2847s; **5** Will Davison, AUS (Ford Falcon BF), 48m 46.5899s; **6** Russell Ingall, AUS (Ford Falcon BF), 48m 47.1434s; **7** Mark Winterbottom, AUS (Ford Falcon BF), 48m 48.4405s; **8** Mark Skaife, AUS (Holden Commodore VE), 48m 48.8247s; **9** Paul Morris, AUS (Holden Commodore VE), 48m 55.1308s; **10** Lee Holdsworth, AUS (Holden Commodore VE), 48m 55.4786s.
**Fastest race lap:** Tander, 1m 11.2398s, 98.157 mph/157.967 km/h.
**Pole position:** Tander.

**Race 3 (73.811 miles/118.788 km).**
**1** Garth Tander, AUS (Holden Commodore VE), 50m 1.0691s, 88.542 mph/142.494 km/h; **2** Craig Lowndes, AUS (Ford Falcon BF), 50m 2.2412s; **3** Jamie Whincup, AUS (Ford Falcon BF), 50m 7.6878s; **4** Will Davison, AUS (Ford Falcon BF), 50m 9.6688s; **5** Mark Winterbottom, AUS (Ford Falcon BF), 50m 11.4424s; **6** Rick Kelly, AUS (Holden Commodore VE), 50m 13.5928s; **7** Greg Murphy, NZ (Holden Commodore VE), 50m 16.9791s; **8** Jason Richards, NZ (Holden Commodore VE), 50m 19.4764s; **9** Russell Ingall, AUS (Ford Falcon BF), 50m 19.9088s; **10** Lee Holdsworth, AUS (Holden Commodore VE), 50m 20.8901s.
**Fastest race lap:** Jason Bright, AUS (Ford Falcon BF), 1m 11.3791s, 97.965 mph/157.659 km/h.
**Pole position:** Tander.

**JIM BEAM 400, Oran Park Raceway, Narellan, New South Wales, Australia, 18/19 August. Round 8. 3 x 46 laps of the 1.628-mile/2.620-km circuit.**
**Race 1 (74.888 miles/120.520 km).**
**1** Mark Skaife, AUS (Holden Commodore VE), 56m 37.0949s, 79.361 mph/127.718 km/h; **2** Rick Kelly, AUS (Holden Commodore VE), 56m 37.7425s; **3** Jamie Whincup, AUS (Ford Falcon BF), 56m 38.1338s; **4** Mark Winterbottom, AUS (Ford Falcon BF), 56m 47.4268s; **5** Steven Richards, NZ (Ford Falcon BF), 56m 48.2025s; **6** Will Davison, AUS (Ford Falcon BF), 56m 55.3141s; **7** Craig Lowndes, AUS (Ford Falcon BF), 56m 56.3251s; **8** Todd Kelly, AUS (Holden Commodore VE), 57m 3.1738s; **9** Greg Murphy, NZ (Holden Commodore VE),

57m 5.6650s; **10** Lee Holdsworth, AUS (Holden Commodore VE), 57m 6.1404s.
**Fastest race lap:** Kelly (Todd), 1m 9.4559s, 84.381 mph/135.798 km/h.
**Pole position:** Kelly (Todd), 1m 8.4388s, 85.635 mph/137.816 km/h.

**Race 2 (74.888 miles/120.520 km).**
**1** Craig Lowndes, AUS (Ford Falcon BF), 1h 3m 25.7192s, 70.840 mph/114.005 km/h; **2** Todd Kelly, AUS (Holden Commodore VE), 1h 3m 28.7095s; **3** Mark Winterbottom, AUS (Ford Falcon BF), 1h 3m 29.6706s; **4** Lee Holdsworth, AUS (Holden Commodore VE), 1h 3m 30.1319s; **5** Jason Richards, NZ (Holden Commodore VE), 1h 3m 47.0663s; **6** Steven Richards, NZ (Ford Falcon BF), 1h 3m 50.9642s; **7** James Courtney, AUS (Ford Falcon BF), 1h 3m 52.5771s; **8** Will Davison, AUS (Ford Falcon BF), 1h 3m 59.9984s; **9** Russell Ingall, AUS (Ford Falcon BF), 1h 4m 6.1539s; **10** Simon Wills, AUS (Ford Falcon BF), 1h 4m 11.1235s.
**Fastest race lap:** Winterbottom, 1m 18.3951s, 74.759 mph/120.313 km/h.
**Pole position:** Skaife.

**Race 3 (74.888 miles/120.520 km).**
**1** Lee Holdsworth, AUS (Holden Commodore VE), 1h 11m 3.3513s, 63.236 mph/101.767 km/h; **2** Garth Tander, AUS (Holden Commodore VE), 1h 11m 9.6915s; **3** Russell Ingall, AUS (Ford Falcon BF), 1h 11m 11.5806s; **4** Jamie Whincup, AUS (Ford Falcon BF), 1h 11m 11.8101s; **5** Steven Richards, NZ (Ford Falcon BF), 1h 11m 12.3154s; **6** Jason Richards, NZ (Holden Commodore VE), 1h 11m 17.4624s; **7** Andrew Jones, AUS (Ford Falcon BF), 1h 11m 18.3592s; **8** Steve Owen, AUS (Holden Commodore VZ), 1h 11m 19.5806s; **9** Max Wilson, BR (Ford Falcon BF), 1h 11m 19.8198s; **10** Paul Dumbrell, AUS (Holden Commodore VE), 1h 11m 23.1873s.
**Fastest race lap:** Holdsworth, 1m 18.5971s, 74.567 mph/120.004 km/h.
**Pole position:** Lowndes.

**JUST CAR INSURANCE 500, Sandown International Motor Raceway, Melbourne, Victoria, Australia, 16 September. Round 9. 161 laps of the 1.926-mile/3.100-km circuit, 310.126 miles/499.100 km.**
**1** Jamie Whincup/Craig Lowndes, AUS/AUS (Ford Falcon BF), 3h 23m 16.5157s, 91.539 mph/147.317 km/h; **2** Rick Kelly/Paul Radisich, AUS/AUS (Holden Commodore VE), 3h 23m 19.2330s; **3** Steven Richards/Owen Kelly, NZ/AUS (Ford Falcon BF), 3h 23m 29.5846s; **4** Garth Tander/Craig Baird, AUS/AUS (Holden Commodore VE), 3h 23m 52.1448s; **5** Lee Holdsworth/Dean Canto, AUS/AUS (Holden Commodore VZ), 3h 23m 56.8118s; **6** Paul Dumbrell/Paul Weel, AUS/AUS (Holden Commodore VE), 3h 24m 16.2350s; **7** Russell Ingall/Luke Youlden, AUS/AUS (Ford Falcon BF), 3h 23m 20.0221s; **8** Mark Winterbottom/Matthew Halliday, AUS/NZ (Ford Falcon BF), 3h 23m 26.1611s; **9** Todd Kelly/Nathan Pretty, AUS/AUS (Holden Commodore VE), 3h 23m 33.1986s; **10** Richard Lyons/Allan Simonsen, GB/DK (Ford Falcon BF), 3h 23m 34.0068s.
**Fastest race lap:** Kelly (Todd), 1m 12.0409s, 96.258 mph/154.912 km/h.
**Pole position:** Winterbottom, 1m 10.6405s, 98.166 mph/157.983 km/h.

**SUPERCHEAP AUTO BATHURST 1,000, Mount Panorama, Bathurst, New South Wales, Australia, 7 October. Round 10. 161 laps of the 3.861-mile/6.213-km circuit, 621.553 miles/1000.293 km.**
**1** Craig Lowndes/Jamie Whincup, AUS/AUS (Ford Falcon BF), 6h 29m 10.1985s, 95.828 mph/154.219 km/h; **2** James Courtney/David Besnard, AUS/AUS (Ford Falcon BF), 6h 29m 10.8223s; **3** Steven Johnson/Will Davison, AUS/AUS (Ford Falcon BF), 6h 29m 11.0145s; **4** Greg Murphy/Jason Richards, NZ/NZ (Holden Commodore VE), 6h 29m 11.3697s; **5** Allan Simonsen/Richard Lyons, DK/GB (Ford Falcon BF), 6h 29m 18.5113s; **6** Steve Owen/Tony D'Alberto, AUS/AUS (Holden Commodore VZ), 6h 29m 19.5279s; **7** Max Wilson/Jason Bargwanna, BR/AUS (Ford Falcon BF), 6h 29m 22.0323s; **8** Alex Davison/Andrew Thompson, AUS/AUS (Ford Falcon BF), 6h 29m 24.8447s; **9** Greg Ritter/Cameron McLean, AUS/AUS (Holden Commodore VE), 6h 29m 28.0785s; **10** Steven Richards/Mark Winterbottom, AUS/AUS (Ford Falcon BF), 6h 29m 28.5564s.
**Fastest race lap:** Lowndes/Whincup, 2m 8.4651s, 108.186 mph/174.107 km/h.
**Pole position:** Mark Winterbottom, AUS (Ford Falcon BF), 2m 7.0908s, 109.356 mph/175.990 km/h.

**V8 SUPERCAR CHALLENGE, Surfer's Paradise Steet Circuit, Queensland, Australia, 20/21 October. Round 11. 3 x 27 laps of the 2.794-mile/4.496-km circuit.**
**Race 1 (75.429 miles/121.392 km).**
**1** Garth Tander, AUS (Holden Commodore VE), 52m 35.5753s, 86.053 mph/138.488 km/h; **2** Jamie Whincup, AUS (Ford Falcon BF), 52m 35.9827s; **3** Craig Lowndes, AUS (Ford Falcon BF), 52m 36.9792s; **4** Russell Ingall, AUS (Ford Falcon BF), 52m 38.4403s; **5** Greg Murphy, NZ (Holden Commodore VE), 52m 38.4473s; **6** James Courtney, AUS (Ford Falcon BF), 52m 38.8810s; **7** Rick Kelly, AUS (Holden Commodore VE), 52m 39.6331s; **8** Steven Johnson, AUS (Ford Falcon BF), 52m 40.5402s; **9** Dean Canto, AUS (Holden Commodore VE), 52m 42.0108s; **10** Jason Richards, NZ (Holden Commodore VE), 52m 42.5921s.
**Fastest race lap:** Whincup, 1m 49.9198s, 91.496 mph/147.249 km/h.
**Pole position:** Mark Winterbottom, AUS (Ford Falcon BF), 1m 48.4819s, 92.709 mph/149.200 km/h.

**Race 2 (75.429 miles/121.392 km).**
**1** Garth Tander, AUS (Holden Commodore VE), 50m 44.6631s, 89.188 mph/143.533 km/h; **2** Jamie Whincup, AUS (Ford Falcon BF), 50m 47.9659s; **3** Russell Ingall, AUS (Ford Falcon BF), 50m 59.5920s; **4** Greg Murphy, NZ (Holden Commodore VE), 51m 0.8806s; **5** Steven Richards, NZ (Ford Falcon BF), 51m 4.0491s; **6** Jason Richards, NZ (Holden Commodore VE), 51m 11.1145s; **7** Jason Bargwanna, AUS (Ford Falcon BF), 51m 24.6200s; **8** Mark Skaife, AUS (Holden Commodore VE), 51m 25.1149s; **9** Max Wilson, BR (Ford Falcon BF), 51m 34.7815s; **10** Cameron McConville, AUS (Holden Commodore VE), 51m 34.9989s.
**Fastest race lap:** Whincup, 1m 49.9905s, 91.438 mph/147.154 km/h.
**Pole position:** Tander.

**Race 3 (75.429 miles/121.392 km).**
**1** Steven Richards, NZ (Ford Falcon BF), 53m 42.3815s, 84.269 mph/135.617 km/h; **2** Jason Richards, NZ (Holden Commodore VE), 53m 44.9037s; **3** Russell Ingall, AUS (Ford Falcon BF), 53m 49.0928s; **4** James Courtney, AUS (Ford Falcon BF), 53m 58.7275s; **5** Mark Winterbottom, AUS (Ford Falcon BF), 54m 1.2305s; **6** Rick Kelly, AUS (Holden Commodore VE), 54m 3.4955s; **7** Craig Lowndes, AUS (Ford Falcon BF), 54m 3.6534s; **8** Garth Tander, AUS (Holden Commodore VE), 54m 5.8979s; **9** Cameron McConville, AUS (Holden Commodore VE), 54m 7.6813s; **10** Max Wilson, BR (Ford Falcon BF), 54m 12.5434s.
**Fastest race lap:** Tander, 1m 49.8352s, 91.567 mph/147.362 km/h.
**Pole position:** Tander.

**Provisional championship points**
**Drivers**
**1** Jamie Whincup, AUS, 501; **2** Garth Tander, AUS, 492; **3** Craig Lowndes, AUS, 473; **4** Rick Kelly, AUS, 466; **5** Todd Kelly, AUS, 324; **6** Steven Richards, NZ, 299; **7** Mark Skaife, AUS, 283; **8** Mark Winterbottom, AUS, 271; **9** Russell Ingall, AUS, 263; **10** James Courtney, AUS, 257; **11** Will Davison, AUS, 257; **12** Steven Johnson, AUS, 221; **13** Greg Murphy, NZ, 208; **14** Jason Richards, NZ, 193; **15** Lee Holdsworth, AUS, 175; **16** Max Wilson, BR, 108; **17** Steve Owen, AUS, 101; **18** Paul Radisich, NZ, 96; **19** Jason Bargwanna, AUS, 86; **20** Dean Canto, AUS, 85.

**Teams**
**1** Toll HSV Dealer Team, 958; **2** Team Vodafone, 893; **3** Holden Racing Team, 637.

*Results of the Bahrain, Symmons Plains and Phillip Island races will be given in AUTOCOURSE 2008–2009.*

## FIA World Touring Car Championship 2006

The following races were run after AUTOCOURSE 2006–2007 went to press.

**FIA WORLD TOURING CAR CHAMPIONSHIP, Circuito Da Guia, Macau, 19 November. 9 and 11 laps of the 3.803-mile/6.120-km circuit.**
**Round 19 (34.225 miles/55.080 km).**
**1** Andy Priaulx, GB (BMW 320si), 23m 44.490s, 86.494 mph/139.199 km/h; **2** Duncan Huisman, NL (BMW 320si), 23m 45.510s; **3** Yvan Muller, F (SEAT Leon), 23m 45.875s; **4** Fabrizio Giovanardi, I (Honda Accord Euro R), 23m 47.151s; **5** Augusto Farfus Jr, BR (Alfa Romeo 156), 23m 54.086s; **6** Jörg Müller, D (BMW 320si), 23m 54.985s; **7** Tom Coronel, NL (SEAT Leon), 23m 55.579s; **8** Peter Terting, D (SEAT Leon), 24m 04.267s; **9** Robert Huff, GB (Chevrolet Lacetti), 24m 11.121s; **10** James Thompson, GB (SEAT Leon), 24m 14.549s.
**Fastest race lap:** Menu, 2m 34.249s, 88.753 mph/142.833 km/h.
**Fastest qualifying lap:** Priaulx, 2m 33.318s, 89.292 mph/143.701 km/h.

**Round 20 (41.831 miles/67.320 km).**
**1** Jörg Müller, D (BMW 320si), 36m 1.074s, 69.683 mph/112.144 km/h; **2** Yvan Muller, F (SEAT Leon), 36m 3.176s; **3** Tom Coronel, NL (SEAT Leon), 36m 3.771s; **4** James Thompson, GB (SEAT Leon), 36m 5.547s; **5** Andy Priaulx, GB (BMW 320si), 36m 6.347s; **6** Fabrizio Giovanardi, I (Honda Accord Euro R), 36m 7.198s; **7** André Couto, MAC (SEAT Leon), 36m 11.418s; **8** Dirk Müller, D (BMW 320si), 36m 12.482s; **9** Alessandro 'Alex' Zanardi, I (BMW 320si), 36m 12.908s; **10** Alain Menu, CH (Chevrolet Lacetti), 36m 20.450s.
**Fastest race lap:** Muller (Yvan), 2m 34.394s, 88.670 mph/142.699 km/h.
**Pole position:** Terting.

**Final championship points**
**Drivers**
**1** Andy Priaulx, GB, 73; **2** Jörg Müller, D, 72; **3** Augusto Farfus Jr, BR, 64; **4** Yvan Muller, F, 62; **5** Gabriele Tarquini, I, 57; **6** Dirk Müller, D, 54; **7** Rickard Rydell, S, 54; **8** James Thompson, GB, 54; **9** Peter Terting, D, 49; **10** Jordi Gené, E, 36; **11** Alessandro 'Alex' Zanardi, I, 26; **12** Nicola Larini, I, 24; **13** Duncan Huisman, NL, 22; **14** Gianni Morbidelli, I, 22; **15** Alain Menu, CH, 21; **16** Robert Huff, GB, 20; **17** Tom Coronel, NL, 20; **18** Salvatore Tavano, I, 15; **19** Luca Rangoni, I, 14; **20** Fabrizio Giovanardi, I, 8; **21** Ryan Sharp, GB, 6; **22** Alessandro Balzan, I, 5; **23** André Couto, MAC, 2.

**Independents' Trophy**
**1** Tom Coronel, NL, 178; **2** Luca Rangoni, I, 100; **3** Stefano d'Aste, I, 93; **4** Ryan Sharp, GB, 75; **5** Maurizio Ceresoli, I, 69.

**Manufacturers**
**1** BMW, 254; **2** SEAT, 235; **3** Alfa Romeo, 154; **4** Chevrolet, 128.

**Teams**
**1** GR Asia, 247; **2** Proteam Motorsport, 192; **3** JAS Motorsport, 132; **4** Wiechers-Sport, 90; **5** DB Motorsport, 25.

## 2007

**FIA WORLD TOURING CAR CHAMPIONSHIP, Autódromo Internacional de Curitiba, Brazil, 11 March. 16 and 14 laps of the 2.291-mile/3.695-km circuit.**
**Round 1 (36.735 miles/59.120 km).**
**1** Jörg Müller, D (BMW 320si), 25m 38.208s, 85.975 mph/138.363 km/h; **2** Andy Priaulx, GB (BMW 320si), 25m 38.629s; **3** Augusto Farfus Jr, BR (BMW 320si), 25m 39.442s; **4** Gabriele Tarquini, I (SEAT Leon), 25m 47.084s; **5** Robert Huff, GB (Chevrolet Lacetti), 25m 47.909s; **6** Tom Coronel, NL (SEAT Leon), 25m 48.532s; **7** Alessandro 'Alex' Zanardi, I (BMW 320si), 25m 49.216s; **8** Yvan Muller, F (SEAT Leon), 25m 51.488s; **9** Jordi Gené, E (SEAT Leon), 25m 51.757s; **10** Pierre-Yves Corthals, B (SEAT Leon), 26m 01.959s.
**Fastest race lap:** Müller (Jörg), 1m 25.469s, 96.707 mph/155.635 km/h.
**Fastest qualifying lap:** Müller (Jörg), 1m 24.769s, 97.506 mph/156.920 km/h.

**Round 2 (32.144 miles/51.730 km).**
**1** Augusto Farfus Jr, BR (BMW 320si), 20m 20.148s, 94.838 mph/152.627 km/h; **2** Andy Priaulx, GB (BMW 320si), 20m 24.526s; **3** Jörg Müller, D (BMW 320si), 20m 25.839s; **4** Yvan Muller, F (SEAT Leon), 20m 27.111s; **5** Gabriele Tarquini, I (SEAT Leon), 20m 27.627s; **6** Alessandro 'Alex' Zanardi, I (BMW 320si), 20m 30.454s; **7** Luca Rangoni, I (BMW 320si), 20m 30.642s; **8** Tom Coronel, NL (SEAT Leon), 20m 32.221s; **9** Pierre-Yves Corthals, B (SEAT Leon), 20m 37.492s; **10** Nicola Larini, I (Chevrolet Lacetti), 20m 38.573s.
**Fastest race lap:** Müller (Jörg), 1m 25.914s, 96.206 mph/154.829 km/h.
**Pole position:** Muller (Yvan).

**FIA WORLD TOURING CAR CHAMPIONSHIP, Circuit Park Zandvoort, Netherlands, 6 May. 13 and 12 laps of the 2.676-mile/4.307-km circuit.**
**Round 3 (34.791 miles/55.991 km).**
**1** Alain Menu, CH (Chevrolet Lacetti), 25m 12.863s, 82.789 mph/133.235 km/h; **2** Nicola Larini, I (Chevrolet Lacetti), 25m 13.514s; **3** Luca Rangoni, I (BMW 320si), 25m 13.850s; **4** Tiago Monteiro, P (SEAT Leon), 25m 15.221s; **5** Augusto Farfus Jr, BR (BMW 320si), 25m 15.868s; **6** Roberto Colciago, I (SEAT Leon), 25m 18.484s; **7** Gabriele Tarquini, I (SEAT Leon), 25m 18.876s; **8** Andy Priaulx, GB (BMW 320si), 25m 19.287s; **9** Jordi Gené, E (SEAT Leon), 25m 20.097s; **10** Jörg Müller, D (BMW 320si), 25m 20.483s.
**Fastest race lap:** Rangoni, 1m 48.858s, 88.505 mph/142.435 km/h.
**Fastest qualifying lap:** Menu, 1m 47.044s, 90.005 mph/144.848 km/h.

**Round 4 (32.115 miles/51.684 km).**
**1** Gabriele Tarquini, I (SEAT Leon), 22m 6.110s, 87.183 mph/140.306 km/h; **2** Augusto Farfus Jr, BR (BMW 320si), 22m 6.559s; **3** Jörg Müller, D (BMW 320si), 22m 6.784s; **4** Nicola Larini, I (Chevrolet Lacetti), 22m 7.088s; **5** Andy Priaulx, GB (BMW 320si), 22m 7.824s; **6** Luca Rangoni, I (BMW 320si), 22m 8.392s; **7** Roberto Colciago, I (SEAT Leon), 22m 9.574s; **8** Felix Porteiro, E (BMW 320si), 22m 11.328s; **9** Tiago Monteiro, P (SEAT Leon), 22m 12.461s; **10** Jordi Gené, E (SEAT Leon), 22m 13.904s.
**Fastest race lap:** Tarquini, 1m 49.243s, 88.193 mph/141.933 km/h.
**Pole position:** Priaulx.

**FIA WORLD TOURING CAR CHAMPIONSHIP, Circuit de la Comunitat Valenciana Ricardo Tormo, Cheste, Valencia, Spain, 20 May. 15 and 13 laps of the 2.489-mile/4.005-km circuit.**
**Round 5 (37.329 miles/60.075 km).**
**1** James Thompson, GB (Alfa Romeo 156), 29m 37.113s, 75.619 mph/121.697 km/h; **2** Nicola Larini, I (Chevrolet Lacetti), 29m 39.952s; **3** Yvan Muller, F (SEAT Leon), 29m 41.350s; **4** Jordi Gené, E (SEAT Leon), 29m 41.923s; **5** Andy Priaulx, GB (BMW 320si), 29m 42.605s; **6** Michel Jourdain Jr, MEX (SEAT Leon), 29m 45.996s; **7** Luca Rangoni, I (BMW 320si), 29m 47.013s; **8** Jörg Müller, D (BMW 320si), 29m 48.886s; **9** Alain Menu, CH (Chevrolet Lacetti), 29m 53.329s; **10** Sergio Hernández, E (BMW 320si), 29m 56.323s.
**Fastest race lap:** Thompson, 1m 44.260s, 85.929 mph/138.288 km/h.
**Fastest qualifying lap:** Thompson, 1m 43.954s, 86.182 mph/138.695 km/h.

**Round 6 (32.352 miles/52.065 km).**
**1** James Thompson, GB (Alfa Romeo 156), 23m 12.920s, 83.613 mph/134.561 km/h; **2** Jörg Müller, D (BMW 320si), 23m 14.731s; **3** Andy Priaulx, GB (BMW 320si), 23m 15.186s; **4** Yvan Muller, F (SEAT Leon), 23m 16.144s; **5** Nicola Larini, I (Chevrolet Lacetti), 23m 17.636s; **6** Jordi Gené, E (SEAT Leon), 23m 21.744s; **7** Luca Rangoni, I (BMW 320si), 23m 23.562s; **8** Sergio Hernández, E (BMW 320si), 23m 24.207s; **9** Michel Jourdain Jr, MEX (SEAT Leon), 23m 24.969s; **10** Augusto Farfus Jr, BR (BMW 320si), 23m 29.961s.
**Fastest race lap:** Robert Huff, GB (Chevrolet Lacetti), 1m 45.902s, 84.596 mph/136.144 km/h.
**Pole position:** Müller (Jörg).

**FIA WORLD TOURING CAR CHAMPIONSHIP, Pau Street Circuit, France, 3 June. 19 and 21 laps of the 1.715-mile/2.760-km circuit.**
**Round 7 (32.585 miles/52.440 km).**
**1** Alain Menu, CH (Chevrolet Lacetti), 26m 42.140s, 73.218 mph/117.832 km/h; **2** Yvan Muller, F (SEAT Leon), 26m 44.400s; **3** Tiago Monteiro, P (SEAT Leon), 26m 45.948s; **4** Robert Huff, GB (Chevrolet Lacetti), 26m 51.334s; **5** Felix Porteiro, E (BMW 320si), 26m 53.515s; **6** Andy Priaulx, GB (BMW 320si), 26m 53.943s; **7** Augusto Farfus Jr, BR (BMW 320si), 26m 54.823s; **8** Jordi Gené, E (SEAT Leon), 27m 1.468s; **9** Tom Coronel, NL (SEAT Leon), 27m 4.557s; **10** James Thompson, GB (Alfa Romeo 156), 27m 6.944s.
**Fastest race lap:** Menu, 1m 23.054s, 74.337 mph/119.633 km/h.
**Fastest qualifying lap:** Menu, 1m 21.930s, 75.356 mph/121.274 km/h.

**Round 8 (36.015 miles/57.960 km).**
**1** Augusto Farfus Jr, BR (BMW 320si), 31m 54.553s, 67.720 mph/108.984 km/h; **2** Andy Priaulx, GB (BMW 320si), 31m 55.015s; **3** Tiago Monteiro, P (SEAT Leon), 31m 59.738s; **4** Robert Huff, GB (Chevrolet Lacetti), 32m 0.178s; **5** Jordi Gené, E (SEAT Leon), 32m 7.571s; **6** Yvan Muller, F (SEAT Leon), 32m 9.029s; **7** James Thompson, GB (Alfa Romeo 156), 32m 15.414s; **8** Alain Menu, CH (Chevrolet Lacetti), 32m 15.713s; **9** Alessandro 'Alex' Zanardi, I (BMW 320si), 32m 17.000s; **10** Jörg Müller, D (BMW 320si), 32m 17.196s.
**Fastest race lap:** Farfus Jr, 1m 24.190s, 73.333 mph/118.018 km/h.
**Pole position:** Gené.

**FIA WORLD TOURING CAR CHAMPIONSHIP, Automotodrom Brno Masaryk Circuit, Brno, Czech Republic, 17 June. 11 and 10 laps of the 3.357-mile/5.403-km circuit.**
**Round 9 (36.930 miles/59.433 km).**
**1** Felix Porteiro, E (BMW 320si), 26m 51.609s, 82.494 mph/132.760 km/h; **2** Jörg Müller, D (BMW 320si), 26m 51.868s; **3** Alessandro 'Alex' Zanardi, I (BMW 320si), 26m 54.894s; **4** Augusto Farfus Jr, BR (BMW 320si), 26m 55.893s; **5** Nicola Larini, I (Chevrolet Lacetti), 27m 5.756s; **6** Yvan Muller, F (SEAT Leon), 27m 6.214s; **7** Gabriele Tarquini, I (SEAT Leon), 27m 6.407s; **8** Alain Menu, CH (Chevrolet Lacetti), 27m 9.179s; **9** James Thompson, GB (Alfa Romeo 156), 27m 11.003s; **10** Massimiliano Pedalà, I (SEAT Leon), 27m 11.235s.
**Fastest race lap:** Farfus Jr, 2m 13.721s, 90.383 mph/145.458 km/h.
**Fastest qualifying lap:** Porteiro, 2m 11.584s, 91.851 mph/147.820 km/h.

**Round 10 (33.573 miles/54.030 km).**
**1** Jörg Müller, D (BMW 320si), 22m 42.008s, 88.738 mph/142.809 km/h; **2** Augusto Farfus Jr, BR (BMW 320si), 22m 42.820s; **3** Felix Porteiro, E (BMW 320si), 22m 46.828s; **4** Gabriele Tarquini, I (SEAT Leon), 22m 49.370s; **5** James Thompson, GB (Alfa Romeo 156), 22m 51.627s; **6** Nicola Larini, I (Chevrolet Lacetti), 22m 52.121s; **7** Andy Priaulx, GB (BMW 320si), 22m 53.033s; **8** Jordi Gené, E (SEAT Leon), 22m 55.466s; **9** Tiago Monteiro, P (SEAT Leon), 22m 56.943s; **10** Stefan d'Aste, I (BMW 320si), 22m 57.298s.
**Fastest race lap:** Zanardi, 2m 14.514s, 89.851 mph/144.600 km/h.
**Pole position:** Menu.

**FIA WORLD TOURING CAR CHAMPIONSHIP, Circuito da Boavista, Porto, Portugal, 8 July. 2 x 13 laps of the 2.933-mile/4.720-km circuit.**
**Round 11 (38.127 miles/61.360 km).**
**1** Alain Menu, CH (Chevrolet Lacetti), 34m 7.853s, 67.026 mph/107.867 km/h; **2** Robert Huff, GB (Chevrolet Lacetti), 34m 8.690s; **3** Nicola Larini, I (Chevrolet Lacetti), 34m 9.471s; **4** Gabriele Tarquini, I (SEAT Leon), 34m 9.782s; **5** Yvan Muller, F (SEAT Leon), 34m 13.271s; **6** Tom Coronel, NL (SEAT Leon), 34m 13.943s; **7** Andy Priaulx, GB (BMW 320si), 34m 14.491s; **8** Jörg Müller, D (BMW 320si), 34m 14.823s; **9** Augusto Farfus Jr., BR (BMW 320si), 34m 15.123s; **10** James Thompson, GB (Alfa Romeo 156), 34m 19.935s.
**Fastest race lap:** Huff, 2m 8.829s, 81.956 mph/131.895 km/h.
**Fastest qualifying lap:** Menu, 2m 6.927s, 83.184 mph/133.872 km/h.

**Round 12 (38.127 miles/61.360 km).**
**1** Andy Priaulx, GB (BMW 320si), 32m 2.175s, 71.408 mph/114.919 km/h; **2** Jörg Müller, D (BMW 320si), 32m 4.232s; **3** Alain Menu, CH (Chevrolet Lacetti), 32m 6.569s; **4** Tom Coronel, NL (SEAT Leon), 32m 6.973s; **5** Yvan Muller, F (SEAT Leon), 32m 8.363s; **6** Augusto Farfus Jr, BR (BMW 320si), 32m 8.672s; **7** Gabriele Tarquini, I (SEAT Leon), 32m 9.181s; **8** Pierre-Yves Corthals, B (SEAT Leon), 32m 11.276s; **9** Michel Jourdain Jr, MEX (SEAT Leon), 32m 15.527s; **10** James Thompson, GB (Alfa Romeo 156), 32m 16.329s.
**Fastest race lap:** Müller (Jörg). 2m 9.875s, 81.296 mph/130.833 km/h.
**Pole position:** Müller (Jörg).

**FIA WORLD TOURING CAR CHAMPIONSHIP, Anderstorp, Sweden, 29 July. 2 x 13 laps of the 2.501-mile/4.025-km circuit.**
**Round 13 (32.513 miles/52.325 km).**
**1** Robert Huff, GB (Chevrolet Lacetti), 23m 51.708s, 81.754 mph/131.570 km/h; **2** Tiago Monteiro, P (SEAT Leon), 23m 52.437s; **3** James Thompson, GB (Alfa Romeo 156), 24m 4.209s; **4** Tom Coronel, NL (SEAT Leon), 24m 10.173s; **5** Gabriele Tarquini, I (SEAT Leon), 24m 12.566s; **6** Yvan Muller, F (SEAT Leon TDI), 24m 12.850s; **7** Nicola Larini, I (Chevrolet Lacetti), 24m 17.529s; **8** Alain Menu, CH (Chevrolet Lacetti), 24m 17.600s; **9** Rickard Rydell, S (Chevrolet Lacetti), 24m 18.145s; **10** Robert Dahlgren, S (Volvo S60), 24m 19.234s.
**Fastest race lap:** Menu, 1m 45.150s, 85.627 mph/137.803 km/h.
**Fastest qualifying lap:** Monteiro, 1m 50.056s, 81.810 mph/131.660 km/h.

**Round 14 (32.513 miles/52.325 km).**
**1** Rickard Rydell, S (Chevrolet Lacetti), 23m 41.120s, 82.363 mph/132.550 km/h; **2** Nicola Larini, I (Chevrolet Lacetti), 23m 42.728s; **3** Alain Menu, CH (Chevrolet Lacetti), 23m 42.976s; **4** Tom Coronel, NL (SEAT Leon), 23m 46.277s; **5** James Thompson, GB (Alfa Romeo 156), 23m 47.190s; **6** Tiago Monteiro, P (SEAT Leon), 23m 47.916s; **7** Gabriele Tarquini, I (SEAT Leon), 23m 49.885s; **8** Robert Dahlgren, S (Volvo S60), 23m 49.904s; **9** Augusto Farfus Jr, BR (BMW 320si), 23m 50.027s; **10** Jörg Müller, D (BMW 320si), 23m 50.226s.
**Fastest race lap:** Alessandro 'Alex' Zanardi, I (BMW 320si), 1m 42.432s, 87.899 mph/141.459 km/h.
**Pole position:** Menu.

**FIA WORLD TOURING CAR CHAMPIONSHIP, Motorsport Arena Oschersleben, Germany, 26 August. 16 and 14 laps of the 2.297-mile/3.696-km circuit.**
**Round 15 (36.745 miles/59.136 km).**
**1** Yvan Muller, F (SEAT Leon TDI), 27m 57.209s, 78.871 mph/126.930 km/h; **2** Gabriele Tarquini, I (SEAT Leon), 27m 57.655s; **3** James Thompson, GB (Alfa Romeo 156), 27m 58.002s; **4** Jörg Müller, D (BMW 320si), 27m 58.465s; **5** Andy Priaulx, GB (BMW 320si), 27m 58.689s; **6** Jordi Gené, E (SEAT Leon TDI), 27m 59.973s; **7** Augusto Farfus Jr, BR (BMW 320si), 28m 0.225s; **8** Roberto Colciago, I (SEAT Leon), 28m 0.586s; **9** Olivier Tielemans, NL (Alfa Romeo 156), 28m 3.191s; **10** Tiago Monteiro, P (SEAT Leon), 28m 5.842s.
**Fastest race lap:** Colciago, 1m 37.262s, 85.005 mph/136.801 km/h.
**Fastest qualifying lap:** Tarquini, 1m 36.291s, 85.862 mph/138.181 km/h.

**Round 16 (32.152 miles/51.744 km).**
**1** Augusto Farfus Jr, BR (BMW 320si), 22m 55.632s, 84.142 mph/135.412 km/h; **2** Andy Priaulx, GB (BMW 320si), 22m 56.196s; **3** Jordi Gené, E (SEAT Leon TDI), 22m 58.136s; **4** James Thompson, GB (Alfa Romeo 156), 22m 58.494s; **5** Yvan Muller, F (SEAT Leon TDI), 22m 59.327s; **6** Robert Huff, GB (Chevrolet Lacetti), 22m 59.704s; **7** Gabriele Tarquini, I (SEAT Leon), 23m 0.270s; **8** Tiago Monteiro, P (SEAT Leon), 23m 5.354s; **9** Michel Jourdain Jr, MEX (SEAT Leon), 23m 5.494s; **10** Alain Menu, CH (Chevrolet Lacetti), 23m 6.392s.
**Fastest race lap:** Thompson, 1m 37.310s, 84.963 mph/136.734 km/h.
**Pole position:** Colciago.

**FIA WORLD TOURING CAR CHAMPIONSHIP, Brands Hatch Grand Prix Circuit, West Kingsdown, Dartford, Kent, Great Britain, 23 September. 2 x 16 laps of the 2.301-mile/3.703-km circuit.**
**Round 17 (36.796 miles/59.278 km).**
**1** Alain Menu, CH (Chevrolet Lacetti), 26m 48.377s, 82.444 mph/132.681 km/h; **2** James Thompson, GB (Alfa Romeo 156), 26m 49.036s; **3** Colin Turkington, GB (BMW 320si), 26m 49.332s; **4** Yvan Muller, F (SEAT Leon TDI), 26m 50.538s; **5** Jordi Gené, E (SEAT Leon TDI), 26m 51.376s; **6** Robert Huff, GB (Chevrolet Lacetti), 26m 51.594s; **7** Andy Priaulx, GB (BMW 320si), 26m 52.645s; **8** Pierre-Yves Corthals, B (SEAT Leon), 26m 53.354s; **9** Felix Porteiro, E (BMW 320si), 26m 55.326s; **10** Gabriele Tarquini, I (SEAT Leon), 26m 56.742s.
**Fastest race lap:** Muller (Yvan), 1m 33.980s, 88.140 mph/141.847 km/h.
**Fastest qualifying lap:** Menu, 1m 33.018s, 89.051 mph/143.314 km/h.

**Round 18 (36.796 miles/59.278 km).**
**1** Andy Priaulx, GB (BMW 320si), 28m 5.811s, 78.657 mph/126.586 km/h; **2** Felix Porteiro, E (BMW 320si), 28m 6.538s; **3** Robert Huff, GB (Chevrolet Lacetti), 28m 6.971s; **4** Colin Turkington, GB (BMW 320si), 28m 7.193s; **5** Yvan Muller, F (SEAT Leon TDI), 28m 11.209s; **6** Jordi Gené, E (SEAT Leon TDI), 28m 11.600s; **7** Jörg Müller, D (BMW 320si), 28m 13.444s; **8** James Thompson, GB (Alfa Romeo 156), 28m 15.580s; **9** Tom Coronel, NL (SEAT Leon), 28m 16.360s; **10** Pierre-Yves Corthals, B (SEAT Leon), 28m 17.098s.
**Fastest race lap:** Turkington, 1m 34.265s, 87.873 mph/141.418 km/h.
**Pole position:** Porteiro.

**FIA WORLD TOURING CAR CHAMPIONSHIP, Autodromo Nazionale di Monza, Milan, Italy, 7 October. 2 x 9 laps of the 3.600-mile/5.793-km circuit.**
**Round 19 (32.204 miles/51.828 km).**
**1** Yvan Muller, F (SEAT Leon TDI), 18m 19.438s, 105.450 mph/169.705 km/h; **2** Jordi Gené, E (SEAT Leon TDI), 18m 19.639s; **3** James Thompson, GB (Alfa Romeo 156), 18m 20.305s; **4** Nicola Larini, I (Chevrolet Lacetti), 18m 20.634s; **5** Alain Menu, CH (Chevrolet Lacetti), 18m 21.854s; **6** Gabriele Tarquini, I (SEAT Leon TDI), 18m 22.446s; **7** Augusto Farfus Jr, BR (BMW 320si), 18m 23.490s; **8** Robert Huff, GB (Chevrolet Lacetti), 18m 24.128s; **9** Tom Coronel, NL (SEAT Leon), 18m 29.367s; **10** Luca Rangoni, I (BMW 320si), 18m 30.114s.
**Fastest race lap:** Gené, 2m 0.864s, 107.216 mph/172.547 km/h.
**Fastest qualifying lap:** Muller (Yvan), 1m 59.487s, 108.452 mph/174.536 km/h.

**Round 20 (32.204 miles/51.828 km).**
**1** Jordi Gené, E (SEAT Leon TDI), 18m 21.957s, 105.209 mph/169.317 km/h; **2** Nicola Larini, I (Chevrolet Lacetti), 18m 22.968s; **3** James Thompson, GB (Alfa Romeo 156), 18m 23.246s; **4** Robert Huff, GB (Chevrolet Lacetti), 18m 24.470s; **5** Yvan Muller, F (SEAT Leon TDI), 18m 29.863s; **6** Alessandro 'Alex' Zanardi, I (BMW 320si), 18m 32.456s; **7** Tom Coronel, NL (SEAT Leon), 18m 32.502s; **8** Tiago Monteiro, P (SEAT Leon), 18m 36.893s; **9** Roberto Colciago, I (SEAT Leon), 18m 38.177s; **10** Stefan d'Aste, I (BMW 320si), 18m 38.178s.
**Disqualified:** Car not equipped with energy-absorbing material inside the doors. Pierre-Yves Corthals, B (SEAT Leon), finished 9th in 18m 37.241s.
**Fastest race lap:** Thompson, 2m 1.055s, 107.047 mph/172.275 km/h.
**Pole position:** Huff.

**Provisional championship points**
**Drivers**
**1** Andy Priaulx, GB, 81; **2** Yvan Muller, F, 81; **3** Augusto Farfus Jr, BR, 71; **4** James Thompson, GB, 69; **5** Jörg Müller, D, 66; **6** Nicola Larini, I, 61; **7** Alain Menu, CH, 59; **8** Gabriele Tarquini, I, 54; **9** Robert Huff, GB, 51; **10** Jordi Gené, E, 50; **11** Felix Porteiro, E, 30; **12** Tiago Monteiro, P, 30; **13** Tom Coronel, NL, 25; **14** Luca Rangoni, I, 15; **15** Alessandro 'Alex' Zanardi, I, 14; **16** Rickard Rydell, S, 10; **17** Roberto Colciago, I, 6; **18** Michel Jourdain Jr, MEX, 3; **19** Pierre-Yves Corthals, B, 3; **20** Sergio Hernández, E, 1.

**Independents' Trophy**
**1** Stefan d'Aste, I, 120; **2** Pierre-Yves Corthals, B, 112; **3** Luca Rangoni, I, 110; **4** Roberto Colciago, I, 78; **5** Sergio Hernández, E, 63.

**Manufacturers**
**1** BMW, 237; **2** SEAT, 227; **3** Chevrolet, 194; **4** Alfa Romeo, 111.

**Teams**
**1** Proteam Motorsport, 176; **2** Exagon Engineering, 133; **3** SEAT Sport Italia, 122; **4** Wiechers-Sport, 120; **5** GR Asia, 103

*Results of the Macau races will be given in AUTOCOURSE 2008–2009.*

## German Touring Car Championship (DTM)

**GERMAN TOURING CAR CHAMPIONSHIP, Hockenheimring Grand Prix Circuit, Heidelberg, Germany, 22 April. Round 1. 27 laps of the 2.842-mile/4.574-km circuit, 76.738 miles/123.498 km.**
**1** Mattias Ekström, S (Audi A4), 1h 10m 16.441s, 65.519 mph/105.443 km/h; **2** Martin Tomczyk, D (Audi A4), 1h 10m 20.267s; **3** Daniel La Rosa, D (Mercedes C-klasse), 1h 10m 23.498s; **4** Alexandros 'Alex' Margaritis, GR (Mercedes C-klasse), 1h 10m 24.892s; **5** Paul di Resta, GB (Mercedes C-klasse), 1h 10m 25.477s; **6** Jamie Green, GB (Mercedes C-klasse), 1h 10m 27.354s; **7** Bernd Schneider, D (Mercedes C-klasse), 1h 10m 30.184s; **8** Gary Paffett, GB (Mercedes C-klasse), 1h 10m 30.901s; **9** Timo Scheider, D (Audi A4), 1h 10m 33.300s; **10** Mika Häkkinen, FIN (Mercedes C-klasse), 1h 10m 33.712s.
**Fastest race lap:** Ekström, 1m 35.188s, 107.492s, 107.490 mph/172.988 km/h.
**Fastest qualifying lap:** Bruno Spengler, CDN (Mercedes C-klasse), 1m 34.369s, 108.423 mph/174.489 km/h.

**GERMAN TOURING CAR CHAMPIONSHIP, Motorsport Arena Oschersleben, Germany, 6 May. Round 2. 44 laps of the 2.297-mile/3.696-km circuit, 101.050 miles/162.624 km.**
**1** Gary Paffett, GB (Mercedes C-klasse), 1h 3m 30.763s, 95.461 mph/153.630 km/h; **2** Paul di Resta, GB (Mercedes C-klasse), 1h 3m 34.516s; **3** Mike Rockenfeller, D (Audi A4), 1h 3m 45.807s; **4** Timo Scheider, D (Audi A4), 1h 3m 50.069s; **5** Martin Tomczyk, D (Audi A4), 1h 3m 50.581s; **6** Bernd Schneider, D (Mercedes C-klasse), 1h 3m 50.806s; **7** Mattias Ekström, S (Audi A4), 1h 3m 53.571s; **8** Alexandros 'Alex' Margaritis, GR (Mercedes C-klasse), 1h 3m 55.409s; **9** Adam Carroll, GB (Audi A4), 1h 3m 56.330s; **10** Christian Abt, D (Audi A4), 1h 3m 58.673s.
**Fastest race lap:** Jamie Green, GB (Mercedes C-klasse), 1m 23.869s, 98.579 mph/158.647 km/h.
**Fastest qualifying lap:** Mika Häkkinen, FIN (Mercedes C-klasse), 1m 22.456s, 100.268 mph/161.366km/h.

**GERMAN TOURING CAR CHAMPIONSHIP, EuroSpeedway Lausitz, Klettwitz, Dresden, Germany, 20 May. Round 3. 48 laps of the 2.161-mile/3.478-km circuit, 103.734 miles/166.944 km.**
**1** Mika Häkkinen, FIN (Mercedes C-klasse), 1h 9m 10.219s, 89.982 mph/144.811 km/h; **2** Paul di Resta, GB (Mercedes C-klasse), 1h 9m 11.898s; **3** Bruno Spengler, CDN (Mercedes C-klasse), 1h 9m 14.394s; **4** Bernd Schneider, D (Mercedes C-klasse), 1h 9m 18.933s; **5** Timo Scheider, D (Audi A4), 1h 9m 23.295s; **6** Jamie Green, GB (Mercedes C-klasse), 1h 9m 24.672s; **7** Mathias Lauda, A (Mercedes C-klasse), 1h 9m 30.326s; **8** Gary Paffett, GB (Mercedes C-klasse), 1h 9m 33.380s; **9** Martin Tomczyk, D (Audi A4), 1h 9m 33.961s; **10** Mattias Ekström, S (Audi A4), 1h 9m 34.290s.
**Fastest race lap:** Ekström, 1m 19.884s, 97.392 mph/156.737 km/h.
**Fastest qualifying lap:** Spengler, 1m 18.408s, 99.225 mph/159.687 km/h.

**GERMAN TOURING CAR CHAMPIONSHIP, Brands Hatch Indy Circuit, West Kingsdown, Dartford, Kent, Great Britain, 10 June. Round 4. 83 laps of the 1.199-mile/1.929-km circuit, 99.486 miles/160.107 km.**
**1** Bernd Schneider, D (Mercedes C-klasse), 1h 5m 10.090s, 91.596 mph/147.410 km/h; **2** Martin Tomczyk, D (Audi A4), 1h 5m 10.633s; **3** Mattias Ekström, S (Audi A4), 1h 5m 11.345s; **4** Mika Häkkinen, FIN (Mercedes C-klasse), 1h 5m 16.272s; **5** Bruno Spengler, CDN (Mercedes C-klasse), 1h 5m 16.567s; **6** Jamie Green, GB (Mercedes C-klasse), 1h 5m 32.575s; **7** Alexandre Prémat, F (Audi A4), 1h 5m 36.915s; **8** Christian Abt, D (Audi A4), 1h 5m 39.811s; **9** Alexandros 'Alex' Margaritis, GR (Mercedes C-klasse), 1h 5m 40.308s; **10** Gary Paffett, GB (Mercedes C-klasse), 1h 5m 43.043s.
**Fastest race lap:** Tomczyk, 43.520s, 99.151 mph/159.568 km/h.
**Fastest qualifying lap:** Häkkinen, 42.660s, 101.150 mph/162.784 km/h.

**GERMAN TOURING CAR CHAMPIONSHIP, Norisring, Nürnberg (Nuremberg), Germany, 24 June. Round 5. 74 laps of the 1.429-mile/2.300-km circuit, 105.757 miles/170.200 km.**
**1** Bruno Spengler, CDN (Mercedes C-klasse), 1h 3m 59.350s, 99.164 mph/159.590 km/h; **2** Bernd Schneider, D (Mercedes C-klasse), 1h 4m 01.153s; **3** Mattias Ekström, S (Audi A4), 1h 4m 01.851s; **4** Gary Paffett, GB (Mercedes C-klasse), 1h 4m 08.510s; **5** Tom Kristensen, DK (Audi A4), 1h 4m 13.100s; **6** Jamie Green, GB (Mercedes C-klasse), 1h 4m 13.551s; **7** Alexandros 'Alex' Margaritis, GR (Mercedes C-klasse), 1h 4m 18.827s; **8** Alexandre Prémat, F (Audi A4), 1h 4m 20.278s; **9** Mika Häkkinen, FIN (Mercedes C-klasse), 1h 4m 21.049s; **10** Christian Abt, D (Audi A4), 1h 4m 35.419s.
**Fastest race lap:** Spengler, 48.792s, 105.447 mph/169.699 km/h.
**Fastest qualifying lap:** Spengler, 55.963s, 91.935 mph/147.954 km/h.

**GERMAN TOURING CAR CHAMPIONSHIP, Autodromo Internazionale del Mugello, Italy, 15 July. Round 6. 33 laps of the 3.259-mile/5.245-km circuit, 107.550 miles/173.085 km.**
**1** Mika Häkkinen, FIN (Mercedes C-klasse), 1h 3m 10.117s, 102.155 mph/164.403 km/h; **2** Mattias Ekström, S (Audi A4), 1h 3m 10.488s; **3** Paul di Resta, GB (Mercedes C-klasse), 1h 3m 13.315s; **4** Bruno Spengler, CDN (Mercedes C-klasse), 1h 3m 18.839s; **5** Daniel La Rosa, D (Mercedes C-klasse), 1h 3m 19.537s; **6** Mike Rockenfeller, D (Audi A4), 1h 3m 20.190s; **7** Alexandre Prémat, F (Audi A4), 1h 3m 22.092s; **8** Tom Kristensen, DK (Audi A4), 1h 3m 22.368s; **9** Markus Winkelhock, D (Audi A4), 1h 3m 26.675s; **10** Susie Stoddart, GB (Mercedes C-klasse), 1h 3m 32.261s.
**Fastest race lap:** Martin Tomczyk, D (Audi A4), 1m 46.126s, 110.555 mph/177.920 km/h.
**Fastest qualifying lap:** Ekström, 1m 43.851s, 112.977 mph/181.818 km/h.

**GERMAN TOURING CAR CHAMPIONSHIP, Circuit Park Zandvoort, Netherlands, 29 July. Round 7. 38 laps of the 2.676-mile/4.307-km circuit, 101.697 miles/163.666 km.**
**1** Martin Tomczyk, D (Audi A4), 1h 2m 31.668s, 97.586 mph/157.050 km/h; **2** Alexandre Prémat, F (Audi A4), 1h 2m 31.965s; **3** Mattias Ekström, S (Audi A4), 1h 2m 33.704s; **4** Timo Scheider, D (Audi A4), 1h 2m 34.081s; **5** Bruno Spengler, CDN (Mercedes C-klasse), 1h 2m 34.662s; **6** Christian Abt, D (Audi A4), 1h 2m 36.637s; **7** Mika Häkkinen, FIN (Mercedes C-klasse), 1h 2m 37.416s; **8** Alexandros 'Alex' Margaritis, GR (Mercedes C-klasse), 1h 2m 38.597s; **9** Gary Paffett, GB (Mercedes C-klasse), 1h 2m 39.550s; **10** Mike Rockenfeller, D (Audi A4), 1h 2m 40.582s.
**Fastest race lap:** Jamie Green, GB (Mercedes C-klasse), 1m 35.395s, 100.996 mph/162.536 km/h.
**Fastest qualifying lap:** Scheider, 1m 32.823s, 103.794 mph/167.040 km/h.

**GERMAN TOURING CAR CHAMPIONSHIP, Nürburgring, Nürburg/Eifel, Germany, 2 September. Round 8. 43 laps of the 2.255-mile/3.629-km circuit, 96.963 miles/156.047 km.**
**1** Martin Tomczyk, D (Audi A4), 1h 2m 39.571s, 92.848 mph/149.424 km/h; **2** Bruno Spengler, CDN (Mercedes C-klasse), 1h 2m 45.788s; **3** Mattias Ekström, S (Audi A4), 1h 3m 0.106s; **4** Timo Scheider, D (Audi A4), 1h 3m 5.930s; **5** Jamie Green, GB (Mercedes C-klasse), 1h 3m 6.539s; **6** Paul di Resta, GB (Mercedes C-klasse), 1h 3m 7.557s; **7** Bernd Schneider, D (Mercedes C-klasse), 1h 3m 10.244s; **8** Tom Kristensen, DK (Audi A4), 1h 3m 10.692s; **9** Alexandre Prémat, F (Audi A4), 1h 3m 15.936s; **10** Mika Häkkinen, FIN (Mercedes C-klasse), 1h 3m 16.430s.
**Fastest race lap:** Spengler, 1m 24.529s, 96.036 mph/154.555 km/h.
**Fastest qualifying lap:** Tomczyk, 1m 23.197s, 97.574 mph/157.029 km/h.

**GERMAN TOURING CAR CHAMPIONSHIP, Circuit de Catalunya, Montmeló, Barcelona, Spain, 23 September. Round 9. 58 laps of the 1.850-mile/2.977-km circuit, 107.290 miles/172.666 km.**
**1** Jamie Green, GB (Mercedes C-klasse), 1h 8m 21.523s, 94.171 mph/151.553 km/h; **2** Bruno Spengler, CDN (Mercedes C-klasse), 1h 8m 33.072s; **3** Paul di Resta, GB (Mercedes C-klasse), 1h 8m 36.162s; **4** Alexandros 'Alex' Margaritis, GR (Mercedes C-klasse), 1h 9m 08.062s; **5** Gary Paffett, GB (Mercedes C-klasse), 1h 9m 11.119s; **6** Mathias Lauda, A (Audi A4), 1h 9m 12.024s; **7** Mike Rockenfeller, D (Audi A4), 49 laps (DNF); **8** Lucas Luhr, D (Audi A4), 49 (DNF); **9** Tom Kristensen, DK (Audi A4), 49 (DNF); **10** Alexandre Prémat, F (Audi A4), 48 (DNF).
**Fastest race lap:** Spengler, 1m 8.669s, 96.978 mph/156.070 km/h.
**Fastest qualifying lap:** Martin Tomczyk, D (Audi A4), 1m 18.689s, 84.629 mph/136.196 km/h.

**GERMAN TOURING CAR CHAMPIONSHIP, Hockenheimring Grand Prix Circuit, Heidelberg, Germany, 14 October. Round 10. 37 laps of the 2.842-mile/4.574-km circuit, 105.160 miles/169.238 km.**
**1** Jamie Green, GB (Mercedes C-klasse), 1h 0m 19.948s, 104.580 mph/168.305 km/h; **2** Timo Scheider, D (Audi A4), 1h 0m 23.644s; **3** Mattias Ekström, S (Audi A4), 1h 0m 27.183s; **4** Bruno Spengler, CDN (Mercedes C-klasse), 1h 0m 27.617s; **5** Bernd Schneider, D (Mercedes C-klasse), 1h 0m 31.027s; **6** Tom Kristensen, DK (Audi A4), 1h 0m 39.606s; **7** Alexandros 'Alex' Margaritis, GR (Mercedes C-klasse), 1h 0m 43.122s; **8** Paul di Resta, GB (Mercedes C-klasse), 1h 0m 49.106s; **9** Martin Tomczyk, D (Audi A4), 1h 0m 53.133s; **10** Daniel la Rosa, D (Mercedes C-klasse), 1h 0m 54.740s.
**Fastest race lap:** Green, 1m 34.413s, 108.372 mph/174.408 km/h.
**Fastest qualifying lap:** Kristensen, 1m 32.862s, 110.182 mph/177.321 km/h.

**Final championship points**
**Drivers**
**1** Mattias Ekström, S, 50; **2** Bruno Spengler, CDN, 47; **3** Martin Tomczyk, D, 40; **4** Jamie Green, GB, 34.5; **5** Paul di Resta, GB, 32; **6** Bernd Schneider, D, 31.5; **7** Timo Scheider, D, 25; **8** Mika Häkkinen, FIN, 22; **9** Gary Paffett, GB, 20.5; **10** Alexandros 'Alex' Margaritis, GR, 16; **11** Alexandre Prémat, F, 13; **12** Mike Rockenfeller, D, 11; **13** Daniel La Rosa, D, 10; **14** Tom Kristensen, DK, 9; **15** Christian Abt, D, 4; **16** Mathias Lauda, A, 4; **17** Lucas Luhr, D, 1.

**Teams**
**1** Audi Sport Team Abt Sportsline, 90; **2** Originalteile/DC Bank AMG Mercedes, 78.5; **3** Salzgitter/AMG Mercedes, 56.5; **4** stern/Laureas AMG Mercedes, 36.5; **5** Audi Sport Team Abt, 34; **6** TV-Spielfilm/JAWA.de AMG Mercedes, 32.

## British Touring Car Championship

**BRITISH TOURING CAR CHAMPIONSHIP, Brands Hatch Indy Circuit, West Kingsdown, Dartford, Kent, Great Britain, 1 April. 27, 24 and 27 laps of the 1.1986-mile/1.929-km circuit.**
**Round 1 (32.363 miles/52.082 km).**
**1** Jason Plato, GB (SEAT Leon), 24m 57.801s, 77.783 mph/125.179 km/h; **2** Colin Turkington, GB (BMW 320si), 24m 59.038s; **3** Matt Neal, GB (Honda Civic), 25m 1.757s; **4** Mike Jordan, GB (Honda Integra), 25m 2.027s; **5** Tom Onslow-Cole, GB (BMW 320si), 25m 2.903s; **6** Tom Chilton, GB (Vauxhall Vectra), 25m 3.451s; **7** Adam Jones, GB (SEAT Toledo Cupra), 25m 5.987s; **8** Gordon Shedden, GB (Honda Civic), 25m 12.149s; **9** Gareth Howell, GB (SEAT Toledo Cupra), 25m 12.632s; **10** Fabrizio Giovanardi, I (Vauxhall Vectra), 25m 12.910s.
**Disqualified:** Car dropping oil and failed to pit at black/yellow flag - Mat Jackson, GB (BMW 320si), finished 3rd in 25m 0.558s.
**Fastest race lap:** Plato, 49.706s, 86.810 mph/139.707 km/h.
**Fastest qualifying lap:** Turkington, 49.532s, 87.115 mph/140.197 km/h.

**Round 2 (28.767 miles/46.294 km).**
**1** Jason Plato, GB (SEAT Leon), 20m 27.095s, 84.392 mph/135.817 km/h; **2** Colin Turkington, GB (BMW 320si), 20m 29.754s; **3** Tom Onslow-Cole, GB (BMW 320si), 20m 31.236s; **4** Darren Turner, GB (SEAT Leon), 20m 31.853s; **5** Matt Neal, GB (Honda Civic), 20m 37.317s; **6** Adam Jones, GB (SEAT Toledo Cupra), 20m 37.765s; **7** Fabrizio Giovanardi, I (Vauxhall Vectra), 20m 39.172s; **8** Mat Jackson, GB (BMW 320si), 20m 40.033s; **9** Matt Allison, GB (SEAT Toledo Cupra), 20m 43.537s; **10** Chris Stockton, GB (Lexus IS200), 20m 49.141s.
**Fastest race lap:** Turner, 50.224s, 85.914 mph/138.266 km/h.
**Pole position:** Plato

**Round 3 (32.363 miles/52.082 km).**
**1** Matt Neal, GB (Honda Civic), 23m 48.564s, 81.553 mph/131.246 km/h; **2** Fabrizio Giovanardi, I (Vauxhall Vectra), 23m 49.712s; **3** Mat Jackson, GB (BMW 320si), 23m 49.800s; **4** Jason Plato, GB (SEAT Leon), 23m 51.031s; **5** Adam Jones, GB (SEAT Toledo Cupra), 23m 52.626s; **6** Tom Onslow-Cole, GB (BMW 320si), 23m 52.861s; **7** Tom Chilton, GB (Vauxhall Vectra), 23m 53.790s; **8** Mike Jordan, GB (Honda Integra), 23m 53.808s; **9** Gareth Howell, GB (SEAT Toledo Cupra), 23m 54.900s; **10** Matt Allison, GB (SEAT Toledo Cupra), 24m 1.217s.
**Disqualified:** Caused accident - Darren Turner, GB (SEAT Leon), finished 3rd.
**Fastest race lap:** Jackson, 49.789s, 86.665 mph/139.474 km/h.
**Pole position:** Giovanardi.

**BRITISH TOURING CAR CHAMPIONSHIP, Rockingham Motor Speedway, Corby, Northamptonshire, Great Britain, 22 April. 15, 19 and 17 laps of the 1.9486-mile/3.136-km circuit.**
**Round 4 (29.229 miles/47.040 km).**
**1** Fabrizio Giovanardi, I (Vauxhall Vectra), 21m 43.800s, 80.706 mph/129.884 km/h; **2** Tom Chilton, GB (Vauxhall Vectra), 21m 47.950s; **3** Jason Plato, GB (SEAT Leon), 21m 48.180s; **4** Gordon Shedden, GB (Honda Civic), 21m 51.310s; **5** Matt Neal, GB (Honda Civic), 21m 51.610s; **6** Mike Jordan, GB Honda Integra), 21m 56.611s; **7** Colin Turkington, GB (BMW 320si), 22m 0.115s; **8** Tom Onslow-Cole, GB (BMW 320si), 22m 0.377s; **9** Eoin Murray, IRL (Alfa Romeo 156), 22m 1.271s; **10** Mat Jackson, GB (BMW 320si), 22m 04.389s.
**Fastest race lap:** Giovanardi, 1m 25.173s, 82.361 mph/132.548 km/h.
**Fastest qualifying lap:** Turner, 1m 24.908s, 132.961 mph/82.618 km/h.

**Round 5 (37.023 miles/59.583 km).**
**1** Fabrizio Giovanardi, I (Vauxhall Vectra), 30m 1.521s, 73.983 mph/119.065 km/h; **2** Tom Onslow-Cole, GB (BMW 320si), 30m 4.405s; **3** Tom Chilton, GB (Vauxhall Vectra), 30m 5.787s; **4** Mat Jackson, GB (BMW 320si),

30m 6.193s; **5** Jason Plato, GB (SEAT Leon), 30m 6.426s; **6** Darren Turner, GB (SEAT Leon), 30m 6.904s; **7** Matt Allison, GB (SEAT Toledo Cupra), 30m 15.877s; **8** David Pinkney, GB (Alfa Romeo 156), 30m 24.371s; **9** Jason Hughes, GB (MG ZS), 30m 27.767s; **10** John George, GB (Honda Integra), 30m 33.666s.
**Fastest race lap:** Turner, 1m 25.648s, 81.905 mph/131.813 km/h.
**Pole position:** Giovanardi.

**Round 6 (33.126 miles/53.311 km).**
**1** Jason Plato, GB (SEAT Leon), 25m 26.790s, 78.107 mph/125.702 km/h; **2** Mat Jackson, GB (BMW 320si), 25m 29.204s; **3** Darren Turner, GB (SEAT Leon), 25m 30.531s; **4** Tom Chilton, GB (Vauxhall Vectra), 25m 31.149s; **5** Fabrizio Giovanardi, I (Vauxhall Vectra), 25m 32.896s; **6** Gordon Shedden, GB (Honda Civic), 25m 33.460s; **7** Matt Neal, GB (Honda Civic), 25m 33.626s; **8** Mike Jordan, GB (Honda Integra), 25m 37.745s; **9** Matt Allison, GB (SEAT Toledo Cupra), 25m 41.333s; **10** Simon Blanckley, GB (Honda Integra), 25m 44.063s.
**Fastest race lap:** Plato, 1m 25.393s, 82.149 mph/132.206 km/h.
**Pole position:** George.

**BRITISH TOURING CAR CHAMPIONSHIP, Thruxton Circuit, Andover, Hampshire, Great Britain, 6 May. 16, 18 and 16 laps of the 2.356-mile/3.792-km circuit.**
**Round 7 (37.696 miles/60.666 km).**
**1** Fabrizio Giovanardi, I (Vauxhall Vectra), 21m 41.754s, 104.248 mph/167.771 km/h; **2** Jason Plato, GB (SEAT Leon), 21m 46.112s; **3** Darren Turner, GB (SEAT Leon), 21m 46.726s; **4** Colin Turkington, GB (BMW 320si), 21m 46.973s; **5** Matt Neal, GB (Honda Civic), 21m 48.180s; **6** Tom Chilton, GB (Vauxhall Vectra), 21m 54.859s; **7** Matt Allison, GB (SEAT Toledo Cupra), 22m 1.209s; **8** Tom Onslow-Cole, GB (BMW 320si), 22m 5.308s; **9** Eoin Murray, IRL (Alfa Romeo 156), 22m 8.598s; **10** Mike Jordan, GB (Honda Integra), 22m 8.883s.
**Fastest race lap:** Chilton, 1m 19.106s, 107.218 mph/172.551 km/h.
**Fastest qualifying lap:** Giovanardi, 1m 17.476s, 109.474 mph/176.181 km/h.

**Round 8 (42.408 miles/68.249 km).**
**1** Fabrizio Giovanardi, I (Vauxhall Vectra), 25m 41.800s, 99.020 mph/159.357 km/h; **2** Matt Neal, GB (Honda Civic), 25m 42.085s; **3** Tom Chilton, GB (Vauxhall Vectra), 25m 46.157s; **4** Mike Jordan, GB (Honda Integra), 25m 49.415s; **5** Colin Turkington, GB (BMW 320si), 25m 50.352s; **6** Jason Plato, GB (SEAT Leon), 25m 50.873s; **7** Tom Onslow-Cole, GB (BMW 320si), 25m 52.041s; **8** Gordon Shedden, GB (Honda Civic), 25m 52.106s; **9** Jason Hughes, GB (MG ZS), 25m 55.245s; **10** David Pinkney, GB (Alfa Romeo 156), 25m 57.430s.
**Fastest race lap:** Giovanardi, 1m 19.791s, 106.298 mph/171.070 km/h.
**Pole position:** Giovanardi.

**Round 9 (37.696 miles/60.666 km).**
**1** Jason Plato, GB (SEAT Leon), 21m 45.119s, 103.979 mph/167.339 km/h; **2** Gordon Shedden, GB (Honda Civic), 21m 46.532s; **3** Mike Jordan, GB (Honda Integra), 21m 50.085s; **4** Fabrizio Giovanardi, I (Vauxhall Vectra), 21m 52.414s; **5** Matt Neal, GB (Honda Civic), 21m 52.591s; **6** Darren Turner, GB (SEAT Leon), 21m 53.000s; **7** Gareth Howell, GB (SEAT Toledo Cupra), 21m 57.578s; **8** Tom Chilton, GB (Vauxhall Vectra), 22m 2.540s; **9** Jason Hughes, GB (MG ZS), 22m 11.761s; **10** Tom Onslow-Cole, GB (BMW 320si), 22m 13.321s.
**Fastest race lap:** Shedden, 1m 19.690s, 106.432 mph/171.286 km/h.
**Pole position:** Pinkney.

**BRITISH TOURING CAR CHAMPIONSHIP, Croft Racing Circuit, Croft-on-Tees, North Yorkshire, Great Britain, 3 June. 15, 18 and 16 laps of the 2.125-mile/3.420-km circuit.**
**Round 10 (31.875 miles/51.298 km).**
**1** Colin Turkington, GB (BMW 320si), 22m 6.494s, 86.506 mph/139.218 km/h; **2** Gordon Shedden, GB (Honda Civic), 22m 10.451s; **3** Matt Neal, GB (Honda Civic), 22m 11.577s; **4** Darren Turner, GB (SEAT Leon), 22m 13.323s; **5** Mike Jordan, GB (Honda Integra), 22m 13.997s; **6** Fabrizio Giovanardi, I (Vauxhall Vectra), 22m 15.988s; **7** Jason Plato, GB (SEAT Leon), 22m 19.190s; **8** Tom Chilton, GB (Vauxhall Vectra), 22m 22.087s; **9** Mat Jackson, GB (BMW 320si), 22m 23.670s; **10** Gareth Howell, GB (SEAT Toledo Cupra), 22m 25.925s.
**Fastest race lap:** Turkington, 1m 27.210s, 87.719 mph/141.171 km/h.
**Fastest qualifying lap:** Shedden, 1m 26.243s, 88.703 mph/142.753 km/h.

**Round 11 (38.250 miles/61.557 km).**
**1** Darren Turner, GB (SEAT Leon), 29m 17.908s, 78.332 mph/126.063 km/h; **2** Jason Plato, GB (SEAT Leon), 29m 18.282s; **3** Mike Jordan, GB (Honda Integra), 29m 21.234s; **4** Mat Jackson, GB (BMW 320si), 29m 23.155s; **5** Gareth Howell, GB (SEAT Toledo Cupra), 29m 25.007s; **6** Fabrizio Giovanardi, I (Vauxhall Vectra), 29m 25.346s; **7** Tom Onslow-Cole, GB (BMW 320si), 29m 29.764s; **8** Jason Hughes, GB (MG ZS), 29m 47.922s; **9** John George, GB (Honda Integra), 29m 57.757s; **10** Chris Stockton, GB (Lexus IS200), 30m 0.381s.
**Fastest race lap:** Turner, 1m 27.482s, 87.447 mph/140.732 km/h.
**Pole position:** Turkington.

**Round 12 (34.000 miles/54.718 km).**
**1** Fabrizio Giovanardi, I (Vauxhall Vectra), 24m 0.874s, 84.948 mph/136.711 km/h; **2** Tom Onslow-Cole, GB (BMW 320si), 24m 4.502s; **3** Mat Jackson, GB (BMW 320si), 24m 9.475s; **4** Gordon Shedden, GB (Honda Civic), 24m 9.941s; **5** Darren Turner, GB (SEAT Leon), 24m 15.005s; **6** Matt Neal, GB (Honda Civic), 24m 15.410s; **7** Tom Chilton, GB (Vauxhall Vectra), 24m 16.168s; **8** Jason Plato, GB (SEAT Leon), 24m 16.945s; **9** Colin Turkington, GB (BMW 320si), 24m 17.693s; **10** Mike Jordan, GB (Honda Integra), 24m 18.673s.
**Fastest race lap:** Giovanardi, 1m 26.817s, 88.116 mph/141.810 km/h.
**Pole position:** George.

**BRITISH TOURING CAR CHAMPIONSHIP, Oulton Park Circuit, Tarporley, Cheshire, Great Britain, 24 June. 15, 15 and 17 laps of the 2.226-mile/3.582-km circuit.**
**Round 13 (33.390 miles/53.736 km).**
**1** Gordon Shedden, GB (Honda Civic), 22m 32.533s, 88.873 mph/143.028 km/h; **2** Fabrizio Giovanardi, I (Vauxhall Vectra), 22m 33.603s; **3** Colin Turkington, GB (BMW 320si), 22m 33.839s; **4** Matt Neal, GB (Honda Civic), 22m 34.244s; **5** Mat Jackson, GB (BMW 320si), 22m 35.482s; **6** Tom Chilton, GB (Vauxhall Vectra), 22m 38.624s; **7** Jason Plato, GB (SEAT Leon), 22m 39.749s; **8** Mike Jordan, GB (Honda Integra), 22m 47.088s; **9** Tom Onslow-Cole, GB (BMW 320si), 22m 47.630s; **10** Gareth Howell, GB (SEAT Toledo Cupra), 23m 02.327s.
**Fastest race lap:** Turkington, 1m 28.831s, 90.212 mph/145.182 km/h.
**Fastest qualifying lap:** Turkington, 1m 28.534s, 90.514 mph/145.669 km/h.

**Round 14 (33.390 miles/53.736 km).**
**1** Colin Turkington, GB (BMW 320si), 32m 24.747s, 61.810 mph/99.473 km/h; **2** Fabrizio Giovanardi, I (Vauxhall Vectra), 32m 24.793s; **3** Mike Jordan, GB (Honda Integra), 32m 25.735s; **4** Matt Neal, GB (Honda Civic), 32m 27.710s; **5** Jason Plato, GB (SEAT Leon), 32m 28.019s; **6** Mat Jackson, GB (BMW 320si), 32m 28.995s; **7** Darren Turner, GB (SEAT Leon), 32m 33.324s; **8** Adam Jones, GB (SEAT Toledo Cupra), 32m 34.395s; **9** Tom Chilton, GB (Vauxhall Vectra), 32m 36.411s; **10** Matt Allison, GB (SEAT Toledo Cupra), 32m 39.114s.
**Fastest race lap:** Jordan & Giovanardi, 1m 39.263s, 80.731 mph/129.924 km/h.
**Pole position:** Shedden.

**Round 15 (37.842 miles/60.901 km).**
**1** Mat Jackson, GB (BMW 320si), 26m 56.440s, 84.279 mph/135.633 km/h; **2** Jason Plato, GB (SEAT Leon), 26m 56.973s; **3** Darren Turner, GB (SEAT Leon), 27m 0.372s; **4** Gordon Shedden, GB (Honda Civic), 27m 0.542s; **5** Adam Jones, GB (SEAT Toledo Cupra), 27m 6.011s; **6** Tom Chilton, GB (Vauxhall Vectra), 27m 7.092s; **7** Tom Onslow-Cole, GB (BMW 320si), 27m 14.674s; **8** Matt Allison, GB (SEAT Toledo Cupra), 27m 15.643s; **9** Mike Jordan, GB (Honda Integra), 27m 16.758s; **10** Martyn Bell, GB (BMW 320i), 27m 37.279s.
**Fastest race lap:** Shedden, 1m 29.085s, 89.955 mph/144.768 km/h.
**Pole position:** Jones.

**BRITISH TOURING CAR CHAMPIONSHIP, Donington Park National Circuit, Castle Donington, Great Britain, 15 July. 19, 16 and 16 laps of the 1.9573-mile/3.150-km circuit.**
**Round 16 (37.189 miles/59.850 km).**
**1** Gordon Shedden, GB (Honda Civic), 30m 19.346s, 73.587 mph/118.427 km/h; **2** Adam Jones, GB (SEAT Toledo Cupra), 30m 26.227s; **3** Matt Neal, GB (Honda Civic), 30m 26.567s; **4** Mike Jordan, GB (Honda Integra), 30m 27.008s; **5** Jason Plato, GB (SEAT Leon), 30m 29.214s; **6** Matt Allison, GB (SEAT Toledo Cupra), 30m 34.586s; **7** Colin Turkington, GB (BMW 320si), 30m 36.791s; **8** Fabrizio Giovanardi, I (Vauxhall Vectra), 30m 41.567s; **9** Mat Jackson, GB (BMW 320si), 30m 43.621s; **10** Tom Onslow-Cole, GB (BMW 320si), 30m 45.974s.
**Fastest race lap:** Neal, 1m 26.348s, 81.603 mph/131.328 km/h.
**Fastest qualifying lap:** Shedden, 1m 13.486s, 95.886 mph/154.314 km/h.

**Round 17 (31.317 miles/50.400 km).**
**1** Jason Plato, GB (SEAT Leon), 23m 11.490s, 81.022 mph/130.392 km/h; **2** Gordon Shedden, GB (Honda Civic), 23m 17.366s; **3** Fabrizio Giovanardi, I (Vauxhall Vectra), 23m 18.778s; **4** Matt Neal, GB (Honda Civic), 23m 23.344s; **5** Adam Jones, GB (SEAT Toledo Cupra), 23m 23.526s; **6** Darren Turner, GB (SEAT Leon), 23m 23.903s; **7** Mike Jordan, GB (Honda Integra), 23m 24.446s; **8** Matt Allison, GB (SEAT Toledo Cupra), 23m 46.283s; **9** Colin Turkington, GB (BMW 320si), 23m 47.532s; **10** Mat Jackson, GB (BMW 320si), 23m 49.963s.
**Fastest race lap:** Plato, 1m 25.172s, 82.730 mph/133.141 km/h.
**Pole position:** Shedden.

**Round 18 (31.317 miles/50.400 km).**
**1** Jason Plato, GB (SEAT Leon), 23m 17.182s, 80.692 mph/129.861 km/h; **2** Matt Neal, GB (Honda Civic), 23m 18.671s; **3** Mike Jordan, GB (Honda Integra), 23m 25.808s; **4** Mat Jackson, GB (BMW 320si), 23m 26.756s; **5** Gordon Shedden, GB (Honda Civic), 23m 27.289s; **6** Colin Turkington, GB (BMW 320si), 23m 27.794s; **7** Tom Chilton, GB (Vauxhall Vectra), 23m 28.579s; **8** Tom Onslow-Cole, GB (BMW 320si), 23m 28.808s; **9** Darren Turner, GB (SEAT Leon), 23m 30.514s; **10** Matt Allison, GB (SEAT Toledo Cupra), 23m 31.597s.
**Fastest race lap:** Neal, 1m 25.122s, 82.779 mph/133.219 km/h.
**Pole position:** Turkington.

**BRITISH TOURING CAR CHAMPIONSHIP, Snetterton Circuit, Thetford, Norfolk, Great Britain, 29 July. 18, 21 and 18 laps of the 1.952-mile/3.141-km circuit.**
**Round 19 (35.136 miles/56.546 km).**
**1** Gordon Shedden, GB (Honda Civic), 22m 5.923s, 95.397 mph/153.527 km/h; **2** Tom Onslow-Cole, GB (BMW 320si), 22m 6.732s; **3** Tom Chilton, GB (Vauxhall Vectra), 22m 7.134s; **4** Mat Jackson, GB (BMW 320si), 22m 7.833s; **5** Fabrizio Giovanardi, I (Vauxhall Vectra), 22m 9.523s; **6** Darren Turner, GB (SEAT Leon), 22m 19.603s; **7** Mike Jordan, GB (Honda Integra), 22m 19.830s; **8** Jason Plato, GB (SEAT Leon), 22m 20.199s; **9** Tom Ferrier, GB (SEAT Toledo Cupra), 22m 28.986s; **10** Jason Hughes, GB (MG ZS), 22m 29.310s.
**Disqualified:** Car under weight - Colin Turkington, GB (BMW 320si), finished 1st in 22m 05.217s.
**Fastest race lap:** Chilton, 1m 12.636s, 96.745 mph/155.697 km/h.
**Fastest qualifying lap:** Turkington, 1m 12.290s, 97.208 mph/156.442 km/h.

**Round 20 (40.992 miles/65.970 km).**
**1** Fabrizio Giovanardi, I (Vauxhall Vectra), 32m 8.399s, 76.525 mph/123.155 km/h; **2** Matt Neal, GB (Honda Civic), 32m 9.597s; **3** Jason Plato, GB (SEAT Leon), 32m 10.076s; **4** Darren Turner, GB (SEAT Leon), 32m 10.832s; **5** Mat Jackson, GB (BMW 320si), 32m 11.093s; **6** Tom Onslow-Cole, GB (BMW 320si), 32m 11.526s; **7** Eoin Murray, IRL (Alfa Romeo 156), 32m 12.172s; **8** Tom Chilton, GB (Vauxhall Vectra), 32m 13.218s; **9** Colin Turkington, GB (BMW 320si), 32m 13.609s; **10** Matt Allison, GB (SEAT Toledo Cupra), 32m 14.636s.
**Fastest race lap:** Neal, 1m 12.784s, 95.549 mph/155.380 km/h.
**Pole position:** Shedden.

**Round 21 (35.136 miles/56.546 km).**
**1** Tom Onslow-Cole, GB (BMW 320si), 22m 7.246s, 95.302 mph/153.374 km/h; **2** Matt Neal, GB (Honda Civic), 22m 9.947s; **3** Fabrizio Giovanardi, I (Vauxhall Vectra), 22m 10.498s; **4** Jason Plato, GB (SEAT Leon), 22m 11.154s; **5** Gordon Shedden, GB (Honda Civic), 22m 12.214s; **6** Colin Turkington, GB (BMW 320si), 22m 12.767s; **7** Mat Jackson, GB (BMW 320si), 22m 12.959s; **8** Tom Chilton, GB (Vauxhall Vectra), 22m 14.239s; **9** Darren Turner, GB (SEAT Leon), 22m 15.782s; **10** Eoin Murray, IRL (Alfa Romeo 156), 22m 17.150s.
**Fastest race lap:** Shedden, 1m 12.398s, 97.063 mph/156.208 km/h.
**Pole position:** Onslow-Cole.

**BRITISH TOURING CAR CHAMPIONSHIP, Brands Hatch Indy Circuit, West Kingsdown, Dartford, Kent, Great Britain, 19 August. 22, 27 andx 27 laps of the 1.1986-mile/1.929-km circuit.**
**Round 22 (26.369 miles/42.437 km).**
**1** Fabrizio Giovanardi, I (Vauxhall Vectra), 20m 0.886s, 79.049 mph/127.216 km/h; **2** Jason Plato, GB (SEAT Leon), 20m 4.005s; **3** Darren Turner, GB (SEAT Leon), 20m 4.994s; **4** Colin Turkington, GB (BMW 320si), 20m 5.413s; **5** Tom Onslow-Cole, GB (BMW 320si), 20m 6.290s; **6** Tom Chilton, GB (Vauxhall Vectra), 20m 8.165s; **7** Adam Jones, GB (SEAT Toledo Cupra), 20m 10.010s; **8** Gavin Smith, GB (SEAT Leon), 20m 17.200s; **9** Matt Allison, GB (SEAT Toledo Cupra), 20m 21.102s; **10** Erkut Kizilirmak, TR (Vauxhall Astra Sport Hatch), 20m 31.329s.
**Fastest race lap:** Turner, 53.401s, 80.803 mph/130.040 km/h.
**Fastest qualifying lap:** Turkington, 49.446s, 87.266 mph/140.441 km/h.

**Round 23 (32.362 miles/52.082 km).**
**1** Fabrizio Giovanardi, I (Vauxhall Vectra), 26m 8.333s, 74.285 mph/119.550 km/h; **2** Jason Plato, GB (SEAT Leon), 26m 17.604s; **3** Gordon Shedden, GB (Honda Civic), 26m 21.652s; **4** Mat Jackson, GB (BMW 320si), 26m 21.801s; **5** Mike Jordan, GB (Honda Integra), 26m 23.007s; **6** Adam Jones, GB (SEAT Toledo Cupra), 26m 37.518s; **7** Gavin Smith, GB (SEAT Leon), 26m 55.704s; **8** Jason Hughes, GB (MG ZS), 27m 1.362s; **9** Colin Turkington, GB (BMW 320si), 26 laps; **10** Erkut Kizilirmak, TR (Vauxhall Astra Sport Hatch), 26.
**Fastest race lap:** Turkington, 50.268s, 85.839 mph/138.145 km/h.
**Pole position:** Giovanardi.

**Round 24 (32.362 miles/52.082 km).**
**1** Colin Turkington, GB (BMW 320si), 23m 54.988s, 81.188 mph/130.659 km/h; **2** Gordon Shedden, GB (Honda Civic), 24m 2.478s; **3** Mat Jackson, GB (BMW 320si), 24m 3.131s; **4** Fabrizio Giovanardi, I (Vauxhall Vectra), 24m 3.701s; **5** Jason Plato, GB (SEAT Leon), 24m 11.097s; **6** Tom Onslow-Cole, GB (BMW 320si), 24m 12.917s; **7** Gavin Smith, GB (SEAT Leon), 24m 13.993s; **8** Mike Jordan, GB (Honda Integra), 24m 14.183s; **9** Tom Chilton, GB (Vauxhall Vectra), 24m 20.600s; **10** John George, GB (Honda Integra), 24m 25.741s.
**Fastest race lap:** Jordan, 49.953s, 86.380 mph/139.016 km/h.
**Pole position:** Jones.

**BRITISH TOURING CAR CHAMPIONSHIP, Knockhill Racing Circuit, Dunfermline, Fife, Scotland, Great Britain, 2 September. 3 x 24 laps of the 1.2713-mile/2.046-km circuit.**
**Round 25 (30.511 miles/49.103 km).**
**1** Darren Turner, GB (SEAT Leon), 21m 45.478s, 84.137 mph/135.406 km/h; **2** Colin Turkington, GB (BMW 320si), 21m 47.132s; **3** Jason Plato, GB (SEAT Leon), 22m 1.113s; **4** Adam Jones, GB (SEAT Toledo Cupra), 22m 2.381s; **5** Mike Jordan, GB (Honda Integra), 22m 2.697s; **6** Fabrizio Giovanardi, I (Vauxhall Vectra), 22m 2.741s; **7** Gavin Smith, GB (SEAT Leon), 22m 4.191s; **8** John George, GB (Honda Integra), 22m 16.599s; **9** Martyn Bell, GB (BMW 320i), 22m 32.753s; **10** Alan Taylor, GB (Honda Integra), 22m 37.180s.
**Disqualified:** Dangerous driving - Tom Onslow-Cole, GB (BMW 320si), finished 4th in 22m 01.469.
**Fastest race lap:** Shedden, 53.313s, 85.845 mph/138.155 km/h.
**Fastest qualifying lap:** Turner, 53.007s, 86.341 mph/138.952 km/h.

**Round 26 (30.511 miles/49.103 km).**
**1** Darren Turner, GB (SEAT Leon), 21m 36.562s, 84.716 mph/136.337 km/h; **2** Colin Turkington, GB (BMW 320si), 21m 37.098s; **3** Fabrizio Giovanardi, I (Vauxhall Vectra), 21m 44.767s; **4** Gordon Shedden, GB (Honda Civic), 21m 45.123s; **5** Jason Plato, GB (SEAT Leon), 21m 45.503s; **6** Matt Neal, GB (Honda Civic), 21m 45.832s; **7** Adam Jones, GB (SEAT Toledo Cupra), 21m 46.709s; **8** Mike Jordan, GB (Honda Integra), 21m 46.944s; **9** Gavin Smith, GB (SEAT Leon), 21m 49.244s; **10** Mat Jackson, GB (BMW 320si), 21m 57.494s.
**Fastest race lap:** Shedden, 53.470s, 85.593 mph/137.749 km/h.
**Pole position:** Turner.

**Round 27 (30.511 miles/49.103 km).**
**1** Gordon Shedden, GB (Honda Civic), 21m 48.929s, 83.916 mph/135.049 km/h; **2** Matt Neal, GB (Honda Civic), 21m 49.423s; **3** Jason Plato, GB (SEAT Leon), 21m 50.075s; **4** Mike Jordan, GB (Honda Integra), 21m 50.858s; **5** Fabrizio Giovanardi, I (Vauxhall Vectra), 21m 51.407s; **6** Colin Turkington, GB (BMW 320si), 21m 52.173s; **7** Darren Turner, GB (SEAT Leon), 21m 53.641s; **8** Adam Jones, GB (SEAT Toledo Cupra), 21m 54.182s; **9** Mat Jackson, GB (BMW 320si), 21m 57.092s; **10** Tom Onslow-Cole, GB (BMW 320si), 22m 04.353s.
**Fastest race lap:** Shedden, 53.340s, 85.802 mph/138.085 km/h.
**Pole position:** Jordan.

**BRITISH TOURING CAR CHAMPIONSHIP, Thruxton Circuit, Andover, Hampshire, Great Britain, 14 October. 16, 16 and 13 laps of the 2.356-mile/3.792-km circuit.**
**Round 28 (37.696 miles/60.666 km).**
**1** Fabrizio Giovanardi, I (Vauxhall Vectra), 21m 33.994s, 104.873 mph/168.777 km/h; **2** Jason Plato, GB (SEAT Leon), 21m 34.998s; **3** Gordon Shedden, GB (Honda Civic), 21m 39.198s; **4** Alain Menu, F (Vauxhall Vectra), 21m 39.656s; **5** Matt Neal, GB (Honda Civic), 21m 40.323s; **6** Colin Turkington, GB (BMW 320si), 21m 40.738s; **7** Mat Jackson, GB (BMW 320si), 21m 41.018s; **8** Tom Coronel, NL (SEAT Leon), 21m 47.411s; **9** Adam Jones, GB (SEAT Toledo Cupra), 21m 52.200s; **10** Tom Onslow-Cole, GB (BMW 320si), 21m 52.549s.
**Fastest race lap:** Chilton, 1m 19.150s, 107.159 mph/172.455 km/h.
**Pole position:** Chilton, 1m 17.269s, 109.767 mph/176.653 km/h.

**Round 29 (37.696 miles/60.666 km).**
**1** Fabrizio Giovanardi, I (Vauxhall Vectra), 21m 35.623s, 104.742 mph/168.565 km/h; **2** Jason Plato, GB (SEAT Leon), 21m 36.456s; **3** Matt Neal, GB (Honda Civic), 21m 37.352s; **4** Colin Turkington, GB (BMW 320si), 21m 43.223s; **5** Mat Jackson, GB (BMW 320si), 21m 43.992s; **6** Alain Menu, F (Vauxhall Vectra), 21m 44.638s; **7** Tom Coronel, NL (SEAT Leon), 21m 45.394s; **8** Mike Jordan, GB (Honda Integra), 21m 45.818s; **9** Tom Chilton, GB (Vauxhall Vectra), 21m 51.430s; **10** Tom Onslow-Cole, GB (BMW 320si), 21m 53.065s.
**Fastest race lap:** Neal, 1m 19.654s, 106.481 mph/171.364 km/h.
**Pole position:** Giovanardi.

**Round 30 (30.628 miles/49.291 km).**
**1** Mat Jackson, GB (BMW 320si), 17m 33.434s, 104.668 mph/168.447 km/h; **2** Fabrizio Giovanardi, I (Vauxhall Vectra), 17m 36.093s; **3** Tom Chilton, GB (Vauxhall Vectra), 17m 36.897s; **4** Jason Plato, GB (SEAT Leon), 17m 37.756s; **5** Matt Neal, GB (Honda Civic), 17m 38.078s; **6** Darren Turner, GB (SEAT Leon), 17m 38.331s; **7** Adam Jones, GB (SEAT Toledo Cupra), 17m 39.530s; **8** Tom Coronel, NL (SEAT Leon), 17m 40.001s; **9** Gordon Shedden, GB (Honda Civic), 17m 40.332s; **10** Rob Collard, GB (SEAT Leon), 17m 48.072s.
**Fastest race lap:** Jordan, 1m 19.288s, 106.972 mph/172.155 km/h.
**Pole position:** Coronel.

**Final championship points**
**Drivers**
**1** Fabrizio Giovanardi, I, 300; **2** Jason Plato, GB, 297; **3** Gordon Shedden, GB, 200; **4** Matt Neal, GB, 195; **5** Colin Turkington, GB, 184; **6** Darren Turner, GB, 160; **7** Mat Jackson, GB, 158; **8** Mike Jordan, GB, 131; **9** Tom Chilton, GB, 130; **10** Tom Onslow-Cole, GB, 109; **11** Adam Jones, GB, 72; **12** Matt Allison, GB, 29; **13** Gavin Smith, GB, 17; **14** Gareth Howell, GB, 16; **15** Jason Hughes, GB, 13; **16** Alain Menu, F, 13; **17** Tom Coronel, NL, 10; **18** Eoin Murray, IRL, 9; **19** John George, GB, 7; **20** David Pinkney, GB, 5; **21** Martyn Bell, GB, 3; **22** Chris Stockton, GB, 2; **23** Tom Ferrier, GB, 2; **24** Erkut Kizilirmak, TR, 2; **25** Simon Blanckley, GB, 1; **26** Alan Taylor, GB, 1; **27** Rob Collard, GB, 1.

**Independent Drivers**
**1** Colin Turkington, GB, 285; **2** Mat Jackson, GB, 270; **3** Mike Jordan, GB, 260; **4** Tom Onslow-Cole, GB, 226; **5** Adam Jones, GB, 164.

**Manufacturers**
**1** Vauxhall, 637; **2** SEAT, 623.

**Teams**
**1** SEAT Sport UK, 446; **2** VX Racing, 421; **3** Team Halfords, 345; **4** Team RAC, 277; **5** Jacksons M.Sport, 155.

**Independent Teams**
**1** Team RAC, 363; **2** Jacksons M.Sport, 274; **3** Team Eurotech, 267.

## Indy Racing League (IRL) IndyCar Series

All cars are Dallara IR4-Honda HI7R unless stated.

**XM SATELLITE RADIO INDY 300, Homestead-Miami Speedway, Florida, USA, 24 March. Round 1. 200 laps of the 1.485-mile/2.390-km circuit, 297.000 miles/ 477.975 km.**
**1** Dan Wheldon, GB, 1h 48m 06.8893s, 164.825 mph/ 265.260 km/h; **2** Scott Dixon, NZ, 1h 48m 13.3886s; **3** Sam Hornish Jr, USA, 1h 48m 24.3647s; **4** Vitor Meira, BR, 1h 48m 29.4266s; **5** Tony Kanaan, BR, 1h 48m 30.0072s; **6** Ed Carpenter, USA, 199 laps; **7** Dario Franchitti, GB, 199; **8** Tomas Scheckter, ZA, 199; **9** Hélio Castroneves, BR, 199; **10** Buddy Rice, USA, 199; **11** Sarah Fisher, USA, 195; **12** Scott Sharp, USA, 194; **13** Darren Manning, GB, 158 (DNF-mechanical); **14** Danica Patrick, USA, 154 (DNF-accident); **15** Marty Roth, USA, 119 (DNF-handling); **16** Kosuke Matsuura, J, 92 (DNF-accident); **17** Jeff Simmons, USA, 90 (DNF-accident); **18** AJ Foyt IV, USA, 90 (DNF-accident); **19** Alex Barron, USA, 86 (DNF-handling); **20** Marco Andretti, USA, 53 (DNF-mechanical).
**Most laps led:** Wheldon, 179.
**Fastest race lap:** Wheldon, 24.9303s, 214.438 mph/ 345.104 km/h.
**Fastest qualifying lap:** Wheldon, 24.9438s, 214.322 mph/344.917 km/h.
**Championship points:** **1** Wheldon, 53; **2** Dixon, 40; **3** Hornish Jr, 35; **4** Meira, 32; **5** Kanaan, 30; **6** Carpenter, 28.

**HONDA GRAND PRIX OF ST. PETERSBURG, Streets of St. Petersburg, Florida, USA, 1 April. Round 2. 100 laps of the 1.800-mile/2.897-km circuit, 180.000 miles/289.682 km.**
**1** Hélio Castroneves, BR, 2h 1m 07.3512s, 89.166 mph/ 143.499 km/h; **2** Scott Dixon, NZ, 2h 1m 07.9519s; **3** Tony Kanaan, BR, 2h 1m 15.2642s; **4** Marco Andretti, USA, 2h 1m 20.8602s; **5** Dario Franchitti, GB, 2h 1m 21.9447s; **6** Tomas Scheckter, ZA, 2h 1m 32.6621s; **7** Sam Hornish Jr, USA, 2h 1m 34.4234s; **8** Danica Patrick, USA, 2h 1m 35.3890s; **9** Dan Wheldon, GB, 2h 1m 41.7411s; **10** Buddy Rice, USA, 2h 1m 54.2692s; **11** Scott Sharp, USA, 2h 1m 55.4492s; **12** Darren Manning, GB, 99 laps; **13** AJ Foyt IV, USA, 98; **14** Jeff Simmons, USA, 97; **15** Sarah Fisher, USA, 97; **16** Vitor Meira, BR, 96; **17** Kosuke Matsuura, J, 83; **18** Ed Carpenter, USA, 45 (DNF-accident).
**Most laps led:** Castroneves, 95.
**Fastest race lap:** Andretti, 1m 2.9653s, 102.914 mph/ 165.624 km/h.
**Fastest qualifying lap:** Castroneves, 1m 1.6839s, 105.052 mph/169.064 km/h.
**Championship points:** **1** Dixon, 80; **2** Wheldon, 75; **3** Castroneves, 75; **4** Kanaan, 65; **5** Hornish Jr, 61; **6** Franchitti, 56.

**INDY JAPAN 300, Twin Ring Motegi, Motegi-machi, Haga-gun, Tochigi Prefecture, Japan, 21 April. Round 3. 200 laps of the 1.520-mile/2.446-km circuit, 304.000 miles/489.241 km.**
**1** Tony Kanaan, BR, 1h 52m 23.2574s, 162.295 mph/ 261.189 km/h; **2** Dan Wheldon, GB, 1h 52m 23.7402s; **3** Dario Franchitti, GB, 1h 52m 34.8112s; **4** Scott Dixon, NZ, 1h 52m 36.3197s; **5** Sam Hornish Jr, USA, 199 laps; **6** Scott Sharp, USA, 199; **7** Hélio Castroneves, BR, 199; **8** Jeff Simmons, USA, 199; **9** Tomas Scheckter, ZA, 199; **10** Buddy Rice, USA, 199; **11** Danica Patrick, USA, 198; **12** Darren Manning, GB, 198; **13** AJ Foyt IV, USA, 197; **14** Sarah Fisher, USA, 197; **15** Ed Carpenter, USA, 192; **16** Marco Andretti, USA, 134 (DNF-accident); **17** Vitor Meira, BR, 50 (DNF-handling); **18** Kosuke Matsuura, J, 0 (DNF-accident).
**Most laps led:** Wheldon, 126.
**Fastest race lap:** Castroneves, 27.1247s, 201.735 mph/ 324.661 km/h.
**Fastest qualifying lap:** Castroneves, 26.6416s, 205.393 mph/330.548 km/h.
**Championship points:** **1** Wheldon, 118; **2** Kanaan, 115; **3** Dixon, 112; **4** Castroneves, 101; **5=** Hornish Jr, 91; **5=** Franchitti, 91.

**KANSAS LOTTERY INDY 300, Kansas Speedway, Kansas City, Kansas, USA, 29 April. Round 4. 200 laps of the 1.520-mile/2.446-km circuit, 304.000 miles/ 489.241 km.**
**1** Dan Wheldon, GB, 1h 36m 56.0586s, 188.169 mph/ 302.828 km/h; **2** Dario Franchitti, GB, 1h 37m 14.5416s; **3** Hélio Castroneves, BR, 1h 37m 29.2866s; **4** Scott Dixon, NZ, 1h 37m 30.4794s; **5** Tomas Scheckter, ZA, 199 laps; **6** Sam Hornish Jr, USA, 199; **7** Danica Patrick, USA, 198; **8** Vitor Meira, BR, 198; **9** AJ Foyt IV, USA, 198; **10** Jeff Simmons, USA, 198; **11** Darren Manning, GB, 198; **12** Sarah Fisher, USA, 196; **13** Scott Sharp, USA, 195 (DNF-accident); **14** Milka Duno, YV, 194; **15** Tony Kanaan, BR, 192; **16** Alex Barron, USA, 191; **17** Ed Carpenter, USA, 99 (DNF-accident); **18** Kosuke Matsuura, J, 57 (DNF-mechanical); **19** Marco Andretti, USA, 43 (DNF-mechanical); **20** Buddy Rice, USA, 37 (DNF- handling); **21** Marty Roth, CDN, 24 DNF - (handling).
**Most laps led:** Wheldon, 177.
**Fastest race lap:** Wheldon, 25.7230s, 212.728 mph/ 342.352 km/h.
**Fastest qualifying lap:** Kanaan, 25.5476s, 214.188 mph/ 344.703 km/h.
**Championship points:** **1** Wheldon, 171; **2** Dixon, 144; **3** Castroneves, 136; **4** Franchitti, 131; **5** Kanaan, 130; **6** Hornish Jr, 119.

**91st INDIANAPOLIS 500, Indianapolis Motor Speedway, Speedway, Indiana, USA, 27 May. Round 5. 166 laps of the 2.500-mile/4.023-km circuit, 415.000 miles/667.878 km.**
**Scheduled for 200 laps, but delayed by heavy rain and stopped early.**
**1** Dario Franchitti, GB, 2h 44m 03.5608s, 151.774 mph/ 244.257 km/h; **2** Scott Dixon, NZ, 2h 44m 3.9218s; **3** Hélio Castroneves, BR, 2h 44m 05.4093s; **4** Sam Hornish Jr, USA, 2h 44m 8.1932s; **5** Ryan Briscoe, AUS, 2h 44m 8.7717s; **6** Scott Sharp, USA, 2h 44m 12.9078s; **7** Tomas Scheckter, ZA, 2h 44m 14.9431s; **8** Danica Patrick, USA, 2h 44m 15.7397s; **9** Davey Hamilton, USA, 2h 44m 18.9724s; **10** Vitor Meira, BR, 2h 44m 21.2599s; **11** Jeff Simmons, USA, 2h 44m 23.2727s; **12** Tony Kanaan, BR, 2h 44m 24.9947s; **13** Michael Andretti, USA, 2h 44m 38.6843s; **14** AJ Foyt IV, USA, 165 laps; **15** Alex Barron, USA, 165; **16** Kosuke Matsuura, J, 165; **17** Ed Carpenter, USA, 164 (DNF-accident); **18** Sarah Fisher, USA, 164; **19** Buddy Lazier, USA, 164; **20** Darren Manning, GB, 164; **21** Roger Yasukawa, USA, 164; **22** Dan Wheldon, GB, 163 (DNF-accident); **23** Richie Hearn, USA, 163; **24** Marco Andretti, USA, 162 (DNF-accident); **25** Buddy Rice, USA, 162 (DNF-accident); **26** Al Unser Jr, USA, 161; **27** Jaques Lazier, USA (Panoz-Honda), 155 (DNF-accident); **28** Marty Roth, CDN, 148 (DNF-accident); **29** Phil Giebler, USA (Panoz DP-Honda), 106 (DNF-accident); **30** John Andretti, USA, 95 (DNF-accident); **31** Milka Duno, YV, 65 (DNF-accident); **32** Jon Herb, USA, 51 (DNF-accident); **33** Robert Moreno, BR (Panoz-Honda), 36 (DNF-accident).
**Did not qualify:** PJ Jones, USA; Jimmy Kite, USA.
**Most laps led:** Kanaan, 83.
**Fastest race lap and fastest leading lap:** Kanaan, 40.2829s, 223.420 mph/359.559 km/h.
**Pole position/Fastest qualifying lap:** Castroneves, 1m 39.4214s, 225.817 mph/363.417 km/h (over four laps).
**Championship points:** **1** Dixon, 184; **2** Wheldon, 183; **3** Franchitti, 181; **4** Castroneves, 171; **5** Kanaan, 151; **6** Hornish Jr, 151.

**ABC SUPPLY/A.J. FOYT INDY 225, The Milwaukee Mile, Wisconsin State Fair Park, West Allis, Wisconsin, USA, 3 June. Round 6. 225 laps of the 1.015-mile/1.633-km circuit, 228.375 miles/367.534 km.**
**1** Tony Kanaan, BR, 1h 47m 42.4393s, 127.220 mph/ 204.740 km/h; **2** Dario Franchitti, GB, 1h 47m 45.0100s; **3** Dan Wheldon, GB, 1h 47m 45.5542s; **4** Scott Dixon, NZ, 1h 47m 45.8419s; **5** Vitor Meira, BR, 1h 47m 47.7257s; **6** Scott Sharp, USA, 1h 47m 49.2752s; **7** Ed Carpenter, USA, 1h 47m 49.4753s; **8** Danica Patrick, USA, 1h 47m 50.4598s; **9** Sam Hornish Jr, USA, 224 laps; **10** Jeff Simmons, USA, 224; **11** Darren Manning, GB, 224; **12** Kosuke Matsuura, J, 223; **13** AJ Foyt IV, USA, 222; **14** Sarah Fisher, USA, 221; **15** Marco Andretti, USA, 209 (DNF-accident); **16** Hélio Castroneves, BR, 201 (DNF-accident); **17** Tomas Scheckter, ZA, 159 (DNF-driveshaft); **18** Buddy Rice, USA, 156 (DNF-accident).
**Most laps led:** Castroneves, 126.
**Fastest race lap:** Wheldon, 22.2017s, 164.582 mph/ 264.869 km/h.
**Fastest qualifying lap:** Castroneves, 21.3596s, 171.071 mph/275.311 km/h.
**Championship points:** **1** Franchitti, 221; **2** Wheldon, 218; **3** Dixon, 216; **4** Kanaan, 201; **5** Castroneves, 188; **6** Hornish Jr, 173.

**BOMBARDIER LEARJET 550k, Texas Motor Speedway, Fort Worth, Texas, USA, 9 June. Round 7. 228 laps of the 1.455-mile/2.342-km circuit, 331.740 miles/ 533.884 km.**
**1** Sam Hornish Jr, USA, 1h 52m 15.2873s, 177.314 mph/ 285.360 km/h; **2** Tony Kanaan, BR, 1h 52m 15.3659s; **3** Danica Patrick, USA, 1h 52m 15.6717s; **4** Dario Franchitti, GB, 1h 52m 19.2638s; **5** Vitor Meira, BR, 1h 52m 19.2892s; **6** Jeff Simmons, USA, 1h 52m 19.9213s; **7** Scott Sharp, USA, 227 laps; **8** Buddy Rice, USA, 225; **9** Kosuke Matsuura, J, 225; **10** Sarah Fisher, USA, 221; **11** Milka Duno, YV, 221; **12** Scott Dixon, NZ, 206; **13** Darren Manning, GB, 200 (DNF-suspension); **14** Tomas Scheckter, ZA, 199; **15** Dan Wheldon, GB, 196 (DNF-accident); **16** Hélio Castroneves, BR, 196 (DNF-accident); **17** AJ Foyt IV, USA, 195 (DNF-accident); **18** Ed Carpenter, USA, 195 (DNF-accident); **19** Marco Andretti, USA, 140 (DNF-gearbox); **20** Jon Herb, USA, 44 (DNF-accident).
**Most laps led:** Hornish Jr, 159.
**Fastest race lap:** Andretti, 24.3289s, 215.299 mph/ 346.491 km/h.
**Fastest qualifying lap:** Sharp, 24.3334s, 215.260 mph/ 346.427 km/h.
**Championship points:** **1** Franchitti, 253; **2** Kanaan, 241; **3** Dixon, 234; **4** Wheldon, 233; **5** Hornish Jr, 226; **6** Castroneves, 202.

**IOWA CORN INDY 250, Iowa Speedway, Newton, Iowa, USA, 24 June. Round 8. 250 laps of the 0.894-mile/ 1.439-km circuit, 223.500 miles/359.688 km.**
**1** Dario Franchitti, GB, 1h 48m 14.1344s, 123.896 mph/ 199.392 km/h; **2** Marco Andretti, USA, 1h 48m 14.2025s; **3** Scott Sharp, USA, 1h 48m 15.1921s; **4** Buddy Rice, USA, 1h 48m 18.3770s; **5** Darren Manning, GB, 1h 48m 19.3500s; **6** Ed Carpenter, USA, 247 laps; **7** Sarah Fisher, USA, 247; **8** Hélio Castroneves, BR, 246; **9** Vitor Meira, BR, 216 (DNF-suspension); **10** Scott Dixon, NZ, 173; **11** Dan Wheldon, GB, 145; **12** AJ Foyt IV, USA, 99 (DNF-accident); **13** Danica Patrick, USA, 99 (DNF-accident); **14** Sam Hornish Jr, USA, 99 (DNF-accident); **15** Kosuke Matsuura, J, 99 (DNF-accident); **16** Tony Kanaan, BR, 85 (DNF-accident); **17** Jeff Simmons, USA, 85 (DNF-accident); **18** Milka Duno, YV, 60 (DNF-handling); **19** Tomas Scheckter, ZA, 0 (DNF-accident).
**Most laps led:** Franchitti, 96.
**Fastest race lap:** Castroneves, 17.5946s, 182.920 mph/ 294.381 km/h.
**Fastest qualifying lap:** Dixon, 17.6486s, 182.360 mph/ 293.480 km/h.
**Championship points:** **1** Franchitti, 306; **2** Kanaan, 255; **3** Dixon, 254; **4** Wheldon, 252; **5** Hornish Jr, 242; **6** Castroneves, 226.

**SUN TRUST INDY CHALLENGE, Richmond International Raceway, Virginia, USA, 30 June. Round 9. 250 laps of the 0.750-mile/1.207-km circuit, 187.500 miles/ 301.752 km.**
**1** Dario Franchitti, GB, 1h 24m 19.6684s, 133.408 mph/ 214.699 km/h; **2** Scott Dixon, NZ, 1h 24m 20.0878s; **3** Dan Wheldon, GB, 1h 24m 21.0313s; **4** Tony Kanaan, BR, 1h 24m 22.5772s; **5** Buddy Rice, USA, 1h 24m 25.5814s; **6** Danica Patrick, USA, 1h 24m 26.0303s; **7** Tomas Scheckter, ZA, 1h 24m 27.2281s; **8** Scott Sharp, USA, 1h 24m 28.2423s; **9** Vitor Meira, BR, 1h 24m 29.1960s; **10** Ed Carpenter, USA, 1h 24m 29.9931s; **11** Hélio Castroneves, BR, 249 laps; **12** Marco Andretti, USA, 249; **13** AJ Foyt IV, USA, 249; **14** Darren Manning, GB, 249; **15** Sam Hornish Jr, USA, 248; **16** Sarah Fisher, USA, 247; **17** Kosuke Matsuura, J, 236 (DNF-accident); **18** Jeff Simmons, USA, 153 (DNF-accident); **19** Milka Duno, YV, 79 (DNF-handling).
**Most laps led:** Franchitti, 242.
**Fastest race lap:** Wheldon, 16.4433s, 164.201 mph/ 264.255 km/h.
**Pole position:** Franchitti (rain prevented qualifying so grid decided by championship placing).
**Championship points:** **1** Franchitti, 359; **2** Dixon, 294; **3** Wheldon, 287; **4** Kanaan, 287; **5** Hornish Jr, 257; **6** Castroneves, 245.

**WATKINS GLEN INDY GRAND PRIX, Watkins Glen International, Watkins Glen, New York, USA, 8 July. Round 10. 60 laps of the 3.370-mile/5.423-km circuit, 202.200 miles/325.409 km.**
**1** Scott Dixon, NZ, 1h 43m 51.5094s, 116.813 mph/ 187.992 km/h; **2** Sam Hornish Jr, USA, 1h 43m 57.7685s; **3** Dario Franchitti, GB, 1h 44m 1.2586s; **4** Tony Kanaan, BR, 1h 44m 5.9924s; **5** Marco Andretti, USA, 1h 44m 6.9843s; **6** Buddy Rice, USA, 1h 44m 18.4265s; **7** Dan Wheldon, GB, 1h 44m 26.8609s; **8** Kosuke Matsuura, J, 1h 44m 32.2131s; **9** Darren Manning, GB, 1h 44m 39.1987s; **10** Jeff Simmons, USA, 1h 44m 46.3989s; **11** Danica Patrick, USA, 1h 44m 48.5927s; **12** Ed Carpenter, USA, 1h 44m 58.4446s; **13** Tomas Scheckter, ZA, 1h 44m 59.2369s; **14** Scott Sharp, USA, 1h 45m 1.8258s; **15** AJ Foyt IV, USA, 1h 45m 16.7947s; **16** Sarah Fisher, USA, 58 laps; **17** Vitor Meira, BR, 58; **18** Hélio Castroneves, BR, 19 (DNF-accident).
**Most laps led:** Dixon, 23.
**Fastest race lap:** Franchitti, 1m 30.7541s, 133.680 mph/ 215.137 km/h.
**Fastest qualifying lap:** Castroneves, 1m 29.1919s, 136.021 mph/218.905 km/h.
**Championship points:** **1** Franchitti, 394; **2** Dixon, 347; **3** Kanaan, 319; **4** Wheldon, 313; **5** Hornish Jr, 297; **6** Castroneves, 257.

**FIRESTONE INDY 200, Nashville Superspeedway, Lebanon, Tennessee, USA, 15 July. Round 11. 200 laps of the 1.300-mile/2.092-km circuit, 260.000 miles/ 418.429 km.**
**1** Scott Dixon, NZ, 1h 35m 6.2615s, 164.030 mph/ 263.981 km/h; **2** Dario Franchitti, GB, 1h 35m 8.5015s; **3** Danica Patrick, USA, 1h 35m 9.4499s; **4** Sam Hornish Jr, USA, 1h 35m 9.5529s; **5** Marco Andretti, USA, 1h 35m 10.4024s; **6** Hélio Castroneves, BR, 1h 35m 10.7713s; **7** Scott Sharp, USA, 1h 35m 11.5064s; **8** Dan Wheldon, GB, 1h 35m 12.0196s; **9** Darren Manning, GB, 199 laps; **10** Vitor Meira, BR, 199; **11** Tomas Scheckter, ZA, 199; **12** AJ Foyt IV, USA, 198; **13** Ed Carpenter, USA, 197; **14** Jeff Simmons, USA, 196; **15** Sarah Fisher, USA, 194; **16** Kosuke Matsuura, J, 182 (DNF-accident); **17** Buddy Rice, USA, 166 (DNF-handling); **18** Tony Kanaan, BR, 35 (DNF-accident).
**Most laps led:** Dixon, 105.
**Fastest race lap:** Wheldon, 23.1841s, 201.862 mph/ 324.866 km/h.
**Fastest qualifying lap:** Dixon, 22.8947s, 204.414 mph/ 328.973 km/h.
**Championship points:** **1** Franchitti, 434; **2** Dixon, 400; **3** Wheldon, 337; **4** Kanaan, 331; **5** Hornish Jr, 329; **6** Castroneves, 285.

**HONDA 200, Mid-Ohio Sports Car Course, Lexington, Ohio, USA, 22 July. Round 12. 85 laps of the 2.258-mile/3.634-km circuit, 191.930 miles/308.881 km.**
**1** Scott Dixon, NZ, 1h 47m 24.0663s, 107.222 mph/ 172.558 km/h; **2** Dario Franchitti, GB, 1h 47m 26.7580s; **3** Hélio Castroneves, BR, 1h 47m 32.7446s; **4** Tony Kanaan, BR, 1h 47m 33.0274s; **5** Danica Patrick, USA, 1h 47m 49.3241s; **6** Darren Manning, GB, 1h 47m 54.5269s; **7** Ryan Hunter-Reay, USA, 1h 48m 8.5664s; **8** Buddy Rice, USA, 1h 48m 13.9860s; **9** Tomas Scheckter, ZA, 1h 48m 18.5995s; **10** Dan Wheldon, GB, 1h 48m 19.2496s; **11** Scott Sharp, USA, 84 laps; **12** Kosuke Matsuura, J, 84; **13** AJ Foyt IV, USA, 84; **14** Sam Hornish Jr, USA, 84; **15** Sarah Fisher, USA, 83; **16** Ed Carpenter, USA, 82; **17** Vitor Meira, BR, 54 (DNF-water pressure); **18** Marco Andretti, USA, 0 (DNF-accident).
**Most laps led:** Castroneves, 37.
**Fastest race lap:** Franchitti, 1m 8.0148s, 119.515 mph/ 192.341 km/h.
**Fastest qualifying lap:** Castroneves, 1m 6.8375s, 121.620 mph/195.729 km/h.
**Championship points:** **1** Franchitti, 474; **2** Dixon, 450; **3** Kanaan, 363; **4** Wheldon, 357; **5** Hornish Jr, 345; **6** Castroneves, 323.

**FIRESTONE INDY 400, Michigan International Speedway, Brooklyn, Michigan, USA, 5 August. Round 13. 200 laps of the 2.000-mile/3.219-km circuit, 400.000 miles/643.738 km.**
**1** Tony Kanaan, BR, 2h 49m 38.0509s, 141.481 mph/ 227.691 km/h; **2** Marco Andretti, USA, 2h 49m 38.1104s; **3** Scott Sharp, USA, 2h 49m 38.4376s; **4** Kosuke Matsuura, J, 2h 49m 38.5212s; **5** Buddy Rice, USA, 2h 49m 42.9606s; **6** Ryan Hunter-Reay, USA, 2h 49m 48.0623s; **7** Danica Patrick, USA, 199 laps; **8** AJ Foyt IV, USA, 167 (DNF-mechanical); **9** Sam Hornish Jr, USA, 148 (DNF-accident damage); **10** Scott Dixon, NZ, 145 (DNF-accident damage); **11** Tomas Scheckter, ZA, 144 (DNF-accident); **12** Dan Wheldon, GB, 143 (DNF-accident); **13** Dario Franchitti, GB, 143 (DNF-accident); **14** Ed Carpenter, USA, 143 (DNF-accident); **15** Darren Manning, GB, 113 (DNF-accident); **16** Sarah Fisher, USA, 83 (DNF-accident); **17** Hélio Castroneves, BR, 58 (DNF-accident); **18** Vitor Meira, BR, 58 (DNF-accident); **19** Milka Duno, YV, 43 (DNF-mechanical); **20** Jon Herb, USA, 26 (DNF-accident).
**Most laps led:** Franchitti, 101.
**Fastest race lap:** Patrick, 32.9067s, 218.800 mph/ 352.125 km/h.
**Fastest qualifying lap:** Franchitti, 32.9810s, 218.308 mph/351.332 km/h.
**Championship points:** **1** Franchitti, 494; **2** Dixon, 470; **3** Kanaan, 413; **4** Wheldon, 375; **5** Hornish Jr, 367; **6** Castroneves, 336.

**MEIJER INDY 300, Kentucky Speedway, Fort Mitchell, Kentucky, USA. 11 August. Round 14. 200 laps of the 1.480-mile/2.382-km circuit, 296.000 miles/476.366 km.**
**1** Tony Kanaan, BR, 1h 38m 21.7078s, 180.558 mph/ 290.580 km/h; **2** Scott Dixon, NZ, 1h 38m 23.4535s; **3** AJ Foyt IV, USA, 1h 38m 23.8148s; **4** Marco Andretti, USA, 1h 38m 24.0076s; **5** Tomas Scheckter, ZA, 1h 38m 24.0738s; **6** Scott Sharp, USA, 1h 38m 24.3569s; **7** Ed Carpenter, USA, 1h 38m 24.5228s; **8** Dario Franchitti, GB, 1h 38m 27.9917s; **9** Hélio Castroneves, BR, 199 laps; **10** Vitor Meira, BR, 199; **11** Kosuke Matsuura, J, 199; **12** Buddy Rice, USA, 199; **13** Darren Manning, GB, 198; **14** Sarah Fisher, USA, 197; **15** Ryan Hunter-Reay, USA, 183; **16** Danica Patrick, USA, 180 (DNF-accident); **17** Dan Wheldon, GB, 37 (DNF-accident); **18** Sam Hornish Jr, USA, 35 (DNF-accident).
**Most laps led:** Kanaan, 131.
**Fastest race lap:** Wheldon, 24.3701s, 218.629 mph/ 351.849 km/h.
**Fastest qualifying lap:** Kanaan, 24.4307s, 218.086 mph/ 350.976 km/h.
**Championship points:** **1** Franchitti, 518; **2** Dixon, 510; **3** Kanaan, 466; **4** Wheldon, 388; **5** Hornish Jr, 379; **6** Castroneves, 358.

**MOTOROLA INDY 300, Infineon Raceway, Sears Point, Sonoma, California, USA, 26 August. Round 15. 80 laps of the 2.300-mile/3.701-km circuit, 184.000 miles/296.119 km.**
**1** Scott Dixon, NZ, 1h 51m 58.5533s, 98.593 mph/ 158.669 km/h; **2** Hélio Castroneves, BR, 1h 51m 59.0982s; **3** Dario Franchitti, GB, 1h 52m 06.9347s; **4** Tony Kanaan, BR, 1h 52m 7.5397s; **5** Sam Hornish Jr, USA, 1h 52m 8.5006s; **6** Danica Patrick, USA, 1h 52m 8.9258s; **7** Dan Wheldon, GB, 1h 52m 9.3631s; **8** Tomas Scheckter, ZA, 1h 52m 11.2388s; **9** Vitor Meira, BR, 1h 52m 11.5315s; **10** Kosuke Matsuura, J, 1h 52m 13.5241s; **11** Buddy Rice, USA, 79 laps; **12** Darren Manning, GB, 79; **13** Ed Carpenter, USA, 79; **14** Scott Sharp, USA, 79; **15** AJ Foyt IV, USA, 71 (DNF-accident); **16** Marco Andretti, USA, 68 (DNF-accident); **17** Sarah Fisher, USA, 28 (DNF-gearbox); **18** Ryan Hunter-Reay, USA, 5 (DNF-handling).
**Most laps led:** Franchitti, 62.
**Fastest race lap:** Kanaan, 1m 17.5524s, 106.767 mph/ 171.824 km/h.
**Fastest qualifying lap:** Franchitti, 1m 16.7017s, 107.951 mph/173.730 km/h.
**Championship points:** **1** Dixon, 560; **2** Franchitti, 556; **3** Kanaan, 498; **4** Wheldon, 414; **5** Hornish Jr, 409; **6** Castroneves, 398.

**DETROIT INDY GRAND PRIX, The Raceway at Belle Isle, Detroit, Michigan, USA, 2 September. Round 16. 89 laps of the 2.096-mile/3.331-km circuit, 184.230 miles/296.489 km.**
**1** Tony Kanaan, BR, 2h 11m 50.5097s, 83.841 mph/ 134.930 km/h; **2** Danica Patrick, USA, 2h 11m 50.9962s; **3** Dan Wheldon, GB, 2h 11m 51.7304s; **4** Darren Manning, GB, 2h 11m 52.4314s; **5** Kosuke Matsuura, J, 88 laps; **6** Dario Franchitti, GB, 88; **7** Buddy Rice, USA, 87; **8** Scott Dixon, NZ, 87; **9** AJ Foyt IV, USA, 87; **10** Ed Carpenter, USA, 87; **11** Scott Sharp, USA, 82; **12** Sam Hornish Jr, USA, 75; **13** Tomas Scheckter, ZA, 67 (DNF-accident); **14** Hélio Castroneves, BR, 67 (DNF-accident); **15** Vitor Meira, BR, 31 (DNF-accident); **16** Sarah Fisher, USA, 29 (DNF-accident); **17** Marco Andretti, USA, 27 (DNF-gearbox); **18** Ryan Hunter-Reay, USA, 24 (DNF-input shaft).
**Most laps led:** Franchitti, 27.
**Fastest race lap:** Franchitti, 1m 13.5110s, 101.373 mph/ 163.143 km/h.
**Fastest qualifying lap:** Castroneves, 1m 12.0688s, 103.401 mph/166.408 km/h.
**Championship points:** **1** Franchitti, 587; **2** Dixon, 584; **3** Kanaan, 548; **4** Wheldon, 449; **5** Hornish Jr, 427; **6** Castroneves, 414.

**PEAK ANTIFREEZE INDY 300, Chicagoland Speedway, Chicago, Illinois, USA, 9 September. Round 17. 200 laps of the 1.520-mile/2.446-km circuit, 304.000 miles/489.241 km.**
**1** Dario Franchitti, GB, 1h 44m 53.7950s, 173.886 mph/ 279.842 km/h; **2** Scott Dixon, NZ, 1h 44m 55.6389s; **3** Sam Hornish Jr, USA, 199 laps; **4** Hélio Castroneves, BR, 199; **5** Scott Sharp, USA, 199; **6** Tony Kanaan, BR, 199; **7** Ryan Hunter-Reay, USA, 198; **8** Hideki Mutoh, J, 198; **9** Buddy Rice, USA, 198; **10** AJ Foyt IV, USA, 198; **11** Danica Patrick, USA, 198; **12** Sarah Fisher, USA, 196; **13** Dan Wheldon, GB, 193 (DNF-out of fuel); **14** Marty Roth, CDN, 190; **15** Milka Duno, YV, 184; **16** Ed Carpenter, USA, 164; **17** Kosuke Matsuura, J, 156 (DNF-electrics); **18** Vitor Meira, BR, 133 (DNF-accident); **19** PJ

Chesson, USA, 94; **20** Tomas Scheckter, ZA, 73 (DNF-wheel lost); **21** Darren Manning, GB, 62 (DNF-mechanical); **22** Marco Andretti, USA, 34 (DNF-accident).
**Most laps led:** Hornish Jr, 90.
**Fastest race lap:** Mutoh, 25.2578s, 216.646 mph/ 348.658 km/h.
**Fastest qualifying lap:** Franchitti, 25.4931s, 214.646 mph/345.440 km/h.

**Final championship points**
**Drivers**
**1** Dario Franchitti, GB, 637; **2** Scott Dixon, NZ, 624; **3** Tony Kanaan, BR, 576; **4** Dan Wheldon, GB, 466; **5** Sam Hornish Jr, USA, 465; **6** Hélio Castroneves, BR, 446; **7** Danica Patrick, USA, 424; **8** Scott Sharp, USA, 412; **9** Buddy Rice, USA, 360; **10** Tomas Scheckter, ZA, 357; **11** Marco Andretti, USA, 350; **12** Vitor Meira, BR, 334; **13** Darren Manning, GB, 332; **14** AJ Foyt IV, USA, 315; **15** Ed Carpenter, USA, 309; **16** Kosuke Matsuura, J, 303; **17** Sarah Fisher, USA, 275; **18** Jeff Simmons, USA, 201; **19** Ryan Hunter-Reay, USA, 119; **20** Milka Duno, YV, 96; **21** Marty Roth, CDN, 53; **22** Alex Barron, USA, 41; **23** Jon Herb, USA, 34; **24** Ryan Briscoe, AUS, 30; **25** Hideki Mutoh, J, 24; **26** Davey Hamilton, USA, 22; **27** Michael Andretti, USA, 17; **28** Buddy Lazier, USA, 12; **29** PJ Chesson, USA, 12; **30** Roger Yasukawa, USA, 12; **31** Richie Hearn, USA, 12; **32** Al Unser Jr, 10; **33** Jaques Lazier, USA, 10; **34** Phil Giebler, USA, 10; **35** John Andretti, USA, 10; **36** Roberto Moreno, BR, 10.

**Bombardier Rookie of the Year:** Ryan Hunter-Reay.

**Chassis Manufacturers**
**1** Dallara, 70; **2** Panoz, 7.

## Bridgestone presents The Champ Car World Series Powered by Ford

## 2006

Following publication of AUTOCOURSE 2006–2007, amendments were made to the final driver point standings on the Champcar official website. The standings were:

**Final championship points**
**Drivers:**
**1** Sébastien Bourdais, F, 387; **2** Justin Wilson, GB, 298; **3** AJ Allmendinger, USA, 285; **4** Nelson Philippe, F, 231; **5** Bruno Junqueira, BR, 219; **6** Will Power, AUS, 213; **7** Paul Tracy, CDN, 209; **8** Alex Tagliani, CDN, 205; **9** Màrio Dominguez, MEX, 202; **10** Andrew Ranger, CDN, 200; **11** Oriol Servià, E, 197; **12** Dan Clarke, GB, 175; **13** Charles Zwolsman, NL, 162; **14** Jan Heylen, B, 140; **15** Cristiano da Matta, BR, 134; **16** Katherine Legge, GB, 133; **17** Nicky Pastorelli, NL, 73; **18** Antonio Pizzonia, I, 43; **19** Tonis Kasemets, EE, 34; **20** Andreas Wirth, D, 19; **21** Ryan Briscoe, AUS, 17; **22** David Martinez, MEX, 13; **23** Buddy Rice, USA, 11; **24** Jimmy Vasser, USA, 7; **25** Juan Cáceres, ROU, 6.

## 2007

All cars are Panoz DP01-Ford Cosworth XFE.

**VEGAS GRAND PRIX, Downtown Las Vegas Street Circuit, Nevada, USA, 8 April. Round 1. 68 laps of the 2.440-mile/3.927-km circuit, 165.920 miles/267.022 km.**
**1** Will Power, AUS, 1h 45m 13.637s, 94.607 mph/ 152.255 km/h; **2** Robert Doornbos, NL, 1h 45m 30.424s; **3** Paul Tracy, CDN, 1h 45m 40.993s; **4** Alex Tagliani, CDN, 1h 46m 2.618s; **5** Tristan Gommendy, F, 1h 46m 24.033s; **6** Katherine Legge, GB, 1h 46m 34.898s; **7** Bruno Junqueira, BR, 67 laps; **8** Alex Figge, USA, 63; **9** Màrio Dominguez, MEX, 57; **10** Neel Jani, CH, 56 (DNF-mechanical); **11** Ryan Dalziel, GB, 52; **12** Simon Pagenaud, F, 47 (DNF-engine); **13** Sébastien Bourdais, F, 30 (DNF-accident); **14** Justin Wilson, GB, 20 (DNF-input shaft); **15** Dan Clarke, GB, 13 (DNF-accident); **16** Matthew Halliday, NZ, 3 (DNF-accident); **17** Graham Rahal, USA, 1 (DNF-accident).
**Most laps led:** Power, 38.
**Fastest race lap:** Power, 1m 19.934s, 109.891 mph/ 176.852 km/h.
**Fastest qualifying lap:** Power, 1m 17.629s, 113.154 mph/182.103 km/h.
**Championship points: 1** Power, 33; **2** Doornobs, 27; **3** Tracy, 26; **4** Tagliani, 23; **5** Gommendy, 21; **6** Legge, 19.

**TOYOTA GRAND PRIX OF LONG BEACH, Long Beach Street Circuit, California, USA, 15 April. Round 2. 78 laps of the 1.968-mile/3.167-km circuit, 153.504 miles/247.041 km.**
**1** Sébastien Bourdais, F, 1h 40m 43.975s, 91.432 mph/ 147.146 km/h; **2** Oriol Servià, E, 1h 40m 46.589s; **3** Will Power, AUS, 1h 40m 47.842s; **4** Justin Wilson, GB, 1h 40m 49.301s; **5** Alex Tagliani, CDN, 1h 40m 50.155s; **6** Bruno Junqueira, BR, 1h 40m 50.370s; **7** Neel Jani, CH, 1h 40m 51.686s; **8** Graham Rahal, USA, 1h 40m 52.243s; **9** Ryan Dalziel, GB, 1h 40m 52.938s; **10** Katherine Legge, GB, 1h 40m 53.862s; **11** Tristan Gommendy, F, 1h 40m 54.311s; **12** Dan Clarke, GB, 77 laps; **13** Robert Doornbos, NL, 74; **14** Simon Pagenaud, F, 73; **15** Matthew Halliday, NZ, 72 (DNF-mechanical); **16** Alex Figge, USA, 69 (DNF-accident); **17** Màrio Dominguez, MEX, 7 (DNF-accident).
**Did not start:** Paul Tracy, CDN (injured in practice).
**Most laps led:** Bourdais, 58.
**Fastest race lap:** Pagenaud, 1m 8.594s, 103.286 mph/ 166.223 km/h.
**Fastest qualifying lap:** Bourdais, 1m 7.546s, 104.889 mph/168.802 km/h.
**Championship points: 1** Power, 59; **2** Tagliani, 44; **3** Bourdais, 40; **4** Junqueira, 36; **5** Doornbos, 35; **6** Gommendy, 31.

**GRAND PRIX OF HOUSTON, JAGFlo Speedway at Reliant Park, Houston, Texas, USA, 22 April. Round 3. 93 laps of the 1.683-mile/2.709-km circuit, 156.519 miles/251.893 km.**
**1** Sébastien Bourdais, F, 1h 45m 32.136s, 88.986 mph/ 143.208 km/h; **2** Graham Rahal, USA, 1h 45m 36.955s; **3** Robert Doornbos, NL, 1h 45m 39.197s; **4** Oriol Servià, E, 1h 45m 40.886s; **5** Simon Pagenaud, F, 1h 45m 41.590s; **6** Màrio Dominguez, MEX, 1h 45m 51.215s; **7** Bruno Junqueira, BR, 1h 45m 51.917s; **8** Ryan Dalziel, GB, 1h 45m 52.465s; **9** Alex Tagliani, CDN, 1h 45m 57.199s; **10** Justin Wilson, GB, 1h 46m 00.676s; **11** Will Power, AUS, 92 laps; **12** Roberto Moreno, BR, 90; **13** Tristan Gommendy, F, 85 (DNF-out of fuel); **14** Matthew Halliday, NZ, 77; **15** Neel Jani, CH, 67 (DNF-accident); **16** Katherine Legge, GB, 67 (DNF-accident); **17** Dan Clarke, GB, 67 (DNF-accident).
**Did not start:** Alex Figge, USA.
**Most laps led:** Bourdais, 62.
**Fastest race lap:** Bourdais, 58.018s, 104.430 mph/ 168.063 km/h.
**Fastest qualifying lap:** Will Power, AUS, 57.405s, 105.545 mph/169.858 km/h.
**Championship points: 1** Bourdais, 73; **2** Power, 70; **3** Doornbos, 61; **4** Tagliani, 57; **5** Junqueira, 53; **6** Servià, 51.

**MAZDA CHAMP CAR GRAND PRIX OF PORTLAND, Portland International Raceway, Oregon, USA, 10 June. Round 4. 103 laps of the 1.964-mile/3.161-km circuit, 202.292 miles/325.557 km.**
**1** Sébastien Bourdais, F, 1h 45m 42.774s, 114.816 mph/ 184.778 km/h; **2** Justin Wilson, GB, 1h 45m 56.311s; **3** Robert Doornbos, NL, 1h 46m 17.925s; **4** Will Power, AUS, 1h 46m 26.112s; **5** Alex Tagliani, CDN, 1h 46m 44.170s; **6** Dan Clarke, GB, 1h 46m 44.819s; **7** Tristan Gommendy, F, 102 laps; **8** Simon Pagenaud, F, 102; **9** Graham Rahal, USA, 102; **10** Paul Tracy, CDN, 102; **11** Oriol Servià, E, 102; **12** Neel Jani, CH, 102; **13** Bruno Junqueira, BR, 102; **14** Ryan Dalziel, GB, 101; **15** Jan Heylen, B, 100 (DNF-out of fuel); **16** Alex Figge, USA, 100; **17** Katherine Legge, GB, 99 (DNF-out of fuel).
**Most laps led:** Wilson, 51.
**Fastest race lap:** Bourdais, 59.331s, 119.169 mph/ 191.783 km/h.
**Fastest qualifying lap:** Wilson, 58.000s, 121.903 mph/ 196.185 km/h.
**Championship points: 1** Bourdais, 105; **2** Power, 94; **3** Doornbos, 87; **4** Tagliani, 78; **5** Wilson, 69; **6** Servià, 61.

**THE GRAND PRIX OF CLEVELAND, Burke Lakefront Airport, Cleveland, Ohio, USA, 24 June. Round 5. 89 laps of the 2.106-mile/3.389-km circuit, 187.434 miles/301.646 km.**
**1** Paul Tracy, CDN, 1h 45m 10.860s, 106.921 mph/ 172.072 km/h; **2** Robert Doornbos, NL, 1h 45m 11.373s; **3** Neel Jani, CH, 1h 45m 16.265s; **4** Justin Wilson, GB, 1h 45m 16.809s; **5** Simon Pagenaud, F, 1h 45m 17.171s; **6** Alex Tagliani, CDN, 1h 45m 28.610s; **7** Oriol Servià, E, 1h 45m 34.514s; **8** Graham Rahal, USA, 1h 45m 35.550s; **9** Ryan Dalziel, GB, 1h 45m 38.677s; **10** Will Power, AUS, 1h 46m 06.071s; **11** Dan Clarke, GB, 88 laps; **12** Sébastien Bourdais, F, 67 (DNF-engine); **13** Tristan Gommendy, F, 34 (DNF-accident); **14** Jan Heylen, B, 34 (DNF-accident); **15** Katherine Legge, GB, 32 (DNF-handling); **16** Bruno Junqueira, BR, 6 (DNF-accident); **17** Alex Figge, USA, 3 (DNF-gearbox).
**Most laps led:** Power, 32.
**Fastest race lap:** Bourdais, 57.601s, 131.623 mph/ 211.826 km/h.
**Fastest qualifying lap:** Bourdais, 56.363s, 134.514 mph/ 216.479 km/h.
**Championship points: 1** Bourdais, 117; **2** Doornbos, 114; **3** Power, 105; **4** Tagliani, 97; **5** Wilson, 92; **6** Servià, 78.

**GRAND PRIX OF MONT-TREMBLANT, Circuit Mont-Tremblant, St. Jovite, Quebec, Canada, 1 July. Round 6. 62 laps of the 2.621-mile/4.218-km circuit, 162.502 miles/261.522 km.**
**1** Roberto Doornbos, NL, 1h 45m 41.899s, 92.245 mph/ 148.454 km/h; **2** Sébastien Bourdais, F, 1h 45m 44.788s; **3** Will Power, AUS, 1h 45m 49.209s; **4** Simon Pagenaud, F, 1h 45m 52.465s; **5** Justin Wilson, GB, 1h 45m 53.188s; **6** Neel Jani, CH, 1h 45m 54.246s; **7** Graham Rahal, USA, 1h 45m 54.690s; **8** Alex Tagliani, CDN, 1h 45m 55.322s; **9** Oriol Servià, E, 1h 46m 08.641s; **10** Ryan Dalziel, GB, 1h 46m 14.848s; **11** Katherine Legge, GB, 1h 46m 28.490s; **12** Tristan Gommendy, F, 60 laps; **13** Alex Figge, USA, 56 (DNF-brakes); **14** Dan Clarke, GB, 34 (DNF-drivetrain); **15** Paul Tracy, CDN, 28 (DNF-engine); **16** Jan Heylen, B, 24 (DNF-spin); **17** Bruno Junqueira, BR, 5 (DNF-gearbox).
**Most laps led:** Bourdais, 27.
**Fastest race lap:** Bourdais, 1m 17.327s, 122.022 mph/ 196.375 km/h.
**Fastest qualifying lap:** Gommendy, 1m 16.776s, 122.898 mph/197.785 km/h.
**Championship points: 1** Bourdais, 145; **2** Doornobs, 145; **3** Power, 131; **4** Wilson, 113; **5** Tagliani, 112; **6** Pagenaud, 97.

**THE GRAND PRIX OF TORONTO, Exhibition Place Circuit, Toronto, Ontario, Canada, 8 July. Round 7. 73 laps of the 1.755-mile/2.824-km circuit, 128.115 miles/ 206.181 km.**
**1** Will Power, AUS, 1h 45m 58.568s, 72.534 mph /116.733 km/h; **2** Neel Jani, CH, 1h 46m 1.540s; **3** Justin Wilson, GB, 1h 46m 2.048s; **4** Simon Pagenaud, F, 1h 46m 4.211s; **5** Bruno Junqueira, BR, 1h 46m 19.306s; **6** Robert Doornbos, NL, 72 laps; **7** Ryan Dalziel, GB, 72; **8** Alex Tagliani, CDN, 71; **9** Sébastien Bourdais, F, 67 (DNF-accident); **10** Oriol Servià, E, 56 (DNF-accident); **11** Graham Rahal, USA, 52 (DNF-accident); **12** Dan Clarke, GB, 43 (DNF-accident); **13** Jan Heylen, B, 1 (DNF-accident); **14** Paul Tracy, CDN, 0 (DNF-accident); **15** Tristan Gommendy, F, 0 (DNF-accident); **16** Katherine Legge, GB, 0 (DNF-accident); **17** Alex Figge, USA, 0 (DNF-accident).
**Most laps led:** Servià, 34.
**Fastest race lap:** Bourdais, 1m 0.083s, 105.155 mph/ 169.230 km/h.
**Fastest qualifying lap:** Bourdais, 58.288s, 108.393 mph/ 174.441 km/h.
**Championship points: 1** Doornbos, 164; **2** Power, 162; **3** Bourdais, 161; **4** Wilson, 138; **5** Tagliani, 127; **6** Pagenaud, 120.

**REXALL GRAND PRIX OF EDMONTON, Rexall Speedway, Edmonton, Alberta, Canada, 22 July. Round 8. 96 laps of the 1.973-mile/3.175-km circuit, 189.408 miles/ 304.823 km.**
**1** Sébastian Bourdais, F, 1h 45m 41.953s, 107.517 mph/ 173.032 km/h; **2** Justin Wilson, GB, 1h 45m 45.900s; **3** Graham Rahal, USA, 1h 45m 48.598s; **4** Simon Pagenaud, F, 1h 46m 6.761s; **5** Paul Tracy, CDN, 1h 46m 10.097s; **6** Oriol Servià, E, 1h 46m 11.968s; **7** Bruno Junqueira, BR, 1h 46m 12.657s; **8** Dan Clarke, GB, 1h 46m 17.286s; **9** Neel Jani, CH, 1h 46m 19.735s; **10** Jan Heylen, B, 1h 46m 40.700s; **11** Robert Doornbos, NL, 95 laps; **12** Ryan Dalziel, GB, 95; **13** Alex Figge, USA, 95; **14** Alex Tagliani, CDN, 69 (DNF-accident); **15** Will Power, AUS, 69 (DNF-steering); **16** Katherine Legge, GB, 36 (DNF-gearbox/throttle); **17** Màrio Dominguez, MEX, 32 (DNF-driveline).
**Did not start:** Tristan Gommendy, F (injured in qualifying).
**Most laps led:** Bourdais, 49.
**Fastest race lap:** Bourdais, 58.653s, 121.099 mph/ 194.889 km/h.
**Fastest qualifying lap:** Power, 58.403s, 121.617 mph/ 195.724 km/h.
**Championship points: 1** Bourdais, 194; **2** Doornbos, 174; **3** Power, 169; **4** Wilson, 165; **5** Pagenaud, 143; **6** Tagliani, 134.

**SAN JOSE GRAND PRIX, Redback Raceway, San Jose, California, USA, 29 July. Round 9. 107 laps of the 1.443-mile/2.322-km circuit, 154.401 miles/248.484 km.**
**1** Robert Doornbos, NL, 1h 45m 7.617s, 88.123 mph/ 141.820 km/h; **2** Neel Jani, CH, 1h 45m 13.762s; **3** Oriol Servià, E, 1h 45m 14.522s; **4** Will Power, AUS, 1h 45m 15.105s; **5** Sébastien Bourdais, F, 1h 45m 15.651s; **6** Graham Rahal, USA, 1h 45m 17.217s; **7** Bruno Junqueira, BR, 1h 45m 21.568s; **8** Tristan Gommendy, F, 1h 45m 26.855s; **9** Jan Heylen, B, 1h 45m 36.149s; **10** Simon Pagenaud, F, 1h 45m 56.046s; **11** Paul Tracy, CDN, 105 laps; **12** Màrio Dominguez, MEX, 104; **13** Justin Wilson, GB, 87; **14** Alex Figge, USA, 84 (DNF-accident); **15** Alex Tagliani, CDN, 83 (DNF-gearbox valve); **16** Katherine Legge, GB, 13 (DNF-accident); **17** Dan Clarke, GB, 6 (DNF-accident).
**Most laps led:** Servià, 42.
**Fastest race lap:** Wilson, 49.584s, 104.768 mph/ 168.607 km/h.
**Fastest qualifying lap:** Wilson, 49.039s, 105.932 mph/ 170.481 km/h.
**Championship points: 1** Bourdais, 216; **2** Doornbos, 206; **3** Power, 192; **4** Wilson, 175; **5** Jani, 156; **6** Pagenaud, 154.

**GENERAC POWER WEEKEND, Road America, Elkhart Lake, Wisconsin, USA, 12 August. Round 10. 53 laps of the 4.048-mile/6.515-km circuit, 214.544 miles/ 345.275 km.**
**1** Sébastain Bourdais, F, 1h 40m 58.596s, 127.481 mph/ 205.161 km/h; **2** Dan Clarke, GB, 1h 41m 8.348s; **3** Graham Rahal, USA, 1h 41m 10.803s; **4** Oriol Servià, E, 1h 41m 19.457s; **5** Alex Tagliani, CDN, 1h 41m 49.300s; **6** Jan Heylen, B, 1h 41m 58.649s; **7** Tristan Gommendy, F, 1h 42m 0.938s; **8** Justin Wilson, GB, 1h 42m 1.557s; **9** Bruno Junqueira, BR, 1h 42m 3.121s; **10** Neel Jani, CH, 1h 42m 11.563s; **11** Simon Pagenaud, F, 1h 42m 27.537s; **12** Paul Tracy, CDN, 1h 42m 33.647s; **13** Alex Figge, USA, 52 laps; **14** Robert Doornbos, NL, 49; **15** Katherine Legge, GB, 36 (DNF-engine fire); **16** Will Power, AUS, 25 (DNF-gearbox); **17** Ryan Dalziel, GB, 15 (DNF-fuel pump).
**Most laps led:** Bourdais, 51.
**Fastest race lap:** Bourdais, 1m 44.346s, 139.658 mph/ 224.758 km/h.
**Fastest qualifying lap:** Bourdais, 1m 41.535s, 143.525 mph/230.981 km/h.
**Championship points: 1** Bourdais, 250; **2** Doornbos, 213; **3** Power, 197; **4** Wilson, 190; **5** Rahal, 170; **6** Servià, 170.

**CHAMP CAR GRAND PRIX OF BELGIUM, Zolder Circuit, Heusden-Zolder, Belgium, 26 August. Round 11. 71 laps of the 2.492-mile/4.010-km circuit, 176.932 miles/284.744 km.**
**1** Sébastien Bourdais, F, 1h 45m 21.997s, 100.752 mph/ 162.145 km/h; **2** Bruno Junqueira, BR, 1h 45m 35.652s; **3** Graham Rahal, USA, 1h 45m 36.455s; **4** Will Power, AUS, 1h 45m 37.144s; **5** Justin Wilson, GB, 1h 45m 37.969s; **6** Oriol Servià, E, 1h 45m 39.147s; **7** Robert Doornbos, NL, 1h 45m 40.366s; **8** Neel Jani, CH, 1h 45m 41.070s; **9** Alex Tagliani, CDN, 1h 45m 45.831s; **10** Paul Tracy, CDN, 1h 45m 46.498s; **11** Katherine Legge, GB, 1h 45m 50.840s; **12** Simon Pagenaud, F, 1h 45m 55.185s; **13** Jan Heylen, B, 1h 46m 34.095s; **14** Alex Figge, USA, 70 laps; **15** Ryan Dalziel, GB, 67; **16** Tristan Gommendy, F, 60 (DNF-oil leak); **17** Màrio Dominguez, MEX, 47 (DNF-wheel/input shaft).
**Excluded:** Dan Clarke, GB (caused accident during practice).
**Most laps led:** Bourdais, 51.
**Fastest race lap:** Bourdais, 1m 14.089s, 121.087 mph/ 194.870 km/h.
**Fastest qualifying lap:** Bourdais, 1m 12.821s, 123.195 mph/198.264 km/h.
**Championship points: 1** Bourdais, 283; **2** Doornbos, 230; **3** Power, 221; **4** Wilson, 211; **5** Rahal, 196; **6** Servià, 189.

**BAVARIA CHAMP CAR GRAND PRIX, TT-Circuit Assen, Assen, Netherlands. 2 September. Round 12. 69 laps of the 2.830-mile/4.554-km circuit, 195.270 miles/ 314.257 km.**
**1** Justin Wilson, GB, 1h 46m 2.236s, 110.491 mph/ 177.819 km/h; **2** Jan Heylen, B, 1h 46m 9.463s; **3** Bruno Junqueira, BR, 1h 46m 10.655s; **4** Tristan Gommendy, F, 1h 46m 11.273s; **5** Neel Jani, CH, 1h 46m 24.498s; **6** Simon Pagenaud, F, 1h 46m 24.934s; **7** Sébastien Bourdais, F, 1h 46m 25.191s; **8** Oriol Servià, E, 1h 46m 25.642s; **9** Graham Rahal, USA, 1h 46m 26.185s; **10** Ryan Dalziel, GB, 1h 46m 31.790s; **11** Dan Clarke, GB, 1h 46m 41.139s; **12** Katherine Legge, GB, 1h 46m 47.096s; **13** Robert Doornbos, NL, 1h 47m 02.874s; **14** Will Power, AUS, 1h 47m 03.440s; **15** Alex Tagliani, CDN, 68 laps; **16** Alex Figge, USA, 68; **17** Paul Tracy, CDN, 14 (DNF-oil pressure).
**Most laps led:** Wilson, 39.
**Fastest race lap:** Clarke, 1m 20.727s, 126.203 mph/ 203.104 km/h.
**Fastest qualifying lap:** Bourdais, 1m 18.765s, 129.347 mph/208.163 km/h.
**Championship points: 1** Bourdais, 301; **2** Wilson, 243; **3** Doornbos, 238; **4** Power, 228; **5** Rahal, 209; **6** Servià, 204.

**LEXMARK INDY 300, Surfer's Paradise Steet Circuit, Queensland, Australia, 21 October. Round 13. 61 laps of the 2.795-mile/4.498-km circuit, 170.495 miles/ 274.385 km.**
**1** Sébastien Bourdais, F, 1h 45m 49.318s, 96.669 mph/ 155.574 km/h; **2** Justin Wilson, GB, 1h 45m 56.094s; **3** Bruno Junqueira, BR, 1h 46m 40.214s; **4** Robert Doornbos, NL, 1h 46m 51.959s; **5** Simon Pagenaud, F, 1h 46m 52.729s; **6** Nelson Philippe, F, 1h 46m 58.329s; **7** Alex Tagliani, CDN, 1h 47m 1.609s; **8** Neel Jani, CH, 1h 47m 19.107s; **9** Paul Tracy, CDN, 1h 47m 37.932s; **10** David Martinez, MEX, 60 laps; **11** Graham Rahal, USA, 60; **12** Màrio Dominguez, MEX, 59; **13** Alex Figge, USA, 59; **14** Oriol Servià, E, 58; **15** Katherine Legge, GB, 26 (DNF-steering/accident); **16** Will Power, AUS, 18 (DNF-accident); **17** Dan Clarke, GB, 12 (DNF-accident).
**Most laps led:** Bourdais, 30.
**Fastest race lap:** Rahal, 1m 31.093s, 110.459 mph/ 177.766 km/h.
**Fastest qualifying lap:** Power, 1m 30.054s, 111.733 mph/ 179.817 km/h.

**Provisional championship points**
**Drivers**
**1** Sébastien Bourdais, F, 332; **2** Justin Wilson, GB, 270; **3** Robert Doornbos, NL, 262; **4** Will Power, AUS, 234; **5** Graham Rahal, USA, 220; **6** Neel Jani, CH, 218; **7** Bruno Junqueira, BR, 216; **8** Simon Pagenaud, F, 213; **9** Oriol Servià, E, 212; **10** Alex Tagliani, CDN, 197; **11** Paul Tracy, CDN, 150; **12** Tristan Gommendy, F, 140; **13** Dan Clarke, GB, 125; **14** Ryan Dalziel, GB, 116; **15** Jan Heylen, B, 104; **16** Katherine Legge, GB, 102; **17** Alex Figge, USA, 85; **18** Màrio Dominguez, MEX, 62; **19** Nelson Philippe, F, 19; **20** Matthew Halliday, NZ, 18; **21** David Martinez, MEX, 11; **22** Roberto Moreno, BR, 9.

**Rookie of the Year:** Robert Doornbos.

*Result of the Mexico City race will be given in AUTOCOURSE 2008–2009.*

## NASCAR Nextel Cup Series

## 2006

The following races were run after AUTOCOURSE 2006–2007 went to press.

**DICKIE'S 500, Texas Motor Speedway, Fort Worth, Texas, USA, 5 November. Round 34. 339 laps of the 1.500-mile/2.414-km circuit, 508.500 miles/818.351 km.**
**1** Tony Stewart, USA (Chevrolet Monte Carlo), 3h 46m 11.0s, 134.891 mph/217.085 km/h; **2** Jimmie Johnson, USA (Chevrolet Monte Carlo), 3h 46m 11.272s; **3** Kevin Harvick, USA (Chevrolet Monte Carlo), 339 laps; **4** Kyle Busch, USA (Chevrolet Monte Carlo), 339; **5** Clint Bowyer, USA (Chevrolet Monte Carlo), 339; **6** Dale Earnhardt Jr, USA (Chevrolet Monte Carlo), 339; **7** Casey Mears, USA (Dodge Charger), 339; **8** Kurt Busch, USA (Dodge Charger), 339; **9** Jeff Gordon, USA (Chevrolet Monte Carlo), 339; **10** Denny Hamlin, USA (Chevrolet Monte Carlo), 339.
**Pole position:** Brian Vickers, USA (Chevrolet Monte Carlo).
**Drivers' championship points: 1** Johnson, 6,157; **2** Kenseth, 6,140; **3** Earnhardt Jr, 6,079; **4** Hamlin, 6,077; **5** Harvick, 6,052; **6** Gordon (Jeff), 6,000.

**CHECKER AUTO PARTS 500, Phoenix International Raceway, Arizona, USA, 12 November. Round 35. 312 laps of the 1.000-mile/1.609-km circuit, 312.000 miles/502.115 km.**
**1** Kevin Harvick, USA (Chevrolet Monte Carlo), 3h 14m 44.0s, 96.131 mph/154.709 km/h; **2** Jimmie Johnson, USA (Chevrolet Monte Carlo), 3h 14m 44.250s; **3** Denny Hamlin, USA (Chevrolet Monte Carlo), 312 laps; **4** Jeff Gordon, USA (Chevrolet Monte Carlo), 312; **5** Carl Edwards, USA (Ford Fusion), 312; **6** Mark Martin, USA (Ford Fusion), 312; **7** Kasey Kahne, USA (Dodge Charger), 312; **8** Kurt Busch, USA (Dodge Charger), 312; **9** Dale Earnhardt Jr, USA (Chevrolet Monte Carlo), 312; **10** Jeff Burton, USA

(Chevrolet Monte Carlo), 312.
**Pole position:** Gordon (Jeff).
**Drivers' championship points: 1** Johnson, 6,332; **2** Kenseth, 6,269; **3** Harvick, 6,242; **4** Hamlin, 6,242; **5** Earnhardt Jr, 6,217; **6** Gordon (Jeff), 6,165.

**FORD 400, Homestead-Miami Speedway, Florida, USA, 19 November. Round 36. 268 laps of the 1.500-mile/2.414-km circuit, 402.000 miles/646.956 km.**
**1** Greg Biffle, USA (Ford Fusion), 3h 12m 23.0s, 125.375 mph/201.771 km/h; **2** Martin Truex Jr, USA (Chevrolet Monte Carlo), 3h 12m 23.389s; **3** Denny Hamlin, USA (Chevrolet Monte Carlo), 268 laps; **4** Kasey Kahne, USA (Dodge Charger), 268; **5** Kevin Harvick, USA (Chevrolet Monte Carlo), 268; **6** Matt Kenseth, USA (Ford Fusion), 268; **7** Scott Riggs, USA (Dodge Charger), 268; **8** Carl Edwards, USA (Ford Fusion), 268; **9** Jimmie Johnson, USA (Chevrolet Monte Carlo), 268; **10** Clint Bowyer, USA (Chevrolet Monte Carlo), 268.
**Pole position:** Kahne.

**Final championship points**
**Drivers**
**1** Jimmie Johnson, USA, 6,475; **2** Matt Kenseth, USA, 6,419; **3** Denny Hamlin, USA, 6,407; **4** Kevin Harvick, USA, 6,397; **5** Dale Earnhardt Jr, USA, 6,328; **6** Jeff Gordon, USA, 6,256; **7** Jeff Burton, USA, 6,228; **8** Kasey Kahne, USA, 6,183; **9** Mark Martin, USA, 6,168; **10** Kyle Busch, USA, 6,027.

**Not involved in Chase for the Nextel Cup**
**11** Tony Stewart, USA, 4,727; **12** Carl Edwards, USA, 4,428; **13** Greg Biffle, USA, 4,075; **14** Casey Mears, USA, 3,914; **15** Brian Vickers, USA, 3,906; **16** Kurt Busch, USA, 3,900; **17** Clint Bowyer, USA, 3,833; **18** Ryan Newman, USA, 3,748; **19** Martin Truex Jr, USA, 3,673; **20** Scott Riggs, USA, 3,619; **21** Bobby Labonte, USA, 3,567; **22** Elliott Sadler, USA, 3,469; **23** Dale Jarrett, USA, 3,438; **24** Reed Sorensen, USA, 3,434; **25** Jamie McMurray, USA, 3,405; **26** Dave Blaney, USA, 3,259; **27** Joe Nemechek, USA, 3,255; **28** Jeff Green, USA, 3,253; **29** JJ Yeley, USA, 3,220; **30** Robby Gordon, USA, 3,113.

**Raybestos Rookie of the Year:** Denny Hamlin.

**Manufacturers**
**1** Chevrolet, 279; **2** Dodge, 203; **3** Ford, 202.

**Bud Pole Award winner:** Kurt Busch and Kasey Kahne, 6 poles each.

## 2007

**48th DAYTONA 500, Daytona International Speedway, Daytona Beach, Florida, USA, 18 February. Round 1. 202 laps of the 2.500-mile/4.023-km circuit, 505.000 miles/812.719 km.**
**1** Kevin Harvick, USA (Chevrolet Impala SS), 3h 22m 54.0s, 149.335 mph/240.331 km/h; **2** Mark Martin, USA (Chevrolet Impala SS), 3h 22m 54.020s; **3** Jeff Burton, USA (Chevrolet Impala SS), 202 laps; **4** Mike Wallace, USA (Chevrolet Impala SS), 202; **5** David Ragan, USA (Ford Fusion), 202; **6** Elliott Sadler, USA (Dodge Avenger), 202; **7** Kasey Kahne, USA (Dodge Avenger), 202; **8** David Gilliland, USA (Ford Fusion), 202; **9** Joe Nemechek, USA (Chevrolet Impala SS), 202; **10** Jeff Gordon, USA (Chevrolet Impala SS), 202.
**Pole position:** Gilliland.
**Drivers' championship points: 1** Harvick, 190; **2** Martin, 175; **3** Burton (Jeff), 165; **4** Wallace, 160; **5** Ragan, 155; **6** Gilliland, 147.

**AUTO CLUB 500, California Speedway, Fontana, California, USA, 25 February. Round 2. 250 laps of the 2.000-mile/3.219-km circuit, 500.000 miles/804.672 km.**
**1** Matt Kenseth, USA (Ford Fusion), 3h 36m 41.0s, 138.451 mph/222.815 km/h; **2** Jeff Gordon, USA (Chevrolet Impala SS), 3h 36m 41.679s; **3** Jimmie Johnson, USA (Chevrolet Impala SS), 250 laps; **4** Jeff Burton, USA (Chevrolet Impala SS), 250; **5** Mark Martin, USA (Chevrolet Impala SS), 250; **6** Clint Bowyer, USA (Chevrolet Impala SS), 250; **7** Kurt Busch, USA (Dodge Avenger), 250; **8** Tony Stewart, USA (Chevrolet Impala SS), 250; **9** Kyle Busch, USA (Chevrolet Impala SS), 250; **10** Brian Vickers, USA (Toyota Camry), 250.
**Pole position:** Gordon (Jeff).
**Drivers' championship points:** 1 Martin, 335; **2** Burton (Jeff), 330; **3** Gordon (Jeff), 309; **4** Harvick, 307; **5** Ragan, 270; **6** Bowyer, 264.

**UAW-DAIMLER CHRYSLER 400, Las Vegas Motor Speedway, Nevada, USA, 11 March. Round 3. 267 laps of the 1.500-mile/2.414-km circuit, 400.500 miles/644.542 km.**
**1** Jimmie Johnson, USA (Chevrolet Impala SS), 3h 7m 28.0s, 128.183 mph/206.290 km/h; **2** Jeff Gordon, USA (Chevrolet Impala SS), 3h 7m 30.795s; **3** Denny Hamlin, USA (Chevrolet Impala SS), 267 laps; **4** Matt Kenseth, USA (Ford Fusion), 267; **5** Mark Martin, USA (Chevrolet Impala SS), 267; **6** Carl Edwards, USA (Ford Fusion), 267; **7** Tony Stewart, USA (Chevrolet Impala SS), 267; **8** Ryan Newman, USA (Dodge Avenger), 267; **9** Kyle Busch, USA (Chevrolet Impala SS), 267; **10** Jamie McMurray, USA (Ford Fusion), 267.
**Pole position:** Kasey Kahne, USA (Dodge Avenger).
**Drivers' championship points: 1** Martin, 495; **2** Gordon (Jeff), 489; **3** Burton (Jeff), 453; **4** Johnson, 406; **5** Kenseth, 397; **6** Harvick, 389.

**KOBALT TOOLS 500, Atlanta Motor Speedway, Hampton, Georgia, USA, 18 March. Round 4. 325 laps of the 1.540-mile/2.478-km circuit, 500.500 miles/805.477 km.**
**1** Jimmie Johnson, USA (Chevrolet Impala SS), 3h 16m 23.0s, 152.915 mph/246.093 km/h; **2** Tony Stewart, USA (Chevrolet Impala SS), 3h 16m 24.311s; **3** Matt Kenseth, USA (Ford Fusion), 325 laps; **4** Jeff Burton, USA (Chevrolet Impala SS), 325; **5** Juan Pablo Montoya, CO (Dodge Avenger), 325; **6** Clint Bowyer, USA (Chevrolet Impala SS), 325; **7** Carl Edwards, USA (Ford Fusion), 325; **8** Martin Truex Jr, USA (Chevrolet Impala SS), 325; **9** Reed Sorensen, USA (Dodge Avenger), 325; **10** Mark Martin, USA (Chevrolet Impala SS), 325.
**Pole position:** Ryan Newman, USA (Dodge Avenger).
**Drivers' championship points: 1** Martin, 629; **2** Gordon (Jeff), 621; **3** Burton (Jeff), 618; **4** Johnson, 601; **5** Kenseth, 567; **6** Stewart, 507.

**FOOD CITY 500, Bristol Motor Speedway, Tennessee, USA, 25 March. Round 5. 504 laps of the 0.533-mile/0.858-km circuit, 268.632 miles/432.321 km.**
**1** Kyle Busch, USA (Chevrolet Impala SS), 3h 16m 38.0s, 81.969 mph/131.917 km/h; **2** Jeff Burton, USA (Chevrolet Impala SS), 3h 16m 38.064s; **3** Jeff Gordon, USA (Chevrolet Impala SS), 504 laps; **4** Kevin Harvick, USA (Chevrolet Impala SS), 504; **5** Greg Biffle, USA (Ford Fusion), 504; **6** Jeff Green, USA (Chevrolet Impala SS), 504; **7** Dale Earnhardt Jr, USA (Chevrolet Impala SS), 504; **8** Clint Bowyer, USA (Chevrolet Impala SS), 504; **9** Jamie McMurray, USA (Ford Fusion), 504; **10** Casey Mears, USA (Chevrolet Impala SS), 504.
**Pole position:** Gordon (Jeff).
**Drivers' championship points: 1** Gordon (Jeff), 791; **2** Burton (Jeff), 788; **3** Johnson, 716; **4** Kenseth, 697; **5** Harvick, 647; **6** Busch (Kyle), 639.

**GOODY'S COOL ORANGE 500, Martinsville Speedway, Virginia, USA, 1 April. Round 6. 500 laps of the 0.526-mile/0.847-km circuit, 263.000 miles/423.257 km.**
**1** Jimmie Johnson, USA (Chevrolet Impala SS), 3h 44m 36.0s, 70.258 mph/113.070 km/h; **2** Jeff Gordon, USA (Chevrolet Impala SS), 3h 44m 36.065s; **3** Denny Hamlin, USA (Chevrolet Impala SS), 500 laps; **4** Kyle Busch, USA (Chevrolet Impala SS), 500; **5** Dale Earnhardt Jr, USA (Chevrolet Impala SS), 500; **6** Jeff Burton, USA (Chevrolet Impala SS), 500; **7** Tony Stewart, USA (Chevrolet Impala SS), 500; **8** Scott Riggs, USA (Dodge Avenger), 500; **9** Jamie McMurray, USA (Ford Fusion), 500; **10** Matt Kenseth, USA (Ford Fusion), 500.
**Pole position:** Hamlin.
**Drivers' championship points: 1** Gordon (Jeff), 966; **2** Burton (Jeff), 938; **3** Johnson, 906; **4** Kenseth, 836; **5** Busch (Kyle), 804; **6** Hamlin, 776.

**SAMSUNG 500, Texas Motor Speedway, Fort Worth, Texas, USA, 15 April. Round 7. 334 laps of the 1.500-mile/2.414-km circuit, 501.000 miles/806.281 km.**
**1** Jeff Burton, USA (Chevrolet Impala SS), 3h 29m 41.0s, 143.358 mph/230.714 km/h; **2** Matt Kenseth, USA (Ford Fusion), 3h 49m 41.410s; **3** Mark Martin, USA (Chevrolet Impala SS), 334 laps; **4** Jeff Gordon, USA (Chevrolet Impala SS), 334; **5** Jamie McMurray, USA (Ford Fusion), 334; **6** Greg Biffle, USA (Ford Fusion), 334; **7** Martin Truex Jr, USA (Chevrolet Impala SS), 334; **8** Juan Pablo Montoya, CO (Dodge Avenger), 334; **9** Denny Hamlin, USA (Chevrolet Impala SS), 334; **10** David Stremme, USA (Dodge Avenger), 334.
**Pole position:** Gordon (Jeff).
**Drivers' championship points: 1** Gordon (Jeff), 1,136; **2** Burton (Jeff), 1,128; **3** Kenseth, 1,011; **4** Johnson, 955; **5** Hamlin, 914; **6** Bowyer, 866.

**SUBWAY FRESH FIT 500, Phoenix International Raceway, Arizona, USA, 21 April. Round 8. 312 laps of the 1.000-mile/1.609-km circuit, 312.000 miles/502.115 km.**
**1** Jeff Gordon, USA (Chevrolet Impala SS), 2h 53m 48.0s, 107.710 mph/173.342 km/h; **2** Tony Stewart, USA (Chevrolet Impala SS), 2h 53m 48.697s; **3** Denny Hamlin, USA (Chevrolet Impala SS), 312 laps; **4** Jimmie Johnson, USA (Chevrolet Impala SS), 312; **5** Matt Kenseth, USA (Ford Fusion), 312; **6** Jeff Green, USA (Chevrolet Impala SS), 312; **7** Kyle Busch, USA (Chevrolet Impala SS), 312; **8** Bobby Labonte, USA (Dodge Avenger), 312; **9** Johnny Sauter, USA (Chevrolet Impala SS), 312; **10** Kevin Harvick, USA (Chevrolet Impala SS), 312.
**Pole position:** Gordon (Jeff).
**Drivers' championship points: 1** Gordon (Jeff), 1,326; **2** Burton (Jeff), 1,252; **3** Kenseth, 1,166; **4** Johnson, 1,115; **5** Hamlin, 1,084; **6** Busch (Kyle), 1,002.

**AARON'S 499, Talladega Superspeedway, Alabama, USA, 29 April. Round 9. 192 laps of the 2.660-mile/4.281-km circuit, 510.720 miles/821.924 km.**
**1** Jeff Gordon, USA (Chevrolet Impala SS), 3h 18m 46.0s, 154.167 mph/248.107 km/h; **2** Jimmie Johnson, USA (Chevrolet Impala SS), 192 laps (under caution); **3** Kurt Busch, USA (Dodge Avenger), 192; **4** David Gilliland, USA (Ford Fusion), 192; **5** Jamie McMurray, USA (Ford Fusion), 192; **6** Kevin Harvick, USA (Chevrolet Impala SS), 192; **7** Dale Earnhardt Jr, USA (Chevrolet Impala SS), 192; **8** David Stremme, USA (Dodge Avenger), 192; **9** Ryan Newman, USA (Dodge Avenger), 192; **10** Martin Truex Jr, USA (Chevrolet Impala SS), 192.
**Pole position:** Gordon (Jeff).
**Drivers' championship points: 1** Gordon (Jeff), 1,521; **2** Burton (Jeff), 1,318; **3** Kenseth, 1,292; **4** Johnson, 1,290; **5** Hamlin, 1,189; **6** Stewart, 1,078.

**CROWN ROYAL PRESENTS THE JIM STEWART 400, Richmond International Raceway, Virginia, USA, 6 May. Round 10. 400 laps of the 0.750-mile/1.207-km circuit, 300.000 miles/482.803 km.**
**1** Jimmie Johnson, USA (Chevrolet Impala SS), 3h 17m 13.0s, 91.270 mph/146.885 km/h; **2** Kyle Busch, USA (Chevrolet Impala SS), 3h 17m 13.723s; **3** Denny Hamlin, USA (Chevrolet Impala SS), 400 laps; **4** Jeff Gordon, USA (Chevrolet Impala SS), 400; **5** Kurt Busch, USA (Dodge Avenger), 400; **6** Ryan Newman, USA (Dodge Avenger), 400; **7** Kevin Harvick, USA (Chevrolet Impala SS), 400; **8** Tony Stewart, USA (Chevrolet Impala SS), 400; **9** Clint Bowyer, USA (Chevrolet Impala SS), 400; **10** Matt Kenseth, USA (Ford Fusion), 400.
**Pole position:** Gordon (Jeff).
**Drivers' championship points: 1** Gordon (Jeff), 1,691; **2** Johnson, 1,480; **3** Kenseth, 1,431; 4 Hamlin, 1,359; **5** Burton (Jeff), 1,352; **6** Busch (Kyle), 1,229.

**DODGE AVENGER 500, Darlington Raceway, South Carolina, USA, 13 May. Round 11. 367 laps of the 1.366-mile/2.198-km circuit, 501.322 miles/806.800 km.**
**Scheduled for 12 May, but postponed due to rain.**
**1** Jeff Gordon, USA (Chevrolet Impala SS), 4h 1m 51.0s, 124.372 mph/200.157 km/h; **2** Denny Hamlin, USA (Chevrolet Impala SS), 4h 1m 51.978s; **3** Jimmie Johnson, USA (Chevrolet Impala SS), 367 laps; **4** Ryan Newman, USA (Dodge Avenger), 367; **5** Carl Edwards, USA (Ford Fusion), 367; **6** Tony Stewart, USA (Chevrolet Impala SS), 367; **7** Matt Kenseth, USA (Ford Fusion), 367; **8** Dale Earnhardt Jr, USA (Chevrolet Impala SS), 367; **9** Clint Bowyer, USA (Chevrolet Impala SS), 367; **10** Jeff Burton, USA (Chevrolet Impala SS), 367.
**Pole position:** Bowyer.
**Drivers' championship points: 1** Gordon (Jeff), 1,881; **2** Johnson, 1,650; **3** Kenseth, 1,582; **4** Hamlin, 1,539; **5** Burton (Jeff), 1,486; **6** Stewart, 1,375.

**COCA-COLA 600, Lowe's Motor Speedway, Concord, Charlotte, North Carolina, USA, 27 May. Round 12. 400 laps of the 1.500-mile/2.414-km circuit, 600.000 miles/965.606 km.**
**1** Casey Mears, USA (Chevrolet Impala SS), 4h 36m 27.0s, 130.222 mph/209.573 km/h; **2** JJ Yeley, USA (Chevrolet Impala SS), 4h 36m 36.561s; **3** Kyle Petty, USA (Dodge Avenger), 400 laps; **4** Reed Sorensen, USA (Dodge Avenger), 400; **5** Brian Vickers, USA (Toyota Camry), 400; **6** Tony Stewart, USA (Chevrolet Impala SS), 400; **7** Ricky Rudd, USA (Ford Fusion), 400; **8** Dale Earnhardt Jr, USA (Chevrolet Impala SS), 400; **9** Denny Hamlin, USA (Chevrolet Impala SS), 400; **10** Jimmie Johnson, USA (Chevrolet Impala SS), 400.
**Pole position:** Ryan Newman, USA (Dodge Avenger).
**Drivers' championship points: 1** Gordon (Jeff), 1,921; **2** Johnson, 1,789; **3** Kenseth, 1,714; **4** Hamlin, 1,682; **5** Burton (Jeff), 1,577; **6** Stewart, 1,530.

**AUTISM SPEAKS 400 PRESENTED BY VISA, Dover International Speedway, Delaware, USA, 4 June. Round 13. 400 laps of the 1.000-mile/1.609-km circuit, 400.000 miles/643.738 km.**
**Scheduled for 3 June, but postponed due to rain.**
**1** Martin Truex Jr, USA (Chevrolet Impala SS), 3h 21m 45.0s, 118.959 mph/191.446 km/h; **2** Ryan Newman, USA (Dodge Avenger), 3h 21m 52.355s; **3** Carl Edwards, USA (Ford Fusion), 400 laps; **4** Denny Hamlin, USA (Chevrolet Impala SS), 400; **5** Matt Kenseth, USA (Ford Fusion), 400; **6** Greg Biffle, USA (Ford Fusion), 400; **7** Mark Martin, USA (Chevrolet Impala SS), 400; **8** Clint Bowyer, USA (Chevrolet Impala SS), 400; **9** Jeff Gordon, USA (Chevrolet Impala SS), 400; **10** Robby Gordon, USA (Ford Fusion), 400.
**Pole position:** Newman.
**Drivers' championship points: 1** Gordon, 2,059; **2** Johnson, 1,907; **3** Kenseth, 1,869; **4** Hamlin, 1,842; **5** Burton (Jeff), 1,704; **6** Edwards, 1,584.

**POCONO 500, Pocono Raceway, Long Pond, Pennsylvania, USA, 10 June. Round 14. 106 laps of the 2.500-mile/4.023-km circuit, 265.000 miles/426.476 km.**
**Rain delayed the start by 2 hours and the race was stopped early.**
**1** Jeff Gordon, USA (Chevrolet Impala SS), 1h 57m 15.0s, 135.608 mph/218.239 km/h; **2** Ryan Newman, USA (Dodge Avenger), 106 laps (under caution); **3** Martin Truex Jr, USA (Chevrolet Impala SS), 106; **4** Casey Mears, USA (Chevrolet Impala SS), 106; **5** Tony Stewart, USA (Chevrolet Impala SS), 106; **6** Denny Hamlin, USA (Chevrolet Impala SS), 106; **7** Mark Martin, USA (Chevrolet Impala SS), 106; **8** Kyle Busch, USA (Chevrolet Impala SS), 106; **9** Matt Kenseth, USA (Ford Fusion), 106; **10** Clint Bowyer, USA (Chevrolet Impala SS), 106.
**Pole position:** Newman.
**Drivers' championship points: 1** Gordon (Jeff), 2,249; **2** Kenseth, 2,007; **3** Hamlin, 2,002; **4** Johnson, 1,944; **5** Burton (Jeff), 1,828; **6** Stewart, 1,733.

**CITIZENS BANK 400, Michigan International Speedway, Brooklyn, Michigan, USA, 17 June. Round 15. 200 laps of the 2.000-mile/3.219-km circuit, 400.000 miles/643.738 km.**
**1** Carl Edwards, USA (Ford Fusion), 2h 42m 5.0s, 148.072 mph/238.299 km/h; **2** Martin Truex Jr, USA (Chevrolet Impala SS), 2h 42m 8.668s; **3** Tony Stewart, USA (Chevrolet Impala SS), 200 laps; **4** Casey Mears, USA (Chevrolet Impala SS), 200; **5** Dale Earnhardt Jr, USA (Chevrolet Impala SS), 200; **6** Kyle Busch, USA (Chevrolet Impala SS), 200; **7** Kevin Harvick, USA (Chevrolet Impala SS), 200; **8** Jamie McMurray, USA (Ford Fusion), 200; **9** Jeff Gordon, USA (Chevrolet Impala SS), 200; **10** Michael Waltrip, USA (Toyota Camry), 200.
**Pole position:** JJ Yeley, USA (Chevrolet Impala SS).
**Drivers' championship points: 1** Gordon (Jeff), 2,392; **2** Hamlin, 2,128; **3** Johnson, 2,055; **4** Kenseth, 2,044; **5** Burton (Jeff), 1,919; **6** Edwards, 1,905.

**TOYOTA/SAVE MART 350, Infineon Raceway, Sears Point, Sonoma, California, USA, 24 June. Round 16. 110 laps of the 1.990-mile/3.203-km circuit, 218.900 miles/352.285 km.**
**1** Juan Pablo Montoya, CO (Dodge Avenger), 2h 56m 11.0s, 74.547 mph/119.972 km/h; **2** Kevin Harvick, USA (Chevrolet Impala SS), 2h 56m 15.097s; **3** Jeff Burton, USA (Chevrolet Impala SS), 110 laps; **4** Clint Bowyer, USA (Chevrolet Impala SS), 110; **5** Greg Biffle, USA (Ford Fusion), 110; **6** Tony Stewart, USA (Chevrolet Impala SS), 110; **7** Jeff Gordon, USA (Chevrolet Impala SS), 110; **8** Kyle Busch, USA (Chevrolet Impala SS), 110; **9** Boris Said, USA (Ford Fusion), 110; **10** Denny Hamlin, USA (Chevrolet Impala SS), 110.
**Pole position:** Jamie McMurray, USA (Ford Fusion).
**Drivers' championship points: 1** Gordon (Jeff), 2,438; **2** Hamlin, 2,267; **3** Kenseth, 2,105; **4** Burton (Jeff), 2,084; **5** Johnson, 2,072; **6** Stewart, 2,058.

**LENOX INDUSTRIAL TOOLS 300, New Hampshire International Speedway, Loudon, New Hampshire, USA, 1 July. Round 17. 300 laps of the 1.058-mile/1.703-km circuit, 317.400 miles/510.806 km.**
**1** Denny Hamlin, USA (Chevrolet Impala SS), 2h 55m 59.0s, 108.215 mph/174.155 km/h; **2** Jeff Gordon, USA (Chevrolet Impala SS), 2h 55m 59.068s; **3** Martin Truex Jr, USA (Chevrolet Impala SS), 300 laps; **4** Dale Earnhardt Jr, USA (Chevrolet Impala SS), 300; **5** Jimmie Johnson, USA (Chevrolet Impala SS), 300; **6** Jeff Green, USA (Chevrolet Impala SS), 300; **7** Jeff Burton, USA (Chevrolet Impala SS), 300; **8** Kevin Harvick, USA (Chevrolet Impala SS), 300; **9** Matt Kenseth, USA (Ford Fusion), 300; **10** Ryan Newman, USA (Dodge Avenger), 300.
**Pole position:** Dave Blaney, USA (Toyota Camry).
**Drivers' championship points: 1** Gordon (Jeff), 2,613; **2** Hamlin, 2,457; **3** Kenseth, 2,248; **4** Johnson, 2,232; **5** Burton (Jeff), 2,230; **6** Stewart, 2,185.

**PEPSI 400, Daytona International Speedway, Daytona Beach, Florida, USA, 7 July. Round 18. 160 laps of the 2.500-mile/4.023-km circuit, 400.000 miles/643.738 km.**
**1** Jamie McMurray, USA (Ford Fusion), 2h 52m 41.0s, 138.983 mph/223.671 km/h; **2** Kyle Busch, USA (Chevrolet Impala SS), 2h 52m 41.005s; **3** Kurt Busch, USA (Dodge Avenger), 160 laps; **4** Carl Edwards, USA (Ford Fusion), 160; **5** Jeff Gordon, USA (Chevrolet Impala SS), 160; **6** Greg Biffle, USA (Ford Fusion), 160; **7** Clint Bowyer, USA (Chevrolet Impala SS), 160; **8** Matt Kenseth, USA (Ford Fusion), 160; **9** Kasey Kahne, USA (Dodge Avenger), 160; **10** Jimmie Johnson, USA (Chevrolet Impala SS), 160.
**Pole position:** Gordon (Jeff).
**Drivers' championship points: 1** Gordon (Jeff), 2,773; **2** Hamlin, 2,496; **3** Kenseth, 2,390; **4** Johnson, 2,366; **5** Burton (Jeff), 2,345; **6** Edwards, 2,308.

**USG SHEETROCK 400, Chicagoland Speedway, Chicago, Illinois, USA, 15 July. Round 19. 267 of the 1.500-mile/2.414-km circuit, 400.500 miles/644.542 km.**
**1** Tony Stewart, USA (Chevrolet Impala SS), 2h 58m 59.0s, 134.258 mph/216.068 km/h; **2** Matt Kenseth, USA (Ford Fusion), 2h 59m 0.727s; **3** Carl Edwards, USA (Ford Fusion), 267 laps; **4** Kevin Harvick, USA (Chevrolet Impala SS), 267; **5** Casey Mears, USA (Chevrolet Impala SS), 267; **6** Kurt Busch, USA (Dodge Avenger), 267; **7** Jeff Burton, USA (Chevrolet Impala SS), 267; **8** Ryan Newman, USA (Dodge Avenger), 267; **9** Jeff Gordon, USA (Chevrolet Impala SS), 267; **10** Clint Bowyer, USA (Chevrolet Impala SS), 267.
**Pole position:** Mears.
**Drivers' championship points: 1** Gordon (Jeff), 2,911; **2** Hamlin, 2,608; **3** Kenseth, 2,565; **4** Burton (Jeff), 2,491; **5** Edwards, 2,473; **6** Stewart, 2,429.

**ALLSTATE 400 AT THE BRICKYARD, Indianapolis Motor Speedway, Speedway, Indiana, USA, 29 July. Round 20. 160 laps of the 2.500-mile/4.023-km circuit, 400.000 miles/643.738 km.**
**1** Tony Stewart, USA (Chevrolet Impala SS), 3h 24m 28.0s, 117.379 mph/188.902 km/h; **2** Juan Pablo Montoya, CO (Dodge Avenger), 3h 24m 30.982s; **3** Jeff Gordon, USA (Chevrolet Impala SS), 160 laps; **4** Kyle Busch, USA (Chevrolet Impala SS), 160; **5** Reed Sorensen, USA (Dodge Avenger), 160; **6** Mark Martin, USA (Chevrolet Impala SS), 160; **7** Kevin Harvick, USA (Chevrolet Impala SS), 160; **8** Jeff Burton, USA (Chevrolet Impala SS), 160; **9** Dave Blaney, USA (Toyota Camry), 160; **10** Matt Kenseth, USA (Ford Fusion), 160.
**Pole position:** Sorensen.
**Drivers' championship points: 1** Gordon (Jeff), 3,076; **2** Hamlin, 2,705; **3** Kenseth, 2,699; **4** Burton (Jeff), 2,633; **5** Stewart, 2,624; **6** Edwards, 2,582.

**PENNSYLVANIA 500, Pocono Raceway, Long Pond, Pennsylvania, USA, 5 August. Round 21. 200 laps of the 2.500-mile/4.023-km circuit, 500.000 miles/804.672 km.**
**1** Kurt Busch, USA (Dodge Avenger), 3h 47m 55.0s, 131.627 mph/211.833 km/h; **2** Dale Earnhardt Jr, USA (Chevrolet Impala SS), 3h 47m 59.131s; **3** Denny Hamlin, USA (Chevrolet Impala SS), 200 laps; **4** Jeff Gordon, USA (Chevrolet Impala SS), 200; **5** Jimmie Johnson, USA (Chevrolet Impala SS), 200; **6** Tony Stewart, USA (Chevrolet Impala SS), 200; **7** Ryan Newman, USA (Dodge Avenger), 200; **8** Clint Bowyer, USA (Chevrolet Impala SS), 200; **9** Mark Martin, USA (Chevrolet Impala SS), 200; **10** Casey Mears, USA (Chevrolet Impala SS), 200.
**Pole position:** Earnhardt Jr.
**Drivers' championship points: 1** Gordon (Jeff), 3,236; **2** Hamlin, 2,870; **3** Kenseth, 2,825; **4** Burton (Jeff), 2,763; **5** Stewart, 2,749; **6** Edwards, 2,682.

**CENTURION BOATS AT THE GLEN, Watkins Glen International, New York, USA, 12 August. Round 22. 90 laps of the 2.450-mile/3.943-km circuit, 220.500 miles/354.860 km.**
**1** Tony Stewart, USA (Chevrolet Impala SS), 2h 50m 38.0s,

77.535 mph/124.780 km/h; **2** Denny Hamlin, USA (Chevrolet Impala SS), 2h 50m 40.460s; **3** Jimmie Johnson, USA (Chevrolet Impala SS), 90 laps; **4** Ron Fellows, USA (Chevrolet Impala SS), 90; **5** Robby Gordon, USA (Ford Fusion), 90; **6** Martin Truex Jr, USA (Chevrolet Impala SS), 90; **7** Kyle Busch, USA (Chevrolet Impala SS), 90; **8** Carl Edwards, USA (Ford Fusion), 90; **9** Jeff Gordon, USA (Chevrolet Impala SS), 90; **10** Greg Biffle, USA (Ford Fusion), 90.

**Pole position:** Gordon (Jeff).

**Drivers' championship points: 1** Gordon, 3,384; **2** Hamlin, 3,040; **3** Kenseth, 2,952; **4** Stewart, 2,939; **5** Edwards, 2,824; **6** Burton (Jeff), 2,806.

**3M PERFORMANCE 400, Michigan International Speedway, Brooklyn, Michigan, USA, 21 August. Round 23. 203 laps of the 2.000-mile/3.219-km circuit, 406.000 miles/653.394 km.**

**Scheduled for 19 August, but postponed due to rain.**

**1** Kurt Busch, USA (Dodge Avenger), 3h 28m 11.0s, 117.012 mph/188.313 km/h; **2** Martin Truex Jr, USA (Chevrolet Impala SS), 3h 28m 11.495s; **3** Jimmie Johnson, USA (Chevrolet Impala SS), 203 laps; **4** Matt Kenseth, USA (Ford Fusion), 203; **5** Denny Hamlin, USA (Chevrolet Impala SS), 203; **6** Dave Blaney, USA (Toyota Camry), 203; **7** Carl Edwards, USA (Ford Fusion), 203; **8** Brian Vickers, USA (Toyota Camry), 203; **9** Bobby Labonte, USA (Dodge Avenger), 203; **10** Tony Stewart, USA (Chevrolet Impala SS), 203.

**Pole position:** Jeff Gordon, USA (Chevrolet Impala SS).

**Drivers' championship points: 1** Gordon (Jeff), 3,471; **2** Hamlin, 3,195; **3** Kenseth, 3,117; **4** Stewart, 3,073; **5** Edwards, 2,970; **6** Johnson, 2,959.

**SHARPIE 500, Bristol Motor Speedway, Tennessee, USA, 25 August. Round 24. 500 laps of the 0.533-mile/0.858-km circuit, 266.500 miles/428.890 km.**

**1** Carl Edwards, USA (Ford Fusion), 2h 59m 39.0s, 89.006 mph/143.242 km/h; **2** Kasey Kahne, USA (Dodge Avenger), 2h 59m 40.405s; **3** Clint Bowyer, USA (Chevrolet Impala SS), 500 laps; **4** Tony Stewart, USA (Chevrolet Impala SS), 500; **5** Dale Earnhardt Jr, USA (Chevrolet Impala SS), 500; **6** Kurt Busch, USA (Dodge Avenger), 500; **7** Ryan Newman, USA (Dodge Avenger), 500; **8** Bobby Labonte, USA (Dodge Avenger), 500; **9** Kyle Busch, USA (Chevrolet Impala SS), 500; **10** Greg Biffle, USA (Ford Fusion), 500.

**Pole position:** Kahne.

**Drivers' championship points: 1** Gordon (Jeff), 3,582; **2** Stewart, 3,233; **3** Hamlin, 3,229; **4** Kenseth, 3,163; **5** Edwards, 3,160; **6** Johnson, 3,059.

**SHARP AQUOS 500, California Speedway, Fontana, California, USA, 2 September. Round 25. 250 laps of the 2.000-mile/3.219-km circuit, 500.000 miles/804.672 km.**

**1** Jimmie Johnson, USA (Chevrolet Impala SS), 3h 48m 8.0s, 131.502 mph/211.632 km/h; **2** Carl Edwards, USA (Ford Fusion), 3h 48m 9.868s; **3** Kyle Busch, USA (Chevrolet Impala SS), 250 laps; **4** Jeff Burton, USA (Chevrolet Impala SS), 250; **5** Dale Earnhardt Jr, USA (Chevrolet Impala SS), 250; **6** Martin Truex Jr, USA (Chevrolet Impala SS), 250; **7** Matt Kenseth, USA (Ford Fusion), 250; **8** Brian Vickers, USA (Toyota Camry), 250; **9** Kurt Busch, USA (Dodge Avenger), 250; **10** Kasey Kahne, USA (Dodge Avenger), 250.

**Pole position:** Busch (Kurt).

**Drivers' championship points: 1** Gordon (Jeff), 3,679; **2** Stewart, 3,362; **3** Hamlin, 3,335; **4** Edwards, 3,330; **5** Kenseth, 3,309; **6** Johnson, 3,249.

**CHEVY ROCK & ROLL 400, Richmond International Raceway, Virginia, USA, 8 September. Round 26. 400 laps of the 0.750-mile/1.207-km circuit, 300.000 miles/482.803 km.**

**1** Jimmie Johnson, USA (Chevrolet Impala SS), 3h 16m 3.0s, 91.813 mph/147.759 km/h; **2** Tony Stewart, USA (Chevrolet Impala SS), 3h 16m 6.007s; **3** David Ragan, USA (Ford Fusion), 400 laps; **4** Jeff Gordon, USA (Chevrolet Impala SS), 400; **5** Johnny Sauter, USA (Chevrolet Impala SS), 400; **6** Denny Hamlin, USA (Chevrolet Impala SS), 400; **7** Kevin Harvick, USA (Chevrolet Impala SS), 400; **8** Kasey Kahne, USA (Dodge Avenger), 400; **9** Kurt Busch, USA (Dodge Avenger), 400; **10** JJ Yeley, USA (Chevrolet Impala SS), 400.

**Pole position:** Johnson.

**Drivers' championship points: 1** Johnson, 5,060; **2** Gordon (Jeff), 5,040; **3** Stewart, 5,030; **4** Edwards, 5,020; **5** Busch (Kurt), 5,020; **6** Hamlin, 5,010.

**SYLVANIA 300, New Hampshire International Speedway, Loudon, New Hampshire, USA, 16 September. Round 27. 300 laps of the 1.058-mile/1.703-km circuit, 317.400 miles/510.806 km.**

**1** Clint Bowyer, USA (Chevrolet Impala SS), 2h 52m 23.0s, 110.475 mph/177.792 km/h; **2** Jeff Gordon, USA (Chevrolet Impala SS), 2h 52m 29.469s; **3** Tony Stewart, USA (Chevrolet Impala SS), 300 laps; **4** Kyle Busch, USA (Chevrolet Impala SS), 300; **5** Martin Truex Jr., USA (Chevrolet Impala SS), 300; **6** Jimmie Johnson, USA (Chevrolet Impala SS), 300; **7** Matt Kenseth, USA (Ford Fusion), 300; **8** Casey Mears, USA (Chevrolet Impala SS), 300; **9** Ryan Newman, USA (Dodge Avenger), 300; **10** J.J. Yeley, USA (Chevrolet Impala SS), 300.

**Pole position:** Bowyer.

**Drivers' championship points: 1** Johnson, 5,210; **2** Gordon (Jeff), 5,210; **3** Stewart, 5,200; **4** Bowyer, 5,195; **5** Busch (Kyle), 5,175; **6** Truex Jr, 5,170.

**DODGE DEALERS 400, Dover International Speedway, Dover, Delaware, USA, 23 September. Round 28. 400 laps of the 1.000-mile/1.609-km circuit, 400.000 miles/643.738 km.**

**1** Carl Edwards, USA (Ford Fusion), 3h 55m 39.0s, 101.846 mph/163.905 km/h; **2** Greg Biffle, USA (Ford Fusion), 3h 55m 39.671s; **3** Dale Earnhardt Jr, USA (Chevrolet Impala SS), 400 laps; **4** Mark Martin, USA (Chevrolet Impala SS), 400; **5** Kyle Busch, USA (Chevrolet Impala SS), 400; **6** Casey Mears, USA (Chevrolet Impala SS), 400; **7** Jeff Burton, USA (Chevrolet Impala SS), 400; **8** Jamie McMurray, USA (Ford Fusion), 400; **9** Tony Stewart, USA (Chevrolet Impala SS), 400; **10** Juan Pablo Montoya, CO (Dodge Avenger), 400.

**Pole position:** Jimmie Johnson, USA (Chevrolet Impala SS).

**Drivers' championship points: 1** Gordon (Jeff), 5,340; **2** Stewart, 5,338; **3** Johnson, 5,336; **4** Busch (Kyle), 5,330; **5** Bowyer, 5,322; **6** Edwards, 5,312.

**LIFELOCK 400, Kansas Speedway, Kansas City, Kansas, USA, 30 September. Round 29. 210 laps of the 1.500-mile/2.414-km circuit, 315.000 miles/506.943 km.**

**1** Greg Biffle, USA (Ford Fusion), 3h 00m 2.0s, 104.981 mph/168.950 km/h; **2** Clint Bowyer, USA (Chevrolet Impala SS), 210 laps (under caution); **3** Jimmie Johnson, USA (Chevrolet Impala SS), 210; **4** Casey Mears, USA (Chevrolet Impala SS), 210; **5** Jeff Gordon, USA (Chevrolet Impala SS), 210; **6** Kevin Harvick, USA (Chevrolet Impala SS), 210; **7** Reed Sorensen, USA (Dodge Avenger), 210; **8** Elliott Sadler, USA (Dodge Avenger), 210; **9** Kasey Kahne, USA (Dodge Avenger), 210; **10** Dale Earnhardt Jr, USA (Chevrolet Impala SS), 210.

**Pole position:** Johnson.

**Drivers' championship points: 1** Johnson, 5,506; **2** Gordon, 5,500; **3** Bowyer, 5,492; **4** Stewart, 5,389; **5** Harvick, 5,380; **6** Busch (Kyle), 5,370.

**UAW-FORD 500, Talladega Superspeedway, Alabama, USA, 7 October. Round 30. 188 laps of the 2.660-mile/4.281-km circuit, 500.080 miles/804.801 km.**

**1** Jeff Gordon, USA (Chevrolet Impala SS), 3h 29m 11.0s, 143.438 mph/230.841 km/h; **2** Jimmie Johnson, USA (Chevrolet Impala SS), 3h 29m 11.066s; **3** Dave Blaney, USA (Toyota Camry), 188 laps; **4** Denny Hamlin, USA (Chevrolet Impala SS), 188; **5** Ryan Newman, USA (Dodge Avenger), 188; **6** Casey Mears, USA (Chevrolet Impala SS), 188; **7** Kurt Busch, USA (Dodge Avenger), 188; **8** Tony Stewart, USA (Chevrolet Impala SS), 188; **9** Tony Raines, USA (Chevrolet Impala SS), 188; **10** Reed Sorensen, USA (Dodge Avenger), 188.

**Pole position:** Waltrip.

**Drivers' championship points: 1** Gordon (Jeff), 5,690; **2** Johnson, 5,681; **3** Bowyer, 5,627; **4** Stewart, 5,536; **5** Harvick, 5,488; **6** Edwards, 5,485.

**BANK OF AMERICA 500, Lowe's Motor Speedway, Concord, Charlotte, North Carolina, USA, 13 October. Round 31. 337 laps of the 1.500-mile/2.414-km circuit, 505.500 miles/813.523 km.**

**1** Jeff Gordon, USA (Chevrolet Impala SS), 4h 0m 58.0s, 125.868 mph/202.565 km/h; **2** Clint Bowyer, USA (Chevrolet Impala SS), 4h 0m 58.579s; **3** Kyle Busch, USA (Chevrolet Impala SS), 337 laps; **4** Jeff Burton, USA (Chevrolet Impala SS), 337; **5** Carl Edwards, USA (Ford Fusion), 337; **6** Dave Blaney, USA (Toyota Camry), 337; **7** Tony Stewart, USA (Chevrolet Impala SS), 337; **8** Kasey Kahne, USA (Dodge Avenger), 337; **9** David Stremme, USA (Dodge Avenger), 337; **10** Michael Waltrip, USA (Toyota Camry), 337.

**Pole position:** Newman.

**Drivers' championship Points: 1** Gordon (Jeff), 5,880; **2** Johnson, 5,812; **3** Bowyer, 5,802; **4** Stewart, 5,682; **5** Edwards, 5,640; **6** Busch (Kyle), 5,600.

**SUBWAY 500, Martinsville Speedway, Virginia, USA, 21 October. Round 32. 506 laps of the 0.526-mile/0.847-km circuit, 266.156 miles/428.337 km.**

**1** Jimmie Johnson, USA (Chevrolet Impala SS), 3h 59m 45.0s, 66.608 mph/107.196 km/h; **2** Ryan Newman, USA (Dodge Avenger), 506 laps (under caution); **3** Jeff Gordon, USA (Chevrolet Impala SS), 506; **4** Kyle Busch, USA (Chevrolet Impala SS), 506; **5** Matt Kenseth, USA (Ford Fusion), 506; **6** Denny Hamlin, USA (Chevrolet Impala SS), 506; **7** Greg Biffle, USA (Ford Fusion), 506; **8** Juan Pablo Montoya, CO (Dodge Avenger), 506; **9** Clint Bowyer, USA (Chevrolet Impala SS), 506; **10** Kevin Harvick, USA (Chevrolet Impala SS), 506.

**Pole position:** Gordon (Jeff).

**Drivers' championship points: 1** Gordon (Jeff), 6,055; **2** Johnson, 6,002; **3** Bowyer, 5,940; **4** Stewart, 5,806; **5** Edwards, 5,770; **6** Busch (Kyle), 5,765.

**PEP BOYS AUTO 500, Atlanta Motor Speedway, Hampton, Georgia, USA, 28 October. Round 33. 329 laps of the 1.540-mile/2.478-km circuit, 506.660 miles/815.390 km.**

**1** Jimmie Johnson, USA (Chevrolet Impala SS), 3h 44m 45.0s, 135.260 mph/217.679 km/h; **2** Carl Edwards, USA (Ford Fusion), 329 laps (under caution); **3** Reed Sorensen, USA (Dodge Avenger), 329; **4** Matt Kenseth, USA (Ford Fusion), 329; **5** Jeff Burton, USA (Chevrolet Impala SS), 329; **6** Clint Bowyer, USA (Chevrolet Impala SS), 329; **7** Jeff Gordon, USA (Chevrolet Impala SS), 329; **8** Kurt Busch, USA (Dodge Avenger), 329; **9** Kasey Kahne, USA (Dodge Avenger), 329; **10** Brian Vickers, USA (Toyota Camry), 329.

**Pole position:** Greg Biffle, USA (Ford Fusion).

**Provisional championship points**

**Drivers**

**1** Jeff Gordon, USA, 6,201; **2** Jimmie Johnson, USA, 6,192; **3** Clint Bowyer, USA, 6,090; **4** Carl Edwards, USA, 5,940; **5** Tony Stewart, USA, 5,879; **6** Kyle Busch, USA, 5,873; **7** Kevin Harvick, USA, 5,809; **8** Jeff Burton, USA, 5,801; **9** Kurt Busch, USA, 5,782; **10** Denny Hamlin, USA, 5,777; **11** Matt Kenseth, USA, 5,753; **12** Martin Truex Jr, USA, 5,688.

**Not involved in chase for the Nextel Cup**

**13** Dale Earnhardt Jr, USA, 3,714; **14** Casey Mears, USA, 3,635; **15** Greg Biffle, USA, 3,633; **16** Ryan Newman, USA, 3,612; **17** Kasey Kahne, USA, 3,246; **18** Bobby Labonte, USA, 3,199; **19** Jamie McMurray, USA, 3,198; **20** Juan Pablo Montoya, CO, 3,164; **21** JJ Yeley, USA, 3,153; **22** Reed Sorensen, USA, 3,024; **23** David Ragan, USA, 2,993; **24** David Stremme, USA, 2,890; **25** Elliott Sadler, USA, 2,882; **26** Robby Gordon, USA, 2,774; **27** Mark Martin, USA, 2,761; **28** Jeff Green, USA, 2,704; **29** David Gilliland, USA, 2,699; **30** Tony Raines, USA, 2,689.

**Raybestos Rookie of the Year:** Juan Pablo Montoya.

**Manufacturers**

**1** Chevrolet, 268; **2** Ford, 187; **3** Dodge, 164; **4** Toyota, 107.

**Bud Pole Award winner:** Jeff Gordon, 10 poles.

*Results of the Texas, Phoenix and Homestead races will be given in AUTOCOURSE 2008–2009.*

## Other NASCAR Races

**BUDWEISER SHOOTOUT, Daytona International Speedway, Daytona Beach, Florida, USA, 10 February. 70 laps of the 2.500-mile/4.023-km circuit, 175.000 miles/281.635 km.**

**1** Tony Stewart, USA (Chevrolet Monte Carlo), 70 laps; **2** Dave Gillilasnd, USA (Ford Fusion), 70; **3** Kurt Busch, USA (Dodge Charger), 70; **4** Jimmie Johnson, USA (Chevrolet Monte Carlo), 70; **5** Kevin Harvick, USA (Chevrolet Monte Carlo), 70; **6** Mark Martin, USA (Chevrolet Monte Carlo), 70; **7** Kyle Busch, USA (Chevrolet Monte Carlo), 70; **8** Brian Vickers, USA (Toyota Camry), 70; **9** Jeff Buton, USA (Chevrolet Monte Carlo), 70; **10** Scott Riggs, USA (Dodge Charger), 70.

**NASCAR NEXTEL ALL-STAR CHALLENGE, Lowe's Motor Speedway, Concord, Charlotte, North Carolina, USA, 19 May. 80 laps of the 1.500-mile/2.414-km circuit, 120.000 miles/193.121 km.**

**1** Kevin Harvick, USA (Chevrolet Impala SS), 80 laps; **2** Jimmie Johnson, USA (Chevrolet Impala SS), 80; **3** Mark Martin, USA (Chevrolet Impala SS), 80; **4** Jeff Burton, USA (Chevrolet Impala SS), 80; **5** Tony Stewart, USA (Chevrolet Impala SS), 80; **6** Johnny Sauter, USA (Chevrolet Impala SS), 80; **7** Matt Kenseth, USA (Ford Fusion), 80; **8** Ryan Newman, USA (Dodge Avenger), 80; **9** Dale Earnhardt Jr, USA (Chevrolet Impala SS), 80; **10** Martin Truex Jr, USA (Chevrolet Impala SS), 80.

## Indy Racing League (IRL) Indy Pro Series

All cars are Dallara IPS-Infiniti.

**MIAMI 100, Homestead-Miami Speedway, Florida, USA, 24 March. Round 1. 57 laps of the 1.485-mile/2.390-km circuit, 84.645 miles/136.223 km.**

**1** Alex Lloyd, GB, 57m 45.9637s, 87.918 mph/141.491 km/h; **2** Chris Festa, USA, 57m 46.7608s; **3** Hideki Mutoh, J, 57 laps; **4** Jaime Câmara, BR, 57; **5** Andrew Prendeville, USA, 57; **6** Bobby Wilson, USA, 57; **7** Mike Potekhen, USA, 57; **8** Robbie Pecorari, USA, 57; **9** CR Crews, USA, 57; **10** Jay Howard, GB, 57.

**Fastest race lap:** Logan Gomez, USA, 28.7290s, 186.084 mph/299.473 km/h.

**Fastest qualifying lap:** Festa, 28.5455s, 187.280 mph/301.398 km/h.

**INDY PRO SERIES GRAND PRIX OF ST. PETERSBURG, Streets of St. Petersburg, Florida, USA, 31 March/1 April. 2 x 40 laps of the 1.800-mile/2.897-km circuit. Round 2 (72.000 miles/115.873 km).**

**1** Alex Lloyd, GB, 56m 59.2976s, 75.805 mph/121.996 km/h; **2** Hideki Mutoh, J, 57m 0.9014s; **3** Jonathan Klein, USA, 40 laps; **4** Stephen Simpson, ZA, 40; **5** Jay Howard, GB, 40; **6** Bobby Wilson, USA, 40; **7** Robbie Pecorari, USA, 40; **8** Chris Festa, USA, 40; **9** Wade Cunningham, NZ, 40; **10** CR Crews, USA, 40.

**Fastest race lap:** Mutoh, 1m 7.6939s, 95.725 mph/154.054 km/h.

**Fastest qualifying lap:** Lloyd, 1m 7.1404s, 96.514 mph/155.325 km/h.

**Round 3 (72.000 miles/115.873 km).**

**1** Alex Lloyd, GB, 58m 35.8707s, 73.723 mph/118.645 km/h; **2** Wade Cunningham, NZ, 58m 36.1249s; **3** Bobby Wilson, USA, 40 laps; **4** Hideki Mutoh, J, 40; **5** Robbie Pecorari, USA, 40; **6** CR Crews, USA, 40; **7** Phil Giebler, USA, 40; **8** Jaime Câmara, BR, 40; **9** Joey Scarallo, USA, 40; **10** Ken Losch, USA, 40.

**Fastest race lap:** Lloyd, 1m 7.8359s, 95.525 mph/153.732 km/h.

**Pole position:** Lloyd.

**FREEDOM 100, Indianapolis Motor Speedway, Speedway, Indiana, USA, 25 May. Round 4. 40 laps of the 2.500-mile/4.023-km circuit, 100.000 miles/160.934 km.**

**1** Alex Lloyd, GB, 46m 39.6029s, 128.590 mph/206.945 km/h; **2** Chris Festa, USA, 40 laps (under caution); **3** Jaime Câmara, BR, 40; **4** Andrew Prendeville, USA, 40; **5** Hideki Mutoh, J, 40; **6** Mike Potekhen, USA, 40; **7** Matt Jaskol, USA, 40; **8** Al Unser III, USA, 40; **9** Jon Brownson, USA, 40; **10** Jonathan Klein, USA, 40.

**Fastest race lap:** Prendeville, 47.6002s, 189.075 mph/304.286 km/h.

**Pole position/Fastest qualifying lap:** Losch, 1m 35.6271s, 188.231 mph/302.928 km/h (over two laps).

**ROAD RUNNER 100, The Milwaukee Mile, Wisconsin State Fair Park, West Allis, Wisconsin, USA, 2 June. Round 5. 100 laps of the 1.015-mile/1.633-km circuit, 101.500 miles/163.348 km.**

**1** Alex Lloyd, GB, 55m 55.5643s, 108.894 mph/175.248 km/h; **2** Mike Potekhen, USA, 55m 57.8469s; **3** Jonathan Klein, USA, 100 laps; **4** Sean Guthrie, USA, 100; **5** Bobby Wilson, USA, 99; **6** Ryan Justice, USA, 99; **7** Al Unser III, USA, 98; **8** Joey Scarallo, USA, 97; **9** Marc Williams, NZ, 97; **10** Brad Jaeger, USA, 93.

**Fastest race lap:** Lloyd, 25.8768s, 141.208 mph/227.252 km/h.

**Fastest qualifying lap:** Lloyd, 25.0142s, 146.077 mph/235.088 km/h.

**LIBERTY CHALLENGE, Indianapolis Motor Speedway (Road Course), Speedway, Indiana, USA, 16/17 June. 2 x 18 laps of the 2.600-mile/4.184-km circuit. Round 6 (46.800 miles/75.317 km).**

**1** Hideki Mutoh, J, 26m 09.8910s, 107.320 mph/172.714 km/h; **2** Alex Lloyd, GB, 26m 16.1640s; **3** Jaime Câmara, BR, 18 laps; **4** Wade Cunningham, NZ, 18; **5** Stephen Simpson, ZA, 18; **6** Richard Antinucci, USA, 18; **7** Bobby Wilson, USA, 18; **8** Ryan Justice, USA, 18; **9** Logan Gomez, USA, 18; **10** Mike Potekhen, USA, 18.

**Fastest race lap:** Mutoh, 1m 26.556s, 108.138 mph/174.031 km/h.

**Fastest qualifying lap:** Mutoh, 1m 25.281s, 109.755 mph/176.733 km/h.

**Round 7 (46.800 miles/75.317 km).**

**1** Bobby Wilson, USA, 28m 40.9170s, 97.901 mph/157.557 km/h; **2** Alex Lloyd, GB, 28m 51.4430s; **3** Hideki Mutoh, J, 18 laps; **4** Ryan Justice, USA, 18; **5** Jaime Câmara, BR, 18; **6** Logan Gomez, USA, 18; **7** Jonathan Klein, USA, 18; **8** Mike Potekhen, USA, 18; **9** Richard Antinucci, USA, 18; **10** Daniel Herrington, USA, 18.

**Fastest race lap:** Wilson, 1m 26.194s, 108.592 mph/174.756 km/h.

**Fastest qualifying lap:** Justice.

**IOWA 100, Iowa, USA, 23 June. Round 8. 115 laps of the 0.894-mile/1.439-km circuit, 102.810 miles/165.457 km.**

**1** Alex Lloyd, GB, 53m 18.7234s, 115.707 mph/186.213 km/h; **2** Wade Cunningham, NZ, 53m 19.1161s; **3** Hideki Mutoh, J, 115; **4** Ryan Justice, USA, 115; **5** Robbie Pecorari, USA, 115; **6** Logan Gomez, USA, 115; **7** Al Unser III, USA, 115; **8** Marc Williams, NZ, 115; **9** Bobby Wilson, USA, 115; **10** Ben Petter, USA, 115 laps.

**Fastest race lap:** Lloyd, 19.7912s, 162.618 mph/261.708 km/h.

**Fastest qualifying lap:** Cunningham, 19.9522s, 161.306 mph/259.596 km/h.

**CORNING TWIN 100s, Watkins Glen International, New York, USA, 7 8 July. 2 x 29 laps of the 3.370-mile/5.423-km circuit.**

**Round 9 (97.730 miles/157.281 km).**

**1** Wade Cunningham, NZ, 55m 19.2394s, 105.997 mph/170.585 km/h; **2** Hideki Mutoh, J, 55m 19.3152s; **3** Alex Lloyd, GB, 29 laps; **4** Phil Giebler, USA, 29; **5** Bobby Wilson, USA, 29; **6** Daniel Herrington, USA, 29; **7** Jaime Câmara, BR, 29; **8** Richard Antinucci, USA, 29; **9** Mike Potekhen, USA, 29; **10** Andrew Prendeville, USA, 29.

**Fastest race lap:** Lloyd, 1m 38.2179s, 123.521 mph/198.788 km/h.

**Fastest qualifying lap:** Cunningham, 1m 36.7418s, 125.406 mph/201.821 km/h.

**Round 10 (97.730 miles/157.281 km).**

**1** Alex Lloyd, GB, 52m 28.2245s, 111.754 mph/179.851 km/h; **2** Wade Cunningham, NZ, 52m 32.9439s; **3** Daniel Herrington, USA, 29 laps; **4** Phil Giebler, USA, 29; **5** Richard Antinucci, USA, 29; **6** Hideki Mutoh, J, 29; **7** Mike Potekhen, USA, 29; **8** Andrew Prendeville, USA, 29; **9** Jonathan Klein, USA, 29; **10** Jaime Câmara, BR, 29.

**Fastest race lap:** Lloyd, 1m 38.1898s, 123.557 mph/198.845 km/h.

**Pole position:** Herrington.

**SUNBELT RENTALS 100, Nashville Superspeedway, Lebanon, Tennessee, USA, 14 July. Round 11. 77 laps of the 1.300-mile/2.092-km circuit, 100.100 miles/161.095 km.**

**1** Robbie Pecorari, USA, 52m 56.3282s, 113.452 mph/182.583 km/h; **2** Logan Gomez, USA, 52m 56.5508s; **3** Jaime Câmara, BR, 77 laps; **4** Wade Cunningham, NZ, 77; **5** Jonathan Klein, USA, 77; **6** Hideki Mutoh, J, 77; **7** Stephen Simpson, ZA, 77; **8** Ryan Justice, USA, 77; **9** Chris Festa, USA, 77; **10** Ken Losch, USA, 77.

**Fastest race lap:** Pecorari, 26.2990s, 177.954 mph/286.388 km/h.

**Fastest qualifying lap:** Lloyd, 25.7368s, 181.841 mph/292.644 km/h.

**MID-OHIO 100, Mid-Ohio Sports Car Course, Lexington, Ohio, USA, 22 July. Round 12. 40 laps of the 2.258-mile/3.634-km circuit, 90.320 miles/145.356 km.**

**1** Richard Antinucci, USA, 51m 40.7399s, 104.863 mph/168.760 km/h; **2** Wade Cunningham, NZ, 51m 41.6987s; **3** Stephen Simpson, ZA, 40 laps; **4** Andrew Prendeville, USA, 40; **5** Hideki Mutoh, J, 40; **6** Bobby Wilson, USA, 40; **7** Robbie Pecorari, USA, 40; **8** Jaime Câmara, BR, 40; **9** Mike Potekhen, USA, 40; **10** Logan Gomez, USA, 40.

**Fastest race lap:** Antinucci, 1m 13.2998s, 110.898 mph/178.473 km/h.

**Fastest qualifying lap:** Lloyd, 1m 13.7719s, 110.188 mph/177.331 km/h.

**KENTUCKY 100, Kentucky Speedway, Fort Mitchell, Kentucky, USA, 11 August. Round 13. 67 laps of the 1.480-mile/2.382-km circuit, 99.160 miles/159.583 km.**

**1** Hideki Mutoh, J, 54m 1.6259s, 110.123 mph/177.225

km/h; **2** Alex Lloyd, GB, 54m 01.7282s; **3** Wade Cunningham, NZ, 67 laps; **4** Chris Festa, USA, 67; **5** Jaime Câmara, BR, 67; **6** Sean Guthrie, USA, 67; **7** Mike Potekhen, USA, 67; **8** Robbie Pecorari, USA, 67; **9** Brad Jaeger, USA, 67; **10** Travis Gregg, USA, 67.
**Fastest race lap:** Lloyd, 27.6689s, 192.563 mph/309.000 km/h.
**Fastest qualifying lap:** Mutoh, 27.8551s, 191.276 mph/307.828 km/h.

**CARNEROS 100/VALLEY OF THE MOON 100, Infineon Raceway, Sears Point, Sonoma, California, USA, 25/26 August. 2 x 30 laps of the 2.300-mile/3.701-km circuit. Round 14 (69.000 miles/111.045 km).**
**1** Alex Lloyd, GB, 45m 28.8873s, 91.026 mph/146.492 km/h; **2** Richard Antinucci, USA, 45m 29.7800s; **3** Mike Potekhen, USA, 30 laps; **4** Stephen Simpson, ZA, 30; **5** Jaime Câmara, BR, 30; **6** Logan Gomez, USA, 30; **7** Andrew Prendeville, USA, 30; **8** Ryan Justice, USA, 30; **9** Jonathan Klein, USA, 30; **10** Brad Jaeger, USA, 30.
**Fastest race lap:** Mutoh, 1m 23.8829s, 98.709 mph/158.857 km/h.
**Fastest qualifying lap:** Antinucci, 1m 22.2742s, 100.639 mph/161.963 km/h.

**Round 15 (69.000 miles/111.045 km).**
**1** Richard Antinucci, USA, 42m 20.6464s, 97.770 mph/157.346 km/h; **2** Ryan Justice, USA, 42m 22.3864s; **3** Andrew Prendeville, USA, 30 laps; **4** Logan Gomez, USA, 30; **5** Stephen Simpson, ZA, 30; **6** Jonathan Klein, USA, 30; **7** Matt Jaskol, USA, 30; **8** Mike Potekhen, USA, 30; **9** Brad Jaeger, USA, 30; **10** Hideki Mutoh, J, 30.
**Fastest race lap:** Antinucci, 1m 23.4655s, 99.203 mph/159.651 km/h.
**Pole position:** Justice.

**CHICAGOLAND 100, Chicagoland Speedway, Chicago, Illinois, USA, 9 September. Round 16. 67 of the 1.520-mile/2.446-km circuit, 101.840 miles/163.896 km.**
**1** Logan Gomez, USA, 56m 10.8201s, 108.764 mph/175.039 km/h; **2** Alex Lloyd, GB, 56m 10.8206s; **3** Robbie Pecorari, USA, 67 laps; **4** Bobby Wilson, USA, 67; **5** Mike Potekhen, USA, 67; **6** Sean Guthrie, USA, 67; **7** PJ Abbott, USA, 67; **8** Jon Brownson, USA, 67; **9** Ken Losch, USA, 67; **10** Jimmy Kite, USA, 67.
**Fastest race lap:** Travis Gregg, USA, 28.3736s, 192.855 mph/310.371 km/h.
**Fastest qualifying lap:** Lloyd, 28.7799s, 190.133 mph/305.989 km/h.

**Final championship points**
**1** Alex Lloyd, GB, 652; **2** Hideki Mutoh, J, 481; **3** Wade Cunningham, NZ, 423; **4** Bobby Wilson, USA, 393; **5** Mike Potekhen, USA, 379; **6** Jaime Câmara, BR, 373; **7** Logan Gomez, USA, 368; **8** Robbie Pecorari, USA, 344; **9** Stephen Simpson, ZA, 340; **10** Chris Festa, USA, 313; **11** Andrew Prendeville, USA, 306; **12** Jonathan Klein, USA, 304; **13** Ryan Justice, USA, 276; **14** Sean Guthrie, USA, 274; **15** Richard Antinucci, USA, 273; **16** Brad Jaeger, USA, 260; **17** Ken Losch, USA, 239; **18** Joey Scarallo, AUS, 184; **19** Jon Brownson, USA, 171; **20** Phil Giebler, USA, 163.

## Cooper Tires presents The Champ Car Atlantic Championship powered by Mazda

All cars are Swift 016.a-Mazda Cosworth MZR.

**CHAMP CAR ATLANTIC CHAMPIONSHIP, Las Vegas Motor Speedway, Nevada, USA, 8 April. Round 1. 22 laps of the 2.440-mile/3.927-km circuit, 53.680 miles/86.390 km.**
**1** Raphael Matos, BR, 50m 39.638s, 63.576 mph/102.316 km/h; **2** Robert Wickens, CDN, 50m 39.798s; **3** Jonathan Bomarito, USA, 50m 41.408s; **4** James Hinchcliffe, CDN, 50m 43.594s; **5** Franck Perera, F, 50m 45.149s; **6** Junior Strous, NL, 50m 48.008s; **7** Alan Sciuto, USA, 50m 49.135s; **8** Ronnie Bremer, DK, 50m 50.217s; **9** Justin Sofio, USA, 50m 50.660s; **10** Matt Lee, USA, 51m 01.393s.
**Most laps led:** Wickens, 15.
**Fastest race lap:** Wickens, 1m 31.554s, 95.943 mph/154.406 km/h.
**Fastest qualifying lap:** Wickens, 1m 30.934s, 96.598 mph/155.459 km/h.

**CHAMP CAR ATLANTIC CHAMPIONSHIP, Long Beach Steet Circuit, California, USA, 15 April. Round 2. 31 laps of the 1.968-mile/3.167-km circuit, 61.008 miles/98.183 km.**
**1** Raphael Matos, BR, 46m 29.978s, 78.721 mph/126.689 km/h; **2** Jonathan Bomarito, USA, 46m 31.495s; **3** Robert Wickens, CDN, 46m 34.883s; **4** John Edwards, USA, 46m 36.001s; **5** Franck Perera, F, 46m 38.325s; **6** Giacomo Ricci, I, 46m 42.393s; **7** James Hinchcliffe, CDN, 46m 44.702s; **8** Ronnie Bremer, DK, 46m 45.243s; **9** Carl Skerlong, USA, 46m 45.776s; **10** Justin Sofio, USA, 46m 49.271s.
**Most laps led:** Matos, 31.
**Fastest race lap:** Matos, 1m 16.554s, 92.546 mph/148.939 km/h.
**Fastest qualifying lap:** Matos, 1m 15.724s, 93.561 mph/150.572 km/h.

**CHAMP CAR ATLANTIC CHAMPIONSHIP, Reliant Park, Houston, Texas, USA, 22 April. Round 3. 43 laps of the 1.683-mile/2.709-km circuit, 72.369 miles/116.467 km.**
**1** Raphael Matos, BR, 50m 50.602s, 85.402 mph/137.442 km/h; **2** Carl Skerlong, USA, 50m 51.548s; **3** James Hinchcliffe, CDN, 50m 58.780s; **4** Jonathan Bomarito, USA, 50m 59.991s; **5** Franck Perera, F, 51m 8.846s; **6** Alan Sciuto, USA, 51m 12.984s; **7** JR Hildebrand, USA, 51m 13.390s; **8** Giacomo Ricci, I, 51m 20.153s; **9** Ronnie Bremer, DK, 51m 20.898s; **10** Robert Wickens, CDN, 51m 26.382s.
**Most laps led:** Matos, 43.
**Fastest race lap:** Skerlong, 1m 5.072s, 93.109 mph/149.845 km/h.
**Fastest qualifying lap:** Matos, 1m 4.520s, 93.906 mph/151.127 km/h.

**TRINITY CARPET 100k, Portland International Raceway, Oregon, USA, 9/10 June. 30 and 35 laps of the 1.964-mile/3.161-km circuit.**
**Round 4 (58.920 miles/94.823 km).**
**1** Robert Wickens, CDN, 46m 5.689s, 76.694 mph/123.427 km/h; **2** James Hinchcliffe, CDN, 46m 16.646s; **3** Ryan Lewis, GB, 46m 18.553s; **4** Raphael Matos, BR, 46m 19.147s; **5** Franck Perera, F, 46m 27.297s; **6** JR Hildebrand, USA, 46m 28.120s; **7** Alan Sciuto, USA, 46m 32.463s; **8** Carl Skerlong, USA, 46m 36.039s; **9** Junior Strous, NL, 46m 39.153s; **10** Ronnie Bremer, DK, 46m 41.193s.
**Most laps led:** Hinchcliffe, 23.
**Fastest race lap:** Bomarito, 1m 23.615s, 84.559 mph/136.085 km/h.
**Fastest qualifying lap:** Hinchcliffe, 1m 6.561s, 106.224 mph/170.952 km/h.

**Round 5 (68.740 miles/110.626 km).**
**1** Kevin Lacroix, CDN, 45m 35.561s, 90.462 mph/145.584 km/h; **2** James Hinchcliffe, CDN, 45m 37.033s; **3** Franck Perera, F, 45m 40.351s; **4** Robert Wickens, CDN, 45m 47.204s; **5** Ryan Lewis, GB, 45m 50.570s; **6** Raphael Matos, BR, 45m 51.469s; **7** Jonathan Bomarito, USA, 45m 52.549s; **8** Junior Strous, NL, 45m 59.659s; **9** JR Hildebrand, USA, 46m 0.693s; **10** David Garza, MEX, 46m 1.177s.
**Most laps led:** Lacroix, 30.
**Fastest race lap:** Hinchcliffe, 1m 7.035s, 105.473 mph/169.743 km/h.
**Fastest qualifying lap:** Hinchcliffe, 1m 5.991s, 107.142 mph/172.428 km/h.

**CHAMP CAR ATLANTIC CHAMPIONSHIP, Burke Lakefront Airport, Cleveland, Ohio, USA, 24 June. Round 6. 42 laps of the 2.106-mile/3.389-km circuit, 88.452 miles/142.350 km.**
**1** Raphael Matos, BR, 50m 46.634s, 104.518 mph/168.205 km/h; **2** JR Hildebrand, USA, 50m 47.140s; **3** Franck Perera, F, 50m 55.827s; **4** Giacomo Ricci, I, 51m 0.565s; **5** Robert Wickens, CDN, 51m 0.986s; **6** James Hinchcliffe, CDN, 51m 2.295s; **7** Ronnie Bremer, DK, 51m 8.900s; **8** David Garza, MEX, 51m 13.533s; **9** Alan Sciuto, USA, 51m 19.866s; **10** Justin Sofio, USA, 51m 21.493s.
**Most laps led:** Matos, 42.
**Fastest race lap:** Hinchcliffe, 1m 6.127s, 114.652 mph/184.515 km/h.
**Fastest qualifying lap:** Matos, 1m 5.405s, 115.918 mph/186.552 km/h.

**CHAMP CAR ATLANTIC CHAMPIONSHIP, Circuit Mont-Tremblant, St. Jovite, Quebec, Canada, 1 July. Round 7. 34 laps of the 2.621-mile/4.218-km circuit, 89.114 miles/143.415 km.**
**1** Franck Perera, F, 51m 4.494s, 104.686 mph/168.476 km/h; **2** Raphael Matos, BR, 51m 24.980s; **3** James Hinchcliffe, CDN, 51m 25.337s; **4** Jonathan Bomarito, USA, 51m 26.335s; **5** Robert Wickens, CDN, 51m 26.975s; **6** Giacomo Ricci, I, 51m 27.657s; **7** Simona de Silverstro, I, 51m 28.980s; **8** Kevin Lacroix, CDN, 51m 30.556s; **9** J.R. Hildebrand, USA, 51m 31.341s; **10** Matt Lee, USA, 51m 40.730s.
**Most laps led:** Perera, 34.
**Fastest race lap:** Carl Skerlong, USA, 1m 27.157s, 108.260 mph/174.227 km/h.
**Fastest qualifying lap:** Perera, 1m 26.426s, 109.175 mph/175.701 km/h.

**CHAMP CAR ATLANTIC CHAMPIONSHIP, Exhibition Place Circuit, Toronto, Ontario, Canada, 8 July. Round 8. 28 laps of the 1.755-mile/2.824-km circuit, 49.140 miles/79.083 km.**
**1** Franck Perera, F, 50m 25.137s, 58.478 mph/94.111 km/h; **2** John Edwards, USA, 50m 31.194s; **3** Raphael Matos, BR, 50m 33.136s; **4** Giacomo Ricci, I, 50m 37.839s; **5** Ryan Lewis, GB, 50m 39.741s; **6** Alan Sciuto, USA, 50m 40.366s; **7** Robert Wickens, CDN, 50m 41.528s; **8** Justin Sofio, USA, 50m 42.356s; **9** Frankie Muniz, USA, 51m 01.452s; **10** David Garza, MEX, 26 laps.
**Most laps led:** Perera, 23.
**Fastest race lap:** Perera, 1m 20.636s, 78.352 mph/126.095 km/h.
**Fastest qualifying lap:** Matos, 1m 5.621s, 96.280 mph/154.948 km/h.

**CHAMP CAR ATLANTIC CHAMPIONSHIP, Rexall Speedway, Edmonton, Alberta, Canada, 21/22 July. 34 and 38 laps of the 1.973-mile/3.175-km circuit.**
**Round 9 (67.082 miles/107.958 km).**
**1** Raphael Matos, BR, 45m 17.475s, 88.867 mph/143.018 km/h; **2** Franck Perera, F, 45m 19.722s; **3** James Hinchcliffe, CDN, 45m 21.971s; **4** Robert Wickens, CDN, 45m 22.691s; **5** Giacomo Ricci, I, 45m 33.495s; **6** John Edwards, USA, 45m 34.858s; **7** Adrian Carrio, USA, 45m 35.579s; **8** David Garza, MEX, 45m 36.033s; **9** Ryan Lewis, GB, 45m 40.185s; **10** Justin Sofio, USA, 45m 50.286s.
**Most laps led:** Matos, 20.
**Fastest race lap:** Perera, 1m 6.803s, 106.325 mph/171.113 km/h.
**Fastest qualifying lap:** Hinchcliffe, 1m 6.356s, 107.041 mph/172.265 km/h.

**Round 10 (74.974 miles/120.659 km).**
**1** Raphael Matos, BR, 45m 43.810s, 98.369 mph/158.310 km/h; **2** Jonathan Bomarito, USA, 45m 46.371s; **3** Franck Perera, F, 45m 46.500s; **4** Alan Sciuto, USA, 45m 48.662s; **5** JR Hildebrand, USA, 45m 50.905s; **6** Giacomo Ricci, I, 45m 57.456s; **7** Kevin Lacroix, CDN, 45m 58.156s; **8** John Edwards, USA, 45m 58.918s; **9** James Hinchcliffe, CDN, 46m 0.802s; **10** Robert Wickens, CDN, 46m 12.831s.
**Disqualified:** Car failed post-race technical inspection - Carrio finished 4th in, 45m 46.663s.
**Most laps led:** Perera, 37.
**Fastest race lap:** Sciuto, 1m 6.371s, 107.017 mph/172.227 km/h.
**Fastest qualifying lap:** Matos, 1m 5.750s, 108.027 mph/173.853 km/h.

**CHAMP CAR ATLANTIC CHAMPIONSHIP, San Jose Steet Circuit, California, USA, 29 July. Round 11. 48 laps of the 1.443-mile/2.322-km circuit, 69.264 miles/111.470 km.**
**1** Jonathan Bomarito, USA, 50m 8.871s, 82.872 mph/133.369 km/h; **2** Franck Perera, F, 50m 9.769s; **3** Robert Wickens, CDN, 50m 11.391s; **4** Raphael Matos, BR, 50m 12.485s; **5** Junior Strous, NL, 50m 13.337s; **6** Adrian Carrio, USA, 50m 13.987s; **7** Alan Sciuto, USA, 50m 16.136s; **8** Justin Sofio, USA, 50m 16.531s; **9** Ronnie Bremer, DK, 50m 17.023s; **10** Simona de Silvestro, I, 50m 17.641s.
**Most laps led:** Bomarito, 48.
**Fastest race lap:** Wickens, 55.503s, 93.595 mph/150.626 km/h.
**Fastest qualifying lap:** Bomarito, 55.286s, 93.962 mph/151.218 km/h.

**CHAMP CAR ATLANTIC GRAND PRIX OF ROAD AMERICA, Road America, Elkhart Lake, Wisconsin, USA, 12 August. Round 12. 22 laps of the 4.048-mile/6.515-km circuit, 89.056 miles/143.322 km.**
**1** Franck Perera, F, 50m 24.548s, 106.000 mph/170.590 km/h; **2** Raphael Matos, BR, 50m 25.224s; **3** Carl Skerlong, USA, 50m 26.685s; **4** Jonathan Bomarito, USA, 50m 32.089s; **5** Giacomo Ricci, I, 50m 37.454s; **6** Kevin Lacroix, CDN, 50m 38.210s; **7** Robert Wickens, CDN, 50m 38.652s; **8** John Edwards, USA, 50m 39.027s; **9** JR Hildebrand, USA, 50m 40.766s; **10** Ryan Lewis, GB, 50m 42.407s.
**Most laps led:** Perera, 22.
**Fastest race lap:** Sciuto, 2m 0.463s, 120.973 mph/194.688 km/h.
**Fastest qualifying lap:** Perera, 1m 58.883s, 122.581 mph/197.275 km/h.

**Final championship points**
**1** Raphael Matos, BR, 341; **2** Franck Perera, F, 310; **3** Robert Wickens, CDN, 255; **4** James Hinchcliffe, CDN, 224; **5** Jonathan Bomarito, USA, 207; **6** Giacomo Ricci, I, 188; **7** JR Hildebrand, USA, 140; **8** Alan Sciuto, USA, 140; **9** John Edwards, USA, 125; **10** Carl Skerlong, USA, 114; **11** Justin Sofio, USA, 112; **12** Ryan Lewis, GB, 107; **13** Kevin Lacroix, CDN, 105; **14** Junior Strous, NL, 92; **15** Ronnie Bremer, DK, 92; **16** Matt Lee, USA, 79; **17** David Garza, MEX, 78; **18** Adrian Carro, USA, 77; **19** Simona de Silvestro, I, 69; **20** Adrien Herberts, CDN, 51.

**Rookie of the year:** Franck Perera.

## A1GP World Cup of Motorsport

All cars are A1GP Lola-Zytek ZA1348.

## 2006–2007

The following races were run after AUTOCOURSE 2006–2007 went to press.

**A1GP, Jingkai Convention and Exhibition Centre Circuit, Beijing, China, 12 November. Round 3. 15 and 63 laps of the 1.367-mile/2.200-km circuit.**
**Sprint race (20.505 miles/33.000 km).**
**1** Netherlands-Jeroen Bleekemolen, 20m 28.420s, 60.093 mph/96.709 km/h; **2** Mexico-Salvador Durán, 20m 29.884s; **3** Italy-Enrico Tocaccelo, 20m 30.731s; **4** Canada-James Hinchcliffe, 20m 31.795s; **5** Germany-Nicolas Hülkenberg, 20m 32.363s; **6** Brazil-Raphael Matos, 20m 32.820s; **7** Great Britain-Oliver Jarvis, 20m 35.797s; **8** Czech Republic-Tomás Enge, 20m 36.817s; **9** Switzerland-Neel Jani, 20m 37.269s; **10** New Zealand-Matthew Halliday, 20m 37.685s; **11** USA-Phil Giebler, 20m 38.842s; 12 Australia-Karl Reindler, 20m 40.340s; **13** China-Cong Fu Cheng, 20m 41.636s; **14** Malaysia-Alex Yoong, 20m 45.447s; **15** Indonesia-Ananda Mikola, 20m 46.899s; **16** Singapore-Christian Murchison, 20m 49.079s; **17** France-Nicolas Lapierre, 20m 49.222s; **18** India-Armaan Ebrahim, 20m 50.673s; **19** Lebanon-Basil Shaaban, 20m 51.203s; **20** Ireland-Michael Devaney, 20m 51.667s; **21** Pakistan-Nur Ali, 21m 15.961s; **22** South Africa-Adrian Zaugg, 2 laps (DNF-accident).
**Fastest race lap:** Mexico, 59.329s, 82.949 mph/133.492 km/h.
**Fastest qualifying lap:** Netherlands, 1m 0.093s, 81.894 mph/131.795 km/h (over 2 laps).

**Feature race (86.122 miles/138.600 km).**
**1** Italy-Enrico Tocaccelo, 1h 10m 15.919s, 73.540 mph/118.351 km/h; **2** Great Britain-Oliver Jarvis, 1h 10m 20.427s; **3** Australia-Karl Reindler, 1h 10m 21.836s; **4** France-Nicolas Lapierre, 1h 10m 28.819s; **5** South Africa-Adrian Zaugg, 1h 10m 29.197s; **6** Czech Republic-Tomás Enge, 1h 10m 29.603s; **7** Brazil-Raphael Matos, 1h 10m 30.758s; **8** Singapore-Christian Murchison, 1h 10m 32.405s; **9** New Zealand-Matthew Halliday, 1h 10m 32.924s; **10** Canada-James Hinchcliffe, 62 laps (DNF-accident); **11** India-Armaan Ebrahim, 62; **12** Malaysia-Alex Yoong, 61 (DNF-accident); **13** Lebanon-Basil Shaaban, 61; **14** Netherlands-Jeroen Bleekemolen, 53 (DNF-accident); **15** Germany-Nicolas Hülkenberg, 53 gearbox); **16** Indonesia-Ananda Mikola, 36 (accident damage); **17** China-Cong Fu Cheng, 28 (DNF-accident); **18** USA-Phil Giebler, 21 (DNF-accident); **19** Switzerland-Neel Jani, 20 (DNF-accident); **20** Mexico-Salvador Durán, 14 gearbox); **21** Ireland-Michael Devaney, 3 (DNF-accident); **22** Pakistan-Nur Ali, 1 (DNF-accident).
**Fastest race lap:** Canada, 58.107s, 84.693 mph/136.300 km/h.
**Pole position:** Netherlands.
**Championship points:** **1** Mexico, 24; **2** Germany, 22; **3** Great Britain, 20; **4** Italy, 19; **5** Malaysia, 17; **6** Canada, 16.

**A1GP, Sepang International Circuit, Jalan Pekeliling, Kuala Lumpur, Malaysia, 26 November. Round 4. 10 and 28 laps of the 3.444-mile/5.542-km circuit.**
**Sprint race (34.436 miles/55.420 km).**
**1** Switzerland-Neel Jani, 19m 06.289s, 108.150 mph/174.050 km/h; **2** Germany-Nicolas Hülkenberg, 19m 7.492s; **3** New Zealand-Jonny Reid, 19m 9.890s; **4** Malaysia-Alex Yoong, 19m 18.115s; **5** Great Britain-Robbie Kerr, 19m 19.147s; **6** France-Nicolas Lapierre, 19m 20.020s; **7** Netherlands-Jeroen Bleekemolen, 19m 22.386s; **8** Canada-Sean McIntosh, 19m 23.647s; **9** USA-Phil Giebler, 19m 24.581s; **10** China-Cong Fu Cheng, 19m 27.496s; **11** Mexico-Salvador Durán, 19m 28.861s; **12** Australia-Ryan Briscoe, 19m 29.917s; **13** South Africa-Adrian Zaugg, 19m 30.975s; **14** Ireland-Michael Devaney, 19m 31.722s; **15** Singapore-Christian Murchison, 19m 39.805s; **16** India-Armaan Ebrahim, 19m 41.473s; **17** Lebanon-Khalil Beschir, 19m 51.507s; **18** Pakistan-Nur Ali, 20m 41.862s; **19** Brazil-Raphael Matos, 20m 45.706s; **20** Indonesia-Ananda Mikola, 1 lap (DNF-accident damage); **21** Czech Republic-Tomás Enge, 1 (DNF-accident damage); **22** Italy-Enrico Tocaccelo, 1 (DNF-accident damage).
**Fastest race lap:** New Zealand, 1m 53.343s, 109.377 mph/176.024 km/h.
**Fastest qualifying lap:** Switzerland, 3m 43.014s, 111.178 mph/178.923 km/h (over 2 laps).

**Feature race (96.422 miles/155.176 km).**
**1** Germany-Nicolas Hülkenberg, 1h 10m 54.943s, 81.580 mph/131.290 km/h; **2** Great Britain-Robbie Kerr, 1h 11m 37.792s; **3** France-Nicolas Lapierre, 1h 11m 41.564s; **4** Switzerland-Neel Jani, 1h 11m 57.264s; **5** Canada-Sean McIntosh, 1h 12m 2.552s; **6** USA-Phil Giebler, 1h 12m 3.535s; **7** Malaysia-Alex Yoong, 1h 12m 8.002s; **8** New Zealand-Jonny Reid, 1h 12m 16.275s; **9** Netherlands-Jeroen Bleekemolen, 1h 12m 28.358s; **10** Ireland-Michael Devaney, 1h 12m 31.434s; **11** Singapore-Christian Murchison, 1h 12m 33.238s; **12** South Africa-Adrian Zaugg, 1h 12m 41.211s; **13** Italy-Enrico Tocaccelo, 1h 12m 41.415s; **14** Czech Republic-Tomás Enge, 1h 12m 42.721s; **15** Indonesia-Ananda Mikola, 1h 12m 51.708s; **16** China-Cong Fu Cheng, 1h 12m 56.244s; **17** Australia-Ryan Briscoe, 1h 13m 14.742s; **18** India-Armaan Ebrahim, 27 laps; **19** Lebanon-Khalil Beschir, 27; **20** Pakistan-Nur Ali, 26; **21** Mexico-Salvador Durán, 11 (DNF-puncture).
**Disqualified:** Pitted outside allotted time - Brazil-Raphael Matos, finished 18th (completed 27 laps).
**Fastest race lap:** Italy, 2m 14.790s, 91.973 mph/148.016 km/h.
**Pole position:** Switzerland.
**Championship points:** **1** Germany, 37; **2** Great Britain, 31; **3** Malaysia, 24; **4** Mexico, 24; **5** France, 24; **6** Canada, 22.

**A1GP, Sentul International Circuit, Citeureup, Bogor, West Java, Indonesia, 10 December. Round 5. 15 and 47 laps of the 2.464-mile/3.965-km circuit.**
**Sprint race (36.956 miles/59.475 km).**
**1** New Zealand-Jonny Reid, 19m 41.054s, 112.647 mph/181.287 km/h; **2** Mexico-Salvador Durán, 19m 41.792s; **3** Great Britain-Robbie Kerr, 19m 44.517s; **4** USA-Phil Giebler, 19m 50.134s; **5** Germany-Nicolas Hülkenberg, 19m 51.054s; **6** Australia-Ryan Briscoe, 19m 51.691s; **7** France-Nicolas Lapierre, 19m 53.057s; **8** Canada-Sean McIntosh, 19m 55.420s; **9** South Africa-Alan van der Merwe, 19m 57.043s; **10** Switzerland-Neel Jani, 19m 58.687s; **11** Italy-Enrico Tocaccelo, 19m 59.955s; **12** Malaysia-Alex Yoong, 20m 04.724s; **13** Netherlands-Jeroen Bleekemolen, 20m 5.202s; **14** Indonesia-Ananda Mikola, 20m 7.032s; **15** Brazil-Tuka Rocha, 20m 17.114s; **16** Czech Republic-Jaroslav 'Janek' Janis, 20m 17.835s; **17** Ireland-Richard Lyons, 20m 18.249s; **18** India-Armaan Ebrahim, 20m 25.636s; **19** Lebanon-Basil Shaaban, 20m 26.051s; **20** Pakistan-Nur Ali, 21m 02.745s; **21** China-Ho-Pin Tung, 11 laps (DNF-spin).
**Fastest race lap:** Great Britain, 1m 18.110s, 113.551 mph/182.742 km/h.
**Fastest qualifying lap:** New Zealand, 2m 33.242s, 115.758 mph/186.293 km/h (over 2 laps).

**Feature race (115.796 miles/186.355 km).**
**1** New Zealand-Jonny Reid, 1h 10m 36.607s, 98.396 mph/158.352 km/h; **2** Germany-Nicolas Hülkenberg, 1h 10m 37.785s; **3** France-Nicolas Lapierre, 1h 10m 40.869s; **4** Italy-Enrico Tocaccelo, 1h 10m 45.268s; **5** Malaysia-Alex Yoong, 1h 10m 51.225s; **6** Mexico-Salvador Durán, 1h 10m 51.977s; **7** Czech Republic-Jaroslav 'Janek' Janis, 1h 10m 56.674s; **8** Switzerland-Neel Jani, 1h 10m 59.730s; **9** USA-Phil Giebler, 1h 11m 3.845s; **10** Australia-Ryan Briscoe, 46 laps; **11** Indonesia-Ananda Mikola, 46; **12** Ireland-Richard Lyons, 46; **13** China-Ho-Pin Tung, 46; **14** Brazil-Tuka Rocha, 46; **15** Pakistan-Nur Ali, 43; **16** Great Britain-Robbie Kerr, 39 (DNF-spin); **17** Canada-Sean McIntosh, 38 (DNF-lost wheel); **18** South Africa-Alan van der Merwe, 29 (DNF-gearbox); **19** Lebanon-Basil Shaaban, 7 (DNF-rear suspension).
**Disqualified:** Netherlands-Jeroen Bleekemolen finished 5th in 1h 10m 46.689s (pitted outside allotted time); India-Armaan Ebrahim, 11 laps (black-flagged for incorrect grid slot).
**Fastest race lap:** New Zealand, 1m 20.351s, 110.384 mph/177.645 km/h.
**Pole position:** New Zealand.

**Championship points: 1** Germany, 48; **2** Great Britain, 36; **3** Mexico, 34; **4** France, 32; **5** New Zealand, 31; **6** Malaysia, 30.

**A1GP, Taupo Racetrack, Lake Taupo, New Zealand, 21 January. Round 6. 14 and 50 laps of the 2.063-mile/3.320-km circuit.**
**Sprint race (28.881 miles/46.480 km).**
**1** Germany-Nicolas Hülkenberg, 19m 49.089s, 87.439 mph/140.719 km/h; **2** France-Loïc Duval, 19m 52.836s; **3** New Zealand-Jonny Reid, 19m 53.304s; **4** Netherlands-Jeroen Bleekemolen, 19m 56.621s; **5** Switzerland-Sébastien Buemi, 19m 56.891s; **6** Canada-James Hinchcliffe, 19m 57.898s; **7** South Africa-Alan van der Merwe, 20m 05.413s; **8** Great Britain-Robbie Kerr, 20m 18.182s; **9** Italy-Enrico Tocaccelo, 20m 18.606s; **10** India-Narain Karthikeyan, 20m 18.720s; **11** USA-Ryan Hunter-Reay, 20m 19.226s; **12** Mexico-Salvador Durán, 20m 19.623s; **13** China-Ho-Pin Tung, 20m 20.519s; **14** Australia-Karl Reindler, 20m 20.775s; **15** Indonesia-Ananda Mikola, 20m 21.865s; **16** Brazil-Raphael Matos, 20m 24.896s; **17** Czech Republic-Tomás Enge, 20m 40.636s; **18** Pakistan-Nur Ali, 20m 59.999s; **19** Malaysia-Alex Yoong, 13 laps; **20** Ireland-Richard Lyons, 6 (DNF-driveshaft); **21** Lebanon-Alex Khateeb, 6 (DNF-accident); **22** Singapore-Christian Murchison, 0 (DNF-accident).
**Fastest race lap:** Germany, 1m 14.862s, 99.204 mph/ 159.653 km/h.
**Fastest qualifying lap:** Germany, 2m 28.218s, 100.212 mph/161.275 km/h (over 2 laps).

**Feature race (103.148 miles/166.000 km).**
**1** Germany-Nicolas Hülkenberg, 1h 3m 38.100s, 97.256 mph/156.517 km/h; **2** France-Loïc Duval, 1h 3m 57.611s; **3** New Zealand-Jonny Reid, 1h 3m 58.027s; **4** Switzerland-Sébastien Buemi, 1h 3m 58.956s; **5** Netherlands-Jeroen Bleekemolen, 1h 3m 59.451s; **6** Canada-James Hinchcliffe, 1h 3m 59.908s; **7** India-Narain Karthikeyan, 1h 4m 8.859s; **8** Italy-Enrico Tocaccelo, 1h 4m 9.574s; **9** China-Ho-Pin Tung, 1h 4m 23.837s; **10** USA-Ryan Hunter-Reay, 1h 4m 26.641s; **11** Malaysia-Alex Yoong, 1h 4m 27.335s; **12** Czech Republic-Tomás Enge, 1h 4m 44.205s; **13** Australia-Karl Reindler, 1h 4m 50.728s; **14** Brazil-Raphael Matos, 49 laps; **15** Singapore-Christian Murchison, 49; **16** South Africa-Alan van der Merwe, 49; **17** Lebanon-Alex Khateeb, 48; **18** Pakistan-Nur Ali, 46; **19** Ireland-Richard Lyons, 45 (DNF-suspension); **20** Mexico-Salvador Durán, 42 (DNF-puncture); **21** Great Britain-Robbie Kerr, 40 (DNF-battery); **22** Indonesia-Ananda Mikola, 8 (DNFspin).
**Fastest race lap:** Germany, 1m 14.742s, 99.364 mph/ 159.910 km/h.
**Pole position:** Germany.
**Championship points: 1** Germany, 65; **2** France, 46; **3** New Zealand, 43; **4** Great Britain, 36; **5** Mexico, 34; **6** Malaysia, 30.

**A1GP, Eastern Creek International Raceway, Sydney, New South Wales, Australia, 4 February. Round 7. 14 and 46 laps of the 2.442-mile/3.930-km circuit.**
**Sprint race (34.188 miles/55.020 km).**
**1** Germany-Nicolas Hülkenberg, 20m 13.223s, 101.446 mph/163.260 km/h; **2** New Zealand-Jonny Reid, 20m 15.377s; **3** France-Loïc Duval, 20m 21.054s; **4** Switzerland-Sébastien Buemi, 20m 24.108s; **5** Netherlands-Jeroen Bleekemolen, 20m 25.360s; **6** China-Ho-Pin Tung, 20m 26.315s; **7** Malaysia-Alex Yoong, 20m 26.771s; **8** USA-Phil Giebler, 20m 27.477s; **9** Czech Republic-Tomás Enge, 20m 28.152s; **10** Ireland-Richard Lyons, 20m 29.097s; **11** Mexico-Salvador Durán, 20m 29.559s; **12** Singapore-Christian Murchison, 20m 29.987s; **13** Canada-James Hinchcliffe, 20m 30.834s; **14** Australia-Karl Reindler, 20m 30.919s; **15** Italy-Enrico Tocaccelo, 20m 32.647s; **16** South Africa-Alan van der Merwe, 20m 33.037s; **17** Indonesia-Ananda Mikola, 20m 33.774s; **18** India-Parthiva Sureshwaren, 20m 42.451s; **19** Great Britain-Robbie Kerr, 13 (DNF-puncture); **20** Pakistan-Nur Ali, 12 (DNF-spin); **21** Brazil-Tuka Rocha, 11 (DNF-fuel pressure); **22** Lebanon-Alex Khateeb, 5 (DNF-accident).
**Fastest race lap:** Germany, 1m 19.142s, 111.081 mph/ 178.767 km/h.
**Fastest qualifying lap:** Germany, 2m 36.225s, 112.544 mph/181.123 km/h (over 2 laps).

**Feature race (112.331 miles/180.780 km).**
**1** Germany-Nicolas Hülkenberg, 1h 8m 35.139s, 98.270 mph/158.149 km/h; **2** New Zealand-Jonny Reid, 1h 8m 42.752s; **3** China-Ho-Pin Tung, 1h 9m 01.215s; **4** Netherlands-Jeroen Bleekemolen, 1h 9m 08.841s; **5** Czech Republic-Tomás Enge, 1h 9m 13.416s; **6** Malaysia-Alex Yoong, 1h 9m 17.190s; **7** Switzerland-Sébastien Buemi, 1h 9m 18.790s; **8** USA-Phil Giebler, 1h 9m 19.331s; **9** France-Loïc Duval, 1h 9m 21.376s; **10** Great Britain-Robbie Kerr, 1h 9m 25.240s; **11** Brazil-Tuka Rocha, 1h 9m 26.078s; **12** Italy-Enrico Tocaccelo, 1h 9m 29.408s; **13** Indonesia-Ananda Mikola, 1h 9m 30.834s; **14** Australia-Karl Reindler, 1h 9m 40.332s; **15** Mexico-Salvador Durán, 45 laps; **16** India-Parthiva Sureshwaren, 45; **17** Lebanon-Alex Khateeb, 41; **18** Ireland-Richard Lyons, 22 (DNF-accident); **19** Pakistan-Nur Ali, 6 (DNF-accident); **20** South Africa-Alan van der Merwe, 4 (DNF-accident); **21** Canada-James Hinchcliffe, 0 (DNF-accident); **22** Singapore-Christian Murchison, 0 (DNF-accident).
**Fastest race lap:** Germany, 1m 19.899s, 110.028 mph/ 177.073 km/h.
**Pole position:** Germany.
**Championship points: 1** Germany, 82; **2** New Zealand, 57; **3** France, 52; **4** Great Britain, 37; **5** Switzerland, 36; **6** Malaysia, 35.

**A1GP, Durban Street Circuit, KwaZulu-Natal, South Africa, 25 February. Round 8. 15 and 49 laps of the 1.988-mile/3.200-km circuit.**
**Sprint race (29.826 miles/48.000 km).**
**1** Germany-Nicolas Hülkenberg, 19m 57.070s, 89.696 mph/144.352 km/h; **2** France-Loïc Duval, 19m 59.851s; **3** New Zealand-Matthew Halliday, 20m 0.560s; **4** Netherlands-Jeroen Bleekemolen, 20m 3.426s; **5** Switzerland-Neel Jani, 20m 7.767s; **6** Ireland-Richard Lyons, 20m 11.426s; **7** South Africa-Adrian Zaugg, 20m 14.179s; **8** Portugal-Alvaro Parente, 20m 16.017s; **9** Great Britain-Robbie Kerr, 20m 16.986s; **10** Czech Republic-Tomás Enge, 20m 17.941s; **11** Indonesia-Ananda Mikola, 20m 19.537s; **12** Italy-Enrico Tocaccelo, 20m 20.987s; **13** Canada-James Hinchcliffe, 20m 30.597s; **14** China-Ho-Pin Tung, 20m 39.153s; **15** India-Narain Karthikeyan, 20m 41.155s; **16** Australia-Karl Reindler, 21m 15.050s; **17** Brazil-Bruno Junqueira, 14 laps; **18** Pakistan-Nur Ali, 14; **19** Lebanon-Allam Khodair, 14; **20** USA-Jonathan Summerton, 12 (DNF-driveshaft); **21** Mexico-Salvador Durán, 9 (DNF-driveshaft); **22** Singapore-Christian Murchison, 8 (DNF-accident); **23** Malaysia-Alex Yoong, 0 (DNF-accident damage).
**Fastest race lap:** Germany, 1m 18.701s, 90.954 mph/ 146.376 km/h.
**Fastest qualifying lap:** Germany, 2m 35.404s, 92.124 mph/148.258 km/h (over 2 laps).

**Feature race (97.431 miles/156.800 km).**
**1** Germany-Nicolas Hülkenberg, 1h 10m 35.582s, 82.111 mph/133.270 km/h; **2** Great Britain-Robbie Kerr, 1h 10m 45.138s; **3** New Zealand-Matthew Halliday, 1h 10m 46.101s; **4** Switzerland-Neel Jani, 1h 10m 48.224s; **5** Portugal-Alvaro Parente, 1h 10m 51.557s; **6** Netherlands-Jeroen Bleekemolen, 1h 10m 52.381s; **7** Brazil-Bruno Junqueira, 1h 10m 57.450s; **8** Malaysia-Alex Yoong, 48 laps; **9** India-Narain Karthikeyan, 45 (DNF-driveshaft); **10** Pakistan-Nur Ali, 45 (DNF-running); **11** Mexico-Salvador Durán, 42 (DNF-electrics); **12** Ireland-Richard Lyons, 39 (DNF-accident); **13** USA-Jonathan Summerton, 33 (DNF-accident); **14** China-Ho-Pin Tung, 27 (DNF-gearbox); **15** Lebanon-Allam Khodair, 24 (DNF-injury); **16** Czech Republic-Tomás Enge, 15 (DNF-gearbox); **17** South Africa-Adrian Zaugg, 11 (DNF-accident damage); **18** Australia-Karl Reindler, 8 (DNF-accident); **19** Indonesia-Ananda Mikola, 4 (DNF-accident); **20** France-Loïc Duval, 2 (DNF-driveshaft); **21** Canada-James Hinchcliffe, 0 (DNF-accident damage); **22** Italy-Enrico Tocaccelo, 0 (DNF-accident); **23** Singapore-Christian Murchison, 0 (DNF-accident).
**Fastest race lap:** South Africa, 1m 18.780s, 90.863 mph/146.230 km/h.
**Pole position:** Germany.
**Championship points: 1** Germany, 99; **2** New Zealand, 69; **3** France, 57; **4** Great Britain, 46; **5** Switzerland, 45; **6** Netherlands, 43.

**A1GP, Autfidromo Hermanos Rodríguez, Mexico City, D.F., Mexico, 25 March. Round 9. 12 and 45 laps of the 2.763-mile/4.447-km circuit.**
**Sprint race (33.159 miles/53.364 km).**
**1** Malaysia-Alex Yoong, 17m 44.563s, 112.132 mph/ 180.459 km/h; **2** Great Britain-Oliver Jarvis, 17m 46.701s; **3** Australia-Ian Dyk, 17m 50.909s; **4** South Africa-Adrian Zaugg, 17m 53.786s; **5** USA-Jonathan Summerton, 17m 54.003s; **6** China-Ho-Pin Tung, 17m 56.596s; **7** Italy-Enrico Tocaccelo, 17m 57.660s; **8** Indonesia-Ananda Mikola, 17m 58.795s; **9** Netherlands-Renger van der Zande, 17m 59.318s; **10** Switzerland-Marcel Fassler, 18m 0.263s; **11** India-Narain Karthikeyan, 18m 1.454s; **12** Czech Republic-Jaroslav 'Janek' Janis, 18m 2.484s; **13** Canada-James Hinchcliffe, 18m 11.865s; **14** Portugal-Alvaro Parente, 18m 36.309s; **15** Pakistan-Nur Ali, 18m 40.658s; **16** New Zealand-Jonny Reid, 18m 59.660s; **17** Mexico-Salvador Durán, 19m 04.774s; **18** Lebanon-Allam Khodair, 11 laps; **19** France-Jean-Karl Vernay, 2 (DNF-accident); **20** Brazil-Bruno Junqueira, 0 (DNF-accident); **21** Germany-Christian Vietoris, 0 (DNF-accident); **22** Ireland-Richard Lyons, 0 (DNF-accident).
**Fastest race lap:** Mexico, 1m 27.534s, 113.643 mph/ 182.891 km/h.
**Fastest qualifying lap:** Malaysia, 2m 53.138s, 114.910 mph/184.929 km/h (over 2 laps).

**Feature race (124.346 miles/200.115 km).**
**1** Great Britain-Oliver Jarvis, 1h 7m 37.362s, 110.329 mph/177.557 km/h; **2** USA-Jonathan Summerton, 1h 7m 38.052s; **3** South Africa-Adrian Zaugg, 1h 7m 47.418s; **4** Italy-Enrico Tocaccelo, 1h 7m 51.449s; **5** Malaysia-Alex Yoong, 1h 7m 56.633s; **6** New Zealand-Jonny Reid, 1h 7m 59.003s; **7** Portugal-Alvaro Parente, 1h 8m 0.771s; **8** Australia-Ian Dyk, 1h 8m 11.430s; **9** Germany-Christian Vietoris, 1h 8m 12.673s; **10** China-Ho-Pin Tung, 1h 8m 13.604s; **11** Indonesia-Ananda Mikola, 1h 8m 14.271s; **12** Czech Republic-Jaroslav 'Janek' Janis, 1h 8m 14.773s; **13** Brazil-Bruno Junqueira, 1h 8m 15.239s; **14** Switzerland-Marcel Fassler, 1h 8m 19.600s; **15** Canada-James Hinchcliffe, 1h 8m 28.501s; **16** Ireland-Richard Lyons, 1h 8m 41.340s; **17** Netherlands-Jeroen Bleekemolen, 1h 8m 48.853s; **18** India-Narain Karthikeyan, 44 laps; **19** Lebanon-Allam Khodair, 44; **20** France-Jean-Karl Vernay, 44; **21** Pakistan-Nur Ali, 43; **22** Mexico-Salvador Durán, 14 (DNF-fuel pump).
**Fastest race lap:** USA, 1m 27.841s, 113.246 mph/ 182.252 km/h.
**Pole position:** Malaysia.
**Championship points: 1** Germany, 101; **2** New Zealand, 74; **3** Great Britain, 61; **4** France, 57; **5** Malaysia, 50; **6** Switzerland, 45.

**A1GP, Shanghai International Circuit, Jiading, China, 15 April. Round 10. 10 and 38 laps of the 2.860-mile/ 4.603-km circuit.**
**Sprint race (28.602 miles/46.030 km).**
**1** Great Britain-Robbie Kerr, 16m 4.825s, 106.720 mph/ 171.749 km/h; **2** New Zealand-Jonny Reid, 16m 5.210s; **3** Germany-Nicolas Hülkenberg, 16m 7.340s; **4** Switzerland-Sébastien Buemi, 16m 10.948s; **5** USA-Jonathan Summerton, 16m 11.932s; **6** Malaysia-Alex Yoong, 16m 15.982s; **7** India-Narain Karthikeyan, 16m 16.651s; **8** South Africa-Alan van der Merwe, 16m 21.578s; **9** Netherlands-Renger van der Zande, 16m 21.962s; **10** Italy-Enrico Tocaccelo, 16m 23.026s; **11** China-Cong Fu Cheng, 16m 23.615s; **12** Ireland-Richard Lyons, 16m 24.232s; **13** Indonesia-Ananda Mikola, 16m 26.380s; **14** Brazil-Vitor Meira, 16m 29.056s; **15** Mexico-Sergio Pérez, 16m 29.871s; **16** Australia-Ian Dyk, 16m 33.677s; **17** Czech Republic-Filip Salaquarda, 16m 33.916s; **18** Lebanon-Allam Khodair, 16m 35.307s; **19** Portugal-João Urbano, 16m 38.614s; **20** Pakistan-Nur Ali, 16m 54.258s; **21** Canada-Sean McIntosh, 7 (DNF-accident); 22 France-Jean-Karl Vernay, 7 (DNF-accident).
**Fastest race lap:** New Zealand, 1m 36.033s, 107.220 mph/172.553 km/h.
**Fastest qualifying lap:** Great Britain, 3m 10.138s, 108.306 mph/174.302 km/h (over 2 laps).

**Feature race (108.687 miles/174.914 km).**
**1** New Zealand-Jonny Reid, 1h 8m 13.498s, 95.584 mph/ 153.826 km/h; **2** Great Britain-Robbie Kerr, 1h 8m 15.065s; **3** Germany-Nicolas Hülkenberg, 1h 8m 16.683s; **4** Netherlands-Renger van der Zande, 1h 8m 19.159s; **5** Ireland-Richard Lyons, 1h 8m 23.879s; **6** Canada-Sean McIntosh, 1h 8m 25.796s; **7** Italy-Enrico Tocaccelo, 1h 8m 26.669s; **8** France-Jean-Karl Vernay, 1h 8m 28.441s; **9** Switzerland-Sébastien Buemi, 1h 8m 28.761s; **10** Czech Republic-Filip Salaquarda, 1h 8m 35.283s; **11** Malaysia-Alex Yoong, 1h 8m 35.829s; **12** South Africa-Alan van der Merwe, 1h 8m 39.212s; **13** Portugal-João Urbano, 1h 8m 42.398s; **14** Lebanon-Allam Khodair, 1h 8m 42.774s; **15** China-Cong Fu Cheng, 1h 8m 43.893s; **16** Indonesia-Ananda Mikola, 1h 9m 3.196s; **17** India-Narain Karthikeyan, 1h 9m 8.084s; **18** Pakistan-Nur Ali, 36 laps; **19** Brazil-Vitor Meira, 34; **20** USA-Jonathan Summerton, 24 (DNF-spin); **21** Australia-Ian Dyk, 17 (DNF-damage); **22** Mexico-Sergio Pérez, 2 (DNF-battery).
**Fastest race lap:** New Zealand, 1m 36.961s, 106.193 mph/170.901 km/h.
**Pole position:** Great Britain.
**Championship points: 1** Germany, 113; **2** New Zealand, 90; **3** Great Britain, 76; **4** France, 60; **5** Malaysia, 51; **6** Netherlands, 50.

**A1GP, Brands Hatch Grand Prix Circuit, West Kingsdown, Dartford, Kent, Great Britain, 29 April. Round 11. 15 and 50 laps of the 2.301-mile/3.703-km circuit.**
**Sprint race (34.514 miles/55.545 km).**
**1** Great Britain-Robbie Kerr, 18m 51.354s, 109.825 mph/ 176.745 km/h; **2** Germany-Nicolas Hülkenberg, 18m 59.685s; **3** Italy-Enrico Tocaccelo, 19m 04.877s; **4** France-Loïc Duval, 19m 8.466s; **5** Malaysia-Alex Yoong, 19m 13.089s; **6** Netherlands-Jeroen Bleekemolen, 19m 13.545s; **7** India-Narain Karthikeyan, 19m 13.912s; **8** Ireland-Richard Lyons, 19m 20.539s; **9** USA-Jonathan Summerton, 19m 20.912s; **10** Canada-Sean McIntosh, 19m 21.904s; **11** Portugal-Alvaro Parente, 19m 22.079s; **12** Brazil-Bruno Junqueira, 19m 22.468s; **13** Czech Republic-Jan Charouz, 19m 27.956s; **14** Australia-Ian Dyk, 19m 29.649s; **15** South Africa-Adrian Zaugg, 19m 51.048s*; **16** New Zealand-Matthew Halliday, 19m 56.257s; **17** Indonesia-Moreno Soeprapto, 20m 5.124s; **18** Mexico-Juan Pablo Garcia, 14 laps; **19** Lebanon-Allam Khodair, 11 (DNF-accident); **20** Switzerland-Sébastien Buemi, 8 (DNF-accident); **21** Pakistan-Nur Ali, 4 (DNF-accident); **22** China-Cong Fu Cheng, 2 (DNF-gearbox).
* Includes 25s penalty for causing accident.
**Fastest race lap:** Great Britain, 1m 14.923s, 110.559 mph/177.926 km/h.
**Fastest qualifying lap:** Great Britain, 2m 28.899s, 111.262 mph/179.058 km/h (over 2 laps).

**Feature race (115.047 miles/185.150 km).**
**1** Germany-Nicolas Hülkenberg, 1h 11m 1.907s, 97.179 mph/156.394 km/h; **2** Great Britain-Robbie Kerr, 1h 11m 2.526s; **3** Italy-Enrico Tocaccelo, 1h 11m 20.441s; **4** India-Narain Karthikeyan, 1h 11m 20.704s; **5** Netherlands-Jeroen Bleekemolen, 1h 11m 28.176s; **6** USA-Jonathan Summerton, 1h 11m 30.123s; **7** France-Loïc Duval, 1h 11m 37.155s; **8** New Zealand-Matthew Halliday, 1h 11m 37.392s; **9** Malaysia-Alex Yoong, 1h 11m 39.420s; **10** China-Cong Fu Cheng, 1h 11m 48.328s; **11** Portugal-Alvaro Parente, 1h 11m 52.757s; **12** Canada-Sean McIntosh, 49 laps; **13** Lebanon-Allam Khodair, 49; **14** Mexico-Juan Pablo Garcia, 49; **15** Czech Republic-Jan Charouz, 49; **16** Indonesia-Moreno Soeprapto, 49; **17** Pakistan-Nur Ali, 48; **18** Brazil-Bruno Junqueira, 9 (DNF-accident); **19** Australia-Ian Dyk, 0 (DNF-accident); **20** South Africa-Adrian Zaugg, 0 (DNF-accident).
**Disqualified:** Pitted outside allotted time - Switzerland-Sébastien Buemi (finished 12th in 1h 11m 53.795s); Ireland-Richard Lyons (finished 13th in 1h 11m 54.611s).
**Fastest race lap:** Switzerland, 1m 16.165s, 108.756 mph/175.025 km/h.
**Pole position:** Great Britain.

**Final championship points**
**1** Germany, 128; **2** New Zealand, 93; **3** Great Britain, 92; **4** France, 67; **5** Netherlands, 57; **6** Malaysia, 55; **7** Italy, 52; **8** Switzerland, 50; **9** USA, 42; **10** Mexico, 35; **11** Canada, 33; **12** Czech Republic, 27; **13** Australia, 25; **14** South Africa, 24; **15** China, 22; **16** India, 13; **17** Portugal, 10; **18** Brazil, 9; **19** Ireland, 8; **20** Singapore, 3; **21** Indonesia, 1; **22** Pakistan, 1.

## 2006–2007

All cars are A1GP Lola-Zytek ZA1348

**A1GP, Circuit Park Zandvoort, Netherlands, 30 September. Round 1. 12 and 45 laps of the 2.875-mile/4.627-km circuit.**
**Sprint race (34.501 miles/55.524 km).**
**1** South Africa-Adrian Zaugg, 18m 1.087s, 114.888 mph/ 184.893 km/h; **2** France-Loïc Duval, 18m 8.619s; **3** Netherlands-Jeroen Bleekemolen, 18m 9.184s; **4** Mexico-Salvador Durán, 18m 9.292s; **5** Switzerland-Neel Jani, 18m 9.668s; **6** Germany-Christian Vietoris, 18m 11.431s; **7** Great Britain-Oliver Jarvis, 18m 11.653s; **8** Ireland-Ralph Firman, 18m 13.255s; **9** New Zealand-Jonny Reid, 18m 15.021s; **10** India-Narain Karthikeyan, 18m 19.603s; **11** Portugal-João Urbano, 18m 26.054s; **12** Italy-Enrico Tocaccelo, 18m 26.804s; **13** Brazil-Sérgio Jimenez, 18m 27.131s; **14** Lebanon-Chris Alajajian, 18, 35.634s; **15** Czech Republic-Erik Janis, 18m 36.355s; **16** Malaysia-Alex Yoong, 18m 36.982s; **17** China-Cong Fu Cheng, 18m 37.385s; **18** Pakistan-Adam Khan, 18m 37.597s; **19** Canada-James Hinchcliffe, 18m 40.596s; **20** Indonesia-Satrio Hermanto, 18m 49.019s; **21** Australia-Ian Dyk, 18m 49.070s; **22** USA-Buddy Rice, 18m 49.295s.
**Fastest race lap:** South Africa, 1m 28.353s, 117.147 mph/188.530 km/h.
**Fastest qualifying lap:** South Africa, 1m 45.095s, 98.485 mph/158.496 km/h.

**Feature race (129.379 miles/208.215 km).**
**1** Great Britain-Oliver Jarvis, 1h 9m 51.394s, 111.124 mph/178.836 km/h; **2** South Africa-Adrian Zaugg, 1h 9m 57.136s; **3** Switzerland-Neel Jani, 1h 9m 59.368s; **4** Mexico-Salvador Durán, 1h 10m 2.910s; **5** France-Loïc Duval, 1h 10m 17.183s; **6** Ireland-Ralph Firman, 1h 10m 25.091s; **7** New Zealand-Jonny Reid, 1h 10m 39.029s; **8** Netherlands-Jeroen Bleekemolen, 1h 10m 40.664s; **9** Germany-Christian Vietoris, 1h 10m 41.270s; **10** Czech Republic-Erik Janis, 1h 10m 51.058s; **11** Brazil-Sérgio Jimenez, 1h 10m 51.472s; **12** Australia-Ian Dyk, 1h 11m 21.987s; **13** USA-Buddy Rice, 1h 11m 22.542s; **14** Italy-Enrico Tocaccelo, 44 laps; **15** China-Cong Fu Cheng, 44; **16** Indonesia-Satrio Hermanto, 44; **17** Pakistan-Adam Khan, 43; **18** Canada-James Hinchcliffe, 40 (DNF-accident damage); **19** Lebanon-Chris Alajajian, 40 (DNF-spin); **20** India-Narain Karthikeyan, 13 (DNF-handling); **21** Malaysia-Alex Yoong, 8 (DNF-electronics); **22** Portugal-João Urbano, 2.
**Fastest race lap:** Mexico, 1m 29.181s, 116.060 mph/ 186.779 km/h.
**Fastest qualifying lap:** South Africa, 1m 43.979s, 99.542 mph/160.197 km/h.
**Championship points: 1** South Africa, 28; **2** Great Britain, 19; **3** France, 18; **4** Mexico, 17; **5** Switzerland, 16; **6** Netherlands, 13.

**A1GP, Automotodrom Brno Masaryk Circuit, Brno, Czech Republic, 14 October. Round 2. 10 and 38 and laps of the 3.357-mile/5.403-km circuit.**
**Sprint race (33.573 miles/54.030 km).**
**1** New Zealand-Jonny Reid, 18m 11.609s, 110.719 mph/ 178.184 km/h; **2** Great Britain-Robbie Kerr, 18m 17.561s; **3** Ireland-Adam Carroll, 18m 20.433s; **4** South Africa-Adrian Zaugg, 18m 21.878s; **5** Netherlands-Jeroen Bleekemolen, 18m 23.170s; **6** France-Nicolas Lapierre, 18m 23.412s; **7** Germany-Christian Vietoris, 18m 24.809s; **8** Switzerland-Neel Jani, 18m 25.056s; **9** Portugal-João Urbano, 18m 30.179s; **10** China-Cong Fu Cheng, 18m 30.410s; **11** Brazil-Sérgio Jimenez, 18m 33.781s; **12** Canada-James Hinchcliffe, 18m 35.605s; **13** Mexico-Michel Jourdain Jr, 18m 36.536s; **14** Italy-Enrico Tocaccelo, 18m 37.531s; **15** Pakistan-Adam Khan, 18m 40.372s; **16** USA-Buddy Rice, 18m 42.685s; **17** Malaysia-Alex Yoong, 18m 45.270s; **18** Czech Republic-Erik Janis, 18m 46.324s; **19** Indonesia-Satrio Hermanto, 18m 59.798s; **20** Lebanon-Khalil Beschir, 19m 1.439s; **21** India-Narain Karthikeyan, 19m 49.425s; 22 Australia-Ian Dyk, 3 laps (DNF-gearbox).
**Fastest race lap:** New Zealand, 1m 48.438s, 111.457 mph/179.372 km/h.
**Fastest qualifying lap:** South Africa, 1m 44.859s, 115.261 mph/185.494 km/h.

**Feature race (127.576 miles/205.314 km).**
**1** New Zealand-Jonny Reid, 1h 10m 34.700s, 108.455 mph/174.541 km/h; **2** Netherlands-Jeroen Bleekemolen, 1h 10m 41.846s; **3** Switzerland-Neel Jani, 1h 10m 46.977s; **4** China-Cong Fu Cheng, 1h 10m 47.423s; **5** France-Nicolas Lapierre, 1h 10m 54.139s; **6** Ireland-Adam Carroll, 1h 10m 59.048s; **7** Brazil-Sérgio Jimenez, 1h 11m 04.325s; **8** Germany-Christian Vietoris, 1h 11m 12.649s; **9** India-Narain Karthikeyan, 1h 11m 13.085s; **10** Italy-Enrico Tocaccelo, 1h 11m 24.106s; **11** Canada-James Hinchcliffe, 1h 11m 26.231s; **12** Czech Republic-Erik Janis, 1h 11m 32.499s; **13** Australia-Ian Dyk, 1h 11m 37.248s; **14** Malaysia-Alex Yoong, 1h 11m 37.938s; **15** USA-Buddy Rice, 1h 11m 57.490s; **16** South Africa-Adrian Zaugg, 1h 11m 57.800s; **17** Great Britain-Robbie Kerr, 1h 11m 58.433s; **18** Portugal-João Urbano, 1h 11m 59.618s; **19** Indonesia-Satrio Hermanto, 1h 12m 0.037s; **20** Pakistan-Adam Khan, 1h 12m 06.215s; **21** Lebanon-Khalil Beschir, 37 laps; **22** Mexico-Michel Jourdain Jr, 37.
**Fastest race lap:** China, 1m 47.610s, 112.315 mph/ 180.752 km/h.
**Fastest qualifying lap:** Netherlands, 1m 44.649s, 115.492 mph/185.867 km/h.

**Provisional championship points**
**1** New Zealand, 37; **2** South Africa, 36; **3** Great Britain, 31; **4** Netherlands, 31; **5** France, 29; **6** Switzerland, 29; **7** Ireland, 23; **8** Mexico, 17; **9** Germany, 14; **10** China, 10; **11** Brazil, 4; **12** India, 3; **13** Portugal, 2; **14** Italy, 1; **15** Czech Republic, 1.

*Results of the remaining races will be given in AUTOCOURSE 2008–2009.*